International Law and the Principle of Non-Intervention

International Law and the Principle of Non-Intervention

History, Theory, and Interactions with Other Principles

MARCO ROSCINI
University of Westminster

Great Clarendon Street, Oxford, OX2 6DP,
United Kingdom

Oxford University Press is a department of the University of Oxford.
It furthers the University's objective of excellence in research, scholarship,
and education by publishing worldwide. Oxford is a registered trade mark of
Oxford University Press in the UK and in certain other countries

© Marco Roscini 2024

The moral rights of the author have been asserted

All rights reserved. No part of this publication may be reproduced, stored in
a retrieval system, or transmitted, in any form or by any means, without the
prior permission in writing of Oxford University Press, or as expressly permitted
by law, by licence or under terms agreed with the appropriate reprographics
rights organization. Enquiries concerning reproduction outside the scope of the
above should be sent to the Rights Department, Oxford University Press, at the
address above

You must not circulate this work in any other form
and you must impose this same condition on any acquirer

Public sector information reproduced under Open Government Licence v3.0
(http://www.nationalarchives.gov.uk/doc/open-government-licence/open-government-licence.htm)

Published in the United States of America by Oxford University Press
198 Madison Avenue, New York, NY 10016, United States of America

British Library Cataloguing in Publication Data
Data available

Library of Congress Control Number: 2024931031

ISBN 978–0–19–878689–4

DOI: 10.1093/oso/9780198786894.001.0001

Printed and bound by
CPI Group (UK) Ltd, Croydon, CR0 4YY

Links to third party websites are provided by Oxford in good faith and
for information only. Oxford disclaims any responsibility for the materials
contained in any third party website referenced in this work.

The manufacturer's authorised representative in the EU for product
safety is Oxford University Press España S.A. of el Parque Empresarial San
Fernando de Henares, Avenida de Castilla, 2 – 28830 Madrid
(www.oup.es/en).

Per Mara e Matt

'Madame, non-intervention est un mot diplomatique et énigmatique,
qui signifie à peu près la même chose qu'intervention.'
Charles-Maurice de Talleyrand-Périgord, Prince of Talleyrand[1]

---

[1] Quoted in M Ellery C Stowell, 'La théorie et la pratique de l'intervention' (1932) 40 Recueil des Cours 87, 91–2.

Acknowledgements

I started to study the principle of non-intervention many years ago when I was writing my law degree dissertation at the University of Perugia under the supervision of Professor Giorgio Badiali. It is on that occasion that I first realized the many ramifications and challenges posed by this principle and its fascinating interactions with some of the most fundamental notions of international law, such as sovereignty, the use of force, and self-determination. Throughout the years, I have stumbled over the principle again and again, most recently in my research on the application of international law in cyberspace. After wrestling with it for over twenty years, therefore, I decided that it was time to collect my thoughts and systematize them in a coherent work. This is how the present book was conceived. My hope is that it will contribute to a better understanding of this cardinal principle, which sits at the border between law and politics.

The research to write this book took almost ten years. In 2017–19, Marco Longobardo provided excellent research assistance: I am grateful not only to him but also to the Fritz Thyssen Foundation, which awarded me a three-year grant to hire him. In subsequent phases of the project, I benefitted from the editorial assistance of Angeliki Papantoniou and Jean Paul Moinet. The Geneva Academy of International Humanitarian Law and Human Rights generously provided financial support for the final revision of the manuscript, skilfully carried out by Munizha Ahmad-Cooke, and the University of Westminster bore the cost of the use of the cover image. Nehal Bhuta, Russell Buchan, Marco Longobardo, and Nicholas Tsagourias kindly read previous versions of the manuscript in whole or in part and provided precious comments. Any remaining errors or omissions are of course my sole responsibility. Last but not least, Merel Alstein, Robert Cavooris, Jordan Burke, and Paulina dos Santos Major at Oxford University Press have been supportive and very patient editors throughout different phases of the preparation of the book.

Section 7.5 of Chapter I and its subsections and parts of Section 2 of Chapter IV largely reproduce an article on intervention in the XIXth century that I published in the Israel Yearbook on Human Rights in 2020.[1] Chapter V also develops some ideas that I first presented in my sections of the article 'The Intersections Between the Arms Trade Treaty and the International Law of Foreign Intervention in Situations of Internal Unrest', published in the Israel Yearbook on Human Rights in 2022.[2] I am grateful to the Yearbook's editor, Professor Yoram Dinstein, for the permission to use these articles in the present book.

Marco Roscini
30 June 2023

---

[1] Marco Roscini, 'Intervention in XIXth Century International Law and the Distinction between Rebellions, Insurrections, and Civil Wars' (2020) 50 Israel YBHR 269.

[2] Marco Roscini and Riccardo Labianco, 'The Intersections Between the Arms Trade Treaty and the International Law of Foreign Intervention in Situations of Internal Unrest' (2022) 52 Israel YBHR 365.

Contents

Table of Cases	xv
Select Table of Treaties and Other Instruments	xix
List of Abbreviations	xxxi

Introduction		1
I.	The Development of the Principle of Non-Intervention from the End of the Religious Wars in Europe to the Outbreak of the Second World War	9
1.	Introduction	9
2.	The Emergence of the Idea of Non-Intervention during the 17th and 18th Centuries	10
3.	Classical Scholarship of the 18th Century	17
4.	The Age of Revolutions	24
5.	Intervention in the 19th Century and the Distinction between War and Measures Short of War	28
6.	The Legality of Intervention and the Fundamental Right of States to Independence	35
7.	19th-Century State Practice and *Opinio Juris* Concerning Intervention	40
	7.1 The Holy Alliance: Intervention as a Means to Enforce the Collective Interest in the Peace and Tranquillity of Europe	41
	7.2 The British Position: Intervention as a Means to Protect Essential Interests of the Intervening State	46
	7.3 Intervention 'in the Interests of Humanity'	48
	7.4 The Italian *Risorgimento* and the Principle of Nationalities as a Legal Basis for Intervention	51
	7.5 The Emergence of the Distinction between Rebellions, Insurrections, and Civil Wars in the Second Half of the 19th Century	54
	7.5.1 Rebellions and insurrections	55
	7.5.2 Civil wars resulting in *de facto* secession	57
	7.5.3 Civil wars where belligerency was recognized	59
	7.5.4 Civil wars where recognition of belligerency did not occur	67
	7.5.5 Recognition of insurgency and third-state intervention	69
8.	The Period between the Two World Wars and the Trend towards Negative Equality (1919–39)	70
	8.1 The Spanish Civil War	75
9.	Intervention and Non-Intervention in the Americas	78
	9.1 US Interventionism in Latin America (1823–1933)	78
	9.2 The Reaction to US Interventionism in the Americas: The Non-Intervention and Negative Equality Treaties	84

X CONTENTS

10. The Scholarly Debate on Intervention in the Period between
1815 and 1939   87
11. Conclusions   96

II. The Principle of Non-Intervention in the Framework of the Sources of
Contemporary International Law and in the Current Scholarly Debate   98
1. Introduction   98
2. The Principle of Non-Intervention and Treaty Law   100
   2.1 The Charter of the United Nations   100
   2.2 Regional Treaties   102
      2.2.1 American treaties   102
      2.2.2 African treaties   105
      2.2.3 Asian treaties   107
      2.2.4 European treaties and other documents   108
   2.3 Other Treaties   110
3. The Principle of Non-Intervention and Customary
International Law   112
4. Non-Intervention as a 'Principle' from which Rights and Duties of
States Arise   121
5. Does the Principle of Non-Intervention Create an *Erga Omnes*
Obligation?   122
6. The Principle of Non-Intervention as a *Jus Cogens* Norm?   125
7. Post-1945 Scholarship on Intervention   127
   7.1 The Scholarly Debate on Intervention and International Order   128
      7.1.1 Realist versus liberal approaches   128
      7.1.2 The TWAIL approach to intervention   132
      7.1.3 The feminist approach   133
   7.2 The Scholarly Debate on Intervention by Invitation   134
      7.2.1 The traditional doctrine that conceives the principle of
non-intervention only as a prohibition on supporting
foreign insurgents   134
      7.2.2 The negative equality doctrine   135
      7.2.3 The positive equality doctrine   137
      7.2.4 The consent of all factions doctrine   138
      7.2.5 The purpose-based doctrine   138
      7.2.6 The policy-oriented school   139
      7.2.7 The TWAIL approach   142
8. Conclusions   143

III. The Content of the Principle of Non-Intervention   144
1. Introduction   144
2. Intervention: 'A Monochromatic Term for a Polychromatic Reality'   145
3. Coercion as 'the Very Essence' of Intervention   147
   3.1 Dictatorial Coercion   152
   3.2 Forcible Coercion   155
4. Intent to Coerce and Motive as Elements of the Prohibition of
Intervention   158

5.	The Object Protected by the Principle of Non-Intervention	161
6.	The First Pillar of the Principle of Non-Intervention: The Prohibition of Armed Coercion	169
7.	The Second Pillar of the Principle of Non-Intervention: The Prohibition of Economic and Political Coercion	170
	7.1 Economic Coercion	175
	7.2 Political Coercion	184
8.	The Third Pillar of the Principle of Non-Intervention: The Prohibition of Supporting Subversive, Terrorist, or Armed Activities and of Interfering in Civil Strife in Another State	186
	8.1 The Different Forms of Support for Subversive, Terrorist, or Armed Activities	189
9.	Conclusions	194

IV. The Application of the Principle of Non-Intervention to Civil Strife and the Role of Consent

		196
1.	Introduction	196
2.	Non-Intervention as a Principle Applying Only to Civil Strife which is a Domestic Affair of the Concerned State	196
3.	Non-Intervention as a Principle Prohibiting Only Coercive Interferences in Civil Strife	202
4.	Intervention with the Consent of the Incumbent Government	205
	4.1 Who is the *De Jure* Government of a State?	208
	4.1.1 Domestic legitimacy	208
	4.1.2 Effective control	211
	4.1.3 Recognition	218
	4.2 Form of Consent	219
	4.3 Ad Hoc and Open-Ended Consent	222
	4.4 Validity Requirements of Consent	226
	4.4.1 Error, fraud, and corruption	227
	4.4.2 Coercion	227
	4.4.3 Conflict with a peremptory norm of general international law	228
	4.4.4 Conflict with a provision of internal law regarding competence to grant consent	229
	4.5 Timing of Consent	231
	4.6 Limits to the Scope of Consent	232
	4.7 Withdrawal of Consent	233
	4.8 Consent and UN Security Council Resolutions	235
5.	Intervention with the Consent of Insurrectional Authorities	237
	5.1 Intervention with the Consent of Pro-Democracy Insurgents	240
6.	Conclusions	244

V. The Interaction between the Principle of Non-Intervention and that of Internal Self-Determination

		246
1.	Introduction	246
2.	The Principle of Internal Self-Determination	247

xii CONTENTS

3. Third-State Intervention in Civil Wars 250
   3.1 The Meaning of 'Civil War' in the Context of the Principle of Internal Self-Determination 252
   3.2 State Practice and *Opinio Juris* Concerning the Dispatch of Armed Forces in Support of an Incumbent Government Beset by Civil War 255
      3.2.1 Cases where third states declined to send armed forces in support of an incumbent government beset by civil war 255
      3.2.2 Cases where third states sent armed forces in support of an incumbent government beset by civil war 257
      3.2.3 Evaluation 272
   3.3 Third-State Intervention in a Civil War Other than by Dispatching Armed Forces 278
4. Third-State Intervention by Dispatching Armed Forces in Situations of Internal Unrest Short of Civil War 281
   4.1 Evaluation 292
5. Situations Where Third-State Dispatch of Armed Forces in a Civil War is Not in Conflict with the Principle of Internal Self-Determination 293
   5.1 Counter-Intervention 293
      5.1.1 Counter-intervention in support of an incumbent government 293
      5.1.2 Counter-intervention in support of insurgents 296
   5.2 Counterterrorism Intervention 298
6. Can the UN Security Council Set Aside the Principle of Internal Self-Determination and Intervene, or Authorize an Armed Intervention, in a Civil War? 301
7. Third-State Intervention in Civil Strife Involving Racist Regimes 303
8. Conclusions 305

VI. The Interaction between the Principle of Non-Intervention and that of External Self-Determination 309
1. Introduction 309
2. The Scope of the Principle of External Self-Determination 310
3. Third-State Intervention in Decolonization Conflicts 314
   3.1 Third-State Intervention in Support of a Colonial Power 315
   3.2 Third-State Intervention in Support of a National Liberation Movement 320
      3.2.1 Support by sending armed forces 320
      3.2.2 Other forms of support 325
4. Third-State Intervention in Situations of Alien Domination and Occupation 327
5. Third-State Intervention in Other Secessionist Situations of Internal Unrest 330
   5.1 Third-State Support for a Government against Secessionist Insurgents 330
   5.2 Third-State Support for Secessionist Insurgents 334
6. Conclusions 335

VII. The Interaction between the Principle of Non-Intervention and Respect for International Human Rights Law and International Humanitarian Law 337
1. Introduction 337
2. The Changing Character of Sovereignty 338
3. Human Rights and Domestic Jurisdiction 340
4. Intervention and the Protection of Community Interests 345
5. Third-State Assistance to a Government Responsible for Violations of IHRL and/or IHL 348
6. Third-State Assistance to a Government against an Armed Opposition Group Responsible for Violations of IHL during a Civil War 354
7. Third-State Intervention in Support of Insurgents Fighting against a Government Responsible for Violations of IHRL or IHL 356
   7.1 The Dispatch of Armed Forces 357
       7.1.1 Arguments in favour of the legality of sending armed forces 357
       7.1.2 Arguments against the legality of sending armed forces 361
   7.2 Intervention Other than by Sending Armed Forces 368
8. Intervention in Civil Wars with the Authorization of the UN Security Council in Response to IHRL/IHL Violations 370
9. Conclusions 372

VIII. The Principle of Non-Intervention in the Information Age: Cyber Operations as a New Means of Coercion in the Domestic Affairs of States 374
1. Introduction 374
2. The Different Types of Cyber Operations 376
3. The Application of the Principle of Non-Intervention in Cyberspace 377
4. Domestic Jurisdiction and Cyberspace 381
5. Coercion of State in Cyberspace 382
   5.1 Cyber Operations Causing or Designed to Cause Material Damage to Persons and/or Physical Objects 385
   5.2 Cyber Operations Causing or Designed to Cause Loss of Functionality of Infrastructure 387
   5.3 Cyber Operations Exclusively Involving Unauthorized Extraterritorial Access to Non-Publicly Available Data 390
   5.4 Cyber Influence Operations 396
6. Third-State Cyber Operations in Support of a Government or of Subversive, Terrorist, or Armed Opposition Groups during Civil Strife 400
7. Conclusions 403

xiv CONTENTS

General Conclusions	404
1. History	404
2. Theory	407
3. Interactions	409
4. Epilogue	413
Select Bibliography	415
Index	447

Table of Cases

A. INTERNATIONAL COURTS AND TRIBUNALS

1. European Court of Justice

A Åhlström Osakeyhtiö and others v Commission of the European Communities 119–20
Council of the European Union v Front populaire pour la libération de la saguia-el-hamra et du rio de oro (Front Polisario) 298n.377
Liberation Tigers of Tamil Eelam (LTTE) v Council of the European Union 119n.138, 121–2

2. Inter-American Court of Human Rights

Juan Carlos Abella v Argentina 254n.44

3. International Court of Justice

Accordance with International Law of the Unilateral Declaration of Independence in Respect of Kosovo 310n.6, 331n.145, 356n.121, 357
Allegations of Genocide under the Convention on the Prevention and Punishment of the Crime of Genocide (Ukraine v Russian Federation) 347n.71–8, 359n.147, 359n.148, 365–6
Alleged Violations of the 1955 Treaty of Amity, Economic Relations, and Consular Rights (Islamic Republic of Iran v USA) 101n.13, 160n.108, 179–80
Appeal Relating to the Jurisdiction of the ICAO Council under Article 84 of the Convention on International Civil Aviation (Bahrain, Egypt, Saudi Arabia and United Arab Emirates v Qatar) 115–16n.112, 179–80
Application of the Convention on the Prevention and Punishment of the Crime of Genocide (Bosnia and Herzegovina v Serbia and Montenegro) 115–16n.112, 119n.136, 347–8n.71, 349n.81
Application of the International Convention on the Elimination of All Forms of Racial Discrimination (Azerbaijan v Armenia) 400n.239
Application of the International Convention on the Elimination of All Forms of Racial Discrimination (Qatar v United Arab Emirates) 160n.107, 179–80
Application of the International Convention for the Suppression of the Financing of Terrorism and of the International Convention on the Elimination of All Forms of Racial Discrimination (Ukraine v Russian Federation) 115–16n.112
Armed Activities on the Territory of the Congo (Democratic Republic of the Congo v Uganda).................. 115–16n.112, 118–19, 125n.176, 169, 187, 187n.297, 191–2, 221, 232–3, 234, 238n.317, 274–5, 277, 323, 341–2, 362–4, 378–9
Armed Activities on the Territory of the Congo (New Application: 2002) (Democratic Republic of the Congo v Rwanda) 206–7n.68, 341n.30
Asylum Case (Colombia/Peru).......................................78n.492, 104, 156
Barcelona Traction, Light and Power Company, Limited (Belgium v Spain) 122–3, 313n.25, 343n.38
Case Concerning Aerial Herbicide Spraying (Ecuador v Colombia)......115–16n.112, 166n.140
Case Concerning the Application of Article 11(1) of the Interim Accord of 13 September 1995 (The Former Yugoslav Republic of Macedonia v Greece)....... 119n.136
Case Concerning the Land and Maritime Boundary between Cameroon and Nigeria (Cameroon v Nigeria: Equatorial Guinea intervening) 115–16n.112, 119n.136, 206–7n.68, 210, 230

xvi TABLE OF CASES

*Case Concerning Military and Paramilitary Activities in and against Nicaragua
(Nicaragua v USA)* 2n.6, 4n.14, 5–6, 7, 101, 102, 109, 115–16n.112, 116–19, 120,
123–4, 125–6, 134–5, 146, 147, 148, 155n.72, 156, 158, 159, 161–2, 162n.121,
165–6, 168–9, 171–2, 174, 177n.225, 182, 186–7, 189–90, 192, 197–8,
222n.190, 237–9, 237–8n.311, 241–2, 243, 246, 247, 249–50, 257, 277,
278, 294–5, 296n.367, 312–13, 320n.77, 325–6, 338n.2, 340–1, 343,
351n.91, 364–6, 368–9, 378–9, 380, 385, 387, 391, 400, 401
*Certain Activities Carried Out by Nicaragua in the Border Area
(Costa Rica v Nicaragua)* 159–60, 384, 388n.130, 393n.182
Certain Questions Concerning Diplomatic Relations (Honduras v Brazil) 100n.6,
111–12, 119n.136
Corfu Channel (United Kingdom of Great Britain and Northern Ireland v Albania) 118–19,
126n.186, 146, 158–9
Delimitation of the Maritime Border in the Gulf of Maine Area (Canada/USA). 121n.151
Dispute Regarding Navigational and Related Rights (Costa Rica v Nicaragua) 375
East Timor (Portugal v Australia) 298n.377, 313n.25
Fisheries Jurisdiction (United Kingdom v Iceland) 148
Immunities and Criminal Proceedings (Equatorial Guinea v France) 119n.136, 156–8
*Legal Consequences of the Construction of a Wall in the Occupied Palestinian
Territory* 185n.285, 298n.377, 313n.25, 319n.70, 328–9, 343n.38, 365–6
*Legal Consequences of the Separation of the Chagos Archipelago from Mauritius
in 1965* 100, 152, 248, 298n.377, 313n.25
*Legal Consequences for States of the Continued Presence of South Africa in
Namibia (South West Africa) notwithstanding Security Council
Resolution 276 (1970)*. 65n.400, 199, 304–5, 317n.54, 324–5, 328–9
Legality of the Threat or Use of Nuclear Weapons. 116–18, 183n.272, 386
Legality of Use of Force (Yugoslavia v Belgium) 341n.30, 360, 364n.182
Legality of the Use of Force (Yugoslavia v France). 365–6
Legality of Use of Force (Yugoslavia v Netherlands) .227–8, 360, 364n.182
Legality of Use of Force (Yugoslavia v Spain). 227–8
Legality of Use of Force (Yugoslavia v USA) 119n.136
*North Sea Continental Shelf Cases (Federal Republic of Germany v
Denmark/The Netherlands)*. 4n.14, 6, 112n.88, 178–9, 237–9, 257, 393–4, 399–400
Questions Related to the Obligation to Prosecute or Extradite (Belgium v Senegal) 343n.38
*Sovereignty over Pedra Branca/Pulau Batu Puteh, Middle Rocks and
South Ledge (Malaysia/ Singapore)*. 5–6
United States Diplomatic and Consular Staff in Tehran (USA v Iran) 148
Western Sahara 168–9, 249–50, 314n.33

4. International Criminal Tribunal for the former Yugoslavia

Prosecutor v Duško Tadić 56n.332, 254n.47, 338
Prosecutor v Limaj et al. 253n.41

5. Permanent Court of Arbitration

Affaire de l'indemnité russe (Russie, Turquie). 35n.191
Chagos Marine Protected Area Arbitration (Mauritius v United Kingdom) 312n.24
Island of Palmas Case (Netherlands, United States). 36n.199, 161n.115, 247, 392–3

6. Permanent Court of International Justice

The Case of the S.S. 'Lotus' (France v Turkey) 5, 155–6, 220n.176, 255–6, 392–3
Case of the S.S. 'Wimbledon' (United Kingdom, France, Italy and Japan v Germany) 203n.46
Customs Regime between Germany and Austria 12n.16
Nationality Decrees Issued in Tunis and Morocco 162–3

TABLE OF CASES xvii

7. Special Tribunal for Lebanon

Interlocutory Decision on the Applicable Law: Terrorism, Conspiracy, Homicide, Perpetration, Cumulative Charging 300

8. Other Arbitral Tribunals

Aguilar-Amory and Royal Bank of Canada Claims (Great Britain v Costa Rica) 45–6, 45n.262, 219n.167
Case of Charles J Jansen v Mexico 45–6
Case of Melville E. Day and David E. Garrison, as surviving executors of Cornelius K. Garrison v Venezuela 46n.266
Cuculla v Mexico 45–6
Dubai-Sharjah Border Arbitration 148n.22
French Claims against Peru (France v Peru) 46n.266
Responsabilité de l'Allemagne à raison des dommages causés dans les colonies portugaises du sud de l'Afrique (sentence sur le principe de la responsabilité) (Portugal contre Allemagne) 34
Sambiaggio Case (Italy v Venezuela) 64–5
The United States of America on Behalf of George W Hopkins, Claimant, v The United Mexican States 46n.266

B. NATIONAL COURTS AND TRIBUNALS

1. Canada

Hape v Her Majesty the Queen, Supreme Court 101n.13, 155–6, 161n.114
Re Secession of Québec, Supreme Court 248n.14, 310n.6, 327–8n.126, 330–1

2. Federal Republic of Germany

Spanish Civil War Pension Entitlement Case, Federal Social Court 76n.475

3. Latvia

Judgment on behalf of the Republic of Latvia on Case No 2007-10-0102, Constitutional Court 109n.64, 119–20, 154, 165–6, 174, 205n.60

4. Norway

Tidal Music AS v The Public Prosecution Authority, Supreme Court 384, 395

5. United Kingdom

Buck v Attorney General, England and Wales Court of Appeal 119–20
Deutsche Bank AG London Branch v Receivers Appointed By the Court & Ors, England and Wales High Court 184–5
The 'Maduro Board' of the Central Bank of Venezuela v The 'Guaidó Board' of the Central Bank of Venezuela, England and Wales Court of Appeal 184–5
'Maduro Board' of the Central Bank of Venezuela (Respondent/Cross-Appellant) v 'Guaidó Board' of the Central Bank of Venezuela (Appellant/Cross-Respondent), Supreme Court 185n.283
R (on the application of Smith) (FC) (Respondent) v Secretary of State for Defence (Appellant) and another, Supreme Court 231–2
R v Zardad (Faryadi), England and Wales High Court 254n.45
Republic of Somalia v Woodhouse Drake & Carey (Suisse) S.A. and Others (The "Mary"), England and Wales High Court 208n.77, 212–13

xviii   TABLE OF CASES

Sierra Leone Telecommunications Co Ltd v Barclays Bank plc, England and
  Wales High Court. 212–13

6. United States

The Ambrose Light (United States v The Ambrose Light etc),
  New York District Court 56n.332, 59–61, 62–3, 64–5, 66n.404
Banco Nacional de Cuba v Sabbatino, Court of Appeals 181
The Divina Pastora, Supreme Court. 57n.342
Ford v Surget, Supreme Court 65, 66
Prize Cases, Supreme Court. 57–8, 60–1, 60n.364, 63–4
The Santissima Trinidad, Supreme Court 58–9
The Scotia, Supreme Court. 29n.144
The Three Friends, Supreme Court 59–60, 65, 68n.414, 69, 79
United States v Palmer, Supreme Court 58–9
Williams v Bruffy, Supreme Court 58n.347, 60–1

Select Table of Treaties and Other Instruments

A. TREATIES

Additional Protocol Relative to Nonintervention (Buenos Aires, 23 December 1936) 243
Art 1(1) 84–5, 103, 162n.118
Art 1(2) 84–5

African Charter on Human and Peoples' Rights (Banjul, 27 June 1981)
Art 20(1) 248n.17, 249n.19
Art 20(3) 320–1n.78
Art 21 . . . . .106n.41

African Union Non-Aggression and Common Defence Pact (Abuja, 31 January 2005)
Art 1 (c)(ix) 393n.185
Art 1(k) 339–40
Art 5(b) 105–6, 188

Agreement between Angola, Cuba, and South Africa on Principles for a Peaceful Settlement in Southwestern Africa (Geneva, 5 August 1988)
Principle E 110

Agreement between the Government of Australia and the Government of Solomon Islands Concerning the Basis for Deployment of Police, Armed Forces, and other Personnel to Solomon Islands (Canberra, 14 August 2017) 288

Agreement between NATO and Yugoslavia to establish a NATO air verification regime in Kosovo (Belgrade, 15 October 1998) 227–8

Agreement between the Republic of India and the People's Republic of China on Trade and Intercourse between Tibet Region of China and India (Beijing, 29 April, 1954)
Preamble 110, 113–14

Agreement between the Russian Federation and Ukraine on the Status and Conditions of the Russian Federation Black Sea Fleet's Stay on Ukrainian Territory (Kharkiv, 21 April, 2010)
Art 6 110

Agreement between the United Kingdom and Brunei on Defence and External Affairs (Brunei, 29 September 1959) 285n.284
Art 3(5)(a) 222–4

Agreement concerning Aid to Greece (Athens, 20 June 1947)
Art 10(1) 233
Art 10(2) .235n.296

Agreement concerning Aid to Turkey (Ankara, 12 July 1947)
Art VI(2) .235n.296

Agreement concerning the Settlement of Mutual Financial and Property Claims arising before 1939 (London, 15 July, 1986) 74n.463

Agreement on Ending the War and Restoring Peace in Viet Nam (Paris Peace Accords) (Paris, 27 January 1973)
Art 4 110
Arts 20(c) and (d) 110
Art 22 110

Agreement Establishing the Inter-Governmental Authority on Development (Nairobi, 21 March 1996)
Art 6A(b) 106–7

Agreement for Lasting Peace through a Permanent Cessation of Hostilities between the Government of the Federal Democratic Republic of Ethiopia and the Tigray People's Liberation Front (Pretoria, 2 November 2022) 271

Agreement on Political Principles (3 June 1999) 227–8

Agreement respecting Internal Revolutions and Neutrality between Bolivia, Colombia, Ecuador, Peru and Venezuela (Caracas, 18 July 1911) 85–6

American Treaty on Pacific Settlement
(Pact of Bogotá) (Bogotá,
30 April 1948)
Art I 102
Anti-War Treaty of Non-aggression and
Conciliation (Saavedra-Lamas Pact)
(Rio de Janeiro, 10 October 1933)
Art III.................... 30–1, 72, 85
Arab Charter on Human Rights
(Tunis, 22 May 2004)
Art 2(1) 248n.17
Art 2(3) 312
Art 2(4) 327–8n.126
Arms Trade Treaty (New York,
2 April 2013)
Art 6....................... 190, 350
Art 7 350
Bangui Agreements/Accords
(Bangui, 25 January 1997)......... 287
Basic Treaty of Friendship and
Cooperation between Australia
and Japan (Tokyo, 16 June 1976)
Art II........................... 110
Bilateral Agreement between the
Republic of Afghanistan and the
Islamic Republic of Pakistan on
the Principles of Mutual Relations,
in particular on Non-Interference
and Non-Intervention (Geneva,
14 April 1988)
Arts I–II........................ 110
Ceasefire Agreement (Lusaka Agreement)
(Lusaka, 10 July 1999) 221
Central American Treaty of Peace,
Friendship and Trade (1887)
Art 3............................ 85
Charter of the Association of Southeast
Asian Nations (Singapore,
20 November 2007)
Art 2(2)(e)..................... 107–8
Art 2(2)(f) 107–8
Charter of the Collective Security Treaty
Organization (Chisinau,
7 October 2002)
Art 5 107–8
Charter of the Commonwealth of
Independent States (Minsk,
22 January 1993)
Art 3 107–8
Charter of the Conseil de l'Entente
(Cotonou, 5 December 2011)
Art 3 106–7

Charter of the Council for Mutual
Economic Assistance (Sofia,
14 December 1959)
Art 1(2) 108–9
Charter of the Organisation of African
Unity (Addis Ababa, 25 May 1963)
Art II(1)(d) 312
Arts III(2) and III(3) 105–6
Art III(5) 188
Charter of the Organisation of Islamic
Cooperation (Dakar, revised
14 March 2008)
Art 1(3) 312
Art 2(4) 107–8
Art 2(5) 107–8
Art 2(6) 107–8
Art 8........................... 312
Charter of the Organization of
American States (Bogotá, 30 April
1948) 4, 102–6, 145–6, 160–1,
171–2, 174–5, 182–3, 188–9, 190,
196n.2, 240–1, 242–3, 281, 378–9, 381
Art 2 105
Art 2(b) 243
Art 3 ....105, 247n.9
Art 3(e)................... 247, 399–400
Art 19 .... 102–3, 104, 122, 124, 145,
154–6, 161–2, 171–3, 179n.236,
181, 188–9, 191–2, 243,
258–9, 362n.170, 378–9
Art 20 .... 103–5, 145, 158–9, 160–1,
171–3, 175, 179n.236, 181
Art 21 ....179n.236, 186n.288
Art 23 .... 103, 104–5
Charter of the Shanghai Cooperation
Organisation (St Petersburg,
7 June 2002)
Art 2........................... 107–8
Charter of the United Nations (San
Francisco, 26 June 1945) 1–2, 10,
72, 100–1, 103, 108–9, 137, 147–8,
171–2, 178–9, 200, 201n.39, 207–8,
224n.211, 231–2, 235–6, 240–1, 244,
244n.360, 258, 262–3, 286, 291–2, 298,
300–1, 302–3, 304–5, 312, 320, 322–3,
325–6, 327, 331, 337, 357–8, 364–5
Art 1(2) 101, 302–3, 310–12
Art 1(3) 341–2
Art 2(1) 101
Art 2(4) 5, 101, 153, 161–2,
169–70, 189–90, 197–8, 200,
296, 314, 320–1, 322–4, 329,

SELECT TABLE OF TREATIES AND OTHER INSTRUMENTS   xxi

357–8, 365–6, 368–9, 373,
386–7, 388–9–, 401, 412
Art 2(5) 235–6
Art 2(7) 1n.2, 100–1,
107n.50, 235–6, 370
Art 25...................... 219, 235–6
Art 39......................... 165–6
Art 41........................... 318
Art 42........................... 386
Art 51 .... 169–70, 200, 213–15, 236,
260–1, 262–3, 267n.153, 270–1, 284,
287–8, 294–5, 324–5, 329, 386, 387
Art 52........................... 102
Art 53..................... 276–7, 366–7
Art 55.................... 310–12, 340–1
Art 56.................... 340–1
Art 78.......................... 101
Art 103............. 235–6, 318–19, 349
Ch VI........................... 301
Ch VII 100–1, 161, 164, 165–6, 200,
213–14, 217–18, 225, 235–6,
244–5, 301, 317n.55, 364–5,
370, 373, 387, 408–9, 412
Collective Security Treaty (Tashkent, 15
May 1992) 291–2
Constitutive Act of the African Union
(Lomé, 11 July 2000)
Art 4(g) 105–6
Art 4(h) 105–6, 225–6, 366–7
Art 4(j).................. 105–6, 276–7
Art 4(o) 105–6, 188
Convenio para que el Gobierno de
Bolivia preste auxilios militares al
del Perú (Arequipa, 24 June 1835)
Art 1 56–7
Convention between the United States
of America and the Dominican
Republic providing for the
assistance of the United States
in the collection and application
of the customs revenues of the
Dominican Republic, The Enabling
Act, and other correspondence
relative to the interpretation and
enforcement of the treaty (Santo
Domingo, 8 February 1907) 83
Convention (XIII) Concerning the
Rights and Duties of Neutral
Powers in Naval War (The Hague,
18 October 1907) 308n.a
Convention on Cybercrime (Budapest,
23 November 2001) 375n.5
Art 32........................ 395–6

Art 32(b) 395–6
Ch II, Section 1, Title 1............. 377
Convention for the Definition of
Aggression (London, 3 July 1933) 72
Art II........................... 72
Art III.......................... 72
Convention on the Duties and Rights
of States in the Event of Civil Strife
(Havana Convention) (Havana,
20 February 1928).............196–7,
243, 300n.388, 308n.b
Art 1 191–2
Art 1(3) 56n.336, 85–6, 190, 196–7
Art 1(4) 191–2
Art 3 .... 57, 85n.536, 191–2
Convention for the Pacification of the
Levant (London, 15 July 1840)
Preamble 42–3, 49–50
Art 4........................... 42–3
Convention on the Prevention and
Punishment of the Crime of
Genocide (Paris, 9 December 1948)
Art I 349–50, 351
Convention (III) Relative to the
Opening of Hostilities (The Hague
18 October 1907)
Art 1............................ 33
Convention (II) Respecting the
Limitation of the Employment of
Force for the Recovery of Contract
Debts (Drago-Porter Convention)
(The Hague, 18 October 1907)
Art 1 .... 70–1n.439
Convention (V) Respecting the Rights
and Duties of Neutral Powers and
Persons in Case of War on Land
(The Hague, 18 October 1907)..... 308n.a
Convention on the Rights and Duties
of States (Montevideo,
26 December 1933) 161–2
Art 1 ....200n.32
Art 8 .... 84–5, 103n.21, 162n.118
Art 11 .... 30–1, 184, 186n.288
Conventions on the Protection
of Victims of War (Geneva
Conventions) (Geneva,
12 August 1949) 199, 326n.120
Common Art 1.... 343–4, 349–50, 351, 365–6
Common Art 2 .... 211, 233
Common Art 3 343
Covenant of the League of Nations
(Paris, 28 April 1919) 70–1, 100–1
Art 11(1) 75

xxii SELECT TABLE OF TREATIES AND OTHER INSTRUMENTS

Art 11(2) 75n.467
Arts 12–15 70–1
Art 21 81
Defence Agreement between France
  and Cameroon (1960) 282
Defence Agreement between France,
  Central African Republic,
  Congo and Chad (Brazzaville,
  15 August 1960) 260
Defence Agreement between France
  and Gabon (Libreville,
  17 August 1960) 222–3, 285
  Preamble 223–4
  Art 3 223–4
Defence Agreement between France
  and Madagascar (Antananarivo,
  27 June 1960). 222–3
Defence Agreement between France
  and Mali (1960) 222–3
Defence Agreement between France
  and Togo (Paris, 10 July 1963). 286
Economic Agreement of Bogotá
  (Bogotá, 2 May 1948) 163–4n.128
  Art 8 . . . . .104n.31
General Agreement on Tariffs and Trade
  (Geneva, 30 October 1947) 164
General Agreement on Technical
  Military Co-operation (Kinshasa,
  22 May 1974). 223n.193
General Treaty of Peace and
  Amity (Washington, DC,
  7 February, 1923) 405
  Art II. 86
  Art IV. 85–6
  Art XIV 86n.538
General Treaty of Peace and Amity and
  Additional Convention between
  Costa Rica, Guatemala, Honduras,
  Nicaragua and El Salvador
  (Washington, DC,
  20 December 1907) 86, 97, 405
  Art I (Additional Convention) 86
  Art II (Additional Convention) 85–6
General Treaty for the Re-Establishment
  of Peace between Austria, France,
  Great Britain, Prussia, Sardinia,
  and Turkey, and Russia (Paris,
  30 March 1856) 44n.255
General Treaty for the Renunciation of
  War as an Instrument of National
  Policy (Pact of Paris/Kellogg–
  Briand Pact) (Paris,
  27 August 1928)
  Arts I and II. 71–2

Geneva Agreements (Geneva,
  20–21 July 1954) 201–2, 259–60
Hay-Bunau-Varilla Treaty (Washington,
  DC, 18 November 1903)
  Art I 83n.523
  Art XXIII. 83
Holbrooke–Milošević Agreement
  (Belgrade,16 October 1998) 227–8
Holy Alliance Treaty (Paris,
  18/26 September 1815) 41n.235, 167–8
Indo–Sri Lanka Accord (Colombo,
  29 July 1987) 332–3
  Art 2.16(c) 223–4
Inter-American Treaty of Reciprocal
  Assistance (Rio Treaty) (Rio de Janeiro,
  2 September 1947) 102, 243n.354
  Art 12 102
Interim Accord Between the Hellenic
  Republic and the Former Yugoslav
  Republic of Macedonia, (New York,
  13 September 1995)
  Art 6(2) 110
Interim Agreement for Peace and
  Self-Government in Kosovo
  (Rambouillet Accords)
  (18 March 1999) 227–8
International Convention on the
  Elimination of All Forms of Racial
  Discrimination (New York,
  29 December 1965) 304–5
International Convention on the
  Suppression and Punishment of
  the Crime of Apartheid (New York,
  30 November 1973) 304–5
International Covenant on Civil and
  Political Rights (New York,
  16 December 1966)
  Art 1 249
  Art 1(1) 248n.17
  Art 1(3) 310–12
International Covenant on Economic,
  Social and Cultural Rights (New
  York, 16 December 1966)
  Art 1 249
  Art 1(1) 248n.17
  Art 1(3) 310–12
Memorandum on Security Assurances
  in Connection with Ukraine's
  Accession to the Treaty on the
  Non-Proliferation of Nuclear
  Weapons (Budapest, 5 December
  1994) 178–9
Memorandum of Understanding
  Between the Government of

the Republic of Turkey and the Government of National Accord-State of Libya on Delimitation of the Maritime Jurisdiction Areas in the Mediterranean (Istanbul, 27 November 2019) 280–1

Memorandum of Understanding Between the Government of the Republic of Turkey and the Government of National Accord-State of Libya on Security and Military Cooperation (Istanbul, 27 November 2019)
Art IV 222–3

Military Cooperation Agreement between Russia and Central African Republic (Moscow, 21 August 2018) 289

Military Technical Agreement between the International Security Force ("KFOR") and the Governments of the Federal Republic of Yugoslavia and the Republic of Serbia (Kumanovo Agreement) (Kumanovo, 9 June 1999) 227–8

Mutual Assistance Pact between Member States of the Economic Community of Central African States (Malabo, 24 February 2000)
Art 8(2) 225–6, 366–7
Art 9 . . . . 206, 220n.170

Mutual Defence Agreement between Gambia and Senegal (1965) 285–6

Nyon Agreement (Nyon, 14 September 1937) 77

Pacte de Famille (Paris, 15 August 1761) 15–16

Pact of Mutual Cooperation Between the Kingdom of Iraq, the Republic of Turkey, the United Kingdom, the Dominion of Pakistan, and the Kingdom of Iran (Baghdad Pact) (Baghdad, 24 February 1955)
Art 3 110

Pact of Mutual Defence between Sierra Leone and Guinea (1971) 285
Art 2 222–3

Pact of the League of Arab States (Cairo, 22 March 1945)
Art 8 . . . . 107–8, 188

Panama Canal Treaty (Washington, DC, 7 September 1977) 213–14, 241–2
Art IV 225n.214
Art V 110
Art 4 . . . . .60n.364

Peace Treaty of Versailles (Paris, 28 June 1919). 67n.409

Protocol to the 1928 Havana Convention on Duties and Rights of States in the Event of Civil Strife (Washington, DC, 1 May 1957). 105, 196–7, 306
Art 1 190
Art 2 . . . . 190, 196–7, 199
Art 5 . . . . 190, 191–3

Protocol Additional to the Geneva Conventions of 12 August 1949, and relating to the Protection of Victims of International Armed Conflicts (Protocol I) (Geneva, 8 June 1977). 310n.5, 320, 327–8, 327–8n.126
Art 1(1) 365–6
Art 89 365–6

Protocol Additional to the Geneva Conventions of 12 August 1949, and relating to the Protection of Victims of Non-International Armed Conflicts (Protocol II) (Geneva, 8 June 1977) 293, 343
Art 2(1) 252n.38
Art 3 . . . . 110–11, 197–8
Art 3(2) 162n.118, 365–6

Protocol of Aix-la-Chapelle (Aix-la-Chapelle, 9 October 1818) 41n.234
Art 4 42–3

Protocol of Amendment to the Inter-American Treaty of Reciprocal Assistance (San José, Costa Rica, 26 July 1975) 102

Protocol of Amendments to the Charter of the Organization of American States (Protocol of Cartagena de Indias) (Cartagena de Indias, 12 May 1985). 105

Protocol on Non-Aggression and Mutual Defence in the Great Lakes Region (Nairobi, 30 November 2006)
Art 1(3)(i) .393n.185
Art 2(1) 188
Art 2(6) 188
Art 3(3) 188
Art 3(4) 188
Art 4 106–7
Art 4(2) 162–3
Art 4(4) 188
Art 4(8) 345n.52, 367n.207
Art 8(2) 188

SELECT TABLE OF TREATIES AND OTHER INSTRUMENTS

Art 8(4) 188
Art 10(3) 367n.207
Protocol on Prohibitions or Restrictions
on the Use of Mines, Booby-Traps
and Other Devices as amended
on 3 May 1996 (Protocol II, as
amended on 3 May 1996) annexed
to the Convention on Prohibitions
or Restrictions on the Use of
Certain Conventional Weapons
Which May be Deemed to be
Excessively Injurious or to have
Indiscriminate Effects (Geneva,
3 May 1996)
Art I(5).................. 111, 162n.118
Protocol Relating to the Council for
Peace and Security of Central
Africa (Libreville,
18 December 2019)
Art 3 ....106–7, 225–6, 366–7
Protocol Relating to the Council for
Peace and Security of Central
Africa (COPAX) (Malabo,
24 February 2000)
Art 25 276–7
Protocol Relating to the Establishment
of the Peace and Security Council
of the African Union (Durban,
9 July 2002)
Art 4 (f), (j) and (k)............... 105–6
Art 13(3)(c)..................... 105–6
Art 25 ......107n.47, 225–6, 276–7, 366–7
Protocol Relating to Mutual Assistance
in Defence (Freetown, 29 May 1981)
Art 4(b) 276–7
Art 18......................... 276–7
Protocols of the Conferences between
Austria, France, Great Britain,
Prussia, Russia, and Turkey
Relative to the Pacification of Syria
(Paris, 3 August 1860) 49–50
Quadruple Alliance Treaty (Paris,
20 November 1815) 41n.234
Revised Treaty of the Economic
Community of West African States
(ECOWAS) (Cotonou, 24 July 1993)
Art 4......................... 106–7
Revised Treaty Instituting the
Economic Community of the
Central African States (Libreville,
18 December 2019)
Art 3......................... 106–7
Second Protocol to The Hague
Convention of 1954 for the

Protection of Cultural Property in
the Event of Armed Conflict (The
Hague, 26 March, 1999)
Art 22(5) 111, 162n.118
Security Agreement between the
People's Republic of China and the
Solomon Islands (April 2022).... 222–3
Security and Defense Cooperation
Agreement Between the United
States of America and the Islamic
Republic of Afghanistan (Kabul,
30 September 2014) 264–5
Preamble and Art 2(1) 264–5
Art 1 .... 223–4, 223n.194
Sino-British Joint Declaration on the
Question of Hong Kong (Beijing,
19 December 1984) 179–80
Southern African Development
Community Mutual Defence Pact
(Dar es Salaam, 26 August 2003)
Art 7(1) 106–7
Southern African Development
Community Protocol on Politics,
Defence and Security Co-operation
(Blantyre, 14 August 2001)........276–7
Art 11(2)(b)(i).............225–6, 366–7
Soviet–Iranian Treaty (1941)......224n.211
Status of Forces Agreement between
the Government of the Republic
of Uganda and the Government of
the Republic of South Sudan
(10 January 2014) 269
Status of Forces Agreement between
the Republic of Iraq and the
United States (Baghdad,
17 November 2008) 266–7
Art 27......................... 222–4
Status of Forces Agreement between
Sierra Leone and Nigeria........ 287–8
Statute of the International Court of
Justice (San Francisco, 26 June 1945)
Art 36(2) 255
Art 38(1) 4, 5–6
Statute of the International Criminal
Court (Rome Statute) (Rome,
17 July 1998)
Art 8(3) 111
Statute of the Permanent Court of
International Justice (Geneva,
13 December 1920)
Art 38......................... 28–9
Technical Military Cooperation
Agreement (N'Djamena,
19 June 1976)........ 223n.193, 260–1

SELECT TABLE OF TREATIES AND OTHER INSTRUMENTS xxv

Treaties of Alliance between the United
Provinces of the Netherlands,
Great Britain, and Prussia (Berlin
and The Hague, 15 April 1788) . . . 15–16
Treaty of Amity and Commerce (Paris,
6 February 1778). 24–5
Treaty of Amity and Cooperation in
Southeast Asia (Denpasar,
24 February 1976)
Art 2 107–8
Treaty between Austria-Hungary,
France, Germany, Great Britain
and Ireland, Italy, Russia, and
the Ottoman Empire for the
Settlement of Affairs in the East
(Berlin, 13 July 1878)
Art LXI–LXII 50n.288
Treaty between Poland and the
Ottoman Empire (1790) 15–16
Treaty between Poland and Russia
(Warsaw, 18 September 1773)
Art VII 15–16
Treaty between the United States and
Great Britain (Treaty of Washington)
(Washington, DC, 8 May 1871) 308n.a
Treaty Between the United States and
the Republic of Haiti (Port-au-
Prince, 16 September 1915). 83
Treaty between the United States of
America and the Republic of
Columbia (Thomson-Urrutia
Treaty) (Bogotá, 6 April 1914) 84n.525
Treaty Concerning the Permanent
Neutrality and Operation of the
Panama Canal (Washington, DC, 7
September 1977). 213–14,
223n.193, 241–2
Treaty of Confederation between the
Republics of Peru, Bolivia, Chile,
Ecuador, and New Granada (Lima,
8 February 1848). 84n.526
Treaty of Constantinople
(Constantinople, 21 July 1832) . . . 48n.280
Treaty for the Definitive Separation of
Belgium from Holland between
Austria, France, Great Britain,
Prussia and Russia, and Belgium
(London, 15 November 1831)
Arts 7 and 25 . . . . .67n.409
Treaty Establishing the Organisation
of Eastern Caribbean States
(Basseterre, 18 June 1981) 286
Treaty on the Establishment of the Union
State (Moscow, 8 December 1999). . . . 291

Treaty of Friendship and Alliance
between Libya and Chad (Tripoli,
15 June 1980). 260–1
Treaty of Friendship, Alliance and
Mutual Assistance between the
People's Republic of China and
the Soviet Union (Moscow,
14 February 1950)
Art 5 . . . . .113n.98
Treaty of Friendship and Alliance
with Spain (Madrid,
5 July 1814) 78n.494
Treaty of Friendship, Assistance
and Cooperation between
Belgium and Congo (Leopoldville,
29 June 1960)
Art 6 . . . . 206, 223–4
Treaty of Friendship and Collaboration
Between the Turkish Republic,
the Kingdom of Greece, and
the Federal People's Republic of
Yugoslavia (Balkan Pact) (Ankara,
28 February 1953)
Art 5 110
Treaty of Friendship and Cooperation
between Pakistan and Turkey
(Ankara, 28 February 1954)
Art 1 110
Art 8 108–9
Treaty of Friendship,
Good-Neighbourliness and
Cooperation (Moscow,
5 December 1978) 222n.191
Art 1 110
Treaty of Guarantee (Nicosia,
16 August 1960) 222n.191
Art IV. 224n.212
Art IV(2) 224–5n.213
Treaty of Havana (Havana,
22 May 1903)
Art III. 83
Treaty Intended to Adapt and
Strengthen Friendship and
Cooperation Relations between
the Principality of Monaco and
the French Republic (Paris, 24
October 2002)
Art 4 . . . . 206, 222–4
Treaty of Kadesh (1278 BC) C1P1
Treaty of London between France,
Great Britain, and Russia for the
Pacification of Greece (London
6 July 1827) 48–9
Additional Article. 32n.170

xxvi SELECT TABLE OF TREATIES AND OTHER INSTRUMENTS

Treaty of Mutual Cooperation and Security
between Japan and the United
States of America (San Francisco, 8
September 1951)................ 223
Treaty of Paris (Paris, 30 March 1856)
Art VII......................44n.255
Art IX........................50n.288
Treaty of Paris (Paris, 20 November
1815) 44–5
Treaty of Paris (Paris, 3 September 1783) 25
Treaty of Paris (Paris, 10 February 1763)...... 25
Treaty of Peace and Alliance Between
Philip IV, King of Spain, and
Charles I, King of Great Britain
(Treaty of Madrid) (Madrid,
15 November 1630)
Art IV......................... 15–16
Treaty of Peace, Amity, Commerce and
Navigation between the Argentine
Confederation and Brazil (Paraná,
7 March 1856)................... 85
Treaty of Peace, Amity, Navigation and
Commerce between New Granada and
the United States (Bogotá,
12 December 1846)
Art XXXV 84
Arts 2–3....................... 15–16
Treaty of Peace between France and the
Empire (Münster, 14 (24)
October 1648)................12n.18
Arts CXXIII and CXXIV.........15n.39
Treaty of Peace Between Frederick
I, King of Sweden, and Peter I,
Emperor of Russia (Nystad
10 September 1721)
Art VII....................... 15–16
Treaty of Peace between Spain and the
Netherlands (Münster, 30 January
1648) 12n.18
Treaty of Peace between Sweden and
the Empire (Osnabrück, 14 (24)
October 1648)................12n.18
Art 17 §§5–6 ....15n.39
Treaty of Peace and Friendship between
Great Britain and Spain (Utrecht,
11 April 1713)................13n.20
Treaty for the Perpetual Imprisonment
of Napoleon (Paris, 2 August
1815) 26
Treaty of the Pyrenees (Pheasant Island,
7 November 1659)
Art LXVIII..................... 15–16

Treaty Relative to the Grand Duchy of
Luxembourg (London, 11 May 1867)
Art 2.........................67n.409
Treaty of Union, Concert and Subsidy
between Austria, Great Britain,
Prussia, and Russia (Chaumont,
1 March 1814)
Art 1.........................41n.234
Troppau Protocol (Troppau,
19 November 1820) 41–2
United Nations Convention against
Illicit Traffic in Narcotic Drugs and
Psychotropic Substances (Vienna,
20 December 1988)
Art 2(2) 111–12
United Nations Convention against
Transnational Organized Crime
(Palermo, 12 December 2000)
Art 4(1) 111–12
Vienna Convention on Consular
Relations (Vienna, 24 April 1963)
Art 55(1) 111–12
Vienna Convention on Diplomatic
Relations (Vienna, 18 April 1961)
Art 41 .... 111–12, 184n.275
Vienna Convention on the Law of Treaties
(Vienna, 23 May 1969) 170–1,
226–7, 234–5, 318–19, 328–9,
335–6, 349, 372–3, 410–12
Preamble 101n.14
Art 7(2) 206–7n.68
Arts 31–33.......................4
Art 46................ 230, 233–4n.284
Art 46(2) 230
Art 47.......................230n.251
Art 48.......................227n.229
Art 49.......................227n.229
Art 50.......................227n.229
Art 51 227
Art 52.......... 147n.19, 171, 227–8
Art 53....... 125–6, 222n.191, 228–9, 319
Art 64.................... 228–9, 319

B. OTHER INTERNATIONAL INSTRUMENTS

Charter of Paris for a New Europe (Paris,
21 November 1990) 109
Declaration of the Heads of States or
Government of Non-Aligned
Countries (Belgrade,
6 September 1961) 112–13

SELECT TABLE OF TREATIES AND OTHER INSTRUMENTS xxvii

Declaration of Mexico (1945)
Art 3 102
Declaration of the People's Republic of
China and the Russian Federation
on the Promotion of International
Law (Beijing, 25 June 2016) . . . 114, 178–9
Declaration on the Problem of
Subversion (Accra, 24 October
1965) 106n.41, 12–13
Declaration of Reciprocal Assistance
and American Solidarity by the
Governments Represented at the
Inter-American Conference on War
and Peace (Act of Chapultepec)
(Mexico City, 3 March 1945)
Preamble 102
Draft Instrument of Instances of Violation
of the Principle of Nonintervention
and Statement of Reasons Approved
by the Inter-American Juridical
Committee at Its Regular Meeting
Held in January– February 1974 (5
December 1974) 45n.6,
147–8, 158n.91
ECOWAS Conflict Prevention
Framework (Ouagadougou,
16 January 2008) . . . 225–6, 345n.52, 365–6
EU Council Common Position 2008/
944/CFSP of 8 December 2008
defining common rules governing
control of exports of military
technology and equipment
Arts 1(1) and 2(2) 350–1
EU Council Decision 2013/255/CFSP of
31 May 2013 concerning restrictive
measures against Syria
Art 6 . . . . .369n.223
EU Council Decision 2013/109/CFSP
of 28 February 2013 Amending
Decision 2012/739/CFSP
concerning restrictive measures
against Syria 369n.224
EU Council Decision 2011/273/CFSP of
9 May 2011 concerning restrictive
measures against Syria
Art 1 . . . . .239n.320
Art 2(1)(b) .189n.308
Final Act of the Conference on Security
and Co-operation in Europe
(Helsinki Final Act) (Helsinki,
1 August 1975) 4, 108–9, 114, 45–6,
160–1, 182–3, 187, 196n.2, 281, 378–9

Principle VI 108–9, 145–6, 153, 158–9,
162–4, 167–8, 174–5, 187, 190,
237, 247, 378–9
Principle VII 342n.31, 362
Principle VIII 248, 312
Final Communiqué of the Asian-
African Conference of Bandung
(Bandung, 24 April 1955) 112–14
Section D(1)(b), ...311n.10
Libyan Political Agreement (Skhirat,
17 December 2015)
Article 8(2)(f) 229–30
Lima Declaration of Principles of the
Solidarity of America (Lima,
24 December 1938) 84–5
Non-Aligned Movement's Programme
for Peace and International
Co-operation (Cairo,
10 October 1964) 112–13
Organization of American States'
Declaration of San José
(San José, Costa Rica,
28 August 1960) 81n.510, 124n.169
Taif Agreement (Taif, 22 October 1989). . 261

C. SELECT UN DOCUMENTS

General Assembly

Declaration on the Elimination of All
Forms of Racial Discrimination
(GA Res 1904 (XVIII), 20
November 1963) 304
Declaration on the Enhancement of the
Effectiveness of the Principle of
Refraining from the Threat or
Use of Force in International
Relations (GA Res 42/22, 18
November 1987) 116–18, 174n.201
Declaration on the Granting of
Independence to Colonial
Countries and Peoples
(Decolonization Declaration)
(GA Res 1514 (XV), 14 December
1960) 99n.4, 116–18, 249,
310–12, 313–14
Declaration on the Inadmissibility
of Intervention in the Domestic
Affairs of States and the Protection
of their Independence and
Sovereignty (GA Res 2131 (XX), 21
December 1965) 4, 101, 116–18,
122, 145–6, 147–8, 153, 154–5, 158–9,

160–1, 170, 172–5, 176, 178–9, 182–3, 187–8, 190, 196–7, 202–3, 237, 247, 275, 281, 301, 304–5, 310–12, 313–14, 315–16, 362, 378–9, 381

Declaration on the Inadmissibility of Intervention and Interference in the Internal Affairs of States, (GA Res 36/103, 9 December 1981) 116–18, 122, 125–6, 147n.18, 151, 192, 342–3, 378–9n.22

Declaration on Measures to Eliminate International Terrorism (GA Res 49/60, 9 December 1994). 299

Declaration on Non-interference in the Internal Affairs of States (GA Res 31/91, 14 December 1976) 378–9n.22

Declaration on Principles of International Law Concerning Friendly Relations and Co-operation among States in Accordance with the Charter of the United Nations (GA Res 2625 (XXV), 24 October 1970) 4, 101, 114, 115–16n.112, 116–18, 123–4, 125, 126, 145–6, 147–8, 160–1, 166n.146, 169n.167, 170, 171–2, 173–5, 178–9, 182–3, 187–8, 190, 192–3, 196–7, 202–3, 237, 246n.4, 247, 272–3, 275, 281, 301, 313–14, 322–3, 325–6, 342n.31, 344, 356, 381, 399–400

First principle 314

Third principle 122n.157, 145, 153, 154–5, 158–9, 162–3, 187, 192, 362, 378–9, 378–9n.22, 383n.77

Fourth principle 304–5

Fifth principle 247n.9, 248, 309n.1, 310–12, 315–16, 321–2, 324–5, 330n.143, 334n.173, 341n.27, 356

Declaration on the Rights of Indigenous Peoples (GA Res 61/295, 13 September 2007)

Art 3 . . . . .249n.19

Definition of Aggression (GA Res 3314 (XXIX), 14 December 1974) . . . 173n.195, 220n.170, 324–5

Art 1 . . . . .200n.33

Art 3 321–2

Art 3(e). 233, 276

Art 3(f). 228–9

Art 5(1) 362n.170

Art 6 322–3

Art 7 321–3

Essentials of Peace (GA Res 290 (IV), 1 December 1949) 187n.293, 196–7

Peace Through Deeds (GA Res 380 (V), 17 November 1950) 116–18, 172–3, 196–7

Principles which should guide Members in determining whether or not an obligation exists to transmit the information called for under Article 73e of the Charter of the United Nations (GA Res 1541 (XV), 15 December 1960)

Principle IV .315n.40

Principle V 315n.40

Principle VI 309

Resolution on the Status of the Implementation of the Declaration on the Inadmissibility of Intervention in the Domestic Affairs of States and the Protection of Their Independence and Sovereignty (GA Res 2225 (XXI), 19 December 1966) 116–18, 123–4

Resolution on the Strict Observance of the Prohibition of the Threat or Use of Force in International Relations and of the Right of Peoples to Self-Determination (GA Res 2160 (XXI), 30 November 1966) 116–18, 311n.13, 313–14

United Nations Millennium Declaration (GA Res 55/2, 18 September 2000) 114

World Summit Outcome (GA Res 60/1, 16 September 2005) 114

Human Rights Council

Resolution 9/9, 18 September 2008, Protection of the Human Rights of Civilians in Armed Conflict 344

International Law Commission

Articles on the Responsibility of States for Internationally Wrongful Acts, 2001 . . . . 122, 203–4

Art 2 158

Art 4 205–6

Art 16 . . . . 318n.63, 348–9

Art 18 . . . . . . .147n.19, 155n.71, 163–4n.128

Art 20 . . . . . 203–5, 206, 220–1, 230, 231–2, 232n.271, 232n.273

Art 25 . . . . .324n.104, 358n.131

SELECT TABLE OF TREATIES AND OTHER INSTRUMENTS xxix

Art 41(2) 185–6
Art 42 .... 164n.130, 381
Art 43 .... 164n.130
Art 45 .... 221n.181, 231–2
Arts 49–54 .... 164n.130, 381
Art 50(1) 324–5, 326n.115
Art 50(1)(a) 170n.169, 298
Art 51 .... 164n.130
Art 54 ...... 244n.361, 298n.378, 327n.121
Part One, Ch II 377
Draft Code of Crimes against the
  Peace and Security of
  Mankind, 1996 127
Draft Code of Crimes against
  the Peace and Security of
  Mankind, 1991 .... 148n.22
Draft Art 17(2) 127
Draft Code of Offences against the
  Peace and Security of Mankind,
  1954 126–7
Art 2(4) 127
Art 2(5) 127
Art 2(9) 126–7
Draft Conclusions on Identification
  of Customary International
  Law, 2018 ..... 4n.14, 5, 8n.37, 192n.328
Conclusion 10 .... 5–6, 257n.66
Conclusion 10(3) 6n.24, 257
Conclusion 11(2) 116n.113
Conclusion 12 7
Draft Declaration on Rights and Duties
  of States, 1949 .... 247n.8
Art 3 .... 116n.114, 162n.118
Art 4 .... 116n.114

Security Council

Resolution 2304, 12 August
  2016 .... 345n.53, 370–1
Resolution 2259, 23 December
  2015 .... 219n.168, 267–8, 302
Resolution 1973, 17 March 2011 237–9,
                        362–4, 371–2
Resolution 1970, 26 February
  2011 .... 189n.308, 230n.250,
                    236n.300, 267–8
Resolution 1296, 19 April 2000 344
Resolution 1199, 23 September
  1998 227–8
Resolution 955, 8 November 1994 344
Resolution 929, 22 June 1994. 370–1
Resolution 808, 22 February 1993 344
Resolution 794, 3 December
  1992 .... 344n.46, 370–1

Resolution 169, 24 November
  1961 .... 235n.297, 301–2, 332
Resolution 146, 9 August 1960 ... 301–2, 332

D. NATIONAL CONSTITUTIONS

Brazil
  Art 4 .... 115n.110
Central African Republic
  Art 28 229–30
Gambia. 210
Grenada 208–9
Lesotho
  Art 92 229
Mexico
  Art 89(x) 115n.110
North Macedonia
  Art 49(1) 115n.110
People's Republic of China
  Preamble 115n.110
Philippines
  Section 25 229
Qatar
  Art 7 .... 115n.110
Romania
  Art 14 .... 115n.110
South Africa 229–30
Ukraine 208–9, 229–30
  Art 85(23) 229
Venezuela. 211–12
  Art 233 208–9

E. OTHER NATIONAL LEGISLATION

France

Décret sur le droit de guerre et de
  paix, 22 May 1790. .... 25n.122

Hungary

Law on the Transparency of Organizations
  Receiving Support from Abroad,
  13 June 2017 186

Russia

Federal Law Introducing Amendments
  to Certain Legislative Acts of the
  Russian Federation Regarding
  the Regulation of Activities of
  Non-Commercial Organizations
  Performing the Function of
  Foreign Agents, 20 July 2012. 186

SELECT TABLE OF TREATIES AND OTHER INSTRUMENTS

United Kingdom

Foreign Enlistment Act,
3 July 1819 . . . . 62–3, 78–9
Foreign Enlistment Act, 9 August 1870 62–3

United States

Cuban Democracy Act,
24 September 1992 . . . . .160n.104
Instructions for the Government of
Armies of the United States in the
Field, General Orders No. 100
(Lieber Code), 24 April 1863 55–6
Art 149 55
Art 150 55
Art 151 55
Arts 152 and 153 . . . . .60n.363
Iraq Liberation Act, 31 October
1998 . . . . 156–8, 240–1
National Defense Authorization
Act for Fiscal Year 2015,
19 December 2014 . . . . 237–8n.320
Neutrality Act, 5 June 1794 62–3

Venezuela

Law on Defence of Political Sovereignty and
National Self-Determination,
21 December 2010 186

F. NATIONAL MILITARY MANUALS

Canada

Law of Armed Conflict at the Operational
and Tactical Levels, Joint Doctrine
Manual, 2001 . . . . .115n.111

Denmark

Military Manual on International
Law Relevant to Danish Armed
Forces in International
Operations, 2016 . . . . 115n.111, 359,
361, 367–8

France

Manuel de droit des opérations militaires,
2023 . . . . 115n.111, 387–8

Germany

Law of Armed Conflict—
Manual, 2013 . . . . .190n.313

New Zealand

Manual of Armed Forces Law,
2nd edn, 2017 . . . . 115n.111, 239–40

Norway

Manual of the Law of Armed
Conflict, 2013 . . . . .115n.111

United Kingdom

The Manual of the Law of Armed
Conflict, 2004 . . . . 189–90, 198

United States

Law of War Manual, 2015 (updated
December 2016) 115n.111, 199,
273–4n.204, 358

List of Abbreviations

ACDI	*Anuario colombiano de derecho internacional*
AdV	*Archiv des Völkerrechts*
AFDI	*Annuaire français de droit international*
AF L Rev	*Air Force Law Review*
African YBIL	*African Yearbook of International Law*
Afr J Intl & Comp L	*African Journal of International and Comparative Law*
AHLADI	*Anuario Hispano-Luso-Americano de Derecho Internacional*
AHRLJ	*African Human Rights Law Journal*
AIDI	*Annuaire de l'Institut de droit international*
AJIL	*American Journal of International Law*
Annuaire de l'AAA	*Annuaire de l'Association des auditeurs et anciens auditeurs de l'Académie de droit international de La Haye*
ARIEL	*Austrian Review of International and European Law*
Ariz J Int'l & Comp L	*Arizona Journal of International and Comparative Law*
ARSIWA	Articles on the Responsibility of States for Internationally Wrongful Acts
ASEAN	Association of Southeast Asian Nations
Asian JIL	*Asian Journal of International Law*
Asian-Pacific L & PJ	*Asian-Pacific Law & Policy Journal*
Asian YBIL	*Asian Yearbook of International Law*
ASIL Proceedings	*Proceedings of the American Society of International Law at its Annual Meeting*
AU	African Union
AU Intl L Rev	*American University International Law Review*
Australian YBIL	*Australian Yearbook of International Law*
Baltic YBIL	*Baltic Yearbook of International Law*
BU Int'l LJ	*Boston University International Law Journal*
BULR	*Boston University Law Review*
BYBIL	*British Yearbook of International Law*
Cambridge J Int'l & Comp L	*Cambridge Journal of International and Comparative Law*
CAR	Central African Republic
Case Western Reserve JIL	*Case Western Reserve Journal of International Law*
CEDAM	Casa Editrice Dott. Antonio Milani
Chi J Int'l L	*Chicago Journal of International Law*
CJCL	*Chinese Journal of Comparative Law*
CJIL	*Chinese Journal of International Law*
CLJ	*Cambridge Law Journal*
Colum Hum Rts L Rev	*Columbia Human Rights Law Review*
Colum J Transnat'l L	*Columbia Journal of Transnational Law*

LIST OF ABBREVIATIONS

Colum L Rev	*Columbia Law Review*
Comp & Int'l LJ S Afr	*Comparative and International Law Journal of Southern Africa*
Conn J Int'l L	*Connecticut Journal of International Law*
Cornell Int'l LJ	*Cornell International Law Journal*
CPE	*Chronique de politique étrangère*
CRIA	*Cambridge Review of International Affairs*
CSCE	Conference on Security and Co-operation in Europe
CSTO	Collective Security Treaty Organization
CTS	*The Consolidated Treaty Series* (Clive Parry ed, Oceana Publications 1969)
CUP	Cambridge University Press
CYBIL	*Canadian Yearbook of International Law*
Dept St Bull	*Department of State Bulletin*
DUDI	*Diritti umani e diritto internazionale*
DoS/DDoS	Denial of service/distributed denial of service attacks
DRC	Democratic Republic of the Congo
Duke J Comp & Intl L	*Duke Journal of Comparative and International Law*
ECCAS	Economic Community of Central African States
ECOMOG	Economic Community of West African States Monitoring Group
ECOWAS	Economic Community of West African States
EJIL	*European Journal of International Law*
Ethiopian YBIL	*Ethiopian Yearbook of International Law*
FCO	Foreign and Commonwealth Office
Fordham Int'l LJ	*Fordham International Law Journal*
Foreign Aff	*Foreign Affairs*
FROLINAT	Front de libération nationale du Tchad
FYIL	*Finnish Yearbook of International Law*
Ga J Intl & Comp L	*Georgia Journal of International and Comparative Law*
GLJ	*German Law Journal*
GNA	Government of National Accord (Libya)
GPO	United States Government Printing Office
GR2P	*Global Responsibility to Protect*
GYBIL	*German Yearbook of International Law*
Harv Intl LJ	*Harvard International Law Journal*
Harv L Rev	*Harvard Law Review*
Harv NSJ	*Harvard National Security Journal*
Hast LJ	*Hastings Law Journal*
Hastings Int'l & Comp L Rev	*Hastings International and Comparative Law Review*
How LJ	*Howard Law Journal*
HRLJ	*Human Rights Law Journal*
HRLR	*Human Rights Law Review*
HRQ	*Human Rights Quarterly*
IACHR	Inter-American Court of Human Rights
ICISS	International Commission on Intervention and State Sovereignty

LIST OF ABBREVIATIONS   xxxiii

ICJ	International Court of Justice
ICJ Rep	*Reports of Judgments, Advisory Opinions and Orders of the International Court of Justice*
ICRC	International Committee of the Red Cross
IFFMCG	Independent Fact-Finding Mission on the Conflict in Georgia
IHL	International humanitarian law
IHRL	International human rights law
IHRR	*International Human Rights Reports*
IJIL	*Indian Journal of International Law*
ILA	International Law Association
ILC	International Law Commission
ILM	*International Legal Materials*
ILR	*International Law Reports*
ILS	*International Law Studies*
ILT	*International Legal Theory*
Ind LJ	*Indiana Law Journal*
Indonesian J Int'l L	*Indonesian Journal of International Law*
Indon J Int'l & Comp L	*Indonesian Journal of International and Comparative Law*
Int'l Comm L Rev	*International Community Law Review*
Intl & Comp LQ	*International and Comparative Law Quarterly*
Int'l Crim L Rev	*International Criminal Law Review*
Intl J HR	*International Journal of Human Rights*
IRRC	*International Review of the Red Cross*
ISIL	Islamic State in Iraq and the Levant
Israel LR	*Israel Law Review*
Israel YBHR	*Israel Yearbook on Human Rights*
IYIL	*Italian Yearbook of International Law*
J Conflict Resol	*Journal of Conflict Resolution*
JCSL	*Journal of Conflict & Security Law*
JDIP	*Journal de droit international privé*
J His Intl L	*Journal of the History of International Law*
JILE	*Journal of International Law and Economics*
J Int'l Crim Just	*Journal of International Criminal Justice*
JNSLP	*Journal of National Security Law and Policy*
JSS	*Journal of Strategic Studies*
J Transnat'l L & Pol'y	*Journal of Transnational Law and Policy*
JUFIL	*Journal on the Use of Force and International Law*
Keesing's	*Keesing's Contemporary Archives/Keesing's Record of World Events*
Law Guild Rev	*Lawyers Guild Review*
Lewis & Clark L Rev	*Lewis & Clark Law Review*
LGDJ	Librairie générale de droit et de jurisprudence
Liverpool LR	*Liverpool Law Review*
LJIL	*Leiden Journal of International Law*
LNOJ	*League of Nations Official Journal*
LNTS	*League of Nations Treaty Series*

xxxiv LIST OF ABBREVIATIONS

LTTE	Liberation Tigers of Tamil Eelam
Max Planck YB UN L	*Max Planck Yearbook of United Nations Law*
McGill L J	*McGill Law Journal*
Melb J Int'l L	*Melbourne Journal of International Law*
Mich J Intl L	*Michigan Journal of International Law*
Mich L Rev	*Michigan Law Review*
Mich St Int'l L Rev	*Michigan State International Law Review*
Mil L Rev	*Military Law Review*
Mizan LR	*Mizan Law Review*
MPEPIL	*Max Planck Encyclopedia of Public International Law*
NC J Int'l L	*North Carolina Journal of International Law*
ND J Intl & Comp L	*Notre Dame Journal of International and Comparative Law*
New Eng L Rev	*New England Law Review*
NIAC	Non-international armed conflict
NILR	*Netherlands International Law Review*
Nordic J Int'l L	*Nordic Journal of International Law*
NRHDFE	*Nouvelle revue historique de droit français et étranger*
NYBIL	*Netherlands Yearbook of International Law*
NYU J Intl L & Pol	*New York University Journal of International Law and Politics*
NYU L Rev	*New York University Law Review*
NZYBIL	*New Zealand Yearbook of International Law*
OAS	Organization of American States
OAU	Organization of African Unity
OECS	Organisation of Eastern Caribbean States
Ohio St LJ	*Ohio State Law Journal*
OIC	Organisation of Islamic Cooperation
ONUC	Opération des Nations Unies au Congo
OUP	Oxford University Press
PCIJ	Permanent Court of International Justice
Phil ILJ	*Philippines International Law Journal*
Phil LJ	*Philippine Law Journal*
Pol Sci Q	*Political Science Quarterly*
PRC	People's Republic of China
PYIL	*Polish Yearbook of International Law*
Quest Intl L	*Questions of International Law*
RBDI	*Revue belge de droit international*
RCL	*Review of Contemporary Law*
RDC	*Revue de droit contemporain*
RDI	*Rivista di diritto internazionale*
RDILC	*Revue de droit international et de législation comparée*
RDMDG	*Revue de droit militaire et de droit de la guerre*
Recueil des Cours	*Recueil des Cours de l'Académie de droit international de La Haye (Collected Courses of The Hague Academy of International Law)*
REDI	*Revue égyptienne de droit international*
REEI	*Revista electrónica de estudios internacionales*

LIST OF ABBREVIATIONS xxxv

Rev Intl Stud	*Review of International Studies*
Rev Jur UPR	*Revista Jurídica de la Universidad de Puerto Rico*
RGDIP	*Revue générale de droit international public*
RIAA	*Reports of International Arbitral Awards*
RJPEF	*Revue juridique et politique des États francophones*
RREI	*Revue roumaine d'études internationales*
RSDIDE	*Revue suisse de droit international et de droit européen*
Rutgers LR	*Rutgers Law Review*
SADC	Southern African Development Community
SALJ	*South African Law Journal*
SAYBIL	*South African Yearbook of International Law*
SOFA	Status of Forces Agreement
Sri Lanka J Int'l L	*Sri Lanka Journal of International Law*
Stan J Intl Stud	*Stanford Journal of International Studies*
Suffolk Transnat'l L Rev	*Suffolk Transnational Law Review*
SYBIL	*Spanish Yearbook of International Law*
Temp Int'l & Comp LJ	*Temple International and Comparative Law Journal*
Tex Intl LJ	*Texas International Law Journal*
Tex L Rev	*Texas Law Review*
TFG	Transitional Federal Government (Somalia)
Tul L Rev	*Tulane Law Review*
TWAIL	Third World Approaches to International Law
UAE	United Arab Emirates
UAR	United Arab Republic
U Chi L Rev	*University of Chicago Law Review*
UCLA J Int'l L Foreign Aff	*UCLA Journal of International Law & Foreign Affairs*
U Miami Inter-Am L Rev	*University of Miami Inter-American Law Review*
UNSWLJ	*University of New South Wales Law Journal*
UNTS	United Nations Treaty Series
U Pa J Int'l L	*University of Pennsylvania Journal of International Law*
U Pa L Rev	*University of Pennsylvania Law Review*
U Pitt L Rev	*University of Pittsburgh Law Review*
Va J Intl L	*Virginia Journal of International Law*
Va L Rev	*Virginia Law Review*
Vand J Transnat'l L	*Vanderbilt Journal of Transnational Law*
VCLT	Vienna Convention on the Law of Treaties
Washburn LJ	*Washburn Law Journal*
Wash & Lee L Rev	*Washington and Lee Law Review*
Wash L Rev	*Washington Law Review*
Wis Int'l LJ	*Wisconsin International Law Journal*
Yale JIL	*Yale Journal of International Law*
Yale LJ	*Yale Law Journal*
YB ILC	*Yearbook of the International Law Commission*
YB UN	*Yearbook of the United Nations*
ZaöRV	*Zeitschrift für ausländisches öffentliches Recht und Völkerrecht*

Introduction

The principle of non-intervention in the domestic affairs of states is one of the most venerable principles of international law: as Vattel famously wrote in 1758, '[i]t is an evident consequence of the liberty and independence of nations, that all of them have a right to be governed as they think proper, and that no state has the smallest right to interfere in the government of another'.[1] Although not expressly mentioned in the Charter of the United Nations (UN), at least as an inter-state prohibition,[2] the principle currently appears in a plethora of treaties and UN General Assembly resolutions and has been invoked like a mantra by states of all geographical and political denominations. In spite of this, the determination of its exact content has remained an enigma which has haunted generations of international lawyers: writing in the 1920s, P. H. Winfield posited that '[a] reader, after perusing Phillimore's chapter upon intervention, might close the book with the impression that intervention may be anything from a speech of Lord Palmerston's in the House of Commons to the partition of Poland'.[3]

This book's main objective is to solve this enigma and identify what the customary principle of non-intervention specifically prohibits, and what it does not. As I show, the principle in question is strictly linked to some fundamental notions of international law, such as sovereignty, use of force, and self-determination: its study, therefore, is of great significance as it offers a fascinating opportunity to explore the macrostructures of international law. Indeed, as a commentator notes, '[i]f intervention is a transgression of political authority, then it is a potentially illuminating window on the distribution and legitimation of such authority in different international orders. And to the extent that interventionary ideas and practices challenge these distributions, they may also illuminate processes of fundamental international change'.[4]

While there have been recent books on the narrower topic of 'intervention by invitation' or 'military assistance on request',[5] contemporary international legal scholarship has curiously ignored the broader issues arising from the principle of

---

[1] Emer de Vattel, *Le droit des gens ou Principes de la loi naturelle appliqués à la conduite et aux affaires des nations et des souverains* (1758), tr by Béla Kapossy and Richard Whatmore as *The Law of Nations, Or, The Principles of the Law of Nature, Applied to the Conduct and Affairs of Nations and Sovereigns, with three Early Essays on the Origin and Nature of Natural Law and on Luxury* (Liberty Fund 2008) 289.

[2] Charter of the United Nations (San Francisco, 26 June 1945). The principle appears, however, as a limit to the UN organs' competences in Art 2(7).

[3] PH Winfield, 'The History of Intervention in International Law' (1922–1923) 3 BYBIL 130, 130.

[4] Christian Reus-Smit, 'The Concept of Intervention' (2013) 39 Rev Intl Stud 1057, 1064.

[5] See eg Eliav Lieblich, *International Law and Civil Wars. Intervention and Consent* (Routledge 2013); Christina Nowak, *Das Interventionsverbot im Bürgerkrieg: Darstellung eines Wandels durch die Bürgerkriege in Libyen, Syrien, Irak, Jemen und Ukraine seit 2011* (Peter Lang 2018); Erika de Wet, *Military Assistance on Request and the Use of Force* (OUP 2020); Chiara Redaelli, *Intervention in Civil Wars: Effectiveness, Legitimacy, and Human Rights* (Bloomsbury 2021); Seyfullah Hasar, *State Consent to Foreign Military Intervention during Civil Wars* (Brill/Nijhoff 2022).

International Law and the Principle of Non-Intervention. Marco Roscini, Oxford University Press. © Marco Roscini 2024.
DOI: 10.1093/oso/9780198786894.003.0001

non-intervention. What has been missing, then, is a scholarly work approaching in a systematic and coherent fashion the multifarious theoretical and practical legal problems raised by it. One of the reasons for this lack of interest can be ascribed to the fact that, since 1945, the use of armed force has been prohibited by the UN Charter. This book shows, however, that this important development has not made the principle of non-intervention redundant as it only concerns one means of coercion. The principle is in fact even more relevant today, as economic globalization and the digitization of societies have significantly increased the opportunities for states to interfere in the domestic affairs of other states. A book that addresses the principle of non-intervention from a legal perspective in a comprehensive and innovative manner, as well as its interactions with other fundamental principles of contemporary international law, is therefore badly needed.

The key research questions this book addresses are: What constitutes an 'intervention' in international law and when is such intervention unlawful? The approach is from three different perspectives, which are reflected in the book's structure: historical, theoretical, and systemic. The first two chapters trace the history of the principle of non-intervention throughout the centuries. More specifically, Chapter I explores its emergence in the 1700s as a corollary of 'Westphalian' sovereignty and its morphing from a political concept into a discrete international legal rule in the 19th century and the first half of the 20th. Research questions specifically addressed in Chapter I thus include: When did the principle of non-intervention turned into a legal norm of the law of nations? What did it aim to protect? How did the main actors of the time conceive and apply it? Did its application depend on the qualification of the situation of internal unrest in the country where the intervention was conducted? How was the principle of non-intervention reconciled with the fundamental right of states to independence? In order to properly address these questions, Chapter I situates the evolution of the law of intervention in the broader political and intellectual context of the time. Chapter II considers the status of the principle of non-intervention in the framework of the sources of contemporary international law and identifies the post-1945 treaties in which it has been incorporated. It also investigates whether, in the UN era, the principle continues to reflect customary international law and whether it constitutes a *jus cogens* norm and/or an *erga omnes* obligation. Furthermore, the main lines of thoughts of contemporary legal scholarship in regard to our topic are surveyed.

The theory of the principle of non-intervention is discussed in Chapters III, IV, and VIII. Chapter III determines the specific conduct that falls under its prohibitive scope by analysing the constitutive elements of a prohibited intervention, namely, the coercive character of the interference and the fact that it bears on 'matters in which each State is permitted, by the principle of State sovereignty, to decide freely.'[6] The chapter demonstrates that non-intervention is not only a general principle prohibiting coercion in the domestic affairs of other states, but also consists of more specific rules of application that prohibit certain means and methods of coercion. The research questions addressed in Chapter III include: What constitute coercion of state and domestic jurisdiction in the context of the law of intervention? What is the relevance of

---

[6] *Case Concerning Military and Paramilitary Activities in and against Nicaragua (Nicaragua v USA)* (Merits) [1986] ICJ Rep 3, para 205 (hereafter *Nicaragua v USA*).

intent and motive as elements of the wrongful act of intervention? What forms of coercion are prohibited by the customary principle of non-intervention? In particular, is economic coercion unlawful when it aims to coerce a state into doing something it does not have an obligation to do, or into not doing something it has the right to do? Chapter IV builds on the analysis conducted in the previous chapter and explores the role played by consent in excluding the coercive nature of the interference: if coercion is characterized by compulsion or imposition, then the presence of valid consent is a normative game changer that turns what would have otherwise been an intervention into cooperation. The chapter addresses the following research questions: Who is entitled under international law to consent to intervention on behalf of a state? What validity requirements must this consent possess? Can insurrectional authorities ever validly consent to an intervention, in particular when they aim to overthrow an authoritarian regime? Finally, Chapter VIII examines whether the digitization of today's societies has contributed to the emergence of a new form of intervention in addition to those identified in Chapter III, that is, cyber operations, and whether at least some of them can be considered coercive interferences falling under the prohibitive scope of the principle of non-intervention.

After history and theory, the book explores the application of the principle of non-intervention against the broader background of international law, that is, in its interactions with other principles and rules that have emerged or consolidated during the UN Charter era and which have moved away from a purely statist idea of sovereignty. Indeed, it is one of this book's theses that the problem of third-state intervention in situations of internal unrest is one of systemic integration. In particular, this book investigates whether different situations of internal unrest remain a domestic affair of the concerned state in contemporary international law and, therefore, whether the principle of non-intervention still fully applies to them.[7] Chapter V examines the interaction between the principle of non-intervention and that of internal self-determination, that is, the right of a people to choose their own political, economic, social, and cultural systems without external interferences. Questions addressed in this chapter include: What situations of internal unrest trigger the application of the principle of internal self-determination? Does this principle preclude any coercive interference or only the direct use of force? Does the obligation of 'negative quality' in civil wars reflect customary international law? Are the UN organs also constrained by it? Are there any situations where third-state pro-government intervention in a civil war furthers internal self-determination instead of undermining it? Chapter VI examines the interaction between the principle of non-intervention and the principle of self-determination in its external dimension, that is, the right of a people to choose its international status: the overall question is whether, in situations where a people is unlawfully prevented from exercising external self-determination, third states are still permitted to intervene in support of the oppressive government and/or are still prohibited from assisting the opposition groups. In particular, the chapter explores the legality of third-state intervention in three contexts: colonial domination, alien

---

[7] 'Situations of internal unrest' is used in this book not as a technical legal expression, but rather to refer to situations where a more or less ample group of individuals challenge the incumbent governmental authorities by violent means.

occupation, and other secessionist situations of internal unrest. Last but not least, Chapter VII considers how the notion of sovereignty has changed in contemporary discourse and what consequences this has had on the principle of non-intervention. More specifically, the chapter discusses whether violations of international human rights law (IHRL) and/or international humanitarian law (IHL) committed by a government during a situation of internal unrest prevent third states from intervening in its support; and, conversely, whether the principle of internal self-determination, which displaces that of non-intervention in case of civil war and which prohibits sending armed forces also on the side of the incumbent, can be set aside when it is the insurgents who are responsible for the violations in question. The chapter also addresses the problem of the legality of different forms of intervention in support of opposition groups in response to the violations of IHRL and/or IHL committed by the governmental authorities.

The research to write this book was conducted over almost ten years and was predominantly desk- and library-based, involving rigorous analysis of primary materials and qualitative data evidencing the practice of states and relevant international organizations. Through a comprehensive survey of primary documents, as well as through an extensive evaluation of state practice and literature search, the book thus provides a systematic and coherent analysis of the principle of non-intervention. The sources used are mainly those listed in Article 38(1) of the Statute of the International Court of Justice (ICJ), that is, treaties (including the resolutions of treaty-based international organizations), customary international law, general principles of law, and, in a subsidiary role, the 'judicial decisions and the teachings of the most highly qualified publicists of the various nations'.[8] The analysis of the relevant treaty provisions, in particular, was conducted by employing the interpretative criteria identified in Articles 31–3 of the 1969 Vienna Convention on the Law of Treaties (VCLT).[9] I also extensively researched the *travaux préparatoires* of the relevant parts of the core documents, namely, the 1948 Charter of the Organization of American States (OAS),[10] the UN General Assembly's Resolutions 2131 (XX) of 21 December 1965[11] and 2625 (XXV) of 24 October 1970,[12] and the 1975 Helsinki Final Act.[13]

In regard to customary international law, I side with those who see it as resulting from the convergence of two elements, that is, general and uniform state practice and *opinio juris sive necessitatis*: among many others, the ICJ has explicitly rejected the opposite view that considers the latter element unnecessary.[14] In fact, *opinio juris* is of

---

[8] Statute of the International Court of Justice (San Francisco, 26 June 1945), Art 38(1), 33 UNTS 993.

[9] Vienna Convention on the Law of Treaties (VCLT) (Vienna, 23 May 1969) 1155 UNTS 331.

[10] Charter of the Organization of American States (Bogotá, 30 April 1948) 119 UNTS 47.

[11] GA Res 2131 (XX) of 21 December 1965 adopting the Declaration on the Inadmissibility of Intervention in the Domestic Affairs of States and the Protection of Their Independence and Sovereignty.

[12] GA Res 2625 (XXV) of 24 October 1970 containing the Declaration on Principles of International Law Concerning Friendly Relations and Co-operation among States in Accordance with the Charter of the United Nations.

[13] Final Act of the 1st CSCE Summit of Heads of State or Government (Helsinki, 1 August 1975) (1975) 14 ILM 1292.

[14] See eg *North Sea Continental Shelf (Federal Republic of Germany/Denmark; Federal Republic of Germany/Netherlands)* (Judgment) [1969] ICJ Rep 3, para 77 (hereafter *North Sea Continental Shelf*); *Nicaragua v USA*, para 207. See also Conclusion 2, Draft Conclusions on Identification of Customary International Law [2018] YB ILC, vol II, part two, 93.

INTRODUCTION 5

particular relevance for any research on the principle of non-intervention, as this is a negative rule: a focus only on what states do would lead to the overemphasis of cases of violation and the overlooking of those of compliance.[15]

The practice examined in this book consists of more than 200 cases of intervention from the mid-18th century to the present day. Unlike other works, therefore, I have chosen not to limit the scope of the enquiry to post-Cold War interventions. Indeed, it is my conviction that these more recent cases can be properly understood only by adopting a historical approach, and not a 'snapshot' one: to assess the Western states' intervention in the ongoing Syrian Civil War, for instance, one necessarily has to start the analysis from the numerous interventions of the European powers in the Ottoman Empire in the 1800s. A historical approach allows us to establish whether earlier versions and practices find resonance in today's arguments on intervention and its contours and helps us elucidate dimensions of the logic of the principle of non-intervention so to better identify its content. Furthermore, the book does not exclusively address intervention in civil wars (as defined in Section 3.1 of Chapter V), but also in other, less serious situations of internal unrest, namely mutinies, coups d'état, mob violence, popular uprisings, and low-intensity internal armed conflicts. Finally, again differently from other authors, I have opted to address not only armed intervention (or 'military assistance') in the form of sending troops and/or arms and war *matériel*, but all forms of coercive interference in the domestic affairs of states (economic, political, and cyber). This book, therefore, is not a study of Article 2(4) of the UN Charter, but rather of the broader principle of non-intervention. While it would be pretentious to claim that *all* cases of intervention have been examined (particularly when it comes to economic and political interventions), I am confident that the research has covered the most significant ones.

Practice consists not only of physical acts 'on the ground', but also of verbal acts, such as '[d]iplomatic statements (including protests), policy statements, press releases, official manuals (e.g. on military law), instructions to armed forces, comments by governments on draft treaties, legislation, decisions of national courts and executive authorities, pleadings before international tribunals, statements in international organizations'.[16] In this context, I have mostly avoided the use of documents not for public release, like internal memoranda, and of classified materials, as the customary formation process is one of claim and response.[17] To the best of my capacity, when I have used the same materials both as verbal practice and as evidence of *opinio juris*, I have examined them as separate inquiries.[18] Finally, inaction by states has been considered practice only when deliberate and 'based on their being conscious of having a duty to abstain'.[19]

Evidence of *opinio juris sive necessitatis* can be deduced from, inter alia, 'public statements made on behalf of States; official publications; government legal opinions;

---

[15] Draft Conclusions, 95.
[16] Statement of Principles Applicable to the Formation of (General) Customary International Law, in International Law Association (ILA), Report of the Sixty-Ninth Conference (London 2000) 14 <www.ila-hq.org/en_GB/documents/conference-report-london-2000-2>.
[17] Draft Conclusions, 98; Statement of Principles, 15.
[18] Draft Conclusions, 96.
[19] *The Case of the SS 'Lotus' (France v Turkey)*, Judgment of 7 September 1927, PCIJ Series A No 10, 2, 28. See also Draft Conclusions, 99.

diplomatic correspondence; decisions of national courts; treaty provisions; and conduct in connection with resolutions adopted by an international organization or at an intergovernmental conference'.[20] For each case of intervention, the research identified both the legal justifications advanced by the intervening state(s) (if any) and the reaction of other states and international organizations.[21] Particularly useful in this context were the letters sent by the intervening states to the UN Security Council on the occasion of an intervention, as well as the debates in the UN political organs. The research, however, considered not only the *opinio juris* expressed in relation to specific cases of intervention, but also more general statements on the content of the principle of non-intervention. In fact, positions adopted in the abstract can be even more valuable than those adopted ad hoc, as the latter more than the former might be influenced by political interests and emotional impulses. As Article 38(1) of the ICJ Statute indicates, practice must be 'accepted *as law*' to create customary international law:[22] I have therefore privileged statements phrased in legal terms, that is, those that use legal language and/or refer to sources of international law and thus make a legal claim, over mere policy statements.[23] Statements made in international fora have also been given more weight than those before domestic audiences, as it is in the former case that states 'speak' directly to other states. *Opinio juris* has been deduced from the lack of reactions to interventions only with great caution: as the ICJ has found, 'silence may also speak, but only if the conduct of the other State calls for a response'.[24] The state(s) in question must also have had knowledge of the conduct and been in a position to react.[25] Furthermore, 'the inaction should derive from a sense of legal obligation or right, rather than non-legal considerations, such as resource constraints, international or domestic political calculations, or diplomatic relations'.[26]

Both practice and *opinio juris* must be general and uniform to create or modify customary international law. The research thus covered states from different continents and political affiliations, as the general character is more a qualitative than a quantitative requirement.[27] Representativeness, in other words, matters.[28] In particular, it has been one of my objectives to include as much practice and *opinio juris* from the 'Global South' as possible. When appropriate, I have emphasized the position of 'States whose interests were specially affected'.[29]

---

[20] Conclusion 10, Draft Conclusions, 103.

[21] *Nicaragua v USA*, para 207.

[22] Art 38(1), ICJ Statute, emphasis added.

[23] *Nicaragua v USA*, para 206.

[24] *Sovereignty over Pedra Branca/Pulau Batu Puteh, Middle Rocks and South Ledge (Malaysia/Singapore)* (Judgment) [2008] ICJ Rep 12, para 121. For the International Law Commission (ILC), '[f]ailure to react over time to a practice may serve as evidence of acceptance as law (*opinio juris*), provided that States were in a position to react and the circumstances called for some reaction' (Conclusion 10(3), Draft Conclusions, 103).

[25] Conclusion 10, Draft Conclusions,103.

[26] Dustin A Lewis, Naz K Modirzadeh, and Gabriella Blum, 'Quantum of Silence: Inaction and *Jus ad Bellum*', The Harvard Law School Program on International Law and Armed Conflict (HLS PILAC), 2019, 30 <https://pilac.law.harvard.edu/quantum-of-silence>.

[27] Statement of Principles, 26.

[28] See *North Sea Continental Shelf*, Dissenting Opinion of Judge Lachs, 227.

[29] *North Sea Continental Shelf*, para 73.

State practice and *opinio juris* must be not only general but also uniform, that is, both the same state over time and different states must not have conducted themselves in a substantially different manner on the same matter.[30] Inconsistencies, however, do not necessarily prevent the formation of customs: as the ICJ noted

> [i]n order to deduce the existence of customary rules ... it [is] sufficient that the conduct of States should, in general, be consistent with such rules, and that instances of State conduct inconsistent with a given rule should generally have been treated as breaches of that rule, not as indications of the recognition of a new rule. If a State acts in a way prima facie incompatible with a recognized rule, but defends its conduct by appealing to exceptions or justifications contained within the rule itself, then whether or not the State's conduct is in fact justifiable on that basis, the significance of that attitude is to confirm rather than to weaken the rule.[31]

This confirms the importance of *opinio juris* for the identification of customary international law: 'actual practice merely provides an opportunity to ascertain the legal convictions of the States concerned by analysing the discourse to which it gives rise'.[32]

Resolutions of international organizations can have a double relevance for the identification of customary international law: they can contribute to its formation and can be evidence of the existence of a customary rule when they declare the law and are adopted unanimously or by consensus.[33] General and uniform practice, however, is also necessary.[34] Note that '[i]t is only when a resolution claims (explicitly or by implication) to enunciate binding rules that the question of customary law even arises, for only these resolutions pass the threshold test of being what one might term "legal pronouncements"'.[35] This is the case, for instance, with the UN General Assembly's Friendly Relations Declaration, to which frequent reference is made in this book. General Assembly resolutions are more significant than those of the Security Council for the identification of customary international law because of the broader membership of the former organ and its more equalitarian voting system.[36]

Resort to primary sources has been supplemented with the use of relevant scholarly literature. I have tried to give a voice to scholars from diverse legal cultures and jurisdictions, particularly those who have written in those languages I am able to read other than English (French, Spanish, and Italian). I hope I have succeeded in this endeavour. Of particular significance were the works of the Institut de droit international, which has adopted four resolutions concerning the principle of non-intervention: the Resolution on Droits et devoirs des Puissances étrangères, au cas de mouvement insurrectionnel, envers les gouvernements établis et reconnus qui sont aux prises avec l'insurrection (adopted at the Neuchâtel Session in 1900), the Resolution on

---

[30] Statement of Principles, 21.

[31] *Nicaragua v USA*, para 186.

[32] Olivier Corten, *The Law Against War: The Prohibition on the Use of Force in Contemporary International Law* (2nd edn, Hart Publishing 2021) 42.

[33] Conclusion 12, Draft Conclusions, 107; Statement of Principles, 57–61.

[34] Draft Conclusions, 108.

[35] Statement of Principles, 55–6.

[36] Draft Conclusions, 107.

The Principle of Non-Intervention in Civil Wars (adopted at the Wiesbaden Session in 1975), the Resolution on The Protection of Human Rights and the Principle of Non-intervention in Internal Affairs of States (adopted at the Santiago de Compostela Session in 1989), and the Resolution on Military Assistance on Request (adopted at the Rhodes Session in 2011). The extensive reports of the special rapporteurs and their discussion by the Institut's members offer important perspectives on our topic.[37]

While this book primarily adopts a doctrinal methodology, it goes beyond the strict black-letter texts and complements their interpretation with a contextual approach to legal interpretation that also considers history and politics. A historical reading of the principle of non-intervention is necessitated to properly understand its current connotations: without it, 'we have no way of knowing whether contemporary ideas and practices are novel and potentially revolutionary or merely the most recent examples of practices that have long characterized International Relations'.[38] As the principle is a corollary of state sovereignty, in particular, it is essential to map the evolution of this notion through time and its reverberations on the law of intervention. It would also be impossible to make sense of individual cases of intervention without considering the political context in which they occurred. While I mainly look at the *lex lata* and how it formed, considerations *de lege ferenda* are also made where appropriate, for instance, in regard to economic coercion and to the application of the principle of non-intervention in cyberspace.

One final word on what this book does *not* do. The book does not look at the *jus in bello* aspects of foreign intervention in situations of internal unrest, in particular those related to the classification (or reclassification) of such situations as a consequence of the intervention. It also does not scrutinize all instances and justifications for the use of armed force in international law, for instance the right of states to self-defence and operations to protect nationals abroad: *jus contra bellum* analysis is undertaken only when relevant for the discussion of the principle of non-intervention.[39]

The law is stated as of 30 June 2023 and all websites were also last consulted on that date.

---

[37] The usefulness of the works of the Institut de droit international for the identification of customary international law has been highlighted by the ILC (Draft Conclusions, 110).

[38] Reus-Smit, 'The Concept', 1061–2.

[39] I use the expression *jus contra bellum* instead of the more traditional *jus ad bellum* to emphasize the fact that international law now prohibits the use of armed force as a means to settle international disputes and does not merely restrict it. The expression *jus ad bellum* is employed when referring to the rules on the use of force in existence before the UN Charter.

I

The Development of the Principle of Non-Intervention from the End of the Religious Wars in Europe to the Outbreak of the Second World War

1. Introduction

What we now call 'intervention' is by no means a recent phenomenon. A treaty concluded around 1278 BC between Ramses II, pharaoh of Egypt, and Hattousilis III, king of the Hittites, provided that the two rulers would assist each other with infantry and chariots in case their subjects revolted against them.[1] The Greek historian Thucydides also gives an accurate account of Corcyra and Corinth's interferences in the civil strife occurring in Epidamnus between the democratic and aristocratic parties of that city.[2] Epidamnus's ruling democratic faction first sent ambassadors to Corcyra, their mother city, asking for help to reestablish order, but the request was declined. After consulting the oracle in Delphi, the Epidamnians appealed for assistance from Corinth, the city of their founder, which responded positively not only because of the 'equity of the cause' but also 'for hatred of the Corcyræans'.[3] Corinth's intervention led to counter-intervention by Corcyra to restore Epidamnus's exiled aristocrats in power. Other Greek *póleis* joined the quarrel on one side or the other by sending ships, money, or troops, which eventually led to the Great Peloponnesian War (431–404 BC). In Thucydides's account, however, the discussion is limited to whether it was the mother city or the founder's city that was entitled to intermeddle in Epidamnus's affairs: the permissibility of the intervention is not questioned as such.[4]

---

[1] The so-called Treaty of Kadesh is the oldest peace treaty known to date. Read the text in Boutros Boutros-Ghali, *Contribution à une théorie générale des alliances* (Pedone 1963) 15–16.

[2] Thucydides, *The History of the Grecian War* (431 BC) (Thomas Hobbes of Malmesbury tr, John Bohn 1843) vol I, 27 ff.

[3] ibid, 29.

[4] Indeed, it is doubtful that an 'international law' as we presently conceive it already existed in antiquity. In particular, while it is correct that the relations among the Greek *póleis* and between the Roman Empire and its rivals were regulated by certain rules (Carlo Focarelli, *Introduzione storica al diritto internazionale* (Giuffrè 2012) 54, 82–3), there was still 'no conception of an international community of states co-existing within a defined framework' (Malcolm N Shaw, *International Law* (9th edn, CUP 2021) 13). See Mario Giuliano, 'Rilievi sul problema storico del diritto internazionale' (1950) 3 Comunicazioni e studi dell'Istituto di diritto internazionale dell'Università di Milano 107; Wolfgang Preiser, 'History of International Law, Ancient Times to 1648' in *MPEPIL Online* (last updated 1984); Carlo Focarelli, 'The Early Doctrine of International Law as a Bridge from Antiquity to Modernity and Diplomatic Inviolability in the 16th- and 17th-Century European Practice' in Randall Lesaffer (ed), *The Twelve Years Truce (1609): Peace, Truce, War and Law in the Low Countries at the Turn of the 17th Century* (Brill/Nijhoff 2014) 210, 213–16.

International Law and the Principle of Non-Intervention. Marco Roscini, Oxford University Press. © Marco Roscini 2024.
DOI: 10.1093/oso/9780198786894.003.0002

10 INTERNATIONAL LAW AND THE PRINCIPLE OF NON-INTERVENTION

Indeed, as I demonstrate in the following pages, non-intervention as a legal obligation of states did not start to emerge until the 17th century. It is from this period, therefore, that this chapter begins its analysis: the main purpose is not to identify the exact moment in time *when* the principle of non-intervention emerged, but *how* it sedimented before the adoption of the Charter of the United Nations (1945). This objective is achieved by examining both the most representative scholarship and the state practice of the time: the latter, in particular, has been often overlooked by the historiography of international law, even though resort to arms in or against another state was often accompanied by declarations, pamphlets, manifestos, and other official statements that, far from being mere propaganda, can reveal the normative beliefs of the concerned actors.[5]

After examining the appearance of the idea of non-intervention during the 17th and 18th centuries in Europe, the chapter explores its consolidation in the 1800s. It first identifies what was meant by 'intervention' in this period and how the notion was different from that of 'war'. It next contextualizes the problem of the legality of intervention in the framework of the doctrine of the fundamental rights of states before proceeding to analyse the practice and *opinio juris* of the main actors of the time both in Europe and in the Americas. The chapter also examines whether different rules applied depending on the type of internal unrest in which the intervention took place. The emergence of a prohibition of war after the First World War and its consequences on the law of intervention is explored in Section 8. Finally, the chapter undertakes a survey of the most representative Anglo-Saxon, continental European, and Latin American legal scholarship of the 19th century and of the first half of the 20th to detect the main lines of thought in regard to the legality of intervention.

2. The Emergence of the Idea of Non-Intervention during the 17th and 18th Centuries

As Ward's *History of the Law of Nations* reminds us, one of the foundations of the feudal order dominant in the Middle Ages in Europe was 'the right to interfere with one another, which the states of Europe mutually assumed in consequence of the divisions and subdivisions into which they had fallen'.[6] Indeed, a principle of non-intervention in the internal affairs of others did not make much sense in the *jus commune* of the *Respublica christiana*, a society conceived as a unit ruled by the Holy Roman Emperor as *dominus mundi* and by the Roman pontiff as the earthly representative of Christ, on whose behalf vicars administered their lands.[7] In this vertical system, the Pope claimed

---

[5] Pärtel Piirimäe, 'Just War in Theory and Practice: The Legitimation of Swedish Intervention in the Thirty Years War' (2002) 45 The Historical Journal 499, 500–1. By the late 17th century, custom was considered a formative source of the law of nations, based on tacit consent (Randall Lesaffer, 'Sources in the Modern Tradition: The Nature of Europe's Classical Law of Nations' in Samantha Besson and Jean d'Aspremont (eds), *The Oxford Handbook of the Sources of International Law* (OUP 2017) 99, 112–13).

[6] Robert Ward, *An Enquiry into the Foundation and History of the Law of Nations*, vol I (Butterworth 1795) 367.

[7] According to Johannes Teutonicus (d 1245), in particular, the Emperor was 'super omnes reges ... et omnes naciones sunt sub eo' (quoted in Gaines Post, 'Two Notes on Nationalism in the Middle Ages' (1953) 9 *Traditio* 281, 299).

DEVELOPMENT OF THE PRINCIPLE OF NON-INTERVENTION 11

the power to adjudicate disputes between Christian princes, depose the illegitimate or heretical ones, and release subjects from their duties towards their rulers, while the Emperor interfered in the affairs of the Empire's polities and possessed the prerogative 'to wage war against the internal and external enemies of Christendom'.[8] The Emperor's vassals could thus invoke his assistance when they felt threatened by other vassals or by popular revolts.[9] Feudal laws did not exclusively apply to the relations between the Emperor and the Pope on one side and their direct vassals on the other, as a lord could have been the vassal of another overlord through subinfeudation.[10] Princes, republics, and free cities also did not have exclusive *dominium* over their territories and populations internally: different social groups (clergy, Jews, infidels, etc.) were subject to different rules and certain prerogatives could be exercised by a prince in a territory formally ruled by another.[11] No affairs, therefore, were properly internal, and the distinction between international war and civil war was difficult to make.[12] The important classification, in the Middle Ages, was rather that between public and private wars.[13]

The consolidation of national kingdoms *superiorem non recognoscentes* started in the 15th century (or even earlier)[14] and led to the progressive dismantling of the idea of universal monarchy and to the formation of the modern notion of 'state'.[15] Kings

[8] Wilhelm G Grewe, *Epochen der Völkerrechtsgeschichte* (Nomos 1984), tr and rev by Michael Byers as *The Epochs of International Law* (Walter de Gruyter 2000) 110. There was of course another emperor who had universalistic claims and who was not subordinated (in fact he claimed to be superior) to the Holy Roman Emperors: it was the emperor of the Eastern Roman Empire, who had a much more direct ascendancy from the old Roman Empire than his Western counterpart. In its heyday, the Byzantine Empire (as it became known) took up the role of defender of Christianity in the East: when the Armenians rebelled against the Persians in AD 562, for instance, Emperor Justin invoked the right to assist them (Arthur Nussbaum, *A Concise History of the Law of Nations* (rev edn, Macmillan 1954) 49).

[9] As has been pointed out, however, not all vassalage relationships were the same: some vassals were properly subordinated to their feudal overlordship, while for others the subordination was only in name (Giorgio Badiali, *Il diritto di pace di Alberico Gentili* (Il Sirente 2010) 82–3).

[10] Nussbaum, *A Concise History*, 22.

[11] Focarelli, *Introduzione storica*, 113. Some vassals of the king of France, for instance, were at the same time vassals of the English Crown (Preiser, 'History of International Law', para 48). The king of England was also a vassal of the king of France in his capacity as duke of Normandy (Nussbaum, *A Concise History*, 22).

[12] Stefan Oeter, 'Civil War, Humanitarian Law and the United Nations' (1997) 1 Max Planck YB UN L 195, 196; Focarelli, *Introduzione storica*, 115–16. As Nussbaum points out, in the universal monarchy 'there could not be "international" relations among its members (princes or free cities)' (Nussbaum, *A Concise History*, 21).

[13] See eg Hugo Grotius, *De jure belli ac pacis* (1625) (Richard Tuck ed, Jean Barbeyrac tr, Liberty Fund 2005) 240: 'Private War is that which is made between private Persons, without publick Authority. Mixed War is that which is made on one Side by publick Authority, and on the other by mere private Persons'. Quoting Cicero, Grotius adds that '[h]e is an Enemy … Who has the Government of publick Affairs, a publick Council, a Treasury, the Right of commanding the People by Vertue of their Consent and Union, the Power of making peace and War, when necessary' (ibid, 1247).

[14] Grewe, *The Epochs*, 164. The maxim *rex superiorem non recognoscens in regno suo est imperator* is thought to have been developed in the 13th century by the glossators of the School of Bologna and, during that century, it became the foundation of the early claims to independence from the Empire of the Sicilian, French, and Spanish monarchies (Francesco Calasso, *I glossatori e la teoria della sovranità* (3rd edn, Giuffrè 1957) 34–6). The formula is composed of two parts of different origin: the denial of a superior authority by the *reges liberi* (*rex superiorem non recognoscens*) and the attribution to them, in their respective kingdoms, of the *plenitudo potestatis* of the Emperor (*rex in regno suo est imperator*). See ibid, 39–41.

[15] Francisco Suárez, for instance, writes that 'there exists within the Church no one supreme temporal prince over that whole body, that is to say, over all the kingdoms of the Church; but that, on the contrary, there are as many princes as there are kingdoms, or sovereign states' (Francisco Suárez, 'A Defence of the Catholic and Apostolic Faith—In Refutation of the Errors of the Anglican Sect with a Reply to the Apologie

gradually became free to exercise their prerogatives within their territories as they deemed fit and without external interferences from the Pope, the Emperor, or other monarchs. Modern sovereignty in its external aspect began to take shape, while internal sovereignty would consolidate at least a century later.[16] The emancipation process was accelerated in the 16th century by the Protestant Reformation, which broke up the Christian unity of Europe and undermined the spiritual supremacy of the Pope. If the Reformation contributed to the formation of national sovereign states in Europe, however, at the same time it opened the door to confessional wars often accompanied by foreign intervention on grounds of religious solidarity.[17]

By putting an end to the religious wars in Europe, the Peace of Westphalia (1648) helped create the conditions for a new and more stable international order founded on the divine right of monarchs to rule and the respect for succession rules.[18] The subsequent period is thus characterized by the consolidation of absolute monarchies and of a pluralistic community of states with exclusive jurisdiction in their own territorial sphere.[19] The *jus publicum europæum* formed a set of rules to regulate the

---

for the Oath of Allegiance and to the Admonitory Preface of His Most Serene Majesty James, King of England (1613)' in Gwladys L Williams, Ammi Brown, and John Waldron (eds), *Selection from Three Works of Francisco Suárez, SJ*, vol II (Humphrey Milford 1944) 766).

[16] Randall Lesaffer, 'Paix et guerre dans les grands traités du dix-huitième siècle' (2005) 7 J His Intl L 25, 40. It is well known that the expression 'sovereignty' is thought to have been used for the first time by Jean Bodin, who defined it as the 'puissance absolue et perpetuelle d'une République' (Jean Bodin, *Les six Livres de la République* (Imprimerie de Jean de Tournes 1579) 85). As Judge Anzilotti puts it in the Advisory Opinion on the *Customs Regime between Germany and Austria*, external sovereignty means that 'the State has over it no other authority than that of international law' (*Customs Regime between Germany and Austria*, Advisory Opinion of 5 September 1931, PCIJ Series A/B No 41, Individual Opinion by Judge Anzilotti, 57). Internal sovereignty, on the other hand, is the condition where 'the central ruler is the sole power within his territories who enjoy an original legitimization of power and ... all other territorial and functional public authorities—such as the nobility, clergy and towns—derive their powers from the central ruler' (Randall Lesaffer, 'The Grotian Tradition Revisited: Change and Continuity in the History of International Law' (2002) 73 BYBIL 103, 116).

[17] As Lesaffer notes, '[r]eligious intervention was an act of "collective defence", rather than intervention on behalf of a third party' (Randall Lesaffer, 'Between Faith and Empire: The Justification of the Spanish Intervention in the French Wars of Religion in the 1590s' in Martti Koskenniemi, Walter Rech, and Jiménez Fonseca (eds), *International Law and Empire: Historical Explorations* (OUP 2017) 101, 117). Defensive wars of religion in support of persecuted foreign subjects on grounds of confessional solidarity had to be distinguished from offensive religious wars to propagate a faith, which were unequivocally condemned by all major scholars of the time.

[18] The Peace of Westphalia ended the Thirty Years' War (1618–48) in the Holy Roman Empire and the Eighty Years' War (1568–1646) between Spain and the United Provinces of the Netherlands. The settlement, signed on 24 October 1648, included the Treaty of Münster between the Holy Roman Emperor and France and the Treaty of Osnabrück between the Emperor and Sweden, in addition to a separate treaty, signed in Münster on 30 January of the same year, between Spain and the Dutch Republic. See Treaty of Peace between Sweden and the Empire (Osnabrück, 14 (24) October 1648) 1 CTS 198; Treaty of Peace between France and the Empire (Münster, 14 (24) October 1648) 1 CTS 319; Treaty of Peace between Spain and the Netherlands (Münster, 30 January 1648) 1 CTS 70. The Treaties of Westphalia settled religious and territorial disputes within the Empire, redefined several borders, and reduced the number of polities within the Empire from about 900 to about 300. All the major European powers were represented at Westphalia, with the notable exceptions of England and Poland (Nussbaum, *A Concise History*, 115). Pope Innocent X famously declared the Treaties of Westphalia 'null, void, invalid, inequitable, unjust, condemned, reprobated, frivolous, of no force or effect' (ibid, 116).

[19] There were, of course, important exceptions to absolutism, like post-Stuart England and the Netherlands.

DEVELOPMENT OF THE PRINCIPLE OF NON-INTERVENTION 13

co-existence of and maintain a balance of power among these sovereign entities (*principe d'équilibre*).[20] In this scenario, non-intervention started to be seen as a corollary of the sovereign equality of states and as a normative shield against the hegemonic ambitions of the great power of the day: as Rainer Grote notes, 'the recognition that the government of each country is supreme within its territory implies that no external authority, be it universal or national in character, should interfere with its exercise of governmental powers on domestic matters since this would undermine the very basis of its sovereignty'.[21] Intervention in the affairs of other states, therefore, came to be considered impermissible not because it was prohibited by a discrete rule, but because it encroached on state sovereignty. In fact, there was still no identifiable notion of 'intervention' in this period.[22] The word rarely appeared in the diplomatic and scholarly language of the time and, when it did, it was not employed in any technical sense: expressions more frequently used were *s'ingérer* and *ne pas se mêler des affaires domestiques d'autrui*, which included not only the use of armed force but also any unauthorized exercise of jurisdiction on the territory of another sovereign.[23] When conducted by armed force, what we now call intervention overlapped with the notion of 'war' and, therefore, the scholars of the time discussed it in the context of the just causes of war.[24]

As said, the idea of non-intervention was born as a corollary of 'Westphalian' sovereignty as embodied in the person of the monarch, who ruled 'by grace of God' and whose legitimacy depended on his or her divine right to rule in accordance with succession rules. Inherent in this construction was the principle of the continuity of legitimate power, which was an essential feature of the 18th century's *jus publicum europæum* and which required that 'sovereignty might not be taken away from

---

[20] The expression 'balance of power' was used for the first time by Francesco Guicciardini in the 16th century in relation to the states of the Italian peninsula (Detlev Vagts, 'Balance of Power' in *MPEPIL Online* (last updated September 2007) para 2). The balance of power, which sees the *agrandissement* of one power as a destabilizing factor in Europe, was explicitly mentioned in the Peace Treaty of Utrecht (1713) between Spain and Britain, which ended the War of Spanish Succession (Art II, Treaty of Peace and Friendship between Great Britain and Spain (Utrecht, 11 April 1713) 28 CTS 297). As Lassa Oppenheim observes, however, the principle in question 'is not a legal principle and therefore not one of International Law, but one of International policy; it is a political principle indispensable to the existence of International Law in its present condition' (Lassa Oppenheim, *International Law: A Treatise*, vol I: Peace (2nd edn, Longmans, Green and Co 1912) 193, fn 1). The balance-of-power language has occasionally resurfaced in contemporary diplomatic parlance. The letter addressed to the Czechoslovak communists by the five Warsaw Pact states that intervened in the Eastern European country in 1968, for instance, rejected imperialist attempts 'to make a breach in the socialist system and change the balance of power in Europe' (reproduced in Kazimierz Grzybowski, *Soviet Public International Law: Doctrines and Diplomatic Practice* (Sijthoff/Rule of Law Press 1970) 118).

[21] Rainer Grote, 'Westphalian System' in *MPEPIL Online* (last updated June 2006) para 7.

[22] Ian Brownlie, 'The Use of Force in Self-Defence' (1961) 37 BYBIL 183, 187.

[23] PH Winfield, 'The History of Intervention in International Law' (1922–1923) 3 BYBIL 130, 134; Rosario Sapienza, *Il principio del non intervento negli affari interni. Contributo allo studio della tutela giuridica internazionale della potestà di governo* (Giuffrè 1990) 42–50.

[24] Edward Keene, 'International Hierarchy and the Origins of the Modern Practice of Intervention' (2013) 39 Rev Intl Stud 1077, 1081. Under the scholastic doctrine of just war, based on natural law, war was an enforcement action: following Thomas Aquinas (1225–74), a war was just, and thus not a sin, when it was waged by a proper authority (ie, a sovereign), had a just cause, and a righteous intention (Lesaffer, 'Between Faith', 103–4). A just cause, in particular, implied that a war had to be based on a valid claim (Stephen C Neff, *War and the Law of Nations: A General History* (CUP 2005) 51).

legitimate sovereigns without their consent'.[25] Said otherwise, no conquest or revolution could have been a legitimate title to sovereignty: '[n]o crown and no territory could be declared in abeyance if the legitimate sovereign had not formally abdicated; every state and every government established in opposition to the will of the legitimate sovereign of the territory might not be internationally recognized'.[26] The doctrine of resistance to tyranny developed by the Christian theologians of the Middle Ages and championed by the Protestant writers of the 16th and 17th centuries, therefore, gradually faded away with the internal pacification and consolidation of the nation states, as the state itself became the guarantor of law and order: those who resisted the established authority were by definition mere criminals.[27] As a result, no intervention was conceivable on their side: disputes between a sovereign and their subjects always remained an internal affair of the concerned state, even when the ruler was tyrannical.[28]

The role played by recognition in this context is also of interest for our purposes, as it is in the works of the jusnaturalists and early positivists of the 18th century that the first separate treatment of this subject appears.[29] What emerges from their works is that, both under the law of nature and the law of nations, sovereignty was now seen as originating from within, and not from without, the state: said otherwise, the title and rank of hereditary and elective sovereigns did not depend on their recognition by other states or even less by a universal authority (at least when succession rules were respected). The refusal to recognize a legitimate monarch was in fact a delictual act,

---

[25] Angelo Piero Sereni, *The Italian Conception of International Law* (Columbia University Press 1943) 155.

[26] ibid. See also Daniel Emilio Rojas Castro, 'La reconnaissance des gouvernements ibéro-américains: Histoire du droit international et histoire transnationale au XIXᵉ siècle' (2015/2) 162 *Relations internationales* 9, 13.

[27] Oeter, 'Civil War', 197.

[28] Sapienza, *Il principio*, 136; Jean Siotis, *Le droit de la guerre et les conflits armés d'un caractère non-international* (R Pichon et R Durand-Auzias 1958) 19; Erik Castrén, *Civil War* (Suomalainen Tiedeakatemia 1966) 39; Lindsay Moir, *The Law of Internal Armed Conflict* (CUP 2007) 3. The contrast with Hugo Grotius's thought is evident. Although he denies that subjects possess a right to revolt against their sovereign, even when he is tyrannical (Grotius, *De jure belli*, 338–42, 365–72), Grotius (1583–1645) admits, like Bodin before him, that other sovereigns can intervene to defend them: this is in fact a just cause of war. He famously explains his argument in the 'Chapter on the Causes for which War is to be Undertaken on the Account of Others': 'if the Injustice be visible, as if a *Busiris*, a *Phalaris*, or a *Thracian Diomedes* exercise such Tyrannies over Subjects, as no good Man living can approve of, the Right of human Society shall not be therefore excluded' (ibid, 1161, italics in the original, footnotes omitted). He concludes that 'tho' it were granted that Subjects ought not, even in the most pressing Necessity, to take up Arms against their Prince ... we should not yet be able to conclude from thence, that others might not do it for them' (ibid, 1161–2). This right to exact punishment for the benefit of human society, however, only 'reside[s] in those who are possessed of the supreme Power, and that properly, not as they have an Authority over others, but as they are in Subjection to none' (ibid, 1021). As has been observed, Grotius 'granted external players—that is, third states endowed with sovereign power—the right that he denied to internal players (ie, the subjects), who did not have sovereign power' (Daniele Archibugi, Mariano Croce, and Andrea Salvatore, 'Law of Nations or Perpetual Peace? Two Early International Theories on the Use of Force' in Marc Weller (ed), *The Oxford Handbook of the Use of Force in International Law* (OUP 2015) 56, 74). This has earned Grotius the reputation of 'father of solidarist international society theory' (Nicholas Wheeler, *Saving Strangers: Humanitarian Intervention in International Society* (OUP 2000) 45).

[29] CH Alexandrowicz, 'The Theory of Recognition *in fieri* (1958)' in CH Alexandrowicz, *The Law of Nations in Global History* (David Armitage and Jennifer Pitts eds, OUP 2017) 354. Alexandrowicz refers to the works of Johann Heinrich Gottlieb von Justi, Johann Christian Wilhelm von Steck, and Georg Friedrich von Martens, as well as early 19th-century writers like Jean Louis Klueber, Friedriech Saalfeld, and Henry Wheaton.

as it contradicted the principle of the sovereign equality of states.[30] The same logic applied to secessionist struggles: when the parent state had recognized the independence of the rebellious province, foreign powers had no right to take action to force the newly independent state into submitting to their former overlord.[31] Foreign powers, however, had to abstain from recognizing the secessionist province and providing support to it until the previous sovereign had agreed to transfer sovereignty.[32]

These considerations explain why most interventions which took place from the second half of the 17th century to the outbreak of the American War of Independence were in support of sovereigns facing rebellions. In 1731, for instance, the Republic of Genoa asked Emperor Charles VI for military assistance to quell an insurrection in Corsica.[33] During the Swedish Revolution of 1772, France promised support to King Gustav III to re-establish monarchical rule.[34] Louis XIV also sent 3,000 livres to King James II of England (James VII of Scotland and James II of Ireland) who was facing the Glorious Revolution, although the latter declined the former's offer of military support.[35] Russia and, to a lesser extent, Prussia and Austria participated in quelling the insurrection of Tadeusz Kościuszko in Poland in 1794, which led to the third and final partition of the Polish–Lithuanian Commonwealth.[36] In 1787, Prussia also sent an expeditionary force to the United Provinces of the Netherlands to restore the authority of the Stadtholder during the Batavian Revolution. Prussia's official reason for its intervention was to obtain satisfaction for the offence caused by the arrest of the Stadtholder's wife (who was also the Prussian king's sister) by the forces of the States of Holland.[37] While France protested against the Prussian interference, Britain declared that it would support the Stadtholder.[38]

The claimed legal basis of these interventions was often the existence of alliance treaties by which one or more powers committed to guarantee the thrones of royal dynasties or the constitution of states. In addition to the 1648 Peace Treaties of Westphalia,[39] one could recall, among many, the 1761 'family compact' between

---

[30] ibid, 356–8.

[31] ibid, 360. Other states also did not need to formally recognize the new state's independence, it being sufficient that they treated it as such (ibid).

[32] ibid, 360–1, 363–4.

[33] Peter Hamish Wilson, *German Armies: War and German Society, 1648–1806* (Routledge 1998) 208. In a second insurrection in 1734, the insurgents appealed for the assistance of Spain against Genoa, but none arrived.

[34] Brendan Simms, '"A False Principle in the Law of Nations": Burke, State Sovereignty, (German) Liberty, and Intervention in the Age of Westphalia' in Brendan Simms and DJB Trim (eds), *Humanitarian Intervention* (CUP 2011) 89, 98.

[35] John R Western, *Monarchy and Revolution: The English State in the 1680s* (Blandford Press 1972) 259.

[36] Łukasz Kadziela and Robert Strybel, 'The 1794 Kościuszko Insurrection' (1994) 39 The Polish Review 387.

[37] Grewe, *The Epochs*, 336.

[38] Thomas Baty observes that 'it was, at that date at all events, not considered an improper intervention in the affairs of a foreign country to support a friendly government against reaction or revolution' and the Stadtholder was 'an established element of the Dutch Government' (Thomas Baty, 'Can an Anarchy be a State?' (1934) 28 AJIL 444, 448).

[39] Under the treaties, in particular, Catholic France and Protestant Sweden committed to guarantee the privileges and immunities acquired by the Empire's princes and free cities and, therefore, acquired a right to intervene in the affairs of the Empire (Arts CXXIII and CXXIV of the Treaty of Münster and Art XVII §5 and §6 of the Treaty of Osnabrück). This has led a commentator to brand the Westphalian Treaties as a 'charter for intervention' (Simms, '"A False Principle in the Law of Nations"', 92).

16   INTERNATIONAL LAW AND THE PRINCIPLE OF NON-INTERVENTION

the Bourbons of France and Spain, later extended to those of the Two Sicilies and Parma,[40] the 1773 Treaty between Russia and Poland, by which the former guaranteed the constitution of the latter,[41] and the 1788 Treaties of Alliance between the United Provinces, Great Britain, and Prussia, by which the latter two guaranteed the hereditary stadtholderate in the House of Orange.[42] Certain treaties also contained an explicit obligation not to interfere in the internal affairs of other states and/or a mutual obligation to abstain from providing assistance to rebels. Examples are the 1629 Treaty of Lübeck between the Holy Roman Empire and Denmark,[43] the 1630 Treaty of Madrid between Spain and Great Britain,[44] the 1659 Peace of the Pyrenees between Spain and France,[45] the 1721 Treaty of Nystad between Russia and Sweden,[46] and the 1790 Treaty between Poland and the Ottoman Empire.[47]

Compared to those on the side of sovereigns, interventions in support of foreign insurgents were rare in this period and were normally accompanied by caveats and qualifications. The Swedish intervention in the Thirty Years War, for instance, was not presented as a war against the Empire, but as a military operation to protect the Protestant princes from privateers, whose actions the Emperor was unable or unwilling to prevent.[48] In the 1688 Glorious Revolution, the Dutch Stadtholder, William III of Orange-Nassau, landed with his fleet in England following a letter of invitation from leading members of both the ruling Tory party and the Whig opposition (the 'Immortal Seven') in order to help them overthrow King James II.[49] The letter, dated 30 June 1688, referred to the dissatisfaction of the population with James's government 'in relation to their religion, liberties and properties.'[50] In the Declaration of The Hague, William stated that his only aim was 'to preserve the established Laws,

---

[40] Pacte de Famille (Paris, 15 August 1761) in *British and Foreign State Papers 1812–1814*, vol I, Part I (1841) 276.

[41] Art VII, Treaty between Poland and Russia (Warsaw, 18 September 1773) 45 CTS 250. The provision was reaffirmed in Art III of the Separate Acts between Poland and Russia (Warsaw, 15 March 1775) 46 CTS 7.

[42] Wheaton, *History*, 286.

[43] Arts II and III, Treaty of Peace Between Ferdinand II, Emperor of the Romans, and Christian IV, King of Denmark (Lübeck, 27 May 1629) in Jean Dumont, *Corps universel diplomatique du droit des gens*, vol V, part II (P Brunel et al 1728) 584.

[44] Art IV, Treaty of Peace and Alliance Between Philip IV, King of Spain, and Charles I, King of Great Britain (Madrid, 15 November 1630) in *A General Collection of Treaties, Manifesto's, Contracts of Marriage, Renunciations, And other Publick Papers. From 1495 to the Present Time*, vol II (1713) 275.

[45] The parties committed to refuse any assistance to another party's subjects in rebellion (Art LXVIII, Treaty of the Pyrenees (Pheasant Island, 7 November 1659) 5 CTS). See Robert R Wilson, 'Recognition of Insurgency and Belligerency' (1937) 31 ASIL Proceedings 136, 137.

[46] Art VII, Treaty of Peace Between Frederick I, King of Sweden, and Peter I, Emperor of Russia (Nystad, 10 September 1721) 31 CTS 345.

[47] Quoted in Victor Kattan, 'To Consent or Revolt? European Public Law, the Three Partitions of Poland (1772, 1793, and 1795) and the Birth of National Self-Determination' (2015) 17 J His Intl L 247, 267.

[48] Piirimäe, 'Just War', 517. The only invitation to intervene came from Stralsund, which was not part of the Empire (ibid, 505). Using an argument that would be invoked again a few centuries later to exonerate Japan's Emperor Hirohito of any responsibility in the Second World War, Sweden's intervention was claimed to be against the imperial general Wallenstein, who allegedly acted against the command of the emperor and against the laws of the Empire (ibid). The Catholic electors, however, accused King Gustav Adolphus of interfering in the affairs of the Empire.

[49] The 'revolution' was in fact more a coup supported by a foreign invasion than a popular rebellion.

[50] John Dalrymple, *Memoirs of Great Britain and Ireland: From the Dissolution of the Last Parliament of Charles II till the Capture of the French and Spanish Fleets at Vigo*, vol II (A Strahan, T Cadell, J Bell, W Creech, and E Balfour 1790) 107.

Liberties and Customs, and, above all, the Religion and Worship of God'.[51] Besides the propaganda language, what is significant, in addition to the emphasis on the Immortal Seven's letter of invitation as a legitimizing ground, is that, even though the expedition was conducted with the consent and support of the Dutch Republic, the Prince of Orange acted in his personal capacity as nephew and son-in-law to James II, and not as Stadtholder.[52] At least initially, his declared intention was also not to dethrone the English king but solely to secure the call of a free and lawful parliament.[53]

3. Classical Scholarship of the 18th Century

In the scholarly works of the 18th century, considerations based on the law of nature, particularly those based on the just war doctrine, continue to play an important role. After finding that '[e]very nation ought to perfect itself and its form of government',[54] for instance, Christian Wolff (1679–1754) posits that '[b]y nature no nation has the right to any act which belongs to the exercise of the sovereignty of another nation' as 'the perfection of sovereignty consists in its exercise independently of the will of any other'.[55] The foundation of this obligation of non-interference (Wolff does not use the expression 'intervention') is still natural law: '[t]o interfere in the government of another, in whatever way indeed that may be done, is opposed to the natural liberty of nations, by virtue of which one nation is altogether independent of the will of other nations in its action'.[56] He concludes that '[a] perfect [that is, enforceable] right belongs to every nation not to allow any other nation to interfere in any way in its government. For if a nation interferes with the government of another, it does this in contravention of the other's right'.[57]

Wolff also distinguishes between rebellion and civil war depending on whether the subjects have (the latter) or do not have (the former) a just cause to take up arms against their sovereign.[58] It is the law of nature that determines whether or not rebels have a just cause: as other nations do not have a right to interfere in the relations between a ruler and his subjects, they should avoid qualifying the situation as a 'rebellion'

---

[51] William Arthur Speck, *Reluctant Revolutionaries: Englishmen and the Revolution of 1688* (OUP 1989) 74.

[52] Wout Troost, *William III the Stadtholder-King: A Political Biography* (JC Grayson tr, Ashgate 2005) 193, 198. Stowell claims that, even if James II's actions justified an internal revolution against him, they were not a sufficient ground for an intervention by other states, and, therefore, William of Orange's expedition was contrary to the law of nations (Ellery C Stowell, *Intervention in International Law* (John Byrne & Co 1921) 352–3).

[53] Troost, *William III*, 198–9. The real aim, however, was another: to prevent James II from siding with Louis XIV of France against the Dutch Republic (ibid, 199).

[54] Christian Wolff, *Jus gentium methodo scientifica pertractatum* (1749), Joseph H Drake tr, *The Law of Nations: Treated According to a Scientific Method*, vol II (Clarendon Press/Humphrey Milford 1934) 24.

[55] ibid, 130.

[56] ibid, 131. He adds that '[e]very ruler of a state ought to consider the ruler of another state as his equal by nature. For by nature all nations are equal' (ibid, 128).

[57] ibid, 137. In the chapter dedicated to the methods of settling disputes between nations, Wolff confirms that 'if the ruler of a state interferes with the government of another, that is a just cause of grievance' (ibid, 289).

[58] ibid, 513–14. A civil war is a 'mixed war', ie 'one which is public as to one party, private as to the other' (ibid, 311–12).

unless the wrong of the subjects is 'perfectly plain', and use more neutral expressions like 'internal unrest' and 'malcontents using force against a ruler'.[59] Wolff also refers to 'riots', a notion linked not to the just or unjust cause pursued by the subjects but to the fact that they rise, or threaten to rise, against 'minor powers or private individuals' and their property, instead of against 'sovereign power'.[60] He considers riot a crime or a public wrong that cannot be justified by any cause.

Unlike in Vattel, however, Wolff's classification of different situations of internal unrest does not affect the operation of the obligation of non-interference: manifesting a disdain for insurgents typical of his period, he argues that in no case is support for foreign subjects against their legitimate sovereign permissible, including when they have a just cause of complaint. Even when a ruler 'should burden his subjects too heavily or treat them too harshly', another ruler may offer his good offices ('intercede in their behalf') and prayers but may not use force against the tyrant.[61] Only an intervention by the *civitas maxima*, a sort of universal supreme state, would be permissible in order to punish the wrongs of nations.[62]

Emer de Vattel (1714–67) wrote his *Le Droit des Gens* while the Seven Years' War (1756–63) was still raging in Europe and was heavily influenced by Wolff's work. Vattel is widely considered the father of the principle of non-intervention and is arguably the first author to have employed the expression 'intervenir', if only twice and not in any technical sense.[63] He rejects Wolff's idea of the *civitas maxima* as unnecessary and incompatible with the internal and external sovereignty of states, which admits no superior authority.[64] He also famously affirms the legal equality of all nations regardless of their size ('[a] dwarf is as much a man as a giant; a small republic is no less a sovereign state than the most powerful kingdom')[65] and, like Wolff, sees non-interference as a corollary of the independence, that is, the external sovereignty, of states:

---

[59] ibid, 514.

[60] ibid, 514–15.

[61] ibid, 132. Similarly, force cannot be used to educate barbarous and uncultivated nations (ibid, 89) or to introduce a religion into another state (ibid, 132).

[62] ibid, 14.

[63] Expressions that Vattel uses more frequently are *s'en mêler* et *s'ingérer* (Winfield, 'The History', 133). In the English translation of *The Law of Nations*, 'intervenir' has been translated as 'intermeddle' and 'interpose' (Emer de Vattel, *Le droit des gens ou Principes de la loi naturelle appliqués à la conduite et aux affaires des nations et des souverains* (1758), tr by Béla Kapossy and Richard Whatmore as *The Law of Nations, Or, The Principles of the Law of Nature, Applied to the Conduct and Affairs of Nations and Sovereigns, with Three Early Essays on the Origin and Nature of Natural Law and on Luxury* (Liberty Fund 2008) 96, 498).

[64] ibid, 14. Like Wolff, Vattel sees the law of nations as formed of both natural law (the 'necessary law of nations': ibid, 70) and positive law (comprising the voluntary, conventional and customary laws of nations). The three laws forming the positive law of nations 'all proceed from the will of nations—the *voluntary* from their presumed consent, the *conventional* from an express consent, and the *customary* from tacit consent' (ibid, 78, emphasis in the original). Customary law, then, 'is not obligatory except on those nations who have adopted it, and … is not universal, any more than the *conventional law*' (ibid, 77, emphasis in the original). Leo Gross observes that '[a]lthough he does not rank as a strict positivist, Vattel prepared the ground for the era of uninhibited positivism' (Leo Gross, 'The Peace of Westphalia, 1648–1948' (1948) 42 AJIL 3, 36).

[65] Vattel, *The Law of Nations*, 75. Vattel is not, however, the first to do so: Vitoria and Pufendorf had already maintained that states, like men, are equal by nature (Juliane Kokott and Lauri Mälksoo, 'States, Sovereign Equality' in *MPEPIL Online* (last updated March 2023) para 9).

It is an evident consequence of the liberty and independence of nations, that all have a right to be governed as they think proper, and that no state has the smallest right to interfere in the government of another. Of all the rights that belong to a nation, sovereignty is, doubtless, the most precious, and that which other nations ought the most scrupulously to respect, if they would not do her an injury.[66]

He concludes that 'no foreign power has a right to interfere [*se mêler*] in [affairs being solely a national concern], nor ought to intermeddle [*intervenir*] with them otherwise than by its good offices, unless requested to do it, or induced by particular reasons'.[67] The violation of the obligation of non-interference is, in Vattel as in Wolff, a wrongful act: 'If any intrude [*s'ingère*] in the domestic concerns of another nation, and attempt to put a constraint on its deliberations, they do it an injury'.[68] Among these domestic concerns is the choice of a government: 'If a people, after having expelled their prince, submit to another—if they change the order of succession, and acknowledge a sovereign to the prejudice of the natural and appointed heir—foreign powers may, in this instance also, consider what has been done as lawful; it is no quarrel or business of theirs'.[69] Vattel, therefore, repudiates the principle of continuity of legitimate power based on dynastic succession, at least with regard to internal governmental changes, and thus anticipates the developments of the Age of Revolutions.

Unlike Wolff, however, Vattel does not see the obligation of non-interference as absolute but identifies an exception based on the voluntary law of nations: a foreign power can intermeddle in the internal unrest occurring in another state if it constitutes a civil war, mediation has proved fruitless, the assisted party has justice on its side and has requested help, and there are no treaties of alliance prohibiting the interference.[70] With regard to the first element, Vattel develops Wolff's classification of internal unrest and distinguishes between popular commotion ('a concourse of people who assemble in a tumultuous manner, and refuse to listen to the voice of their superiors'), sedition ('[i]f the rage of the malcontents be particularly levelled at the magistrates, or others vested with the public authority, and they proceed to a formal disobedience or acts of open violence'), insurrection (a serious case of sedition 'when it infects the majority of the inhabitants of a city or province, and gains such strength that even the sovereign himself is no longer obeyed'),[71] and civil war ('[w]hen a party is formed in a state, who no longer obey the sovereign, and are possessed of sufficient strength to oppose him,—or when, in a republic, the nation is divided into two opposite factions, and both sides take up arms').[72] The difference between civil war and other forms of

---

[66] Vattel, *The Law of Nations*, 289. Winfield argues that this passage contains 'the germ of the modern rule of non-intervention' (Winfield, 'The History', 133).

[67] Vattel, *The Law of Nations*, 96.

[68] ibid. When Vattel refers to 'another nation', he refers to sovereign states, namely 'those that without dependency upon any foreign State, govern themselves under any form whatsoever' (ibid, 83).

[69] ibid, 689.

[70] ibid, 290–1. It has been argued that the exception to non-intervention is so broad in Vattel that it overturns the rule (Andre Mallarmé, 'Emer de Vattel' in Antoine Pillet (ed), *Les fondateurs du droit international* (Giard et Brière 1904) 481, 545). For Koskenniemi, however, this exception is not necessarily an inconsistency in Vattel's thought (Marti Koskenniemi, *From Apology to Utopia: The Structure of International Legal Argument* (CUP 2005) 115–16).

[71] Vattel, *The Law of Nations*, 641–2.

[72] ibid, 644.

20 INTERNATIONAL LAW AND THE PRINCIPLE OF NON-INTERVENTION

internal unrest is that, in the latter case, the rebellion against lawful authority is 'void of all appearance of justice'.[73] Unlike in Wolff, however, other factors also play a role in Vattel's classification of situations of internal unrest, namely their target (superiors, magistrates, or the sovereign) and their magnitude: in a civil war, the insurgents 'have acquired sufficient strength to give [the sovereign] effectual opposition, and to oblige him to carry on the war against them according to the established rules'.[74] He famously adds: 'when a nation becomes divided into two parties absolutely independent, and no longer acknowledging a common superior, the state is dissolved, and the war between the two parties stands on the same ground, in every respect, as a public war between two different nations'.[75] At that point, the conflict is a civil war regardless of whether the rebels initially had a just cause to revolt or not.[76] What matters is that the sovereign is forced to resort to warfare to restore internal order.[77]

Unlike popular commotion, sedition, and insurrection, which 'disturb the public order, and are state crimes, even when arising from just causes of complaint', civil war has for Vattel two important consequences: the first is that the laws of war apply to the conflict and the second is that the obligation of non-interference is lifted and any foreign power may take part in the civil strife.[78] More specifically, Vattel affirms the right of foreign powers to assist the party in a civil war 'which appears ... to have justice on its side, in case that party requests their assistance or accepts the offer of it', although only after an attempt to mediate between the parties has proved unsuccessful.[79] It is important to stress that, for Vattel, a just cause is necessary but not sufficient to justify third-state intervention in a civil war: the request of the party on whose side the intervention takes place or its acceptance of an offer of assistance is also required.[80]

In regard to intervention on the side of the incumbent government, Vattel distinguishes personal from real treaties of alliance. In the case of a 'real' alliance concluded with the state, and not with a monarch for the protection of his person, revolts that lead to the deposition of a king or to the expulsion of a republic's magistrates are 'domestic regulations' and opposing them 'would be interfering in the government of another nation, and doing her an injury'.[81] In cases of alliances concluded for the defence of a king and his family, on the other hand, Vattel argues that a king unlawfully dethroned 'does not forfeit the character of royalty merely by the loss of his kingdom' and 'still preserves his rights, among which are to be reckoned his alliances'.[82] The condition is that the king must have been *unjustly* deprived of his throne: 'If the body of

---

[73] ibid, 645.

[74] ibid, 645.

[75] ibid, 648. In Carl Schmitt's view, Vattel sees civil war as 'an anticipation of *possible* statehood' (Carl Schmitt, *The Nomos of the Earth in the International Law of the* Jus Publicum Europaeum (first published 1950, GL Ulmen tr, Telos Press 2003) 167, emphasis in the original).

[76] Alberto Carrera, 'Tra dovere di obbedienza e diritto di resistenza. La figura del ribelle nel pensiero giuridico di Vattel' in Giuseppina De Giudici, Dante Fedele, and Elisabetta Fiocchi Malaspina (eds), *Soggettività contestate e diritto internazionale in età moderna* (Historia et ius 2023) 177, 188 <www.histor iaetius.eu/uploads/5/9/4/8/5948821/de_giudici_ebook.pdf>.

[77] ibid,194.

[78] Vattel, *The Law of Nations*, 645–7, 648–9.

[79] ibid, 291. See also ibid, 649.

[80] ibid, 649.

[81] ibid, 364–5. The alliance, however, could be terminated because of the change of government.

[82] ibid, 363.

DEVELOPMENT OF THE PRINCIPLE OF NON-INTERVENTION   21

the nation declare that the king has forfeited his right by the abuse he has made of it, and depose him, they may justly do it when their grievances are well founded'.[83] In such case, '[t]he personal ally of this king ought not ... to assist him against the nation who have made use of their right in deposing him'.[84] When the ruler has been overthrown unjustly, on the other hand, the loss of effective control of the state does not remove his legitimacy and he remains entitled to request foreign assistance to regain his throne: indeed, it would be 'absurd' if the alliance was 'dissolved at the moment when [the king and his family] stand in need of it, and by the very event which it was intended to guard against'.[85]

As said, however, for Vattel foreign intervention in a civil war is also permissible on the side of insurgents if they have justice on their side. After recognizing that, in extreme circumstances, subjects have the right to take up arms against a tyrannical government like those of Philip II in the Low Countries and James II in England,[86] he maintains that 'if the prince, by violating the fundamental laws, gives his subjects a legal right to resist him, —if tyranny becoming insupportable obliges the nation to rise in their own defence, —every foreign power has a right to succour an oppressed people who implore their assistance', providing that the people have taken up arms against the tyrant and have good reasons to do so.[87] The Neuchâtel writer, therefore, still relies on the old doctrine of resistance to tyranny but with a caveat: he denies that persecution on grounds of religion can on its own justify foreign intervention in support of the subjects of another sovereign unless the persecution reaches intolerable excesses, in which case it becomes 'manifest tyranny, in opposition to which all nations are allowed to assist an unhappy people'.[88]

Wolff and Vattel are not the only scholars of this period to address the problem of intervention in the internal troubles of other states. The Swiss Jean-Jacques Burlamaqui (1694–1748) distinguishes an ordinary war from an imperfect one, the latter being 'that which does not intirely interrupt the peace, but only in certain particulars, the public tranquillity being in other respects undisturbed'.[89] While this seems to anticipate the distinction between wars and measures short of war which would become popular in the 19th century,[90] Burlamaqui does not treat intervention in the context of imperfect wars, as he identifies this category with reprisals.[91] Similarly to Wolff, Burlamaqui also distinguishes 'wars' from 'revolts or insurrections' depending on whether the subjects have or do not have a just cause to take up arms against their prince:

---

[83] ibid.

[84] ibid. In doubtful cases, the presumption works in favour of the deposed king (ibid, 364).

[85] ibid, 363.

[86] ibid, 104–5, 108, 110–12, 290. This right arises only in extreme situations where there are no 'means of resisting and curbing [the tyrant], without exposing the state to violent shocks' (ibid, 108–9, 110–12). In the 'Chapter on Civil War', Vattel affirms that '[e]very citizen should even patiently endure evils which are not insupportable, rather than disturb the public peace' (ibid, 642).

[87] ibid, 290.

[88] ibid, 295.

[89] Jean-Jacques Burlamaqui, *Principes du droit naturel* (1747 and 1751), tr by Thomas Nugent as *The Principles of Natural and Political Law* (Liberty Fund 2006) 475.

[90] See Section 5 of this chapter.

[91] Burlamaqui, *The Principles*, 475.

> [I]f the subjects have just reason to resist the sovereign, it is strictly a war; since, in such a crisis, there are neither sovereign nor subjects, all dependance and obligation having ceased. The two opposite parties are then in a state of nature and equality, trying to obtain justice by their own proper strength, which constitutes what we understand properly by the term *war*.[92]

Burlamaqui suggests that, in the case of succession disputes, 'other nations, who were not concerned in the war, ... have no more authority to examine the validity of the acquisitions, than they have to be judges of a war made between two different states'.[93] The same conclusion applies to the case of 'an insurrection of a considerable part of the state against the reigning prince' resulting from tyranny or from the violation of the fundamental laws of the kingdom where 'the government is ... dissolved, and the state is actually divided into two distinct and independent bodies'.[94]

That said, Burlamaqui accepts that a state can wage war in defence of foreign subjects oppressed by their prince on the basis of the principle of humanity, although 'only in cases where the tyranny is risen to such a height, that the subjects themselves may lawfully take up arms, to shake off the yoke of the tyrant ... '.[95] In such situation

> the subjects, on the one hand, re-enter into the several rights of natural liberty, which authorises them to seek assistance wherever they can find it; and, on the other hand, those who are in a condition of giving it them, without any considerable damage to themselves, not only may, but ought to do all they can to deliver the oppressed; for the single consideration of pity and humanity.[96]

He cautions, however, that 'the presumption ought to be in favour of the sovereign, and a foreign power has no right to intermeddle with what passes in another state'.[97]

Non-intervention also plays an important role in the thought of Immanuel Kant (1724–1804). In his *Zum ewigen Frieden* ('Towards perpetual peace', first published in 1795), he distances himself from the just-war tradition of 'Job's comforters' like Grotius, Pufendorf, and Vattel[98] and instead identifies positive and negative conditions for perpetual peace among nations. One of the negative conditions is his Fifth Preliminary Article, which prescribes that '[n]o state shall violently interfere with the constitution and government of another'.[99] Like Vattel, he admits an exception to this principle: when 'a State ... has become split up through internal corruption into two parts, each of them representing by itself an individual state which lays claim to the whole', assistance to either party cannot be considered interference in the constitution of another state.[100] This exception, however, is limited to situations of internal unrest

---

[92] ibid, 479, emphasis in the original.
[93] ibid, 509.
[94] ibid.
[95] ibid, 465.
[96] ibid, 466.
[97] ibid, 465–6.
[98] Immanuel Kant, *Perpetual Peace: A Philosophical Essay* (first published 1795), M Campbell Smith tr, George Allen & Unwin/Macmillan 1903) 131.
[99] ibid, 112.
[100] ibid, 113.

that have reached the critical point of anarchy leading to the *de facto* dismemberment of the country. Interference of foreign powers in less serious situations 'would be a violation of the rights of an independent nation which is only struggling with internal disease [and] would therefore itself cause a scandal, and make the autonomy of all states insecure'.[101] Kant's non-intervention principle must be read in conjunction with his affirmation, in the positive conditions for perpetual peace, that the constitution of all nations should be republican.[102] It is, therefore, only a prohibition of interfering with the government of republican states and does not rule out intervention to overthrow monarchical governments, as this would ultimately contribute to the establishment of a cosmopolitan order and to the end of all wars.[103]

The German jurist Georg Friedrich von Martens (1756–1821) follows Vattel in his main conclusions about foreign meddling in the internal affairs of other countries and affirms that, as a rule, the internal constitution of a state is a domestic matter in which foreign powers cannot interfere in case of an internal dispute apart from certain exceptional cases.[104] These exceptions include the offer or interposition of good offices if they are accepted; the request of assistance by the party to the internal dispute that has a lawful claim; the existence of a positive title to intermeddle (like a treaty of guarantee or a treaty preserving rights of succession); and the self-preservation of the intervening state.[105] Martens acknowledges, however, that these exceptions, in particular the latter two, are so broad that it is difficult to find a situation which would not offer a pretext to intervene.[106] If the internal dispute between the sovereign and his subjects becomes a 'rupture ouverte' and the latter manage to factually acquire the freedom they claim, Martens (again echoing Vattel) posits that the struggle becomes the equivalent of one between states and therefore

> il est permis de prêter secours à celui qui a le bon droit de son côté, qu'on y soit obligé ou non par des traités faits avec le souverain ou avec le peuple, pourvu qu'on n'ait pas promis la neutralité; il n'est pas permis au contraire d'épouser une cause injuste.[107]

If the embattled sovereign renounces his throne or accepts the independence of the secessionist state, however, third states have no right to oppose the new situation and its recognition by them is not necessary.[108]

To conclude, 18th-century writers do not see the obligation of non-interference as a discrete rule of the law of nations but rather conceive it as directly emanating from

---

[101] ibid, 113–14.

[102] ibid, 120.

[103] Richard B Lillich, 'Kant and the Current Debate over Humanitarian Intervention' (1997) 6 J Transnat'l L & Pol'y 397, 401–2.

[104] Georg Friedrich von Martens, *Précis du droit des gens moderne de l'Europe fondé sur les traités et l'usage*, vol I (Jean Chret Dieterich 1789) 76, 86. As Nussbaum notes, '[a]s a writer, von Martens belongs to the pre-Napoleonic period, during which his literary opus was virtually completed' (Nussbaum, *A Concise History*, 179). Martens's *Précis* is considered one of the earliest positivist treatises, as it identifies legal principles from the practice of states and not from dogmatic assertions.

[105] Martens, *Précis*, 77, 86–7.

[106] ibid, 77.

[107] ibid, 88–9.

[108] ibid, 89–90.

24   INTERNATIONAL LAW AND THE PRINCIPLE OF NON-INTERVENTION

sovereignty and the equality of states. In their view, the internal constitution of a state is a domestic affair in which other powers have no title to interfere and which, therefore, they cannot change forcibly. With the exception of Wolff, mainstream scholarship of this period also posits that, in the case of civil war that has led the state to divide into two parts, it becomes permissible to assist the faction that has justice on its side if it has appealed for help and consistently with treaties of alliance and guarantee: an intervention in support of insurgents, therefore, cannot be ruled out, particularly when the ruler is a tyrannical one. As discussed in Section 2, however, this view was not reflected in the state practice of the time.

4. The Age of Revolutions

Before the 18th century could end its run, the American War of Independence and the French Revolution challenged the established European order and the existing balance of power.[109] They violently rejected the absolutist form of government based on the divine right to rule predominant at the time and, with it, several principles of the *jus publicum europæum*. Practice related to the two revolutions also seemed, at least at first sight, to undermine the clear disfavour towards supporting foreign insurgents that had characterized the previous decades.

The struggle for independence of the North American colonies from Britain started in 1774 and concluded successfully in 1783 with the Paris Peace Conference.[110] During the conflict, most European states did not support the colonies and either refused to give rights of war to them (Denmark and Portugal) or opted for a neutral position (Prussia, Sweden, Russia, and the Netherlands).[111] France, however, adopted a different attitude and, after an initial prudent approach, started to assist the North American rebels with arms, soldiers, and loans and concluded a Treaty of Amity and Commerce with them on 6 February 1778.[112] The Court of Versailles justified its recognition of and support for the colonies claiming that they were *de facto* independent, regardless of whether this independence had been acquired lawfully or not.[113] This was proved—the French argued—by the fact that Britain had ceased to

---

[109] Armitage notes that '[t]he nascent category of revolution was designed, in part, to repress memories of civil war and to replace them with something more constructive, more hopeful, and more forward-looking' (David Armitage, *Civil Wars: A History of Ideas* (Yale University Press 2017) 120). The expression, however, never became a term of art in the law of nations and was often used interchangeably with civil war.

[110] Certain contemporary commentators referred to the struggle as a 'civil war' (ibid, 140).

[111] John Bassett Moore, *A Digest of International Law*, vol I (GPO 1906) 169. Portugal closed its ports to the insurgent ships and to those that had visited insurgent ports and Denmark denied the insurgents' right to take prizes, giving rise to a dispute with the United States (Arnold D McNair, 'The Law Relating to the Civil War in Spain' (1937) 53 LQR 471, 478; Siotis, *Le droit de la guerre*, 62–3). See also Sam Foster Halabi, 'Traditions of Belligerent Recognition: The Libyan Intervention in Historical and Theoretical Context' (2011–2012) 27 AU Int'l L Rev 321, 336–7.

[112] Sir Robert Phillimore, *Commentaries upon International Law*, vol I (3rd edn, Butterworths 1879) 26. The recognition of independence and the signing of a treaty with the insurgent colonies was deemed too rushed by Harcourt, as Britain 'was still being engaged in a contest for their subjugation' (Sir William Vernon Harcourt, *Letters by Historicus on Some Questions of International Law* (Macmillan 1863) 9). Calvo agreed: for him the French support to the insurgents provided Britain with 'un juste sujet de plainte' (Charles Calvo, *Le droit international théorique et pratique*, vol I (4th edn, Guillaumin et al 1887) 241).

[113] Wheaton, *History*, 291, 293.

DEVELOPMENT OF THE PRINCIPLE OF NON-INTERVENTION   25

treat them as rebels and observed the ordinary laws of war between nations during the conflict.[114] As a result, the French king 'was bound neither to assist England against the colonies, nor to repulse the colonies when they presented themselves to him as an independent people'.[115] France also used self-preservation language by claiming that it acted together with Spain 'pour venger leurs griefs respectifs, et pour mettre un terme à l'empire tyrannique que l'Angleterre a usurpé et prétend conserver sur toutes les mers'.[116]

The American War of Independence constitutes the first high-profile case where the principle of continuity of legitimate power, according to which a secessionist revolt could not lead to the formation of a new state until the previous sovereign had accepted to renounce and transfer his rights over the territory to a new sovereign, was set aside because of the *de facto* success of the secessionists.[117] The British government strongly protested, arguing that disputes within an independent and sovereign state were an internal matter and, therefore, they were not subject to the jurisdiction of another state: the French actions constituted a dangerous precedent that could have backfired on France in possible future rebellions in its own colonies.[118] Britain also accused France of breaching Article I of the 1763 Treaty of Paris between the two countries, which required a party not to support or protect, directly or indirectly, those who wanted to injure the other.[119] War with France and Spain ensued in 1777 and 1779, respectively, and in 1780 Britain also declared war on the Dutch Republic, alleging that the latter had recognized the independence of the United States and intended to conclude a trade agreement with it.[120] Britain, however, was eventually forced to accept the independence of its former American colonies with the signing of the Treaty of Paris on 3 September 1783. Several countries had already recognized the United States *de facto* or *de jure* without waiting for the conclusion of the peace treaty.[121]

The French Revolution broke out in 1789. In spite of the revolutionaries' early reassuring declarations committing to non-intervention,[122] in the Pillnitz Declaration of 27 August 1791 the Holy Roman Emperor Leopold II and King Frederick William II of Prussia declared that the troubles of France and of its monarch were 'an object of common interest to all sovereigns of Europe' and not a purely internal French matter, and asked all European powers to assist the imprisoned king.[123] Military action against

---

[114] ibid, 293. Both France and Spain accepted insurgent ships in their ports and treated them as if they belonged to a belligerent (Antoine Rougier, *Les guerres civiles et le droit des gens* (Larose & Forcel 1903) 374).

[115] Wheaton, *History*, 294.

[116] Karl von Martens, *Nouvelles Causes Célèbres du Droit des Gens*, vol I (FA Brockhaus/Brockhaus & Avenarius 1843) 435.

[117] Rojas Castro, 'La reconnaissance', 14. See also John Fischer Williams, 'La doctrine de la reconnaissance en droit international et ses développements récents' (1933) 44 Recueil des Cours 199, 218–19.

[118] Martens, *Nouvelles Causes*, 456–7.

[119] ibid, 446–7.

[120] Grewe, *The Epochs*, 386.

[121] In addition to France, this was the case for Morocco, the Netherlands, Spain, Sweden, and the Republics of Ragusa and Venice.

[122] Art 4 of the Décret sur le droit de guerre et de paix (adopted 22 May 1790) proclaimed that '[l]a nation française renonce à entreprendre aucune guerre dans la vue de faire des conquêtes, et ... elle n'emploiera jamais ses forces contre la liberté d'aucun peuple' (*Archives Parlementaires de 1787 à 1860—Première série (1787–1799)*, Tome XV—Du 21 avril au 30 mai 1790 (Librairie Administrative P Dupont 1883) 661–2).

[123] Read the text of the Pillnitz Declaration in JM Roberts, *French Revolution Documents*, vol I (Basil Blackwell 1966) 439. The manifesto issued on 25 July 1792 by the Duke of Brunswick, commander of the

revolutionary France was thus conceived as a police operation to restore the legitimate sovereign to his throne: Prussia and Austria presented themselves not as states at war with France but as acting on behalf of its legitimate government, that of Louis XVI, to stop internal anarchy and the spread of subversive ideas.[124]

Britain's position, on the other hand, was more cautious. Prime Minister Pitt pointed out that, as Britain had not been attacked, it could not interfere in the internal affairs of France and that the restoration of the monarchy was not an essential condition for peace.[125] In his view, only 'if the continuance of a particular system was the ground of that enmity, would an interference to destroy that system be justifiable'.[126] It is also noteworthy that the deposed French king himself recommended that his allies declare that 'they had no intention of intermeddling in any form with the internal government of the nation, but only desired to restore to it the power of choosing that which really was in accordance with the wishes of the great majority'.[127] A few years later, his successor, Louis XVIII, similarly stressed that he had accepted the help of the allied sovereigns after Napoleon had come back from Elba only because they had given him 'the most solemn assurances' not to intermeddle with France's internal government.[128] In his legal opinion on the British acceptance of the 1815 Treaty for the Perpetual Imprisonment of Napoleon, Lord Chancellor Eldon explained Britain's standing on the matter: the general rule was that foreign states had no right 'to prevent [a] People from choosing their own Government', but the case of France was an exception based on the 'absolute necessity' of preventing the former emperor returning to power and disturbing peace again.[129] As will be seen, this position would be at the core of British foreign policy for the entire 19th century.[130]

What the American War of Independence did for secessionist struggles, therefore, the French Revolution did for the violent overthrow of governments: it repudiated

allied Austrian and Prussian armies, and addressed to the population of Paris threatened collective intervention and retaliations against civilians if the French royal family were harmed.

[124] Paul Bastid, 'La révolution de 1848 et le droit international' (1948) 72 Recueil des Cours 167, 240–1; Wheaton, *History*, 354–5.

[125] Wheaton, *History*, 365, 369.

[126] ibid. 368. George Canning would later explain that his country 'had made war against France, not because she had altered her own government, or even dethroned her own king, but because she had invaded Genoa, Savoy, and Avignon; because she had overrun Belgium, and threatened to open the mouth of the Scheldt in defiance of treaties; and because she openly announced, and acted upon the determination to revolutionize every adjoining state' (Henry Wager Halleck, *International Law or, Rules Regulating the Intercourse of States in Peace and War* (1st edn, Brancroft & Co 1861) 341–2). Compare this view with those of the Anglo-Irish statesman Edmund Burke (1729–1797), who, rejecting Austria and Prussia's initial reluctance to engage in a war against revolutionary France and calling for intervention against what he deemed an abusive government, argued that the doctrine of non-intervention in the internal affairs of other states was 'a false principle in the Law of Nations' (Edmund Burke, 'Heads for Consideration on the Present State of Affairs' in LG Mitchell (ed), *The Writings and Speeches of Edmund Burke*, vol VIII: *The French Revolution* (OUP 1989) 392–3).

[127] Quoted in Winfield, 'The History', 142.

[128] Proclamation du Roi de France, Gand, 2 May 1815, quoted in James Crawford, 'Napoleon 1814–1815: A Small Issue of Status' in Inge Van Hulle and Randall CH Lesaffer (eds), *International Law in the Long Nineteenth Century* (Brill/Nijhoff 2019) 3, 6–7.

[129] John Hall Stewart, 'The Imprisonment of Napoleon: A Legal Opinion by Lord Eldon' (1951) 45 AJIL 571, 575.

[130] See Section 7.2 this chapter.

DEVELOPMENT OF THE PRINCIPLE OF NON-INTERVENTION 27

the dynastic principle founded on the divine right to rule as the source of political legitimacy and replaced it with the consent of the governed as expressed in a social contract.[131] As a result, the identification of the party on whose side intervention was permissible came to depend not on compliance with succession rules and formal transfer of sovereignty, but on the factual success of the challenge to the established authority by the nation. The French revolutionaries initially also claimed an unfettered right to support popular insurrections against dynastic rulers in other countries: on 19 November 1792, in particular, the French Convention adopted a decree that ordered the French generals to provide 'fraternité et secours à tous les peuples qui voudront recouvrer leur liberté'.[132] In the end, however, the decree was never put into practice and republican France soon adopted a more prudent approach. The Convention's decree of 13 April 1793 repealed the Girondin global war against tyrants and proclaimed, in the name of the French people, that the Convention 'ne s'immiscera d'aucune façon dans le government des autres puissances'.[133] Similarly, if Article 118 of the Jacobin Constitution of 1793 affirmed that '[l]e peuple français est l'ami et l'allié naturel des peuples libres', the following article cautioned that the French people would not interfere in the government of other nations and would not tolerate others interfering in theirs.[134] British Prime Minister Pitt would later point out that revolutionary France had dropped its interventionist policy 'upon the express ground ... that such interference, and such attempts, would be a violation of the law of nations'.[135]

To conclude, the American and French Revolutions did not undermine the prohibition of intervention on the side of insurgents that had consolidated during the 18th century. Indeed, most states either supported Britain or remained neutral during the American War of Independence, and France's siding with the colonies was founded not on a rejection of the respect for sovereignty and non-intervention, but rather on the claim that they had become *de facto* independent. As to the French Revolution, the republicans' initial proclamations of support for peoples revolting against their autocratic rulers were met with general condemnation, were not put into practice, and were eventually abandoned in favour of non-interventionist policies. The contribution of the Age of Revolutions to the development of the principle of non-intervention is rather to be found in the emerging reluctance of states to explicitly claim a right to intervene to maintain a ruler in power if his authority was successfully challenged by the nation. Uprisings that had led to the *de facto* independence of secessionist provinces also began to be treated as interstate conflicts and no longer as an internal affair of the parent state, which allowed foreign powers to choose between neutrality and

---

[131] It is with John Locke's *Two Treatises of Government* (1689) and Jean-Jacques Rousseau's *The Social Contract* (1762) that sovereignty starts to be theorized as pertaining to the people, on behalf and to the benefit of whom the ruler must exercise it (John B Noone, Jr, 'The Social Contract and the Idea of Sovereignty in Rousseau' (1970) 32 The Journal of Politics 696–708).

[132] Text in Charles Rousseau, *Droit international public*, vol IV (Sirey 1980) 41.

[133] Text in NA Ouchakov, 'La compétence interne des Etats et la non-intervention dans le droit international contemporain' (1974) 141 Recueil des Cours 1, 5–6.

[134] Text in Alexandre-Charles Kiss, *Répertoire de la pratique française en matière de droit international public*, vol II (Editions du Centre National de la Recherche Scientifique 1966) 69. The 1793 Constitution never entered into force.

[135] Quoted in Arthur Larson, 'The Present Status of Propaganda in International Law' (1966) 31 LCP 39, 442.

28 INTERNATIONAL LAW AND THE PRINCIPLE OF NON-INTERVENTION

co-belligerency. In spite of the major setback suffered during the Restoration years, this double trend would become predominant in Europe and the Americas from the 1830s.

5. Intervention in the 19th Century and the Distinction between War and Measures Short of War

Unlike the 18th century, the 19th is characterized by a proliferation of situations of internal unrest: in European national states, subjects frequently rose against their rulers to obtain constitutional reforms or to overthrow the governments installed or reinstated by the Congress of Vienna in 1815 after the end of the Napoleonic Wars, while in multinational empires like the Austrian, Russian, and Ottoman, nationalities insurged to break free. In this period, revolutions, insurrections, and civil wars were also a frequent phenomenon in Latin America, first in the context of the struggle for independence of the Spanish colonies and then within the newly independent, but highly unstable, republics.[136] A civil war would eventually break out even in the United States (1861–5).

Because of the increasing interconnectedness of the 'family of nations' and the globalization of commercial interests, many of these situations of internal unrest were accompanied by external interferences.[137] It is not surprising, therefore, that it is in this period that intervention becomes a proper legal notion. Indeed, most international law treatises published in the second half of the 19th century contain a lengthy chapter on this topic, often found in the section on the fundamental rights and duties of states.[138] Monographs and pamphlets in several languages were also written on the specific subject of intervention[139] and leading legal scholars delivered public lectures on this topic, including Oxford professor Mountague Bernard (All Soul's College, 3 December 1860) and the Italian Giuseppe Carnazza Amari (University of Catania, 16

---

[136] Neff, *War*, 165.

[137] ibid.

[138] See eg Pasquale Fiore, *Nouveau droit international public suivant les besoins de la civilisation moderne*, vol I (Charles Antoine tr, 2nd edn, A Durand et Pedone-Lauriel 1885) 497 ff; William Edward Hall, *A Treatise on International Law* (3rd edn, Clarendon Press 1890) 281 ff. Halleck distinguishes between 'pacific interference', which he treats in the chapter on the rights of states to independence and self-preservation, and 'war of intervention', which he discusses in that on the different types of war (Halleck, *International Law*, 81, 334).

[139] See eg Laurent-Basile Hautefeuille, *Le principe de non-intervention et ses applications* (Jouaust et fils 1863); Ercole Vidari, *Del principio di intervento e di non intervento* (Amministrazione del Politecnico 1868); Jean Tanoviceano, *De l'intervention au point de vue du droit international* (L Larose et Forcel 1884); Friedrich Heinrich Geffcken, *Das Recht der Intervention* (JF Richter 1887); Adolph von Floecker, *De l'intervention en droit international* (Pedone 1896); Carlos Wiesse, *Le droit international appliqué aux guerres civiles* (2nd edn, B Benda 1898; 1st edn: *Reglas de derecho internacional aplicables a las guerras civiles* (Viuda Galland 1893)); Antonio L Valverde, *La intervención: estudio de derecho internacional público* (Ruis y Hermano 1902); Charles de Morillon, *Du principe d'intervention en droit international public et des modifications qu'il a subies au cours de l'histoire* (Imprimerie régionale 1904); Arrigo Cavaglieri, *L'intervento nella sua definizione giuridica: Saggio di diritto internazionale* (Beltrami 1913), and *Nuovi studi sull'intervento* (Società Anonima Editrice 1928); Henry G Hodges, *The Doctrine of Intervention* (Banner Press 1915); Stowell, *Intervention*; Hermann Mosler, *Die Intervention im Völkerrecht* (Junker and Dünnhaupt 1937).

November 1872).[140] In spite of this, in 1885 Pradier-Fodéré still noted that 'toute est contradiction et confusion' in the matter of intervention.[141] This was, however, an exaggeration. Treaties were adopted to regulate foreign intervention and certain rules also consolidated in customary international law: indeed, in this period custom, based on the 'common consent' of the Family of Nations, became an established source of international law,[142] as testified by its eventual inclusion in Article 38 of the 1920 Statute of the Permanent Court of International Justice (PCIJ) among the sources applied by the Court[143] and by the references made to it by domestic judges.[144]

It is thought that the term 'intervention' started to be used in a technical sense in the years 1817–30 to refer to measures characterized by the use of coercion.[145] In 1905, the German, later British,[146] scholar Lassa Oppenheim (1858–1919) would eventually conceive what has probably remained the most cited definition of 'intervention' to this day, namely a 'dictatorial interference by a State in the affairs on another State for the purpose of maintaining or altering the actual condition of things'.[147] As in the 18th century, this 'dictatorial interference' was essentially identified with diplomatic and armed coercion: economic pressures were not normally discussed in the framework of intervention.[148] The trade dispute between the Austro-Hungarian Empire and the Kingdom of Serbia from 1906 to 1909 (the 'Pig War'), in which the former

---

[140] The lectures have been published as Mountague Bernard, *On the Principle of Non-Intervention* (JH and Jas Parker 1860); and Giuseppe Carnazza Amari, *Nuova esposizione del principio del non intervento* (Stabilimento Tipografico Caronda 1873).

[141] Paul Pradier-Fodéré, *Traité de droit international public européen et américain*, vol I (Durand et Pedone-Lauriel 1885) 547.

[142] See eg Robert Phillimore, *Commentaries*, 68; Lassa Oppenheim, *International Law: A Treatise*, vol I: Peace (1st edn, Longmans, Green and Co 1905) 15–25. 'Common consent' refers to 'the express or tacit consent of such an overwhelming majority of the members that those who dissent are of no importance whatever and disappear totally from the view of one who looks for the will of the community as an entity in contradistinction with its single members' (ibid, 15). The role of *opinio juris* as an element of custom, however, was still uncertain in this period (J Patrick Kelly, 'Customary International Law in Historical Context: The Exercise of Power Without General Acceptance' in Brian D Lepard (ed), *Reexamining Customary International Law* (CUP 2017) 47, 72), and non-European views were completely ignored in the identification of customs (ibid, 49). Natural law also did not completely disappear as a source: Phillimore, for instance, still included 'Divine Law' and 'the Revealed Will of God' among the sources of international law (Phillimore, *Commentaries*, 68). 'Reason' was considered a source of law by Phillimore (ibid) and John Westlake, *International Law*, Part I (CUP 1904) 14–15.

[143] Art 38, Statute of the Permanent Court of International Justice (Geneva, 13 December 1920) PCIJ Series D No 1, 7.

[144] See eg US Supreme Court, *The Scotia*, 81 U.S. 170 (1871), where the Court held that certain rules of navigation 'by common consent of mankind ... have been acquiesced in as of general obligation': ibid, 188.

[145] Winfield, 'The History', 134. The importance of coercion is affirmed by, among others, August Wilhelm Heffter, *Le droit international public de l'Europe* (Jules Bergson tr, 3rd edn, E-H Schrœder/Cotillon Editeur 1857) 103; FF de Martens, *Traité de droit international* (Alfred Léo tr, Librairie A Maresco Ainé, 1883) 394; Oppenheim, *International Law*, vol I, 1st edn, 182–3; Pradier-Fodéré, *Traité*, 551–2; Edwin DeWitt Dickinson, *The Equality of States in International Law* (Harvard University Press 1920) 260; Paul Fauchille, *Traité de droit international public*, vol I, Première partie (Rousseau 1922) 539–40; Fiore, *Nouveau droit international*, 500; Charles Dupuis, 'Liberté des voies de communication' (1924) 2 Recueil des Cours 127, 369; Santi Romano, *Corso di diritto internazionale* (CEDAM 1926) 127; Pitman B Potter, 'Intervention en droit international moderne' (1930) 32 Recueil des Cours 607, 617; J-M Yepes, 'Les problèmes fondamentaux du droit des gens en Amérique' (1934) 47 Recueil des Cours 1, 69–70.

[146] Nussbaum refers to him as 'English in spirit and German in method' (Nussbaum, *A Concise History*, 247).

[147] Oppenheim, *International Law*, vol I, 1st edn, 181.

[148] Grewe, *The Epochs*, 596–7; Sapienza, *Il principio*, 111.

30 INTERNATIONAL LAW AND THE PRINCIPLE OF NON-INTERVENTION

imposed a customs blockade on the latter, offers an illustrative example. After Serbia started to import French rather than Austrian munitions in 1904 and agreed to a customs union with Bulgaria the following year, Austria-Hungary responded by closing its borders to Serbia's major export good, pork (97% of Serbian exports were towards its powerful neighbour). The Dual Monarchy also blocked the transit of Serbian agricultural products towards Western Europe and threatened to increase the tariffs for the export and transit of Serbian wheat on its territory so as to compel the Balkan state to renounce its claims over Bosnia and Herzegovina, which the Habsburgs wanted to annex.[149] While the pressures were ultimately unsuccessful, no claims of a violation of the principle of non-intervention in the internal affairs of Serbia were raised against Austria-Hungary: as Hersch Lauterpacht notes, 'in the absence of explicit conventional obligations, particularly those laid down in commercial treaties, a state is entitled to prevent altogether goods from a foreign state from coming into its territory'.[150] The permissibility of economic coercion would start to be questioned only in the interwar period, when the newly formed Soviet Union campaigned for the substantive, and not only formal, equality of states.[151]

If intervention did not include economic coercion, it could certainly consist of dictatorial interferences exercised by diplomatic means.[152] Diplomatic intervention consisted of hortatory representations (typically accompanied by a threat of force), imposed mediation, or premature recognitions and was considered as unlawful as its armed counterpart because it too involved the unauthorized exercise of sovereign powers in the sphere of exclusive jurisdiction of another sovereign. Calvo explains that

> [l]a forme sous laquelle a lieu l'intervention n'en altère pas le caractère. L'intervention se produisant par l'emploi des procédés diplomatiques, n'en est pas moins une intervention; c'est une ingérence plus ou moins directe, plus ou moins dissimulée, qui très souvent n'est que le prélude de l'intervention armée.[153]

As Fauchille notes, however, 'il doit y avoir avis comminatoire exprès ou implicite pour contraindre le pays à se soumettre aux observations présentées; sinon il n'y aurait pas volonté d'un gouvernement imposée à un autre: il s'agirait alors d'une offre de conseils, de bons offices ou de médiation, mais non pas d'une intervention'.[154] Article III of the 1933 Anti-War Treaty of Non-aggression and Conciliation (the Saavedra-Lamas Pact) confirmed that it was prohibited to 'resort to intervention, either diplomatic or

---

[149] Guido Napoletano, *Violenza nei trattati* (Giuffrè 1977) 518, fn 59.

[150] Hersch Lauterpacht, 'Boycott in International Relations' (1933) 14 BYBIL 125, 130.

[151] Paola Gaeta, Jorge E Viñules & Salvatore Zappalà, *Cassese's International Law* (3rd edn, OUP 2020) 33.

[152] Stowell's influential monograph *Intervention in International Law* (1921), for instance, addresses not only intervention by armed force but also other forms of interference.

[153] Calvo, *Le droit international*, 267. Bonfils uses almost exactly the same words: Henry Bonfils, *Manuel de droit international public (Droit des gens)* (Paul Fauchille ed, 7th edn, Rousseau 1914) 186. See also Augusto Pierantoni, *Storia degli studi del diritto internazionale in Italia* (Carlo Vincenzi 1869) 241; Fiore, *Nouveau droit international*, 513. According to Britain's Foreign Secretary, Palmerston, '[i]n an ordinary case of civil war between a sovereign and his subjects, foreign states can have no grounds for interference, even by advice or remonstrance' (Palmerston to Lord Heytesbury, 22 March 1831, *British and Foreign State Papers, 1849–1850*, vol XXXVIII, 1416).

[154] Fauchille, *Traité*, 543.

armed'[155] and the Montevideo Convention on the Rights and Duties of States, adopted the same year, indicated 'threatening diplomatic representations' as a case of 'coercive measure'.[156] Mexico's 'Carranza Doctrine' also explicitly condemned the use of diplomacy as a means of coercion.[157]

Most visibly, a dictatorial interference would have occurred by military means. If the jusnaturalists of the Early Modern Age did not distinguish it from (just) war, in the 19th century armed intervention came to be seen as a 'measure short of war', a notion developed in this period as a result of weaponry becoming more sophisticated and war turning into a phenomenon that affected not only professional armies, but also the entire political, economic, and cultural life of a society as well as international trade. Its appeal was that it allowed some limited use of armed force by a state in or against another state without triggering the disruptive legal and political consequences of a state of war. Indeed, in addition to the severance of diplomatic relations, the establishment of a state of war in the legal sense also entailed that treaties between belligerents and contracts between their nationals were suspended or terminated, emergency powers could be exercised at the domestic level, and the laws of war (between belligerents) and neutrality (between belligerents and third states) started to apply.[158]

Foreign armed interventions like those of the Holy Alliance in Spain and in the Italian peninsula,[159] of Britain, France, and Russia in the Greek War of Independence (1821–33),[160] of France in the Mount Lebanon Civil War (1860–61),[161] of the European powers in China against the Boxers (1900),[162] and of the United States in Central America between 1898 and 1934[163] were thus not normally considered as establishing a state of war between the concerned states even when they occurred without the consent of the territorial sovereign. No state of war also arose between France and Britain on one side and the Netherlands on the other in spite of the British and French active support for the Belgian secessionists in 1832: the blockade of the Dutch ports by the two powers was claimed to be a 'pacific' one.[164] The only examples of armed support

---

[155] Anti-War Treaty of Non-Aggression and Conciliation (Rio de Janeiro, 10 October 1933) 163 LNTS 393–413. The treaty was signed by the representatives of Argentina, Brazil, Chile, Mexico, Paraguay, and Uruguay. The US government acceded on 10 August 1934.

[156] Art 11, Convention on the Rights and Duties of States (Montevideo, 26 December 1933) 165 LNTS 19.

[157] Jürgen Buchenau, *In the Shadow of the Giant: The Making of Mexico's Central America Policy, 1876–1930* (The University of Alabama Press 1996) 122. The doctrine is contained in the State of the Union address delivered by Mexico's President Venustiano Carranza in September 1918. On the Carranza Doctrine, see Juan Pablo Scarfi, 'Mexican Revolutionary Constituencies and the Latin American Critique of US Intervention' in Kathryn Greenman, Anne Orford, Anna Saunders, and Ntina Tzouvala (eds), *Revolutions in International Law: The Legacies of 1917* (CUP 2021) 218.

[158] Quincy Wright, 'When Does War Exist?' (1932) 26 AJIL 362, 363; Marina Mancini, *Stato di guerra e conflitto armato nel diritto internazionale* (Giappichelli 2009) 24 ff.

[159] Davide Rodogno, *Against Massacre: Humanitarian Interventions in The Ottoman Empire 1815–1914* (Princeton University Press 2012) 22.

[160] Wright, 'When Does War Exist?', 365.

[161] Davide Rodogno, 'The "Principles of Humanity" and the European Powers' Intervention in Ottoman Lebanon and Syria in 1860–1861' in Simms and Trim (eds), *Humanitarian Intervention*, 159, 181.

[162] In order not to declare war on China, the intervening states claimed that they were acting in support of the government to suppress the insurrection (Fauchille, *Traité*, 583). The British prime minister, Lord Salisbury, argued for instance that, as the Boxers' actions were not attributable to the Chinese imperial government, there was no conflict between the armed forces of the two countries (Neff, *War*, 244).

[163] Alexandre Alvarez, *Le droit international américain* (Pedone 1910) 176; Neff, *War*, 223.

[164] Grewe, *The Epochs*, 527.

32   INTERNATIONAL LAW AND THE PRINCIPLE OF NON-INTERVENTION

for insurgents that resulted in *de jure* wars were Russia's participation in the Greek War of Independence after 14 April 1828 and the US resort to force against Spain during the Second Cuban Civil War in 1898.

Armed measures short of war were '*acts* of war taking place during a *state* of peace'.[165] Even though the distinction between war and armed measures short of war was generally accepted, there was no consensus among publicists on the criteria to differentiate them.[166] For Hall, armed measures short of war were unilateral acts which occurred when there was resort to armed force by one state only.[167] This view was not supported by state practice, which shows that a reaction to an armed intervention might have established a state of war in the material (*de facto*) sense, but was not sufficient to establish a state of war in the legal (*de jure*) sense if the concerned states did not so intend.[168] In spite of the blockade of Greece culminating in the Battle of Navarino (20 October 1827) and subsequent occupation of the Morea, for instance, the European states (apart from Russia)[169] and the Ottoman Empire never considered themselves at war with each other during the Greek War of Independence.[170] As Yepes correctly points out, the essential element of intervention was 'l'action coercitive de l'Etat qui agit et non la résistance de celui qui subit l'action'.[171]

Other scholars posited that what distinguished armed measures short of war from war proper was their purpose. Oppenheim's famous definition of war refers to the belligerents' 'purpose of overpowering each other and imposing such conditions of peace as the victor pleases'.[172] Armed measures short of war, on the other hand, were thought to have a more limited aim. For Winfield, in particular, the practice of the 19th century suggests that intervention includes three different situations: 'that of interference in the relations of two other states, that of interference in the internal disputes of a single state, and that of some measure of redress falling short of war directed by one state against another for some alleged breach of international law committed by the latter'.[173] While there is no legal ground for differentiating the first type from

---

[165] Neff, *War*, 216, emphasis in the original.

[166] In fact, for some writers the differentiation between the two notions was unsustainable. Halleck, for instance, identifies war with armed intervention: in his view, armed intervention 'is virtually a *war*, and must be justified or condemned upon the same general principles as other wars' (Halleck, *International Law*, 335, emphasis in the original). The rule of non-interference, therefore, 'must be resolved upon the general principles upon which war is in any case justified' (ibid, 341). See also Arrigo Cavaglieri, 'Note critiche su la teoria dei mezzi coercitivi al difuori della guerra' (1915) 9 RDI 23, 339.

[167] Hall, *A Treatise*, 281–2.

[168] Hersh Lauterpacht, '"Resort to War" and the Interpretation of the Covenant during the Manchurian Dispute' (1934) 28 AJIL 43, 47–8. On the distinction between war in the technical and material senses, see Yoram Dinstein, *War, Aggression and Self-Defence* (6th edn, CUP 2017) 11–13.

[169] Russia declared war on the Ottoman Empire on 14 April 1828 (*British and Foreign State Papers 1827–1828*, vol XV (1829) 656–62).

[170] Ian Brownlie, *International Law and the Use of Force by States* (Clarendon Press 1963) 30–1; Will Smiley, 'War Without War: The Battle of Navarino, the Ottoman Empire, and the Pacific Blockade' (2016) 18 J His Intl L 42, 57. The Additional Article to the 1827 Treaty of London between Britain, France, and Russia specified that 'all the means' adopted by the three states to enforce the armistice provided in the treaty would occur 'without ... taking any part in the hostilities between the Two Contending Parties' (Treaty of London between Britain, France, and Russia for the Pacification of Greece (London 6 July 1827) 77 CTS 314).

[171] Yepes, 'Les problèmes', 70.

[172] Lassa Oppenheim, *International Law: A Treatise*, vol II: *War and Neutrality* (Longmans, Green and Co 1906) 56.

[173] Winfield, 'The History', 131. Winfield describes the different meanings given to intervention (external and internal) as 'unfortunate' (ibid, 148).

DEVELOPMENT OF THE PRINCIPLE OF NON-INTERVENTION   33

war,[174] he argues that, when it comes to the second, its object is 'as a rule, not the in-fliction of a blow upon the resources of a state, but the usurpation of some part of its powers of government, in the course of which bloodshed becomes an undesirable but inevitable incident'.[175] The classification based on the limited purpose pursued by the intervening state, however, never gained broad consensus and was criticized for being too political.[176]

For the majority of writers, the existence of a state of war in the legal sense required an *animus bellandi*, that is, the intention to establish it: *de jure* war, therefore, could only start with an 'overt act' through which at least one state manifests its intention to turn a state of peace into a state of war.[177] An armed measure short of war, on the other hand, occurred when there was no such intention even though some use of armed force had taken place.[178] The *animus bellandi* could be manifested explicitly through a declaration of war, as required by Article 1 of the 1907 Hague Convention (III) Relative to the Opening of Hostilities.[179] It could also be implied in certain conduct, normally the exercise of belligerent rights that are only permissible in a state of war, such as the promulgation of a belligerent blockade,[180] or a use of force accompanied by an invitation to other states to observe the international laws of neutrality.[181]

It is important to emphasize that the intention of one belligerent was considered sufficient to establish a state of war in the legal sense: the other state could have been dragged into it without having such intention itself.[182] An act of war, then, established a state of *de jure* war instead of being a mere peacetime armed intervention if: 1) the state resorting to armed force expressly declared war on the target state; 2) it resorted to armed force without a declaration of war, but its *animus bellandi* could be implied from its conduct; or 3) it resorted to armed force without *animus bellandi*, but the target state decided to treat the resort to force as establishing a state of war, either by declaring war itself or by expressing its *animus bellandi* in alternative ways.[183] Even if

---

[174] ibid, 147.

[175] ibid, 142.

[176] Cavaglieri, 'Note critiche', 46.

[177] Wright, 'When Does War Exist?', 363. See also John A Cohan, 'Legal War: When Does It Exist and When Does It End?' (2003–4) 27 Hastings Int'l & Comp L Rev 222, 242; Angelo Piero Sereni, 'Il concetto di guerra nel diritto internazionale contemporaneo' (1963) 46 RDI 537, 556.

[178] Sereni, 'Il concetto', 558; Dionisio Anzilotti, *Corso di diritto internazionale*, vol III (Athenæum 1915) 164–5; Gabriella Venturini, *Necessità e proporzionalità nell'uso della forza militare in diritto internazionale* (Giuffrè 1988) 6. As the Secretary-General of the League of Nations pointed out in 1927, 'from the legal point of view the existence of a state of war between two States depends upon their intention and not upon the nature of their acts. Accordingly measures of coercion, however drastic, which are not intended to create and are not regarded by the State to which they are applied as creating a state of war, do not legally establish a relation of war between the States concerned' (Report by the Secretary-General, 15 June 1927 in (1927) 8 LNOJ 834).

[179] Convention (III) Relative to the Opening of Hostilities (The Hague 18 October 1907) (1908) 2 AJIL Supplement 85.

[180] A 'pacific blockade', on the other hand, did not imply *animus bellandi* and was 'enforced only against ships of the country whose territory was being invested, i.e., there was no interference with third-state vessels [and] ships of the target country, when captured, would only be sequestered, pending resolution of the crisis', and not confiscated through prize proceedings (Neff, *War*, 234). See the Declaration of the Institut de droit international on the matter adopted at the 1887 Heidelberg Session (text in (1888) 9 AIDI 300).

[181] Cohan, 'Legal War', 254.

[182] Wright, 'When Does War Exist?', 363.

[183] JL Brierly, 'International Law and Resort to Armed Force' (1930–1932) 4 CLJ 308, 311–12.

34   INTERNATIONAL LAW AND THE PRINCIPLE OF NON-INTERVENTION

no belligerents manifested an *animus bellandi*, a third state could have always recognized the existence of a state of war, thus indicating its intention to conduct itself on the basis of the law of neutrality.[184]

In the 19th century, armed intervention was seen as different not only from war but also from reprisals adopted in response to a previous wrongful act.[185] Like intervention, peacetime reprisals belonged to the category of coercive measures short of war: as such, they did not trigger the application of the law of neutrality for third states.[186] The *Naulilaa* arbitration famously defined them as 'un acte de propre justice (Selbsthilfehandlung) de l'État lésé, acte répondant—*après sommation restée infructueuse*—à un acte contraire au droit des gens de l'État offenseur'.[187] Although the two notions had in common the element of coercion, reprisals could have only been adopted by a state in response to the breach of its own *rights* or the rights of its nationals in order to obtain redress for it, while intervention had a broader scope and could have also been undertaken to protect individual and community *interests* (as evidenced by the state practice which is examined later)[188] or when the breached obligation was not owed to the intervening state but to another state. While a reprisal was lawful per se as it was a response to a previous wrongful act, then, an intervention to protect mere interests or obligations not owed to the intervening state needed a valid legal basis. Unlike reprisals, the purpose of intervention was also not limited to obtaining reparation for a wrongful act, but normally had more far-reaching political purposes. When both reprisals and intervention aimed to enforce a right, however, the distinction between the two was very thin: it has been suggested that, while in an intervention the violation of another state's rights was a means to an end, namely coercing the target state into doing or not doing something (including providing reparations), in a reprisal the violation was an end in itself, that is, it *was* the reparation for the wrong suffered.[189] Be that as it may, a reprisal, unlike intervention, had to be preceded by an attempt to obtain redress and had to be proportionate to the gravity of the wrong that justified it.[190]

---

[184] Marina Mancini, 'The Effects of a State of War or Armed Conflict' in Weller (ed), *The Oxford Handbook of the Use of Force in International Law*, 988, 990–1; Arnold McNair and AD Watts, *The Legal Effects of War* (4th edn, CUP 1966) 10.

[185] Georg Schwarzenberger, *International Law as Applied by International Courts and Tribunals*, vol II (Stevens & Sons 1968) 675. The state against which the reprisal was directed could have of course treated it as an act of war and a state of *de jure* war would have ensued.

[186] Neff, *War*, 232.

[187] *Responsabilité de l'Allemagne à raison des dommages causés dans les colonies portugaises du sud de l'Afrique (sentence sur le principe de la responsabilité) (Portugal contre Allemagne)*, 31 July 1928, 2 RIAA 1011, 1026, emphasis in the original. On peacetime reprisals, see also the resolution of the Institut de droit international adopted at the 1934 Paris Session (text in (1934) 38 AIDI 708).

[188] See Sections 7.1, 7.2, and 7.3 this chapter.

[189] Giorgio Balladore Pallieri, *Diritto internazionale pubblico* (2nd edn, Giuffrè 1938) 341–2. In an intervention, therefore, if the measures initially adopted did not reach their coercive effect, further action could have been taken, while the reprisal had to terminate with the completion of the act and the infliction of the damage on the state responsible for the wrongdoing.

[190] McNair and Watts, *The Legal Effects*, 16.

6. The Legality of Intervention and the Fundamental Right of States to Independence

Establishing whether a resort to armed force was an act of war establishing a state of war or a peacetime intervention was important to determine its permissibility. For the positivists of the 19th century, war was neither just nor unjust, as there was no longer an authority superior to states, like that of the Pope, that could decide which belligerent had justice on its side: war was rather a 'duel', a Darwinist means to settle disputes between states on the basis of naked force.[191] In this non-discriminatory construction, the restrictions on the *jus ad bellum* of states could have only been procedural: as Wheaton puts it, '[a] war in form, or duly commenced, is to be considered, as to its effects, as just on both sides'.[192]

If one accepts the view that war is either a right inherent in state sovereignty or an extra-legal phenomenon, the problem of the legality of armed intervention during the 19th century presented itself only in peacetime, that is, in the case of armed intervention without *animus bellandi*.[193] Certain scholars claimed that, if war was not prohibited and if intervention was a lesser form of resort to armed force, then intervention should have also always been considered permissible: as Dupuis explains, '[q]ui peut le plus peut le moins. Si l'État a le droit de faire la guerre quand il veut et pour le motif qu'il veut, il a le droit d'intervenir quand il veut et pour le motif qu'il veut'.[194] In the 1915 edition of his international law treatise, Anzilotti also makes the point that, as states may resort to war, *a fortiori* they may resort to lesser uses of armed force.[195] For the Italian writer, what is not prohibited is permitted: it is not necessary to demonstrate the existence of a customary norm that allows armed measures short of war; on the contrary, what needs to be identified is a norm that prohibits them, which—the

---

[191] In the *Russian Indemnities* Award, the Permanent Court of Arbitration depicted war as a 'fait international au premier chef' (*Affaire de l'indemnité russe (Russie, Turquie)*, 11 November 1912, 11 RIAA 421, 433).

[192] Henry Wheaton, *Elements of International Law* (William Beach Lawrence ed, 6th edn, Little, Brown & Co 1855) 364.

[193] A minority of scholars, however, considered war neither a right inherent in sovereignty nor an extra-legal fact of life and claimed that, even in the 19th century, states had to possess a legal title not only to conduct intervention, but also to resort to war against other states. Floeckher, for instance, argues that war is permissible only when the purpose is to repel an attack, to defend oneself against hostilities, to obtain the execution of a treaty, and to protect justified interests (Adolphe de Floeckher, 'Les conséquences de l'intervention' (1896) 3 RGDIP 329, 332). For Despagnet, a war is just if it meets three conditions: 1) it is in response to the unjustified attack, or threat of attack, by another state, which is serious enough to justify war as a response; 2) the reaction is proportionate to the attack; 3) peaceful solutions are pointless, impossible, or dangerous (Frantz Despagnet, *Cours de droit international public* (3rd edn, Larose & Tenin 1905) 609–10). See also Heffter, *Le droit international*, 221–2; Halleck, *International Law*, 312–17; Vidari, *Del principio*, 10. The supporters of this view relied on the fact that states felt the need to justify the initiation of a war, in particular by claiming that it was a defensive one, although 'defence' was intended very broadly as including the protection of both rights and interests (Randall Lesaffer, 'Too Much History: From War as Sanction to the Sanctioning of War' in Weller (ed), *The Oxford Handbook of the Use of Force in International Law*, 35, 46). If one accepts this alternative construction, most of the following considerations on the legality of intervention as a peacetime coercive measure can also be extended to that amounting to a *de jure* war.

[194] Dupuis, 'Liberté', 373. See also Antoine Pillet, *Recherches sur les droits fondamentaux des États dans l'ordre des rapports internationaux et sur la solution des conflits qu'ils font naître* (Pedone 1899) 29; Anzilotti, *Corso*, 156.

[195] ibid, 156.

36 INTERNATIONAL LAW AND THE PRINCIPLE OF NON-INTERVENTION

practice of states suggested—did not exist.[196] Limits to the resort to armed measures short of war, therefore, could only derive from treaties.[197]

Most commentators of the time, however, disagree with these views: being a more serious event than intervention, war is an *extrema ratio* which determines the establishment of special relations between the belligerents.[198] Whenever armed intervention does not take the form of a *de jure* war, it has to be reconciled with the law applicable in peacetime, including the obligation to respect the fundamental right of other states to independence.[199] This essentially means that intervention has either to take place by right as in the cases of suzerainty and of a treaty of guarantee,[200] or, lacking such a right, that there must be at least a 'just cause' that can be invoked to justify the violation of the independence of the victim state.[201] Winfield explains:

[If] the causes of war are practically infinite and are beyond the scope of international law, apart from the exceptional case of a clear breach of it ... the causes which confer upon one state the right of intervening in another are regarded as clearly definable by nearly every modern jurist, —though little agreement exists as to what precisely these causes are. Yet they are regarded as comparatively few in number, —certainly not identical with the causes which justify war.[202]

---

[196] ibid, 172.

[197] ibid, 165.

[198] Heffter, for instance, sees war as the 'extreme remedy' if other peaceful remedies have failed to achieve the purpose of the intervention (Heffter, *Le droit international*, 105).

[199] Bernard, *On the Principle*, 9; Gustave Rolin-Jaequemyns, 'Note sur la théorie du droit d'intervention. A propos d'une lettre de M. le Professeur Arntz' (1876) 8 RDILC 673, 676–7; Théophile Funck-Brentano and Albert Sorel, *Précis du droit des gens* (Plon 1877) 216; Pradier-Fodéré, *Traité*, 547; Hall, *A Treatise*, 50, 281; Thomas Joseph Lawrence, *The Principles of International Law* (3rd edn, Heath & Co 1895) 115; Alphonse Rivier, *Principes du droit des gens*, vol I (Rousseau 1896) 390; Pasquale Fiore, *International Law Codified and its Legal Sanction, or The Legal Organization of the Society of States*, tr from the 5th Italian edn by Edwin M Borchard (Baker, Voorhis & Co 1918) 265–6; Charles Dupuis, *Le droit des gens et les rapports des grandes puissances avec les autres États avant le Pacte de la Société des Nations* (Plon-Nourrit 1921) 128. As the *Island of Palmas* arbitration famously found in 1928, '[s]overeignty in the relations between States signifies independence. Independence in regard to a portion of the globe is the right to exercise therein, to the exclusion of any other State, the functions of a State' (*Island of Palmas Case (Netherlands, United States)*, 4 April 1928, 2 RIAA 829, 838). The fundamental rights of states were 'des droits qui appartiennent à tout État du fait de son existence même, qui sont inhérents à lui et qui présentent le triple caractère d'être absolus, inviolables, inaliénables. Ils sont absolus en ce sense que l'État perdrait ses caractères distinctifs s'ils venaient à manquer et cesserait d'être une «personne du droit international»' (Gilbert Gide, 'Droits et devoirs des nations: La théorie classique des droits fondamentaux des États' (1925–V) 10 Recueil des Cours 537, 542). See also Marco Roscini and Daniel H Joyner, 'Is There Any Room for the Doctrine of Fundamental Rights of States in Today's International Law?' (2015) 4 Cambridge J Int'l & Comp L 467.

[200] Art 3 of the 1863 Treaty of London between Great Britain, France, and Russia, for instance, provided that 'Greece, under the sovereignty of Prince William of Denmark, and the guarantee of the three courts, forms a monarchical, independent, and constitutional State' (text in 12 AJIL Supplement 1918, 75). Some writers, however, criticize treaty-based interventions as incompatible with the sovereignty and independence of states (see eg Carnazza Amari, *Nuova esposizione*, 80; Pradier-Fodéré, *Traité*, 605–6; Fiore, *International Law*; 266–7; Stowell, *Intervention*, 438–46).

[201] For Lesaffer, 'the just war retained its relevance for those cases of "imperfect" war in which the conditions of formal war were not fulfilled, such as self-defence, reprisal, or intervention' (Lesaffer, 'Between Faith', 105).

[202] Winfield, 'The History', 131.

DEVELOPMENT OF THE PRINCIPLE OF NON-INTERVENTION   37

The list of just causes for intervention varies from author to author but the one on which virtually all publicists agree is based on another fundamental right of states, the right to self-preservation (or, as the French doctrine call it, *droit de conservation*), which is in turn based on the right of states to existence.[203] The notion of self-preservation is much broader than that of self-defence, as it includes the right to use forcible measures not only to react against an attack, but in any situation where the rights and even the essential interests of a state are in danger.[204] As such, it tends to merge with self-help.[205]

If non-intervention was a corollary of the fundamental right of states to independence, intervention was a manifestation of the right to self-preservation.[206] How could the two rights be reconciled so that at least certain cases of peacetime intervention could be admitted? In the *Caroline* correspondence, the British diplomat Lord Ashburton reminded US Secretary of State Webster that, however important the duty to respect the territory of another state might be, 'it is admitted by all writers, by all jurists, by the occasional practice of all nations ... that a strong overpowering necessity may arise when this great principle may and must be suspended' as '[s]elf-defence is the first law of our nature'.[207] President Buchanan's 1857 inaugural address also stressed that the United States would 'cherish a sacred regard for the independence of all nations, and never attempt to interfere in the domestic concerns of any unless this shall be imperatively required by the great law of self-preservation'.[208] Most writers concur with these views and posit that, although both rights are of a fundamental nature, the right to self-preservation prevails over that to independence in the case of conflict between the two.[209] Some, however, express a more cautious view: after arguing that 'almost the whole of the duties of states are subordinated to the right of self-preservation',[210] Hall warns that

---

[203] Pierluigi Lamberti Zanardi, *La legittima difesa nel diritto internazionale* (Giuffré 1972) 9; Stanimir A Alexandrov, *Self-Defense Against the Use of Force in International Law* (Kluwer Law International 1996) 23.

[204] Brownlie, 'The Use of Force', 185. Even though originally intended as a 'legal principle of limitation' in the 19th century self-preservation became a 'principle for potential domination', as it included 'whatever tended to preserve [the state's] natural being and therefore extended to the limits of its natural free determination and of its prerogatives, or even beyond them' (Emmanuelle Jouannet, *The Liberal-Welfarist Law of Nations: A History of International Law* (CUP 2012) 128).

[205] Brownlie, *International Law*, 42. For Haggenmacher, however, self-preservation is different from self-help: '[w]hile self-preservation has a mainly defensive connotation, self-help is distinctly active since it aims at the pursuit of a right' (Peter Haggenmacher, 'Self-Defence as a General Principle of Law and its Relation to War' in Arthur Eyffinger, Alan Stephens, and Sam Muller (eds), *Self-Defence as a Fundamental Principle* (Hague Academic Press 2009) 3, 9).

[206] Wheaton, *Elements*, 87.

[207] Lord Ashburton to Mr Webster, 28 July 1842, *British and Foreign State Papers 1841–1842*, vol XXX (1858) 196.

[208] James D Richardson (ed), *A Compilation of the Messages and Papers of the Presidents, 1789–1902*, vol V (GPO 1902) 78.

[209] Wheaton, *Elements*, 87; Halleck, *International Law*, 91–2; Phillimore, *Commentaries*, 314; Pradier-Fodéré, *Traité*, 552–3; Calvo, *Le droit international*, 352; Lawrence, *The Principles*, 117; Rivier, *Principes*, 397–8; Despagnet, *Cours*, 209. Certain authors specifically claim that self-preservation can also justify an intervention in support of foreign insurgents (John Stuart Mill, 'A Few Words on Non-Intervention', Fraser's Magazine, December 1859, reproduced in (2003) 27 New Eng L Rev 252, 262–3; Luigi Casanova, *Del diritto internazionale*, vol I (2nd edn, Eugenio e Filippo Cammelli 1870) 94; Theodore D Woolsey, *Introduction to the Study of International Law* (5th edn, Sampson Low, Marston, Searle, & Livington 1879) 44).

[210] Hall, *A Treatise*, 265.

38 INTERNATIONAL LAW AND THE PRINCIPLE OF NON-INTERVENTION

[t]he right of independence is so fundamental a part of international law, and respect for it so essential to the existence of legal restraint, that any action tending to place it in a subordinate position must be looked upon with disfavour, and any general grounds of intervention pretending to be sufficient, no less than their application in particular cases, may properly be judged with an adverse bias.[211]

That said, only Carnazza Amari entirely rejects self-preservation as a valid justification for intervention in a civil war.[212]

An alternative construction is put forward by the French and Belgian scholars. As Arntz puts it, 'quelque respectables que ce soient les droits de souveraineté et d'indépendance des États, il y a quelque chose de plus respectable encore, c'est le droit de l'humanité, ou de la *société humaine*, qui ne doit pas être outragé'.[213] The respect for other states' right to independence, therefore, is not unqualified: sovereignty implies responsibility and its protection needs to be deserved.[214] As a consequence, states, as members of the human family, can intervene collectively, or individually with a collective mandate, when the rights of humankind have been breached.[215] Intervention on grounds of humanity is thus for these authors not a violation of the right of the victim state to independence. Section 7.3 of this chapter, however, shows that this view was never reflected in state practice and *opinio juris*.[216]

It is worth recalling that, for most of the 19th century, peripheral or semiperipheral actors like the Ottoman Empire and China were not considered to possess a full right to independence, as they were not deemed to have yet the necessary maturity to make good use of it.[217] The application of the principle of non-intervention to them was thus conditional upon their compliance with the international law of the civilized states of Europe, particularly the protection of the Christian minorities living on their territory.[218] Phillimore, for instance, candidly comments that the Porte was 'by reason of the religious difference between the followers of Christ and of Mahomet, placed in an anomalous and inferior condition to that of other European States, and subjected with

---

[211] ibid, 282. For Basdevant, the independence of a state could be bent in some cases to allow the intervention of another state, but only when other non-coercive measures had failed (Jules Basdevant, 'L'action coercitive anglo-germano-italienne contre le Vénézuela 1902–1903)' (1904) 11 RGDIP 362, 373–4).

[212] Carnazza Amari, *Nuova esposizione*, 51, 53–4.

[213] In Rolin-Jaequemyns, 'Note', 675, emphasis in the original.

[214] Dupuis, *Le droit*, 130.

[215] Rougier, *Les guerres civiles*, 344.

[216] See Section 7.3 of this chapter.

[217] As Koskenniemi points out, '[a] right or duty to intervene outside Europe was routinely asserted ... If the lawyers sometimes disagreed on the opportunity or manner of conducting intervention, they never doubted its principle' (Martti Koskenniemi, *The Gentle Civilizer of Nations: The Rise and Fall of International Law 1870–1960* (CUP 2001) 131). John Stuart Mill, for instance, explains that non-intervention only applied among civilized nations, and not where 'one of the parties to the situation is of a high, and the other of a very low, grade of social improvement' (Mill, 'A Few Words', 259). This was because barbarian states were incapable of exercising self-determination: '[i]ndependence and nationality, so essential to the due growth and development of a people further advanced in improvement, are generally impediments to theirs' (ibid, 259). There were, however, also dissenting views, including Carnazza Amari, *Nuova esposizione*, 77; Pradier-Fodéré, *Traité*, 646–7, and Johann Caspar Bluntschli, *Le droit international codifié* (MC Lardy and Alphonse Rivier tr, 5th edn, Guillaumin & Co 1895) 60.

[218] Luigi Nuzzo, 'Territory, Sovereignty, and the Construction of Colonial Space' in Koskenniemi, Rech, and Fonseca (eds), *International Law and Empire*, 263, 269.

DEVELOPMENT OF THE PRINCIPLE OF NON-INTERVENTION

respect to this right of Intervention to exceptional rules of international treatment'.[219] Others refer to the failed character of certain states and argue that international law and the principle of non-intervention do not protect 'un cadavre politique en décomposition' like the Ottoman Empire.[220]

While apparently pluralistic, therefore, the principle of non-intervention was only applied in the intra-European order: it was indeed a corollary of sovereignty, but sovereignty was a 'gift of civilization',[221] which pertained almost exclusively to the European family of nations. The distinction between states according to their level of civilization is probably best epitomized in the works of James Lorimer (1818–1890), 'the foremost intellectual heretic of the 19th-century international legal thought'.[222] For him, the doctrines of recognition, intervention, and neutrality constitute 'the *corpus juris inter gentes*'.[223] The doctrine of intervention, in particular, results from that of recognition.[224] Indeed, '[i]ntervention and recognition are relations which are mutually exclusive ... and the former will supply the rule of action when the latter fails'.[225] He identifies different types of recognition: plenary political recognition, which extends to all European states and the independent states of North and South America (civilized humanity); partial political recognition, which pertains to Turkey and the Asian states which have not become European dependencies, like Persia, Siam, Japan, and China (barbarous humanity); and natural or mere human recognition, which is that of the rest of humankind, as distinguished between progressive and non-progressive races (savage humanity).[226] The law of nations only fully applies to the relations between entities belonging to the first category. In Lorimer's view,

[t]he simple fact that savages behave themselves as such — that they enslave, and murder, and eat each other — creates neither rights nor duties towards them on the

---

[219] Phillimore, *Commentaries*, 635. See also Martens, *Traité*, 398; Despagnet, *Cours*, 237. These views are criticized by Pradier-Fodéré, for whom the European interventions in the Middle East could be justified 'par le droit international réel, pratique', but 'le droit international théorique [les] condamne au nom des principes, qui ne sont pas autres pour les pays chrétiens et autres pour les pays mahométans' (Pradier-Fodéré, *Traité*, 646–7). Bluntschli agrees: '[u]n État n'acquiert pas des droits spéciaux vis-à-vis d'un autre, parce que l'un d'eux est chrétien et l'autre mahométan' (Bluntschli, *Le droit international*, 60).

[220] Gustave Rolin-Jaequemyns, 'Le droit international et la phase actuelle de la question d'Orient' (1876) 8 RDILC 293, 369.

[221] Koskenniemi, *The Gentle Civilizer*, 98.

[222] Stephen C Neff, 'Heresy in Action: James Lorimer's Dissident Views on War and Neutrality' (2016) 27 EJIL 477, 477.

[223] James Lorimer, *The Institutes of the Law of Nations: A Treatise of the Jural Relations of Separate Political Communities* vol II (William Blackwood and Sons 1884) 52.

[224] ibid, 42. Lorimer distinguishes two types of intervention: double, ie, 'coming between two States which stand to each other in an abnormal relation', and single, ie, 'professedly and avowedly taking part with the one against the other' (ibid, 53). An example of double intervention is that of France and England between Belgium and Holland in 1830, while the intervention of the Allied powers against Napoleon's France is a case of single intervention (ibid, 53).

[225] ibid, 49, emphasis omitted.

[226] James Lorimer, *The Institutes of the Law of Nations: A Treatise of the Jural Relations of Separate Political Communities*, vol I (William Blackwood and Sons 1883) 101–2. Two situations, then, must be distinguished: that of communities which could not be recognized, ie those 'incapable of expressing or realising their reciprocating will under any form of internal government' (further distinguished in nonage, imbecility, and criminality: ibid, 157 ff) and those with personal or class governments (ibid, 162 ff); and that of states entitled to recognition, which have 'the capacity for self-support and self-government' (ibid, 23).

40 INTERNATIONAL LAW AND THE PRINCIPLE OF NON-INTERVENTION

part of civilised men. It is in the power to help them that the duty and even the right to interfere with them originates; and the right and the duty are measured by the power.[227]

In the relations between states entitled to recognition, on the other hand, 'the rule must be in favour of non-interference'.[228] Even in this case, however, intervention becomes permissible when states breach the conditions for recognition 'on which their proximate freedom, or, in other words, their independence by the positive law of nations, depended'.[229] Lorimer concludes that

> [s]o long as the facts or conditions on which the right of recognition depends are present ... the relation of belligerency, whether in the form of intervention or any other, can have no place. When intervention comes into play, recognition disappears, whilst neutrality becomes jural only on the failure of the former. Neutrality, or abnormal peace, is thus the converse of intervention; but its attitude towards recognition is an attitude of hesitation, not of negation.[230]

7. 19th-Century State Practice and *Opinio Juris* Concerning Intervention

As the practice examined in this section demonstrates, the principle of non-intervention, as a discrete rule of international law, consolidated in the 19th century out of the great powers' preoccupation with constitutional changes in Europe: after the political and administrative uniformity that had characterized Napoleonic rule in Europe, each state was 'deliberately cut adrift from each other under profoundly different governments ... Their borders and rulers thus fixed, the post-Napoleonic states of Europe were left to go their own ways'.[231] Like the law of occupation, the principle of non-intervention thus created 'a spatial regime which permitted the coexistence of absolutism, liberal parliamentarism and enlightened authoritarianism, in a kind of *complexio oppositorium*, preserved by a system of treaties that "legalized" the hegemony of the Great Powers'.[232] At least during the first decades of the 19th century, however, the right of each state to choose its form of government was not an unconditional one: 'existing rulers could not be overthrown by their own subjects or an outside power, and in no circumstances could they be replaced by anything resembling the revolutionary regimes of pre-1814'.[233] Nowhere were these limitations more evident than in the Holy Alliance's doctrine of intervention.

---

[227] ibid, 227.
[228] ibid, 231.
[229] Lorimer, *The Institutes*, vol II, 54.
[230] ibid, 52.
[231] Michael Broers, *Europe After Napoleon; Revolution, Reaction and Romanticism, 1814–1848* (Manchester University Press 1996) 11.
[232] Nehal Bhuta, 'The Antinomies of Transformative Occupation' (2005) 16 EJIL 721, 731–2.
[233] Broers, *Europe After Napoleon*, 11.

7.1 The Holy Alliance: Intervention as a Means to Enforce the Collective Interest in the Peace and Tranquillity of Europe

From 1 November 1814 to 9 June 1815, the delegates of most European states gathered in Vienna to redesign the political map of Europe after the French Revolution and the Napoleonic Wars. The following decades were thus characterized by the interventions of the great powers, grouped together in the 'Concert of Europe', to secure the unstable thrones of the restored rulers.[234]

Within the Concert of Europe, closer ties existed among the autocratic monarchies of Central and Eastern Europe (Austria, Prussia, and Russia). By a treaty signed in Paris on 14/26 September 1815,[235] the three powers formed a 'Holy Alliance' founded on the divine right of sovereigns to rule, on the solidarity among them, and on the total rejection of liberal ideas and revolutionary changes of government.[236] The Troppau Protocol of 19 November 1820 delineated the Holy Alliance's doctrine of intervention: states where a dynastic ruler had been overthrown would cease to be members of the European alliance and intervention could be carried out to restore the legitimate order, although only as an *extrema ratio* after diplomatic means had failed.[237] On this basis, several interventions were planned, and in most cases executed, by the Holy Alliance powers, collectively or individually, with the mandate of the Concert of Europe in support of monarchs who faced, or had been ousted by, revolutions, insurrections, or civil wars. The Congress of Laybach (1821), in particular, mandated Austria to intervene in Naples and Piedmont,[238] while in Verona (1822) France was entrusted with sending its forces to Spain in support of King Ferdinand VII.[239] Austria

---

[234] The first reference to the Concert of Europe appeared in the Treaty of Union, Concert and Subsidy between Austria, Great Britain, Prussia, and Russia (Chaumont, 1 March 1814) where the powers agreed to act 'dans un parfait concert afin de se procurer à elles-mêmes et à l'Europe une paix générale' (Art 1, 63 CTS 83). The Quadruple Alliance Treaty (Paris, 20 November 1815) provided for periodic congresses in order to consider questions related to peace in Europe (65 CTS 296). At Aix-la-Chapelle (1818), the four main powers that had defeated Napoleon were joined by a normalized France and became the 'Pentarchy' (the text of the Protocol of Aix-la-Chapelle (9 October 1818) is in 69 CTS 365). Other congresses were held in Troppau (1820), Laybach (1821), and Verona (1822). Minor powers were not invited.

[235] The Holy Alliance Treaty (Paris, 18/26 September 1815) 65 CTS 199.

[236] As emphasized in the circular dispatch of 12 May 1821 at the end of the Congress of Laybach, '[l]es changements utiles et nécessaires dans la Législation et dans l'Administration des Etats, ne doivent émaner que de la volonté libre, de l'impulsion réfléchie et éclairée de ceux que Dieu a rendus responsables du pouvoir ... Pénétrés de cette vérité éternelle, les Souverains ... ont déclaré qu'en respectant les droits et l'indépendance du pouvoir légitime, ils [regardaient] comme légalement nulle et désavouée par les principes qui constituent le droit public de l'Europe, toute prétendue réforme opérée par la révolte et la force ouverte' (Circular to the Austrian, Prussian, and Russian Ministers at Foreign Courts, Laybach, 12 May 1821, *British and Foreign State Papers 1820–1821*, vol VIII (1830) 1203 (hereafter Laybach Circular)). The French minister of foreign affairs, Pasquier, branded the circular 'a novelty introduced into the law of nations' (quoted in William Ezra Lingelbach, 'The Doctrine and Practice of Intervention in Europe' (1900) 16 *Annals of the American Academy of Political and Social Science* 1, 13).

[237] The text of the Troppau Protocol (19 November 1820) is in F Martens, *Recueil des traités conclus par la Russie avec les Puissances étrangères*, vol IV (*Traités avec l'Autriche 1815–1849*) (Devrient 1878) 281.

[238] See Laybach Circular, 1201–5. Britain did not sign the document, while France did but specified that its signature implied only the consent to, and not cooperation with, the intervention in the Kingdom of the Two Sicilies (Dupuis, *Le droit*, 107).

[239] Read the text of the Verona Resolution of 19 November 1822 in Tanoviceano, *De l'intervention*, 106–7. Britain refused to sign it. At Verona, Austria also unsuccessfully proposed the creation of a committee of inquiry based in Piacenza to deal with liberal movements in the Italian peninsula (Sereni, *The Italian Conception*, 183).

also intervened in the Papal States in 1831 upon request of Pope Gregory XVI, claiming that the insurgents' propaganda threatened Austrian Lombardy.[240] At the Congress of Aix-la-Chapelle (1818), the Alliance's members also discussed a possible intervention in the rebellious Spanish colonies in America, but the proposal met with the strong opposition of Britain and the United States and, therefore, never went ahead.[241]

The Holy Alliance attempted to use intervention as an instrument to restore and maintain the 18th century's *ancien régime* founded on the divine right to rule that had been wiped out by the French Revolution and the Napoleonic Wars. The main features of the Alliance's doctrine of intervention can be summarized as follows: 1) intervention was permissible only in favour of the legitimate government; 2) this was so whatever the qualification of the situation of internal unrest, and regardless of the success of the insurgents in overthrowing the incumbent or establishing a *de facto* administration; and 3) consent to intervention by the legitimate government was desirable but not necessary if the collective interest in preventing the contagion of revolution required action. Starting from the first point, the government that could request and receive support from other states was not deemed to be that in effective control of a country: rather, it was the one that had the right to rule as determined at Vienna in 1815, 'ceux que Dieu a rendus responsables du pouvoir', to use the Laybach circular's language.[242] The principle of continuity of legitimate power that characterized the 18th century was thus strongly reaffirmed by the Holy Alliance during the first decades of the 19th century and entailed an obligation of non-recognition of any government borne out of revolutions or in violation of dynastic succession rules, as well as the right to intervene to restore the monarch who had been illegally overthrown.[243] The *de facto* situation did not have any relevance: interventions were undertaken also in favour of ousted monarchs to reinstate them on their thrones.

The second point was a consequence of the previous one and entailed that, in the Holy Alliance's view, there could be no distinction between situations of rebellion, insurrection, or civil war: the presumption in favour of the legitimate government operated regardless of the level reached by the internal unrest. Interventions, then, took place both in situations of mere revolutions and coups d'état that had overthrown a monarch (as in the cases of the interventions in Naples, Piedmont, Spain, and the Papal Legations) and in full-blown civil wars (namely the Hungarian War of Independence of 1848–49 and the Oriental Crisis of 1840).

As to the third point, interventions normally took place at the request of those the Holy Alliance considered to be the legitimate authorities of the concerned state, even if they had been ousted. The need for consent was highlighted at the Congress of Aix-la-Chapelle, where the Powers agreed that meetings to address crises would only 'take place in pursuance of a formal invitation on the part of such of those states as the said affairs may concern'.[244] Austria's interventions in Naples and in Piedmont

---

[240] PH Winfield, 'The Grounds of Intervention in International Law' (1924) 5 BYBIL 149, 152.

[241] Ann Van Wynen Thomas and AJ Thomas, Jr, *Non-Intervention; The Law and Its Import in the Americas* (Southern Methodist University Press 1956) 12; John B Whitton, 'La doctrine de Monroe' (1933) 40 RGDIP 5, 12–14.

[242] Laybach Circular, 1203.

[243] Rojas Castro, 'La reconnaissance', 15–16.

[244] Art 4, Protocol of Aix-la-Chapelle.

DEVELOPMENT OF THE PRINCIPLE OF NON-INTERVENTION 43

were thus solicited by King Ferdinand I of the Two Sicilies and King Charles Felix of Sardinia, respectively.[245] The Austrian chancellor, Prince Metternich, also secured the conclusion of treaties of alliance with the Duke of Modena and the Duchess of Parma by which the latter two committed not to change the constitution of their states and which led to Austria's anti-revolution intervention in the two duchies in 1831.[246] France's expedition in Spain in 1823 (the 'Hundred Thousand Sons of Saint Louis') was invited by the Spanish King Ferdinand VII, while its occupation of Ancona and Rome in 1831 and 1849, respectively, were at the request of Popes Gregory XVI and Pius IX.[247] When, in 1849, Tsar Nicholas I sent troops to support Emperor Franz Josef of Austria who was struggling to quell a national revolt in Hungary, the Russian government justified the intervention on the basis of the emperor's invitation and on self-preservation arguments by pointing the finger at the infiltration of Polish elements among the Hungarian insurgents and the risk that the troubles could spread to Congress Poland.[248] The European powers' intervention against Egypt's governor, Muhammad Ali, to maintain 'the integrity and independence of the Ottoman empire, as a security for the peace of Europe' was also 'at the express demand of the Sultan, and solely for his defence'.[249]

The absence of consent, however, did not necessarily preclude an intervention: in a dispatch to his generals in Italy dated 29 April 1822, Metternich instructed them to militarily intervene in the Italian states either at the request of their rulers *or* on their own initiative.[250] Austria also prolonged its military presence in Piedmont until October 1823 regardless of King Charles Felix's request to end it,[251] whereas French troops occupied Ancona from 1832 to 1838 in spite of Pope Gregory XVI's protests so to forestall a possible Austrian intervention in the Legations.[252] All in all, the main title to intervention was not consent but the right to self-preservation against revolutionary contagion, as the survival of one monarchy was seen as depending on that of all others.[253] In the Holy Alliance's missionary vision, the intervening powers did not need to be directly endangered by the internal situation in other states: they could intervene to enforce a collective interest (the maintenance of the tranquillity of Europe) against the resurgence of the revolutionary ideas that had plagued the continent at the end of the 18th century and had led to the Napoleonic Wars.[254] Exactly because it served a

---

[245] Fauchille, *Traité*, 541; Giorgio Cansacchi, *Storia dei trattati e politica internazionale. I principi informatori delle relazioni internazionali* (Giappichelli 1965) 106.

[246] Tanoviceano, *De l'intervention*, 96, 128–9.

[247] Fauchille, *Traité*, 541.

[248] Bastid, 'La révolution', 245–7. There were no official protests against the intervention (ibid, 248).

[249] Convention for the Pacification of the Levant (London, 15 July 1840), Preamble and Art 4, cited in Wheaton, *History*, 579, 581.

[250] Quoted in Tanoviceano, *De l'intervention*, 105.

[251] Vidari, *Del principio*, 22.

[252] ibid, 22–3; Tanoviceano, *De l'intervention*, 129.

[253] Woolsey, *Introduction*, 48. The point was clearly made in the circular dispatch of 8 December 1820 from the Courts of Austria, Prussia, and Russia in relation to the intervention in the Kingdom of the Two Sicilies: 'The powers have exercised an uncontestable right in occupying themselves with taking in common measures of security against states in which the overthrow of government by a revolt, even could it be considered only as a dangerous example, must have for its consequences a hostile attitude against all constitutions and legitimate governments' (quoted in Westlake, *International Law*, Part I, 305).

[254] For Metternich, the principle of non-intervention was anathema: '[c]e sont les brigands qui récusent la gendarmerie, et les incendiaries qui protestent contre les pompiers' (quoted in Dupuis, 'Liberté', 385–6).

44 INTERNATIONAL LAW AND THE PRINCIPLE OF NON-INTERVENTION

collective interest, however, intervention had to be conducted collectively through the Concert of Europe: this is why, at the congresses, one or more powers were mandated to act on behalf of all others to maintain or restore the legitimate internal order in the European states, and with it, peace on the continent. This mandate was a stronger legitimizing factor than the consent of the territorial sovereign.

The three waves of liberal revolutions that characterized the first half of the 19th century (1820, 1830, 1848), however, soon demonstrated that the Holy Alliance's project was an anachronistic one. The Alliance, in particular, was unable to prevent the change of government in France in 1830 or to recover Spain's American colonies.[255] In the Belgian War of Independence (1830), the Dutch king also unsuccessfully appealed for the intervention of Britain, Austria, Prussia, and Russia on the basis of the treaties of Paris and Vienna which had attributed Belgium to the Netherlands.[256] In fact, in 1832 Britain and Orléanist France militarily intervened to prevent the reoccupation of Belgium by the Netherlands and to force King Willem I to recognize the independence of the new country.[257] The claims of the Holy Alliance that the legitimate government of a state was the dynastic one were also eventually abandoned: as Emmanuelle Jouannet has pointed out, from the second half of the 19th century 'no basic textbook of international law any longer defended [the] principle of [dynastic] legitimacy and the right of intervention that accompanied it'.[258] The practice of this period confirms this conclusion. In 1830, Austria, Prussia, and Russia were forced to recognize Louis-Philippe of Orléans as the new King of the French after the July Revolution overthrew Charles X and the senior branch of the House of Bourbon.[259] When Louis-Napoleon Bonaparte took the French imperial throne on 2 December 1852, a secret protocol signed by the courts of Austria, Britain, Prussia, and Russia the following day declared that the change of government was an internal affair of France and that the powers remained bound by the principle of non-intervention in spite of the 1815 Treaty of

In 1864, Pope Pius IX still considered the principle of non-intervention one of the principal errors of the time (*Syllabus errorum*, 8 December 1864, Proposition LXII).

[255] The Crimean War (1853–6) saw most European powers opposed to Russia and rang the death knell for the Holy Alliance, which had already been declining after the death of its main inspirator, Tsar Alexander I of Russia, in 1825. After the end of the Alliance, the Concert of Europe continued to operate and opened up to lesser powers, like the Kingdom of Sardinia, and also to non-European states, like the Ottoman Empire (Art VII, General Treaty for the Re-Establishment of Peace between Austria, France, Great Britain, Prussia, Sardinia and Turkey, and Russia (Paris, 30 March 1856) 114 CTS 409). The Concert, however, was weakened by the rivalry between Austria and France over supremacy in Italy and between Austria and Russia in the Balkans. In 1908, the creation of two rival blocs in Europe, the Triple Entente (Britain, France, and Russia) and the Triple Alliance (Germany, Austria-Hungary, and Italy) formally terminated the Concert and eventually resulted in the First World War (Rodogno, *Against Massacre*, 19).

[256] Rougier, *Les guerres civiles*, 366.

[257] Wheaton, *History*, 551–2. France entered Belgium and sieged Antwerp while the British and French fleets blockaded the Dutch ports. The other powers refused to take part. For Stowell, the French and British intervention was an 'abuse of force' (Stowell, *Intervention*, 283). Indeed, Belgium had not yet achieved *de facto* independence and the intervention was a violation of the Final Act of the Congress of Vienna.

[258] Jouannet, *The Liberal-Welfarist Law*, 123. Writing in 1876, Creasy affirms that '[t]he form of a State's government is, in the eye of International Law, absolutely immaterial' (Sir Edward S Creasy, *First Platform of International Law* (John Van Voorst 1876) 99), a conclusion shared, according to Fiore, by all publicists (Fiore, *Nouveau droit international*, 280–1).

[259] Focarelli, *Introduzione storica*, 290–1.

DEVELOPMENT OF THE PRINCIPLE OF NON-INTERVENTION   45

Paris that excluded the Bonapartes from the throne of France.[260] British practice consistently followed the factual approach to the identification of governments,[261] and so did the United States.[262] The recognition of *de facto* independent colonies even before the parent state had agreed to transfer sovereignty also became common practice during the wars of independence in Latin America in the first decades of the 19th century: Britain, for instance, established diplomatic relations and signed friendship treaties with Colombia, Mexico, and Buenos Aires from January 1825 as, after the Battle of Ayacucho, it had become clear that Spain would not be able to recover control over its former territories.[263]

Case-law of the second half of the 19th century confirmed the demise of the dynastic legitimacy doctrine. In *Jansen* (1868), the Mixed Commission established under the 1868 Convention between the United States and Mexico found that 'a government *de facto* is also a government *de jure*' and denied that the government of Emperor Maximilian was the *de facto* government of Mexico, as it lacked 'the element of popular support or habitual obedience from the mass of the people [and] rested alone on the assistance of foreign force'.[264] In the same year, the *Cuculla* arbitration between the United States and Mexico held, quoting Wheaton, that '[h]abitual obedience of the members of a political society (of the "bulk" of them) must, in fact, exist to constitute a government'.[265] These conclusions were subsequently famously reaffirmed in

[260]   Rivier, *Principes*, 394.

[261]   TC Chen, *The International Law of Recognition* (LC Green ed, Stevens & Sons 1951) 107, 118–19.

[262]   ibid, 120; PK Menon, 'Some Thoughts About the Law of Recognition' (1991) 3 Sri Lanka J Int'l L 87, 96. There were, however, occasional departures: during the American Civil War, for instance, Secretary of State Seward affirmed that governmental changes resulting from violence and not constitutional procedures could not be recognized until it was clear that they had been accepted by the people (Noël-Henry, 'La doctrine américaine en matière de reconnaissance de gouvernements étrangers' (1928) 35 RGDIP 201, 257–8). Another departure from the effective control doctrine occurred when, in 1913, President Wilson refused to recognize General Victoriano Huerta as the new head of the Mexican government following the murders of President Madero and Vice President Pino Suárez in the Ten Tragic Days (ibid, 261). The Wilson Doctrine developed in parallel to the analogous Tobar Doctrine in Latin America and also led to the non-recognition of governments in the Dominican Republic (1913–16), Ecuador (1913), Costa Rica (1917), and Cuba (1917): Chen, *The International Law*, 108. It was eventually repudiated by President Hoover in 1931, although not in regard to the United States' immediate neighbours, the Central American states (ibid, 110, 127). In the *Tinoco Claims* arbitration, Judge Taft incidentally noted that, whatever the merits of the United States' national policy of non-recognition, 'it certainly has not been acquiesced in by all the nations of the world, which is a condition precedent to considering it as a postulate of international law' (*Aguilar-Amory and Royal Bank of Canada Claims (Great Britain v Costa Rica)*, 18 October 1923, 1 RIAA 369, 381 ('Tinoco Claims Arbitration')).

[263]   Rojas Castro, 'La reconnaissance', 25. As William Vernon Harcourt noted in his letters to *The Times* under the nom de plume Historicus, '[w]hen a sovereign State, from exhaustion or any other cause, has virtually and substantially abandoned the struggle for supremacy it has no right to complain if a foreign State treats the independence of its former subjects as *de facto* established; nor can it prolong its sovereignty by a mere paper assertion of right' (Harcourt, *Letters by Historicus*, 9). See also Andrès Bello, *Principios de derecho internacional* (first published 1832, 3rd edn, Garnier Hermanos 1873) 27.

[264]   Mixed Commission established under the Convention concluded between the United States of America and Mexico on 4 July 1868, *Case of Charles J Jansen v Mexico*, Opinion of the Commission delivered by the United States Commissioner, Mr Wadsworth, 29 RIAA 159, 186–7.

[265]   *Cuculla v Mexico*, Mexico–United States Claims Commission, Award of 4 July 1868, in John Bassett Moore, *History and Digest of the International Arbitrations to which the United States Has Been a Party*, vol III (GPO 1898) 2877. The arbitration related to the acts of the Mexican insurgents of Zuloaga, who took control of (only) the capital city and were recognized as the new government by several European countries and by the United States. The Award denied that Zuloaga's was the legitimate government of Mexico as it had never achieved *de facto* control of the country.

46   INTERNATIONAL LAW AND THE PRINCIPLE OF NON-INTERVENTION

the 1923 *Tinoco Claims* arbitration between Great Britain and Costa Rica.[266] In the end, the consolidation of the effective control approach to the identification of the government of a state was a result of the replacement of the divine right to rule with popular will as the source of legitimate power: as a commentator has noted, effective control is nothing but 'an application of [popular sovereignty] in those circumstances of ideological pluralism'.[267]

7.2 The British Position: Intervention as a Means to Protect Essential Interests of the Intervening State

As Grewe puts it, the international legal order of the 19th century developed 'under the dominant influence of British world policy';[268] the rules on intervention were no exception. Apart from the United States in the Americas[269] and, at least initially and after the July 1830 Revolution, France,[270] it was indeed mainly Britain that, from the Congress of Verona, persistently objected to the Holy Alliance's claim of a *general* right of intervention aimed at securing not only the territorial integrity of states but also their government on the basis of the principle of dynastic legitimacy: for Britain, foreign intervention was permissible only on grounds of self-preservation in *specific* cases. In a circular dispatch to the British ministers at foreign courts dated 19 January 1821 in response to that sent by Austria, Prussia, and Russia proclaiming their intention to oppose all revolutions in Europe, the Foreign Secretary, Viscount Castlereagh, explained that

> no Government can be more prepared than the British Government is, to uphold the right of any State or States to interfere, *where their own immediate security, or essential interests, are seriously endangered* by the internal transactions of another State. — But, as they regard the assumption of such right, as only to be justified *by the strongest necessity*, and to be limited and regulated thereby, they cannot admit that this right can receive a general and indiscriminate application to all revolutionary movements, *without reference to their immediate bearing upon some particular State or States*, or be made prospectively the basis of an Alliance.[271]

The circular would become the official policy of Britain for the entire 19th century. To be clear, Castlereagh was by no means advocating for an obligation of absolute non-intervention in the internal struggles of other states: he only rejected the abstract, pre-emptive self-preservation arguments of the Holy Alliance. For him, the right to

---

[266] *Tinoco Claims* arbitration, 381. See also the *Case of Melville E Day and David E Garrison, as surviving executors of Cornelius K Garrison v Venezuela*, United States–Venezuela Claims Commission, 5 December 1885, 29 RIAA 227, 231–2; *French Claims against Peru (France v Peru)*, 11 October 1920, 1 RIAA 215, 218–19; *The United States of America on Behalf of George W Hopkins, Claimant, v The United Mexican States* (Opinion and Decision) Mexico–United States Claims Commission, 31 March 1926, 4 RIAA 41, 45–6.
[267] Brad R Roth, *Governmental Illegitimacy in International Law* (OUP 1999) 414.
[268] Grewe, *The Epochs*, 462.
[269] See Section 9.1 of this chapter.
[270] Lingelbach, 'The Doctrine', 13–14.
[271] *British and Foreign State Papers 1820–1821*, vol VIII (1830), 1162, emphasis added.

DEVELOPMENT OF THE PRINCIPLE OF NON-INTERVENTION   47

self-preservation exceptionally permitted intervention, on whichever side, but only in specific cases dictated 'by the strongest necessity' and where the immediate security or other essential interests of the intervening state were seriously affected. The mere adoption of a certain form of government and the risk of revolution contagion to other countries were not sufficient.

Castlereagh's successor as Foreign Secretary, Canning, followed in his footsteps. His letter of 31 March 1823 to the British ambassador to Paris in relation to the French intervention in Spain stressed that 'so long as the troubles and disturbances of Spain should be confined within the circle of her own territory, they could not be admitted by the British Government to afford any plea for foreign interference'.[272] As a consequence, Britain did not participate in the intervention and turned down requests for assistance by both France and the Spanish liberal insurgents.[273] In 1859, another Foreign Secretary, Lord Russell, confirmed that '[w]ith regard to the general question of interference in the internal affairs of other countries, Her Majesty's Government hold that non-intervention is the principle on which the Governments of Europe should act, only to be departed from when the safety of a foreign State, or its paramount interests, require it'.[274]

In addition to self-preservation, Britain also frequently invoked the existence of treaty stipulations between the concerned states to justify its interventions. Those in support of Portugal's Queen Maria II against Dom Miguel's forces in 1834 and in support of Spain's Queen Isabella II and her mother, the Queen Regent Christina, against Don Carlos during the First Carlist War (1833–1840) were, for instance, based on the 1834 Quadruple Treaty for the Pacification of the (Iberian) Peninsula concluded between Britain, France, Spain, and Portugal.[275] Britain's invocation of a treaty-based right to intervene, however, was almost invariably combined with claims of self-preservation.

What the British doctrine had in common with that of the Holy Alliance was that, at least initially, it did not distinguish between different forms of internal unrest: the same rules applied to all. Unlike the Holy Alliance powers, however, Britain saw intervention as an exceptional means to enforce individual, not collective interests: John Stuart Mill was critical of this construction and claimed that 'of all attitudes which a nation can take up on the subject of intervention, the meanest and worst is to profess that it interferes only when it can serve its own objects by it'.[276] The British doctrine of non-intervention also admitted, or at least did not rule out, intervention in support of

---

[272] Quoted in Westlake, *International Law*, Part I, 306.

[273] John Bew, '"From an Umpire to a Competitor": Castlereagh, Canning and the Issue of International Intervention in the Wake of the Napoleonic Wars' in Simms and Trim (eds), *Humanitarian Intervention*, 117, 127.

[274] Quoted in Philip C Jessup, 'The Spanish Rebellion and International Law' (1937) 15 *Foreign Affairs* 260, 264.

[275] Vidari, *Del principio*, 58. The text of the treaty is in *British and Foreign State Papers 1833–1834*, vol XXII (1847) 124. In relation to the intervention in the First Carlist War, in particular, the British Foreign Secretary, Viscount Palmerston, explained that the 'interference' was 'founded on a treaty arising out of the acknowledged right of a sovereign, decided by the legitimate authorities of the country over which she ruled' (Wheaton, *History*, 537).

[276] Mill, 'A Few Words', 255.

48 INTERNATIONAL LAW AND THE PRINCIPLE OF NON-INTERVENTION

insurgents if this was necessary on self-preservation grounds.[277] In the end, the British doctrine was grounded in considerations of opportunity, which left a wide margin of discretionality concerning whether to intervene or not, and on whose side, in each case. After the demise of the Holy Alliance, the British doctrine of non-intervention became the predominant one and was eventually followed not only by France,[278] but also by emerging powers like the United States.[279]

7.3 Intervention 'in the Interests of Humanity'

A limited number of interventions took place in the 19th century in favour of insurgents. Apart from the aforementioned French and British intervention in support of Belgium's independence in 1832 and that of the United States in Cuba against Spain in 1898, they were carried out by the European powers in the Ottoman Empire. The first was the armed intervention in the Greek War of Independence, culminating in the Battle of Navarino (1827) and the French occupation of the Morea (1828–33).[280] With the exception of Austria, all major powers initially adopted an impartial position.[281] In 1827, however, when the ongoing conflict became an obstacle to trade in the eastern Mediterranean and it became clear that the Porte would not be able to put an end to it, Britain, France, and Russia started to support the Greeks and, in the Preamble of the 1827 Treaty for the Pacification of Greece, referred to the following justifications for their determination to act:

> 1st, ... complying with the request of one party [the Greeks]; 2ndly, ... staying the shedding of blood; 3rdly, and *principally*, ... affording protection to the subjects of other Powers who navigated the Levant, in which, for many years, atrocious Piracy

---

[277] This was explicitly affirmed by British Foreign Secretary Lord Russell in 1859: '[t]he best writers on the law of nations allow intervention, where it is rendered necessary for the safety or essential interests of a State, as much in favour of subjects justly discontented, as in favour of a Sovereign, or regular Government' (quoted in Jessup, 'The Spanish Rebellion', 264).

[278] Lingelbach, 'The Doctrine', 30. Defending the intervention in Spain in 1823, for instance, the French foreign affairs minister, Chateaubriand, claimed that 'no Government has a right to interfere in the affairs of another Government, *except in the case where the security and immediate interests of the first Government are compromised*' (quoted in Halleck, *International Law*, 86, emphasis in the original). During the Third Carlist War, another French foreign affairs minister, the Duc de Broglie, also emphasized that France did not intend to intermeddle in the internal affairs of Spain on the side of either party, unless the life or property of its nationals were threatened (Letters of the Duc de Broglie to the French consuls in Spain, 4 and 29 August 1873, in Kiss, *Répertoire*, 403–4).

[279] Already in 1798, US President George Washington wrote that no government could interfere in the internal affairs of other governments unless its own security was at stake (Ernest Nys, *Le droit international: Les principes, les théories, les faits* (Castaigne/Fontemoing 1905) 187).

[280] The War of Greek Independence started in April 1821 and ended in 1832 with the recognition by the Ottoman sultan of Greece's independence in the Treaty of Constantinople of 21 July 1832.

[281] Siotis, *Le droit de la guerre*, 75.

DEVELOPMENT OF THE PRINCIPLE OF NON-INTERVENTION   49

had been exercised, while neither Turkey nor revolted Greece were *de facto* either able or willing to prevent the excesses springing out of this state of anarchy.[282]

Otherwise said, the main ground for the intervention was based on self-preservation, namely the protection of maritime trade interests. All in all, the intervention can be considered an application of the British doctrine and a departure from that of the Holy Alliance.

The intervention in the Greek War of Independence inaugurated a series of interventions by the European states to protect Christian minorities in the Ottoman Empire in the context of the so-called 'Eastern Question'.[283] The conservative powers, however, remained hostile to claims of intervention on humanitarian grounds.[284] In justifying Austria's decision not to participate in the intervention in favour of the Greeks, in particular, Metternich claimed that 'oppressed authority cannot be rescued without a manifest violation of the independence of States'.[285] Prussia also refused to take sides in favour of the insurgents.[286] What is more, even the intervening states never exclusively relied on humanitarian considerations to justify their interventions but accompanied them with other grounds, as clearly shown by the case of the Greek War of Independence.[287] When self-preservation did not play a role, the

---

[282] Phillimore, *Commentaries*, 571, emphasis added. This might be the first reference to the 'unable/unwilling' doctrine in an official document.

[283] In addition to those in Greece (1827) and in Lebanon and Syria (1860–61), other European interventions took place in the context of situations of internal unrest in the Ottoman Empire in the 19th century. During the Great Eastern Crisis (1875–8), the two principalities of Serbia and Montenegro, vassals of Turkey, proclaimed their independence and declared war on the Porte on 18 June 1876. Russia mobilized its army and threatened to declare war on the Ottoman Empire if it did not sign a truce with Serbia and renew the peace negotiations within forty-eight hours. These negotiations lasted until 15 January 1877 and effectively ended the fighting between Serbia and the Porte until the former, having gained financial backing from Russia, again declared war together with Montenegro (see Phillimore, *Commentaries*, 612). When the Christian Cretans insurged in 1866, Greece and Russia armed them, while the European powers set up a naval operation to rescue Christian families (Rodogno, *Against Massacre*, 118). Greece intervened again in support of the Cretan insurgents in 1897 (Prospero Fedozzi, 'Saggio sull'intervento' (1899) 62 *Archivio giuridico Filippo Serafini* 3, 34). The Greek government based the intervention on the anarchy on the island and the need to restore peace and order (Georges Streit, 'La question crétoise au point de vue du droit international' (1897) 4 RGDIP 134, 182). The subsequent landing of European troops and occupation of Crete as well as the blockade of the island for Greek ships were aimed at restoring order and at protecting the civilian population and occurred upon request of the Ottoman government (Arrigo Cavaglieri, 'La questione cretese' (1912) 6 RDI 244, 249; Rodogno, *Against Massacre*, 214, 217). Coercive but non-forcible intervention (with the exception of the brief occupation of the islands of Mytilene and Lemnos in 1905) was also undertaken by Austria-Hungary and Russia following the Macedonian uprisings of 1902–3 and their subsequent repression by the Ottomans (Antoine Rougier, 'L'intervention de l'Europe dans la question de la Macédoine' (1906) 13 RGDIP 178). The Porte protested by invoking the principle of non-intervention and claiming the violation of its sovereignty (Winfield, 'The Grounds', 192). The intervening powers did not offer justifications (ibid, 193).

[284] The expression 'humanitarian intervention' is of relatively recent coinage. In the 19th century, states referred to interventions 'on grounds of humanity', 'in the interests of humanity', or 'to prevent the effusion of blood'. Massacres, atrocities, horrors, and exterminations were also terms used in this period to describe the situations that triggered an intervention on grounds of humanity (Rodogno, *Against Massacre*, 4).

[285] Letter of Richard Klemens von Metternich to Apponyi, 17 October 1826, reproduced in Agatha Verdebout, 'The Contemporary Discourse on the Use of Force in the Nineteenth Century: A Diachronic and Critical Analysis' (2014) 1 JUFIL 223, 230.

[286] Rodogno, *Against Massacre*, 81.

[287] Russia's justifications for its 1877 declaration of war on the Ottoman Empire, for instance, included not only the protection of the Christian populations of Turkey, but also a reference to the Tsar's duties to protect 'the interests of Russia, whose peaceful development is hindered by the permanent disturbances of

50 INTERNATIONAL LAW AND THE PRINCIPLE OF NON-INTERVENTION

interventions in the Ottoman Empire were based on consent provided either ad hoc or in previous treaties.[288] The European powers, for instance, intervened during the Oriental Crisis of 1840 against Muhammad Ali's Egypt upon the request of the sultan 'to prevent the effusion of blood' caused by the continuation of hostilities.[289] Before sending an expeditionary force of up to 12,000 men in the Mount Lebanon Civil War to stop the massacre of Christian Maronites by Druze and Sunni paramilitary groups and 'to contribute towards the re-establishment of tranquillity' (1860), the powers forced Turkey to sign two protocols which authorized the operation.[290] Without the sultan's consent—the British ambassador to France claimed—no intervention would have been possible on Ottoman territory.[291] The French foreign affairs minister, de Thouvenel, concurred.[292] In both their military interventions in Crete (1867 and 1896), the powers also sought to secure the consent of the Porte or acted upon its request.[293]

The lack of clear *opinio juris*, therefore, prevented the formation of a customary rule allowing foreign intervention 'in the interest of humanity' without the consent of the territorial sovereign. That not only was there no right but even less a duty to intervene in the interests of humanity, at least by military means, is demonstrated by the fact that

the East' as well as 'the sentiments and interests of Europe' (Gortchakoff's circular dispatch of 7–19 April 1877, reproduced in Stowell, *Intervention*, 131–2). The main case of intervention on grounds of humanity in a civil war outside Europe, the American intervention in Cuba and subsequent war against Spain (1898), was justified by the need to protect US interests, and not only on humanitarian grounds. In particular, the justifications for the US intervention were: 'to put an end to the barbarities, bloodshed, starvation, and horrible miseries now existing there, and which the parties to the conflict are either unable or unwilling to stop or mitigate'; protection of US citizens in Cuba; the damage to US commerce, trade, and business and the wanton destruction of property on the island; the constant threat to US security and peace (Statement of President McKinley, 11 April 1898, quoted in Charles Cheney Hyde, *International Law Chiefly as Interpreted and Applied by the United States*, vol I (2nd edn, Little, Brown & Co 1947) 259).

[288] By the second half of the 19th century, the status of minorities in the Ottoman Empire was no longer an internal affair, but a matter of international obligation. Art IX of the 1856 Treaty of Paris expressed the will of the Sultan to ameliorate the conditions of his subjects 'without distinction of Religion or of race' and referred to a firman (imperial decree) 'which records his generous intentions towards the Christian population of his Empire', although at the same time it reaffirmed that this did not give the European powers the right to interfere in the domestic affairs of the Porte (the firman referred to is the Imperial Reform Edict (*hatti-houmayoun*) declared by Sultan Abdülmecid on 18 February 1856). Under the Treaty between Austria-Hungary, France, Germany, Great Britain and Ireland, Italy, Russia, and the Ottoman Empire for the Settlement of Affairs in the East (Berlin, 13 July 1878), the Armenians were put under the collective protection of the European powers, which acquired the right to receive periodic reports, evaluate the measures adopted, and superintend their application (Arts LXI and LXII, text in Wilhelm G Grewe (ed), *Fontes Historiae Iuris Gentium* vol III/1 (Walter de Gruyter 1992) 50). Rolin-Jaequemyns notes that the great powers acquired not only a right, but also a duty to ensure the correct implementation of the provisions of the Treaty of Berlin (Gustave Rolin-Jaequemyns, *Armenia, The Armenians, and the Treaties* (John Heywood 1891) 40). See Marco Roscini, 'Establishing State Responsibility for Historical Injustices: The Armenian Case' (2014) 14 Int'l Crim L Rev 291, 305–9.

[289] Preamble, Convention for the Pacification of the Levant, as reproduced in Wheaton, *History*, 579.

[290] Protocols of the Conferences between Austria, France, Great Britain, Prussia, Russia, and Turkey Relative to the Pacification of Syria (Paris, 3 August 1860) in Charles Samwer, *Nouveau Recueil Général de Traités*, vol XVI, Part II (Librairie de Dieterich 1860) 638–40. Stowell points out that the sultan's consent was obtained 'through constraint and a desire to avoid worse' (Stowell, *Intervention*, 66).

[291] Letter of Earl Cowley to Lord John Russell, 31 July 1860, quoted in Verdebout, 'The Contemporary Discourse', 230.

[292] Rodogno, *Against Massacre*, 104.

[293] ibid, 131, 214

no intervention took place in relation to the insurrection in Bosnia and Herzegovina (1875–77), the 'Bulgarian horrors' (1876), or the massacres of the Armenians (1886–1909). Interventions on grounds of humanity were also never carried out, or even contemplated, when massacres took place on the territory of one of the European powers or their colonies.

7.4 The Italian *Risorgimento* and the Principle of Nationalities as a Legal Basis for Intervention

The principle of nationalities (*principio di nazionalità*) took centre stage during the European revolutions of 1848–49 (the 'Springtime of Peoples') and played an important role in the formation of the new states of Italy and Germany, as well as in the wars of independence in the Balkans. In his famous *prelezione* (inaugural lecture) at the University of Turin on 22 January 1851, Pasquale Stanislao Mancini (1817–1888) identified the principle of nationalities as the foundation of the law of nations.[294] For Mancini, who was influenced by the works of the philosopher, historian, and lawyer Giambattista Vico (1668–1744),[295] when a people became a nation it acquired the right to independence.[296] Mancini argued that it was the nation, and not the state, that was the fundamental and original subject of international law and that the perfect state of a nation emerged from the combination of two elements: the internal constitution that it freely gave itself and its independence from other nations.[297] Nations, like individuals, were all equal and had the right to be free and to organize themselves independently: all interventions of one in the affairs of another were thus prohibited.[298]

The Italian writers of the time relied on Mancini's principle of nationalities to both delegitimize Austria's interventions in the Italian states to maintain the local rulers in power and to greenlight France's intervention in support of the Kingdom of Sardinia's efforts to unify the peninsula. Terenzio Mamiani, for instance, posits that the military support by a state in favour of a people under foreign rule (like the Dutch under the Spaniards or the Greeks under the Turks) does not amount to an intervention as

---

[294] Pasquale Stanislao Mancini, *Della nazionalità come fondamento del diritto delle genti* (1851) (Erik Jayme ed, Giappichelli 2000) 26.

[295] Sereni, *The Italian Conception*, 161–2.

[296] To turn a people into a nation, common geography, race, language, customs, history, laws, and religion were not sufficient: what was needed was the *coscienza della nazionalità*, that is, the social conscience of a people that saw themselves as a nation (Mancini, *Della nazionalità*, 45). Mancini's idea of 'nation', therefore, was more spiritual than racial (Arthur Nussbaum, *A Concise History*, 242). For the same view in French scholarship, see Despagnet, *Cours*, 119. German theorists, on the other hand, privileged natural factors for the identification of nations, such as blood and race (Sereni, *The Italian Conception*, 176).

[297] Mancini, *Della nazionalità*, 48–50. Bernard, however, remains unconvinced: for him, '[n]ationality is far from being unreal, but practically, and in the great multitude of cases, it is mere matter of opinion, and wherever the nation is not conterminous with a State, is wholly out of the grasp of law' (Bernard, *On the Principle*, 28). A contemporary commentator has noted that 'Mancini's thesis lacks the fundamental element of a rigorous demonstration ... because concepts such as nation and nationality are intrinsically meta-legal and lack a juridical foundation' (Edoardo Greppi, 'The *Risorgimento* and the "Birth" of International Law in Italy' in Giulio Bartolini (ed), *A History of International Law in Italy* (OUP 2020) 79, 88).

[298] Sereni, *The Italian Conception*, 163.

52   INTERNATIONAL LAW AND THE PRINCIPLE OF NON-INTERVENTION

it supports a nation against its oppressors.[299] For Carnazza Amari, however, the request of the oppressed people for external support is necessary, as one cannot help those who do not want to be helped.[300] When two peoples have been coerced into co-existing in one state but want to separate (like the Belgians from the Dutch), he deems that they too could require foreign assistance to secede, and this again could not be qualified as intervention.[301]

The principle of nationalities was at the same time a centrifugal and centripetal force, as it entailed the right to independence of nations under foreign domination but also promoted the unification of the various parts of the same fragmented nation.[302] It also had both a prohibitive and a permissive dimension: the former prevented states from assisting another to maintain its rule over a subjugated nation, while the latter justified third-state intervention in support of a nation fighting against foreign domination upon its request. Pro-nationality interventions could first and foremost be conducted by a state that shared a nationality link with the oppressed people.[303] When, in 1849, the grand duke was ousted, the Kingdom of Sardinia's prime minister, Gioberti, so justified a possible intervention in Tuscany:

> En vertu du droit national, qui domine tous les autres et qui en est le fondement, les diverses provinces italiennes ne sont, ni séparées, ni indépendantes, ni sans lien entre elles ... Un peuple ne peut intervenir dans les affaires d'un autre; mais les chefs d'une nation peuvent rappeler au devoir les membres qui s'en écartent ... L'intervention nationale est non-seulement permise, mais elle devient un devoir si elle est réclamée pour échapper à l'étranger, ou l'empêcher de se précipiter en masse et en armes sur le pays même.[304]

For Gioberti, therefore, 'national intervention' found its legal basis in 'national law', which took priority over international law. Although Gioberti's proposal to intervene in Tuscany was rejected by his ministers,[305] Sardinia later supported the insurrections in the Italian states, which eventually led to the creation of the unified Kingdom of Italy in 1861. In response to the protests of the Prussian government against the occupation of the Papal States and the Two Sicilies, Sardinia's Prime Minister Cavour argued that

---

[299] Terenzio Mamiani, *D'un nuovo diritto europeo* (4th edn, Tipografia Scolastica—Seb Franco e Figli 1861) 159. Sardinia's intervention in the states of Central Italy, therefore, was not a real 'intervention', as it was part of the struggle of one people (the Italians) to become an independent nation (ibid, 216–17). The only limit to external support in this case was the existence of treaties prohibiting it (ibid, 160).

[300] Carnazza Amari, *Nuova esposizione*, 109.

[301] ibid.

[302] Luigi Palma, *De' principio di nazionalità nella moderna società europea* (Editori della Biblioteca Utile 1867) 77.

[303] Bernard defines this case as '[t]he interference of one people in the domestic politics of another whose blood and language are the same, and who share with them ... that common sentiment, real though indefinable, which constitutes the unity of a nation' (Bernard, *On the Principle*, 25).

[304] Quoted in Pradier-Fodéré, *Traité*, 609.

[305] ibid, 610.

DEVELOPMENT OF THE PRINCIPLE OF NON-INTERVENTION 53

le droit public de tous les temps a reconnu a chaque nation la faculté de régler ses propres destinées, de se donner des institutions conformes à chaque nation, de se constituer en un mot de la manière qu'elle juge la plus propre à sauvegarder la sécurité et la prospérité de l'État. Ce droit n'a jamais été dénoncé comme contraire aux lois internationales.[306]

The principle of nationalities was invoked to allow third-state intervention in support of a nation under foreign domination even in the absence of a nationality link.[307] At least in the first part of his reign, in particular, France's Emperor Napoleon III used the principle as leverage for his political ambitions in the Italian peninsula to the detriment of Austria.[308] His policy, however, was not always consistent. In 1849, he intervened in the State of the Church against the Roman Republic at the request of the ousted Pope Pius IX and occupied Rome and part of the Papal States.[309] The intervention was presented as a pre-emptive counter-intervention to deter Austrian involvement.[310] In July 1860, on the other hand, Napoleon III's foreign minister, de Thouvenel, stressed that the dispute between King Francis II of the Two Sicilies and his people was an internal political matter that had to be settled without external interventions.[311]

Beyond the Italian peninsula, the principle of nationalities was generally not received well.[312] Oppenheim branded it as 'a political doctrine without any legal basis whatever'[313] and Bernard saw it as 'subversive of morality [and] dangerous to freedom'.[314] For Funck-Brentano and Sorel, the fact that the insurgents represented a nation trying to obtain independence did not change the fact that foreign intervention

---

[306] Note of Count Cavour to Count de Launay, Minister of Sardinia in Berlin, 9 November 1860, in Luigi Zini, *Storia d'Italia dal 1850 al 1866*, vol II (Guigoni 1869) 701. Sardinia's interventions in and subsequent annexation of the Italian states were criticized by Britain, France, Prussia, and Russia (Sir Sherston Baker (ed), *Halleck's International Law*, vol I (3rd edn, Kegan Paul, Trench, Trübner & Co 1893) 102; Zini, *Storia d'Italia*, 691–6). Britain's position, however, was not without ambiguities: in a letter sent to the British ambassador in Turin, the British Foreign Secretary, Lord Russell, cited Vattel's argument in favour of the Prince of Orange's invasion of England during the Glorious Revolution to express his sympathies for the insurrection in the Kingdom of the Two Sicilies (Francis Wharton, 'De l'assistance prêtée à une insurrection étrangère' (1885) 10 JDIP 375, 375–6).

[307] Winfield, 'The Grounds', 160. In an 1848 circular, for instance, the French Second Republic's foreign minister, Lamartine, pointed out that 'la République française se croirait en droit d'armer elle-même pour protéger ces mouvements légitimes de croissance et de nationalisation des peuples' (Alphonse de Lamartine, Manifeste à l'Europe: circulaire du ministre des Affaires étrangères aux agents diplomatiques de la République française, Paris, 1848, quoted in Sergio Marchisio, 'The Unification of Italy and International Law' in Giulio Bartolini (ed), *A History*, 285, 292).

[308] Grewe, *The Epochs*, 436.

[309] Bastid, 'La révolution', 252. The occupation of Rome was justified on the basis of the request of the Pope (Le Duc de Gramont to the Marquis de Moustier, 1 December 1967, in Viktor Bruns (ed), *Fontes Juris Gentium* (Carl Heymanns Verlag 1932), Series B, Section 1, Tome I, Part 1, 273) and as a 'regrettable but necessary' exception to the principle of non-intervention due to the exceptional circumstances of the Holy See (Drouyn de Lhuys to Baron de Malaret, 10 November 1864, in Bruns (ed), *Fontes Juris Gentium*, Series B, Section I, Tome I, Part 1, 294).

[310] Bastid, 'La révolution', 256.

[311] Letter to the Comte de Persigny, French Ambassador in London, 24 July 1860, in Kiss, *Répertoire*, 398.

[312] An exception is Tanoviceano , *De l'intervention*, 32–3. Sereni also criticized the doctrine, which in his view was mainly political and prevented 'international lawyers in Italy from absorbing the influence of other doctrines and so shutting out all fruitful clashes of ideas' (Sereni, *The Italian Conception*, 194–5).

[313] Oppenheim, *International Law*, vol I, 1st edn, 182, fn 1.

[314] Bernard, *On the Principle*, 26. See similarly Pradier-Fodéré, *Traité*, 608–10; Despagnet, *Cours*, 123.

54   INTERNATIONAL LAW AND THE PRINCIPLE OF NON-INTERVENTION

in their support remained a violation of international law.[315] In the end, the principle never became an accepted legal title for intervention. Several states, including Austria and Prussia, were explicitly hostile to it and the United States' attitude remained one of little interest.[316] The number of foreign interventions where the principle of nationalities was invoked by the intervening states (be they co-national or other states) remained extremely limited, and even then, considerations of self-preservation played a more important role.[317] As *Halleck's International Law* reports, for instance, in 1860 Sardinia provided logistical support to Garibaldi's *Spedizione dei Mille* (the 'Expedition of the Thousand') in the Kingdom of the Two Sicilies and directly intervened in the states of Northern and Central Italy 'on the ground of the dangers to which northern Italy was exposed owing to the state of affairs on the Papal territory, of the desire of the inhabitants for a change of government, of the obligations on Sardinia, and on Europe respectively, to influence the national movements to repress disorder'.[318] Although in theory applicable, the principle of nationalities was also not an official justification for France and Britain's intervention in the Belgian War of Independence, as they relied on the invitation of the Belgian provisional government, on the maintenance of the general security of Europe and the preservation of the European equilibrium, and on humanitarian grounds.[319] All in all, the principle was a political and not a juridical one and 'expressed only an aspiration and a political program: that humanity should be organized in national states'.[320]

7.5 The Emergence of the Distinction between Rebellions, Insurrections, and Civil Wars in the Second Half of the 19th Century

Although classifications of different forms of internal unrest had already appeared in 18th-century scholarship,[321] the European powers did not distinguish between them when it came to justifying intervention.[322] Put otherwise, states claimed they could or could not intervene in a situation of internal unrest in other countries regardless of its qualification or magnitude. This changed, however, in the second half of the 19th century.

---

[315] Funck-Brentano and Sorel, *Précis*, 221.

[316] Bastid, 'La révolution', 221–2; Marchisio, 'The Unification', 295.

[317] In a communication to the French ambassador in London dated 30 January 1860, for instance, de Thouvenel explained that '[l]e principe de non-intervention est une règle internationale dont personne n'apprécie plus que nous l'importance et l'autorité, et, dans notre pensée, il forme l'un des éléments les plus essentiels de tout règlement sérieux et définitif de la question italienne. Si le Gouvernement de l'Empereur est lui-même intervenu, il ne l'a fait *qu'en cédant à des circonstances impérieuses, parce que, dans l'état de choses en Italie, ses intérêts lui en imposaient la nécessité*' (text in Kiss, *Répertoire*, 105, emphasis added).

[318] Baker (ed), *Halleck's International Law*, 101–2.

[319] Phillimore, *Commentaries*, 593–5. The French minister of foreign affairs, Molé, explained to the Prussian representative that his country intervened not to support the Belgians, but because it could not tolerate an intervention by the other powers in support of the Dutch (Dupuis, 'Liberté', 385).

[320] Sereni, *The Italian Conception*, 174.

[321] See Section 3 of this chapter.

[322] McNair and Watts, *The Legal Effects*, 30.

7.5.1 Rebellions and insurrections

The Lieber Code, adopted on 24 April 1863 as instructions given to the Union's forces during the American Civil War, is arguably the first official document that identifies and defines discrete situations of internal unrest. In particular, the Code distinguishes between insurrection ('the rising of people in arms against their government, or a portion of it, or against one or more of its laws, or against an officer or officers of the government. It may be confined to mere armed resistance, or it may have greater ends in view'),[323] rebellion ('an insurrection of large extent, ... a war between the legitimate government of a country and portions of provinces of the same who seek to throw off their allegiance to it and set up a government of their own'),[324] and civil war ('war between two or more portions of a country or state, each contending for the mastery of the whole, and each claiming to be the legitimate government').[325] In the Code, then, the difference between rebellion and insurrection is based on scale, but that between rebellion and civil war is mainly based on purpose: while, in a rebellion, the rebels try to escape the sovereignty of a state, in a civil war the factions compete for sovereignty over the whole country.[326] Apart from that, as David Armitage observes, the difference between rebellion and civil war is evanescent, with 'wars of rebellion' being a type of civil war.[327] In any case, the Lieber Code does not address third-state obligations and the permissibility of intervention in relation to the several forms of internal unrest it identifies.

Unlike its rules on the conduct of hostilities, the definitions of different forms of internal unrest adopted by the Lieber Code did not have a significant impact on either state practice or scholarship. 'Rebellion' never turned into a term of art in international law and came to be occasionally used descriptively to refer not to a large-scale secessionist insurrection as suggested in the Code, but to its specular opposite, that is, 'a sporadic challenge to the legitimate government by a faction within a state for the purpose of seizing power'.[328] Insurrection (or insurgency), on the other hand, was normally employed to refer to a factual situation where, even though belligerency was not recognized, there was 'a more sustained and substantial internal conflict when the groups in revolt against the government of the state are sufficiently well-organized to offer effective resistance with the object of obtaining control of the government and to prevent the access of supplies from outside states'.[329] Differently from what the Lieber Code provided, then, what came to distinguish an insurrection from a mere rebellion

---

[323] Art 149, Instructions for the Government of Armies of the United States in the Field, General Orders No. 100 (Lieber Code), 24 April 1863. The text can be read in Dietrich Schindler and Jiri Toman (eds), *The Laws of Armed Conflicts* (Martinus Nijhoff Publishers 1988) 3.

[324] Lieber Code, Art 151.

[325] Lieber Code, Art 150.

[326] Neff, *War*, 257. The umpire's preliminary report on the Tehuantepec Claim also distinguished between rebellion and revolution: in the latter case, the individuals acted as authorities of a political party, while in the former as mere individuals (Moore, *History*, vol III, 2863).

[327] David Armitage, *Civil Wars*, 190. See Art 150 of the Lieber Code: '[t]he term [civil war] is also sometimes applied to war of rebellion, when the rebellious provinces or portions of the state are contiguous to those containing the seat of government'.

[328] RP Dhokalia, 'Civil Wars and International Law' (1971) 11 IJIL 219, 224. See similarly Rosalyn Higgins, 'Internal War and International Law' in Cyril E Black and Richard A Falk (eds), *The Future of the International Legal Order*, vol III: *Conflict Management* (Princeton University Press 1971) 81, 86.

[329] Dhokalia, 'Civil Wars', 225.

56 INTERNATIONAL LAW AND THE PRINCIPLE OF NON-INTERVENTION

was the fact that, in the former, the situation had gone 'beyond the control of the *de jure* government, by the magnitude of the hostilities and the consequent uncertainty of the result'.[330]

As US Secretary of State Seward noted on 19 June 1861, the employment of force by a government to suppress an insurrection 'by no means constitutes a state of war impairing the sovereignty of the government, creating belligerent sections, and entitling foreign States to intervene or to act as neutrals between them, or in any other way to cast off their lawful obligations to the nation thus for the moment disturbed'.[331] Said otherwise, a dispute between the government and the rebels/insurgents continued to be an exclusively internal matter of the concerned state to which the principle of non-intervention applied.[332] As a consequence, third states were prohibited from supporting the insurgents directly or indirectly[333] and had the option to support the incumbent government upon its request (unless a treaty prohibited it).[334] Certain treaties explicitly recognized that a government could or even had to be assisted when facing an insurrection: under the 1835 Treaty between Bolivia and Peru, for instance, the former committed to support the latter to quell General Salaverry's revolt.[335] The Resolution on the rights and duties of foreign powers and their ressortissants towards the established and recognized governments in case of insurrection, adopted at the 1900 Session of Neuchâtel by the Institut de droit international, confirmed that third states could continue to support incumbent governments facing civil strife at least until the insurgents had been recognized as belligerents.[336] In addition, the resolution affirmed an obligation for third states not to interfere with the measures taken by a government to restore internal tranquillity and not to provide the insurgents with

---

[330] Quincy Wright, 'International Law and the American Civil War' (1967) 61 ASIL Proceedings 50, 51.

[331] Mr Seward to Mr Adams (London), 19 June 1861, in Bruns (ed), *Fontes Juris Gentium*, Series B, Section 1, Tome I, Part 2, 109.

[332] McNair and Watts, *The Legal Effects*, 31. As the New York District Court found, '[i]nternational law has no place for rebellion; and insurgents have strictly no legal rights, as against other nations, until recognition of belligerent rights is accorded to them' (*The Ambrose Light (United States v The Ambrose Light etc)*, New York District Court, 30 September 1885, 25 *Federal Reporter*, First Series 408, 412). According to the International Criminal Tribunal for the former Yugoslavia (ICTY), the dichotomy belligerency-insurgency 'was clearly sovereignty-oriented and reflected the traditional configuration of the international community, based on the coexistence of sovereign States more inclined to look after their own interests than community concerns or humanitarian demands' (*Prosecutor v Duško Tadić*, Appeals Chamber, Decision on the Defence Motion for Interlocutory Appeal on Jurisdiction, IT-94-1-AR72, 2 October 1995, para 96 <www. icty.org/x/cases/tadic/acdec/en/51002.htm>).

[333] This was so unless the third state declared war on the state in civil war or could justify the support as a reprisal, on grounds of self-preservation, or on a treaty-based right.

[334] See the treaties concluded among the Central American states discussed in this chapter in Section 9.2.

[335] Art 1, Convenio para que el Gobierno de Bolivia preste auxilios militares al del Perú (Arequipa, 24 June 1835) in Juan Oviedo (ed), *Colección de leyes, decretos y órdenes publicadas en el Perú desde en año 1821 hasta 31 diciembre de 1859*, vol XIII (Felipe Bailly 1865) 163.

[336] Arts 2 and 7, Resolution on the Droits et devoirs des Puissances étrangères, au cas de mouvement insurrectionnel, envers les gouvernements établis et reconnus qui sont aux prises avec l'insurrection (Neuchâtel Resolution), 8 September 1900, text in French in (1900) 18 AIDI 227 (the unofficial English translation is in James Brown Scott (ed), *Resolutions of the Institute of International Law dealing with the Law of Nations with an historical introduction and explanatory notes* (OUP 1916) 157–9). Art 1(3) of the Convention on the Duties and Rights of States in the Event of Civil Strife (Havana, 20 February 1928) 134 LNTS 45 (Havana Convention), also allows the supply of arms and war materials to the government facing the civil strife until recognition of belligerency has occurred.

arms, ammunition, military *matériel*, or financial aid.[337] States were further required not to allow a hostile military expedition against an 'established and recognized' government to be organized on their territory.[338]

In the absence of a treaty providing otherwise, states could have also adopted a position that can be called, for want of a better expression, of 'negative equality' with respect to the foreign rebellion or insurrection, where they remained mere spectators and refrained from assisting *any* of the parties involved in the internal unrest.[339] Negative equality could have been an obligation assumed by treaty but was more frequently a unilateral decision made on the basis of political considerations, and should not be confused with neutral status in a technical sense or with non-intervention *stricto sensu*.[340] If '[t]he two pillars of the laws of neutrality are non-participation and non-discrimination'[341] and if the principle of non-intervention allows both participation and discrimination in favour of one party (the incumbent government), negative equality only means that, in addition to not supporting the insurgents, the third state has opted not to assist the government in spite of its request: it entails, therefore, non-participation on either side but not necessarily non-discrimination as the insurgents still do not have belligerent rights. While a neutral power can allow both belligerents to equip their vessels of war on its territory without abandoning its status,[342] for instance, in the case of negative equality the third state can only deny, but not grant, such permission to both the governmental and rebel ships, as it is still required to deliver the war or merchant ships equipped by the rebels that enter its ports to the government of the state in civil strife.[343] Furthermore, the limitations to their freedoms and those of their nationals that neutral states have to accept, in particular the right of the belligerents to visit and search neutral ships on the high seas, to blockade, and to confiscate contraband, do not apply in a negative equality regime as they are triggered only in case of war.[344]

7.5.2 Civil wars resulting in *de facto* secession

In theory, 'a civil war … was, by *definition*, a conflict that was fully the equal of an interstate war and hence was a war in the true sense'.[345] By the mid-19th century, this most visibly occurred when a secessionist armed conflict had successfully led to the

---

[337] Arts 2(1) and (2). The supply of arms, ammunition, military *matériel*, or financial aid by third-state nationals, however, is not prohibited.

[338] Art 2(3).

[339] The expression 'negative equality' is employed by the International Fact-Finding Commission on the Conflict in Georgia and is often used in contemporary scholarship on intervention by invitation to refer to an obligation not to assist either the government or the armed opposition group(s) when a civil war breaks out. See Report of the Independent International Fact-Finding Mission on the Conflict in Georgia, September 2009, vol II, 278 <www.mpil.de/files/pdf4/IIFFMCG_Volume_II1.pdf>.

[340] While the principle of non-intervention and neutrality are, respectively, an obligation and a status under customary international law, negative equality can only result from a treaty or unilateral declaration.

[341] Dinstein, *War*, 27.

[342] US Supreme Court, *The Divina Pastora*, 17 U.S. 52, 71 (1819).

[343] Art 3, 1928 Havana Convention.

[344] Montague Bernard, *A Historical Account of the Neutrality of Great Britain During the American Civil War* (Longmans 1870) 113. The use of 'neutrality' in a technical sense, therefore, should not be confused with its popular meaning: the former entails not only non-participation and non-discrimination, but also the acquiescence in the exercise of belligerent rights by the parties in conflict beyond their territory.

[345] Neff, *War*, 257, emphasis in the original.

58   INTERNATIONAL LAW AND THE PRINCIPLE OF NON-INTERVENTION

de facto independence of the rebellious provinces, regardless of whether their *de jure* independence had been recognized by the parent state.[346] As Justice Grier, writing for the majority in the 1863 US Supreme Court's judgment on the *Prize Cases*, found, '[w]hen the party in rebellion occupy and hold in a hostile manner a certain portion of territory; have declared their independence; have cast off their allegiance; have organized armies; have commenced hostilities against their former sovereign, the world acknowledges them as belligerents, and the contest a *war*'.[347]

As has been seen, Vattel had already claimed that 'when a nation becomes divided into two parties absolutely independent, and no longer acknowledging a common superior', foreign powers could 'assist the party which they shall judge to have right on its side, in case that party requests their assistance or accepts the offer of it', although only after an attempt to mediate between the belligerents has proved unsuccessful.[348] Vattel's argument resonated in 19th-century scholarship.[349] In his public lecture on the principle of non-intervention delivered in 1860, Mountague Bernard argued that when 'a successful revolt makes two States out of one ... interference ceases to be intervention' as there are 'two nations in arms against each other'.[350] Andrès Bello, who briefly taught *El Libertador* of Spanish America, Simón Bolívar, agrees: when, in a civil war, an insurrectional faction succeeds in securing control of some part of the national territory, establishes a government, administers justice, in other words exercises sovereign prerogatives, it becomes a subject of international law and the conflict must be treated by third states as if it were an interstate one.[351] Hence, third states can remain neutral, intervene on the side of either belligerent, or offer their mediation, the only criteria to guide their decision being justice and their own interests.[352] These views find support in the practice of the time. During the wars of independence of the Spanish colonies in the Americas in the first decades of the 19th century, for instance, the United States and the United Kingdom chose to apply their neutrality legislations on the basis of the *de facto* independence achieved by the Latin American republics.[353]

---

[346] In this period, the expression 'civil war' was used to refer not only to conflicts within a state, but also to those between the metropolis and its colonies (Siotis, *Le droit de la guerre*, 48–50). Conflicts between a suzerain state and its vassals and between protected and protector states, on the other hand, were of an international or a civil character depending on the nature of the relationship (Despagnet, *Cours*, 604). As to unions of states, the conflict between two countries joined in a personal union was considered international, while if the union was real, it rather constituted a civil war (ibid).

[347] *The Prize Cases*, 67 U.S. 635, 666–7 (1863), emphasis in the original. The Court had to decide whether the armed conflict between the Union and the Confederation was a war in the legal sense, thus triggering the application of prize law. See also US Supreme Court, *Williams v Bruffy*, 96 U.S. 176, 186 (1877).

[348] Vattel, *The Law of Nations*, 648–9.

[349] Not everyone, however, was an admirer: the Marquis de Olivart saw Vattel's theory of intervention in civil wars as 'funestísima, madre de abusivas intervenciones' (El Marqués de Olivart, *Del reconocimiento de Beligerancia: Y Sus Efectos Inmediatos* (Tipolitografía de L Péant e hijos 1895) 7).

[350] Bernard, *On the Principle*, 22. See also Pradier-Fodéré, *Traité*, 590–1.

[351] Bello, *Principios*, 299. Phillimore warned that the country must really be divided and thus '[n]o mere temporary outbreak, no isolated resistance to authority, no successful skirmish, is sufficient' (Phillimore, *Commentaries*, 571).

[352] Bello, *Principios*, 301.

[353] See Canning's speech of 16 April 1823, quoted in Hersch Lauterpacht, *Recognition in International Law* (CUP 1947) 187. US President Monroe's message of 2 December 1817 affirmed that the United States 'regarded the contest not in the light of an ordinary insurrection or rebellion, but as a civil war between parties nearly equal, having as to neutral powers equal rights' (Moore, *A Digest*, vol I, 173). In his 1822 message, Monroe repeated that '[a]s soon as the [revolutionary] movement assumed such a steady and consistent form as to make the success of the provinces probable, the rights to which they were entitled by the law

DEVELOPMENT OF THE PRINCIPLE OF NON-INTERVENTION   59

It should however be emphasized that, as noted by Bello, the United States and Britain had the *option*, but not the obligation, to remain neutral: they could have also taken sides and become co-belligerents, exactly as in an international war. This was clearly stated by the US Supreme Court in the 1818 *Palmer* case, where the Chief Justice found that, in conflicts where parts of a foreign empire are trying to assert their independence, 'a nation may engage itself with one party or the other — may observe absolute neutrality — may recognize the new state absolutely — or may make a limited recognition of it'.[354] The point was confirmed in subsequent judgments, including that on the *Santissima Trinidad* (1822).[355]

Apart from secessionist conflicts that led to the *de facto* independence of new states, however, the problem was how to distinguish civil wars from lesser forms of internal unrest like rebellions and insurrections, which continued to be an internal affair of the concerned state and to which the principle of non-intervention (intended as a prohibition of assistance to insurgents) still applied. As practice was confused and language employed inconsistently, resort to a practical tool was frequently made in the second half of the 19th century: recognition of belligerency.

7.5.3 Civil wars where belligerency was recognized

'Belligerency' is a status arising from a situation of internal unrest where the parties are entitled to exercise the full spectrum of belligerent rights, including beyond the concerned state's territory. Although logic suggested that belligerency would automatically be triggered once the threshold of a civil war had been reached,[356] in practice states exercised significant discretion and decided on a case-by-case basis.[357] The decision of a state to consider a situation of internal unrest in another state as a *de jure* war came to be known as recognition of belligerency. Recognition of belligerency in relation to civil wars started to develop during the wars of independence of the Latin American colonies from Spain as a consequence of the disruption to maritime communications caused by these conflicts, which led to the application by Britain and the United States of their domestic neutrality acts.[358] A proper doctrine of recognition of belligerency, however, was elaborated only in the second half of the 19th century

---

of nations, as equal parties to a civil war, were extended to them' (Message to Congress, 8 March 1822, in Moore, *A Digest*, vol I, 174). The United States also proclaimed its neutrality in the conflict between Mexico and the secessionist Texas because the latter 'had declared its independence and at the time was actually maintaining it' (Mr Forsyth, Secretary of State, to Mr Gorostiza, Mexican minister, 20 September 1836, in Moore, *A Digest*, vol I, 176).

[354] *United States v Palmer*, 16 U.S. 610, 634 (1818).
[355] *The Santissima Trinidad*, 20 U.S. 283, 337 (1822).
[356] In regard to the Greek War of Independence, for instance, Canning explained that belligerency 'is not so much a principle as a fact. A certain degree of force and consistency acquired by any mass of population engaged in war entitles that population to be treated as a belligerent' (quoted in *The Ambrose Light*, 440). Hall, however, noted that '[i]t is impossible to be certain on the terms of the dispatch to Mr Stratford Canning whether the British government intended to convey an impression that the Greek insurgents merely deserved, or that they had a legal right to, belligerent recognition' (Hall, *A Treatise*, 34).
[357] Neff, *War*, 261.
[358] Hans Wehberg, 'La guerre civile et le droit international' (1938) 63 Recueil des Cours 1, 15–18; Lauterpacht, *Recognition*, 176–82; Jorge L Esquirol, 'Latin America' in Bardo Fassbender and Anne Peters (eds), *The Oxford Handbook of the History of International Law* (OUP 2012) 553, 554–6.

by the US Supreme Court in its judgments related to events that occurred during the American Civil War, as several European states had recognized the Confederates as belligerents and declared their neutrality.[359] The doctrine was eventually codified in the aforementioned Neuchâtel Resolution of the Institut de droit international, which distinguishes between the recognition of belligerency by the government facing the internal unrest and that by third states. The former, granted by the political and executive departments and not by the judiciary,[360] is the counterpart in a civil war of a declaration of war in an international one and establishes a state of *de jure* war: even though it is a unilateral act, recognition of belligerency produces constitutive effects for other subjects (the insurgents and third states) because a customary rule so provides. These effects are that the entire spectrum of the laws of war becomes applicable to the conflict between the government and the insurgents, who may at that point exercise belligerent rights also beyond the national territory including 'rights of blockade, visitation, search and seizure of contraband articles on the high seas',[361] and that the law of neutrality can regulate the relations between the belligerents and third states. After recognition, the incumbent government is also no longer responsible for the acts of the insurgents towards third states and their nationals.[362]

Recognition by the government could take place explicitly 'by a categorical declaration' or, more frequently, implicitly through the exercise of belligerent rights beyond national territory (particularly on the high seas) that leave no doubt as to the intention to recognize.[363] The proclamation by the government of a (belligerent) blockade of the coasts controlled by the insurgents which extended to the high seas, for instance, normally entailed their recognition as belligerents, providing that the blockade was effectively maintained.[364] There was no obligation on the government to grant recognition of belligerency to insurgents and the recognition was also not subject to any requirements: as the US Supreme Court noted, 'to what extent [belligerent rights] shall

---

[359] De Olivart, *Del reconocimiento*, 2. It appears that the first reference to 'recognition of belligerency' as a discrete legal status is contained in the 8th edition of Wheaton's *Elements of International Law* (1866): Roscoe Ralph Oglesby, *Internal War and the Search for Normative Order* (Nijhoff 1971) 33.

[360] *The Ambrose Light*, 412; US Supreme Court, *The Three Friends* 166 U.S. 1, 63 (1897). Courts, however, can assess the existence of belligerent status when the executive is silent, particularly in the context of prize claims (Robert McLaughlin, *Recognition of Belligerency and the Law of Armed Conflict* (OUP 2020) 132).

[361] *The Three Friends*, 63.

[362] Rougier, *Les guerres civiles*, 409. The legal personality of the recognized belligerents is imperfect, temporary, limited to the rights and duties arising from the conduct of hostilities, and does not extend to peacetime activities such as trade or the *jus legationis* (Wiesse, *Le droit international*, 10).

[363] Art 4(1), Neuchâtel Resolution. The application of certain laws of war for humanitarian purposes, however, does not in itself amount to recognition of belligerency (Art 4(2)). See, in this sense, Arts 152 and 153 of the Lieber Code.

[364] *The Ambrose Light*, 443. In relation to the American Civil War, the US Supreme Court found that '[t]he proclamation of blockade is itself official and conclusive evidence ... that a state of war existed' (*The Prize Cases*, 670). In 1874, in response to the intention of the Serrano government to blockade the northern coast of Spain during the Third Carlist War, the British Foreign Office's legal advisors noted that '[a]ssuming the blockade to be effective Her Majesty's Government must ... recognize the fact that it exists de facto and de jure. The result, however, will be that the Carlists henceforth become belligerents' (Henry James, WV Harcourt, and J Parker Deane, 6 February 1874, in Lord McNair, *International Law Opinions*, vol II (CUP 1956) 389). A blockade is effective when it is 'maintained by a force sufficient really to prevent access to the coast of the enemy' (Art 4, Paris Declaration respecting Maritime Law, 16 April 1856, text in Edward Herstlet, *The Map of Europe by Treaty; Showing the Various Political and Territorial Changes Which Have Taken Place Since the General Peace of 1814*, vol II (Butterworths/Harrison 1875) 1283).

DEVELOPMENT OF THE PRINCIPLE OF NON-INTERVENTION   61

be accorded to insurgents depends upon the considerations of justice, humanity, and policy controlling the government'.[365] The fact that the incumbent authorities recognized the insurgents as belligerents, however, stopped them from complaining against a similar measure adopted by third states.[366] At the outbreak of the American Civil War, for instance, President Lincoln proclaimed the blockade of the ports controlled by the Confederacy.[367] Although Lincoln always denied that the blockade amounted to recognition of belligerency, Britain proclaimed its neutrality a month later, on 13 May 1861, and recognized the existence of hostilities between the United States and the Confederate States, claiming that its interests were gravely affected by the war.[368] Brazil, France, the Netherlands, Hawaii, and Spain followed suit.[369] The US government complained, arguing that British recognition was unnecessary and premature and thus constituted 'an act of wrongful intervention, a departure from the obligations of existing Treaties, and without sanction of the law of nations'.[370] The United States did not contest the right to recognize, only the fact that recognition of belligerency was granted too early, when its conditions did not exist yet.[371] In the *Prize Cases*, however, the Supreme Court disagreed and found that, once the government had recognized belligerency by blockading the coasts controlled by the insurgents, a civil war was turned into a war in the legal sense with effects *erga omnes*, whether or not the conditions for recognition of belligerency by third states had also been met.[372]

Similarly to what happened in interstate wars, where the existence of a state of *de jure* war could be recognized by the parties to the conflict or, with the limited effect of triggering the law of neutrality, by other countries,[373] recognition of belligerency could have also been granted by third states and resulted from their acceptance of, or acquiescence in, the exercise of belligerent rights by all parties to the civil war, particularly

---

[365] *Williams v Bruffy*, 187.

[366] Hyde, *International Law*, 201.

[367] Read the text of the proclamation in Hall, *A Treatise*, 40–1. The blockade ended on 23 June 1865.

[368] The text of the proclamation is reproduced in Théodore Ortolan, *Règles internationales et diplomatie de la mer*, vol II (Librairie de Henri Plon 1864) 502–4.

[369] Castrén, *Civil War*, 45; Neff, *War*, 262. The text of France's declaration and Spain's decree are in Ortolan, *Règles*, 500–1 and 504–5, respectively. Russia, the German Confederation, and Austria-Hungary refused recognition (Quincy Wright, 'The American Civil War, 1861–1865' in Richard Falk (ed), *The International Law of Civil War* (Johns Hopkins Press 1971) 30, 82).

[370] Letter of Mr Seward to Mr Adams, 27 August 1866, in Bruns (ed), *Fontes Juris Gentium*, Series B, Section I, Tome I, Part 1, 266.

[371] Siotis, *Le droit de la guerre*, 85. According to the US secretary of state, the conflict in North America was 'an armed sedition seeking to overthrow the government, and the government [was] employing military and naval forces to repress it. But these facts do not constitute a war presenting two belligerent powers' (Letter or Mr Seward to Mr Dayton, 17 June 1861, in Bruns (ed), *Fontes Juris Gentium*, Series B, Section I, Tome I, Part 2, 108).

[372] *The Prize Cases*, 669. The Law Officers of the Crown also noted that, if the government 'declared a formal blockade, it would have no reason to complain if foreign States simply recognized the rebels as belligerents' (JB Karslake, CJ Selwyn, and R Phillimore, 14 August 1867, in Lord McNair, *International Law Opinions*, vol I (CUP 1956) 144). The French minister of foreign affairs, de Thouvenel, made the same point (Letter of M de Thouvenel à M Mercier, 11 May 1861, in Bruns (ed), *Fontes Juris Gentium*, Series B, Section I, Tome I, Part 2, 105). It has been argued that, in the *Prize Cases*, the US Supreme Court elaborated a dual-theory of civil war: it found that the Confederacy was an unlawful rebellion against the legitimate authorities but at the same time concluded that its soldiers were combatants with belligerent rights as in *de jure* wars (James G Randall, *Constitutional Problems Under Lincoln* (revised edn, University of Illinois Press 1951) 72–3).

[373] Mancini, 'The Effects', 990–1; McNair and Watts, *The Legal Effects*, 10.

62 INTERNATIONAL LAW AND THE PRINCIPLE OF NON-INTERVENTION

outside the territory of the concerned state.[374] The conflict, in other words, was treated *as if* it were a conflict between states.[375] Care should be taken, however, to distinguish recognition of belligerency from recognition of statehood and of government. Indeed, recognition of belligerency merely takes formal notice of the existence of a war without taking a position on the legitimacy of a government or the independence of a state.[376] While recognition of belligerency is granted *during* a civil war, therefore, recognition of independence of a new state or of a new *de jure* government can only occur *after* it has ended. Recognition of government also does not involve any acceptance of the exercise of belligerent rights by the new government against the former one.[377]

Like that granted by the government, recognition of belligerency by third states is a unilateral act that produces effects for the incumbent authorities and the insurgents involved in a civil war because of a customary rule—arguably formed by the 1860s—creating such effects, namely the applicability of the law of neutrality. Differently from that by the government, however, recognition of belligerency by third states has effects only *inter partes* (that is, between the belligerents and the recognizing state) and does not prejudice the position of other states or the relations between the incumbent and the insurgents.[378] It also has no retroactive effects.[379] Under Article 9 of the Neuchâtel Resolution, once granted the recognition may be withdrawn, even if the situation has not changed, although the withdrawal does not operate retroactively.[380]

Declarations by third states adopted specifically to recognize insurgents as belligerents have been rare in practice: examples are those made by Peru with respect to the Cuban insurgents in 1869 and by Bolivia in relation to the Chilean insurgents in

---

[374] In relation to Garibaldi's expedition to the Kingdom of the Two Sicilies, for instance, the Queen's Advocate advised that '[i]f Her Majesty's Government considers that a Civil War actually exists between the 'Dictatorial Government of Southern Italy' and that of His Majesty the King of the Two Sicilies, in which Great Britain is to be strictly neutral, and that the Dictatorial Government has in fact attained (howsoever) an independent and Sovereign existence and governs 'de facto' a portion of the Neapolitan dominions', then Britain could recognize the validity of a blockade proclaimed by the *de facto* government so long as it was effective (reproduced in HA Smith, 'Some Problems of the Spanish Civil War' (1937) 18 BYBIL 17, 19). The fact that third states have not recognized belligerency does not deprive the government of its belligerent rights if it decides to exercise them. It only means that the insurgents cannot exercise them if neither the government nor third states have recognized belligerency (Schwarzenberger, *International Law*, 704).

[375] McNair and Watts, *The Legal Effects*, 32. In relation to the American Civil War, where Britain had recognized the insurgents as belligerents, the British Foreign Secretary, Lord Russell, explained that 'there is, as regards neutral nations, no difference between civil war and foreign war' (quoted in Lorimer, *The Institutes*, vol I, 147).

[376] Dhokalia, 'Civil Wars', 228. See the diplomatic correspondence in relation to the American Civil War, where the states recognizing the belligerency of the Confederates cautioned that this did not equate to recognition of statehood (in Bruns (ed), *Fontes Juris Gentium*, Series B, Section I, Tome I, Part 2, 126–7). During the Spanish Civil War, British Foreign Secretary Anthony Eden also argued that '[r]ecognition of belligerency is, of course, quite distinct from recognizing any one to whom you give that right as being the legitimate Government of the Country. It has nothing to do with it. It is a conception simply concerned with granting rights of belligerency which are of convenience to the donor as much as they are to the recipients' (quoted in Heather A Wilson, *International Law and the Use of Force by National Liberation Movements* (Clarendon Press 1988) 27).

[377] McNair and Watts, *The Legal Effects*, 34.

[378] Yoram Dinstein, *Non-International Armed Conflicts in International Law* (2nd edn, CUP 2021) 144–5.

[379] Siotis, *Le droit de la guerre*, 172; Castrén, *Civil War*, 42; Sapienza, *Il principio*, 140.

[380] Some authors, however, disagree with this view and argue that recognition may not be retracted unless it was conditional and the conditions were not fulfilled (Rougier, *Les guerres civiles*, 396–7; Castrén, *Civil War*, 192, 194). Others claim that the withdrawal may take place only if the circumstances that founded the recognition have changed (Wiesse, *Le droit international*, 35).

DEVELOPMENT OF THE PRINCIPLE OF NON-INTERVENTION   63

1891.[381] Far more frequent are recognitions resulting implicitly from the third state's conduct with regard to the parties of the civil war.[382] As Dinstein has noted, in these cases 'instead of neutrality flowing from "recognition of belligerency" … it is the other way around'.[383] Not all proclamations of neutrality, however, imply recognition of belligerency: the mere application of domestic neutrality legislation, like the US Neutrality Act 1794 and the British Foreign Enlistment Acts 1819 and 1870, might for instance not be sufficient if it is not accompanied by the third state's acceptance of the exercise of belligerent rights beyond national territory by the parties of the civil war and/or by the request that they respect the rights of neutrals.[384]

Unlike that by the government, recognition of belligerency can only be granted by third states when certain requirements are met by the insurgents: due to the detrimental effects arising from the application of the law of neutrality for the government beset by civil war, a premature recognition would amount to an intervention in its internal affairs. The requirements for recognition of belligerency by third states are factual and do not take into account the purpose of the insurgents: as British Foreign Secretary Lord Russell, quoting Canning, stated, 'the size and strength of the party contending against a Government, and not the goodness of their cause, entitle them to the character and treatment of belligerents'.[385] The requirements, which largely correspond to those identified by the US Supreme Court for the existence of a civil war,[386] have been codified in Article 8 of the Neuchâtel Resolution: the insurgents must have gained control of a certain part of the national territory, set up a provisional government that exercises the rights attached to sovereignty over that territory, and conduct hostilities with organized troops, subject to military discipline, and consistently with the laws and customs of war.[387] In the January Uprising of 1863–4, for instance, France refused to recognize the Polish insurgents as belligerents because, in addition to lacking stable control of territory, they also had no *de facto* government, no common direction, and no single superior.[388] In spite of their request, no state granted recognition of belligerency to the pro-monarchy insurgents of Admiral de Mello in the Brazilian revolt of 1893–4 on the ground that they consisted only of some units of the navy and had not established and maintained a political organization.[389] In the

---

[381] Rougier, *Les guerres civiles*, 399–400. Read the text of Peru's recognition in de Olivart, *Del reconocimiento*, 33.

[382] *The Ambrose Light*, 443. The Court found that the United States had granted 'implied recognition' of belligerency to the Colombian insurgents in a note of the US secretary of state to the Colombian minister in Washington of 24 April 1885 (ibid, 443–5).

[383] Dinstein, *Non-International Armed Conflicts*, 148.

[384] McNair and Watts, *The Legal Effects*, 452. The British Foreign Enlistment Act 1870, for instance, was applied during the Spanish Civil War, even though no recognition of belligerency ever occurred. In 1817, the US Neutrality Act was amended so as to extend its application to conflicts involving unrecognized entities like a 'colony, district, or people' (Eliav Lieblich, *International Law and Civil Wars. Intervention and Consent* (Routledge 2013), 85).

[385] Letter of Lord Russell to Lord Lyons, 21 June 1861, in Bruns (ed), *Fontes Juris Gentium*, Series B, Section 1, Tome I, Part 2, 109.

[386] *The Prize Cases*, 666–7.

[387] With regard to the requirement of compliance with the laws and customs of war, certain authors have interpreted it as actual compliance, while others as mere capacity to comply (Sandesh Sivakumaran, *The Law of Non-International Armed Conflicts* (OUP 2012) 12).

[388] Statement of President Stourm to the French Senate, reproduced in Charles Zorgbibe, 'Sources of the Recognition of Belligerent Status' (1977) 17 IRRC 111, 121.

[389] Moore, *A Digest*, vol I, 202–3.

64   INTERNATIONAL LAW AND THE PRINCIPLE OF NON-INTERVENTION

First Cuban Civil War (1868–78), the United States also considered but eventually did not grant recognition of belligerency to the rebels as they lacked the necessary conditions.[390]

Recognition of belligerency is a political act that normally occurs when third states decide that they would benefit from it, for instance when the hostilities approach their borders or in the case of a maritime war that negatively affects foreign trade.[391] US courts confirmed that it 'may rightfully be given or withheld by other nations, according to their views of their own interests, their moral sympathies, their ties of blood, or their treaty obligations; or according to their views of the merits or demerits of the revolt, its extent, or probabilities of success'.[392] There is, in other words, a negative obligation not to grant recognition until the conflict meets certain characteristics, but no positive obligation to grant it, not even if those characteristics exist.[393] The opposite view, championed by Lauterpacht,[394] is at odds with state practice. In the Polish insurrection of 1830–1, for example, the insurgents were not recognized as belligerents even if they had a provisional government in Warsaw, control of some territory, and observed the laws and customs of war since, the conflict being limited to land, the interests of other states were not affected.[395] Similarly, in the Hungarian insurrection of 1848–49 against Austrian rule, the insurgents arguably met the conditions for

[390] See President Grant's messages of 6 December 1869 (ibid, 194), 13 June 1870 (ibid, 194–5), and 7 December 1875 (ibid, 196–7) as well as President McKinley's message of 6 December 1897 (ibid, 200). Certain Latin American states (Peru, Bolivia, Colombia, Venezuela) recognized the belligerency of the Cuban insurgents and Venezuela, Peru, Mexico, and Chile even recognized the independence of the island (Marquis de Olivart, 'Le différend entre l'Espagne et les États-Unis au sujet de la question cubaine' (1897) 4 RGDIP 577, 618; Wehberg, 'La guerre civile', 33; Castrén, Civil War, 47).

[391] Hall, A Treatise, 36–7. As US Secretary of State Fish noted on 25 September 1869, 'every sovereign power decides for itself, on its responsibility, the question whether or not it will, a given time, accord the status of belligerency to the insurgent subjects of another power' (Moore, A Digest, vol I, 192).

[392] The Ambrose Light, 419. Some writers have argued that the existence of an interest in recognizing the insurgents as belligerents is a legal requirement for the recognition. McNair, for instance, requires that 'the recognizing State and its people [be] closely affected by the hostilities', which normally occurs when the civil war takes place in a neighbouring country or is wholly or partly maritime (McNair, 'The Law', 476). See also Calvo, Le droit international, 238; Louis-Joseph-Delphin Féraud-Giraud, 'De la reconnaissance de la qualité de belligérants dans les guerres civiles' (1896) 3 RGDIP 277, 285; Rougier, Les guerres civiles, 384; Despagnet, Cours, 607. The 'practical necessity for third states to define their attitude to the civil war', however, cannot be seen as a legal condition for recognition of belligerency: it is rather the political reason (Lauterpacht, Recognition, 176). In a number of cases, insurgents were recognized by third states as belligerents without the existence of a specific interest: Peru, for instance, recognized the Cuban insurgents in 1869 'simply because of its openly proclaimed intention to cause trouble for Spain' (Zorgbibe, 'Sources', 124). Desjardin's Draft Art 9, which required, for a third state to recognize insurgents, that the recognition was necessary to safeguard a national interest, was also not included in the final version of the Neuchâtel Resolution ((1898) 17 AIDI 89).

[393] Olivier Corten, 'La rébellion et le droit international: le droit de neutralité en tension' (2015) 374 Recueil des Cours 53, 94. This view was incorporated in Arts 4 and 9 of the Neuchâtel Resolution.

[394] For Lauterpacht, third states have an obligation to recognize belligerency when the required conditions are present, as '[t]he law cannot refuse to acknowledge the legal consequences of facts which are not in themselves unlawful and which, as between sovereign States, normally give rise to legal rights and obligations' (Lauterpacht, Recognition, 175). See similarly Giorgio Balladore Pallieri, 'Quelques aspects juridiques de la non-intervention en Espagne' (1937) 18 RDILC, 285, 287–8; Bluntschli, Le droit international, 291; Bernard, A Historical Account, 115–16.

[395] Oglesby, Internal War, 24–5. Read the text of France's refusal to recognize the belligerency of the Poles in Balladore Pallieri, 'Quelques aspects', 307–8.

DEVELOPMENT OF THE PRINCIPLE OF NON-INTERVENTION   65

belligerency but were nevertheless not recognized.[396] Neither Spain nor the United States granted belligerent rights to the Cuban insurgents in 1898 despite the magnitude of the hostilities.[397] Also, no state recognized the belligerency of the insurgents in the 1891 Chilean Civil War (with the exception of Bolivia)[398] even though they had gained control of part of the national territory, established a government at Iquique, and controlled the navy.[399]

Even if recognition of belligerency could take the form of, or result from, a proclamation of neutrality, neutrality was not an *obligation* automatically arising from it as assumed by so many commentators.[400] Put otherwise, if a request to respect the rights of neutrals necessarily implied recognition of belligerency (as there cannot be neutrality in a technical sense without at least two belligerents),[401] a recognition of belligerency by third states in other forms (for instance, a declaration of recognition *expressis verbis*, or the acquiescence in the exercise of belligerent rights by the parties of the civil war beyond national territory), and all the more a recognition of belligerency by the government, did not necessarily result in an obligation to observe neutrality. Indeed, recognition of belligerency merely acknowledged the existence of a war in the legal sense between a government and its subjects and considered it 'as much as if it was waged between two independent nations'.[402] If the civil war had to be treated 'as if' it was an international conflict, third states could then either remain neutral *or* support one of the belligerents and come to be at war with the other.[403] The immediate consequence of recognition of belligerency, therefore, was the displacement of the principle of non-intervention as the regime regulating the relations between the state in civil war and other states: the latter no longer had the option of discriminating in favour of the government, but had to choose between neutrality and co-belligerency as in interstate wars. Although he does not refer to recognition of belligerency (his *Elements of International Law* was first published in 1836), Wheaton, citing Vattel, so explains it:

---

[396] Oglesby, *Internal War*, 24. All states considered the conflict between Austria and Hungary as a civil, not international, war (Wehberg, 'La guerre civile', 26).

[397] *Sambiaggio Case*, Italy–Venezuela Claims Commission, Opinion of Umpire Ralston, 13 February and 7 May 1903, 10 RIAA 499, 515.

[398] The insurgents were in control of the routes that Bolivia had to use to reach the sea (Wiesse, *Le droit international*, 25).

[399] Wehberg, 'La guerre civile', 34; Castrén, *Civil War*, 48.

[400] See eg Despagnet, *Cours*, 605–6; Rosalyn Higgins, 'Intervention and International Law' in Hedley Bull (ed), *Intervention in World Politics* (OUP 1984) 30, 40; Siobhan Wills, 'The Legal Characterization of the Armed Conflicts in Afghanistan and Iraq: Implications for Protection' (2011) 58 NILR 173, 181; Sivakumaran, *The Law*, 15; Judge Ammoun's Separate Opinion in *Legal Consequences for States of the Continued Presence of South Africa in Namibia (South West Africa) notwithstanding Security Council Resolution 276* (1970) (Advisory Opinion) [1971] ICJ Rep 16, para 13.

[401] *The Three Friends*, 76.

[402] US Supreme Court, *Ford v Surget*, 97 U.S. 594, 611 (1878).

[403] This appears to also be the view of some contemporary scholars, including Richard A Falk, 'Janus Tormented: The International Law of Internal War' in James N Rosenau (ed), *International Aspects of Civil Strife* (Princeton University Press 1964) 185, 203; Schwarzenberger, *International Law*, 573; Alberto Miele, *L'estraneità ai conflitti armati secondo il diritto internazionale*, vol II (CEDAM 1970) 495; Mohamed Bennouna, *Le consentement à l'ingérence militaire dans les conflits internes* (Librairie générale de droit et de jurisprudence 1976) 18; James Crawford, *The Creation of States in International Law* (2nd edn, OUP 2006) 381; Rosario Sapienza, *La guerra civile nell'evoluzione del diritto internazionale* (Editpress 2010) 64.

whilst the civil war involving the contest for the government continues, other States may remain indifferent spectators of the controversy, still continuing to treat the ancient government as sovereign, and the government *de facto* as a society entitled to the rights of war against the enemy; or may espouse the cause of the party which they believe to have justice on its side. ... In the latter case, it becomes, of course, the enemy of the party against whom it declares itself, and the ally of the other; and as the positive law of nations makes no distinction, in this respect, between a just and an unjust war, the intervening State becomes entitled to all the rights of war against the opposite party.[404]

Wheaton's views heavily influenced the US Supreme Court's case-law. In *Ford v Surget*, for instance, the Court found that, after a blockade on the ports controlled by the insurgents had been proclaimed and enforced by a government, a third state 'may assist the government *de jure* as an independent power, or it may assist the insurgents, in either of which cases it becomes a party to the war, or it may remain impartial, still continuing to treat the government *de jure* as an independent power whilst it treats the insurgents as a community entitled to the rights of war against its adversary'.[405] In a lesser known passage of the *Caroline* correspondence, US Secretary of State Webster also pointed out that

when civil wars break out in other countries, [a government] may decide on all circumstances of the particular case upon its own existing stipulations; on probable results, on what its own security requires, and on many other considerations. It may be already bound to assist one party, or it may become bound, if it so chooses, to assist the other, and to meet the consequences of such assistance.[406]

The United States was not the only country to adopt this position. Justifying Britain's intervention in support of Queen Isabella in the First Carlist War, Foreign Secretary Viscount Palmerston stressed that '[i]n the case of a civil war, proceeding either from a disputed succession, or from a long revolt no writer on international law denied that other countries had a right, if they chose to exercise it, to take part with either of the two belligerent parties'.[407]

Recognition of belligerency, then, did not compel third states to observe neutrality: it only required the belligerents to treat the recognizing state and its nationals as neutrals to the extent that they did not engage in non-neutral activities.[408] Whether

---

[404] Wheaton, *Elements*, 32. Woolsey also notes that '[n]o rule of international law forces a neutral state into an impartial attitude. It has the choice between aiding the parent state, and entire neutrality' (quoted in *The Ambrose Light*, 435).

[405] *Ford v Surget*, 610.

[406] Letter of Mr Webster to Mr Fox, 24 April 1841, *British and Foreign State Papers 1840–1841*, vol XXIX (1857) 1135.

[407] Quoted in Wheaton, *History*, 537. Even though Palmerston did not mention recognition of belligerency, he referred to the parties of the civil war as 'belligerents'.

[408] Art 7 of the Neuchâtel Resolution does not refer to neutrality as an *obligation* arising from recognition of belligerency: it merely emphasizes the default option for third states (or, to put it differently, it provides for a rebuttable presumption of neutral status), which could however be reverted should they decide to take sides and declare war.

DEVELOPMENT OF THE PRINCIPLE OF NON-INTERVENTION 67

or not third states could use armed force in support of one of the belligerents was not determined by the occurrence of recognition of belligerency but by the customary and treaty rules that regulated resort to war: intervention by invitation of an incumbent government as a measure short of war was no longer an option.[409]

7.5.4 Civil wars where recognition of belligerency did not occur

What remained unclear throughout the period under consideration was whether the consequences of belligerency for the incumbent government and third states would be triggered exclusively by its recognition or would *ipso facto* arise when a civil war met the requirements for recognition regardless of whether it had been granted or not. For the Law Officers of the Crown,

> the question, whether a state of war does or does not exist between insurgents holding possession of a particular territory, and a Government claiming their allegiance and attempting to subdue them, is one of fact, quite as much as of law; and, if the facts are such as really to constitute a state of war between the contending parties, according to the law of nations, it is not, we think, competent, by law, to any neutral Power, to withdraw its ships and subjects, upon the high seas, from the operation of the ordinary laws incident to that state of things, merely by declining to acknowledge its existence.[410]

The same view was adopted by US Secretary of State Cass during the Vivanco insurrection in Peru (1856–8): when the Peruvian minister to the United States, Osma, stressed that a formal recognition of civil war was necessary before US nationals could avail themselves of neutral status,[411] Cass replied that whether a civil war existed in Peru was a question of fact and that, therefore, recognition was not needed 'unless in the progress of the contest their interests were brought into question'.[412]

An intermediate, and isolated, position was that espoused by the Law Officers of the Crown in relation to the Second Franco-Hova War (1894–5) between France and Madagascar (then a French protectorate), which distinguished between the belligerents' duties (for instance, treating captured soldiers as prisoners of war) and the rights and obligations related to neutral status: while the former were not deemed to depend on recognition of belligerency but only on the factual existence of a war, the latter arose from recognition of belligerency which third states could grant when it was in their interest.[413]

---

[409] An obligation to remain neutral, however, could have arisen from neutralization treaties. Belgium, for instance, was neutralized by the Treaty for the Definitive Separation of Belgium from Holland between Austria, France, Great Britain, Prussia and Russia, and Belgium (London, 15 November 1831) 82 CTS 255 (Arts 7, 25) and Luxembourg by the Treaty Relative to the Grand Duchy of Luxembourg (London, 11 May 1867) 135 CTS 1 (Art 2). The neutralized status of both countries was abrogated by the Peace Treaty of Versailles (Paris, 28 June 1919).

[410] Quoted in Jessup, 'The Spanish Rebellion', 267. See also Bello, *Principios*, 299; Bluntschli, *Le droit international*, 291.

[411] Note of the Peruvian Minister to the United States, Osma, to the US Secretary of State, Cass, quoted in Oglesby, *Internal War*, 29.

[412] Letter of Mr Cass to Mr Osma, 22 May 1858, in Moore, *A Digest*, vol I, 182–3.

[413] Report by RT Reid and Franck Lockwood, 26 April 1895, in McNair, *International Law Opinions*, vol II, 371.

68   INTERNATIONAL LAW AND THE PRINCIPLE OF NON-INTERVENTION

The mainstream view, however, was that the law of neutrality, with its customary rights and obligations for both belligerents and neutral states, could only become applicable in a civil war when recognition of belligerency had occurred and a state of war in the legal sense was established.[414] If recognition of belligerency had not been granted, the law of peace continued to regulate the relations between third states and the parties of the civil war, with the result that the principle of non-intervention still applied and no exercise of belligerent rights beyond the territorial sea was permissible.[415] The state practice of the time confirms this conclusion. In the Polish insurrection of 1830-1, for instance, Austria transferred to the Russians the cannons and war *matériel* of a Polish expedition that had been found on its territory.[416] Similarly, in spite of its efforts, the Paris Commune (1871) did not manage to obtain recognition of belligerency from Germany, which therefore returned those captured while trying to leave the city to the French government.[417] During the Third Carlist War (1872–6), the Law Officers of the Crown advised that coals could continue to be provided to the Spanish government's ships until the insurgents had been recognized as belligerents either by the Madrid authorities or by Her Majesty's Government.[418] The French Minister of Foreign Affairs also authorized not treating the Carlist ships as pirates because Spain was 'en pleine guerre civile',[419] but warned that this was not a consequence arising from neutrality, as none of the insurrectional parties had reached the conditions for recognition of belligerency.[420] During the civil war in Chile between the forces of President Balmaceda and those of the Congress (1891), the Italian minister of foreign affairs, di Rudinì, declined the request of the provisional government to prevent the *Presidente Pinto* cruiser from being equipped and armed while in Genoa, as the insurgents had not been recognized as belligerents.[421] Spain's instructions in relation to the war with the United States over Cuba provided that the right to visit foreign merchant ships could only be exercised when a third state had recognized the belligerent status of the insurrectional party.[422] In his message to Congress of 7 December 1911, President Taft also affirmed that no neutrality obligations bound the United States with regard to the factions of the Mexican Revolution as there had been no official recognition of belligerency.[423] Finally, during the 1930 Brazilian Revolution, the US Department of State

---

[414] Wehberg, 'La guerre civile', 40. As the US Supreme Court found, 'the maintenance unbroken of peaceful relations between two powers when the domestic peace of one of them is disturbed is not neutrality in the sense in which the word is used when the disturbance has acquired such head as to have demanded the recognition of belligerency' (*The Three Friends*, 2).

[415] Balladore Pallieri points out, for instance, that, if the insurgents have not been recognized as belligerents, the governmental ships cannot be subject to special restrictions apart from those provided for foreign ships under customary international law (Balladore Pallieri, 'Quelques aspects', 290).

[416] Wehberg, 'La guerre civile', 24.

[417] A Wilhelm, 'Protectorat et neutralité' (1895) 22 JDIP 760, 768.

[418] JD Coleridge, Henry James, J Parker Deane, 28 October 1873, in Lauterpacht, *Recognition*, 269.

[419] Note of the French Foreign Affairs Minister, the Duc de Broglie, to the French consuls in Spain, 4 August 1873, in Kiss, *Répertoire*, 433.

[420] Note of the French Foreign Affairs Minister, the Duc de Broglie, to the French consuls in Spain, 11 August 1873, ibid.

[421] Società Italiana per l'Organizzazione Internazionale/Consiglio Nazionale delle Ricerche, *La prassi italiana di diritto internazionale*, Seconda Serie (1887–1918), vol I (Oceana Publications 1979) para 1599.

[422] Instructions de 24 avril 1898 pour l'exercice du droit de visite à l'occasion de la guerre hispano-américaine, reproduced in (1898) 5 RGDIP, Documents, 7.

[423] Quoted in Jessup, 'The Spanish Rebellion', 263.

DEVELOPMENT OF THE PRINCIPLE OF NON-INTERVENTION 69

prohibited the sale of arms to rebels but not to the government and explained that '[u]ntil belligerency is recognised, and the duty of neutrality arises, all the humane predispositions towards stability of government, the preservation of international amity, and the protection of established intercourse between nations are in favour of the Existing Government.'[424] The Neuchâtel Resolution reflected this practice.

7.5.5 Recognition of insurgency and third-state intervention

Between the end of the 19th and the beginning of the 20th century, a doctrine of recognition of insurgency (as distinguished from that of belligerency) developed on the basis of the practice of the United States and, to a lesser extent, Britain in relation to the internal strife in the Latin American states, in particular Cuba (1895–8),[425] Haiti (1888-9),[426] Bolivia (1899),[427] Chile (1891),[428] and Brazil (1893–4).[429] In the *Three Friends* case, in particular, the US Supreme Court found that the attitude of the United States with regard to the 1895 Cuban insurrection perfectly illustrated '[t]he distinction between recognition of belligerency and recognition of a condition of political revolt, between recognition of the existence of war in the material sense and of war in a legal sense', as 'the political department has not recognized the existence of a *de facto* belligerent power engaged in hostility with Spain, but has recognized the existence of insurrectionary warfare.'[430] According to Castrén, recognition of insurgency entails 'acknowledgment of the existence of an armed revolt of grave character and the incapacity, at least temporarily, of the lawful government to maintain public order and exercise authority over all parts of the territory.'[431] For him, recognition of insurgency has constitutive effects like that of belligerency and confers certain specific rights to the insurgents (but does not trigger the application of the entire spectrum of the law of armed conflict, as in recognition of belligerency) within the territory of the state in internal unrest, including its territorial waters (but not on the high seas).[432] On the other hand, recognition of insurgency does not affect the rights of third states as in the case of recognition of belligerency.[433] Castrén concedes, however, that it is difficult to distinguish it in practice from recognition of belligerency.[434]

---

[424] Quoted in Tom J Farer, 'The Regulation of Foreign Intervention in Civil Armed Conflict' (1974) 142 Recueil des Cours 289, 322.

[425] Moore, *A Digest*, vol I, 242–3. See, for instance, President Cleveland's message of 2 December 1895 and presidential proclamation of 12 June 1895, in (1907) 1 AJIL 48, 50–1.

[426] Moore, *A Digest*, vol I, 201.

[427] ibid, 243.

[428] The British government did not recognize the insurgents as belligerents although it allowed them to exercise certain belligerent rights (McNair, 'The Law', 485–6).

[429] Moore, *A Digest*, vol I, 204–5; Sivakumaran, *The Law*, 17; Castrén, *Civil War*, 209–10.

[430] *The Three Friends*, 63–4.

[431] Erik Castrén, 'Recognition of Insurgency' (1965) 5 IJIL 443, 445–6. See also Vernon A O'Rourke, 'Recognition of Belligerency and the Spanish War' (1937) 31 AJIL 398, 403. Lauterpacht identified the reasons why third states might have had an interest in recognizing insurgency: '[i]t may prove expedient to enter into contact with insurgent authorities with a view to protecting national interest in the territory occupied by them, to regularizing political and commercial intercourse with them, and to interceding with them in order to ensure a measure of humane conduct of hostilities' (Lauterpacht, *Recognition*, 270).

[432] Castrén, 'Recognition', 446.

[433] ibid.

[434] ibid.

70 INTERNATIONAL LAW AND THE PRINCIPLE OF NON-INTERVENTION

In reality, one can doubt that a customary norm providing for 'recognition of insurgency' from which specific legal consequences ensue ever existed in international law. The expression itself was an oxymoron: insurgency was, by definition, a factual situation which occurred regardless of it being recognized by the government or by third states. When it took place, then, recognition was merely declarative and could not have a constitutive character like recognition of belligerency. Relevant practice was inconsistent and limited to a couple of states, influential as they might have been. There is also no mention of recognition of insurgency in the Neuchâtel Resolution. In any case, even the supporters of the doctrine of recognition of insurgency agreed that it did not displace the application of the principle of non-intervention: in particular, it did not impose an obligation of negative equality or make the law of neutrality applicable.[435] Third states, therefore, remained free to choose between assisting the incumbent government at its request and not intervening on any side on the basis of their interests or treaty obligations.

8. The Period between the Two World Wars and the Trend towards Negative Equality (1919–39)

As Nehal Bhuta has noted, '[t]he First World War shattered what remained of the Vienna settlement ... the "well-ordered police state" of the 19th century had given way to a range of interventionist state-forms, from social democracy to fascism and communism ... '.[436] During the conflict, in particular, the belligerent states often fomented insurrections in enemy territory and supported insurgents in order to destabilize their adversaries. The Finnish Civil War, for instance, broke out on 27 January 1918 and ended on 15 May of the same year during Finland's transition from a grand duchy under Russian sovereignty to independence. The conflict was fought between the Reds (social-democrat insurgents) and the Whites (government) factions. The former were supplied with weapons and a limited number of troops by Soviet Russia, while Germany sent forces upon request of the latter.[437] Germany also attempted to support the 1916 Irish rebellion whereas Britain fomented Arab nationalism in the Ottoman Empire.[438] As these interventions took place between states already at war, however, they were not a violation of the principle of non-intervention.

The interwar period is characterized by three main normative developments. The first is the adoption of treaties limiting the right of states to use armed force against each other.[439] More specifically, the 1919 Covenant of the League of Nations imposed

---

[435] As Hyde writes, '[r]ecognition of a condition of insurgency within a foreign country is an official reckoning with a state of facts. In one sense such action does not strengthen the legal position already attained by the insurgents; it does not necessarily manifest a design to aid them; it does not impose upon the outside State the technical burdens of a neutral or serve to increase the load of obligations already resting upon it in consequence of the contest' (Hyde, *International Law*, 203).

[436] Bhuta, 'The Antinomies', 733.

[437] Castrén, *Civil War*, 51; Rousseau, *Droit international public*, 47.

[438] Cansacchi, *Storia*, 214.

[439] For Brownlie, 'the practice of states between 1920 and 1945, and more particularly between 1928 and 1934, provides adequate evidence of a customary rule that the use of force as an instrument of national policy otherwise than under a necessity of self-defence was illegal' (Brownlie, *International Law*, 110). The 1907 Convention (II) Respecting the Limitation of the Employment of Force for the Recovery of Contract

procedural limitations on the right to wage war but did not expressly deal with coercive measures short of war.[440] The question, therefore, was whether the member states had at least to resort to the procedure provided in Articles 12 to 15 before conducting an armed intervention.[441] The answer depended on whether the expression 'resort to war' in Article 12 could be interpreted broadly as 'resort to armed force', as suggested by Cavaglieri and Brierly.[442] For Lauterpacht, however, the narrower interpretation was preferable, as during the negotiations the expression 'resort to war' was preferred to 'resort to armed force' which appeared in an earlier draft.[443] A special Commission of Jurists set up by the League's Council after Italy's armed reprisal in response to the killing of General Tellini in Corfu (1923) unhelpfully opted for a case-by-case approach and found that '[c]oercive measures which are not intended to constitute acts of war may or may not be consistent with the provisions of Articles 12 to 15 of the Covenant.'[444]

Under Article I of the 1928 General Treaty for the Renunciation of War (more succinctly known as the Pact of Paris or the Kellogg–Briand Pact), the states parties also 'condemn recourse to war for the solution of international controversies, and renounce it, as an instrument of national policy in their relations with one another'.[445] For the states that ratified the treaty, then, an armed intervention in another state party is illegal when it is an act of war, at least to the extent that it is used as 'an instrument of national policy'.[446] As to armed interventions short of war, Article II provides that the parties must settle 'all disputes or conflicts of whatever nature or of whatever origin they may be, which may arise among them' exclusively by pacific means: the question is whether 'pacific means' should be understood as non-armed means or as means short of war. For Brierly, the latter interpretation is preferable, as—there not being an

---

Debts (Drago-Porter Convention) (The Hague, 18 October 1907) had already prohibited the resort to force by states in at least one case, namely, to recover contract debts owed by a state to the nationals of another (Art 1, text in (1908) 2 AJIL Supplement 81). The prohibition did not apply if the debtor state had not replied to an offer of arbitration, had prevented an agreement on a *compromis* after the acceptance of the offer of arbitration, or had failed to implement the arbitral award. The Convention was not ratified by any European country.

[440] Covenant of the League of Nations (Paris, 28 April 1919). For Lauterpacht, however, when 'recourse to force short of war is in fact so comprehensive as to leave no doubt that it actually approaches or constitutes war the resort to armed force will as a rule amount to a violation of the territorial integrity and political independence, and will thus fall under the provisions of Art 10 of the Covenant which ... does not require formal recourse to war as a condition of its applicability' (Lauterpacht, ' "Resort to War" ', 59).

[441] Art 12 provided that in no case could member states 'resort to war until three months after the award by the arbitrators or the judicial decision, or the report by the Council'. Art 13 required member states not to 'resort to war' against any other member that complied with an award or decision, and Art 15 committed members not to 'go to war' with any disputant which complied with the recommendations contained in a council report unanimously adopted.

[442] Cavaglieri, *Nuovi studi*, 19–21; Brierly, 'International Law', 314.

[443] Lauterpacht, ' "Resort to War" ', 49–50.

[444] Report of the Special Commission of Jurists, 24 January 1924, para IV (1924) 5 LNOJ 523, 524.

[445] Art 1, General Treaty for the Renunciation of War as an Instrument of National Policy (Paris, 27 August 1928) 94 LNTS 57. As Dinstein points out, the Pact marks the transition from the *jus ad bellum* to the *jus contra bellum* (Dinstein, *War*, 87). It is still in force.

[446] Germany maintained that it was permissible to resort to war as 'a means of international action which may be considered necessary for the maintenance of order in international life' ('Amendment of the Covenant of the League of Nations in Order to Bring It into Harmony with the Pact of Paris' (1930) 11 LNOJ 353, 368).

72 INTERNATIONAL LAW AND THE PRINCIPLE OF NON-INTERVENTION

intermediate state between war and peace—all measures that do not amount to war must necessarily qualify as 'pacific'.[447] In Lesaffer's view, on the other hand, the practice of the 1930s suggests that states interpreted the Pact as also prohibiting uses of force other than formally declared wars.[448]

Unlike the Covenant of the League of Nations and the Pact of Paris, certain regional treaties concluded between the two world wars expressly prohibited intervention in its different forms: in addition to those that will be examined later,[449] one could recall the already mentioned Article III of the 1933 Saavedra-Lamas Pact, which provided that the parties 'will in no case resort to intervention, either diplomatic or armed'.[450] The London Convention for the Definition of Aggression, adopted the same year, was an initiative of the Soviet Union which sought to ban interferences like those conducted by foreign powers during the Russian Civil War. Unsurprisingly, therefore, it identified a state responsible for aggression as that which first carried out certain acts normally associated with intervention, such as the '[p]rovision of support to armed bands formed in its territory which have invaded the territory of another State, or refusal, notwithstanding the request of the invaded State, to take, in its own territory, all the measures in its power to deprive those bands of all assistance or protection'.[451] Article III of the Convention also specified that '[n]o political, military, economic or other considerations may serve as an excuse or justification for the aggression referred to in Article 2': among the examples of unacceptable grounds for aggression, an annex to the treaty listed the internal condition of a state, namely 'disturbances due to strikes, revolutions, counter-revolutions, or civil war'.

The second normative development that characterizes the interwar period is that, concurrently with the emergence of the aforementioned treaty-based limitations on the use of armed force, the fundamental right of states to self-preservation (which constituted the main ground for intervention in the 19th century) also starts to be restricted.[452] This evolution, which had begun with the *Caroline* incident,[453] would eventually culminate with the adoption of the Charter of the United Nations, when the narrower right of self-defence against an armed attack became the only permissible form of use of force in self-preservation.[454]

---

[447] Brierly, 'International Law', 314.

[448] Randall Lesaffer, 'Kellogg–Briand Pact (1928)' in *MPEPIL Online* (last updated October 2010) para 11. Brownlie also contends that the pact prohibits 'any substantial use of force' but does not clarify when a use of force is 'substantial' (Brownlie, 'The Use of Force', 192–3).

[449] See Section 9.2 of this chapter.

[450] For Cançado Trindade, the crystallization of a customary norm prohibiting resort to war as an instrument of national policy occurred as a consequence of the cumulative effects of the Pact of Paris and the Saavedra-Lamas Pact (Antonio Augusto Cançado Trindade, 'The Contribution of Latin American Doctrine to the Progressive Development of International Law' (2015) 376 Recueil des Cours 9, 34).

[451] Art II, Convention for the Definition of Aggression (London, 3 July 1933) 147 LNTS 68. The Convention was ratified by Afghanistan, Czechoslovakia, Estonia, Finland, Latvia, Lithuania, Persia, Poland, Romania, Turkey, the USSR, and Yugoslavia.

[452] Writing in 1905, Oppenheim recalls that '[s]uch acts of violence in the interest of self-preservation are exclusively excused as are necessary in self-defence' (Oppenheim, *International* Law, vol I, 1st edn, 178). Hyde concurs and argues that it is only on the 'narrower yet firmer basis of one form of self-preservation, that of self-defense' that intervention can be justified (Hyde, *International Law*, 248). See also Westlake, *International Law*, Part I, 248.

[453] See Robert Y Jennings, 'The *Caroline* and McLeod Cases' (1938) 32 AJIL 82.

[454] Rosalyn Higgins, *The Development of International Law Through the Political Organs of the United Nations* (OUP 1963) 216.

DEVELOPMENT OF THE PRINCIPLE OF NON-INTERVENTION   73

Thirdly and finally, the practice of states between the two world wars evidences a noticeable trend towards not supporting any faction, not even the incumbent government, when civil wars and popular uprisings broke out in other countries. In 1919, for instance, Italy's Prime Minister Nitti gave instructions to the Italian armed forces not to sell any arms and war *matériel* to either of the fighting parties in the Russian Civil War and declared Italy's resolution not to take a position in the internal conflict, as all the *de facto* governments that had formed were to be considered equally.[455] During the 1911 Xinhai Revolution that led to the abdication of Emperor Pu Yi and the establishment of the Republic of China, France refused to financially support the imperial party and deemed any intervention inadmissible 'tant que les deux partis en présence respectent la vie et les biens des étrangers'.[456] In 1919, Britain, Spain, Portugal, the United States, Brazil, France, and Japan prohibited the export of arms and munitions towards China 'until the establishment of a government whose authority is recognized throughout the whole country'.[457] The same position was adopted by France in 1914 with regard to the different factions of the Mexican Revolution.[458] In the 1924 Albanian revolution, which led to the proclamation of the republic the following year with Ahmed Bey Zogu as president, the Italian government instructed the navy to maintain a 'neutral' attitude and not to support any faction.[459] Two warships were dispatched for the exclusive purpose of the protection of nationals and of Albanians in imminent danger of life. Finally, the US Department of State declared that the position of the American government in regard to the 1927 Portuguese Revolution was 'one of hands off. The uprising is regarded as distinctly one concerning Portugal alone'.[460]

The trend towards negative equality, which started in the Age of Revolutions,[461] had continued during the 19th century as a consequence of the decline of dynastic legitimacy and its replacement with popular sovereignty: if a ruler was such 'by the will of the Nation' and not 'by the grace of God', then the nation could have always revoked their mandate and no states could have interfered with this decision. What is new in the interwar period is that what we now call 'internal self-determination', namely the right of a state to choose its political system without external interferences, starts to be seen as a discrete principle of international law. In 1938, the British Secretary, Lord Halifax, so described it before the Council of the League of Nations:

> [o]ne of the fundamental principles governing the relations of States to one another is that each independent State has the right to determine for itself its own form of Government ... It follows from the right of self-determination that when a dispute arises in one State as to how the people should be governed, other States should

---

[455] Sergio Marchisio, Ornella Ferrajolo, Viviana Javicoli, Fabio Marcelli (eds), *La prassi italiana di diritto internazionale, Terza serie (1919-1925)*, vol III (Consiglio Nazionale delle Ricerche 1995) 1755.

[456] Note for the President of the Republic, 13 January 1912, in Kiss, *Répertoire*, 401. See also the minister of foreign affairs' statements (Kiss, *Répertoire* 401–2).

[457] Lauterpacht, *Recognition*, 231.

[458] Statement of the Prime Minister Doumergue at the Chamber of Deputies, 10 March 1914, in Kiss, *Répertoire*, 404.

[459] Mussolini to Durazzo, Rome, 26 December 1924, in Marchisio, Ferrajolo, Javicoli, Marcelli (eds), *La prassi italiana*, vol VI, 3577–8.

[460] Quoted in Jessup, 'The Spanish Rebellion', 265.

[461] See Section 4 of this chapter.

74   INTERNATIONAL LAW AND THE PRINCIPLE OF NON-INTERVENTION

refrain from exercising any pressure upon the people of that State in one direction or in the other.[462]

A resolution adopted by the Allied powers in Cannes on 6 January 1922 in regard to future relationships with Soviet Russia also stressed that '[t]he nations cannot claim the right to dictate one another the principles according to which they intend to organize their interior property regime, their economy, and their government. It belongs to each country to choose for itself the system it prefers in this respect.'[463] What is even more remarkable is that this right began to be occasionally attached to peoples and not only to states, as in the aide-mémoire of 17 July 1918 issued by US Secretary of State Lansing with regard to the Russian Civil War (1917–22).[464] It is true that, according to the International Committee of Jurists' report on the Åland Islands question, the principle of self-determination of peoples was not yet 'a positive rule of the Law of Nations'.[465] What the Committee was referring to, however, was self-determination in its *external* dimension, that is, a right of secession, and not in its internal one, namely the right of a people to choose its political system without external interferences.

---

[462] (1938) 19 LNOJ 324, 330. Since the Restoration years that saw it opposing the Holy Alliance's policies, Britain had always been careful not to appear as intermeddling with the choice of the government of another state unless this represented an actual and immediate threat to its security as in the case of revolutionary France. When he sent troops to Portugal in 1826, for instance, Canning explained that this was motivated by the fact that Miguelist deserters had entered the Iberian country from Spain and cautioned that 'it never has been the wish or the pretension of the British Government to interfere in the internal concerns of the Portuguese nation. Questions of that kind the Portuguese nation must settle among themselves' (Parliamentary Debates, XVI, 12 December 1826, 360, reproduced in Richard Little, *Intervention: External Involvement in Civil Wars* (Martin Robertson & Co 1975) 25).

[463] Art 1, quoted in Alexander N Sack, 'The Truman Doctrine in International Law' (1947) 7 Law Guild Rev 141, 160. The French prime minister, Briand, also declared in 1921 that '[l]e bolschevisme est affaire russe tant qu'il reste confiné dans ses frontières, et nous n'avons pas à intervenir dans les affaires intérieures de la Russie' (quoted in Paul Fauchille, *Droit international public*, vol I, Première partie: Paix (8th edn, Rousseau & Co 1922) 557–8). See also the words of Britain's Foreign Secretary Balfour (17 February 1919), reproduced in Little, *Intervention*, 26, and those of the Italian government, in Marchisio, Ferrajolo, Javicoli, Marcelli (eds), *La prassi italiana*, vol III, 1763–8. At the same time, however, France, Great Britain, and the United States intervened politically and militarily in Russia in support of the White forces in 1918–20 (Rousseau, *Droit international public*, 43). Other states also sent troops, including Japan, Italy, Romania, Greece, and China. Even though, after 1918, the intervention could no longer be justified by the war against Germany, it received little attention, as the international community was essentially focused on post-war reconstruction. The Soviet Union committed not to pursue claims related to the 1918–21 British intervention in Russia in Art 2 of the Agreement concerning the Settlement of Mutual Financial and Property Claims arising before 1939 (London, 15 July 1986), reproduced in (1986) 57 BYBIL 622.

[464] The document affirmed that the United States, Britain, and France 'recognize[d] the absolute right of the Russian people to direct their own affairs without dictation or direction of any kind from outside ... They recognize[d] the revolution without reservation and [would] in no way, and in no circumstances, aid or give countenance to any attempt at a counter-revolution' (text in *Papers Relating to the Foreign Relations of the United States, The Paris Conference 1919*, vol III (GPO 1943) 691).

[465] Report of the International Committee of Jurists entrusted by the Council of the League of Nations with the Task of Giving an Advisory Opinion upon the Legal Aspects of the Aaland Islands Question, 5 September 1920 (1920) 3 LNOJ Special Supplement 2, 5.

DEVELOPMENT OF THE PRINCIPLE OF NON-INTERVENTION   75

8.1 The Spanish Civil War

The Spanish Civil War (1936–9) started with a *pronunciamiento* led by General Francisco Franco against the Republican government in the Spanish territories in Morocco. After a series of victories over the governmental forces, Franco gained control of a significant portion of the Spanish territory and set up a government in Burgos.[466] Spain appealed to the Council of the League of Nations in September 1936 on the basis of Article 11(1) of the League's Covenant and the Council adopted three resolutions: the first (December 1936) affirming the obligation of states not to intervene in the internal affairs of other states, but without censoring any specific state for its violation; the second (February 1937) banning foreign volunteers; and the third (May 1937) urging the withdrawal of all foreign troops from Spain and condemning the bombardment of open cities.[467]

No explicit recognition of belligerency ever occurred during the Spanish Civil War in spite of both parties claiming certain belligerent rights and of the International Committee of the Red Cross organizing exchanges of prisoners of war.[468] In August 1936, the Republican government hinted that it would blockade all ports controlled by the Nationalists,[469] but France, the United States, and Britain protested arguing that the measure was not effectively enforced, with France instructing its warships not to allow merchant ships to be diverted.[470] In 1937, Franco's insurgents also declared a blockade off the port of Bilbao, and, subsequently, Barcelona, but Britain and the United States again objected.[471] The Republican government always insisted that it had not recognized the Nationalists as belligerents, and so did most states.[472] Between 1936 and 1938, however, Germany, Italy, Guatemala, El Salvador, Nicaragua, Albania, Portugal, Japan, Manchukuo, Austria, Hungary, and the Holy See recognized the insurgents not as belligerents, but as the new *de jure* government of Spain.[473] Other states, including Britain, France, Czechoslovakia, Greece, the Netherlands, Romania,

---

[466] Castrén, *Civil War*, 52.

[467] Council Resolutions of 12 December 1936, 29 May 1937, and 1 October 1938, text in (1937) 18 LNOJ 18; (1937) 18 LNOJ 334; (1938) 19 LNOJ 882. A civil war could have amounted to a 'threat of [international] war', making it 'a matter of concern to the whole League' under Art 11(1) of the League of Nations Covenant (Wehberg, 'La guerre civile', 118). Art 11(2) also provided that each member of the League could 'bring to the attention of the Assembly or of the Council any circumstance whatever affecting international relations which threatens to disturb international peace or the good understanding between nations upon which peace depends'. The Spanish government claimed that there was a 'danger to peace arising out of a new form of aggression, which consisted in a State making war to all intents and purposes, but without declaring war, by first provoking a rebellion within another State and then giving military assistance to the rebels' ((1937) 18 LNOJ 7, 8).

[468] Alfred de Zayas, 'Spanish Civil War (1936–1939)' in *MPEPIL Online* (last updated July 2013) paras 10, 13.

[469] Castrén, *Civil War*, 54.

[470] O'Rourke, 'Recognition', 412; Lauterpacht, *Recognition*, 250.

[471] Castrén, *Civil War*, 56–7.

[472] ibid, 55.

[473] De Zayas, 'Spanish Civil War', para 8. Britain, the United States, France, and Australia recognized Franco as the new *de jure* government only in the last days of the war (ibid, para 8). For Sereni, Franco's government was more stable and effective, and it controlled more territory and population than the Republicans: as a consequence, it should have been considered the legitimate government of Spain, and the Republicans the insurgents (Angelo Sereni, 'La cessione delle miniere spagnole da parte dei rossi' (1938) 318 *Nuova Antologia* 319, 320).

76 INTERNATIONAL LAW AND THE PRINCIPLE OF NON-INTERVENTION

Turkey, and Yugoslavia, recognized the Nationalists as *de facto* authorities exercising administrative control over part of the Spanish territory, but no belligerent rights at sea were granted.[474] Mexico and the Soviet Union continued to recognize the Republican government as the only lawful authority in Spain until the end of the conflict, with the Soviet Union sending funds in response to the violations of the 'non-intervention agreement' by Germany and Italy.[475]

At the outbreak of the conflict, the French Ministry of Foreign Affairs' Legal Office gave the following advice to its government:

> Il n'y a pas lieu de parler pour la France d'une attitude de neutralité: celle-ci signifierait que la France traite sur le même pied le Gouvernement ... avec qui elle entretient des relations diplomatiques, et les rebelles. En réalité, il n'y a neutralité que s'il y a guerre au sens du droit international, ce qui n'est pas le cas actuellement. Selon le droit international, la France est tenue de ne pas faciliter aux rebelles leurs entreprises, mais il ne lui est pas interdit d'aider le gouvernement légal dans l'accomplissement de sa tâche.[476]

The Legal Office, then, initially applied the 19th-century rule that distinguished between insurgency and belligerency and between non-intervention and neutrality. The concern that the civil war would turn into a proxy war and then into an international conflict, however, led several states to commit to strictly abstaining from intervention on either side even in the absence of recognition of belligerency. On 15 August 1936, France unilaterally declared that it would not intervene in any manner, direct or indirect, in the internal affairs of Spain and that it would prohibit all exports and transit of arms, ammunition, war *matériel*, aircraft, and warships destined for Spain, its possessions, and the Spanish territories in Morocco.[477] On the same day, Britain made an analogous declaration.[478] Twenty-seven European states adhered to it, with Switzerland applying it in practice.[479] Turkey and Yugoslavia appended reservations warning that the commitment was 'not to constitute a precedent, or result in even the

---

[474] Castrén, *Civil War*, 59–60; Siotis, *Le droit de la guerre*, 164. Britain, in particular, entertained certain official relations with the Nationalists for the protection of its commercial interests and agents were exchanged (Hersch Lauterpacht, 'Recognition of Insurgents as a *de facto* Government' (1939) 3 MLR 1, 4). English courts found that Britain had recognized the Nationalists as a *de facto* government: see *Government of Republic of Spain v SS Arantzazu Mendi and others* (1939) 33 AJIL 583; *Banco de Bilbao v Sancha and Rey* (1942) 9 *Annual Digest and Reports of Public International Law Cases* 75).

[475] Germany and Italy sent troops and weapons to the Falangists (Siotis, *Le droit de la guerre*, 159; Castrén, *Civil War*, 58–9). In 1978, a decision of the Federal Republic of Germany's Federal Social Court found that, as no recognition of belligerency had occurred, the Spanish Civil War was not a war within the meaning of international law and, therefore, Germany's support for the Nationalists did not turn it into a belligerent (Federal Republic of Germany, Federal Social Court, *Spanish Civil War Pension Entitlement Case*, 14 December 1978, 80 ILR 666, 668–9).

[476] Note of the Legal Office, 12 March 1935, in Kiss, *Répertoire*, 412.

[477] Text of the declaration in (1937) 44 RGDIP 250.

[478] ibid, 251.

[479] Norman J Padelford, 'The International Non-intervention Agreement and the Spanish Civil War' (1937) 44 RGDIP 252–6. The Polish government explained its participation on the basis that 'it was a cardinal principle of Polish foreign policy to refrain from interference in the internal affairs of other states' (quoted in Little, *Intervention*, 28).

DEVELOPMENT OF THE PRINCIPLE OF NON-INTERVENTION 77

implicit recognition of a principle that a government can not render a legal government on the demand of the latter, aid in the struggle against rebellion.[480] The United States did not join in but declared that it would abstain from any interference in the Spanish situation.[481] A committee was set up in London on 9 September 1936 to monitor the implementation of the declarations, but without sanctioning powers.[482]

In spite of the name under which it has gone down in history, the Spanish 'non-intervention agreement' was neither a formal multilateral treaty, as it consisted of a series of unilateral declarations adhering to the initial French declaration,[483] nor provided for non-intervention.[484] Indeed, the principle of non-intervention, in its traditional meaning, would have allowed support for the Republican government upon its request and prohibited only that for the insurgents. Instead, the agreement contained a comprehensive obligation of negative equality, that is, a prohibition of any direct or indirect assistance to all parties, which also extended to the nationals of the participating states (the so-called 'double embargo'). The agreement, therefore, had the opposite effect of a recognition of belligerency: instead of accepting the exercise of belligerent rights by the parties to the civil war, it rejected it, at least beyond the Spanish land territory and territorial waters.[485] The agreement was also not a proclamation of neutrality in any technical sense and this expression never appears in the unilateral declarations submitted by the participating states or in the Nyon Agreement.

The Republicans repeatedly claimed that the non-intervention agreement was a 'legal monstrosity' and an intervention in the internal affairs of Spain, as it put on equal footing government and rebels and deprived the former of foreign assistance.[486] The Soviet Union concurred and condemned it as a 'breach of the principles of international law.'[487] The same position was taken by Mexico, which continued to supply arms and ammunition to the Spanish Republic because of 'a petition made by a constituted Government'.[488] It is however difficult to see how the agreement could have been a violation of international law: states do not have an obligation to support a government facing internal unrest unless a treaty provides otherwise.[489] Also, the agreement

---

[480] Quoted in Padelford, 'The International Non-Intervention Agreement', 581.

[481] Department of State Press Release, 29 August 1936, quoted in Hyde, *International Law*, 254.

[482] A further agreement, concluded at Nyon, aimed at protecting freedom of navigation of neutral ships in the Mediterranean (Nyon Agreement (Nyon, 14 September 1937) 181 LNTS 137).

[483] Padelford, 'The International Non-Intervention Agreement', 580.

[484] The Italian declaration interestingly put 'non-intervention' between guillemets ((1937) 44 RGDIP 253).

[485] Under the Preamble of the Nyon Agreement, neither party to the civil war was recognized as having the right 'to exercise belligerent rights or to interfere with merchant ships on the high seas even if the laws of warfare at sea are observed'.

[486] Ignacio de la Rasilla del Moral, *In the Shadow of Vitoria: A History of International Law in Spain (1770–1953)* (Brill/Nijhoff 2017) 230–1.

[487] Padelford, 'The International Non-Intervention Agreement', 585.

[488] Statement of Mexican President Cárdenas to the Mexican Congress, quoted in Jessup, 'The Spanish Rebellion', 266.

[489] As McNair writes, it was within Britain's sovereign rights to give up the option of assisting the Republican government by signing the non-intervention agreement (McNair, 'The Law', 498). It was not the non-intervention agreement as such that was unlawful, therefore, but the non-compliance with it by Germany and Italy: at that point, the Spanish government had the right to react in self-defence against their aggression, a right that was prejudiced by the continued application of the agreement. This was, apparently, Mexico's position (Fabia Fernandes Carvalho Veçoso, 'Mexican Post-Revolutionary Foreign Policy and the

78 INTERNATIONAL LAW AND THE PRINCIPLE OF NON-INTERVENTION

bound only the states voluntarily adhering to it and did not prevent others from assisting the Republicans.[490] All in all, the Spanish non-intervention agreement was not a game changer. It fitted with the aforementioned trend towards negative equality, but it was not dictated by a sense of legal obligation: it was rather a collective political decision not to recognize belligerency and not to support the government beset by civil war, motivated by the potentially incendiary circumstances and adopted with an understanding that it would not constitute a precedent.[491]

9. Intervention and Non-Intervention in the Americas

The 19th century also saw the extension of the application of the principle of non-intervention, originally devised to regulate the relations among European states, to the American continent: the principle in fact became one of the foundations of 'American international law'.[492] Without taking a position on whether an 'American' international law ever existed,[493] the application of the principle of non-intervention in the Americas in the period 1815–1939 is explored in the following sections. The first focuses on the practice of the United States, while the second analyses that of the Latin American states.

9.1 US Interventionism in Latin America (1823–1933)

After the return of absolutist monarchy in Spain following the French intervention of 1823, the possible restoration of Spanish rule over its former American empire was considered by the Holy Alliance members. The plan, however, was strongly opposed by Britain and the United States. The former, in particular, was interested in averting the re-establishment of Madrid's monopoly on Latin American trade, in preventing the cession of Spanish colonies to France, and, ultimately, in weakening the policies of the Holy Alliance in Europe.[494] At the same time, however, Britain was reluctant to recognize the independence of the new republics and to openly support their armed struggle, as Spain was considered an important barrier against the possible resurgence

---

Spanish Civil War' in Greenman, Orford, Saunders, and Tzouvala (eds), *Revolutions in International Law*, 242, 261).

[490] Castrén, *Civil War*, 65.
[491] Alice Riccardi, 'Sull'esistenza di un obbligo generale di prevenire e reprimere il fenomeno dei *foreign fighters* alla luce della vicenda della guerra civile spagnola' (2017) 72 *La Comunità internazionale* 213, 234.
[492] See the declaration of the Mexican delegate to the Second Pan-American Conference (Mexico, 1901), quoted in Isidro Fabela, *Intervention* (Pedone 1961) 144. The International Court of Justice has also found that non-intervention is 'one of the most firmly established traditions of Latin America' (*Asylum Case (Colombia/Peru)* (Judgment) [1950] ICJ Rep 266, 285).
[493] The existence of an American international law applicable on the American continent and which contained certain rules different from the 'European' international law, is championed by Alvarez, *Le droit international*. Oppenheim, however, disagrees and argues that international law rules are the same for both European and American states (Oppenheim, *International Law*, vol I, 1st edn, 190).
[494] Whitton, 'La doctrine', 13.

DEVELOPMENT OF THE PRINCIPLE OF NON-INTERVENTION   79

of French expansionist policies on the continent.[495] In 1819, the Foreign Enlistment Act was eventually passed by parliament, which made service of British subjects in foreign militaries a crime punishable by fines and imprisonment.[496]

The United States also had a strong strategic interest in weakening European influence on the American continent. In his first annual message to Congress as president (1817), James Monroe had already recognized the existence of a civil war between Spain and its American territories, the parties being 'nearly equal, having as to neutral powers equal rights', and affirmed the 'impartial neutrality' of the United States, thus committing to not providing troops, funds, ships, or munitions to either side, and to opening its ports to the ships of both.[497] In the message of 8 March 1822, Monroe proposed the *de jure* recognition of the independence of the Spanish provinces, already reached *de facto*, but noted that this would not change the neutral position of the United States with respect to the parties.[498] The message that Monroe issued the following year, on 2 December 1823, was meant to address, among others, the growing concerns about a possible intervention by the Holy Alliance powers in the Americas in support of Spain.[499] The message, which has gone down in history as the 'Monroe Doctrine', proclaims in its relevant parts:

With the existing colonies or dependencies of any European power we have not interfered and shall not interfere. But with the Governments who have declared their independence and maintain it, and whose independence we have, on great consideration and on just principles, acknowledged, we could not view any interposition for the purpose of oppressing them, or controlling in any other manner their destiny, by any European power in any other light than as the manifestation of an unfriendly disposition toward the United States. In the war between those new Governments and Spain we declared our neutrality at the time of their recognition, and to this we have adhered, and shall continue to adhere, provided no change shall occur which, in the judgement of the competent authorities of this Government, shall make a corresponding change on the part of the United States *indispensable to their security*...

Our policy in regard to Europe, which was adopted at an early stage of the wars which have so long agitated that quarter of the globe, ... remains the same, which is, not to interfere in the internal concerns of any of its powers; *to consider the government de facto as the legitimate government for us*; to cultivate friendly relations with it, and to preserve those relations by a frank, firm, and manly policy, meeting in all instances

---

[495] DAG Waddell, 'British Neutrality and Spanish-American Independence: The Problem of Foreign Enlistment' (1987) 19 Journal of Latin American Studies 1, 1. In the additional articles to the 1814 Treaty of Friendship and Alliance with Spain, Britain committed 'to take the most effectual measures for preventing his Subjects from furnishing Arms, Ammunition, or any other warlike article to the revolted in America' (Treaty of Friendship and Alliance with Spain (Madrid, 5 July 1814), Art III). The text of the articles is in *British and Foreign State Papers 1812–1814*, vol I—Part I (1841) 292.

[496] Stephen C Neff, *The Rights and Duties of Neutrals* (Manchester University Press 2000) 104.

[497] Quoted in *The Three Friends*, 74.

[498] Papers Relating to the Foreign Relations of the United States, Part II (GPO 1869) 907. As a consequence, in the same year the US Congress recognized the independence of Buenos Aires, Chile, Venezuela, New Granada, Mexico, and Peru (Alvarez, *Le droit international*, 131).

[499] In fact, the Monroe message confirms policies that had already been formulated by Presidents Jefferson and Madison and by Secretary of State Adams (Fauchille, *Traité*, 595).

80   INTERNATIONAL LAW AND THE PRINCIPLE OF NON-INTERVENTION

the just claims of every power, submitting to injuries from none. But in regard to those continents circumstances are eminently and conspicuously different.

It is impossible that the allied powers should extend their political system to any portion of either continent *without endangering our peace and happiness*; nor can anyone believe that our southern brethren, if left to themselves, would adopt it of their own accord. It is equally impossible, therefore, that we should behold such interposition in any form with indifference.[500]

Two points are important for our purposes. First, Monroe rejected the principle of dynastic legitimacy purported by the Holy Alliance and claimed that the legitimate government of a state is the *de facto* one, or—to use Bernard's words—the 'one which is really in possession of [the powers of sovereignty], although the possession may be wrongful or precarious'.[501] Secondly, the Monroe Doctrine did not rule out US interventions in America or European interventions in Europe. It only entailed a commitment of the United States not to intervene in Europe and, with regard to the intervention of the European powers in the Americas, it distinguished two situations: that of territories still under European rule and that of territories that had declared independence and whose independence had been recognized by the United States. While Monroe proclaimed that the United States would not interfere in the internal affairs of the former, European interventions in the latter were disallowed in all cases: neither considerations of self-preservation nor the consent of the legitimate government could justify them, which led the German Chancellor Bismarck to brand the doctrine as 'une impertinence internationale'.[502] At the same time, Monroe invoked self-preservation arguments, namely the danger to the United States' peace and security, to justify the possible counter-intervention of the United States against European interventions in the American countries.[503]

If the Monroe Doctrine initially aimed at maintaining the geopolitical status quo as it existed in 1823, its application was later extended to reject any European intervention on the American continent, even when the territories had not yet achieved *de facto* independence. In the Cuban insurrection of 1851, for instance, the United States

---

[500] Text in Moore, *A Digest*, vol VI, 401–3, emphasis added. At the 1826 Congress of Panama, the newly independent Latin American republics tried to incorporate the Monroe Doctrine into a collective declaration, but the United States opposed the project (Yepes, 'Les problèmes', 53).

[501] A *de jure* government, on the other hand, 'is one which, in the opinion of the person using the phrase, ought to possess the powers of sovereignty, though at the time it may be deprived of them' (Bernard, *A Historical Account*, 108).

[502] Quoted in Alvarez, *Le droit international*, 38. In 1858, for instance, the United States opposed a naval intervention by Britain and France in Nicaragua even though the intervention had been requested by its government to suppress an insurrection (John B Whitton, 'La doctrine de Monroe—suite' (1933) 40 RGDIP 140, 144). When the French Emperor Napoleon III installed Archduke Maximilian of Austria on the throne of the re-established Mexican Empire, the Chilean parliament also refused to recognize 'comme conforme au droit international américain les actes d'intervention européenne en Amérique [et] les gouvernements qui se constituent en vertu de cette intervention, *quoique celle-ci soit sollicitée*' (quoted in Fauchille, *Traité*, 632, emphasis added).

[503] The European states did not significantly criticize the Monroe Doctrine, at least in its original version (Nussbaum, *A Concise History*, 189). Whitton, however, warns against reading too much in the European silence: this might have been due to mere disinterest and to the conviction that the Monroe message was essentially aimed at an internal audience (Whitton, 'La doctrine', 26).

opposed a proposed intervention by Britain and France in support of Spain[504] and, in 1898, it intervened in the Second Cuban Civil War in support of the insurgents: after the sinking of the *USS Maine* on 25 January, the US government sent an ultimatum to the Spanish authorities asking them to leave the island, the rejection of which led to a declaration of war by the United States and, eventually, to Cuba's independence.[505]

It has long been debated whether the Monroe Doctrine is a mere political principle or a legal rule.[506] President Theodore Roosevelt saw it as having merely a political value.[507] Roosevelt's secretary of state, Elihu Root, more cautiously concluded that 'the doctrine is not international law but it rests upon the right of self-protection and that right is recognized by international law'.[508] For Alvarez, the doctrine was a cardinal rule of American international law which regulated the relations between the European and American states.[509] Be that as it may, Monroe's message constitutes an element of verbal state practice useful for identifying the customary international law of the time. It was also mentioned in Article 21 of the Covenant of the League of Nations, which declared its compatibility with the Covenant.[510] The Doctrine has continued to occasionally resurface in the UN Charter era: during the Cold War, for instance, it was invoked to forestall possible communist takeovers on the continent.[511] In 2019, the White House national security advisor, Bolton, claimed that the Monroe Doctrine was still 'alive and well' when he announced new economic measures against Cuba, Nicaragua, and Venezuela.[512]

After the independence of the Spanish colonies, the United States' focus shifted to consolidating its hegemony on the continent: as Carl Schmitt notes, '[t]he Monroe Doctrine turned from a principle of non-intervention and the rejection of foreign interference to become a justification for imperialistic interventions of the United States in other American states'.[513] In his message to Congress of 2 December 1845,

---

[504] Rousseau, *Droit international public*, 78.

[505] Alvarez, *Le droit international*, 157–8. Spain's responsibility for blowing up the *Maine*, however, was never proved.

[506] See Fauchille, *Traité*, 646 and the bibliography cited there.

[507] ibid, 642. Of the same view, Despagnet, *Cours*, 226; Indeed, the doctrine was never promulgated by Act or Resolution of Congress (A Pearce Higgins, 'The Monroe Doctrine' (1924) 5 BYBIL 103, 113).

[508] Elihu Root, 'The Real Monroe Doctrine' (1914) 8 AJIL 427, 432.

[509] Alvarez, *Le droit international*, 139. For a discussion of Alvarez's views, see Juan Pablo Scarfi, *The Hidden History of International Law in the Americas: Empire and Legal Networks* (OUP 2017) 74–8.

[510] Art 21 provided that '[n]othing in this Covenant shall be deemed to affect the validity of international engagements, such as treaties of arbitration or regional understandings like the Monroe Doctrine, for securing the maintenance of peace'. Latin American scholars criticized the inclusion of this article in the League of Nations Covenant as a legitimization of US supremacy in Latin America (Juan Pablo Scarfi, 'Camilo Barcia Trelles on the Meaning of the Monroe Doctrine and the Legacy of Vitoria in the Americas' (2021) 31 EJIL 1463, 1469–70).

[511] The 1960 Declaration of San José adopted by the Seventh Meeting of Consultation of the Organization of American States' Ministers of Foreign Affairs, for instance, '[c]ondemns emphatically the intervention or the threat of intervention, even when conditional, from an extracontinental power in the affairs of the American republics and declares that the acceptance of a threat of extracontinental intervention by any American state jeopardizes American solidarity and security' (Marjorie Millace Whiteman, *Digest of International Law*, vol V (Department of State 1965) 437).

[512] Kori Schake, 'Let the Monroe Doctrine Die' (*Foreign Policy*, 29 May 2019) <https://foreignpolicy.com/2019/05/29/let-the-monroe-doctrine-die-venezuela-bolton/>.

[513] Carl Schmitt, 'The *Großraum* Order of International Law with a Ban on Intervention for Spatially Foreign Powers: A Contribution to the Concept of *Reich* in International Law (1939–1941)' in Carl Schmitt, *Writings on War* (Timothy Nunan tr and ed, Polity Press 2011) 86.

82 INTERNATIONAL LAW AND THE PRINCIPLE OF NON-INTERVENTION

in particular, President James Polk reinterpreted the Monroe Doctrine in the light of the 'Manifest Destiny' of American settlers to expand westwards and reach the Pacific coast, and warned the European states against interfering with this objective.[514] The United States also claimed for itself the role of *gendarme* in Latin America in the same way as the Holy Alliance had done in Europe in the first decades of the 19th century. President Theodore Roosevelt's Corollary to the Monroe Doctrine, articulated in his 1904 State of the Union address, famously proclaimed:

> Chronic wrongdoing, or an impotence which results in a general loosening of the ties of civilized society, may in America, as elsewhere, ultimately require intervention by some civilized nation, and in the Western Hemisphere the adherence of the United States to the Monroe Doctrine may force the United States, however reluctantly, in flagrant cases of such wrongdoing or impotence, to the exercise of an international police power.[515]

He however cautioned:

> We would interfere with them only in the last resort, and then only if it became evident that their inability or unwillingness to do justice at home and abroad had violated the rights of the United States or had invited foreign aggression to the detriment of the entire body of American nations.[516]

The address followed the 1902–3 Venezuelan crisis and, therefore, envisaged possible US action to stabilize the insolvent economies of the Latin American states and to forestall European intervention to recover debts.[517] As a result, in the years 1898–1933 the United States carried out several interventions in Central America and the Caribbean which went down in history under the collective name of 'Banana Wars' and which often led to the occupation of the concerned country (Cuba, Nicaragua, Haiti, Dominican Republic). The vast majority of these interventions took place in support of the constitutional governments and often relied on the incumbent authorities' consent.[518]

---

[514] President James K Polk's First Annual Message, 2 December 1845 <www.gutenberg.org/files/12463/12463-h/12463-h.htm>.

[515] Message of President Theodore Roosevelt to the US Congress, 6 December 1904, in US Congress, *A Compilation of the Messages and Papers of the Presidents*, vol 14, 6923–4.

[516] ibid.

[517] From December 1902 to February 1903, Germany, Italy, and the United Kingdom imposed a pacific naval blockade on Venezuela after President Cipriano Castro refused to pay foreign debts and damages suffered by European citizens in the previous civil war (Yepes, 'Les problèmes', 61–2) The episode contributed to the adoption of the Drago Doctrine and of the Roosevelt Corollary to the Monroe Doctrine, which would lead to the United States acquiring control of the finances of Haiti, Nicaragua, and the Dominican Republic (ibid, 62–6).

[518] This was the case, for instance, of the 1906 intervention in Cuba and of the 1912 and 1927 interventions in Nicaragua (Thomas and Thomas, *Non-Intervention*, 26, 42, 44). These military interventions were in most cases carried out by the United States Marine Corps. On occasion, the navy provided gunfire support and limited army troops were also used. The Banana Wars ended with the Good Neighbor Policy announced by Franklin D Roosevelt in his 1933 inaugural address.

DEVELOPMENT OF THE PRINCIPLE OF NON-INTERVENTION   83

Like Britain, however, the United States justified its interventions not only on the basis of considerations of self-preservation, but also on the existence of treaty-based rights. Indeed, a number of treaties were signed between the United States and Latin American countries providing for a broad right of intervention of the former on the territory of the latter. Article III of the Treaty of Havana of 22 May 1903 between the United States and Cuba famously incorporated the so-called 'Platt Amendment', which allowed the United States to

> exercise the right to intervene for the preservation of Cuban independence, the maintenance of a government adequate for the protection of life, property, and individual liberty, and for discharging the obligations with respect to Cuba imposed by the Treaty of Paris on the United States, now to be assumed and undertaken by the Government of Cuba.[519]

The United States intervened several times in Cuba in support of its government on the basis of this provision in order to put down rebellions.[520] In May 1916, the United States also intervened in the Dominican Republic in support of President Jiménez against a military revolt, removed the newly elected President Henríquez from office, and occupied the island for eight years claiming that the Dominican government had breached Article III of the 1907 treaty between the two countries, which prohibited any increase of the Caribbean country's public debt without US agreement.[521] No recognition of a state of war occurred.[522] A treaty between the United States and Haiti, concluded in 1915 after the intervention on the island following disorders that had led to the assassination of the Haitian president, also contained the Platt Amendment language,[523] and the 1903 Hay-Bunau-Varilla Treaty between the United States and Panama granted intervention rights to the former if it became necessary for the protection of the Panama Canal.[524]

---

[519] Text in Charles I Bevans (ed), *Treaties and Other International Agreements of the United States of America 1776–1949*, vol 6 (Department of State 1971) 1116. The Platt Amendment was also incorporated in the Cuban Constitution.

[520] Thomas and Thomas, *Non-Intervention*, 26–8. The 1903 treaty, including the Platt Amendment clause, was abrogated by a new treaty signed between the United States and Cuba in 1934.

[521] Emilio Roig de Leuchsenring, *La ocupación de la República Dominicana por los Estados Unidos y el derecho de las pequeñas nacionalidades de América* (El Siglo XX 1919) 44–8. The treaty, an application of the Roosevelt Corollary, gave the US government control over the administration of Dominican customs to pay off foreign creditors and forestall possible European interventions to recover credits (Yepes, 'Les problèmes', 63–4). For Philip Marshall Brown, '[t]here is nothing illegal or reprehensible in intervention of this character in the defence of special rights and the general interests of international law and order' (Philip Marshall Brown, 'The Armed Occupation of Santo Domingo' (1917) 11 AJIL 394, 399.

[522] Brown, 'The Armed Occupation', 397.

[523] Treaty Between the United States and the Republic of Haiti (Port-au-Prince, 16 September 1915), Art XIV. See Thomas and Thomas, *Non-Intervention*, 39. The treaty expired in 1936.

[524] Hay-Bunau-Varilla Treaty (Washington, DC, 18 November 1903), Art XXIII, text in (1905) 31 *Nouveau Recueil de Traités* 2nd Ser 599. Under Art I of the Treaty, the United States also committed to guarantee and maintain the independence of the Central American country. This led to the armed intervention in Panama City upon request of the Panamanian government to quell the *Movimento Inquilinario* riots in October 1925 (Luis Guillermo Zuñiga, *El principio de no intervención* (Tibás 1991) 127). The right of intervention was relinquished in 1939.

It should be noted that, although these treaties were normally invoked to justify support for a government facing internal unrest, they did not in principle rule out intervention on the side of insurgents if this was dictated by the security or economic interests of the United States: during Panama's War of Independence from Colombia (1903), for instance, the United States prevented the landing of Colombian forces in Panama, sent forces to protect US citizens, and recognized the new republic.[525] To justify the intervention, President Roosevelt invoked treaty provisions that entrusted the United States with securing the right of free and open transit across the Isthmus and with preventing the commission of belligerent acts therein (in particular, Article XXXV of the 1846 Treaty between the United States and the Republic of New Granada), the security of the United States, and the interests of the civilized world.[526]

9.2 The Reaction to US Interventionism in the Americas: The Non-Intervention and Negative Equality Treaties

Treaties that contained the idea of non-intervention had already been concluded among the Latin American states in the first decades of the 19th century, although early attempts failed to enter into force for lack of sufficient ratifications.[527] It was however only at the turn of the 20th century that, in response to the increasing US interventionism, the Pan-American conferences started to focus their attention on the principle of non-intervention. At the Seventh Pan-American Conference, held in Montevideo in 1933, the principle of non-intervention was eventually accepted by all American states in Article 8 of the Convention on the Rights and Duties of States ('No state has the right to intervene in the internal or external affairs of another').[528] Article 1(1) of the Additional Protocol Relative to Nonintervention, adopted at the Inter-American Conference for the Maintenance of Peace held in Buenos Aires in 1936,[529]

---

[525] Thomas and Thomas, *Non-Intervention*, 28–9.

[526] Hyde, *International Law*, 260. Secretary of State Root would later also add that Panama was an ancient state that had preserved its sovereignty within the Republic of New Granada and was therefore entitled to demand independence from tyrannical rule (Note of 10 February 1906, reproduced in James Brown Scott, 'The Treaty between Colombia and the United States' (1921) 15 AJIL 430, 436–7). In the 1914 Thomson-Urrutia Treaty with Colombia, the United States under Woodrow Wilson eventually expressed regret for the role played in the separation of Panama (Treaty of 6 April 1914 between the United States and Colombia, Art I, in William K Jackson, 'Proposed Treaty between the United States and the Republic of Colombia' (1917–18) 5 Va L Rev 247, 248). At the moment of the ratification in 1921, however, the US Senate rejected Art I of the original treaty containing the expression of regret (Scott, 'The Treaty', 432).

[527] See Thomas and Thomas, *Non-Intervention*, 56; J Irizarry y Puente, 'The Doctrines of Recognition and Intervention in Latin America' (1954) 28 Tul L Rev 316, 327–8. It appears that the principle of non-intervention in Latin America was first affirmed in the 1826 Congress of Panama, convened on the initiative of Simón Bolívar (Statement of the Peruvian delegate, Belaúnde, at the Bogotá Conference (1948), in Novena Conferencia Internacional Americana, *Actas y Documentos*, vol III (Ministerio de Relaciones Exteriores de Colombia, 1953) 150–1). See also Art 12 of the Treaty of Confederation between the Republics of Peru, Bolivia, Chile, Ecuador, and New Granada (Lima, 8 February 1848) <www.oas.org/sap/peacefund/ VirtualLibrary/CongressofLima1847/Treaty/TratadoConfederacionPeruBoliviaChileEcuadorNuevaGran ada.pdf>.

[528] This formula was first proposed by the Argentinian international lawyer Luis Podestá Costa at the 1927 meeting of the International Commission of American Jurists in Rio de Janeiro and was eventually incorporated in the Montevideo Convention (UN Doc A/C.1/SR.1398, 6 December 1965, para 39). Thanks to the change of attitude of the Roosevelt administration, the United States also signed the Convention.

[529] The Conference was convened after the end of the Chaco War between Paraguay and Bolivia (1932–5).

also declared inadmissible the intervention of any of the parties 'directly or indirectly, and for whatever reason, in the internal or external affairs of any other of the Parties'.[530] A violation of this provision triggered a mutual consultation mechanism in order to settle the dispute peacefully.[531] The Eighth Pan-American Conference reaffirmed the non-intervention principle in the Lima Declaration of Principles of the Solidarity of America (24 December 1938).[532]

Other treaties incorporating the principle of non-intervention or certain aspects of it were concluded outside the framework of the Pan-American Conferences. The treaty between Argentina and Brazil of 7 March 1856 provided for a mutual obligation not to support insurgents (Article 2).[533] The 1887 Central American Treaty of Peace, Friendship and Trade contained an obligation to abstain from all interference, be it direct or indirect, in the internal affairs of the other parties and to solemnly respect the principle of non-intervention.[534] An agreement signed in 1911 between Bolivia, Colombia, Ecuador, Peru, and Venezuela required the contracting parties to prevent their territories from being used to foment revolutions, recruit troops or supply arms destined to be used against any of them.[535] As already mentioned, Article III of the 1933 Saavedra-Lamas Pact also stipulated that the states parties 'will in no case resort to intervention, either diplomatic or armed'.[536]

If the abovementioned agreements essentially reaffirmed the customary principle of non-intervention in its general terms or as a specific obligation not to foment/ support rebellions in other countries, the Havana Convention on the Duties and Rights of States in the Event of Civil Strife (1928), adopted at the Sixth Pan-American Conference, distinguished between civil strife where recognition of belligerency had occurred and that where it had not: in the former case, the parties were required to forbid the traffic of arms and war material also in favour of the incumbent government.[537] Other treaties contained an obligation of negative equality regardless of whether recognition of belligerency had been granted in a civil war. In addition to the abovementioned 1911 agreement between Bolivia, Colombia, Ecuador, Peru, and Venezuela, Article II of the 1907 Additional Convention to the General Treaty of Peace and Amity, adopted at the Central American Peace Conference, provided that '[n]o Government of Central America shall in case of civil war intervene in favor of

---

[530] Additional Protocol Relative to Nonintervention (Buenos Aires, 23 December 1936) (1937) 31 AJIL Supplement 57. The Protocol was signed by the United States without reservations.

[531] Art 1(2).

[532] Text reproduced in Fabela, *Intervention*, 163.

[533] Treaty of Peace, Amity, Commerce and Navigation between the Argentine Confederation and Brazil (Paraná, 7 March 1856), cited in Rougier, *Les guerres civiles*, 400–1.

[534] Tratado de Paz, Amistad y Comercio, Art 3 (Guatemala City, 10 February 1887) <http://legislacion.asamblea.gob.ni/Normaweb.nsf/%28$All%29/5E95AB10EE9A102E062577AD00618025?OpenDocument>.

[535] Arts 1, 2, and 3 of the Agreement respecting Internal Revolutions and Neutrality between Bolivia, Colombia, Ecuador, Peru and Venezuela (Caracas, 18 July 1911) 214 CTS 128.

[536] The Treaty was signed by the representatives of Argentina, Brazil, Chile, Mexico, Paraguay, and Uruguay. The United States acceded on 10 August 1934, but appended a reservation according to which '[i]n adhering to this Treaty the United States does not thereby waive any rights it may have under other treaties or conventions or under international law' (text in Whiteman, *Digest*, vol V, 879).

[537] Art 1(3), Havana Convention. Most American states are parties to the Convention. The United States attached a reservation to Art 3, affirming that it does not apply 'where a state of belligerency has been recognised' (Green Haywood Hackworth, *Digest of International Law*, vol II (GPO 1941) 696).

or against the Government of the country where the struggle takes place'.[538] Almost identical language is contained in Article IV of the 1923 General Treaty of Peace and Amity, signed by the five Central American republics.[539] These provisions are yet another manifestation of the aforementioned trend towards negative equality that developed in the first half of the 20th century.[540]

Some of these treaties also touched upon the question of the legitimacy of governments. Under Article I of the 1907 Additional Convention to the General Treaty of Peace and Amity, the parties were required not to 'recognize any other Government which may come into power in any of the five Republics as a consequence of a coup d'état, or of a revolution against the recognized Government, so long as the freely elected representatives of the people thereof, have not constitutionally reorganized the country'. The same language appeared in Article II of the 1923 General Treaty of Peace and Amity, which replaced the former and added that, even when the country had been constitutionally reorganized by freely elected representatives, recognition could not be granted if the new president, vice president, or chief of state were individuals who had played a leadership role in the coup or revolution or were members of their family. These provisions incorporated the doctrine enunciated by Ecuador's minister of foreign affairs, Carlos Tobar, proscribing the extension of recognition to any government that had come to power by unconstitutional means regardless of the *de facto* situation.[541] The Tobar Doctrine was a constitutional revisitation of the old principle of dynastic legitimacy championed by the Holy Alliance in the first decades of the 19th century and it met with the same criticism and, ultimately, the same fate: Costa Rica and El Salvador repudiated it in 1933[542] and the 1923 General Treaty of Peace and Amity was denounced by most of its parties in the 1930s thus coming to an end in 1934. In 1930, Mexico also adopted the Estrada Doctrine, named after its minister of foreign affairs, according to which states should not judge, positively or negatively, the governments or changes of government in other states, as this would entail a breach of their sovereignty.[543] In spite of occasional departures, therefore, by the outbreak of the Second World War it was generally accepted that effective control of territory was the essential factor that determined governmental status in international law and thus entitlement to consent to foreign intervention, not only in Europe but also on the American continent.

---

[538] General Treaty of Peace and Amity and Additional Convention between Costa Rica, Guatemala, Honduras, Nicaragua and El Salvador (Washington, DC, 20 December 1907) (1908) 2 AJIL Supplement 229.

[539] General Treaty of Peace and Amity (Washington, DC, 7 February 1923) (1923) 17 ASIL Supplement 117. In addition, under Art XIV, '[e]ach of the Governments of the Republics of Central America, in the desire to maintain a permanent peace, agree ... not to permit any person, whether a national, Central American or foreigner, to organize or foment revolutionary activities within its territory against a recognized government of any other Central American Republic. None of the contracting governments will permit the persons under its jurisdiction to organize armed expeditions or to take part in any hostilities which may arise in a neighboring country, or to furnish money or war supplies to the contending parties ...'.

[540] See Section 8 of this chapter.

[541] Read Tobar's letter of 15 March 1907 delineating the Doctrine in (1914) 21 RGDIP 482.

[542] Thomas and Thomas, *Non-Intervention*, 43.

[543] The text of Estrada's declaration of 27 September 1930 is in (1931) 25 AJIL Supplement 203.

10. The Scholarly Debate on Intervention in the Period between 1815 and 1939

The problem of intervention was very much en vogue among the legal scholars of the 19th and early 20th century: as already noted, most international law treatises of the time contained a lengthy chapter on this topic and a number of monographs were also published in several languages. In the period between the two world wars, the focus gradually shifts from intervention to the emerging legal limitations on war. Writing in 1937, however, Arnold McNair still maintains that 'the law on [intervention] is not well settled'.[544]

Some scholars argued that intervention is a mere fact or political matter, either in whole or in part. Sir William Vernon Harcourt (1827–1904), the first Whewell Professor of International Law at the University of Cambridge,[545] posits for instance that '[i]ntervention is a question rather of policy than of law. It is above and beyond the domain of law, and when wisely and equitably handled by those who have the power to give effect to it, may be the highest policy of justice and humanity'.[546] Paul Pradier-Fodéré (1827–1904) is of the same persuasion: '[l]'intervention et la non-intervention ne sont pas des principes; l'intervention n'est qu'un fait politique résultant de la souveraineté des États; la non-intervention est l'abstention de ce fait'.[547] For the Belgian Égide Arntz (1812–1884), the law of nations does not provide for an obligation of non-intervention and, therefore, the task is to reconcile the right of intervention with the need to limit it and prevent abuses.[548] Georges Scelle (1878–1961) is perhaps the harshest critic of the principle of non-intervention: for him, '[l]e célèbre principe de non-intervention est, en politique, une chimère. En technique juridique, il est faux. Il serait incompatible avec un ordre juridique quel qu'il fût et, dans l'ordre international, il est la négation même de l'internationalité'.[549] Non-intervention is thus an anarchic principle, a false doctrine born out of the abuses of intervention for political purposes.[550] In Scelle's solidarist view, intervention is a physiological phenomenon in both the domestic and the international legal orders and its lawfulness depends on its purpose, namely on whether it aims to enforce the law or not.[551] In

---

[544] McNair, 'The Law', 474.

[545] Apart from his Cambridge chair, Harcourt was also Solicitor-General (1873–4), Home Secretary (1880–85), and Chancellor of the Exchequer (1886).

[546] Harcourt, *Letters by Historicus*, 14.

[547] Pradier-Fodéré, *Traité*, 548. Pradier-Fodéré's words remind us of those which the French diplomat and politician François-René de Chateaubriand pronounced at the 1822 Congress of Verona in regard to the proposed French intervention in Spain: 'l'intervention ou la non-intervention ... est ... une puérilité absolutiste ou libérale, dont aucune tête puissante ne s'embarrassera: en politique, il n'y a point de principe exclusif; on intervient ou l'on n'intervient pas, selon les exigences de son pays' (M de Chateaubriand, *Congrès de Vérone. Guerre d'Espagne, Négociations: Colonies Espagnoles* (Delloye/Brockhaus et Avenarius 1838) 314).

[548] Rolin-Jaequemyns, 'Note', 675–6.

[549] Georges Scelle, 'La guerre civile espagnole et le droit des gens (suite)' (1939) 46 RGDIP 197, 197.

[550] Georges Scelle, 'Règles générales du droit de la paix' (1933) 46 Recueil des Cours 331, 665.

[551] ibid, 664. Scelle distinguishes intervention from sanction: '[l]a *sanction* proprement dite dépasse l'intervention, parce qu'elle crée une nouvelle situation juridique, modifie l'ordonnancement juridique tandis que l'intervention n'a pour but que de la réaliser' (ibid, 669, emphasis in the original). Intervention, in other words, does not entail the replacement of the authority against which it takes place with that of the intervenor, but limits itself to demand the correct use of its competences (ibid, 668).

88   INTERNATIONAL LAW AND THE PRINCIPLE OF NON-INTERVENTION

particular, intervention is lawful 'toutes les fois que l'ordre public international se trouve menacé ou affecté par les contingences de la politique intérieure ou extérieure d'une des circonscriptions étatiques'.[552]

Most writers of this period, however, analysed the topic of intervention in the context of the fundamental rights of states. Both jusnaturalists and positivists, in particular, associated the principle of non-intervention with the fundamental right of states to independence: while for the former this right is an axiom dictated by reason (states are born equal like individuals), for the latter it derives from state practice and is a customary right.[553] Section 6 of this chapter explored how different authors attempted to reconcile the fundamental right of states to independence with the equally fundamental right of self-preservation, which constituted the main ground invoked to justify interventions until at least the First World War.

With specific regard to foreign intervention in situations of internal unrest, four main schools of thought can be identified in the period under consideration: 1) that which interprets non-intervention as an absolute prohibition on third states to intervene on any side; 2) that for which non-intervention only entails a prohibition on supporting insurgents, but not the legitimate government upon its request; 3) that which allows intervention only when it has been consented to by all the parties of a civil war; and 4) that for which it is permissible to intervene in support of whichever party has justice on its side.

For the *first school of thought*, negative equality is not only an option, but also an obligation arising from the fundamental right of states to independence and the doctrine of popular sovereignty. Most authors belonging to this school limit the application of the absolute prohibition on intervention to the case of civil wars and do not extend it to lesser forms of internal unrest.[554] The British writer Thomas Joseph Lawrence (1849–1920), for instance, contends that foreign interventions in internal struggles are 'an attempt to prevent the people of a state from settling their own affairs in their own way, and, as such, a gross violation of national independence'.[555] In the case of civil wars, in particular, the request of one of the parties, be it the incumbent government or the rebels, cannot make lawful what is contrary to the fundamental principles of the law of nations.[556] For Henri Bonfils (1835–1897), the author of 'perhaps the most widely used French textbook' of his time,[557] no foreign intervention is permissible in a civil war, not even at the invitation of the government, as, by asking for external help, the incumbent has manifested its failure: third states would commit an impermissible interference in

---

[552] Scelle, 'La guerre civile espagnole', 200.

[553] RJ Vincent, *Nonintervention and International Order* (Princeton University Press 1974) 39.

[554] There were, however, also alternative views. For Hyde, in the case of either revolution or civil war no intervention is admissible, either to aid or suppress the revolt, not even if it is requested by a party to the conflict or is provided for in a treaty of guarantee, unless a valid ground can be invoked (Hyde, *International Law*, 253–4). Pradier-Fodéré also maintains that 'quels que soient les évènements intérieurs qui agitent les Etats, quels que soient le caractère et la durée de ces évènements', foreign powers cannot intervene by force under any pretext (Pradier-Fodéré, *Traité*, 582–3). For Smith, even in the case of internal disturbances not recognized as war there is a duty on third states to remain impartial, so as to allow the people of that country to settle the dispute in their own way (Smith, 'Some Problems', 23).

[555] Lawrence, *The Principles*, 126. Foreign interventions aiming at supporting or quelling a revolution, therefore, are impermissible (ibid, 130).

[556] ibid, 126.

[557] Koskenniemi, *The Gentle Civilizer*, 280.

DEVELOPMENT OF THE PRINCIPLE OF NON-INTERVENTION   89

the internal affairs of the concerned country if they impose such government on its people.[558] Using language that preconizes the contemporary principle of internal self-determination, the Peruvian Carlos Wiesse (1859–1945), who published one of the first legal monographs on civil wars, agrees: 'Toute intervention dans une guerre civile constitue une atteinte au droit des peuples de régler eux-mêmes leurs propres affaires avec une entière indépendance. Le fait que l'un des partis sollicite l'intervention n'est nullement de nature à la rendre légitime, alors même que la demande émanerait du gouvernement établi'.[559] Another Latin American, the Colombian diplomat and international law professor Jesús María Yepes (1892–1962), so explains the rationale of the prohibition of intervention on any side:

> Ce qu'il faut à chaque peuple, c'est une liberté complète dans son territoire, avec une juridiction unique, et sous la souveraineté nationale, souveraineté qui sera unitaire ou multiple, barbare ou civilisée, conservatrice ou libérale, démocrate ou autoritaire, pacifique ou belliqueuse, mais qui seule, et toujours seule, a le droit de gouverner l'Etat.[560]

For Mountague Bernard (1820–1882), the first Chichele Professor of International Law at the University of Oxford, who delivered a public lecture on the principle of non-intervention in 1860, the situation is more complex. He agrees that no evidence of usage in favour of a general right of intervention or of exceptions to non-intervention can be identified.[561] Only if a revolution becomes aggressive does the matter cease to be purely internal and 'the measures of self-defence which it justified are not intervention, but war'.[562] Bernard, however, distinguishes between different situations of internal unrest for the purposes of intervention, not on the basis of their magnitude but of their purpose: '[a] successful rebellion changes a government or a dynasty; a successful revolt makes two States out of one'.[563] In the former case, third states have a duty to abstain from interfering on either side, as 'both parties, though struggling with each other, are all the while integral parts of one State, which does not cease to be one because a change in its constitution is being wrought out by the sharp agony of intestine discord instead of being conducted peaceably'.[564] In the latter case, on the other hand, 'interference ceases to be intervention' as there are 'two nations in arms against each other'.[565] Finally, Antoine Rougier (1877–1927), who authored an influential

---

[558] Bonfils, *Manuel*, 202. See also Bernard, *On the Principle*, 15–18; Lawrence, *The Principles*, 126; Funck-Brentano and Sorel, *Précis*, 219; Stowell, *Intervention*, 330–1; Fauchille, *Traité*, 575.

[559] Wiesse, *Le droit international*, 86.

[560] Yepes, 'Les problèmes', 77.

[561] Bernard, *On the Principle*, 22–3. The fact that '[a] few irregularities' occurred as a consequence of religious (in the 16th and 17th centuries) and political (from the end of the 18th century) movements does not undermine the force of the prohibitive rule (ibid, 23). In fact, such 'petty transgressions ... are just exceptions as prove a rule' (ibid, 35).

[562] ibid, 13.

[563] ibid, 22.

[564] ibid, 21.

[565] ibid, 22. It should be noted that Bernard's doctrine of absolute non-intervention does not apply to 'Governments which labour under an incurable incapacity to govern, and which a make-shift policy keeps alive under an irregular and capricious tutelage' (Bernard is referring, without mentioning it, to the Ottoman Empire): ibid, 7–8.

90 INTERNATIONAL LAW AND THE PRINCIPLE OF NON-INTERVENTION

monograph on civil wars published in French in 1910, posits that foreign intervention, be it direct or indirect, is entirely impermissible in a civil war unless an exceptional ground can be invoked.[566] The request of one of the factions does not make any difference: such a request would be a violation of national sovereignty, as the insurgents do not have legal personality and the government facing the insurrection no longer can be said to represent the whole country.[567] In fact, intervention in civil wars is a 'double' intervention, as it occurs not only in the affairs of another state, but also in those of the insurrectional party, whose independence also needs to be protected until the question of sovereignty has been resolved by its victory or defeat.[568]

Absolute non-intervention was also enthusiastically championed by the Italian international lawyers of the 19th century. Pellegrino Rossi (1787–1848) writes that, in the case of civil war, an obligation of 'neutrality' arises for foreign states as any intervention constitutes an obstacle to the free exercise of the national will, although he identifies several exceptions to the prohibition.[569] Terenzio Mamiani della Rovere (1799–1885) agrees: in a civil war occurring in a foreign state, it is not possible to intervene either in favour of the government or of the insurgents, as a nation needs to decide its fate without external interferences.[570] Unlike Rossi, however, he only identifies one admissible exception, that is, the case of an intervention to oppose an unlawful intervention.[571] Apart from that, intervention is never permissible, not even in the case of a humanitarian crisis: only good offices and mediation are allowed.[572] Assistance for a nation fighting against foreign rule, on the other hand, does not constitute an intervention in the internal affairs of the oppressor state and is thus lawful because it protects the subjugated nation.[573] When nationality is not relevant, namely in the case of a civil war where the parties aim for the dismemberment of the state, or a civil war between suzerain and vassal states, absolute non-intervention continues to apply.[574] Giuseppe Carnazza Amari (1837–1911), a disciple of Mamiani's, agrees and posits that intervention is never permissible, either as a rule or as an exception: a people must be entirely free within their territory, whatever form of government they have given themselves.[575] Carnazza Amari, then, criticizes interventions in civil wars based on considerations of self-preservation[576] and on grounds of humanity, as states do not have sovereign powers over each other.[577] Invitation by any party in a civil war also does not make the intervention lawful, as the nation is not identifiable with any

---

[566] Rougier, Les guerres civiles, 352, 369–70.

[567] ibid, 361–2.

[568] ibid, 328.

[569] Pellegrino Rossi, 'Droit des gens. Intervention' (1837) 1 Archives de droit et de législation 353, 364.

[570] Mamiani, D'un nuovo diritto, 157.

[571] ibid, 215.

[572] ibid, 158.

[573] ibid, 159. The only limit to external support in this case is the existence of treaties that prohibit it (ibid, 160),

[574] ibid, 160–2.

[575] Carnazza Amari, Nuova esposizione, 123. See the critical remarks of Rolin-Jaequemyns, for whom absolute non-intervention is an obstacle to the development of the international community of states and is the temporary result of a reaction against the selfish applications of the doctrine of intervention by the Holy Alliance (Rolin-Jaequemyns, 'Note', 676).

[576] Carnazza Amari, Nuova esposizione, 51, 53–4.

[577] ibid, 72–3.

DEVELOPMENT OF THE PRINCIPLE OF NON-INTERVENTION 91

faction or a monarch.[578] Accordingly, even if the latter invites a foreign state to intervene, or the intervention is based on a treaty, the intervention is still unlawful and the treaty invalid, as it alienates what is inalienable, that is, sovereignty.[579] Carnazza Amari is a true non-interventionist: in his view, the absolute prohibition of intervention also extends to the relationship with 'barbarian' nations.[580] For Pasquale Fiore (1837–1914), the duty of non-intervention is the necessary complement of the right to autonomy and independence of every state.[581] Intervention, then, 'must be considered absolutely unlawful.'[582] He writes that not even a treaty or the consent of the government can justify intervention in a civil war, as this would be 'a palpable violation of the international rights of the people.'[583] Fiore, however, is critical of Mamiani and Carnazza Amari's doctrine of absolute non-intervention.[584] For him, intervention is exceptionally permissible if the political system of a state causes 'real and actual injury' to the rights of another, which can thus defend itself and treat it as a *casus belli*.[585] Furthermore, collective intervention can in certain cases be required and in others be admissible. It is 'obligatory when its object is to protect the rights of the persons and legal entities who are members of the international society.'[586] As such, intervention becomes 'a form of protection of international law' against its violations.[587] Collective intervention is also obligatory when it aims to terminate a prolonged state of anarchy that is highly prejudicial to international trade, industry, and general interests.[588] Although not obligatory, collective intervention is admissible when it aims

> *a.* to prevent or to put an end to a state of affairs contrary to law: such as the incorporation of a territory by conquest, the execution of a treaty imposed by violence on the vanquished by the victor and any acts which must be deemed unjust and illegitimate under 'common' law; *b.*. . . . to repress the violation of an order of things previously established by a general treaty, a violation arbitrarily committed by one of the contracting parties to the detriment of the other parties; *c.* When one of the parties fails to carry out the particular stipulations of a general treaty, thus violating the right of those for whose benefit the stipulations were made, provided the wrongdoing party acts arbitrarily and in bad faith.[589]

Writers belonging to the *second school of thought* identify non-intervention as the rule but interpret it only as a prohibition on assisting insurgents: support for a legitimate government at its request for the purposes of suppressing an insurrection is thus not

---

[578] ibid, 54. From the moment the Pope needed foreign intervention to maintain his secular power, then, he ceased to be a legitimate sovereign, as legitimacy can only derive from the will of the people (ibid, 66–7).
[579] ibid, 80.
[580] ibid, 77.
[581] Fiore, *Nouveau droit international*, 498.
[582] Fiore, *International Law*, 265.
[583] ibid, 266–7.
[584] Fiore, *Nouveau droit international*, 501.
[585] Fiore, *International Law*, 266. An example of the latter is when the revolutionaries try to overthrow the institutions of a neighbouring country.
[586] ibid, 268.
[587] ibid, 269.
[588] ibid.
[589] ibid, 270.

92 INTERNATIONAL LAW AND THE PRINCIPLE OF NON-INTERVENTION

intervention but cooperation.[590] The Swiss jurist Johann Kaspar Bluntschli (1808–1881), for instance, included the principle of non-intervention in his code of the international law of civilized states.[591] Bluntschli sees intervention in civil strife occurring in another country not only as an attack on the independence of states but also as a threat to world peace.[592] He however admits that the intervention can be justified by the invitation of a government that is still in control of the state and has the support of the nation.[593] Paul Fauchille (1858–1926) considers intervention as 'une ingérence exercée d'autorité par un État dans les affaires intérieures ou extérieures d'un autre État qui n'est point placé sous sa dépendance politique et qui n'a pas consenti à cette ingérence'.[594] That said, a state which responds to the appeal for help of another state does not commit an act of intervention, providing that the request originates from the legitimate government and not from an ousted prince or an insurrectional party.[595] Santi Romano (1875–1947) agrees: intervention that is founded on the request of a legitimate authority or on a treaty, as well as offers of mediation, good offices, or cooperation, are not real 'interventions', as they lack the necessary element of coercion.[596] Like Fauchille, he concludes that intervention upon invitation of or authorised by an ousted monarch or by rebels is unlawful.[597] It is worth noting that the majority of those who argue in favour of treaty-based intervention by invitation claim that a contracting party also needs to request it in each specific case.[598]

Certain authors belonging to the second school of thought circumscribe the third-state support that a government beset by civil war can receive to the supply of arms and funds, but not troops.[599] Ludovico (Luigi) Casanova (1799–1853), for instance, distinguishes two situations: that of a civil war where one of the parties can still be identified as the legitimate government, and that of a civil war among different factions none of which can claim to be the government.[600] In the latter case, third states have to remain strictly neutral, which entails—for Casanova—a prohibition of direct support and the choice between prohibiting or allowing their citizens to assist the parties of the civil war.[601] In the former case, third states have an obligation to abstain from supporting in any form the insurgents but they can supply arms and funds to the government.[602]

A *third group of scholars* requires that intervention be consented to by all factions of a civil war. Henry W. Halleck (1815–1872), who served as a general in the Union

---

[590] Woolsey, *Introduction*, 42–3; Vidari, *Del principio*, 12–13.

[591] Bluntschli, *Le droit international*, 90, 271.

[592] ibid, 271.

[593] ibid, 273.

[594] Fauchille, *Traité*, 542. Fauchille distinguishes between positive or negative intervention depending on whether it takes place directly or prevents other states from intervening (ibid, 543).

[595] ibid, 541.

[596] Romano, *Corso*, 127–8.

[597] ibid, 128.

[598] See eg Éd Engelhardt, 'Le droit d'intervention et la Turquie' (1880) 12 RDILC 363, 365; Bernard, *On the Principle*, 14.

[599] Wehberg, 'La guerre civile', 55, 57. The supply can be delivered by a state either directly or by allowing its nationals to provide it.

[600] For Casanova, the *de facto* government of a state, that is, the one that is recognized and obeyed by the nation, is also the legitimate government (Casanova, *Del diritto*, 86).

[601] ibid, 92.

[602] ibid, 91.

DEVELOPMENT OF THE PRINCIPLE OF NON-INTERVENTION   93

Army during the American Civil War, criticizes Vattel's and Wheaton's claims that third states can support the party in a civil war that has a just cause: he maintains that, as a rule, foreign states are bound not to intervene on any side, not even when the insurgents have achieved *de facto* statehood, because no foreign power can become the judge of the justice of war and, in any case, the justice or injustice of the cause cannot be a sufficient reason for third-state intervention.[603] It is only when it has been invited by all contending factions that intervention becomes permissible.[604] In a mere insurrection, on the other hand, the rebels do not have international legal personality and, therefore, in such a situation only the invitation from the government is legally meaningful.[605] Like Halleck, Sir Robert Phillimore (1810–1892) argues that, to be a valid ground for foreign intervention in a civil war, the invitation must come from both contending parties.[606] Paul Pradier-Fodéré (1827–1904) is of the same opinion.[607] William Edward Hall (1835–1894)—according to Koskenniemi the author of 'perhaps the most influential English-language textbook of the period'[608]—also posits that, in the specific context of a civil war, foreign intervention can take place exclusively at the invitation of all parties.[609] Indeed, if the intervention is directed against the government, 'independence is violated by an attempt to prevent the regular organ of the state from managing the state affairs in its own way'.[610] If the intervention is against the insurgents, 'the fact that it has been necessary to call in foreign help is enough to show that the issue of the conflict would without it be uncertain, and consequently that there is a doubt as to which side would ultimately establish itself as the legal representative of the state'.[611] In Hall's view, however, intervention that is impermissible for individual states can be carried out by a group of states acting together in the general interest of Europe, for instance to end a protracted civil war, but the ground would only be a moral, not legal, one.[612]

Finally, a *fourth school of thought* is influenced by the jusnaturalists of the 16th–18th centuries and gives a prominent role to the just cause of the party in support of which the intervention takes place. The American Henry Wheaton (1785–1848) claims that '[n]on-interference is the general rule, to which cases of justifiable interference form exceptions limited by the necessity of each particular case'.[613] With specific regard to intervention in civil wars, Wheaton, echoing Vattel, opines that third states 'may remain indifferent spectators of the controversy ... or may espouse the cause of the party which they believe to have justice on its side'.[614] In the former case, the third

---

[603] Halleck, *International Law*, 73–4. Halleck sees Vattel and Wheaton's view 'as not only erroneous, but exceedingly dangerous, from the fact that it justifies the most objectionable species of intervention in the internal affairs of states' (ibid, 74).

[604] ibid, 339.

[605] ibid.

[606] Phillimore, *Commentaries*, 569.

[607] Pradier-Fodéré, *Traité*, 591.

[608] Koskenniemi, *The Gentle Civilizer*, 81.

[609] Hall, *A Treatise*, 290–91.

[610] ibid, 291.

[611] ibid.

[612] ibid, 291–2.

[613] Wheaton, *Elements*, 106. Koskenniemi reads this sentence as the exception that overturns the rule: '[t]he system simply does not allow the hierarchization of the freedom to intervene and the freedom of not to be intervened against' (Koskenniemi, *From Apology to Utopia*, 150).

[614] Wheaton, *Elements*, 32.

94   INTERNATIONAL LAW AND THE PRINCIPLE OF NON-INTERVENTION

state has to conduct itself impartially according to its neutral status, while in the latter case it becomes a party to the conflict.[615] The same view is adopted by the German scholar August Wilhelm Heffter (1796–1880)[616] and the Italian Ercole Vidari (1836–1916). For the latter, in particular, to be lawful the intervention must first of all be requested, as only in this way can the right to independence be preserved.[617] In addition, intervention needs a just cause, namely self-defence or the enforcement of a right.[618] Intervention requested by a tyrannical government against oppressed populations, on the other hand, is unlawful.[619] The same principles apply to foreign intervention in civil wars: third states can intervene, provided that they are requested to do so and only on the side of the faction that has a just cause.[620] Finally, the Venezuelan Andrès Bello (1781–1865) points out that when, in a civil war, an insurrectional faction achieves control of some part of the national territory, establishes a government, administers justice and, therefore, exercises sovereignty, it becomes a subject of international law and the conflict has to be treated by external states as if it is one between two states.[621] Third states, therefore, can remain neutral, intervene on the side of either belligerent, or offer their mediation.[622] The only criteria are justice and one's own interests.[623]

In the interwar period, the scholarly debate on the principle of non-intervention assumes strong ideological connotations. Russian writers of the early Soviet period, in particular, admit intervention in support of socialist revolutions during the transitional period from a capitalist to a communist society.[624] In the relations between communist states, the principle of sovereignty, an expression of the 'old international law', is in their view destined to be eventually replaced by that of proletarian dictatorship, which does not leave much room for independence and non-interference.[625] German scholarship between the two world wars also shifts away from the traditional notion of non-intervention as an interstate principle in an attempt to justify Germany's expansionist policies.[626] Explaining the Nazi conception of non-intervention, in particular, Carl Schmitt (1888–1985) argues that 'the principle of non-interference of spatially alien powers has triumphed as the valid principle of current international

---

[615] ibid.

[616] Heffter, Le droit international, 107. Heffter's views are criticized in Concepción Arenal, Ensayo sobre el derecho de gentes (Imprenta de la Revista de Legislación 1879) 14, one of the first international law treatises authored by a woman.

[617] Vidari, Del principio, 12–13.

[618] ibid, 10–11.

[619] ibid, 39. He concludes that Sardinia's interventions in the Italian states in 1859–60 were lawful because they were requested by the de facto governments which had overthrown the previous despotic rulers (ibid, 28).

[620] ibid, 41–2, 63–5.

[621] Bello, Principios, 299.

[622] ibid, 301.

[623] ibid.

[624] Nussbaum, A Concise History, 288. As has been observed, 'in Russian revolutionary doctrine, which had substituted class for nation, [the principle of non-intervention] appeared to find no place at all' (Vincent, Nonintervention, 147). In Stalin's view, in particular, the Soviet Union had a duty to support the proletariat 'starting revolts against the capitalists in these countries, and, in case of necessity, even sending its military forces against the exploiting classes and their states' (quoted in Mintauts Chakste, 'Soviet Concepts of the State, International Law and Sovereignty' (1949) 43 AJIL 21, 36).

[625] Chakste, 'Soviet Concepts', 34–5.

[626] Virginia L Gott, 'National Socialist Theory of International Law' (1938) 32 AJIL 704, 714, 717–8.

law with respect to national group law.'[627] Schmitt considers the notion of 'state as the central concept of international law' an obsolete concept that 'no longer corresponds to truth and reality'[628] and replaces it with that of *Reich*.[629] In his view, 'every *Reich* has a *Großraum* [great space] into which its political idea radiates and which is not to be confronted with foreign interventions'.[630] As a consequence, *Reiche* are entitled to intervene in the affairs of subordinate polities within their *Großraum* but at the same time they are prohibited from intervening in other *Reiche's Großräume*.[631] It is only when '*Großräume* of international law with bans on intervention by spatially alien powers are recognised and the sun of the concept of *Reich* rises [that] a fenced-off co-existence on a sensibly divided earth will become thinkable and the principle of non-intervention may unfold its developing effect into a new international law'.[632] Other German scholars of the Nazi period employ the notion of *Lebensraum* (living space) instead of that of *Großraum* but the purpose is the same, namely to justify the right of a racially superior state to expand at the expenses of inferior ones.[633]

The Spanish Civil War offered the opportunity for passionate scholarly debates on the legality of intervention. The Frenchman Louis Le Fur (1870–1943), in particular, depicts the Iberian conflict as a struggle 'entre la civilisation chrétienne et le communisme athée'[634] and claims that what makes a government legitimate is not necessarily its origin but 'le bon exercice du pouvoir'.[635] As a result, he denies that the Republicans, unable to maintain law and order in the zone under their control and in fact responsible for the violence occurring therein, can be considered the legitimate government of Spain.[636] He concludes that third states are, as a minimum, under an obligation to recognize the Nationalists as belligerents but that, in their own interest, they should recognize them also as a legitimate government.[637] Coming from a different ideological position, Le Fur's compatriot, Scelle, disagrees and writes that, under customary international law, 'les gouvernements tiers ne doivent intervenir *en aucune façon* en faveur des rebelles; ils peuvent intervenir *de toute façon* en faveur du gouvernement légal'.[638] For him, the Spanish non-intervention agreement, by depriving the Madrid authorities of their right to buy arms and ammunition and by creating a mechanism to enforce the embargo, put on an equal legal footing the Nationalist insurgents and the legitimate Republican government, removed the civil war from the domestic jurisdiction of Spain, and thus amounted to an unlawful intervention.[639]

[627] Schmitt, 'The *Großraum* Order', 101.
[628] ibid, 104.
[629] ibid, 112.
[630] ibid, 101.
[631] François Rigaux, 'L'histoire du droit international revue par Carl Schmitt' (2007) 9 J His Intl L 233, 246.
[632] Schmitt, 'The *Großraum* Order', 101.
[633] Detlev F Vagts, 'International Law in the Third Reich' (1990) 84 AJIL 661, 689.
[634] Louis Le Fur, *La Guerre d'Espagne et le Droit* (Les Éditions Internationales 1938) 70.
[635] ibid, 8.
[636] ibid, 24.
[637] ibid, 66. The Italian fascist scholars of the time also argue that the denial of belligerent rights to the Nationalists is a violation of international law (see eg Giacinto Bosco, 'La guerra civile in Spagna e il diritto internazionale' (1938) 5 *Civiltà fascista* 504, 511).
[638] Scelle, 'La guerre civile espagnole', 227, emphasis in the original.
[639] ibid. For further discussion of Le Fur and Scelle's positions in regard to the Spanish Civil War, see Koskenniemi, *The Gentle Civilizer*, 338–42.

11. Conclusions

During the 18th century in Europe, non-intervention became a corollary of state sovereignty as vested in the person of the monarch: as such, it constituted an instrument for states to shield themselves from external interferences and to consolidate internal sovereignty within their borders. States could have thus intervened only in support of a legitimate sovereign at their request, while support for rebels was in all cases impermissible. Mainstream scholarship of the time, however, claimed that, when the internal unrest had reached the threshold of a civil war and the insurgents were successful in *de facto* dividing a country, it was allowed to assist the party which had justice on its side at its request as in interstate wars, consistently with applicable treaties of alliance and guarantee.

The American and French Revolutions repudiated the dynastic principle as the source of political legitimacy and replaced it with the consent of the governed, with the result that the permissibility of intervention in support of a monarch facing internal unrest depended no longer on compliance with succession rules and formal transfer of sovereignty, but on the factual success of the challenge to the established authority by the insurgents. The two revolutions, on the other hand, did not alter the matrix that had consolidated during the 18th century and that proscribed any support for foreign insurgents. Indeed, the majority of states either sided with Britain or remained neutral during the American War of Independence, and France's support for the colonies was grounded not in a rejection of the respect for sovereignty and non-intervention but rather in the claim that they had become *de facto* independent. The French Revolution's initial proclamations of support for peoples revolting against their dynastic rulers also met with general condemnation and the revolutionaries' interventionist foreign policies were eventually repealed in favour of more cautious positions.

By the 1830s, the principle of non-intervention, as a balancing mechanism ensuring the co-existence of different forms of political legitimacies in Europe, had become a well-established rule of the *jus publicum europæum* and even those powers that were often interfering in the internal affairs of other states, like the Holy Alliance members, paid lip service to it. In the second half of the 19th century, a distinction between different situations of internal unrest also emerged. At this point, two factors determined the legality of armed intervention: the context in which the use of force occurred (rebellion/insurrection as opposed to civil war) and the form it took (war or measure short of war). In situations of mere rebellion and insurrection, third states were required to comply with the principle of non-intervention, which essentially entailed that they were prohibited from supporting the insurgents but could assist the incumbent government upon its request with troops or, for some scholars, only by supplying arms and other military *matériel*. The restraining impact of the principle of non-intervention, however, was significantly limited by the fact that—if one accepts the view that war, in this period, was either a right inherent in state sovereignty or an extra-legal phenomenon—a state could have always militarily supported foreign insurgents after declaring war on the government they opposed. If they decided to intervene without establishing a state of war, however, third states needed to have either a treaty-based right to do so or at least a justification which excused the violation of the fundamental right of independence of the victim state. Self-preservation, in particular, was a catch-all notion that justified action for the protection of both the rights and the essential interests of states. Different actors interpreted self-preservation in different ways, from the abstract and pre-emptive notion of the Holy Alliance to the narrower one adopted by Britain, which required that the immediate security or essential interests of the intervening state were seriously threatened in each specific case. On the other hand, it does not seem that the international law of the time permitted interventions to stop massacres, to terminate a prolonged civil war, or to support nations under foreign rule to gain independence.

In two cases, civil war was treated as an interstate war: when the secessionist insurgents had managed to achieve *de facto* statehood and when recognition of belligerency had been granted by the incumbent government and/or by third states. In these cases, the principle of non-intervention was displaced and the same rules that applied to *de jure* wars were triggered, with the consequence that third states had the option of either remaining neutral or becoming involved in the conflict on either side as co-belligerents: whether the latter option was permissible was determined by the customary and treaty rules on the resort to war, and not by the recognition of belligerency.

In the period between the two world wars, states often adopted a position of negative equality with respect to situations of internal unrest in foreign countries, particularly in civil wars, regardless of whether belligerency had been recognized or not. This was a consequence of the emerging treaty restrictions on the states' *jus ad bellum*, of the limitation of the right of self-preservation to the narrower case of self-defence, and of the consolidation of the right of each state to determine its own political system without external interferences. While negative equality with respect to civil wars was undoubtedly a trend detectable in the state practice of the time, however, it was not yet an obligation under customary international law: indeed, treaties had to be concluded to prohibit intervention also on the side of incumbent governments, the most noticeable examples being the Spanish 'non-intervention agreement' and the General Treaties of Peace and Amity among the Central American republics.

II
The Principle of Non-Intervention in the Framework of the Sources of Contemporary International Law and in the Current Scholarly Debate

1. Introduction

The period that followed the end of the Second World War was no longer characterized by a plurality of competing political legitimacies, but by 'a global order of two domains, and a series of proxy confrontations in the hinterlands of each'.[1] During the Cold War (1947–91), in particular, the Soviet Union and the United States frequently intervened, with mixed results, to overthrow hostile regimes or to keep in power friendly ones in states situated within their respective spheres of influence, as in the case of the US interventions in Guatemala (1954), Cuba (1961), Dominican Republic (1965), Nicaragua (1981–9), Grenada (1983), and Panama (1989–90), and the Soviet interventions in East Germany (1953), Hungary (1956), and Czechoslovakia (1968). The decline of the European colonial empires also led to the proliferation of wars of national liberation fought by peoples in Africa and Asia, often with the support of the Soviet Union and other members of the communist bloc. Even after achieving independence, the new states witnessed regular interventions by the former colonial powers, like those of France in the *Françafrique*.

After the end of the Cold War, the United Nations and regional organizations have played an active role in the maintenance of peace and the restoration of constitutional governments. Civil wars, insurgencies, and revolutions, however, have continued to occur, particularly in Eastern European, African, and Middle Eastern countries, as a consequence of the collapse of state structures as in Somalia (1991–present) and Libya (2014–20); internal or regional power struggles as in Zaire (later renamed the Democratic Republic of the Congo (DRC): 1996–2003), Sierra Leone (1991–2002), Liberia (1989–97 and 1999–2003), Central African Republic (2004–7 and 2012–present), Yemen (2015–present), Ethiopia (2020–2), and Sudan (2023–present); secessionist aspirations as in the former Yugoslavia (1991–5), Sudan (1983–2005), Chechnya (1994–6 and 2000–9), Mali (2012–present), and Ukraine (2014–present);

---

[1] Nehal Bhuta, 'The Antinomies of Transformative Occupation' (2005) 16 EJIL 721, 734. Morgenthau notes that 'the cold war has not only been a conflict between two world powers but also a contest between two secular religions. And like the religious wars of the seventeenth century, the war between communism and democracy does not respect national boundaries. It finds enemies and allies in all countries, opposing the one and supporting the other regardless of the niceties of international law' (Hans J Morgenthau, 'To Intervene or Not to Intervene' (1967) 45 Foreign Affairs 425, 429).

International Law and the Principle of Non-Intervention. Marco Roscini, Oxford University Press. © Marco Roscini 2024.
DOI: 10.1093/oso/9780198786894.003.0003

CONTEMPORARY INTERNATIONAL LAW AND CURRENT SCHOLARLY DEBATE 99

and claims for democracy as in the 2011 Arab Spring uprisings, particularly in Tunisia, Egypt, Bahrain, Libya, and Syria.[2] Post-1991 interventions have been based less on ideology and more on the claimed protection of community interests, such as the protection of human rights, the fight against international terrorism, and the enforcement of disarmament obligations.

In this volatile scenario, the principle of non-intervention has continued to play an important balancing role as it did in the 19th century. During the Cold War, in particular, it was one of the principles on which the peaceful coexistence of states with different political, social, and economic systems was based: the Berlin Wall, built by the German Democratic Republic in 1961, was its most graphic representation. The interdependence of states in an increasingly globalized world economy and the economic gap between the North and the South of the world have also brought to the forefront the question of whether forms of coercion other than military, in particular economic coercion, can constitute an unlawful intervention.[3] Finally, technological developments and the digitization of societies have resulted in the further extension of the scope of the principle of non-intervention so as to cover new forms of interferences in the domestic affairs of states, namely those conducted in and through cyberspace.

This chapter begins the analysis of the principle of non-intervention in the UN era (1945–present) by discussing its status in the framework of the sources of contemporary international law. It starts by identifying the treaties which explicitly or implicitly contain a reaffirmation of the principle in question and by investigating whether this reflects customary international law. The chapter then examines whether the principle of non-intervention establishes an obligation owed *erga omnes* and whether it constitutes a *jus cogens* norm. It concludes by conducting a survey of the international legal scholarship on intervention in order to identify the main post-1945 schools of thought.

Before proceeding, a word of caution about language. For the sake of simplicity, I use the expressions 'socialist' and 'communist' states as interchangeable to indicate those countries where the central government, normally ruled by a party that identifies itself as communist, controls all aspects of the economic and political systems. Note, however, that no country has ever achieved the elimination of personal property, money, and class system that the communist ideology requires: from a social-structure perspective, therefore, communist countries were in fact 'socialist'. Furthermore, I employ the expression 'Western states' as including those states with a capitalist economic system that were, one way or the other, allied with the United States during the Cold War. The expression does not include states that officially adopted a non-aligned position, whatever their economic or political systems.[4]

---

[2] As the International Commission on Intervention and State Sovereignty (ICISS) has observed, '[t]he most marked security phenomenon since the end of the Cold War has been the proliferation of armed conflict within states … more often than not with ugly political and humanitarian repercussions' (ICISS, The Responsibility to Protect: Report of the International Commission on Intervention and State Sovereignty, December 2001, para 1.16).

[3] Wilhelm G Grewe, *Epochen der Völkerrechtsgeschichte* (Nomos 1984), tr and rev by Michael Byers as *The Epochs of International Law* (Walter de Gruyter 2000) 658.

[4] The Non-Aligned Movement was established in 1961 after the adoption of the Decolonization Declaration (GA Res 1514 (XV), 14 December 1960).

2. The Principle of Non-Intervention and Treaty Law

The decades that followed the end of the Second World War were characterized by a trend towards multilateralism and international governance, with the conclusion of several treaties establishing international organizations for the maintenance of international peace and security. These and other treaties often contain a reference to the principle of non-intervention in addition to reiterating the prohibition of the threat and use of force contained in the UN Charter.

Relevant treaties concluded in this period can be classified as those that merely imply the principle of non-intervention through references to broader notions like the sovereign equality of states, those that expressly mention it as a general principle, and those that also list specific forms of prohibited intervention.

2.1 The Charter of the United Nations

Even though Brazil's draft of Article 2(4) contained a prohibition of intervention together with that of the use of force,[5] the final text of the UN Charter, which superseded the Covenant of the League of Nations, does not include explicit references to it, nor does it employ the term 'intervention' or 'to intervene' anywhere apart from Article 2(7). According to this provision, '[n]othing contained in the present Charter shall authorize the United Nations to intervene in matters which are essentially within the domestic jurisdiction of any state or shall require the Members to submit such matters to settlement under the present Charter'. The position of the Western states has always been that Article 2(7) is not a codification of the customary principle of non-intervention applicable between states, as it operates exclusively in the relations between UN organs and member states and only constitutes a limit to the competences of the former.[6] The scope of the prohibition of intervention incumbent on the United Nations is at the same time broader and narrower than that applicable between states. It is broader because it is not limited to coercive conduct and also includes the exercise of the normal powers of the organs in matters falling under the domestic jurisdiction of states, such as the adoption of a recommendation addressed to a specific state or even the discussion of a question (although not merely placing it on the agenda).[7] It is

---

[5] Documents of the United Nations Conference on International Organization, vol III (United Nations Information Organizations 1945) 237 ('All members of the Organization shall refrain in their international relations from any intervention in the foreign or domestic affairs of any other member of the Organization, and from resorting to threats or use of force, if they are not in accord with the methods and decisions of the Organization. In the prohibition against intervention there shall be understood to be included any interference that threatens the national security of another member of the Organization, directly or indirectly threatens its territorial integrity, or involves the exercise of any excessively foreign influence on its destinies').

[6] See eg France, UN Doc A/C.1/SR.1405, 9 December 1965, para 39. For other states, however, Art 2(7) applies *a fortiori* to the relations among states (A/6799, 26 September 1967, para 313). Honduras invoked a violation of Art 2(7) when Brazil allowed its embassy in Tegucigalpa to be used by the ousted Honduran president to foment an insurrection (*Certain Questions Concerning Diplomatic Relations (Honduras v Brazil)*, Application instituting proceedings, 28 October 2009, paras 8–9 <www.icj-cij.org/case/147> (hereafter *Honduras v Brazil*)).

[7] Quincy Wright, 'Is Discussion Intervention?' (1956) 50 AJIL 102, 106–7; Oscar Schachter, 'The United Nations and Internal Conflict' in John Norton Moore (ed), *Law and Civil War in the Modern World* (Johns

narrower because, as the last part of Article 2(7) makes clear, it does not prevent the Security Council from intervening in a state under Chapter VII of the Charter even without the consent of its government.

The International Court of Justice (ICJ) has confirmed that the principle of non-intervention 'is not, as such, spelt out in the Charter'.[8] The Court explains this omission with the fact that 'it was never intended that the Charter should embody written confirmation of every essential principle of international law in force'.[9] It has been argued that, even if it is not expressly stated, an obligation of non-intervention in the domestic affairs of other states results implicitly from Articles 1(2) (which includes, among the UN purposes, '[t]o develop friendly relations among nations based on respect for the principle of equal rights and self-determination of peoples')[10] and 2(1) (which provides that '[t]he Organization is based on the principle of the sovereign equality of all its Members') of the Charter, in addition to Article 2(4) itself.[11] Articles 1(2) and 2(1), however, address the Organization and not its member states and the obligation contained in Article 2(4) is narrower in scope than the principle of non-intervention as it only prohibits one form of coercion: that by armed means.[12] A better candidate for an implicit recognition of the principle of non-intervention in the Charter is Article 78, which requires that the relations among member states be 'based on respect for the principle of sovereign equality'.[13] Be that as it may, both the 1965 General Assembly's Declaration on the Inadmissibility of Intervention and the 1970 Declaration on Principles of International Law Concerning Friendly Relations and Co-operation among States in Accordance with the Charter of the United Nations (the latter being an interpretation of the Charter by the General Assembly) proclaim that 'any form of intervention ... violates the spirit and letter of the Charter'.[14]

Hopkins University Press 1974) 401, 421–2; Benedetto Conforti and Carlo Focarelli, *Le Nazioni Unite* (11th edn, Wolters Kluwer/CEDAM 2017) 194–5.

[8] *Case Concerning Military and Paramilitary Activities in and against Nicaragua (Nicaragua v United States of America)* (Merits) [1986] ICJ Rep 3, para 202 (hereafter *Nicaragua v USA*).

[9] ibid.

[10] Joyner and Grimaldi argue that self-determination as provided in Art 1(2) of the UN Charter entails a right of states to choose a government and adopt laws without external pressures, which translates into a prohibition to assist 'civilians' in an internal war in another state (Christopher C Joyner and Michael A Grimaldi, 'The United States and Nicaragua: Reflections on the Lawfulness of Contemporary Intervention' (1985) 25 Va J Intl L 621, 643).

[11] For France, Art 2(1) of the Charter 'applied to all cases in which constraint was exercised on one State to compel it to subordinate its domestic jurisdiction to the interests of another State', while Art 2(4) 'referred more specifically to cases in which force was used to violate a State's sovereignty' (UN Doc A/C.1/SR.1405, para 39).

[12] See Chapter III, Section 6.

[13] As Judge Momtaz notes, the principle of non-intervention is the 'first natural consequence' of the sovereign equality of states (*Alleged Violations of the 1955 Treaty of Amity, Economic Relations, and Consular Rights (Islamic Republic of Iran v USA)* (Provisional Measures) [2018] ICJ Rep 623, Declaration of Judge ad hoc Momtaz, para 18). See also Supreme Court of Canada, *Hape v Her Majesty the Queen* [2007] 2 SCR 292, paras 45–6 (LeBel J) (hereafter *Hape v Her Majesty the Queen*).

[14] GA Resolutions 2131 (XX), 21 December 1965, para 4, and 2625 (XXV), 24 October 1970, Preamble. See also the Preamble of the 1969 Vienna Convention on the Law of Treaties (VCLT), which affirms that the principle of 'non-interference' in the domestic affairs of states is one of those principles of international law 'embodied' in the UN Charter (1155 UNTS 331).

102   INTERNATIONAL LAW AND THE PRINCIPLE OF NON-INTERVENTION

2.2 Regional Treaties

The conclusion of regional arrangements for the maintenance of international peace and security is endorsed by the UN Charter.[15] These agreements have been adopted in all regions of the world and provide for different degrees of cooperation and integration. Several of them contain references, at different levels of detail, to the principle of non-intervention.

2.2.1 American treaties

Post-Second World War American treaties on hemispheric security were adopted at a time when the United States increasingly felt the need for the support of the Latin American states against communist infiltrations on the continent: as Nicaragua has pointed out, the reaffirmation of a comprehensive prohibition of intervention was thus 'the *quid pro quo* of Latin American participation in regional organization'.[16] The Preamble of the Act of Chapultepec and Article 3 of the Declaration of Mexico, both adopted in 1945, thus included the condemnation of intervention in the internal and external affairs of other states among the principles of international law of the American states.[17] The Act of Chapultepec ushered the way to the 1947 Inter-American Treaty of Reciprocal Assistance (Rio Treaty) and to the Ninth International Conference of American States, held at Bogotá from 30 March to 2 May 1948. The original version of the Rio Treaty did not contain express references to intervention, but its Protocol of Amendment, adopted at San Josè de Costa Rica on 26 July 1975, later added a new Article 12 providing that '[n]othing stipulated in [the Rio Treaty] shall be interpreted as limiting or impairing in any way the principle of nonintervention and the right of all states to choose freely their political, economic and social organization'.[18]

Article I of the American Treaty on Pacific Settlement (the Pact of Bogotá), adopted at the Ninth International Conference of American States, does not explicitly mention the principle of non-intervention, but states that '[t]he High Contracting Parties ... agree to refrain from the threat or the use of force, or from any other means of coercion for the settlement of their controversies, and to have recourse at all times to pacific procedures'.[19] The principle of non-intervention was explicitly incorporated in Article 19 (originally Article 15) of the Charter of the Organization of American States (OAS), also adopted at Bogotá in 1948, in the chapter on the fundamental rights and duties of states:

---

[15] Art 52, UN Charter.

[16] *Nicaragua v USA*, Memorial of Nicaragua (Merits), 30 April 1985, ICJ Pleadings, vol IV, para 331.

[17] Declaration of Reciprocal Assistance and American Solidarity by the Governments Represented at the Inter-American Conference on War and Peace (Mexico City, 3 March 1945) para 5(B) (1945) 108 World Affairs 119; Declaration of Mexico, Art 3, UN Doc A/CN.4/2, 15 December 1948, 64.

[18] Protocol of Amendment to the Inter-American Treaty of Reciprocal Assistance (San Josè of Costa Rica, 26 July 1975) in Eleanor C McDowell (ed), *Digest of United States Practice in International Law 1975* (GPO 1976) 19. An amendment to the Rio Treaty that would have added intervention to the cases that the Organ of Consultation could characterize as aggression was proposed by the Colombian Senate for consideration by the 1948 Bogotá Conference (Novena Conferencia Internacional Americana, *Actas y Documentos*, vol IV (Ministerio de Relaciones Exteriores 1948) 60–1). The amendment, however, was not adopted.

[19] American Treaty on Pacific Settlement (Bogotá, 30 April 1948) 30 UNTS 55.

CONTEMPORARY INTERNATIONAL LAW AND CURRENT SCHOLARLY DEBATE   103

No State or group of States has the right to intervene, directly or indirectly, for any reason whatever, in the internal or external affairs of any other State. The foregoing principle prohibits not only armed force but also any other form of interference or attempted threat against the personality of the State or against its political, economic, and cultural elements.[20]

The first sentence is clearly modelled on Article 1(1) of the Additional Protocol Relative to Nonintervention adopted at the Inter-American Conference for the Maintenance of Peace held in Buenos Aires in 1936.[21] A novelty, however, is the reference to 'group of states' in addition to individual states, which was intended 'to put an end to the doctrinal and the practical movements that were favoring collective intervention during the [Second World] war' and made clear that 'multilateral intervention is as harmful and unacceptable as is unilateral'.[22] The second sentence was contained in the joint Chilean/Peruvian draft submitted at the Bogotá Conference.[23] It appears that the reference to the political, economic, and cultural elements of a state was included with the threat of communist infiltrations in mind, which were not expected to materialize in the form of an invasion.[24] The draft of the provision adopted by the Juridical Subcommittee first and then by the Committee for the Organization of the Inter-American System, which served as the initial negotiating basis at Bogotá, also contained a safety clause ruling out that collective actions undertaken on the basis of the OAS or UN Charters could be considered unlawful interventions.[25] The clause, rephrased, was in the end included in a separate provision (now Article 23).[26]

Unlike Article 19, Article 20 (originally Article 16) of the OAS Charter is not a rule codifying pre-existing customary international law.[27] For the first time, economic coercion is explicitly prohibited in the text of a treaty: 'No State may use or encourage the use of coercive measures of an economic or political character in order to force the

[20] Charter of the Organization of American States (OAS Charter) (Bogotá, 30 April 1948) 119 UNTS 47. The Inter-American Conference on the Problems of War and Peace, which was held at Chapultepec Castle, Mexico City, in 1945 and which started the process of formulating a new pact to strengthen the Inter-American system with a view to submitting it at the Ninth International Conference of American States, envisaged that the fundamental rights and duties of states would be included in a separate annex to the OAS Charter. The Bogotá Conference, however, decided to incorporate them in the main text of the treaty, in what is now Chapter 4. The principle of non-intervention was included in the second draft adopted by the Juridical Subcommittee first and then by the Committee for the Organization of the Inter-American System (CB-10): see Novena Conferencia Internacional Americana, *Actas y Documentos*, vol III, 8.

[21] See Chapter I, Section 9.2. This is expressly stated in Art F of the Mexican draft of the chapter on the fundamental rights and duties of states (CB-130/C.I-10, in Novena Conferencia Internacional Americana, *Actas y Documentos*, vol III, 66). The Buenos Aires formulation was preferred to the more succinct one contained in Art 8 of the Convention on the Rights and Duties of States (Montevideo, 26 December 1933) 165 LNTS 19 ('no state has the right to intervene in the internal or external affairs of another').

[22] Inter-American Juridical Committee, Instrument Relating to Violations of the Principle of Nonintervention, Draft and Report prepared in accordance with Resolution VII of the Fifth Meeting of Consultation of Ministers of Foreign Affairs, CIJ-51, Pan-American Union, General Secretariat, Organization of American States, Washington, DC, 1959, 4.

[23] Anteproyecto de la primera parte de la Carta de la Organización de los Estados Americanos (CB-256/C.I-Sub A-2), Art 11, in Novena Conferencia Internacional Americana, *Actas y Documentos,* vol III, 90.

[24] Comments of the Peruvian delegate, ibid, 221–2.

[25] Proyecto de Pacto Constitutivo del Sistema Interamericano (CB-10), ibid, 8.

[26] ibid, 200–1.

[27] See Chapter I, Section 5.

104   INTERNATIONAL LAW AND THE PRINCIPLE OF NON-INTERVENTION

sovereign will of another State and obtain from it advantages of any kind.'[28] The text was drafted by the special subcommittee appointed by the Committee on Initiatives of the Bogotá Conference to study the topic of economic aggression.[29] The chairman of the subcommittee explained that the provision

> condemns every action or attempted action that tends to force a State, in spite of its sovereignty, to adopt any attitude which that State believes contrary to its interests ... such condemnation is in no wise [*sic*] affected by the nature of the advantages sought by the State that takes or stimulates the coercive action.[30]

Strictly speaking, however, the inclusion of Article 20 was not necessary, as measures 'against the personality of [another state] or against its political, economic, and cultural elements' were already prohibited by the broad language of Article 19: the provision was meant to strengthen the condemnation of economic and political coercion in response to the 'dollar diplomacy' of the United States in the first decades of the 20th century.[31]

Articles 19 and 20 constitute the end result of the efforts to codify the principle of non-intervention started by the Latin American states in the early 19th century as a reaction first to the interventions of the European powers and then to those of the United States, efforts which have led the ICJ to conclude that non-intervention is 'one of the most firmly established traditions of Latin America'.[32] The formulation contained in the OAS Charter would later be used as a model by the UN General Assembly in its resolutions on the principle under examination.

While excluding unilateral interventions, the OAS Charter does not rule out an intervention by the Organization aimed at enforcing the OAS principles. This is implied in Article 23, according to which '[m]easures adopted for the maintenance of peace and security in accordance with existing treaties do not constitute a violation of the principles set forth in Articles 19 and 21'. Such institutionalized intervention

---

[28] The condemnation of economic coercion was contained in the Brazilian and Cuban drafts of the OAS Charter (Novena Conferencia Internacional Americana, *Actas y Documentos*, vol III, 48, 83, 94). The Brazilian draft Declaration on the Rights and Duties of the American States, which, in the original idea, was to be annexed to the OAS Charter, referred to the obtainment of advantages of any kind, but not to the coercion of the sovereign will of another state: 'Es prohibido a un Estado ejercer or amparar presión económica o política sobre cualquier otro, a fin de obtener ventajas de cualquier naturaleza de ese otro, no incluyéndose, entretanto, en la categoría de presión las sanciones adoptadas en obediencia a una determinación de un órgano internacional competente' (Art XII(1) of the Proyecto de Declaración de los Derechos y Deberes de los Estados Americanos, ibid, 83). According to the Cuban draft, '[n]ingun Estado Americano podrá aplicar unilateralmente a otro medidas coercitivas de carácter económico que constituyan una represalia o que tiendan a forzar la voluntad soberana del Estado a que se apliquen' (ibid, 94). For the Cuban delegate, economic aggression was the 'last rampart' of interventionism (ibid, 156).

[29] ibid, 222.

[30] Reproduced in FV García-Amador (ed), *The Inter-American System: Treaties, Conventions & Other Documents*, vol 1, part I (Oceana Publications 1983) 92.

[31] See Chapter I, Section 9.1. The language of Art 20 was also incorporated, at the suggestion of the Cuban delegation, in Art 8 of the Economic Agreement of Bogotá (Novena Conferencia Internacional Americana, *Actas y Documentos*, vol IV, 646–7). Read the texts proposed by Cuba, Chile, and Colombia in ibid, 258–9. The Economic Agreement has not entered into force.

[32] *Asylum Case (Colombia/Peru)* (Judgment) [1950] ICJ Rep 266, 285.

requires a decision by the competent collective organ and cannot be conducted by a member state or group of states acting on their own initiative.[33] Even though Article 20 is not recalled in Article 23, it was agreed at the Bogotá Conference that the prohibition contained therein would not affect the adoption of economic sanctions by international organizations according to their statutes.[34]

The 1985 Protocol of Cartagena de Indias has added further references to the principle of non-intervention in the OAS Charter. It has amended Article 2 (originally Article 4) so as to include the promotion and consolidation of 'representative democracy, with due respect for the principle of nonintervention' among the purposes of the Organization, and has added another principle among those reaffirmed in Article 3 (formerly Article 5), according to which '[e]very State has the right to choose, without external interference, its political, economic, and social system and to organize itself in the way best suited to it, and has the duty to abstain from intervening in the affairs of another State'.

Finally, in 1957 the American states adopted a Protocol to the 1928 Havana Convention on Duties and Rights of States in the Event of Civil Strife, which is examined in the following chapters.[35]

2.2.2 African treaties

In the 1960s, the principle of non-intervention also became popular among the newly independent states of Africa as a safeguard against the neo-colonialist policies of their former metropolises, the interferences of the United States and the Soviet Union, and the subversive activities of neighbouring states. The principle is thus included in both Pan-African and sub-regional agreements.

Article III of the now terminated 1963 Charter of the Organization of African Unity (OAU) identified 'non-interference' in the internal affairs of states as one of the foundational principles of the Organization together with the '[r]espect for the sovereignty and territorial integrity of each State and for its inalienable right to independent existence', and condemned all subversive activities.[36] These principles have been incorporated in the 2000 African Union (AU)'s Constitutive Act (Article 4(g) and (o)), although the respect for the sovereignty and territorial integrity of each state has been omitted.[37] This can be explained in light of the fact that the AU Constitutive Act provides for 'the right of the Union to intervene in a Member State pursuant to a decision of the Assembly in respect of grave circumstances, namely: war crimes, genocide and crimes against humanity' (Article 4(h)) and for 'the right of Member States to request intervention from the Union in order to restore peace and security' (Article 4(j)), which reflects the non-indifference policy of the new organization. The African Union's right of intervention and the member states' obligation of non-interference are reiterated in the 2002 Protocol Relating to the Establishment of the Peace and Security Council

---

[33] Ernesto Dihigo, 'Legality of Intervention under the Charter of the Organization of American States' (1957) 51 ASIL Proceedings 91, 94.

[34] Novena Conferencia Internacional Americana, *Actas y Documentos*, vol III, 222.

[35] See Chapter III, Section 8.1; Chapter V, Table 1.

[36] Art III (2) and (3), Charter of the Organization of African Unity (Addis Ababa, 25 May 1963) 479 UNTS 39.

[37] Constitutive Act of the African Union (Lomé, 11 July 2000) 2158 UNTS 3.

106 INTERNATIONAL LAW AND THE PRINCIPLE OF NON-INTERVENTION

of the African Union,[38] while the 2005 Non-Aggression and Common Defence Pact requires each party to 'prevent its territory and its people from being used for encouraging or committing acts of subversion, hostility, aggression and other harmful practices that might threaten the territorial integrity and sovereignty of a Member State or regional peace and security.'[39] The present Pan-African security system, therefore, is structured around the strict prohibition of 'interference' by individual states and the right of the African Union to 'intervene' on their territory in certain exceptional circumstances through an African Standby Force.[40] Unlike in the OAS Charter, there is no mention of economic coercion in the AU Constitutive Act, which however contains an explicit condemnation of subversive activities absent in the American treaty.[41]

As to treaties adopted at the African sub-regional level, the 2006 Protocol on Non-Aggression and Mutual Defence in the Great Lakes Region requires the parties 'strictly to abide by the duty of non-interference in matters which are within the domestic jurisdiction of any State, in accordance with international law, the Charter of the United Nations, and the Constitutive Act of the African Union' and then proscribes specific conduct that constitutes a violation of the principle of non-intervention as well as of the prohibition of the threat and use of force.[42] Article 3 of the 2019 Protocol Relating to the Peace and Security Council of Central Africa (COPAX), concluded under the framework of the Economic Community of Central African States (ECCAS), also contains the principle of non-interference and the obligation of the states parties not to tolerate or favour the creation or operation on their territory of mercenary, terrorist, subversive, or rebel groups directed against another state.[43] Other African sub-regional treaties only contain a reaffirmation, in general terms, of the prohibition of interference (*ingérence* in the French texts) in the internal affairs of another state (Article 6A(b) of the 1996 Agreement Establishing the Inter-Governmental Authority on Development (IGAD),[44] Article 3 of the 2019 Revised Treaty Instituting ECCAS,[45]

---

[38] Art 4(f), (j), and k, Protocol Relating to the Establishment of the Peace and Security Council of the African Union (Durban, 9 July 2002) <https://au.int/en/treaties/protocol-relating-establishment-peace-and-security-council-african-union>.

[39] Art 5(b), African Union Non-Aggression and Common Defence Pact (Abuja, 31 January 2005) 2656 UNTS 285.

[40] Art 13(3)(c), Protocol Relating to the Establishment of the Peace and Security Council of the African Union.

[41] Art 4(o). See also the OAU Declaration on the Problem of Subversion, which includes, as condemned cases of subversion, 'the use of ... territories for any subversive activity directed from outside Africa against any Member States of the Organization of African Unity', 'press or radio campaigns against any Member States of the Organization of African Unity', and 'fomenting or aggravating racial, religious, linguistic, ethnic or other differences' (paras 2, 4(b), 5(a) of the OAU Declaration on the Problem of Subversion (Accra, 24 October 1965) (1966) 5 ILM 138). The right of peoples to dispose of their wealth and natural resources against external economic exploitation is spelt out in Art 21 of the African Charter on Human and Peoples' Rights (Banjul, 27 June 1981) 1520 UNTS 217.

[42] Art 4, Protocol on Non-Aggression and Mutual Defence in the Great Lakes Region (Nairobi, 30 November 2006) <https://icglr.org/ova_doc/protocol-on-non-aggression-and-mutual-defence-in-the-great-lakes-region/>.

[43] Art 3, Protocol Related to Peace and Security Council of Central Africa (COPAX) (Libreville, 18 December 2019) <www.labase-lextenso.fr/sites/lextenso/files/lextenso_upload/protocole_du_copax.pdf>.

[44] Agreement Establishing the Inter-Governmental Authority on Development (Nairobi, 21 March 1996) <http://treaties.mfa.go.ke/download/231>.

[45] Revised Treaty Instituting the Economic Community of the Central African States (Libreville, 18 December 2019) <www.sgg.cg/JO/2020/congo-jo-2020-27.pdf>. The reference was also contained in the original 1983 version.

CONTEMPORARY INTERNATIONAL LAW AND CURRENT SCHOLARLY DEBATE   107

and Article 7(1) of the 2003 Southern African Development Community (SADC)'s Mutual Defence Pact).[46] Finally, the 1993 Revised Treaty of the Economic Community of West African States (ECOWAS) mentions non-aggression between member states as a fundamental principle of the Organization (Article 4), but not non-intervention.[47] The 2011 Charter of the Conseil de l'Entente also does not mention the principle of non-intervention, although the Organization is founded, inter alia, on the sovereign equality and independence of all member states.[48]

2.2.3 Asian treaties

Article 8 of the 1945 Pact of the League of Arab States does not expressly mention the principle of non-intervention, although it commits the member states to respect the form of government of the other member states and not to take any action to change it.[49] The other regional treaties concluded among the Asian countries employ the expression 'non-interference' instead of 'non-intervention' like their African counterparts. The language, for instance, is incorporated in Article 2 of the 2008 Charter of the Organisation of Islamic Cooperation (formerly known as the Organisation of the Islamic Conference), which defers to 'the Charter of the United Nations, international law and international humanitarian law' for the definition of its scope.[50] Article 2 of the 1976 Treaty of Amity and Cooperation in Southeast Asia states that the contracting parties will be guided by, inter alia, the '[m]utual respect for the independence, sovereignty, equality, territorial integrity and national identity of all nations; ... The right of every State to lead its national existence free from external interference, subversion or coercion; ... Non-interference in the internal affairs of one another'.[51] The principle of non-interference is reaffirmed in Article 2(2)(e) of the 2007 Charter of the Association of Southeast Asian Nations (ASEAN), although only towards other member states.[52]

---

[46] SADC Mutual Defence Pact (Dar es Salaam, 26 August 2003) <www.sadc.int/document/sadc-mutual-defence-pact-2003>.

[47] Revised Treaty of the Economic Community of West African States (ECOWAS) (Cotonou, 24 July 1993) <https://ecowas.int/wp-content/uploads/2022/08/Revised-treaty-1.pdf>. The previous version of the Treaty, adopted in Lagos in 1975, also did not mention the principle of non-intervention. The intervention of ECOWAS in internal conflicts is envisaged in Art 25 of the 1999 Protocol Relating to the Mechanism for Conflict Prevention, Management, Resolution, Peace-Keeping and Security (Lomé, 10 December 1999) (2000) 5 JCSL 231.

[48] Art 3, Charter of the Conseil de l'Entente (Cotonou, 5 December 2011) <www.conseildelentente.org/images/pdf/charte/charte_du_conseil_de_lentente.pdf>.

[49] Pact of the League of Arab States (Cairo, 22 March 1945) 70 UNTS 237.

[50] Charter of the Organisation of Islamic Cooperation (Dakar, revised 14 March 2008), Art 2(4): 'All Member States undertake to respect national sovereignty, independence and territorial integrity of other Member States and shall refrain from interfering in the internal affairs of others'. Art 2(5): 'All Member States undertake to contribute to the maintenance of international peace and security and to refrain from interfering in each other's internal affairs as enshrined in the present Charter, the Charter of the United Nations, international law and international humanitarian law'. Art 2(6) also refers to Art 2(7) of the UN Charter and imposes an obligation of non-intervention in the domestic affairs of member states on the Organisation and its organs. The English text of the Charter is at <www.oic-oci.org/page/?p_id=53&p_ref=27&lan=en>.

[51] Treaty of Amity and Cooperation in Southeast Asia (Denpasar, 24 February 1976) <https://treaties.un.org/doc/Publication/UNTS/Volume%201025/volume-1025-I-15063-English.pdf>.

[52] Charter of the Association of Southeast Asian Nations (ASEAN) (Singapore, 20 November 2007) 2624 UNTS 223. On non-interference in the ASEAN framework, see Eric Corthay, 'The ASEAN Doctrine of Non-Interference in Light of the Fundamental Principle of Non-Intervention' (2015) 17 Asian-Pacific L & PJ, 1; Tom Ginsburg, *Democracies and International Law* (CUP 2021) 198–203.

108 INTERNATIONAL LAW AND THE PRINCIPLE OF NON-INTERVENTION

Article 2(2)(f) of the same treaty also includes the 'respect for the right of every Member State to lead its national existence free from external interference, subversion and coercion' among the principles in accordance with which the Association and its members act. Article 2 of the 2002 Charter of the Shanghai Cooperation Organisation (SCO) provides that its member states shall comply with, among other things, 'non-interference in internal affairs'[53] and similar language is contained in Article 3 of the 1993 Charter of the Commonwealth of Independent States.[54] Finally, the principle of non-interference in matters falling within the national jurisdiction of the member states is included in Article 5 of the 2002 Charter of the Collective Security Treaty Organization as a limit to the powers of the Organization.[55]

It has been suggested that the non-interference language indicates that, in the aforementioned treaties, the prohibition of intervention is conceived more broadly as also encompassing non-coercive acts like criticism of the policies of another state, in particular those affecting human rights.[56] The difference between interference and intervention is explored in Chapter III.[57]

2.2.4 European treaties and other documents

Most European regional treaties do not contain explicit references to the principle of non-intervention. The only exceptions were contained in treaties signed among the Eastern European states during the Cold War, namely Article 8 of the now-defunct 1955 Warsaw Pact and Article 1(2) of the 1959 Charter of the Council for Mutual Economic Assistance (COMECON).[58] Indeed, as I show later,[59] it was the socialist bloc that became, after the adoption of the UN Charter, the most fervent supporter of the principle of non-intervention, while the Western states tended to see it as co-terminous with the prohibition of the use of force: as this was already contained in the Charter, for them the inclusion of a separate prohibition of intervention in the regional treaties was not necessary.[60] It was only in the mid-1970s, in a period of détente between the two blocs, that the European states from both East and West adopted a

---

[53] Charter of the Shanghai Cooperation Organisation (St Petersburg, 7 June 2002) 2896 UNTS 245 (English translation).

[54] Charter of the Commonwealth of the Independent States (Minsk, 22 January 1993) 1819 UNTS 58 (English translation).

[55] Charter of the Collective Security Treaty Organization (Chisinau, 7 October 2002) 2235 UNTS 89 (English translation).

[56] Hitoshi Nasu, 'Revisiting the Principle of Non-Intervention: A Structural Principle of International Law or a Political Obstacle to Regional Security in Asia?' (2013) 3 Asian JIL 25, 36–7. See, for instance, ASEAN's failure to condemn the 2021 military coup in Myanmar (Vanessa Chong and Tanyalak Thongyoojaroen, 'Beyond the Coup in Myanmar: The ASEAN Way Must Change' (*Just Security*, 14 May 2021) <www.justsecurity.org/76126/beyond-the-coup-in-myanmar-the-asean-way-must-change/>).

[57] See Chapter III, Section 3.

[58] Treaty of Friendship, Cooperation and Mutual Assistance Between the People's Republic of Albania, the People's Republic of Bulgaria, the Hungarian People's Republic, the German Democratic Republic, the Polish People's Republic, the Rumanian People's Republic, the Union of Soviet Socialist Republics and the Czechoslovak Republic (Warsaw Pact) (Warsaw, 14 May 1955) <https://avalon.law.yale.edu/20th_cent ury/warsaw.asp> (English translation); Charter of the Council for Mutual Economic Assistance (Sofia, 14 December 1959) 368 UNTS 264 (English translation). The violation of Art 8 of the Warsaw Pact was claimed by several states on the occasion of the 1956 Soviet intervention in Hungary (see eg the statements by France and Cuba in UN Doc S/PV.746, 28 October 1956, paras 91, 119).

[59] See Chapter III, Section 7.

[60] ibid.

non-binding document that expressly includes non-intervention among the ten principles guiding their mutual relations. Principle VI of the Final Act of the Conference on Security and Co-operation in Europe (CSCE), signed in Helsinki on 1 August 1975 by thirty-five countries, thus provides that '[t]he participating States will refrain from any intervention, direct or indirect, individual or collective, in the internal or external affairs falling within the domestic jurisdiction of another participating State, regardless of their mutual relations.'[61] After this general reaffirmation of the principle, the Helsinki Final Act specifically condemns not only armed intervention, but also economic and political coercion and subversion, thus combining both the American and African experiences.[62]

Although it is not a treaty and is therefore not binding on its signatories,[63] the Helsinki Final Act reflects the *communis opinio* of all European states as well as that of the United States and Canada: in the *Nicaragua* Judgment (Merits), the ICJ noted that 'while these principles were presented as applying to the mutual relations among the participating States, it can be inferred that the text testifies to the existence, and the acceptance ... of a customary principle which has universal application.'[64] The continuing relevance of the Helsinki Final Act was reaffirmed after the end of the Cold War in the Charter of Paris for a New Europe, adopted at the Meeting of the Heads of State or Government of the participating states of the CSCE in 1990.[65]

---

[61] Final Act of the 1st CSCE Summit of Heads of State or Government (Helsinki, 1 August 1975) (1975) 14 ILM 1292. Although it saw the participation of thirty-five states across blocs, the CSCE (1972–5) was originally an idea of the socialist bloc and aimed to produce a declaration of principles governing relations between states in the field of security (Basket I) and to deal with cooperation between states in the economic, technical, and humanitarian fields (Baskets II and III): Foreign and Commonwealth Office (FCO), *Documents on British Policy Overseas*, Series III, vol II (The Stationary Office 1997) 250–1. The Russians' main purpose was the maintenance of the status quo in Europe, hence, the most important principles for them were that of the inviolability of frontiers and of non-intervention (ibid, 319). The ten principles were drafted by Sub-Committee 1 and were adopted by consensus.

[62] The attempts by the Soviet Union to also include references to 'hostile propaganda' and to the 'respect for the cultural foundations of states' were unsuccessful (FCO, *Documents*, 297). See also the Finnish proposal, inspired by the Russians but not adopted, which provided that the participants would 'respect the political, economic and cultural foundations of other participating States as well as their right to determine their own legislative and regulatory systems' (ibid, 298). The Soviet Union also wanted a reference to the principle of non-intervention in the Preamble of Basket III of the Act, which was unacceptable for the Western states: as a compromise solution, a clause was added at the end of the Declaration stating that all the principles 'are of primary significance and, accordingly, they will be equally and unreservedly applied, each of them being interpreted taking into account the others' (Richard Tötterman, 'Some Principles of International Law as Reflected in the Final Act of the CSCE' in Essays in Honour of Erik Castrén (Finnish Branch of the International Law Association 1979) 241, 246–7).

[63] It was particularly the Western states that were keen on ensuring that the Final Act was not binding (FCO, *Documents*, 454).

[64] *Nicaragua v USA*, para 204. The Latvian Constitutional Court has also found that, although the Final Act is not a treaty, 'it can be used to determine the content of the principles of international law' (The Constitutional Court of the Republic of Latvia, Judgment on behalf of the Republic of Latvia, 29 November 2007, Case No 2007-10-0102, para 71.1, English translation at <www.satv.tiesa.gov.lv/web/wp-content/uplo ads/2007/04/2007-10-0102_Spriedums_ENG.pdf>). For Cassese, the Helsinki Final Act has three effects. First, states are politically accountable for disregarding the standards provided therein. Secondly, the signatory states are estopped from challenging the validity of the content of the principles included in the Final Act. Thirdly, the Final Act might be a powerful factor in the formation of customary international law (Antonio Cassese, *Self-Determination of Peoples: A Legal Reappraisal* (CUP 1995) 291–2).

[65] Charter of Paris for a New Europe (Paris, 21 November 1990) 5 <www.osce.org/mc/39516?download= true>.

110 INTERNATIONAL LAW AND THE PRINCIPLE OF NON-INTERVENTION

2.3 Other Treaties

References to the principle of non-intervention have also been added in bilateral and multilateral cooperation treaties and peace agreements, including Article 5 of the 1953 Treaty of Friendship and Collaboration between Yugoslavia, Greece, and Turkey,[66] Article 1 of the 1954 Treaty of Friendship and Cooperation between Pakistan and Turkey,[67] the Preamble of the 1954 Agreement between India and the People's Republic of China (PRC) on Trade and Intercourse between the Tibet Region of China and India,[68] Article 3 of the 1955 Baghdad Pact,[69] Articles 4, 20(c) and (d), and 22 of the 1973 Agreement on Ending the War and Restoring Peace in Viet-Nam,[70] Article II of the 1976 Basic Treaty of Friendship and Cooperation between Australia and Japan,[71] Article V of the 1977 Panama Canal Treaty,[72] Article 1 of the 1978 Soviet–Afghan Treaty of Friendship, Good-neighbourliness and Cooperation,[73] Articles I and II of the 1988 Bilateral Agreement between Afghanistan and Pakistan on the Principles of Mutual Relations, in particular on Non-Interference and Non-Intervention,[74] Principle E of the 1988 Agreement between Angola, Cuba, and South Africa on Principles for a Peaceful Settlement in Southwestern Africa,[75] Article 6(2) of the 1995 Interim Accord Between the Hellenic Republic and the Former Yugoslav Republic of Macedonia (FYROM),[76] and Article 6 of the 1997 Agreement between the Russian Federation and Ukraine on the Status and Conditions of the Russian Federation Black Sea Fleet's Stay on Ukrainian Territory.[77]

Furthermore, international humanitarian law treaties applicable to non-international armed conflicts (NIACs) have reaffirmed the principle of

---

[66] Treaty of Friendship and Collaboration between the Turkish Republic, the Kingdom of Greece, and the Federal People's Republic of Yugoslavia (Ankara, 28 February 1953) <https://avalon.law.yale.edu/20th_cent ury/eu001.asp>.

[67] Treaty of Friendship and Cooperation between Pakistan and Turkey (Karachi, 2 April 1954), Italian translation of the text in (1954) 18 *Relazioni internazionali* 458.

[68] Agreement between the Republic of India and the People's Republic of China on Trade and Intercourse between Tibet Region of China and India (Beijing, 29 April 1954) 299 UNTS 70.

[69] Pact of Mutual Cooperation Between the Kingdom of Iraq, the Republic of Turkey, the United Kingdom, the Dominion of Pakistan, and the Kingdom of Iran (Baghdad, 24 February 1955) <https://ava lon.law.yale.edu/20th_century/baghdad.asp>.

[70] Agreement on Ending the War and Restoring Peace in Viet-Nam (Paris, 27 January 1973) 935 UNTS 4.

[71] Basic Treaty of Friendship and Cooperation between Australia and Japan (Tokyo, 16 June 1976) <www. dfat.gov.au/geo/japan/Pages/basic-treaty-of-friendship-and-co-operation-between-australia-and-japan>.

[72] Panama Canal Treaty (Washington, DC, 7 September 1977) 1280 UNTS 3.

[73] Treaty of Friendship, Good-neighbourliness and Cooperation (Moscow, 5 December 1978) (1980) 19 ILM 1.

[74] Bilateral Agreement between the Republic of Afghanistan and the Islamic Republic of Pakistan on the Principles of Mutual Relations, in particular on Non-Interference and Non-Intervention (Geneva, 14 April 1988) (1988) 27 ILM 578.

[75] Agreement between Angola, Cuba, and South Africa on Principles for a Peaceful Settlement in Southwestern Africa (Geneva, 5 August 1988) <https://digitalarchive.wilsoncenter.org/document/118287. pdf?v=a87b1e203ac5f6080d1f6b8c5c19a1b0>.

[76] Greece and The Former Yugoslav Republic of Macedonia Interim Accord (with related letters and translations of the Interim Accord in the languages of the Contracting Parties) (New York, 13 September 1995) 1891 UNTS 3.

[77] Agreement between the Russian Federation and Ukraine on the Status and Conditions of the Russian Federation Black Sea Fleet's Stay on Ukrainian Territory (Kharkiv, 21 April, 2010) <https://cis-legislation. com/document.fwx?rgn=31091>. Russia unilaterally terminated the treaty on 31 March 2014.

CONTEMPORARY INTERNATIONAL LAW AND CURRENT SCHOLARLY DEBATE 111

non-intervention in order to avoid that they might be invoked to legitimize armed opposition groups. Article 3 of the 1977 Protocol II additional to the 1949 Geneva Conventions on the Protection of Victims of War, in particular, provides that

1. Nothing in this Protocol shall be invoked for the purpose of affecting the sovereignty of a State or the responsibility of the government, by all legitimate means, to maintain or re-establish law and order in the State or to defend the national unity and territorial integrity of the State.
2. Nothing in this Protocol shall be invoked as a justification for intervening, directly or indirectly, for any reason whatever, in the armed conflict or in the internal or external affairs of the High Contracting Party in the territory of which that conflict occurs.[78]

The reference to 'legitimate means' in paragraph 1 limits the powers of a government to maintain and restore internal law and order: a state, therefore, could not claim that the choice of means and methods of warfare used to quell an insurrection in a NIAC is a purely internal affair.[79] Paragraph 2 applies not only to states but also to international organizations, although it leaves unaffected the UN collective security mechanism.[80] The language of paragraph 2 is also incorporated in Article I(5) of the Protocol on Prohibitions or Restrictions on the Use of Mines, Booby-Traps and Other Devices to the 1980 UN Weapons Convention (as amended in 1996)[81] and Article 22(5) of the 1999 Second Hague Protocol for the Protection of Cultural Property in the Event of Armed Conflict,[82] while text similar to that of paragraph 1 is contained in Article 8(3) of the 1998 Rome Statute of the International Criminal Court (ICC).[83]

Finally, the principle of non-intervention appears in a number of thematic treaties. Article 2(2) of the 1988 Narcotics Convention, for instance, indicates the principle of non-intervention as one of the limits that the parties must observe when adopting measures to address illicit trafficking in narcotic drugs and psychotropic substances having an international dimension more effectively.[84] Likewise, Article 4(1) of the 2000 UN Convention against Transnational Organized Crime provides that 'States Parties shall carry out their obligations under this Convention in a manner consistent with the principles of sovereign equality and territorial integrity of States

---

[78] Protocol Additional to the Geneva Conventions of 12 August 1949, and relating to the Protection of Victims of Non-International Armed Conflicts (Protocol II) (Geneva, 8 June 1977) 1125 UNTS 609.

[79] Yves Sandoz, Christophe Swinarski, and Bruno Zimmermann (eds), *Commentary on the Additional Protocols of 8 June 1977 to the Geneva Conventions of 12 August 1949* (Nijhoff 1987) para 4501.

[80] ibid, paras 4503–4. The provision also does not prevent the International Committee of the Red Cross from offering its services and assistance, although the parties remain free to turn them down (ibid, para 4505).

[81] Protocol on Prohibitions or Restrictions on the Use of Mines, Booby-Traps and Other Devices as amended on 3 May 1996 (Protocol II) annexed to the Convention on Prohibitions or Restrictions on the Use of Certain Conventional Weapons Which May be Deemed to be Excessively Injurious or to have Indiscriminate Effects 2048 UNTS 93.

[82] Second Protocol to The Hague Convention of 1954 for the Protection of Cultural Property in the Event of Armed Conflict (The Hague, 26 March 1999) 2253 UNTS 212.

[83] Statute of the International Criminal Court (Rome, 17 July 1998) 2187 UNTS 90.

[84] UN Convention against Illicit Traffic in Narcotic Drugs and Psychotropic Substances (Vienna, 20 December 1988) 1582 UNTS 95.

and that of non-intervention in the domestic affairs of other States'.[85] Article 41(1) of the 1961 Vienna Convention on Diplomatic Relations (VCDR) and Article 55(1) of the 1963 Vienna Convention on Consular Relations (VCCR) also recall that diplomatic and consular agents and all other persons enjoying diplomatic and consular privileges and immunities have an obligation not to interfere in the internal affairs of the receiving state.[86] The former provision was debated before the ICJ: when, in 2009, the ousted president of Honduras, Zelaya, returned to his country on the eve of presidential elections and found refuge in the Brazilian Embassy in Tegucigalpa, Honduras filed an application instituting proceedings against Brazil claiming a breach of, inter alia, Article 41 of the VCDR based on the fact that the diplomatic premises were being used 'to conduct illegal activities against the lawful and legitimate Government of Honduras by calling for insurrection by Honduran nationals against the constitutionally established authority'.[87] The case was discontinued by Honduras in 2010.

3. The Principle of Non-Intervention and Customary International Law

As shown in Chapter I, the principle of non-intervention was already a customary international law rule by the mid-19th century at the latest. This status does not change after 1945. During the Cold War, in particular, all three main groups of states (Western, socialist, and non-aligned) converged on non-intervention as a general principle, even though they disagreed on its exact content.[88] For the non-aligned countries, the principle of non-intervention was 'an article of faith'[89] and a legal shield against possible resurgences of European colonialism and against American and Soviet interferences. Unsurprisingly, therefore, the Declarations of the 1955 Asian–African Conference at Bandung and of the 1961 First Conference of Heads of State or Government of Non-Aligned Countries at Belgrade, the 1964 Programme for Peace and International Co-operation adopted at the end of the Second Conference of Heads of State or Government of Non-Aligned Countries at Cairo, and the 1965 Declaration on the Problem of Subversion adopted at Accra by the Heads of State and Government

---

[85] United Nations Convention against Transnational Organized Crime (Palermo, 12 December 2000) 225 UNTS 209.

[86] Vienna Convention on Diplomatic Relations (Vienna, 18 April 1961) 500 UNTS 95; Vienna Convention on Consular Relations (Vienna, 24 April 1963) 596 UNTS 261. The prohibition applies to a diplomat's comments and activities undertaken in their personal capacity (Eileen Denza, *Diplomatic Law: Commentary on the Vienna Convention on Diplomatic Relations* (4th edn, OUP 2016) 377).

[87] *Honduras v Brazil*, para 6.

[88] As Judge Lachs points out in the *North Sea Continental Shelf Cases*, 'a general rule of international law [cannot] be established by the fiat of one or of a few, or—as it was once claimed—by the consensus of European States only' (*North Sea Continental Shelf Cases (Federal Republic of Germany v Denmark; Federal Republic of Germany v Netherlands)* (Judgment) [1969] ICJ Rep 3, Dissenting Opinion of Judge Lachs, 228).

[89] UN Doc A/C.1/SR.1403, para 32.

CONTEMPORARY INTERNATIONAL LAW AND CURRENT SCHOLARLY DEBATE   113

of the African States all reaffirmed the principle of non-intervention.[90] The principle was also reiterated by the OAS General Assembly[91] and Permanent Council.[92]

In the post-Stalin Soviet Union, non-intervention was considered a fundamental principle of both the international law applicable among socialist states and the international law aimed at the peaceful coexistence of states with different social and economic systems.[93] That said, it had two significant limitations. First, in the relations among socialist states, it had a position subordinated to socialist internationalism and international proletarian solidarity, which justified interventions to suppress counter-revolutionary movements.[94] Even when intervening in Hungary, Czechoslovakia, and Afghanistan, however, the Soviet Union paid formal deference to the principle of non-intervention by relying on the (dubious) invitation of the local authorities.[95] Secondly, the law of peaceful coexistence, including the principle of non-intervention, was not considered applicable in regard to relations between colonial powers and non-independent peoples: the latter could thus be lawfully supported by other states in their struggle for self-determination.[96]

The PRC has also been a strong supporter of the doctrine of sovereignty and of its corollary, the principle of non-intervention (or rather of non-interference, as the Chinese prefer to call it).[97] The Five Principles of Peaceful Coexistence (known as *Pancha Shila* in their Indian denomination), enunciated in the Preamble of the 1954 Agreement on Trade and Intercourse between the Tibet Region of China and India, include, in addition to mutual respect for each state's territorial integrity and sovereignty, also mutual non-aggression and non-interference in internal affairs.[98] The Five

---

[90] The Ten Bandung Principles, in particular, include not only '[a]bstention from intervention or interference in the internal affairs of another country', but also the much broader '[a]bstention by any country from exerting pressures on other countries'. The text of the Final Communiqué of the Asian-African Conference of Bandung (Bandung, 24 April 1955) is available at <www.cvce.eu/en/obj/final_communique_of_the_asian_african_conference_of_bandung_24_april_1955-en-676237bd-72f7-471f-949a-88b6ae513585.html>.

[91] AG/RES. 78 (II-0/72) on Strengthening of the Principles of Nonintervention and the Self-Determination of Peoples and Measures to Guarantee Their Observance, 21 April 1972, OEA/Ser.P/II-0.2, 28 April 1972, vol II, Corr. 1, 43–5; AG/RES. 128 (III-0/73) on Principles Governing Relations Among the American States, 15 April 1973, OEA/Ser.P/III-0.2, 15 April 1973, vol I, 137–8; AG/RES. 782 (XV-0/85) on the Reaffirmation of the Principle of Nonintervention, 9 December 1985, OEA/Ser.P/XV.0.2, 2 April 1986, vol I, 44–5. The first two resolutions were referred to by the ICJ in *Nicaragua v USA*, para 204.

[92] Resolution CP/RES. 424 (612/85) on the Reaffirmation of the Principle of Nonintervention, 1 May 1985.

[93] Serge Krylov, 'Les notions principales du droit des gens (la doctrine soviétique du droit international)' (1947) 70 Recueil des Cours 407, 428–9, 434; RJ Vincent, *Nonintervention and International Order* (Princeton University Press 2015) 183.

[94] Kazimierz Grzybowski, 'Soviet Theory of International Law for the Seventies' (1983) 77 AJIL 862, 867–8.

[95] Vincent, *Nonintervention*, 178.

[96] Grzybowski, 'Soviet Theory', 865. See Brezhnev's speech at the Twenty-Third Congress of the Communist Party (1966), quoted in Stephen M Schwebel, 'The Brezhnev Doctrine Repealed and Peaceful Co-Existence Enacted' (1972) 66 AJIL 816, 818–19.

[97] Jiangyu Wand and Huaer Cheng, 'China's Approach to International Law: From Traditional Westphalianism to Aggressive Instrumentalism in the Xi Jinping Era' (2022) 10 CJCL 140, 141. Like other communist countries, however, China was in favour of supporting national liberation movements in the context of decolonization (Vincent, *Nonintervention*, 172).

[98] Lazar Focsaneanu, 'Les "cinq principes" de coexistence et le droit international' (1956) 2 AFDI 150, 150. The principles, including that of non-intervention, were already contained in Art 5 of the Treaty of Friendship, Alliance and Mutual Assistance between the People's Republic of China and the Soviet Union (Focsaneanu, 'Les "cinq principes"', 150–1).

114 INTERNATIONAL LAW AND THE PRINCIPLE OF NON-INTERVENTION

Principles of Peaceful Coexistence were incorporated in a Joint Statement by the prime ministers of the PRC and India on 28 June 1954,[99] in the Joint Statement by the prime ministers of the PRC and Burma issued the following day, and in the abovementioned Bandung Declaration. It has been observed that 'Chinese scholars of international law regard the Five Principles as having a high degree of normative weight because they sum up the most basic principles of international law and are recognized by all States'.[100] The Five Principles were reaffirmed by India, China, and Myanmar in 2014 on the 60th anniversary of their adoption.[101]

As for the Western states, they never seriously questioned the general obligation not to intervene in the domestic affairs of other countries, although they were initially reluctant to extend its scope to forms of coercion other than armed force and subversion.[102] In the end, the Western states did not oppose the broad language prohibiting all forms of coercion contained in the General Assembly's Declaration on Friendly Relations and the Helsinki Final Act.

After the fall of the Berlin Wall and the dismantlement of the communist bloc, reaffirmations of the principle of non-intervention have continued, most prominently in the UN Millennium Declaration[103] and in the 2005 World Summit Outcome Document,[104] which both use the 'non-interference' language. In the 2016 Declaration on the Promotion of International Law, Russia and China also stressed that they 'fully support the principle of non-intervention in the internal or external affairs of States'.[105] The 2018 Qingdao Declaration of the Council of Heads of State of the SCO affirms the commitment of the member states

> to strict compliance with the goals and principles of the UN Charter, primarily ... non-interference in their internal affairs ... and other universally recognised norms of international law aimed at the maintenance of peace and security, ... [and] the right of nations to determine their future and to choose their political, socioeconomic and cultural path.[106]

It additionally condemns 'the interference in the domestic affairs of other states under the pretence of combatting terrorism and extremism ... as well as the use of terrorist, extremist and radical groups for one's own purposes'.[107] On 23 June 2020, Iran and Russia stressed their endorsement of the principle of non-intervention and condemned as a violation of this principle 'any interference by States in the internal

---

[99] Eric Yong-Joong Lee, 'Early Development of Modern International Law in East Asia—With Special Reference to China, Japan and Korea' (2002) 4 J His Intl L 42, 70.

[100] Björn Ahl, 'China' in *MPEPIL Online* (last updated January 2008) para 9.

[101] 'Xi's speech at "Five Principles of Peaceful Coexistence" anniversary', 7 July 2014 <www.china.org.cn/world/2014-07/07/content_32876905.htm>.

[102] See Chapter III, Section 7.

[103] GA Res 55/2, 18 September 2000, para 4.

[104] GA Res 60/1, 16 September 2005, para 6.

[105] Declaration of the People's Republic of China and the Russian Federation on the Promotion of International Law (Beijing, 25 June 2016) para 4 <www.fmprc.gov.cn/mfa_eng/wjdt_665385/2649_665393/201608/t20160801_679466.html>.

[106] Qingdao Declaration of the Council of Heads of State of Shanghai Cooperation Organisation (10 June 2018) 2 <www.iri.edu.ar/wp-content/uploads/2018/09/a2018eurasiaDoc2QingdaoDeclaration.pdf>.

[107] ibid, 3.

CONTEMPORARY INTERNATIONAL LAW AND CURRENT SCHOLARLY DEBATE   115

or external affairs of other States with the aim of forging change of legitimate governments', 'any action or attempt in whatever form or under whatever pretext to destabilize or to undermine the stability of another State or of any of its institutions', the 'extraterritorial application of national law by States not in conformity with international law', and attempts at prejudicing

> the sovereign and inalienable right of a State to determine its own political, economic, cultural and social system, to develop its international relations and to exercise permanent sovereignty over its natural resources in accordance with the will of its people, without outside intervention, interference, subversion, coercion or threat in any form whatsoever.[108]

The Non-Aligned Movement has also reiterated its commitment to non-intervention and its rejection of regime change from outside.[109] Finally, several countries have incorporated the principle of non-intervention in their constitution[110] and military manuals[111] and have explicitly stated that it reflects customary international law.[112]

---

[108] UN Doc A/74/930-S/2020/588, 25 June 2020, Annex, paras 4–7.

[109] See eg XVII Ministerial Conference of the Non-Aligned Movement (Algiers, 26–29 May 2014), Final Document, UN Doc A/68/966-S/2014/573, 19 August 2014, 13.

[110] See eg Art 89(x) of the 1917 Constitution of Mexico (as amended); Art 4 of the 1988 Constitution of Brazil (as amended through 2017); Art 7 of the 2004 Constitution of Qatar; Art 14 of the 1965 Constitution of Romania (the present Constitution, adopted in 1991, no longer mentions the principle of non-intervention); the Preamble of the 1982 Constitution of the PRC; and Art 49(1) of the 1991 Constitution of the Republic of North Macedonia (as amended in 1992).

[111] Ministère des Armées, Manuel de droit des opérations militaires (2 February 2023) 67, 77 <www.defense.gouv.fr/actualites/droit-operations-militaires-manuel-inedit-au-service-armees-francaises>; US Department of Defense, Law of War Manual, June 2015 (updated December 2016), 1047, 1064–5; New Zealand Defence Force, Manual of Armed Forces Law, 2nd edn, vol 4: Law of Armed Conflict, DM 69, 2017, para 16.2.3; Norwegian Ministry of Defence, Manual of the Law of Armed Conflict, 2013 (English edn 2018) para 1.4; Danish Ministry of Defence—Defence Command Denmark, Military Manual on International Law Relevant to Danish Armed Forces in International Operations, September 2016, 33; Canada's Office of the Judge Advocate General, Law of Armed Conflict at the Operational and Tactical Levels, Joint Doctrine Manual, B-GJ-005-104/FP-021, 2001, para 1703.

[112] See Cameroon (*Case Concerning the Land and Maritime Boundary between Cameroon and Nigeria (Cameroon v Nigeria: Equatorial Guinea intervening)* (Counter-claims) [2002] ICJ Rep 303, para 310 (hereafter *Cameroon v Nigeria*)); DRC (*Armed Activities on the Territory of the Congo (Democratic Republic of the Congo v Uganda)* (hereafter *DRC v Uganda*), Memorial of the DRC (Merits), 6 July 2000, vol I, para 3.36); Nicaragua (*Nicaragua v USA*, Memorial of Nicaragua, para 459); Bosnia and Herzegovina (*Application of the Convention on the Prevention and Punishment of the Crime of Genocide (Bosnia and Herzegovina v Serbia and Montenegro)* (hereafter *Bosnian Genocide*), Application instituting proceedings, 20 March 1993, para 135(i) and (j)); Ecuador (*Case Concerning Aerial Herbicide Spraying (Ecuador v Colombia)*, Reply of Ecuador, vol I, 31 January 2011, paras 5.8–5.9 <www.icj-cij.org/case/138>); Romania (UN Doc A/C.1/1403, 9 December 1965, 301); Yugoslavia (A/C.6/1178, 23 September 1970, 7); Thailand (A/C.1/1398, 6 December 1965, 264); United Arab Republic (UAR) (A/C.1/1403, 299); Bahrain, Egypt, Saudi Arabia, and United Arab Emirates (UAE) (*Appeal Relating to the Jurisdiction of the ICAO Council under Article 84 of the Convention on International Civil Aviation (Bahrain, Egypt, Saudi Arabia and UAE v Qatar)*, Joint Application instituting proceedings, 4 July 2018, para 8 <www.icj-cij.org/case/173>); Iran (Declaration of General Staff of the Armed Forces of the Islamic Republic of Iran Regarding International Law Applicable to the Cyberspace, July 2020, Art III(1) <https://nournews.ir/n/53144>); Ministry for Foreign Affairs of Finland, 'International Law and Cyberspace—Finland's National Positions', 15 October 2020, 3 <https://um.fi/documents/35732/0/KyberkannatPDF_EN.pdf/12bbbbde-623b-9f86-b254-07d5af3c6d85?t=1603097522727>); Costa Rica (Ministerio de Relaciones Exteriores y Culto, Costa Rica's position on the application of international law in cyberspace, 2023, para 23 <https://docs-library.unoda.org/Open-Ended_

The existence of 'an extensive pattern of treaties in the same terms' is also an indication of the customary status of an international law rule.[113] As the previous section shows, there is a long list of treaties, in all regions of the world, that have incorporated the obligation not to intervene in the domestic affairs of other states and that have been broadly ratified. Numerous UN General Assembly resolutions have also reaffirmed the principle of non-intervention.[114] Their sheer number makes their enumeration pointless. The most significant ones include Resolution 290 (IV) of 1 December 1949 (Essentials of Peace);[115] Resolution 380 (V) of 17 November 1950 (Peace Through Deeds);[116] Resolution 1514 (XV) of 14 December 1960 containing the Declaration on the Granting of Independence to Colonial Countries and Peoples;[117] Resolution 2131 (XX) of 21 December 1965 adopting the Declaration on the Inadmissibility of Intervention in the Domestic Affairs of States and the Protection of Their Independence and Sovereignty;[118] Resolution 2160 (XXI) of 30 November 1966 on the Strict Observance of the Prohibition of the Threat or Use of Force in International Relations and of the Right of Peoples to Self-Determination;[119] Resolution 2225 (XXI) of 19 December 1966 on the Status of the Implementation of

Working_Group_on_Information_and_Communication_Technologies_-_(2021)/Costa_Rica_-_Position _Paper_-_International_Law_in_Cyberspace.pdf>); Denmark (Jeppe Mejer Kjelgaard and Ulf Melgaard, 'Denmark's Position Paper on the Application of International Law in Cyberspace' (2023) 92 Nordic J Int'l L 1, 4 (advance access)); Germany (A/76/136, 13 July 2021, 34); Switzerland (A/76/136, 87); United Kingdom (A/76/136, 116); United States (A/76/136, 139); and Russia (Application of the International Convention for the Suppression of the Financing of Terrorism and of the International Convention on the Elimination of All Forms of Racial Discrimination (Ukraine v Russian Federation), Oral proceedings, CR 2017/4, 9 March 2017, 10 am, 25, 37 <www.icj-cij.org/case/166>). Other states have qualified all principles contained in the Declaration on Friendly Relations as 'general principles of international law' binding on all states (see eg Kenya, UN Doc A/C.6/1182, 25 September 1970, para 60; Hungary, A/C.6/SR.1179, 24 September 1970, para 35).

[113] James Crawford, Brownlie's Principles of Public International Law (9th edn, OUP 2019) 22. More cautiously, the ILC's draft Conclusion 11(2) on the identification of customary international law states that '[t]he fact that a rule is set forth in a number of treaties may, but does not necessarily, indicate that the treaty rule reflects a rule of customary international law' ([2018] YB ILC, vol II, part two, 105).

[114] The ILC's Draft Declaration on Rights and Duties of States (1949) also contains a general duty of states not to intervene in the internal or external affairs of other states (Art 3) and a more specific duty not to foment civil strife and prevent the organization of activities to that aim within a state's own territory (Art 4) ([1949] YB ILC 286, 287). Even though for two years the draft Declaration was considered and commented on by states at the UN General Assembly, no further official action was ever taken, and the Declaration has remained to this day unadopted by the Assembly.

[115] The resolution calls upon states 'to refrain from any threat or acts, direct or indirect, aimed at impairing the freedom, independence or integrity of any State, or at fomenting civil strife and subverting the will of the people in any State' (para 3). It was adopted by fifty votes to five with one abstention.

[116] This early resolution espoused the narrow notion of non-intervention limited to the use of force that was endorsed by the Western states. The resolution was adopted by fifty-three votes to five with one abstention.

[117] The principle of 'non-interference' in the internal affairs of all states is recalled in para 7. Eighty-nine countries voted in favour of the resolution, none voted against, and nine abstained.

[118] The resolution was adopted by 109 votes to none, with one abstention. The topic had been included in the agenda of the 20th session of the General Assembly upon request of the Soviet Union (UN Doc A/5977, 24 September 1965) in reaction to the US interventions in the Dominican Republic, Congo, and Vietnam. The final text was adopted by the General Assembly only eighteen days after the tabling of the Soviet Union's initial draft resolution.

[119] Like the previous Resolution 2131, Resolution 2160 qualifies the use of force to deprive peoples of their national identity as, inter alia, a violation of the principle of non-intervention (para 1(b)).

the Declaration on the Intervention in the Domestic Affairs of States;[120] Resolution 2625 (XXV) of 24 October 1970 containing the Declaration on Principles of International Law Concerning Friendly Relations and Co-operation among States in Accordance with the Charter of the United Nations;[121] Resolution 2734 (XXV) of 16 December 1970 on the Strengthening of International Security;[122] Resolution 3171 (XXVII) of 17 December 1973 on Permanent Sovereignty over Natural Resources;[123] Resolution 31/91 of 14 December 1976 on Non-interference in the Internal Affairs of States;[124] Resolution 34/103 of 14 December 1979 on the Inadmissibility of the Policy of Hegemonism in International Relations;[125] Resolution 36/103 of 9 December 1981 adopting the Declaration on the Inadmissibility of Intervention and Interference in the Internal Affairs of States;[126] and Resolution 42/22 of 18 November 1987 containing

[120] The resolution urged 'the immediate cessation of intervention, in any form whatever, in the domestic or external affairs of States; [condemned] all forms of intervention in the domestic or external affairs of States as a basic source of danger to the cause of world peace' and called upon all states to comply with the Charter and with Resolution 2131. The resolution was adopted by a majority of 114 to none with two abstentions. The topic was again included in the agenda of the General Assembly upon request of the Soviet Union (UN Doc A/6397, 23 September 1966).

[121] The Declaration on Friendly Relations, the aim of which was to elaborate on seven principles contained in the UN Charter considering the post-1945 practice within the organization, was drafted by the Special Committee established by GA Res 1966 (XVIII) in 1963 and composed of 'qualified jurists' appointed by twenty-seven (thirty-one from 1966) states. The Committee held six sessions between 1964 and 1970. The final text of the Declaration was eventually adopted by consensus without a vote at the twenty-fifth anniversary session of the General Assembly after nine years of work. The expression 'friendly relations', which derives from the UN Charter, was used upon request of the Western states, who preferred it to that of 'peaceful coexistence' endorsed by the socialist states (Robert Rosenstock, 'The Declaration of Principles of International Law Concerning Friendly Relations: A Survey' (1971) 65 AJIL 713, 713). 'In Accordance with the Charter' was added to emphasize that the purpose was not to revise, but to interpret the UN Charter provisions (ibid).

[122] The resolution was adopted to complement the Friendly Relations Declaration. In addition to reaffirming the principles of the latter, including non-intervention (para 2), Resolution 2734 reiterates that 'States must fully respect the sovereignty of other States and the right of peoples to determine their own destinies, free of external intervention, coercion or constraint, especially involving the threat or use of force, overt or covert, and refrain from any attempt aimed at the partial or total disruption of the national unity and territorial integrity of any other State or country' (para 4) and that 'every State has the duty to refrain from organizing, instigating, assisting or participating in acts of civil strife or terrorist acts in another State' (para 5).

[123] According to the resolution, all states have a duty 'to refrain in their international relations from military, political, economic or any other form of coercion aimed against the territorial integrity of any State and the exercise of its national jurisdiction'. The resolution was adopted by a vote of 108 in favour to one against, with sixteen abstentions.

[124] The resolution, sponsored by the non-aligned countries, focuses particularly on indirect intervention. It denounces 'any form of interference, overt or covert, direct or indirect, including recruiting and sending mercenaries, by one State or group of States and any act of military, political, economic or other form of intervention in the internal or external affairs of other States, regardless of the character of their mutual relations or their social and economic systems' and condemns 'all forms of overt, subtle and highly sophisticated techniques of coercion, subversion and defamation aimed at disrupting the political, social or economic order of other States or destabilizing the Governments seeking to free their economies from external control or manipulation' (paras 3 and 4). The resolution was adopted by a majority of ninety-nine to one with eleven abstentions. Paras 3 and 4 of the resolution were reaffirmed in the subsequent Resolution 32/153 of 19 December 1977 on Non-Interference in the Internal Affairs of States.

[125] The resolution, inter alia, '[r]esolutely condemns policies of pressure and use or threat of use of force, direct or indirect aggression, occupation and the growing practice of interference and intervention, overt or covert, in the internal affairs of States' (para 4, emphasis omitted).

[126] The Declaration was the brainchild of the socialist bloc and listed duties that proved to be unacceptable to the Western states, including '[t]he duty of States to refrain from any measure which would lead to the strengthening of existing military blocs or the creation or strengthening of new military alliances,

118 INTERNATIONAL LAW AND THE PRINCIPLE OF NON-INTERVENTION

the Declaration on the Enhancement of the Effectiveness of the Principle of Refraining from the Threat or Use of Force in International Relations.[127] As the ICJ noted in the *Nicaragua* Judgment, the vote in favour of certain General Assembly resolutions, in particular Resolution 2625, is not a mere ' "reiteration or elucidation" of the treaty commitment undertaken in the Charter', but 'an acceptance of the validity of the rule or set of rules declared by the resolution by themselves'.[128] In the *Nuclear Weapons* Advisory Opinion, the Court added that

> General Assembly resolutions, even if they are not binding, may sometimes have normative value. They can, in certain circumstances, provide evidence important for establishing the existence of a rule or the emergence of an *opinio juris*. [...] Or a series of resolutions may show the gradual evolution of the *opinio juris* required for the establishment of a new rule.[129]

In the *Chagos* Advisory Opinion, the ICJ further suggested that the high number of votes in favour of a General Assembly resolution, the absence of votes against, the declarations of the abstaining states when voting, and the normative character of the wording used might all be indications of the fact that a resolution is declarative of customary international law.[130]

Finally, the customary status of the principle of non-intervention has been affirmed by international and domestic courts. In the *Corfu Channel* case before the ICJ, the United Kingdom sought to present 'a new and special application of the theory of intervention', where a state could intervene to secure possession of evidence to submit to an international tribunal.[131] In the Judgment, the Court rejected this argument and

---

interlocking arrangements, the deployment of interventionist forces or military bases and other related military installations conceived in the context of great-Power confrontation'; '[t]he duty of a State to abstain from any defamatory campaign, vilification or hostile propaganda for the purpose of intervening or interfering in the internal affairs of other States'; and '[t]he duty of a State to refrain from the exploitation and the distortion of human rights issues as a means of interference in the internal affairs of States, of exerting pressure on other States or creating distrust and disorder within and among States or groups of States'. GA Res 36/103 (9 December 1981) was adopted by 120 to twenty-two with six abstentions and it is not generally considered to reflect customary international law. On the history of the resolution, see Michel Vincineau, 'Quelques commentaires à propos de la «Déclaration sur l'inadmissibilité de l'intervention et de l'ingérence dans les affaires intérieures des États» (Résolution 36/103 du décembre 1981)' in *Mélanges offerts à Charles Chaumont—Le droit des peuples à disposer d'eux-mêmes. Méthodes d'analyse du droit international* (Pedone 1984) 555.

[127] See paras I(6), (7), and (8). Other relevant resolutions include the Resolutions on (Unilateral) Economic Measures as a Means of Political and Economic Coercion against Developing Countries, those on Respect for the Principles of National Sovereignty and Non-Interference in the Internal Affairs of States in Electoral Processes, and Resolution 56/154 (2001) on Respect for the Principles of National Sovereignty and Non-interference in the Internal Affairs of States in Electoral Processes as an Important Element for the Promotion and Protection of Human Rights.

[128] *Nicaragua v USA*, para 188.

[129] *Legality of the Threat or Use of Nuclear Weapons* (Advisory Opinion) [1996] ICJ Rep 226, para 70.

[130] *Legal Consequences of the Separation of the Chagos Archipelago from Mauritius in 1965* (Advisory Opinion) [2019] ICJ Rep 95, paras 152–3.

[131] *Corfu Channel (United Kingdom of Great Britain and Northern Ireland v Albania)* (Merits) [1949] ICJ Rep 4, 34 (hereafter *Corfu Channel*).

held that the 'alleged' right of intervention 'has, in the past, given rise to the most serious abuses and such as cannot, whatever be the present defects in international organization, find a place in international law'.[132] The Court also did away with the 19th century's self-help/self-preservation justification for intervention by finding that respect for territorial sovereignty is 'an essential foundation of international relations'.[133] In *Nicaragua*, the ICJ explicitly noted that 'though examples of trespass against [the principle of non-intervention] are not infrequent ... it is part and parcel of customary international law'.[134] In the Court's view, '[e]xpressions of an *opinio juris* regarding the existence of the principle of non-intervention in customary international law are numerous and not difficult to find' and this *opinio juris* 'is backed by established and substantial practice'.[135] In *DRC v Uganda*, the ICJ reiterated the customary status of the relevant paragraphs of the Declaration on Friendly Relations.[136]

In addition to the ICJ, the European Court of Justice (ECJ) referred to the principle of 'non-interference' in the *Ahlström* case although it did not find it necessary to investigate whether it existed in international law, as the conditions for its applicability in the case were not deemed to have occurred.[137] In another case, however, it concluded that the principle reflects customary international law.[138] The principle of non-intervention has also been applied in domestic judgments.[139] The Supreme Court of Canada, in particular, saw it as functional to the preservation of the 'organizing principles of the relationships between independent states', namely sovereignty and equality, and found that the principle of non-intervention is supported by state practice and *opinio juris* and is therefore a 'firmly established' rule of customary

---

[132] ibid, 35. The Court particularly disagreed with the special right of intervention to secure evidence for international tribunals, as this would be 'reserved to the most powerful States' and would eventually lead 'to perverting the administration of international justice itself' (ibid).

[133] ibid.

[134] *Nicaragua v USA*, para 202. In his Dissenting Opinion, Judge Jennings agreed that '[t]here can be no doubt that the principle of non-intervention is an autonomous principle of customary law; indeed it is very much older than any of the multilateral treaty régimes in question. It is, moreover, a principle of law which in the inter-American system has its own peculiar development, interpretation and importance' (*Nicaragua v USA*, Dissenting Opinion of Judge Jennings, 534–5).

[135] *Nicaragua v USA*, para 202.

[136] *DRC v Uganda* (Merits) [2005] ICJ Rep 168, paras 162–3, 300. A violation of the principle of non-intervention was also claimed by Yugoslavia against the United States before the ICJ for 'financing, arming, training and equipping the so-called "Kosovo Liberation Army"' (*Legality of Use of Force (Yugoslavia v USA)*, Application instituting proceedings, 29 April 1999 <www.icj-cij.org/case/114> —the case did not reach the merits stage); by Cameroon against Nigeria (*Cameroon v Nigeria*, para 310—the ICJ did not explicitly adjudicate on Cameroon's claim: ibid, para 319); by Bosnia and Herzegovina against Serbia and Montenegro in the *Bosnian Genocide* case (Merits) [2007] ICJ Rep 43, para 64; by Honduras against Brazil (*Honduras v Brazil*, paras 8–9, 15); by Equatorial Guinea against France (*Immunities and Criminal Proceedings (Equatorial Guinea v France)* (Preliminary Objections) [2018] ICJ Rep 292, para 50); and by Greece against FYROM (*Case Concerning the Application of Article 11(1) of the Interim Accord of 13 September 1995 (The Former Yugoslav Republic of Macedonia v Greece)* (Judgment) [2011] ICJ Rep 644, paras 140–1 (non-intervention was invoked in this case not as a customary rule, but as a provision of the 1995 Interim Accord)).

[137] *A Åhlström Osakeyhtiö and others v Commission of the European Communities*, Joined cases 89, 104, 114, 116, 117 and 125 to 129/85, Judgment of 27 September 1988, ECLI:EU:C:1988:447, paras 19–20.

[138] *Liberation Tigers of Tamil Eelam (LTTE) v Council of the European Union*, Joined Cases T-208/11 and T-508/11, Judgment of 16 October 2014, ECLI:EU:T:2014:885, para 69 (hereafter *Liberation Tigers of Tamil Eelam v EU Council*).

[139] See eg *Buck v Attorney General* [1965] EWCA Civ J0212-3, para 769.

120 INTERNATIONAL LAW AND THE PRINCIPLE OF NON-INTERVENTION

international law.[140] The Constitutional Court of Latvia reached the same conclusion in 2007.[141]

Granted, there have been numerous cases of intervention since 1945, but no state has ever claimed that the principle under consideration has been abrogated.[142] This is a particularly important point, as non-intervention is a rule requiring a negative conduct: in such cases, 'identifying actual State practice by merely analysing concrete situations in the field is highly challenging because such an analysis would lead to highlighting essentially the situations where the rule has been breached, and not the situations where the rule has been respected'.[143] It is necessary, therefore, to give special relevance to the element of *opinio juris*.[144] From this perspective, as the ICJ notes, '[i]t is not to be expected that in the practice of States the application of the rules in question should have been perfect, in the sense that States should have refrained, with complete consistency, from the use of force or from intervention in each other's internal affairs'.[145] For the Court, it is

> sufficient that the conduct of States should, in general, be consistent with such rules, and that instances of State conduct inconsistent with a given rule should generally have been treated as breaches of that rule, not as indications of the recognition of a new rule. If a State acts in a way prima facie incompatible with a recognized rule, but defends its conduct by appealing to exceptions or justifications contained within the rule itself, then whether or not the State's conduct is in fact justifiable on that basis, the significance of that attitude is to confirm rather than to weaken the rule.[146]

As I discuss later, this is exactly the case with the principle of non-intervention.[147]

If there is general consensus on the existence and binding character of the principle of non-intervention in current customary international law, the exact content of the prohibition has however remained controversial, in particular whether it is limited to armed intervention or also extends to other forms of coercion: this question is addressed in Chapter III.[148]

---

[140] *Hape v Her Majesty the Queen*, para 46.
[141] The Constitutional Court of the Republic of Latvia, Judgment on behalf of the Republic of Latvia, para 26.
[142] As Vaughan Lowe puts it, '[i]nterventions have not, in general, been presented as exercises of naked power in total disregard of international law. They have been justified as exercises of power in pursuit of exceptions to that principle, which exceptions are accepted in international law' (Vaughan Lowe, 'The Principle of Non-intervention: Use of Force' in Vaughan Lowe and Colin Warbrick (eds), *The United Nations and the Principles of International Law: Essays in Memory of Michael Akehurst* (Routledge 1994) 66, 73–4).
[143] Corthay, 'The ASEAN Doctrine', 37.
[144] ibid.
[145] *Nicaragua v USA*, para 186.
[146] ibid.
[147] See Chapter IV, Section 5.
[148] See Chapter III, Sections 7, 7.1, and 7.2.

4. Non-Intervention as a 'Principle' from which Rights and Duties of States Arise

Non-intervention is traditionally referred to as a 'principle'. As Antonio Cassese notes, principles are

> the expression and result of conflicting views of States on matters of crucial importance. When States cannot agree upon definite and specific standards of behaviour because of their principled, opposing attitudes, but need, however, some sort of basic guideline for their conduct, their actions and discussions eventually lead to the formulation of principles.[149]

As a consequence, 'unlike rules, which are fairly specific in content and normally do not lend themselves to contradictory interpretations, principles are loose, sweeping, and do not prescribe any given conduct in precise and unequivocal terms'.[150] While it is undoubtedly true that the 'principle' of non-intervention is characterized by a certain vagueness, this fact alone does not prevent it from being construed in terms of the Hohfeldian dichotomy right/duty: in other words, it encompasses the right of every state to conduct its domestic affairs without external intervention and the corresponding duty of other states to refrain from such intervention.

As the principle is a corollary of state sovereignty, the right holders are only states: international organizations do not have a right to non-intervention under customary international law, although their constitutive act could require their member states to respect the exclusive competence of the organization in certain areas.[151] National liberation movements are also not protected by the principle of non-intervention. In 2011, the Liberation Tigers of Tamil Eelam (LTTE) applied to the ECJ for the annulment of an EU Council regulation including the insurgent group in a list of restrictive measures adopted with a view to combating terrorism. The LTTE claimed to be a liberation movement involved in an armed conflict against an 'oppressive government' and not a terrorist organization and, as such, the freezing of its funds was 'an infringement of the principle of non-interference under international humanitarian law' (*sic*).[152] The ECJ found that the 'customary international law principle, also called

---

[149] Cassese, *Self-Determination*, 128.

[150] ibid, 320. Gaja agrees: '[w]hile the distinction between principles and rules has not been elaborated in judicial or arbitral decisions, the use of the term principles denotes the general nature of the norm in question' (Giorgio Gaja, 'General Principles of Law' in *MPEPIL Online* (last updated April 2020) para 31). See also *Delimination of the Maritime Border in the Gulf of Maine Area (Canada/USA)* (Judgment) [1984] ICJ Rep 246, para 79 ('the association of the terms "rules" and "principles" is no more than the use of a dual expression to convey one and the same idea, since ... "principles" clearly means principles of law, that is, it also includes rules of international law in whose case the use of the term "principles" may be justified because of their more general and more fundamental character').

[151] But see the recent EU Commission's proposal on economic coercion by third countries, according to which economic coercion occurs when 'a third country:—interferes in the legitimate sovereign choices *of the Union* or a Member State by seeking to prevent or obtain the cessation, modification or adoption of a particular act by the Union or a Member State —by applying or threatening to apply measures affecting trade or investment' (Art 2(1), European Commission's Proposal for a Regulation of the European Parliament and of the Council on the protection of the Union and its Member States from economic coercion by third countries, COM/2021/775 final, 8 December 2021, emphasis added).

[152] *Liberation Tigers of Tamil Eelam v EU Council*, para 54.

122 INTERNATIONAL LAW AND THE PRINCIPLE OF NON-INTERVENTION

the principle of non-intervention, concerns the right of any sovereign State to conduct its affairs without external interference and constitutes a corollary of the principle of sovereign equality of States' and that the principle 'is set out for the benefit of sovereign States, and not for the benefit of groups or movements'.[153] The restrictive measures adopted against the LTTE, therefore, did not infringe it.

States are not only the right holders but also the bearers of the corresponding obligation of non-intervention under customary international law. Whether or not a state is responsible for an unlawful intervention is determined by the rules on state responsibility, in particular the rules on attribution codified in Articles 4 to 11 of the Articles on the Responsibility of States for Internationally Wrongful Acts drafted by the UN International Law Commission (ILC) and adopted by the General Assembly in 2001.[154] It is, however, not only states that are required not to intervene in the domestic affairs of other states but international organizations as well—first towards their own members under their respective statutes[155] and second towards non-member states under the customary principle of non-intervention. The OAS Charter and General Assembly Resolutions 2131 and 2625, in particular, make clear that the principle of non-intervention binds not only individual states but also groups of states.[156] Intervention by individuals and corporations, on the other hand, is regulated by internal laws, not international law, unless the individual or corporation's conduct can be attributed to a state under the law of state responsibility.[157] General Assembly Resolution 36/103 affirms the duty of states 'to prevent the use of transnational and multinational corporations under its jurisdiction and control as instruments of political pressure or coercion against another State, in violation of the Charter of the United Nations', but the resolution does not reflect customary international law.[158]

5. Does the Principle of Non-Intervention Create an *Erga Omnes* Obligation?

Anne Peters posits that 'the obligation not to intervene coercively is owed both to individual states ... and to the international community as a whole' as its abandonment 'would lead to a global instability of living conditions and to massive human suffering through interventionist and imperialist wars'.[159] In the *Barcelona Traction* Judgment,

---

[153] ibid, para 69.

[154] [2001] YB ILC, vol II, part two, 26. It should be stressed that a state that supports foreign insurgents will be responsible for a violation of the principle of non-intervention regardless of whether the support also results in attributing the conduct of the insurgents to the state in question (Rosario Sapienza, *Il principio del non intervento negli affari interni. Contributo allo studio della tutela giuridica internazionale della potestà di governo* (Giuffrè 1990) 156).

[155] See eg Art 2(7), UN Charter; Art I(3), Constitution of the United Nations Educational, Scientific and Cultural Organization (UNESCO) (London, 16 November 1945) 4 UNTS 275; Art 1(2), OAS Charter (as amended by the 1985 Cartagena Protocol); and Art IV, Section 10, Articles of Agreement of the International Bank for Reconstruction and Development (Washington, DC, 27 December 1945) 2 UNTS 134.

[156] Art 19, OAS Charter; GA Res 2131 (XX), para 7; GA Res 2625 (XXV), Annex, third principle, para 1.

[157] See Jean Charpentier, 'Pratique française du droit international public' (1959) 5 AFDI 877, 892.

[158] GA Res 36/103, para k.

[159] Anne Peters, 'Humanity as the A and Ω of Sovereignty' (2009) 20 EJIL 513, 534. Sperduti is another author who has argued in favour of the *erga omnes* character of the principle of non-intervention, although without much argumentation (Giuseppe Sperduti, *Il dominio riservato* (Giuffrè 1970) 13). Oppenheim also

the ICJ identified as obligations *erga omnes* those assumed 'toward the international community as a whole' that are 'the concern of all States' and in the protection of which '[i]n view of the importance of the rights involved, all States can be held to have a legal interest ... '.[160] Norms creating obligations *erga omnes* are thus those rules of customary international law reflecting community values and which are characterized by a special title to react in case of their violation, that is, by the fact that not only do they create obligations owed to all states but also that any state is entitled to invoke the consequences of their violation.[161] Said otherwise, the obligations in question do not find a counterpart in individual rights of other states, but impose a positive or negative conduct that can be demanded by all states.[162] Obligations *erga omnes* must thus be distinguished from *jus cogens* norms: while both protect fundamental values of the international community, only rules creating obligations *erga omnes* allow all states to invoke the legal consequences of their violation.[163]

As said, obligations *erga omnes* are characterized by two elements: they are owed to the international community as a whole as they express values that are the concern of all states *and*, because of the importance of the rights involved, all states have a right to demand compliance with them.[164] This means that the customary nature of a rule is necessary (due to the first requirement)[165] but not sufficient (due to the additional requirement of the entitlement of all states to invoke the legal consequences of their violation) to create *erga omnes* obligations.[166] The principle of non-intervention undoubtedly protects interests that transcend those of the victim state.

maintains that 'any unjustifiable intervention by one State in the affairs of another gives a right of intervention to all other States' because the interests of all states are involved (Lassa Oppenheim, *International Law: A Treatise*, vol I: Peace (2nd edn, Longmans, Green & Co 1912) 196).

[160] *Barcelona Traction, Light and Power Company, Limited (Belgium v Spain)* (Preliminary Objections, Second phase) [1970] ICJ Rep 3, para 33 (hereafter *Barcelona Traction*). For the Institut de droit international, an obligation *erga omnes* is 'an obligation under general international law that a State owes in any given case to the international community, in view of its common values and its concern for compliance, so that a breach of that obligation enables all States to take action' (Resolution on Obligations and Rights *Erga Omnes* in International Law (Krakow Resolution), 27 August 2005, Krakow Session, Art 1(a) <www.idi-iil. org/app/uploads/2017/06/2005_kra_01_en.pdf>).

[161] Marco Longobardo, 'Genocide, Obligations *Erga Omnes*, and the Responsibility to Protect: Remarks on a Complex Convergence' (2015) 19 Intl J HR 1199, 1202.

[162] Paolo Picone, 'Obblighi reciproci e obblighi *erga omnes* degli Stati nel campo della protezione internazionale dell'ambiente marino dall'inquinamento' in Vincenzo Starace and Paolo Picone (eds), *Diritto internazionale e protezione dell'ambiente marino* (Giuffrè 1983) 15, 27. In the *Barcelona Traction* Judgment, the ICJ juxtaposed *erga omnes* obligations with those assumed 'vis-à-vis another State', like those in the area of diplomatic protection (*Barcelona Traction*, para 33).

[163] Paolo Picone, 'La distinzione tra norme internazionali di *jus cogens* e norme che producono obblighi *erga omnes*' (2008) 91 RDI 5, 17, 22.

[164] Ragazzi highlights that the two characteristics of obligations *erga omnes* are '*universality*, in the sense that obligations *erga omnes* are binding on all States without exceptions' and '*solidarity*, in the sense that every State is deemed to have a legal interest in their protection' (Maurizio Ragazzi, *The Concept of International Obligations* Erga Omnes (OUP 1997) 17, emphasis in the original).

[165] The fact that, in *Barcelona Traction*, the ICJ asserted that obligations *erga omnes* can arise not only from general international law but also from 'international instruments of a universal or quasi-universal character' (*Barcelona Traction*, para 34) should be interpreted in the sense that obligations *erga omnes* are also incorporated in certain treaties (Christian J Tams, *Enforcing* Erga Omnes *Obligations* (CUP 2005) 122–3).

[166] Paolo Picone, 'Obblighi *erga omnes* e codificazione della responsabilità degli Stati' (2005) 88 RDI 893, 899, fn 8.

General Assembly Resolution 2131 on the Inadmissibility of Intervention, for instance, emphasizes that '[t]he strict observance of [the obligations arising from the principle of non-intervention] is an essential condition to ensure that nations live together in peace with one another',[167] and Resolution 2225 condemns 'all forms of intervention in the domestic or external affairs of States as a basic source of danger to the cause of world peace'.[168] In his Separate Opinion appended to the *Nicaragua* Judgment, Judge Nagendra Singh also sees the principle in question as 'a sanctified absolute rule of law whose non-observance could lead to disastrous consequences causing untold misery to humanity'.[169] As I discuss later, however, at present the principle of non-intervention reflects customary international law not in its entirety, but only where it prohibits armed and political forms of coercion and subversion.[170] In addition, reactions by states not specially affected by a breach of the principle in question have occurred only when the breach consisted in an unlawful use of force, as in the case of the Soviet Union's occupation of Afghanistan (1979) and of Russia's invasion of Crimea (2014) and Donbass (2022). The *erga omnes* character of the principle of non-intervention, therefore, appears to be presently limited to the pillar that prohibits the most serious form of intervention: that involving the use of armed force.

On the other hand, the principle of non-intervention contained in Article 19 of the OAS Charter arguably has an *erga omnes partes* character, that is, it creates an obligation owed to the group of the states parties as a whole.[171] This conclusion has been implicitly confirmed by the OAS General Assembly, which has emphasized that there is a 'duty of each state to respect the principles of nonintervention and self-determination of peoples *and the right to demand compliance with those principles by other states*'.[172]

---

[167] GA Res 2131 (XX), para 4.

[168] GA Res 2225 (XXI), 19 December 1966, para (b). At the Security Council, Colombia also noted that '[s]overeignty, territorial integrity, political independence, non-interference in the internal affairs of States, the prohibition of the use or threat of use of force and the peaceful settlement of international disputes are the fundamental pillars underpinning international law and international relations' (UN Doc S/PV.7621, 15 February 2016, 50). Other countries made similar statements (Guyana, S/PV.7621, 15 February 2016, 80; Azerbaijan, S/PV.7621, 15 February 2016, 87; Greece, A/32/164, 2 September 1977, 4; Qatar, A/33/216, 21 September 1978, 30; United States, ibid, 32; Chile, A/8018, 1970, 74). In its statement attached to the 1960 Declaration of San José, Mexico also declared that the principle of non-intervention is 'the irreplaceable basis of peace and understanding among states' (Declaration of San José, adopted at the Seventh Meeting of Consultation of Ministers of Foreign Affairs, held at San José, Costa Rica, 28 August 1960 <http://avalon. law.yale.edu/20th_century/intam13.asp>).

[169] *Nicaragua v USA*, Separate Opinion of President Nagendra Singh, 156.

[170] See Chapter III, Sections 6, 7.1, 7.2, and 8.

[171] The aforementioned Institut de droit international's Krakow Resolution defines an *erga omnes partes* obligation as 'an obligation under a multilateral treaty that a State party to the treaty owes in any given case to all the other States parties to the same treaty, in view of their common values and concern for compliance, so that a breach of that obligation enables all these States to take action' (Art 1(b)).

[172] OAS General Assembly, Principles Governing Relations Among the American States, 15 April 1973 (1973) 68 Dept St Bull 685, para 3, emphasis added.

6. The Principle of Non-Intervention as a *Jus Cogens* Norm?

It has been claimed that the principle of non-intervention not only has customary status, but is also a *jus cogens* norm.[173] Judge Sette-Camara, for instance, found that 'the non-use of force as well as non-intervention—the latter as a corollary of equality of States and self-determination—are not only cardinal principles of customary international law but could in addition be recognized as peremptory rules of customary international law which impose obligations on all States'.[174] Some states have also claimed that the principle of non-intervention is a *jus cogens* norm.[175] Others have affirmed that all the principles contained in the Declaration on Friendly Relations, including that of non-intervention, are of a peremptory character.[176]

The defining characteristics of a *jus cogens* rule are that a) it is a norm of general international law, and b) that it is 'accepted and recognized by the international community of States as a whole as a norm from which no derogation is permitted *and* which can be modified only by a subsequent norm of general international law having the same character' (Article 53 of the VCLT).[177] With regard to the second element, in particular, the ICJ has found that the principle of non-intervention can have exceptions.[178] This fact alone is not sufficient to conclude that it does not have a peremptory character. Indeed, even the prohibition of the use of force has exceptions although it is generally considered a *jus cogens* rule: as Jean d'Aspremont notes, 'the situations where the use of force is allowed do not, strictly speaking, derogate from the prohibition. They

---

[173] George B Zotiades, 'Intervention by Treaty Right' (1964) 34 *Yearbook of the Association of Attenders and Alumni of the Hague Academy of International Law* 153, 167; Mohamed Bennouna, *Le consentement à l'ingérence militaire dans les conflits internes* (Librairie générale de droit et de jurisprudence 1974) 79 (who however appears to limit the *jus cogens* character to the prohibition of armed intervention); Ion Diaconu, 'La non-immixtion dans les affaires intérieures des États — principe fondamental du droit international contemporain' (1980) 50 RREI 331, 336; Jacques Noël, *Le principe de non-intervention. Théorie et pratique dans les relations inter-américaines* (Editions de l'Université de Bruxelles/Bruylant 1981) 143; Victor Carlos García Moreno, 'El principio de la no intervención en los conflictos internos de los Estados soberanos' (1983) 52 Rev Jur UPR 97, 110; Antonio Cassese, *International Law in a Divided World* (Clarendon Press 1986) 47; Dino Kritsiotis, 'Reappraising Policy Objections to Humanitarian Intervention' (1998) 19 Mich J Intl L 1005, 1042–3; Jianming Shen, 'The Non-Intervention Principle and Humanitarian Interventions under International Law' (2001) 7 ILT 1, 2–8; Amy Eckert, 'The Non-Intervention Principle and International Humanitarian Interventions', ibid, 49, 51. Šahović (the Yugoslav member of the Special Committee on Friendly Relations) also posits that all the principles contained in the 1970 Declaration, including that of non-intervention, constitute *jus cogens* rules (Milan Šahović, 'Codification des principes du droit international des relations amicales et de la coopération entre les Etats' (1972) 137 Recueil des Cours 243, 306–7).

[174] *Nicaragua v USA*, Separate Opinion of Judge Sette-Camara, 193.

[175] *DRC v Uganda*, DRC Memorial, para 3.37; Ecuador, UN Doc A/C.6/SR.849, 13 October 1965, 61; Ceylon, United Nations Conference on the Law of Treaties, Official Records, First Session, Vienna, 26 March–24 May 1968 (United Nations 1969) 219.

[176] UN Doc A/8018, 77 (Venezuela); A/C.6/SR.1180, 24 September 1970, para 6 (Iraq); A/C.6/SR.1182, 25 September 1970, para 49 (Ethiopia); A/72/307, 9 August 2017, para 9 (Guatemala). More ambiguously, Greece affirmed that the seven principles of the Declaration 'furnished greatly needed clarification of the content of the related *jus cogens* provisions of the Charter' (A/C.6/SR.1181, 25 September 1970, para 31).

[177] Emphasis added. Linderfalk explains that the fact that no derogation is permitted means that '[i]rrespective of the situation, there will never be a legally valid reason to depart from a rule of *jus cogens*' (Ulf Linderfalk, 'What Is So Special About *Jus Cogens*? On the Difference between the Ordinary and the Peremptory International Law' (2012) 14 Int'l Comm L Rev 3, 12).

[178] *Nicaragua v USA*, para 207.

simply *limit* its ambit'.[179] A *jus cogens* rule, therefore, can have *exceptions*, but cannot be subject to *derogation* by custom or treaty. The principle of non-intervention's resistance to derogation by treaty has been affirmed on certain occasions. In the *Nicaragua* case, Judge Sette-Camara found that any treaty where states agree to intervene in the internal or external affairs of another state would be null and void as a consequence of the application of Article 53 of the VCLT.[180] General Assembly Resolution 36/103 emphasizes '[t]he duty of states to refrain from concluding agreements with other States designed to intervene or interfere in the internal and external affairs of third States'.[181] Cyprus has also repeatedly claimed that a treaty containing a provision conferring a right of intervention in the internal affairs of another state would be void because it would conflict with *jus cogens*.[182]

Apart from Cyprus, however, not many states have qualified the principle of non-intervention as *jus cogens* and 'it may be questioned whether silence is enough to bestow supernorm status on a rule'.[183] Certain states have in fact explicitly declared that the seven principles contained in the Friendly Relations Declaration are not of peremptory character[184] and at least one has argued that intervention can be a lawful means of policy in specific circumstances.[185] The 'as a whole' requirement, therefore, is far from being met. The controversy about the broad and narrow scope of the customary principle of non-intervention, discussed in Chapter III, makes this conclusion even more persuasive in regard to economic intervention.[186] All that can be safely said at this point is that *jus cogens* only prohibits that form of intervention amounting to an act of aggression.[187]

It is also symptomatic that, unlike most *jus cogens* rules, the violation of the principle of non-intervention does not give rise to individual criminal liability in addition to state responsibility. The history of the rule in the ILC's Draft Code of Offences against the Peace and Security of Mankind is instructive. The 1954 version of the Draft Code included '[t]he intervention by the authorities of a State in the internal or external affairs of another State, by means of coercive measures of an economic or

---

[179] Jean d'Aspremont, 'Mapping the Concepts Behind the Contemporary Liberalization of the Use of Force in International Law' (2009–2010) 31 U Pa J Int'l L 1089, 1106, emphasis in the original.

[180] *Nicaragua v USA*, Separate Opinion of Judge Sette-Camara, 199–200. See also Sixth Report on the Draft Code of Crimes against the Peace and Security of Mankind, by Mr Doudou Thiam, Special Rapporteur [1998] YB ILC, vol II, part one, 199.

[181] GA Res 36/103, para II(h).

[182] See eg UN Doc A/C.6/SR.783, 3 October 1963, para 18.

[183] James A Green, 'Questioning the Peremptory Status of the Prohibition of the Use of Force' (2011) 32 Mich J Intl L 215, 253–4. Cassese notes, however, that 'it is not always necessary for all States to say in so many words that they consider that norm [of *jus cogens*] as existing. Although such formal "labelling" proves important and in some cases indispensable, there may be instances where the upgrading of a rule to *jus cogens* may result *implicitly* from the attitude taken by States in their international dealings and in collective fora' (Cassese, *Self-Determination*, 139, emphasis in the original).

[184] See eg United States (UN Doc A/8018, 119); Hungary (A/C.6/SR.1179, para 35).

[185] See the United Kingdom's line of defence in the *Corfu Channel* case, ICJ Pleadings, vol II, 282–3.

[186] Andrea De Guttry, *Le rappresaglie non comportanti la coercizione militare nel diritto internazionale* (Giuffrè 1985) 208–9.

[187] On the *jus cogens* character of the prohibition of aggression, see Roberto Ago, Addendum to the eighth Report on State Responsibility [1980] YB ILC, vol II, part one, 44; Rein Müllerson, '*Jus ad bellum*: Plus Ça Change (Le Monde) Plus C'Est la Même Chose (Le Droit)?' (2002) 7 JCSL 149, 169; Natalino Ronzitti, *Diritto internazionale dei conflitti armati* (7th edn, Giappichelli 2021) 33.

political character, in order to force its will and thereby obtain advantages of any kind' in the list of crimes codified therein.[188] Draft Articles 2(4) and 2(5) also criminalized specific cases of intervention as acts of aggression, in particular

[t]he organization, or the encouragement of the organization, by the authorities of a State, of armed bands within its territory or any other territory for incursions into the territory of another State, or the toleration of the organization of such bands in its own territory, or the toleration of the use by such armed bands of its territory as a base of operations or as a point of departure for incursions into the territory of another State, as well as direct participation in or support of such incursions [and] [t]he undertaking or encouragement by the authorities of a State of activities calculated to foment civil strife in another State, or the toleration by the authorities of a State of organized activities calculated to foment civil strife in another State.

Draft Article 17(2) of the Draft Code of Crimes against the Peace and Security of Mankind, adopted at first reading by the ILC in 1991, still included in the list of crimes the '[i]ntervention in the internal or external affairs of a State' consisting 'of fomenting [armed] subversive or terrorist activities or by organizing, assisting or financing such activities, or supplying arms for the purpose of such activities, thereby [seriously] undermining the free exercise by that State of its sovereign rights'.[189] The reference to economic and political coercion present in the 1954 Draft Code, however, no longer appeared in the 1991 version, as several members of the Commission were concerned that it would criminalize 'perfectly legitimate and normal manifestations of international life'.[190] The article on intervention was eventually entirely dropped in the final version of the Code adopted by the Commission in 1996 because of its vagueness, which was deemed inconsistent with the *nullum crimen sine lege* principle.[191] It also does not seem that there was ever a proposal to include a crime of intervention in the ICC Statute.

7. Post-1945 Scholarship on Intervention

In the UN Charter era, it has been primarily international relations scholars who have explored the principle of non-intervention from a broad perspective, including

---

[188] Art 2(9), text in [1954] YB ILC, vol II, 151. The draft article was originally proposed by the Cuban delegate, García Amador, and was modelled on the relevant provisions of the OAS Charter (EY Benneh, 'Economic Coercion, The Non-Intervention Principle and the Nicaragua Case' (1994) 6 Afr J Intl & Comp L 235, 246). On the works of the ILC on the crime of intervention, see John Linarelli 'An Examination of the Proposed Crime of Intervention in the Draft Code of Crimes Against the Peace and Security of Mankind' (1995) 18 Suffolk Transnat'l L Rev 1. During the debates in the UN General Assembly's First Committee that would lead to the adoption of Resolution 2131, Uganda referred to intervention as a crime against humanity (UN Doc A/C.1/SR.1399, 7 December 1965, 273).

[189] [1995] YB ILC, vol II, part two, 22. The terms in brackets are those on which the members of the Commission disagreed (Linarelli, 'An Examination', 35).

[190] See comments by Lauterpacht in [1954] YB ILC, vol I, 151.

[191] Maziar Jamnejad and Michael Wood, 'The Principle of Non-intervention' (2009) 22 LJIL 345, 359.

128 INTERNATIONAL LAW AND THE PRINCIPLE OF NON-INTERVENTION

its place in the international order. With few exceptions,[192] international lawyers have exclusively focussed on *armed* intervention and, therefore, have approached the topic from the point of view of the *jus contra bellum*. In particular, a number of monographs on intervention by invitation, or, as is now more fashionably called, 'military assistance on request', have been published in different languages in recent decades.[193]

7.1 The Scholarly Debate on Intervention and International Order

Does intervention play a positive or destabilizing role in international relations? Is there, or should there be, a norm of non-intervention? These questions, which already troubled writers of previous centuries, continue to be debated in the UN Charter era. While the limited bounds of this book do not allow an in-depth account of all approaches and authors, the most representative ones will be summarized in the following pages.

7.1.1 Realist versus liberal approaches

Realist scholars stress the importance of power relations among states, their inequality, and the inevitability of power struggles: they question, therefore, the enforceability of international law due to the lack of a vertical structure in the international legal order. For Hans Morgenthau, the leading academic representative of realism in the post-Second World War United States and a disillusioned international lawyer,[194] this results in the futility of any norm of non-intervention aimed at distinguishing between legitimate and illegitimate interventions:

> All nations will continue to be guided in their decisions to intervene and their choice of the means of intervention by what they regard as their respective national interests. There is indeed an urgent need for the governments of the great powers to abide by certain rules according to which the game of intervention is to be played. But these rules must be deduced not from abstract principles which are incapable of controlling

---

[192] An exception is Sapienza, *Il principio*. See also the bibliography on the legality of the Arab oil embargo in the 1970s cited in Chapter III, Section 7.1.

[193] Cástor Miguel Díaz Barrado, *El consentimiento, causa de exclusión de la ilicitud del uso de la fuerza, en Derecho Internacional* (Universidad de Zaragoza 1989); Antonio Tanca, *Foreign Armed Intervention in Armed Conflict* (Nijhoff 1993); Valentina Grado, *Guerre civili e terzi Stati* (CEDAM 1998); Georg Nolte, *Eingreifen auf Einladung. Zur völkerrechtlichen Zulässigkeit des Einsatzes fremder Truppen im internen Konflikt auf Einladung der Regierung* (Springer 1999); Eliav Lieblich, *International Law and Civil Wars. Intervention and Consent* (Routledge 2013); Christina Nowak, *Das Interventionsverbot im Bürgerkrieg: Darstellung eines Wandels durch die Bürgerkriege in Libyen, Syrien, Irak, Jemen und Ukraine seit 2011* (Peter Lang 2018); Erika de Wet, *Military Assistance on Request and the Use of Force* (OUP 2020); Chiara Redaelli, *Intervention in Civil Wars: Effectiveness, Legitimacy, and Human Rights* (Bloomsbury 2021); Seyfullah Hasar, *State Consent to Foreign Military Intervention during Civil Wars* (Brill/Nijhoff 2022).

[194] David Armstrong, Theo Farrell and Hélène Lambert, *International Law and International Relations* (CUP 2007) 16.

CONTEMPORARY INTERNATIONAL LAW AND CURRENT SCHOLARLY DEBATE 129

the actions of governments, but from the interests of the nations concerned and from their practice of foreign policy reflecting those interests.[195]

It is national interest, therefore, that should guide foreign policy: '[i]ntervene we must where our national interest requires it and where our power gives us a chance to succeed'.[196] In Morgenthau's rule-scepticist vision, legalistic, moralistic, or utopian notions like non-intervention are not only ineffectual, but also harmful as they can be used to provide an ideological cover for crusading politics.[197]

Adopting a softer approach that admits the existence of an international society and, at least in part, the efficacy of international law, writers belonging to the English school of realism reach a different conclusion. For them, a minimum public order can be achieved only by maintaining a balance of power among states, a result that the principle of non-intervention can help to achieve by insulating their territories from destabilizing foreign interferences.[198] Hedley Bull, in particular, considers the principle of non-intervention to be one of the rules that set out the minimum conditions for the coexistence of the members of the international society and a corollary (or 'near-corollary') of the central 'duty to respect the sovereignty or supreme jurisdiction of every other state over its own citizens and domain'.[199] He concludes that '[p]roposals to abandon the rule of non-intervention ... are in effect proposals to abandon the principle that states have rights to independence, and to construct the world order upon a quite different basis.'[200] The rejection of interventions, however, only applies to unilateral ones and not those conducted collectively on behalf of the international community to protect shared values. The idea, which is not new,[201] is so explained by Bull:

we have a rule of non-intervention because unilateral intervention threatens the harmony and concord of the society of sovereign states. If, however, an intervention

---

[195] Morgenthau, 'To Intervene', 430.

[196] ibid, 436.

[197] Martti Koskenniemi, *The Gentle Civilizer of Nations. The Rise and Fall of International Law 1870–1960* (CUP 2001) 438. See also ibid, 480–1. That said, Morgenthau concedes that international law can play a restraining role, if limited, in matters like 'the limits of territorial jurisdiction, the rights of vessels in foreign waters, and the status of diplomatic representatives.' (Hans J Morgenthau, *Politics among Nations. The Struggle for Power and Peace* (Knopf 1948) 211).

[198] Ravi Mahalingam, 'The Compatibility of the Principle of Nonintervention with the Right of Humanitarian Intervention' (1996) 1 UCLA J Int'l L Foreign Aff 221, 230.

[199] Hedley Bull, *The Anarchical Society. A Study of Order in World Public Politics* (4th edn, Macmillian-Red Globe Press 2012) 67. Bull juxtaposes rules of coexistence to those aimed at cooperation among states (ibid).

[200] Hedley Bull, 'Conclusions' in Hedley Bull (ed), *Intervention in World Politics* (Clarendon 1984) 181, 185. Rolando Quadri, the founder of the Italian school of legal realism, agrees: for him, allowing states to intervene to protect their own rights and/or interests would ultimately mean negating the existence of the international legal order (Rolando Quadri, *Diritto internazionale pubblico* (5th edn, Liguori 1968) 276).

[201] Think, for instance, of Christian Wolff's *civitas maxima*, on which see Chapter I, Section 3.

itself expresses the collective will of the society of states, it may be carried out without bringing that harmony and concord into jeopardy.[202]

In the absence of general consensus, however, 'it is the proponents of intervention who wish to threaten peace, and they are moved by considerations not of peace but of justice.'[203] Ultimately, 'the crux of the realist legacy', including with regard to the principle of non-intervention, is that 'international law is at once both relevant and irrelevant, because it is conveniently conceived of as a formal law one day and as an informal regime of like-minded states the next.'[204]

Intervention and non-intervention also play a major role in liberal thought, although for different reasons. Martti Koskenniemi notes that, as the ultimate purpose of the liberal international order is to protect the freedom of individual states, the principle of 'non-interference', founded on the delimitation between a private sphere of domestic jurisdiction and matters of public concern, exists to protect such freedom.[205] Grounded in what Gerry Simpson calls 'Charter liberalism', in particular, the present international legal order is pluralistic and its point is 'to treat all states equally, to allow them each the same rights afforded to individuals in a liberal society (i.e. domestic jurisdiction, equality, non-intervention) and to, if not celebrate, at least tolerate the diversity produced by these norms.'[206] The consequence is that internal self-determination takes priority over democracy and human rights protection.[207] Michael Walzer famously explains the argument by asking a rhetorical question: should the Swedish government use a chemical at its disposal which can turn all Algerians into social-democrats and thus create a regime where political and civil rights are respected without distinctions?[208] In his view, the (negative) answer would be the same if the dilemma concerned not the use of a chemical but support for a pro-democratic or feminist movement in the North African country:

> For foreigners cannot judge the relative strength of such movements or allow them to substitute themselves for the people as a whole, not until they have won sufficient support to transform Algerian politics on their own. That may be a long process; it will certainly involve compromises of different sorts; and the movements if and when they win will be different from what they were when they began. All that is Algerian self-determination, a political process that also has value, even if it isn't always pretty,

---

[202] Bull, 'Conclusions', 195. See also Pasquale Paone, 'Intervento (diritto internazionale)' in *Enciclopedia del diritto*, vol XII (Giuffrè 1972) 512, 526; Quadri, *Diritto*, 277

[203] Bull, *The Anarchical Society*, 92. The way forward, therefore, 'lies not in seeking to replace the rule of non-intervention with some other rule, but rather in considering how it should be modified and adapted to meet the particular circumstances and needs of the present time' (Bull, 'Conclusions', 187).

[204] Oliver Jütersonke, 'Realist Approaches to International Law' in Anne Orford and Florian Hoffman (eds), *The Oxford Handbook of the Theory of International Law* (OUP 2016) 327, 342.

[205] Martti Koskenniemi, *From Apology to Utopia. The Structure of International Legal Argument* (CUP 2005) 93.

[206] Gerry Simpson, 'Two Liberalisms' (2001) 12 EJIL 537, 541.

[207] Michael Walzer, 'The Moral Standing of States: A Response to Four Critics' (1980) 9 *Philosophy and Public Affairs* 209, 215–16.

[208] ibid, 225–6.

and even if its outcome doesn't conform to philosophical standards of political and social justice.[209]

His argument inevitably results in 'the right to be ruled by domestic thugs rather than by foreigners announcing benevolent intentions.'[210] Walzer, however, does not exclude that intervention can be legitimate in extreme cases such as massacres and enslavement of minorities or political opponents.[211]

A very different, and very critical, view of the principle of non-intervention is propounded by cosmopolitan (or, as Simpson brands them, liberal anti-pluralist)[212] scholars like Fernando Tesón.[213] For them, human beings and not states should be the subjects of international law and human rights should take priority over state rights.[214] If the protection of human beings is the ultimate purpose of both the domestic and international legal orders, then the principle of non-intervention cannot be used as a cloak behind which governments can hide when human rights violations are committed. Sovereignty, in particular, should be seen not as a dogma but as a privilege that states and governments must deserve by protecting the rights of individuals: failure to do so results in the removal of the protection from interferences when they are based on humanitarian grounds.[215] Tesón criticizes Walzer's view of a pluralistic legal order: for him, '[c]ultural differences are not sufficient grounds for prohibiting humanitarian intervention. No cultural tradition can justify a violation of basic human rights.'[216] As a consequence, 'we must accord respect to different customs, ways of life, and institutional arrangements, as long as they consistently *do not* impinge upon basic human rights.'[217] He concludes that non-intervention is

the one doctrine whose origin, design, and effect is to protect established political power and render persons defenseless against the worst forms of human evil. The principle of non-intervention denies victims of tyranny and anarchy the possibility of appealing to people other than their tormentors. It condemns them to fight unaided or die. Rescuing others will always be onerous, but if we deny the moral duty and legal

---

[209] ibid, 226.

[210] Brad R Roth, *Governmental Illegitimacy in International Law* (OUP 1999) 415.

[211] Michael Walzer, *Just and Unjust Wars. A Moral Argument with Historical Illustrations* (5th edn, Basic Books 2015) 101.

[212] Simpson, 'Two Liberalisms', 537.

[213] See Tesón's conception of the cosmopolitan interest of humanity in Fernando R Tesón, 'The Vexing Problem of Authority in Humanitarian Intervention: A Proposal' (2006) 24 Wis Int'l LJ 761.

[214] Fernando R Tesón, *Humanitarian Intervention: An Inquiry into Law and Morality* (3rd edn, Transnational Publishers 2005) 416. See also Mahalingam, 'The Compatibility', 235–6.

[215] Tesón, *Humanitarian Intervention*, 143–50. See also Fernando R Tesón, 'The Kantian Theory of International Law' (1992) 92 Colum L Rev 53, 92 ('Sovereignty is to be respected only when it is justly exercised.')

[216] Tesón, *Humanitarian Intervention*, 54.

[217] ibid, 55. Emphasis in the original.

132 INTERNATIONAL LAW AND THE PRINCIPLE OF NON-INTERVENTION

right to do so, we deny not only the centrality of justice in political affairs, but also the common humanity that binds us all.[218]

7.1.2 The TWAIL approach to intervention

As one of its most prominent representatives explains, the Third World Approaches to International Law (TWAIL) project is a 'loose network of third world scholars who articulate a critique of the history, structure and process of contemporary international law from the standpoint of third world peoples, in particular its marginal and oppressed groups'.[219] TWAIL scholars therefore aim, in the words of Antony Anghie, to view international law 'from the position of the objects of colonialism' and to develop alternative visions of justice.[220]

TWAILers put a strong emphasis on sovereignty. As Georges Abi-Saab notes:

> [f]or the newly independent states, sovereignty is the hard won prize of their long struggle for emancipation. It is the legal epitome of the fact that they are masters in their own house. It is the legal shield against any further domination or intervention by stronger states. They are very aware of its existence and importance for, until recently, they were deprived of it.[221]

Unsurprisingly, therefore, TWAILers generally see intervention as an instrument to maintain the subordination of the 'Global South' to the political and economic hegemony of the 'Global North'.[222] Both Abi-Saab and James Thuo Gathii, for instance, denounce the illusionary end of colonialism and warn of its continuation under different forms.[223] Neoliberal values like democracy and human rights, in particular, are accused of being a new standard of civilization the violation of which serves as a legitimizing ground for coercive action, as in the case of the 'war on terror'.[224] This leads Anghie to wonder 'whether international law and the UN system can resist this drive towards a new imperialism even while adapting to the new challenges facing the international community' like terrorism.[225]

---

[218] ibid, 420. He cautions, however, that '[i]t would be wrong to interfere, even peacefully, before making sure that the practice one objects to cannot be justified by an appropriate account of permissible variations. And, at any rate, it is always wrong to intervene by force to stop a practice that, while objectionable, falls short of tyranny.' (ibid, 55).

[219] Bhupinder S Chimni, *International Law and World Order: A Critique of Contemporary Approaches* (2nd edn, CUP 2017) 15.

[220] Antony Anghie, 'Imperialism and International Legal Theory' in Orford and Hoffmann, *The Oxford Handbook of the Theory of International Law*, 156, 165.

[221] Georges M Abi-Saab, 'The Newly Independent States and the Rules of International Law: An Outline' (1962) 8 How LJ 95, 103.

[222] Antony Anghie and BS Chimni, 'Third World Approaches to International Law and Individual Responsibility in Internal Conflicts' (2003) 2 CJIL 77, 85.

[223] Georges Abi-Saab, 'The Third World and the Future of the International Legal Order' (1973) 29 *Revue égyptienne de droit international* 27, 31; James Thuo Gathii, *War Commerce, and International Law* (OUP 2010) 185, 189.

[224] Antony Anghie, 'The Evolution of International Law: Colonial and Postcolonial Realities' (2006) 27 *Third World Quarterly* 739, 749–51.

[225] Antony Anghie, *Imperialism, Sovereignty and the Making of International Law* (CUP 2004) 309.

CONTEMPORARY INTERNATIONAL LAW AND CURRENT SCHOLARLY DEBATE   133

TWAILers also conceive intervention broadly as including all forms of coercion, particularly economic ones: as Gathii notes, '[t]he failure to read nonintervention as prohibiting economic coercion underscores the selective reading of the norm of non-intervention by an overwhelming majority of Western public international lawyers'.[226] Chimni also questions the role played by international institutions, which he considers 'a *nascent global state* whose function is to realize the interests of transnational capital and powerful states in the international system to the disadvantage of third world states and peoples'.[227] This is particularly the case of international trade and financial institutions like the World Trade Organization (WTO), the International Monetary Fund (IMF), and the World Bank.[228] The 'New International Economic Order' was the flagship initiative of both third world states and scholars that, in the 1970s, attempted to establish more balanced and fair economic relations between developed and less-developed countries.[229]

7.1.3 The feminist approach
In feminist legal theory, the dichotomy intervention/non-intervention (and coercive/non-coercive measures) is among those framed 'in a gendered way, with the first term connected with "male" characteristics and the second "female"'.[230] Anne Orford has used the metaphor of the 'white knight':

> Intervention narratives are premised on the notion of an international community facing new dangers, acting to save the oppressed and to protect values such as democracy and human rights. The reader of intervention literature is asked to identify with the active hero of the story, be that the international community, the UN or the USA, at the cost of the violence done to the imagined objects who form the matter of the hero's quest. This is a dream of heroic masculinity, where the colonial subject as coloniser recognises itself as a white knight riding to the rescue of beleaguered victims, across devastated landscapes of destruction and death. The hero possesses the attributes of that version of aggressive white masculinity produced in late twentieth-century US culture, a white masculinity obsessed with competitive militarism and the protection of universal (read imperial) values.[231]

At the same time, feminist international lawyers have denounced the invisibility of gender issues in the *jus contra bellum* rules. Christine Chinkin, in particular, notes that '[t]he denial to women of the freedom to determine their own economic, social and cultural development is irrelevant to States when they are determining the legitimacy of claims for assistance in achieving self-determination or for the use of

---

[226] James Thuo Gathii, 'Neoliberalism, Colonialism and International Governance: Decentering the International Law of Governmental Legitimacy' (2000) 98 Mich L Rev 1996, 2028.

[227] BS Chimni, 'International Institutions Today: An Imperial Global State in the Making' (2004) 15 EJIL 1, 1–2, emphasis in the original.

[228] Anghie, 'The Evolution', 749; Gathii, 'Neoliberalism', 2028–9.

[229] Anghie and Chimni, 'Third World Approaches', 82.

[230] Hilary Charlesworth and Christine Chinkin, *The Boundaries of International Law: A Feminist Analysis* (Manchester University Press 2000) 260.

[231] Anne Orford, *Rethinking Humanitarian Intervention: Human Rights and the Use of Force in International Law* (CUP 2003) 170.

force'.[232] This is because their right to self-determination has been subsumed in that of the broad notion of 'people'.[233] While American support for the *mujahidin* resistance in the 1980s was aimed at protecting the Afghani people's right of self-determination against the Soviet invasion of their country and the instalment of a puppet government, for instance, no consideration was given to the situation of women and to the fact that 'the *mujahidin* insurgents were committed to an oppressive, rural, unambiguously patriarchal form of society'.[234] In more recent years, the Western states continued to support the government of Hamid Karzai in Afghanistan in spite of its adoption of measures that restricted the freedom of women.[235] Decisions to intervene in unstable countries also do not normally take into account the post-conflict scenario and the fact that, once completed, interventions 'regularly reinforce the unequal and oppressive political and social systems that have caused and sustained the immediate conflict'.[236] When women's rights are indeed invoked to legitimize an intervention, it is only 'as a complement to militarism by enabling the deployment of normative arguments ... to support military campaigns'.[237]

Feminist international lawyers, therefore, advocate for a rethinking of current international law rules on the use of force in a way that does not ignore the marginalization of women, even if this might challenge the established notions of authority and sovereignty and might require a reconsideration of the sources of international law.[238]

7.2 The Scholarly Debate on Intervention by Invitation

As did those in the previous century, post-1945 scholars have continued to disagree on how the principle of non-intervention specifically applies in situations of internal unrest, that is, whether third-state intervention is prohibited only on the side of opposition groups or also in support of an incumbent government the authority of which is challenged from within the country.

7.2.1 The traditional doctrine that conceives the principle of non-intervention only as a prohibition on supporting foreign insurgents

For some writers, the occurrence of a situation of internal unrest does not change the rules of the game: the principle of non-intervention continues to apply as in all other contexts, with the consequence that third states can (or have an obligation to, if so provided in a treaty) assist the incumbent government to restore internal order upon its valid request. Scholars of this persuasion include, among others, Dinstein,[239]

---

[232] Christine Chinkin, 'A Gendered Perspective to the International Use of Force' (1988–1989) 12 Australian YBIL 279, 290.

[233] ibid, 289.

[234] ibid, 287.

[235] Hilary Charlesworth, 'Feminist Reflections on the Responsibility to Protect' (2010) 2 GR2P 232, 244.

[236] ibid, 247.

[237] Dianne Otto, 'Feminist Approaches to International Law' in Orford and Hoffman, *The Oxford Handbook of the Theory of International Law*, 488, 496.

[238] Chinkin, 'A Gendered Perspective', 292–3.

[239] Yoram Dinstein, *Non-International Armed Conflicts in International Law* (2nd edn, CUP 2021) 98–102.

CONTEMPORARY INTERNATIONAL LAW AND CURRENT SCHOLARLY DEBATE 135

Castrén,[240] De Wet,[241] Lieblich,[242] Ronzitti,[243] and Pustorino.[244] In his oral arguments before the ICJ in the *Nicaragua* case, Alain Pellet, as legal counsel for Nicaragua, also reminds us that mainstream doctrine supports the legality of foreign assistance to an incumbent government facing an 'insurrection'.[245]

These scholars posit that, since 1945, there have been many cases of military intervention on the side of governments facing internal unrest, including civil wars, which have often met with little criticism. In support of their views, these writers also invoke the dictum of the ICJ in the *Nicaragua* Judgment where the Court explains that 'intervention ... is ... allowable at the request of the government of a State'.[246]

The traditional doctrine has been criticized for being 'a Maginot line for vested privileges, deterring necessary reforms in feudal or totalitarian societies'[247] and for focusing exclusively on the element of state practice in the identification of customary international law to the detriment of *opinio juris*. In particular, by putting too much emphasis on what states *do* and too little on what they *say*, the claim is that the scholars under consideration overlook the fact that, when third states do get involved in an internal armed conflict, they either downplay their role in the conflict or claim that the insurgents have been unlawfully supported from abroad.[248]

7.2.2 The negative equality doctrine

If the traditional doctrine gives priority to state practice in the identification of customary international law, the negative equality scholars privilege *opinio juris*. For them, even when the existence and validity of consent was not in doubt, states qualified their pro-government interventions by invoking certain special circumstances, which arguably reflects the legal conviction that, in their absence, an incumbent government involved in a civil war could not be assisted by other states in spite of its request.[249] While the idea is not new,[250] the expression 'negative equality' was employed for the first time in the Report of the Independent International Fact-Finding Mission on the Conflict in Georgia (IIFFMCG) to refer to a situation where no invitation by any party can justify a military intervention by a third state in a country torn by civil war.[251] An obligation of negative equality in civil wars has also been famously

---

[240] Erik Castrén, *Civil War* (Suomalainen Tiedeakatemia 1966) 110.

[241] De Wet, *Military Assistance*, 76–83.

[242] Lieblich, *International Law*, 138–40.

[243] Natalino Ronzitti, 'Non-ingerenza negli affari interni di un altro Stato' in *Digesto delle discipline pubblicistiche*, vol X (UTET 1995) 159, 165.

[244] Pietro Pustorino, *Movimenti insurrezionali e diritto internazionale* (Cacucci 2018) 248–52.

[245] Plaidoirie de M Pellet, *Nicaragua v USA*, ICJ Pleadings, vol V, 218.

[246] *Nicaragua v USA*, para 246.

[247] John Norton Moore, 'Intervention: A Monochromatic Term for a Polychromatic Reality' in Richard A Falk (ed), *The Vietnam War and International Law*, vol 2 (Princeton University Press 1969) 1061, 1065.

[248] Théodore Christakis and Karine Bannelier, '*Volenti non fit injuria*? Les effets du consentement à l'intervention militaire' (2004) 50 AFDI 102, 128.

[249] See eg Karine Bannelier-Christakis, 'Military Intervention Against ISIL in Iraq, Syria and Libya, and the Legal Basis of Consent' (2016) 29 LJIL 743, 748.

[250] See Chapter I, Section 10.

[251] Report of the Independent International Fact-Finding Mission on the Conflict in Georgia, September 2009, vol II, 178 <www.mpil.de/files/pdf4/IIFFMCG_Volume_II1.pdf>. The report notes that 'the legal solution to prohibit intervention in a civil war ... is prudent from a policy perspective, because it removes the pretext of "invitation" relied on by third states in order to camouflage interventions motivated by their own policy objectives' (ibid, 279).

136 INTERNATIONAL LAW AND THE PRINCIPLE OF NON-INTERVENTION

endorsed by the Institut de droit international in its 1975 Wiesbaden Resolution on the Principle of Non-Intervention in Civil Wars (Wiesbaden Resolution), which affirms that third states must refrain from giving any assistance to parties to a civil war with the exception of humanitarian aid, technical or economic aid not likely to have any substantial impact on the outcome of the conflict, and of assistance prescribed, authorized, or recommended by the United Nations.[252]

Within this school, however, disagreement exists on the legal basis of the obligation of negative equality. For some writers, it is the consequence of the loss of effective territorial control by the government, which is inherent in the occurrence of a civil war or in a request for assistance.[253] Others focus on the principle of self-determination and/ or on the political independence of states: for Charles Chaumont, for instance, foreign intervention on any side in an internal armed conflict by definition deprives a people of the right to choose its political system.[254] Jacques Noël adds that it does not matter whether or not the insurgents have managed to control territory for the application of negative equality: indeed, '[a]dmettre l'intervention dans ses phases initiales ne peut que priver un peuple de son droit de choisir son destin'.[255] What these authors do not clarify is 'whether the idea is for the logic of self-determination to bolster the argument for an absolute prohibition of intervention in the event of civil war or whether it is intended as a separate and parallel limitation—one that, presumably, applies to non-international armed conflicts more generally'.[256]

The negative equality doctrine has been accused of overlooking state practice and of not giving sufficient weight to the undeniable fact that recent and less recent history has been plagued with numerous interventions. The link between self-determination and compulsory negative equality has also been criticized. Roger Pinto, for instance, observes that the prohibition of all interventions in a civil war does not uphold the popular will when the insurgents are trying to overthrow a democratically elected government.[257] For Gregory Fox, the doctrine of compulsory negative equality leads

[252] Arts 2 and 3, Resolution on the Principle of Non-Intervention in Civil Wars of the Institut de Droit International (Wiesbaden Resolution) 14 August 1975 <www.idi-iil.org/app/uploads/2017/06/1975_wies_03_en.pdf>.

[253] Ann Van Wynen Thomas and AJ Thomas, Jr, *Non-Intervention: The Law and Its Import in the Americas* (Southern Methodist University Press 1956) 94; Quincy Wright, 'United States Intervention in the Lebanon' (1959) 53 AJIL 112, 121; Eric David, *Mercenaires et volontaires internationaux en droit des gens* (Editions de l'Université de Bruxelles 1978) 79; Louise Doswald-Beck, 'The Legal Validity of Military Intervention by Invitation of the Government' (1985) 56 BYBIL 189, 196; Tanca, *Foreign Armed Intervention*, 22; Enzo Cannizzaro, *Diritto internazionale* (3rd edn, Giappichelli 2016), 59–60 (who concedes, however, that state practice is still inconclusive).

[254] Charles Chaumont, 'Analyse critique de l'intervention américaine au Vietnam' (1968) 4 RBDI 61, 75. Of the same persuasion are, among others, Wolfgang Friedmann, 'United States Policy and the Crisis of International Law: Some Reflections on the State of International Law in "International Co-operation Year"' (1965) 59 AJIL 857, 866; Quincy Wright, 'Non-Military Intervention' in Karl W Deutsch and Stanley Hoffman (eds), *The Relevance of International Law. Essays in Honor of Leo Gross* (Schenkman 1968) 5, 17–18; Oscar Schachter, 'International Law: The Right of States to Use Armed Force' (1984) 82 Mich L Rev 1620, 1641; Doswald-Beck, 'The Legal Validity', 243; Rein Mullerson, 'Intervention by Invitation' in Lori Fisler Damrosch and David J Scheffer (eds), *Law and Force in the New International Order* (Westview Press 1991) 127, 132; Mary Ellen O'Connell, *The Art of Law in the International Community* (CUP 2019) 234.

[255] Noël, *Le principe*, 145.

[256] Dino Kritsiotis, 'Interrogations of Consent: A Reply to Erika de Wet' (2015) 26 EJIL 999, 1007–8.

[257] Roger Pinto, 'Les règles du droit international concernant la guerre civile' (1965) 114 Recueil des Cours 451, 483. See in the same vein Roberto Barsotti, 'Insorti' in *Enciclopedia del diritto*, vol XXI (Giuffrè 1971) 796, 811.

CONTEMPORARY INTERNATIONAL LAW AND CURRENT SCHOLARLY DEBATE   137

to the perpetuation of the status quo as it advantages the stronger party, which is normally the incumbent authority.[258] In his characteristically colourful language, John Norton Moore also rejects the 'Alice-in-Wonderland search for neutral principles'[259] and criticizes the 'Darwinian definition of self-determination as survival of the fittest within the national boundaries, even if fittest means most adept in the use of force'.[260]

7.2.3 The positive equality doctrine

In his 1965 Hague Academy course, Pinto taught his students that, state practice being contradictory, it is not possible to demonstrate the existence of a customary rule that prohibits intervention either on any side in a civil war or even only in support of insurgents.[261] In the absence of a treaty providing otherwise, therefore, third states may assist whichever faction they favour.[262] The only exceptions are situations of colonial domination and racist regimes, where it is impermissible to assist the colonial or racist governments but support for the insurgents continues to be allowed.[263] John Lawrence Hargrove agrees and posits that the consent of any faction is sufficient to justify third-state intervention, although only on the condition that it has certain specific purposes, namely, to stop human rights abuses or allow the population to choose a new government.[264] In an article written for the *New York University Law Review*, Thomas Franck and Nigel Rodley also claim that it is better to focus on 'realistic limits' rather than continue to insist on the 'futile and counterproductive' illegality of all interventions.[265] The two authors predict that, according to the emerging international law of foreign intervention in civil war, '[a]id to any rebellious movement, to the extent that it cannot be prevented by the status quo regime, will be legal': the principle of non-intervention thus only applies as an inter-bloc norm by prohibiting a superpower from supporting revolutionary movements with troops or military *matériel* in a state within the sphere of influence of the other.[266]

The positive equality doctrine has remained a minority one: it is inconsistent with contemporary state practice and *opinio juris* and with the *jus contra bellum* rules codified in the UN Charter. It is indicative that, in the debates that led to the adoption of the Wiesbaden Resolution, no member of the Institut de droit international maintained that assistance to insurgents is permissible.[267]

---

[258] Gregory H Fox, 'Intervention by Invitation' in Marc Weller (ed), *The Oxford Handbook of the Use of Force in International Law* (OUP 2015) 816, 829.

[259] John Norton Moore, 'The Lawfulness of Military Assistance to the Republic of Viet-Nam' (1967) 61 AJIL 1, 31.

[260] John Norton Moore, 'International Law and the United States Role in the Viet Nam War: A Reply' (1967) 76 Yale LJ 1051, 1081.

[261] Pinto, 'Les règles', 488–9.

[262] ibid, 490.

[263] ibid, 495.

[264] John Lawrence Hargrove, 'Intervention by Invitation and the Politics of the New World Order' in Fisler Damrosch and Scheffer (eds), *Law and Force*, 113, 121–2.

[265] Thomas M Franck and Nigel S Rodley, 'Legitimacy and Legal Rights of Revolutionary Movements with Special Reference to the Peoples' Revolutionary Government of South Viet Nam' (1970) 45 NYU L Rev 679, 689.

[266] ibid, 687–8.

[267] Rapport supplémentaire de Dietrich Schindler (1975) 56 AIDI 127.

7.2.4 The consent of all factions doctrine

As in the 19th century, some contemporary scholars have argued that consent by *all* factions is necessary for a foreign intervention in a situation of internal unrest. Thomas and Thomas, for instance, maintain that, if both government and insurgents accept it, its legality 'would then be based upon the total consent of the state'.[268] More recently, David Wippman has claimed that, when a political community is split between two or more opposing factions, consent to intervention, either ad hoc or by treaty, as well as its revocation, should reflect the concurrent will of all the factions.[269]

This school differs from the positive equality doctrine in that the latter allows intervention with the consent of *any* faction, while the present one requires the consent of *all* of them for the intervention to be lawful. By its very own logic, however, this doctrine can only make sense in the case of non-partisan operations, and not of interventions that aim to support one of the parties.

7.2.5 The purpose-based doctrine

The purpose-based doctrine is a variant of the negative equality doctrine as it assumes that any third-state intervention in civil wars is in principle impermissible. For these scholars, however, intervention can become lawful in certain situations because of the purpose pursued by the intervening states.[270] Théodore Christakis and Karine Bannelier, in particular, distinguish between situations of internal unrest where the insurgents are a genuine expression of popular aspirations and other situations where the insurgents do not embody internal self-determination instances, as in the case of terrorist groups. In the former, in order to be lawful the intervention must have a legitimate purpose, that is, it must not aim at influencing the outcome of the internal struggle.[271] In the latter, on the other hand, interventions in support of a government are generally permissible.[272] Georg Nolte agrees and posits that intervention can be based on consent only when it does not aim to influence the outcome of an internal armed conflict, as in the case of intervention to protect nationals.[273]

As Antoine Rougier already affirmed at the beginning of the 20th century, however, '[u]ne bonne intention ne suffit pas à légitimer une illégalité'.[274] Critics of the purpose-based approach have pointed out that the motivations or reasons for an intervention are not the same as its legal justifications and, therefore, do not equate with *opinio juris*.[275] It is also unclear whether it is the *declared* or the *real* purpose of an

---

[268] Thomas and Thomas, *Non-Intervention*, 215. President Compaoré of Burkina Faso, for instance, criticized the ECOWAS intervention in Liberia because, in his view, it could have only taken place with the consent of all factions (David Wippman, 'Enforcing the Peace: ECOWAS and the Liberian Civil War' in Lori Fisler Damrosch (ed), *Enforcing Restraint: Collective Intervention in Internal Conflicts* (Council of Foreign Relations Press 1993) 157, 168).

[269] David Wippman, 'Treaty-Based Intervention: Who Can Say No?' (1995) 62 U Chi L Rev 607, 630, 650.

[270] Hasar, *State Consent*, 309.

[271] Christakis and Bannelier, '*Volenti non fit injuria?*', 120.

[272] ibid, 124–6.

[273] Nolte, *Eingreifen*, 562–3.

[274] Antoine Rougier, *Les guerres civiles et le droit des gens* (Larose & Forcel 1903) 362.

[275] In Kolb's view, states normally invoke governmental consent as the legal basis for their interventions, while other factors 'are rather adduced to politically strengthen and colour the claims, but they are not legally necessary to justify the use of force' (Robert Kolb, *International Law on the Maintenance of Peace:* Jus Contra Bellum (Edward Elgar 2018) 453).

CONTEMPORARY INTERNATIONAL LAW AND CURRENT SCHOLARLY DEBATE   139

intervention that would be relevant and how the latter could be established with suffi-cient certainty.[276] Finally, even when the third state genuinely intervenes to, say, pro-tect nationals or for humanitarian reasons and thus does not intend to influence the outcome of civil strife, the intervention could still result in advantaging one faction to the detriment of the other, as in the case of the 1964 joint US–Belgium operation in Stanleyville (now Kisangani).[277]

7.2.6 The policy-oriented school

For Myres S. McDougal and Harold D. Lasswell, the founders of the policy-oriented New Haven School of International Law, law is an instrument aimed at promoting human welfare: for them, it is fundamental to identify the base values towards the real-ization of which the law must be directed, and not just formal rules detached from the reality in which they are supposed to operate.[278] Once such values are identified, the role of law, including international law, is to contribute to the realization of as many of them as possible. The scholars belonging to this school, therefore, do not identify the rules on foreign intervention on the basis of state practice and *opinio juris*, but by focusing on how well they conform to and support the base values at the core of the international order.[279]

In his influential 1969 article published in the *Virginia Journal of International Law* on the legality of the US intervention in the Second Indochina War, John Norton Moore, a former student of McDougal's at Yale in the 1960s, condemns the 'abstrac-tions of the Charter'[280] and argues that the non-intervention standards must be ac-ceptable, workable, certain, and effective.[281] He criticizes the debate between the non-intervention and negative equality doctrines because it distracts attention from the real issues, namely identifying 'limitations on types of assistance, area limitations, international procedural processes, or conditioning external assistance on willingness to hold free elections'.[282] 'Loosely' applying McDougal and Lasswell's policy-oriented approach to the problem of intervention,[283] Moore frowns upon attempts to regulate it by identifying a single rigid rule and argues for a more flexible approach, centred on the function that the norms on intervention must perform, which can be accept-able to states, reasonably workable, and reasonably certain.[284] From this perspective,

---

[276] Veronika Bílková, 'Reflections on the Purpose-Based Approach' (2019) 79 ZaöRV 681, 681–2; Christian Henderson, 'A Countering of the Asymmetrical Interpretation of the Doctrine of Counter-Intervention' (2021) 8 JUFIL 34, 38.

[277] See Chapter V, Section 3.2.2.

[278] Harold D Lasswell and Myres S McDougal, *Jurisprudence for a Free Society: Studies in Law, Science and Policy*, vols I and II (New Haven Press/Nijhoff 1992). See also Myres McDougal and Florentino P Feliciano, *Law and Minimum World Public Order. The Legal Regulation of International Coercion* (Yale University Press 1961).

[279] Farer suggests that these values are revealed in 'multilateral and bilateral treaties, decisions of inter-national tribunals, resolutions of authoritative organs of the United Nations, writings of journalists, publi-cists, and propagandists, and the writings, statements, and actions of national decisionmakers' (Tom J Farer, 'Problems of an International Law of Intervention' (1968) 3 Stan J Intl Stud 20, 22).

[280] John Norton Moore, 'The Control of Foreign Intervention in Internal Conflict' (1969) 9 Va J Intl L 205, 211.

[281] ibid, 253.

[282] Moore, 'Intervention', 1088.

[283] Moore, 'The Control', 221.

[284] ibid, 253.

140   INTERNATIONAL LAW AND THE PRINCIPLE OF NON-INTERVENTION

he identifies three basic community policies at stake in the case of intervention: self-determination (intended broadly as 'the freedom of a people to choose their own government and institutions and to control their own resources'),[285] minimum human rights, and minimum public order.[286] He then categorizes six situations, characterized by the increasing threat they present to these community policies: non-authority oriented intervention; anti-colonial wars; wars of secession; indigenous conflicts for control of internal authority structures; external imposition of authority structures; and Cold-War divided nation conflicts.[287] These situations are subdivided into twenty-one claims of intervention: their admissibility essentially depends on whether or not the claim implements most, and preferably all, of the community policies.[288] In an indigenous insurgency for the control of internal authority structures, in particular, Moore suggests that all interventions, including those in support of a widely recognized government, should be prohibited with the exception of the case where the insurgents are receiving unlawful external assistance, which allows proportionate counter-intervention.[289] Pre-insurgency assistance to the government, however, remains permissible, as its interruption would result in an unfair advantage for the insurgents.[290] Overall, a government's authority to request external assistance is reduced when it lacks 'rightness to govern' or effective control of territory, or both: the former is relevant from the perspective of the self-determination community policy, the latter from that of minimum public order.[291] Moore's theory has been criticized for being based on information that is not easily available, for being too subjective, and for allowing states to pursue their own political agendas.[292]

Similarly to Moore, Tom Farer identifies four core values in the contemporary international society: minimum public order (i.e. the avoidance of conduct that might lead to general war), self-determination (as limited to decolonization), minimum human rights, and modernization (that is, the need to raise the standards of living).[293] Unlike Moore, however, he identifies a single categorical rule on intervention, which maximizes the abovementioned values and is 'more likely to win the support of the international community and become incorporated into customary international law'.[294]

---

[285] ibid, 247.

[286] ibid, 246–53. Moore concludes that self-determination and minimum public order support more the US intervention on the side of South Vietnam than North Vietnam's military assistance to the Việt Cộng (John Norton Moore, 'Law and Politics in the Vietnamese War: A Response to Professor Friedmann' (1967) 61 AJIL 1039, 1049).

[287] Moore, 'The Control', 256.

[288] ibid, 256–7.

[289] ibid, 272.

[290] ibid, 272–3.

[291] Moore, 'Intervention', 1081.

[292] Tom J Farer, 'Harnessing Rogue Elephants: A Short Discourse on Foreign Intervention in Civil Strife' (1969) 82 Harv L Rev 511, 522–4. For Friedmann, 'in the absence of third-party determination, "minimum public order" means, Humpty-Dumpty like, what the policy-maker wants it to mean, a catch-all phrase to justify whatever action the writer wishes to justify' (Wolfgang Friedmann, 'Law and Politics in the Vietnamese War: A Comment' (1967) 61 AJIL 776, 783).

[293] Farer, 'Problems', 22–4. In his Hague course, however, he argues that the two overriding values in international society are the preservation of the nation-state and the avoidance of armed conflict between states, to which other values, like self-determination, are subordinated (Tom J Farer, 'The Regulation of Foreign Intervention in Civil Armed Conflict' (1974) 142 Recueil des Cours 291, 335–7).

[294] Farer, 'Problems', 22.

In his view, this rule is 'a flat prohibition of participation in tactical operations, either openly or through the medium of advisors or volunteers', although third states remain free to provide other types of support to any side, be they the incumbent government or the insurgents.[295] In Farer's view, the proposed rule avoids the risks of the escalation and internationalization of the conflict (minimum public order) and also reduces the level of damage in the country torn by civil strife (minimum human rights).[296] Farer's views have been criticized by Moore, who sees them as 'undesirable, both in permitting a wide variety of activities that would now be regarded as impermissible intervention and, conversely, in overly-broadly prohibiting some forms of intervention, such as counter-intervention and humanitarian intervention, which may sometimes require participation in tactical operations if they are to be effective'.[297]

For his part, Michael Reisman, the Myres McDougal Professor Emeritus of Law at Yale Law School, claims that a degree of coercion is inevitable in social life and that the critical question is 'whether it has been applied in support of or against community order and basic policies, and whether it was applied in ways whose net consequences include increased congruence with community goals and minimum order'.[298] On this basis, he concludes that it is not impermissible to forcefully intervene to replace a despotic government with a democratic one, as the United States did in Grenada and Panama.

Distancing himself from both the New Haven and the more formalist Columbia scholars, Richard Falk, another of McDougal's students, criticizes what he calls the 'rule-oriented legalism' and the 'policy-oriented reductionism' and proposes 'an intermediate approach ... through the identification of critical thresholds, the advocacy of frameworks of guidance, and the emphasis on obligations to provide a public accounting of action undertaken'.[299] For him, '[t]he task of legal analysis is to find a middle ground, conjoining law to politics without collapsing the one into the other and attaining a realism that neither expects law to guarantee a peaceful world nor concludes that law is irrelevant to international peace'.[300] In Falk's view, states can be expected to comply with a non-intervention rule only if it reflects two 'structural needs' of the international community: it must not endanger national security and it must be supplemented by the establishment of effective ways to achieve peaceful changes to the existing status quo.[301] He identifies four patterns of civil strife: civil strife without significant foreign intervention; civil strife with foreign intervention by states other than great powers or their surrogates; civil strife with foreign intervention

---

[295] Tom J Farer, 'Intervention in Civil Wars: A Modest Proposal' (1967) 67 Colum L Rev 266, 275.

[296] Farer, 'Harnessing Rogue Elephants', 532–5. For him, 'the staffing of military schools and the delivery of matériel to either side in zones not contested by the other with ground forces' are examples of assistance short of tactical support (Farer, 'Problems', 26).

[297] John Norton Moore, 'Towards an Applied Theory for the Regulation of Intervention' in Moore (ed), *Law and Civil War*, 3, 31.

[298] W Michael Reisman, 'Coercion and Self-Determination: Construing Article 2(4)' (1984) 78 AJIL 642, 645.

[299] Richard A Falk, 'Introduction' in Richard A Falk (ed), *The International Law of Civil War*, vol I (The Johns Hopkins Press 1971) 1, 28. For him, in the policy-oriented approach 'the choice of action is left indeterminate, no fixed guidelines are hazarded, and the only imperative is the rhetorical one that a government explain its policy preferences by reference to world-community values' (ibid).

[300] Richard A Falk, *The Status of Law in International Society* (Princeton University Press 1970) 51.

[301] Richard A Falk, *Legal Order in a Violent World* (Princeton University Press 1968) 165–6.

by great powers or their surrogates (within or outside their sphere of influence); and civil strife where foreign intervention is claimed to constitute an armed attack.[302] In relation to each of them, he identifies rules that are in his view compatible with international law: in the first case, either non-discrimination or discrimination in favour of the incumbent government; in the second, either counter-intervention by a regional power or international peacekeeping; in the third, counter-intervention; and in the fourth, (collective) self-defence or counter-intervention.[303] Falk also argues that, while the incumbent government can be presumed to be legitimate, the presumption is rebutted if it is founded on colonial domination or racial discrimination, in which case the rules on non-intervention are suspended.[304] If the conflict becomes a 'major civil war between two rivals who each govern a portion of the disputed state (the factual conception of belligerency)', both administrations are legitimate and the 'most orderly disposition' is non-intervention on either side apart from the case of counter-intervention.[305] All in all, Falk criticizes the rigidity of the principle of non-intervention, which is 'inappropriate for a world of growing interdependence' and for 'the need to centralize authority and control with respect to internal war, to substitute community management for domestic autonomy, and to entrust supranational actors with gradually increasing competence and responsibility for the regulation of an internal war'.[306] Falk's views have been criticized by B. S. Chimni for being 'too broad, lacking the specificity of Farer's suggestion'.[307]

7.2.7 The TWAIL approach

Painted with a broad brush, the TWAIL approach to intervention by invitation is grounded in three main propositions. First, as Chimni points out, 'no assistance can be provided to the established government to crush a rebellion at any stage'.[308] Like Farer, he argues for 'a flat prohibition of participation in tactical operations'[309] but, unlike the American scholar, he extends it to arms transfers. In Chimni's view, this comprehensive prohibition does not result in supporting the insurgents: '[i]f the masses are with the established government then it has nothing to fear'.[310] Farideh Shaygan has also stressed that intervention by invitation cannot constitute an exception to the principle of self-determination as it is against the political independence of the state and against the purposes of the United Nations.[311] For her, self-determination is

---

[302] Richard A Falk, 'The New States and International Legal Order' (1966) 118 Recueil des Cours 1, 67–9.

[303] ibid, 69.

[304] Falk, *Legal Order*, 151.

[305] ibid, 152. On this basis, Falk concludes that the Việt Cộng had acquired enough '*de facto* sovereignty' in South Vietnam to be treated on an equal footing to the Saigon government for the purposes of intervention (Richard A Falk, 'International Law and the United States Role in Viet Nam: A Response to Professor Moore' (1967) 76 Yale LJ 1095, 1136).

[306] Falk, *Legal Order*, 147, 149.

[307] Bhupinder Singh Chimni, 'Towards a Third World Approach to Non-Intervention: Through the Labyrinth of Western Doctrine' (1980) 20 IJIL 243, 262.

[308] Chimni, 'Towards a Third World Approach', 263.

[309] ibid.

[310] ibid, 264.

[311] Farideh Shaygan, 'Intervention by Invitation as a Tool of New Colonialism' in James Crawford, Abdul G Koroma, Said Mahmoudi, and Alain Pellet (eds), *The International Legal Order: Current Needs and Possible Responses: Essays in Honour of Djamchid Momtaz* (Brill/Nijhoff, 2017) 767, 770.

breached not only when a state intervenes in a civil war occurring in another country, but also in other less serious situations of internal unrest if the aim is to support a government against its own population.[312] The record of the intervening state should be looked at, in particular whether it has an interventionist policy history, it enjoys democratic legitimacy, or it is suspected of supporting terrorist organizations or dictatorial regimes.[313]

Second, several TWAIL scholars advocate a central role to be played by the United Nations. For Shaygan, for instance, the determination of the legality of invited interventions should be entrusted to an impartial body set up by the United Nations.[314] Chimni also proposes that intervention in civil strife should be the exclusive prerogative of the international community and should be exercised through the United Nations: to be permissible, therefore, it should need the authorization of the Security Council or the General Assembly.[315]

Third, and finally, TWAILers have claimed that an intervention in support of national liberation movements against colonial or racist governments constitutes an admissible exception to the negative equality rule and is thus lawful even when it consists of military assistance. This view is explored in Chapter VI.[316]

8. Conclusions

This chapter showed that, in the UN Charter era, the principle of non-intervention has continued to enjoy good health: not only has it remained at the focus of scholarly interest, particularly when applied to situations of internal unrest, but it also has been incorporated in a plethora of global, regional, sub-regional, and thematic treaties and it undeniably reflects customary international law. Indeed, states of all ideological and geographical affiliations, both during and after the end of the Cold War, have considered it a beneficial instrument protecting both their individual security interests and the general cause of world peace. Conduct inconsistent with the principle has been justified by the intervening states on the basis of alleged exceptions or has been denied, thus confirming the principle's validity. Only the narrower prohibition of armed intervention, however, is an obligation *erga omnes*, and only those armed interventions qualifying as acts of aggression constitute *jus cogens* violations.

If its existence can hardly be doubted, it is undeniable that, as demonstrated by this chapter's survey of scholarship, the exact normative content of the principle of non-intervention has remained the object of contention. Two issues, in particular, remain unsettled: whether the principle under consideration only prohibits armed intervention or also other forms of coercion; and whether, in a civil war, it exclusively prohibits intervention in support of insurgents or also that to assist the incumbent government. The former problem is examined in Chapter III, the latter in Chapter V.

---

[312] ibid, 780.
[313] ibid, 782.
[314] ibid.
[315] Chimni, 'Towards a Third World Approach', 263.
[316] See Chapter VI, Section 3.2.1.

III
The Content of the Principle of Non-Intervention

1. Introduction

Chapter II showed how the principle of non-intervention is not only contained in several treaties but is also reflected in customary international law. But what does 'intervention' mean? The question has fascinated, and troubled, generations of international lawyers. Seeing the difficulties as insurmountable, a former US member of the Inter-American Juridical Committee reached the conclusion that intervention cannot be defined because it covers situations that 'are so varied that a definition may be too broad or too narrow to anticipate cases that arise'.[1] Rosalyn Higgins is of the same persuasion: 'intervention can mean many different things to many people'.[2] For her, 'not only is it not profitable to seek such definition, but ... really one is dealing with a spectrum'.[3]

In John Norton Moore's view, however, although '[t]he normative aspects of interventionary behavior present a great puzzle, [it is] not one that is incapable of solution'.[4] This chapter takes up Moore's challenge and explores what the principle of non-intervention exactly prohibits on the basis of an in-depth analysis of the relevant primary sources and of the post-1945 practice and *opinio juris* of states. It starts by discussing what constitutes coercion of state in the present context and whether intent and motive are elements of the notion of 'intervention'. It then investigates what the principle under examination protects. Finally, it distinguishes different forms of coercion and establishes whether they are all prohibited by the customary principle of non-intervention.

---

[1] Dissenting Statement of Dr James Oliver Murdock, US member of the Inter-American Juridical Committee, in Inter-American Juridical Committee, Instrument Relating to Violations of the Principle of Nonintervention: Draft and Report Prepared in Accordance with Resolution VII of the Fifth Meeting of Consultation of Ministers of Foreign Affairs (Pan-American Union 1959) 19, 22. For a summary of the debates in the Special Committee on Friendly Relations on the opportunity to define 'intervention', see UN Doc A/5746, 16 November 1964, paras 230–4.

[2] Rosalyn Higgins, 'Intervention and International Law' in Hedley Bull (ed), *Intervention in World Politics* (Clarendon Press 1984) 29, 29.

[3] ibid, 30.

[4] John Norton Moore, 'Legal Standards for Intervention in Internal Conflicts' (1983) 13 Ga J Intl & Comp L 191, 191.

International Law and the Principle of Non-Intervention. Marco Roscini, Oxford University Press. © Marco Roscini 2024.
DOI: 10.1093/oso/9780198786894.003.0004

2. Intervention: 'A Monochromatic Term for a Polychromatic Reality'[5]

The primary sources that contain elements helpful to identify what conduct the principle of non-intervention proscribes are the Charter of the Organization of American States (OAS), General Assembly Resolutions 2131 (XX) and 2625 (XXV), the Helsinki Final Act, and the jurisprudence of the International Court of Justice (ICJ).[6] After reaffirming it in its general terms, Article 19 of the 1948 OAS Charter specifies that the principle of non-intervention 'prohibits not only armed force but also any other form of interference or attempted threat against the personality of the State or against its political, economic, and cultural elements'.[7] Article 20 specifically addresses 'coercive measures of an economic or political character' and forbids them when they are used or encouraged 'in order to force the sovereign will of another State and obtain from it advantages of any kind'.

The language of Article 19 of the OAS Charter is reproduced in General Assembly Resolutions 2131 (1965) and 2625 (1970) with minor adjustments,[8] while Article 20 is incorporated with more noticeable modifications: it is not only economic and political coercion that is condemned in the resolutions but also 'any other type of [coercive] measures', and the subjective element is rephrased to read 'in order to obtain from [the victim state] the subordination of the exercise of its sovereign rights *or* to secure advantages of any kind'.[9] Furthermore, a sentence condemning subversion is added: 'no State shall organize, assist, foment, finance, incite or tolerate subversive, terrorist or armed activities directed towards the violent overthrow of the regime of another State, or interfere in civil strife in another State'. Last but not least, in the General Assembly resolutions the 'use of force to deprive peoples of their national identity' is singled out as a discrete case of prohibited intervention.[10]

Principle VI of the 1975 Helsinki Final Act employs partly innovative language with respect to the previous documents.[11] The first paragraph is more concise than its

---

[5] John Norton Moore, 'Intervention: A Monochromatic Term for a Polychromatic Reality' in Richard Falk (ed), *The Vietnam War and International Law*, vol 2 (Princeton University Press 1969) 1061, 1061–2.

[6] Attempts to identify the conduct prohibited by the principle of non-intervention were also made by the Inter-American Juridical Committee (on two occasions) and by the International Law Commission (ILC). In 1959, at the request of the Fifth Meeting of Consultation of Ministers of Foreign Affairs, the Inter-American Juridical Committee produced a report containing a list of cases of prohibited intervention (Inter-American Juridical Committee, Instrument Relating to Violations). The document was expanded and updated in 1974 upon request of the OAS General Assembly and Permanent Council (OAS, Draft Instrument of Instances of Violation of the Principle of Nonintervention and Statement of Reasons Approved by the Inter-American Juridical Committee at Its Regular Meeting Held in January–February 1974, OEA/Ser.G, CP/doc 388/74, 5 December 1974). For the ILC's works on the principle of non-intervention in the context of the Draft Code on Offences against the Peace and Security of Mankind, see Chapter II, Section 6.

[7] Charter of the Organization of American States (Bogotá, 30 April 1948) 119 UNTS 47.

[8] Apart from the sentence structure, the only difference is that, in the General Assembly resolutions, 'armed force' is replaced by 'armed intervention'.

[9] GA Resolutions 2131 (XX), 21 December 1965, paras 1–2, and 2625 (XX), 24 October 1970, Annex, third principle, paras 1–2, emphasis added. The Special Committee on Friendly Relations explained that the replacement of 'and' with 'or' was aimed at making the text consistent with Art 19 (now 20) of the OAS Charter and was not meant to restrict the meaning or scope of the 1965 Declaration on Intervention (UN Doc A/8018, 1970, para 88).

[10] This aspect of the principle of non-intervention is explored in Chapter VI, Section 2.

[11] Principle VI, Final Act of the 1st CSCE Summit of Heads of State or Government (Helsinki, 1 August 1975) (1975) 14 ILM 1292.

counterparts in the OAS Charter and the General Assembly resolutions as it omits the reference to 'other forms of interference or attempted threats against the personality of the State or against its political, economic and cultural elements'. Also omitted is 'for any reason whatever', arguably to avoid that resort to countermeasures can be considered a prohibited intervention.[12] As to non-armed intervention, intent is worded more elegantly than in the General Assembly resolutions: coercion must be 'designed to subordinate to their own interest the exercise by another participating State of the rights inherent in its sovereignty and thus to secure advantages of any kind'. Finally, in the Helsinki Final Act the condemnation of direct and indirect assistance to subversive, terrorist or other activities directed towards the violent overthrow of the government in another state is shortened and simplified by omitting the list of individual acts. The reference to the use of force to deprive peoples of their national identity also does not appear in Principle VI.

The ICJ has had more than one opportunity to express its views on the content of the principle of non-intervention. In the *Corfu Channel* Judgment, it found that intervention is a 'manifestation of a policy of force'.[13] Although the Court did not expand on the point, this seems to suggest that an act of intervention has two components: first, there must be some force involved, which is not necessarily armed;[14] and second, this force must be manifested to the victim state. Taken literally, this would exclude that covert subversive operations constitute an intervention, a conclusion that would be at odds with the letter of General Assembly Resolutions 2131 and 2625 and of the Helsinki Final Act, as well as with the subsequent jurisprudence of the Court, all of which do not make distinctions on that basis. It is plausible, therefore, that what the ICJ meant by 'manifestation' was simply that intervention is an act, covert or not, which *embodies* a policy of force.

It is mainly in the *Nicaragua* Merits Judgment that the Court elaborated on the notion of intervention. More specifically, it found that '[t]he principle of non-intervention involves the right of every sovereign State to conduct its affairs without outside interference'[15] and that a prohibited intervention consists in the use of methods of coercion in regard to 'matters in which each State is permitted, by the principle of State sovereignty, to decide freely', including—but not limited to—'the choice of a political, economic, social and cultural system, and the formulation of foreign policy'.[16] Like the General Assembly resolutions, the Court specified that coercion can occur not only directly through military action, but also indirectly by supporting 'subversive or terrorist armed activities within another State'.[17]

Taken together, the aforementioned sources suggest that non-intervention is not only a general principle prohibiting coercion in regard to matters in which a state is

---

[12] Gaetano Arangio-Ruiz, 'Human Rights and Non-Intervention in the Helsinki Final Act' (1977) 157 Recueil des Cours 195, 275.

[13] *Corfu Channel (United Kingdom of Great Britain and Northern Ireland v Albania)* (Merits) [1949] ICJ Rep 4, 35 (hereafter *Corfu Channel*).

[14] As the following sentence makes clear, the Court saw Operation Retail, ie an armed operation, only as a 'particular form' that an intervention can assume (ibid).

[15] *Case Concerning Military and Paramilitary Activities in and against Nicaragua (Nicaragua v United States of America)* (Merits) [1986] ICJ Rep 3, para 202 (hereafter *Nicaragua v USA*).

[16] ibid, para 205.

[17] ibid.

CONTENT OF THE PRINCIPLE OF NON-INTERVENTION   147

entitled to decide freely, but also consists of more specific rules of application that prohibit certain means and methods of coercion.[18] It is helpful to visualize it as Greek temple, where the tympanum representing the general principle surmounts three pillars: 1) the prohibition of armed coercion exercised towards another state or to deprive peoples of their national identity (now also banned by the prohibition of the use of force and the principle of self-determination, respectively); 2) the prohibition of economic and political measures designed to obtain the subordination of the exercise of the sovereign rights of the target state to the interests of the coercing state and secure advantages; and 3) the prohibition of the organization, assistance, fomentation, financing, incitement, or toleration of subversive, terrorist, or armed activities directed towards the overthrow of a foreign government, as well as of any interference in the civil strife occurring in another state.

The two elements of the general principle of non-intervention identified by the ICJ in *Nicaragua* (coercion and 'matters in which each State is permitted, by the principle of State sovereignty, to decide freely') as well as the relevance of intent and motive as possible further elements of the principle under examination are analysed in the following sections before we look at the rules of application prohibiting specific means and methods of coercion.

3. Coercion as 'the Very Essence' of Intervention

Let us assume that State A wants to annex a region of State B. In order to achieve its purpose, State A can: a) send its army and take control of the region; b) support secessionist insurgents operating thereby who, once they manage to take control of the region, will hold a referendum and ask for its annexation to State A; c) demand that State B surrender the region otherwise it will dramatically cut its import of State B's main export and will thus cause its economic collapse; d) threaten State B with breaking off diplomatic relations unless negotiations are initiated with regard to the status of the disputed territory; e) prematurely recognize the independence of the disputed territory and then accept its request of becoming part of State A. Assuming that the status of the territory is a domestic matter of State B, which of the above situations can be considered coercive and thus lead to a violation of the principle of non-intervention?

To answer this question, we need to take a step back. Identifying coercion as the core feature of the notion of 'intervention' is not a new idea, as most writers had already reached this conclusion well before the adoption of the UN Charter.[19] Coercion goes 'beyond the limits of persuasion and good counsel as between governments

---

[18] After reaffirming the principle of non-intervention in the usual general terms, GA Res 36/103 of 9 December 1981 containing the Declaration on the Inadmissibility of Intervention and Interference in the Internal Affairs of States also lists a long series of additional rights and duties claimed to be 'comprehended' by the principle in question. The resolution, however, met with the opposition of the Western states, which voted against it, and cannot be used to identify customary international law.

[19] See Chapter I, Section 10. Coercion can also be a ground for excluding state responsibility under Art 18 of the ILC's Articles on the Responsibility of States for Internationally Wrongful Acts (ARSIWA) [2001] YB ILC, vol II, part two, 26, and a ground for the invalidity of treaties under Art 52, Vienna Convention on the Law of Treaties (VCLT) (Vienna, 23 May 1969) 1155 UNTS 331.

148 INTERNATIONAL LAW AND THE PRINCIPLE OF NON-INTERVENTION

associated in a common cause'.[20] As the Inter-American Juridical Committee notes, '[i]t is … a distortion of the normal relations between states and a deviation from the regular means of negotiation, which perturb the usual channels of international relations'.[21] To coerce, in other words, is not the same as to influence: during the drafting of the Friendly Relations Declaration, it was proposed that the latter language should replace the former in a revised text of the principle of non-intervention contained in Resolution 2131 to be incorporated in Resolution 2625. Certain representatives, however, observed that this would have resulted in abolishing the diplomatic profession and would have made 'normal and customary diplomatic intercourse between States impossible'.[22] 'Coerce', therefore, was retained.

The ICJ has referred to the notion of coercion of state on a couple of occasions, but without shedding much light on it. In the *Tehran Hostages* case, the Court qualified the continued detention of US diplomatic staff as 'a means of coercing the sending State'.[23] In *Nicaragua*, the ICJ did not define coercion even though it deemed it to be the key element of intervention. The Court only stated that a 'particularly obvious' example of coercion is an intervention that employs the use of force 'either in the direct form of military action, or in the indirect form of support for subversive or terrorist armed activities within another State'.[24] Coercion, however, can also consist of methods other than the direct and indirect use of armed force: as Judge Padilla Nervo wrote in his Dissenting Opinion in the *Fisheries Jurisdiction* case, '[a] big power can use force and pressure against a small nation in many ways, even by the very fact of diplomatically insisting in having its view recognized and accepted … certain "Notes" delivered by the government of a strong power to the government of a small nation, may have the same purpose and the same effect as the use or threat of force'.[25]

Not many international lawyers have devoted their attention to the notion of coercion of state. Among them are Myres McDougal and Florentino Feliciano, who see it not as an act but as a *process* that leads to the creation or reaffirmation of norms and involves 'certain participants applying to each other coercion of alternatively accelerating and decelerating intensity, for a whole spectrum of objectives, by methods which include the employment of all available instruments of policy, and under all the continually changing conditions of a world arena'.[26] The two authors explain that

---

[20] Note from the British Foreign Office dated 5 July 1928, in GH Hackworth, *Digest of International Law*, vol V (GPO 1943) 704.

[21] OAS, Draft Instrument of Instances of Violation, 6.

[22] UN Doc A/6799, 26 September 1967, para 353. In the *Dubai-Sharjah Border Arbitration*, the arbitral tribunal confirmed that '[m]ere influence and pressures cannot be equated with the concept of coercion as it is known in international law' (*Dubai-Sharjah Border Arbitration*, Award of 19 October 1981, 91 ILR 543, 571). During the works on the Draft Code of Offences against the Peace and Security of Mankind, several ILC members also highlighted the need to distinguish 'intervention' as a term of art from other forms of relations between states that are not characterized by an element of coercion ([1984] YB ILC vol II, part two, 61).

[23] *United States Diplomatic and Consular Staff in Tehran (USA v Iran)* (Judgment) [1980] ICJ Rep 1980 3, para 87 (hereafter *USA v Iran*).

[24] *Nicaragua v USA*, para 205.

[25] *Fisheries Jurisdiction (United Kingdom v Iceland)* (Jurisdiction) [1973] ICJ Rep 3, Dissenting Opinion of Judge Padilla Nervo, 47.

[26] Myres S McDougal and Florentino P Feliciano, 'International Coercion and World Public Order: The General Principles of the Law of War' (1958) 67 Yale LJ 771, 779. As Koskenniemi notes, both the Yale and Columbia internationalists 'agreed that international law was not merely formal diplomacy or cases from

CONTENT OF THE PRINCIPLE OF NON-INTERVENTION 149

the process of coercion is based on three dimensions of consequentiality, that is, 'the importance and number of values affected, the extent to which such values are affected and the number of participants whose values are so affected'.[27] The demands can range 'from such limited ones as the payment of a debt owed by the target state or its nationals ... to the complete absorption of the target state, the annihilation of its people and the establishment of a universal empire'.[28] As to the methods employed, they can be diplomatic (e.g. 'a threat of grievous deprivations', a refusal of recognition or the suspension/termination of diplomatic relations),[29] ideological (i.e. 'the selective manipulation and circulation of symbols, verbal or nonverbal, calculated to alter the patterns of identifications, demands and expectations of mass audiences in the target-state and thereby to induce or stimulate politically significant attitudes and behavior favorable to the initiator-state', including propaganda, infiltration, subversion, and coups d'état),[30] economic ('the management of access to a flow of goods, services and money, as well as to markets, with the end of denying the target-state such access while maintaining it for oneself')[31] and military.[32] McDougal and Feliciano, therefore, distinguish coercion from the narrower notions of force ('the infliction of severe deprivations of the value well-being through uses of the military instrument') and violence ('the most intense attacks on well-being by means of military weapons').[33]

States, however, have identified methods of coercion on the basis of the impact that they can have on the target state's agency.[34] A document on intervention prepared by the British Foreign and Commonwealth Office (FCO) in 1984, for instance, borrows Lassa Oppenheim's language and defines intervention as 'forcible or dictatorial interference by a state in the affairs of another state, calculated to deprive that state of control of the matter in question'.[35] In 2022, the UK Attorney General confirmed that coercion includes depriving the target state of its 'freedom of control' over matters in which it can decide freely.[36] For Canada, an activity breaches the principle of non-intervention when it 'would cause coercive effects that deprive, compel, or impose an outcome on

---

the International Court of Justice but that—if it were to be relevant—it had to be conceived in terms of broader political processes or techniques that aimed towards policy "objectives" ' (Martti Koskenniemi, *The Gentle Civilizer of Nations: The Rise and Fall of International Law 1870–1960* (CUP 2001) 479).

[27] McDougal and Feliciano, 'International Coercion', 782.

[28] ibid, 782–3, footnotes omitted.

[29] ibid, 792.

[30] ibid, 793.

[31] ibid, 794.

[32] ibid, 795.

[33] ibid, 779, fn 25.

[34] Jean Charpentier, 'Les effets du consentement sur l'intervention' in *Mélanges Seferiades*, vol II (De Ange Ath Klissounis 1961) 489–90; HG de Jong, 'Coercion in the Conclusion of Treaties: A Consideration of Articles 51 and 52 of the Convention on the Law of Treaties' (1984) 15 NYIL 209, 220–4; Gary P Corn, 'Covert Deception, Strategic Fraud, and the Rule of Prohibited Intervention', Hoover Working Group on National Security, Technology, and Law, Aegis Series Paper No 2005 (18 September 2020) 12 <www.hoover. org/sites/default/files/research/docs/corn_webready.pdf>.

[35] Foreign Office, 'Is Intervention Ever Justified?' in Geoffrey Marston (ed), 'United Kingdom Materials on International Law 1986' (1986) 57 BYBIL 487, 615.

[36] Attorney General's Office and The Rt Hon Suella Braverman KC MP, 'International Law in Future Frontiers', Speech at Chatham House, 19 May 2022 (hereafter Braverman, 'International Law') <www.gov. uk/government/speeches/international-law-in-future-frontiers>.

the affected State on matters in which it has free choice',[37] and in the Netherlands' view coercion 'means compelling a state to take a course of action (whether an act or an omission) that it would not otherwise voluntarily pursue'.[38] The Australian government sees coercive means as those which 'effectively deprive or are intended to deprive the State of the ability to control, decide upon or govern matters of an inherently sovereign nature'.[39] For New Zealand, an act breaches the principle of non-intervention if 'there is an intention to deprive the target state of control over matters falling within the scope of its inherently sovereign functions'.[40] Costa Rica's position is that coercion can be exercised 'in a multitude of ways where one State ... deprives another State of the capacity to make free and informed choices pertaining to its internal or external affairs.'[41] Finally, Germany has claimed that 'coercion implies that a State's internal processes regarding aspects pertaining to its *domaine réservé* are significantly influenced or thwarted and that its will is manifestly bent by the foreign State's conduct'.[42]

These statements suggest that, to be coercive, a measure must be able to undermine the agency of the target state and impair its decisional sovereignty: as noted, 'coercion is present if intervention cannot be terminated at the pleasure of the state that is subject to intervention'.[43] Decisional sovereignty can be impaired as a result of an individual act or of a combination of acts: to illustrate this point, Andrea Bianchi posits that, while the unilateral sanctions adopted by the United States against Cuba taken separately do not breach the principle of non-intervention, they do if considered as a whole because of their cumulative effects on the island's economy.[44] The same conclusion can be extended to the restrictive measures adopted by several Gulf states against Qatar in 2017: in light of their cumulative effect and considering that Qatar is dependent on imports by land and sea for the basic needs of its population, and about forty per cent of its food comes in through the land border with Saudi Arabia, it is clear that the measures were capable of having a coercive effect. Whether such measures constitute a violation of the principle of non-intervention, therefore, essentially

---

[37] Government of Canada, 'International Law Applicable in Cyberspace', 2022, para 22 <www.internatio nal.gc.ca/world-monde/issues_development-enjeux_developpement/peace_security-paix_securite/cyb erspace_law-cyberespace_droit.aspx?lang=eng>.

[38] UN Doc A/76/136, 13 July 2021, 57.

[39] ibid, 5.

[40] New Zealand Department of the Prime Minister and Cabinet (DPMC), 'The Application of International Law to State Activity in Cyberspace', 1 December 2020, para 9 <https://dpmc.govt.nz/publi cations/application-international-law-state-activity-cyberspace>.

[41] Ministerio de Relaciones Exteriores y Culto, Costa Rica's position on the application of international law in cyberspace, 2023, para 24 <https://docs-library.unoda.org/Open-Ended_Working_Group_on_ Information_and_Communication_Technologies_-_(2021)/Costa_Rica_-_Position_Paper_-_Internat ional_Law_in_Cyberspace.pdf> (hereafter Costa Rica's position).

[42] UN Doc A/76/136, 34.

[43] Edwin DeWitt Dickinson, *The Equality of States in International Law* (Harvard University Press 1920) 260. As Stefan Talmon suggests, '[t]he requirement of coercion is to be determined from the view of the target state. It depends on the impact of the measure on the target State' (Stefan Talmon, *Recognition of Governments in International Law: With Particular Reference to Governments in Exile* (OUP 1998) 248).

[44] Andrea Bianchi, 'Le recenti sanzioni unilaterali adottate dagli Stati Uniti nei confronti di Cuba e la loro liceità internazionale' (1998) 81 RDI 313, 335. Nigel White also argues that the Cuban embargo breaches the principle of non-intervention as it is coercive (Nigel D White, *The Cuban Embargo under International Law: El Bloqueo* (Routledge 2015) 142).

depends on whether they bear on 'matters in which each State is permitted, by the principle of State sovereignty, to decide freely'.

Even though the two expressions are often used interchangeably in diplomatic interactions, coercion is what distinguishes intervention from a mere interference.[45] The 'principle of non-interference' is frequently invoked by certain countries to censor other states' criticism of their policies or when foreign authorities meet with separatists.[46] As seen in Chapter II, in particular, the 'non-interference' language is frequently used in the African and Asian regional treaties.[47] General Assembly Resolution 36/103 (1981) on the Inadmissibility of Intervention and Interference in the Internal Affairs of States also condemns a long list of cases of interference. The resolution was essentially the brainchild of the Soviet Union and the communist bloc and, because of the significant number of abstentions and votes against at the moment of its adoption, cannot be used as declarative of customary international law.[48] All in all, it does not seem that this broader principle of 'non-interference' reflects customary international law.[49]

An important consequence derives from coercion as the core element of the principle of non-intervention: when a state has, through its competent organs, validly consented to a certain condition of things, the acts of another state that procured it are not an intervention. As Chapter IV shows, in particular, the deployment of troops in another state's territory at the request of its government is a case of cooperation, not intervention: it is correct to say, therefore, that the expression 'intervention by invitation' is an oxymoron and only makes sense if 'intervention' is used as a factual and not

[45] See eg Natalino Ronzitti, 'Non-ingerenza negli affari interni di un altro Stato' in *Digesto delle discipline pubblicistiche*, vol X (UTET 1995) 159, 161; Sean Watts, 'Low-Intensity Cyber Operations and the Principle of Non-Intervention' (2014) 14 Baltic YBIL 137, 144; Christian Henderson, *The Use of Force and International Law* (CUP 2018) 51. Alternative definitions of interference have also been suggested. At the 1977 Geneva Conference on the reaffirmation of international humanitarian law, for instance, a delegation affirmed that '"intervention" refers to subversive or terrorist activities, whereas the word "interference" may be used for ordinary "démarches" or protests' (Yves Sandoz, Christophe Swinarski, and Bruno Zimmermann (eds), *Commentary on the Additional Protocols of 8 June 1977 to the Geneva Conventions of 12 August 1949* (Nijhoff 1987) para 45069). For Niki Aloupi, intervention affects the territorial integrity of the target state, interference its political independence and domestic affairs (Niki Aloupi, 'The Right to Non-intervention and Non-interference' (2015) 4 Cambridge J Int'l & Comp L 566, 571–2). It does not seem, however, that these distinctions are reflected in state practice or diplomatic language.

[46] See eg Stefan Talmon, 'Meeting with Hong Kong Activist as Interference in China's Internal Affairs?' (*GPIL—German Practice in International Law*, 17 November 2020) <https://gpil.jura.uni-bonn.de/2020/11/meeting-with-hong-kong-activist-as-interference-in-chinas-internal-affairs/>. When, in August 2020, Argentina's minister for women, gender and diversity signed a letter sent by NGO Progressive International to the United Nations calling for democracy and transparency in Bolivia after former president Evo Morales had fled to Argentina and the undersecretary of public works tweeted his support for Morales and for the participation of Bolivian migrants in the presidential election, the Bolivian government formally complained claiming that these statements, made in an official capacity, had been made with the intention to influence the outcome of the elections in Bolivia 'in patent violation of international law and the principles of non-intervention and non-interference in the internal affairs of other States' (UN Doc A/74/1009, 15 September 2020, 2).

[47] See Chapter II, Sections 2.2.2 and 2.2.3.

[48] The resolution was adopted by 120 to twenty-two with six abstentions.

[49] Ido Kilovaty, 'Doxfare: Politically Motivated Leaks and the Future of the Norm on Non-Intervention in the Era of Weaponized Information' (2018) 9 Harv NSJ 146, 167.

152 INTERNATIONAL LAW AND THE PRINCIPLE OF NON-INTERVENTION

legal notion.[50] Whether or not consent can operate at all with regard to intervention at the request of a foreign government engulfed in a civil war is a question explored in Chapter V.

Note that, for the ICJ, a special standard of coercion applies in the decolonization context. In the *Chagos* Advisory Opinion, the Court found that 'heightened scrutiny should be given to the issue of consent in a situation where a part of a non-self-governing territory is separated to create a new colony' and that such consent must be 'based on the free and genuine expression of the will of the people concerned'.[51] Even if consent to a certain condition of things had been granted, therefore, coercion would still be present if said consent did not reflect the true aspirations of the concerned people. This special threshold, however, is applied by the Court only in the relations between the colony and the administering power and only with regard to 'consent in a situation where a part of a non-self-governing territory is separated to create a new colony'.[52]

3.1 Dictatorial Coercion

Coercion can assume two different forms: it can consist in compelling another state to do or not to do something *or* in taking control of a certain matter and forcibly imposing a condition of things.[53] For want of better expressions, I use Oppenheim's language and refer to the former as 'dictatorial' coercion and to the latter as 'forcible' coercion.[54] By causing or threatening to cause a certain harm to another state, dictatorial coercion *bends* the will of the victim state so to make it do or not do something: in our initial list of scenarios, this case corresponds to scenario (c), where a state is coerced into ceding part of its territory in order to avoid economic strangulation. The coercing state, therefore, does not achieve the intended condition of things itself, but compels the target state into procuring it. It is not that the target state's will is absent (as in the case of forcible coercion); rather, the will is deflected, and the internal decision-making process distorted, by a significant external pressure. The EU Commission describes this situation as follows:

---

[50] In his Preliminary Report to the Institut de droit international, Hafner notes that ' "intervention by invitation" is a *contradiction in se*' (Gerhard Hafner, Preliminary Report, Present Problems of the Use of Force in International Law—Sub-group: Intervention by Invitation (2009) 73 AIDI 310–11).

[51] *Legal Consequences of the Separation of the Chagos Archipelago from Mauritius in 1965* (Advisory Opinion) [2019] ICJ Rep 95, para 172 (hereafter *Chagos*). In 1965, the United Kingdom subordinated the granting of independence to Mauritius to the separation of the Chagos Archipelago (*Chagos*, Written statement of the Republic of Mauritius, vol I, 1 March 2018, 91–100).

[52] *Chagos*, para 172.

[53] The distinction corresponds to that between direct and indirect coercion contained in "Projet de règlement sur le régime des représailles en temps de paix" and "Observations de Henri Rolin' (1934) 38 AIDI 7, 126.

[54] Sir Robert Y Jennings and Sir Arthur Watts (eds), *Oppenheim's International Law*, vol 1: Peace (9th edn, Longman 1992) 432 ('intervention is forcible or dictatorial interference by a state in the affairs of another state, calculated to impose certain conduct or consequences on that other state'). Interestingly, Oppenheim's original definition only referred to 'dictatorial' coercion (Lassa Oppenheim, *International Law: A Treatise*, vol I: Peace (Longmans, Green and Co 1905) 181).

CONTENT OF THE PRINCIPLE OF NON-INTERVENTION   153

> Coercion is prohibited under international law when a country deploys measures ... in order to obtain from another country an action or inaction which that country is not internationally obliged to perform and which falls within its sovereignty, when the coercion reaches a certain qualitative or quantitative threshold, depending on both the ends pursued and the means deployed.[55]

Dictatorial coercion implies first of all making a demand either explicitly or implicitly, an element reflected in General Assembly Resolutions 2131 and 2625 in the language 'to obtain from [the victim state] the subordination of the exercise of its sovereign rights and [or] to secure advantages of any kind'.[56] To be able to impair the agency of the victim state, however, the demand must be accompanied by a threat, that is, an explicit or implicit promise of harm the realization of which depends on whether the target state complies with the demands of the threatening state.[57] The threat must be clear, specific, and credible enough to intimidate the victim and genuinely reduce 'the range of choices otherwise available to states'.[58] The threatened harm, whatever its nature, must also be sufficiently serious. It would be difficult to claim, for instance, that a threat of armed force, to the extent that it is credible, is not coercive: Principle VI of the Helsinki Final Act explicitly prohibits 'any form of armed intervention' *and* the 'threat of such intervention against another participating State'. Threats of the use of armed force are also prohibited by Article 2(4) of the UN Charter and its customary counterpart.[59] A threat to sever diplomatic relations as in our scenario (d), on the other hand, is unlikely to ever have coercive effects. During the Cold War, the socialist states and certain non-aligned countries attempted to include the threat to break off diplomatic relations in order to force a state not to recognize another state in the condemnation of intervention contained in the Declaration on Friendly Relations,[60] but the attempt, which targeted West Germany's Hallstein Doctrine, did not manage to obtain enough support and was ultimately unsuccessful.[61] Between these two extremes, whether or not the threatened harm is sufficiently serious to be able to undermine the agency of the victim state is necessarily a case-by-case evaluation: the threshold of coercion is crossed only when the target cannot make a meaningful decision.[62]

---

[55] European Commission, Proposal for a Regulation of the European Parliament and of the Council on the protection of the Union and its Member States from economic coercion by third countries, COM/2021/775 final, 8 December 2021, para 11 of the Preamble.

[56] GA Resolutions 2131 (XX), paras 1–2, and 2625 (XX), Annex, third principle, paras 1–2. Analogous language is contained in Art 20 of the OAS Charter.

[57] As Stowell observes, '[t]he mere fact that a particular course is adopted by a small state from fear that otherwise the great neighbor will make it suffer does not constitute an act of interference unless the great state has given an intimation or warning which thereby attaches to the act a greater certainty of a disagreeable consequence' (Ellery C Stowell, *Intervention in International Law* (J Bryne & Company 1921) 318).

[58] Romana Sadurska, 'Threats of Force' (1988) 82 AJIL 239, 242.

[59] Nikolas Stürchler notes that '[a]pplying the coercion criterion to Article 2(4), the no-threat rule would be identical to the non-intervention rule but for the difference that coercion needs to involve a military dimension' (Nikolas Stürchler, *The Threat of Force in International Law* (CUP 2007) 60).

[60] See Czechoslovakia's proposal, UN Doc A/AC.119/L.6, 29 August 1964, 2–3; and Mexico's proposal, A/AC.119/L.24, 21 September 1964, 2.

[61] The Hallstein Doctrine, named after the state secretary of the German Federal Republic (GFR)'s Foreign Office, aimed at isolating the German Democratic Republic (GDR) and provided that the GFR would not establish or maintain diplomatic relations with any state that recognized the GDR.

[62] Steven Wheatley, 'Foreign Interference in Elections under the Non-Intervention Principle: We Need to Talk About "Coercion"' (2020) 31 Duke J Comp & Intl L 161, 180.

154   INTERNATIONAL LAW AND THE PRINCIPLE OF NON-INTERVENTION

To be coercive, a threat does not necessarily have to be explicit as long as it is sufficiently clear and specific. On 16 June 1940, for instance, the USSR people's commissar for foreign affairs, Molotov, sent a note to Latvia's ambassador in Moscow demanding the immediate formation of a new government that could implement the 1939 Pact of Mutual Assistance between Latvia and the USSR (which the latter accused the former of violating) and an immediate guarantee of the free entrance of Soviet troops on Latvia's territory in numbers sufficient to implement said pact.[63] The statement gave a specific timeframe for the Latvian government to respond but did not indicate the possible consequences of a refusal to accept the demands.[64] The same day, the government in Riga decided to submit to them, which eventually led to the occupation and annexation of the Baltic state by the USSR.[65] Even though the Soviet statement did not specify the consequences of a refusal, the Latvian Constitutional Court found in 2007 that it was clear from the 'historical context', and in particular from the previous uses of force by the Soviet Union against its neighbours, that Soviet troops would have entered the territory of Latvia with or without its consent.[66] The consent, therefore, was invalid as given under duress.[67]

Note that it is not essential that the threat reaches its objective for the principle of non-intervention to be breached: it is sufficient that unlawful coercion is exercised, whether or not the victim state actually submits to it or decides to resist and stoically endure the harm.[68] Indeed, even if the attempted coercion fails and the coerced conduct does not occur, the harm to the target state still materializes and an obligation to provide full reparation for any consequences that are the proximate effect of the coercing state's conduct arises.[69] This results clearly from the text of Article 19 of the OAS Charter and General Assembly Resolutions 2131 and 2625, which also condemn the 'attempted threat against the personality of the State or against its political, economic, and cultural elements'.[70] The higher threshold for coercion in the context of the law of treaties and the law of state responsibility, which requires an inability to resist the

---

[63] The Constitutional Court of the Republic of Latvia, Judgment on behalf of the Republic of Latvia, 29 November 2007, Case No 2007-10-0102, para 24.2 (hereafter Latvia's Constitutional Court Judgment), English translation at <www.satv.tiesa.gov.lv/web/wp-content/uploads/2007/04/2007-10-0102_Spriedums_ENG.pdf>.

[64] ibid.

[65] ibid, para 24.3.

[66] ibid, para 25.6.

[67] ibid.

[68] Ann Van Wynen Thomas and AJ Thomas, Jr, *Non-Intervention: The Law and Its Import in the Americas* (Southern Methodist University Press 1956) 72; Rosario Sapienza, *Il principio del non intervento negli affari interni. Contributo allo studio della tutela giuridica internazionale della potestà di governo* (Giuffrè 1990) 83–4. As the Argentinian delegate on the Special Committee on Friendly Relations noted, '[e]ven if that State refused to be coerced or intimidated by threats, there might be an intention on the part of the intervening State to coerce the sovereign will of the other State' (UN Doc A/AC.119/SR.28, 23 October 1964, 5, emphasis omitted).

[69] Proximate causation requires that 'there is an "unbroken connection" between the coercing state's act and the injury suffered that can be "clearly, unmistakably, and definitely traced" to the coercing state's act' (James D Fry, 'Coercion, Causation, and the Fictional Elements of Indirect State Responsibility' (2007) 40 Vand J Transnat'l L 611, 637 (quoting Bin Cheng's *General Principles of Law as Applied by International Courts and Tribunals*)).

[70] Art 19, OAS Charter; GA Res 2131 (XX), para 1; GA Res 2625 (XXV), Annex, third principle, para 1, emphasis added.

CONTENT OF THE PRINCIPLE OF NON-INTERVENTION 155

pressures, does not therefore extend to coercion as an element of the primary rule of non-intervention.[71]

3.2 Forcible Coercion

The scholarly analysis of the principle of non-intervention normally stops here. Not all forms of coercion, however, aim at compelling the victim state to do or not to do something: as Titus Komarnicki explains, the object of intervention is 'soit de se substituer à l'Etat victime dans l'exercice de ses droits souverains, soit de le forcer à suivre une certaine ligne de conduite, tant dans les affaires intérieures que dans les rapports avec d'autres Etats'.[72] In the case of forcible coercion, in particular, the intervening state *replaces* the will of the victim state with its own by carrying out the unauthorized act itself instead of pressuring someone else to do anything. Note that 'forcible' in this context does not refer exclusively to the use of armed force but to the fact that a certain condition of things has been imposed on the victim state against its will, whatever the means employed to achieve this result. The UK Attorney General so explains it in relation to cyber operations:

> Some have characterised coercion as forcing a State to act differently from how it otherwise would—that is, compelling it into a specific act or omission. [...] But I want to be clear today that coercion can be broader than this. In essence, an intervention in the affairs of another State will be unlawful if it is forcible, dictatorial, or otherwise coercive, depriving a State of its freedom of control over matters which it is permitted to decide freely by the principle of State sovereignty. While the precise boundaries of coercion are yet to crystallise in international law, we should be ready to consider whether disruptive cyber behaviours are coercive even where it might not be possible to point to a specific course of conduct which a State has been forced into or prevented from taking.[73]

Indeed, case-law as well as state practice and *opinio juris* show that the principle of non-intervention has been conceived more broadly than mere 'dictatorial interference' as also prohibiting the direct exercise of power in the territory of another state without its valid consent or a permissive rule of international law.[74] When in 2008

---

[71] The Special Rapporteur on the Law of Treaties, Sir Hersch Lauterpacht, pointed out that a treaty is void if the coerced state 'as the result of unlawful use of force, has been reduced to such a degree of impotence as to be *unable to resist* the pressure to become a party to a treaty' (Sir Hersch Lauterpacht, First Report on the Law of Treaties [1953] YB ILC, vol II, 147, emphasis added). The Commentary on Art 18 of ARSIWA also explains that '[c]oercion for the purpose of article 18 has the same essential character as *force majeure* under article 23. Nothing less than conduct which forces the will of the coerced State will suffice, giving it *no effective choice but to comply* with the wishes of the coercing State' ([2001] YB ILC, vol II, part two, 69, emphasis added).

[72] Titus Komarnicki, 'L'intervention en droit international moderne' (1956) 60 RGDIP 521, 523–4. Corn also notes that 'nothing in the [*Nicaragua*] judgment or international law more broadly requires that an intervention be [only] effected by threat of consequences, lawful or otherwise.' (Corn, 'Covert Deception', 12).

[73] Braverman, 'International Law'.

[74] *The Case of the SS 'Lotus' (France v Turkey)*, Judgment of 7 September 1927, PCIJ Rep Series A No 10, 2, 18 (hereafter *Lotus*).

156   INTERNATIONAL LAW AND THE PRINCIPLE OF NON-INTERVENTION

Colombian armed forces attacked a camp of the Fuerzas Armadas Revolucionarias de Colombia (FARC) in Ecuador, for instance, the Declaration of the XXth Summit of the Rio Group reaffirmed, inter alia, the principle of non-intervention as codified in Article 19 of the OAS Charter.[75] In a case involving the collection of evidence by Canadian authorities on the territory of Turks and Caicos, the Canadian Supreme Court also found that

[a]ccording to the principle of non-intervention, states must refrain from exercising extraterritorial enforcement jurisdiction over matters in respect of which another state has, by virtue of territorial sovereignty, the authority to decide freely and autonomously ... absent either the consent of the other state or, in exceptional cases, some other basis under international law.[76]

In the *Asylum* case, the ICJ considered Colombia's decision to grant diplomatic asylum to a Peruvian dissident leader in its Lima embassy as an 'intervention in its least acceptable form, one which implies foreign interference in the administration of domestic justice and which could not manifest itself without casting some doubt on the impartiality of that justice'.[77] It therefore found it illegal 'unless its legal basis is established in each particular case'.[78] In the *Nicaragua* Judgment, the Court added that an intervention that employs the use of force 'either in the direct form of military action, or in the indirect form of support for subversive or terrorist armed activities within another State' is a 'particularly obvious' example of coercion (the aforementioned scenarios (a) and (b)).[79] In none of these cases is the binomial 'threats + demands' present.

As Alexander Mann notes, therefore, extraterritorial (or international) jurisdiction 'is an aspect or an ingredient or a consequence of sovereignty (or of territoriality or of the principle of non-intervention, —the difference is merely terminological)'.[80] While the unauthorized extraterritorial exercise of enforcement (or 'executive') jurisdiction, that is, 'the power to ensure through coercive means that legal commands and entitlements are complied with',[81] is undoubtedly a form of forcible coercion prohibited by the principle of non-intervention,[82] however, the situation is more uncertain with regard to the exercise of other forms of jurisdiction.[83] In the *Immunities and Criminal*

---

[75]   Declaración de la XX Cumbre del Grupo de Río, 7 March 2008, para 6 <https://es.wikisource.org/wiki/Declaraci%C3%B3n_de_la_XX_Cumbre_del_Grupo_de_R%C3%ADo>.

[76]   Supreme Court of Canada, *Hape v Her Majesty the Queen* [2007] 2 SCR 292, para 65 (hereafter *Hape v Her Majesty the Queen*).

[77]   *Asylum Case (Colombia/Peru)* (Judgment) [1950] ICJ Rep 266, 285.

[78]   ibid, 275.

[79]   *Nicaragua v USA*, para 205.

[80]   Frederick Alexander Mann, 'The Doctrine of International Jurisdiction Revisited After Twenty Years' (1984) 186 Recueil des Cours 9, 20.

[81]   Paola Gaeta, Jorge E Viñuales, and Salvatore Zappalà, *Cassese's International Law* (3rd edn, OUP 2020) 50.

[82]   Maziar Jamnejad and Michael Wood, 'The Principle of Non-intervention' (2009) 22 LJIL 345, 372.

[83]   The UN General Assembly has called all states 'to refrain from promulgating and applying laws and measures', 'the extraterritorial effects of which affect the sovereignty of other States, the legitimate interests of entities or persons under their jurisdiction and the freedom of trade and navigation' (see eg GA Res 72/4, 1 November 2017, Preamble and para 4). The Collective Security Treaty Organization (CSTO) has also

CONTENT OF THE PRINCIPLE OF NON-INTERVENTION   157

Proceedings case before the ICJ, for instance, Equatorial Guinea accused France of interfering in its internal affairs 'by permitting its courts to initiate criminal legal proceedings against the Second Vice President of Equatorial Guinea for alleged offences which, even if they were established ... would fall solely within the jurisdiction of the courts of Equatorial Guinea'.[84] For Cedric Ryngaert, a mere jurisdictional assertion is not per se unlawful under international law and '[o]nly the exercise of extraterritorial enforcement jurisdiction—the carrying out of certain *material* acts on another State's territory—has been deemed to infringe upon the principle of non-intervention'.[85] He acknowledges, however, that the principle in question might play a role in restraining other jurisdictional claims by requiring an interest-balancing test: '[o]nly if the asserting State's interests in having its laws applied to a foreign situation outweigh the interests of another involved State will a jurisdictional assertion respect the principle of non-intervention'.[86] Even if 'the mere prescription of a norm is far less coercive than actual enforcement of that norm',[87] Ascensio also does not exclude that '[a] normative fact may constitute a kind of immaterial intervention ... if it necessarily implies a material implementation in a foreign country, without the agreement of the territorial authorities, or a strong pressure over that country with considerable negative consequences'.[88] Examples of the exercise of prescriptive jurisdiction which can constitute an 'immaterial' intervention include the adoption by a state of a law which grants funds to an armed opposition group fighting a foreign government, like the US Iraq Liberation Act 1998 (to the extent that it is implemented) or the premature recognition of statehood, government, or belligerency (see scenarios (b) and (e) above). Ukraine has also condemned the Russian presidential decree of 24 April 2019 allowing residents in the Donbass region to obtain Russian citizenship through a simplified procedure as an interference in its internal affairs and a violation of its sovereignty, territorial integrity, and independence, and Poland branded 'the widespread naturalization by a State of

---

indicated, as an example of the violation of the principle of 'non-interference', the extra-territorial application of national law by states (A/74/901-S/2020/534, 17 June 2020, 2).

[84] *Immunities and Criminal Proceedings (Equatorial Guinea v France)* (Preliminary Objections) [2018] ICJ Rep 399, para 50. Equatorial Guinea submitted that, under the Palermo Convention, it had exclusive jurisdiction against Transnational Organized Crime to establish whether the offence in question (money laundering) had been committed, that France should have therefore deferred to the report of Equatorial Guinea's public prosecutor who had found no evidence of the commission of the offence, and that it should have put an end to its own criminal proceedings (ibid, para 71). The ICJ found that it lacked jurisdiction to adjudicate on this aspect of the dispute (ibid, para 117).

[85] Cedric Ryngaert, *Jurisdiction in International Law* (2nd edn, OUP 2015) 155 (emphasis added). It is unclear, therefore, whether issuing subpoenas of individuals or ordering the production of documents when such individuals or documents are located abroad is a violation of the principle of non-intervention (see the different positions of the United States and the EU states ibid, 89-94). It has been suggested that '[t]he international jurisdiction to adjudicate is ... not a separate type of jurisdiction, but merely an emanation of the international jurisdiction to legislate: a State's right of regulation is exercised by legislative jurisdiction which includes adjudication' (Frederick Alexander Mann, 'The Doctrine of International Jurisdiction Revisited After Twenty Years' (1984) 186 Recueil des Cours 9, 67).

[86] Ryngaert, *Jurisdiction*, 155.

[87] Cedric Ryngaert, 'Extraterritorial Enforcement Jurisdiction in Cyberspace: Normative Shifts' (2023) 24 GLJ 537, 528. Indeed, '[p]rescription does not lead the prescribing State to enter the territory of another State, whereas enforcement may well have this consequence' (ibid).

[88] Hervé Ascensio, 'Are Spanish Courts Backing Down on Universality? The Supreme Tribunal's Decision in *Guatemalan Generals*' (2003) 1 J Int'l Crim Just 690, 699.

158 INTERNATIONAL LAW AND THE PRINCIPLE OF NON-INTERVENTION

nationals of another State residing in the latter State's territory [as] a clearly illegal act of coercion' prohibited by international law.[89]

4. Intent to Coerce and Motive as Elements of the Prohibition of Intervention

According to the International Law Commission (ILC), intent is necessary for the commission of an internationally wrongful act whenever it constitutes an element of the breached primary rule.[90] The question, therefore, is whether the intent to bring about the coercion of the victim state is a component of the principle of non-intervention. In his oral statement in the *Nicaragua* Merits proceedings, for instance, Alain Pellet, counsel for Nicaragua, argued that intervention requires both a *corpus* and an *animus*: the former is one or more acts of coercion, while the latter is constituted by the intent of bending the victim state's will.[91] During the debates on the Friendly Relations Declaration, some delegates also noted that 'the legal concept of non-intervention related largely to the intention of one State to coerce another State to change its internal order', although 'the intention by itself was not enough without any effect'.[92] More recently, Germany has pointed out that, without requiring an intent to coerce, the scope of the principle of non-intervention would be too broad.[93]

My view is that, to establish whether intent to coerce is a necessary element of the notion of intervention, forcible and dictatorial forms of coercion must be distinguished. When the coercing state directly engages in unauthorized conduct on foreign territory, intent to coerce is presumed and no demonstration of its existence is required to establish the commission of the wrongful act: 'one who does an act wilfully intends the natural and proximate consequences of the act'.[94] Not only intent but also motive is irrelevant in this case: in the *Corfu Channel* Judgment, the ICJ refused to accept the British claim that an armed intervention to 'secure possession of evidence in the territory of another State, in order to submit it to an international tribunal and thus facilitate its task' was lawful in international law.[95] In *Nicaragua*, the Court also found that 'a strictly humanitarian objective' like the protection of human rights is not compatible with the mining of ports, the destruction of oil installations, or the arming, training, and equipping of foreign armed opposition groups.[96]

The intent to coerce, on the other hand, must be demonstrated in the case of dictatorial coercion, that is, when a state does not carry out the unauthorized act itself but compels the victim state into doing something it would have not done or into not doing something it would have done. Article 20 of the OAS Charter explicitly requires

---

[89] UN Doc S/PV.8516, 25 April 2019, 2, 12, 18.
[90] Commentary on Art 2 ARSIWA [2001] YB ILC, vol II, part two, 34. Intent denotes the determination to bring about a certain result, regardless of the underlying motive for this.
[91] *Nicaragua v USA*, ICJ Pleadings, vol V, 216. The same point has been made by the OAS Juridical Committee (OAS, Draft Instrument of Instances of Violation, 6).
[92] UN Doc A/6230, 27 June 1966, para 309.
[93] UN Doc A/76/136, 34.
[94] Thomas and Thomas, *Non-Intervention*, 73.
[95] *Corfu Channel*, 34–5.
[96] *Nicaragua v USA*, para 268.

CONTENT OF THE PRINCIPLE OF NON-INTERVENTION   159

that, to be prohibited, coercive measures of an economic or political character must be adopted 'in order to force the sovereign will of another State'. Using similar language, General Assembly Resolutions 2131 and 2625 condemn economic, political, or other coercive measures only when they are adopted 'in order to obtain from [another state] the subordination of the exercise of its sovereign rights' and Principle VI of the Helsinki Final Act requires the participating states to refrain from acts of coercion 'designed to subordinate to their own interest the exercise by another participating State of the rights inherent in its sovereignty'. In the *Corfu Channel* case, the ICJ also found that the mere display of force by the United Kingdom in Operation Retail, however large, was not per se unlawful as it did not amount to 'a demonstration of force for the purpose of exercising political pressure on Albania'.[97]

Evidence of an intent to coerce is particularly important to distinguish normal economic interactions between states from economic coercion: indeed, a state might adopt certain restrictive trade measures that cause harm to another state (like the reduction of imports or the imposition of tariffs on certain goods) in order to support domestic production or protect its own economy.[98] In Derek Bowett's view, therefore, economic pressures constitute intervention only if their 'predominant purpose' is to dictate the policy of another state by injuring its economic interests rather than to protect one's own.[99] Several states have espoused this view. For the former US assistant legal adviser for Near Eastern and South Asian affairs, 'two types of economic measures are prohibited: that which attempts to coerce a state not to exercise its legal rights and that which attempts to extort advantages'.[100] A Canadian Legal Bureau's memorandum dated 15 November 1973 cautions that 'both the treaties and the Friendly Relations Declaration condemn the use of economic pressure, not *per se*, but only when used to achieve a particular objective'.[101] Cuba highlighted that political intervention and economic aggression are characterized by their 'unilateral character' and their 'coercive intent'.[102] Nicaragua also accused the United States of breaching the principle of non-intervention by engaging in activities that were meant to substantially damage its economy and weaken its political system 'in order to coerce the Government of Nicaragua into the acceptance of United States policies and political demands'.[103]

It is true that providing evidence of intent is often a diabolical task when it comes to immaterial entities like states. The coercive intent, however, is self-evident when

---

[97] *Corfu Channel*, 35.

[98] As Bowett notes, the promotion of one's economy might often result in prejudice towards another's and it is thus necessary to identify unlawful economic measures 'by their intent rather than their effect'. (Derek W Bowett, 'Economic Coercion and Reprisals by States' (1972) 13 Va J Intl Law 1, 5). For the relevance of coercive intent for economic forms of intervention, see also Sapienza, *Il principio*, 122–5.

[99] Bowett, 'Economic Coercion', 5. For the same view, see Dire Tladi, 'The Duty Not to Intervene in Matters within Domestic Jurisdiction' in Jorge E Viñuales (ed), *The UN Friendly Relations Declaration at 50* (CUP 2020) 87, 100–1; Sapienza, *Il principio* 122–3. Other authors maintain that damaging the economy of another state must be the 'sole' purpose of the adopted measures for them to be unlawful coercion (Thomas and Thomas, *Non-Intervention*, 410–1).

[100] Eleanor C McDowell (ed), *Digest of United States Practice in International Law 1976* (GPO 1977) 578.

[101] Text in [1974] 12 CYBIL 296.

[102] UN Doc S/PV.874, 18 July 1960, para 69.

[103] *Nicaragua v USA*, Nicaragua's Memorial (Merits), 30 April 1985, ICJ Pleadings, vol IV, para 465.

160 INTERNATIONAL LAW AND THE PRINCIPLE OF NON-INTERVENTION

a state makes explicit demands, as in the case of the US embargo on Cuba[104] and Nicaragua,[105] the Organization of Arab Petroleum Exporting Countries (OAPEC)'s oil embargo on the Western states,[106] the Gulf countries' embargo on Qatar,[107] and the resumption of US sanctions against Iran.[108] In other cases, it can be inferred, as Judge Robinson found in another context, 'from a State's actions, including their gravity, as well as statements made by the State and the relevant context'.[109] The burden of proving its existence rests of course on the state claiming that an intervention has occurred.

The language of the OAS Charter, General Assembly Resolutions 2131 and 2625, and the Helsinki Final Act suggests that, in the case of dictatorial coercion exercised by economic, political, or other means, not only intent but also motive is relevant. More specifically, all the aforementioned documents condemn such measures when they are used to secure advantages of any kind from another state. State practice and *opinio juris* confirm this conclusion. The United States, for instance, claimed that, as the economic measures it adopted against Nicaragua did not aim to obtain advantages of any kind from the Central American country, they were outside the scope of Article 20 of the OAS Charter.[110] The same argument was used by Washington to justify the

---

[104] The Cuban Democracy Act of 24 September 1992 (the Torricelli Act) provides that the US sanctions will be lifted if 'free, fair and internationally supervised elections' were to take place (quoted in White, *The Cuban Embargo*, 105). According to White, after the fall of the Soviet Union 'the continuation and tightening of the embargo was a deliberate act aimed at the removal of the Cuban government by deepening the suffering of the Cuban people thereby provoking change from within' (ibid, 122).

[105] (1985) 85 Dept St Bull 74–7.

[106] In the communiqué dated 17 October 1973, the OPAEC countries explained that the embargo would last 'until such a time as the international community compels Israel to relinquish our occupied territories' (reproduced in Ibrahim FI Shihata 'Destination Embargo of Arab Oil: Its Legality under International Law' (1974) 68 AJIL 591, 593).

[107] Saudi Arabia, United Arab Emirates (UAE), Bahrain, and Egypt submitted a list of thirteen demands and six principles that Qatar had to accept in order for the measures to be revoked (*Application of the International Convention on the Elimination of All Forms of Racial Discrimination (Qatar v UAE)*, Application instituting proceedings, 11 June 2018, paras 26–8 <www.icj-cij.org/case/172> (hereafter *Qatar v UAE*)). Among the demands was that Qatar stop interfering in the internal affairs of other states. Before the ICJ, legal counsel for Qatar claimed that the 'real purpose' of the restrictive measures was 'to undermine Qatar's sovereignty by seeking to interfere with its internal affairs and dictate its international relations' (*Qatar v UAE*, Oral proceedings, CR 2018/12, 27 June 2018, 17).

[108] President Trump declared that the sanctions' 'objective is to force the [Iranian] regime into a clear choice: either abandon its destructive behavior or continue down the path toward economic disaster' (Statement by the President Regarding the Reimposition of Nuclear-Related Sanctions on Iran, 2 November 2018 <https://trumpwhitehouse.archives.gov/briefings-statements/statement-president-regarding-reimposition-nuclear-related-sanctions-iran/>). For Judge Momtaz, however, the resumption of the US unilateral sanctions against the Islamic Republic in 2018 constitutes coercion aimed at influencing the formulation of the external relations of sovereign states, and thus amounts to a violation of the principle of non-intervention (*Alleged Violations of the 1955 Treaty of Amity, Economic Relations, and Consular Rights (Islamic Republic of Iran v USA)* (Provisional Measures) [2018] ICJ Rep 623 (hereafter *Iran v USA*), Declaration of Judge ad hoc Momtaz, para 20).

[109] *Certain Activities Carried Out by Nicaragua in the Border Area (Costa Rica v Nicaragua)* (Merits) [2015] ICJ Rep 665, Separate Opinion of Judge Robinson, para 54. For New Zealand, '[w]hile the coercive intention of the state actor is a critical element of the [the principle of non-intervention], intention may in some circumstances be inferred from the effects of cyber activity' (DPMC, 'The Application of International Law', para 9).

[110] The US representative claimed that the measures were not a violation of Art 20 of the OAS Charter 'because that article describes as coercive only those measures directed to force the sovereign will of another State and obtain from it advantages of any kind' and the United States was not trying to obtain advantages from Nicaragua. The measures—he continued—were 'primarily intended to prevent Nicaragua from deriving benefits from its trade with the United States; and to manifest support for the achievement of the

consistency with Article 20 of its economic measures against Argentina after the invasion of the Falklands/Malvinas.[111] The next section discusses how the expression 'advantages of any kind' should be interpreted as 'undue advantages', that is, 'any kind of advantage that the intervenor would not be entitled to as a matter of right under international law'.[112]

5. The Object Protected by the Principle of Non-Intervention

Coercion is as such neither lawful nor unlawful: it is a method that states, like individuals, use in order to achieve a certain objective. In a decentralized legal system like international law, it can play an important law enforcement role, both when exercised unilaterally by states and through institutionalized mechanisms like that delineated in Chapter VII of the UN Charter. As the ICJ notes, it is only when it bears on 'matters in which each State is permitted, by the principle of State sovereignty, to decide freely'[113] that coercion is prohibited by the principle of non-intervention and thus becomes an internationally wrongful act.

As seen in Chapter I, the principle of non-intervention was born as, and remains to this day, a corollary of state sovereignty.[114] Oppenheim famously defined sovereignty as '*independence*. It is *external* independence with regard to the liberty of action outside its borders. It is *internal* independence with regard to the liberty of action of a state inside its borders.'[115] It is this 'liberty of action' that the principle of non-intervention protects from coercion. The *Nicaragua* Merits Judgment calls it 'political integrity', which the ICJ considers as essential a foundation of international relations together with territorial integrity.[116] The expression can also be considered equivalent to that of 'political independence' used in Article 2(4) of the UN Charter, which has been defined as 'the autonomy in the affairs of the State with respect to its institutions, freedom of political decisions, policy making, and in matters pertaining to its domestic and foreign affairs'.[117] Indeed, the reference to domestic (internal) and/or foreign (external) affairs has formed part of the formulation of the principle of non-intervention since at least the 1933 Montevideo Convention on the Rights and Duties

---

objectives embodied in the 1983 Contadora Document of Objectives' (EY Benneh, 'Economic Coercion, The Non-Intervention Principle and the Nicaragua Case' (1994) 6 Afr J Intl & Comp L 235, 241–2).

[111] ibid, 243.

[112] Arangio-Ruiz, 'Human Rights', 262.

[113] *Nicaragua v USA*, para 205.

[114] The Supreme Court of Canada has noted that the principle of non-intervention sits 'at the apex' of the duties that protect sovereignty and equality (*Hape v Her Majesty the Queen*, para 45).

[115] Jennings and Watts (eds), *Oppenheim's International Law*, 382 (emphasis in the original). The definition evokes Judge Huber's famous words in the *Island of Palmas Case*: '[s]overeignty in the relations between States signifies independence. Independence in regard to a portion of the globe is the right to exercise therein, to the exclusion of any other State, the functions of a State' (*Island of Palmas Case (Netherlands, United States)*, 4 April 1928, 2 RIAA 829, 838).

[116] *Nicaragua v USA*, para 202.

[117] Samuel KN Blay, 'Territorial Integrity and Political Independence' in *MPEPIL Online* (last updated March 2010) para 1.

162 INTERNATIONAL LAW AND THE PRINCIPLE OF NON-INTERVENTION

of States.[118] Internal affairs concern the relations between a state on the one hand and its citizens and national territory on the other, while external affairs include the relations that a state has with other states and international organizations.[119]

If the principle of non-intervention protected the 'liberty of action' of states without further qualifications, however, it would result in prohibiting all enforcement measures aimed to secure compliance with international law. It cannot thus be *all* external and internal affairs that the principle of non-intervention shields, but only those where the concerned state is free of international obligations: as Arangio-Ruiz puts it, this principle 'would *not* condemn actions concerning matters in which the victim State was *not exempt* from international legal obligations'.[120] Said otherwise, the principle of non-intervention protects the liberty of action that states have *within international law*, and not regardless of it, and prohibits a state from coercing another into doing something it does not have an obligation to do, or into not doing something it has the right to do.[121] The matters where a state is free of international obligations are normally referred to as 'domestic jurisdiction', an expression that appears in the title of the principle of non-intervention in Resolution 2625 and in the text of Principle VI of the Helsinki Final Act as well as in the formulation of the principle in more recent treaties like the 2006 Protocol on Non-Aggression and Mutual Defence in the Great Lakes Region.[122] 'Domestic jurisdiction' is coterminous with the older French expression *domaine réservé*, defined in the *Dictionnaire de droit international public* as the '[d]omaine d'activités dans lequel l'Etat, n'étant pas lié par le droit international, jouit d'une compétence totalement discrétionnaire et, en conséquence, ne doit subir aucune immixtion de la part des autres Etats ou des organisations internationales'.[123]

---

[118] See Art 8, Convention on the Rights and Duties of States (Montevideo, 26 December 1933) 165 LNTS 19; Art 1(1), Additional Protocol Relative to Nonintervention (Buenos Aires, 23 December 1936) (1937) 31 AJIL Supplement 57; and Art 19, OAS Charter. See also Art 3 of the 1949 ILC Draft Declaration on Rights and Duties of States, which was heavily influenced by the American experience ([1949] YB ILC 286, 287). The American formulation is also incorporated in Art 3(2) of the Protocol Additional to the Geneva Conventions of 12 August 1949, and relating to the Protection of Victims of Non-International Armed Conflicts (Protocol II) (Geneva, 8 June 1977) 1125 UNTS 609; Art I(5) of the Protocol on Prohibitions or Restrictions on the Use of Mines, Booby-Traps and Other Devices (Protocol II, as amended on 3 May 1996) annexed to the Convention on Prohibitions or Restrictions on the Use of Certain Conventional Weapons which may be deemed to be Excessively Injurious or to have Indiscriminate Effects 2048 UNTS 93; and Art 22(5) of the Second Protocol to The Hague Convention of 1954 for the Protection of Cultural Property in the Event of Armed Conflict (The Hague, 26 March 1999) 2253 UNTS 212.

[119] It should be noted that the expression 'internal affairs' is often employed to refer to matters where a state is free of international obligations: in this sense, it is a synonym for domestic jurisdiction (Sapienza, *Il principio*, 12).

[120] Arangio-Ruiz, 'Human Rights', 279, emphasis in the original.

[121] As Judge Schwebel puts it, the United States did not 'intervene' in the internal or external affairs of Nicaragua, because its demands were 'legally well-grounded efforts to induce Nicaragua to perform its legal obligations' (*Nicaragua v USA*, Dissenting Opinion of Judge Schwebel, para 246). While the US efforts were not so well-grounded as argued by Schwebel, his point about non-intervention only referring to domestic affairs is correct.

[122] Art 4(2). The title of GA Res 2131 also refers to 'domestic affairs of States'.

[123] Jean Salmon (ed), *Dictionnaire de droit international public* (Bruylant 2001) 356. See also Art 1 of the Resolution on the determination of the 'reserved domain' and its effects, adopted by the Institut de droit international at the Aix-en-Provence session in 1954: 'The "reserved domain" is the domain of State activities where the jurisdiction of the State is not bound by International Law.' (English text of the resolution in (1954) 45 AIDI 299). For Robert Kolb, the notion of *domaine réservé* is 'l'*alter ego* de la souveraineté et de l'indépendance étatique, autour desquelles il accomplit ses révolutions en orbite géostationnaire'

CONTENT OF THE PRINCIPLE OF NON-INTERVENTION 163

'Domestic jurisdiction', however, is more accurate: the idea of domains 'reserved' to states and which international law cannot regulate was purported by the Soviet international legal scholarship during the Cold War and has now been discarded.[124] Indeed, as the Permanent Court of International Justice (PCIJ) found, '[t]he question whether a certain matter is or is not solely within the jurisdiction of a State is an essentially relative question; it depends upon the development of international relations'.[125] Whenever a binding source of international law imposes a positive or negative obligation on a state, therefore, the matter ceases to be a domestic affair of that state.

That the principle of non-intervention only protects the liberty of action that states possess within the limits of international law and not regardless of them results clearly from the language of Principle VI of the Helsinki Final Act, which requires the participating states to refrain from intervention 'in the internal or external affairs *falling within the domestic jurisdiction of another participating State*'.[126] The fact that coercion must be exercised in a matter where the target state does not have an obligation under international law to conduct itself in a certain way is what distinguishes a violation of the principle of non-intervention from a countermeasure: even though it can be coercive,[127] the latter, unlike the former, aims to induce a state that has committed an internationally wrongful act to cease it and provide full reparation, and is therefore lawful.[128] The formulation of Principle VI of the Helsinki Final Act reflects this difference by juxtaposing the intervening state's *interests* with the target state's *rights* thus implying that coercion must not necessarily be refrained from when

(Robert Kolb, 'Du domaine réservé: réflexions sur la théorie de la compétence nationale' (2006) 110 RGDIP 597, 628).

[124] See Tomislav Mitrović, 'Non-Intervention in the Internal Affairs of States' in Milan Šahović (ed), *Principles of International Law Concerning Friendly Relations and Cooperation* (The Institute of International Politics and Economics/Oceana Publications 1973) 219, 245–6; Nicolai A Ouchakov, 'La compétence interne des Etats et la non-intervention dans le droit international contemporain' (1974) 141 Recueil des Cours 1, 46, 49.

[125] *Nationality Decrees Issued in Tunis and Morocco*, Advisory Opinion of 7 February 1923, PCIJ Series B No 4, 6, 24.

[126] Helsinki Final Act, Principle VI, para 1, emphasis added.

[127] The Commentary on Art 18 ARSIWA, 70, notes that coercion could take the form of a threat or use of force, an intervention ('a coercive interference') in the affairs of another state, a countermeasure, or 'serious economic pressure, provided that it is such as to deprive the coerced State of any possibility of conforming with the obligation breached'.

[128] The Commentary on Art 18, ARSIWA specifies that the function of countermeasures, unlike that of intervention in the domestic affairs of states, 'is to induce a wrongdoing State to comply with obligations of cessation and reparation towards the State taking the countermeasures' (ibid). The *travaux préparatoires* of the OAS Charter confirm this conclusion: a proposal by Cuba at the 1948 Bogotá Conference that aimed at prohibiting coercive economic measures constituting reprisals was not included in the final text (Novena Conferencia Internacional Americana, *Actas y Documentos*, vol III (Ministerio de Relaciones Exteriores de Colombia, 1953) 4). Cuba submitted the same proposal in relation to the Economic Agreement of Bogotá at the Ninth International Conference of American States, but it was again not adopted (ibid, vol IV, 341). That countermeasures are coercive measures not constituting unlawful intervention was a point also made by certain representatives in the Special Committee on Friendly Relations (UN Doc A/5746, para 264). According to a Dutch report, the prohibition of intervention 'does not affect the institutions of retorsion and reprisals, which are recognised by international law, albeit subject to certain rules' (Report of the Advisory Committee on Questions of International Law on measures against South Africa and the non-intervention duty to Parliament, 27 May 1982 (1983) 14 NYIL 246, 248). See also Department of Foreign

164 INTERNATIONAL LAW AND THE PRINCIPLE OF NON-INTERVENTION

it consists in acts that breach the victim state's rights in order to protect the intervening state's rights.[129]

When coercion is not exercised in regard to a matter in which the target state can decide freely, therefore, it escapes the prohibitive scope of the principle of non-intervention and is either a lawful measure per se or, if it is prohibited by another primary rule of international law, it can potentially constitute a lawful countermeasure. To be clear, the mere fact that a matter does not belong to a state's domestic jurisdiction does not automatically mean that other states can resort to coercion in regard to it: this would only be lawful when coercive means not otherwise prohibited are employed or, if the coercive act was wrongful, when it is aimed at enforcing compliance with the breached obligation by the target state, it is commensurate with the injury suffered, it does not entail the breach of an obligation that cannot be affected by countermeasures, and the coercing state is entitled to react.[130] Armed coercion, in particular, is now allowed exclusively within the narrow limits of Chapter VII of the UN Charter and it is no longer permissible to use it to, say, recover debts or secure compliance with a judgment as in the 19th century. When the means of coercion are already unlawful under other primary rules (e.g. the prohibition of the use of armed force or a cooperation treaty like the General Agreement on Tariffs and Trade (GATT) and the World Trade Organization (WTO) agreements), the relevance of the principle of non-intervention is limited.[131] If the means used are not otherwise prohibited, on the other hand, the coercive act might still constitute a violation of the principle of non-intervention if it is exercised in regard to a matter in which the target state does not have an obligation to conduct itself in a certain way.[132]

Affairs, Ireland: Position paper on the application of international law in cyberspace, 2023, para 10 <https://www.dfa.ie/media/dfa/ourrolepolicies/internationallaw/Ireland---National-Position-Paper.pdf>.

[129] Helsinki Final Act, Principle VI, para 3. An author has thus distinguished between 'sanctioning coercion' and 'aggressive coercion' (Georges Ténékidés, 'Les effets de la contrainte sur les traités à la lumière de la Convention de Vienne du 23 mai 1969' (1974) 20 AFDI 79, 93).

[130] See Arts 42, 43, 49–54 ARSIWA. It is worth recalling that the 1996 version of Draft Art 50 prohibited countermeasures involving 'extreme economic or political coercion designed to endanger the territorial integrity or political independence of the State which has committed the internationally wrongful act'. The language was dropped from the final version as the reference to proportionality in Art 51 was deemed sufficient (David J Bederman, 'Counterintuiting Countermeasures' (2002) 96 AJIL 817, 831).

[131] Verhoeven points out that 'il est sans intérêt de se référer à la règle de non-intervention pour condamner une ingérence, si les moyens utilisés à cette fin sont de toute manière illicites' (Joe Verhoeven, 'Non-intervention: "affaires intérieures" ou "vie privée"?' in Le droit international au service de la paix, de la justice et du développement. Mélanges Michel Virally (Pedone 1991) 495). For him, '[c]e n'est plus la contrainte objectivement exercée mais la finalité subjectivement poursuivie qui est … déterminante: l'acte est illicite non pas parce qu'il est en soi interdit mais parce que l'objectif qui l'inspire est incompatible avec le respect dû à la souveraineté' (ibid, 496).

[132] For Giegerich, therefore, even a retorsion, when used for an illegitimate purpose, could be an unlawful intervention 'if its coercive force is strong enough to pose a serious threat to the self-determination of the target State with regard to its domaine réservé' (Thomas Giegerich, 'Retorsion' in MPEPIL Online (last updated September 2020) para 24). See also Eric David, 'Portée et limite du principe de non-intervention' (1990) 23 RBDI 350, 360. It has been suggested that, in these cases, an intervention is in fact an abuse of right, ie 'an action which is described as lawful [and which] may cease to be so if pursued in an unsocial manner or in a manner contrary to the purpose for which it has been allowed' (Hersch Lauterpacht, 'General Rules of the Law of Peace' in Elihu Lauterpacht (ed), International Law, Being the Collected Papers of Hersch Lauterpacht, vol I: General Works (CUP 1970) 384). The reference to the abuse of right was indeed made by two delegates in the debates at the Friendly Relations Special Committee to justify the unlawfulness of

It has been claimed that the principle of non-intervention does not protect the entire sphere of the domestic jurisdiction of states as defined here, but only certain aspects of sovereignty. Rosario Sapienza, for instance, posits that what the principle under consideration prohibits is not any offence against the freedom of states, but only conduct that hampers another state's exercise of governmental powers on its territory.[133] According to Tom Farer, an unlawful intervention occurs 'only when one state seeks to affect the "authority structure" of another state rather than specific policies; when, in other words, the coercion is directed at the identity of policymakers or the processes of policymaking'.[134] The UK Attorney General has also noted that the principle of non-intervention prohibits coercive acts 'in the matters of government which are at the heart of state's sovereignty, such as the freedom to choose its own political, social, economic and cultural system',[135] and other states have linked the principle of non-intervention to the free exercise of 'inherently sovereign functions' by a state.[136] These views arguably originate from the misleading language of the *Nicaragua* judgment, where the ICJ holds that '[a] prohibited intervention must ... be one bearing on matters in which each state is permitted, *by the principle of state sovereignty*, to decide freely'.[137] In the same paragraph, however, the Court clarifies that 'the generally accepted formulation' of the principle of non-intervention 'forbids all States or groups of States to intervene directly or indirectly in internal or external affairs of other States' without further qualifications.[138] As Brad Roth notes, '[t]his is a limitation, not on the permissible subject matter of international legal obligations—which nowadays pertain to every aspect of internal governance—but on the permissible extent of cross-border exercises of power'.[139] What the principle of non-intervention

economic coercion and of the Hallstein Doctrine ([1964] YB UN 142–3). The applicability of the doctrine of abuse of right in international law, however, is disputed: it has been observed that 'harm caused by the exercise of sovereignty [is] best resolved not by invoking abuse, but rather positive obligations created by international agreements, or interpretation of the inherent limits of rights in specific contexts' (Jan Paulsson, *The Unruly Notion of Abuse of Rights* (Cambridge University Press 2020) 125). In other words, '[t]hese matters are more soundly dealt with by the process of negotiation and accretion of custom backed by *opinio juris*', which establishes whether a right exists or not, rather than whether it has been used or 'abused' (ibid, 123).

[133] Sapienza, *Il principio*, 81.

[134] Tom J Farer, 'Problems of an International Law of Intervention' (1968) 3 Stan J Intl Stud 20, 21. See also Verhoeven, 'Non-intervention', 499; RJ Vincent, *Nonintervention and International Order* (Princeton University Press 2015) 13.

[135] 'Cyber and International Law in the 21st Century', Speech by the Attorney General Jeremy Wright at Chatham House, 23 May 2018 <www.gov.uk/government/speeches/cyber-and-international-law-in-the-21st-century>.

[136] Government of Canada, 'International Law', para 22; Ministry for Foreign Affairs of Finland, 'International Law and Cyberspace: Finland's National Positions', 15 October 2020, 3 <https://um.fi/documents/35732/0/Cyber+and+international+law%3B+Finland%27s+views.pdf/41404cbb-d300-a3b9-92e4-a7d675d5d585?t=1602758856859>; DPMC, 'The Application of International Law', para 9. Inherently sovereign functions are those 'functions that the state cannot, *under international law*, validly [devolve] to other actors' (Frédéric Mégret, 'Are There "Inherently Sovereign Functions" in International Law?' (2021) 115 AJIL 452, 454, emphasis in the original). For Mégret, only some functions (use of force, legislation, and adjudication) can never be outsourced without a state losing its 'governmentality' (ibid, 491).

[137] *Nicaragua v USA*, para 205, emphasis added.

[138] ibid.

[139] Brad R Roth, 'Legitimacy in the International Order: The Continuing Relevance of Sovereign States' (2021) 11 ND J Intl & Comp L 60, 76.

ultimately protects, therefore, is the decisional sovereignty of a state in all its facets and manifestations *in the absence of international obligations*.

In the *Nicaragua* Judgment, the ICJ singled out 'the choice of a political, economic, social and cultural system, and the formulation of foreign policy' as one of the matters 'in which each State is permitted, by the principle of State sovereignty, to decide freely'.[140] In 2007, Latvia's Constitutional Court also found that the 1940 ultimatum by the Soviet Union demanding, inter alia, that the Baltic state immediately form a new government able to implement the Pact of Mutual Assistance between the two countries was an intervention in Latvia's internal affairs.[141] A state's choice of its political, economic, social, and cultural systems, and the formulation of its policies, however, is a domestic matter only to the extent that there are no international obligations limiting it.[142] A state, for instance, could commit by treaty to adopt a certain form of government, or to hold multi-party elections.[143] A state could also prevent itself from joining a military alliance by ratifying a neutralization treaty[144] or entrust its defence or foreign policy to another state as in the case of the compacts signed by several South Pacific Ocean countries with the United States.[145] In addition, customary international law can restrict the right of a state to formulate its domestic policies in certain cases, for instance when this results in an apartheid regime.[146] Finally, a certain policy could be qualified as a threat to the peace by the UN Security Council under Chapter VII of the Charter.[147]

Cold War interventionist doctrines attempted to remove the choice of a state's political system from its domestic jurisdiction on ideological grounds, and not on the basis of its international law obligations. Borrowing from the Monroe Doctrine and adapting it to the new threats, the US presidents, from Truman to Reagan, denied that the establishment of a communist regime in the Americas and in other key areas of the world like the Middle East was a domestic affair of the concerned states.[148] According

[140] *Nicaragua v USA*, para 205. It is in fact not only the formulation of the foreign policy that falls within the domestic jurisdiction of a state but also of other policies, including national defence (*Nuclear Tests (Australia v France)* (Judgment) [1974] ICJ Rep 253, Separate Opinion of Judge Gros, para 12) and environmental and health standards (*Case Concerning Aerial Herbicide Spraying (Ecuador v Colombia)*, Reply of Ecuador, vol I, 31 January 2001, paras 5.10, 5.12 <www.icj-cij.org/case/138>) to the extent that a state has not assumed international obligations in relation to them.

[141] Latvia's Constitutional Court Judgment, para 26.

[142] In *Nicaragua v USA*, the ICJ held that '[a] state's domestic policy falls within its exclusive jurisdiction, provided of course that it does not violate any obligation of international law' (*Nicaragua v USA*, para 258).

[143] ibid, para 259. See also Judge Schwebel's Dissenting Opinion in the same case, paras 241–6.

[144] See examples in Natalino Ronzitti, *Diritto internazionale dei conflitti armati* (7th edn, Giappichelli 2021) 125–8.

[145] On the compacts between the United States and the South Pacific countries, see Marco Roscini, 'On the "Inherent" Character of the Right of States to Self-Defence' (2015) 4 Cambridge J Int'l & Comp L 634, 649–51.

[146] A report from the Dutch government's Advisory Committee on Questions of International Law, for instance, concluded that the restrictive economic measures that the Netherlands intended to adopt against South Africa were not contrary to the Declaration on Friendly Relations, as the policy of apartheid constituted a flagrant violation of human rights and was therefore not protected by the norm on non-intervention (Report of the Advisory Committee on Questions of International Law on measures against South Africa, 247–9).

[147] Art 39, UN Charter.

[148] See eg Harry S Truman, Special Message to the Congress on Greece and Turkey, 12 March 1947 (1947) 16 Dept St Bull 829, 831; John Fitzgerald Kennedy, 'The Lesson of Cuba', 8 May 1961 (1961) 44 Dept St Bull

CONTENT OF THE PRINCIPLE OF NON-INTERVENTION   167

to President Johnson, in particular, while '[r]evolutions in any country is a matter for that country to deal with [i]t becomes a matter calling for hemispheric action ... when the object is the establishment of a Communist dictatorship.[149] In the 1980s, President Reagan championed 'the proposition that the United States is politically and morally justified in providing economic and military support to indigenous insurgencies fighting totalitarian governments dependent on the Soviet bloc' and authorized destabilization operations in several countries, normally conducted covertly.[150]

In the communist bloc, the so-called Brezhnev Doctrine proclaimed that '[t]he sovereignty of each socialist country cannot be opposed to the interests of the world of socialism, of the world revolutionary movement.[151] Otherwise said, in the reciprocal relations among socialist countries the principle of non-intervention was subordinated to the collective obligation to prevent imperialist counterrevolutions. In a letter sent to the Czechoslovak communists before the intervention in Czechoslovakia, five members of the Warsaw Pact warned:

> we cannot assent to hostile forces pushing your country off the path of socialism and creating the threat that Czechoslovakia may break away from the socialist commonwealth. This is no longer your affair alone. It is the common affair of all Communist and Workers' Parties and states that are united by alliance, cooperation and friendship. It is the common affair of our countries.[152]

Similarly, in an address in Warsaw in November 1968 after the end of the 'Prague Spring', the USSR Communist Party's General Secretary, Leonid Brezhnev, declared:

> when the internal and external forces hostile to socialism seek to revert the development of any socialist country toward the restoration of the capitalist order, when a threat to the cause of socialism in that country, a threat to the security of the socialist community as a whole, emerges, this is no longer only a problem of the people of that country but also a common problem ... for all socialist states.[153]

By invading Czechoslovakia, then, the Soviet troops were allegedly not intervening in that country's internal affairs, but were protecting its sovereignty against imperialism: Grewe notes that the Brezhnev Doctrine 'was comparable to the right of intervention claimed and exercised by the Holy Alliance, after the Congress of Vienna

---

659, 659. The Truman Doctrine found its first application in the support to the Greek government against the communist insurgency in the second half of the 1940s.

[149] Address to the Nation, 2 May 1965 in *Public Papers of the Presidents of the United States: Lindon B Johnson* (1965, Book I) 472–3. The Johnson Doctrine led to intervention in the Dominican Republic in 1965.

[150] David P Fidler, 'War, Law, and Liberal Thought: The Use of Force in the Reagan Years' (1994) 11 Ariz J Int'l & Comp L 45, 105.

[151] '*Pravda* Article Justifying Intervention in Czechoslovakia' (1968) 7 ILM 1323, 1323.

[152] The five members were Bulgaria, Hungary, the German Democratic Republic, Poland, and the Soviet Union. The text of the letter is in (1968) 6 ILM 1265.

[153] Quoted in Stephen M Schwebel, 'The Brezhnev Doctrine Repealed and Peaceful Co-Existence Enacted' (1972) 66 AJIL 816, 816–17.

168   INTERNATIONAL LAW AND THE PRINCIPLE OF NON-INTERVENTION

of 1815, to protect «legitimate» monarchs against revolutionary attempts at their removal'.[154] In fact, the socialist states claimed not only a right but even a duty to intervene to prevent counterrevolutions: in the relations within the socialist commonwealth, therefore, the principle of non-intervention also entailed a positive obligation.[155] Brezhnev's doctrine of limited sovereignty and the Soviet Union's intervention in Czechoslovakia, however, were condemned not only by the Western bloc and the non-aligned states, but even by certain socialist countries, including Yugoslavia, Romania, Albania, and the People's Republic of China (PRC).[156] The Soviet Union itself was reluctant to exclusively rely on the doctrine of limited sovereignty as a legal justification for its interventions: in Hungary, Czechoslovakia, and Afghanistan, it paid formal deference to the principle of non-intervention by invoking the (dubious) invitation of those who were claimed to be the legitimate representatives of the concerned state.[157] In the end, at the instance of the Western states, language was added in Principle VI of the Helsinki Final Act to specify that the prohibition of intervention applies between the participating states 'regardless of their mutual relations', thus delegitimizing any claims of intrabloc intervention based on limited sovereignty arguments.[158] On 7 December 1988, Chairman Mikhail Gorbachev eventually reaffirmed at the UN General Assembly that changes to political and social systems were an internal affair of each state[159] and, in 1989, the Soviet Union acknowledged the illegality of its interventions in Eastern Europe.[160]

The American and Soviet doctrines of limited sovereignty have also been discounted by the ICJ. In the Advisory Opinion on *Western Sahara*, the Court affirmed that '[n]o rule of international law ... requires the structure of a State to follow any particular pattern, as is evident from the diversity of the forms of State found in the world today'.[161] In the *Nicaragua* Judgment, it confirmed that 'adherence by a State to any particular doctrine does not constitute a violation of customary international law; to hold otherwise would make nonsense of the fundamental principle of State sovereignty, on which the whole of international law rests, and the freedom of choice of the political, social, economic and cultural system of a State'.[162] The ICJ then concluded that it could 'not contemplate the creation of a new rule opening up a right of intervention by one State against another on the ground that the latter has opted for some

---

[154] Wilhelm G Grewe, *Epochen der Völkerrechtsgeschichte* (Nomos 1984), tr and rev by Michael Byers as *The Epochs of International Law* (Walter de Gruyter 2000) 657. See also Kazimierz Grzybowski, 'Soviet Theory of International Law for the Seventies' (1983) 77 AJIL 862, 870. The same has been said of American interventionism (Richard A Falk, 'The United States and the Doctrine of Nonintervention' (1959) 5 How LJ 163, 183).

[155] Arangio-Ruiz, 'Human Rights', 283–4.

[156] Mario Bettati, '«Souveraineté limitée» ou «internationalisme prolétarien»? Les liens fondamentaux de la communauté des Etats socialistes' (1972) 8 RBDI 455, 459–64. The Western and non-aligned states overwhelmingly deplored the intervention in Czechoslovakia. See eg United States (UN Doc S/PV.1441, 21 August 1968, 4, 17), Canada (S/PV.1441, 5, 18), United Kingdom (S/PV.1441, 5), Paraguay (S/PV.1441, 10), France (S/PV.1441, 18), Denmark (S/PV.1441, 19), and Brazil (S/PV.1441, 20).

[157] Vincent, *Nonintervention*, 178.

[158] Gaetano Arangio-Ruiz, 'Droits de l'homme et non intervention: Helsinki, Belgrade, Madrid' (1980) 35 *La Comunità internazionale* 453, 485.

[159] Grewe, *The Epochs*, 657.

[160] Keesing's 1989, 36982.

[161] *Western Sahara* (Advisory Opinion) [1975] ICJ Rep 12, para 94.

[162] *Nicaragua v USA*, para 263.

particular ideology or political system'.[163] Finally, the Court dismissed the role that these doctrines can play in the formation of customary international law by qualifying them as mere 'statements of international policy, and not an assertion of rules of existing international law'.[164]

6. The First Pillar of the Principle of Non-Intervention: The Prohibition of Armed Coercion

As mentioned in Section 2 of this chapter, non-intervention consists not only of a general principle prohibiting coercion in matters in which each state is permitted to decide freely, but also of a set of more specific rules of application prohibiting discrete means and methods of coercion. The first of these rules prohibits armed coercion: indeed, as the ICJ has famously held, '[t]he element of coercion ... is particularly obvious in the case of an intervention which uses force ... in the direct form of military action'.[165] If, in the 19th century, intervention was ontologically different from war in the legal sense,[166] therefore in the UN Charter era the use of armed force, as an instrument to coerce another state, constitutes a species of the broader genus of intervention.[167] A use of armed force can amount to either forcible or dictatorial coercion: in the former case, a state takes by force what it wants (for instance, a disputed territory), while in the latter the continuation of a military operation is employed as leverage to secure the acceptance of the aggressor state's demands.

Since 1945, armed coercion has been prohibited not only by the principle of non-intervention but also by the customary rule codified in Article 2(4) of the UN Charter, according to which '[a]ll Members [of the United Nations] shall refrain in their international relations from the threat or use of force against the territorial integrity or political independence of any state, or in any other manner inconsistent with the

---

[163] ibid. For Michael Reisman, however, 'there is a core in both the Brezhnev and Reagan doctrines that contributes, and indeed may be indispensable to, the maintenance of current minimum world order' (W Michael Reisman, 'Old Wine in New Bottles: The Reagan and Brezhnev Doctrines in Contemporary International Law and Practice' (1988) 13 Yale JIL 171, 185). It is only when the doctrines are abused that they become unlawful (ibid).

[164] Nicaragua v USA, para 207.

[165] ibid, para 205. In DRC v Uganda, the ICJ also found that Uganda's actions in the DRC were at the same time a violation of the latter's sovereignty and territorial integrity, of the principle of 'non-interference' in the internal affairs of the DRC, and a grave violation of the prohibition of the use of force as contained in Art 2(4) of the UN Charter (Armed Activities on the Territory of the Congo (Democratic Republic of the Congo v Uganda) (Merits) [2005] ICJ Rep 168, para 165 (hereafter DRC v Uganda)).

[166] Chapter I showed that, in the 19th century, intervention was considered a coercive measure short of war, 'a coercive action, limited in scope and duration' (Davide Rodogno, Against Massacre: Humanitarian Interventions in The Ottoman Empire 1815–1914 (Princeton University Press 2012) 20). Intervention, then, was not defined by the means employed (both intervention and war consisted in the use of armed force) or by the gravity of its effects (both intervention and war could cause serious consequences for the victim state, or be limited to 'surgical operations': in the case of a declaration of war not followed by actual hostilities, war in the legal sense might have even occurred without the causation of any material damage). What distinguished an act of intervention from war was essentially the lack of animus bellandi, that is, of the intention to establish a state of war between the concerned states (see Chapter I, Section 5).

[167] During the debates on the Declaration on Friendly Relations, for instance, some representatives observed that 'military intervention was only one of the possible forms of intervention' (UN Doc A/6955, 11 December 1967, para 92).

Purposes of the United Nations'. This provision, however, does not entirely overlap with the first pillar of the principle of non-intervention for two reasons. First, the principle of non-intervention only prohibits armed coercion when it bears 'on matters in which each State is permitted, by the principle of State sovereignty, to decide freely'[168] and thus does not rule out the permissibility of armed countermeasures. Apart from Security Council authorization, on the other hand, the only case where resort to armed force is permitted under the Charter is in the case of self-defence against an armed attack (Article 51). Armed coercion to enforce compliance with international law obligations, therefore, is beyond the prohibitive reach of the principle of non-intervention, but it remains unlawful under the *jus contra bellum* codified in the UN Charter.[169] Secondly, the principle of non-intervention only prohibits coercion, that is, *non-consensual* acts: the presence and operation of foreign troops on the territory of a state with the valid consent of its government is entirely permissible.[170] In contrast, Article 2(4) prohibits not only non-consensual uses of armed force, but also certain consensual ones if they are inconsistent with the UN purposes.[171] An intervention in support of an apartheid regime, for instance, would arguably still be a violation of that provision regardless of whether or not the racist regime has granted its consent.

7. The Second Pillar of the Principle of Non-Intervention: The Prohibition of Economic and Political Coercion

Whether other forms of coercion also fall under the prohibitive scope of the principle of non-intervention was an issue hotly debated during the Cold War: commentators in favour of a narrow notion of intervention limited to the use of armed force included writers of the calibre of Hans Kelsen[172] and James Brierly,[173] while Wolfgang Friedmann was among the supporters of a broader version including other forms of coercion.[174] Soviet scholars also championed an unconditional and comprehensive prohibition of intervention, including indirect, economic, and ideological aggression.[175]

The debate on the narrow and broad scope of the principle of non-intervention, that is, on the forms of coercion it prohibits, took centre stage during the drafting of the Vienna Convention on the Law of Treaties (VCLT) and of General Assembly Resolutions 2131 and 2625.[176] The fourth Special Rapporteur on the Law of Treaties, Sir Humphrey Waldock, explained that forms of political and economic coercion

---

[168] *Nicaragua v USA*, para 205.

[169] Art 50(1)(a) ARSIWA.

[170] See Chapter IV, Section 3.

[171] Patrick M Butchard, 'Territorial Integrity, Political Independence, and Consent: The Limitations of Military Assistance on Request under the Prohibition of the Use of Force' (2020) 7 JUFIL 35, 72.

[172] Hans Kelsen, 'The Draft Declaration on Right and Duties of States' (1950) 44 AJIL 259, 268.

[173] James Leslie Brierly, *The Law of Nations* (Clarendon Press 1955) 308 (intervention 'must either be forcible or backed by the threat of force.').

[174] Wolfgang Friedmann, *The Changing Structure of International Law* (Stevens & Sons 1964) 270–2.

[175] Vincent, *Nonintervention*, 182–3.

[176] During the drafting of the Declaration on the Rights and Duties of States at the ILC, Brierly also noted that 'an act of intervention was an act of dictation by one State to another with regard to its internal or

CONTENT OF THE PRINCIPLE OF NON-INTERVENTION 171

are much less capable of definition and much more liable to subjective appreciations. Moreover, the operation of political and economic pressures is part of the normal working of the relations between States, and international law does not yet seem to contain the criteria necessary for formulating distinctions between the legitimate and illegitimate uses of such forms of pressure as a means of securing consent to treaties.[177]

For these reasons, the Western states, including the Netherlands, the United States, and the United Kingdom, opposed the incorporation of economic and political coercion in the VCLT as a ground for invalidating treaties.[178] Even though other states disagreed,[179] Article 49 of the 1966 draft, which only referred to the threat and use of force in violation of the principles of the UN Charter, was eventually adopted.[180] At the 1968–9 Vienna Conference, a group of nineteen developing and non-aligned countries proposed an amendment to Draft Article 49 to specify that the threat and use of force also included economic and political pressures.[181] As the opposition to the amendment jeopardized the success of the conference, it was decided not to put it to the vote and economic and political forms of coercion were condemned in a separate declaration annexed to the Convention, but not in Article 52 of the final text of the treaty.[182] The drafting history of the VCLT, therefore, does not support the existence of a broad prohibition of any form of coercion under customary international law. At the same time, it does not necessarily reject it: the VCLT only addresses coercion as a ground for invalidating treaties, and not as an element of the principle of non-intervention.

The only post-1945 treaty rules that expressly prohibit not only armed but also economic and political forms of coercion are contained in the OAS Charter (Articles 19 and 20). In his Separate Opinion in the *Nicaragua* Merits Judgment, however, Judge Ago doubted that, as of 1986, these provisions reflected customary international law.[183] Judge Schwebel agreed: in his view, 'dictatorial interferences' by one state in the affairs of another are prohibited by customary international law, but the same cannot be said of the 'much more pervasive' prohibition of intervention contained in the OAS

---

external policy backed by the use or threat of force, express or implied ... if there was no force or threat of force any action, however improper or unfriendly, could not be qualified as intervention' ([1949] YB ILC 90). Among the other members of the ILC, Scelle supported Brierly's view, but for François, Yépès, and Amado this interpretation of the notion of intervention, limited to the threat or use of armed force, was too narrow: [1949] YB ILC 91–2.

[177] Sir Humphrey Waldock, Second Report on the Law of Treaties [1963] YB ILC, vol II, 52.
[178] Sir Humphrey Waldock, Fifth Report on the Law of Treaties [1966] YB ILC, vol II, 16.
[179] See eg Algeria, Byelorussia, Czechoslovakia, Ecuador, Ghana, Hungary, Indonesia, Iraq, Jamaica, the Philippines, Poland, Venezuela, and Yugoslavia (ibid, 15–18).
[180] On the different positions, see [1966] YB ILC vol II, 16–18.
[181] United Nations Conference on the Law of Treaties, Official Records, First and Second Sessions, UN Doc A/CONF.39/11/Add.2, 26 March–24 May 1968 and 9 April–22 May 1969, 172.
[182] Art 52 VCLT. The Declaration, which is not binding, condemns 'the threat or use of pressure in any form, whether military, political, or economic, by any State, in order to coerce another State to perform any act relating to the conclusion of a treaty in violation of the principle of the sovereign equality of States and freedom of consent' (text in Mark E Villiger, *Commentary on the 1969 Vienna Convention on the Law of Treaties* (Brill 2009) 651).
[183] *Nicaragua v USA*, Separate Opinion of Judge Ago, para 6.

172   INTERNATIONAL LAW AND THE PRINCIPLE OF NON-INTERVENTION

Charter.[184] A violation of Articles 19 and/or 20 in relation to acts of economic co-ercion has been invoked on at least three occasions.[185] The first was on 11 July 1960 when Cuba accused the United States of 'economic aggression' for reducing its sugar imports from the latter, cancelling Cuban credits, and freezing its bank accounts. For Havana, the US measures were prohibited by Articles 19 and 20 of the OAS Charter (then 15 and 16) 'because of its unilateral character and its coercive aggression'.[186] While Cuba did not file a complaint to the OAS, it brought the matter to the attention of the UN Security Council.[187] No resolution was however adopted either at the UN or OAS levels. In 1985, Nicaragua filed a complaint with the OAS protesting against the total trade embargo adopted by the United States against the Central American country.[188] Nine OAS member states presented a draft resolution condemning the US measures as a violation of international law, in particular the UN and OAS Charters, and urging Washington to repeal them and not adopt them again in the future.[189] The nine-country resolution was not put to the vote because of lack of quorum. The third situation—and the only in which the Organization took a position—was the adoption of restrictive economic measures by the United States against Argentina during the Falkland/Malvinas crisis of 1982: on 9 October 1982, the Inter-American Economic and Social Council declared that the measures were in violation of the OAS Charter (particularly of what is now Article 20), the Friendly Relations Declaration, and other international instruments.[190]

The relevant resolutions of the UN General Assembly also espouse the broad version of the principle of non-intervention. Resolution 380 (V) of 17 November 1950 still limited the condemnation of intervention to situations implying the use of force, but Resolution 2131 containing the Declaration on the Inadmissibility of Intervention, adopted in 1965, rejects 'armed intervention and all other forms of interference or attempted threats against the personality of the State or against its political, economic and cultural elements'.[191] As already noted, this paragraph is taken almost verbatim from Article 19 of the OAS Charter (the compromise draft that was eventually adopted had been prepared by an informal working group consisting of Asian, African, and Latin American states and merged elements from the previous Latin American and Asian-African drafts).[192] The following paragraph is also heavily based on Article 20

[184] *Nicaragua v USA*, Dissenting Opinion of Judge Schwebel, paras 98–9. Schwebel, in particular, points out that '[t]here is no universal treaty which has incorporated those provisions into the body of general international law. There is hardly sign of custom—of the practice of States—which suggests, still less demonstrates, a practice accepted as law which equates with the standards of non-intervention prescribed by the OAS Charter' (ibid, para 98). The US assistant secretary of state for congressional relations also claimed that Art 18 (now 19) of the OAS Charter is only binding on the states that have ratified the Charter (McDowell (ed), *Digest 1976*, 8).

[185] The United States has also referred to these provisions in relation to military operations: see Chapter V, Section 3.2.2 (intervention in the Dominican Republic).

[186] Quoted in Benneh, 'Economic Coercion', 239.

[187] UN Doc S/4378, 11 July 1960. The US response rejecting the allegations is in S/4388, 15 July 1960.

[188] Benneh, 'Economic Coercion', 240.

[189] ibid, 241.

[190] ibid, 242.

[191] GA Res 2131 (XX), para 1.

[192] Nicholas Greenwood Onuf, 'The Principle of Nonintervention, the United Nations, and the International System' (1971) 25 International Organization 209, 216–17.

CONTENT OF THE PRINCIPLE OF NON-INTERVENTION   173

of the OAS Charter, with the difference that the Charter only contemplates coercive measures of an economic and political character, while Resolution 2131 also condemns 'any other type of measures to coerce another State in order to obtain from it the subordination of the exercise of its sovereign rights or to secure from it advantages of any kind'.[193] The resolution was adopted by 109 votes to none, with one abstention.

The status of Resolution 2131 was discussed during the drafting of what would become Resolution 2625 by the Special Committee on Principles of International Law concerning Friendly Relations and Co-operation among States, as the socialist, Latin American, and Asian-African countries endorsed the incorporation of the broad formulation of the principle of non-intervention contained in the former, as well as the inclusion of a list of prohibited cases, in the latter.[194] In fact, for some states political and economic coercion should have even been included in the section on the prohibition of the threat and use of force.[195] The Western bloc, on the other hand, considered Resolution 2131 as a mere political statement rather than a formulation of legal principles and saw the principle of non-intervention as limited in scope to prohibiting the direct and indirect use of armed force.[196] These states deemed it impossible to give an exhaustive definition of what constitutes intervention[197] and were concerned that too broad or too detailed a formulation would result in prohibiting activities that are normal intercourse between states.[198] At its 1966 session, the Special Committee on Friendly Relations eventually adopted a resolution that considered Resolution 2131 'by virtue of the number of States which voted in its favour, the scope and profundity of its contents and, in particular the absence of opposition' as reflecting 'a universal legal

---

[193] GA Res 2131 (XX), para 2.

[194] See eg Romania, UN Doc A/AC.119/SR.26, 23 October 1964, 6–7. See also the proposals by Yugoslavia (A/AC.119/L.7, 31 August 1964, 2–3); Mexico (A/AC.119/L.24, 1–2); and Ghana, India, and Yugoslavia (A/AC.119/L.27, 21 September 1964, para 2).

[195] See the proposals by Czechoslovakia (UN Doc A/AC.119/L.6, 1) and Yugoslavia (A/AC.119/L.7, 1). See also the comments by Indonesia (A/C.6/SR.809, 12 November 1963, para 7) and Algeria (A/C.6/SR.809, para 24). Subsequent attempts by the Latin American and socialist states to have economic aggression included in the General Assembly's Declaration on the Definition of Aggression (GA Res 3314 (XXIX), 14 December 1974) were also unsuccessful (Gaetano Arangio-Ruiz, Fourth Report on State Responsibility [1992] YB ILC, vol II, 28).

[196] See UN Doc A/6230, paras 297–8; Foreign Office, 'Is Intervention Ever Justified?', 620. The Western states were also keen on including a reaffirmation of the right of self-defence against intervention: see joint draft presented by Australia, Canada, France, Italy, United Kingdom, and United States, A/6230, para 279. See also Australia and Italy's joint proposal (A/6230, para 280) and the commentary accompanying the British proposal (A/AC.119/L.8, 31 August 1964, 7–8).

[197] See eg the United Kingdom's position, UN Doc A/AC.119/L.8, 7.

[198] The commentary attached to the British draft of the principle of non-intervention submitted at the Friendly Relations Special Committee's 1964 session, in particular, posited that '[i]n considering the scope of "intervention", it should be recognized that in an interdependent world, it is inevitable and desirable that States will be concerned with and will seek to influence the actions and policies of other States, and that the objective of international law is not to prevent such activity but rather to ensure that it is compatible with the sovereign equality of States and self-determination of their peoples' (UN Doc A/AC.119/L.8, 7). See also the statement of the Dutch representative (A/AC.119/SR.7, 2 September 1964, 8–9). A joint proposal by Australia, Canada, France, Italy, and the United States cautioned that nothing in the Declaration could be construed as derogating from 'the generally recognized freedom of States to seek to influence the policies and actions of other States, in accordance with international law and settled international practice and in a manner compatible with the principle of sovereign equality of States and the duty to co-operate in accordance with the Charter' (A/6799, para 303). See also the joint proposal by Australia and Italy (A/6799, para 305). This language, however, was seen by the developing countries as legitimizing intervention (A/6230, para 133) and was eventually not incorporated in the final text of the Declaration.

conviction which qualifies it to be regarded as an authentic and definite principle of international law'.[199] The disagreement, however, persisted: nine representatives from the Western bloc voted against or abstained as, in their view, Resolution 2131 did not contain a legal definition of the principle of non-intervention.[200]

After a four-year stalemate with no substantial discussion of non-intervention, the text of the principle was agreed at the last session of the Special Committee in 1970, when the position of the socialist and non-aligned states eventually prevailed and it was agreed to incorporate the language of paragraphs 1, 2, 3, 5, and 8 of Resolution 2131 in the final text of Resolution 2625 with only minor variations.[201] Unlike Resolution 2131, the Declaration on Friendly Relations expressly states that it is not merely a political document, as it embodies the principles of the UN Charter which constitute 'basic principles of international law'.[202] The ICJ also found that the acceptance of the text of the Declaration by the General Assembly's member states reveals their *opinio juris*, that is, their recognition of the legal force of the principles contained therein.[203]

The broader notion of non-intervention prohibiting all forms of coercion is reflected not only in the OAS Charter and General Assembly Resolutions 2131 and 2625, but also in the 1975 Helsinki Final Act, which requires the participating states to refrain 'from any ... act of military, or of political, economic or other coercion designed to subordinate to their own interest the exercise by another participating State of the rights inherent in its sovereignty and thus to secure advantages of any kind'.[204] In *Nicaragua*, the ICJ held that the text of the Final Act 'testifies to the existence ... of a customary principle which has universal application'.[205] In 2007, the Latvian Constitutional Court also found that, although the Final Act is not a treaty, 'it can be used to determine the content of the principles of international law'.[206]

The next two sections verify whether the broad version of the principle of non-intervention contained in the OAS Charter, General Assembly Resolutions 2131 and

---

[199] UN Doc A/6230, para 341.

[200] See the statements by the representatives of France, Japan, the United Kingdom, Sweden, Australia, and the United States, UN Doc A/6230, paras 343–4, 348, 350–52.

[201] The language of Resolutions 2131 (XX) and 2625 (XXV) is also contained in other landmark resolutions, including: GA Res 3171 (XXVIII) of 11 December 1973 on the Permanent Sovereignty over Natural Resources; Art 32 of the Charter of Economic Rights and Duties of States (GA Res 3281 (XXIX), 4 December 1974); and GA Res 42/22 of 18 November 1987 containing the Declaration on the Enhancement of the Effectiveness of the Principle of Refraining from the Threat or Use of Force in International Relations. Other important resolutions condemning economic coercion or certain aspects of it include the Declaration on the Establishment of a New International Economic Order (GA Res 2103 (S-VI), 1 May 1974), para 4(e)) and GA Res 36/103, 9 December 1981, para 2(II)(k).

[202] GA Res 2625 (XXV), para 3. Mali, for instance, observed that the Declaration 'was a recommendation which interpreted the Charter and consequently no State which adopted it could evade its responsibilities' (UN Doc A/C.6/SR.1181, 25 September 1970, para 38). Others referred to the *jus cogens* or customary nature of the principles contained therein (see Chapter II, Section 6). It is true that the Declaration was adopted by the General Assembly's Political Committee, but a number of representatives observed that it was immaterial which committee recommended the adoption of the resolution (A/6799, para 326).

[203] *Nicaragua v USA*, para 188.

[204] Helsinki Final Act, Principle VI, para 3.

[205] *Nicaragua v USA*, para 204.

[206] Latvia's Constitutional Court Judgment, para 71.1.

2625, and the Helsinki Final Act does reflect customary international law: as the ILC observed,

> provisions of resolutions adopted by an international organization or at an intergovernmental conference cannot in and of themselves serve as conclusive evidence of the existence and content of rules of customary international law. This follows from the indication that, for the existence of a rule to be demonstrated, the *opinio juris* of States, as may be evidenced by a resolution, must be borne out by practice; other evidence is thus required, in particular to show whether the alleged rule is in fact observed in the practice of States.[207]

7.1 Economic Coercion

Inspired by Lenin's doctrine of substantive, and not merely formal, equality, it was mainly the Soviet Union that, during the Cold War, took the diplomatic initiative to extend the principle of non-intervention to *all* forms of coercion.[208] In fact, the idea was not new: a broad notion of the principle of non-intervention also encompassing economic coercion had already been championed by the Latin American states since the beginning of the 20th century in response to the Unites States' 'dollar diplomacy' and eventually materialized in Article 20 (originally Article 16) of the OAS Charter, but it had remained limited in its application to the American continent. After the creation of the United Nations, the USSR and the socialist bloc joined forces with the Third World countries to adopt a resolution that would reaffirm the principle of non-intervention in its broad incarnation at the global level. The newly independent states were particularly interested in this endeavour as they considered their continued economic dependence from their former metropolis as a vehicle for neo-colonialist policies and an obstacle to real emancipation.[209] As seen, these efforts led to the adoption of, among others, General Assembly Resolutions 2131 and 2625.

Economic coercion is different from coercion for economic purposes.[210] In the latter, states intervene by armed, economic, political, or other means to obtain economic advantages.[211] The former, on the other hand, is the use of economic means of pressure to coerce another state and secure advantages which might be of economic or other nature: as the US national security adviser, John Bolton, colourfully put it to explain the US government's economic sanctions against the Venezuelan government, '[i]t is like in Star Wars, when Darth Vader constricts somebody's throat;

---

[207] Commentary on Draft Conclusion 12 [2018] YB ILC, vol II, part two, 108.

[208] Gaeta, Viñules, and Zappalà, *Cassese's International Law*, 33.

[209] Antony Anghie and BS Chimni, 'Third World Approaches to International Law and Individual Responsibility in Internal Conflicts' (2003) 2 CJIL 77, 82.

[210] Thomas and Thomas, *Non-Intervention*, 410.

[211] See eg the naval blockade from December 1902 to February 1903 imposed on Venezuela by Britain, Germany, and Italy over President Cipriano Castro's refusal to pay foreign debts and damages suffered by European citizens in the Venezuelan Civil War and the interventions of the European great powers in China in the 19th century that coerced the Asian country into opening its ports to foreign trade.

176 INTERNATIONAL LAW AND THE PRINCIPLE OF NON-INTERVENTION

that is what we are doing to the regime economically'.[212] Using more technical language, the EU Commission has clarified that economic coercion occurs when 'a third country: —interferes in the legitimate sovereign choices of the Union or a Member State by seeking to prevent or obtain the cessation, modification or adoption of a particular act by the Union or a Member State—by applying or threatening to apply measures affecting trade or investment'.[213]

Thomas and Thomas usefully distinguish three main forms of economic intervention: through trade relations, through public financial relations, and through private financial relations.[214] Economic intervention through trade relations includes the manipulation of tariffs, the imposition of an embargo, and the imposition of a boycott.[215] Although boycott is normally an act of individuals, it could potentially fall under the principle of non-intervention if the government instructs its citizens to adopt it.[216] In economic intervention through public financial relations, a state could refuse to grant loans to another, freeze its public assets, manipulate the control of exchange, or devaluate or inflate its currency in relation to the currency of the other state.[217] Finally, economic intervention through private financial relations occurs

> when a state prohibits all private banking and lending institutions from granting credits to another nation or its citizens; when it prohibits the sale of stocks or bonds of that nation or of its corporate citizens within its territory; and when it suspends all existing clearing or payment agreements between its citizens and the citizens or government of the other state.[218]

To these a fourth form of economic coercion can be added: the suspension or drastic reduction of economic aid on which another state depends.[219] Indeed, the *travaux* of Resolution 2131 suggest that what the socialist and developing states had in mind as the typical case of economic coercion was the subordination of the supply of economic aid to conditions like the acceptance of military bases on the territory of the receiving state, the adoption of domestic legislation favouring foreign private investments, or the waiver of the right of nationalizing and expropriating foreign property.[220]

The aforementioned measures can be adopted as either primary or secondary sanctions.[221] While the former are aimed at putting pressure directly on the target state,

---

[212] Quoted by the Venezuelan delegate at the Security Council, UN Doc S/PV.8506, 10 April 2019, 23.

[213] European Commission, Proposal for a Regulation, Art 2(1).

[214] Thomas and Thomas, *Non-Intervention*, 410.

[215] ibid.

[216] ibid, 411. The Chinese boycott of US goods in 1905 in reaction to the mistreatment of Chinese workers in the United States, for instance, was supported by the Qing government (Christopher C Joyner, 'Boycott' in *MPEPIL Online* (last updated March 2009) para 3).

[217] Thomas and Thomas, *Non-Intervention*, 411.

[218] ibid.

[219] Gaeta, Viñuales, and Zappalà, *Cassese's International Law*, 55.

[220] See eg Soviet Union (UN Doc A/C.1/SR.1395, 3 December 1965, para 18); Ghana (A/C.1/SR.1402, 8 December 1965, para 13); Bulgaria (A/C.1/SR.1405, 9 December 1965, para 16); and Sudan (A/C.1/SR.1405, para 23).

[221] Mohamed S Helal, 'On Coercion in International Law' (2019) 52 NYU J Intl L & Pol 1, 103. On secondary sanctions, see Tom Ruys and Cedric Ryngaert, 'Secondary Sanctions: A Weapon out of Control? The International Legality of, and European Responses to, US Secondary Sanctions' (2020) BYBIL (advance access).

the latter intend to coerce third parties not to do business with the state which is the ultimate object of the coercion. The United States, for instance, has famously adopted secondary sanctions against states and foreign nationals not complying with its restrictive measures against Cuba and Iran.[222] These sanctions

> aim to replace [other states'] foreign policy choices with US foreign policy preferences, and they put pressure on foreign actors to change their foreign policies towards both Iran and Cuba in line with US foreign policy goals through the medium of natural and legal persons that are constrained by the extra-territorial legislation.[223]

The European Union considers extraterritorial sanctions a violation of international law because of the absence of a sufficient jurisdictional nexus between the target and the sanctioning states.[224]

To be coercive, economic measures must have sufficient impact on the target state to impair its decisional sovereignty: J Dapray Muir notes that '[c]learly, it is appropriate to distinguish between a boycott in bananas and one on petroleum or wheat.'[225] In the end, whether an economic measure is of magnitude sufficient to have a coercive effect is necessarily a contextual assessment: a state where the economy entirely depends on the export of one good (including bananas) might be severely affected by an embargo on that good, while countries with a more diversified economic system would not. Factors to consider can include the effects on the target state's finances, whether the target state protested at the time, whether it tried to avoid the consequences after the coercive conduct occurred, and whether there was any realistic alternative to submission.[226] The EU Commission's proposal for a regulation on the protection of the Union and its member states from economic coercion by third countries also suggests the following factors, which is worth reproducing in full:

(a) the intensity, severity, frequency, duration, breadth and magnitude of the third country's measure and the pressure arising from it;
(b) whether the third country is engaging in a pattern of interference seeking to obtain from the Union or from Member States or other countries particular acts;
(c) the extent to which the third-country measure encroaches upon an area of the Union's or Member States' sovereignty;
(d) whether the third country is acting based on a legitimate concern that is internationally recognised;

---

[222] See Julia Schmidt, 'The Legality of Unilateral Extra-Territorial Sanctions under International Law' (2022) 27 JCSL 53, 61–4.

[223] ibid, 70.

[224] Tom Ruys and Felipe Rodriguez Silvestre, 'L'Union contre-attaque—La proposition d'instrument anti-coercition (IAC) vue sous l'angle du droit international' (2021) 67 AFDI 143, 155.

[225] J Dapray Muir, 'The Boycott in International Law' (1974) JILE 187, 203. See also Ignaz Seidl-Hohenveldern, 'The United Nations and Economic Coercion' (1984) 18 RBDI 9, 12; Philip Kunig, 'Intervention, Prohibition of' in MPEPIL Online (last updated April 2008) para 25; Jamnejad and Wood, 'The Principle', 348. During the ICJ proceedings, Nicaragua also defined economic coercion as 'substantial damaging of the economy' (Nicaragua v USA, Nicaragua's Memorial, para 465, emphasis added).

[226] These factors are borrowed from the treatment of economic duress in contract law (Janet O'Sullivan, O'Sullivan & Hilliard's The Law of Contract (8th edn, OUP 2018) 264–5).

178 INTERNATIONAL LAW AND THE PRINCIPLE OF NON-INTERVENTION

(e) whether and in what manner the third country, before the imposition of its measures, has made serious attempts, in good faith, to settle the matter by way of international coordination or adjudication, either bilaterally or within an international forum.[227]

The mere fact that economic coercion is widely practised does not necessarily mean that it is allowed under customary international law since practice is in itself insufficient to generate customary rules if not accompanied by *opinio juris*.[228] A significant number of states have indeed expressed themselves against the legality of economic coercion in the debates on General Assembly Resolutions 2131 and 2625.[229] In 1960, Cuba also claimed that the discontinuation by the United States of sugar purchases was 'an attempt to strangle Cuba's economy' and, therefore, was 'at variance with the rules of international law' and that the economic 'blockade' was 'a direct intervention in Cuba's domestic affairs and a clear violation of its national sovereignty for aggressive purposes'.[230] The Preamble of the General Assembly resolutions calling for an end to the US economic, commercial, and financial embargo against Cuba reaffirms the principle of non-intervention, with several member states referring to it in the discussions that led to their adoption.[231] The 1984 FCO memorandum on intervention concedes that intervention also includes economic coercion and propaganda.[232] In the 1994 Memorandum on Security Assurances in Connection with Ukraine's Accession to the Treaty on the Non-Proliferation of Nuclear Weapons signed by Ukraine, the Russian Federation, the United Kingdom, and the United States, the latter three states also use language borrowed from General Assembly Resolutions 2131 and 2625 to reaffirm their commitment 'to refrain from economic coercion designed to subordinate to their own interest the exercise by Ukraine of the rights inherent in its sovereignty and thus to secure advantages of any kind'.[233] US President Obama's executive order imposing financial sanctions on Venezuelan officials in March 2015 was reacted to by the Union of South American Nations (UNASUR) with a statement that criticized the interventionist threat to sovereignty and to the principle of 'non-interference' in the internal affairs of other states.[234] The Venezuelan delegate at the Security Council claimed that it was 'illegal for acts of economic war to be perpetrated against' his country[235] and denounced the 'deliberate economic destruction, the systematic implementation of the policy of aggression through the use of financial instruments,

---

[227] European Commission, Proposal for a Regulation, Art 2(2).

[228] *North Sea Continental Shelf Cases (Federal Republic of Germany/Denmark; Federal Republic of Germany/Netherlands)* (Judgment) [1969] ICJ Rep 3, para 77.

[229] See eg Ceylon (UN Doc A/C.6/SR.1180, 24 September 1970, paras 11–6); Bolivia (A/C.6/SR.1181, paras 21–5); Jordan (A/C.1/SR.1405, paras 1–5); and Bulgaria (A/C.1/SR.1405, paras 11–16).

[230] UN Doc S/PV.876, 19 July 1960, 8.

[231] See eg GA Res 47/19, 24 November 1992. These resolutions are usually adopted with only the United States and Israel's negative votes (in 2016, the two countries abstained for the first time).

[232] Foreign Office, 'Is Intervention Ever Justified?', 614. The document, however, is ambiguous on whether economic and political measures are prohibited (ibid, 615).

[233] UN Doc A/49/765-S/1994/1399, 19 December 1994, Annex I, para 3.

[234] UNASUR, Comunicado de la Unión de Naciones Suramericanas sobre el Derecho Ejecutivo del Gobierno de los Estados Unidos sobre Venezuela, Quito, 14 March 2015 <www.cancilleria.gob.bo/webmre/node/917>.

[235] UN Doc S/PV.8476, 28 February 2019, 11–12.

CONTENT OF THE PRINCIPLE OF NON-INTERVENTION 179

through the application of undue pressure and through the use of market dominance to influence the banking sector, private enterprise and other nations that engage in legal trade with Venezuela.[236] In 2016, the PRC, India, and Russia jointly condemned the use of 'unilateral coercive measures not based on international law' as a violation of the principle of non-intervention,[237] and so did the African Union.[238] At the Human Rights Council's 44th session, the PRC, backed by several other Council members, denounced the sanctions adopted or threatened by certain Western countries in response to the repressive measures of the Chinese government in Hong Kong as an interference in its internal affairs, an infringement of its legislative sovereignty, and a breach of the UN Charter.[239] In its recent position document on the application of international law in cyberspace, Costa Rica posits that the exercise of 'significant political or economic pressure on another State' is a form of coercion for the purposes of the principle of non-intervention.[240] Finally, the EU Commission has claimed that '[c]oercive [economic] measures by third countries targeting the EU or Member States can be considered a breach of customary international law, which prohibits certain forms of interference in the affairs of another subject of international law when there is no basis in international law for doing so'.[241]

In addition to these statements of condemnation, justificatory countermeasure language has often been used by the states that have adopted unilateral coercive economic measures against other countries.[242] The United States has linked its embargo on all exports to Cuba to the lack of adequate compensation received for the expropriation of US property and assets by the Caribbean state in 1959–60 and to its violations of human rights.[243] When President Allende denounced the cutting of lines of credit to Chile by the United States as 'a form of intervention in the internal affairs of a sovereign

---

[236] UN Doc S/PV.8506, 24. The Venezuelan representative claimed that the sanctions could have only been imposed with the express authorization of the Security Council (S/PV.8506, 25). In the Security Council debates, certain states declared that the economic strangulation of Venezuela was at odds with the OAS Charter but oddly referred to Art 21, instead of Arts 19 or 20 (S/PV.8472, 26 February 2019, 35 (Suriname); S/PV.8472, 45 (Dominica)).

[237] Joint Communiqué of the 14th Meeting of the Foreign Ministers of the Russian Federation, the Republic of India and the PRC, Moscow, 19 April 2016, para 6 <www.fmprc.gov.cn/eng/wjdt_665385/2649 _665393/201604/t20160419_679455.html>; Declaration of the People's Republic of China and the Russian Federation on the Promotion of International Law (Beijing, 25 June 2016) para 6 <www.fmprc.gov.cn/eng/ wjdt_665385/2649_665393/201608/t20160801_679466.html>.

[238] Resolution on the Impact of Sanctions and Unilateral Coercive Measures on African Union Member States, Assembly/AU/Res.1 (XXXV), 5–6 February 2022; Resolution on the Lifting of the Economic, Commercial and Financial Blockade Imposed on the Republic of Cuba by the United States, Assembly/AU/ Res.2 (XXXV), 5–6 February 2022.

[239] Statement by the Permanent Mission of the People's Republic of China to the United Nations Office at Geneva and Other International Organizations in Switzerland (30 June 2020), quoted in Stefano Saluzzo, 'The Principle of Non-Intervention and the Battle over Hong Kong' (2021) 79 Quest Intl L 27, 32.

[240] Costa Rica's position, para 24.

[241] Commission Staff Working Document, Impact Assessment Report Accompanying the Document Proposal for a Regulation of the European Parliament and of the Council on the protection of the Union and its Member States from economic coercion by third Countries, 8 December 2021, SWD (2021) 371 final, 8.

[242] For Flavia Lattanzi, states always try to justify their resort to economic and political coercion and no state has admitted the legality of measures aimed at subordinating the exercise of another state's sovereign rights or at securing advantages of any kind (Flavia Lattanzi, *Garanzie dei diritti dell'uomo nel diritto internazionale generale* (Giuffrè 1983) 284).

[243] Bianchi, 'Le recenti sanzioni', 355–60.

180 INTERNATIONAL LAW AND THE PRINCIPLE OF NON-INTERVENTION

state',[244] the US government claimed again that it was a response to the expropriation of American property in Chile without adequate compensation.[245] The UK boycott of the purchase of Iranian oil in the 1950s was also presented as a reaction to the nationalization of the oil industry by Iran's Prime Minister Mossadegh.[246] When OAPEC reduced oil supplies to Europe and Japan and cut them off entirely from the United States and the Netherlands as a consequence of Western support for Israel during the Yom Kippur War (1973), the Arab countries justified it as an exercise of the right of self-defence, as a lawful belligerent measure, and as a reaction to a previous violation of international law.[247] Similarly, the US economic sanctions against the Soviet Union after the invasion of Afghanistan were adopted in response to what President Carter qualified as a 'gross interference in the internal affairs of Afghanistan ... in blatant violation of accepted international rules of behavior'.[248] In 2017, Saudi Arabia, the United Arab Emirates (UAE), Bahrain, and Egypt closed their airspace to Qatari aircraft, Saudi Arabia closed Qatar's only land border, and ships flying the Qatari flag or those serving Qatar were prohibited from docking at many regional ports: the UAE explained that such measures were a last-resort reaction against Qatar's 'unlawful conduct', that is, its 'support for terrorism, its interference in the affairs of its neighbours, and its dissemination of hate speech',[249] and that the measures had the 'aim of inducing compliance by Qatar'.[250] The United States referred to Iran's 'unlawful and threatening conduct' as the reason for which the sanctions against the Islamic Republic were resumed in August 2018.[251] The Western states also indicated that the restrictive measures adopted against the PRC in 2020 were a response to its violation of human rights and democracy in Hong Kong as well as of the 1984 Sino-British Joint Declaration on the Question of Hong Kong.[252] Finally, the economic sanctions adopted by the United States, the European Union members, and other states against Russia's financial system, energy sector, and international trade have been justified with the invasion of Ukraine in February 2022 and the violations of international humanitarian law committed by the Russian forces.[253]

[244] Speech at the UN General Assembly, quoted in Harmut Brosche, 'The Arab Oil Embargo' (1974) 7 Case Western Reserve JIL 3, 11.

[245] ibid, 12.

[246] Muir, 'The Boycott', 189.

[247] James A Boorman III, 'Economic Coercion in International Law: The Arab Oil Weapon and the Ensuing Juridical Issues' (1974) 9 JILE 205, 208–9. The Arab countries subordinated the end of the restrictive measures to Israel's withdrawal from territories occupied during the 1967 Six-Day War and to the restoration of the Palestinians' rights (Brosche, 'The Arab Oil Embargo', 9–10).

[248] Speech of 28 December 1979, quoted in Sapienza, *Il principio*, 114.

[249] *Qatar v UAE*, Oral proceedings, CR 2018/13, 28 June 2018, 11–12.

[250] *Appeal Relating to the Jurisdiction of the ICAO Council under Article 84 of the Convention on International Civil Aviation (Bahrain, Egypt, Saudi Arabia and UAE v Qatar)*, Joint Application instituting proceedings, 4 July 2018, para 9 <www.icj-cij.org/case/173>.

[251] *Iran v USA*, Oral Proceedings, CR 2018/19, 30 August 2018, 19. The alleged violations include the export of arms in breach of UN Security Council resolutions, the non-suspension by Iran of its ballistic missile programme, the intervention in regional states to create instability, and the secret storage of nuclear-weapon-related documents in contravention of the Joint Comprehensive Plan of Action (ibid, CR 2018/19, 19–20).

[252] Saluzzo, 'The Principle', 41. For the PRC's contrary view, see Jia Guide, 'New China and International Law: Practice and Contribution in 70 Years' (2019) 18 CJIL 727, 735–7.

[253] Elena Chachko and J Benton Heath, 'A Watershed Moment for Sanctions? Russia, Ukraine, and the Economic Battlefield' (2022) 116 AJIL Unbound 135, 138.

CONTENT OF THE PRINCIPLE OF NON-INTERVENTION   181

At the same time, however, there are powerful arguments against the inclusion of economic coercion in the customary version of the principle of non-intervention.[254] Indeed, the Western states, and the United States in particular, have long supported the legality of economic sanctions: these states' concern is that the qualification of economic coercion as a violation of the principle of non-intervention coupled with the present lack of generally accepted criteria to distinguish it from normal business interactions between states would provide an excuse to adopt unjustifiable counter-measures in response to it. A 1974 memorandum of law prepared by the acting legal adviser of the US Department of State points out that the negotiating history of Article 18 (now 19) of the OAS Charter does not support the view that it prohibits decreasing or increasing bilateral assistance to a country, sending diplomatic notes, restricting or encouraging exports of US products, or supporting one government at the expense of another.[255] In 1980, the United States also argued that its economic measures against Nicaragua were not a violation of Article 19 (now 20) of the OAS Charter because, among others, 'there is no general principle of customary law which obliges one State to trade with another. The OAS Charter did not, and was not intended to, create such a rule'.[256] In the *Sabbatino* case, the US Court of Appeals for the Second Circuit could not 'find any established principle of international jurisprudence that requires a nation to continue buying commodities from an unfriendly source'.[257]

It is therefore not surprising that the UN resolutions on 'Human rights and unilateral coercive measures' and on 'Unilateral economic measures as a means of political and economic coercion against developing countries' have been adopted with the negative vote of the Western states.[258] While it is true that unilateral economic

---

[254] There is no consensus in scholarship on whether economic coercion is lawful or not under customary international law. It has been observed that '[t]he use of export controls for political purposes is so widespread that no general rule of international custom could have developed to the contrary' (Ibrahim FI Shihata, 'Arab Oil Policies and the New International Economic Order' (1975) 16 Va J Intl L 261, 267). Other commentators are of the same view (Wolfgang Friedmann, 'Intervention, Civil War and the Role of International Law' (1965) 59 ASIL Proceedings 67, 69; Omer Yusif Elagab, *The Legality of Non-Forcible Counter-Measures in International Law* (Clarendon Press 1988) 208; Benneh, 'Economic Coercion', 249–52; Antonios Tzanakopoulos, 'The Right to Be Free from Economic Coercion' (2015) 4 Cambridge J Int'l & Comp L 616, 630–33; Ori Pomson, 'The Prohibition on Intervention Under International Law and Cyber Operations' (2022) 99 ILS 180, 210). Clive Parry, however, is not entirely convinced: 'the abrupt termination of or interference with an established trade pattern may approach the impermissible and may be capable of adequate enough definition' (Clive Parry, 'Defining Economic Coercion in International Law' (1977) 12 Tex Intl LJ 1, 4). White also affirms that '[t]he sovereign freedom of a state must always be balanced against the infringement of the sovereignty of other states' (White, *The Cuban Embargo*, 96). For Farer, 'under some conceivable conditions, economic coercion can be a violation of international law even where the means employed do not themselves violate any treaty' (Tom J Farer, 'Political and Economic Coercion in Contemporary International Law' (1985) 79 AJIL 405, 411). He concludes, however, that economic coercion might be an act of aggression only when its objective is 'to liquidate an existing state or to reduce that state to the position of a satellite' (ibid, 413). If it is only aimed at influencing foreign policy, it is 'a legitimate act of coercion within a decentralized international system' (ibid). Roth also considers 'unilaterally-imposed economic sanctions' as a case of illegal coercion 'where they assert extraterritorial effect or involve secondary boycotts—ie interference with a foreign state's trade relations through pressures (other than moral suasion) on its trading partners' or when the economies of the coercing and target state are intertwined (Brad R Roth, *Governmental Illegitimacy in International Law* (OUP 1999) 169).

[255] Eleanor C McDowell (ed), *Digest of United States Practice in International Law 1974* (GPO 1975) 6.

[256] Benneh, 'Economic Coercion', 241–2.

[257] *Banco Nacional de Cuba v Sabbatino*, Court of Appeals, 307 F.2d 845 (2d Cir 1962) 866.

[258] Alexandra Hofer, 'The Developed/Developing Divide on Unilateral Coercive Measures: Legitimate Enforcement or Illegitimate Intervention?' (2017) 16 CJIL 175, 188. Read the position of states in Unilateral

182 INTERNATIONAL LAW AND THE PRINCIPLE OF NON-INTERVENTION

measures have often been justified using countermeasure language, it is also unclear whether states did so because they considered the measures a treaty breach or a violation of the principle of non-intervention.[259] In the end, the reluctance of the Western liberal states to accept limitations to economic interactions betrays their long-standing conception of the principle of non-intervention as 'freedom to act instead of freedom from the acts of others',[260] a conception that, in the economic sphere, continues to play into the hands of the developed countries at the expense of the developing ones. As James Thuo Gathii notes, the rules regulating economic relations 'continue to perpetuate the subordinate position of [the] formerly colonial countries in a manner that uncannily reflects the imbalances that characterized colonial rule'.[261]

Any conclusion that the customary version of the principle of non-intervention prohibits economic coercion also flies in the face of the ICJ's findings in the *Nicaragua* case, where the Court held that '[a] State is not bound to continue particular trade relations longer than it sees fit to do so, in the absence of a treaty commitment or other specific legal obligation'.[262] The Court was thus unable to find that the US discontinuation of economic aid to Nicaragua, the drastic reduction (ninety per cent) of sugar imports from Nicaragua, and the trade embargo adopted against the Central American country by the United States constituted a breach of the customary principle of non-intervention, as argued by counsel for Nicaragua.[263] UN Secretary-General Boutros-Ghali was of the same opinion: in a 1993 report, he concluded that '[t]here is no clear consensus in international law as to when coercive economic measures are improper, despite relevant treaties, declarations and resolutions adopted in international organizations which try to develop norms limiting the use of such measures'.[264] His words remain true to this day.

When it comes to extending the customary principle of non-intervention to economic coercion, then, the risk is—to use Martti Koskenniemi's famous image—to indulge in either apology or utopia.[265] On the one hand, it is tempting to lean towards apology and conclude that the use of economic coercion is never a violation of the principle under examination as several states, namely the developed ones, still see it as a lawful means to pursue their foreign policy and to enforce community interests.[266]

Economic Measures as a Means of Political and Economic Coercion Against Developing Countries, Report of the Secretary-General, UN Doc A/72/307, 9 August 2017.

[259] Ronzitti, 'Non-ingerenza', 168.
[260] Greenwood Onuf, 'The Principle', 224.
[261] James Thuo Gathii, *War Commerce, and International Law* (OUP 2010) 189.
[262] *Nicaragua v USA*, para 276.
[263] ibid, paras 244–5.
[264] Economic Measures as a Means of Political and Economic Coercion against Developing Countries: Note by the Secretary-General, UN Doc A/48/535, 25 October 1993, para 2(a).
[265] Martti Koskenniemi, *From Apology to Utopia: The Structure of International Legal Argument* (CUP 2006) 17.
[266] Hofer, 'The Developed/Developing Divide', 196. That said, it has been suggested that even the Western states are now starting to oppose the use of unilateral coercive measures (Anh Nguyen, 'The G7 Fear of Economic Coercion through Weaponised Interdependence — Geopolitical Competition Cloaked in International Law?' (*EJIL:Talk!*, 22 June 2023) <www.ejiltalk.org/the-g7s-fear-of-economic-coercion-through-weaponised-interdependence-geopolitical-competition-cloaked-in-international-law/>). The European Commission's Proposal for a Regulation of the European Parliament and of the Council on the protection of the Union and its Member States from economic coercion by third countries has already been mentioned. In May 2023, the G7 Leaders' Statement on Economic Resilience and Economic Security also

CONTENT OF THE PRINCIPLE OF NON-INTERVENTION   183

When enforcing community interests, in particular, economic coercion seems to now perform the role that was played, in the 19th century, by armed measures short of war.[267] On the other hand, if we look at the black-letter texts (the OAS Charter, General Assembly Resolutions 2131 and 2625, and the Helsinki Final Act) we might find ourselves in the realm of utopia, namely, of rules that are not sufficiently reflected in the general practice and *opinio juris* of states.[268] It is indeed undeniable, as Nigel White has observed, that, in this area, 'there is a clear gap between the normative prescriptions of the General Assembly and the consistent practice of powerful states'.[269] All that can be said at this stage is that, while before 1945 the customary principle of non-intervention was limited to prohibiting the use of armed coercion and coercive diplomatic representations,[270] in the Charter era there have been increasing indications of a *trend* towards its broadening in scope so as to also include economic coercion.[271] The 'naked prohibition'[272] of economic coercion, however, already plays an important role at the level of burden of proof by making it more difficult for states to justify the adoption of unilateral coercive economic measures to protect their interests (as opposed to their rights).[273]

noted 'a disturbing rise in incidents of economic coercion that seek to exploit economic vulnerabilities and dependencies and undermine the foreign and domestic policies and positions of G7 members as well as partners around the world' and condemned the use of economic coercion which 'infringes upon the international order centered on respect for sovereignty and the rule of law' (G7 Leaders' Statement on Economic Resilience and Economic Security, 20 May 2023, 3 <www.consilium.europa.eu/media/64501/g7-statement-on-economic-resilience-and-economic-security.pdf>).

[267] Richard Lillich, for instance, maintains that economic coercion is 'a form of permissible self-help only when it is also compatible with the overall interests of the world community, as manifested in the principles of the UN Charter or in decisions taken or documents promulgated thereunder' (Richard B Lillich, 'Economic Coercion and the International Legal Order' (1975) 51 International Affairs 358, 366–7).

[268] Reviewing Roth's *Governmental Illegitimacy in International Law*, Gathii suggests that the General Assembly resolutions should be considered binding sources of international law, which would allow to construe the principle of non-intervention as prohibiting economic coercion (James Thuo Gathii, 'Neoliberalism, Colonialism and International Governance: Decentering the International Law of Governmental Legitimacy' (2000) 98 Mich L Rev 1996, 2028, 2031–2).

[269] White, *The Cuban Embargo*, 96–7. For the same opinion, see Lori Fisler Damrosch, 'Politics Across Borders: Nonintervention and Nonforcible Influence over Domestic Affairs' 1989 (83) AJIL 1, 2. To borrow Antonio Cassese's remarks made in another context, we are 'faced with elements (or fragmentary expressions) of *opinio juris* unattended by corresponding State practice, or *usus*' (Antonio Cassese, *Self-Determination of Peoples: A Legal Reappraisal* (CUP 1995) 309).

[270] See Chapter I, Section 5. See also Christian Tomuschat, 'International Law: Ensuring the Survival of Mankind on the Eve of a New Century' (1999) 281 Recueil des Cours 77, 231.

[271] Arangio-Ruiz, Fourth Report, 30. See also Paola Anna Pillitu, *Lo stato di necessità nel diritto internazionale* (Edizioni Scientifiche Italiane 1981) 238. According to a former assistant legal adviser for Near Eastern and South Asian affairs, 'existing international law can probably best be described as narrowing only slightly the permissive legal regime of the past. The direction of development of the law is toward greater restriction on the use of economic coercion, but it has been a slow movement with, thus far, limited effects' (McDowell (ed), *Digest 1976*, 578).

[272] I borrow the reference to the 'naked prohibition' which cannot be implemented because of the inconsistent practice of states from Judge Ferrari Bravo's Declaration appended to the ICJ's *Nuclear Weapons Advisory Opinion* (*Legality of the Threat or Use of Nuclear Weapons* (Advisory Opinion) [1996] ICJ Rep 226, Declaration of Judge Ferrari Bravo, 286).

[273] ibid.

7.2 Political Coercion

Political (or diplomatic) coercion is the quintessential means of dictatorial coercion and involves the use of political means of pressure to coerce another state into doing or not doing something: historically, it has been seen as consisting of threats communicated through diplomatic channels (the 'threatening diplomatic representations' mentioned in Article 11 of the 1933 Montevideo Convention on the Rights and Duties of States).[274] The threatened harm must of course be credible, specific, and serious enough to be able to impair the agency of the target state: public criticism of its policies, expressions of support for an opposition party, or the threat to break off diplomatic relations would arguably not suffice.[275] When the threatened harm is of an armed or economic nature, political coercion tends to merge with armed and economic forms of coercion.

Political coercion, however, can consist not only in demands accompanied by threats, but also in the premature recognition of belligerency, government, and statehood (scenario (e) above).[276] More specifically, coercion is present in two situations. First, a premature recognition is coercive to the extent that it results in preventing a state from exercising its sovereign prerogatives in the recognizing state, such as accessing financial assets or diplomatic premises or enjoying immunity from foreign jurisdiction and execution.[277] This is particularly evident when the recognizing state adopts the 'one voice' principle, that is, when the judiciary must conform to the political decision of the executive in relation to recognition.[278] The Venezuelan case well

---

[274] Sapienza, *Il principio*, 85; Rolando Quadri, *Diritto internazionale pubblico* (5th edn, Liguori 1968) 275.

[275] Talmon notes, however, that criticism expressed by diplomats with regard to the policies of the receiving state cannot be expressed through social media without breaching Art 4(1) of the Vienna Convention on Diplomatic Relations: '[w]hile a small group of Western States ... may consider Twitter, blogs, and other social media as just another means of communicating their foreign policy objectives, the majority of States still prefers the traditional, more discreet means of diplomacy' (Stefan Talmon, 'Iran Condemns German Ambassador's Tweets as Interference in Internal Affairs' (*GPIL—German Practice in International Law*, 13 July 2021) <https://gpil.jura.uni-bonn.de/2021/07/iran-condemns-german-ambassadors-tweets-as-interference-in-internal-affairs/>).

[276] See Art 2(f) of the Resolution of the Institut de droit international on 'Le principe de non-intervention dans les guerres civiles', Session of Wiesbaden, 13 August 1975 (1975) 56 AIDI 544 (hereafter Wiesbaden Resolution). See also, among many, Sir Hersch Lauterpacht, *Recognition in International Law* (CUP 1947) 94–5; Joe Verhoeven, 'La reconnaissance internationale: déclin ou renouveau?' (1993) 39 AFDI 7, 25; Yoram Dinstein, *Non-international Armed Conflicts in International Law* (2nd edn, CUP 2021) 132. The Southern African Development Community (SADC) has condemned the recognition by several states of Guaidò as the president of Venezuela as an interference in the internal affairs of the South American state and as a violation of international law (SADC Solidarity Statement with the Bolivarian Republic of Venezuela, 10 February 2019 <www.sadc.int/latest-news/solidarity-statement-bolivarian-republic-venezuela-issued-sadc-chairperson-his>).

[277] This is what Talmon calls the 'negatory effect' of recognition (Stefan Talmon, 'The Constitutive versus the Declaratory Theory of Recognition: *Tertium Non Datur?*' (2004) 75 BYBIL 101, 144). With regard to recognition of government, see eg the freezing of Libyan assets in Italy and their transfer to the National Transitional Council following the recognition of insurgency by the Italian government, as well as the cases related to the right to represent Libya before English courts (Marco Pertile, *Diritto internazionale e rapporti economici nelle guerre civili* (Editoriale Scientifica 2020) 214–15, 229–30).

[278] While only a limited number of states adopt the 'one voice' principle (eg the United Kingdom), it has been observed that '[f]ew courts, if any, ignore entirely whether or not the executive offices of the State have recognized (or declined to recognize) the entity in question' (Tom Grant, 'How to Recognise a State (and Not); Some Practical Considerations' in Christine Chinkin and Freya Baetens (eds), *Sovereignty, Statehood and State Responsibility: Essays in Honour of James Crawford* (CUP 2015) 192, 194–5).

illustrates this scenario. Following the 2018 presidential crisis, a legal dispute arose between the 'Maduro Board' and the 'Guaidó Board' of the Central Bank of Venezuela about the entitlement to give instructions to financial institutions on behalf of Venezuela with regard to its foreign currency reserves in England.[279] In first instance, the High Court of Justice decided the case in favour of Guaidó on the basis of his recognition as *de jure* Interim President of Venezuela by the UK government (even though he had no effective control of his country's territory).[280] In the appeals proceedings, the 'Maduro Board' claimed that, if Britain had recognized Guaidó as *de facto* president of Venezuela and not only *de jure* in spite of his total lack of effectiveness, this would have been unlawful because it would amount to a 'coercive intervention in the internal affairs of a foreign state which is prohibited by customary international law'.[281] Writing for the majority, Lord Justice Males disagreed and, quoting *Oppenheim's International Law*, found that *de facto* recognition is not an unlawful intervention in a foreign state's internal affairs because it 'does not imply any approval of the head of state or government thus recognised, but is merely the result of an assessment of which person or entity is in fact exercising effective control over the territory in question'.[282] This argument, however, misses the point: as already said, what makes recognition coercive is not its *de jure* or *de facto* character, but whether it results in preventing the prematurely derecognized entity from exercising its sovereign prerogatives on the territory of the recognizing state. In the case in question, the *de jure* recognition of Guaidó by the British government was not a coercive interference in Venezuela's internal affairs because, under English law, 'the acts of a *de jure* ruler (in the sense of a ruler who is entitled to be so regarded) have to be treated as a nullity', unlike those of a government that maintains effective control of its country.[283]

Secondly, premature recognition of belligerency, government, and statehood can constitute an unlawful intervention to the extent that it is aimed to assist, foment, or incite subversive, terrorist, or armed activities or at interfering in civil strife in another state. This aspect is examined in Section 8.

The refusal to recognize a situation that exists *de facto* is coercive in the same situations as those related to premature recognitions.[284] Note, however, that states have an obligation not to recognize situations arising from a serious breach of a peremptory norm of general international law.[285] This would be the case, for instance, of the

---

[279] Like the British government, the United States also certified Guaidó to control Venezuelan Central Bank assets, although Maduro was still in control of the government (Statement by Robert Palladino, Deputy Spokesperson, U.S. Department of State, 29 January 2019 <https://br.usembassy.gov/statement-by-robert-palladino-protecting-venezuelas-assets-for-benefit-of-venezuelan-people>).

[280] *Deutsche Bank AG London Branch v Receivers Appointed By the Court & Ors* [2020] EWHC 1721 (Comm).

[281] The *'Maduro Board' of the Central Bank of Venezuela v The 'Guaidó Board' of the Central Bank of Venezuela* [2020] EWCA Civ 1249, para 54(5) (hereafter *The 'Maduro Board' v The 'Guaidó Board'*).

[282] ibid, paras 135–6.

[283] ibid, para 125. The Supreme Court eventually found that Guaidó had been recognized by the British government as Venezuela's president for all purposes (*'Maduro Board' of the Central Bank of Venezuela (Respondent/Cross-Appellant) v 'Guaidó Board' of the Central Bank of Venezuela (Appellant/Cross-Respondent)* [2021] UKSC 57, paras 99–101).

[284] Alessandra Annoni, *Il riconoscimento come atto unilaterale dello Stato* (Jovene 2023) 61–4.

[285] Art 41(2) ARSIWA; *Legal Consequences of the Construction of a Wall in the Occupied Palestinian Territory* (Advisory Opinion) [2004] ICJ Rep 136, para 159. See Annoni, *Il riconoscimento*, 116–44.

secession of a territory achieved with the support of a foreign intervention (as in the case of Crimea and the Donbass People's republics), of a government that takes power thanks to an unlawful foreign military intervention (as in the case of the People's Republic of Kampuchea),[286] of states or governments that breach the principle of self-determination and in particular the prohibition of apartheid (as in the case of Rhodesia and the *bantustans*), and of the recognition of belligerency or governmental status of insurgents responsible for *jus cogens* violations like the self-styled 'Islamic State in Iraq and the Levant'.[287] The non-recognition of these and analogous situations, therefore, cannot be considered an intervention in the domestic affairs of the concerned state regardless of the factual situation.[288]

Finally, it is worth recalling that certain governments have recently condemned a further means of political coercion, the foreign funding of non-governmental organizations (NGOs), which is based on the assumption that 'the civil society in their state is not representing the view of "the people" but, rather, is influenced, or even controlled by, external powers'.[289] Examples include Venezuela's Law on Defence of Political Sovereignty and National Self-Determination (2010), Russia's Federal Law Introducing Amendments to Certain Legislative Acts Regarding the Regulation of Activities of Non-Commercial Organizations Performing the Function of Foreign Agents (2012), and Hungary's Law on the Transparency of Organizations Receiving Support from Abroad (2017).[290] As Heike Krieger notes, there is no international jurisprudence so far on the legality under international law of domestic restrictions on foreign NGO funding.[291]

8. The Third Pillar of the Principle of Non-Intervention: The Prohibition of Supporting Subversive, Terrorist, or Armed Activities and of Interfering in Civil Strife in Another State

In *Nicaragua*, the ICJ found that not only 'military action', but also 'support for subversive or terrorist armed activities within another State' is a 'particularly obvious' example of coercion.[292] Indeed, support for subversive, terrorist, or armed activities

---

[286] ibid, 136.

[287] Pertile, *Diritto internazionale*, 181–4.

[288] An obligation not to recognize territorial acquisitions or special advantages resulting not only from armed force but also other forms of coercion is contained in Art 11 of the Montevideo Convention and in Art 21 of the OAS Charter.

[289] Heike Krieger, 'Populist Governments and International Law' (2019) 30 EJIL 971, 991.

[290] ibid, 991–2.

[291] ibid, 993.

[292] *Nicaragua v USA*, para 205. The United Kingdom has pointed out that the duty not to foment civil disturbances in other states is 'a particular and important aspect of the more general principle' of non-intervention (UN Doc A/CN.4/2, 15 December 1948, 59). In a memorandum of law dated 25 October 1974, the acting legal adviser of the US State Department also noted that '[t]he threat or use of force, assistance to armed revolutionaries, and coercion designed to secure advantages from a state in contravention of its rights are the only state acts clearly and expressly prohibited by' the legal principle of non-intervention, although he conceded that the practice of states might lead to an extension of the scope of acts covered (McDowell (ed), *Digest 1974*, 8). See also Costa Rica's position, para 24.

CONTENT OF THE PRINCIPLE OF NON-INTERVENTION

can constitute a forcible form of coercion (for instance, by overthrowing a state's government) as well as a dictatorial one (by using the actual or threatened support for an armed opposition group as leverage to obtain certain concessions).

This third pillar of the principle of non-intervention is spelt out in General Assembly Resolutions 2131 and 2625, which include, as a case of prohibited intervention, the organization, assistance, fomentation, financing, incitement or toleration of 'subversive, terrorist or armed activities directed towards the violent overthrow of the regime of another State'.[293] For the ICJ, this language reflects customary international law.[294] Similarly, Principle VI of the Helsinki Final Act requires the participating states to 'refrain from direct or indirect assistance to terrorist activities, or to subversive or other activities directed towards the violent overthrow of the regime of another participating State'. Unlike with economic coercion, there was broad consensus already during the Cold War among countries of different political and geographical affiliations that support for subversive, terrorist, or armed activities in another state constituted a case of prohibited intervention, as this reflected the preoccupations of the Western countries with communist infiltrations, of the socialist bloc with counter-revolutionary activities, and of the newly independent states of Africa and Asia with neo-colonial policies.[295]

General Assembly Resolutions 2131 and 2625 and the Helsinki Final Act require that subversive, terrorist or armed activities be directed towards the *violent* overthrow of a foreign government. During the debates on the Friendly Relations Declaration, however, some states rejected the possible *a contrario* interpretation of this language which would permit such activities when aimed at the non-violent overthrow of a government.[296] The ICJ has also pointed out that it is only the terrorist, subversive, or armed group that must aim to overthrow a government:

> in international law, if one State, with a view to the coercion of another State, supports and assists armed bands in that State whose purpose is to overthrow the government of that State, that amounts to an intervention by the one State in the internal affairs of the other, whether or not the political objective of the State giving such support and assistance is equally far-reaching.[297]

Motive, therefore, is relevant for the conduct of the armed opposition groups, but not for that of the state that supports them.

The last part of the paragraph on subversive intervention as it appears in General Assembly Resolutions 2131 and 2625 condemns any interference in civil strife in

---

[293] The formulation was almost entirely identical in all drafts (Robert Rosenstock, 'The Declaration of Principles of International Law Concerning Friendly Relations: A Survey' (1971) 65 AJIL 713, 727). See also the previous GA Res 290 (IV) on the Essentials of Peace (1 December 1949) which called upon states to 'refrain from any threats or act, direct or indirect, aimed at ... fomenting civil strife and subverting the will of the people in any State'.

[294] *DRC v Uganda*, para 162.

[295] See eg Canada's statement, UN Doc A/C.6/SR.1178, 23 September 1970, 8.

[296] See eg the Netherlands, UN Doc A/C.6/SR.1183, 28 September 1970, para 32.

[297] *Nicaragua v USA*, para 241. In *DRC v Uganda*, the Court also found that Uganda had breached the principles of non-intervention and of the non-use of force even if its motive was not to overthrow the DRC's President Kabila, but to protect its security interests (*DRC v Uganda*, para 163).

188 INTERNATIONAL LAW AND THE PRINCIPLE OF NON-INTERVENTION

another state. Whether this entails not only a prohibition of supporting insurgents but also the incumbent government in at least certain circumstances is a problem explored in the following chapters.[298]

The prohibition of subversive activities is also a clause included in several bilateral and regional cooperation and non-aggression treaties. Under Article 8 of the Pact of the League of Arab States, for instance, the member states pledge not to take any action to change the form of government of another member state.[299] Like the Charter of the Organization of African Unity before it,[300] the African Union (AU)'s Constitutive Act indicates that the condemnation of political assassinations, acts of terrorism, and subversive activities is one of the principles on which the organization is founded.[301] The AU Non-Aggression and Common Defence Pact also requires each party to 'prevent its territory and its people from being used for encouraging or committing acts of subversion ... that might threaten the territorial integrity and sovereignty of a Member State or regional peace and security'.[302] Finally, subversion is prohibited in the Protocol on Non-Aggression and Mutual Defence in the Great Lakes Region, which devotes to it several provisions.[303]

On the other hand, there is no express prohibition of support for subversive or terrorist activities in the OAS Charter, which is surprising if one considers that the Bogotá Conference, which started on 30 March 1948, had to be suspended from 9 to 14 April because of the assassination of Colombian presidential candidate Jorge Eliécer Gaitán and of the resulting Bogotazo riots.[304] Article 19 of the Charter, however, specifies that the principle of non-intervention prohibits not only armed force, but also 'any other form of interference or attempted threat against the personality of the State or against its political, economic, and cultural elements'. The *travaux préparatoires* of the article suggest that these words were added to extend the scope of the principle of

---

[298] See Chapters IV and V.

[299] Art 8, Pact of the League of Arab States (Cairo, 22 March 1945) 70 UNTS 237.

[300] Art III(5), Charter of the Organization of African Unity (Addis Ababa, 25 May 1963) 479 UNTS 39.

[301] Art 4(o), Constitutive Act of the African Union (Lomé, 11 July 2000) 2158 UNTS 3.

[302] Art 5(b), African Union Non-Aggression and Common Defence Pact (Abuja, 31 January 2005) 2656 UNTS 285. Art 1(a) defines subversion as 'any act that incites, aggravates or creates dissension within or among Member States with the intention or purpose to destabilize or overthrow the existing regime or political order by, among other means, fomenting racial, religious, linguistic, ethnic and other differences, in a manner inconsistent with the Constitutive Act, the Charter of the United Nations and the Lomé Declaration'.

[303] Arts 2(1), 2(6), 3(3), 3(4), 4(4), 8(2), 8(4), Protocol on Non-Aggression and Mutual Defence in the Great Lakes Region (Nairobi, 30 November 2006) <https://peacemaker.un.org/sites/peacemaker.un.org/files/061130_ProtocolofNonAgressionGreatLakes.pdf>.

[304] The Panamanian draft of the OAS Charter contained an article that provided for the obligation of member states to prevent the organization of activities on their respective territories aimed at fomenting civil strife in another state, but the provision was not included in the final text adopted at Bogotá (Art 22 of the Panamanian draft project, in Novena Conferencia Internacional Americana, *Actas y Documentos*, 57). In Resolution XXXII, however, the American states agreed '[t]o adopt, within their respective territories and in accordance with the constitutional provisions of each state, the measures necessary to eradicate and prevent activities directed, assisted, or instigated by foreign governments, organizations, or individuals, that tend to overthrow their institutions by violence, to foment disorder in their domestic political life, or to disturb, by means of pressure, subversive propaganda, threats or by any other means, the free and sovereign right of their peoples to govern themselves in accordance with their democratic aspirations' (text in <https://history.state.gov/historicaldocuments/frus1948v09/d161>).

CONTENT OF THE PRINCIPLE OF NON-INTERVENTION   189

non-intervention to forms of coercion other than armed force.[305] As economic and political coercion are specifically prohibited by the subsequent article, the sentence, not to be redundant, should be interpreted as referring to subversive activities other than the direct use of armed force.[306]

8.1 The Different Forms of Support for Subversive, Terrorist, or Armed Activities

Support for subversive, terrorist, or armed activities can take different forms. Most obviously, it can consist in sending regular and irregular combat troops or, less visibly, in supplying arms, ammunition, and military training. In both cases, the intervention is not only a breach of the principle of non-intervention, but also of the treaty and customary prohibition contained in Article 2(4) of the UN Charter.[307] What is doubtful is whether the same conclusion applies to the supply of non-lethal military equipment. Although they did not provide a legal justification, for instance, the United Kingdom, the United States, France, Qatar, Turkey, Australia, and the Netherlands all acknowledged supplying bulletproof vests, helmets, uniforms, night-vision devices, satellite phones, and communication equipment to the moderate opposition forces in the Syrian Civil War.[308] Only Syria, Iran, and Russia expressed criticism.[309] In order to approach the question correctly, two situations must be distinguished. The supply of non-lethal equipment which constitutes a *weapon*, that is, is 'explicitly designed and developed to incapacitate or repel [persons], with a low probability of fatality or permanent injury, or to disable equipment, with minimal undesired damage or impact on the environment',[310] constitutes a violation of both the principle of non-intervention and the prohibition of the use of force: the ICJ's *Nicaragua* Judgment does not

---

[305] The Peruvian delegate, Víctor Andrés Belaúnde, whose delegation proposed the text together with Chile, referred to interventions that take place 'financiando agentes; creando situaciones; pretendiendo modificar, desde el exterior, directa o indirectamente, la estructura económica de un país, o influir por medio de la coacción o mediante la amenaza de uso de la fuerza, o simplemente por una presión en su política interior y en los rumbos que quiera seguir' (Novena Conferencia Internacional Americana, *Actas y Documentos*, vol III, 222). In the General Assembly debates on the Declaration on the Inadmissibility of Intervention, El Salvador also noted that the OAS Charter 'defined intervention in clear and comprehensive terms, covering every form of direct and indirect intervention and coercive action' (UN Doc A/C.1/SR.1403, 9 December 1965, 301).

[306] Arangio-Ruiz, 'Human Rights', 259. It is one of the customary rules of legal interpretation that 'a clause must be so interpreted as to give it a meaning rather than so as to deprive it of meaning' (*Cayuga Indians (Great Britain v United States)*, 22 January 1926, RIAA, vol VI, 173, 184).

[307] *Nicaragua v USA*, para 228. For Switzerland's Department of Foreign Affairs, however, the supply of arms to insurgents can be assimilated to the use of force only if it reaches a certain level (Lucius Caflisch, 'La pratique suisse en matière de droit international public 1999' (2000) 10 RSDIDE 627, 669, 673).

[308] Christina Nowak, 'The Changing Law of Non-Intervention in Civil Wars—Assessing the Production of Legality in State Practice After 2011' (2018) 5 JUFIL 40, 73–4. The UN Security Council and the EU Council excluded non-lethal military equipment from the arms embargoes on Libya and Syria (SC Res 1970, 26 February 2011; EU Council Decision 2011/273/CFSP of 9 May 2011 concerning restrictive measures against Syria, Art 2(1)(b), OL 2011 L 121/11). On the Dutch non-lethal assistance programme in support of Syrian rebels, see Tom Ruys and Luca Ferro, 'The Enemy of My Enemy: Non-Lethal Assistance for "Moderate" Syrian Rebels and the Multilevel Violation of International Law' (2019) 50 NYIL 333.

[309] Nowak, 'The Changing Law', 75.

[310] UK Ministry of Defence, The Manual of the Law of Armed Conflict (OUP 2004) para 6.18.1.

differentiate between types of arms on the basis of their lethality. The provision of military equipment designed to protect its bearer and not to cause harmful effects on a target, on the other hand, cannot be considered a violation of the prohibition of the use of force but still breaches the principle of non-intervention as, by strengthening the defensive capabilities of a party, it disadvantages the other and thus interferes with the civil strife.[311]

It is unclear whether the principle of non-intervention not only prohibits third states to arm insurgents but also requires them to prevent those under their jurisdiction from doing so. The OAS Charter, Resolutions 2131 and 2625, and the Helsinki Final Act are silent on this point. Applying the law of neutrality to internal armed conflicts, Erik Castrén suggests that, under customary international law, states are not required to prohibit military assistance of a private nature to foreign insurgents.[312] It has, however, been counterargued that, as arms exports are now subordinated to a licence system in virtually all states, the distinction between public and private transfers is difficult to maintain and 'private arms exports proper are virtually nonexistent'.[313] An obligation for states to prevent the traffic of arms and war material intended for foreign insurgents is contained in the 1928 Havana Convention on Duties and Rights of States in the Event of Civil Strife,[314] its 1957 Protocol,[315] and, at least in certain circumstances, in the 2013 Arms Trade Treaty (ATT).[316] The Institut de droit international's Wiesbaden Resolution on the Principle of Non-Intervention in Civil Wars also affirms that third states are required not to allow weapons or other war material to be supplied to any party to a civil war.[317] It is difficult, however, to conclude with sufficient confidence that these rules reflect customary international law as, if it is true that states no longer unconditionally defend their nationals' right to sell weapons, 'the sentiment of legal obligation ... seems diluted in considerations of moral dictate or political suitability'.[318] All in all, limitations to private arms transfers can derive from treaties or Security Council resolutions, but not yet from the customary principle of non-intervention.

---

[311] Christine Gray, 'The Limits of Force' (2016) 376 Recueil des Cours 93, 68.

[312] Erik Castrén, *Civil War* (Suomalainen Tiedeakatemia 1966) 125–6.

[313] George P Politakis, 'Variations on a Myth: Neutrality and the Arms Trade' (1992) 35 GYBIL 435, 494. See also Michael Bothe, 'The Law of Neutrality' in Dieter Fleck (ed), *The Handbook of International Humanitarian Law* (4th edn, OUP 2021) 602, 615–16. According to the German Manual of the Law of Armed Conflict, '[s]tate practice has modified the former contractual rule that a neutral State is not called upon to prevent the export and transport of war materiel by private persons for the benefit of one of the Parties to a conflict ... If the export of war materiel is State controlled, allowing such export is considered an unneutral service' (Joint Service Regulation (ZDv) 15/2, Law of Armed Conflict—Manual, May 2013, para 1209).

[314] Art 1(3), Convention on Duties and Rights of States in the Event of Civil Strife (Havana, 20 February 1928) 134 LNTS 45 (Havana Convention).

[315] Arts 1, 2, 5, Protocol to the Convention on Duties and Rights of States in the Event of Civil Strife (Washington, DC, 1 May 1957) 284 UNTS 201.

[316] Art 6, Arms Trade Treaty (ATT) (New York, 2 April 2013) 3013 UNTS 269. On the relation between the principle of non-intervention and the ATT, see Marco Roscini and Riccardo Labianco, 'The Intersections Between the Arms Trade Treaty and the International Law of Foreign Intervention in Situations of Internal Unrest' (2022) 52 Israel YBHR 365.

[317] Art 2(2)(c), Wiesbaden Resolution.

[318] Politakis, 'Variations', 506.

The principle of non-intervention additionally requires states not to tolerate or acquiesce in subversive, terrorist, or armed activities directed towards the overthrow of a foreign government.[319] The Wiesbaden Resolution confirms that 'making ... territories available to any party to a civil war, or allowing them to be used by any such party, as bases of operations or of supplies, as places of refuge, for the passage of regular or irregular forces, or for the transit of war material' is a violation of the principle of non-intervention.[320] In *DRC v Uganda*, for instance, Uganda argued that the support of the Democratic Republic of the Congo (DRC)'s authorities for the anti-Ugandan armed groups was a violation of the prohibition of the use of force and of the principle of non-intervention and claimed that the Congolese authorities had a 'duty of vigilance' that entailed the non-toleration on its territory of the groups' activities.[321] The Court accepted this view, but did not consider the inability of Zaire (as the DRC was known at the time) to first take *any* action (until May 1997) and then any *successful* action (May 1997 till August 1998) against the armed groups operating in its eastern regions equivalent to toleration or acquiescence, as the failure to do so was due to the 'difficulty and remoteness of the terrain'.[322]

As a minimum, the obligation not to tolerate or acquiesce in subversive, terrorist, or armed activities directed towards the overthrow of a foreign government requires the state that is aware of such activities to inform the target state.[323] Article 1 of the 1928 Havana Convention adds that rebel forces crossing the border must be disarmed and interned, their arms seized by the government granting asylum and returned only at the end of the civil strife.[324] Insurgent vessels must also be prevented from being equipped, armed, or adapted for warlike purposes and, if they are found in the third state's waters, they must be delivered to the government of the state in civil strife even before the conflict has ended, although their crew can be granted political refugee status.[325] During the Algerian War of Independence, France referred to Article 1 of the Havana Convention to denounce Tunisia's support for the Algerian Front de libération nationale (FLN) on its territory, even though neither Tunisia nor France were parties to it.[326] Reacting to the ill-fated Bay of Pigs operation, Cuba also accused the United

---

[319] Chile, for instance, has affirmed that the toleration or failure to prevent activities directed against another state, including those by private individuals or groups, constitutes an 'illegal intervention' (UN Doc A/33/216, 21 September 1978, 7).

[320] Art 2(2)(e).

[321] *DRC v Uganda*, para 277. The Friendly Relations Declaration considers a state's acquiescence in organized activities involving a threat or use of force directed towards the commission of acts of civil strife or terrorist acts in another state also a breach of the prohibition codified in Art 2(4) of the UN Charter. In the *Nicaragua* Judgment, the ICJ qualified this case as a 'less grave' form of the use of force (*Nicaragua v USA*, para 191).

[322] ibid, paras 301, 303. Judge Tomka, however, dissented on this point: for him, '[t]he geomorphological features or size of the territory does not relieve a State of its duty of vigilance nor render it less strict. Nor does the absence of central governmental presence in certain areas of a State's territory set aside the duty of vigilance for a State in relation to those areas' (*DRC v Uganda*, Declaration of Judge Tomka, para 4). Tom Ruys suggests that what counts is whether the territorial state had the necessary means to prevent the unlawful activities and whether it was aware of them (Tom Ruys, *'Armed Attack' and Article 51 of the UN Charter: Evolutions in Customary Law and Practice* (CUP 2010) 376).

[323] Marco Pertile, *La relazione tra risorse naturali e conflitti armati nel diritto internazionale* (CEDAM 2012) 147.

[324] Art 1(2), Havana Convention.

[325] Arts 1(4), 3, ibid.

[326] UN Doc S/PV.819, 2 June 1958, para 75.

States of breaching Article 5 of the 1957 Protocol to the Havana Convention, which contains a due diligence obligation to prevent, in the areas subject to a state party's jurisdiction, 'any person, national or alien, from deliberately participating in the preparation, organization, or carrying out of a military enterprise that has as its purpose the starting, promoting or supporting of civil strife in another Contracting State, whether or not the government of the latter has been recognized'.[327] As the United States had not ratified the Protocol, Cuba clearly implied that it reflected customary international law.[328] A memorandum prepared by the US Assistant Attorney General, on the other hand, claims that the reference to 'indirect' intervention in Article 15 (now 19) of the OAS Charter prohibits the *active* supply of weapons, money, or governmental facilities by a state to foreign revolutionary forces but not a mere omissive conduct, that is, the failure to take measures to prevent revolutionary activities within its borders (apart from the case when such activities amount to an armed attack).[329] The memorandum cites with approval Hersch Lauterpacht's view that international law requires a state to prevent only 'organized acts of force in the form of hostile expeditions against the territory of' other states as well as attempts against the life of political opponents from its territory, but not other activities.[330] This narrow view, however, appears isolated and does not find confirmation in the ICJ jurisprudence.[331]

Finally, in their codification of the principle of non-intervention, both the Declaration on the Inadmissibility of Intervention and that on Friendly Relations condemn financing subversive, terrorist or armed activities.[332] The *Nicaragua* Judgment confirmed that the supply of funds to the Contras was 'undoubtedly an act of intervention in the internal affairs of Nicaragua'.[333] Financing insurgents can occur not only when a state directly transfers funds but also when it purchases resources from them to the extent that the resources are actually transferred and/or the payment made.[334]

It has been suggested that customary international law is developing towards an obligation of states to prohibit their nationals from purchasing resources controlled by foreign insurgents: this rule is allegedly based on the Friendly Relations Declaration and on the due diligence obligation of states not to knowingly allow their territory to be used to commit hostile acts against other states.[335] The Protocol to the Havana

[327] UN Doc A/C.1/SR.1150, 17 April 1961, para 5.
[328] According to the ILC, 'when States act in conformity with a treaty provision by which they are not bound, or apply conventional provisions in their relations with non-parties to the treaty, this may evidence the existence of acceptance as law (*opinio juris*) in the absence of any explanation to the contrary' (Draft Conclusions on Identification of Customary International Law, with Commentaries [2018] YB ILC, vol II, part two, 102).
[329] Nicholas deB Katzenbach, 'Intervention by States and Private Groups in the Internal Affairs of Another State', Memorandum for the Attorney General, 12 April 1961, in Nathan A Forrester (ed), *Supplemental Opinions of the Office of Legal Counsel of the United States Department of Justice*, vol I (2013) 225, 228 <www.justice.gov/sites/default/files/olc/legacy/2013/07/26/op-olc-supp.pdf>.
[330] ibid.
[331] *DRC v Uganda*, para 162.
[332] GA Res 36/103, para II(m) and GA Res 2625 (XXV), Annex, third principle, para 2.
[333] *Nicaragua v USA*, para 228.
[334] Pertile, *La relazione*, 129. Indeed, an important source of funding for insurgents with control of territory is the sale of the key resources located therein, for instance diamonds, timber, oil, coal, gas, drugs, and valuable cultural property, as well as 'security payments' made by companies to local militias to protect or avoid attacks against their personnel and installations (Pertile, *Diritto internazionale*, 56–8, 80–1).
[335] Marco Pertile, 'On the Financing of Civil Wars through Natural Resources: Is There a Duty of Vigilance for Third States on the Activities of Trans-National Corporations?' in Francesca Romanin Jacur, Angelica

Convention also requires the states parties, in areas subject to their jurisdiction, to 'use all appropriate means to prevent any person, national or alien, from' providing or receiving 'money, by any method, intended for the military enterprise'.[336] As with private arms transfers, however, an examination of state practice and *opinio juris* does not lead to conclusive results about the customary status of this obligation, as evidenced by the following cases.

Congo. After the proclamation of the independence of Katanga, the Belgian Union Minière du Haut-Katanga (UMHK) opted to pay the concessions to the secessionist authorities instead of the central government.[337] As the UMHK was a Belgian corporation with its headquarters in Brussels, the UN Secretary-General, U Thant, requested Belgium's government to 'exert all possible influence on the Union Minière to cause it to desist forthwith from paying revenues to Katanga province'.[338] Similar letters were sent by the Secretary-General and by Congo to the states through which the resources would transit.[339]

Nigeria. After Biafra declared its independence from Nigeria on 30 May 1967, the secessionist authorities demanded oil royalties from the oil companies operating in the region.[340] While Shell–BP was initially in favour of making the payment, under pressure from the British government it first proposed to transfer the money into a suspense account pending clarification of the situation and then, given the lack of interest in this proposal by both the federal and the secessionist leaders, to pay a token sum, which was accepted by the Biafrans (the British government requested that the payment be accompanied by a letter specifying that it was made under duress).[341] In response, the Nigerian government declared the blockade of Port Harcourt and the prohibition of oil exports and warned that concessions would be lost if payments were not made to the federal authorities. The British secretary of state attempted to persuade Nigeria's head of state, General Gowon, that under international law royalties could be paid to *de facto* local governments in effective control of disputed territory, but the Nigerian government did not change its demand that royalties be paid to Lagos immediately.[342] After the Biafran forces took over the oil installations and detained their personnel, Shell–BP made no further payments to the secessionists.[343]

Libya. In the First Libyan Civil War (2011), Qatar claimed that it could buy or act as an intermediary in the sale of oil from the territory controlled by the Transitional National Council (TNC) as the Council was 'the legal authority with effective control over the territories under its jurisdiction'.[344] After the start of the Second Civil War

---

Bonfanti, and Francesco Seatzu (eds), *Natural Resource Grabbing: An International Law Perspective* (Brill/Nijhoff 2015) 383, 405.

[336] Art 5, Protocol to the Havana Convention.
[337] Pertile, 'On the Financing', 403.
[338] UN Doc S/5053/Add.14, 11 January 1963, Annex XIII, 1.
[339] ibid, Annexes XIV, XV and XVI.
[340] Chibuike Uche, 'Oil, British Interests and the Nigerian Civil War' (2008) 49 Journal of African History 111, 123.
[341] ibid, 123–4.
[342] ibid, 125.
[343] Rosalyn Higgins, 'Internal War and International Law' in Cyril E Black and Richard A Falk (eds), *The Future of the International Legal Order*, vol III (Princeton University Press 1971) 81, 113.
[344] UN Doc S/2011/346, 7 June 2011, Annex 2.

(2014–20) and the formation of the Government of National Accord (GNA) endorsed by the UN Security Council, however, several states expressed themselves against the sale of the oil controlled by the Tobruk authorities.[345] The application of the March 2019 agreement signed by Federpesca (the Italian association representing the fishing industry) with the Tobruk-based Libyan Investment Authority allowing a certain number of Italian boats to fish in Libyan waters was also suspended as a consequence of the protests raised by the GNA.[346]

Syria. In August 2020, the Syrian government sent a letter to the United Nations denouncing the signature of a contract between the American company Delta Crescent Energy and the Syrian Democratic Forces to develop and export the region's oil. For Damascus, the agreement was 'a blatant assault against the sovereignty of the Syrian Arab Republic and the life-sustaining resources of the Syrian people' and thus 'null and void'.[347]

Overall, this fluid practice, mainly dictated by economic interests and not by legal considerations, does not provide sufficient evidence that customary international law requires states to prohibit *private* commercial transactions with local *de facto* authorities.[348] This conclusion is corroborated by the Wiesbaden Resolution, wherein third states cannot give 'any party to a civil war any financial or economic aid likely to influence the outcome of that war' but, unlike in the case of the supply of arms and war material, they are not required to prevent private funding initiatives.[349]

9. Conclusions

During the Cold War, several attempts were made at codifying the principle of non-intervention and clarifying its content: regionally, these attempts took place in the OAS framework whereas those at the global level were inspired by the socialist bloc, which saw them as part of its strategy to gain influence over the Third World countries. What emerges from the examination of the resulting documents is that, in the UN Charter era, treaties, resolutions, and state practice have determined the coexistence of two sets of legal standards: a general principle that prohibits the use of coercion in matters in which each state is permitted to decide freely and a number of rules of application prohibiting specific means and methods of coercion, some of which have customary status while others are still controversial.

The analysis conducted in this chapter demonstrated that, to be coercive, an act must be designed and able to undermine the agency of the target state and impair its decisional sovereignty. Coercion of state can assume two forms: forcible or dictatorial. Dictatorial interferences consist in the binomial 'demands + threats': by causing or threatening to cause a certain harm, they bend the will of the victim state so as to

---

[345] Pertile, *Diritto internazionale*, 277–8.
[346] ibid, 72–3.
[347] UN Doc S/2020/775, 6 August 2020, 1–2.
[348] Pertile, 'On the Financing', 405. See also Sir Gerald Fitzmaurice, 'The General Principles of International Law Considered from the Standpoint of the Rule of Law' (1957) 92 Recueil des Cours 1, 180–1; Castrén, *Civil War*, 126.
[349] Art 2(2)(d), Wiesbaden Resolution.

make it do or not do something. A demand is coercive when it is accompanied by a clear, specific, and credible threat and the threatened harm, whatever its nature, is sufficiently serious. Forcible interferences, on the other hand, consist in the exercise of power in the territory of another state without its valid consent or a permissive international law rule. In this case, the coercing state imposes a certain condition of things on the victim state by carrying out the unauthorized act itself instead of compelling someone else to do anything. By prohibiting both forms of coercion, the principle of non-intervention protects state sovereignty in all its aspects, that is, decisional and territorial. The existence of an intent to coerce must be demonstrated in the case of dictatorial coercion, while it is presumed in forcible coercion.

Coercion constitutes a violation of the principle of non-intervention only when it bears on matters in which each state is permitted to decide freely. The fact that coercion is exercised in a matter where the target state does not have an obligation under international law to conduct itself in a certain way is what distinguishes a violation of the principle of non-intervention from a countermeasure: even though it can be coercive, the latter, unlike the former, aims to induce a state that has committed a violation of international law to cease it and provide full reparation, and is therefore lawful. The mere fact that a matter does not belong to a state's domestic jurisdiction, however, does not automatically mean that other states can resort to coercion in regard to it. This would only be permissible when the coercive means are not prohibited by other primary rules or, if the coercive means are unlawful, when their use was aimed at enforcing compliance by the target state with the breached obligation, they did not entail the breach of an obligation that cannot be affected by countermeasures, and the coercing state was entitled to react.

This chapter also identified the following rules of application that flow from the general principle of non-intervention: 1) the prohibition of armed coercion exercised towards another state or to deprive peoples of their national identity; 2) the prohibition of economic and political measures designed to obtain the subordination of the exercise of the sovereign rights of the target state to the interests of the coercing state and secure advantages; and 3) the prohibition of supporting subversive, terrorist or armed activities and of interfering in civil strife in another state. While the rules of application of the principle of non-intervention prohibiting armed coercion, political coercion in the form of the threat of armed force and of the premature recognition of statehood, government, and belligerency, and support for subversive, terrorist, and armed activities in another state are well established in customary international law, the situation is less clear with regard to economic coercion. Because of the inconsistent practice and *opinio juris* of states, therefore, we could only conclude that there are indications of a trend towards its inclusion in the customary content of the principle of non-intervention.

IV

The Application of the Principle of Non-Intervention to Civil Strife and the Role of Consent

1. Introduction

As seen in Chapter III, one of the rules of application of the principle of non-intervention is that prohibiting 'interference in civil strife'.[1] Neither the UN General Assembly's Declaration on the Inadmissibility of Intervention nor that on Friendly Relations and Cooperation among States, however, specify the exact contours of this prohibition.[2] It is unclear, therefore, whether, when, and how the government of the state in civil strife can validly consent to interference by another state, and whether support for opposition groups is always prohibited.

This chapter aims to address these questions. It first ascertains when the principle of non-intervention does *not* apply, that is, when the civil strife is no longer a domestic affair of the concerned state. It then discusses the role played by consent in excluding the coercive nature of the interference and identifies the authority entitled under international law to grant it as well as the requirements that consent must possess in order to produce its effects. Finally, the chapter explores whether consent by insurrectional authorities can ever be a valid legal basis for an intervention in their support, particularly when they aim to overthrow an authoritarian regime.

A word of caution on terminology. Unless otherwise specified, expressions like 'rebels' and 'insurgents' are employed in this chapter not in the technical sense en vogue in the 19th century but as referring generally to any armed opposition group, and 'incumbent' government is used to indicate the government that was effectively in office at the beginning of the civil strife.

2. Non-Intervention as a Principle Applying Only to Civil Strife which is a Domestic Affair of the Concerned State

General Assembly Resolutions 2131 and 2625 use the expression 'civil strife' but do not define it. The language, which is also contained in earlier General Assembly

---

[1] See Chapter III, Section 8.
[2] GA Resolutions 2131 (XX), 21 December 1965, and 2625 (XX), 24 October 1970. The prohibition of interference in civil strife does not appear in the Charter of the Organization of American States (OAS) or in the Helsinki Final Act.

International Law and the Principle of Non-Intervention. Marco Roscini, Oxford University Press. © Marco Roscini 2024.
DOI: 10.1093/oso/9780198786894.003.0005

resolutions,[3] finds its roots in the 1928 Havana Convention on Duties and Rights of States in the Event of Civil Strife and its 1957 Protocol.[4] While the Convention and the Protocol also do not contain an explicit definition, it is clear from the content of the obligations contained therein and from their object and purpose that 'civil strife' is conceived as any armed struggle within a state between governmental authorities and 'rebels' (or, it can be added, between different groups of rebels). The expression is thus broader than 'civil war', as the two treaties distinguish civil strife where the belligerency of the rebels has been recognized (that is, the traditional case of civil war) from that where it has not.[5] This interpretation finds confirmation in the *travaux préparatoires* of the Declaration on Friendly Relations. During the works of the Special Committee, the United Kingdom proposed to replace 'civil strife' with 'civil war' in the formulation of the principle of non-intervention.[6] What the United Kingdom was concerned about was 'an unduly broad definition of "civil strife"' which would prevent 'a Government in temporary difficulties [to] seek and receive assistance from a friendly State which it trusted to render aid with full respect for the territorial integrity and political independence of the recipient State'.[7] Clearly, therefore, the United Kingdom saw civil strife as potentially a much broader notion than civil war. The British proposal was eventually not adopted.

To fall under the scope of the principle of non-intervention, civil strife must be and remain a domestic affair of the concerned state, that is, it must be a matter in which it can decide freely.[8] Even though there are now international law rules limiting *how* states can use armed force internally, Article 2(4) of the UN Charter only outlaws the use of force in 'international relations' and neither a government nor an insurgent group are required by it not to use armed force against each other.[9] The result is that 'it is the "excessive" use of force—i.e. in violation of international humanitarian law or of international human rights obligations — that [is] condemned, not the *resort* to force as such'.[10] Article 3 of the 1977 Protocol II additional to the 1949 Geneva

---

[3] See GA Res 290 (IV), 1 December 1949 ('Essentials of Peace'), para 3; GA Res 380 (V), 17 November 1950 ('Peace Through Deeds') para 1.

[4] Convention on Duties and Rights of States in the Event of Civil Strife (Havana, 20 February 1928) 134 LNTS 45 (Havana Convention); Protocol to the Convention on Duties and Rights of States in the Event of Civil Strife (Washington, DC, 1 May 1957) 284 UNTS 201. The Argentine delegation successfully proposed at the Sixth Pan-American Conference at Havana that 'civil war' be replaced with 'civil strife' (Report of the Delegates of the United States of America to the Sixth International Conference of American States (US Government Printing Office (GPO) 1928) 19–20).

[5] Art 1(3), Havana Convention; Art 2, Protocol to the Havana Convention.

[6] UN Doc A/6799, 26 September 1967, para 306. A joint proposal by Argentina, Chile, Guatemala, Mexico, and Venezuela also contained the expression 'civil war' instead of 'civil strife' (A/6799, para 27).

[7] UN Doc A/AC.125/SR.57, 29 November 1967, 5.

[8] *Case Concerning Military and Paramilitary Activities in and against Nicaragua (Nicaragua v United States of America)* (Merits) [1986] ICJ Rep 3, para 205 (hereafter *Nicaragua v USA*).

[9] Olivier Corten, *The Law Against War: The Prohibition on the Use of Force in Contemporary International Law* (2nd edn, Hart Publishing 2021) 138–40. There is, however, an emerging *de lege ferenda* debate in scholarship on a *jus contra bellum internum*: see eg Eliav Lieblich, 'Internal *Jus ad Bellum*' (2016) 67 Hast LJ 687; Jan Arno Hessbruegge, *Human Rights and Personal Self-Defense in International Law* (OUP 2017) 293–344; Tom Ruys, 'The Quest for an Internal *Jus Ad Bellum*: International Law's Missing Link, Mere Distraction, or Pandora's Box?' in Claus Kreß and Robert Lawless (eds), *Necessity and Proportionality in International Peace and Security Law* (OUP 2020) 169.

[10] Olivier Corten, 'The Russian Intervention in the Ukrainian Crisis: Was *Jus Contra Bellum* "Confirmed Rather than Weakened"?' (2015) 2 JUFIL 17, 23, emphasis in the original.

198   INTERNATIONAL LAW AND THE PRINCIPLE OF NON-INTERVENTION

Conventions on the Protection of Victims of War confirms that states have not only a right but also a responsibility 'by all legitimate means, to maintain or re-establish law and order in the State or to defend the national unity and territorial integrity of the State'.[11] If quelling an insurrection is not prohibited as such by international law, therefore, there are no legal obstacles for foreign states to assist a government in that endeavour under the principle of non-intervention. In the subsequent chapters, I explore whether customary rules and principles that have consolidated after 1945 have altered this paradigm.[12]

As seen in Chapter I, civil strife is no longer a domestic affair if the insurgents have been recognized as belligerents.[13] The doctrine of recognition of belligerency has not had many applications after 1865. The current British Manual on the Law of Armed Conflict concedes that the doctrine 'has declined to the point where recognition of belligerency is almost unknown today'.[14] The Turkel Commission's report on the *Mavi Marmara* incident also found that the doctrine of recognition of belligerency 'has become less important and today is almost irrelevant'.[15] It is a fact that no government beset by civil strife has explicitly recognized the insurgents as belligerents in the 20th and 21st centuries. In some cases, however, they adopted measures that might imply a recognition of belligerency, as in the case of Nigeria's blockade of the ports controlled by the Biafrans and their treatment as prisoners of war during the Nigerian Civil War (1967–70),[16] the boarding and searching of vessels on the high seas by France during the Algerian War of Independence (1954–62),[17] and Israel's naval blockade of Gaza in 2007.[18] The Nigerian, French, and Israeli governments, however, refused to consider such measures as entailing recognition of belligerency.[19] As to third states, the only unequivocal post-1945 case is that which occurred on 17 June 1979, when the members of the Andean Group (Bolivia, Colombia, Ecuador, Peru, and Venezuela) recognized the armed opposition against Somoza's dictatorship in Nicaragua as belligerents.[20]

---

[11] Protocol Additional to the Geneva Conventions of 12 August 1949, and relating to the Protection of Victims of Non-International Armed Conflicts (Protocol II) (Geneva, 8 June 1977) 1125 UNTS 609.

[12] See Chapters V (principle of internal self-determination), VI (principle of external self-determination), and VII (respect for international human rights law and international humanitarian law).

[13] See Chapter I, Section 7.5.3.

[14] UK Ministry of Defence, The Manual of the Law of Armed Conflict (OUP 2004) para 15.1.2.

[15] The Turkel Commission, Report of the Public Commission to Examine the Maritime Incident of 31 May 2010, 2011, 46 <www.gov.il/BlobFolder/generalpage/alternatefiles/he/turkel_eng_a_0.pdf>.

[16] Charles Rousseau, 'Chronique des faits internationaux' (1968) 72 RGDIP 145, 234. See also EI Nwogugu, 'The Nigerian Civil War: A Case Study in the Law of War' (1974) 14 IJIL 13, 24–5, 29–30. It is not clear, however, whether the 'blockade' was a municipal act within the territorial sea or a proper law of armed conflict measure.

[17] See Mohammed Bedjaoui, *La révolution algérienne et le droit* (Éditions de l'Association internationale des juristes democrats 1961) 154–5, 161; Robert McLaughlin, *Recognition of Belligerency and the Law of Armed Conflict* (OUP 2020) 232–5.

[18] Iain Scobbie, 'Gaza' in Elizabeth Wilmshurst (ed), *International Law and the Classification of Conflicts* (OUP 2012) 280, 302.

[19] Mohamed Bennouna, *Le consentement à l'ingérence militaire dans les conflits internes* (Librairie générale de droit et de jurisprudence 1974) 29.

[20] Joint Declaration of the Foreign Ministers of Member States of the Cartagena Agreement on the Situation in Nicaragua, 16 June 1979, reproduced in Rafael Nieto Navia, '¿Hay o no hay conflicto armado en Colombia?' (2008) 1 ACDI 139, 147. The 1981 Joint Franco-Mexican Declaration on El Salvador recognized the Salvadorian opposition as 'une force politique représentative, disposée à assumer les obligations et à exercer les droits qui en découlent' (text of the Declaration in Jean Charpentier, 'Pratique française de droit international—1981' (1981) 27 AFDI 855, 904). It is doubtful, however, that this statement implied

NON-INTERVENTION AND THE ROLE OF CONSENT   199

This paucity of contemporary practice, however, does not necessarily mean that the doctrine of recognition of belligerency has fallen into desuetude.[21] All in all, the doctrine has succeeded in cheating death: military manuals, including the US Law of War Manual, still refer to it,[22] and so does the 1957 Protocol to the Havana Convention.[23] The records of the Diplomatic Conference that adopted the 1949 Geneva Conventions also suggest that the Conventions were not intended to touch upon the issue of recognition of belligerency and left it to the regulation of customary international law.[24] References to recognition of belligerency are still occasionally made by international courts. In the *South West Africa* Advisory Opinion, for instance, Judge Ammoun found that '[t]he recognition by the United Nations of the legitimacy of the Namibian people's struggle against the South African aggression is nothing less than a recognition of belligerency'.[25]

The doctrine of recognition of belligerency also makes occasional appearances in the practice of states. A 1954 British Foreign Office memorandum on the US military aid in Indochina noted that the Việt Minh had not been recognized by Britain or the United States as belligerents and, therefore, the support provided by the latter to France could not be considered unneutral service.[26] When, on 31 January 1956, a Kuomintang jet fighter was forced to land in Hong Kong and the People's Republic of China (PRC) asked the British authorities to detain the vehicle and its pilot, the request was rejected because belligerency had not been recognized in the Chinese Civil War.[27] In 1958, the United States and Britain also explored the option of recognizing the Sumatran rebellion in Indonesia, although they eventually desisted from proceeding to it.[28] Finally, in 2008 the Venezuelan National Assembly supported President Chavez's call for Colombia to recognize the belligerent status of the Revolutionary Armed Forces of Colombia (FARC) and of the National Liberation Army.[29]

recognition of belligerency. On 10 April 2015, Pakistan's parliament voted that 'Pakistan should maintain neutrality in the Yemen conflict so as to be able to play a proactive diplomatic role to end the crisis' (quoted in McLaughlin, *Recognition*, 239). It is unclear whether neutrality was meant in a technical sense, thus entailing recognition of belligerency.

[21] Yoram Dinstein, *Non-international Armed Conflicts in International Law* (2nd edn, CUP 2021) 146. Of the same opinion are Scobbie, 'Gaza', 304; Kubo Mačák, *Internationalized Armed Conflicts in International Law* (OUP 2018) 77–8; and McLaughlin, *Recognition*, 265.
[22] US Department of Defense, Law of War Manual (June 2015, updated December 2016) 75–6 <www.hsdl.org/c/abstract/?docid=797480>.
[23] Art 2, Protocol to the Havana Convention.
[24] Final Record of the Diplomatic Conference of Geneva of 1949, vol II, Section B, 336.
[25] *Legal Consequences for States of the Continued Presence of South Africa in Namibia (South West Africa) notwithstanding Security Council Resolution 276 (1970)* (Advisory Opinion) [1971] ICJ Rep 16, Separate Opinion of Vice-President Ammoun, 92.
[26] Memorandum from the UK delegation to the Geneva Conference to the Foreign Office on United States Military Aid in Indo–China: Questions of Belligerency (17 May 1954), quoted in McLaughlin, *Recognition*, 41–2.
[27] Elihu Lauterpacht, 'The Contemporary Practice of the United Kingdom in the Field of International Law—Survey and Comment' (1956) 5 Intl & Comp LQ 405, 487.
[28] Keesing's 1957–1958, 16083 (United States); McLaughlin, *Recognition*, 79–80 (United Kingdom).
[29] 'Venezuelan Legislature Supports Belligerent Status for Colombian Rebels', *Venezuelanalysis*, 18 January 2008, <https://venezuelanalysis.com/news/3080>. The call, however, fell on deaf ears: Colombia considered it an interference in its internal affairs.

It cannot be entirely ruled out, therefore, that insurgents might still be recognized as belligerents. As seen in Chapter I, this would displace the principle of non-intervention as the legal regime regulating the relations between the state in civil strife and other states: the latter would no longer have the option of discriminating in favour of the incumbent government but would have to choose between neutrality and co-belligerency as in interstate conflicts.[30] That said, the co-belligerency option is now severely curtailed by the *jus contra bellum* rules codified in the UN Charter: third states could intervene by sending armed forces or supplying arms in support of one of the belligerents only with the authorization of the UN Security Council.[31] Forms of support short of armed force, on the other hand, remain permissible unless prohibited by treaties or by Security Council resolutions, although they could also constitute an unneutral act that might lead the targeted belligerent to retaliate.

Civil strife also ceases to be a domestic affair when the rebels succeed in establishing a new state on the territory they control.[32] In this case, the prohibition of the use of force codified in Article 2(4) of the UN Charter becomes applicable between the parent and the breakaway states regardless of whether the former has recognized the independence of the latter.[33] As in recognition of belligerency, the principle of non-intervention is superseded by the *jus contra bellum* rules and intervention by invitation to restore authority over the lost territory is no longer permissible. Third states can adopt a position of neutrality with regard to the conflict, providing that the Security Council has not identified an aggressor and adopted measures under Chapter VII against it. Third states can also intervene on the side of either belligerent if this is consistent with the Charter: in the absence of Security Council authorization, co-belligerency would be permissible only on the side of the state acting in self-defence.[34]

---

[30] Lord McNair and AD Watts usefully explain the different effects of recognition of government and recognition of belligerency on third-state intervention. When the insurgents are recognized as *de jure* government and such recognition is withdrawn from the previous government, it is only the former that can request and obtain third-state assistance. If the insurgents are recognized as belligerents, on the other hand, the choice is between neutrality or co-belligerency on either side consistently with the *jus ad bellum* (Lord McNair and AD Watts, *The Legal Effects of War* (CUP 1966) 34).

[31] Collective self-defence would arguably be difficult to apply, as it is a right of states against *external* armed attacks and not also of non-state actors, even if they have been recognized as belligerents.

[32] Antonello Tancredi, *La secessione nel diritto internazionale* (CEDAM 2001) 650. Whether an entity has become a state depends on whether it meets the customary requirements detailed in Art 1 of the Convention on the Rights and Duties of States (Montevideo, 26 December 1933) 165 LNTS 19. Of course, the secession must not be fomented or supported by another state or be inconsistent with *jus cogens* rules, as in the case of the 1965 declaration of independence of apartheid Rhodesia or the 2014 secession of Crimea.

[33] See Georg Nolte, 'Secession and External Intervention' in Marcelo Kohen (ed), *Secession: International Law Perspectives* (CUP 2006) 65, 79–80. The Wiesbaden Resolution excludes 'armed conflicts between political entities which are separated by an international demarcation line or which have existed de facto as States over a prolonged period of time, or conflicts between any such entity and a State' from its definition of 'civil war' (Art 1(2)(b), Resolution on the Principle of Non-Intervention in Civil Wars of the Institut de droit international, 14 August 1975 (Wiesbaden Resolution) <www.idi-iil.org/app/uploads/2017/06/1975_wies_03_en.pdf>). For the application of Art 2(4) of the UN Charter, it is irrelevant that the two entities recognize each other as states or that the separation is temporary: Art 1 of the Declaration on the Definition of Aggression cautions that the term 'state' as used in the resolution is 'used without prejudice to questions of recognition or to whether a State is a member of the United Nations' (GA Res 3314 (XXIX), 14 December 1974, Annex, Art 1).

[34] Art 51, UN Charter.

NON-INTERVENTION AND THE ROLE OF CONSENT   201

Statehood arguments have been invoked on a number of occasions to justify or condemn armed interventions in civil strife. When, in July 1957, Britain sent troops to the Sultanate of Muscat and Oman at the request of the sultan against the Jebel Akhdar rebellion, several Arab countries claimed that the Imamate of Oman was an independent state and not an insurgency and that, therefore, the British intervention was a violation of its independence.[35] Statehood claims were also at the core of the US legal justifications for its involvement in the Second Indochina War (1955–75).[36] As Louis Henkin usefully points out, the conflict could have been considered: a) an internal armed conflict within the Republic of Vietnam (South Vietnam), with the Democratic Republic of Vietnam (North Vietnam) intervening in support of the Việt Cộng insurgency; b) an internal armed conflict between the North and the South within the single state of Vietnam; or c) an international armed conflict between two states, North Vietnam and South Vietnam.[37] For North Vietnam, the conflict should have been regarded as civil strife and a domestic affair of the Vietnamese state, the legitimate government of which sat in Hanoi: as a consequence, the US support for South Vietnam was an unlawful intervention on the side of insurgents.[38] The United States, on the other hand, rejected this view and argued that, whatever its status under the 1954 Geneva Agreements, South Vietnam had become a separate state by 1965.[39] The situation, therefore, was initially a civil war within South Vietnam, in which North Vietnam unlawfully assisted the Việt Cộng insurgents, and subsequently an international armed conflict triggered by the armed attack by the North against the South that had started by February 1965.[40] This—it was claimed—allowed the United States

[35] UN Doc S/3865, 15 August 1957; S/PV.783, 20 August 1957, para 8; S/PV.784, 20 August 1967, paras 40–43. For the United Kingdom, however, Oman was only a district of the dominions of the sultan of Muscat and Oman and the matter fell within his domestic jurisdiction. The sultan, therefore, was entitled to request assistance to restore order in the face of a revolt supported from abroad (S/PV.783, para 35; S/PV.784, paras 78–80). France expressed a similar view (S/PV.784, paras 26–7). The Report of the UN Ad Hoc Committee on Oman found that the British operation was difficult to justify because, inter alia, it 'was taken against a people who believed that they were part of an independent State and that they had an agreement with their neighbour that this independence would be respected' (A/5846, 22 January 1965, para 671).

[36] During the First Indochina War (1946–54), the conflict between Hồ Chí Minh's Democratic Republic of Vietnam (Việt Minh) and Bảo Đại's Republic of Viet-Nam (supported by France) was regarded as internal by the involved parties (Quincy Wright, 'Legal Aspects of the Viet-Nam Situation' (1966) 60 AJIL 750, 756). After the 1954 Geneva Conference, the South, under Ngô Đình Diệm, declared independence and was recognized by a number of states and international organizations, although it was not admitted to the United Nations. From 1956, the Diệm government faced the Việt Cộng insurgency (as the Việt Minh were called in the South). The Việt Cộng eventually organized themselves into the South Vietnam National Liberation Front (NLF), which controlled much of the countryside, while the Saigon government received military and financial support from the United States.

[37] Louis Henkin, How Nations Behave (2nd edn, Columbia University Press 1979) 306–8.

[38] Wright, 'Legal Aspects', 753. Wright concludes that the situation was one of civil strife under the domestic jurisdiction of Vietnam as it was a resumption of the hostilities for the control of the state of Vietnam that had been suspended by the Geneva Agreements: as the South breached the agreement by not conducting the planned elections in 1956, the North was no longer obliged to respect the ceasefire and could therefore resume its military efforts to unify Vietnam (ibid, 762).

[39] This conclusion was based on the fact that South Vietnam had been recognized by a significant number of countries (sixty at the time of the memorandum) and had been admitted to several UN specialized agencies (Leonard C Meeker, 'The Legality of United States Participation in the Defense of Viet-Nam' (1966) 54 Dept St Bull 474, 477). The memorandum subsequently concedes that South Vietnam 'may lack some of the attributes of an independent sovereign state' but at the same time affirms that the UN Charter does not prevent states from defending 'a recognized international entity' against an armed attack (ibid, 478).

[40] ibid, 475.

202 INTERNATIONAL LAW AND THE PRINCIPLE OF NON-INTERVENTION

to justify its attacks on North Vietnam and Việt Cộng positions in Laos and Cambodia as measures in South Vietnam's collective self-defence.[41]

More recently, statehood has played an important role in Russia's legal justifications for its use of force in support of secessionist entities in neighbouring countries. While the independence of South Ossetia and Crimea was recognized only after the armed interventions in Georgia (2008) and Ukraine (2014), respectively, and thus the argument was used to legitimize the *continued* presence of Russian troops in those territories and the annexation of Crimea,[42] the invasion of Ukraine in late February 2022 started the day after the recognition of the independence of the self-proclaimed People's Republics of Donetsk and Lugansk: this enabled Russia to (unpersuasively) claim that it acted in collective self-defence in response to Ukraine's armed attack against the newly independent states.[43]

3. Non-Intervention as a Principle Prohibiting Only Coercive Interferences in Civil Strife

In spite of the language employed in General Assembly Resolutions 2131 and 2625, the customary principle of non-intervention does not prohibit any third-state 'interference' in civil strife but only those of a coercive character, be they armed, economic, political, or of other nature.[44] As explained in Chapter III, to be coercive, a measure

---

[41] UN Doc S/6174, 8 February 1965. A famous debate on the legality of the US role in the Vietnam War took place between John Norton Moore and Richard Falk. The former argued that the conflict could not be considered a civil war between the North and the South as the South had been a separate *de facto* entity since the 1954 Geneva Agreements, had been recognized by several states, was a member of several international organizations, and its admission to the United Nations had been prevented only by the Soviet veto (John Norton Moore, 'The Lawfulness of Military Assistance to the Republic of Viet-Nam' (1967) 61 AJIL 1, 2–3). The two entities also had 'separate governments, separate international representation, separate constitutions, separate territories, separate populations, separate armies, and have developed for a substantial period of time along separate ideological lines' (ibid, 4). As a result of the armed attack carried out by the North against the South through the Việt Cộng, therefore, the latter was entitled to exercise its right of individual self-defence and the United States could come to its assistance in collective self-defence (ibid, 12–13). For Moore, even if the conflict within the South were to be characterized as a civil war, the fact that the Việt Cộng received substantial military assistance from the North cast doubts on the fact that they could be considered a genuine indigenous movement and that, therefore, third states should be bound to adopt a negative equality attitude (ibid, 29–30). Falk, on the other hand, saw the Vietnam War as a secessionist struggle of the South from the North and claimed that, when there are two competing governments within one state, third states can treat either as legitimate, as occurred in the Spanish Civil War (Richard A Falk, *The Six Legal Dimensions of the Vietnam War* (Princeton Center for International Studies 1968) 238). He disagreed that North Vietnam's involvement could be characterized as an armed attack against South Vietnam: for him, the situation in South Vietnam was one of strife 'between factions contending for control of the southern zone, whether or not the zone is considered a nation' (Richard A Falk, *Legal Order in a Violent World* (Princeton University Press 1968) 234). Falk concluded that 'as of 1962 the N.L.F. enjoyed enough de facto sovereignty in South Viet Nam to allow North Viet Nam to furnish military assistance on the same legal premises as relied upon by the United States vis-à-vis Saigon' (Richard A Falk, 'International Law and the United States Role in Viet Nam: A Response to Professor Moore' (1967) 76 Yale LJ 1095, 1136).

[42] Report of the Independent International Fact-Finding Mission on the Conflict in Georgia, September 2009, vol II, 440–1 <www.mpil.de/files/pdf4/IIFFMCG_Volume_II1.pdf> (hereafter IIFFMCG Report) (South Ossetia); UN Doc S/PV.7144, 19 March 2014, 8 (Crimea).

[43] UN Doc S/2022/154, 24 February 2022, 6. See the request of the self-proclaimed Republics of Donetsk and Lugansk in A/76/740-S/2022/179, 7 March 2022, Annexes III and IV.

[44] See Chapter III, Section 3.

must be able to undermine the agency of the target state and impair its decisional sovereignty, either by compelling it to do or not to do something or by taking control of a certain matter and forcefully imposing a condition of things.[45] If coercion is characterized by compulsion or imposition, then the presence of valid consent is a normative game changer which turns what would have otherwise been an intervention into cooperation.

The fact that a state may consent to third-state interference in civil strife occurring in its territory assumes that such consent is a manifestation of sovereignty, of which the principle of non-intervention is a corollary: in the same way states, as sovereigns, can consent to assume international obligations,[46] they can also allow the suspension of the performance of obligations that other states have towards them. Consent can originate from a request of the state in civil strife, which is accepted by the intervening state, or be solicited by the intervening state and then granted by the state in civil strife. In both cases, consent is not a unilateral act but an agreement between the consenter and the consentee, as it necessitates the convergence of two manifestations of will to produce its effects.[47] Indeed, if a state requests another to intervene in its territory but the requested state declines, consent evidently does not form, and if the state that intends to intervene solicits consent but the other state does not grant it, the interference, should it be carried out, remains coercive.

Consent can be seen as a defence which transforms what would have otherwise been a wrongful act into a non-wrongful one (if a state intervenes with the valid consent of the target state, the unlawful act becomes lawful),[48] as an exception to the primary rule prohibiting intervention (intervention is prohibited apart from when it is validly consented to), or as an element of the primary rule the presence of which situates the conduct outside the scope of the prohibition and thus characterizes it as lawful *ab initio* (the principle of non-intervention only prohibits coercive, i.e. non-consensual, interferences). The International Law Commission (ILC)'s second Special Rapporteur on state responsibility, Roberto Ago, favoured the first option: he did not see significant differences between consent and other circumstances precluding wrongfulness and, therefore, supported its inclusion among these circumstances in the ILC's Articles on Responsibility of States for Internationally Wrongful Acts (ARSIWA). Adopting a *lex specialis* approach, in particular, Ago saw consent as an agreement leading to the non-application of a certain rule between the concerned states *in a specific case* (but not to its amendment or termination).[49] The final Special Rapporteur on state responsibility, James Crawford, took a different approach and recommended its deletion from

---

[45] ibid.

[46] *Case of the S.S. 'Wimbledon' (United Kingdom, France, Italy & Japan v Germany)*, Judgment of 17 August 1923, PCIJ Series A No 1, 15, 25 ('the right of entering into international engagements is an attribute of State sovereignty').

[47] Maria Luisa Alaimo, 'Natura del consenso nell'illecito internazionale' (1982) 65 RDI 257, 270–2.

[48] Defences can either preclude wrongfulness (justifications) or responsibility (excuses): Laura Visser, 'May the Force Be with You: The Legal Classification of Intervention by Invitation' (2019) 66 NILR 21, 35. On the debate about the nature of consent as a justification or excuse, see Federica Paddeu, *Justification and Excuse in International Law: Concept and Theory of General Defences* (CUP 2018) 131–74.

[49] Roberto Ago, Eighth Report on State Responsibility, UN Doc A/CN.4/318 and add 1–4, 24 January 1979, para 57. The ILC Commentary on Draft Art 29 (now Art 20), adopted in 1979, incorporated Ago's views and noted that '[i]f a State (or any other subject of international law) consents to another State's committing an act that, without such consent, would constitute a breach of an international obligation towards the first State, that consent really amounts to an agreement between the two subjects, an agreement which

204   INTERNATIONAL LAW AND THE PRINCIPLE OF NON-INTERVENTION

the Articles as, in his view, 'to treat consent in advance as a circumstance precluding wrongfulness is to confuse the content of the substantive obligation with the operation of the secondary rules of responsibility'.[50] For him, consent is a negative element of a primary rule: when it is absent, the conduct falls under the rule's prohibitive scope. Ago's concern that 'it would be more dangerous to remain silent than to try to prevent abuses by a well-drafted article',[51] however, eventually prevailed and the rule on consent was retained in the final version of ARSIWA (Article 20). The 2001 commentary explains:

> States have the right to dispense with the performance of an obligation owed to them individually, or generally to permit conduct to occur which (absent such permission) would be unlawful so far as they are concerned. In such cases, the primary obligation continues to govern the relations between the two States, but it is displaced on the particular occasion or for the purposes of the particular conduct by reason of the consent given.[52]

In the final analysis, both Ago and Crawford were right: the fact that consent can be a secondary rule providing for a defence in certain contexts does not necessarily exclude that it can also be an element of a primary rule in others, namely when the rule incorporates a non-consensual element.[53] When it comes to the principle of non-intervention, in particular, lack of consent is the prerequisite for the occurrence of the prohibited conduct, that is, coercion: in the same way consensual sexual intercourse between adults is not 'lawful rape', a use of force based on consent is not 'lawful aggression' or 'lawful intervention', as it is not aggression or intervention at all. Seen from this perspective, there is no rule displacement or suspension as a result of consent as there is no conflict or even overlap between the different laws: whenever there is a valid agreement between the intervening state and that where the intervention takes place, the conduct falls outside the primary rule's prohibitive scope and is thus lawful *ab initio*.[54]

That being said, it should be recalled that the distinction between primary and secondary rules was adopted by the ILC for pragmatic, and not conceptual, reasons, as it merely allowed the Commission to delimit the scope of the codification.[55] As Ago himself noted, it must be understood 'rather loosely' and not as 'a Great Wall of China'.[56]

---

has the effect of rendering the obligation inoperative in that particular case' ([1979] YB ILC, vol II, part II, 109).

[50] James Crawford, Second Report on State Responsibility, UN Doc A/CN.4/498 and Add.1–4, 17 March 1999, para 241.
[51] [1979] YB ILC, vol I, 54.
[52] Commentary on Art 20 ARSIWA [2001] YB ILC, vol II, part two, 73.
[53] Paddeu, *Justification*, 165–6.
[54] Théodore Christakis and Karine Bannelier, '*Volenti non fit injuria*? Les effets du consentement à l'intervention militaire' (2004) 50 AFDI 102, 111.
[55] Paddeu, *Justification*, 55.
[56] [1969] YB ILC, vol I, 117.

Rigid classifications should thus be avoided as '[t]he so-called secondary rules may become primary rules and vice-versa'.[57] Federica Paddeu so explains it:

> Exceptions can be incorporated into the definition of the offence or be stated as defences, depending on the messages that the relevant rules are intended to convey to their addressees. If we can identify a general reason not to perform certain actions, then any permissions to perform that action must be stated as defences. Otherwise, they can be stated as definitional elements qualifying the scope of the rule.[58]

For these reasons, the following pages will often refer to Article 20 of ARSIWA and its commentary whenever they are pertinent to explaining consent not only as a defence but also as a negative element of the primary rule prohibiting intervention. While the coercive interference in civil strife can also occur by other means (for instance, by adopting restrictive economic measures against one of the factions), the analysis will focus on territorially intrusive forms of intervention, and particularly the dispatch of armed forces, as it is in this case that the consent of the territorial state is most evidently required.

4. Intervention with the Consent of the Incumbent Government

Identifying the authority entitled to consent to foreign intervention on behalf of a state is a question different from that of the attribution of conduct under the law of state responsibility: local authorities and low-rank officials, for example, attribute their acts and omissions to their state under Article 4 of ARSIWA but are unable to validly consent to foreign intervention.[59] It is the government of a state that holds the *jus repræsentationis omnimodæ*, that is, 'the plenary and exclusive competence in international law to represent its State in the international sphere',[60] and that, as a result, is the authority entitled to grant consent to the presence and operation of foreign forces

---

[57] Eric David, 'Primary and Secondary Rules' in James Crawford, Alain Pellet, and Simon Olleson (eds), *The Law of International Responsibility* (OUP 2010) 27, 32. Giorgio Gaja concurs: '[w]hatever characterization is given to the rules contained in Part One as primary or secondary, they contribute to determine whether a State is responsible or not' (Giorgio Gaja, 'Primary and Secondary Rules in the International Law on State Responsibility' (2014) 97 RDI 981, 990).

[58] Federica Paddeu, 'Military Assistance on Request and General Reasons Against Force: Consent as a Justification for the Use of Force' (2020) 7 JUFIL 227, 240–1.

[59] Commentary on Art 20 ARSIWA [2001] YB ILC, vol II, part two, 73. See also the United Kingdom's comments on draft Art 29, in ILC, Comments and Observations Received by Governments (25 March, 30 April, 4 May, 20 July 1998), UN Doc A/CN.4/488 and Add 1–3, 131.

[60] Stefan Talmon, *Recognition of Governments in International Law: With Particular Reference to Governments in Exile* (OUP 2011) 115. The point has been made by Latvia's Constitutional Court in 2007 (The Constitutional Court of the Republic of Latvia, Judgment on Behalf of the Republic of Latvia, 29 November 2007, Case No 2007-10-0102, para 43.1, English translation at <www.satv.tiesa.gov.lv/web/wp-content/uploads/2007/04/2007-10-0102_Spriedums_ENG.pdf>). See also Hans Kelsen, 'Recognition in International Law: Theoretical Observations' (1941) 35 AJIL 605, 615; Bin Cheng, *General Principles of Law as Applied by International Courts and Tribunals* (Stevens & Sons 1953) 184; Enzo Cannizzaro, *Diritto internazionale* (3rd edn, Giappichelli 2016) 159.

206   INTERNATIONAL LAW AND THE PRINCIPLE OF NON-INTERVENTION

on the state's territory.[61] It is however important to emphasize that, while governmental status is a necessary condition to express valid consent to foreign intervention under international law, it is not also sufficient. Said otherwise, the authority to consent to foreign intervention always implies governmental status, but governmental status does not always entail authority to consent to foreign intervention: governments might be precluded from validly consenting to foreign intervention by certain treaties, such as those providing for neutralization or demilitarization,[62] or by the customary rules which will be explored in the following chapters.[63]

The specific governmental organ entitled to express consent on behalf of a state under international law depends on the primary rule that will be affected: '[i]t is one thing to consent to a search of embassy premises, another to the establishment of a military base on the territory of a State'.[64] Treaties occasionally indicate the governmental organ competent to grant consent to armed intervention: the 1960 Treaty of Friendship and Cooperation between Belgium and Congo, for instance, provided that Belgian forces stationed in the African country could intervene only at the express request of the Congolese Minister of National Defence,[65] while under the 2002 Treaty between France and Monaco the former can intervene in the Principality 'à la demande ou avec l'agrément du Prince'.[66] Article 9 of the 2000 Economic Community of Central African States (ECCAS) Pact of Mutual Assistance also specifies that, when an aggression or threat thereof against a member state originates from outside the Community, the head of state of the concerned member sends a written request for assistance to the President of the Conference of Heads of State and Government and a copy to the other member states.[67]

In the absence of specific treaty provisions, the authority to consent to intervention on a state's territory rests by default with its government's highest office, namely the head of state or, when the head of state is a mere ceremonial role, the head of government.[68] If the head of state/government is unable to exercise their powers, consent to

---

[61] Consent to intervention granted by a government on the eve of elections, however, can be controversial: see the USSR's criticism of President Chamoun's request for UN intervention in Lebanon in 1958 (UN Doc S/PV.835, 21 July 1958, para 66).

[62] Roger Pinto, 'Les règles du droit international concernant la guerre civile' (1965) 114 Recueil des Cours 451, 495–6.

[63] See Chapters V, VI, and VII. In the 1950s–1960s, the PRC argued that whether or not a government can invite intervention also depended on whether 'that request coincides with the genuine desires of the ... people' (Jerome Alan Cohen, 'China and Intervention: Theory and Practice' (1973) 121 U Pa L Rev 471, 483–4). The fact that Ti-Chiang Chen, the author of an important monograph on recognition published in English in 1951, had unconditionally supported the Soviet intervention in Hungary without conditioning it on the fact that the requesting authorities represented the 'genuine desires' of the Hungarians was one of the reasons for his purge during Chairman Mao's 1957 'anti-rightist' campaign (ibid, 483).

[64] Commentary on Art 20 ARSIWA [2001] YB ILC, vol II, part two, 73.

[65] Art 6, Treaty of Friendship, Assistance and Cooperation (Léopoldville, 29 June 1960) (1960) 13 CPE 627. The treaty was never ratified by Congo and thus never entered into force.

[66] Art 4 of the Treaty Intended to Adapt and Strengthen Friendship and Cooperation Relations between the Principality of Monaco and the French Republic (Paris, 24 October 2002) <https://legimonaco.mc/tai/traite/2002/10-24-tail1010453/>.

[67] Art 9, Mutual Assistance Pact between Member States of ECCAS (Malabo, 24 February 2000) <www.droitcongolais.info/files/0.42.02.00-Pacte-d-assistance-mutuelle-du-24-fevrier-2000-entre-les-Etat-membres-de-la-CEEAC.pdf>.

[68] Art 7(2) of the Vienna Convention on the Law of Treaties (VCLT) provides that '[i]n virtue of their functions and without having to produce full powers, the following are considered as representing their State: (a) Heads of State, Heads of Government and Ministers for Foreign Affairs, for the purpose of

NON-INTERVENTION AND THE ROLE OF CONSENT 207

intervention can be provided by the highest surviving governmental official.[69] This point was made by the United States in relation to its intervention in Grenada (1983)[70] and by Belgium in Congo (1960).[71] The 1964 French intervention in Gabon was also at the request of the vice president of the African country as President M'ba had been ousted by a coup,[72] and France and South Africa's 1989 intervention in the Comoros was solicited by the president of the Supreme Court, who was interim head of state after the killing of President Abdallah by a group of mercenaries.[73] The authority of these organs to request the intervention was not criticized by other countries.

As there can only be one government representing each state, local or *de facto* administrations are not entitled to consent to foreign intervention: the US representative in the Security Council has noted that '[t]he prohibition on the use of force would be rendered moot were subnational authorities able to unilaterally invite military intervention by a neighbouring State.'[74] Despite referring to the approval of Katanga's President Tshombe, 'the lawful, constitutional head of a provincial government constituted in accordance with the fundamental law of the Congolese State', to justify its 1960 armed operation in Congo, Belgium at the same time noted that Congo's prime minister, Lumumba, had not objected to the intervention or to the agreement between Tshombe and Belgium, and that Lumumba and President Kasa-Vubu had countersigned an agreement requesting Belgium to intervene to restore security in the troubled region.[75] More recently, Somalia has denounced an agreement between the United Arab Emirates (UAE) and Somaliland, which allows the former to establish

performing all acts relating to the conclusion of a treaty' (VCLT (Vienna, 23 May 1969) 1155 UNTS 331). See also *Case Concerning the Land and Maritime Boundary between Cameroon and Nigeria (Cameroon v Nigeria: Equatorial Guinea intervening)* (Counter-claims) [2002] ICJ Rep 303, para 265 (hereafter *Cameroon v Nigeria*). In *DRC v Rwanda*, the DRC confirmed that 'it is a well-established rule of international law that the Head of State, the Head of Government and the Minister for Foreign Affairs are deemed to represent the State merely by virtue of exercising their functions, including for the performance, on behalf of the said State, of unilateral acts having the force of international commitments' (*Armed Activities on the Territory of the Congo (New Application: 2002) (Democratic Republic of the Congo v Rwanda)* (Questions of Jurisdiction and/or Admissibility) [2006] ICJ Rep 6, para 46). Ministries of foreign affairs have normally limited themselves to transmit the request for or the consent to intervention (Cástor Miguel Díaz Barrado, *El consentimiento, causa de exclusión de la ilicitud del uso de la fuerza, en Derecho Internacional* (Universidad de Zaragoza 1989) 311–12).

[69] UN Doc A/68/382, 13 September 2013, para 82.
[70] The invitation came from Grenada's governor-general, whose office was essentially ceremonial but who was claimed to be 'the sole source of governmental legitimacy on the island in the wake of the tragic events' that occurred there (Marian Nash Leich (ed), 'Contemporary Practice of the United States Relating to International Law' (1984) 78 AJIL 200, 203). At the United Nations, however, the United States only invoked, as legal justifications, the protection of its citizens and the Organisation of Eastern Caribbean States (OECS) Treaty (UN Doc S/PV.2487, 25 October 1983, paras 189–96; S/PV.2491, 27 October 1983, paras 65–75).
[71] UN Doc S/PV.873, 13/14 July 1960, para 187.
[72] Bennouna, *Le consentement*, 48.
[73] Tom Masland, 'French Troops End Reign of Mercenary in Comoros' (*Chicago Tribune*, 16 December 1989) <www.chicagotribune.com/news/ct-xpm-1989-12-16-8903180553-story.html>.
[74] UN Doc S/PV.7125, 3 March 2014, 5.
[75] UN Doc S/PV.873, paras 187–8.

208 INTERNATIONAL LAW AND THE PRINCIPLE OF NON-INTERVENTION

a military base in the latter, as a 'clear' violation of international law and of the UN Charter.[76]

4.1 Who is the *De Jure* Government of a State?

A problem arises when civil strife determines the emergence of rival administrations all claiming to be the *de jure* government of a state. In this scenario, three factors have been suggested by international legal scholarship to identify the authority entitled to represent the concerned state in its relations with other states: domestic legitimacy, effectiveness, and recognition.[77] The next sub-sections address them in turn.

4.1.1 Domestic legitimacy

As seen in Chapter I, the doctrine of legitimacy has assumed different connotations throughout the centuries.[78] Jean d'Aspremont has usefully distinguished 'between the legitimacy pertaining to the source of power and the legitimacy related to the exercise of power': while the qualification of governmental legitimacy depends on the former, its disqualification arises from the latter.[79] The disqualification of governments based on their conduct is examined in later chapters.[80] Here I focus on legitimacy pertaining to the source of power, that is, its origin.

According to the doctrine of domestic legitimacy, international law limits itself to refer to each domestic legal order to identify the authority entitled to speak on behalf of a state and, thus, 'every government that comes to power in a country depends for its legality, not upon mere *de facto* possession, but upon its compliance with the established legal order of that country'.[81] The latter point is a reaffirmation of the old

---

[76] UN Doc S/PV.8215, 27 March 2018, 3. Somaliland is a *de facto* self-governing entity within the internationally recognized borders of Somalia. The IIFFMCG confirmed that 'a secessionist party cannot validly invite a foreign state to use force against the army of the metropolitan state' (IIFFMCG Report, vol II, 279).

[77] Sir Robert Y Jennings and Sir Arthur Watts, *Oppenheim's International Law*, vol 1: Peace (9th edn, Longman 1992) 435–8. In *Republic of Somalia v Woodhouse Drake & Carey*, an English court had to determine whether there was a government in the war-torn African country. Judge Hobhouse found that the factors that needed to be taken into account to answer this question were '(a) whether it is the constitutional government of the state; (b) the degree, nature and stability of administrative control, if any, that it of itself exercises over the territory of the state; (c) whether Her Majesty's Government has any dealings with it and if so what is the nature of those dealings; and (d) in marginal cases, the extent of international recognition that it has as the government of the state' (*Republic of Somalia v Woodhouse Drake & Carey (Suisse) SA and Others (The 'Mary')*, Hobhouse J, Judgment of 13 March 1992, reprinted in (1994) 94 ILR 608, 622 (hereafter *Republic of Somalia v Woodhouse Drake & Carey*)).

[78] See Chapter I, Sections 2, 4, 7.1. Zaire's representative at the UN Security Council noted that '[o]ne must not confuse legality with legitimacy. Legitimacy is a sociological concept whereas legality has more to do with legal forms. Thus, a Government can be legal without necessarily being legitimate, and vice versa. Naturally it would be ideal for a Government to be both legitimate and legal. After all, it is not because one country denies the legitimacy of another Government that it loses its status' (UN Doc S/PV.2463, 11 August 1983, para 56).

[79] Jean d'Aspremont, 'Legitimacy of Governments in the Age of Democracy' (2005) 38 NYU J Intl L & Pol 877, 880–1.

[80] See Chapters VI and VII.

[81] Ti-Chiang Chen, *The International Law of Recognition with Special Reference to Practice in Great Britain and the United States* (Frederick A Praeger 1951) 105. See also David Wippman, 'Pro-Democratic Intervention in Africa' (2002) 96 ASIL Proceedings 143, 145; Yejoon Rim, 'Two Governments and One Legitimacy: International Responses to the Post-Election Crisis in Côte d'Ivoire' (2012) 25 LJIL 683, 694;

principle of continuity of legitimate power that characterized the law of nations of the 18th century and which required that the legitimacy of a new legal order derive from that of the previous.[82] In several cases, the intervening states have stressed the constitutional credentials of the authorities requesting the intervention. This was done, for instance, by the United States in the 1958 intervention in Lebanon[83] and by the United Kingdom in the intervention in Jordan of the same year.[84] The US State Department's Legal Advisor also referred to the Constitution of Grenada to justify the authority of the governor-general to invite American troops to restore internal order on the Caribbean island.[85] During the political crisis of 2014, Russia claimed that Ukraine's President Yanukovych had been overthrown unconstitutionally as the two-third majority required by the Ukrainian Constitution to remove sitting presidents from office had not been reached: for Moscow, therefore, Yanukovych remained the legitimate president of Ukraine and the only authority entitled to request foreign intervention.[86] More recently, when, on 23 January 2019, the president of the Venezuelan National Assembly, Juan Guaidó, proclaimed himself president of the republic on the basis of Article 233 of the Venezuelan Constitution, Poland was one of the states that recognized him as 'the only legitimate power in Venezuela' on the basis of his 'democratic mandate, won in free and fair elections, in line with the Venezuelan Constitution'.[87] The Lima Group states also affirmed that the recognition of Guaidó as the legitimate interim president of Venezuela was 'based firmly on Venezuela's own Constitution'.[88]

The doctrine of domestic legitimacy, however, raises several normative and practical problems. To start with, identifying the authority entitled to grant consent to foreign intervention on the basis of domestic legitimacy would be equivalent to prohibiting revolutions and coups, which, if successful, result by definition in an unconstitutional change of government. As already said, however, customary international law does not yet prohibit such events, at least to the extent that they have not been fomented or supported by foreign states.[89] While coups d'état in member states are frequently censored by regional organizations,[90] condemnations should be read in the context of treaty regimes and not necessarily, in the absence of further indications, as expressions of *opinio juris* of their illegality in general terms. The many inconsistencies of the attitudes of states and international organizations, which have led to the

---

Themistoklis Tzimas, 'Legal Evaluation of the Saudi-Led Intervention in Yemen: Consensual Intervention in Cases of Contested Authority and Fragmented States' (2018) 78 ZaöRV 147, 159, 161. Domestic legitimacy should not be confused with democratic legitimacy: an autocracy could be perfectly constitutional while a pro-democracy *coup* would establish an unconstitutional, if democratic, government.

[82] See Chapter I, Section 2.
[83] UN Doc S/PV.827, 15 July 1958, paras 43–4.
[84] UN Doc A/3877, 18 August 1958.
[85] Nash Leich (ed), 'Contemporary Practice', 662.
[86] UN Doc S/PV.7124, 1 March 2014, 5.
[87] UN Doc S/PV.8472, 26 February 2019, 8. See similar references to the Venezuelan Constitution as the basis of the legitimacy of Guaidó by France (S/PV.8506, 10 April 2019, 14) and the United Kingdom (S/PV.8476, 28 February 2019, 6).
[88] UN Doc S/PV.8472, 39.
[89] Section 2 of this chapter.
[90] See the analysis in Rafâa Ben Achour, 'Changements anticonstitutionnels de gouvernement en droit international' (2016) 379 Recueil des Cours 397.

condemnation of certain coups or fraudulent elections and to the acceptance (if reluctantly) of others, as well as the lack of any justifications for such inconsistencies, also prevent the consolidation of a normative pattern that can lead to the establishment of a customary rule prohibiting such events.[91]

Secondly, as the International Court of Justice (ICJ) found in *Cameroon v Nigeria*, 'there is no general legal obligation for States to keep themselves informed of legislative and constitutional developments in other States which are or may become important for the international relations of these States'.[92] Two examples can illustrate why. During the Ivorian crisis of 2010–11, the preliminary results announced by the Ivorian Commission Electorale Indépendante indicated that President Gbagbo had lost in favour of his rival, Ouattara. The Constitutional Council, however, declared that the Electoral Commission had no authority to announce any results because it had already missed the deadline to do so and, consequently, the results were invalid. The Council declared Gbagbo the winner, charging the northern departments controlled by the rebels of the Forces Nouvelles de Côte d'Ivoire with massive fraud.[93] The other example concerns The Gambia. In 2017, the troops of the Economic Community of West African States (ECOWAS) briefly entered the West African country in order to force President Jammeh, who had lost the presidential elections, to step down in favour of President-elect Adama Barrow, who had requested the intervention (Operation Restore Democracy). At the moment the threat of intervention was made, however, Jammeh was still head of state, as the Gambian Constitution provides that a new president takes office sixty days after they are elected and that, before assuming office, they need to take the required oaths.[94] To complicate matters even further, President Jammeh's mandate had been extended by The Gambia's National Assembly for an additional three months so that the Constitutional Court could decide on the regularity of the elections.[95] The Ivorian and Gambian examples demonstrate how intricate the assessment of the constitutional situation in a country can be, particularly for external actors.

Thirdly and finally, leaving to other states the determination of whether a certain country's government has come to power constitutionally or not can constitute in itself an interference in its domestic affairs and might even be at odds with the principle of internal self-determination.[96] The interactions of the latter principle with that of non-intervention are explored in Chapter V.

---

[91] Seyfullah Hasar, *State Consent to Foreign Military Intervention during Civil Wars* (Brill/Nijhoff 2022) 115.

[92] *Cameroon v Nigeria*, para 266. See Hannah Woolaver, 'From Joining to Leaving: Domestic Law's Role in the International Legal Validity of Treaty Withdrawal' (2019) 30 EJIL 73, 85–6.

[93] Rim, 'Two Governments', 684–5.

[94] Andrew G Jones, 'Intervening for Democracy: The Threat or Use of Force and Crisis in The Gambia' (2018) 51 Comp & Int'l LJ S Afr 241, 254.

[95] ibid, 255. In the end, the UN Security Council, while not authorizing the use of force, endorsed Barrow's legitimacy (SC Res 2337, 19 January 2017, para 2).

[96] Chen, *The International Law*, 111; Alessandra Annoni, *Il riconoscimento come atto unilaterale dello Stato* (Jovene 2023) 168.

4.1.2 Effective control

In order to avoid these problems, the authority internationally entitled to speak on behalf of a state has been identified not on the basis of domestic law but of the fact that it is able to exercise effective control over its country with a sufficient degree of stability and permanence (*ex factis jus oritur*).[97] As Kelsen explains, 'victorious revolutions or successful *coups d'état* are to be interpreted as procedures by which a national legal order can be changed. Both events are, viewed in the light of international law, law-creating facts'.[98] A new order is effective when there is no significant internal opposition to it, that is, when 'the individuals whose behavior [it] regulates actually behave, by and large, in conformity with [it]'.[99] Unlike that of legitimacy, the effective control doctrine does not pass judgment on the origin of governments: it merely takes note of a factual situation, namely the capacity of an authority to exercise legislative, executive, and judicial powers that are met with the obedience of the community and to apply coercion in case of disobedience.[100]

As seen in Section 7.1 of Chapter I, the effective control doctrine has been the dominant one since at least the end of the 19th century and can be considered 'an application of [popular sovereignty] in those circumstances of ideological pluralism'.[101] Post-1945 state practice and *opinio juris* continue to corroborate the view that, if domestic legitimacy and effective control lead to different results in the identification of the authority entitled to speak on behalf of a state, the latter prevails. When the Libyan representative at the Security Council claimed that the Chadian government headed by Hissein Habré, which Zaire was supporting, was illegitimate, Zaire pointed out that

> in public international law there exists what is known as the theory of effectiveness [...] According to that theory the effective Government of the Libyan Arab Jamahiriya is the one which rules in effect in Tripoli and governs Libya. The same applies to other countries.[102]

During the 2011 Libyan Civil War, the US Department of State legal advisor noted that 'international law focuses on the question of recognition, and recognition tends to follow facts on the ground, particularly control over territory'.[103] Commenting on the request for Russian intervention in Ukraine by President Yanukovych in 2014,

---

[97] According to the 2016 ICRC Commentary on Common Art 2 of the 1949 Geneva Conventions, '[u]nder international law, the key condition for the existence of a government is its effectiveness, that is, its ability to exercise effectively functions usually assigned to a government within the confines of a State's territory, including the maintenance of law and order. Effectiveness is the ability to exert State functions internally and externally, i.e. in relations with other States' (2016 ICRC Commentary, para 234 <https://ihl-databases.icrc.org/en/ihl-treaties/gci-1949/article-2/commentary/2016?activeTab=undefined>).

[98] Hans Kelsen, *General Theory of Law and State* (Russell & Russell 1961) 221.

[99] ibid, 118.

[100] Carlo Focarelli, *International Law as Social Construct* (OUP 2012) 44. Jean Salmon agrees: 'the triumph of the principle of effectiveness in the wider context stems from the pluralism of the existing systems' (Jean Salmon, 'Internal Aspects of the Right to Self-Determination: Towards a Democratic Legitimacy Principle?' in Christian Tomuschat (ed), *Modern Law of Self-Determination* (Nijhoff 1993) 253, 263).

[101] Brad R Roth, *Governmental Illegitimacy in International Law* (OUP 1999) 414.

[102] UN Doc S/PV.2463, para 55.

[103] US Senate, Committee on Foreign Relations, Libya and War Powers, Hearing, S Hrg 112189, 28 June 2011, 39.

212 INTERNATIONAL LAW AND THE PRINCIPLE OF NON-INTERVENTION

the British foreign secretary also emphasized that, even assuming that Yanukovych had been unconstitutionally removed from power, '[i]n law and as a matter of logic it is clearly ludicrous to argue that a President who abandoned his post and fled the country has any right whatsoever to make decisions about the future of that country let alone inviting foreign troops into it'.[104] When Canada's delegate to the Security Council affirmed that his country's recognition of Guaidó as the legitimate interim president of Venezuela was 'based firmly on Venezuela's own Constitution',[105] Venezuela responded that, by recognizing him, states were recognizing 'a new puppet Government that does not even control a single street in Venezuela'.[106] In fact, only a minority of states and international organizations have formally accredited Guaidó's envoys as representatives of the Venezuelan government and have withdrawn *de jure* recognition from Maduro's,[107] while many others have reaffirmed the principle of non-intervention in the internal affairs of the South American country and the right of each state to choose its political, economic, social, and cultural system without external interferences.[108] The same fact-based approach was adopted after the Taliban's violent takeover of Afghanistan in August 2021 despite the fact that the ousted government had been democratically elected and was recognized by the international community.[109] A further example is that of the 2021 Myanmar coup. After elections in November 2020 assigned the National League for Democracy 396 out of 476 seats in the country's parliament, Myanmar's military junta staged a coup in February 2021 before the new government could take office, removed President U Win Myint from office, and established the State Administration Council. In response, parliamentary members formed a National Unity Government (NUG) headed by the ousted president and by State Counsellor Aung San Suu Kyi. The Western states have condemned the coup and adopted sanctions against Myanmar and the junta but have stopped short of recognizing the NUG as the Southeast Asian country's government. The Association of Southeast Asian Nations (ASEAN) states have characterized the coup as an internal matter and have refrained from taking sides.[110]

Domestic tribunals have also confirmed the vitality of the effective control doctrine. In *Republic of Somalia v Woodhouse Drake & Carey*, for instance, an English court found that 'if an interim government is to be treated as the Government of Somalia,

---

[104] Foreign and Commonwealth Office (FCO) and The Rt Hon William Hague, Oral Statement to Parliament: Russia's Actions in Crimea, 18 March 2014 <www.gov.uk/government/speeches/russias-acti ons-in-crimea>. See also the US statement (UN Doc S/PV.7125, 18).

[105] UN Doc S/PV.8472, 39.

[106] UN Doc S/PV.8506, 27.

[107] Federica Paddeu and Alonso Gurmendi Dunkelberg, 'Recognition of Governments: Legitimacy and Control Six Months after Guaidó' (*Opinio Juris*, 18 July 2019) <https://opiniojuris.org/2019/07/18/recognit ion-of-governments-legitimacy-and-control-six-months-after-guaido//18/recognition-of-governments-legitimacy-and-control-six-months-after-guaido>.

[108] In addition to Venezuela's (UN Doc S/PV.8476, 12), see the statements of Kuwait (S/PV.8506, 18), Russia (S/PV.8506, 10), China (S/PV.8506, 13), Indonesia (S/PV.8472, 11), Bolivia (S/PV.8472, 24), Cuba (S/ PV.8472, 28), Nicaragua (S/PV.8472, 33–4), Saint Vincent and the Grenadines (S/PV.8472, 38–9), Belize (S/ PV.8472, 40), Ecuador (S/PV.8472, 41), Antigua and Barbuda (S/PV.8472, 42), El Salvador (S/PV.8472, 42), and Dominica (S/PV.8472, 45).

[109] Hasar, *State Consent*, 114.

[110] 'West Condemns Myanmar Coup but Thailand, Cambodia Shrug' (*Bangkok Post*, 1 February 2021) <www.bangkokpost.com/world/2060651/west-condemns-myanmar-coup-but-thailand-cambo dia-shrug>.

it must be able to show that it is exercising administrative control over the territory of the Republic': absent such control, 'international recognition of an unconstitutional regime should not suffice'.[111] The Queen's Bench Division of the High Court also held that the junta that took power in Sierra Leone after the 1997 coup was not in effective control of the country and, therefore, was not its government because looting and robbery in the capital Freetown were widespread, the judicial system, schools, the banking, and manufacturing sectors were all paralyzed, and the junta did not control more than two thirds of the national territory.[112]

It is true that interventions have occasionally helped restore *elected* governments ousted or prevented from taking office by coups. In these cases, however, the intervening state(s) have not exclusively relied on the consent of the non-effective authorities to justify the intervention (if at all). The United States, for instance, justified its 1989 invasion of Panama claiming it was an exercise of individual self-defence under Article 51 of the UN Charter against the attacks on American citizens and also invoked the obligation to defend the integrity of the 1977 Panama Canal treaties: the 'democratically-elected leaders of Panama', who had been unable to assume power as General Noriega refused to recognize the results of the national elections, were only 'consulted'.[113] The ousted Haitian President Aristide's consent was also not considered a sufficient legal basis for the 1994 OECS intervention that restored him to office, as Security Council Resolution 940 (1994) was adopted under Chapter VII of the UN Charter.[114] When a group of disgruntled army officers staged a coup against Sierra Leone's President Kabbah, ECOWAS intervened in February 1998 and restored him to power.[115] The Economic Community of West African States Monitoring Group (ECOMOG), however, was already present in Sierra Leone with the consent of both parties of the civil war as formalized in the 1997 Conakry Communiqué and claimed it was acting in self-defence and to enforce the arms and oil embargo imposed by Security Council Resolution 1132 (1997).[116] The resolution had also demanded that 'the military junta take immediate steps to relinquish power in Sierra Leone and make way for the restoration of the democratically elected Government and a return to constitutional order'.[117] During the constitutional crisis of 2010–11 in Côte d'Ivoire in which President-elect Ouattara was prevented from taking office by the incumbent Gbagbo, the French forces intervened and facilitated the resolution of the crisis in favour of Ouattara. France, however, acted on the basis of Security Council Resolution 1975 (2011) and the request of the UN Secretary-General to protect civilians, not of the consent of the president-elect, and repeatedly affirmed that it would

---

[111] *Republic of Somalia v Woodhouse Drake & Carey*, 621–2.
[112] *Sierra Leone Telecommunications Co Ltd v Barclays Bank plc* (1999) 114 ILR 466, 476–7.
[113] UN Doc S/21035, 20 December 1989. See Louis Henkin, 'The Invasion of Panama Under International Law: A Gross Violation' (1991) 29 Colum J Transnat'l L 293, 299–300.
[114] Corten, *The Law Against War*, 285–6. Aristide was ousted in the 1991 coup that installed a military regime.
[115] Karsten Nowrot and Emily W Schabacker, 'The Use of Force to Restore Democracy: International Legal Implications of the ECOWAS Intervention in Sierra Leone' (1998) AU Intl L Rev 327.
[116] UN Doc S/1996/1034, 11 December 1996, Annex; S/1997/824, 28 October 1997, Annex I.
[117] SC Res 1132, 8 October 1997, para 1.

214 INTERNATIONAL LAW AND THE PRINCIPLE OF NON-INTERVENTION

not take sides.[118] The French forces had also been in the country since 2002 under a 1961 bilateral defence agreement and had been mandated by the Security Council to assist the United Nations Operation in Côte d'Ivoire (UNOCI) to protect civilians.[119] The only case of intervention which exclusively relied on the consent of an elected but non-effective authority is that of ECOWAS in The Gambia in 2017 on the appeal of President-elect Adama Barrow after sitting President Jammeh refused to accept the results of the elections.[120] As in the case of Sierra Leone and Côte d'Ivoire, however, the inviting authorities had been endorsed by the Security Council and by regional organizations, a factor that, in the eyes of the international community, seems to have compensated for the lack of effectiveness.[121] Even though it did not authorize the use of force, the Council also welcomed the decision of the Fiftieth Ordinary Session of the ECOWAS Authority to take all necessary actions to enforce the results of the 1 December 2016 elections.[122] In the end, the ECOWAS operation in The Gambia was halted to allow for a final round of negotiations, which led to Jammeh stepping down voluntarily and going into exile. All in all, the aforementioned cases do not constitute convincing evidence against resorting to the effective control doctrine for the identification of governments in international law.

A government must owe its effectiveness to its own forces, and not to those of another country.[123] While a certain degree of interdependence is physiological in international relations, this cannot go beyond a reasonable measure: this would occur, for instance, when a government maintains its grip on power exclusively thanks to external support.[124] Interventions criticized for having been invited by 'puppet governments' include those of the United States in South Vietnam[125] and in Lebanon,[126] that of Vietnam in Kampuchea,[127] and that of Russia in South Ossetia.[128] All the more, when a government has been installed in power by a foreign armed intervention as in the case of those headed by János Kádár and Babrak Karmal in Hungary and

---

[118] Declaration of the French President, 4 April 2011, in Frédérique Coulée and Hélène Picot, 'Pratique française du droit international' (2011) 57 AFDI 757, 764.

[119] SC Res 1464, 4 February 2003, para 9.

[120] UN Doc S/PV.7866, 19 January 2017, 2.

[121] SC Res 2337, para 2. See Gregory H Fox, 'Intervention by Invitation' in Marc Weller (ed), *The Oxford Handbook of the Use of Force in International Law* (OUP 2015) 812, 837; Corten, *The Law Against War*, 289–91.

[122] SC Res 2337, para 4.

[123] Dietrich Schindler, 'Le principe de non-intervention dans les guerres civiles', Rapport provisoire (1973) 55 AIDI 416, 446; Maria Luisa Alaimo, 'La questione dell'Afghanistan alle Nazioni Unite e il problema del consenso nell'illecito internazionale' (1981) 64 RDI 287, 298.

[124] Jennings and Watts, *Oppenheim's International Law*, 435–8.

[125] The Soviet Union, for instance, claimed that the 'Saigon régime' 'was a puppet of the United States itself and would collapse if the United States withdrew its troops. It was therefore in no position to make an independent appeal to another Government that reflected the will of the people and was designed to support a movement of national self-determination' (UN Doc A/AC.125/SR.65, 4 December 1967, 10).

[126] For the Soviet Union, Lebanon's President Chamoun was a 'political puppet' of the United States (UN Doc S/PV.827, para 214).

[127] UN Doc S/PV.2108, 11 January 1979, para 100.

[128] According to the IIFFMCG, 'Russia's influence on and control of the decision-making process in South Ossetia concerned a wide range of matters with regard to the internal and external relations of the entity. The influence was systematic, and exercised on a permanent basis. Therefore the *de facto* Government of South Ossetia was not "effective" on its own' (IIFFMCG Report, vol II, 133).

NON-INTERVENTION AND THE ROLE OF CONSENT 215

Afghanistan (respectively)[129] and of the 'Free Provisional Government' in Kuwait,[130] it is not the authority *in situ* but the ousted one that is entitled to consent to foreign intervention in collective self-defence.[131] The Kuwaiti government in exile in Saudi Arabia, in particular, successfully requested other states, under Article 51 of the Charter, to take all steps necessary to implement Security Council Resolution 661 (1990) and its entitlement to do so was not questioned by any state.[132]

4.1.2.1 How much effective control is necessary?
As shown in the previous sub-section, an authority can successfully claim to be the government of a state under international law to the extent that it is able to effectively exercise governmental functions over the state's territory. The challenge is to establish until when a government can still be considered in effective control of its state during civil strife. According to Georg Nolte, this is so until it is in 'control over a sufficiently representative part of the State territory'.[133] For some authors, this implies control of the country's capital.[134] Yoram Dinstein, on the other hand, stresses that effective control depends on topography and not only on demography.[135] Control of territory, in other words, must be reconciled with control of the population: in prevalently desert countries like Libya where the majority of the inhabitants live along the coast, effective control of that relatively small area means control of most of the country's population and, therefore, might be sufficient evidence of effectiveness.[136]

Hersch Lauterpacht identifies an effective government by resorting to a legal rebuttable presumption: the *de jure* government of a state is presumed to be that in effective control at the beginning of the civil strife until it 'offers resistance which is not ostensibly hopeless or purely nominal'.[137] As long as it still has the means and reasonable chances to re-establish its authority, therefore, the mere occurrence of civil strife or a request for external assistance to quell it are not per se sufficient to deprive

---

[129] According to the chairman of the UN Special Committee on the Problem of Hungary, 'it cannot be denied that, but for this military action by the Soviet Union, it would not have been possible for Mr. Kadar to establish his régime' (UN Doc A/PV.677, 13 September 1957, 1453). Reactions to the Soviet invasion of Afghanistan also were overwhelmingly negative, with states doubting that there had been an external threat and questioning the validity of consent (S/PV.2185-2190; A/ES.6/PV.1-7). Read the USSR's reference to Karmal's consent in the framework of the 1978 Treaty of Friendship, Good Neighbourliness and Cooperation between the two countries in A/ES-6/PV.2, 11 January 1980, para 76; S/PV.2186, 5 January 1980, para 17. For Karmal's consent, see A/35/PV.11, 221, para 142.

[130] UN Doc S/PV.2932, 2 August 1990, 11.

[131] Talmon, *Recognition*, 146.

[132] Letter to the President of the UN Security Council, 12 August 1990, quoted ibid, 147.

[133] Georg Nolte, 'Intervention by Invitation', in *MPEPIL Online* (last updated January 2010) para 18.

[134] See eg David Wippman, 'Military Intervention, Regional Organizations, and Host-State Consent' (1996) 7 Duke J Comp & Intl L 209, 220; Stefan Talmon, 'Recognition of Opposition Groups as the Legitimate Representative of a People' (2013) 12 CJIL 219, 232–3; Mačák, *Internationalized Armed Conflicts*, 118. For Roth, however, control of the capital only has factual relevance (Roth, *Governmental Illegitimacy*, 183). In relation to Vietnam's intervention in Kampuchea, China affirmed that '[t]he temporary setbacks on the battlefield and the temporary loss of the capital in no way affects the legal status of the Government of Democratic Kampuchea' (UN Doc S/PV.2108, 2).

[135] Dinstein, *Non-International Armed Conflicts*, 128.

[136] It has also been noted that the Northern regions controlled by insurgents in Mali were prevalently a desert area (Laura Magi, 'Sulla liceità dell'intervento militare francese in Mali' (2013) 96 RDI 551, 560).

[137] Hersch Lauterpacht, *Recognition in International Law* (CUP 1947) 93–4. See also Tom J Farer, 'The Regulation of Foreign Intervention in Civil Armed Conflict' (1974) 142 Recueil des Cours 291, 354.

216   INTERNATIONAL LAW AND THE PRINCIPLE OF NON-INTERVENTION

an incumbent government of its effective character.[138] From a practical perspective, Lauterpacht's presumption has the double advantage of largely avoiding the difficulties related to the identification of the exact threshold of control that must be lost for an authority to forfeit its entitlement to invite foreign intervention and of ensuring that there are no accountability gaps in the transition to a new regime. As has been observed, '[t]he international system's preference for order seems to make some presumption in favor of the established government inevitable'.[139] The unappealing alternative is shifting governmental status back and forth from faction to faction depending on the military situation on the battlefield.[140]

The presumption should of course not be applied too rigidly: as Lauterpacht himself stresses, '[t]o maintain that the lawful government holding out in one isolated fortress is entitled to continued recognition *de jure* is to strain to breaking point an otherwise unimpeachable rule'.[141] The 'hopeless or purely nominal' resistance offered by the incumbent government can be evidenced by an evaluation of different *juris tantum* indicia, including, but not limited to, the loss of control of the capital, of the army's loyalty or of the country's financial institutions, the flight of the incumbent government's head from the national territory, the derecognition by other states, or the expulsion of delegates from international organizations.[142]

Lauterpacht's presumption is reflected in the general practice of states, which have normally continued to consider the authority in office at the beginning of the civil strife as the government of the concerned state (and thus that entitled to request foreign intervention) even if it has lost control of most of the territory: the cases of Traoré's, Assad's, and Hadi's governments in Mali, Syria, and Yemen, respectively, are the most illustrative recent examples. The only situation in which states departed from the Lauterpacht presumption appears to be that of the First Libyan Civil War, when the National Transitional Council (NTC) was recognized as 'the governing authority in Libya' on 15 July 2011 by the thirty-two-member Libya Contact Group even though the civil war was still in full progress.[143]

If no effective authority can be identified because the incumbent government has collapsed but no opposition group has managed to replace it with a sufficient degree of stability, different solutions have been suggested. For some, if the purpose of an intervention in a 'failing state' is limited (e.g. the restoration of internal law and order, or to avert a humanitarian crisis), it can be conducted at the request of *any* of the factions.[144]

---

[138] Sir Gerald Fitzmaurice agrees: 'so long as there exists a substantial prospect, or even a reasonable hope, of retrieving the situation, assistance or support can lawfully be given, or continue to be given, to a legitimate authority' (Gerald Fitzmaurice, 'The General Principles of International Law Considered from the Standpoint of the Rule of Law' (1957) 92 Recueil des Cours 1, 178).

[139] Roth, *Governmental Illegitimacy*, 183.

[140] ibid.

[141] Lauterpacht, *Recognition*, 97.

[142] Ángel Sánchez Legido, '¿Podemos armar a los rebeldes? La legalidad internacional del envío de armas a grupos armados no estatales a la luz de los conflictos libio y sirio' (2015) 29 REEI 9, 31.

[143] See Chapter VII, Section 7.2. The early recognition of the NTC as the new government of Libya in 2011, granted by several states, was motivated not by the loss of effectiveness of the previous government, but rather by the atrocities committed by the Ghaddafi regime.

[144] David Wippman, 'Enforcing the Peace: ECOWAS and the Liberian Civil War' in Lori Fisler Damrosch (ed), *Enforcing Restraint: Collective Intervention in Internal Conflicts* (Council on Foreign Relations Press 1993) 157, 182. The author, however, concedes that this position 'has not yet gained acceptance as an exception to the usual rules governing intervention' (ibid).

This was, for instance, one of Belgium's claims in relation to its 1960 intervention in Congo, where it argued that the state of anarchy existing at the time in the African country allowed the local authorities of Katanga to consent to an operation to evacuate foreign nationals.[145]

Alternatively, it has been suggested that, in the case of anarchy, consent is unnecessary or presumed if the intervention aims to restore a functioning state.[146] When South Africa controversially intervened in war-torn Angola in the 1970s, for instance, it explained that its limited purpose was to 'secure for the people of Angola the necessary time to reach a peaceful political settlement for themselves around the conference table, or, failing that, an opportunity for the Organization of African Unity to find a political solution without interference from outside'.[147] The second phase of the 1965 US intervention in the Dominican Republic was also based on the claim that it had the purpose of 'preserving the capacity of the OAS [Organization of American States] to ... achieve peace and justice through securing a cease-fire and through re-establishing orderly political processes within which Dominicans could choose their own government, free from outside interferences'.[148] In Grenada, the United States referred to 'the absence of a minimally responsible Government' and the request of the OECS 'to restore minimal conditions of law and order' as a consequence of the governmental authority vacuum.[149] Finally, ECOWAS did not officially rely on the request of the Doe government to justify its 1990 intervention in Liberia and instead emphasized 'a state of anarchy and the total break-down of law and order in' the African country.[150]

The third and, in my view, preferable solution is that, in cases where the incumbent government has been vanquished and no other faction has managed to achieve sufficient effective control of the country in civil strife to be able to claim governmental status, no authority embodies state sovereignty and can thus validly grant consent to foreign intervention.[151] This is because the absence of a government entitled to

---

[145] UN Doc S/PV.873, para 187.

[146] In its comments on the ILC Draft Articles on the Protection of Persons in the Event of Disasters, for instance, the United States observed that, in 'a scenario involving a State in which the Government had completely collapsed and where it was not possible to find authorities who could provide consent', the non-consensual provision of assistance for disaster relief or disaster risk reduction would not necessarily violate the principle of non-intervention (UN Doc A/CN.4/696/Add.1, 28 April 2016, 16). For Thomas and Thomas, however, intervention would be lawful without consent 'only where there is a prolonged entire absence of government' (Ann Van Wynen Thomas and AJ Thomas, Jr, *Non-Intervention: The Law and Its Import in the Americas* (Southern Methodist University Press 1956) 221).

[147] UN Doc S/PV.1904, 30 March 1976, para 119. See China's critical comments (S/PV.1900, 26 March 1976, paras 55–6). The Security Council condemned South Africa's aggression against Angola (SC Res 387, 31 March 1976).

[148] Leonard C Meeker, 'The Dominican Situation in the Perspective of International Law' (1965) 53 Dept St Bull 60, 62.

[149] UN Doc S/PV.2491, paras 65, 72. The UN General Assembly condemned the intervention as 'a flagrant violation of international law and of the independence, sovereignty and territorial integrity of [Grenada]' (GA Res 38/7, 2 November 1983, para 1). Condemnation by the Security Council was avoided only thanks to the US veto.

[150] ECOWAS Standing Mediation Committee, Final Communiqué of the First Session, 7 August 1990, para 7, in Marc Weller (ed), *Regional Peace-Keeping and International Enforcement: The Liberian Crisis* (CUP 1994) 72.

[151] Dinstein, *Non-International Armed Conflicts*, 108; Corten, *The Law Against War*, 285–8. See also John Norton Moore, 'The Control of Foreign Intervention in Internal Conflict' (1969) 9 Va J Intl L 205, 278; Schindler, 'Le principe', 487.

represent the state in its international relations temporarily prevents that state from assuming new obligations towards or granting new rights to other states. As a result, interventions to restore a functioning state or protect civilians can only be conducted with the authorization of the Security Council under Chapter VII of the UN Charter. This conclusion finds support in state practice (Corten makes the examples of the interventions in Somalia (1992), Haiti (1994), Albania (1996), and Côte d'Ivoire (2011))[152] and *opinio juris*.[153] In 1992, the UN Secretary-General also stressed the need for Security Council authorization in the case of an armed intervention in Somalia, as no government existed at the time in the troubled Eastern African country.[154]

4.1.3 Recognition

De jure recognition of a government is a unilateral act entailing that 'in the opinion of the recognizing State, the government so recognized is a sovereign authority, i.e. the government of a sovereign State, and/or indicates the recognizing State's willingness to enter into relations with it on the basis of sovereign equality'.[155] In the debates on the Resolution on Military Assistance on Request (Rhodes Resolution), certain members of the Institut de droit international maintained that a government in exile can continue to request foreign intervention if it has been recognized by a majority of democratic states[156] or if it remains recognized *de jure* by the government from which intervention is requested.[157] Stefan Talmon more prudently claims that, if recognition by the intervening state alone is not sufficient, 'widespread recognition, especially by the United Nations or regional organizations, of the requesting authority in exile as a government will normally secure that a request is regarded as a valid justification of the military intervention to (re-)install the government in exile'.[158] For other commentators, both 'general' recognition and effectiveness are necessary for a government to be able to consent to foreign intervention.[159]

---

[152] Corten, *The Law Against War*, 285–8.

[153] The United States, for instance, has argued on at least one occasion that 'where there is total absence of an established government, and factions are striving for control of the people and territory as well as recognition of legitimacy from the outside world, foreign intervention in terms of troops, supply of arms, military equipment, and financing of the military action as assistance to any faction would appear to violate the heart of the legal rationale of the nonintervention principle—to prohibit interference that would prejudice the outcome of the internal struggle' (Memorandum of the Attorney Adviser in the Office of the Department of State's Legal Adviser dated 20 February 1976, reproduced in Eleanor C McDowell (ed), *Digest of United States Practice in International Law 1976* (GPO 1977) 3). For Canada, 'when two rival factions are competing over control, neither of which has established effective control over the territory or over a substantial part of it ... acceptance of a request to intervene by one of the factions might well constitute an intervention in the domestic affairs of the state, and in some cases be inconsistent with the principle of self-determination.' (LH Legault, 'Canadian Practice in International Law During 1983—At the Department of External Affairs' (1984) 22 CYBIL 321, 324).

[154] UN Doc S/24868, 30 November 1992, 3.

[155] Talmon, *Recognition*, 76.

[156] Comments by Jeanette Irigoin-Barrenne (2009) 73 AIDI, parts I & II, 354.

[157] Comments by Edward McWhinney, ibid, 358.

[158] Talmon, *Recognition*, 149.

[159] Antonello Tancredi, 'The Russian Annexation of the Crimea: Questions Relating to the Use of Force' (2014) 1 Quest Intl L 5, 17; Tom Ruys and Luca Ferro, 'Weathering the Storm: Legality and Legal Implications of the Saudi-Led Military Intervention in Yemen' (2016) 65 Intl & Comp LQ 65, 81; Robert Kolb, *International Law on the Maintenance of Peace*: Jus Contra Bellum (Edward Elgar 2018) 448; Christian Henderson, *The Use of Force and International Law* (CUP 2018) 356–7.

The recognition doctrine, however, involves circular reasoning: it argues that a government is such because it is recognized by other states but at the same time that recognition can lawfully occur only when the recognized entity has become a government.[160] It is also at odds with contemporary state practice: the official policy of many states, including the United Kingdom,[161] Belgium,[162] France,[163] Switzerland, Australia, Canada, New Zealand, Italy, and the Netherlands,[164] is not to recognize governments, but states. What is more, as Roger Fisher notes, 'all the rules about intervention are meaningless if every nation can decide for itself which governments are legitimate and how to characterize particular limited conflict'.[165] In the final analysis, recognition by other states is neither necessary nor sufficient for the identification of governments under current international law,[166] although it might have the practical effect of evidencing or consolidating their effectiveness.[167]

That said, in recent decades the UN Security Council has frequently endorsed authorities of countries in civil strife that received a popular mandate through free and fair elections or that resulted from an inclusive national reconciliation process, as in the case of the Government of National Accord (GNA), President Hadi, and President-elect Barrow in Libya, Yemen, and The Gambia, respectively.[168] It has therefore been suggested that, 'in the absence of any body able to assert control, a body that emerges from a national reconciliation process with UN-backing will be identified as the authoritative government of the state even before it is established, with full capacity to exercise the state's rights under international law'.[169] It is worth recalling that 'recognitions' contained in Security Council decisions adopted in accordance with the UN Charter are binding on the UN member states under Article 25 of the Charter.

4.2 Form of Consent

As shown in Section 3, consent to intervention is an agreement formed by two concurring manifestations of will, that of the intervening state and that of the state where the intervention takes place. As for any other agreement, international law does not

---

[160] Stefan Talmon, 'The Constitutive Versus the Declaratory Theory of Recognition: *Tertium Non Datur?*' (2004) 75 BYBIL 101, 116.

[161] Geoffrey Marston (ed), 'United Kingdom Materials on International Law 1980' (1980) 51 BYBIL 355, 367.

[162] MJ Peterson, 'Recognition of Governments Should Not Be Abolished' (1983) 77 AJIL 31, 42–3.

[163] Jean Charpentier, 'Pratique française de droit international' (1973) 19 AFDI 1026, 1059.

[164] Peterson, 'Recognition', 43; Malcolm N Shaw, *International Law* (9th edn, CUP 2021) 340.

[165] Roger Fisher, 'Intervention: Three Problems of Policy and Law' in Richard A Falk (ed), *The Vietnam War and International Law*, vol I (Princeton University Press 1968) 135, 144.

[166] Wippman, 'Military Intervention', 223; Talmon, *Recognition*, 271; Dinstein, *Non-International Armed Conflicts*, 129. See also 2016 ICRC Commentary on Common Art 2, para 235 <https://ihl-databases.icrc.org/en/ihl-treaties/gci-1949/article-2/commentary/2016?activeTab=undefined>.

[167] *Aguilar-Amory and Royal Bank of Canada Claims (Great Britain v Costa Rica)*, 18 October 1923, 1 RIAA 369, 381.

[168] See SC Resolutions 2259 (23 December 2015) and 2238 (10 September 2015) for Libya; 2051 (12 June 2012), 2140 (26 February 2014), 2201 (15 February 2015), 2216 (14 April 2015) for Yemen; and 2337 (19 January 2017) for The Gambia.

[169] Hannah Woolaver, 'State Failure, Sovereign Equality and Non-Intervention: Assessing Claimed Rights to Intervene in Failed States' (2014) 32 Wis Int'l LJ 595, 608.

prescribe a specific form of consent to intervention. The two manifestations of will can thus be expressed either orally or in writing unless otherwise provided.[170] Consent to intervention can even be granted secretly.[171] The United States, for instance, claimed that the consent to the OECS intervention in Grenada granted by the governor-general, initially not disclosed, could only be made public after his safety was ensured.[172] More recently, leaked classified memos suggest that, in 2004, Pakistan secretly consented to US drone strikes on its territory for several years until eventually protesting in June 2013 and, in August 2014, accusing the American government of violating Pakistan's sovereignty and territorial integrity.[173] Yemen's Presidents Saleh and Hadi also secretly consented to the counterterrorism operations conducted by the United States in their country since 2002, with Hadi acknowledging it only in September 2012.[174] While secret consent is not invalid per se, it might need to be evidenced should a dispute arise over its existence and scope.[175]

Whatever the form, consent must be 'clearly established' and not merely presumed.[176] Ago explains that presumed consent is different from tacit consent in that in the former case 'there is actually no consent by the injured party; it is simply presumed that the State concerned would have consented to the conduct adopted in the case in question if it had been possible to request its consent'.[177] Lack of protest against an intervention by the territorial state, in particular, is not equivalent to consent. Even though Cambodia had not objected to the ground operations against North Vietnamese and Việt Cộng sanctuaries conducted by American and South Vietnamese troops on its territory in April 1970,[178] the United States relied not on presumed consent to justify

---

[170] President Nyerere of Tanganyika's request to the British government for an intervention in January 1964, for instance, was first made orally, given the urgency of the situation, and then confirmed in writing two hours later at the instance of the British, who were keen to avoid any doubts about its existence (Christopher MacRae and Tony Laurence, 'The 1964 Tanganyka Rifles Mutiny and the British Armed Intervention that Ended It' (2007) 152 RUSI Journal 96, 97, 99). A treaty, however, can require a specific form. Art 9 of the ECCAS Pact of Mutual Assistance, for instance, specifies that, when an aggression or threat thereof originates from outside the Community against a member state, a request for assistance must be sent in writing by the head of state of the concerned member. During the drafting of the Definition of Aggression, Ceylon unsuccessfully proposed that a state would be considered an aggressor if 'its weapons or military or para-military forces enter another State otherwise than in accordance with the laws of that State or without the express written consent of the Government of that State' (UN Doc A/C.6/SR.1081, 26 November 1968, para 11).

[171] What can be kept secret is the existence of consent itself or its content.

[172] Statement by Deputy Secretary of State Dam before the House Committee on Foreign Affairs, 2 November 1983, in Nash Leich (ed), 'Contemporary Practice', 203. See also Dominica's statement at the Security Council, UN Doc S/PV.2489, 26 October 1983, para 9.

[173] Max Brookman-Byrne, 'Intervention by (Secret) Invitation: Searching for a Requirement of Publicity in the International Law on the Use of Force with Consent' (2020) 7 JUFIL 74, 83–6.

[174] Hasar, State Consent, 59–60.

[175] Brookman-Byrne, 'Intervention', 88–9.

[176] Commentary on Art 20 ARSIWA [2001] YB ILC, vol II, part two, 73. In the Lotus case, the Permanent Court of International Justice famously found that '[r]estrictions upon the independence of States cannot ... be presumed' (The Case of the SS 'Lotus' (France v Turkey), Judgment of 7 September 1927, PCIJ Series A No 10, 2, 18). For the UN Special Committee set up to investigate the Hungarian events of 1956, '[t]he act of calling in the forces of a foreign State for the repression of internal disturbances is an act of so serious a character as to justify the expectation that no uncertainty should be allowed to exist regarding the actual presentation of such a request by a duly constituted government' (Report of the Special Commission on the Problem of Hungary, UN Doc A/3592, 1957, para 266).

[177] Ago, Eighth Report, para 69.

[178] Richard A Falk, 'The Cambodian Operation and International Law' (1971) 65 AJIL 1, 10.

NON-INTERVENTION AND THE ROLE OF CONSENT   221

them but on the collective self-defence of South Vietnam.[179] From September 2014 to September 2015, Syria also did not protest against the US airstrikes against Islamic State in Iraq and the Levant (ISIL) on its territory although it vehemently opposed Turkey and Israel's incursions on its territory.[180] As in Cambodia, the United States and its allies never invoked the presumed consent of Syria to justify their strikes. All in all, absence of objections to an intervention can at best constitute implied waiver or acquiescence resulting in the loss of the right to invoke the consequences of the wrongful act but it leaves the wrongfulness unaffected.[181]

If consent to intervention cannot be presumed, it does not necessarily have to be explicit. In *DRC v Uganda*, for instance, the ICJ found that the ambiguous language of the 1998 Protocol on Security along the Common Border could be interpreted as permitting the continued presence of Ugandan troops in the Democratic Republic of the Congo (DRC) because of 'both the absence of any objection to the presence of Ugandan troops in the DRC in the preceding months, and the practice subsequent to the signing of the Protocol'.[182] Note that the Court used the DRC's active and passive attitude as an instrument to interpret the treaty and establish whether the treaty (and not the absence of objections) amounted to consent. The Lusaka Ceasefire Agreement of 10 July 1999 also did not mention the DRC's consent to Uganda's intervention as it merely referred to a foreign troops' withdrawal schedule. The ICJ, therefore, had to interpret it to establish whether the third phase of Uganda's intervention in the DRC (from 10 July 1999) could have been justified on the basis of the DRC's implicit consent as claimed by the respondent state. For the Court, the provisions of the Agreement

> stipulated how the parties should move forward. They did not purport to qualify the Ugandan military presence in legal terms. In accepting this *modus operandi* the DRC did not 'consent' to the presence of Ugandan troops. It simply concurred that there should be a process to end that reality in an orderly fashion.[183]

As a result, neither the Lusaka Agreement nor the subsequent bilateral treaties between the DRC and Uganda that revised the withdrawal timetable could be interpreted as implicitly consenting to the presence of Ugandan troops on DRC territory after July 1999.[184] Even though it reached a negative conclusion in this specific instance, what matters for our purposes is that the Court, by proceeding to interpret the Lusaka Agreement, appears to have accepted that consent to intervention does not necessarily have to be explicitly stated, as long as it can be 'clearly established'.

---

[179] UN Doc S/9781, 5 May 1970, 1–2.

[180] See eg UN Doc S/2014/874, 8 December 2014; S/2015/132, 25 February 2015. In September 2015, Syria started to send letters to the Security Council denouncing the airstrikes (S/2015/719, 21 September 2015; S/2015/727, 22 September 2015, 2).

[181] Commentary on Art 20 ARSIWA [2001] YB ILC, vol II, part two, 73. See also Art 45 ARSIWA [2001] YB ILC, vol II, part two, 26. Acquiescence is different from implied waiver because the loss of the right derives from the mere conduct of the relevant state, regardless of the element of will (Alaimo, 'Natura del consenso', 268–9).

[182] *Armed Activities on the Territory of the Congo (Democratic Republic of the Congo v Uganda)* (Merits) [2005] ICJ Rep 168, para 46 (hereafter *DRC v Uganda*).

[183] ibid, para 99.

[184] ibid, para 105.

4.3 Ad Hoc and Open-Ended Consent

Consent can be provided either ad hoc with regard to a specific intervention or be open-ended, that is, in relation to possible future events.[185] We have already mentioned the treaties concluded between the United States and certain Central American and Caribbean countries in the first half of the 20th century, which provided for a broad right of intervention by the former on the territory of the latter.[186] France's policy towards what it considers its *pré carré* since the 1960s has also been founded on the conclusion of agreements with the former colonies. These agreements are of two types: technical military agreements allowing the presence of French military advisors, training, and equipment; and defence agreements allowing the presence and operation of French troops. Between 1960 and 1961, twelve agreements were signed and two more (with Djibouti and the Comoros) in 1977–8.[187] The agreements were subsequently revised in the 2000s and 2010s.[188]

For most authors, as states can even extinguish themselves by treaty, they can all the more grant other states an open-ended treaty-based right to intervene in their territory.[189] Others, however, disagree and maintain that treaties providing for such a right are inconsistent with the political independence of the state where the intervention takes place and with *jus cogens*.[190] In my view, two problems should be distinguished when it comes to treaties granting an open-ended right of intervention. The first is establishing whether they are reconcilable with the prohibition of the use of armed force and with the principle of internal self-determination, that is, the right of states and peoples to choose their political system without external interference.[191] The former does not appear to be an obstacle as it only prohibits the use of force against a state, and not with its consent (at least to the extent that the use of force is

---

[185] Section 4.3 focuses on treaties contemplating intervention in support of a government to maintain internal order and not treaties of mutual assistance in case of external aggression, which are based on collective self-defence.

[186] See Chapter I, Section 9.1.

[187] Victor-Manuel Vallin, 'France as the Gendarme of Africa, 1960–2014' (2015) 130(1) Pol Sci Q 79, 81.

[188] ibid, 94.

[189] Thomas and Thomas, *Non-Intervention*, 91–2. For Farer, 'international agreements authorizing intervention are neither void nor voidable if the objective is legitimate under international law and consent has not been coerced by one means or another' (Tom J Farer, 'The United States as Guarantor of Democracy in the Caribbean Basin: Is There a Legal Way?' (1988) (10) *Human Rights Quarterly* 157, 168).

[190] See eg Bennouna, *Le consentement*, 79–80; W Michael Reisman, 'Termination of the USSR's Treaty Right of Intervention in Iran' (1980) 74 AJIL 144, 152; *Nicaragua v USA*, Separate Opinion of Judge Sette-Camara, 199–200; Christakis and Bannelier, '*Volenti not fit injuria?*', 135; Giorgio Gaja, Fourth Report on Responsibility of International Organizations', UN Doc A/CN.4/564, 28 February 2006, para 48. For Corten, whenever the consented-to conduct consists in a use of armed force and not in the mere presence or passage of troops, ad hoc consent is also required in order to avoid conflict with *jus cogens* (Corten, *The Law Against War*, 255).

[191] States normally refer to the prohibition of the use of force as the relevant *jus cogens* rule that renders these treaties null and void. See, for instance, Cyprus's position on the validity of the 1960 Treaty of Guarantee, UN Doc S/PV.1098, 27 February 1964, paras 95–8. In a 1979 memorandum, the US State Department's Legal Advisor also noted that, if the 1978 Treaty of Friendship, Good-Neighbourliness and Cooperation between Afghanistan and the Soviet Union provided for a right of intervention to depose one ruler and replace it with another, it would be void as in conflict with a peremptory norm of general international law (that contained in Art 2(4)) under Art 53 of the VCLT (Marian Nash Leich (ed), 'Contemporary Practice of the United States Relating to International Law' (1980) 74 AJIL 418, 419). The same point was made by Panama (S/PV.2190, 7 and 9 January 1980, paras 13–19).

NON-INTERVENTION AND THE ROLE OF CONSENT   223

not inconsistent with UN purposes). On the other hand, a treaty the object and purpose of which is to keep a regime in power might not always be consistent with the principle of internal self-determination.[192] From this perspective, it is interesting that certain military cooperation treaties explicitly caution that they do not authorize foreign forces to participate in the maintenance of internal order and/or that they cannot be interpreted as permitting interferences in internal affairs.[193] Others envisage military assistance in civil strife but only if third states are involved in it.[194] In some cases, however, intervention is contemplated even in purely internal situations of unrest: examples are the 1959 Agreement between the United Kingdom and Brunei,[195] the 1960 defence agreements between France and Gabon, between France and Mali, and between France and Madagascar,[196] the 1971 Pact of Mutual Defence between Sierra Leone and Guinea,[197] the 2002 Treaty between France and Monaco,[198] the 2008 Status of Forces Agreement (SOFA) between the United States and Iraq,[199] the 2019 Memorandum of Understanding between Turkey and the GNA on behalf of Libya,[200] and the leaked 2022 security agreement between the PRC and the Solomon Islands.[201] For the reasons explained in Chapter V, these treaties must be interpreted as allowing the dispatch of armed forces in support of a government facing internal unrest only if the unrest has not become a civil war.[202]

The second question is whether ad hoc consent to an intervention is *also* necessary in addition to the treaty-based open-ended right.[203] In several treaties, this is expressly

[192]   On the principle of internal self-determination, see Chapter V.

[193]   Art 4 of the Technical Military Cooperation Agreement between France and Chad (N'Djamena, 19 June 1976) and Art 5(2) of the General Agreement on Technical Military Co-operation between France and Zaire (Kinshasa, 22 May 1974), for instance, provide that France can supply instructors and military equipment and *matériel* but cannot participate in military operations or contribute to the maintenance or restoration of internal order in the African counterpart (cited in Aleth Manin, 'L'intervention française au Shaba (19 mai–14 juin 1978)' (1978) 24 AFDI 159, 174). Similarly, the US Instrument of Ratification with Amendments, Conditions and Reservations to the 1977 Treaty Concerning the Permanent Neutrality and Operation of the Panama Canal specifies that the treaty 'shall not have as its purpose or be interpreted as a right of intervention in the internal affairs of the Republic of Panama or interference with its political independence or sovereign integrity' (text in (1978) 17 ILM 827). Panama made an identical statement.

[194]   See eg Art 1 of the Treaty of Mutual Cooperation and Security between Japan and the United States of America (San Francisco, 8 September 1951) 136 UNTS 211.

[195]   Agreement between the United Kingdom and Brunei on Defence and External Affairs (Brunei, 29 September 1959), Art 3(5)(a) (cited in Elihu Lauterpacht, *The Contemporary Practice of the United Kingdom in the Field of International Law—1962*, vol II (British Institute of International and Comparative Law 1963) 143).

[196]   Text of the treaty between France and Gabon in (1961) 14 CPE 446.

[197]   Art 2, mentioned in Díaz Barrado, *El consentimiento*, 170.

[198]   Art 4, 2002 Treaty between France and Monaco.

[199]   Art 27, Status of Forces Agreement (SOFA) between the Republic of Iraq and the United States (Baghdad, 17 November 2008) <www.dcaf.ch/sites/default/files/publications/documents/US-Iraqi_S OFA-en.pdf>.

[200]   Art IV, Memorandum of Understanding Between the Government of the Republic of Turkey and the Government of National Accord-State of Libya on Security and Military Cooperation (Istanbul, 27 November 2019) <www.nordicmonitor.com/2019/12/full-text-of-new-turkey-libya-sweeping-security-military-cooperation-deal-revealed>.

[201]   Patricia M Kin, 'Does the China-Solomon Islands Security Pact Portend a More Interventionist Beijing?' (*Brookings*, 6 May 2022) <www.brookings.edu/blog/order-from-chaos/2022/05/06/does-the-china-solomon-islands-security-pact-portend-a-more-interventionist-beijing/>.

[202]   See Chapter V, Section 3.2.3.

[203]   The Rhodes Resolution affirms that '[i]f military assistance is based on a treaty, an *ad hoc* request is required for the specific case' (Art 4 of the Resolution on Military Assistance on Request of the Institut de

224 INTERNATIONAL LAW AND THE PRINCIPLE OF NON-INTERVENTION

required. Under the 1960 Treaty of Friendship and Cooperation between Belgium and Congo, for instance, Belgian forces stationed in the African country could intervene only at the express request of the Congolese minister of national defence.[204] The 2002 Treaty between France and Monaco also provides that the former can intervene in the Principality 'à la demande ou avec l'agrément du Prince', although this consent is not necessary 'lorsque l'indépendance, la souveraineté ou l'intégrité du territoire de la Principauté de Monaco sont menacées d'une manière grave et immédiate et que le fonctionnement régulier des pouvoirs publics est interrompu'.[205] Other treaties that also require ad hoc consent include the 1951 Treaty of Mutual Cooperation and Security between Japan and the United States of America,[206] the 1960 Defence Agreement between France and Gabon,[207] the 1987 Indo–Sri Lanka Accord,[208] and the abovementioned 2008 SOFA between the United States and Iraq.[209] The 1959 Agreement between the United Kingdom and Brunei subordinates the access of British troops to the territory of the Sultanate for the purposes of defending it not to ad hoc consent but to prior consultation with the Standing Advisory Council consisting of representatives of both states 'except when there exists a state of emergency of such nature as to make such prior consultation clearly impracticable'.[210]

An examination of state practice also shows that the post-1945 cases in which a state has justified an armed intervention in another state exclusively on the basis of open-ended treaty-based consent are limited to the 1946 Soviet Union's intervention in Iran[211] and Turkey's interventions in Cyprus in 1964[212] and 1974,[213] which took

---

Droit International (Rhodes Resolution), 8 September 2011 <www.idi-iil.org/app/uploads/2017/06/2011 _rhodes_10_C_en.pdf>). Dinstein considers this part of the Resolution an accurate statement of the law (Dinstein, *Non-International Armed Conflicts*, 105). For some commentators, it is sufficient that the consent contained in the previous treaty is not withdrawn (Schindler, 'Le principe', 494; David Wippman, 'Treaty-Based Intervention: Who Can Say No?' (1995) 62 U Chi L Rev 607, 623; Visser, 'May the Force', 30).

[204] Art 6.
[205] Art 4.
[206] Art 1.
[207] Preamble and Art 3.
[208] Art 2.16(c), Indo–Sri Lanka Accord (Colombo, 29 July 1987) (1987) 26 ILM 1175.
[209] Art 27.
[210] Art 3(5)(a), in Lauterpacht, *The Contemporary Practice*, 143.
[211] When the Azerbaijan People's Government and the Kurdish Republic of Mahabad attempted to secede from Iran, Soviet forces prevented the Iranian army from reaching the northern province where the revolt was taking place. The USSR first denied that the intervention took place (UN Doc S/3, Appendix A, no 8, 26 November 1945, 53) and then justified the presence of its troops on the basis of the 1941 Soviet–Iranian Treaty (S/3, Appendix A, no 11, 29 November 1945, 59). Iran claimed that this treaty was contrary to the spirit of the UN Charter and that it did not apply to the situation in its northern province (S/1, 26 January 1946, 7).
[212] Turkey conducted airstrikes against the Greek Cypriot positions. In the letter addressed to the Security Council before the intervention, the Turkish government claimed that the intervention was justified by Art IV of the 1960 Treaty of Guarantee (UN Doc S/5596, 13 March 1964, 4). In the letter sent after the intervention, however, Turkey referred to the intervention as 'a limited police action in self-defence pending the decisions of the [UN Security] Council' (S/5904, 18 August 1964, 4).
[213] Turkey invoked Art IV(2) of the 1960 Treaty of Guarantee and intervened in Cyprus as a result of the internal unrest caused by the coup that ousted the island's President Makarios (UN Doc S/PV.1781, 20 July 1974, para 226). Note that, regardless of whether the consent contained in the treaty, and the treaty itself, were lawful, Turkey exceeded the limits under which the unilateral intervention could have been carried out, as Art IV(2) subordinates it to the fact that 'common and concerted action' is not possible and to the fact that such action must have the sole purpose of re-establishing the state of affairs created by the treaty. The

place *against* the incumbent governments. In all other cases, the intervening states either invoked additional justifications[214] or also referred to the ad hoc consent of the government of the day, as France did in its former colonies (Cameroon (1960), Chad (1969, 1978, 1983–4, 2006), Gabon (1964 and 1990), Togo (1986), and Comoros (1995)); the Soviet Union in Hungary (1956), Czechoslovakia (1968), and Afghanistan (1979–80); Guinea in Sierra Leone (1971); Papua New Guinea in Vanuatu (1980); Libya in Chad (1980); India in Sri Lanka (1987); Senegal and Guinea in Guinea-Bissau (1998); the Gulf Cooperation Council in Bahrain (2011); Turkey in Libya (2019); and the Collective Security Treaty Organization member states in Kazakhstan (2022).

All in all, therefore, state practice suggests that, if ad hoc consent has not been granted or has been revoked, the intervention cannot lawfully occur or continue exclusively on the basis of the treaty containing open-ended consent.[215] Although it is not sufficient on its own to legitimize an intervention, however, a treaty providing for an open-ended right of intervention can produce certain effects. From a legal point of view, it can establish competences, conditions, formalities, and procedures for ad hoc consent to be granted, which reduces the risk of abuses. From a political perspective, the existence of a previous treaty in addition to ad hoc consent can provide stronger legitimacy to the intervention by situating it in the context of an institutionalized co-operation between the concerned states.[216]

Does the same conclusion apply to treaties establishing the competence of an international organization to intervene on the territory of its members if specific circumstances occur? The most famous example is of course Chapter VII of the UN Charter, which grants enforcement powers to the Security Council in case of a threat to the peace, breach of the peace, or act of aggression. In this case

> [s]tates that have committed themselves to the Charter have agreed to allow the Security Council to authorize an intervention on their territory when warranted under Chapter VII. A state may not prevent an intervention under Chapter VII by revoking consent to the U.N. Charter on the event of the planned intervention.[217]

Other examples exist at the African regional and sub-regional level. The Constitutive Act of the African Union (AU), for instance, provides for 'the right of the Union to intervene in a Member State pursuant to a decision of the Assembly in respect of grave circumstances, namely: war crimes, genocide and crimes against humanity'.[218]

UN Security Council and General Assembly condemned the unilateral action and called for the withdrawal of foreign forces from the island and the cessation of all interferences in the internal affairs of Cyprus (SC Res 360, 16 August 1974, para 1, and Res 367, 12 March 1975, para 1; GA Res 3212 (XXIX), 1 November 1974, para 2).

[214] In the case of its 1989 intervention in Panama, for instance, the United States did rely on its right and duty under Art IV of the Panama Canal Treaty (Washington, DC, 7 September 1977) to protect and defend the Canal and its availability to all nations but also invoked other justifications (UN Doc S/21035; S/PV.2899, 20 December 1989, 31, 34; S/PV.2902, 23 December 1989, 13).

[215] Dinstein, *Non-International Armed Conflicts*, 106.

[216] Díaz Barrado, *El consentimiento*, 188.

[217] Oona A Hathaway, Julia Brower, Ryan Liss, Tina Thomas, and Jacob Victor, 'Consent-Based Intervention: Giving Sovereign Responsibility Back to the Sovereign' (2013) 46 Cornell Int'l LJ 499, 561.

[218] Art 4(h), Constitutive Act of the African Union (Lomé, 11 July 2000) 2158 UNTS 3.

Intervention by a sub-regional organization is also envisaged in the 2000 ECCAS Pact of Mutual Assistance,[219] the 2019 ECCAS Protocol Relating to the Peace and Security Council of Central Africa (COPAX),[220] the 2001 Southern African Development Community (SADC) Protocol on Politics, Defence and Security Co-operation,[221] the 1999 ECOWAS Protocol Relating to the Mechanism for Conflict Prevention, Management, Resolution, Peace-Keeping and Security,[222] and the 2008 ECOWAS Conflict Prevention Framework.[223] In all these cases, requiring ad hoc consent before the organization's intervention can take place appears incompatible with the object and purpose of the treaty, which is to act if certain events occur *even when it is the member state's government that is responsible for them.* By ratifying these treaties, the member states have thus accepted to transfer the competence to enforce certain obligations to a regional body: this partial transfer of sovereignty does not appear to be inconsistent with statehood—rather, it is a phenomenon that characterizes many contemporary international organizations.

That said, regional organizations have so far refrained from exclusively relying on a treaty-based right to intervene in the territory of a member state and from conducting operations therein without also obtaining ad hoc consent in the absence of UN Security Council authorization.[224] The only case in which the AU came close to intervening on the basis of Article 4(h) of its Constitutive Act, in particular, was when, in 2015, the Peace and Security Council threatened Burundi with military intervention should it not accept the deployment of an operation to protect civilians on its territory.[225] The Burundian government, however, refused to accept the ultimatum and the intervention never took place.[226] It is unclear whether this negative practice is supported by *opinio juris* or is merely due to considerations of political opportunity.

4.4 Validity Requirements of Consent

Consent might be a wrongful act in itself.[227] States that have a neutralized status by treaty, for instance, are prevented from consenting to the presence of foreign troops on their territory.[228] In most cases, however, consent is not an unlawful act but can

---

[219] Art 8(2), ECCAS Pact of Mutual Assistance.

[220] Art 3, Protocol Relating to the Peace and Security Council of Central Africa (COPAX) (Libreville, 18 December 2019) <www.labase-lextenso.fr/sites/lextenso/files/lextenso_upload/protocole_du_copax.pdf>).

[221] Art 11(2)(b)(i), SADC Protocol on Politics, Defence and Security Co-operation (Blantyre, 14 August 2001) <www.sadc.int/document/protocol-politics-defence-and-security-2001>.

[222] Art 25, ECOWAS Protocol Relating to the Mechanism for Conflict Prevention, Management, Resolution, Peace-Keeping and Security (Lomé, 10 December 1999) (2000) 5 JCSL 231.

[223] The ECOWAS Conflict Prevention Framework, Regulation MSC/REG.1/01/08 (16 January 2008) paras 26, 41 <https://au.int/sites/default/files/documents/39184-doc-140._the_ecowas_conflict_p revention_framework.pdf>.

[224] Erika De Wet, *Military Assistance on Request and the Use of Force* (OUP 2020) 173–4, 177.

[225] Nina Wilén and Paul D Williams, 'The African Union and Coercive Diplomacy: The Case of Burundi' (2018) 56 Journal of Modern African Studies 673, 682.

[226] ibid.

[227] Ago, Eighth Report, 37.

[228] Pinto, 'Les règles', 495–6.

NON-INTERVENTION AND THE ROLE OF CONSENT   227

be vitiated by the presence of certain grounds of invalidity. These grounds are codified in the 1969 Vienna Convention on the Law of Treaties (VCLT) and apply, at least *qua* customary international law, also to consent to intervention as an oral or written agreement between the intervening state and that where the intervention takes place.

4.4.1 Error, fraud, and corruption

To the best of my knowledge, error, fraud, and corruption of a representative have never been invoked as grounds to condemn consent to intervention.[229] It is not unthinkable, however, that a state representative can be bribed into providing consent or that a state's request for an authorization to intervene is accompanied with misleading and incorrect information in order to obtain the other state's consent on the basis of false assumptions.[230]

4.4.2 Coercion

Coercion finalized to the conclusion of an agreement can be exercised on a state representative or on a state itself. Coercion of state representative as a ground for the invalidity of treaties is contemplated in Article 51 of the VCLT. In 1968, for instance, the United States claimed that the invitation by Czechoslovak party and state leaders to the Warsaw Pact countries to invade Czechoslovakia in 1968 was 'invented and written by frightened men in Moscow reacting to their own dark nightmares'.[231]

Under Article 52 of the VCLT, coercion of state can be invoked to invalidate a treaty when it consists of a threat or use of armed force in breach of the UN Charter. An illustration is President Nyerere of Tanganyka's claim that he was forced to grant consent to the 1964 UK intervention in its country by the acting British high commissioner, as he was told that the operation would be carried out anyway.[232] A more recent instance comes from the Kosovo crisis of the late 1990s. On 13 October 1998, the North Atlantic Council issued an Activation Order for Phased Air Operation and Limited Air Option to begin in ninety-six hours should the Federal Republic of Yugoslavia not fully comply with Security Council Resolution 1199 of 23 September 1998 (NATO had already issued an Activation Warning on 24 September). Under such threat of force, Yugoslavia signed two documents: one with NATO on 15 October, which established a NATO air surveillance mission over Kosovo and defined the technical aspects of the operation, and another the following day with the Organization for Security and Co-operation in Europe (OSCE) establishing the Kosovo Verification Mission in order to monitor compliance with Resolution 1199 (the Holbrooke–Milošević Agreement). The agreements were subsequently endorsed by the Security Council in Resolution 1203 of 24 October 1998. Yugoslavia initially complied with the agreements and Resolution 1199, but later its security forces started to re-enter Kosovo. The North Atlantic Council thus decided to maintain the Activation Order for airstrikes. Notwithstanding the ongoing threat of force,[233] Yugoslavia did not sign the Rambouillet Interim Agreement for Peace and Self-Government in Kosovo of

---

[229] See Arts 48, 49, and 50 VCLT.
[230] Díaz Barrado, *El consentimiento*, 291.
[231] UN Doc S/PV.1441, 21 August 1968, para 41.
[232] MacRae and Laurence, 'The 1964 Tanganyka Rifles Mutiny', 99.
[233] See NATO Press Release (99) 11, 28 January 1999, paras 6–7 <www.nato.int/docu/pr/1999/p99-011e. htm>; Press Release (99) 12, 30 January 1999, para 5 <www.nato.int/docu/pr/1999/p99-012e.htm>; Press

228   INTERNATIONAL LAW AND THE PRINCIPLE OF NON-INTERVENTION

March 1999. After the start of Operation Allied Force, threats were accompanied by the use of force: in particular, the threat was to continue the use of force should Yugoslavia not accept a detailed schedule of withdrawals.[234] Yugoslavia eventually accepted the Kumanovo Agreement for the withdrawal of all security forces from Kosovo and the deployment of a NATO-led military force as well as the Agreement on Political Principles of 3 June 1999. In the *Legality of Use of Force* proceedings before the ICJ, Yugoslavia claimed the violation of Article 52 of the VCLT only in relation to the attempts to coerce it into signing the draft Interim Agreement for Peace and Self-Government in Kosovo, and not the Holbrooke–Milošević, Kumanovo, or 3 June Agreements.[235] The Court did not pronounce on the merits but, in the decision on provisional measures, declared itself to be 'profoundly concerned with the use of force in Yugoslavia [which] raises very serious issues of international law'.[236]

It is worth pointing out that coercion of state as a ground for the invalidity of treaties is different from coercion of state as an element of the principle of non-intervention, for two reasons. First, as has been seen, coercion under Article 52 of the VCLT exclusively consists of the threat and use of force in violation of the UN Charter, while the principle of non-intervention proscribes all means and methods of coercion.[237] Secondly, Article 52 requires that a treaty be 'procured' by coercion for it to be invalid. Special Rapporteur Lauterpacht explained that a treaty is void only if the coerced state 'as the result of unlawful use of force, has been reduced to such a degree of impotence as to be *unable to resist* the pressure to become a party to a treaty'.[238] In the context of the principle of non-intervention, on the other hand, coercion does not have to be irresistible, it being sufficient that unlawful coercion is exercised, whether or not the victim state actually submits to it or decides to resist and stoically endure the harm.[239]

4.4.3 Conflict with a peremptory norm of general international law

Consent to intervention is also null and void if it conflicts with *jus cogens* rules.[240] This would be the case, for instance, of 'the action of a State in allowing its territory, which it has placed at the disposal of another State, to be used by that other State for perpetrating an act of aggression against a third State'.[241] A request by a state to another for assistance to exterminate a national, ethnical, racial, or religious group would also be in conflict with the peremptory rule prohibiting genocide.[242] Finally, as Chapter VI

Release (99) 20, 19 February 1999 <www.nato.int/docu/pr/1999/p99-020e.htm>; and Press Release (99) 21, 23 February 1999 <www.nato.int/docu/pr/1999/p99-021e.htm>.

[234] The NATO spokesman's statement of 6 June 1999 can be read at <https://web.archive.org/web/201 00523010131/www.cnn.com/world/europe/9906/06/kosovo.04/index.html>.

[235] See *Legality of Use of Force (Yugoslavia v Netherlands)*, Oral proceedings, CR 99/14, 10 May 1999, 41–4, 60.

[236] *Legality of Use of Force (Yugoslavia v Spain)* (Order on Provisional Measures) [1999] ICJ Rep 761, para 16.

[237] See Chapter III, Section 2.

[238] Sir Hersch Lauterpacht, First Report on the Law of Treaties [1953] YB ILC, vol II, 147 (emphasis added).

[239] See Chapter III, Section 3.1.

[240] Arts 53 and 64 VCLT.

[241] GA Res 3314 (XXIX), Annex, Art 3(f).

[242] See comments by Mr Schwebel [1979] YB ILC, vol I, 46.

discusses, colonial or occupying powers and racist regimes cannot validly request foreign intervention in order to suppress a people's efforts to decide their own destiny and third states are under an obligation not to accept such request.[243]

4.4.4 Conflict with a provision of internal law regarding competence to grant consent

Section 4 of this chapter showed how, in the absence of specific treaty provisions, international law grants the authority to consent to foreign intervention to the incumbent government's highest office, namely the head of state or, when the head of state is a mere ceremonial role, the head of government, and, in case of their inability, to the highest surviving governmental official. Do limitations to their competence to express consent under the domestic law of the concerned state invalidate it? Domestic legislations do not normally regulate the competence to request foreign intervention or the necessary procedure, but there are exceptions. Section 25 of the Constitution of the Philippines, for instance, provides that foreign military bases, troops, or facilities can only be allowed on the national territory 'under a treaty duly concurred in by the Senate and, when the Congress so requires, ratified by a majority of the votes cast by the people in a national referendum held for that purpose'.[244] Under Article 85(23) of the Ukrainian Constitution, the decision to admit units of the armed forces of foreign states onto Ukraine's territory pertains to the Verkhovna Rada (parliament) and not the president.[245] In other cases, procedural requirements may derive from more general constitutional provisions as in the case of the Constitution of Lesotho, which prescribes that the prime minister must consult with the king on all matters concerning government.[246]

The claim of a breach of internal rules on competence to grant consent to intervention has been invoked in certain cases. After the 2014 Maidan Revolution, for instance, the British foreign secretary emphasized that Ukraine's President Yanukovych was not entitled to request Russia's intervention in his country 'since the Ukrainian Constitution is clear that only the Ukrainian Parliament has the authority to approve decisions on admitting foreign troops'.[247] In January 2013, additional South African National Defence Special Forces were dispatched to the Central African Republic (CAR) at the request of embattled President Bozizé against the Séléka rebels: criticism was raised as Bozizé sent the request to President Zuma without going through his own country's national assembly as required by Article 28 of CAR's Constitution.[248]

---

[243] See Chapter VI, Section 3.1.

[244] Text at <www.officialgazette.gov.ph/constitutions/the-1987-constitution-of-the-republic-of-the-phil ippines/the-1987-constitution-of-the-republic-of-the-philippines-article-xviii>.

[245] Art 85(23) of the Ukrainian Constitution states that '[t]he authority of the Verkhovna Rada of Ukraine comprises: ... approving decisions on ... admitting units of armed forces of foreign states onto the territory of Ukraine' (unofficial English translation at <https://rm.coe.int/constitution-of-ukraine/168071f58b>).

[246] Art 92, text at <www.constituteproject.org/constitution/Lesotho_2018.pdf?lang=en>. In 1998, Prime Minister Pakalitha Mosisili did not consult with King Letsie III before requesting Botswana and South Africa to intervene to quell a mutiny by military officers in the capital Maseru, as the monarch was suspected of sympathizing with the protesters (Fako Johnson Likoti, 'The 1998 Military Intervention in Lesotho: SADC Peace Mission or Resource War?' (2007) 14 *International Peacekeeping* 251, 253).

[247] FCO and The Rt Hon William Hague, Oral Statement to Parliament. The same point was made by the US delegate to the Security Council (UN Doc S/PV.7125, 5).

[248] 'South Africa to send 400 soldiers to CAR' (*Al Jazeera*, 6 January 2013) <www.aljazeera.com/news/ 2013/1/6/south-africa-to-send-400-soldiers-to-car>; David L Smith, 'CAR: Bozizé, Zuma in backroom

Zuma also failed to inform parliament of his decision to send troops in spite of South Africa's Constitution requiring so.[249] More recently, Egypt noted that the 2019 memorandum of understanding on military cooperation between Libya and Turkey was null and void because it was concluded by the president of the Presidency Council without the endorsement of the House of Representatives, in breach of Article 8(2)(f) of the Libyan Political Agreement concluded in Skhirat on 17 December 2015.[250]

Article 46 of the VCLT adopts an intermediary position between the internationalist theory, which allocates treaty-making power exclusively on the basis of international law, and the constitutionalist theory, according to which international law limits itself to referring to domestic law for the regulation of the competence to bind a state towards other states.[251] Under the VCLT regime, consent given in 'manifest violation' of a rule of internal law 'of fundamental importance' on competence to conclude treaties is exceptionally voidable at the instance of the consenting state.[252] Article 46(2) specifies that '[a] violation is manifest if it would be objectively evident to any State conducting itself in the matter in accordance with normal practice and in good faith': in *Cameroon v Nigeria*, the ICJ found that 'a limitation of a Head of State's capacity in this respect is not manifest in the sense of Article 46, paragraph 2, unless at least properly publicized.'[253] This entails that a specific warning must have been given of the domestic provision unless it was common knowledge.[254] All in all, good faith and constructive knowledge play an essential role in this context: a state could claim that its consent to foreign intervention was invalid because it was granted in manifest violation of its internal law on competence to conclude treaties only when 'the lack of that authority was known or ought to have been known to the acting State.'[255] The burden of proof falls on the state claiming the invalidity of consent.[256]

troops deal' (*Mail & Guardian*, 12 April 2013) <https://mg.co.za/article/2013-04-12-00-bozize-zuma-in-backroom-deal>. A memorandum of understanding had been signed in 2007 but did not expressly provide for the dispatch of troops (text at <www.politicsweb.co.za/documents/sas-2007-mou-with-car-on-defence-cooperation>).

[249] Smith, 'CAR'.
[250] UN Doc S/2019/951, 17 December 2019. For Egypt, the memorandum of understanding was also in breach of para 9 of SC Res 1970, 26 February 2011.
[251] Art 46 is declaratory of customary international law (Mark Eugen Villiger, *Commentary on the 1969 Vienna Convention on the Law of Treaties* (Brill/Nijhoff 2009) 594). If the authority of a competent organ to express the consent of a state has been subjected to specific restrictions, the representative's omission to comply with such restrictions does not constitute a ground to invalidate the consent unless the other state was notified of the restrictions before the expression of consent (Art 47 VCLT). See Hannah Woolaver, 'From Joining to Leaving', 84–5.
[252] Art 46 VCLT.
[253] *Cameroon v Nigeria*, para 265.
[254] Woolaver, 'From Joining to Leaving', 92.
[255] Commentary on Art 20 ARSIWA [2001] YB ILC, vol II, part two, 73. See also Villiger, *Commentary*, 592.
[256] ibid.

4.5 Timing of Consent

Consent must precede or be simultaneous to the commission of the act in order to produce its effects.[257] Cases where consent was granted after an intervention had already begun, such as the Soviet Union's interventions in Hungary[258] and Afghanistan,[259] were met with widespread criticism. These two examples also suggest that consent provided after the intervention has started is often an indication that such consent has been coerced or has been granted by the authority installed by the intervention.

If valid, consent granted after the start of the intervention can have the double nature of waiver for the conduct that has already taken place and of consent to its continuation.[260] Unlike consent, waiver merely results in the loss of the right to invoke the consequences of the wrongful act but does not remove its wrongfulness. While consent is an agreement, waiver is normally a unilateral act as its legal effects are produced by the mere manifestation of will of the right holder, which leads to the extinction of the right.[261] If, however, the waiver aims at transferring a right to another state, it becomes the element of an agreement as the acceptance of the beneficiary is also necessary.[262] It goes without saying that the waiver must be valid to produce its effects: authorities installed by the intervening state, for instance, are unable to waive the legal consequences of an intervention or consent to its continuation.[263] The problem has arisen with regard to the validity of the consent to the continued presence of foreign forces in Afghanistan and Iraq granted by governments that came to power as a consequence of the armed intervention by those same forces. It has been noted that, in Afghanistan, the intervention that led to the replacement of the Taliban regime with the Transitional Authority in 2002 was a lawful use of force in self-defence (although one might question the proportionality of the defensive reaction).[264] It has also been argued that power was transferred to the West-supported authorities not from the Taliban, but from the government that the Taliban had overthrown in 1996 and that continued to be recognized by the international community as the legitimate representative of the Central Asian country.[265] Finally and most importantly, the election of Hamid Karzai as president was legitimized first by the 2002 nationwide Loya Jirga

---

[257] Commentary on Art 20 ARSIWA [2001] YB ILC, vol II, part two, 73.

[258] The second intervention started on 4 November 1956, but Kádár, who requested it, took power only on 7 November.

[259] The Afghani government that requested the USSR intervention was formed at the earliest on 27 December 1979, while the intervention had started on 24 December. The Soviet Union claimed that consent to the presence of its troops in Afghanistan had already been granted in December 1978 by Karmal's predecessor, Amin (UN Doc S/PV.2185, 5 January 1980, para 100).

[260] Commentary on Art 20 ARSIWA [2001] YB ILC, vol II, part two, 73; Díaz Barrado, *El consentimiento*, 386.

[261] Alaimo, 'Natura del consenso', 263. Special Rapporteur Crawford noted that the organ with authority to waive might not necessarily be the same as that which has authority to consent (Crawford, Second Report, para 240, fn 456).

[262] Alaimo, 'Natura del consenso', 264.

[263] Commentary on Art 45 ARSIWA [2001] YB ILC, vol II, part two, 122.

[264] Hasar, *State Consent*, 91–2. See the US and British letters to the UN Security Council (UN Doc S/2001/946, 7 October 2001; S/2001/947, 7 October 2001).

[265] Hasar, *State Consent*, 91.

232 INTERNATIONAL LAW AND THE PRINCIPLE OF NON-INTERVENTION

and then by the 2004 presidential elections.[266] In Iraq, on the other hand, the use of force that led to the overthrow of Saddam Hussein's regime was undoubtedly a violation of the UN Charter.[267] Furthermore, as the US-controlled Coalition Provisional Authority (CPA) was 'the creature of the occupying forces' (to use the words of the UK Supreme Court), its consent to the presence of the foreign armed forces in Iraq could not change the fact that the United Kingdom and the United States technically were occupying powers.[268] The CPA's 'invitation', therefore, did not remove the coercive character of the intervention. Security Council Resolution 1546 (2004) eventually noted that 'the presence of the multinational force in Iraq is at the request of the incoming Interim Government of Iraq', which replaced the CPA on 28 June 2004.[269] The Interim Government, however, did not have effective control of large parts of the country, was unelected, and had not received any legitimization from the Iraqi people.[270] It is at least questionable, therefore, that it had the right to validly consent to the continued presence and operation of foreign forces on the territory of Iraq.

4.6 Limits to the Scope of Consent

Consent only legitimizes an intervention within the limits it sets.[271] Some limits are inherent in the nature of consent, that is, a state can only consent to intervention on its territory (as consent only operates in the relations between the consenter and the consentee) and to acts that it could itself lawfully undertake.[272] Specific limits can also be enunciated in the statement or treaty containing consent: the intervention, for instance, could be allowed only in a certain area, for a certain period or a certain purpose, or under certain conditions.[273] State practice confirms the relevance of these limits. In 1964, Congo's Prime Minister Tshombe authorized Belgium and the United States to provide necessary assistance to conduct a humanitarian operation 'solely for the limited period necessary to make possible the evacuation of [foreign hostages], whose lives are in grave danger'.[274] The intervention could not 'lead to any solutions with regard to the rebels different from those which it rests with the Government of the Congo to seek in the exercise of its full sovereignty'.[275] After its end, therefore, the

[266] Andrea Carcano, 'End of the Occupation in 2004? The Status of the Multinational Force in Iraq After the Transfer of Sovereignty to the Interim Iraqi Government' (2006) 11 JCSL 41, 57.

[267] Marc Weller, 'The Iraq War—2003' in Tom Ruys and Olivier Corten with Alexandra Hofer (eds), *The Use of Force in International Law. A Case-based Approach* (OUP 2018) 639, 651-5.

[268] *R (on the application of Smith) (FC) (Respondent) v Secretary of State for Defence (Appellant) and another* (Judgment of 30 June 2010) 30 June 2010 [2010] UKSC 29, para 186.

[269] SC Res 1546, 8 June 2004, para 9. The Preamble of the resolution also recalls 'the importance of the consent of the sovereign Government of Iraq for the presence of the multinational force'.

[270] Carcano, 'End of the Occupation', 49.

[271] Art 20 of ARSIWA indicates that consent precludes the wrongfulness of conduct only 'to the extent that the act remains within the limits of that consent'.

[272] John A Perkins, 'The Right of Counterintervention' (1987) 17 Ga J Intl & Comp L 171, 189.

[273] The ILC Commentary on Art 20 of the ARSIWA notes that the non-observance of conditions placed on consent does not always result in situating the conduct in question outside the scope of such consent, for instance, in the case of the non-payment of the rent for a military base (Commentary on Art 20 ARSIWA [2001] YB ILC, vol II, part two, 74).

[274] UN Doc S/6060, 24 November 1964.

[275] UN Doc S/6062, 24 November 1964, 4.

NON-INTERVENTION AND THE ROLE OF CONSENT   233

Belgian minister of foreign affairs reported that the operation did not intermeddle in the conflict in the Congo but limited itself to save between 1,500 and 2,000 persons in danger.[276] In *DRC v Uganda*, the ICJ also found that the DRC's consent to the presence and operation of Uganda's troops on its territory was not 'open-ended' and was limited both in its geographic location and objectives, namely, it only allowed Uganda to 'act, or assist in acting, against rebels on the eastern border and in particular to stop them operating across the common border'.[277] A more recent example comes from the on-going armed conflict in Yemen. Even though, on 24 March 2015, the Yemeni government had requested the intervention of the Gulf Cooperation Council states against the Houthi militia, in May 2018 it denounced the deployment of UAE troops and armoured vehicles to the Yemeni island of Socotra as an 'unjustified military action' because such deployment was outside the scope of its consent.[278] The UAE minimized the event and reassured Yemen that it had 'no intention or ambition to maintain a long-term presence in Socotra Island'.[279]

4.7 Withdrawal of Consent

As the Institut de droit international's Rhodes Resolution points out, a state can always withdraw the consent it has granted to an intervention.[280] The International Committee of the Red Cross (ICRC)'s 2016 Commentary on Common Article 2 of the 1949 Geneva Conventions also notes that 'if the territorial State has explicitly protested against the intervention and this protest has been made by authorities that are entitled to give or withdraw the consent, it should be presumed that the consent did not exist in the first place or has been withdrawn'.[281] Article 3(e) of the General Assembly's Definition of Aggression adds that the presence of troops on the territory of another state 'beyond the termination of the agreement' which authorized such presence amounts to an act of aggression.[282] Limits to the right to withdraw consent, however, can be provided by treaty as in the case of the 1947 agreement on US aid to Greece, which stipulated that US assistance would be withdrawn only '[i]f requested by the Government of Greece representing a majority of the Greek people'.[283]

As the ICRC Commentary points out, withdrawal of consent must come from authorities that are entitled to grant consent in the first place: the considerations developed in Section 4 of this chapter and its subsections, therefore, apply *mutatis mutandis* here as well.[284] On 28 October 1956, for instance, Hungary's Prime Minister Nagy

---

[276] UN Doc S/PV.1173, 11 December 1964, para 9.
[277] *DRC v Uganda*, para 52.
[278] UN Doc S/2018/440, 14 May 2018, Annex 2.
[279] UN Doc S/2018/490, 22 May 2018, 2.
[280] Art 5, Rhodes Resolution.
[281] 2016 ICRC Commentary on Common Art 2, para 263 <https://ihl-databases.icrc.org/en/ihl-treaties/gci-1949/article-2/commentary/2016?activeTab=undefined>.
[282] GA Res 3314, Art 3(e).
[283] Art 10(1), Agreement Concerning Aid to Greece (Athens, 20 June 1947) in *A Decade of American Foreign Policy: Basic Documents 1941–1949 (Revised Edition)* (Department of State 1985) 542.
[284] In the letter sent to the president of the UN General Assembly in relation to the 1958 intervention in Jordan, for instance, the British foreign affairs secretary promised that 'United Kingdom forces will be withdrawn from Jordan whenever this is requested by the duly constituted Government of Jordan' (UN Doc A/

234 INTERNATIONAL LAW AND THE PRINCIPLE OF NON-INTERVENTION

demanded the withdrawal of all Soviet forces from Hungary, repudiated the Warsaw Pact, and declared his country's neutrality.[285] The Soviet Union responded that Nagy's communications to the United Nations were invalid, as they had been disavowed by the Revolutionary Workers and Peasants' Government that replaced him.[286] For Moscow, the only lawful authority was 'the revolutionary Hungarian Government, set up by virtue of the Constitution of the Hungarian People's Republic and enjoying the support of the whole Hungarian people'.[287] At the moment of the request for withdrawal, however, Nagy was still the effective prime minister of Hungary and was thus still entitled to terminate his country's consent to the presence of the Soviet troops.

Is withdrawal of consent subordinated to any specific form? Article 5 of the Institut de droit international's Rhodes Resolution seems to suggest a negative answer where it affirms that '[t]he requesting State is free to terminate its request or to withdraw its consent to the provision of military assistance at any time, irrespective of the expression of consent through a treaty'. The question was briefly addressed by the ICJ in *DRC v Uganda*. Uganda justified its military activities in the DRC between May 1997 and 11 September 1998 and then again from July 1999 on the basis of the consent of the Congolese president, Laurent-Désiré Kabila.[288] According to Uganda, upon taking office on 29 May 1997 Kabila invited it to deploy its troops in the eastern regions of the country to stop the anti-Ugandan insurgency, which the DRC was unable to prevent. The consent was reaffirmed in a Protocol on Security along the Common Border signed by the two countries on 27 April 1998.[289] The DRC responded that consent to the deployment of Ugandan forces on its territory had been withdrawn when, in an official statement published on 28 July 1998, Kabila called for the withdrawal of Rwanda's troops from his country and proclaimed 'the end of the presence of all foreign military forces in the Congo'.[290] Uganda interpreted the statement as not addressing its forces as they were not expressly mentioned.[291] The ICJ found that the initial (informal) consent to the presence of foreign troops contained in the 1997 Kabila statement could be 'withdrawn at any time ... without further formalities being necessary',[292] but did not specifically address Uganda's claim that withdrawal of consent also required a formal denunciation of the 1998 Protocol that reaffirmed it.

In my view, to correctly address the problem two situations must be distinguished: that of a treaty containing ad hoc consent to intervention and that of a treaty providing for an open-ended right of intervention. As seen in Section 4.3, open-ended consent is not on its own a sufficient legal basis for an intervention as ad hoc consent is

---

3877). It has been argued that, even though Art 46 of the VCLT only expressly applies to joining treaties, it should also apply by analogy to withdrawal from them (Woolaver, 'From Joining to Leaving', 104).

[285] UN Doc A/3251, 1 November 1956, 1.
[286] (1956) YB UN 67, 70.
[287] UN Doc A/PV.677, para 190.
[288] *DRC v Uganda*, para 42.
[289] ibid, para 36.
[290] ibid, para 49.
[291] ibid, para 50.
[292] ibid, para 47. The Court also held that, whatever the interpretation of Kabila's July 1998 statement, the DRC consent was withdrawn at the latest by 8 August 1998, when, at the Victoria Falls Summit, the DRC accused Uganda and Rwanda of invading its territory (ibid, para 53).

also necessary (unless this is incompatible with the object and purpose of the treaty): if the latter has been granted without formalities, it can also be withdrawn without formalities, at which point the intervention can no longer take place regardless of whether or not the treaty containing open-ended consent has also been denounced. If, on the other hand, it is ad hoc consent itself that has been formalized in a written treaty, the only way to withdraw it would be to denounce the treaty according to its own terms or on the grounds contained in the VCLT: nowhere does the law of treaties suggest that agreements granting consent to intervention are regulated by special rules on termination, suspension, and invalidity.

4.8 Consent and UN Security Council Resolutions

Article 2(7) of the San Francisco Charter excludes that the United Nations can intervene in matters falling 'essentially' within the domestic jurisdiction of any states.[293] In two cases, however, the Security Council's involvement in civil strife is permissible: when the incumbent government consents to it and when, in the Council's view, the civil strife constitutes a threat to international peace and security thus justifying the adoption of enforcement measures under Chapter VII.[294] As the Charter obligations, including those contained in Articles 2(5) and 25,[295] prevail over the obligations of the member states 'under any other international agreement' (Article 103), any third-state intervention in civil strife, even those with the consent of the incumbent government, would have to be terminated or suspended if they got in the way of the Security Council action to maintain international peace and security.[296] This scenario first materialized in Congo in 1960, where the United Nations Operation in the Congo (Opération des Nations Unies au Congo—ONUC) was deployed and both the Security Council and the General Assembly prohibited all unilateral military assistance to the parties to the conflict for the duration of the UN operation.[297] In

---

[293] As seen in Chapter II, the meaning of 'intervention' under Art 2(7) is broader than under the customary principle of non-intervention, which is limited to coercive acts (Chapter II, Section 2.1).

[294] See Art 2(7), last sentence, of the UN Charter.

[295] Art 2(5) requires the member states to 'give the United Nations every assistance in any action it takes in accordance with the present Charter, and ... refrain from giving assistance to any state against which the United Nations is taking preventive or enforcement action'. Under Art 25, the member states 'agree to accept and carry out the decisions of the Security Council in accordance with the present Charter'.

[296] See Art 3(2), Rhodes Resolution. When in 1958 it intervened in Jordan, for instance, the United Kingdom explained that the intervention would end if the Security Council took measures to protect the Jordanian government from external threats (UN Doc S/PV.831, 17 July 1958, para 30). The 1947 Agreements between the United States and Turkey and Greece also provided that aid to the latter two states would be withdrawn '[i]f the Security Council of the United Nations finds (with respect to which finding the United States waives the exercise of any veto) or the General Assembly of the United Nations finds that action taken or assistance furnished by the United Nations makes the continuance of assistance by the Government of the United States pursuant to this Agreement unnecessary or undesirable' (Art 10(2), Agreement Concerning Aid to Greece; Art VI(2), Agreement Concerning Aid to Turkey (Ankara, 12 July 1947) in *A Decade of American Foreign Policy*, 546).

[297] GA Res 1474 (ES-IV), 20 September 1960, para 6, in particular, prohibited 'the direct and indirect provision of arms or other materials of war and military personnel and other assistance for military purposes in the Congo during the temporary period of military assistance through the United Nations', unless requested by the United Nations. See also SC Res 169, 24 November 1961, paras 6, 11.

236 INTERNATIONAL LAW AND THE PRINCIPLE OF NON-INTERVENTION

Resolution 1725 (2006), the Council also endorsed the Intergovernmental Authority on Development (IGAD)'s plan that ruled out any neighbouring states' deployment of troops in war-torn Somalia,[298] and in Resolution 2509 (2020) on Libya it called 'on all Member States not to intervene in the conflict or take measures that exacerbate the conflict'.[299] In other cases, the Security Council has imposed arms embargoes on all factions during internal armed conflicts.[300]

The fact that the Security Council can prohibit assistance to a government, however, has not gone uncriticized. The Soviet Union, for instance, noted that the Council's resolutions on the Congo crisis 'do not contain any provisions restricting in any way the right of the Congolese Government to request assistance directly from the Governments of other countries and to receive such assistance, just as they do not and cannot restrict the rights of states to render assistance to the Republic of the Congo'.[301] When Resolution 1559 (2004) called on all remaining foreign forces in Lebanon to withdraw from its territory, Lebanon also protested, claiming that the resolution was an interference in its internal affairs and that the Syrian troops were on its territory at its invitation.[302] In a 2000 letter to the Security Council, Libya's GNA, while 'mindful of all its commitments in relation to the relevant Security Council resolutions' on the arms embargo, reiterated 'its legitimate right under international law and international norms to defend the sovereignty and territory of Libya and protect the country's citizens by entering, as required to exercise that right, into openly declared alliances, in accordance with international law and through legitimate and transparent channels'.[303] In one case these protests are sound: when the insurgents are supported by another state and this support constitutes an armed attack under Article 51 of the UN Charter. If, in this scenario, the Council's measures resulted in depriving a state of its right to defend itself without at the same time providing it with effective protection, they would be superseded by the 'inherent' right of states to self-defence, which—according to Article 51 itself—is not 'impaired' by any Charter provision, including Chapter VII or Article 103.[304] Whether the principle of internal self-determination also constitutes a limit for Security Council involvement in a civil war is explored in Chapter V.[305]

---

[298] SC Res 1725, 6 December 2006, para 4. On this basis, it has been claimed that Ethiopia's intervention of December 2006 was unlawful (Ahmed Ali M Khayre, 'Self-Defence, Intervention by Invitation, or Proxy War? The Legality of the 2006 Ethiopian Invasion of Somalia' (2014) 22 Afr J Intl & Comp L 208, 230–1).

[299] SC Res 2509, 11 February 2020, para 6, italics omitted.

[300] As noted, if the Security Council adopts a comprehensive arms embargo against all factions in a civil war a direct intervention in support of the government would be *a fortiori* impermissible (Karine Bannelier and Theodore Christakis, 'Under the UN Security Council's Watchful Eyes: Military Intervention by Invitation in the Malian Conflict' (2013) 26 LJIL 855, 869). The Security Council, for instance, imposed an arms embargo on all factions in the conflicts in Yugoslavia (SC Res 713, 25 September 1991), Somalia (SC Res 733, 23 January 1992), Liberia (SC Res 788, 19 November 1992), Rwanda (SC Res 918, 17 May 1994), Libya (SC Res 1970), and South Sudan (SC Res 2428, 13 July 2018).

[301] UN Doc S/4503, 11 September 1960, 3.

[302] UN Doc S/PV.5028, 2 September 2004, 3. Algeria, Brazil, Pakistan, and the Philippines, which abstained from the voting, criticized the Security Council's interference in a Lebanese internal matter and in its bilateral relations with Syria without an identifiable threat to international peace and security (S/PV.5028, 5–7).

[303] UN Doc S/2020/269, 1 April 2020, Annex, 2.

[304] See Marco Roscini, 'On the "Inherent" Character of the Right of States to Self-Defence' (2013) 4 Cambridge J Int'l & Comp L 634, 658.

[305] See Section 6 of Chapter V.

5. Intervention with the Consent of Insurrectional Authorities

As Chiara Redaelli notes, '[i]t would ... be a critical inconsistency if international law protected both sovereignty and the right to rebel against it.'[306] Any consent granted by insurrectional authorities, therefore, is unable to remove the coercive character of the interference, as it is only the incumbent government that under international law is entitled to speak on behalf of a state in its relations with other states.[307] This results clearly from the formulation of the principle of non-intervention contained in the Declarations on the Inadmissibility of Intervention and on Friendly Relations, which explicitly condemn organizing, assisting, fomenting, financing, inciting, or tolerating subversive, terrorist, or armed activities directed towards the violent overthrow of the regime of another state, as well as from the similar language contained in Principle VI of the Helsinki Final Act.[308] It also emerges clearly from the *Nicaragua* Judgment, where the Court found that

> it is difficult to see what would remain of the principle of non-intervention in international law if intervention ... were also to be allowed at the request of the opposition. This would permit any State to intervene at any moment in the internal affairs of another State, whether at the request of the government or at the request of its opposition. Such a situation does not in the Court's view correspond to the present state of international law.[309]

The mere fact that states have frequently intervened in support of foreign insurgents does not contradict this conclusion: practice is in itself insufficient to generate customary rules if not accompanied by *opinio juris*.[310] Indeed, in most (if not all) cases when third states have assisted armed opposition groups, they never invoked a right to do so, but rather acted covertly and did not acknowledge the intervention.[311] When

---

[306] Chiara Redaelli, *Intervention in Civil Wars: Effectiveness, Legitimacy, and Human Rights* (Hart 2020) 255.

[307] Talmon, *Recognition*, 86.

[308] See Chapter III, Section 8.

[309] *Nicaragua v USA*, para 246.

[310] *North Sea Continental Shelf Cases (Federal Republic of Germany/Denmark; Federal Republic of Germany/The Netherlands)* (Judgment) [1969] ICJ Rep 3, para 77.

[311] See eg the logistical and territorial support provided by Yugoslavia, Albania, and Bulgaria to communist insurgents in the Greek Civil War (1946–9) (UN Doc S/PV.83, 12 December 1946, 577, 581 (Yugoslavia), S/PV.84, 16 December 1946, 595 (Albania), and S/PV.84, 597–8 (Bulgaria)); the 1946 USSR armed intervention in the Azerbaijan revolt in Iran (S/3, Appendix A, no 8, 28 January 1946, 53); the 1954 intervention of the United States, Nicaragua, and Honduras in Guatemala (S/3239, 21 June 1954; S/3242, 23 June 1954; S/3243, 24 June 1954; Arthur Mark Weisburd, *Use of Force: The Practice of States Since World War II* (Penn State University Press 1997) 211); North Vietnam's armed support for the Pathet Lao in the Laotian Civil War (1959–75) (S/4236, 5 November 1959, Annex 2, 2–3); the infiltration of United Arab Republic (UAR) forces in Lebanon (1958) (S/PV.823, 6 June 1958, paras 84, 108–9); North Vietnam's support for the Việt Cộng in South Vietnam (provision of arms, training and logistical support from 1958, sending of regular units by late 1964) (Keesing's 1961–1962, 18614); Libya's armed interventions in the civil war in Chad in 1978 and 1983 (S/12560, 14 February 1978; S/15844, 27 June 1983); the 1961 Bay of Pigs operation in Cuba (A/C.1/SR.1150, 17 April 1961, para 21); the supply of arms by Pakistan to the Jammu and Kashmir Liberation Front in India (Ko Swan Sik, 'Chronicle of Events and Incidents Relating to Asia with Relevance to International Law' (1994) 4 Asian YBIL 407, 475); Nicaragua's support of the Farabundo Martí National Liberation Front in El Salvador in the 1980s (*Nicaragua v USA*, paras 132–3); Ethiopia's support for

238 INTERNATIONAL LAW AND THE PRINCIPLE OF NON-INTERVENTION

they admitted it, they claimed that the insurgents were the legitimate government of the state in question,[312] that the incumbent government was responsible for atrocities,[313] that the conflict was a war of national liberation,[314] and that the operation had the limited purpose of protecting their nationals[315] or was non-partisan.[316] On other occasions, they relied on individual self-defence,[317] collective self-defence,[318] or a UN Security Council resolution.[319] As the ICJ found, '[i]f a State acts in a way prima facie

anti-government armed groups in Somalia in the 1980s (Weisburd, *Use of Force*, 40); Uganda's military and non-military assistance for the Rwandese Patriotic Front in Rwanda in the 1990s (S/25356, 3 March 1993); Burundi and Rwanda's intervention in the DRC at the beginning of the Second Congo War (A/53/PV.9, 22 September 1998, 3 (Burundi); A/53/PV.12, 23 September 1998, 44 (Rwanda)); Rwanda's direct intervention in the conflict in Kivu in 2004 (A/C.3/59/SR.54, 30 November 2004, para 50); Eritrea's support for the Union of Islamic Courts and al-Shabaab in Somalia (S/2006/913, 22 November 2006, Annex V, 57); Liberia and Sierra Leone's involvement in attacks carried out by armed insurgents in Guinea in 2000 (S/2000/1055, 31 October 2000, para 5; S/2000/1199, 15 December 2000, para 10); Guinea's support for Liberian dissidents carrying out attacks in Nimba County in November 2000 (S/2000/1199, para 10); Liberia's support for rebels in Sierra Leone (S/1999/17, 7 January 1999, Annex, 2; S/1999/193, 23 February 1999, Annex, 2); Pakistan's support for the Taliban against Afghanistan's government in the mid-1990s (S/1995/786, 12 September 1995, Annex, 2, 3); Russia's support for the secessionists in Donbass (2014–present) (S/PV.7253, 28 August 2014, 13); Qatar and Sudan's supply of weapons to Haftar's rebels in Libya (Tom Ruys and Nele Verlinden (eds), 'Digest of State Practice 1 July–31 December 2014' (2015) 2 JUFIL 119, 128); and Iran's support for the Houthi militia in Yemen (S/2015/207, 23 March 2015; A/71/617, 16 November 2016; S/2017/936, 7 November 2017).

[312] See eg Cuba's dispatch of military instructors and equipment and, from 5 November 1975, combat troops in support of the Movimento Popular de Libertação de Angola (MPLA) in the civil war in the African country (1966–88) (UN Doc S/11941, 24 January 1976) and the USSR's moral and material support for the MPLA (S/11947, 27 January 1976, 1–2).

[313] See Chapter VII, Section 7 and its subsections.

[314] The four African countries that recognized Biafra, for instance, referred to its struggle for self-determination and the conflict between West and East Pakistan was qualified as a war of national liberation by India and the Soviet Union (Natalino Ronzitti, 'Wars of National Liberation—A Legal Definition' (1975) 1 IYIL 192, 202–3).

[315] When Belgium sent paratroopers to Congo in 1960 with the consent of the head of the provincial government of Katanga, it cautioned that the operation was for the sole purpose of 'ensuring the safety of European and other members of the population and of protecting human lives in general' in the face of the inability of the Congolese government to protect its inhabitants and that it 'refrained from any interference in the internal policies of the Republic of the Congo' (UN Doc S/PV.873, paras 183–4, 192–3). SC Res 143 of 14 July 1960 demanded that Belgium withdraw its troops and authorized a UN operation to replace them (ONUC).

[316] See Russia's interventions in Transnistria (UN Doc A/49/114, S/1994/357, 30 March 1994; A/52/PV.16, 29 September 1997, 30–1), Tajikistan (S/24725, 28 October 1992, Annex), and Kazakhstan (Shaun Walker and Naubet Bisenov, 'Russia Paratroopers Arrive in Kazakhstan as Unrest Continues' (*The Guardian*, 6 January 2022) <www.theguardian.com/world/2022/jan/06/shots-heard-in-kazakhstan-as-protests-enter-third-day>).

[317] See India's intervention in East Pakistan in 1971 (UN Doc S/10445, 12 December 1971); Tanzania's intervention in Uganda in 1978–9 (Nicholas J Wheeler, *Saving Strangers: Humanitarian Intervention in International Society* (OUP 2003) 127); Vietnam's intervention in Kampuchea in 1978–9 (S/PV.2108, para 12; S/13011, 8 January 1979, 2); Burundi and Rwanda's intervention in the Second Congo War (S/2001/472, 11 May 2001, 6 (Burundi), S/2002/420, 15 April 2002 (Rwanda)); Uganda's intervention in the DRC from 11 September 1998 to the Lusaka Agreement (A/53/PV.95, 23 March 1999, 14; *DRC v Uganda*, paras 39, 122); the US armed intervention in Afghanistan in 2001 (S/2001/946); and Russia's intervention in Georgia in 2008 (S/2005/545, 11 August 2008; S/PV.5953, 10 August 2008, 8).

[318] See eg the US direct and indirect support of the Contras in Nicaragua in the 1980s (*Nicaragua v USA*, para 24) and Russia's 2022 intervention in Ukraine (UN Doc S/2022/154, 24 February 2022, 6).

[319] NATO's 2011 intervention in Libya (Operation Unified Protector) was based on SC Res 1973 of 17 March 2011 (Dapo Akande, 'Which Entity is the Government of Libya' (*EJIL:Talk!*, 16 June 2011) <www.ejiltalk.org/which-entity-is-the-government-of-libya-and-why-does-it-matter/>).

incompatible with a recognized rule, but defends its conduct by appealing to exceptions or justifications contained within the rule itself, then whether or not the State's conduct is in fact justifiable on that basis, the significance of that attitude is to confirm rather than to weaken the rule'.[320]

It is also not difficult to find explicit official affirmations of the illegality of interventions in any form in support of opposition groups. In the New Zealand military manual, the principle of non-intervention 'precludes States from interfering on behalf of armed groups in rebellion against the government'.[321] With regard to the 1964 operation in Stanleyville (now Kisangani), Belgium's foreign affairs minister declared that '[t]here is no interference in the domestic affairs of a country when the lawful Government of that country is given the assistance for which it asks. There is interference in the domestic affairs of a country when support is given to rebellion or revolution against the lawful Government'.[322] According to the United States, '[i]t is a universally accepted principle of international law that for one nation to arm or otherwise assist rebellious forces against another government is a hostile and aggressive act'.[323] For Côte d'Ivoire, the principle of non-intervention entails that '[n]o State has the right to send organized or unorganized armed elements into the territory of another country unless it has been requested to do so by the legally constituted Government'.[324] In Thailand's view, '[s]ince the essence of the notion of intervention [is] the usurpation of sovereignty, aid supplied to a de jure government [is] not

---

[320] *Nicaragua v USA*, para 186. An exception seems to be the support provided by several states to the Syrian opposition during the Syrian Civil War. On 19 December 2014, the US Congress adopted the National Defense Authorization Act 2015, which authorized the State and Defense Departments to supply 'assistance ... and sustainment, to appropriately vetted elements of the Syrian opposition' with the purpose of 'securing territory controlled by the Syrian opposition' and '[p]romoting the conditions for a negotiated settlement to end the conflict in Syria' (National Defense Authorization Act for Fiscal Year 2015, 19 December 2014, H.R. 3979, P.L. 113–291, Section 1209(a) <www.congress.gov/bill/113th-congress/house-bill/3979>). Other states, including the United Kingdom, France, Germany, Italy, Canada, Australia, and the Netherlands, acknowledged their supply of weapons and non-lethal aid, funding, training, and intelligence to the Syrian opposition and the Kurds (Ruys and Verlinden (eds), 'Digest of State Practice', 133–4). The EU Council initially adopted a comprehensive embargo on 'arms and related matériel of all types' to Syria (EU Council Decision 2011/273/CFSP of 9 May 2011 concerning restrictive measures against Syria, Art 1, OJ 2011 L 121/11). At the end of May 2013, the embargo was lifted in favour of the Syrian opposition under pressure from France and the United Kingdom (EU Foreign Affairs Council, Council Declaration on Syria, 27 May 2013 <www.consilium.europa.eu/uedocs/cms_data/docs/pressdata/en/foraff/137315.pdf>). The support for the Syrian opposition, however, was not uncontroversial. Unsurprisingly, Syria sent several letters to the Security Council protesting against the supply of arms and military equipment to the opposition groups (see, among many, UN Doc S/2013/533, 6 September 2013; S/2013/766, 27 December 2013). Russia did the same (Christian Henderson, 'The Provision of Arms and "Non-Lethal" Assistance to Governmental and Opposition Forces' (2013) 36 UNSWLJ 642, 679). Austria also pointed out that the provision of arms to the Syrian opposition was a breach of the principle of non-intervention and of the prohibition of the use of force (Syria: Austrian Position on Arms Embargo, 13 May 2013, 2 <www.documentcloud.org/documents/700784-austrian-position-on-arms-embargo.html>).

[321] New Zealand Defence Force, Manual of Armed Forces Law, DM 69, vol 4: Law of Armed Conflict (2nd edn, 2017) para 16.2.3.

[322] UN Doc S/PV.1173, para 73.

[323] UN Doc A/PV.82, 17 September 1947, 20.

[324] UN Doc S/PV.1203, 7 May 1965, para 21.

240 INTERNATIONAL LAW AND THE PRINCIPLE OF NON-INTERVENTION

intervention, whereas aid supplied to rebels [is] intervention, because it infringe[s] the sovereignty of the established Government'.[325]

5.1 Intervention with the Consent of Pro-Democracy Insurgents

Does the prohibition of supporting insurgents find an exception when they aim to overthrow an authoritarian regime and establish a democratic government? It is mainly (although by no means exclusively) the US government and scholarship that have championed pro-democratic intervention.[326] In his 1947 message to Congress, President Truman proclaimed that 'it must be the policy of the United States to support free peoples who are resisting attempted subjugation by armed minorities or by outside pressures'.[327] Far from alleging a right to intervene in support of foreign insurgents, however, this statement could be construed as a claim to assist governments representing the majority of the population facing (communist) armed opposition.[328] President Reagan went further and asserted that '[s]upport for freedom fighters is self-defense and totally consistent with the OAS and U.N. charters'.[329] This is because '[a] government is not legitimate merely because it exists, nor merely because it has independent rulers': legitimacy depends 'on the consent of the governed and in its respect for the rights of citizens'.[330] The US government openly funded, among others, the guerrilla forces in Afghanistan after the Soviet invasion of December 1979 and the anti-communist forces fighting the Vietnamese-backed government of Kampuchea in the 1980s.[331] More recently, the 1998 Iraq Liberation Act allocated five million US dollars to support the opposition in the Middle Eastern country in order 'to remove the regime headed by Saddam Hussein from power in Iraq and to promote the emergence of a democratic government to replace that regime'.[332] Groups eligible for support had to be 'committed to democratic values, to respect for human rights ... and to fostering cooperation among democratic opponents of the Saddam Hussein regime'.[333] In 2014,

---

[325] UN Doc A/C.1/SR.1398, 6 December 1965, para 31. See also the Legal Opinion given by the International Law Department of Switzerland's Department of Foreign Affairs, 6 May 1999, in Lucius Caflisch, 'La pratique suisse en matière de droit international public 1999' (2000) 10 RSDIDE 627, 670.

[326] For a European scholar who has supported this view, see Pietro Pustorino, *Movimenti insurrezionali e diritto internazionale* (Cacucci 2018) 251, where he argues for the existence of a special legal regime for insurgents fighting dictatorial governments.

[327] Special Message to the Congress on Greece and Turkey, 12 March 1947 (1947) 16 Dept St Bull 829, 831. See Doris A Graber, 'The Truman and Eisenhower Doctrines in the Light of the Doctrine of Non-Intervention' (1958) 73 Pol Sci Q 321, 322.

[328] The Truman Doctrine resulted in financial and military aid to the governments of Greece and Turkey against communist insurgencies in the second half of the 1940s.

[329] State of the Union Address, 6 February 1985, in *Public Papers of the Presidents of the United States, Ronald Reagan*, Book I (GPO 1985) 135. See Jeane J Kirkpatrick and Allan Gerson, 'The Reagan Doctrine, Human Rights, and International Law' in Louis Henkin and others (eds), *Right v. Might: International Law and the Use of Force* (2nd edn, Council on Foreign Relations Press 1991) 19, 23, 31–2.

[330] Kirkpatrick and Gerson, 'The Reagan Doctrine', 23.

[331] Keesing's 1987, 35121; Keesing's 1990, 37777.

[332] Iraq Liberation Act (1998), Pub L No 105-338, 112 Stat 3178 (1998).

[333] ibid, para 5(c)(2).

the US Congress also authorized aid to vetted elements of the opposition in the on-going Syrian Civil War to help them secure the territory they controlled.[334]

American scholars have provided the theoretical framework for pro-democratic intervention. In his pioneering article published in the *American Journal of International Law* in 1992, Thomas Franck famously argues for the existence of a customary right to a democratically elected government, although he stops short of claiming that unilateral pro-democratic intervention is permissible.[335] Other writers do not consider the US military operations in Central America in the 1980s inconsistent with the UN Charter.[336] For Michael Reisman, in particular, the 1989–90 intervention in Panama to put in power the democratically elected president ended the violation of the political independence of the Panamanian people by the Noriega regime.[337] Criticizing 'statist conceptions of international law', Anthony D'Amato also contends that there was no violation of Panama's territorial integrity as no parts of its territory were annexed by the United States as a consequence of the operation.[338] He concludes that interventions against tyranny are now lawful under customary international law, although he cites only two cases in support, namely, the US interventions in Grenada and Panama.[339] All in all, for the American scholars 'the objective of instituting—even imposing—a democratic governance regime where previously there was none is asserted as the value relative to which positive legal rules should be adapted'.[340]

Leaving aside the Gordian knot of what 'democracy' presently means,[341] arguing for the legality of intervention on the side of pro-democracy insurgents would have to demonstrate that 1) customary international law provides for the obligation of states to embrace a democratic form of government; and 2) compliance with this obligation may be secured through intervention and/or the use of armed force. In *Nicaragua*, the ICJ dismissed the first point and found that 'adherence by a State to any particular doctrine does not constitute a violation of customary international law'.[342] Even assuming

---

[334] HJ Res 124 Sec 149, 19 September 2014. Syria protested (see eg UN Doc S/2014/372, 28 May 2014; S/2017/183, 7 March 2017).

[335] Thomas Franck, 'The Emerging Right to Democratic Governance' (1992) 86 AJIL 46, 46, 84–5. See, more recently, Ben Achour, 'Changements', 445.

[336] W Michael Reisman, 'Coercion and Self-Determination: Construing Charter Article 2(4)' (1984) 78 AJIL 642, 642–5; Anthony D'Amato, 'The Invasion of Panama Was a Lawful Response to Tyranny' (1990) 84 AJIL 516, 520.

[337] For Reisman, 'a jurist rooted in the late twentieth century can hardly say that an invasion by outside forces to remove the caudillo and install the elected government is a violation of national sovereignty' (W Michael Reisman, 'Sovereignty and Human Rights in Contemporary International Law' (1990) 84 AJIL 866, 871).

[338] D'Amato, 'The Invasion', 520.

[339] ibid, 523.

[340] Nehal Bhuta, 'The Antinomies of Transformative Occupation' (2005) 16 EJIL 721, 723.

[341] Two notions of 'democratic government' have been proposed. The first, procedural, requires that a government be the result of free and fair elections: for Gregory Fox, for instance, democracy requires, as a minimum, 'universal and equal suffrage; a secret ballot; elections at reasonable periodic intervals; and an absence of discrimination against voters, candidates, or parties' (Gregory H Fox, 'The Right of Political Participation in International Law' (1992) 17 Yale JIL 539, 570). The second, substantive, expects a government to comply with fundamental human rights (Eliav Lieblich, *International Law and Civil Wars. Intervention and Consent* (Routledge 2013) 218–19). These two dimensions of democracy can be seen either as alternative or cumulative.

[342] *Nicaragua v USA*, para 263. See also Chapter III, Section 5.

242 INTERNATIONAL LAW AND THE PRINCIPLE OF NON-INTERVENTION

for the sake of argument that an international obligation to hold periodic and genuine elections existed, it does not automatically follow from this that states have the right to intervene in support of foreign insurgents to overthrow a dictatorial regime.[343] In fact, state practice and *opinio juris* militate against such a conclusion. Interventions that took place to enforce the results of elections, such as those in Haiti (1994), Sierra Leone (1998), and The Gambia (2017), did not rely on a right of pro-democracy intervention but on other more traditional grounds, and/or the authorities in support of which the intervention took place had been legitimized by the UN Security Council.[344] Even the United States did not resort to the democracy argument as a legal basis for its interventions in Central America.[345] In Panama, in particular, the United States indicated the defence of democracy as one of the objectives of the operation[346] but did not use this as a legal justification and relied instead on the exercise of individual self-defence against the attacks on American citizens and on the obligation to defend the integrity of the Panama Canal treaties.[347] In spite of the unpopularity of the ousted Noriega regime, the intervention was condemned as a violation of international law by many states as well as by the UN General Assembly and the OAS.[348] More recently, the states and international organizations that contested the legitimacy of the elections that confirmed Venezuela's President Maduro in office at the same time rejected the option of a military intervention to promote and defend democracy.[349]

Furthermore, several states, including France,[350] Switzerland,[351] and Uganda,[352] have explicitly expressed themselves against a right of pro-democracy intervention, and the Non-Aligned Movement members have 'rejected the illegal policies of regime

---

[343] *Nicaragua v USA*, para 262.

[344] Hasar, *State Consent*, 108–10. See also Section 4.1.2 of this chapter.

[345] In 1970, the US delegate to the Special Committee on the Definition of Aggression also argued that the doctrine of pro-democratic intervention in support of an oppressed people against a dictatorial state 'was false, both in law and in politics, and it had never been recognized by the United Nations' (UN Doc A/AC.134/SR.67-78, 19 October 1970, 98).

[346] UN Doc A/44/PV.88, 10 January 1990, 22.

[347] UN Doc S/21035, 20 December 1989.

[348] See GA Res 44/240, 29 December 1989; OAS Permanent Council Resolution 534, 22 December 1989. China, Ukraine, and Albania specifically rejected any justification based on the restoration of democracy (UN Doc A/44/PV.88, 6, 12, 16). Mexico and Colombia, among others, demanded respect for the principle of non-intervention and the self-determination of the Panamanian people (A/44/PV.88, 11, 18). Only the British delegate to the Security Council affirmed that '[f]orce was used ... only as a last resort, and against a régime which had itself turned to force to subvert the democratic process [and] with the agreement and support of the Panamanian leaders who had won last May's election' (S/PV.2899, 26), whereas Canada appreciated that the United States used force 'as a last resort, and only after the failure of numerous attempts to resolve the situation in Panama peacefully' (S/PV.2899, 28). El Salvador more cautiously welcomed the regime change without taking an express position on the legality of the intervention (S/PV.2900, 21 December 1989, 47).

[349] See Ecuador (UN Doc S/PV.8472, 41), Costa Rica (S/PV.8472, 44), China (S/PV.8506, 13), Saint Vincent and the Grenadines (S/PV.8472, 38), Germany (S/PV.8452, 26 January 2019, 15), France (S/PV.8476, 7–8), Russia (S/PV.8452, 13), the Dominican Republic (S/PV.8476, 5), Suriname (S/PV.8452, 32), Uruguay (S/PV.8452, 38-9), and the Caribbean Community (Statement by the Conference of Heads of CARICOM on the Latest Developments in the Bolivarian Republic of Venezuela, 25 January 2019 <https://web.archive.org/web/20190206024847/https://caricom.org/media-center/communications/press-relea ses/statement-by-the-conference-of-heads-of-government-of-caricom-on-the-latest-developments-in-the-situation-in-the-bolivarian-republic-of-venezuela>).

[350] UN Doc A/C.1/SR.1405, 9 December 1965, para 43.

[351] Caflisch, 'La pratique', 670.

[352] UN Doc A/C.1/SR.1399, 9 December 1965, para 36.

NON-INTERVENTION AND THE ROLE OF CONSENT   243

change aimed at overthrowing constitutional Governments, in contravention of inter-national law'.[353] In 1950, the OAS Council, acting as Provisional Organ of Consultation in the Haiti–Dominican Republic case,[354] also warned that the principles of representative democracy contained in the OAS Charter

> do not in any way and under any concept authorize any Government or group of Governments to violate the inter-American commitments relative to the principle of non-intervention or to give the appearance of legitimacy to violations of the rules contained in Article 1 of the Habana Convention of 1928 on Duties and Rights of States in the Event of Civil Strife, the Protocol Relative to Non-Intervention (Buenos Aires, 1936), and Article 15 [now 19] of the Charter of the Organization of American States.[355]

Added in 1985, Article 2(b) of the OAS Charter cautions that the Organization's new purpose 'to promote and consolidate representative democracy' can only be pursued 'with due respect for the principle of nonintervention'.

It is hardly surprising, therefore, that, in the *Nicaragua* Judgment, the ICJ could not 'contemplate the creation of a new rule opening up a right of intervention by one State against another on the ground that the latter has opted for some particular ideology or political system'.[356] All in all, Oscar Schachter spoke for many when he affirmed that this 'would introduce a new normative basis for recourse to war that would give powerful states an almost unlimited right to overthrow governments alleged to be un-responsive to the popular will or to the goal of self-determination'.[357] His conclusion remains valid to this day.[358]

That said, it has been suggested that, although states cannot intervene by using armed force in support of foreign pro-democracy movements, they can at least adopt arms embargoes and use economic coercion against a dictatorial government or its members.[359] In 2020, for instance, the United States adopted unilateral coercive measures, including the revocation of export licenses, the suspension of international agreements, and the freezing of assets of certain individuals, after protests erupted in Hong Kong in reaction to the restrictions of democratic processes imposed by the

---

[353] See eg the Declaration of the 17th Summit of Heads of State and Government of the Non-Aligned Movement, para 2 <www.pambazuka.org/global-south/declaration-17th-summit-heads-state-and-gov ernment-non-aligned-movement>.

[354] In 1950, Haiti claimed that the Dominican Republic had breached the 1947 Inter-American Treaty of Reciprocal Assistance (Rio Treaty) by attempting to overthrow its government. The Dominican Republic made similar claims against Haiti, Cuba, Guatemala, and other states (Thomas and Thomas, *Non-Intervention*, 238).

[355] ibid, 366.

[356] *Nicaragua v USA*, para 263.

[357] Oscar Schachter, 'The Legality of Pro-Democratic Invasion' (1984) 78 AJIL 645, 649.

[358] As recent history shows, 'the notion of democracy per se refuses implantation if it means to be a real democracy, which can only be grown spontaneously through a bottom-up approach' (Rim, 'Two Governments', 705). Anne Peters has also highlighted the 'potentially detrimental consequences for human security both in the concerned state and elsewhere' that might arise from considering the Western model of liberal, pluralist democracy as the only one that entitles states to full external sovereignty (Anne Peters, 'Humanity as the A and Ω of Sovereignty' (2009) 20 EJIL 513, 521).

[359] Gaetano Arangio-Ruiz, 'Autodeterminazione (diritto dei popoli alla)' in *Enciclopedia giuridica*, vol IV (Treccani 1988) 1, 10.

244 INTERNATIONAL LAW AND THE PRINCIPLE OF NON-INTERVENTION

Chinese government.[360] Sanctions have also been adopted against Belarus, Venezuela, and Myanmar for their repression of pro-democracy movements. This argument would be defensible in the framework of a treaty regime providing both for an obligation to commit to democratic principles and for enforcement measures in case of its violation (or, lacking the latter element, if the treaty obligation were an *erga omnes partes* one and all states parties were entitled under the law of state responsibility to adopt countermeasures in response to its violation). Under customary international law, however, whenever the sanction involves the breach of international law, the claim would only be supportable if there were an obligation to adopt a democratic form of government beyond treaty obligations (a conclusion that has already been discarded), the obligation were an *erga omnes* one, and any state were entitled under the law of state responsibility to adopt countermeasures to enforce compliance with it.[361]

6. Conclusions

The analysis conducted in this chapter started from two basic premises. First, the principle of non-intervention only shields a state from other states' coercive interferences in matters in which it can decide freely, that is, in its domestic affairs. Although there are now international law rules limiting how states can use force in their own territory, none exists yet to specifically regulate whether a state can do so. As a result, a state, through its government, does not in principle breach international law for the mere fact of using armed coercion to maintain or restore internal order and third states are equally free to assist it if so requested (unless prevented from doing so by a UN resolution or a treaty). It is only when the insurgents succeed in establishing a new state or are recognized as belligerents that the application of the principle of non-intervention is displaced: the use of force in support of *any* party must at this point be consistent with the *jus contra bellum* rules codified in the UN Charter. Forms of intervention short of armed force, on the other hand, are permissible unless prohibited by treaties or by Security Council resolutions, although they could constitute an unneutral act that might lead the affected belligerent to retaliate.

Secondly, the principle of non-intervention prohibits interventions *against* a state but leaves unaffected those to which it consents. Unlike in a neutrality regime, therefore, third states are not required to treat equally the different factions of the civil strife: they can support the incumbent government upon its request and are at the same time prohibited from giving any assistance to opposition groups in spite of their appeal. In the case of rival governmental administrations, the one that was in effective

---

[360] Stefano Saluzzo, 'The Principle of Non-Intervention and the Battle over Hong Kong' (2021) 79 Quest Intl L 27, 31. In a statement backed by fifty-three countries in the UN Human Rights Council, China replied by accusing the Western states of interfering in its internal affairs and of breaching the UN Charter (Statement by the Permanent Mission of the People's Republic of China to the United Nations Office at Geneva and Other International Organizations in Switzerland (30 June 2020), quoted ibid, 32).

[361] Art 54 of ARSIWA does not take position on whether states can adopt countermeasures in response to the violation of *erga omnes* and *erga omnes partes* obligations when they are not specially affected by their breach. The case of a government that is not only authoritarian but also commits serious international human rights law and international humanitarian law violations is examined in Chapter VII.

control of the state's territory, population, and apparatus at the beginning of the civil strife continues to be entitled to consent to foreign intervention until it is defeated or until its resistance becomes merely nominal: the unworkable alternative would be that governmental status shifts from faction to faction depending on the military situation on the field. If the incumbent has been defeated and no other faction has sufficient effective control of the country to be able to claim governmental status, the preferable view is that an intervention to restore a functioning state or protect civilians can only be carried out with the authorization of the Security Council under Chapter VII of the UN Charter.

Consent to intervention constitutes an agreement between the intervening state and that where the intervention takes place and can be granted in writing or orally, publicly or secretly, expressly or implicitly, but cannot be presumed. State practice shows that treaty-based open-ended consent needs to be confirmed before each intervention can validly take place, unless the object and purpose of the treaty is to allow interventions (normally to be undertaken by or through an international organization) if certain events occur even when it is the target state's government that is responsible for them. Furthermore, a state may only consent to intervention on its territory (as consent exclusively operates in the relations between the consenter and the consentee) and only to acts that it could itself lawfully undertake. Last but not least, consent must be valid and the limits attached to it must be respected for it to produce its effects.

V

The Interaction between the Principle of Non-Intervention and that of Internal Self-Determination

1. Introduction

As seen in Chapter III, the principle of non-intervention prohibits interferences when 1) they are coercive and 2) fall 'on matters in which each State is permitted, by the principle of State sovereignty, to decide freely'.[1] The first element entails that an intervention in another state by invitation of its government is not unlawful (in fact, it is not even an 'intervention'), while any assistance for opposition groups is impermissible despite their request.[2] As to the second element, the UN Charter era has seen the emergence and consolidation of new customary rules and principles that have moved away from a purely statist idea of sovereignty and (at least in certain circumstances) have lifted the veil of domestic jurisdiction over the maintenance of internal order.[3] The question is whether these rules and principles have affected the normal application of the principle of non-intervention by allowing third states to support insurgents and/or by preventing them from intervening on the side of an incumbent government.[4]

This chapter starts the analysis of these rules and principles from that of internal self-determination. It begins by clarifying the scope of this principle and by distinguishing it from the principle of non-intervention. It next identifies the situations of internal unrest to which it applies, namely civil wars, and its consequences for pro-government intervention. The chapter continues by exploring the situations where third- state dispatch of armed forces in a civil war is not at odds with the principle of internal self-determination, that is, counter-intervention and counterterrorism. The final part discusses whether the United Nations can set aside the principle of internal self-determination and intervene, or authorize an intervention, in a civil war. While

---

[1] *Case Concerning Military and Paramilitary Activities in and against Nicaragua (Nicaragua v United States)* (Merits) [1986] ICJ Rep 3, para 205 (hereafter *Nicaragua v USA*).

[2] See Chapter IV, Section 3.

[3] Valentina Grado, *Guerre civili e terzi stati* (CEDAM 1998) 105–6. The application of the principle of non-intervention can also be affected by certain treaties but the present analysis focuses on the interaction between customary rules.

[4] Para 2 of the Friendly Relations Declaration stresses that the principles contained therein, including that of non-intervention, 'are interrelated and each principle should be construed in the context of the other principles.' See GA Res 2625 (XXV), 24 October 1970, para 2. According to the Netherlands, in particular, the principle of non-intervention must be reconciled with 'other fundamental principles such as the right of self-determination and the respect for human rights' (UN Doc A/32/164, 2 September 1977, 7).

International Law and the Principle of Non-Intervention. Marco Roscini, Oxford University Press. © Marco Roscini 2024.
DOI: 10.1093/oso/9780198786894.003.0006

briefly introduced, third-state intervention in civil strife involving a racist regime is more comprehensively addressed, together with colonial domination, in Chapter VI.

2. The Principle of Internal Self-Determination

As seen in Chapter I, the principle of non-intervention formed as a corollary of the sovereign equality of states.[5] In particular, it is one of the legal instruments protecting state sovereignty, which has both a territorial and decisional dimension: the former is a state's exclusive jurisdiction in a defined portion of the globe (territorial inviolability),[6] while the latter entails that a state may 'conduct its affairs without outside interference' (political independence).[7] Political independence includes the right to 'internal' self-determination,[8] that is, to determine one's own political, economic, social, and cultural system without external interferences, a right of states that formed before the UN Charter and is now incorporated in Article 3(e) of the Charter of the Organization of American States (OAS), General Assembly Resolutions 2131 and 2625 (which qualify it as 'inalienable')[9] and other resolutions,[10] as well as in the Helsinki Final Act.[11]

The main difference between the principle of non-intervention and that of internal self-determination is that the former prohibits coercive acts in the domestic affairs of another state while the latter proscribes all interferences, although only in the choice of the political, economic, social, and cultural systems. The principle of internal self-determination, therefore, is broader than that of non-intervention with regard to the prohibited conduct, but narrower in respect of the protected object. That said, as the UN Committee on Human Rights has highlighted, the two principles are closely interrelated and an intervention in the domestic affairs of other states will likely also adversely affect the right to self-determination.[12] A state invading another in order to

---

[5] See Chapter I, Section 2. See also *Nicaragua v USA*, para 202.

[6] *Island of Palmas Case (Netherlands, United States)*, 4 April 1928, 2 RIAA 829, 838.

[7] *Nicaragua v USA*, para 202. See Rosario Sapienza, *Il principio del non intervento negli affari interni. Contributo allo studio della tutela giuridica internazionale della potestà di governo* (Giuffrè 1990) 164–5.

[8] The International Law Commission (ILC)'s Draft Declaration on Rights and Duties of States, for instance, affirms that '[e]very State has the right to independence and hence to exercise freely, without dictation by any other state, all its legal powers, *including* the choice of its own form of government' ([1949] YB ILC 286, 287, emphasis added).

[9] GA Resolutions 2131 and 2625 contain a more succinct version of Art 3(e) of the OAS Charter and add the cultural system to those that every state has the right to freely choose without external interferences. See GA Resolutions 2131 (XX), 21 December 1965, para 1, and 2625 (XXV), Annex, fifth principle, para 1, and Art 3 of the Charter of the Organization of American States (Bogotá, 30 April 1948) 119 UNTS 3. Gaetano Arangio-Ruiz finds the reference to the right of a state to choose its cultural system contained in the Friendly Relations Declaration 'appalling' (Gaetano Arangio-Ruiz, 'Human Rights and Non-Intervention in the Helsinki Final Act' (1977) 157 Recueil des Cours 195, 271). In his view, this must be understood as a freedom of individuals or groups (ibid).

[10] See, in particular, the resolutions on the elimination of coercive economic measures as a means of political and economic compulsion, such as GA Resolutions 51/22, 6 December 1996, para 1, and 53/10, 3 November 1998, para 2.

[11] Principle I, Final Act of the 1st CSCE Summit of Heads of State or Government (Helsinki, 1 August 1975) (1975) 14 ILM 1292. The Helsinki Final Act also refers to the right of a state to determine its own laws and regulations.

[12] UN Doc A/39/40, 20 September 1984, 143. Several states have also noted that the principles of non-intervention and self-determination, although distinct, are closely interconnected, including Bolivia (A/PV.677, 13 September 1957, para 168), Denmark (A/PV.677, para 141), Belgium (S/PV.746, 28 October

248 INTERNATIONAL LAW AND THE PRINCIPLE OF NON-INTERVENTION

impose a certain political regime, for instance, would breach not only the principle of non-intervention and the prohibition of the use of force, but also the principle of internal self-determination.[13]

The other important difference between the principles of non-intervention and of internal self-determination is that, although they both act as shields from external interferences, the main purpose of the latter is now not to protect states but their peoples.[14] Said otherwise, '[i]nternal self-determination is ... a concept that seeks to protect the internal sovereignty of the state by protecting the sovereignty of the people within'.[15] This explicitly results from the Declaration on Friendly Relations, which includes the right of 'all peoples ... freely to determine, without external interference, their political status and to pursue their economic, social and cultural development' under the principle of equal rights and self-determination.[16] Analogous language is contained in Principle VIII of the Helsinki Final Act.[17] It is important to note that, in its internal dimension, 'the bearer of the right to self-determination (and consequently the right to freedom from foreign intervention) is the entire population living on the territory of the state and not "the people" as a group with distinctive ethnic or cultural characteristics'.[18]

1956, para 185), Cuba (S/PV.752, 2 November 1956, para 96), France (S/PV.752, para 110), the United States (A/33/216, 21 September 1978, 32), Chile (A/C.1/SR.1402, 8 December 1965, para 44), El Salvador (A/44/PV.88, 10 January 1990, 33), and the United Arab Republic (UAR) (A/C.1/SR.1403, 9 December 1965, para 3, and A/C.6/SR.875, 15 November 1965, para 40).

[13] Antonio Cassese, *Self-Determination of Peoples: A Legal Reappraisal* (CUP 1995) 138. France, for instance, noted that the Warsaw Pact's 1968 intervention in Czechoslovakia was not only an 'open intervention in the internal affairs of a State', but also an infringement of the right of peoples to self-determination (UN Doc S/PV.1441, 21 August 1968, para 175). In a memorandum dated 29 December 1979, the legal adviser of the US State Department also argued that '[t]he use of Soviet troops forcibly to depose one ruler and substitute another clearly is a use of force against the political independence of Afghanistan; and it just as clearly contravenes the principle of Afghanistan's equal international rights and the self-determination of the Afghan people' (text in Marian Nash Leich (ed), 'Contemporary Practice of the United States Relating to International Law' (1980) 74 AJIL 418, 418). With regard to the US invasion of Grenada, the violation of the right of self-determination of the Grenadian people was emphasized by Nicaragua (S/16069, 25 October 1983, Annex), Madagascar (S/16088, 28 October 1983, Annex), and Yugoslavia (S/16086, 26 October 1983, Annex). Nigel White also notes that the US embargo on Cuba breaches the principle of non-intervention because of its coercive nature *and* amounts to a denial of the self-determination of Cuba and of the Cuban people because it aims at preventing the economic development of the island and at removing its government (Nigel D White, *The Cuban Embargo under International Law: El Bloqueo* (Routledge 2016) 142).

[14] See *Reference re Secession of Québec* [1998] 2 SCR 217, paras 113 ff; Report of the Independent International Fact-Finding Mission on the Conflict in Georgia, September 2009, vol II, 277 (fn 180) <www.mpil.de/files/pdf4/IIFFMCG_Volume_II1.pdf> (hereafter IIFFMCG Report).

[15] Kalana Senaratne, *Internal Self-Determination in International Law: History, Theory, and Practice* (CUP 2021) 18.

[16] GA Res 2625 (XXV), Annex, fifth principle, para 1.

[17] Helsinki Final Act, Principle VIII, para 2. The right of peoples to internal self-determination has also been incorporated in Art 1(1) of the 1966 International Covenant on Civil and Political Rights (New York, 16 December 1966) 999 UNTS 171; Art 1(1) of the International Covenant on Economic, Social and Cultural Rights (New York, 16 December 1966) 993 UNTS 3; Art 20(1) of the African Charter on Human and Peoples' Rights (Banjul, 27 June 1981) 1520 UNTS 217; and Art 2(1) of the Arab Charter on Human Rights (Tunis, 22 May 2004) (2005) 12 International Human Rights Reports 893.

[18] Wouter G Werner, 'Self-Determination and Civil War' (2001) 6 JCSL 171, 189. Whether peoples are really the holders of a 'right' to self-determination or merely the beneficiaries of a rule that exclusively addresses states is a question that exceeds the bounds of this book. In favour of self-determination as a right of peoples proper, see, among many, Stefan Oeter, 'Self-Determination' in Bruno Simma and others (eds), *The Charter of the United Nations: A Commentary*, vol I (3rd edn, OUP 2012) 313, 325–7. Against, see

NON-INTERVENTION AND INTERNAL SELF-DETERMINATION   249

In the aforementioned instruments, the principle of internal self-determination only proscribes *external* interferences in the choice by a people of its political, economic, social, and cultural systems, that is, those by other states. Reproducing verbatim the language of the Declaration on the Granting of Independence to Colonial Countries and Peoples,[19] however, Article 1 of the 1966 International Covenants on Civil and Political Rights and on Economic, Social and Cultural Rights defines the right of self-determination as the right of peoples to 'freely determine their political status and freely pursue their economic, social and cultural development' without distinguishing between internal and external interferences. As Antonio Cassese notes, 'freely' in this context has a twofold meaning: it 'requires that a State's domestic political institutions must be free from outside interference' and 'that the people choose their legislators and political leaders free from any manipulation or undue influence from the domestic authorities themselves'.[20] As the Italian scholar himself concedes, however, this broader version of the right of internal self-determination, supported by the Western states during the Cold War, is not sufficiently reflected in the general practice and *opinio juris* of states.[21] Judge Yusuf concurs: in his view, 'we have not yet reached the stage when the denial of the will of the people [by their own government] is considered an infringement of the right to self-determination, even though certain standards and criteria are slowly developing which would result in reaching that stage'.[22]

The right of internal self-determination, therefore, is not coterminous with a right to a democratically elected government and merely involves an obligation on states to abstain from interfering in the choice of another country's political, economic, social, and cultural system by its people, whatever that system might be.[23] In other words,

---

Gaetano Arangio-Ruiz, *The United Nations Declaration on Friendly Relations and the System of the Sources of International Law* (Sijthoff & Noordhoff 1979) 141; Daniel Thürer and Thomas Burri, 'Self-Determination' in *MPEPIL Online* (last updated December 2008) para 26; Giuseppe Palmisano, 'Autodeterminazione dei popoli' in *Enciclopedia del diritto*, vol V (Giuffrè 2012) 82, 121; Carlo Focarelli, *International Law* (Elgar 2019) 67. Applying Hohfeld's classification, Anthony Whelan concludes that self-determination is a 'power' (Anthony Whelan, 'Wilsonian Self-Determination and the Versailles Settlement' (1994) 43 Intl & Comp LQ 99, 106–10).

[19] Declaration on the Granting of Independence to Colonial Countries and Peoples (GA Res 1514 (XV), 14 December 1960, para 2. The 1960 Declaration's language is also reproduced in Art 3 of the 2007 UN Declaration on the Rights of Indigenous Peoples (GA Res 61/295, 13 September 2007) and, with minor variations, in Art 20(1) of the African Charter on Human and Peoples' Rights.
[20] Cassese, *Self-Determination*, 53, 55, emphasis omitted.
[21] ibid, 102. As Jean Salmon points out, '[t]he right to self-determination was conceived as an exogenous right, protecting the people from outside interference. It was not an endogenous right protecting the rights of the people against its own government' (Jean Salmon, 'Internal Aspects of the Right to Self-Determination: Towards a Democratic Legitimacy Principle?' in Christian Tomuschat (ed), *Modern Law of Self-Determination* (Nijhoff 1993) 253, 265). See also Mohamed Bennouna, *Le consentement à l'ingérence militaire dans les conflits internes* (Libraire générale de droit et de jurisprudence 1974) 57–8; Théodore Christakis and Karine Bannelier, '*Volenti non fit injuria*? Les effets du consentement à l'intervention militaire' (2004) 50 AFDI 102, 119–20; Louise Doswald-Beck, 'The Legal Validity of Military Intervention by Invitation of the Government' (1985) 56 BYBIL 189, 203.
[22] Abdulqawi A Yusuf, 'The Role That Equal Rights and Self-Determination of Peoples Can Play in the Current World Community' in Antonio Cassese (ed), *Realizing Utopia: The Future of International Law* (OUP 2012) 375, 385.
[23] Doswald-Beck, 'The Legal Validity', 207. This means that 'the right of self-determination may amount, as a matter of practical application, to the right to be ruled by domestic thugs rather than by foreigners announcing benevolent intentions' (Brad R Roth, *Governmental Illegitimacy in International Law* (OUP 1999)

the principle of internal self-determination is politically neutral and only prescribes *how* an internal system must (not) be chosen or modified, but not *which* one: as the UN General Assembly declared, 'there is no single political system or single model for electoral processes equally suited to all nations and their peoples'.[24] In the Advisory Opinion on *Western Sahara*, the International Court of Justice (ICJ) confirmed that '[n]o rule of international law ... requires the structure of a state to follow any particular pattern, as is evident from the diversity of the forms of State found in the world today'.[25] This view was restated in *Nicaragua*, where the Court emphasized that

> adherence by a State to any particular doctrine does not constitute a violation of customary international law; to hold otherwise would make nonsense of the fundamental principle of State sovereignty, on which the whole of international law rests, and the freedom of choice of the political, social, economic and cultural system of a State.[26]

Indeed, while it is true that the democratic form of government has spread across most continents since the end of the Cold War, there is still not sufficient evidence that its adoption is considered by states the object of an international obligation beyond specific treaty regimes. If anything, the continued existence of a significant number of authoritarian regimes, as well as the emergence of 'illiberal democracies' in certain countries in the last two decades, is evidence to the contrary. At best, one can say that the principle of internal self-determination now requires that a government be *representative* of the whole population of the concerned state, although international law still presumes the representative character from the capacity of an authority to exercise legislative, executive, and judicial powers that are met with the obedience of the community and to apply coercion in case of disobedience.[27] The presumption, however, is reversed if the incumbent has been voted out as a result of free and fair elections. It is also under stress for the whole duration of a civil war, as popular sovereignty is in the process of being redetermined by violent means: it is to this situation that the analysis now turns.

3. Third-State Intervention in Civil Wars

A people can choose their state's political system peacefully, namely, through some formal decision-making procedure by which a group, more or less ample, chooses

---

415). Anne Peters agrees: the principle of self-determination must 'be understood to protect the capacity to choose a political system commensurate with one's national culture, even if this results in an illiberal and authoritarian regime' (Anne Peters, 'Humanity as the A and Ω of Sovereignty' (2009) 20 EJIL 513, 541). For Salmon, the only exception to the irrelevance of the characteristics of an internal regime for international law is that of Nazi-Fascist regimes (Salmon, 'Internal Aspects', 260). To these situations, one can add that of an apartheid regime (see Section 7 of this chapter).

[24] GA Res 45/150, 18 December 1990, Preamble. See also GA Res 45/151, 18 December 1990, Preamble.
[25] *Western Sahara* (Advisory Opinion) [1975] ICJ Rep 12, para 94.
[26] *Nicaragua v USA*, para 263.
[27] Roth, *Governmental Illegitimacy*, 414.

individuals to hold public office,[28] or through violence. In both situations, a normative conflict can emerge between the principle of non-intervention, which prohibits third-state support for opposition groups but not that for the incumbent government upon its request, and the principle of internal self-determination, which proscribes all external interferences. Regardless of whether or not one considers it a *jus cogens* rule,[29] the latter principle takes priority over the former on the basis of both the *lex posterior derogat priori* and *lex specialis derogat generali* maxims. Indeed, as has been seen, internal self-determination, as a principle protecting peoples, is of far more recent coinage than the principle of non-intervention.[30] It also constitutes the special law applicable to processes for the determination of the political system of a state by its people, while the principle of non-intervention generally protects all matters in which a state can decide freely.

What results from the application of the principle of internal self-determination is an obligation of 'negative equality', which prevents states from interfering not only to impose a new government in another state but also to maintain an incumbent one in power notwithstanding its request of assistance: if internal self-determination is a right of peoples, then a government cannot dispose of it by consenting to external interferences when a process for the determination of the political, economic, social, or cultural system of a state has been set in motion, either by ballot or by bullet.[31] This is because 'the displacement of the internal political structure [must] be an authentic decision of the sovereign political community'.[32] It is important to point out that, unlike in the situations that are explored in Chapters VI and VII, the illegality of an intervention in support of a government in this case is not a sanction for a violation of international law, but the result of a normative conflict between the principle of non-intervention and that of internal self-determination which, as mentioned in Section 3, must be settled in favour of the latter.

To be clear, the principle of internal self-determination does not prohibit *any* involvement in a situation of internal unrest in another state, but only those that can affect the outcome of a process for the modification of a state's political system. What counts is not the purpose of the intervention as argued by some commentators,[33] but its *impact*: even assuming that the intervening state did not intend to influence the internal political struggle for power, its actual conduct might still result in advantaging one faction to the detriment of another.[34] This was the case, for instance, of the

---

[28] As has been observed, 'China, Singapore and Vietnam are all well-known for their authoritarian orientation and one-party regimes. Yet, these countries also employ different types of popular electoral processes to justify their role in their internal politics' (Quoc Tan Trung Nguyen, 'Rethinking the Legality of Intervention by Invitation: Toward Neutrality' (2019) 24 JCSL 201, 214).

[29] For Cassese, the entire principle of self-determination, in both its external and internal aspects, now belongs to the body of peremptory norms as, when states have referred to self-determination as *jus cogens*, they have not made any distinctions (Cassese, *Self-Determination*, 140). Matthew Craven, on the other hand, is more cautious (Matthew Craven, 'The European Community Arbitration Commission on Yugoslavia' (1995) 66 BYBIL 333, 382–3).

[30] See Chapter I, Section 8.

[31] Gerhard Hafner, Final Report, in (2009) 73 AIDI 364, 410.

[32] Brad R Roth, 'Legitimacy in the International Order: The Continuing Relevance of Sovereign States' (2021) 11 ND J Intl & Comp L 60, 73.

[33] See Chapter II, Section 7.2.5.

[34] Olivier Corten, 'Is an Intervention at the Request of a Government Always Allowed? From a "Purpose-Based Approach" to the Respect of Self-Determination' (2019) 79 ZaöRV 677, 679; Veronika Bílková,

252 INTERNATIONAL LAW AND THE PRINCIPLE OF NON-INTERVENTION

joint Belgian–US operation in Stanleyville (now Kisangani) in 1964, the Economic Community of West African States (ECOWAS) intervention in Liberia in 1990, the French intervention in Côte d'Ivoire in 2011, and the NATO airstrikes in Libya of the same year: in spite of their declared purposes (evacuation of nationals, protection of civilians), their consistency with the principle of internal self-determination can be doubted.

The crux of the matter is to identify exactly what situations of internal unrest trigger the application of the principle of internal self-determination and result in an obligation of negative equality, as clearly not any street demonstration constitutes a process for the modification of a state's political system.[35] As seen in Chapter I, since at least the 19th century, the idea of third-state 'neutrality' with respect to civil strife occurring in another country has been linked to the occurrence of a civil war, seen as the quintessential attempt to change the political system of a state by violent means.[36] What remains controversial, however, is what 'civil war' means in the context of the law of intervention, a question that is addressed in the following pages.

3.1 The Meaning of 'Civil War' in the Context of the Principle of Internal Self-Determination

As is well known, contemporary international humanitarian law (IHL) has dropped the use of the 'civil war' language in favour of the more objective (but less catchy) expression 'non-international armed conflict' (NIAC).[37] In order to define the threshold for the application of the principle of internal self-determination, however, one should resist the temptation of mechanically importing notions employed in other legal regimes.[38] Indeed, if, in IHL, the definition of NIAC has emerged *in opposition* to that of international armed conflict, the notion of civil war in the law of intervention has always been based on its *similarity* to a war between states: as Emer de Vattel puts it,

---

'Reflections on the Purpose-Based Approach' (2019) 79 ZaöRV 681, 683; Patrick M Butchard, 'Territorial Integrity, Political Independence, and Consent: The Limitations of Military Assistance on Request under the Prohibition of Force' (2020) 7 JUFIL 35, 65–6.

[35] As has been noted, '[i]f, in the event of even the slightest symptoms of an internal conflict, relations with the government were to be suspended, inter-state contacts would be virtually impossible' (Henk J Leurdijk, 'Civil War and Intervention in International Law' (1977) 24 NILR 143, 146).

[36] Grado, *Guerre civili*, 149.

[37] David Armitage notes that '[t]he reluctance to call the conflict a civil war has become typical of international organizations in the twenty-first century because so much—politically, militarily, legally, and ethically—now hangs on the use or withholding of the term' (David Armitage, *Civil Wars: A History in Ideas* (Yale University Press 2017) 208). For Andrew Clapham, however, the language of 'civil war' is still widely used by media and government authorities (Andrew Clapham, *War* (OUP 2021) 257).

[38] In the Institut de droit international's Rhodes Resolution, for instance, the threshold is whether or not the situation of internal unrest falls under the scope of application of the Protocol Additional to the Geneva Conventions of 12 August 1949, and relating to the Protection of Victims of Non-International Armed Conflicts (Protocol II) (Art 2(1) of the Resolution on Military Assistance on Request of the Institut de droit international (Rhodes Resolution), 8 September 2011 <www.idi-iil.org/app/uploads/2017/06/2011 _rhodes_10_C_en.pdf>).

NON-INTERVENTION AND INTERNAL SELF-DETERMINATION   253

a civil war 'stands on the same ground, in every respect, as a public war between two different nations'.[39]

A 2007 note to the UN assistant secretary-general for political affairs usefully defines civil war as 'a notion of two warring factions within a State ... fighting for the control of the political system or secession, each having effective control over parts of the State territory'.[40] This definition differs from that of NIAC in two important respects. First, if the purpose pursued by the armed group is irrelevant for the application of the *jus in bello* rules (apart from the case of 'national liberation movements', to which we return in Chapter VI),[41] in the context of the law of intervention a civil war has been conceived as a conflict where one of the parties is an organized armed group with political objectives (typically to overthrow the incumbent government or to secure secession or autonomy of part of the state's territory).[42] The pursuit of a political objective is what links civil wars to the principle of internal self-determination, as the latter only becomes relevant when a process for the modification of a state's political system has been set in motion. Whatever its intensity, therefore, civil strife exclusively involving criminal organizations, like the 'drug wars' in Mexico, is not a civil war for the purposes of the law of intervention, although it might constitute a NIAC under the *jus in bello*.

The political objectives of the insurgents, however, are insufficient on their own to trigger an obligation of negative equality under the principle of internal self-determination: a small group of pro-democracy protesters clearly does not represent a sufficient challenge to the incumbent's authority so as to start a process for the modification of their state's political system. The intensity of the internal unrest, therefore, also plays an important role in this context: the more widespread and serious the political opposition to the government, the more under threat the principle of internal self-determination in the case of foreign intervention. At least since the second half

---

[39] Emer de Vattel, *Le droit des gens ou Principes de la loi naturelle appliqués à la conduite et aux affaires des nations et des souverains* (1758), tr by Béla Kapossy and Richard Whatmore as *The Law of Nations, Or, The Principles of the Law of Nature, Applied to the Conduct and Affairs of Nations and Sovereigns, with three Early Essays on the Origin and Nature of Natural Law and on Luxury* (Liberty Fund 2008) 648.

[40] (2007) United Nations Juridical Yearbook 458, 459.

[41] The International Criminal Tribunal for the Former Yugoslavia (ICTY), in particular, has found that '[t]he determination of the existence of an armed conflict is based solely on two criteria: the intensity of the conflict and organization of the parties, the purpose of the armed forces to engage in acts of violence or also achieve some further objective is, therefore, irrelevant' (*Prosecutor v Limaj et al*, Trial Chamber, Judgment, IT-03-66-T, 30 November 2005, para 170 <https://www.icty.org/x/cases/limaj/tjug/en/lim-tj051 130-e.pdf>).

[42] Art 1 of the Institut de droit international's Wiesbaden Resolution defines a civil war as 'opposition between established government and one or more insurgent movements whose aim is to overthrow the government or the political, economic or social order of the State, or to achieve secession or self-government for any part of that State', or between such armed groups in the absence of an established government (Resolution on the Principle of Non-Intervention in Civil Wars of the Institut de droit international (Wiesbaden Resolution), 14 August 1975 <www.idi-iil.org/app/uploads/2017/06/1975_wies_03_en.pdf>). Several scholars have also emphasized the political objectives pursued by the insurgents in civil wars. See eg Roger Pinto, 'Les règles du droit international concernant la guerre civile' (1965) 114 Recueil des Cours 451, 464; Ross R Oglesby, 'A Search for Legal Norms in Contemporary Situations of Civil Strife' (1970) 3 Case Western Reserve JIL 30, 34; Ramaa P Dhokalia, 'Civil Wars and International Law' (1971) 11 IJIL 219; Bennouna, *Le consentement*, 14; Peter Malanczuk, *Akehurst's Modern Introduction to International Law* (7th edn, Routledge 1997) 318; Marco Pertile, *Diritto internazionale e rapporti economici nelle guerre civili* (Editoriale Scientifica 2020) 111.

254 INTERNATIONAL LAW AND THE PRINCIPLE OF NON-INTERVENTION

of the 19th century,[43] the most significant indicators of such intensity have been the loss of effective control by the incumbent government over parts of the national territory[44] and the establishment therein of a *de facto* administration through which the insurgents exercise some form of governance over a collectivity of people.[45] Partial loss of effective territorial control by the incumbent does not per se result in loss of its governmental status (at least until it continues to offer more than nominal resistance),[46] but is the strongest indication that an internal process for the modification of a state's political system is under way. This is the second difference between the notion of NIAC under IHL and that of civil war in the law of intervention: the former does not necessarily require for its existence that the insurgents have any stable control of territory as long as they are organized and able to conduct hostilities of a sufficient intensity.[47]

Whenever insurgents with political objectives succeed 'in controlling a modicum of territory and setting up an operational structure capable of effectively wielding authority over the individuals living there',[48] therefore, they acquire international legal personality and the internal unrest becomes a civil war, that is, 'a process of competitive state building'.[49] The following sections examine whether, in this scenario, there is general state practice and *opinio juris* confirming that, under existing customary international law, third states are under an obligation not to intervene on the side of

[43] Art 8 of the Neuchâtel Resolution of the Institut de droit international, for instance, requires that the insurgents have gained control of a certain part of the national territory, set up a provisional government that exercises the rights normally attached to sovereignty over that territory, and conduct hostilities with organized troops, subject to military discipline, and consistently with the laws and customs of war (Institut de droit international, Resolution on the Droits et devoirs des Puissances étrangères, au cas de mouvement insurrectionnel, envers les gouvernements établis et reconnus qui sont aux prises avec l'insurrection (Neuchâtel, 8 September 1900) (1900) AIDI 227). See also the analysis of the doctrine of recognition of belligerency developed in Chapter I, Section 7.5.3.

[44] That this indicator is still relevant has been confirmed by the Inter-American Commission on Human Rights (IACHR) in the *Abella* case, where the IACHR found that a situation 'in which dissident armed groups exercise control over parts of national territory' is 'comparable to a civil war' (IACHR, *Juan Carlos Abella v Argentina*, Case 11.137 (Judgment) 18 November 1997, para 152 <https://www.cidh.oas.org/annualrep/97eng/argentina11137.htm>).

[45] This scenario has been termed 'rebelocracy' (Ana Arjona, 'Wartime Institutions: A Research Agenda' (2014) 58 J Conflict Resol 1360, 1375) and occurs 'only after an insurgent organization gains control over territory that contains civilians and decides to create or encourage civilian structures … to organize civilians living within rebel territory' (Nelson Kasfir, 'Rebel Governance—Constructing a Field of Inquiry: Definitions, Scope, Patterns, Order, Causes' in Ana Arjona, Nelson Kasfir, and Zacharaiah Mampilly (eds), *Rebel Governance in Civil War* (CUP 2015) 21, 27). As an English court has noted, the notion of government does not necessarily need to correspond to 'Western ideas', as 'different types of a structure may exist … which may legitimately come within the ambit of an authority, which wields power sufficient to constitute an official body' (*R v Zardad (Faryadi)*, Judgment and Rulings Pursuant to First Preparatory Hearing, Case No T2203 7676, ILDC 95 (UK 2004), 7 April 2004, para 33).

[46] See Chapter IV, Section 4.1.2.1. The view that, in a NIAC, neither the government nor the opposition are entitled to represent the state would lead to the undesirable result that such state would be left without representation in its international relations.

[47] *Prosecutor v Duško Tadić*, Appeals Chamber, Decision on the Defence Motion for Interlocutory Appeal on Jurisdiction, IT-94-1-AR72, 2 October 1995, para 70 <www.icty.org/x/cases/tadic/acdec/en/51002.htm> (hereafter *Prosecutor v Tadić*). Control of territory by the armed groups, however, is necessary for the application of Additional Protocol II (Art 1(1)).

[48] Paola Gaeta, Jorge E Viñuales, and Salvatore Zappalà, *Cassese's International Law* (3rd edn, OUP 2020) 167.

[49] Stathis N Kalyvas, *The Logic of Violence in Civil War* (CUP 2006) 218.

NON-INTERVENTION AND INTERNAL SELF-DETERMINATION   255

any faction, including the incumbent government.[50] Section 3.2 discusses intervention by sending armed forces, while Section 3.3 addresses other forms of intervention. The analysis in this chapter mainly focuses on civil wars aimed at *internal* political changes, while secessionist civil wars are analysed in Chapter VI.[51]

3.2 State Practice and *Opinio Juris* Concerning the Dispatch of Armed Forces in Support of an Incumbent Government Beset by Civil War

As seen in Chapter I, at the dawn of the UN Charter era the customary international law of intervention provided as follows: in the absence of recognition of belligerency, a situation of rebellion or insurrection continued to be regulated by the principle of non-intervention and third states were thus permitted to assist the incumbent government at its valid request but were prohibited from assisting the insurgents in any form. When recognition of belligerency was granted, on the other hand, the internal unrest became a *de jure* war, with the result that third states had the choice between taking either side and becoming co-belligerents (consistently with the *jus ad bellum* rules in force at the time) or applying the law of neutrality.

Has the consolidation of the principle of internal self-determination as a legal rule had an impact on post-1945 state practice and *opinio juris*? In particular, is there any 'general practice accepted as law'[52] in favour of a prohibition on intervening in support of *any* faction in a civil war, and not only the insurgents? What needs to be demonstrated is not that a right exists to assist a government in a civil war: indeed, a government, in the exercise of its sovereignty, can in principle authorize a foreign state to exercise power on its territory.[53] Rather, what needs to be dug up is evidence proving that the *lex generalis* of non-intervention is now set aside in the case of civil war and replaced by the *lex specialis* of internal self-determination entailing an obligation of negative equality.

3.2.1 Cases where third states declined to send armed forces in support of an incumbent government beset by civil war

The fact that, in certain cases, no state has intervened in support of an incumbent government involved in a civil war does not per se constitute an argument in favour of negative equality 'for only if such abstention were based on their being conscious of having a duty to abstain would it be possible to speak of an international custom'.[54] This would arguably happen if the incumbent had requested a third state to intervene,

---

[50] As Michael Wood reminds us, 'a *methodologically sound assessment* of practice, and of evidence of *opinio juris*, is essential in relation to intervention by invitation, as in relation to all aspects of customary international law' (Michael Wood, 'Assessing Practice on the Use of Force' (2019) 79 ZaöRV 655, 657, emphasis in the original).

[51] See Chapter VI, Section 5 and its subsections.

[52] Art 36(2), Statute of the International Court of Justice (San Francisco, 26 June 1945) 33 UNTS 993.

[53] See Chapter IV, Section 3.

[54] *The Case of the SS 'Lotus' (France v Turkey)*, Judgment of 7 September 1927, PCIJ Rep Series A No 10, 2, 28.

256 INTERNATIONAL LAW AND THE PRINCIPLE OF NON-INTERVENTION

or the third state had committed to intervene under a treaty, *and* the third state based its refusal on self-determination arguments and not only on treaty obligations or political considerations.

This was the case, for instance, in the Chinese Civil War (1946–9), during which the United States provided funds and arms[55] to the Nationalist government against the Communists but excluded any direct military assistance,[56] with President Truman declaring that support will 'not extend to United States military intervention to influence the course of any Chinese internal strife' because '[i]n line with its often expressed views regarding self-determination ... the detailed steps necessary to the achievement of political unity in China must be worked out by the Chinese themselves'.[57] The British foreign secretary also qualified the civil war as 'a Chinese domestic affair in which His Majesty's Government cannot properly interfere'.[58]

France has also on several occasions turned down requests to intervene in its former colonies by their embattled presidents. When in 1966 President Tombalbaye requested assistance against the Front de libération nationale du Tchad (FROLINAT) during the initial phases of the First Chadian Civil War (1965–79), for instance, the French government declined to intervene as it deemed the conflict to be merely internal and only provided limited administrative and advisory assistance.[59] France adopted the same approach when, in 2002, the internal situation in Côte d'Ivoire deteriorated, with rebels controlling the northern half of the country and establishing a *de facto* administration therein.[60] At least initially, the French government refused to apply its defence agreement with the African country and to intervene in support of President Gbagbo in spite of his request and of the claim that the rebels were assisted by foreign countries: for Paris, the agreement was not applicable as the situation was a purely internal conflict to be handled within the African security framework.[61] France was again put on the spot when, on 27 December 2012, the Central African Republic (CAR)'s President Bozizé appealed for assistance against the coalition of armed groups known as the Séléka: President Hollande eventually turned down the request, claiming that the French troops stationed at Bangui's international airport under a previous agreement between the two countries did not intend 'to intervene in the internal affairs of the State' and that the French forces were merely deployed to protect French citizens.[62] After the Séléka took Bangui and overthrew Bozizé in March 2013,

---

[55] See Keesing's 1946–1948, 7775, 8017, 9252.

[56] ibid, 7709.

[57] Marjorie M Whiteman (ed), *Digest of International Law* (GPO 1965) 597.

[58] ibid, 460. The non-interference policy in China was also affirmed on 27 December 1945 at the Moscow meeting between the foreign ministers of the United States, United Kingdom, and Soviet Union (ibid, 599).

[59] Christopher J LeMon, 'Unilateral Intervention by Invitation in Civil Wars: The Effective Control Test Tested' (2003) NYU J Intl L & Pol 757, 769. FROLINAT, an Islamic-socialist armed group which aimed to overthrow Tombalbaye and establish a coalition government, controlled areas of northern Chad.

[60] Till Förster, 'Dialogue Direct: Rebel Governance and Civil Order in Northern Côte d'Ivoire' in Arjona, Kasfir, and Mampilly (eds), *Rebel Governance in Civil War*, 203, 206.

[61] Gilles Cottereau, 'Une Licorne en Côte d'Ivoire au service de la paix: Avant Marcoussi et jusqu'à la reconciliation' (2003) 49 AFDI 176, 188.

[62] Frédérique Coulée, 'Pratique française de droit international' (2013) 59 AFDI 535, 562; Maria-Daniella Marouda and Vasiliki Saranti, 'From Ukraine and Yemen to CAR, Mali and Syria: Is Third Country Intervention by Invitation Reshaped in the Aftermath of Recent Practice?' (2016) 3 Ordine internazionale e diritti umani 556, 574 <www.rivistaoidu.net/rivista-oidu-n-3-2016-15-luglio2016/>.

NON-INTERVENTION AND INTERNAL SELF-DETERMINATION   257

France also declined a request for assistance by the new government.[63] This French practice of declining invitations to intervene, however, has limited significance for the identification of customary international law, as they have usually been justified on the basis of the defence agreements signed with the African countries.

3.2.2 Cases where third states sent armed forces in support of an incumbent government beset by civil war

It is undeniable that, since 1945, there have been many cases of states sending armed forces in support of a foreign government engulfed in a civil war. This mere fact, however, is in itself insufficient to generate customary rules if not accompanied by *opinio juris*.[64] In fact, from a methodological perspective, in our context *opinio juris* has more significance than usual, as it is a negative that must be proved (the prohibition of intervening in support of a government involved in a civil war).[65] What needs to be ascertained, therefore, is whether any justifications have been offered by the intervening state(s) and whether they have been based on legal arguments.[66] By the same token, condemnations of the interventions by other states and international organizations must have made reference to the impermissibility of the intervention itself (and not, say, to how it was conducted or to the existence/validity of consent) and also need to be grounded in international law. Absence of condemnations does not per se amount to acquiescence unless '[s]tates were in a position to react and the circumstances called for some reaction.'[67] Recall also that, as the International Law Association has pointed out,

> it is not so much a question of what a State really believes (which is often undiscoverable, especially since a State is a composite entity involving many persons with possibly different beliefs), but rather a matter of what it *says* it believes, or what can reasonably be implied from its conduct. In other words, it is a matter of what it *claims*.[68]

On these methodological premises, the following pages will analyse post-1945 cases of states dispatching armed forces in support of a foreign government beset by civil war as defined in Section 3.1 of this chapter.

North Yemen. In the civil war between Royalists and Republicans (1962–70), the United Arab Republic (UAR) claimed that its intervention had been requested by the

---

[63] Marouda and Saranti, 'From Ukraine', 575.

[64] *North Sea Continental Shelf Cases (Federal Republic of Germany/Denmark; Federal Republic of Germany/The Netherlands)* (Judgment) [1969] ICJ Rep 3, para 77.

[65] Commentary on Draft Conclusion 3 [2018] YB ILC, vol II, part two, 95.

[66] *Nicaragua v USA*, para 207. According to the ILC, '[a]mong the forms of evidence of acceptance as law (*opinio juris*), an express public statement on behalf of a State that a given practice is permitted, prohibited or mandated under customary international law provides the clearest indication that the State has avoided or undertaken such practice (or recognized that it was rightfully undertaken or avoided by others) out of a sense of legal right or obligation' (Commentary on Draft Conclusion 10 [2018] YB ILC, vol II, part two, 103).

[67] Draft Conclusion 10(3) [2018] YB ILC, vol II, part two, 140.

[68] Final Report of the Committee on Formation of Customary (General) International Law, in International Law Association, Report of the Sixty-Ninth Conference 712, 744, emphasis in the original.

258   INTERNATIONAL LAW AND THE PRINCIPLE OF NON-INTERVENTION

Yemen Arab Republic under a mutual defence pact in order to repel Saudi Arabia's aggression.[69] Accused of providing covert military support to the Royalists,[70] Britain replied that it only acted to eject Republican forces from the Federation of South Arabia in accordance with the 1959 Treaty of Friendship and Protection and that its position in relation to the internal dispute in Yemen remained 'one of strict non-involvement'.[71]

Congo-Léopoldville. After ONUC (Opération des Nations Unies au Congo) had left the country (1964), Belgium and the United States conducted a joint military operation in Stanleyville (Operation Dragon Rouge), where a rebel government had been established by followers of the former Congolese leader Lumumba during the Simba rebellion (1963–5).[72] The United States, which provided air transport for Belgian paratroopers, claimed that, although the operation had been authorized by the controversial Congolese prime minister (and former president of Katanga), Moïse Tshombe, it was merely meant to assist in the evacuation of civilians from the Stanleyville area, while avoiding interferences in the civil strife.[73] It also accused several countries of supporting the rebellion.[74] Belgium affirmed that the operation was a 'humanitarian action' undertaken with the Congolese government's agreement for the mere purpose of saving human lives in danger.[75] The Belgian minister of foreign affairs also stressed that '[i]t was not a matter of helping the Congolese National Army. It was not a matter of conquering or retaining any particular territory. It was a question of saving between 1,500 and 2,000 persons whose lives were in danger'.[76] Britain specified that it had granted the use of its facilities on Ascension Island '[i]n the light of the humanitarian objective' of the intervention.[77] As the operation facilitated the advance of the governmental forces and resulted in Tshombe's forces taking Stanleyville without fighting, however, the representatives of sixteen countries accused it of being 'an intervention in African affairs [and] a flagrant violation of the Charter of the United Nations'.[78] For Tanzania, in particular, the operation was 'a conspiracy to impose upon the people of the Congo the disputed authority of the Tshombé government'.[79]

Dominican Republic. Explaining the US intervention in the civil war between Constitutionalists and Loyalists triggered by the coup led by Colonel Caamaño Deñó,

---

[69] UN Doc S/5336, 21 June 1963, 1. The UN General Assembly approved the Credential Committee's recommendation to seat the Republican delegates as the official representatives of Yemen following their recognition by several states, including the United States and the Soviet Union (GA Res 1871 (XVII), 20 December 1962).

[70] See Yemen's allegations in UN Doc S/5248, 28 February 1963.

[71] UN Doc S/5250, 4 March 1963, 2. See also S/5343, 2 July 1963; S/5424, 10 September 1963.

[72] Congo claimed, however, that the rebellion was not a civil war as it was limited to a very small part of the country and, without outside aid, it would have already been put down (UN Doc S/PV1184, 23 December 1964, paras 32, 35; S/PV.1189, 30 December 1964, para 44).

[73] UN Doc S/6062, 24 November 1964, 2. See Tshombe's request in S/6060, 24 November 1964. Tshombe warned that the humanitarian mission could not 'lead to any solutions with regard to the rebels different from those which it rests with the Government of the Congo to seek in the exercise of its full sovereignty' (S/6062, 4).

[74] UN Doc S/PV.1174, 14 December 1964, para 55.

[75] UN Doc S/6063, 24 November 1964, 1.

[76] UN Doc S/PV.1173, 11 December 1964, para 9.

[77] UN Doc S/6059, 24 November 1964.

[78] UN Doc S/6076, 1 December 1964, 3. The socialist countries were equally critical: see eg Soviet Union (S/PV.1170, 9 December 1964, paras 3–4) and Czechoslovakia (S/PV.1189, para 84).

[79] UN Doc S/PV.1178, 17 December 1964, para 23.

a Department of State's legal memorandum claimed that the initial landing of US forces on the night between 28 and 29 April 1965 was carried out to protect the lives of American and other nationals, while the continued presence of US troops was justified by the need to maintain order after the collapse of local authority, to preserve the situation so that the OAS organs could carry out their responsibilities, and to allow the Dominicans to choose their government without external interferences.[80] The United States pointed out that it did not interfere or intervene in 'the personality of the Dominican State' or act against its 'political, economic and cultural elements' in breach of Article 15 (now 19) of the OAS Charter, but simply took urgent measures to protect human lives.[81] Even though the military junta which had proclaimed itself the government of the Caribbean state had addressed a request to the United States to send in armed forces against the rebels, the US government did not base its intervention on such a request 'because it would have amounted to taking sides in the internal struggle and would, therefore, have resulted in actual interference with the freedom of the Dominican people to choose their own government'.[82] Criticism of the operation focused on the lack of evidence of external subversion. Condemning the intervention, the USSR implicitly referred to the principle of internal self-determination by pointing out that '[t]he question of the internal structure of the Dominican Republic, its Government and the settlement of differences within that country can and must be decided by the Dominican people themselves without any kind of outside interference'.[83] In 2016, the OAS General Assembly '[e]xpresse[d] regret to the Dominican people for the actions of April 1965, which disrupted the process of restoration of the constitutional order in the Dominican Republic'.[84]

South Vietnam. After the State of Vietnam (South Vietnam) refused to carry out general elections in 1956 as provided in the 1954 Geneva Agreements, a civil war broke out between the Saigon government, backed by the United States, and the Việt Cộng insurgency (National Liberation Front) supported by the Democratic Republic of Vietnam (North Vietnam). Although at some point they controlled most of South Vietnam's territory and population and participated in the creation of a provisional revolutionary government, the United States always insisted that the Việt Cộng were not a spontaneous indigenous rebellion. When, in February 1965, the US airstrikes began and regular combat units were dispatched to South-East Asia, a legal memorandum prepared by the Department of State's legal advisor claimed that, whatever its status under the Geneva Agreements, South Vietnam had become a separate state entitled to defend itself against the armed attack carried out by North Vietnam and to

---

[80] Department of State, 'Legal Basis for United States Actions in the Dominican Republic' in Abram Chayes, Thomas Ehrlich, and Andreas F Lowenfeld, *International Legal Process: Materials for an Introductory Course*, vol II (Little, Brown and Co 1969) 1179. The US operation was followed by the deployment of an Inter-American Armed Force by the OAS in late May 1965.

[81] UN Doc S/PV.1198, 4 May 1965, para 156.

[82] Department of State, 'Legal Basis', 1180. The US government made clear that its purpose was not to 'dictate the political future of the Dominican Republic' as 'the Dominican people, under the established principle of self-determination, should select their own government through free elections' (UN Doc S/PV.1196, 3 May 1965, para 89).

[83] UN Doc S/PV.1212, 19 May 1965, para 113.

[84] Declaration on the Dominican Republic, 16 June 2016, AG/DEC. 94 (XLVI-O/16), para 2.

260   INTERNATIONAL LAW AND THE PRINCIPLE OF NON-INTERVENTION

request the United States to intervene in collective self-defence, even though it was not a UN member.[85]

Chad. Chad has had a long history of foreign interventions in its internal troubles. In April 1969, the French Foreign Legion and other units joined Chadian forces in military operations against the FROLINAT rebels at the request of President Tombalbaye on the basis of the 1960 quadripartite defence agreement between France, Chad, CAR, and Congo-Brazzaville (Operation Bison).[86] In 1978, France initially denied sending combat troops,[87] then admitted their presence but excluded that they were participating in the hostilities.[88] When it finally conceded that its troops were engaged in fighting,[89] the French government relied on the request of President Malloum in line with the 1976 cooperation agreements, but specified that the intervention was directed against external aggression and to protect nationals.[90]

Libya intervened in Chad in 1980 at the request of the new Chadian president (and former FROLINAT leader) Goukouni Oueddei against the then Minister of Defence Hissène Habré's insurgents in line with a newly signed Treaty of Friendship and Alliance between the two countries.[91] After a failed attempt to merge Chad with Libya, Libyan forces withdrew in November 1981 at the request of Goukouni, which led to Habré eventually taking control of N'Djamena in June 1982 and becoming the new Chadian president.[92] In 1983, France launched Operation Manta in response to the use by Libya of mechanized battalions in support of Goukouni and to the bombing of the oasis of Faya-Largeau.[93] France relied on the request of President Habré under the framework of the 1976 cooperation agreement but also on Article 51 of the UN Charter and Security Council Resolution 387 (1976),[94] claiming that the purpose was not to meddle in the civil war but to respond to Libya's direct support for Goukoni's insurgents.[95] The operation ended in November 1984 after securing Habré's position. In 1986, Chad reported to the Security Council that, in accordance with Article 51

---

[85] Leonard C Meeker, 'The Legality of United States Participation in the Defense of Viet-Nam' (1966) 54 Dept St Bull 474, 474. North Vietnam's armed attack was said to consist of 'externally supported subversion, clandestine supply of arms, infiltration of armed personnel, and most recently the sending of regular units of the North Vietnamese army into the South' (ibid).

[86] Jean Charpentier, 'Pratique française du droit international' (1970) 16 AFDI 941, 989. Operation Bison ended in September 1972.

[87] Keesing's 1978, 28977.

[88] Keesing's 1979, 29398.

[89] ibid, 29399.

[90] Jean Charpentier, 'Pratique française de droit international' (1978) 24 AFDI 1083, 1092; Jean Charpentier, 'Pratique française de droit international' (1979) 25 AFDI 905, 908.

[91] UN Doc S/14767, 24 November 1981, 1. As a result of the intervention, Libya occupied and annexed the Aozou Strip, claiming it was an integral part of Libya's territory.

[92] Thomas Collelo (ed), *Chad—A Country Study* (GPO 1990) 192.

[93] ibid, 193. In the Security Council, Libya argued that Goukouni's was the legitimate government of Chad even though it had been forced to move its capital to the northern city of Bardai, and that Habré's was a rebel regime (UN Doc S/PV.2462, 3 August 1983, para 41). It also stressed that it took a 'neutral' position among the Chadian factions (S/PV.2462, para 82). Libya's position was only supported by the USSR, while Zimbabwe, China, and Togo called for an end to all foreign interventions.

[94] UN Doc S/PV.2465, 12 August 1983, paras 134–6. Zaire, which intervened alongside France, also referred to self-defence (S/PV.2463, 11 August 1983, para 66). For Chad's request, see S/15897, 1 August 1983, 1.

[95] Jean Charpentier, 'Pratique française de droit international' (1983) 29 AFDI 850, 916; Jean Charpentier, 'Pratique française de droit international' (1984) 30 AFDI 943, 1024–5.

NON-INTERVENTION AND INTERNAL SELF-DETERMINATION   261

of the UN Charter, President Habré had again requested a military intervention by France to repel Libya's 'overt military aggression' in support of Goukouni.[96] France then launched Operation Épervier. While French forces did not interfere in the subsequent power struggle between Habré and Idriss Déby, which ended with the latter's victory in December 1990,[97] in 2008 they evacuated foreigners during the Battle of N'Djamena between governmental forces and the United Front for Change rebels but denied taking part in combat operations.[98] On 1 August 2014, Operation Épervier was replaced by Operation Barkhane, a joint force against terrorism in the region composed of French and G5 Sahel countries' (Burkina Faso, Chad, Mali, Mauritania, and Niger) military personnel. Operation Barkhane was formally terminated on 9 November 2022.

Lebanon. In late spring 1976, Syria sent troops in the Lebanese Civil War (started the previous year) against Palestinian and leftist militias at the invitation of President Suleiman Franjieh.[99] In October 1976, the Syrian troops were incorporated in an Arab Deterrent Force tasked by the Arab League with restoring calm in the Mediterranean country. Syria's continued military presence in Lebanon was authorized by the 1989 Taif Accords which ended the civil war.[100]

Kampuchea. When Vietnam invaded Kampuchea in 1978–9, it emphasized that a 'clear distinction' should be made between 'the border war started by the Pol Pot–Ieng Sary clique against Viet Nam' and 'the revolutionary war of the Kampuchean people against the dictatorial rule of the Pol Pot–Ieng Sary clique, which is an instrument in the hands of the reactionary ruling circles of Peking' and claimed that it was involved exclusively in the former in the exercise of its right of self-defence.[101]

Angola. During the civil war which followed the country's independence (1975–2002), South Africa affirmed that the limited purpose of its Operation Savannah (1975–6) was to 'secure for the people of Angola the necessary time to reach a peaceful political settlement for themselves around the conference table, or, failing that, an opportunity for the Organization of African Unity to find a political solution without interference from outside'.[102] More importantly, it also claimed that '[a]t no stage did South Africa become involved, nor did it desire to become involved, in the civil war as such'.[103] The Soviet Union asserted that its involvement in the civil war was

---

[96] UN Doc S/17837, 18 February 1986, 1. See also Collelo (ed), *Chad*, 195.

[97] Jean Charpentier, 'Pratique française du droit international—1991' (1991) 37 AFDI 933, 985.

[98] Emizet F Kisangani and Jeffrey Pickering, *African Interventions: State Militaries, Foreign Powers, and Rebel Forces* (CUP 2022) 96; 'Paris dément à nouveau toute participation aux combats' (*Le Parisien*, 5 February 2008) <www.leparisien.fr/international/paris-dement-a-nouveau-toute-participation-aux-comb ats-05-02-2008-3296032436.php>.

[99] UN Doc S/2005/662, 20 October 2005, 14. While the intervention was initially at the invitation of the Lebanese Maronite President, Syrian forces subsequently acted alternatively in support of one or another of the several factions in the civil war.

[100] Fouad Ilias, *The Evolving Patterns of Lebanese Politics in Post-Syria Lebanon: The Perceptions of Hizballah among Members of the Free Patriotic Movement* (Graduate Institute Publications 2010) 59.

[101] UN Doc S/PV.2108, 11 January 1979, paras 115, 126. The UN General Assembly and the Association of Southeast Asian Nations (ASEAN) condemned the intervention (GA Res 34/22, 14 November 1979; S/13025, 12 January 1979, Annex). Resolution 34/22, in particular, emphasized that the Cambodian people are entitled 'to decide their own future and destiny free from outside interference, subversion or coercion' (GA Res 34/22, para 9).

[102] UN Doc S/PV.1904, 30 March 1976, para 119.

[103] ibid.

262 INTERNATIONAL LAW AND THE PRINCIPLE OF NON-INTERVENTION

at the request of what it considered the lawful government of the People's Republic of Angola (the Movimento Popular de Libertação de Angola—MPLA) but it specified that the purpose was to repel the aggression of 'racist and imperialist forces' and that no combat troops had been sent.[104] Cuba invoked the same justification but, unlike the Soviet Union, acknowledged sending military combat personnel to Angola.[105] While South Africa's intervention was overwhelmingly condemned, including by the UN Security Council,[106] several African states defended the Cuban and Soviet involvement. Tanzania, for instance, claimed that this was at the request of the legitimate Angolan government and motivated by the external threats to the country's territorial integrity.[107]

Liberia. In August 1990, Nigeria, Ghana, Gambia, Guinea, and Sierra Leone intervened under the framework of ECOWAS in the First Liberian Civil War (1989–97) after a group of rebels led by Charles Taylor (the National Patriotic Front of Liberia—NPFL) entered the country from Côte d'Ivoire with the purpose of overthrowing President Samuel Doe.[108] Although Doe, who by June 1990 only controlled parts of the capital Monrovia, appealed to ECOWAS to send a peacekeeping force to 'forestall increasing terror and tension',[109] the Organization never officially relied on his consent as a legal basis for the operation.[110] Rather, Nigeria's minister of external affairs stated that the main purpose of the intervention was 'to stop the senseless killing of innocent civilian nationals and foreigners, and to help the Liberian people to restore their democratic institutions' and was 'in no way designed to save one part or punish another'.[111] Only Burkina Faso condemned the intervention.[112] The UN Security Council commended 'ECOWAS for its efforts to restore peace, security and stability in Liberia'.[113]

Somalia. Several states have been involved in various forms in the civil war in Somalia. In December 2006, Ethiopian troops intervened against the Union of the Islamic Courts (UIC) invoking an invitation of the Transitional Federal Government of Somalia (TFG) and its own inherent right of self-defence under the UN Charter.[114]

---

[104] UN Doc S/11947, 27 January 1976, 1–2.

[105] UN Doc S/11941, 24 January 1976, 2.

[106] SC Res 387, 31 March 1976, para 1.

[107] UN Doc A/33/131-S/12732, 9 June 1978, Annex, 1.

[108] After being removed from office in the government by Doe for embezzlement and imprisoned in the United States, Taylor escaped in 1989 and set up a militia to overthrow Liberia's president. When ECOWAS took control of Monrovia, Taylor established a *de facto* government in Gbargna (David Wippman, 'Enforcing the Peace: ECOWAS and the Liberian Civil War' in Lori Fisler Damrosch (ed), *Enforcing Restraint: Collective Intervention in Internal Conflicts* (Council on Foreign Relations Press 1993) 157, 158). In 1989, Prince Johnson's Independent National Patriotic Front of Liberia separated from the NPFL and engaged in fighting against both the NPFL and the Armed Forces of Liberia (ibid, 163–4).

[109] Letter addressed by President Samuel K Doe to the Chairman and Members of the Ministerial Meeting of the ECOWAS Standing Mediation Committee, 14 July 1990, in Marc Weller (ed), *Regional Peacekeeping and International Enforcement: The Liberian Crisis* (CUP 1994) 60–1.

[110] Georg Nolte, 'Restoring Peace by Regional Action: International Legal Aspects of the Liberian Conflict' (1993) 23 ZaöRV 603, 621–2.

[111] UN Doc S/21485, 10 August 1990, Annex, 3. In spite of the claim to be a peacekeeping force, however, ECOWAS engaged in offensive operations against the NPFL and allowed the instalment of an interim government led by Amos Sawyer (Wippman, 'Enforcing the Peace', 169).

[112] UN Doc S/PV.3138, 19 November 1992, 33.

[113] SC Resolutions 788, 19 November 1992, para 1, and 813, 26 March 1993, para 2.

[114] UN Doc S/2007/436, 18 July 2007, Annex VII, 44. It is unclear, however, whether the TFG really consented to the intervention (Ahmed Ali M Khayre, 'Self-Defence, Intervention by Invitation, or Proxy

Ethiopia's Prime Minister Zenawi confirmed that his country had 'taken self-defensive measures and started counter-attacking the aggressive extremist forces of the Islamic Courts and foreign terrorist groups'.[115] The operation led to the TFG taking control of Mogadishu. In October 2011, Kenya took 'robust, targeted measures to protect and preserve [its] integrity ... and the efficacy of the national economy and to secure peace and security in the face of the al-Shabaab terrorist militia attacks emanating from Somalia'.[116] The operations were conducted 'with the concurrence of the' TFG.[117] A subsequent joint communiqué of the Kenyan and Somali government also referred to the right of self-defence under Article 51 of the UN Charter.[118] A month later, Ethiopian troops again crossed the border with Somalia to conduct operations against al-Shabaab. Even though Ethiopia did not offer any official legal justifications, it appears that the intervention had been consented to by the TFG through its participation in the adoption of the Intergovernmental Authority on Development (IGAD) Assembly of the Heads of State and Government's Final Communiqué which called upon Ethiopia to support Kenya's and the African Union Mission to Somalia (AMISOM)'s efforts against al-Shabaab.[119] The US counterterrorism strikes against al-Shabaab in Somalia have also been carried out with the consent and in support of the TFG.[120] In 2017, the United States also invoked collective self-defence.[121]

Sierra Leone. The 2000 British intervention in the civil war in Sierra Leone consisted of four distinct operations (Operations Palliser, Basilica, Barras, and Silkman) and followed the withdrawal of the Economic Community of West African States Monitoring Group (ECOMOG) forces and the deployment of the UN Mission in Sierra Leone (UNAMSIL) peacekeeping force.[122] Of the four operations, two—Palliser and Barras—involved violent engagements against the Revolutionary United Front insurgents, who controlled almost half the country's territory and were responsible for brutal attacks on the population. With regard to Operation Palliser of May 2000, the Foreign and Commonwealth Office explained that the British forces were in the African country 'at the request of the Government of Sierra Leone and with the blessing of the United Nations' and that they were evacuating British nationals

---

War? The Legality of the 2006 Ethiopian Invasion of Somalia' (2014) 22 Afr J Intl & Comp L 208, 227–30). Although it controlled a minimal part of the country, the TFG, established in October 2004, was recognized by the United Nations, the African Union, and the League of Arab States.

[115] UN Doc S/PV.5614, 26 December 2006, 3.
[116] UN Doc S/2011/646, 18 October 2011, 1. Al-Shabaab is a radical splinter group of the UIC.
[117] UN Doc S/2011/646, 1.
[118] Mentioned in Seyfullah Hasar, *State Consent to Foreign Military Intervention during Civil Wars* (Brill/Nijhoff 2022) 226.
[119] Jean-Christophe Martin, 'The Ethiopian Military Intervention in Somalia—2011' in Tom Ruys and Olivier Corten with Alexandra Hofer (eds), *The Use of Force in International Law: A Case-Based Approach* (OUP 2018) 803, 808–9.
[120] The White House, Report on the Legal and Policy Frameworks Guiding the United States' Use of Military Force and Related National Security Operations, December 2016, 17 <www.justsecurity.org/wp-content/uploads/2016/12/framework.Report_Final.pdf>.
[121] Tom Ruys, Nele Verlinden, Carl Vander Maelen, and Sebastiaan Van Severen (eds), 'Digest of State Practice: 1 July 2017–31 December 2017' (2018) 5 JUFIL 145, 155.
[122] UNAMSIL was created by SC Res 1270, 22 October 1999, para 8.

264   INTERNATIONAL LAW AND THE PRINCIPLE OF NON-INTERVENTION

while 'complying fully with domestic and international law'.[123] Operation Barras of 10 September 2000 was essentially a rescue operation following the abduction of British soldiers by the West Side Boys armed group.[124]

Côte d'Ivoire. When in September 2002 France sent reinforcements to its troops already stationed in the African country on the basis of a 1961 defence agreement (Operation Licorne), it did so exclusively in order to rescue French and other nationals and to act as an interposition force between the Ivorian armed forces and the rebels: the situation was considered by Paris to be a merely internal one, in spite of the claims to the contrary by Côte d'Ivoire's President Gbagbo.[125] A few months later ECOWAS also deployed a peacekeeping force at the request of President Gbagbo and all the parties to the conflict (ECOFORCE, later renamed ECOMICI).[126] Both ECOWAS and French forces were subsequently authorized by the UN Security Council to take the necessary steps to guarantee their own security and freedom of movement and to protect civilians.[127] Security Council Resolution 1528 (2004) eventually established the United Nations Operation in Côte d'Ivoire (UNOCI), which integrated the ECOWAS forces, and authorized France to use all necessary means to support it.[128]

The Democratic Republic of the Congo (DRC). The African states that intervened in support of the DRC government in the 1998–2003 Second Congo War (Angola, Namibia, and Zimbabwe) invoked collective self-defence under the Southern African Development Community (SADC) framework against rebels supported by Rwanda and Uganda.[129] Zimbabwe pointed out that '[t]he Congolese, and only they, should determine their destiny'.[130] In 2004, Uganda also intervened in support of the DRC government against the Forces démocratiques de libération du Rwanda, an armed rebel group responsible for attacks on Tutsi forces and civilians both in eastern DRC and across the border into Rwanda. Uganda affirmed that 'the conflict in the Democratic Republic of the Congo was exclusively internal, and Uganda had only intervened at the behest of the President of that country who had appealed for its assistance in bringing an end to the conflict, notably in the eastern part of the country'.[131]

Afghanistan. After being overthrown by Operation Enduring Freedom in 2001, the Taliban reorganized themselves as an insurgency against the pro-Western government of Hamid Karzai. Alongside troops contributed to NATO's Resolute Support Mission, which had been established at the invitation of the Afghan government and in accordance with UN Security Council Resolution 2189 of 2014, the United States maintained forces in the Central Asian country on the basis of the Bilateral Security Agreement concluded with Karzai's successor, Ashraf Ghani, in order to conduct attacks against

---

[123] Geoffrey Marston (ed), 'United Kingdom Materials on International Law 2000' (2000) 71 BYBIL 517, 645.

[124] David H Ucko, 'Can Limited Intervention Work? Lessons from Britain's Success Story in Sierra Leone' (2016) 39 JSS 847, 858. The West Side Boys were known for their eccentric clothing and their proneness to drunkenness and hostage-taking (ibid, 860).

[125] Cottereau, 'Une Licorne', 188.

[126] UN Doc S/2002/1386, 19 December 2002, Annex, para 11; S/2003/472, 23 April 2003, Annex, 2.

[127] SC Res 1464, 4 February 2003, para 9.

[128] SC Res 1528, 27 February 2004, paras 1, 16.

[129] UN Doc S/1998/891, 23 September 1998, 3; A/53/PV.95, 23 March 1999, 20.

[130] UN Doc S/1998/891, 4.

[131] UN Doc A/C.3/59/SR.54, 30 November 2004, para 41.

NON-INTERVENTION AND INTERNAL SELF-DETERMINATION   265

the Taliban and the Islamic State-Khorasan Province armed group.[132] The Agreement reaffirmed the commitment 'to refrain from interfering in Afghanistan's internal affairs and democratic processes' and provided that the American forces would not engage in combat operations unless otherwise mutually agreed.[133] Washington did not describe these operations as involvement in the armed conflict, but as counterterrorism measures undertaken with the consent of the Afghan government and aimed at protecting the United States from terrorist attacks.[134] The civil war ended with the return of the Taliban to power after the withdrawal of the US and NATO forces in August and September 2021, respectively.

Mali. In 2012, the interim president and prime minister of Mali, Dioncounda Traoré, requested ECOWAS's help against 'armed groups including terrorists, drug traffickers and criminals of every sort' for 'the liberation of the northern territories and the fight against terrorism and other illicit activities'.[135] As the deployment of the ECOWAS force was delayed, in 2013 France launched Operation Serval upon Traoré's request in order to assist the Malian forces to combat 'terrorist elements' in the north of the country, claiming that '[t]he operation [was] in conformity with international law'.[136] More specifically, France declared that it was acting against three terrorist organizations (the Movement for Oneness and Jihad in West Africa, al-Qaeda in the Islamic Maghreb, and Ansar Dine) but not against the Tuareg secessionists.[137] In addition, it referred to the 'accelerated implementation' of Security Council Resolution 2085 (2012)[138] and, in later statements, to collective self-defence.[139] Chad also sent a military contingent of 2,000 men 'to halt the southward progression of the terrorists' in accordance with Security Council Resolution 2085 (2012)[140] and the United Kingdom provided logistic support in the form of two transport aircraft at the request of Mali's

---

[132] Security and Defense Cooperation Agreement Between the United States of America and the Islamic Republic of Afghanistan (Kabul, 30 September 2014) (2015) 54 ILM 275.

[133] ibid, Preamble and Art 2(1).

[134] Peter M Olson, 'Introductory Note to Security and Defense Cooperation Agreement between the United States of America and the Islamic Republic of Afghanistan & Agreement between the North Atlantic Treaty Organization and the Islamic Republic of Afghanistan on the Status of NATO Forces and NATO Personnel Conducting Mutually Agreed NATO-led Activities in Afghanistan' (2015) 54 ILM 272, 272–3.

[135] UN Doc S/2012/727, 1 October 2012, Annex. Following Mali's request, SC Res 2085 authorized the African-led International Support Mission in Mali (AFISMA) to use all necessary means in support of the Malian authorities 'in recovering the areas in the north of its territory under the control of terrorist, extremist and armed groups and in reducing the threat posed by terrorist organizations ... ' (SC Res 2085, 20 December 2012, para 9(b)).

[136] UN Doc S/2013/17, 14 January 2013.

[137] Karine Bannelier and Theodore Christakis, 'Under the UN Security Council's Watchful Eyes: Military Intervention by Invitation in the Malian Conflict' (2013) 26 LJIL 855, 866–7. At the moment of the intervention, Ansar Dine and AQMI controlled a large area of the country and had established a *de facto* government in Timbuktu.

[138] UN Doc S/2013/17. On whether the French intervention can be justified on the basis of Resolution 2085, see Massimo Starita, 'L'intervento francese in Mali si basa su un'autorizzazione del Consiglio di sicurezza?' (2013) 96 RDI 561; Bannelier and Christakis, 'Under the UN', 868–70.

[139] Laura Magi, 'Sulla liceità dell'intervento militare francese in Mali' (2013) 96 RDI 551, 554. See also Niger's comments, UN Doc S/PV.6905, 22 January 2013, 15. It is not clear, however, how self-defence could be invoked in the absence of an armed attack by an *external* actor: indeed, this legal basis is not mentioned in the identical letters sent to the UN Secretary-General and to the President of the Security Council (Magi, 'Sulla liceità', 554).

[140] UN Doc S/PV.6905, 12.

266   INTERNATIONAL LAW AND THE PRINCIPLE OF NON-INTERVENTION

transitional government and France.[141] The intervention met with little criticism, with numerous countries and the Security Council explicitly praising it.[142] By April 2013, most of the northern regions had fallen back under the control of the Bamako authorities: the Security Council then established the United Nations Multidimensional Integrated Stabilization Mission in Mali (MINUSMA) mandated to stabilize the situation in the country with the support of the French forces.[143] In 2021, Russian mercenaries from the Wagner Group were deployed in Mali, as well as soldiers from Russia's regular army in charge of logistics and training.[144] Mali also asked for a revision of its defence agreements with France. On 15 August 2022, French troops completed their withdrawal from Mali.[145]

CAR. In addition to providing logistics and intelligence to the Bangui government, in 2006 the French forces stationed in the African country reacted in self-defence against attacks by the Union of Democratic Forces for Unity rebels who had taken control of the northern regions of the country.[146] In January 2013, South African National Defence Special Forces were sent to the CAR allegedly at the request of embattled President Bozizé to assist forces already present in the country against the Séléka rebels.[147] Troops were also sent by Cameroon, Gabon, the Republic of the Congo, and Chad. In April of the same year, the government installed after the Séléka had overthrown Bozizé was consensually replaced by a transitional council, but by the end of summer the situation deteriorated again and assumed genocidal aspects. At that point, UN Security Council Resolution 2127 (2013) authorized the deployment of an African-led Mission internationale de soutien à la Centrafrique sous conduite africaine (MISCA) and also mandated the French forces in the CAR to take all necessary measures in its support.[148] Although President Bozizé had asked for France's help before he was ousted, the French government did not justify Operation Sangaris (2013–16) on the basis of either his request or that of the transitional council, but only on the authorization contained in Resolution 2127.[149]

Iraq. The 2008 Status of Forces Agreement (SOFA) between Iraq and the United States contained the former's request for 'the temporary assistance of the United States Forces for the purposes of supporting Iraq in its efforts to maintain security and

---

[141] UN Doc S/2013/58, 25 January 2013.

[142] See eg Senegal (UN Doc S/PV.6905, 11); Niger (S/PV.6905, 14); Nigeria (S/PV.6905, 17–18); Burkina Faso (S/PV.6905, 13); Côte d'Ivoire (S/PV.6905, 9–10); United States (John R Crook (ed), 'Contemporary Practice of the United States Relating to International Law' (2013) 107 AJIL 431, 467–8); and Australia (Michael Hertel (ed), 'Australian Practice in International Law 2013' (2014) 32 Australian YBIL 399, 463). The Preamble of SC Res 2100, 25 April 2013 '[w]elcom[ed] the swift action by the French forces, at the request of the transitional authorities of Mali, to stop the offensive of terrorist, extremist and armed groups towards the south of Mali'.

[143] SC Res 2100, para 7.

[144] Raphael Parens, 'The Wagner Group's Playbook in Africa: Mali', Foreign Policy Research Institute, 18 March 2022 <www.fpri.org/article/2022/03/the-wagner-groups-playbook-in-africa-mali/>.

[145] Annie Risemberg, 'French Forces Complete Departure from Mali' (*VOA*, 15 August 2022) <www.voanews.com/a/french-forces-complete-departure-from-mali-/6702201.html>.

[146] 'French Army Clash with CAR Rebels' (*BBC News*, 29 November 2006) <http://news.bbc.co.uk/1/hi/world/africa/6191754.stm>.

[147] 'South Africa to Send 400 Soldiers to CAR' (*Al Jazeera*, 6 January 2013) <www.aljazeera.com/news/2013/1/6/south-africa-to-send-400-soldiers-to-car>.

[148] SC Res 2127, 5 December 2013, para 50.

[149] Coulée, 'Pratique française de droit international', 564–5.

NON-INTERVENTION AND INTERNAL SELF-DETERMINATION   267

stability in Iraq, including cooperation in the conduct of operations against al-Qaeda and other terrorist groups, outlaw groups, and remnants of the former regime.[150] In August 2014, a coalition of states including the United States, Australia, Belgium, Britain, Canada, Denmark, France, Jordan, and the Netherlands started to conduct airstrikes against the self-styled Islamic State in Iraq and the Levant (ISIL), a terrorist group that controlled the north of the country and had established a brutal *de facto* administration therein.[151] Iran and Russia also separately intervened in support of the Iraqi government.[152] The legal basis for the intervention in Iraq (as opposed to that against ISIL in Syria from September 2014) was the consent of its government.[153] At the same time, all the intervening states stressed that the purpose of the intervention was to defeat the terrorist group.[154]

Libya. In 2014, post-Ghaddafi Libya became engulfed in a second civil war among several factions, the most prominent being the Tripoli-based, UN-recognized Government of National Accord (GNA), with little effective territorial control beyond the capital, and the Tobruk-based House of Representatives' *de facto* government supported by the Benghazi-based Libyan National Army (LNA) of General Khalifa Haftar, a former official of Ghaddafi's regime. Turkey supported the GNA against the LNA by supplying drones, weapons, and trucks in spite of the arms and military equipment embargo imposed by Security Council Resolution 1970 (2011). It also deployed regular and irregular troops in Libya against the 'war criminal' Haftar and terrorist groups on the basis of a memorandum of understanding on military cooperation signed with the GNA in late 2019 and of a specific request by Prime Minister al-Sarraj in line with Security Council Resolution 2259 (2015).[155] Several states and

---

[150] 'White House Statement, November 27, 2008' in (2009) 19 Foreign Policy Bulletin 10, 11.

[151] The Security Council had qualified ISIL and the Al-Nusrah Front (al-Sham from July 2016) as a threat to international peace and security (SC Res 2249, 20 November 2015, Preamble).

[152] Tom Ruys and Nele Verlinden (eds), 'Digest of State Practice 1 January–30 June 2014' (2014) 1 JUFIL 323, 357.

[153] The United Kingdom, for instance, affirmed that 'the consent of Iraq in these terms provides a clear and unequivocal legal basis for the deployment of UK forces and military assets to take military action to strike ISIL sites and military strongholds in Iraq' (Prime Minister's Office, Summary of the Government Legal Position on Military Action in Iraq Against ISIL, 25 September 2014 <www.gov.uk/government/publications/military-action-in-iraq-against-isil-government-legal-position/summary-of-the-governm ent-legal-position-on-military-action-in-iraq-against-isil>). See also the US State Department legal adviser's speech at the American Society of International Law ('International Law, Legal Diplomacy, and the Counter-ISIL Campaign,' 1 April 2016 <https://2009-2017.state.gov/s/l/releases/remarks/255493. htm>) and the statements by France (Déclaration de M François Hollande, Président de la République, sur l'intervention militaire française en Irak, 19 September 2014 <www.vie-publique.fr/discours/192 317-declaration-de-m-francois-hollande-president-de-la-republique-sur-li>), the Netherlands (Letter of Government to Parliament, in Tom Ruys and Nele Verlinden (eds), 'Digest of State Practice 1 July–31 December 2014' (2015) 2 JUFIL 119, 141–2), and Iran (Julian Borger, 'Iran Air Strikes Against Isis Requested by Iraqi Government, Says Tehran' (*The Guardian*, 6 December 2014) <www.theguardian.com/world/2014/dec/05/iran-conducts-air-strikes-against-isis-exremists-iraq>). Iraq's request for assistance in June 2014, however, does not refer to self-defence or Art 51 of the UN Charter (UN Doc S/2014/440, 25 June 2014, Annex). The letter sent in September of the same year mentions the fact that 'ISIL has established a safe haven outside Iraq's borders' and the need 'to regain control of Iraq's borders', although self-defence is again not expressly mentioned (S/2014/691, 22 September 2014, Annex).

[154] Karine Bannelier-Christakis, 'Military Interventions against ISIL in Iraq, Syria and Libya, and the Legal Basis of Consent' (2016) 29 LJIL 743, 755.

[155] UN Doc S/2020/227, 24 March 2020, 2. SC Res 2259, 23 December 2015, para 5, calls on member states to engage with the GNA and to cease support for any other institutions claiming legitimacy.

268 INTERNATIONAL LAW AND THE PRINCIPLE OF NON-INTERVENTION

organizations, however, denounced the Turkish intervention as an interference in Libya's internal affairs and a violation of international law, the UN-imposed arms embargo, and the Skhirat Agreement of 17 December 2015.[156] The GNA responded that the plans to monitor Libya's maritime border were inadequate as evidence showed that Haftar was receiving arms from foreign states by air and land: it reiterated, therefore, 'as the legitimate and internationally recognized Government, its legitimate right under international law and international norms to defend the sovereignty and territory of Libya and protect the country's citizens and vital institutions by entering, as required to exercise that right, into openly declared alliances, in accordance with international law'.[157] In the Conclusions of the 2020 Berlin Conference on Libya, the eleven participating states emphasized the need for 'a Libyan-led and Libyan owned political process' to bring the conflict to an end and committed not to interfere 'in the armed conflict or in the internal affairs of Libya'.[158] The same conclusions were reaffirmed a year later at the Second Berlin Conference, although Turkey introduced a reservation to the call for the withdrawal of all foreign forces without delay.[159] The Security Council has repeatedly called upon 'all Member States not to intervene in the conflict or take measures that exacerbate the conflict'.[160]

In February 2015, the Libyan government also requested Egypt's support to eradicate the terrorist organizations operating on its territory.[161] Calling for the UN arms embargo to be lifted, Egypt noted that '[s]tates wishing to assist the legitimate Libyan Government in confronting terrorism ... should be allowed to do so ... with the condition that such assistance be provided in coordination with the Libyan Government and with its approval'.[162] The Egyptian airstrikes were commended by the Arab League, which confirmed the need for coordination and cooperation with the Libyan authorities.[163] Qatar was the only country to explicitly deplore the operation as an interference in the armed conflict in support of one side.[164] The United States has also

---

[156] See eg Saudi Arabia ('Saudi Arabia Condemns Turkish Escalation in Libya—Statement' (*Reuters*, 5 January 2020) <www.reuters.com/article/libya-security-turkey-saudi-idUSL8N2990NJ>); Bahrain ('Bahrain Condemns Turkish Decision to Send Troops to Libya' (*Bahrain News Agency*, 5 January 2020) <https://bna.bh/en/BahraincondemnsTurkishdecisiontosendtroopstoLibya.aspx?cms=q8FmFJgiscL2 fwIzON1%2bDrwspe0GNJDRUW6p3X50RLY%3d>); and Syria (UN Doc A/74/898, 17 June 2020, 1). Egypt denounced Turkey's intervention not on the basis of a violation of the principle of internal self-determination, but as support for terrorism (S/2020/196, 11 March 2020, 2–3).

[157] UN Doc S/2020/269, 2 April 2020, Annex.

[158] UN Doc S/2020/63, 22 January 2020, Annex I, paras 3, 6. The Security Council endorsed the Berlin Conference's conclusions in SC Res 2510, 12 February 2020, paras 2, 10.

[159] UN Doc S/2021/595, 24 June 2021, Annex, paras 5, 7, 8.

[160] SC Resolutions 2510, para 10; 2542, 15 September 2020, para 7; 2570, 16 April 2021, para 13.

[161] UN Doc S/PV.7387, 18 February 2015, 5, 7.

[162] UN Doc S/PV.7387, 7.

[163] Press Statement by the Consultative Meeting of the League of Arab States Council, 18 February 2015, quoted in Raphaël Van Steenberghe, 'Les interventions militaires étrangères récentes contre le terrorisme international. Première partie: fondements juridiques' (2015) 61 AFDI 145, 154.

[164] Van Steenberghe, 'Les interventions', 154; Ahmed Tolba, 'Egypt, Qatar Trade Barbs in Dispute Over Libya Strikes' (*Reuters*, 19 February 2015) <www.reuters.com/article/us-mideast-crisis-egypt-qatar-idUSKBN0LN07520150219>.

NON-INTERVENTION AND INTERNAL SELF-DETERMINATION   269

repeatedly conducted airstrikes against the 'Islamic State' in Libya upon request of the GNA.[165]

South Sudan. A failed coup attempt against President Salva Kiir Mayardit allegedly orchestrated by Vice President Riek Machar in December 2013 led to the defection of army divisions to the latter and the outbreak of a civil war between governmental forces and the Sudan People's Liberation Movement/Army-in-Opposition (SPLM/A-IO), with the latter gaining control of the state capitals of Bor and Bentiu.[166] Uganda initially denied and then admitted sending troops in support of President Kiir.[167] In a letter to the Parliament's speaker, President Museveni explained that his country's forces had intervened with the agreement of President Kiir and that the operation's limited purpose was to protect Juba airport and facilitate the evacuation of Ugandan nationals.[168] As the actual existence of Kiir's consent was dubious, Uganda later concluded a SOFA with the South Sudanese government that allowed the operations of the Uganda People's Defence Force in South Sudan.[169] In the Ugandan parliament, Uganda's minister of defence explained that the intervention followed a request of the 'democratically elected leader of the Republic of South Sudan' and that it had the purpose '1. To save Ugandans and assist to prevent genocide. 2. Avert negative developments in national and regional security. 3. Protect constitutionalism. 4. Respond to dangers to a fraternal neighbour'.[170] While the intervention was not discussed by the Security Council, criticism from Ethiopia, Sudan, and the United States and accusations of ulterior motives led to Uganda's refusal to intervene again in 2017.[171]

Nigeria and Cameroon. In 2015, the Multinational Joint Task Force (MNJTF), formed of units from Nigeria, Niger, Chad, Cameroon, and Benin, was expanded in order to more effectively support the Nigerian government against Boko Haram, an ISIL-affiliated armed group operating in the Lake Chad basin which had established control of a significant amount of territory in northeast Nigeria and declared it a caliphate.[172] The MNJTF's counterterrorism operations were conducted under the aegis of the Peace and Security Council of the African Union at the request of Nigeria and were welcomed by the UN Security Council, which had condemned Boko Haram's terrorist attacks as well as its violations of IHL and human rights.[173] In 2015, Cameroon

---

[165] Spencer Ackerman, Chris Stephen, and Ewen MacAskill, 'US Launches Airstrikes Against Isis in Libya' (*The Guardian*, 1 August 2016) <www.theguardian.com/world/2016/aug/01/us-airstrikes-against-isis-libya-pentagon>.

[166] Douglas H Johnson, 'Briefing: The Crisis in South Sudan' (2014) 113 African Affairs 300, 300–1. The SPLM/A-IO secured control of large areas in the northeast of South Sudan.

[167] 'Uganda Admits Combat Role in South Sudan' (*Al Jazeera*, 16 January 2014) <www.aljazeera.com/news/2014/1/16/uganda-admits-combat-role-in-south-sudan>.

[168] Kasaija Phillip Apuuli, 'Explaining the (Il)legality of Uganda's Intervention in the Current South Sudan Conflict' (2014) 23 African Security Review 352, 357.

[169] ibid, 356, 358.

[170] Parliament of Uganda, Hansards, 14 January 2014, 3 <www.parliament.go.ug/documents/132/hansards-2014-january>.

[171] 'Uganda Rules Out Military Intervention in South Sudan' (*Reuters*, 2 February 2017) <www.reuters.com/article/us-uganda-southsudan-idUSKBN15H1VL>. For criticism of the 2013 intervention, see Johnson, 'Briefing', 308; 'Tragedy Averted: On Uganda's Involvement in S Sudan' (*Al Jazeera*, 19 February 2014) <www.aljazeera.com/opinions/2014/2/19/tragedy-averted-on-ugandas-involvement-in-s-sudan/>.

[172] 'Who Are Nigeria's Boko Haram Islamist group?' (*BBC News*, 24 November 2016) <www.bbc.co.uk/news/world-africa-13809501>.

[173] Communiqué of the 484th Meeting of the AU's Peace and Security Council on the Boko Haram Terrorist Group, 29 January 2015 <www.peaceau.org/en/article/communique-of-the-484th-meet

270 INTERNATIONAL LAW AND THE PRINCIPLE OF NON-INTERVENTION

also consented to the presence of Chadian troops on its territory in order to assist its armed forces against the 'terrorist sect' Boko Haram.[174]

Yemen. Since 2015, a coalition headed by Saudi Arabia has intervened directly and in other forms in the civil war between, among others, President Hadi's government and the Houthi militias.[175] Even though the intervening states noted that 'President Hadi ... appealed for help in confronting terrorist organizations',[176] the Houthi have not been designated as such by the Security Council.[177] Reference was also made to the fact that the Houthi militias were supported by 'regional Powers' and to the fact that Saudi Arabia had been attacked on its territory, and might be attacked again, by the Houthi.[178] In 2016, a letter sent by the coalition to the UN Secretary-General explicitly pointed the finger at Iran and indicated that the Yemeni government's request for intervention was in conformity with the right of self-defence under Article 51.[179] In response, Iran sent a letter to the Security Council stressing that '[f]oreign interfering powers and terrorist groups should not be allowed to have any say in the future of Yemen'.[180] The Council reaffirmed its support for President Hadi and did not censor the coalition's intervention, although it also did not authorize it.[181] In addition to supporting the coalition, the United States has conducted counterterrorism operations against al-Qaeda in the Arabian Peninsula and, in October 2016, carried out strikes in response to missile launches perpetrated by the Houthi that threatened US warships in the Red Sea. The operations were justified on the basis of the consent of the government of Yemen as well as self-defence.[182]

Syria. Since 2011, the Syrian government has been fighting a civil war against several armed groups, including the Free Syrian Army (which is linked to the Syrian National Council—later renamed Syrian Opposition Coalition), the Islamic Front, al-Nusrah

---

ing-of-the-psc-on-the-boko-haram-terrorist-group>; SC Res 2349, 31 March 2017, Preamble, paras 1, 4. See also Christophe Châtelot, 'Le Tchad se porte au secours du Cameroun contre Boko Haram' (*Le Monde*, 16 January 2015) <www.lemonde.fr/afrique/article/2015/01/16/le-tchad-se-porte-au-secours-du-cameroun-contre-boko-haram_4558067_3212.html>; Van Steenberghe, 'Les interventions', 154–6.

[174] Châtelot, 'Le Tchad'.
[175] Operation Decisive Storm was launched on 26 March 2015 and ended on 22 April 2015. It was replaced by Operation Renewal of Hope. The United States has provided logistic assistance, intelligence, surveillance, and arms to the coalition, the United Kingdom and France logistic assistance, and Somalia allowed the use of its territory, airspace, and ports (Benjamin Nußberger, 'Military Strikes in Yemen in 2015: Intervention by Invitation and Self-Defence in the Course of Yemen's "Model Transitional Process"' (2017) 4 JUFIL 110, 118).
[176] UN Doc S/2015/217, 27 March 2015, 5. See also S/2015/279, 27 April 2015, 3; S/2017/937, 15 November 2017, 1. Saudi Arabia and the UAE have officially classified the Houthi as a terrorist organization.
[177] Concerns have however been expressed that the chaos in Yemen could play into the hands of terrorist organizations like al-Qaeda and ISIL (UN Doc S/PV.7426, 14 April 2015, 2 (United Kingdom), 3 (Russia), 5 (Venezuela), 6 (France), 8 (Angola)).
[178] UN Doc S/2015/217, 4–5. See also S/2016/786, 16 September 2016; S/2017/937.
[179] UN Doc A/71/581, 31 October 2016, 2–3. Art 51 of the UN Charter had already been invoked in the Final Communiqué of the 26th Arab League Summit, 29 March 2015 <www.saudiembassy.net/statements/final-communique- 26th-arab-league-summit>. In the Security Council debates Jordan also pointed to Art 51 of the Charter as the legal basis of the intervention (S/PV.7430, 21 April 2015, 11). Iran denied the allegations (A/71/617, 17 November 2016; S/2017/936, 7 November 2017).
[180] UN Doc S/2015/207, 24 March 2015.
[181] SC Res 2216, 14 April 2015.
[182] The White House, Report on the Legal and Policy Frameworks, 18; UN Doc S/2016/869, 17 October 2016.

NON-INTERVENTION AND INTERNAL SELF-DETERMINATION 271

(al-Sham from July 2016), ISIL, and the Kurdistan Workers' Party (PKK). All these factions have at some point established some form of *de facto* administration on the territory under their control.[183] When Russia began its airstrikes on 30 September 2015, it referred to 'a request from the President of the Syrian Arab Republic, Bashar al-Assad, to provide military assistance in combating the terrorist group ISIL and other terrorist groups operating in Syria'.[184] At the Security Council, the Russian delegate also stressed that the legitimate government of Syria was 'conducting a legitimate fight against international terrorism'.[185] In an article published by *The Guardian*, the Russian ambassador to the United Kingdom was clear: 'Russia did not come to Syria to fight the war. We came to deliver the country from terrorists and extremists, and to create conditions for a peace process'.[186] Other states criticized Russia's intervention when it was directed against the moderate opposition and accused it of violations of IHL, but did not censure the intervention against ISIL as such.[187] Iran claimed that its 'military advisory assistance' to the government of Syria was based on a request by the latter under Article 51 of the Charter in order to help it fight terrorist groups responsible for the killing of civilians.[188] On 1 October 2018, it acknowledged taking 'limited and measured military action' in individual self-defence against terrorist elements linked to an attack in Iran that had taken place the previous month.[189]

Ethiopia. Eritrean armed forces heavily intervened in the Tigray War between the Ethiopian government and Tigray People's Liberation Front (TPLF) (2020–22) on the side of the former, although official acknowledgement only occurred in April 2021.[190] The TPLF have established a *de facto* administration in the Tigray region.[191] In a letter to the Security Council, Eritrea justified its involvement as a measure of self-defence against a possible invasion by the TPLF.[192] In a subsequent letter, it also referred to TPLF missile attacks against its territory in the early days of the conflict and to the US support for the insurgents.[193] The Ethiopia–Tigray Peace Agreement, signed in November 2022, has established a permanent ceasefire between Ethiopia and Tigray, although Eritrea is not a party to it.

---

[183] David Wallace, Amy McCarthy, and Shane Reeves, 'Trying to Make Sense of the Senseless: Classifying the Syrian War under the Law of Armed Conflict' (2017) 25 Mich St Int'l L Rev 555, 562–9.

[184] UN Doc S/2015/792, 15 October 2015, Annex. Syria's request is in S/2015/789, 16 October 2015.

[185] UN Doc S/PV.8727, 19 February 2020, 15.

[186] Alexander Yakovenko, 'Russia Went to Syria to Fight Terrorists. We Are Succeeding' (*The Guardian*, 16 October 2016) <www.theguardian.com/commentisfree/2016/oct/15/syria-russian-ambassador-ale ppo-isis>.

[187] See eg Foreign and Commonwealth Office, Joint Declaration on Recent Military Actions of the Russian Federation in Syria, 2 October 2015 <www.gov.uk/government/news/joint-declaration-on-recent-military-actions-of-the-russian-federation-in-syria>. See also Bannelier-Christakis, 'Military Interventions', 763–4.

[188] UN Doc S/2016/369, 22 April 2016; A/71/617, para 5.

[189] UN Doc S/2018/891, 3 October 2018, 2.

[190] UN Doc S/2021/378, 19 April 2021, 1.

[191] Marishet Mohammed Hamza, 'The Tigray People's Liberation Front: A Provincial Ruling Political Party Turned into a Rebel Government' (*Armed Groups and International Law*, 14 October 2022) <www. armedgroups-internationallaw.org/2022/10/14/the-tigray-peoples-liberation-front-a-provincial-ruling-political-party-turned-into-a-rebel-government/>.

[192] ibid.

[193] UN Doc S/2021/510, 1 June 2021, 2–3.

3.2.3 Evaluation

The analysis conducted in Section 3.2.2 clearly shows that states have intervened by sending armed forces in support of a foreign government beset by civil war on a regular basis. If one looks at this practice in the light of the statements that accompanied the interventions, however, it is equally clear that 'by the early 1970s a formal request by the recognised government of a state was no longer deemed sufficient to justify an outside intervention in civil war situations'.[194] Indeed, even when the existence and validity of consent was not in doubt, states qualified their pro-government interventions by referring to the unlawful conduct of the insurgents (that is, the fact that they engaged in terrorist acts or violations of international human rights law (IHRL) and IHL), the conduct of other states (namely their unlawful support for the insurgents), the non-partisan character of the operation and its non-involvement in the hostilities, or the fact that the operation had been authorized by the UN Security Council. The only cases in which I have not been able to find any qualifications attached to the intervening state's reliance on the incumbent's consent are the French and Libyan interventions in Chad in 1969 and 1980 (respectively), Syria's intervention in Lebanon in 1976, Uganda's interventions in the DRC in 2004 and in South Sudan in 2013, and South Africa and other countries' intervention in the CAR in 2013.

At the end of the day, therefore, whether or not the principle of non-intervention is now at least partly displaced by that of internal self-determination in the case of civil war under customary international law, with the consequent prohibition for third states to send armed forces in support of any factions, essentially depends on the weight to be given to the above statements.[195] Whereas some commentators maintain that, absent an explicit reliance on internal self-determination, they have limited evidentiary value as they are grounded in political considerations,[196] others see them as reflecting the legal conviction that, if the claimed circumstances had not been present, the foreign dispatch of troops upon invitation of an incumbent government involved in a civil war would have been unlawful.[197]

I find the latter view more persuasive for several reasons. The first is logical: if internal self-determination, at least in its exogenous dimension, is a binding rule of international law—which it is because, as shown in Section 2, it is contained in several treaties and is also undoubtedly reflected in customary international law[198]—then it is difficult to see what meaning it would have if it did not preclude at least the most intrusive form of foreign intervention in the most dramatic process for the determination of a state's political system, that is, a civil war.

Secondly, the argument that states do not refer to internal self-determination in their statements concerning specific cases of intervention in civil war is contradicted

---

[194] Patrick CR Terry, 'Afghanistan's Civil War (1979–1989): Illegal and Failed Interventions' (2011) 31 PYIL 107, 125.

[195] Hasar, *State Consent*, 3.

[196] See eg Erika De Wet, *Military Assistance on Request and the Use of Force* (OUP 2020) 115–16, 119; Bílková, 'Reflections', 682–3; Dapo Akande and Zachary Vermeer, 'The Airstrikes against Islamic State in Iraq and the Alleged Prohibition on Military Assistance to Governments in Civil Wars' (*EJIL:Talk!*, 2 February 2015) <www.ejiltalk.org/the-airstrikes-against-islamic-state-in-iraq-and-the-alleged-prohibition-on-military-assistance-to-governments-in-civil-wars/>.

[197] See eg Bannelier-Christakis, 'Military Interventions', 748.

[198] Section 2 of this chapter.

NON-INTERVENTION AND INTERNAL SELF-DETERMINATION 273

by the many situations identified in Section 3.2.2 where this has in fact occurred. In addition, there are several explicit manifestations of *opinio juris* by states from all political and geographical affiliations expressed not in relation to specific interventions but in general terms, claiming the existence of a third-state obligation of negative equality in civil wars. Starting from the Western countries, during the debates on the Friendly Relations Declaration the British delegate on the Sixth Committee stressed that 'if civil war broke out in a State and the insurgents did not receive outside help or support, it [would be] unlawful for a foreign State to intervene, even on the invitation of the régime in power, to assist in maintaining law and order'.[199] At the Friendly Relations Special Committee, the United Kingdom cautioned again that, if control of a country is 'divided between warring factions and if no outside intervention [has] taken place, then any form of interference or any encouragement given to any party [is] prohibited by international law', while in other situations 'the right of a legally constituted and internationally recognized Government to seek and receive from a friendly State assistance in preserving internal law and order' remains unprejudiced.[200] The point was reiterated in the Foreign Office internal memorandum on intervention of July 1984.[201]

A 1976 US Department of State memorandum distinguishes a situation where a government is 'beset by civil violence', which corresponds to the old categories of rebellion and insurgency and where armed intervention upon request of the government is lawful, and internal unrest that reaches the threshold of belligerency (that is, a civil war), where third states must choose between neutrality and co-belligerency.[202] The memorandum concludes that intervention in civil strife is permissible in the following cases:

(1) where the legally established government is threatened by outside intervention (infiltration of personnel, supply of arms and ammunition) ... and the legally established government requests the sending of troops and supply of arms; (2) where the lives of our nationals are threatened whether any government exists to request our intervention or not ... (3) where the lives of our nationals and those of other nationals are threatened and the government appears incapable of rendering the required protection whether such intervention is requested by an established government or not ... (4) where there is a total collapse of governmental authority and nonpartisan military intervention helps in an anarchical situation to preserve order so that free elections can be held.[203]

No intervention to influence the outcome of a civil war where no external interferences have occurred, therefore, is envisaged in the memorandum.[204]

---

[199] UN Doc A/C.6/SR.822, 29 November 1963, para 40.

[200] UN Doc A/AC.125/SR.57, 29 November 1967, 5.

[201] British Foreign Office, 'Is Intervention Ever Justified?' in Geoffrey Marston (ed), 'United Kingdom Materials on International Law 1986' (1986) 57 BYBIL 487, 616.

[202] Memorandum of the Attorney Adviser in the Office of the Department of State's Legal Adviser dated 20 February 1976 in Eleanor C McDowell (ed), *Digest of United States Practice in International Law 1976* (GPO 1977) 6.

[203] ibid, 7.

[204] That said, the 2016 US Law of War Manual affirms that '[i]nternational law does not prohibit States from assisting other States in their armed conflicts against non-State armed groups' without further

274   INTERNATIONAL LAW AND THE PRINCIPLE OF NON-INTERVENTION

France's position is on the same lines. In May 1979, the then minister of foreign affairs, Jean François-Poncet, affirmed before the National Assembly that France's principles with respect to Africa had always included the respect for the autonomy of each state to determine their political system and their independence from all external interferences and that his country's interventions on that continent had only been conducted in order to secure a peaceful solution at the request of states unable to deal with conflicts launched or supported from abroad.[205] At the 16th Franco-African summit in La Baule on 20 June 1990, President Mitterrand reiterated that the French position concerning purely internal conflicts in the *Françafrique* was an abstentionist one:

> Je répète le principe qui s'impose à la politique française: chaque fois qu'une menace extérieure poindra, qui pourrait attenter à votre indépendance, la France sera présente à vos côtés. Elle l'a déjà démontré, plusieurs fois et parfois dans des circonstances très difficiles. *Mais notre rôle à nous, pays étranger, fût-il ami, n'est pas d'intervenir dans des conflits intérieurs.* Dans ce cas-là, la France en accord avec les dirigeants, veillera à protéger ses concitoyens, ses ressortissants; mais elle n'entend pas arbitrer les conflits.[206]

Canada is another country that has claimed the existence of an obligation of negative equality in civil wars. In a 1983 memorandum, the Legal Bureau of the Department of External Affairs pointed out that '[t]he mere fact that a government has issued an invitation to intervene, cannot ... be taken in itself as evidence of the legality of a subsequent intervention.'[207] While pro-government intervention is considered permissible when the incumbent government 'is substantially in control of the territory and its existence is not seriously threatened by an insurgent movement',[208] the legal situation changes when it has lost 'effective control over territory or over a substantial part of it'.[209] In this case, 'acceptance of a request to intervene by one of the factions might well constitute an intervention in the domestic affairs of the state, and in some cases be inconsistent with the principle of self-determination'.[210]

During the Cold War, certain non-aligned and socialist countries also expressed themselves in favour of an obligation of negative equality in civil wars. In Chile's view, for instance, 'intervention by a State in the internal or external affairs of another State even at the request of an established government' was prohibited.[211] Commenting on

---

elaboration (US Department of Defense, Law of War Manual (June 2015, updated December 2016) 1068 <www.hsdl.org/c/abstract/?docid=797480>).

[205] Charles Rousseau, 'Chronique des faits internationaux' (1979) 83 RGDIP 998, 1036.
[206] Allocution de M François Mitterrand, Président de la République, sur la situation économique de l'Afrique, les possibilités d'aide des pays les plus riches et la position française en matière de coopération et d'aide financière, La Baule, 20 June 1990, emphasis added <www.vie-publique.fr/discours/127621-allocut ion-de-m-francois-mitterrand-president-de-la-republique-sur-la>.
[207] LH Legault, 'Canadian Practice in International Law During 1983—At the Department of External Affairs' (1984) 22 CYBIL 321, 334.
[208] ibid.
[209] ibid.
[210] ibid.
[211] UN Doc A/C.6/SR.804, 4 November 1963, para 28.

the Soviet intervention in the civil war in Afghanistan in the 1980s, which the USSR controversially justified on the basis of the request of what it claimed to be the government of the Central Asian country, the Venezuelan representative at the Security Council claimed that 'the expression of the will of the people ... should not be interfered with by external actions of the kind which has been denounced here'.[212] After the end of the Cold War, the DRC also claimed that, under customary international law, 'the principle of non-interference in matters within the domestic jurisdiction of States ... includes refraining from extending any assistance to the parties to a civil war operating on the territory of another State'.[213]

Even though, during the debates that led to the adoption of the Declarations on the Inadmissibility of Intervention and on Friendly Relations, several states pointed out that the condemnation of interferences 'in civil strife in another State' could not be read as prejudicing the right of governments to request foreign assistance,[214] it is unclear whether their point extended to direct intervention in civil wars.[215] Other states explicitly opposed such interpretation. Speaking for Finland at the General Assembly's Sixth Committee, for instance, Castrén affirmed that the prevailing opinion today is that 'third States should not interfere, at least by military means, in civil wars, even at the request of the "legal Government"'.[216]

As to the position of regional organizations, OAS General Assembly Resolution 78 (1972) reaffirms the obligation of the member states to refrain 'from intervening in a civil war in another state or in its internal struggles' without distinguishing between government and opposition.[217] The Independent Fact-Finding Mission on the Conflict in Georgia (IFFMCG), established by the Council of the European Union in 2008, has also found that

> in a state of civil war, none of the competing fractions [*sic*] can be said to be effective, stable, and legitimate. Therefore, it is argued that the principle of non-intervention and respect of the international right to self-determination renders inadmissible any type of foreign intervention, be it upon invitation of the previous 'old' government or of the rebels ... military intervention by a third state in a state torn by civil war

---

[212] UN Doc S/PV.2188, 6 January 1980, para 32.

[213] *Armed Activities on the Territory of Congo (Democratic Republic of the Congo v Uganda)* (Merits) [2005] ICJ Rep 168, para 24 (hereafter *DRC v Uganda*).

[214] See eg United States (UN Doc A/C.6/SR.1180, 24 September 1970, para 23; A/8018, 1970, para 259); United Kingdom (A/AC.125/SR.57, 5); Italy (A/C.1/SR.1422, 20 December 1965, para 43); Austria (A/C.1/SR.1422, para 32); Belgium (A/C.1/SR.1405, 9 December 1965, para 19); France (A/C.1/SR.1405, para 43); Jamaica (A/C.1/SR.1406, 10 December 1965, para 32); and Congo (A/C.1/SR.1400, 7 December 1965, para 40).

[215] In fact, there are indications to the contrary. What the United Kingdom was concerned about, for instance, was only 'an unduly broad definition of "civil strife"' which would prevent 'a Government in *temporary* difficulties [to] seek and receive assistance from a friendly State which it trusted to render aid with full respect for the territorial integrity and political independence of the recipient State' (UN Doc A/AC.125/SR.57, 5, emphasis added).

[216] UN Doc A/C.6/SR.1086, 4 December 1968, para 39.

[217] AG/RES.78 (II-0/72) on Strengthening of the Principles of Non-Intervention and the Self-Determination of People's and Measures to Guarantee their Observance, 21 April 1972, OEA/Ser.P/II-0.2, 28 April 1972, vol II, Corr. 1, 43–5.

276   INTERNATIONAL LAW AND THE PRINCIPLE OF NON-INTERVENTION

will always remain an illegal use of force, which cannot be justified by an invitation (doctrine of negative equality).[218]

All in all, therefore, if one reads state practice not in isolation but through the lenses of the *opinio juris* expressed by states of all groups as well as by international organizations both in relation to specific interventions and in more general terms, the conclusion that third states cannot justify sending armed forces in support of a government involved in a civil war exclusively on the basis of the latter's consent is compelling.

While certain objections have been raised against this view, none of them stands up to closer scrutiny. The fact that Article 3(e) of General Assembly Resolution 3314 (XXIX) containing the Definition of Aggression implies that foreign troops can be stationed 'within the territory of another State with the agreement of the receiving State', in particular, does not necessarily undermine the negative equality obligation: the provision does not specify whether the consented presence of foreign troops is also permissible during a civil war and whether 'presence' includes direct involvement in the conflict.

It has also been objected that treaties allowing regional organizations to intervene in a member state when its internal order is under threat are evidence of a presumption in favour of pro-government intervention.[219] Article 4(j) of the African Union's Constitutive Act, for instance, contains the 'the right of Member States to request intervention from the Union in order to restore peace and security'. The operations so far launched by the Organization, however, have only been of a peacekeeping nature, have been deployed in situations of internal instability short of a civil war, or have been conducted against terrorist groups like the Lord Resistance Army.[220] The 1981 ECOWAS Protocol Relating to Mutual Assistance in Defence envisages the Organization's armed intervention in an internal armed conflict occurring in a member state, but only when it has been 'engineered and supported actively from outside' and is 'likely to endanger the security and peace in the entire Community', and cautions that the 'Community forces shall not intervene if the conflict remains purely internal'.[221] The Mechanism for Conflict Prevention, Management, Resolution, Peace Keeping and Security established in 1999 can also be set in motion only if the internal conflict threatens to trigger a humanitarian disaster or poses a serious threat to peace and security in the subregion.[222] Similar language is contained in the 1999 Protocol Relating to the Peace and Security Council of Central Africa (COPAX).[223] The only treaty that appears to grant a regional organization the right to intervene in a 'significant intra-state conflict', including 'a condition of civil war or insurgency', is the 2001 SADC Protocol on Politics,

---

[218] IIFFMCG Report, vol II, 277–8, footnote omitted. See also ibid, 279–80.

[219] Eliav Lieblich, *International Law and Civil Wars: Intervention and Consent* (Routledge 2013) 147.

[220] De Wet, *Military Assistance*, 90–4.

[221] Arts 4(b) and 18, Protocol Relating to Mutual Assistance in Defence (Freetown, 29 May 1981) 1690 UNTS 51.

[222] Art 25 of the Protocol Relating to the Mechanism for Conflict Prevention, Management, Resolution, Peace-Keeping and Security (Lomé, 10 December 1999) (2000) 5 JCSL 231.

[223] Art 25, Protocol Relating to the Peace and Security Council of Central Africa (COPAX) (Malabo, 24 February 2000) <web.archive.org/web/20050603180732/http://www.iss.co.za/AF/RegOrg/unity_to_un ion/pdfs/eccas/copaxfr.pdf>.

Defence and Security Co-operation, but enforcement action can only occur in accordance with Article 53 of the UN Charter, that is, with Security Council authorization.[224] SADC has yet to intervene in a full-fledged civil war, although it has launched operations in response to internal unrest following coups or military mutinies (Lesotho 1998 and 2017) and guerrilla warfare of jihadist inspiration (Mozambique's Cabo Delgado 2021).[225]

Some authors have also claimed that 'the mere fact that a group has the capacity to engage in sustained hostilities against the government or even control parts of the state's territory does not necessarily imply that the population is no longer acquiescing in the authority of the incumbent government'[226] and that a prohibition of intervention on any side does not further genuine self-determination as it only facilitates the victory of the strongest faction, not necessarily the one supported by the population.[227] That might well be correct, but an intervention in support of a government beset by civil war is also no guarantee that popular aspirations will be implemented: at least, an obligation of negative equality favours the faction that it is militarily stronger *because of its own resources*.

It is true that, in *Nicaragua*, the ICJ incidentally affirmed that 'intervention . . . is . . . allowable at the request of the government of a State'.[228] As has been noted, however, the dictum is not an unconditional blessing of third-state pro-government intervention in civil wars: '[t]he fact that such intervention by invitation is *allowable* does not mean that it is authorized in *all* circumstances'.[229] In the *Armed Activities* case, the Court examined the existence and validity of the DRC's consent to the presence of Ugandan troops on its territory to fight insurgents, which might seem to imply that, had such consent been validly granted, it would have constituted a legal basis for the intervention.[230] The DRC, however, had consented to Uganda's military operations on its territory not to influence the outcome of the civil war between the Kabila government and its opposition, but to eradicate *anti-Ugandan* forces operating in the border area between the two countries, as the Congolese army did not have the resources to do so on its own.[231] The Court, therefore, did not address the legality of third-state intervention in support of an incumbent government against armed groups trying to overthrow it and its findings cannot be read as a rebuttal of the application of the doctrine of negative equality in civil wars.

---

[224] Arts 11(2)(b) and 11(3)(d), Protocol on Politics, Defence and Security Co-operation (Blantyre, 14 August 2001) <www.sadc.int/document/protocol-politics-defence-and-security-2001>. See Marko Svicevic, 'Collective Self-Defence or Regional Enforcement Action: The Legality of a SADC Intervention in Cabo Delgado and the Question of Mozambican Consent' (2002) 9 JUFIL 138, 159–60.

[225] Hasar, *State Consent*, 193–4, 255, 264–6.

[226] De Wet, *Military Assistance*, 81–2.

[227] Roger Pinto, 'Les règles du droit international concernant la guerre civile' (1965) 114 Recueil des Cours 451, 483; John N Moore, 'Intervention: A Monochromatic Term for a Polychromatic Reality' in Richard A Falk (ed), *The Vietnam War and International Law*, vol 2 (Princeton University Press 1969) 1061, 1068.

[228] *Nicaragua v USA*, para 246.

[229] Bannelier-Christakis, 'Military Interventions', 745, emphasis in the original.

[230] *DRC v Uganda*, paras 42–54, 92–104.

[231] ibid, para 45.

3.3 Third-State Intervention in a Civil War Other than by Dispatching Armed Forces

If sending armed forces is the most blatant form of third-state intervention in a civil war, it is not also the most common. Indeed, states more frequently intervene by supplying one or more factions with military *matériel*, training, or funding. While this lesser form of support, when in favour of insurgents, is a breach of the principle of non-intervention and, in the case of arming and training, also of the prohibition of the use of force,[232] the question that needs to be addressed is whether customary international law prohibits it even when aimed at helping an incumbent government involved in a civil war.

The Institut de droit international's Wiesbaden Resolution on the Principle of Non-Intervention in Civil Wars affirms that the supply of weapons, war *matériel*, military instructors or technicians to any party of a civil war, or allowing them to be supplied, is prohibited.[233] Indeed, during the Nigerian Civil War, France decided not to accept any new contract for the supply of military *matériel* after the declaration of secession of Biafra on 30 May 1967 and imposed a total embargo on all arms transfers to the region.[234] Czechoslovakia and Belgium did the same from 1968, with the latter suspending the granting of new arms export licenses and noting that this was the approach of the majority of European countries.[235] More recently, Russia's foreign affairs minister, Lavrov, has claimed that his country's supply of arms to Syria aimed 'to support Syria's defense capabilities in the face of external political threat, and not to back Bashar al-Assad'.[236] The legislation of several states also excludes that permits for export of arms to countries in civil war can be granted by the domestic authorities.[237]

The problem is that, unlike that related to the dispatch of armed forces, state practice with regard to this form of intervention is not accompanied by sufficiently clear *opinio juris*. Said otherwise, it remains uncertain whether states actually believe that arming and training foreign governmental forces involved in a civil war is unlawful under international law and whether, when they abstain from supplying them, they do so out of a sense of a legal obligation.[238] A negative answer is suggested by the fact

---

[232] *Nicaragua v USA*, para 228.

[233] Art 2(2). For Bowett, military aid started before the outbreak of the internal conflict must be stopped when the struggle becomes one of self-determination (Derek W Bowett, 'The Interrelation of Theories of Intervention and Self-Defense' in John N Moore (ed), *Law and Civil War in the Modern World* (The Johns Hopkins University Press 1974) 38, 43).

[234] Jean Charpentier, 'Pratique française de droit international' (1968) 14 AFDI 879, 885–6.

[235] Jean JA Salmon and Michel Vincineau (eds), 'La pratique du pouvoir exécutif et le contrôle des chambres législatives en matière de relations internationales (1967–1968)' (1970) RBDI 278, 294–5.

[236] 'Russia Supplying Arms to Syria Under Old Contracts: Lavrov' (*Reuters*, 5 November 2012) <www.reuters.com/article/us-syria-crisis-russia-arms/russia-supplying-arms-to-syria-under-old-contracts-lavrov-idUSBRE8A40DS20121105>.

[237] George P Politakis, 'Variations on a Myth: Neutrality and the Arms Trade' (1992) 35 GYBIL 435, 487, 490.

[238] The case of the Cuban Revolution is instructive. While Britain continued to provide arms to the Batista government against the Castro insurgents in Cuba until a couple of months before its demise, the minister of state defended the sale of seventeen fighter aircraft by arguing that '[a]t the time the sales were approved there was no evidence that the insurgent elements in Cuba had more than a limited measure of support in some parts of the Eastern Provinces of Cuba' (Elihu Lauterpacht, 'The Contemporary Practice of the United Kingdom in the Field of International Law' (1959) 8 Intl & Comp LQ 146, 157). For Lauterpacht, this might suggest that, if the insurgents had had more substantial control of territory or popular support,

that, differently from those in favour of insurgents, pro-government arms transfers in the scenario under consideration are often publicly acknowledged by states, rarely justified in legal terms, and even more rarely condemned.[239] When states do take an official position, the claims of illegality are based on the violation of Security Council resolutions imposing arms embargoes or of treaty obligations, and not on internal self-determination arguments.[240] All in all, states appear reluctant to ban all existing military assistance to a government exactly when it needs it most, as this would result in an advantage for the opposition.[241] That said, the supply of arms to a government still needs to be consistent with applicable treaty obligations concerning arms transfers.[242]

the British government would have felt compelled not to supply the aircraft to the Cuban government (ibid). Lauterpacht acknowledges, however, that the decision could have been made on the basis of political considerations. The US government also initially continued to supply arms to the Batista government, but, after the Cuban dictator suspended the constitution and the insurgents gained control of territory, the shipments were interrupted (14 March 1958) (Roscoe Ralph Oglesby, *Internal War and the Search for Normative Order* (Springer 1971) 120–1). It is however unclear whether the United States stopped the shipments of arms out of a sense of a legal obligation arising from the fact that the insurgency had reached a certain threshold or because of criticism from members of Congress and from the press. The Cuban government claimed that the suspension of the supply of arms was a violation of the Havana Convention on the Duties and Rights of States in the Event of Civil Strife (ibid, 121).

[239] Roth, *Governmental Illegitimacy*, 186. In the Nigerian Civil War, France and other countries denied supplying arms to the Biafran insurgents, while Britain and the USSR officially acknowledged providing them to the Nigerian government (Bennouna, *Le consentement*, 90–1). Britain's Prime Minister Harold Wilson declared that, by sending arms to the Nigerian government, his country was not intervening in the conflict (Harold Wilson, 4 July 1969, quoted in Charles Rousseau, 'Chronique des faits internationaux' (1970) 74 RGDIP 436, 497). In the Congo conflict of the 1960s, the United States provided military *matériel* and training assistance to the Congolese government, claiming that most African countries were also receiving it in the exercise of their own sovereign right (UN Doc S/PV.1174, para 97). Another illustration comes from the Laotian Civil War (1959–75): while the airstrikes against the communist insurgency were not acknowledged by the United States, the supply of military aid to Prince Souvanna Phouma's government and to anti-communist rebels was admitted by the State Department (Keesing's 1961–1962, 17975, 18561). In the Nepalese Civil War (1996–2006), India, the United States, Belgium, and the United Kingdom also provided arms, military equipment, helicopters, and training to the Royal Nepalese Army against the Maoist insurgency (Gyan Pradhan, 'Nepal's Civil War and Its Economic Costs' (2009) 1 Journal of International and Global Studies 114, 118). More recently, no country has suggested that the supply of arms by Russia and Iran to the Assad government in the Syrian Civil War is illegal, although some have considered it politically reproachable (Christian Henderson, 'The Provision of Arms and "Non-Lethal" Assistance to Government and Opposition Forces' (2013) UNSWLJ 642, 669). The US ambassador to the United Nations, in particular, commented that the supply of weapons to the Assad government is 'not technically, obviously, a violation of international law since there's not an arms embargo, but it's reprehensible that arms would continue to flow to a regime that is using such horrific and disproportionate force against its own people' (Louis Charbonneau, 'U.S. Condemns Reported Russian Arms Shipment to Syria' (*Reuters*, 31 May 2012) <www.reuters.com/article/uk-syria-arms-russia/u-s-condemns-reported-russian-arms-shipment-to-syria-idUKBRE84U0X020120531>).

[240] See, for instance, the statements made by Belgium and the United States at the Security Council in relation to the military cooperation between Libya's GNA and Turkey (UN Doc S/PV.8710, 30 January 2020, 8, 14).

[241] Ann Van Wynen Thomas and AJ Thomas, Jr, *Non-Intervention. The Law and Its Import in the Americas* (Southern Methodist University Press 1956) 218; Tom J Farer, 'Harnessing Rogue Elephants: A Short Discourse on Foreign Intervention in Civil Strife' (1969) 82 Harv L Rev 511, 531; Dietrich Schindler, 'Le principe de non-intervention dans les guerres civiles (Huitième Commission), Rapport provisoire et rapport définitif' (1973) 55 AIDI 416, 469–70; Michael J Matheson, 'Practical Considerations for the Development of Legal Standards for Intervention' (1983) 13 Ga J Intl & Comp L 205, 207–8; Roth, *Governmental Illegitimacy*, 180.

[242] Yoram Dinstein, *Non-International Armed Conflicts in International Law* (2nd edn, CUP 2021) 108.

280 INTERNATIONAL LAW AND THE PRINCIPLE OF NON-INTERVENTION

It has been argued that the supply of arms and military equipment to a government beset by civil war must at least remain within the levels existing at the outbreak of the conflict, and not be increased.[243] During the Nigerian Civil War, for instance, the United Kingdom continued to authorize the export of reasonable quantities of arms and ammunition of the same type and quantity that were already being sold to the federal authorities.[244] The British foreign secretary affirmed that, as neutrality was not applicable, Britain could not stop selling arms to the Nigerian government because this would have resulted in supporting the Biafran rebellion.[245] In 1964, Belgium made a similar argument in relation to its technical support and military aid for Congo's government.[246] More recently, Russia's foreign affairs minister, Lavrov, argued that the sale of $1 billion worth of weapons to the Assad government during the Syrian Civil War was in fulfilment of old Soviet contracts and, therefore, did not violate international law.[247] These views, however, are not without problems: states could always pre-emptively increase the level of armaments they send and receive just before the situation of internal unrest becomes a civil war.[248] Furthermore, it is doubtful that the aforementioned cases constitute sufficient evidence of customary international law, particularly given the uncertain *opinio juris*.

As to financial and economic aid, the Wiesbaden Resolution suggests that technical and economic agreements concluded by third states with the government of the state in civil war *before* the civil war started are presumed not to be aimed at influencing its outcome and must thus be respected unless they can 'substantially' impact it. On the other hand, the conclusion of new contracts after the outbreak of the civil war is prohibited even if they are only 'likely' to influence its outcome.[249] But again, no evidence of general *opinio juris* of the illegality of economic and financial support for a government involved in a civil war can be found. This conclusion applies not only to the unilateral transfer of funds but also to the purchase of resources.[250] Russia and

---

[243] Schindler, 'Le principe', 469–70. Moore suggests four criteria to establish when assistance to a government must be frozen at pre-insurgency levels: '(1) the internal conflict must be an authority-oriented conflict aimed at the overthrow of the recognized government and its replacement by a political organization controlled by the insurgents; (2) ... the recognized government is obliged to make continuing use of most of its regular military forces against the insurgents, or a substantial segment of its regular military forces have ceased to accept orders; (3) ... the insurgents effectively prevent the recognized government from exercising continuing governmental authority over a significant percentage of the population; and (4) ... a significant percentage of the population supports the insurgent movement, as evidenced by military or supply of assistance to the insurgents, general strikes, or other actions' (John N Moore, 'The Control of Foreign Intervention in Internal Conflict' (1969) 9 Va J Intl L 205, 275–6).

[244] UK Commonwealth Secretary in the House of Commons, in Charles Rousseau, 'Chronique des faits internationaux' (1968) 72 RGDIP 145, 234. The number of arms supplied to the Nigerian federal government, however, was subsequently increased (Keesing's 1969–1970, 23850).

[245] British Foreign Secretary, House of Commons, 13 March 1969, in AHM Kirk-Green, *Crisis and Conflict in Nigeria—A Documentary Sourcebook 1966–1969*, vol 2 (OUP 1971) 363.

[246] UN Doc S/PV.1173, paras 74–5.

[247] 'Russia Supplying Arms'.

[248] Bhupinder Singh Chimni, 'Towards a Third World Approach to Non-Intervention: Through the Labyrinth of Western Doctrine' (1980) 20 IJIL 243, 253.

[249] Arts 2(2)(d) and 3(b), Wiesbaden Resolution. For Bowett, 'forms of technical or economic assistance which would have no direct bearing on the outcome of the political struggle and which are intended to benefit the state as a continuing entity rather than any particular incumbent government' are, in principle, permissible (Bowett, 'The Interrelation', 42–3). See also Pertile, *Diritto internazionale*, 245–6.

[250] For Tom Ruys, in particular, state practice appears to support the view that crude oil can be purchased from a government involved in a civil war unless it has been prohibited by the UN Security Council (Tom

Iran, for instance, have concluded agreements for oil exploitation and for financial and banking cooperation with the Syrian government.[251] In 2019, Turkey also signed an agreement with the GNA for the delimitation of Libya's exclusive economic zone and for cooperation in its exploitation.[252] In neither case did other states claim that the GNA and Assad could not conclude such agreements because of the civil wars occurring in their respective countries.[253]

To conclude, the principle of internal self-determination as an all-embracing prohibition of any external interference in a civil war is not (yet) customary international law: while the black-letter formulation of the principle as it appears in the OAS Charter, in General Assembly Resolutions 2131 and 2625, and in the Helsinki Final Act is broad enough to prohibit *any* third-state support for a government beset by civil war, this is not reflected in state practice and *opinio juris*, which distinguish between the dispatch of armed forces (prohibited) and other lesser forms of support (tolerated).[254] This results in a paradox where 'providing war *matériel* to the established government in a full-fledged civil war is illegal as a matter of general principle [but] such assistance is almost always deemed lawful in practice'.[255]

4. Third-State Intervention by Dispatching Armed Forces in Situations of Internal Unrest Short of Civil War

States have also sent their armed forces in support of foreign governments in internal armed conflicts falling short of civil war, that is, where the opposition groups only conducted guerrilla warfare and had no stable control over territory, let alone established a *de facto* administration therein.

Greece. In 1944, Britain landed troops in Greece at the request of the National Unity government after the end of German occupation and quickly defeated the communist insurgency.[256] As British troops remained in the Mediterranean country, the Soviet Union lodged a complaint at the UN Security Council claiming that their presence was no longer necessitated by the circumstances and had become a means of pressure in favour of reactionary elements embodied in the Hellenic monarchy.[257] The

---

Ruys, 'Of Arms, Funding and "Non-lethal Assistance"—Issues Surrounding Third-State Intervention in the Syrian Civil War' (2014) 13 CJIL 13, 50).

[251] Pertile, *Diritto internazionale*, 50–1.
[252] ibid, 135–8.
[253] ibid, 138–9.
[254] This is also mainstream scholarship's view: see, among others, Louis B Sohn, 'Gradations of Intervention in Internal Conflict' (1983) 13 Ga J Intl & Comp L 225, 227–8; Rosalyn Higgins, 'Intervention and International Law' in Hedley Bull (ed), *Intervention in World Politics* (Clarendon Press 1984) 29, 41; Doswald-Beck, 'The Legal Validity', 251; Grado, *Guerre civili*, 184–5; Olivier Corten, *The Law Against War: The Prohibition on the Use of Force in Contemporary International Law* (2nd edn, Hart Publishing 2021) 302; Ruys, 'Of Arms', 44; and Hasar, *State Consent*, 300.
[255] Roth, *Governmental Illegitimacy*, 185.
[256] UN Doc S/2, 28 January 1946, 2–3; Stathis N Kalyvas, 'Rebel Governance During the Greek Civil War, 1942–1949' in Arjona, Kasfir, and Mampilly (eds), *Rebel Governance in Civil War*, 119, 124–5.
[257] Communication of the USSR dated 21 January 1946, reproduced in (1946–7) YB UN, 336. In 1946–9, the communist insurgents essentially operated from mountainous areas in Northern Greece and from neighbouring countries and were unable to secure control of urban centres and large populations. Their

282   INTERNATIONAL LAW AND THE PRINCIPLE OF NON-INTERVENTION

Greek government responded that British troops were in Greece at its request and that they would be withdrawn as soon as their obligations had been carried out.[258] From 1947, the United States under President Truman took over Britain's role in support of the Greek government and granted massive financial assistance, military advisors and trainers, arms, ammunition, means of transport, and equipment against the communist Democratic Army of Greece, although no boots on the ground were sent.[259] The UN General Assembly condemned the support to the insurgents provided by Albania, Bulgaria, and Yugoslavia, but not that of the United Kingdom or the United States.[260]

Malaya. Britain, Australia, and New Zealand supported the Malayan federal authorities in different forms against the communist guerrillas during the 'Emergency' (1948–60). The intervention was justified on the basis of the request of the Kuala Lumpur government in line with a defence agreement.[261]

Lebanon. In May 1958, tensions in Lebanon between the Christian Maronites, the Sunnis, and the Druze resulted in an armed rebellion against President Chamoun, who appealed to friendly countries for assistance under Article 51 of the UN Charter.[262] The US government justified its intervention on the basis of 'the specific request of the duly constituted Government of Lebanon' and the inherent right of self-defence against aggression.[263] For the British foreign secretary, the American operation was in accordance with international law because a state has a right to respond to a request for help by another state that is the victim of direct or indirect aggression.[264]

Cameroon. After Cameroon became independent in 1960, it signed a defence agreement with France on the basis of which President Ahmadou Ahidjo requested Paris's assistance in the conflict against the Cameroon Peoples Union guerrilla movement.[265] French forces also intervened in Cameroon under the terms of the 1974 military cooperation pact in support of President Biya in the period of instability that followed the failed coup d'état of April 1984.[266]

Zaire. In the First Shaba War (1977), the 'Safari Club' states (Belgium, France, Morocco, Egypt, Iran, and Saudi Arabia) intervened in various forms at the request of Zaire's President Mobutu against the Front de libération nationale congolaise,

---

provisional government failed to obtain any foreign recognition (Kalyvas, 'Rebel Governance', 125, 132–3). This phase of the conflict, therefore, does not seem to meet the definition of civil war proposed in Section 3.1 of this chapter.

[258] UN Doc S/2, 2–3.
[259] See Andrew Novo, 'Birth of the Cold War: Irregular Warfare First Blood in Greece' (2019) 30 Small Wars & Insurgencies 31. See also the Agreement on Aid to Greece (Athens, 20 June 1947) in *A Decade of American Foreign Policy: Basic Documents 1941–1949 (Revised Edition)* (Department of State 1985) 542.
[260] GA Resolutions 193, 27 November 1948, paras 5–6, and 288, 18 November 1949, paras 2–3. Greece had accused its neighbours of supporting the communist guerrilla forces (UN Doc S/203, 4 December 1946, 3).
[261] Keesing's 1957–1958, 15455, 16105, 16386.
[262] UN Doc S/PV.827, 15 July 1958, para 84.
[263] ibid, para 44.
[264] UK Foreign Secretary, July 1958 in Lauterpacht, 'The Contemporary Practice', 149.
[265] Elizabeth Schmidt, *Foreign Intervention in Africa: From the Cold War to the War on Terror* (CUP 2013) 182.
[266] Kisangani and Pickering, *African Interventions*, 89.

NON-INTERVENTION AND INTERNAL SELF-DETERMINATION 283

which had entered Shaba from eastern Angola in order to overthrow Zaire's government.[267] Only Morocco sent combat troops responding to an appeal addressed to the Organisation of African Unity (OAU) by Mobutu.[268] Belgium affirmed that its involvement was limited to providing instructors for military schools and scholarships to Zaire's officers and that any participation in operational actions was excluded.[269] France's assistance did not include sending soldiers, but only the supply of military *matériel* and transportation at the request of Zaire's president and Morocco's king in order to react against a foreign invasion.[270] Only Cuba, Angola, the USSR, Nigeria, and Algeria criticized the operation.

Republic of the Congo. When Captain Pierre Anga led a rebellion against the Brazzaville government in the northern region of Cuvette (September 1987), French troops intervened at the request of President Sassou-Ngueso. Curiously, the request was addressed to France's Prime Minister, Chirac, instead of President Mitterrand.[271]

Djibouti. In February 1992, French troops were dispatched to Djibouti in support of the governmental forces facing the Afar insurgency (Operation Iskoutir). The intervention, described by France as a 'peace mission', was at the request of the East African country's government.[272]

Guinea-Bissau. In 1998, President Vieira requested Senegal and Guinea to intervene on the basis of a 1975 defence agreement in the conflict which followed the mutiny of troops loyal to the dismissed Chief of Staff Ansumane Mané.[273] At the request of both Vieira and Mané, the intervention was subsequently replaced by an ECOMOG interposition force mandated to monitor the Guinea-Bissau/Senegal border and facilitate the delivery of humanitarian assistance.[274]

Burkina Faso. Since 2014, France has repeatedly intervened against jihadist armed groups in the African country with the consent of the Burkinabe government under the framework of Operation Barkhane. In 2019, in particular, France and the G5 Sahel states committed ground troops to fight against rebel groups like Ansar ul Islam, Jama'at Nasr al-Islam wal Muslimin, and the Islamic State in the Greater Sahara, which have conducted incursions into Burkina Faso from neighbouring Mali. The European Union, the United States, and ECOWAS have also supplied military funding to Burkina Faso.[275]

---

[267] Jean Charpentier, 'Pratique française de droit international' (1977) 23 AFDI 1012, 1013; Aleth Manin, 'L'intervention française au Shaba (19 mai–14 juin 1978)' (1978) 24 AFDI 159, 174.

[268] Charpentier, 'Pratique française' (1977), 1013.

[269] Jean JA Salmon and Michel Vincineau (eds), 'La pratique du pouvoir exécutif et le contrôle des chambres législatives en matière de droit international (1977–1978)' (1980) 15 RBDI 433, 629.

[270] Charpentier, 'Pratique française' (1977), 1014–15.

[271] Kisangani and Pickering, *African Interventions*, 110–11.

[272] '250 French Troops Sent to Djibouti War Zone' (*AP News*, 25 February 1992) <apnews.com/article/d7b4b1b6a29a468f05130adad5ad7975>.

[273] Keesing's 1998, 42323. Senegal sent soldiers and Guinea dispatched 400 troops and helicopters.

[274] UN Doc S/1999/294, 17 March 1999, paras 1–4. SC Res 1216, 21 December 1998, para 4, approved 'the implementation by the ECOMOG interposition force of its mandate ... in a neutral and impartial way and in conformity with United Nations peacekeeping standards.'

[275] Henry Wilkins, 'France Announces Troops Deployment to Burkina Faso' (*Al Jazeera*, 6 November 2019) <www.aljazeera.com/news/2019/11/6/france-announces-troop-deployment-to-burkina-faso>.

284 INTERNATIONAL LAW AND THE PRINCIPLE OF NON-INTERVENTION

Chad. Again under the framework of Operation Barkhane, France conducted airstrikes in 2019 against an armed group who had entered Chad from Libya.[276] The French ministry of defence stated that the strikes had been requested by the Chadian authorities.[277] Paris's minister of foreign affairs subsequently informed the parliament that the operation aimed to prevent a coup d'état to overthrow President Déby.[278]

Mozambique. Since the end of 2017, the ISIS-affiliated Ansar al-Sunna/al-Shabaab armed group has been active in Mozambique's Cabo Delgado. At the request of the Mozambican government, in July 2021 Rwanda deployed a joint force in the province 'affected by terrorism and insecurity' and recalled its commitment to the Responsibility to Protect doctrine.[279] The same year SADC authorized the deployment of troops 'in support of Mozambique to combat terrorism and acts of violent extremism' (Southern African Development Community Mission in Mozambique).[280]

Third states also sent armed forces at the request of an incumbent government in reaction to military coups and mutinies, mercenary attacks, and mob violence, including in the following cases:

Jordan. Immediately after the 1958 Iraqi revolution that led to the overthrow and execution of the royal family, a coup against the Hashemite monarchy was also expected to take place in Jordan.[281] Britain therefore intervened in response to the request of King Hussein under Article 51 of the UN Charter in order to protect the territorial integrity and political independence of the Arab country from external threats.[282] While the contemporaneous American intervention in Lebanon was controversial, that in Jordan met with less criticism.

Guatemala and Honduras. Following an attempted revolt by left-wing military officers in Guatemala which resulted in armed disturbances in that country and in Honduras (November 1960), the two Central American states requested the United States to assist them, should it become necessary, to prevent communist interventions in their internal affairs. Explaining the legal basis of the possible assistance, the US Department of State affirmed that it would be 'in response to a request which the respective governments concerned have every right in their sovereign capacity to make and which the United States in its sovereign capacity has a right to provide.'[283]

Brunei. When a coup led by the North Kalimantan National Army (which enjoyed covert support from Indonesia) with the purpose of overthrowing the government

---

[276] Louis Balmond, 'L'intervention militaire de la France au Tchad en février 2019' (2019) 13 Paix et sécurité européenne et internationale 245, 246–7.

[277] Nathalie Guibert et Christophe Châtelot, 'Tchad: la France vole au secours d'Idriss Déby en bombardant des rebelles' (*Le Monde*, 7 February 2019) <www.lemonde.fr/afrique/article/2019/02/07/tchad-la-france-vole-au-secours-d-idriss-deby-en-bombardant-des-rebelles_5420297_3212.html>.

[278] Balmond, 'L'intervention militaire', 252.

[279] Republic of Rwanda, 'Rwanda Deploys Joint Force to Mozambique', 9 July 2021 <www.gov.rw/blog-detail/rwanda-deploys-joint-force-to-mozambique>.

[280] SADC, Communiqué of the Extraordinary Summit of SADC Heads of State and Government, 23 June 2021, quoted in Svicevic, 'Collective Self-Defence', 144.

[281] Keesing's 1957–1958, 16358.

[282] UN Doc A/3877, 18 August 1958; S/PV.831, 17 July 1958, paras 24–5.

[283] Whiteman (ed), *Digest*, 433.

of Brunei was attempted on 8 December 1962, the sultan requested, and the United Kingdom granted, 'urgent assistance in restoring law and order'.[284]

Gabon. French paratroopers intervened in 1964 at the request of Vice President Yembit, in line with Article 3 of the 1960 defence agreement between the two countries, to restore President M'ba to power after a coup orchestrated by members of the Gabonese military and police.[285] Paris's foreign affairs minister pointed out that the French forces did not have responsibilities in the affairs concerning the internal sovereignty of Gabon.[286] The intervention was commended by many French-speaking African countries (Madagascar, CAR, Chad, Niger, Upper Volta, Côte d'Ivoire), although others denounced it as an intervention in Gabon's internal affairs (Mali, Algeria, Ghana).[287]

Tanganyika, Kenya, and Uganda. In January 1964, Britain accepted a request for intervention by the presidents of the three newly independent African countries after members of their armed forces had almost simultaneously mutinied to obtain a salary increase.[288]

Sierra Leone. In line with a defence agreement signed, but not ratified,[289] by the two countries, Guinea intervened in 1971 with 200 paratroopers upon request of Sierra Leone's President Siaka Stevens after a military mutiny.[290]

Burundi. In response to Hutu-led violence following the return to Burundi and subsequent assassination of former king Ntare V, in 1972 Tutsi President Micombero declared martial law and requested troops from neighbouring Zaire to assist in restoring internal order.[291] In response, Zaire sent arms and a force of paratroopers.[292]

Bermuda. British forces intervened in 1977 at the request of the governor, who is responsible to the British government for Bermuda's internal security, following riots caused by youths attacking property in protest against the execution of two Bermudians found guilty of murdering two supermarket managers in April 1973.[293]

The Gambia. On 30 July 1981, a coup attempted by members of The Gambia Socialist Revolutionary Party and disaffected staff of The Gambia Field Force against President Dawda Jawara, who was in the United Kingdom attending the wedding of the Prince

---

[284] Elihu Lauterpacht (ed), *The Contemporary Practice of the United Kingdom in the Field of International Law—1962*, vol 2 (British Institute of International and Comparative Law 1963) 140. The request was made on the basis of the Agreement between the United Kingdom and Brunei on Defence and External Affairs (Brunei, 29 September 1959).

[285] Jean Charpentier, 'Pratique française de droit international' (1964) 10 AFDI 900, 928; Bennouna, *Le consentement*, 48.

[286] Charpentier, 'Pratique française' (1964), 928.

[287] Immanuel Maurice Wallerstein, *Africa: The Politics of Independence and Unity* (University of Nebraska Press 2005) 78.

[288] Elihu Lauterpacht (ed), *British Practice in International Law 1964* (British Institute of International Law 1965) 22–3.

[289] The agreement was ratified by the Parliament of Sierra Leone two weeks after the intervention (Castor M Díaz Barrado, *El consentimiento, causa de exclusión de la ilicitud del uso de la fuerza, en Derecho Internacional* (Universidad de Zaragoza 1989) 170).

[290] Keesing's 1971–1972, 24559.

[291] ibid, 25323–4.

[292] Bertil Dunér, 'The Many-Pronged Spear: External Military Intervention in Civil Wars in the 1970s' (1983) 20 Journal of Peace Research 59, 63.

[293] Statement by the Secretary of State for Foreign and Commonwealth Affairs (Dr David Owen) in HC Deb 5 December 1977, vol 940, cc1014–24.

of Wales and Lady Diana Spencer, resulted in his request to Senegal to intervene on the basis of the 1965 mutual defence agreement.[294] The coup was quashed after a few days thanks to the intervention.

Grenada. On 25 October 1983, the United States, Barbados, and Jamaica intervened in Grenada under the framework of the Organisation of Eastern Caribbean States (OECS) after Prime Minister Maurice Bishop had been deposed, arrested, and eventually killed in a coup and the Revolutionary Military Council of General Austin had assumed control of the country, causing mass protests. The American intervention resulted in the removal of General Austin from power. The United States invoked three legal grounds for the intervention: the appeal of the government of Grenada represented by the governor general, Sir Paul Scoon, the last remnant of 'legitimate authority' on the island; the decision of the OECS consistent with the UN Charter under the Treaty Establishing the OECS and its appeal for assistance; and the need to protect the hundreds of American students in the Caribbean country.[295] The United States also specified that it did not intend to impose any particular form of government on the Grenadians.[296] Reactions, however, were overwhelmingly negative.[297] The UN General Assembly censored the intervention as 'a flagrant violation of international law and of the independence, sovereignty and territorial integrity of that state'.[298] Condemnation by the Security Council was avoided only thanks to the US veto.

Togo. In September 1986, a French intervention was requested by Togo's President Gnassingbe Eyadema (whose rule was threatened when some fifty armed men tried to take over his government).[299] Eyadema claimed that Ghana was behind the attempted coup, which allowed the intervention to be framed in the context of the 1963 Defence Agreement between France and Togo.[300]

Maldives. In November 1988, after a group of Maldivians assisted by armed mercenaries associated with Tamil secessionists from Sri Lanka attempted a coup to overthrow President Gayoom, India responded to his appeal for help and dispatched paratroopers and naval forces (Operation Cactus). The operation rescued Gayoom and gained control of the capital Malé, thus suppressing the coup.[301] The Western states praised the role played by India in the crisis.

---

[294] 'Senegalese Said to Close in on Gambia Rebels' (*The New York Times*, 2 August 1981) <www.nytimes.com/1981/08/02/world/senegalese-said-to-close-in-on-gambia-rebels.html>.

[295] Statement by Deputy Secretary of State Dam before the House Committee on Foreign Affairs, 2 November 1983, in Marian Nash Leich (ed), 'Contemporary Practice of the United States Relating to International Law' (1984) 78 AJIL 200, 203–4; Letter of the US Department of State's Legal Adviser, Davis R Robinson, to Professor Edward Gordon, 10 February 1984, ibid, 655, 662–5. At the United Nations, however, the United States only invoked, as justifications, the protection of its citizens and the appeal by OECS treaty (UN Doc S/16076, 25 October 1983, Annex). See also the statements of Barbados (S/PV.2491, 27 October 1983, para 148), Saint Lucia (S/PV.2491, paras 23–4), Saint Vincent and the Grenadines (S/PV.2491, paras 325–34), and Dominica (S/PV.2489, 26 October 1983, para 9).

[296] Statement by Deputy Secretary of State Dam before the House Committee on Foreign Affairs, 204.

[297] Doswald-Beck, 'The Legal Validity', 237–9; Roth, *Governmental Illegitimacy*, 307.

[298] GA Res 38/7, 2 November 1983, para 1.

[299] Jean Charpentier, 'Pratique française de droit international' (1986) 32 AFDI 961, 1015–16.

[300] Kisangani and Pickering, *African Interventions*, 100.

[301] 'Operation Cactus: How Indian Troops Went to the Maldives and Helped Quell a Coup' (*The Times of India*, 7 February 2018) <https://timesofindia.indiatimes.com/world/south-asia/operation-cactus-how-indian-troops-went-to-maldives-and-helped-quell-a-coup/articleshow/62816787.cms>.

NON-INTERVENTION AND INTERNAL SELF-DETERMINATION   287

Comoros. After a 1989 coup by mercenaries resulted in the killing of President Abdallah, France and South Africa intervened to force the mercenaries out of the country. The intervention, codenamed Operation Oside, was at the request of the President of the Supreme Court, Djohar, who was interim head of state after the killing of Abdallah.[302] At the United Nations, the Group of Islamic Countries condemned the coup and the assassination of the Comoros' president as a violation of the principle of non-interference.[303] Six years later, on the night between 27 and 28 September 1995, a group of mercenaries and members of the Comorian armed forces launched another coup against President Djohar and took over the islands. A French elite unit intervened to restore constitutional order at the request of Prime Minister Caabi Elyachroutu pursuant to the 1978 defence agreement between the Comoros and France (Operation Azalée).[304]

Gabon. France intervened in 1990 '[e]n accord avec les autorités locales souveraines'[305] and with the purpose of protecting French citizens following internal disorders caused by the mysterious death of an opposition leader. It affirmed, therefore, that the operation could not be considered an interference in the internal affairs of Gabon.[306]

Côte d'Ivoire. Following unrest caused by army conscripts and motivated by low pay levels and poor employment prospects, in 1990 Côte d'Ivoire's President Houphouët-Boigny requested France's intervention on the basis of a 1961 treaty between the two countries. Although France did not eventually intervene, it alerted the troops already deployed in the country.[307]

CAR. In April and May 1996, French forces intervened at the request of President Patassé under the 1960 and 1966 bilateral cooperation agreements in order to evacuate foreigners and to protect governmental buildings following rebellions by members of the armed forces who protested over unpaid salaries (Operation Almandin II).[308] The intervention was commended by seven African states and by the European Union.[309] After the signing of the Bangui Agreements in 1997, Patassé requested the deployment of an inter-African mission to monitor their implementation, and in particular to disarm the ex-rebels and militias (Mission Interafricaine de Surveillance des Accords de Bangui—MISAB). The force was composed of contingents from six African countries logistically supported by France and was mandated to act in a neutral way.[310]

Sierra Leone. When, on 25 May 1997, a group of disgruntled army officers led by Major Johnny Paul Koroma staged a coup against President Ahmad Tejan Kabbah, ECOWAS first imposed an economic embargo on the country and then sent

---

[302] Tom Masland, 'French Troops End Reign of Mercenary in Comoros' (*Chicago Tribune*, 16 December 1989) <www.chicagotribune.com/news/ct-xpm-1989-12-16-8903180553-story.html>.

[303] UN Doc A/44/249, 14 December 1989, Annex.

[304] UN Doc A/50/PV.40, 24 October 1995, 64; Jean-François Dobelle, 'Pratique française de droit international' (1996) 42 AFDI 1011, 1025; Maurice Torrelli, 'Chronique des faits internationaux' (1996) 100 RGIP 197, 206–8.

[305] Jean Charpentier, 'Pratique française de droit international' (1990) 36 AFDI 977, 1058.

[306] ibid.

[307] Keesing's 1990, 37445.

[308] Torrelli, 'Chronique', 812–13.

[309] ibid, 813.

[310] UN Doc S/1997/561, 22 July 1997, 3.

288 INTERNATIONAL LAW AND THE PRINCIPLE OF NON-INTERVENTION

ECOMOG forces stationed in Liberia to reverse the coup and restore Kabbah to power, an objective achieved in February 1998. Kabbah had requested Nigeria's military assistance under the SOFA between Sierra Leone and Nigeria and other bilateral agreements.[311] Sierra Leone's permanent representative to the United Nations, however, referred to self-defence under Article 51 of the UN Charter.[312] The Security Council had demanded that the junta step down and allow the restoration of the elected government.[313] In April 1998, it also commended the ECOWAS efforts in Sierra Leone.[314]

Lesotho. After a mutiny by junior officers in the Lesotho Defence Force followed by violent clashes in the capital Maseru in 1998, Lesotho's Prime Minister Pakalitha Mosisili successfully requested neighbouring Zimbabwe, Botswana, Mozambique, and South Africa to intervene under the aegis of SADC 'to restore public order and the rule of law' (Operation Boleas).[315]

Solomon Islands. After clan-based fighting had overthrown Prime Minister Ulufa'alu, in 2003 the new prime minister, Manasseh Sogovare, requested assistance from Australia, New Zealand, and the Pacific Islands Forum countries to restore internal order.[316] The Regional Assistance Mission in the Solomon Islands (RAMSI) was essentially a policing operation, with police and armed peacekeepers tasked with assisting the Solomon Islands' law enforcement units.[317] The Australian foreign affairs minister, Alexander Downer, called it a case of 'cooperative intervention'.[318] Australia intervened again in the Solomon Islands in 2021 at the request of Prime Minister Manasseh Sogavare under the terms of a 2017 security treaty between the two countries after violent protests targeted parliament, Chinese businesses, and other buildings in the capital, Honiara. The Australian government pointed out that it was assisting with 'riot control' and did not intend to intervene in the internal affairs of the Pacific Ocean country.[319]

East Timor. In 2006, protests by soldiers from the western part of the country claiming that they were being discriminated against in favour of soldiers from the east degenerated into clashes and internal violence, which led President Xanama Gusmao

---

[311] Peter A Dumbuya, 'ECOWAS Military Intervention in Sierra Leone: Anglophone-Francophone Bipolarity or Multipolarity?' (2008) 25(2) Journal of Third World Studies 83, 83.

[312] See United Nations, 'Press Conference by Permanent Representative of Sierra Leone', 9 June 1997 <https://press.un.org/en/1997/19970609.jonah9.jun.html>; United Nations, 'Press Conference by Permanent Representative of Sierra Leone', 18 February 1998 <https://press.un.org/en/1998/19980218.jonah.html>.

[313] SC Res 1132, 8 October 1997, para 1. The OAU also condemned the coup and urged regional states to take 'all necessary measures' to restore Kabbah to power (Eleanor Lumsden, 'An Uneasy Peace: Multilateral Military Intervention in Civil Wars' (2003) 35 NYU J Intl L & Pol 795, 824).

[314] SC Res 1162, 17 April 1998, para 2.

[315] UN Doc A/53/PV.29, 6 October 1998, 3–4.

[316] UN Doc S/2003/753, 22 July 2003, Annex, paras 3, 9; S/2003/799, 11 August 2003, Annex.

[317] UN Doc S/2003/753, Annex, para 8. See Alex Conte, 'New Zealand Defence Force Activity' (2006) 3 NZYBIL 267, 267.

[318] Tarcisius Tara Kabutaulaka, '"Failed State" and the War on Terror: Intervention in Solomon Islands' (2004) 72 Asia-Pacific Issues 1, 3.

[319] 'Australia to Send Troops and Police to Solomon Islands Amid Unrest' (*ABC News*, 25 November 2021) <www.abc.net.au/news/2021-11-25/australia-to-send-defence-police-to-solomon-islands/100651476>; 'Here's What's Behind the Violent Protests in the Solomon Islands Capital, Honiara' (*ABC News*, 25 November 2021) <www.abc.net.au/news/2021-11-25/solomon-islands-protests-explainer-china-taiwan/100648086>.

NON-INTERVENTION AND INTERNAL SELF-DETERMINATION 289

to request the assistance of Portugal, Australia, New Zealand, and Malaysia 'in order to establish measures of security and confidence among the populations so as to restore tranquillity throughout the national territory and promote a climate of dialogue among the various sectors of society'.[320]

Côte d'Ivoire. During the constitutional crisis that led to heavy fighting between the forces of President Gbagbo and President-elect Ouattara, France intervened on the basis of Resolution 1975 (2011) and the request of the UN Secretary-General to protect civilians, not of the consent of President-elect Ouattara, and repeatedly affirmed that it would not take sides.[321] In the end, however, French and UNOCI forces attacked Gbagbo's stronghold and caused the surrender of his forces and the eventual instalment of Ouattara.[322] The Security Council welcomed Ouattara's acquisition of power but did not comment on the intervention.[323]

Lesotho. In 2014, Lesotho's Prime Minister Thabane fled to South Africa after claims of a military coup aimed at overthrowing and killing him and called upon his host country to send peacekeeping troops to re-establish order. A few days later, South African police escorted Thabane back to Maseru.[324] Following the murder of General Motsomotso in September 2017, SADC deployed the Preventive Mission in the Kingdom of Lesotho (SAPMIL) at the request of its government in order to restore stability in the country.[325]

The Gambia. After President Jammeh lost the 2016 elections, ECOWAS troops briefly entered The Gambia the following year at the appeal of President-elect Adama Barrow and under the Lomé Protocol in order to force Jammeh to leave office.[326] In the end, the ECOWAS incursion in The Gambia was halted to allow for a final round of negotiations which led to Jammeh stepping down voluntarily and going into exile. The UN Security Council had backed the legitimacy of the new president.[327]

CAR. In December 2020, Rwanda and Russia sent troops to the CAR at the request of its government (in the case of Russia, under the framework of the 2018 bilateral military cooperation agreement) after an alleged coup orchestrated by former President Bozizé ahead of the presidential and parliamentary elections. Rwanda also claimed that the deployment was in response to the targeting of its troops in the UN peacekeeping force by rebels supported by Bozizé.[328]

---

[320] UN Doc S/2006/319, 24 May 2006, Annex.

[321] Declaration of the French President, 4 April 2011, in Frédérique Coulée and Hélène Picot, 'Pratique française du droit international' (2011) 57 AFDI 757, 764.

[322] Antonios Tzanakopoulos, 'The UN/French Use of Force in Abidjan: Uncertainties Regarding the Scope of UN Authorizations' (*EJIL:Talk!*, 9 April 2011) <www.ejiltalk.org/the-un-use-of-force-in-abidjan/>.

[323] SC Res 1980, 28 April 2011.

[324] David Smith, 'Lesotho "Coup": Thabane Calls on South Africa to Send Peacekeeping Troops' (*The Guardian*, 1 September 2014) <www.theguardian.com/world/2014/sep/01/lesotho-tom-thabane-south-africa>.

[325] 'SADC Secretariat Briefs African Union Peace and Security Council on the Contingent Force Deployment to Lesotho', 25 January 2018 <www.sadc.int/latest-news/sadc-secretariat-briefs-african-union-peace-and-security-council-contingent-force>.

[326] UN Doc S/PV.7866, 19 January 2017, 2.

[327] SC Res 2337, 19 January 2017.

[328] 'Russia, Rwanda Sent Troops to Central African Republic' (*Al Jazeera*, 21 December 2020) <www.aljazeera.com/news/2020/12/21/russia-rwanda-send-troops-to-central-african-republic>.

290 INTERNATIONAL LAW AND THE PRINCIPLE OF NON-INTERVENTION

Finally, states have sent their troops in support of foreign governments facing popular uprisings calling for democratic reforms in the following cases.

Hungary. As a consequence of mass demonstrations against the Communist government, Soviet forces already in Hungary entered Budapest on 24 October 1956 at the request of the Hungarian Working People's Party General Secretary Ernő Gerő under the framework of the Warsaw Pact in order to assist in restoring order against counter-revolutionary attempts.[329] A second intervention, including a full-scale attack on the capital, took place on 4 November after Imre Nagy, who had been appointed prime minister on 24 October in an effort to appease the protesters, abolished the monopoly of the Communist Party, withdrew Hungary from the Warsaw Pact, declared its neutrality, and requested the Soviet troops to leave the country. This second intervention was claimed to be requested by János Kádár, who took effective power only on 7 November, and was widely condemned.[330] For the United Kingdom, the Soviet intervention in Hungary was unlawful because the uprising was spontaneous unlike that in Lebanon in 1958.[331] Iran pointed out that it 'can never agree to the use of such troops to stifle popular movements, even if the government whose territory is occupied has consented to their use or asked for it'.[332] Brazil and Belgium expressed the same view.[333] For France, 'nothing can justify intervention by foreign troops to crush an absolutely peaceful people which merely claims the elementary freedom of reforming its system of government'.[334] Nepal declared that '[t]he armed intervention of a big country in the affairs of a small country, even on the plea that a request came from the latter, is apt to interfere with the free expression of the will of the people, and to that extent it is apt to hinder the process of democracy'.[335]

Jordan. When Britain intervened in 1958 to pre-empt a coup against King Hussein allegedly organized by the UAR, Prime Minister Macmillan emphasized that '[t]he arguments for standing aside and doing nothing would be different if this movement were for genuine, popular, and constitutional change'.[336]

Czechoslovakia. The Soviet Union claimed that the military intervention of the Warsaw Pact forces in Czechoslovakia in 1968 (Operation Danube) was based on the request for assistance of the government of that state and also referred to the right of the socialist countries to individual and collective self-defence.[337] According to the USSR, the unrest in Czechoslovakia was fuelled by external actors.[338] Many states,

---

[329] UN Doc S/PV.746, paras 155–7, 163; A/PV.582, 19 November 1956, para 108; Soviet statement of 30 October 1956 in (1956) 35 Dept St Bull 745, 746. A UN Special Committee set up to investigate the situation found no evidence that the Hungarian government had given consent to the intervention (A/3592, 1957, 39).

[330] UN Doc A/PV.564, 4 November 1956, para 100. The intervention was condemned in GA Resolutions 1004 (ES-II), 4 November 1956; 1005 (ES-II), 9 November 1956; and 1006 (ES-II), 9 November 1956. A Security Council resolution condemning the intervention was not adopted only thanks to the Soviet veto.

[331] Lauterpacht, 'The Contemporary Practice', 150.

[332] UN Doc S/PV.746, para 176.

[333] UN Doc A/PV.569, 8 November 1956, para 89 (Brazil); S/PV.746, para 182 (Belgium).

[334] UN Doc A/PV.583, 19 November 1956, para 253.

[335] UN Doc A/PV.585, 20 November 1956, para 201.

[336] Keesing's 1957–1958, 16359.

[337] UN Doc S/8759, 21 August 1968, 1. See also Poland (S/PV.1443, 22 August 1968, para 441). The Czechoslovak representative at the Security Council, however, denied that his government had consented to the intervention (S/PV.1445, 24 August 1968, para 161).

[338] UN Doc S/PV.1441, paras 76, 78, 82.

however, condemned the intervention and the Security Council was prevented from censoring it only by the Soviet veto.[339] In 1989, the USSR recognized the illegality of the operation.[340]

Tonga. The 2006 Nuku'alofa riots, where democracy advocates took to the streets of Tonga's capital in protest, degenerated into robbery, looting, vehicle theft, arson, and property damage. Prime Minister Sevele successfully requested Australia and New Zealand to send soldiers and police officers to help the local police restore order.[341] The intervention went largely unnoticed by the international community.

Bahrain. Street demonstrations by the Shi'a population against the Sunni ruling minority in 2011 led to a request by the Bahrain government for an intervention by the Peninsula Shield Force set up by the Gulf Cooperation Council in 1984.[342] The intervention's purpose was to contribute 'to the maintenance of order and stability' and to react against the alleged intervention by Iran in the domestic affairs of Bahrain.[343] Iran, however, denied any involvement.[344] There was no discussion of the intervention at the United Nations and the only state to openly condemn it was Iran.[345]

Belarus. After elections were dubiously won for the sixth consecutive time by President Lukashenko in 2020, mass protests erupted mainly in the capital Minsk calling for his resignation. When Lukashenko reached out to Russia's President Putin for possible military support, the latter declared his readiness to give the necessary assistance under the framework of the Treaty on the Establishment of the Union State and through the Collective Security Treaty Organization (CSTO), but also referred to the existence of 'external pressure' following the elections.[346]

Kazakhstan. On 6 January 2022, the CSTO's Collective Security Council decided to dispatch forces to the Central Asian country at the request of President Tokayev in order to curb demonstrations in Almaty and other cities against fuel price rises and the lack of political and economic reforms.[347] Tokayev branded the protestors 'terrorists'

---

[339] See eg ibid, paras 40, 162, 248 (United States), 57 (United Kingdom), 107 (Paraguay), 169 (Canada), 175 (France), 185–6 (Denmark), and 196 (Brazil). See the analysis of the different state positions in Gerhard Hafner, 'The "Soviet" Intervention in Czechoslovakia (1968)' (2016) 21 ARIEL 27, 42–8.

[340] Keesing's 1989, 36982.

[341] Keesing's 2006, 47587.

[342] Note of the Secretary General of the Cooperation Council, 23 March 2011, cited in Agatha Verdebout, 'The Intervention of the Gulf Cooperation Council in Bahrain—2011) in Ruys and Corten (eds), *The Use of Force*, 795, 797; Report of the Bahrain Independent Commission of Inquiry, 23 November 2011, para 1578 <www.bici.org.bh>.

[343] Report of the Bahrain Independent Commission of Inquiry, paras 1566–77.

[344] UN Doc A/65/822-S/2011/253, 19 April 2011, Annex, 2–3.

[345] ibid, Annex, 2.

[346] President of Russia, 'Telephone Conversation with President of Belarus Alexander Lukashenko', 16 August 2020 <http://en.kremlin.ru/events/president/news/63894>.

[347] Florian Kriener and Leonie Brassat, 'Quashing Protests Abroad: The CSTO's Intervention in Kazakhstan' Max Planck Institute for Comparative Public Law & International Law (MPIL) Research Paper No 2023-10 (6 April 2023) 5-8. The vast majority of the forces were from Russia (ibid, 8). In 2010, a Russian intervention was also requested by the interim government of Kyrgyzstan to combat resistance after a popular revolt led to the resignation of President Bakiyev. The Russian President's spokeswoman, however, replied that the situation was 'an internal conflict and for now Russia [did] not see the conditions for taking part in its resolution' (Hulkar Isamova, 'Kyrgyzstan Asks Russia to Help End Ethnic Clashes' (*Reuters*, 12 June 2010) <www.reuters.com/article/oukwd-uk-kyrgyzstan-violence-idAFTRE65A5PA20100612>).

292 INTERNATIONAL LAW AND THE PRINCIPLE OF NON-INTERVENTION

and 'bandits' and claimed that the threat had an external origin.[348] At the Security Council, the Kazakh delegate also qualified the situation as 'a terrorist threat to national security and an act of aggression' and referred to the right of individual and collective self-defence under the UN Charter and the CSTO Treaty.[349] The CSTO troops did not directly participate in the repression but took over certain defensive tasks of the Kazakh forces to allow the latter to focus on crushing the protests.[350] No state at the Security Council questioned the legality of the operation. The United Kingdom 'noted' the deployment of troops by the CSTO and limited itself to stressing that it 'should be proportionate in any use of force and that Kazakhstan's sovereignty must be respected', thus implicitly accepting the legality of the operation.[351]

4.1 Evaluation

What emerges from the above cases is a sliding scale of situations of internal unrest which impacts on the permissibility of third-state armed intervention in support of an incumbent government. At one extreme, there are civil wars, where practice and *opinio juris* clearly show that the incumbent government's consent is an insufficient legal basis for third states to send their armed forces in its support. At the opposite extreme, we have military coups, mutinies, mercenary attacks, and mob violence, where governmental consent has been invoked as the sole ground for third-state intervention (apart from the British intervention in Jordan, the US operation in Grenada, ECOWAS's 1998 intervention in Sierra Leone, and the French interventions in Togo, Gabon, and Côte d'Ivoire 2011). When criticism was raised, it was due to doubts about the competence of the inviting authority to consent, as in the case of Grenada.[352] In between these extremes, state practice and *opinio juris* are more fluid: in seven out of the eleven examined cases of internal armed conflicts short of civil war, the interventions appear to have been exclusively justified on the basis of the incumbent's consent without further specifications (Malaya 1948, Cameroon 1960, Zaire 1977 (Morocco's intervention), Republic of the Congo 1987, Djibouti 1992, Guinea-Bissau 1998, and Chad 2019). There is, therefore, no sufficiently general practice justifying the extension of the principle of internal self-determination and the resulting obligation of negative equality to internal armed conflicts short of civil war. All that can be said is that, in this scenario, the more serious the conflict, the more the incumbent government and third states tend to accompany the intervention with claims of indirect aggression (Greece 1946, Lebanon 1958) or counterterrorism (Burkina Faso 2014, Mozambique 2021).

---

[348] President of the Republic of Kazakhstan 'President Kassym-Jomart Tokayev Held a Session of the Security Council', 6 January 2022 <www.akorda.kz/en/president-kassym-jomart-tokayev-held-a-session-of-the-security-council-705318>.

[349] UN Doc S/PV.8967, 16 February 2022, 20. Russia, Armenia, and Belarus also invoked the request of Kazakhstan's president under the CSTO Treaty as the legal basis of the operation but did not explicitly refer to self-defence (UN Doc S/PV.8967, 6, 20. 23). The CSTO's secretary-general described the operation as 'peacekeeping' (S/PV.3967, 5).

[350] Kriener and Brassat, 'Quashing Protests', 8.

[351] UN Doc S/PV.8967, 8.

[352] Several states emphasized the absence of a request by the Grenadian government (see eg France (UN Doc S/PV.2489, para 146), Algeria (S/PV.2489, para 99), and Afghanistan (S/PV.2491, para 262)).

In the case of pro-democracy popular uprisings, third states are now increasingly reluctant to send troops merely on the basis of an incumbent government's request and frequently claim that the unrest is fomented from abroad (Hungary, Jordan, Czechoslovakia, Bahrain, Belarus, Kazakhstan), or intervene only if the demonstrations degenerate into violent rioting (Tonga). This trend towards extending the application of the principle of internal self-determination to popular uprisings is reflected in the Institut de droit international's Rhodes Resolution, which rules out military assistance upon request even in situations falling below the threshold of Protocol II additional to the 1949 Geneva Conventions 'when its object is to support an established government against its own population.'[353] The main problem with applying an obligation of negative equality to popular uprisings short of civil war, however, is a practical one: it is unclear in such a case where exactly to draw the line between a people's genuine attempt to modify their state's political system and mere street protests or riots. As has been observed, '"[t]he will of the people", not unlike the will of God, is revealed to different observers in different ways.'[354]

5. Situations Where Third-State Dispatch of Armed Forces in a Civil War is Not in Conflict with the Principle of Internal Self-Determination

As shown in Section 3.2.3, third states are prevented by the principle of internal self-determination to send armed forces in support of a foreign government beset by civil war in spite of its request. This section investigates situations where the intervention would not be at odds with the principle under examination. More specifically, two situations are examined: counter-intervention and counterterrorism.

5.1 Counter-Intervention

Counter-intervention can be defined as an intervention in support of a faction undertaken in response to an unlawful intervention in support of another faction. It can occur on the side of the incumbent government or of opposition groups.

5.1.1 Counter-intervention in support of an incumbent government
The problem of the legality of counter-intervention in support of an incumbent government beset by civil war only arises when it takes the form of the dispatch of armed forces by third states, which is prohibited by the principle of internal self-determination: as discussed in the previous sections, other forms of intervention, and

---

[353] Arts 2(1) and 3(1), Rhodes Resolution. See also Georg Nolte, *Eingreifen auf Einladung. Zur völkerrechtlichen Zulässigkeit des Einsatzes fremder Truppen im internen Konflikt auf Einladung der Regierung* (Springer 1999) 638; Sir Gerald Fitzmaurice, 'The General Principles of International Law Considered from the Standpoint of the Rule of Law' (1957) 92 Recueil des Cours 1, 179.

[354] Roth, *Governmental Illegitimacy*, 430.

294   INTERNATIONAL LAW AND THE PRINCIPLE OF NON-INTERVENTION

the dispatch of armed forces in situations of internal unrest other than civil war, are not prohibited under existing international law.

Pro-government counter-intervention in civil war is not a discrete right the existence of which needs to be demonstrated under customary international law and it has not been claimed to be such by the states that intervened.[355] Its legality is rather based on the consent of the government of the state where it takes place, as the application of the principle of non-intervention, and thus of intervention by invitation, is brought back by the unlawful support received by the insurgents so as to re-establish a fair balance between the opposing forces and restore the correct operation of the principle of internal self-determination.[356] The state practice and *opinio juris* examined in the previous sections confirm that both the governments engulfed in a civil war and the states intervening in their support regularly refer to the fact that the insurgents have received unlawful assistance from abroad, with criticism essentially focused on the existence and extent of such assistance and not on the legality of counter-intervention per se.[357] To be consistent with the principle of internal self-determination, however, pro-government counter-intervention must be proportionate to the support unlawfully received by the insurgents, although it does not necessarily have to be in kind.[358] It can of course be practically difficult to assess the exact nature and amount of pro-insurgent support, especially considering that it is often supplied covertly.[359] Providing clear and convincing evidence, therefore, is essential to build a solid case.

Pro-government counter-intervention can take the form of collective self-defence when the support received by the insurgents is an armed attack under Article 51 of the UN Charter and its customary equivalent, that is, it constitutes a serious violation of the prohibition of the use of force.[360] The defensive armed reaction must be

[355] More than claiming a discrete 'right of counter-intervention', the intervening states normally limit themselves to pointing out that the insurgents are supported from other states, so as to validate the consent of the incumbent government as a legal basis for their intervention.

[356] Bennouna, *Le consentement*, 156; Schindler, 'Le principe', 457; Elihu Lauterpacht, 'The Contemporary Practice of the United Kingdom in the Field of International Law. Survey and Comment, V. July 1–December 31, 1957' (1958) 7 Intl & Comp LQ 92, 106.

[357] A 1976 US Department of State memorandum also indicates that intervention in civil strife is lawful 'where the legally established government is threatened by outside intervention (infiltration of personnel, supply of arms and ammunition) ... and the legally established government requests the sending of troops and supply of arms' (Memorandum of the Attorney Adviser, 6–7). During the drafting of the Friendly Relations Declaration, the United Kingdom noted that a State that 'becomes a victim of unlawful intervention' has 'the right to request aid and assistance from third States, which are correspondingly entitled to grant the aid and assistance requested' (UN Doc A/5746, 16 November 1964, para 205). The already mentioned 1984 UK Foreign Office internal memorandum on intervention reiterates that 'it is widely accepted that outside interference in favour of one party to the struggle permits counter-intervention on behalf of the other' (British Foreign Office, 'Is Intervention Ever Justified?', 616).

[358] Moore, 'The Control', 209, 280; Oscar Schachter, 'The Right of States to Use Armed Force' (1984) 82 Mich L Rev 1620, 1644; Christopher C Joyner and Michael A Grimaldi, 'The United States and Nicaragua: Reflections on the Lawfulness of Contemporary Intervention' (1985) 25 Va J Intl L 621, 648; Díaz Barrado, *El consentimiento*, 363; Philip Kunig, 'Intervention, Prohibition of', *MPEPIL Online* (last updated April 2008) para 31; Joseph Klingler, 'Counterintervention on Behalf of the Syrian Opposition? An Illustration of the Need for Greater Clarity in the Law' (2014) 55 Harv Intl LJ 483, 501.

[359] De Wet, *Military Assistance*, 121–3.

[360] *Nicaragua v USA*, para 195. Collective self-defence, in particular, has been invoked to justify, among others, the 1958 US intervention in Lebanon (UN Doc S/PV.827, para 44); the 1958 British intervention in Jordan (S/PV.831, paras 24–5); the US intervention in Vietnam from February 1965 (Meeker, 'The Legality', 474–5); Cuba's intervention in Angola from 1975 to 1991 (S/11941, 2); the Warsaw Pact countries' intervention in Czechoslovakia in 1968 (S/8759; S/PV.1441, paras 90, 93); Zaire and France's 1983 intervention in

NON-INTERVENTION AND INTERNAL SELF-DETERMINATION   295

necessary and proportionate to repelling the armed attack[361] and, at least for the ICJ, the victim state must declare that it has been attacked and request assistance.[362] Counter-intervention based on collective self-defence can take place not only on the territory of the state in civil war, but also in that of the state supporting the insurgents (to the extent that it is necessary and proportionate).[363] This was the crux of the matter in the *Nicaragua* case: the US intervention in Central America in the 1980s involved military and paramilitary activities in support of the Contras in Nicaragua to overthrow the Sandinista government and did not limit itself to assisting the Salvadoran government in El Salvador against the insurgents supported by Nicaragua.[364] The ICJ, therefore, had to establish whether the US operations were justifiable on the basis of the collective self-defence of El Salvador and, in the end, it reached a negative answer as it could find neither an armed attack by Nicaragua against its neighbour nor a request for assistance by El Salvador to the United States at the time the military and paramilitary activities in and against Nicaragua had started.[365]

Chad (S/PV.2463, para 66 (Zaire); A/38/PV.9, 28 September 1983, para 54 (France)); the 1979 Soviet intervention in Afghanistan (S/PV.2185, 5 January 1980, para 13); the US intervention in support of El Salvador, Honduras, and Costa Rica's governments in the 1980s (Affidavit of Secretary of State George P Schultz, 14 August 1984, in *Nicaragua v USA*, Counter-Memorial of the United States of America (Questions of Jurisdiction and/or Admissibility), 17 August 1984, ICJ Pleadings, vol II, 178); Tanzania and Zimbabwe's intervention in Mozambique in the 1980s against South Africa-backed Resistência Nacional Moçambicana (RENAMO) (*The United Nations and Mozambique 1992–5* (United Nations Department of Public Information 1995) 11); Croatia's intervention in Bosnia and Herzegovina (S/1995/647, 4 August 1995, Annex, 3); Zimbabwe, Angola, and Namibia's intervention in the DRC in the 1990s (S/1998/891, Annex, 3); the coalition's airstrikes against ISIL in Syria from 2014 (S/2014/695, 23 September 2014 (United States); S/2014/851, 26 November 2014 (United Kingdom); S/2015/745, 9 September 2015 (France); S/2015/221, 31 March 2015 (Canada); S/2015/693, 9 September 2015 (Australia); S/2016/132, 10 February 2016 (the Netherlands); S/2015/946, 10 December 2015 (Germany); S/2016/34, 13 January 2016 (Denmark); S/2016/513, 3 June 2016 (Norway); S/2016/523, 9 June 2016 (Belgium)); the Saudi-led coalition's intervention in Yemen from 2015 (A/71/581, 2–3); and the 2022 CSTO operation in Kazakhstan (S/PV.8967, 20).

[361] *Nicaragua v USA*, para 237.

[362] ibid, paras 195, 199.

[363] Note, however, that, even when third states invoke collective self-defence as the legal basis of the intervention in support of a government facing an externally supported insurgency, they often limit their operations to the territory of the inviting state. In fact, the only cases where collective self-defence originating from the intervention of a state in the civil strife in another was extended beyond the territory of the requesting state were the US airstrikes against North Vietnam during the Second Indochina War and the US support for the Contras in Nicaragua. The US attacks against Việt Cộng positions in Cambodia and Laos and the coalition's airstrikes against ISIL in Syria also took place beyond the territory of the requesting state but the state where they occurred was not claimed to be responsible for the attacks against South Vietnam and Iraq, respectively.

[364] *Nicaragua v USA*, para 51.

[365] The ICJ found that there was no sufficient evidence to attribute the flow of arms to Nicaragua (*Nicaragua v USA*, para 160) and that, even if there had been, under customary international law the provision of arms to an opposition group could never qualify as an armed attack (ibid, para 230). The same conclusion applies to 'logistical or other support' (ibid, para 195). Judge Schwebel strongly disagreed with the majority's findings: for him, Nicaragua was 'substantially involved' in the sending of armed bands, groups and irregulars to El Salvador and this, coupled with the gravity of its consequences for El Salvador's population, infrastructure, and economy, constituted an armed attack (ibid, Dissenting Opinion of Judge Schwebel, para 166). Judge Jennings concurred: even if the provision of arms cannot be considered an armed attack on its own, it may become one when it is accompanied by logistic or other support (ibid, Dissenting Opinion of Judge Jennings, 543).

296 INTERNATIONAL LAW AND THE PRINCIPLE OF NON-INTERVENTION

Some authors have suggested that, apart from the case of collective self-defence, pro-government counter-intervention can never consist in the direct use of force: according to Louis Henkin, this would breach the territorial integrity and political independence of the state where the civil war is taking place.[366] This opinion, however, is unsupportable. As already said, the legal basis of counter-intervention is the consent of the incumbent governmental authorities of the state where it takes place, as the application of the principle of non-intervention is brought back in spite of the occurrence of the civil war by the external support unlawfully received by the insurgents: nothing under that principle prevents a third state from dispatching armed forces if this has been validly requested by the competent authorities.[367] As the support for the government needs to be proportionate to the unlawful support received by the insurgents, however, when it takes the form of the dispatch of combat troops counter-intervention will in most cases coincide with collective self-defence.

5.1.2 Counter-intervention in support of insurgents

As said, any support for opposition groups in situations of internal unrest is prohibited by the principle of non-intervention and, if it consists in the use of armed force, also by the rule codified in Article 2(4) of the UN Charter. Can it however be argued that, in certain circumstances, pro-insurgent intervention is allowed by the principle of internal self-determination?

Article 5 of the Wiesbaden Resolution affirms that if, during a civil war, an unlawful intervention has taken place, 'third States may give assistance to the other party only in compliance with the Charter and any other relevant rule of international law, subject to any such measures as are prescribed, authorized or recommended by the United Nations'.[368] The Resolution makes no distinction between government and opposition: counter-intervention in favour of the latter, therefore, appears equally permissible, providing that no arms embargo or similar measures have been imposed by the UN Security Council. Certain scholars have also supported the legality of pro-insurgent counter-intervention. Schachter has claimed that, 'if the government is so substantially supported by foreign aid so that it can be regarded as having been imposed by the foreign power against the wishes of the population, the situation is similar to that of external aggression, with the consequence that aid to the rebels would be permissible'.[369] For Falk, North Vietnam's support for the Việt Cộng in the

---

[366] Louis Henkin, 'Use of Force: Law and U.S. Policy' in Louis Henkin and others (eds), *Right v. Might: International Law and the Use of Force* (2nd edn, Council on Foreign Relations Press 1991) 37, 47. See similarly Díaz Barrado, *El consentimiento*, 364.

[367] It is true that, in the *Nicaragua* case, the ICJ concluded that '[s]tates do not have a right of "collective" armed response to acts which do not constitute an "armed attack"' (*Nicaragua v USA*, para 211) and that the only remedy available to the victim state in this case is non-forcible 'proportionate counter-measures on the part of the State which had been the victim of these acts' (ibid, para 249). What the Court was referring to, however, was the case of forcible counter-intervention conducted not on the territory of the inviting state (El Salvador), but on that of the state unlawfully supporting the insurgents (Nicaragua).

[368] Art 5, Rhodes Resolution.

[369] 'Observations des membres de la Huitième Commission sur le rapport provisoire et en réponse au questionnaire de M. Dietrich Schindler du 21 juillet 1971' (1973) 55 AIDI 527, 604. See also Thilo Marauhn and Zacharie F Ntoubandi, 'Armed Conflict, Non-International' in *MPEPIL Online* (last updated July 2016) para 41; John A Perkins, 'The Right of Counterintervention' (1987) 17 Ga J Intl & Comp L 171, 224. For Joyner and Grimaldi, 'if outside assistance to a government is significantly disproportionate to the internal threat posed by the insurgents, then a tenuous case for counter-intervention might be plausible on

Second Indochina War could have been justified as a proportionate response to the US military assistance to South Vietnam.[370] Lloyd Cutler more cautiously admits counter-intervention in support of insurgents only when there is a civil war waged by an indigenous pro-democracy armed group against an oppressive regime *and* a third state has been giving military assistance to the latter.[371] In John Norton Moore's opinion, on the other hand, it would be unwise to extend the counter-intervention option to insurgents as this would 'sanction a spiral of escalation on both sides, and would as a practical matter reduce the non-intervention standard to a non-rule'.[372]

In my view, two situations must be distinguished to correctly address the problem: that of an intervention in support of an incumbent government consisting in the dispatch of armed forces, and that in other forms. It has been seen that, under customary international law, the latter is lawful even during a civil war: as a consequence, there can be no lawful counter-intervention on the side of the insurgents in response to it. Sending armed forces at the request of a foreign government beset by civil war, on the other hand, is unlawful as it breaches the principle of internal self-determination. A counter-intervention in support of insurgents, however, could not be based on collective self-defence, as this is a right of states and not of non-state actors.[373] It also could not be a case of intervention by invitation, as insurgents are not entitled to express the will of the state at the international level and express consent on its behalf. What needs to be demonstrated, therefore, is that, under customary international law, the principle of internal self-determination constitutes an exception to that of non-intervention which allows assistance for insurgents when third states unlawfully send troops in support of a government involved in a civil war. The aforementioned 1984 British Foreign Office internal memorandum on intervention, for instance, argues that 'outside interference in favour of one party to [a civil war] permits counter-intervention on behalf of the other'.[374] During the Angolan Civil War, the United States also claimed that it could supply funds to one of the factions as this was in response to the external support received by other factions and was aimed at re-establishing a balance of forces consistently with the rationale of the principle of non-intervention (*rectius*: internal self-determination).[375] Apart from these statements, however, I have not been able to find other evidence of *opinio juris* suggesting that support for insurgents can be justified on counter-intervention grounds: no state, for instance, has invoked this argument as a legal basis for their assistance to the Syrian opposition in spite of the extensive military support that Russia has provided to the Assad government.

---

humanitarian grounds; such a situation, however, would be only a rare exception with limited applicability' (Joyner and Grimaldi, 'The United States', 648).

[370] Richard Falk, 'International Law and the United States Role in Viet Nam: A Response to Professor Moore' (1967) 76 Yale LJ 1095, 1137.

[371] Lloyd N Cutler, 'The Right to Intervene' (1985) 64 Foreign Aff 96, 106.

[372] 'Panel Two: General Discussion' (1983) 13 Ga J Intl & Comp L 315, 320. See also Schachter, 'The Right of States', 1642; Kunig, 'Intervention', para 35; Klingler, 'Counterintervention', 523.

[373] Marco Roscini, 'On the "Inherent" Character of the Right of States to Self-Defence' (2015) 4 Cambridge J Int'l & Comp L 634.

[374] British Foreign Office, 'Is Intervention Ever Justified?', 616.

[375] Memorandum of the Attorney Adviser, 6–7.

Pro-insurgent counter-intervention could alternatively be justified as a counter-measure adopted by third states in reaction to a breach of the principle of internal self-determination.[376] This obviously presupposes that the principle of internal self-determination is an *erga omnes* obligation[377] and that all states are entitled to adopt countermeasures in response to its violation.[378] Even if this were the case, counter-measures cannot affect the obligation to refrain from the threat or use of force contained in the UN Charter[379] and, therefore, pro-insurgent counter-intervention could never consist in the dispatch of troops or the supply of arms.

5.2 Counterterrorism Intervention

As a commentator notes, international law is neutral towards rebellions but unequivocally condemns terrorism.[380] It is hardly surprising, therefore, that, as the analysis of state practice and *opinio juris* conducted in Section 3.2.2 of this chapter clearly shows, both the governments engulfed in a civil war and the states intervening in their support have frequently claimed that the armed group they are acting against is a 'terrorist' organization. This practice, the statements accompanying it, and the resolutions of the UN political organs all suggest that, because of the extremist ideology they adopt and/or the methods aimed at spreading terror among civilians that they employ, terrorist organizations like ISIL are considered by definition incapable of reflecting popular instances of internal self-determination: the result is that the conflict between them and

---

[376] Schindler, 'Le principe', 484; Christian Henderson, 'A Countering of the Asymmetrical Interpretation of the Doctrine of Counter-Intervention' (2021) 8 JUFIL 34, 54–62.

[377] Gabriella Carella, *La responsabilità dello Stato per crimini internazionali* (Jovene 1985) 198. On the *erga omnes* character of the principle of self-determination in general, see *East Timor (Portugal v Australia)* (Judgment) [1995] ICJ Rep 90, para 29; *Legal Consequences of the Construction of a Wall in the Occupied Palestinian Territory* (Advisory Opinion) [2004] ICJ Rep 136, paras 155–6; *Legal Consequences of the Separation of the Chagos Archipelago from Mauritius in 1965* (Advisory Opinion) [2019] ICJ Rep 95, para 180; *Council of the European Union v Front populaire pour la libération de la saguia-el-hamra et du rio de oro (Front Polisario)*, Case C-104/16 P, Judgment of 21 December 2016, ECLI:EU:C:2016:973, para 88. *Contra*, see Alessandra Annoni, *Il riconoscimento come atto unilaterale dello Stato* (Jovene 2023) 113–4.

[378] While the ILC's Articles on Responsibility of States for Internationally Wrongful Acts (ARSIWA) leave the question unanswered (see Commentary on Art 54 [2001] YB ILC vol II, part two, 137–9), it has been suggested that international law now allows countermeasures for the protection of community interests (Christian J Tams, *Enforcing Obligations* Erga Omnes *in International Law* (CUP 2005) 249–51; Elena Katselli Proukaki, *The Problem of Enforcement in International Law: Countermeasures, the Non-Injured State and the Idea of International Community* (Routledge 2010) 207; Martin Dawidowicz, *Third-Party Countermeasures in International Law* (CUP 2017) 282–4). The 2005 Institut de droit international's Krakow Resolution envisages non-forcible countermeasures adopted by states other than the specially affected one only if the grave breach of an *erga omnes* obligation is 'widely acknowledged' (Art 5, Resolution on Obligations *Erga Omnes* in International Law of the Institut de droit international (Krakow Resolution) 27 August 2005 <www.idi-iil.org/app/uploads/2017/06/2005_kra_01_en.pdf>). For Cassese, the permissibility of countermeasures in response to violations of the principle of self-determination should be subordinated to the fact that a multilateral forum like the UN General Assembly declares the existence of the violation of the principle in question by a certain state and calls on the international community to react. Alternatively, the state that intends to adopt countermeasures should agree to submit the matter to peaceful settlement of dispute mechanisms before actually resorting to them (Cassese, *Self-Determination*, 156).

[379] Art 50(1)(a) ARSIWA.

[380] Hasar, *State Consent*, 291. There are indeed several treaties and resolutions of international organizations, both at the global and regional level, prohibiting acts of terrorism.

a government cannot be considered a genuine process for the modification of the political system of the concerned state, not even if it reaches the threshold of civil war.[381] The dispatch of armed forces upon the invitation of the incumbent authorities against a terrorist organization, therefore, is not at odds with the principle of internal self-determination because such principle would not be applicable.[382] That this is the correct conclusion is further demonstrated by the fact that, when a civil war involves both 'ordinary' and terrorist armed groups (as in the cases of Mali and Syria), third states discriminate between them and caution that their armed intervention is only aimed at assisting the government against the latter.[383] Note that the fact that an armed group is a terrorist organization only has the consequence of allowing pro-government intervention in any form in spite of the occurrence of a civil war and does not legitimize third-state intervention against the terrorist group without the consent of the government of the state from where the group operates.[384]

It has been argued that third states could easily circumvent the obligation of negative equality arising from the principle of internal self-determination by simply branding the armed opposition as terrorist: the permissive exception could thus easily eat up the prohibitive rule.[385] This is a powerful argument: it is of paramount importance, therefore, that the qualification of an armed opposition group as 'terrorist' is not left to the arbitrary appreciation of the government it opposes or of those that intervene on its side, but is based on objective criteria. The problem is that international law has famously struggled to come up with a definition of terrorism.[386] The General Assembly has identified it as '[c]riminal acts intended or calculated to provoke a state of terror in the general public, a group of persons or particular persons for political purposes'.[387] The Security Council has referred to

---

[381] Both the UN General Assembly and the Security Council have affirmed that terrorist acts are 'in any circumstance unjustifiable, whatever the considerations of a political, philosophical, ideological, racial, ethnic, religious or any other nature that may be invoked to justify them' (GA Res 49/60, 9 December 1994, Annex, para 3; see analogous language in SC Res 1566, 8 October 2004, para 3). Terrorism is also a violation of the fundamental human rights of the victims (Luigi Condorelli, 'The Imputability to States of Acts of International Terrorism' (1989) 19 Israel YBHR 233, 235).

[382] This conclusion finds indirect confirmation in the 2005 World Summit Outcome Document where it 'urge[s] the international community ... to assist States in building national and regional capacity to combat terrorism' (GA Res 60/1, 20 October 2005, para 88).

[383] Hasar, *State Consent*, 292–3.

[384] Syria has noted, for instance, that '[i]f any State invokes the excuse of counter-terrorism in order to be present on Syrian territory without the consent of the Syrian Government ... its actions shall be considered a violation of Syrian sovereignty' (UN Doc S/2015/719, 21 September 2015, 2). See also Iraq's statement, S/2015/963, 14 December 2015, 2.

[385] De Wet, *Military Assistance*, 120–1.

[386] Mirko Sossai, *La prevenzione del terrorismo nel diritto internazionale* (Giappichelli 2012) 168–9. For a scholarly proposal for a definition of terrorism under customary international law, see Marcello Di Filippo, 'The Definition(s) of Terrorism in International Law' in Ben Saul (ed), *Research Handbook on International Law and Terrorism* (2nd edn, Edward Elgar 2014) 2.

[387] GA Res 49/60, Annex, para 3. It has been observed that '[t]he Declaration represents as close to a comprehensive ban on terrorism that the UN has come, and as close to a comprehensive definition of terrorism as the General Assembly has come during the many years of negotiations on a variety of international legal instruments' and that it thus reflects customary international law (Jane Boulden, 'The United Nations General Assembly and Terrorism' in Saul (ed), *Research Handbook*, 493, 503).

criminal acts, including against civilians, committed with the intent to cause death or serious bodily injury, or taking of hostages, with the purpose to provoke a state of terror in the general public or in a group of persons or particular persons, intimidate a population or compel a government or an international organization to do or to abstain from doing any act, which constitute offences within the scope of and as defined in the international conventions and protocols relating to terrorism.[388]

For the Appeals Chamber of the Special Tribunal for Lebanon (STL), terrorism in time of peace requires three elements under customary international law:

(i) the perpetration of a criminal act (such as murder, kidnapping, hostage-taking, arson, and so on), or threatening such an act; (ii) the intent to spread fear among the population (which would generally entail the creation of public danger) or directly or indirectly coerce a national or international authority to take some action, or to refrain from taking it; (iii) when the act involves a transnational element.[389]

Finally, the UN Draft Comprehensive Terrorism Convention defines terrorism as the act of a person who

by any means, unlawfully and intentionally, causes:

(a) Death or serious bodily injury to any person; or
(b) Serious damage to public or private property, including a place of public use, a State or government facility, a public transportation system, an infrastructure facility or to the environment; or
(c) Damage to property, places, facilities or systems referred to in paragraph 1 (b) of the present article resulting or likely to result in major economic loss;
  when the purpose of the conduct, by its nature or context, is to intimidate a population, or to compel a Government or an international organization to do or to abstain from doing any act.[390]

Negotiations to turn the draft into a convention, however, are currently at a deadlock.

Until a definition is agreed by states, it would be prudent to leave the qualification of an armed group as terrorist exclusively to the relevant UN organs: as has been noted, 'the UN Charter gives both the Assembly and the Council wide-ranging mandates on issues of international peace and security meaning that both have mandates that allow them to deal with terrorism as a general phenomenon or in response to specific events'.[391] Only when the UN organs have proceeded to such qualification, therefore,

---

[388] SC Res 1566, para 3.

[389] *Interlocutory Decision on the Applicable Law: Terrorism, Conspiracy, Homicide, Perpetration, Cumulative Charging.* Appeals Chamber, STL-1101/I/AC/R176bis, 16 February 2011, para 85. The application of the definition in armed conflict is, for the STL, still not fully settled (ibid, para 109).

[390] UN Doc A/59/894, 12 August 2005, Appendix II, Art 2.

[391] Boulden, 'The United Nations', 502. See also Tom Ruys, 'The Quest for an Internal *Jus Ad Bellum*: International Law's Missing Link, Mere Distraction, or Pandora's Box?' in Claus Kreß and Robert Lawless (eds), *Necessity and Proportionality in International Peace and Security Law* (OUP 2020) 169, 218–19.

NON-INTERVENTION AND INTERNAL SELF-DETERMINATION 301

should states be permitted to disapply the principle of internal self-determination, and the obligation of negative equality that results from it, in regard to a civil war occurring in another country.

6. Can the UN Security Council Set Aside the Principle of Internal Self-Determination and Intervene, or Authorize an Armed Intervention, in a Civil War?

According to Article 3 of the Wiesbaden Resolution, third states may 'give any assistance prescribed, authorized or recommended by the United Nations in accordance with its Charter and other rules of international law'. Both the Declaration on the Inadmissibility of Intervention and that on Friendly Relations also contain a safeguard clause that reaffirms the primacy of the UN Charter, the former specifically referring to the provisions on the maintenance of international peace and security contained in Chapters VI and VII.[392]

Leaving aside peacekeeping operations with a non-partisan mandate, which exceed the scope of this book, the Security Council has directly intervened in civil wars in different ways.[393] First, it has launched stabilization operations with a 'robust' mandate to help governments recover control of their national territory and neutralize armed opposition groups. Even though Resolution 146 (1960) initially stated that 'the United Nations Force in the Congo will not be a party to, or in any way intervene in or be used to influence the outcome of any internal conflict, constitutional or otherwise',[394] the following year the Council declared its 'full and firm support' for the Congolese government and its determination to assist it against Katanga.[395] ONUC, therefore, became actively involved in armed operations against the secessionists.[396] In spite of this, towards the end of the crisis Secretary-General U Thant claimed that the United Nations had 'scrupulously' observed the principle of non-intervention and had 'avoided any intervention in the internal politics of the country beyond the opposition to secession'.[397] He also added that, even though ONUC was in Congo at the request of the Léopoldville government, 'the United Nations ... never used the arms at its disposal to further the political aims of a group or individual in the country, or to interfere with its political processes'.[398] The Soviet Union, among others, was openly critical of ONUC and stigmatized its actions as a 'flagrant' interference in Congo's internal affairs.[399] Fifty years later, the United Nations Organization Stabilization Mission in

---

[392] GA Res 2131 (XX), para 8; GA Res 2625 (XXV), Annex, third principle, para 5.

[393] As the ICTY noted, 'the practice of the Security Council is rich with cases of civil war or internal strife which it classified as a "threat to the peace" and dealt with under Chapter VII, with the encouragement or even at the behest of the General Assembly' (*Prosecutor v Tadić*, para 30).

[394] SC Res 146, 9 August 1960, para 4.

[395] SC Res 169, 24 November 1961, paras 9–10.

[396] Pinto, 'Les règles', 521. The president and prime minister of Congo initially requested UN military assistance to protect the national territory from Belgian aggression, and not to restore internal order in the country (UN Doc S/4382, 13 July 1960).

[397] UN Doc S/5240, 4 February 1963, para 37.

[398] ibid, para 38.

[399] UN Doc S/4506, 13 September 1960, 2. See also Argentina's statement (S/PV.886, 8–9 August 1960, para 70).

the Congo (MONUSCO)'s Force Intervention Brigade was mandated, 'on an exceptional basis and without creating a precedent', with, among others, 'neutralizing armed groups' in the DRC and carrying out 'targeted offensive operations' unilaterally or jointly with the DRC armed forces.[400] Thanks to MONUSCO's support, the DRC army managed to temporarily defeat the Mouvement du 23 mars insurgents.[401]

Secondly, the Security Council has authorized member states and regional organizations to intervene in support of governments beset by civil wars. The Council, for instance, authorized AMISOM 'to take all necessary measures as appropriate in those sectors in coordination with the Somali security forces to reduce the threat posed by al-Shabaab and other armed opposition groups in order to establish conditions for effective and legitimate governance across Somalia'.[402] Before creating MINUSMA, the Security Council also mandated the African-led International Support Mission in Mali (AFISMA) to take all necessary measures, inter alia, '[t]o support the Malian authorities in recovering the areas in the north of its territory under the control of terrorist, extremist and armed groups and in reducing the threat posed by terrorist organizations'.[403]

Thirdly, the Security Council has identified the legitimate government of the state in civil war and/or commended an intervention in its support but without authorizing it. By appointing and deposing rulers in certain circumstances, the Council has played a role reminiscent of that of the Pope and the Holy Roman Emperor until the early modern period.[404] The Council, for instance, confirmed the legitimacy of Yemen's President Hadi in spite of his limited effective control over most of the country, commended the intervening states' efforts in his support, and imposed an arms embargo on the opposition groups.[405] The Council also legitimized Somalia's TFG and Libya's GNA even though they controlled only limited areas in or around their respective capital cities.[406] It has been suggested that, by clarifying the legal status of the parties, and in particular by identifying the legitimate government, the Security Council has been able to use intervention by invitation for democratic or collective security purposes.[407]

All in all, it is remarkable that the Security Council has motivated its forcible support for a government beset by civil war by referring to circumstances analogous to

---

[400] SC Res 2098, 28 March 2013, paras 9, 12(b). MONUSCO was established by SC Res 1925, 28 May 2010.

[401] UN Doc S/2013/757, 17 December 2013, para 97.

[402] SC Res 2036, 22 February 2012, para 1. The Council had previously authorized the African Union's member states to take all necessary measures to protect the TFG (SC Res 1744, 20 February 2007, para 4).

[403] SC Res 2085, para 9(b). The transitional authorities of Mali had requested the deployment of an international military force under Chapter VII of the UN Charter to recover control of the northern regions of the country (SC Res 2071, 12 October 2012, Preamble).

[404] Jonathan Havercroft, 'Was Westphalia 'All That'? Hobbes, Bellarmine, and the Norm of Non-Intervention' (2012) 1 Global Constitutionalism 120, 137. See Chapter 1, Section 2 of this book.

[405] See the Preambles of SC Resolutions 2051, 12 June 2012; 2140, 26 February 2014; 2201, 15 February 2015; and 2216 of 14 April 2015. Hadi resigned (September 2014), fled to Aden (February 2015), rescinded his resignation and requested intervention (24 March 2015), and finally escaped to Saudi Arabia (25 March 2015). The coalition's airstrikes started on 26 March 2015.

[406] SC Res 1587, 15 March 2005 (Somalia); SC Resolutions 2238, 10 September 2015, and 2259 (Libya). Res 2259 also calls upon states 'to cease support to and official contact with parallel institutions that claim to be the legitimate authority but are outside of the [Skhirat] Agreement as specified by it' (SC Res 2259, para 5).

[407] Claus Kreß and Benjamin Nußberger, 'Pro-Democratic Intervention in Current International Law: The Case of The Gambia in January 2017' (2017) 4 JUFIL 239, 250.

those claimed by states, namely, the terrorist character of the armed groups, the foreign support they receive, and their commission of serious violations of IHRL and/or IHL. The non-partisan character of the operations has also been stressed.[408] This is not surprising: developing respect for the principle of self-determination of peoples is one of the purposes of the United Nations and constitutes a limit to the Security Council's powers.[409] As a result, '[a]n intervention by or under the aegis of the United Nations which is aimed at, or has the effect of, depriving the people of a country from freely choosing their government ... should be regarded as incompatible with the basic tenets of the Charter'.[410] The Council could thus intervene by using or authorizing the use of armed force in a civil war to enforce compliance with a settlement accepted by all the parties, but not to impose a political system on a people by keeping in power an incumbent government or by forcing regime change.[411] The principle of internal self-determination, on the other hand, would not limit the powers of the Security Council to adopt measures short of the use of force.[412]

7. Third-State Intervention in Civil Strife Involving Racist Regimes

As has been seen, the principle of internal self-determination only prohibits *external* interferences in the choice by a people of its political, economic, social, and cultural systems. The principle, in other words, is ideologically neutral: it does not require states to adopt a certain form of government, not even a democratic one, but only dictates that a people's choice of their internal system not be interfered with by other states.

The principle of internal self-determination, however, exceptionally protects a people from the imposition of a political, economic, social, or cultural system from within the state in one case, namely, that of institutionalized racial segregation with a ruling racial group preventing other racial groups from having access to government (apartheid).[413] Georges Abi-Saab has highlighted the link between apartheid regimes and colonial domination: in the former case, 'the settlers, while severing their formal

---

[408] In his fourth progress report on UNOCI, for instance, the UN Secretary-General noted that the operation had been 'deployed in Côte d'Ivoire at the request of the national authorities and in support of the peace process and not to impose a partisan solution to the crisis in Côte d'Ivoire' (UN Doc S/2005/186, 18 March 2005, para 87).

[409] Art 1(2), UN Charter.

[410] Oscar Schachter, 'The United Nations and Internal Conflict' in Moore (ed), *Law and Civil* War, 401, 423. See also Mary Ellen O'Connell, 'Continuing Limits on UN Intervention in Civil War' (1992) 67 Ind LJ 903, 911; Steven Wheatley, 'The Security Council, Democratic Legitimacy and Regime Change in Iraq' (2006) 17 EJIL 531, 541; Grado, *Guerre civili*, 342–3.

[411] For Malaysia, '[r]emoving the Head of State or Government of a sovereign State is illegal and against the Charter, and it must never be a project that has the endorsement of [the Security] Council' (UN Doc S/PV.4625 (Resumption 2), 17 October 2002, 7).

[412] See Section 3.3 of this chapter.

[413] On the definition of apartheid, see Miles Jackson, 'The Definition of Apartheid in Customary International Law and the International Convention on the Elimination of All Forms of Racial Discrimination' (2022) 71 Intl & Comp LQ 831.

304 INTERNATIONAL LAW AND THE PRINCIPLE OF NON-INTERVENTION

ties with their other countries, exercise a colonial policy vis-à-vis [local] populations which denies them their right to self-determination'.[414]

The unlawfulness of apartheid as a form of government is now well established. Article 1 of the 1963 Declaration on the Elimination of All Forms of Racial Discrimination condemns

> [d]iscrimination between human beings on the ground of race, colour or ethnic origin ... as a denial of the principles of the Charter of the United Nations, as a violation of the human rights and fundamental freedoms proclaimed in the Universal Declaration of Human Rights, as an obstacle to friendly and peaceful relations among nations and as a fact capable of disturbing peace and security among peoples.[415]

The 1965 Declaration on the Inadmissibility of Intervention proclaims that 'all states shall contribute to the complete elimination of racial discrimination ... in all its forms and manifestations'.[416] The International Convention on the Elimination of All Forms of Racial Discrimination was adopted the same year under the aegis of the United Nations and has now reached 182 ratifications.[417] The 1970 Declaration on Friendly Relations preserves the territorial integrity or political unity of states only to the extent that they possess 'a government representing the whole people belonging to the territory without distinction as to race, creed or colour'.[418] In 1973, a Convention on the Suppression and Punishment of the Crime of Apartheid was also concluded.[419] Last but not least, numerous resolutions condemning the apartheid regimes in South Africa and Southern Rhodesia (today's Zimbabwe) were adopted by the UN General Assembly and Security Council.[420] If, initially, the Western states were reluctant to adopt sanctions against South Africa as they thought this would infringe upon its sovereignty, after the 1960 Sharpeville massacre, where more than 200 people were killed or wounded by the South African police, the Security Council managed to adopt a resolution deploring the policies and actions of the South African government and warning that the continuation of the situation could endanger international peace and security.[421] In 1963, it also adopted a non-binding arms embargo that became binding in 1977, and, in the 1980s, it accompanied it with a comprehensive sanction

---

[414] Georges Abi-Saab, 'Wars of National Liberation in the Geneva Conventions and Protocols' (1979) 165 Recueil des Cours 353, 394. The Preamble of GA Res 2189 (XXI), 13 December 1966, on the Implementation of the the Declaration on the Granting of Independence to Colonial Countries and Peoples also qualifies racism and apartheid as a manifestation of colonialism.

[415] GA Res 1904 (XVIII), 20 November 1963, para 3, Art 1.

[416] GA Res 2131 (XX), para 6. A draft text of the Declaration on the Inadmissibility of Intervention submitted to the First Committee of the UN General Assembly included an express statement that apartheid and racial discrimination are policies inconsistent with the principle of non-intervention, as they deny peoples their inalienable right to freely choose their own political, economic, social, and cultural systems (UN Doc A/6220, 21 December 1965, para 11).

[417] International Convention on the Elimination of All Forms of Racial Discrimination (New York, 29 December 1965) 660 UNTS 1.

[418] GA Res 2625 (XXV), Annex, fourth principle, para 7.

[419] International Convention on the Suppression and Punishment of the Crime of Apartheid (New York, 30 November 1973) 1015 UNTS 243.

[420] See the resolutions listed in Natalino Ronzitti, *Le guerre di liberazione nazionale e il diritto internazionale* (Pacini 1974) 114, fn 11.

[421] SC Res 134, 1 April 1960, paras 1, 3.

regime.[422] In the *Namibia* Advisory Opinion, the ICJ confirmed that South Africa's discriminatory policies were 'a flagrant violation of the purposes and principles of the UN Charter'.[423]

As the legal consequences of apartheid for the principle of non-intervention are the same as those of colonial domination, whether third states can intervene to maintain a racist government in power and whether they are prohibited from supporting the discriminated against racial group in their struggle to exercise self-determination are questions that will be explored in Chapter VI to avoid unnecessary repetitions.

8. Conclusions

In the UN Charter era, the principle of self-determination becomes a discrete rule of international law. In its internal dimension, the principle entails that a people have the right to choose and modify their state's political, economic, social, and cultural systems without external interferences and, correspondingly, third states have an obligation to abstain from any interferences in that choice. While not all situations of internal unrest constitute a process for the redefinition of the political system of a state, this is certainly the case with the most dramatic one, that is, civil war, defined as an internal armed conflict where an organized armed opposition group with political objectives controls a portion of the state's territory and has established a *de facto* administration therein. In this scenario, a normative conflict arises between the principle of non-intervention, which allows third-state intervention on the side of the incumbent government upon its request, and that of internal self-determination, which prohibits interferences on any side, with the latter prevailing over the former as *lex posterior* and *lex specialis*. If negative equality in relation to civil wars was merely an option for third states in the 19th century (unless otherwise provided in a treaty), therefore, it is now compulsory as a result of the application of the principle of internal self-determination.

The obligation of negative equality in civil wars, however, is a 'qualified' one: while it undoubtedly prevents third states from sending armed forces in support of any party, the analysis of state practice and *opinio juris* conducted in this chapter shows that it does not yet extend to lesser forms of intervention. Incumbent governments, in other words, still maintain a privileged position compared to insurgents during a civil war. State practice and *opinio juris* also indicate that the principle of non-intervention continues to apply to other forms of internal unrest, namely, military coups and mutinies, mercenary attacks, and mob violence. In these cases, third states can intervene in support of the incumbent authorities at their valid request in order to restore internal order, including by sending armed forces. In the case of pro-democracy popular uprisings and internal armed conflicts short of civil war, a trend has been detected towards

---

[422] See Ravi Mahakingam, 'The Compatibility of the Principle of Nonintervention with the Right of Humanitarian Intervention' (1996) 1 UCLA J Int'l L Foreign Aff 221, 249–50. The sanctions were lifted with the abandonment of apartheid by the new South African government.

[423] *Legal Consequences for States of the Continued Presence of South Africa in Namibia (South West Africa) Notwithstanding Security Council Resolution 276 (1970)* (Advisory Opinion) [1971] ICJ Rep 16, para 131.

306 INTERNATIONAL LAW AND THE PRINCIPLE OF NON-INTERVENTION

an obligation of negative equality, but it is premature to conclude that this already reflects the *lex lata*.

Even if third states send armed forces in support of an incumbent government beset by civil war, the principle of internal self-determination is not infringed in three cases: 1) when the intervention is of no or only minimal impact on the internal struggle for power, as in the case of evacuation operations and peacekeeping operations; 2) when the insurgents are unlawfully supported by another state, to the extent that the counter-intervention is proportionate to the unlawful support; and 3) when the competent UN organs have certified that the armed opposition group is a terrorist organization and is thus incapable of reflecting a people's genuine choice of a political system.

Finally, the principle of self-determination, as one of the purposes of the United Nations, also constitutes a limit to the powers of the Security Council. The Council, therefore, could only intervene in a civil war by sending armed forces, or authorize member states to do so, if the situation constitutes a threat to the peace, a breach of peace, or an act of aggression *and* only to enforce compliance with a settlement accepted by all the parties, but not to impose a political system on a people by keeping in power an incumbent government or by forcing regime change.

Table 5.1 summarizes third-state obligations in relation to civil wars and other situations of internal unrest.

Table 5.1 Third-state obligations under different legal regimes

	Civil wars where the belligerency of the insurgents has been recognized[a]	Situations of internal unrest short of civil war[b]	Civil wars[c]
Dispatch of armed forces	Neutral states cannot send armed forces in support of any belligerent. However, they are under no obligation to prevent volunteers from crossing the frontier separately to offer their services to one of the belligerents (although states might voluntarily decide to do so).	Allowed only in support of the incumbent government at its valid request. Third states also have an obligation to use all means at their disposal to prevent the inhabitants of their territory, nationals or aliens, from participating in, gathering elements, crossing the boundary, or sailing from their territory for the purpose of starting or promoting civil strife in another state.	Prohibited with respect to all parties under customary international law. The Wiesbaden Resolution also requires third states not to allow armed forces or military volunteers, instructors or technicians to be sent or to set out.

Table 5.1 Continued

	Civil wars where the belligerency of the insurgents has been recognized[a]	Situations of internal unrest short of civil war[b]	Civil wars[c]
Supply of arms and military equipment	Neutral states cannot supply arms and military equipment to any belligerent. However, they can allow the continuation of the private arms trade with the belligerents on a non-discriminatory basis.	Allowed only in support of the incumbent government. Under the Havana Convention and its Protocol, third states also have an obligation to forbid and prevent the traffic in arms and war material, except when intended for the government. However, this obligation does not reflect customary international law.	The Wiesbaden Resolution prohibits it with respect to all parties. The resolution also requires third states not to allow weapons or other war material to be supplied to any party to a civil war. Under customary international law, however, the principle of non-intervention continues to apply to the supply of arms and military equipment in civil wars, with the result that this form of support remains permissible at the request of an incumbent government and is only prohibited when in support of opposition groups.

Continued

308 INTERNATIONAL LAW AND THE PRINCIPLE OF NON-INTERVENTION

Table 5.1 Continued

	Civil wars where the belligerency of the insurgents has been recognized[a]	Situations of internal unrest short of civil war[b]	Civil wars[c]
Economic and financial support	Same rules as the supply of arms: neutral states cannot grant loans to the belligerents but are not required to prevent their nationals from doing so.[d] Supplies furnished or loans made by a neutral person to one of the belligerents are not considered as committed in their favour, provided that the person who furnishes the supplies or makes the loans lives neither in the territory of the other party nor in the territory occupied by them, and that the supplies do not come from these territories.	Allowed only in support of the incumbent government. Under the 1957 Protocol of the Havana Convention, states are also required to use all appropriate means to prevent any person, national or alien, from providing or receiving money, by any method, intended for a military enterprise that has as its purpose the starting, promoting, or supporting of civil strife in another contracting state. However, this obligation does not reflect customary international law.	Under the Wiesbaden Resolution, the continuation of any economic aid that is not likely to have any substantial impact on the outcome of the civil war is allowed. Financial or economic aid started after the beginning of the civil war is prohibited if it is likely to influence its outcome. Third states are not required to prevent the supply of financial and economic aid to the parties of a civil war by private individuals. Under customary international law, the principle of non-intervention continues to apply to economic and financial assistance during civil wars, with the result that this form of intervention remains permissible in favour of an incumbent government and is only prohibited when in support of opposition groups.

[a] Based on Convention (V) Respecting the Rights and Duties of Neutral Powers and Persons in Case of War on Land (The Hague, 18 October 1907) 205 CTS 299, and Convention (XIII) Concerning the Rights and Duties of Neutral Powers in Naval War (The Hague, 18 October 1907) 205 CTS 395. See also the Institut de droit international's Resolution on the Droits et devoirs des Puissances étrangères, au cas de mouvement insurrectionnel, envers les gouvernements établis et reconnus qui sont aux prises avec l'insurrection (Neuchâtel, 8 September 1900) (1900) 18 AIDI 227, and Art VI of the Treaty between the United States and Great Britain (Washington, DC, 8 May 1871) 143 CTS 145.

[b] Based on the Convention on Duties and Rights of States in the Event of Civil Strife (Havana, 20 February 1928) 134 LNTS 45 (Havana Convention), and the Protocol to the Convention on Duties and Rights of States in the Event of Civil Strife (Washington, DC, 1 May 1957) 284 UNTS 201.

[c] Based on the Institut de droit international's 1975 Wiesbaden Resolution.

[d] Fitzmaurice, 'The General Principles', 181. Hague Convention (V) does not address the point.

VI

The Interaction between the Principle of Non-Intervention and that of External Self-Determination

1. Introduction

Previous chapters have demonstrated how the principle of non-intervention allows states to assist a foreign government to maintain internal order and at the same time proscribes any support for opposition groups. Intervention on the side of the government is permissible until the situation of internal unrest becomes a civil war: at that point, the principle of internal self-determination triggers a prohibition on sending armed forces in support of any party, although other forms of assistance for the incumbent authorities remain allowed.

The principle of self-determination, however, has not only an internal dimension, but also an external one. It entails, in other words, that peoples must be allowed to freely choose not only their internal political, economic, social, and cultural systems without external interferences but also, in certain exceptional cases, their *international* status.[1] What needs to be examined here is the interaction between the principle of self-determination in this external dimension and the principle of non-intervention, that is, whether, in situations where a people is unlawfully prevented from exercising external self-determination, third states are still permitted to intervene in support of the oppressive government and are still prohibited from assisting the opposition groups.

The chapter starts by clarifying the scope of the principle of external self-determination and by juxtaposing it to the principle of non-intervention. It then examines the legality of third-state intervention in support of an incumbent government and of armed opposition groups in three contexts: colonial domination, alien occupation, and other secessionist situations of internal unrest. Racist regimes, characterized by institutionalized racial segregation with a ruling group preventing other racial groups from having equal access to government,[2] have been traditionally assimilated to colonial domination for the purposes of the principle of self-determination, even though, in this case, it is not the right to determine a people's international status that

---

[1] GA Res 1541 (XV), 15 December 1960, Annex, Principle VI. The international status could consist in '[t]he establishment of a sovereign and independent State, the free association or integration with an independent State or the emergence into any other political status freely determined by a people' (GA Res 2625 (XXV), 24 October 1970, Annex, fifth principle, para 4). As with internal self-determination, it is controversial whether external self-determination is a right of peoples or an obligation owed by states towards other states and of which peoples are the mere beneficiaries (see Chapter V, Section 2) fn 18.

[2] See Chapter V, Section 7.

International Law and the Principle of Non-Intervention. Marco Roscini, Oxford University Press. © Marco Roscini 2024.
DOI: 10.1093/oso/9780198786894.003.0007

comes into question but the right to fully participate in the government of the concerned state.[3] Unless otherwise specified, therefore, the considerations developed in Section 3 with regard to colonial domination will also extend to third-state intervention in civil strife involving a racist regime.

A word about terminology. 'Wars of national liberation' is employed in this chapter to designate all armed struggles where the insurgents are fighting against colonial domination, racist regimes, and alien occupation, whether or not they constitute civil wars in the sense indicated in Chapter V.[4] Furthermore, the term 'national liberation movement' is used to refer to an organized armed group that represents a people unlawfully prevented from exercising its right to external self-determination and who has been recognized as such by the competent global or regional organizations.[5]

2. The Scope of the Principle of External Self-Determination

It is now uncontroversial that states have an obligation to allow peoples under colonial domination, racist regimes, and alien occupation to freely exercise self-determination.[6] The UN Charter sees respect for the principle of self-determination as a means to develop friendly relations among nations and, therefore, links it to the

---

[3] Maria Irene Papa, 'Autodeterminazione dei popoli e terzi Stati' in Marcella Distefano (ed), *Il principio di autodeterminazione dei popoli alla prova del nuovo millennio* (Wolters Kluwer/CEDAM 2014) 53, 57.

[4] See Chapter V, Section 3.1.

[5] When ratifying Additional Protocol I to the 1949 Geneva Conventions on the Protection of Victims of War (Additional Protocol I), several states have attached reservations claiming that a national liberation movement should be recognized as such by a regional intergovernmental organization (Kubo Mačák, *Internationalized Armed Conflicts in International Law* (OUP 2018) 69). In 1961, the General Assembly established the Special Committee on the Situation with regard to the Implementation of the Declaration on the Granting of Independence to Colonial Countries and Peoples as its subsidiary organ to monitor implementation of the 1960 Declaration and to make recommendations on its application (GA Res 1654 (XVI), 27 November 1961). The Committee annually reviews the list of Non-Self-Governing Territories to which the Declaration is applicable. The Organisation of African Unity (OAU) also created a Liberation Committee entrusted with identifying national liberation movements (Chiara Redaelli, *Intervention in Civil Wars: Effectiveness, Legitimacy, and Human Rights* (Hart 2020) 261, fn 9). Georges Abi-Saab, however, is sceptical about the role that regional organizations can play in this context, as they would likely only recognize national liberation movements fighting adversaries that do not have membership of the concerned organization (Georges Abi-Saab, 'Wars of National Liberation in the Geneva Conventions and Protocols' (1979) 165 Recueil des Cours 353, 408). Certain states also claimed that the recognition of a national liberation movement as the 'sole' representative of a people might breach that people's right to internal self-determination, ie its right to choose its political system without external interferences: the point was jointly made by Britain, France, the Federal Republic of Germany, Canada, and the United States in relation to the recognition of South West African People's Organisation (SWAPO) as the 'sole and authentic representative of the Namibian people' in para 4 of GA Res 35/227 A, 6 March 1981 (UN Doc A/35/PV.109, 5 March 1981, para 125).

[6] In the *Kosovo* Advisory Opinion, the ICJ found that '[d]uring the second half of the twentieth century, the international law of self-determination developed in such a way as to create a right to independence for the peoples of non-self-governing territories and peoples subject to alien subjugation, domination and exploitation' (*Accordance with International Law of the Unilateral Declaration of Independence in Respect of Kosovo* (Advisory Opinion) [2010] ICJ Rep 403, para 79 (hereafter *Kosovo*)). Canada's Supreme Court also found that '[t]he right of colonial peoples to exercise their right to self-determination by breaking away from the "imperial" power is now undisputed' (*Reference re Secession of Québec* [1998] 2 SCR 217, para 132 (hereafter *Québec*)).

maintenance of international peace and security.[7] The watershed moment, however, was the adoption in 1960 of the landmark Declaration on the Granting of Independence to Colonial Countries and Peoples (the Decolonization Declaration) by the fifteenth session of the General Assembly.[8] After reaffirming the link between external self-determination and the maintenance of peace in the Preamble, the Declaration, which is now considered declaratory of customary international law,[9] proclaims that '[t]he subjection of peoples to alien subjugation, domination and exploitation constitutes a denial of fundamental human rights, is contrary to the Charter of the United Nations and is an impediment to the promotion of world peace and co-operation'.[10] The Declaration also calls upon states to cease '[a]ll armed action or repressive measures of all kinds directed against dependent peoples ... in order to enable them to exercise peacefully and freely their right to complete independence'.[11] The Declaration on the Inadmissibility of Intervention, adopted by the General Assembly five years later, urges all states to 'respect the right of self-determination and independence of peoples and nations, to be freely exercised without any foreign pressure, and with absolute respect for human rights and fundamental freedoms'.[12] The 1970 Declaration on Friendly Relations and Cooperation among States additionally requests all states to refrain from any forcible action that deprives peoples of their right to self-determination, freedom, and independence; declares that colonies and other non-self-governing territories have 'a status separate and distinct from that of the State administering it'; and affirms that peoples are entitled to seek and receive support to exercise self-determination in accordance with the UN purposes and principles.[13] Between the adoption of Resolutions 2131 and 2625, the General Assembly also adopted and opened for signature, ratification, and accession the International Covenants on Civil and Political Rights and on Economic, Social and Cultural Rights, Article 1(3) of which requires the parties 'including those having responsibility for the administration of Non-Self-Governing and Trust Territories, [to] promote the realization of the right of self-determination, and [to] respect that right, in conformity with

[7] Arts 1(2) and 55, UN Charter. The Preamble of GA Res 1514 (XV), 14 December 1960, also emphasizes that 'the increasing conflicts resulting from the denial of or impediments in the way of the freedom of [colonial] peoples ... constitute a serious threat to world peace'. As Kattan notes, the UN Charter originally distinguished trust territories from non-self-governing territories: for the former, the goal was independence, while for the latter it was self-government (Victor Kattan, 'Self-Determination in the Third World: The Role of the Soviet Union (1917–1960)' (2023) 8 Jus Gentium 87, 89).

[8] GA Res 1514 (XV). The resolution was adopted by eighty-nine votes to zero and nine abstentions. In the same session, the General Assembly recognized the right of the Algerian people to self-determination and independence (GA Res 1573 (XV), 19 December 1960, para 1). The resolution was adopted by sixty-three votes to eight with twenty-seven abstentions.

[9] Legal Consequences of the Separation of the Chagos Archipelago from Mauritius in 1965 (Advisory Opinion) [2019] ICJ Rep 95, para 152 (hereafter Chagos).

[10] GA Res 1514 (XV), para 1. The language is taken from the Final Communiqué of the Asian-African Conference of Bandung (Bandung, 24 April 1955) Section D(1)(b) <www.cvce.eu/en/obj/final_communique_of_the_asian_african_conference_of_bandung_24_april_1955-en-676237bd-72f7-471f-949a-88b6ae513585.html>.

[11] GA Res 1514 (XV), para 4.

[12] GA Res 2131 (XX), 21 December 1965, para 6.

[13] See GA Res 2625 (XXV), Annex, fifth principle, paras 5 and 6. See also GA Resolutions 2160 (XXI), 30 November 1966, para 1(b); 2734 (XXV), 16 December 1970, para 18; 3171 (XXVIII), 17 December 1973 ('Permanent sovereignty over natural resources'), para 2; 3281 (XXIX), 12 December 1974 ('Charter of Economic Rights and Duties of States'), Art 16(1); 36/103, 9 December 1981, Annex, para II(d).

312 INTERNATIONAL LAW AND THE PRINCIPLE OF NON-INTERVENTION

the provisions of the Charter of the United Nations'.[14] Finally, the General Assembly as well as the Security Council frequently censored Portugal, Rhodesia, and South Africa for their colonialist and apartheid policies,[15] and the General Assembly has reaffirmed the right to external self-determination of the peoples of Western Sahara and of the Palestinian Territories denied by Morocco and Israel, respectively.[16] Even though the decolonization process has now been almost entirely completed, the matter continues to be on the agenda of the UN organs: in Resolution 75/23 of 10 December 2020, the General Assembly declared the period 2021–30 the Fourth International Decade for the Eradication of Colonialism.[17]

It is not only the United Nations that has endorsed the principle of self-determination in its external dimension. The 1963 Charter of the Organisation of African Unity (OAU) indicated the elimination of 'all forms of colonialism from Africa' among the Organisation's purposes.[18] The respect for the right of self-determination, and particularly that of the Palestinian people, is also one of the objectives of the Organisation of Islamic Cooperation.[19] The 2004 Arab Charter on Human Rights condemns foreign occupation and domination and proclaims that 'efforts must be deployed for their elimination'.[20] Finally, the 1975 Helsinki Final Act reaffirms that, '[b]y virtue of the principle of equal rights and self-determination of peoples, all peoples always have the right, in full freedom, to determine, when and as they wish, their internal and external political status, without external interference, and to pursue as they wish their political, economic, social and cultural development'.[21] As Antonio Cassese notes, '[t]his formulation applies to both external and internal self-determination'.[22] Like the UN Charter, the Helsinki Final Act emphasizes the importance that respect for self-determination has in the development of friendly relations among states.[23]

By imposing colonial domination, a racist regime, or alien occupation, therefore, a state undoubtedly breaches the principle of external self-determination, which is not only treaty law, but also customary international law,[24] an obligation owed

---

[14] Art 1(3), International Covenant on Civil and Political Rights (New York, 16 December 1966) 999 UNTS 171; Art 1(3), International Covenant on Economic, Social and Cultural Rights (New York, 16 December 1966) 993 UNTS 3.

[15] See the resolutions listed in Natalino Ronzitti, *Le guerre di liberazione nazionale e il diritto internazionale* (Pacini 1974) 114, fn 11.

[16] See eg GA Res 34/37, 21 November 1979 (Western Sahara) and GA Res 3236 (XXIX) of 22 November 1974 (Palestinian Territories).

[17] See GA Res 75/23, 10 December 2020, para 1.

[18] Art II(1)(d), Charter of the Organization of African Unity (Addis Ababa, 25 May 1963) 479 UNTS 39.

[19] Art 1(3) and (8), Charter of the Organisation of Islamic Cooperation (Dakar, 25 August 1969, revised 14 March 2008) <www.oic-oci.org/page/?p_id=53&p_ref=27&lan=en>.

[20] Art 2(3), Arab Charter on Human Rights (Tunis, 22 May 2004) (2005) 12 IHRR 893. Similar language appeared in the 1994 version of the Charter (Art 1(b)), reproduced in (1997) 18 HRLJ 151.

[21] Principle VIII, para 2, Final Act of the 1st CSCE Summit of Heads of State or Government (Helsinki, 1 August 1975) (1975) 14 ILM 1292.

[22] Antonio Cassese, *Self-Determination of Peoples: A Legal Reappraisal* (CUP 1995) 285.

[23] Helsinki Final Act, Principle VIII, para 3.

[24] Self-determination was arguably a rule of customary international law by 1965 (*Chagos Marine Protected Area Arbitration (Mauritius v United Kingdom)*, Permanent Court of Arbitration, 18 March 2015, Dissenting and Concurring Opinion of Judge Kateka and Judge Wolfrum, para 71 <https://pcacases.com/web/sendAttach/1570>).

NON-INTERVENTION AND EXTERNAL SELF-DETERMINATION   313

erga omnes,[25] and even a *jus cogens* norm.[26] The result is that, whatever a colonial or occupying power or a racist regime might claim,[27] genuine self-determination struggles can no longer be considered a matter 'in which each State is permitted, by the principle of State sovereignty, to decide freely'[28] and thus do not fall under the protective cloak of the principle of non-intervention.[29] Indeed, as Gaetano Arangio-Ruiz notes, this principle 'would *not* condemn actions concerning matters in which the victim State was *not exempt* from international legal obligations'.[30]

Not only does the principle of non-intervention not shield colonial or occupying powers and racist regimes from coercive external interferences aimed at securing compliance with the principle of self-determination, it also prohibits alien subjugation, domination, and exploitation. According to General Assembly Resolutions 2131, 2160, and 2625, at least the use of force to deprive peoples of their national identity constitutes a violation of the principle of non-intervention (lesser forms of coercion are not mentioned in this context).[31] These resolutions, therefore, extend the application of the principle, which traditionally operates in interstate relations, to those between a colonial or occupying power and a colonial or occupied territory. While the principle of non-intervention, as formulated in the aforementioned resolutions, only

---

[25] *East Timor (Portugal v Australia)* (Judgment) [1995] ICJ Rep 90, para 29; *Legal Consequences of the Construction of a Wall in the Occupied Palestinian Territory* (Advisory Opinion) [2004] ICJ Rep 136, paras 88, 155–6 (hereafter *Palestinian Wall*); *Chagos*, para 180. In *Barcelona Traction*, the ICJ found that the protection from racial discrimination is also an obligation *erga omnes* (*Barcelona Traction, Light and Power Company, Limited (Belgium v Spain)* (Preliminary Objections, second phase) [1970] ICJ Rep 3, paras 33–4).

[26] Dire Tladi, Fourth Report on Peremptory Norms of General International Law (*jus cogens*), UN Doc A/CN.4/727, 31 January 2019, paras 48–9; Rafâa Ben Achour, 'Changements anticonstitutionnels de gouvernement et droit international' (2016) 379 Recueil des Cours 337, 473.

[27] For France, for instance, the Algerian question was a domestic affair (Jean Charpentier, 'Pratique française du droit international public' (1956) 2 AFDI 792, 805). The conflict, therefore, was treated at least at first as a police operation against criminals (Eldon Van Cleef Greenberg, 'Law and Conduct of the Algerian Revolution' (1970) 11 Harv Intl LJ 37, 40). The Algerian War of Independence started on the night of 31 October 1954 with a series of coordinated attacks by the Front de libération nationale in the Costantinois and Aurès regions and ended with the conclusion of the Evian Accords in 1962.

[28] *Case Concerning Military and Paramilitary Activities in and against Nicaragua (Nicaragua v United States of America)* (Merits) [1986] ICJ Rep 3, para 205 (hereafter *Nicaragua v USA*).

[29] Abi-Saab, 'Wars', 371. During the drafting of the Friendly Relations Declaration, for instance, a joint proposal by India, Lebanon, the United Arab Republic (UAR), Syria, and Yugoslavia excluded that aid and assistance given to peoples under any form of colonial domination would constitute intervention (UN Doc A/6230, 27 June 1966, para 276). For Nigeria, the condemnation of subversion does not extend to the efforts of peoples to achieve self-determination (A/C.1/SR.1405, 9 December 1965, para 48). See also Kenya (A/C.6/SR.997, 14 November 1967, para 7); Tunisia (A/C.1/SR.1402, 8 December 1965, para 3); Afghanistan (A/C.6/SR.1182 and Corr. 1, 25 September 1970, para 16); Pakistan (A/C.6/SR.1178, 23 September 1970, para 19); Indonesia (A/C.6/SR.935, 22 November 1966, para 30); Tanzania (A/C.1/SR.1401, 8 December 1965, para 5); and Byelorussia (A/C.1/SR.1401, para 12). In the UN General Assembly's Sixth Committee, Bulgaria stressed that 'a State should not be permitted, under cover of the principle of non-intervention, to avoid obligations arising from other principles of international law which had the character of jus cogens. Thus, the principle of non-intervention could not be invoked with respect to massacres, genocide, a policy of extermination, apartheid or various other colonialist or neo-colonialist practices which could not be tolerated by the international community' (A/C.6/SR.807, 8 November 1963, para 27, underlining in the original).

[30] Gaetano Arangio-Ruiz, 'Human Rights and Non-Intervention in the Helsinki Final Act' (1977) 157 Recueil des Cours 195, 279, emphasis in the original.

[31] During the debates on GA Res 2131, the UAR made the point clearly: '[a]rmed intervention ... could be perpetrated not only against States but also against peoples and movements striving to exercise their inherent right to self-determination and independence' (UN Doc A/C.1/SR.1403, 9 December 1965, para 3).

prohibits the use of force to prevent the exercise of self-determination, however, that of external self-determination is broader as it bans *any* act aimed at maintaining colonial, racist, or alien rule (the Decolonization Declaration refers to 'repressive measures of all kinds directed against dependent peoples')[32] and also entails the positive obligation of the colonial or occupying powers to adopt the measures necessary to exercise self-determination, for instance, the organization of a referendum.[33]

Certain commentators have suggested that, if a colonial power employed armed force to maintain colonial rule, it would also breach Article 2(4) of the UN Charter, as the colonial territory has a status separate and distinct from that of the metropolis and the use of force would thus be 'in international relations'.[34] In addition, such use of force would be 'inconsistent with the purposes of the United Nations', in particular with that '[t]o develop friendly relations among nations based on respect for the principle of ... self-determination of peoples'.[35] This opinion finds support in the Friendly Relations Declaration, which includes forcible actions to deprive peoples of their right to self-determination in its elaboration of the principle of the prohibition of the use of force, and not only of the principle of non-intervention.[36] That said, during the Cold War, the Western and Latin American states persistently opposed framing self-determination struggles in the context of the Charter's *jus contra bellum* rules.[37] The Friendly Relations Declaration itself cautions that it cannot be interpreted 'as enlarging or diminishing in any way the scope of the provisions of the Charter concerning cases in which the use of force is lawful'.[38]

3. Third-State Intervention in Decolonization Conflicts

Ved P. Nanda has defined colonialism as 'a political-economic relationship between a dominant Western nation and a subservient non-Western people'.[39] Although not

---

[32] GA Res 1514, para 4.

[33] The ICJ found that 'the application of the right of self-determination requires a free and genuine expression of the will of the peoples concerned' (*Western Sahara* (Advisory Opinion) [1975] ICJ Rep 12, para 55).

[34] Julio Faundez, 'International Law and the Wars of National Liberation: Use of Force and Intervention' (1989) 1 Afr J Intl & Comp L 85, 96; Giuseppe Palmisano, 'Autodeterminazione dei popoli' in *Enciclopedia del diritto. Annali dal 2007*, vol V (Giuffrè 2012) 82, 128; Cassese, *Self-Determination*, 196. During the Cold War, in particular, the Soviet writers argued that peoples are subjects of international law and the relations between the metropolis and the colonial territory are of an international, not internal, character (Jiri Toman, 'La conception soviétique des guerres de libération nationale' in Antonio Cassese (ed), *Current Problems of International Law* (Giuffrè 1975) 358, 372).

[35] Cassese, *Self-Determination*, 196.

[36] See GA Res 2625 (XXV), Annex, first principle, para 6.

[37] See Section 3.2.1 of this chapter. See also Ronzitti, *Le guerre*, 72–80, who argues that the use of force against national liberation movements is prohibited by a discrete customary rule parallel to that contained in Art 2(4). During the debates on the Friendly Relations Declaration, certain Western states also claimed that the principle of self-determination does not prohibit police actions by the administering state to maintain law and order (see eg Australia, A/8018, 1970, para 204; United Kingdom, A/8018, para 234; United States, A/C.6/SR.1180, 24 September 1970, para 25). This view was criticized by the developing countries (see eg Indonesia, A/C.6/SR.1182 and Corr 1, para 75).

[38] GA Res 2625 (XXV), Annex, first principle, para 12.

[39] Ved P Nanda, 'Self-Determination in International Law: The Tragic Tale of Two Cities—Islamabad (West Pakistan) and Dacca (East Pakistan)' (1972) 66 AJIL 321, 321, fn 1.

NON-INTERVENTION AND EXTERNAL SELF-DETERMINATION   315

necessarily limited to the Western/non-Western dichotomy as suggested by Nanda, the situation refers to 'salt-water colonialism', characterized by 'a territory which is geographically separate and is distinct ethnically and/or culturally from the country administering it' (be the latter a European power or not) and by the arbitrary subordination of the former to the latter.[40]

As mentioned in Section 2, it is now undisputed that states have an obligation to allow peoples under colonial domination to freely exercise their right to self-determination. The existence of this obligation removes the matter from the domestic jurisdiction of the colonial power and displaces the application of the principle of non-intervention in the relations between the colonial power and third states with regard to the colonial territory. The two-pronged question that needs to be addressed, therefore, is whether the violation of the principle of external self-determination by the colonial power allows third-state support for the national liberation movement and, if so, in what form, and/or requires third states to abstain from assisting the colonial power to maintain its grip on the colonial territory.

3.1 Third-State Intervention in Support of a Colonial Power

If, as established in Section 2 of this chapter, a colonial power may not prevent a subjugated people from exercising its right to external self-determination, third-state intervention in its support must also be prohibited even if the situation of internal unrest has not reached the threshold of a civil war, that is, whether or not the national liberation movement has secured any effective territorial control or established a *de facto* administration therein.[41] The request of the colonial power does not make any difference in this context. Indeed, a state can only consent to acts that it could itself lawfully undertake: unlawful acts cannot be performed either by the consenting state or by others on its behalf.[42] Both the Declaration on the Inadmissibility of Intervention and that on Friendly Relations are also clear that it is *all* states, and not only the colonial powers, that must respect the principle of self-determination, promote its realization, and refrain from forcible actions aimed at depriving peoples entitled to it of its exercise.[43] The principle, therefore, limits the discretion of third states to accept

---

[40] GA Res 1541 (XV), Annex, Principles IV and V.

[41] Abi-Saab, 'Wars', 409–15. According to the Rhodes Resolution, military assistance is prohibited, inter alia, 'when it is exercised in violation of ... equal rights and self-determination of peoples' (Art 3(1) of the Institut de droit international's Resolution on Military Assistance on Request (Rhodes Resolution), 8 September 2011 <www.idi-iil.org/app/uploads/2017/06/2011_rhodes_10_C_en.pdf>). See Dietrich Schindler, 'Le principe de non-intervention dans les guerres civiles (Huitième Commission) Rapport provisoire et rapport définitif' (1973) 55 AIDI 416; Ronzitti, *Le guerre*, 110; Flavia Lattanzi, 'Autodeterminazione dei popoli' in *Digesto delle discipline pubblicistiche*, vol 2 (4th edn, UTET 1987) 4, 24–5; Rosario Sapienza, *Il principio del non intervento negli affari interni. Contributo allo studio della tutela giuridica internazionale della potestà di governo* (Giuffrè 1990) 52; Antonello Tancredi, *La secessione nel diritto internazionale* (CEDAM 2001) 647.

[42] John A Perkins, 'The Right of Counterintervention' (1987) 17 Ga J Intl & Comp L 171, 189; David Wippman, 'Military Intervention, Regional Organizations and Host-State Consent' (1996) 7 Duke J Comp & Intl L 209, 215.

[43] GA Resolutions 2131 (XX), para 6, and 2625 (XXV), Annex, fifth principle, paras 2, 5. See also *Chagos*, para 180.

316 INTERNATIONAL LAW AND THE PRINCIPLE OF NON-INTERVENTION

the invitation of the state that breaches the principle of self-determination, invitation that—as just said—would in any case be unable to produce any effects.

Sending armed forces in support of a colonial power is thus undoubtedly inconsistent with the principle of self-determination. Indeed, there have been hardly any post-1945 claims of the legality of armed intervention in support of a colonial power or racist regime against a national liberation movement.[44] The first intervention criticized as a violation of the principle of self-determination was the British military assistance for the Netherlands in the Dutch East Indies in 1946.[45] The United Kingdom replied that its troops were necessary to rescue anti-Japanese internees and that the presence was unrelated to the conflict between the Dutch and the Indonesians.[46] Thirty years later, when South Africa intervened in Angola invoking the request of Portugal (August 1975), Portugal denied having made the request and South Africa later resorted to other justifications.[47] More importantly, South Africa contended that '[a]t no stage did [it] become involved, nor did it desire to become involved, in the civil war as such'.[48] The General Assembly also repeatedly condemned South Africa's armed intervention and called upon all states to withhold any assistance and to prevent arms transfers to it.[49] The Security Council did the same.[50] Although with different degrees of conviction, these resolutions were generally not opposed by the Western states.[51] It is true that, in 1965, the Security Council called upon Britain to quell Rhodesia's rebellion, but this endorsement of the administering power was motivated by the racist character of Ian Smith's white minority regime.[52] The real self-determination struggle,

---

[44] Still in 1984, however, the British Foreign Office noted that the view that states may not accede to requests for help by a colonial power against a people struggling for self-determination is 'not ... shared by many international lawyers, and might be problematic for countries such as France or the United Kingdom' (Foreign Office, 'Is Intervention Ever Justified?' in Geoffrey Marston (ed), 'United Kingdom Materials on International Law 1986' (1986) 57 BYBIL 487, 616).

[45] Olivier Corten, *The Law Against War: The Prohibition on the Use of Force in Contemporary International Law* (2nd edn, Hart Publishing 2021) 307–8.

[46] See UN Doc S/PV.12, 7 February 1946, 178–82. Indonesia (formerly known as the Dutch East Indies) unilaterally declared independence in August 1945. The Netherlands accepted it on 27 December 1949.

[47] UN Doc S/12023, 25 March 1976 (Portugal); S/12019, 20 March 1976, Annex I, 1 (South Africa); S/PV.1904, 30 March 1976, para 97 (South Africa).

[48] UN Doc S/PV.1904, para 119.

[49] See eg GA Resolutions 2105 (XX), 20 December 1965, para 11; 2107 (XX), 21 December 1965, paras 7–8; 2184 (XXI), 12 December 1966, para 8; 2189 (XXI), 13 December 1966, paras 9–10; 2262 (XXII), 3 November 1967, paras 9, 11–12; 2383 (XXIII), 7 November 1968, paras 7–8, 10; 2395 (XXIII), 29 November 1968, paras 6–7; 2508 (XXIV), 21 November 1969, paras 4–5, 9; 2548 (XXIV), 11 December 1969, para 6; 2652 (XXV), 3 December 1970, paras 5–6; 2707 (XXV), 14 December 1970, paras 3–4, 7; 2795 (XXVI), 10 December 1971, paras 5, 8, 10; 2796 (XXVI), 10 December 1971, paras 3–4; 2945 (XXVII), 7 December 1972, para 5; 2979 (XXVII), 14 December 1972, paras 8–9; 3151 (XXVIII) G, 14 December 1973, paras 4–5; 34/192, 18 December 1979, paras 5, 7; 38/39 A, 5 December 1983, para 12; 41/95, 4 December 1986, paras 3–4.

[50] SC Resolutions 191, 18 June 1964, para 12; 218, 23 November 1965, para 6; 221, 9 April 1966, paras 2–5; 277, 18 March 1970, para 2; 282, 23 July 1970, para 6; 290, 8 December 1970, para 6; 311, 4 February 1972, para 5; 312, 4 February 1972, para 5; 326, 2 February 1973, para 6; 328, 10 March 1973, paras 4–5.

[51] Ronzitti, *Le guerre*, 114–15.

[52] On 11 November 1965, Rhodesia unilaterally declared independence from the United Kingdom. This was not considered a genuine act of self-determination (GA Resolutions 2151 (XXI), 17 November 1966, para 3; 2383 (XXIII), para 6; 2652 (XXV), para 2). The Security Council condemned the declaration by the 'illegal' regime of Rhodesia and qualified it as a threat to international peace and security (SC Resolutions 216, 12 November 1965; 217, 20 November 1965, para 1; 277, para 1). The General Assembly called upon the United Kingdom 'to take immediately all the necessary measures, including the use of force, to put an end to the illegal racist minority régime in Southern Rhodesia and to ensure the immediate application of

NON-INTERVENTION AND EXTERNAL SELF-DETERMINATION   317

therefore, was that between the Rhodesian government and the two national liberation movements, the Zimbabwe African People's Union and the Zimbabwe African National Union, and not that between Rhodesia and Britain.

The principle of external self-determination bans not only the dispatch of armed forces, but *all* other forms of third-state intervention in support of a colonial power and racist regime.[53] This includes the supply of arms and logistical support, at least to the extent that it allows the colonial power or racist regime to maintain its grip on power.[54] State practice and *opinio juris* confirm this conclusion: during the Cold War, not only the socialist and developing states but also the Western countries supported the restrictive measures adopted by the UN organs against Portugal, Rhodesia, and South Africa and declared that they complied with them.[55] In fact, several countries, including the United States, affirmed that they would have applied the measures even in the absence of the UN resolutions.[56] It is true that some countries, and particularly Portugal's NATO allies, continued to provide arms, military equipment, and training to the Portuguese army: this support, however, was either supplied covertly or it was

General Assembly resolution 1514 (XV) and other relevant resolutions' (GA Res 2262 (XXII), para 7). The reluctance of the United Kingdom to do so was condemned by the Assembly (see eg GA Res 2383 (XXIII), paras 3, 5). The Security Council also called upon the United Kingdom 'to prevent, by the use of force if necessary, the arrival at Beira of vessels reasonably believed to be carrying oil destined for Southern Rhodesia' (SC Res 221, para 5) and imposed economic and other sanctions (SC Resolutions 232, 16 December 1966, and 253, 29 May 1968).

[53] Ronzitti, *Le guerre*, 110–11. See the UN resolutions listed in Valentina Grado, *Guerre civili e terzi Stati* (CEDAM 1998) 131, fns 56 and 57.

[54] Schindler, 'Le principe', 470. US Secretary of State Marshall, for instance, declared that the United States would not provide arms to the Dutch against the Indonesians and that US ships would not transport their arms or troops (Alexander N Sack, 'The Truman Doctrine in International Law' (1947) 7 NLG Rev 141, 143). It is unclear whether it is any support for a colonial power or racist regime that is prohibited, or only that to be used to maintain the oppressive rule. The General Assembly specified that 'the arms embargo against South Africa makes no distinction between arms for external defence and arms for internal repression' (GA Res 2775 (XXVI) A, 29 November 1971, para 2). The same position was adopted with regard to Portugal (GA Resolutions 1807 (XVII), 14 December 1962, 2107 (XX), and 2270 (XXII), 17 November 1967). In his Separate Opinion in *Namibia*, Judge Ammoun also argued that the supply of arms, military equipment, logistic, economic, industrial and financial assistance by certain Western states to South Africa was unlawful even when it was 'not expressly intended to consolidate [South Africa's] presence in Namibia' (*Legal Consequences for States of the Continued Presence of South Africa in Namibia (South West Africa) notwithstanding Security Council Resolution 276 (1970)* (Advisory Opinion) [1971] ICJ Rep 16 (hereafter *Namibia*), Separate Opinion of Vice-President Ammoun, 99-100). Several states, however, distinguished between arms destined to maintain colonial domination or racist regimes and those for lawful purposes (Grado, *Guerre civili*, 132).

[55] Ronzitti, *Le guerre*, 114; Paulette Pierson-Mathy, 'L'embargo international sur les livraisons d'armes au Portugal' (1973) 9 RBDI 107, 130–3. In Res 181 (7 August 1963), the Council called upon all states to cease the sale and shipment of arms, ammunition, and military vehicles to South Africa. Acting under Chapter VII of the UN Charter, the Security Council later imposed a mandatory embargo on arms, ammunition, and military equipment against South Africa (SC Res 418, 4 November 1977, para 2). SC Res 217 (1965) also called 'upon all States to refrain from any action which would assist and encourage the illegal régime and, in particular, to desist from providing it with arms, equipment and military material, and to do their utmost in order to break all economic relations with Southern Rhodesia, including an embargo on oil and petroleum products' (SC Res 217, para 8). The resolution was adopted with no votes against and one abstention.

[56] Ronzitti, *Le guerre*, 115–16; Pierson-Mathy, 'L'embargo', 131. The same occurred for the sanctions against South Africa: Paulette Pierson-Mathy, 'L'action des Nations Unies contre l'apartheid' (1970) 6 RBDI 539, 551.

318 INTERNATIONAL LAW AND THE PRINCIPLE OF NON-INTERVENTION

claimed that it was not destined for the repression of national liberation movements in Africa but rather was a cooperation measure in the NATO framework.[57]

With regard to non-military forms of support for a colonial power or racist regime, the Security Council did not manage to adopt economic sanctions against Portugal based on Article 41 of the Charter, as the Western states opposed them.[58] The same occurred with regard to the imposition of an oil embargo against South Africa.[59] The General Assembly, however, succeeded where the Council had failed and called upon the member states to adopt restrictive economic and trade measures against South Africa and Portugal even in the absence of a Council decision.[60] As a result, many states (including Western ones) adopted measures against South Africa in the 1980s.[61] Such measures are not inconsistent with the principle of non-intervention even if they constituted economic coercion because, as the Dutch Advisory Committee on Questions of International Law correctly concluded, sovereignty has been restricted as a consequence of the violation of human rights and self-determination: a colonial power and an apartheid regime, therefore, cannot be protected by the principle of non-intervention because the matter is not one in which they can decide freely.[62]

If a state is bound by an economic or trade cooperation treaty with the colonial power or is required by treaty to transfer arms to it, a conflict occurs between such obligations and the aforesaid prohibition of any support stemming from the principle of external self-determination. If the UN Security Council has adopted sanctions against a colonial power, the prevalence of the obligations under the Charter, including the binding resolutions adopted by its organs, is ensured by Article 103 of the Charter.[63] In all other cases, treaty obligations owed to the colonial power can (and indeed must) be disregarded as required by the principle of self-determination even when the grounds codified in the 1969 Vienna Convention on the Law of Treaties (VCLT) cannot be invoked, and this without the third state incurring international responsibility for doing so, as the violation of treaty commitments in such case can be seen as a countermeasure adopted in reaction to the breach of an *erga omnes* obligation.[64] As Cassese has cautioned, however, resort to unilateral action should only be permitted when 'a

---

[57] Pierson-Mathy, 'L'embargo', 144–5.

[58] ibid, 110, 117. See GA Res 2107 (XX).

[59] Elena Katselli Proukaki, *The Problem of Enforcement in International Law: Countermeasures, the Non-Injured State and the Idea of International Community* (Routledge 2010) 168.

[60] ibid, 126, 168–9.

[61] ibid, 168–77; Martin Dawidowicz, *Third-Party Countermeasures in International Law* (CUP 2017) 154–9.

[62] The Committee had been asked to advise on whether the restrictive measures on oil supplies to and imports from apartheid South Africa that the Dutch government intended to adopt were an unlawful intervention (Robert CR Siekmann, 'Netherlands State Practice for the Parliament Year 1981–1982' (1983) 14 NYBIL 246, 246–9).

[63] According to Art 103 of the UN Charter, '[i]n the event of a conflict between the obligations of the Members of the United Nations under the present Charter and their obligations under any other international agreement, their obligations under the present Charter shall prevail'. Art 16 of the International Law Commission (ILC)'s Articles on the Responsibility of States for Internationally Wrongful Acts (ARSIWA), on the other hand, is not a conflict rule and neither prohibits nor allows certain conduct but merely establishes the consequences of aiding or assisting in the commission of an internationally wrongful act. See [2001] YB ILC vol II, part two, 26.

[64] On the admissibility of countermeasures in reaction to the breach of *erga omnes* obligations, see Chapter V, Section 5.1.2, fn 378.

multilateral forum ... has declared that a certain State has grossly infringed the principle or a rule on self-determination and has possibly called upon the Member States of the international community to take action against the delinquent State'.[65]

On the other hand, it does not seem that Articles 53 and 64 of the 1969 VCLT can play a role in this context.[66] Indeed, these provisions envisage a conflict between a *jus cogens* rule and a treaty, while in the present case the conflict is with the *application* of the treaty in a particular circumstance, not with the treaty as such: as Martti Koskenniemi notes in his Fragmentation of International Law Report, 'what the concept of *jus cogens* encapsulates is a rule of hierarchy *senso strictu*, not simply a rule of precedence. Hence, the result of conflicts between treaties and *jus cogens* is that the former shall not only be non-applicable, but wholly void, giving rise to no legal consequences whatsoever'.[67] This would occur when the treaty's object and purpose are exactly to maintain colonial rule, in which case it would arguably be null and void *ab initio*.

While it is uncontroversial that states cannot assist a colonial power or racist regime, it is doubtful whether, apart from when the Security Council so decides,[68] they are also under a due diligence obligation to prevent support by those under their jurisdiction.[69] It has been suggested that the principle of external self-determination, as a *jus cogens* rule, requires states at least to reject arms export licence applications when the arms are destined for a colonial power.[70] Apart from the aforementioned lack of opposition to the Security Council resolutions requiring states to take all necessary measures to prevent the sale and supply of arms and military equipment to Portugal, however, not much state practice and *opinio juris* exist to prove or disprove this assertion. I have found a 1974 statement of the British government that distinguishes the sale of arms to apartheid South Africa from the 'civil trade' and that claims that, unlike the former, 'commercial trading relations with other countries should [not] be based on considerations of their internal or external policies':[71] British nationals, therefore, remained free to conclude contracts with South Africa not involving the sale of arms.

---

[65] Cassese, *Self-Determination*, 156. The alternative is that the state intending to adopt countermeasures accepts to submit the question to international conciliation or arbitration or another means of settling the dispute peacefully before or after resorting to coercion (ibid, 156, 184–5).

[66] Arts 53 and 64, Vienna Convention on the Law of Treaties (VCLT) (Vienna, 23 May 1969) 1155 UNTS 331.

[67] Study Group of the International Law Commission, 'Fragmentation of International Law: Difficulties Arising from the Diversification and Expansion of International Law', UN Doc A/CN.4/L.682, 13 April 2006, para 365.

[68] The Security Council, for instance, requested all states not only to refrain from providing any assistance to Portugal themselves, but also to adopt all measures to prevent the sale and supply of arms and military equipment that would enable it to continue its oppression of the territories under its administration (SC Res 180, 31 July 1963, para 6).

[69] Papa, 'Autodeterminazione', 73.

[70] George P Politakis, 'Variations on a Myth: Neutrality and the Arms Trade' (1992) 35 GYBIL 435, 494. See *Palestinian Wall*, para 146. It has been noted that, as arms exports are now subordinated to a licence system in virtually all states, the distinction between public and private transfers is difficult to maintain and 'private arms exports proper are virtually non-existent' (George P Politakis, 'Variations on a Myth, 494).

[71] UN Doc A/9918, 4 December 1974, Annex I, 1. See also Annex II, 2.

320 INTERNATIONAL LAW AND THE PRINCIPLE OF NON-INTERVENTION

3.2 Third-State Intervention in Support of a National Liberation Movement

In their struggle to exercise self-determination, peoples under colonial rule are represented by a national liberation movement.[72] National liberation movements are organized armed groups who differ from traditional insurgents because they do not need to possess effective control of territory or establish a *de facto* administration to acquire international legal personality: their special status depends not on their strength or success but on the cause they pursue.[73] From a *jus in bello* perspective, this special status results, at least for states parties to Protocol I Additional to the 1949 Geneva Conventions on the Protection of Victims of War (Additional Protocol I), in the application of the law of international armed conflicts.[74] The question is whether national liberation movements are also granted a more favourable treatment under the law of intervention, that is, whether third states can intervene on their side in a war of national liberation and, if so, by what means: this problem is addressed in the following pages.

3.2.1 Support by sending armed forces

As shown in Section 2, the principle of non-intervention does not protect colonial powers from third-state coercive interferences aimed at enforcing compliance with the principle of external self-determination (as will be recalled, support of armed opposition groups is a form of coercion of state).[75] When the interference consists in the use of armed force, however, it needs to be reconciled with the *jus contra bellum* rules contained in the UN Charter and customary international law.

The use of force by national liberation movements, like that of any other group of insurgents, is not prohibited by Article 2(4) of the UN Charter and its customary counterpart as this provision only addresses states and not also non-state actors.[76] Third-state armed support to them, on the other hand, is submitted to the *jus contra bellum* rules as it is a use of force 'in international relations'.[77] During the Cold War, its lawfulness was backed by the developing countries and the communist bloc. The Conference of the Non-Aligned Countries held in Cairo in 1964, in particular, urged the participating states 'to afford all necessary material support—financial and military—to the Freedom Fighters in the territories under Portuguese colonial rule'.[78]

---

[72] On the standards for identifying national liberation movements, see Redaelli, *Intervention*, 189–92.

[73] Ronzitti, *Le guerre*, 108–10; Stephen C Neff, *War and the Law of Nations: A General History* (CUP 2005) 374. Several national liberation movements, including SWAPO and the African National Congress, did not have any stable control of territory and mainly operated from neighbouring states.

[74] See Mačák, *Internationalized Armed Conflicts*, 65–74. Art 1(4) of Additional Protocol I does not reflect customary international law (ibid, 73–4).

[75] See Chapter III, Section 8.

[76] Ronzitti, *Le guerre*, 143. This position was expressed, inter alia, by Mexico and Sweden during the drafting of the Friendly Relations Declaration (UN Doc A/AC.125/SR.66, 4 December 1967, 5).

[77] In the *Nicaragua* Merits Judgment, the ICJ avoided addressing the problem *(Nicaragua v USA*, para 206). For Judge Schwebel, however, 'it is lawful for a foreign State or movement to give to a people struggling for self-determination moral, political and humanitarian assistance; but it is not lawful for a foreign State or movement to intervene in that struggle with force or to provide arms, supplies and other logistical support in the prosecution of armed rebellion' (*Nicaragua v USA*, Dissenting Opinion of Judge Schwebel, para 180).

[78] UN Doc A/5763, 29 October 1964, 7. Art 20(3) of the 1981 African Charter on Human and Peoples' Rights (Banjul, 27 June 1981) also provides that '[a]ll peoples shall have the right to the assistance of the

Kenya spoke for many when it advocated the adoption of 'any measures, including the use of force, designed to defeat apartheid and the racial and colonial policies practised in Mozambique, Angola and Southern Rhodesia'.[79] During the chairmanships of Nikita Khrushchev (1953–64) and Leonid Brezhnev (1964–82), the Soviet Union also became the champion of the 'sacred and just struggle of the peoples for their independence' and of the right of third states to support them with moral, material, and other assistance.[80] This support was not inconsistent with another brainchild of Khrushchev's, the peaceful co-existence between states with different political and economic systems: on the contrary, it was aimed at realizing one of its essential conditions, the right of all peoples to decide their own destiny.[81] In this context, the principle of non-intervention was turned upside down and conceived as protecting the peoples entitled to external self-determination from the colonial powers, and not the latter from third states.[82] Soviet writers claimed that states had not only a right, but even a duty, to help peoples struggling to exercise self-determination.[83] Certain post-Soviet Russian scholars continue to claim the existence of a right of oppressed peoples 'to seek support and receive it from other States and international organizations in accordance with the principles and norms of international law'[84] and the Russian government has used this argument, as well as others, in order to justify its intervention in and annexation of Crimea in 2014.[85]

At the United Nations, the communist and developing countries attempted to secure the adoption of resolutions incorporating their position on self-determination struggles. General Assembly Resolution 2105 (XX) on the implementation of Resolution 1514 (XV) for the first time invited 'all states to provide material and moral assistance to the national liberation movements in colonial territories'.[86] The resolution, however, intentionally left unclear whether the people's struggle could be conducted

States parties to the present Charter in their liberation struggle against foreign domination, be it political, economic or cultural', although it does not specify what type of assistance is lawful (1520 UNTS 217).

[79] UN Doc A/C.1/SR.1402, para 20. See also Zambia (A/C.6/SR.1178, para 13); Pakistan (A/C.6/SR.1179, 24 September 1970, para 19); India (A/C.6/SR.1183, 28 September 1970, para 9); and Syria (A/AC.134/SR.67-78, 19 October 1970, 42).

[80] Khrushchev's address to the UN General Assembly, UN Doc A/PV.869, 23 September 1960, para 223. On Soviet scholarship advocating the use of force in support of peoples struggling for self-determination, see Johannes Socher, 'Lenin, (Just) Wars of National Liberation, and the Soviet Doctrine on the Use of Force' (2017) 19 J His Intl L 219, 234–40; Kattan, 'Self-Determination in the Third World', 87.

[81] RJ Vincent, *Nonintervention and International Order* (Princeton University Press 1974) 185. Chinese scholars adopted an analogous position (Jerome Alan Cohen, 'China and Intervention: Theory and Practice' (1973) 121 U Pa L Rev 471, 495–6).

[82] Vincent, *Nonintervention*, 185.

[83] Toman, 'La conception', 358. The 1981 Declaration on the Inadmissibility of Intervention and Interference in the Internal Affairs of States, inspired by the Soviet Union and opposed by the Western states, also affirms '[t]he right and duty of States fully to support the right to self-determination, freedom and independence of peoples under colonial domination, foreign occupation or racist régimes' (GA Res 36/103, Annex, para III(b)).

[84] Valerii I Kuznetsov and Bakhtiar R Tuzmukhamedov (eds), *International Law—A Russian Introduction* (William Butler tr, Eleven International Publishing 2009) 148.

[85] UN Doc S/PV.7134, 13 March 2014, 15.

[86] GA Res 2105 (XX), para 10. The resolution was adopted by a majority of seventy-four votes to six and twenty-seven abstentions.

322 INTERNATIONAL LAW AND THE PRINCIPLE OF NON-INTERVENTION

by force and whether material support included military intervention.[87] The developing and communist states also succeeded in having a clause included in the Friendly Relations Declaration affirming that, in their struggle for self-determination, peoples subject to alien subjugation, domination, and exploitation are 'entitled to seek and to receive support in accordance with the purposes and principles of the Charter',[88] but again the language was intentionally left vague to secure consensus. It was only in 1973 that the General Assembly's annual resolutions on the universal realization of the right of peoples to self-determination started to explicitly refer to the legitimacy of the 'armed struggle' of peoples under colonial and foreign domination and alien subjugation and to call upon member states to supply moral, material 'and any other assistance' to them.[89] The Soviet Union also obtained the inclusion in Article 7 of the 1974 Definition of Aggression of language which could be interpreted as suggesting that the acts listed in Article 3 of the Definition, and in particular the sending of armed bands, groups, or irregulars who carry out acts of armed force, do not constitute an act of aggression when they are taken against a colonial power, a racist regime, or other forms of alien domination.[90]

The persistent opposition of the Western bloc during the Cold War, however, has prevented the formation of a customary exception to Article 2(4) based on external self-determination.[91] The General Assembly resolutions calling for material or other

---

[87] Christine Gray, *International Law and the Use of Force* (4th edn, OUP 2018) 69. The reference to 'material and moral assistance' is also contained in many other resolutions, including GA Resolutions 2189 (XXI), para 7; 2262 (XXII), para 16; 2270 (XXII), para 12; 2307 (XXII), 13 December 1967, para 8; 2326 (XXII), 16 December 1967, para 6; 2372 (XXII), 12 June 1968, para 10; 2446 (XXIII), 19 December 1968, para 6; 2465 (XXIII), 20 December 1968, para 6; 2508 (XXIV), para 10; 2548 (XXIV), para 5; 2646 (XXV), 30 November 1970, para 2; 2649 (XXV), 30 November 1970, para 2; 2678 (XXV), 9 December 1970, para 10; 2704 (XXV), 14 December 1970, para 5; 2708 (XXV), 14 December 1970, para 6; 2787 (XXVI), 6 December 1971, para 3; 2795 (XXVI), para 13; 2796 (XXVI), para 9; 2871 (XXVI), 20 December 1971, para 9; 2908 (XXVII), 2 November 1972, para 8; 2980 (XXVII), 14 December 1972, para 4; 3031 (XXVII), 18 December 1972, para 10; 3111 (XXVIII), 12 December 1973, para 14; 48/47, 10 December 1993, para 9; 49/89, 16 December 1994, para 9; 50/39, 6 December 1995, para 10; 51/146, 13 December 1996, para 10; 52/78, 10 December 1997, para 10; 53/68, 3 December 1998, para 10; 54/91, 6 December 1999, para 13; 55/147, 8 December 2000, para 13; 56/74, 10 December 2001, para 13; 57/140, 11 December 2002, para 13; 58/111, 9 December 2003, para 12; 59/136, 10 December 2004; para 12, 60/119, 8 December 2005, para 12; 61/130, 14 December 2006, para 15; 62/120, 17 December 2007, para 12; 63/110, 5 December 2008, para 12; 64/106, 10 December 2009, para 12; 65/117, 10 December 2010, para 12; 66/91, 9 December 2011, para 12; 67/134, 18 December 2012, para 12; 68/97, 11 December 2013, para 12; 69/107, 5 December 2014, para 12; 70/231, 23 December 2015, para 15; 71/122, 6 December 2016, para 15; 72/111, 7 December 2017, para 16; 73/123, 7 December 2018, para 16; 74/113, 13 December 2019, para 16; 75/122, 10 December 2020, para 16.

[88] See GA Res 2625 (XXV), Annex, fifth principle, para 5.

[89] See GA Res 3070 (XXVIII), 30 November 1973, paras 2, 3. The resolution was adopted by a majority of ninety-seven votes in favour, five against, and twenty-eight abstentions.

[90] See GA Res 3314 (XXIX), 14 December 1974, Annex, Art 7. See also Ronzitti, *Le guerre*, 135; Julius Stone, 'Hopes and Loopholes in the 1974 Definition of Aggression' (1977) 71 AJIL 224, 238. Art 7 of the Definition of Aggression reads as follows: 'Nothing in this Definition, and in particular article 3, could in any way prejudice the right to self-determination, freedom and independence, as derived from the Charter, of peoples forcibly deprived of that right and referred to in the Declaration on Principles of International Law concerning Friendly Relations and Cooperation among States in accordance with the Charter of the United Nations, particularly peoples under colonial and racist regimes or other forms of alien domination; nor the right of these peoples to struggle to that end and to seek and receive support, in accordance with the principles of the Charter and in conformity with the above-mentioned Declaration.'

[91] Antonio Cassese, 'Le droit international et la question de l'assistance aux mouvements de libération nationale' (1986) 19 RBDI 307, 326; Palmisano, 'Autodeterminazione', 129. The US representative at the Security Council commented that Res 1514 'does not authorize the use of force for its implementation ... and

NON-INTERVENTION AND EXTERNAL SELF-DETERMINATION   323

assistance for peoples struggling for self-determination were all adopted with a significant number of negative votes and abstentions. For the Western states, the Friendly Relations Declaration was clear that support for peoples entitled to self-determination could only be provided 'in accordance with the purposes and principles of the [UN] Charter', that is, it could not consist of armed force. They also claimed that Article 7 of the Definition of Aggression only legitimizes the struggle of the national liberation movements and not also third-state support to them, and must in any case be read in conjunction with Article 6, according to which nothing in the Definition can 'be construed as in any way enlarging or diminishing the scope of the Charter, including its provisions concerning cases in which the use of force is lawful'.[92] All in all, the Western view was that violence was not justified even to exercise, or support legitimate instances of, self-determination.[93]

While they all eventually recognized the legitimacy of anti-colonial struggles, therefore, the Western states on the one hand and the communist and developing countries on the other disagreed on *how* these struggles could be supported: for the latter, any assistance, including armed force, was lawful, while for the former it had to be limited to moral and political support. It is not surprising, therefore, that the only General Assembly resolutions on decolonization issues adopted by consensus during the Cold War were those that did not specify the measures that third states could adopt in support of national liberation movements.[94] Since 1991, General Assembly resolutions on 'the universal realisation of the right of peoples to self-determination' have no longer made reference to 'armed struggle'[95] and even certain developing countries have in recent decades argued that support for a national liberation movement cannot go as far as armed intervention.[96]

With regard to state practice, external self-determination has been invoked as a legal basis for sending armed forces in support of national liberation movements only in a couple of cases. Self-determination, in particular, was mentioned by India in relation to its intervention in and subsequent annexation of Portuguese Goa in 1961.[97] As

---

cannot overrule the Charter injunctions against the use of armed force' (UN Doc S/PV.988, 18 December 1961, para 93). The United Kingdom referred to the position of 'most Western writers' to reject the view that national liberation movements could be assisted by other states, at least until they become belligerents by controlling part of the national territory, with the possible exception of economic and humanitarian help (British Foreign Office, 'Is Intervention Ever Justified?', 619). See also Australia (A/8018, para 204), Sweden (A/C.6/SR.886, 1 December 1965, para 16), the Netherlands (A/AC.119/SR.7, 16 October 1964, 12), and South Africa (A/C.6/SR.1184, 28 September 1970, para 16).

[92] See eg United States (UN Doc A/9619, 1974, 24), United Kingdom (A/9619, 32), and Australia (A/9619, 33). The Declaration on Friendly Relations contains an identical formula: according to mainstream scholarship, therefore, the Declaration does not permit armed support for national liberation movements, which remains prohibited by Art 2(4) (Cassese, *Self-Determination*, 200).

[93] According to the US delegate on the Special Committee on the Definition of Aggression, '[t]he saying "the end justifies the means" must certainly not be applied to self-determination' (UN Doc A/AC.134/SR.67-78, 99).

[94] Grado, *Guerre civili*, 141.

[95] Tom Ruys, *'Armed Attack' and Article 51 of the UN Charter* (CUP 2010) 421.

[96] *Armed Activities on the Territory of the Congo (Democratic Republic of the Congo v Uganda)*, Memorial of the DRC (Merits), 6 July 2000, vol I, para 5.74.

[97] UN Doc S/PV.987, 18 December 1961, para 46. India's intervention aimed to 'restore law and order following the collapse of the colonial administration' (S/PV.987, para 55) and 'to assist the freedom movement of Goa, to help the resistance movement of Goa' (S/PV.988, para 83).

324   INTERNATIONAL LAW AND THE PRINCIPLE OF NON-INTERVENTION

Olivier Corten has noted, however, India did not portray itself as a 'third state' but as a state the territory of which was still in part illegally occupied by a colonial power: it was, in other words, using force within its rightful borders.[98] India also invoked other justifications and narrowly escaped condemnation by the UN Security Council thanks to the Soviet veto.[99] The only case of an intervening state exclusively using self-determination arguments to justify its intervention is the 1975 invasion of Timor-Leste by Indonesia, where the latter referred to the request of the people of the former, as represented by the four parties that wanted integration with Indonesia, in order to stop a faction (the *Frente Revolucionária do Timor-Leste Independente*—FRETILIN) that sought independence and allegedly denied the majority of the East Timorese their right of self-determination.[100] The intervention was almost universally condemned, including by the UN organs.[101] Taking everything into account, therefore, one cannot but conclude that, under customary international law, the principle of external self-determination has affected the application of the principle of non-intervention but has not created an exception to Article 2(4) of the UN Charter.[102]

From a secondary rule perspective, armed intervention in support of national liberation movements also cannot be construed as a countermeasure adopted by third states in reaction to the violation of an *erga omnes* obligation, as it is generally agreed that countermeasures cannot affect the prohibition of the use of force.[103] The same applies to the defence of necessity.[104] To circumvent these obstacles, the Afro–Asian states saw wars of national liberation as an exercise of the right of self-defence by a people against the colonial power, entitling third states to intervene in collective self-defence.[105] Different versions of this doctrine can be

[98] Corten, *The Law*, 150–1.
[99] Ronzitti, *Le guerre*, 119.
[100] UN Doc S/PV.1864, 15 December 1975, paras 93–4, and S/PV.1869, 22 December 1975, para 144. No Portuguese authority had been left in East Timor (S/PV.1864, para 91).
[101] See eg SC Resolutions 384, 22 December 1975, and 389, 22 April 1976; GA Resolutions 3485 (XXX), 12 December 1975 and 31/53, 1 December 1976.
[102] Gaetano Arangio-Ruiz, 'Autodeterminazione (diritto dei popoli alla)' in *Enciclopedia giuridica*, vol IV (Treccani 1988) 1, 10.
[103] Art 50(1)(a) ARSIWA.
[104] It has been argued that a limited use of armed force in support of oppressed peoples can be justified on the ground of necessity (Lattanzi, 'Autodeterminazione dei popoli', 25). The ILC, however, has excluded that state of necessity can justify a use of armed force (Commentary on Art 25 ARSIWA [2001] YB ILC vol II, part two, 84, para 21).
[105] The Algerian representative on the Special Committee on the Definition of Aggression noted that 'the exercise of the right of self-determination must be placed on the same footing as self-defense and included not only the right of peoples subject to any form of alien domination to resort to armed force, but also the right and the duty of all States members of the United Nations to assist those peoples' (UN Doc A/AC.134/SR.110-113, 18 July 1974, 49). See also the statements by Bulgaria (A/C.6/SR.891, 6 December 1965, para 7); Hungary (A/C.6/SR.999, 16 November 1967, para 8); and Sudan (A/C.6/SR.1162, 28 November 1969, para 66). For an affirmation of the right of oppressed peoples to self-defence, see Kenya (A/C.6/SR.1442, 20 November 1973, para 23); Soviet Union (A/C.6/SR.1182 and Corr. 1, para 37); Libya (A/C.6/SR.1182 and Corr. 1, para 47); Algeria (A/C.6/SR.761, 16 November 1962, para 19); Tunisia (A/C.6/SR.822, 29 November 1963, para 21); Ukraine (A/C.6/SR.875, 15 November 1965, para 19); UAR (A/C.1/SR.1403, para 3); Upper Volta (A/C.6/SR.888, 2 December 1965, para 16); Mongolia (A/C.6/SR.935, para 25); Poland (A/C.6/SR.997, para 17); Congo-Brazzaville (A/C.6/SR.998, 15 November 1967, para 6); Cameroon (A/C.6/SR.1086, 4 December 1968, para 19); Czechoslovakia (A/C.6/SR.1086, para 31); Kuwait (A/C.6/SR.1094, 12 December 1968, para 38); Iraq (A/C.6/SR.1180, para 7); Yugoslavia (A/AC.119/SR.9, 16 October 1964, 22); Romania (A/AC.119/SR.16, 19 October 1964, 5); and India (A/AC.125/SR.64, 4 December 1967, 5). On self-defence against colonialism, see in literature John Dugard, 'The Organization of African Unity

NON-INTERVENTION AND EXTERNAL SELF-DETERMINATION   325

identified.[106] The first, employed by India to justify its invasion and annexation of Goa, sees colonial conquest as unlawful *ab initio* and, therefore, as a case of continuing aggression.[107] The second posits that, even if colonialism was lawful at the time the Scramble for Africa took place, by the 1960s the legitimacy of the colonial peoples' struggle had been recognized and the European states had lost a valid legal title to rule their overseas dependencies: at that point, by refusing to grant them independence, the occupation became an act of aggression.[108] Finally, it has been more narrowly claimed that it is only when a colonial power uses forcible measures to prevent the exercise of self-determination that armed resistance in the form of individual and collective self-defence becomes permissible.[109] These views, however, never gained sufficient traction. The Western and Latin American states, in particular, strongly criticized them for applying the law retroactively and for being too broad an interpretation of Article 51 of the UN Charter.[110] As a result, drafts that affirmed the right of self-defence against colonialism were not included in the Friendly Relations Declaration or in the Definition of Aggression.[111] The former, in particular, refers to 'actions against, and resistance to' the use of force to prevent a people from exercising their right to self-determination as well as to the entitlement 'to seek and receive support', but falls short of explicitly using self-defence language.[112]

3.2.2 Other forms of support

If third states may not send regular or irregular armed forces in support of a national liberation movement, it is doubtful whether other forms of military assistance, such as the supply of arms and training, are permissible.[113] For the developing and communist countries, the answer was affirmative. As with the sending of troops, however,

---

and Colonialism: An Inquiry into the Plea of Self-Defence as a Justification for the Use of Force in the Eradication of Colonialism' (1967) 16 Intl & Comp LQ 157, 170–1.

[106] For a detailed analysis, see Redaelli, *Intervention*, 214–19.

[107] For India, Portugal's occupation of Goa in 1510 'started in an illegal manner [and] continues to be illegal today' and, therefore, it constitutes an act of aggression (UN Doc S/PV.987, para 46).

[108] *Namibia*, 90.

[109] Abi-Saab, 'Wars', 371–2.

[110] Heather A Wilson, *International Law and the Use of Force by National Liberation Movements* (Clarendon Press 1988) 95. See eg the statement of the Argentinian delegate on the Special Committee on Friendly Relations, UN Doc A/AC.125/SR.70, 4 December 1967, 16–17. See also Legal Opinion of the International Law Department of Switzerland's Department of Foreign Affairs (6 May 1999) in Lucius Caflisch, 'La pratique suisse en matière de droit international public 1999' (2000) 10 RSDIDE 627, 670; and Robert E Gorelick, 'Wars of National Liberation: *Jus Ad Bellum*' (1979) 11 Case Western Reserve JIL 71, 75. For Arangio-Ruiz, 'to apply Article 51 to the struggle of the "liberation movement" before the attainment of that minimum of stability without which statehood is still in question, would mean ... to stretch the meaning of Article 51 beyond any reasonable wide interpretation and open the way ... to a dangerous instability' (Gaetano Arangio-Ruiz, 'The Normative Role of the General Assembly of the United Nations and the Declaration of Principles of Friendly Relations' (1972) 137 Recueil des Cours 419, 569).

[111] UN Doc A/AC.119/L.15, 9 September 1964, para 3 (Ghana, Yugoslavia, and India); A/7326, 1968, para 22 (Czechoslovakia); A/7326, para 26 (Algeria, Cameroon, Ghana, India, Kenya, Madagascar, Nigeria, Syria, UAR, and Yugoslavia). See also the criticism of Guatemala (A/AC.119/SR.14, 21 October 1964, 7), the United States (A/AC.125/SR.68, 4 December 1967, 5), and Venezuela (A/AC.119/SR.16, 17–18).

[112] GA Res 2625 (XXV), Annex, fifth principle, para 5.

[113] In 1974, Ronzitti wrote that a rule allowing the supply of arms to national liberation movements was in the process of forming (Ronzitti, *Le guerre*, 134). Some twenty years later, Cassese and Grado concluded that such rule is now *lex lata* (Cassese, *Self-Determination*, 199–200; Grado, *Guerre civili*, 141–2).

326   INTERNATIONAL LAW AND THE PRINCIPLE OF NON-INTERVENTION

the Western states always interpreted the Friendly Relations Declaration as not permitting the provision of arms and other military *matériel* to national liberation movements, as this was considered inconsistent with the UN Charter.[114] It is worth noting that arming and training national liberation movements cannot be justified as a countermeasure in response to the violation of the principle of self-determination by the colonial power as, according to the ICJ, such conduct constitutes a use of force.[115]

Other forms of support, on the other hand, are permissible.[116] Although it did not take an explicit position on the legality of hosting the national liberation movement's military bases and training camps, the Security Council not only condemned the incursions conducted by South Africa against South West African People's Organisation (SWAPO) positions in Angola, but also commended the Frontline States' 'support of the people of Namibia in their just and legitimate struggle'.[117] States belonging to different Cold War blocs also provided financial support to certain national liberation movements.[118] Unlike arms transfers, this was often publicly acknowledged.[119] In addition, states recognized certain movements as the legitimate representatives of the concerned peoples or even as governments before they had secured territorial control, and international organizations admitted them as full members or as observers.[120] These measures are beyond the reach of the principle of non-intervention, even when they amount to coercion, as they do not bear on a matter in which the colonial power can decide freely. Unless a specific treaty prohibits them, therefore, they are lawful measures to secure compliance with the principle of external self-determination by

---

[114] UN Doc A/8018, para 204 (Australia); A/8018, para 235 (United Kingdom); A/8018, para 269 (United States). When the ship *Athos* was intercepted on the high seas by a French warship with its cargo of arms allegedly destined for Algerian rebels (19 October 1956), for instance, France sent a letter to the Security Council accusing Egypt of 'flagrant violation of the fundamental rules of international law which stipulate non-interference in the internal affairs of another State and respect by a State for the sovereignty of other States' (S/3689, 25 October 1956, 3). Egypt denied knowledge of the matter (Keesing's 1955–1956, 15277).

[115] *Nicaragua v USA*, para 228. See Art 50(1) ARSIWA.

[116] Paola Gaeta, Jorge E Viñuales, and Salvatore Zappalà, *Cassese's International Law* (3rd edn, OUP 2020) 70.

[117] SC Resolutions 428, 6 May 1978, para 6, and 447, 28 March 1979, para 4. See Elena Sciso, 'L'aggressione indiretta nella Definizione dell'Assemblea generale delle Nazioni Unite' (1983) RDI 253, 289. The 'Frontline States' were a coalition of African countries from the 1960s to the early 1990s cooperating to end apartheid in South Africa and Rhodesia. South Africa launched military incursions in Botswana, Zambia, Zimbabwe, and Mozambique and supported rebel groups seeking to overthrow the regimes in Angola (União Nacional para a Independência Total de Angola—UNITA) and Mozambique (Resistência Nacional Moçambicana—RENAMO).

[118] Grado, *Guerre civili*, 141.

[119] In 1963, the OAU even established the African Liberation Committee with the task, among others, to channel funds from member states to the continent's national liberation movements (Hilmi S Yousuf, 'The OAU and the African Liberation Movement' (1985) 38(4) Pakistan Horizon 55, 56–8).

[120] Wilson, *International Law*, 104. In 1950, for instance, the People's Republic of China recognized Hồ Chí Minh's government as 'the legal representative of the will of the Vietnamese people' and the Soviet Union issued a similar declaration (Keesing's 1948–50, 10494). The Provisional Government of the Republic of Algeria (GPRA), based first in Cairo and then Tunis, was also recognized *de facto* or *de jure* by about thirty African and Asian states while France still controlled the Algerian territory (Erik Castrén, *Civil War* (Suomalainen Tiedeakatemia 1966) 75). In 1960, the GPRA became a member of the Arab League and acceded to the 1949 Geneva Conventions on the Protection of Victims of War (Van Cleef Greenberg, 'Law', 44). The UN General Assembly recognized the national liberation movements in the Portuguese colonies as 'the authentic representatives of the aspirations of the peoples of those Territories' (GA Res 2918 (XXVII), 14 November 1972, para 2) and did the same with the national liberation movements in Rhodesia (GA Res 3115 (XXVIII), 12 December 1973, para 2) and South Africa (GA Res 3151 (XXVIII) G)).

NON-INTERVENTION AND EXTERNAL SELF-DETERMINATION   327

the colonial power.[121] Should they conflict with other international law obligations, they can constitute countermeasures adopted in response to the previous violation of an *erga omnes* obligation (to the extent that they meet their substantive and procedural requirements).[122]

4. Third-State Intervention in Situations of Alien Domination and Occupation

Occupation is 'the effective control of a power (be it one or more states or an international organization, such as the United Nations) over a territory to which that power has no sovereign title, without the volition of the sovereign of that territory'.[123] As Yoram Dinstein points out, occupation is 'a natural phenomenon in war' and is a lawful method of warfare in an international armed conflict under international humanitarian law (IHL).[124] States, therefore, can in principle assist an occupying power to maintain the occupation.[125] Any direct assistance through the sending of armed forces, however, will turn the assisting state into a co-belligerent and will have to be reconciled with the *jus contra bellum* rules codified in the UN Charter: said otherwise, third states can support an occupying power with armed force only if the latter is exercising its right of self-defence or if the use of force has been authorized by the Security Council. Assistance to the occupying power short of the use of armed force might constitute unneutral service that exposes the state supplying it to the retaliation of the belligerent whose territory is occupied.

In certain situations, however, occupation can constitute a violation of the principle of external self-determination: it is to these situations that the expressions 'alien occupation' (in Additional Protocol I) and 'alien domination' (in the relevant General Assembly resolutions) refer.[126] For Eyal Benvenisti, this occurs when 'the occupant [is]

[121] Art 54 ARSIWA reaffirms 'the right of any State, entitled under article 48, paragraph 1, to invoke the responsibility of another State, to take lawful measures against that State to ensure cessation of the breach and reparation in the interest of the injured State or of the beneficiaries of the obligation breached'.

[122] Schindler, 'Le principe', 561–2; Ronzitti, *Le guerre*, 151–2; Gabriella Carella, *La responsabilità dello Stato per crimini internazionali* (Jovene 1985) 198.

[123] Eyal Benvenisti, *The International Law of Occupation* (2nd edn, OUP 2012) 3.

[124] Yoram Dinstein, *The International Law of Belligerent Occupation* (CUP 2009) 1–2.

[125] Under Art 43 of the Hague Regulations, '[t]he authority of the legitimate power having in fact passed into the hands of the occupant, the latter shall take all the measures in his power to restore, and ensure, as far as possible, public order and safety, while respecting, unless absolutely prevented, the laws in force in the country'. See Convention (IV) Respecting the Laws and Customs of War on Land (The Hague, 18 October 1907) 205 CTS 277.

[126] For the Canadian Supreme Court, a 'clear case where a right to external self-determination accrues is where a people is subject to alien subjugation, domination or exploitation outside a colonial context' (*Québec*, para 133). Art 2(4) of the 2004 Arab Charter on Human Rights also provides that '[a]ll peoples have the right to resist foreign occupation'. For a list of UN resolutions recognizing the right of external self-determination to peoples in occupied territories, see Marco Longobardo, *The Use of Armed Force in Occupied Territory* (CUP 2018) 150–1. The expression 'alien domination' in the General Assembly resolutions was adopted to cover 'colonies of settlement', that is, situations 'when the settlers, while severing their formal ties with their mother countries, exercise a colonial policy vis-à-vis these populations which denies them their right to self-determination' and systematically discriminates against them (Abi-Saab, 'Wars', 394–5). The language of 'alien occupation' was included in Art 1(4) of Additional Protocol I at the instance of five Latin American states so as to prevent an interpretation that would allow dissident movements to claim that their government was under 'foreign domination' and thus legitimize insurrections (Abi-Saab,

328 INTERNATIONAL LAW AND THE PRINCIPLE OF NON-INTERVENTION

holding out in bad faith, refusing to negotiate for its withdrawal in return for peace'.[127] In Cassese's view, the violation of the principle of self-determination in the case of occupation essentially depends on the violation of the *jus contra bellum*:

> [S]elf-determination is violated whenever there is a military invasion or belligerent occupation of a foreign territory, except where the occupation—although unlawful— is of a minimal duration or is solely intended as a means of repelling, under Article 51 of the UN Charter, an armed attack initiated by the vanquished Power and consequently is not protracted.[128]

Aeyal Gross has usefully suggested three normative factors to consider in order to differentiate occupation as a lawful method of warfare from conquest, colonialism, and apartheid: '(1) non-acquisition of sovereignty, (2) management of the territory for the benefit of the local population, (3) temporariness rather than indefinite prolongation'.[129] For Lieblich and Benvenisti, indicia that an occupation has become annexation include economic and legal integration with the occupant, passportization, infrastructural and demographic changes in the occupied territory, and the extraterritorial application of the occupant's domestic laws.[130]

Be that as it may, all the aforementioned authors agree that occupations of indefinite duration, like the cases of Namibia (formerly Southwest Africa, occupied by South Africa in 1966–90),[131] East Timor (occupied by Indonesia from 1975 to 1999),[132] the Palestinian Territories (occupied by Israel since 1967),[133] and Western Sahara (occupied by Morocco since 1975),[134] are clearly problematic from a self-determination perspective. If in these situations the concerned peoples have the right of external self-determination (as indeed they do), then the occupant must allow its exercise and, if it does not comply with this obligation, third states may not render aid or assistance to it in order to maintain the unlawful situation, exactly as happens in the case of colonial domination.[135] Consent by the occupant would not make the intervention lawful under the principle of non-intervention, as a state can only consent to acts that it could itself lawfully perform. Not only the dispatch of armed forces, but *any* support

'Wars', 395). For the International Committee of the Red Cross (ICRC), alien occupation only 'covers cases of partial or total occupation of a territory which has not yet been fully formed as a state' (Yves Sandoz, Christophe Swinarski, and Bruno Zimmermann (eds), *Commentary on the Additional Protocols of 8 June 1977 to the Geneva Conventions of 12 August 1949* (Nijhoff 1987) para 112). It should be noted that control over a territory can also be exercised through a 'puppet' government (W Michael Reisman, 'The Resistance in Afghanistan is Engaged in a War of National Liberation' (1987) 81 AJIL 906, 909).

[127] Benvenisti, *The International Law*, 17.

[128] Cassese, *Self-Determination*, 99, emphasis in the original. For him, 'the breach of external self-determination is simply an unlawful use of force looked at from the perspective of the victimized *people* rather than from that of the besieged sovereign State or territory' (ibid, emphasis in the original). See also Yaël Ronen, 'Illegal Occupation and Its Consequences' (2008) 41 Israel LR 201, 210.

[129] Aeyal Gross, *The Writing on the Wall: Rethinking the International Law of Occupation* (CUP 2017) 35.

[130] Eliav Lieblich and Eyal Benvenisti, *Occupation in International Law* (OUP 2022) 30.

[131] *Namibia*, paras 52–3.

[132] GA Res 3485 (XXX).

[133] *Palestinian Wall*, para 88.

[134] GA Res 34/37, 21 November 1979.

[135] Gross, *The Writing*, 21–2.

to maintain a situation of alien occupation would be inconsistent with the principle of self-determination, as the ICJ found in both the *Namibia* and the *Palestinian Wall* Advisory Opinions.[136] Even if the interruption of military and economic cooperation constituted an exercise of coercion on the target state, it would not fall under the prohibitive scope of the principle of non-intervention as the international status of the occupied territory is not a matter in which the occupant can decide freely. Disregarding treaty obligations of cooperation towards the occupant even when the grounds codified in the VCLT cannot be invoked can be justified as a countermeasure adopted in response to the violation of an *erga omnes* obligation (the principle of self-determination) by the occupying power.

The occupant could also not rely on the principle of non-intervention as a legal shield against third-state intervention in support of resistance movements in territories under alien occupation, as the international status of the territories in question is not a domestic jurisdiction matter. Military forms of assistance, however, must be reconciled with the prohibition of the use of force contained in the UN Charter. As in colonial domination, there is no general practice accepted as law that allows to consider the principle of external self-determination an exception to Article 2(4) in the case of alien occupation.[137] In the *Namibia* Advisory Opinion, ICJ Vice-President Ammoun contended that armed support for national liberation movements is lawful as 'once the Security Council proclaims the legitimacy of a defence or of a struggle against a foreign occupier, it is an armed attack *[agression armée]* which is in question, and the occupier's act cannot consequently be anything other than an aggression *[agression]*'.[138] Ammoun's argument, however, appears to have been implicitly rejected by the ICJ in the *Palestinian Wall* Advisory Opinion, where the Court found that Article 51 of the Charter has 'no relevance' in the relations between the Occupied Palestinian Territories and Israel.[139]

On the other hand, assistance short of the use of armed force in support of a national liberation movement fighting against alien occupation, including financial support and premature recognition of statehood or government, is a lawful measure in spite of its possible coercive nature as it escapes the prohibitive scope of the principle of non-intervention.[140] Even if it were in conflict with other international law obligations, such assistance could be justified as a countermeasure adopted in response to the violation of an *erga omnes* obligation by the occupying power.

---

[136] *Namibia*, para 119; *Palestinian Wall*, para 159. See also Art 41(2) ARSIWA. As with colonial domination, it has been suggested that it is only support to the occupant finalized to maintain alien occupation, and not in other contexts, that is prohibited: Britain, for instance, affirmed that its 'policy of strict impartiality over the western Sahara does not preclude the sale of conventional military equipment to friendly Governments in the region' (Geoffrey Marston (ed), 'United Kingdom Materials on International Law 1988' (1988) 59 BYBIL 421, 582). Of course, it might be difficult to clearly distinguish between the two situations.

[137] See Section 3.2.1 of this chapter.

[138] *Namibia*, Separate Opinion of Vice-President Ammoun, 90.

[139] *Palestinian Wall*, para 139. This conclusion was criticized by Judge Higgins, who noted that 'Palestine cannot be sufficiently an international entity to be invited to these proceedings, and to benefit from humanitarian law, but not sufficiently an international entity for the prohibition of armed attack on others to be applicable' (*Palestinian Wall*, Separate Opinion of Judge Higgins, para 34).

[140] The Sahrawi Arab Democratic Republic, for instance, was admitted as a member of the OAU in 1982, which led to Morocco's withdrawal from the Organization in 1984.

330 INTERNATIONAL LAW AND THE PRINCIPLE OF NON-INTERVENTION

5. Third-State Intervention in Other Secessionist Situations of Internal Unrest

Chapter V showed that, when insurgents aim at overthrowing a government, the principle of internal self-determination partly displaces that of non-intervention whenever the situation of internal unrest becomes a civil war, with the consequence that third states are prohibited from sending armed forces even in support of the incumbent authorities although other forms of support remain permissible.[141] The present chapter has demonstrated that, in the case of an armed struggle against colonial domination, racist regimes, and alien occupation, this prohibition, as well as that of any other form of assistance, applies regardless of whether the situation of unrest has reached the threshold of a civil war. What is left to examine is whether the latter conclusion extends to secessionist conflicts beyond the decolonization and alien occupation contexts.[142] There are three questions, in particular, that need to be addressed. Firstly, are third states prevented from assisting a government fighting against secessionist insurgents even when the situation is short of civil war as a consequence of the principle of external self-determination? Or vice versa, can a government fighting a secessionist armed group receive foreign assistance even if the situation of internal unrest has become a civil war? And finally, can third states support secessionist armed groups?

5.1 Third-State Support for a Government against Secessionist Insurgents

While the principle of internal self-determination protects all peoples, that of external self-determination only applies to situations of colonial domination and alien occupation: as the Friendly Relations Declaration emphasizes and as the *Québec* precedent confirms, a state which acts in compliance with the principles of equal rights and self-determination and whose government represents the whole population is entitled to its territorial integrity.[143] In other words, under current international law not all peoples have the right to external self-determination for the mere fact of being a 'people' and, therefore, not all secessionist struggles are wars of national liberation in the technical sense of the expression. Cassese explains the reasons very clearly: 'self-determination is attractive so long as it has not been attained; alternatively, it is attractive so long as it

---

[141] See Chapter V, Section 3.2.3.

[142] Moore has noted that '[a]nti-colonial wars differ from wars of secession in the lesser degree to which internal authority structures of the break-away regime have participated in decision-making for the entity and in the greater clarity of separation of the dominant and subordinate entities prior to break-away' (John N Moore, 'The Control of Foreign Intervention in Internal Conflict' (1969) 9 Va J Intl L 205, 265).

[143] *Québec*, para 154. The safeguard clause contained in the Friendly Relations Declaration reads as follows: 'Nothing in the foregoing paragraphs shall be construed as authorizing or encouraging any action which would dismember or impair, totally or in part, the territorial integrity or political unity of sovereign and independent States conducting themselves in compliance with the principle of equal rights and self-determination of peoples as described above and thus possessed of a government representing the whole people belonging to the territory without distinction as to race, creed or colour'. See GA Res 2625 (XXV), Annex, fifth principle, para 7.

NON-INTERVENTION AND EXTERNAL SELF-DETERMINATION   331

is applied to others. Once realized, enthusiasm dies fast, since henceforth it can only be used to undermine perceived internal and external stability.'[144]

If a state does not breach international law by the mere fact of using force internally to prevent secession beyond the colonial and alien occupation contexts, third states also do not commit an internationally wrongful act by assisting it in this task. In other words, the principle of non-intervention continues to apply with the result that the government can request and receive external help to defend its territorial integrity, at least until the internal unrest becomes a civil war. It goes without saying that, if the secessionist insurgents are successful in creating a new state without unlawful external support, the conflict would no longer be internal, and third-state armed intervention would be regulated by the *jus contra bellum* rules codified in the UN Charter whereas the law of neutrality would apply to other forms of support.[145]

Chapter V showed that the principle of internal self-determination requires states not to dispatch armed forces on any side in a civil war occurring in another country.[146] Several writers have argued that this rule only applies when the insurgents' political objective is to overthrow the incumbent authorities but not when it is the secession of part of the state's territory, as there is no right to secede in international law outside the colonial and alien occupation contexts.[147] Third states, therefore, could send their armed forces in support of a foreign government beset by a secessionist civil war. This argument, however, fails to persuade. It is indeed correct that there is no right of secession in international law, but neither is there a right to overthrow a government: any differentiation between the two situations, therefore, cannot be justified on that basis. State practice and *opinio juris* also do not uphold the aforementioned view, as the following cases demonstrate.

Oman. In the Djebel Akhdar War (1954–9), Britain intervened directly at the request of the sultan of Muscat and Oman against the forces of the imam of Oman in order to assist him in restoring his authority over the whole country but claimed that the revolt had been encouraged and supported from outside.[148] France also emphasized that the rebels were receiving external assistance and that the British intervention was aimed at counterbalancing it.[149]

---

[144] Cassese, *Self-Determination*, 5–6.

[145] See Chapter IV, Section 2. The secession, however, must not be in conflict with *jus cogens* rules, as in the case of the 1965 declaration of independence of apartheid Rhodesia and of the so-called *bantustans*. In the *Kosovo* Advisory Opinion, the ICJ explained that the illegality of declarations of independence derives 'from the fact that they were, or would have been, connected with the unlawful use of force or other egregious violations of norms of general international law, in particular those of a peremptory character (*jus cogens*)' (*Kosovo*, para 81).

[146] Chapter V, Section 3.2.3.

[147] See eg Castrén, *Civil War*, 22–3; 'Observations de membres de la Huitième Commission en réponse à l'exposé préliminaire et au questionnaire de M. Schindler, du 24 mai 1969' in Schindler, 'Le principe', 531; Grado, *Guerre civili*, 173–4; Georg Nolte, 'Secession and External Intervention' in Marcelo Kohen (ed), *Secession: International Law Perspectives* (CUP 2006) 65, 83; Antonello Tancredi, 'Sulla liceità dell'intervento su richiesta alla luce del conflitto in Mali' (2013) 96 RDI 946, 947; Seyfullah Hasar, *State Consent to Foreign Military Intervention during Civil Wars* (Brill/Nijhoff 2022) 149–52.

[148] UN Doc S/PV.783, 20 August 1957, para 35; Elihu Lauterpacht, 'The Contemporary Practice of the United Kingdom in the Field of International Law: Survey and Comment, V. July 1–December 31, 1957' (1958) 7 Intl & Comp LQ 92, 101–2. Britain bombed the capital of the secessionist imamate, Nizwa. See Ali Hammoudi, 'The International Law of Informal Empire and the "Question of Oman"' (2020) 1 TWAIL Review 121–51.

[149] UN Doc S/PV.784, 20 August 1957, para 27.

332 INTERNATIONAL LAW AND THE PRINCIPLE OF NON-INTERVENTION

Congo. Even though Resolution 146 (1960) initially stated that 'the United Nations Force in the Congo [would] not be a party to, or in any way intervene in or be used to influence the outcome of any internal conflict, constitutional or otherwise',[150] the following year the Security Council declared its 'full and firm support' for the Congolese government and its determination to assist it against Katanga.[151] ONUC (Opération des Nations Unies au Congo), therefore, became actively involved in armed operations against the secessionists.[152] Secretary-General U Thant, however, claimed that 'the employment of the Force [was] in the most limited manner, with limited objectives, without the Force itself taking any military initiatives, and only then as a last resort'.[153] The Soviet Union, among others, was openly critical of ONUC and stigmatized its actions as a 'flagrant' interference in Congo's internal affairs.[154] Argentina also noted that '[n]either the United Nations nor any State has the right to meddle in the problem of Katanga, in so far as domestic jurisdiction is concerned, either to recommend or order integration or to encourage secession'.[155]

Ethiopia. In 1977, during the armed conflict between Ethiopia and the Ogaden-based Western Somali Liberation Front, Cuban and Soviet troops were dispatched to assist the military government of Addis Ababa (the *Derg*).[156] At first, Ethiopia denied their presence on its territory.[157] The Soviet Union and Cuba subsequently claimed that they had intervened to react against Somalia's aggression against Ethiopia.[158] In the secessionist armed conflict between the Popular Front for the Liberation of Eritrea and the Ethiopian government (1961–91), Cuba also explained that it could not engage its troops deployed in the Ogaden region against the Eritrean rebels as a struggle for self-determination should not be interfered with.[159]

Sri Lanka. From 1983, Tamil militant groups, of which the most prominent was the Liberation Tigers of Tamil Eelam (LTTE), engaged in armed operations against the Colombo government in order to establish an independent Tamil state in the northeast of the country. After the conclusion of the Indo–Sri Lanka Accord of 29 July 1987,[160] Sri Lanka requested and India sent 65,000 troops in order to regain control of Jaffna and secure the LTTE's disarmament as provided in the Accord (Operation Pawan).[161] India continued to support the government with military *matériel* through

---

[150] SC Res 146, 9 August 1960, para 4.

[151] SC Res 169, 24 November 1961, paras 9–10.

[152] Roger Pinto, 'Les règles du droit international concernant la guerre civile' (1965) 114 Recueil des Cours 451, 521. The president and prime minister of Congo initially requested UN military assistance to protect the national territory from Belgian aggression, and not to restore internal order in the country (UN Doc S/4382, 13 July 1960).

[153] UN Doc S/5240, 4 February 1963, para 38.

[154] UN Doc S/4506, 13 September 1960, 2.

[155] UN Doc S/PV.886, 8–9 August 1960, para 70.

[156] Emizet F Kisangani and Jeffrey Pickering, *African Interventions: State Militaries, Foreign Powers, and Rebel Forces* (CUP 2022) 56.

[157] Keesings, 1978, 28990–91.

[158] Keesings, 1978, 28991. While no UN organ discussed the intervention, the United States and the United Kingdom criticized it (A Mark Weisburd, *Use of Force: The Practice of States Since World War II* (Penn State University Press 1997) 38–9; Keesings, 1978, 28992 and 28994–5).

[159] Keesing's 1978, 28994–5.

[160] Text in (1987) 26 ILM 1175.

[161] UN Doc S/19355, 17 December 1987.

the 1990s.[162] Both countries argued that the intervention was lawful because it had been requested by the government in Colombo.[163] The intervention, however, was portrayed as a peacekeeping operation aimed at securing the implementation of the peace agreement.[164]

Papua New Guinea. After reaffirming Australia's commitment to the territorial integrity of Papua New Guinea, Australian Prime Minister Bob Hawke declined 'to intervene in solving Papua New Guinea's problems' in the secessionist conflict with the Bougainville Revolutionary Army (1988–98) and declared that the matter was an internal affair.[165] A peacekeeping force composed of Fiji, Tonga, Vanuatu and the support of Australia and New Zealand was eventually deployed in 1994.

Mali. In January 2012, the National Movement for the Liberation of Azawad (Mouvement Nationale de Libération de l'Azawad – MNLA), mainly formed of ethnic Tuareg, started its armed struggle to obtain the independence of the Azawad region from Mali and, in April of the same year, declared it an independent state, a move that the Security Council considered null and void.[166] When France intervened in Mali in 2013 at the request of its interim president, Dioncounda Traoré, (Operation Serval), it stressed that it was acting against three terrorist organizations (Mouvement pour l'unicité et le jihad en Afrique de l'Ouest, Ansar Dine, and Al-Qaeda au Maghreb islamique), but not against the MNLA.[167]

As the Independent International Fact-Finding Mission on the Conflict in Georgia (IIFFMCG) notes, therefore, '[t]hird parties have not availed themselves of a right to intervene in any instances of attempted secession solely on the grounds that the government had asked them to intervene and to fight against the seceding parties'.[168] Indeed, the states that intervened in secessionist civil wars in support of the incumbent authorities claimed that the insurgents were supported by other states, that the intervention was a peacekeeping operation or was only directed against terrorist groups, or declined to intervene altogether. This suggests that, as in any other situations of internal unrest, the principle of self-determination in its internal dimension prevents third states from sending armed forces when the secessionist struggle has become a civil war: if territorial integrity is under threat from within the country and not from without, it is not the role of third states to defend it.[169] It is only when the secessionist unrest is below the threshold of a civil war that a government may request and receive

---

[162] Ko Swan Sik, 'Chronicle of Events and Incidents Relating to Asia with Relevance to International Law' (1995) 5 Asian YBIL 383, 425; Ko Swan Sik, 'Chronicle of Events and Incidents Relating to Asia with Relevance to International Law' (1996) 6 Asian YBIL 331, 395.

[163] UN Doc S/19354, 17 December 1987 (India); S/19355 (Sri Lanka).

[164] Corten, *The Law*, 296, fn 408. The operation was not criticized by other states (Nolte, 'Secession', 78).

[165] Jonathan Brown (ed), 'Australian Practice in International Law 1990 and 1991' (1992) 13 Australian YBIL 195, 218.

[166] SC Res 2056 (2012), Preamble. See Amy Laird, 'Mali: A Legally Justifiable Intervention by France?' (2012) 10 NZYBIL 123, 123.

[167] Raphaël Van Steenberghe, 'Les interventions françaises et africaines au Mali au nom de la lutte armée contre le terrorisme' (2014) 118 RGDIP 273, 280.

[168] Report of the Independent International Fact-Finding Mission on the Conflict in Georgia, September 2009, vol II, 277 <www.mpil.de/files/pdf4/IIFFMCG_Volume_II1.pdf> (hereafter IIFFMCG Report).

[169] Mohamed Bennouna, *Le consentement à l'ingérence militaire dans les conflits internes* (Librairie générale de droit et de jurisprudence 1974) 62.

334 INTERNATIONAL LAW AND THE PRINCIPLE OF NON-INTERVENTION

armed support in order to preserve the country's territorial integrity.[170] The legal matrix, therefore, is the same in internal unrest aimed at overthrowing a government and in that aimed at secession.[171]

5.2 Third-State Support for Secessionist Insurgents

As Heather Wilson puts it, a group within an established state 'does not have a right to sever its ties with the established government solely because they are ethnically, culturally, or linguistically different'.[172] As external self-determination is not applicable to secessionist conflicts beyond the colonial and alien occupation scenarios, at least until the government equally represents all the peoples of a multinational state.[173] The principle of non-intervention continues to apply as in any other situation of internal unrest, with the result that any assistance to the insurgents is prohibited despite their invitation. This finds confirmation in state practice and *opinio juris*. When states did intervene in support of the separatist forces, they officially denied it,[174] claimed that the secessionist region was a state,[175] or stressed that the intervention was not aimed

---

[170] Immediately after Vanuatu's independence (30 July 1980), for instance, Papua New Guinea intervened with Australian support to quell the secessionist Nagriamel rebels fighting for the independence of the island of Espiritu Santo, resulting in a brief clash between the Papua New Guinean soldiers and the rebels, who were armed only with bows and arrows, rocks, and slings. The intervention was requested by Prime Minister-elect Walter Lini in accordance with a bilateral agreement between Vanuatu and Papua New Guinea. See Norman MacQueen, 'Beyond Tok Win: The Papua New Guinea Intervention in Vanuatu, 1980' (1988) 61 Pacific Affairs 235, 244. See also Keesing's 1981, 30643. Another example comes from the African continent. When Anjouan's controversial leader, Colonel Mohamed Bacar, was re-elected in fraudulent elections in June 2007 and, the following month, declared the independence of the island from Comoros, the Comorian government appealed to the African Union to help re-establish law and order (Assembly/AU/Dec.186 (X), 2 February 2008). The AU Peace and Security Council authorized Operation Democracy in Comoros in March 2008, consisting of amphibious operations led by Comoros with the support of troops from Sudan, Tanzania, and Senegal and logistical support from Libya, France, and the United States. None of these interventions sparked condemnation from other states or international organizations.

[171] As Oscar Schachter puts it, 'when an organized insurgency occurs on a large scale involving a substantial number of people or control over significant areas of the country, neither side, government or insurgency, should receive outside military aid' and it is immaterial whether the insurgents are fighting to overthrow the government or for secession (Oscar Schachter, 'International Law: The Right of States to Use Armed Force' (1984) 82 Mich L Rev 1620, 1642).

[172] Wilson, *International Law*, 84.

[173] GA Res 2625 (XXV), Annex, fifth principle, para 7.

[174] The Soviet Union, for instance, denied that it intervened on the side of Kurdish secessionists in Iran in 1946 (UN Doc S/3, Appendix A, n 8, 26 November 1945, 53). At least initially, Russia also denied any direct intervention in support of the armed groups in Ukraine's Donbass region and claimed that only volunteers were involved (S/PV.7253, 28 August 2014, 13). Many states criticized Russia for arming, equipping, and training the separatists in violation of international law and the UN Charter (see the Security Council debates in S/PV.7154, 13 April 2014; S/PV.7576, 11 December 2015; S/PV.7683, 28 April 2016).

[175] Russia's invasion of Ukraine in late February 2022 started the day after the recognition of the independence of the self-proclaimed People's Republics of Donetsk and Lugansk: this enabled Russia to (unpersuasively) claim that it acted in collective self-defence in response to Ukraine's armed attack against the new states (UN Doc S/2022/154, 24 February 2022, 6). In the Djebel Akhdar War, the Arab countries also claimed that the Imamate of Oman was a separate state, not a secessionist province of the Sultanate of Muscat and Oman (UN Doc S/3865, 15 August 1957; S/PV.783, 2; S/PV.784, para 8).

NON-INTERVENTION AND EXTERNAL SELF-DETERMINATION   335

at supporting the secessionist struggle but had a purely humanitarian or peacekeeping nature.[176] It is therefore difficult to disagree with the IIFFMCG where it concludes that

[t]here is no support in state practice for the right to use force to attain self-determination outside the context of decolonization or illegal occupation. Still less is there support by states for the right of ethnic groups to use force to secede from existing states ... This also means that a secessionist party cannot validly invite a foreign state to use force against the army of the metropolitan state.[177]

The same conclusion applies to lesser forms of intervention.

6. Conclusions

While a government's efforts to suppress an insurgency and restore internal order normally fall under its domestic jurisdiction, in cases of colonial domination and alien occupation the principle of external self-determination demands that the colonial and occupying powers not prevent the concerned people from choosing their international status, including by creating a new state if they so wish. A state breaching this *erga omnes* obligation can no longer hide behind the principle of non-intervention by claiming that the situation is a purely domestic affair.

The consequences for the rights and obligations of third states are momentous. If the principle of non-intervention third-state support for opposition groups but not that for an incumbent government upon its request, the principle of external self-determination proscribes any assistance to a colonial or occupying power in order to maintain its rule, regardless of whether or not the unrest has reached the threshold of a civil war. Even if the interruption of military and economic cooperation constituted an exercise of coercion on the colonial or occupying power, it would not fall under the prohibitive scope of the principle of non-intervention, as the international status of the colonial or occupied territory is not a matter in which the colonial or occupying

---

[176] Belgium explained that its 1960 military operation in Katanga had an exclusively humanitarian purpose and did not aim to support the secessionist province, thus emphasizing 'the complete absence of interference by the Belgian Government in the internal affairs of the Republic of the Congo' (UN Doc S/PV.873, 13–14 July 1960, para 193). Tunisia was one of the many African and communist countries which noted that a request for intervention cannot originate from a provincial authority and that the real reason of the Belgian intervention was not to save lives, but to enable the secession of Katanga (S/PV.878, 21 July 1960, paras 33, 37). See also S/PV.873, paras 79–80, 105, 156, 158–9. During the Sri Lankan Civil War, India initially covertly supplied the LTTE with arms and training and then airdropped food and medicines to Tamil-controlled Jaffna (Shah Alam, 'Indian Intervention in Sri Lanka and International Law' (1991) 38 NILR 346, 353–4). India, however, never advocated for the creation of a separate state and was careful to stress the humanitarian character of the operation, which met with general acquiescence (ibid, 359). In the 1999 Kosovo conflict, the NATO states conducted airstrikes against Yugoslavia not to support the secessionist cause, but to stop the gross violations of fundamental human rights committed by Serbia against ethnic Albanians (Tancredi, *La secessione*, 641). In Transnistria, Russia claimed to be involved in a peacekeeping mission with the consent of the territorial state and the parties to the conflict (A/49/114-S/1994/357, 30 March 1994, Annex; A/52/PV.16, 29 September 1997, 30–1). For Moldova, however, by arming the secessionists and participating in their actions Moscow committed an indirect aggression and an intervention in its domestic affairs (S/24041, 30 May 1992, Annex I; S/24138, 22 June 1992, 3).

[177] IIFFMCG Report, 279.

power can decide freely. If an obligation to support a colonial or occupying power arises from a treaty of cooperation not specifically finalized at the maintenance of the illegal situation and there is no sanction regime imposed by the UN Security Council, compliance with it can be suspended and/or terminated even when the grounds codified in the VCLT cannot be invoked: the suspension or termination would constitute a countermeasure adopted in reaction to the breach of an *erga omnes* obligation, providing that the necessary substantive and procedural requirements are met.

The principle of external self-determination also has another important consequence. While the principle of non-intervention normally prohibits all assistance to insurgents, consensus formed during the Cold War that at least some support could be granted to a people struggling to free itself from colonial rule or alien occupation. What blocs disagreed on was what type of support was lawful. The opposition of the Western states has prevented the formation of a customary rule based on the principle of external self-determination allowing direct or indirect military assistance to national liberation movements. Financial and political support, on the other hand, was considered permissible by the vast majority of states: such measures are not proscribed by the principle of non-intervention when they aim at terminating the unlawful situation as they do not bear on a matter in which the target state can decide freely. Even if they were in conflict with other international law obligations, they could constitute countermeasures adopted in response to the violation of an *erga omnes* obligation.

Finally, the principle of non-intervention continues to apply to secessionist armed struggles beyond the colonial and alien occupation contexts, as no right of external self-determination exists under current international law in such cases. Third states are thus prohibited from supporting foreign secessionist groups but remain allowed to intervene in support of a government's efforts to maintain its territorial integrity, at least until the unrest becomes a civil war: at that point, the application of the principle of self-determination in its internal dimension is triggered, resulting in the obligation not to send armed forces on any side, while other support for the incumbent authorities remains permissible. In the final analysis, therefore, the rights and obligations of states with regard to situations of internal unrest occurring in another country do not change depending on whether the insurgents' political objective is to overthrow a government or establish a new state.

VII

The Interaction between the Principle of Non-Intervention and Respect for International Human Rights Law and International Humanitarian Law

1. Introduction

The principle of non-intervention can be an obstacle to the protection of human rights: by allowing support for a government upon its valid request and by prohibiting any assistance to opposition groups, it does not distinguish between actors who respect and do not respect them. It has been observed, however, that, in the UN Charter era, '[t]he normative gap between the principle of non-intervention and the protection of human rights appear[s] to be narrowing through a gradual redefinition of the parameters of sovereignty'.[1] This chapter intends to test this statement by examining whether the application of the principle of non-intervention also depends on compliance with international human rights law (IHRL) and, when the unrest becomes an armed conflict, international humanitarian law (IHL).

As a first step, the chapter considers how the notion of sovereignty has changed in contemporary discourse and what consequences this has had on the principle of non-intervention. Following that, it explores whether violations of IHRL and/or IHL committed by a government during a situation of internal unrest prevent third states from intervening in its support; and, conversely, whether the principle of internal self-determination, which displaces that of non-intervention in the case of civil war and which also prohibits the sending of armed forces on the side of the incumbent authorities, can be set aside when it is the insurgents who are responsible for the violations in question. The chapter then addresses the problem of the legality of different forms of intervention in support of opposition groups in response to the violations of IHRL and/or IHL committed by the governmental authorities. It concludes by examining whether the UN Security Council can authorize an intervention in a civil war on humanitarian grounds or whether it is restricted in its action by the principle of internal self-determination. Before starting, however, a caveat. The analysis in this chapter focuses on third-state intervention in a situation of internal unrest in

---

[1] S Neil MacFarlane, 'Intervention in Contemporary World Politics', The Adelphi Papers, vol 42, issue 350 (2002) 55. See also Christian Tomuschat, 'International Law: Ensuring the Survival of Mankind on the Eve of a New Century. General Course on Public International Law' (1999) 281 Recueil des Cours 9, 237 ('No single rule of international law has suffered, under the impact of human rights, as incisive an amputation *ratione materiae* as the principle of non-intervention').

International Law and the Principle of Non-Intervention. Marco Roscini, Oxford University Press. © Marco Roscini 2024.
DOI: 10.1093/oso/9780198786894.003.0008

338 INTERNATIONAL LAW AND THE PRINCIPLE OF NON-INTERVENTION

support of a faction as a reaction to the violations of IHRL and/or IHL committed by another: non-partisan peacekeeping operations and the provision of humanitarian assistance, therefore, are not considered unless otherwise indicated.[2]

2. The Changing Character of Sovereignty

Chapter I discussed how the principle of non-intervention emerged as a corollary of what has become the predominant version of sovereignty, that characterized by a state's exclusive jurisdiction over a specific territory, a duty not to exercise jurisdiction in the sphere of exclusive jurisdiction of others without their consent, and the consensual nature of all obligations assumed by states.[3] While it undoubtedly remains the cornerstone of contemporary international relations, the 'Westphalian' model of sovereignty is a social construct and not a dogma: as such, it can be reinterpreted when circumstances and values change and it can thus morph into alternative normative conceptions. As the International Criminal Tribunal for the former Yugoslavia (ICTY) notes, in particular, '[a] State-sovereignty-oriented approach has been gradually supplanted by a human-being-oriented approach.'[4] This humanistic shift permeates both sovereignty's source of legitimacy and its function. With regard to the former, the end of the Second World War has seen the culmination of a centuries-long process that has recalibrated sovereignty from being embodied in the person of a God-anointed monarch to being based on popular will, that is, on a social contract between the ruled and their ruler.[5] Sovereignty's main function, therefore, is no longer to protect a state and its ruling authorities from external or internal threats, but has become—as Martti Koskenniemi puts it—'the fulfilment of the wishes, desires, or preferences of the people.'[6] What results from this shift is a 'conditional' model of state sovereignty, that is, a sovereignty that 'has a legal value only to the extent that it respects human rights, interests, and needs.'[7]

---

[2] As the International Court of Justice (ICJ) has found, 'the provision of strictly humanitarian aid to persons or forces in another country, whatever their political affiliations or objectives, cannot be regarded as unlawful intervention, or as in any other way contrary to international law' as long as it is provided in a non-discriminatory manner (*Case Concerning Military and Paramilitary Activities in and against Nicaragua (Nicaragua v United States of America)* (Merits) [1986] ICJ Rep 3, para 242 (hereafter *Nicaragua v USA*)).

[3] James Crawford, *Brownlie's Principles of Public International Law* (9th edn, OUP 2019) 431.

[4] *Prosecutor v Duško Tadić*, Appeals Chamber, Decision on the Defence Motion for Interlocutory Appeal on Jurisdiction, IT-94-1-AR72, 2 October 1995, para 97 <www.icty.org/x/cases/tadic/acdec/en/51002.htm>. Anne Peters has posited that 'the normative status of sovereignty is derived from humanity, understood as the legal principle that human rights, interests, needs, and security must be respected and promoted, and that this humanistic principle is also the *telos* of the international legal system' (Anne Peters, 'Humanity as the A and Ω of Sovereignty' (2009) 20 EJIL 513, 514).

[5] One of the late manifestations of this change was the imperial rescript issued by Japan's Emperor Hirohito on 1 January 1946 where the emperor renounced his divine nature.

[6] Martti Koskenniemi, 'What Use for Sovereignty Today?' (2011) 1 Asian JIL 61, 66. A commentator has observed that, in fact, the Westphalian notion of sovereignty has always been split between that 'of a territorially delimited entity with monopoly over force, and ... of a diverse population that was seeking security and freedom within that entity ... The notion of responsibility was always wedded to the concept of sovereignty' (Kalana Senaratne, *Internal Self-Determination in International Law: History, Theory, and Practice* (CUP 2021) 17).

[7] Peters, 'Humanity', 514. According to the Dutch representative at the Security Council, '[t]oday, human rights have come to outrank sovereignty. Increasingly, the prevailing interpretation of the Charter

This re-characterization of sovereignty has been famously advocated in the Report on the Responsibility to Protect (R2P) prepared by the International Commission on Intervention and State Sovereignty (ICISS).[8] According to the Commission, the change does not dilute the fundamental features of sovereignty but involves three consequences:

> First, it implies that the state authorities are responsible for the functions of protecting the safety and lives of citizens and promotion of their welfare. Secondly, it suggests that the national political authorities are responsible to the citizens internally and to the international community through the UN. And thirdly, it means that the agents of state are responsible for their actions; that is to say, they are accountable for their acts of commission and omission.[9]

The ICISS links this recalibration of sovereignty with the notion of human security, which 'has created additional demands and expectations in relation to the way states treat their own people'.[10] The notion first appeared in the United Nations Development Programme (UNDP)'s Human Development Report 1994 on 'New Dimensions of Human Security'.[11] If security was traditionally identified with defending the state and its territory from external threats, the new concept makes individuals the focus of protection: the basic idea is that 'there is no secure state with insecure people living in it'.[12] The broader view of human security, adopted in the UNDP Report, in the ICISS R2P Report,[13] and in the Non-Aggression and Common Defence Pact of the African Union (AU),[14] associates it with development and the environment and contends that it includes not only 'protection from sudden and hurtful disruptions in the patterns of daily life' such as violent threats, conflicts, or natural disasters, but also safety from chronic threats like hunger, disease, and repression ('freedom from fear and want').[15]

---

is that it aims to protect individual human beings, not to protect those who abuse them. Today, we regard it as a generally accepted rule of international law that no sovereign State has the right to terrorize its own citizens. Indeed, if the Charter were to be written today, there would be an Article 2.8 saying that nothing contained in the present Charter shall authorize Member States to terrorize their own people' (UN Doc A/54.PV.13, 24 September 1999, 23).

[8] The Commission was established by the Canadian government in response to the UN Secretary-General's Millennium Report ('We the Peoples: The Role of the United Nations in the Twenty-First Century', Report of the Secretary-General, UN Doc A/54/2000, 27 March 2000 (hereafter Millennium Report)).
[9] ICISS, The Responsibility to Protect: Report of the International Commission on Intervention and State Sovereignty, December 2001, para 2.15 (hereafter ICISS R2P Report).
[10] ibid, para 1.33.
[11] United Nations Development Programme, Human Development Report 1994 (OUP 1994) (hereafter UNDP Report).
[12] Gerd Oberleitner, 'Human Security: A Challenge to International Law?' (2005) 11 Global Governance 185, 190.
[13] ICISS R2P Report, para 2.21.
[14] Art 1(k), African Union Non-Aggression and Common Defence Pact (Abuja, 31 January 2005) 2656 UNTS 285.
[15] UNDP Report, 23. The United Nations has embraced the notion of human security in the 2005 World Summit Outcome Document qualifying it as 'freedom from fear and want', where 'fear' refers to security and 'want' to development, and has pledged to discuss and define it (GA Res 60/1, 24 October 2005, para 143). The concept also permeates the UN Secretary-General's 2000 Millennium Report, the UN Secretary-General's High-Level Panel on Threats, Challenges and Change's Report, A More Secure World: Our Shared

340 INTERNATIONAL LAW AND THE PRINCIPLE OF NON-INTERVENTION

The proponents of the narrower view, on the other hand, claim that such a broad approach renders the concept of human security meaningless[16] and suggest that it should be limited to the protection from violent threats ('freedom from fear') and focus only on the human consequences of (especially internal) armed conflicts, state failure, and repressive governments.[17]

Whichever version is preferred, the human-centred notion of security has consequences not only for the understanding of sovereignty, but also for the principle of non-intervention. Lithuania has put it in crystal clear terms at the UN General Assembly:

> There is a universal principle of non-interference and State sovereignty. But there are other universal principles underlying international relations, including respect for human rights. The principle of non-interference is universal, but not absolute. [...] International relations are increasingly based on something else, more human, more reasonable and more progressive than the divinity of the principle of State sovereignty. Equally important is the supremacy of a human being over the State ... States cannot do whatever they please with individuals within their jurisdiction. New tones in international relations tend to justify involvement from the outside to stop flagrant violations of human rights.[18]

Otherwise said, respect for external sovereignty, and thus the relevance of the principle of non-intervention, have come to depend on how a state exercises its sovereignty internally.[19] The result is that '[s]tates that are not in "a rightful condition" arguably forfeit their right to protest alleged violations of their sovereignty'.[20]

3. Human Rights and Domestic Jurisdiction

The decreasing protective role played by the principle of non-intervention with regard to sovereignty mirrors the progressive curtailment of the scope of domestic jurisdiction (as the reader will remember, the principle of non-intervention only prohibits coercion exercised on matters in which the target state is permitted under international law to decide freely).[21] Whereas, until at least the beginning of the 20th century, the relations between a state and its citizens were as a rule considered a purely

---

Responsibility (UN Doc A/59/565, 2 December 2004), and the 2005 UN Secretary-General's Report In Larger Freedom: Towards Development, Security and Human Rights for All (A/59/2005, 21 March 2005).

[16] Andrew Mack, 'A Signifier of Shared Values' (2004) 35 Security Dialogue 366, 367.

[17] See ibid, 366–7, and, more broadly, Human Security Centre, *The Human Security Report 2005: War and Peace in the 21st Century* (OUP 2005).

[18] UN Doc A/54/PV.35, 20 October 1999, 19.

[19] Peters, 'Humanity', 517; Chiara Redaelli, *Intervention in Civil Wars: Effectiveness, Legitimacy, and Human Rights* (Hart 2020) 79.

[20] Cedric Ryngaert, *Selfless Intervention: The Exercise of Jurisdiction in the Common Interest* (OUP 2020) 55, 57.

[21] *Nicaragua v USA*, para 205. See Chapter III, Section 5.

internal matter to which the principle of non-intervention fully applied,[22] the situation changes significantly in the United Nations era and even more visibly after the fall of the Berlin Wall.[23] In particular, while there are still no rules regulating *whether* states can use force internally,[24] there are now limitations on *how* this force can be used: as the UN Secretary-General observed in regard to the Kosovo crisis of the late 1990s, for instance, '[t]he authorities of the Federal Republic of Yugoslavia have the inherent right, as well as the duty, to maintain public order and security and to respond to violent acts of provocation. However, this can in no way justify the systematic terror inflicted on civilians'.[25]

In the San Francisco Charter, respect for human rights and fundamental freedoms is one of the purposes of the United Nations.[26] Member states also commit, under Articles 55 and 56, 'to take joint and separate action in co-operation with the Organization for the achievement of', inter alia, 'universal respect for, and observance of, human rights and fundamental freedoms for all without distinction as to race, sex, language, or religion'.[27] As a result, a plethora of human rights treaties and resolutions have been adopted both at the global and regional level since 1948.[28] Furthermore, under customary international law states are bound to abstain 'from seriously and repeatedly infringing a basic right ... and from trampling upon a whole series of rights (e.g. the fundamental civil and political rights, or social, economic, and cultural rights)'.[29] The norms forbidding grave and systematic violations, including slavery, genocide, crimes against humanity, racial discrimination, and torture, are even considered to have evolved into *jus cogens* rules.[30] All in all, there is little doubt that human rights protection is now a 'conglomeration' and 'foundational' principle that characterizes the contemporary international community and which determines

---

[22] This was so unless treaties provided otherwise, as in the case of those protecting the Christian minorities in the Ottoman Empire: see Chapter I, Section 7.3.

[23] Louis Henkin, *The Rights of Man Today* (Westview Press 1978) 94.

[24] See Chapter IV, Section 2.

[25] UN Doc S/1998/912, 3 October 1998, para 29.

[26] Art 1(3), UN Charter.

[27] The point is reiterated in the General Assembly's Declaration on Principles of International Law Concerning Friendly Relations and Co-operation among States in Accordance with the Charter of the United Nations (GA Res 2625 (XXV), 24 October 1970, Annex, fifth principle, para 3).

[28] Eibe Riedel, 'Human Rights Protection as a Principle' in Jorge E Viñuales (ed), *The UN Friendly Relations Declaration at 50* (OUP 2020) 213, 234–40.

[29] Paola Gaeta, Jorge E Viñuales, and Salvatore Zappalà, *Cassese's International Law* (3rd edn, OUP 2020) 72. Customary international law, in particular, prohibits 'grave, repeated, and systematic violations of human rights', as well as slavery, genocide, racial discrimination, and torture (ibid, 420).

[30] Dire Tladi, Fourth Report on Peremptory Norms of General International Law (*jus cogens*), UN Doc A/CN.4/727, 31 January 2019, paras 52–4. The White Paper attached to the Democratic Republic of the Congo (DRC)'s Application instituting proceedings against Rwanda before the ICJ, for instance, argues that 'States that commit human rights violations cannot cite the principle of "non-interference in the internal affairs" of a State that is a member of the international community for the simple reason that this is a matter which is part of jus cogens (peremptory international law)' (*Armed Activities on the Territory of the Congo (New Application: 2002) (Democratic Republic of the Congo v Rwanda)*, White Paper Annexed to the Application instituting proceedings of the Government of the Democratic Republic of the Congo filed in the Registry of the Court on 23 June 1999, vols I and II, para 38, underlining in the original). See the similar points made by Bulgaria at the UN General Assembly's Sixth Committee (A/C.6/SR.807, 8 November 1963, 140) and by Belgium before the ICJ (*Legality of Use of Force (Yugoslavia v Belgium)*, Oral proceedings, CR 99/15, 10 May 1999, 15–16 <www.icj-cij.org/case/105>).

342 INTERNATIONAL LAW AND THE PRINCIPLE OF NON-INTERVENTION

what state conduct is perceived as acceptable.[31] This conclusion has been recently confirmed by the International Court of Justice (ICJ) in the *Armed Activities* Judgment on Reparations.[32]

During the Cold War, however, disagreement existed on *who* was entitled to secure compliance with human rights: the socialist states as well as some developing countries insisted that, apart from the case of massive violations arising from colonialist or neo-colonialist policies,[33] the matter fell under the exclusive jurisdiction of the territorial state and often invoked the principle of non-intervention as a shield from external interferences in this context.[34] Unsurprisingly, therefore, the Declaration on the Inadmissibility of Intervention and Interference in the Internal Affairs of States, adopted by the UN General Assembly in 1981 and inspired by the Soviet Union, still stressed that states have the right and duty to observe, promote, and defend all human rights and fundamental freedoms only 'within their own national territories'[35] and must 'refrain from the exploitation and the distortion of human rights issues as a means of interference in the internal affairs of States, of exerting pressure on other States or of creating distrust and disorder within and among States or groups of States'.[36] As noted by a former UN Secretary-General, with the end of the Cold War and the disappearance of the socialist bloc the principle of non-intervention can no longer 'be regarded as a protective barrier behind which human rights [can] be massively or systematically violated with impunity'.[37] Indeed, there is now broad consensus that 'the principles

---

[31] Art 2(1), Institut de droit international's Resolution on the Protection of Human Rights and the Principle of Non-Intervention in Internal Affairs of States (Santiago de Compostela Resolution), 13 September 1989 (1990) 63(II) AIDI 338; Eliav Lieblich, *International Law and Civil Wars: Intervention and Consent* (Routledge 2013); 178; Riedel, 'Human Rights', 233; Gaeta, Viñuales, and Zappalà, *Cassese's International Law*, 71–2. While the protection of human rights does not appear as a separate principle in the Friendly Relations Declaration, Principle VII of the Helsinki Final Act proclaims 'the universal significance of human rights and fundamental freedoms, respect for which is an essential factor for the peace, justice and well-being necessary to ensure the development of friendly relations and co-operation among themselves as among all States' (Principle VII, para 5, Final Act of the 1st CSCE Summit of Heads of State or Government (Helsinki, 1 August 1975) (1975) 14 ILM 1292).

[32] *Armed Activities on the Territory of the Congo (Democratic Republic of the Congo v Uganda)* (hereafter *DRC v Uganda*) (Judgment on Reparations of 9 February 2022) para 65 <www.icj-cij.org/case/116/judgments>.

[33] See eg Bulgaria's statement at the General Assembly's Sixth Committee, UN Doc A/C.6/SR.807, 140.

[34] See eg Ion Diaconu, 'La non-immixtion dans les affaires intérieures des États—Principe fondamental du droit international contemporain' (1980) 50 RREI 331, 336. See also Tomuschat, 'International Law', 236.

[35] GA Res 36/103, 9 December 1981, Annex, para 2(III)(c). The resolution was adopted by 120 to twenty-two, with six abstentions and it is not considered to reflect customary international law.

[36] GA Res 36/103, para 2(II)(l).

[37] Report of the Secretary-General on the Work of the Organization, UN Doc A/46/1, 1991, 5. In the 1991 Luxembourg Declaration, the EU member states committed 'to pursue their policy of promoting and safeguarding human rights and fundamental freedoms throughout the world [as] [t]his is the legitimate and permanent duty of the world community and of all States acting individually or collectively' and recalled 'that the different ways of expressing concern about violations of rights, as well as requests designed to secure those rights, cannot be considered as interference in the internal affairs of a State' (European Council (Luxembourg, 28 and 29 June 1991), Presidency Conclusions, Annex V (Declaration on Human Rights) 25 <www.consilium.europa.eu/media/20528/1991_june_-_luxembourg__eng_.pdf>). The 1993 Vienna Declaration and Programme of Action also recognizes that 'the promotion and protection of all human rights is a legitimate concern of the international community' (World Conference on Human Rights, Vienna Declaration and Programme of Action (Vienna, 25 June 1993) para I(4) <www.ohchr.org/en/instruments-mechanisms/instruments/vienna-declaration-and-programme-action>). The 1991 Document of the Moscow Meeting of the Conference on the Human Dimension of the CSCE and the 1992 Document of the CSCE Helsinki Summit both confirm that 'the commitments undertaken in the field of the human

and rules concerning the basic rights of the human person' are obligations *erga omnes*, that is, owed to the international community as a whole, with the consequence that all states have a legal interest in their compliance, and other treaty-based human rights are obligations *erga omnes partes*, that is, owed to all states that have ratified the treaty concerned.[38]

This curtailment of the domestic jurisdiction of states has occurred with regard to the protection of individuals not only in peacetime but also in situations of internal unrest qualifying as non-international armed conflicts. Common Article 3 of the 1949 Geneva Conventions on the Protection of Victims of War, in particular, constitutes a 'minimum yardstick' of protective regulation applicable to all armed conflicts regardless of their classification.[39] In 1977, an Additional Protocol (II) was also adopted to specifically regulate the conduct of hostilities in armed conflicts of a non-international character.[40] Securing compliance with these obligations is entrusted not only to the parties to the conflict: Common Article 1 of the Geneva Conventions commits all states parties 'to respect *and* to ensure respect for the present Convention[s] in all circumstances'.[41] As the International Committee of the Red Cross (ICRC)'s 2016 Commentary explains,

dimension of the CSCE are matters of direct and legitimate concern to all participating States and do not belong exclusively to the internal affairs of the State concerned' (CSCE, Document of the Moscow Meeting of the Conference on the Human Dimension of the CSCE, 4 October 1991, 29 <www.osce.org/it/odihr/elections/14310>; CSCE, Helsinki Summit Declaration, 9 July 1992, para 8 <www.osce.org/files/f/docume nts/7/c/39530.pdf>). See also the statements listed in Jean d'Aspremont, *L'Etat non démocratique en droit international. Etude critique du droit international positif et de la pratique contemporaine* (Pedone 2008) 87, fn 411.

[38] *Barcelona Traction, Light and Power Company, Limited (Belgium v Spain)* (Preliminary Objections, second phase) [1970] ICJ Rep 3, paras 33–4; *Legal Consequences of the Construction of a Wall in the Occupied Palestinian Territory* (Advisory Opinion) [2004] ICJ Rep 136, paras 155, 157 (hereafter *Palestinian Wall*); *Questions Related to the Obligation to Prosecute or Extradite (Belgium v Senegal)* (Judgment) [2012] ICJ Rep 422, para 68. See also Human Rights Committee, General Comment No 31, UN Doc CCPR/C/21/Rev.1/Add.13, 26 May 2004, para 2; Art 1(2), Santiago de Compostela Resolution. However, states like China (Shitong Qiao, 'Whither China's Non-Interference Principle?' ESIL Conference Paper No 2/2011, 14), the Association of Southeast Asian Nations (ASEAN) member states (Vanessa Chong and Tanyalak Thongyoojaroen, 'Beyond the Coup in Myanmar: The ASEAN Way Must Change' (*Just Security*, 14 May 2021) <www.justsecurity.org/76126/beyond-the-coup-in-myanmar-the-asean-way-must-change/>), and Zimbabwe (UN Doc S/PV.3046, 31 January 1992, 131) still protest against foreign interferences in their domestic human rights policies. Egypt has also warned against using the 'shared goal of promoting human rights as a back door for interfering in the internal affairs of States' (S/PV.7926, 18 April 2017, 9). That said, in recent times even the Beijing government seems to have cautiously endorsed the R2P doctrine, although at the same time reaffirming that any action based on it has to go through the Security Council (Jiangyu Wang and Huarer Cheng, 'China's Approach to International Law: From Traditional Westphalianism to Aggressive Instrumentalism in the Xi Jinping Era' (2022) 10 CJCL 140, 147–8).

[39] *Nicaragua v USA*, paras 218, 220.

[40] Protocol Additional to the Geneva Conventions of 12 August 1949, and relating to the Protection of Victims of Non-International Armed Conflicts (Protocol II) (Geneva, 8 June 1977) 1125 UNTS 609.

[41] Emphasis added. The duty to ensure respect for IHRL and IHL is one of due diligence: as the ICRC has noted, 'its content depends on the specific circumstances, including the gravity of the breach, the means reasonably available to the State, and the degree of influence it exercises over those responsible for the breach' (2016 ICRC Commentary on Common Art 1, para 165 <https://ihl-databases.icrc.org/en/ihl-treaties/gci-1949/article-1/commentary/2016?activeTab=undefined>). The broader interpretation of Common Art 1, which also addresses states not involved in the armed conflict, finds support in Resolution 2444 (XXIII) on Human Rights and Armed Conflict, adopted by the 1968 International Conference on Human Rights with no vote against (GA Res 2444 (XXIII), 19 December 1968, para 1) and in the ICJ's *Palestinian Wall* Advisory Opinion, para 158. In the ICRC's Study on Customary International Humanitarian Law, the obligation to

344 INTERNATIONAL LAW AND THE PRINCIPLE OF NON-INTERVENTION

[t]he principle of non-intervention is not as such an impediment to the taking of measures by third States pursuant to common Article 1. It follows from the *erga omnes partes* nature of the obligations under the Conventions that violations of their provisions by a High Contracting Party should not be seen as the exclusive internal affair of that Party, even if the violations took place in the context of a non-international armed conflict.[42]

It is true that the San Francisco Charter does not contain any express reference to IHL, but 'human rights' has been interpreted broadly in UN fora since the 1960s: the notion of 'human rights in armed conflict' was first put forward at the 1968 UN International Conference on Human Rights in Tehran and was later reaffirmed in several General Assembly resolutions.[43] Resolution 9/9 (2008) of the Human Rights Council confirms that 'conduct that violates international humanitarian law ... may also constitute a gross violation of human rights'.[44] After the end of the Cold War, the Security Council has also frequently become involved in internal armed conflicts where violations of IHL were committed and considered them a threat to international peace and security for the first time in Resolution 808 (1993) on Bosnia and Herzegovina.[45] The following year, Resolution 955 (1994) considered violations of IHL committed in an internal armed conflict (Rwanda) as a threat to international peace and security.[46] In Resolution 1296 (2000) on the protection of civilians in armed conflict, systematic, flagrant, and widespread violations of IHL were qualified as potentially constituting threats to the peace without reference to any specific conflict.[47]

---

respect and ensure respect is not limited to the Geneva Conventions but extends to the entire body of IHL binding on a state (Rule 139, in Jean-Marie Henckaerts and Louise Doswald-Beck, *Customary International Humanitarian Law*, vol I (ICRC/CUP 2005) 495).

[42] 2016 ICRC Commentary on Common Art 1, para 177. See also Luigi Condorelli and Laurence Boisson de Chazournes, 'Quelques remarques à propos de l'obligation des Etats de «respecter et faire respecter» le droit international humanitaire «en toute circonstances»' in Christophe Swinarski (ed), *Studies and Essays on International Humanitarian Law and Red Cross Principles in Honour of Jean Pictet* (ICRC/Nijhoff 1984) 17, 26–31.

[43] The first was GA Res 2444 (XXIII).

[44] UN Doc A/HRC/RES/9/9, 18 September 2008, para 1.

[45] SC Res 808, 22 February 1993, Preamble. On the broad interpretation of the notion of 'threat to the peace' by the Security Council, see Marco Roscini, 'The United Nations Security Council and the Enforcement of International Humanitarian Law' (2010) 43 Israel LR 330, 332–7.

[46] SC Res 955, 8 November 1994, Preamble. The Preamble of SC Res 918, 17 May 1994, had already qualified 'the magnitude of the human suffering caused by the [Rwandan] conflict' as a threat to peace and security in the region. Similarly, in SC Res 794 with regard to Somalia, it was the consequences ('human tragedy') of the violations of IHL and of the armed violence, rather than the violations themselves, that were qualified as a threat to the peace (SC Res 794, 3 December 1992, Preamble). See also SC Res 733, 23 January 1992, Preamble.

[47] SC Res 1296, 19 April 2000, para 5.

4. Intervention and the Protection of Community Interests

Even though it is at odds with the Westphalian notion of sovereignty characterized by the state's exclusive authority over its territory, the idea of intervention to protect community interests is not new: Grotius already claimed that

> Kings, and those who are invested with a Power equal to that of Kings, have a Right to exact Punishments, not only for Injuries committed against themselves, or their Subjects, but likewise, for those which do not peculiarly concern them, but which are, in any Persons whatsoever, grievous Violations of the Law of Nature or Nations.[48]

As a proper legal concept, however, intervention for the protection of community interests finds its most immediate roots in the 19th century's notion of measures short of war and in the military expeditions of the European states in the Ottoman Empire to protect Christian minorities.[49] In recent decades, the idea has come back to the forefront thanks to the success of the R2P doctrine. According to the ICISS, '[w]here a population is suffering serious harm, as a result of internal war, insurgency, repression or state failure, and the state in question is unwilling or unable to halt or avert it, the principle of non-intervention yields to the international responsibility to protect'.[50] More specifically, this 'fallback' responsibility of the international community involves a responsibility to react to an 'actual or apprehended human catastrophe', to prevent it, and to rebuild after the event, and can be exercised by adopting political, economic, judicial and, in extreme cases, military measures.[51] This subsidiary role of the international community to protect human beings has been explicitly or implicitly endorsed in instruments adopted by African regional organizations[52] and in several UN Security Council resolutions.[53]

The question is, of course, who the 'international community' is. In Paolo Picone's view, the enforcement of community interests reflected in *erga omnes* obligations can be undertaken either through forms of partial institutionalization of the international community, namely the United Nations, or by any state acting *uti universi*. In the former case, the Organization acts as the material organ of the international

---

[48] Hugo Grotius, *De jure belli ac pacis* (1625) (Richard Tuck ed, Jean Barbeyrac tr, Liberty Fund 2005) 1021. See also the Belgian and French scholarship mentioned in Chapter I, Section 6. A commentator has noted that '[i]nternational law has never accepted a positivist norm of absolute sovereignty and nonintervention, nor has it accepted the Kantian norm of a free right of intervention to protect human rights despite concerns about sovereignty. Rather, it has strived for balance' (Ravi Mahalingam, 'The Compatibility of the Principle of Nonintervention with the Right of Humanitarian Intervention' (1996) 1 UCLA J Int'l L Foreign Aff 221, 258).

[49] Chapter I, Section 7.3. See also Stephen C Neff, *War and the Law of Nations: A General History* (CUP 2005) 217.

[50] ICISS R2P Report, xi.

[51] ibid, paras 2.31–2.32.

[52] See Art 4(8), Protocol on Non-Aggression and Mutual Defence in the Great Lakes Region (Nairobi, 30 November 2006) <https://icglr.org/ova_doc/protocol-on-non-aggression-and-mutual-defence-in-the-great-lakes-region/>; The ECOWAS Conflict Prevention Framework, Regulation MSC/REG.1/01/08 (Ouagadougou, 16 January 2008) paras 26, 41 <https://au.int/sites/default/files/documents/39184-doc-140._the_ecowas_conflict_prevention_framework.pdf>).

[53] See eg SC Resolutions 1674, 28 April 2006; 1706, 31 August 2006; 1970, 26 February 2011; 1973, 17 March 2011; 1975, 30 March 2011; 1996, 8 July 2011; 2014, 21 October 2011; 2304, 12 August 2016.

community, and thus not in the framework of the San Francisco Charter but of customary international law and within the limits set therein.[54] This accessory role of the United Nations is reflected in the broadening of the concept of threat to the peace following the end of the Cold War, which has allowed the Security Council to act beyond its original peace enforcer function and to activate itself for the protection of other fundamental values of the international community.[55] With regard to armed responses adopted unilaterally by states, Picone cautions that not every violation of *erga omnes* obligations justifies them: they can be undertaken only to the extent that they are consistent with customary international law (as he claims is the case with humanitarian intervention) and exclusively in the event of the Security Council's inaction.[56]

In a recent book, Cedric Ryngaert has gone further and has highlighted the positive 'cosmopolitan' role that forms of 'regulatory unilateralism that enhances global welfare' can play.[57] In his view, 'hegemonic states, that is, internationally leading states, may, under certain circumstances, harness their power and capacities to extend their sovereignty with a view to protecting global values and common interests.'[58] In fact, 'precisely because they have more power and capacity, in accordance with the principle of common but differentiated responsibilities, it may be *incumbent* on [powerful states acting as benevolent hegemons] to do more than others to further the global interest.'[59] Instead of banning it, therefore, 'cosmopolitan intervention' should be submitted to procedural and material conditions and limitations.[60] To this benevolent role of the hegemonic powers corresponds the relaxation of formal consent as the ultimate foundation of international obligations: what matters is not its actual provision but the fact that 'in the original position, states, for reasons of rational morality, would have given their consent if their vision had not been clouded by particularist considerations.'[61] Ryngaert concludes that the exercise of enforcement jurisdiction in another state should be permissible even without the territorial state's actual consent if it contributes to the prevention and repression of human rights violations or of terrorism.[62]

Like Ryngaert, Monica Hakimi has attempted to highlight the positive role that 'unfriendly unilateralism' can play not only in the enforcement of international law but also in international lawmaking by compensating for the shortcomings of the legal order's formal processes and thus by allowing it to stay relevant.[63] Hakimi argues that, of the different forms that unfriendly unilateralism can assume, not only the use of lawful ones (namely retorsions and countermeasures), but also those that do not

---

[54] Paolo Picone, 'Interventi delle Nazioni Unite e obblighi *erga omnes*' in Paolo Picone (ed), *Interventi delle Nazioni Unite e diritto internazionale* (CEDAM 1995) 517, 554–6.

[55] Paolo Picone, 'Nazioni Unite e obblighi *erga omnes*' (1993) 48 La Comunità internazionale (1993) 709, 716.

[56] Paolo Picone, 'La guerra contro l'Iraq e le degenerazioni dell'unilateralismo' (2003) 86 RDI 329, 338.

[57] Ryngaert, *Selfless Intervention*, 54.

[58] ibid, 38.

[59] ibid, 40, emphasis in the original.

[60] ibid, 37–8.

[61] ibid, 53.

[62] ibid, 54–5.

[63] Monica Hakimi, 'Unfriendly Unilateralism' (2014) 55 Harv Intl LJ 105, 126. She describes 'unfriendly unilateralism' as follows: 'A state acts *unilaterally* when it does not channel through a formal international process the decision to act ... *Unfriendliness* deprives a specific state of some benefit' (ibid, 111–12, emphasis in the original).

comply with international law and cannot be excused on the basis of a circumstance precluding wrongfulness ('disobedient measures') can be beneficial as 'inaction can be worse for the legal order than is unfriendly, unilateral, and even disobedient action'.[64] Disobedient measures can thus induce compliance with international law rules and prevent their erosion.[65]

The 'benevolent hegemon' narrative aims to alleviate the fundamental problem of the international legal order, namely the limited accountability of states, but presents obvious risks. As Carl Schmitt famously noted, '[t]he concept of humanity is an especially useful ideological instrument of imperialist expansion, and in its ethical-humanitarian form it is a specific vehicle of economic imperialism. Here one is reminded of a somewhat modified expression of Proudhon's: whoever invokes humanity wants to cheat.'[66]

More recently, Antony Anghie warned that '[t]he fact that a state is democratic and proclaims itself to be acting from the highest motives does not make its violation of international law any the less excusable.'[67] In his view, '[i]nternational law is now being subjected to various pressures that might ultimately result in the emergence of an international system that permits, if not endorses and adopts, quite explicitly imperial practices'.[68] Anne Orford also stresses the authoritarian risks connected to the 'turn to protection' and points out that, so far, there has been little discussion of the legal limits to the international community's actions to protect populations in danger.[69]

Be that as it may, coercive measures adopted to enforce community interests reflected in *erga omnes* or *erga omnes partes* obligations, including those arising from IHRL and IHL, are not prohibited by the principle of non-intervention: if compliance with IHRL and IHL is not a matter in which each state can decide freely, then coercion exercised to enforce it does not fall under the prohibitive scope of the principle.[70] Of course, this fact alone does not per se allow *any* coercive interference: the coercive measures adopted to secure compliance with IHRL and IHL must also not be prohibited by other primary rules of international law.[71] Indeed, the UN Charter era is characterized by an inherent contradiction: it has seen not only the protection of human

---

[64] ibid, 126.

[65] ibid, 126–9.

[66] Carl Schmitt, *The Concept of the Political* (Georg Schwab tr, The University of Chicago Press 2007) 54.

[67] Antony Anghie, *Imperialism, Sovereignty and the Making of International Law* (CUP 2004) 308.

[68] ibid, 274.

[69] Anne Orford, *International Authority and the Responsibility to Protect* (CUP 2011) 137–8. For Nicholas Tsagourias, however, 'sovereignty is organically tied to the welfare of the state's population and small states as well as large ones can be guilty of abuses or crimes against their inhabitants. Even if the concepts of human rights and humanitarianism are "bound to be abused", one could equally argue that sovereignty and non-intervention are "bound to be abused" by those committing human rights abuses or genocide' (Nicholas Tsagourias, 'Humanitarian Intervention and Legal Principles' (2001) 7 ILT 83, 85).

[70] Art 2(2), Santiago de Compostela Resolution. The gravity of the violations, therefore, would affect not whether an interference can take place, but how: the more serious the violation, the more intrusive the permissible response.

[71] In response to Bosnia and Herzegovina's claim that all parties to the Genocide Convention had an obligation to react against its violations, by military means if necessary, the ICJ for instance recalled that the duty to prevent genocide can only be exercised 'respecting the United Nations Charter' and 'within the limits permitted by international law' (*Application of the Convention on the Prevention and Punishment of the Crime of Genocide (Bosnia and Herzegovina v Serbia and Montenegro)* (Merits) [2007] ICJ Rep 43, paras 427, 430 (hereafter *Bosnian Genocide*)). The point was made again by the Court in *Allegations of Genocide under the Convention on the Prevention and Punishment of the Crime of Genocide (Ukraine v Russian Federation)* (Order of 16 March 2022) para 59 <www.icj-cij.org/case/182/orders> (hereafter *Allegations of*

348 INTERNATIONAL LAW AND THE PRINCIPLE OF NON-INTERVENTION

rights acquire international relevance and sovereignty relativized, but also the right of states to use coercion against other states circumscribed.[72] As Vera Gowlland-Debbas has noted, therefore, the whole debate on humanitarian intervention should not be 'stated as a choice between protection of human rights on the one hand and state sovereignty on the other—it is really a debate over the means not the ends, for remedial action can encompass a number of reactions to human rights violations'.[73] It is with this in mind that the following sections explore what forms of coercion can be exercised on the party which, in a situation of internal unrest, has committed violations of IHRL and/or IHL.

5. Third-State Assistance to a Government Responsible for Violations of IHRL and/or IHL

As seen in Chapter IV, the principle of non-intervention does not prohibit states to support the incumbent government of another state at its request. If, in the traditional version of sovereignty that triumphed in the 19th century, '[t]he factual powers of a government form part of its output legitimacy, and thereby not only constitute sovereignty, but also justify it',[74] the sovereignty as responsibility model attaches normative requirements to the idea of government and considers it legitimate only to the extent that it possesses them.[75] It has been claimed, therefore, that one of the consequences of the lack of legitimacy is a government's inability to exercise certain prerogatives of sovereignty, including that of receiving assistance from other states in the case of internal unrest in spite of its request.[76]

In order to correctly assess this view, it is helpful to distinguish the situation where states have the mere *option* to assist a foreign government facing internal unrest from that where they have a treaty *obligation* to do so. In the former case, states can always decline requests for assistance as well as suspend/terminate existing voluntary cooperation whether in reaction to IHRL/IHL violations or for any other reasons. States that opt to provide assistance, however, do so at their own risk as they might be found co-responsible for the violations committed by the assisted state under Article 16 of the ILC's Articles on Responsibility of States for Internationally Wrongful Acts (ARSIWA).[77] Note that the suspension or termination of voluntary cooperation would

---

Genocide). See also Gaetano Arangio-Ruiz, 'Human Rights and Non-Intervention in the Helsinki Final Act' (1977) 157 Recueil des Cours 195, 279.

[72] MacFarlane, 'Intervention', 37.

[73] Vera Gowlland-Debbas, 'The Limits of Unilateral Enforcement of Community Objectives in the Framework of UN Peace Maintenance' (2000) 11 EJIL 361, 379.

[74] Peters, 'Humanity', 519.

[75] Cóman Kenny and Seán Butler, 'The Legality of "Intervention by Invitation" in Situations of R2P Violations' (2018) 51 NYU J Intl L & Pol 135, 152.

[76] ibid, 159. As seen in Chapter V, third states are prohibited from sending armed forces in support of a government involved in a civil war by the principle of internal self-determination (see Chapter V, Section 3.2.3). Compliance with IHRL and/or IHL by the incumbent authorities, therefore, has relevance only in relation to other forms of intervention in a civil war and to intervention in situations of internal unrest short of civil war.

[77] Claus Kreß, 'Major Post-Westphalian Shifts and Some Important Neo-Westphalian Hesitations in the State Practice on the International Law on the Use of Force' (2014) 1 JUFIL 11, 30. Under Art 16, ancillary

not breach the principle of non-intervention even if it constituted coercion, as respect for IHRL/IHL is not a matter in which the target state can decide freely.

When states are under a treaty obligation to support a foreign government, would they incur international responsibility if they opted to suspend compliance with such treaty in response to the violations committed by the incumbent authorities during the internal unrest? If the UN Security Council has imposed such measures against the wrongdoer, the prevalence of the obligations arising from the Charter, including the binding resolutions adopted by its organs, over conflicting treaty obligations is ensured by Article 103 of the Charter. In other cases, the non-performance of the treaty beyond the grounds codified in the 1969 Vienna Convention on the Law of Treaties (VCLT) can be construed as a countermeasure adopted in response to the violation of *erga omnes* or *erga omnes partes* obligations arising from IHRL and IHL, assuming, of course, that it is accepted that all states are entitled to adopt countermeasures in such case and that their material and procedural requirements are met.[78] This conclusion finds support in the 2016 ICRC Commentary on Common Article 1 of the Geneva Conventions, which includes, among the measures that the states parties can adopt to ensure respect for the Conventions, 'lawful countermeasures such as arms embargoes, trade and financial restrictions, flight bans and the reduction or suspension of aid and cooperation agreements' and 'conditioning, limiting or refusing arms transfers'.[79]

Are third states *required* to cease existing assistance or to decline a request for assistance by a government facing internal unrest if the latter has committed IHRL or IHL violations? This appears to be the position of the 2011 Institut de droit international's Rhodes Resolution on Military Assistance on Request, which affirms that military assistance to another state is prohibited 'when it is exercised in violation of ... generally accepted standards of human rights and in particular when its object is to support an established government against its own population'.[80] Such an obligation might indeed result from a treaty. More specifically, the 1948 Genocide Convention calls upon the states parties to prevent the commission of the acts listed in its Article I,[81] and Common Article 1 of the 1949 Geneva Conventions contains an obligation 'to ensure respect for the present Convention[s] in all circumstances'. The 2016 ICRC

responsibility arises when the state which aids or assists another state in the commission of an internationally wrongful act 'does so with knowledge of the circumstances of the internationally wrongful act'. The Commentary points out that the relevant state organ must have 'intended, by the aid or assistance given, to facilitate the occurrence of the wrongful conduct' (Commentary on Art 16 ARSIWA [2001] YB ILC vol II, part two, 66).

[78] See Chapter V, Section 5.1.2, fn 378.

[79] 2016 ICRC Commentary on Common Article 1, para 181. In literature, see Evan J Criddle, 'Humanitarian Financial Intervention' (2013) 24 EJIL 583, 595–9.

[80] Art 3, Resolution on Military Assistance on Request of the Institut de droit international (Rhodes Resolution), 8 September 2011 <www.idi-iil.org/app/uploads/2017/06/2011_rhodes_10_C_en.pdf>.

[81] Art I, Convention on the Prevention and Punishment of the Crime of Genocide (Paris, 9 December 1948), text in GA Res 260 (III), 9 December 1948, Annex. For the ICJ, factors for establishing the violation of the duty to prevent genocide include 'the capacity to influence effectively the action of persons likely to commit, or already committing, genocide. This capacity itself depends, among other things, on the geographical distance of the State concerned from the scene of the events, and on the strength of the political links, as well as links of all other kinds, between the authorities of that State and the main actors in the events' (*Bosnian Genocide*, para 430).

Commentary on Common Article 1 explains that this provision entails both negative and positive obligations:

> Under the negative obligation, High Contracting Parties may neither encourage, nor aid or assist in violations of the Conventions by Parties to a conflict. Under the positive obligation, they must do everything reasonably in their power to prevent and bring such violations to an end. This external dimension of the obligation to ensure respect for the Conventions goes beyond the principle of *pacta sunt servanda*.[82]

With regard to the negative obligation, in particular, the Commentary observes that

> [f]inancial, material or other support [to a party to an armed conflict] in the knowledge that such support will be used to commit violations of humanitarian law would ... violate common Article 1, even though it may not amount to aiding or assisting in the commission of a wrongful act by the receiving States for the purposes of State responsibility.[83]

The parties to the Geneva Conventions are specifically required 'to refrain from transferring weapons if there is an expectation, based on facts or knowledge of past patterns, that such weapons would be used to violate the Conventions'.[84]

Article 6(3) of the 2013 Arms Trade Treaty also prohibits a state party from authorizing arms transfers

> if it has knowledge at the time of authorization that the arms or items would be used in the commission of genocide, crimes against humanity, grave breaches of the Geneva Conventions of 1949, attacks directed against civilian objects or civilians protected as such, or other war crimes as defined by international agreements to which it is a Party.[85]

Article 7 addresses arms exports that are not prohibited under Article 6 and bans those that fail to pass a pre-export assessment on the basis of several criteria, including, among others, 'the potential that the conventional arms or items ... could be used to ... commit or facilitate a serious violation of' IHL or IHRL, as well as acts of terrorism.[86]

In addition, an obligation not to provide and to prevent the provision of arms and war *matériel* when it could contribute to IHRL and/or IHL violations could exist in

---

[82] 2016 ICRC Commentary on Common Art 1, para 154.

[83] ibid, para 160.

[84] ibid, para 162.

[85] Art 6(3), Arms Trade Treaty (New York, 2 April 2013) 3013 UNTS 269. See Marco Roscini and Riccardo Labianco, 'The Intersections Between the Arms Trade Treaty and the International Law of Foreign Intervention in Situations of Internal Unrest' (2002) 52 Israel YBHR 365, 382–5.

[86] While Art 6 applies to 'any transfer', Art 7 only applies to exports, which, although not defined in the treaty itself, has been interpreted as '[t]he act of taking out or causing to be taken out any goods from the Customs territory' (World Customs Organization, 'Glossary of International Customs Terms', December 2018 <www.wcoomd.org/-/media/wco/public/global/pdf/topics/facilitation/instruments-and-tools/tools/glossary-of-international-customs-terms/glossary-of-international-customs-terms.pdf>).

the framework of international organizations. The UN Security Council, in particular, has often demanded that member states refrain from supplying or allowing the supply of arms to states where serious violations of fundamental human rights law and/or IHL were being committed.[87] On 8 December 2008, the EU Council also adopted Common Position 2008/944/CFSP requiring each member state to assess arms export licence applications on a case-by-case basis taking into account, inter alia, '[r]espect for human rights and fundamental freedoms in the country of final destination as well as respect by that country for international humanitarian law'.[88] The EU member states must 'deny an export licence if there is a clear risk that the military technology or equipment to be exported might be used in the commission of serious violations of international humanitarian law'.[89]

It is more doubtful that an obligation to refuse or stop assistance to a foreign government responsible for IHRL and/or IHL violations exists in customary international law.[90] While it is arguable that Article I of the Genocide Convention and Common Article 1 of the Geneva Conventions are binding on all states,[91] both the duty to prevent and the duty to ensure respect contained therein have been interpreted as only entailing a *faculty* to adopt measures in response to the violations of the conventions in question, and not a legal obligation to do so.[92]

True, the domestic legislations of certain states exclude that arms export licences may be granted when the weapons are expected to be employed to commit human rights violations.[93] States have also often declined to provide or have interrupted assistance to foreign governments responsible for gross violations of IHRL and IHL.[94] The United States and other countries, for instance, suspended economic and military

---

[87] Motivated by IHRL and IHL violations, for instance, in 2018 the Security Council requested all member states to 'take the necessary measures to prevent the direct or indirect supply, sale or transfer to the territory of South Sudan from or through their territories or by their nationals, or using their flag vessels or aircraft, of arms and related materiel of all types, including weapons and ammunition, military vehicles and equipment, paramilitary equipment, and spare parts for the aforementioned; and technical assistance, training, financial or other assistance, related to military activities or the provision, maintenance or use of any arms and related materiel, including the provision of armed mercenary personnel whether or not originating in their territories' (SC Res 2428, 13 July 2018, para 4).

[88] EU Council Common Position 2008/944/CFSP of 8 December 2008 defining common rules governing control of exports of military technology and equipment, Arts 1(1) and 2(2).

[89] ibid, Art 2(2)(c).

[90] A commentator has suggested that it is only gross and large-scale violations of human rights that result in the prohibition of third states intervening in support of the wrongdoer under customary international law (Lieblich, *International Law*, 204).

[91] For Art I of the Genocide Convention, see Orna Ben-Naftali, 'The Obligation to Prevent and Punish Genocide' in Paola Gaeta (ed), *The UN Genocide Convention* (OUP 2009) 27, 43–4; Giorgio Gaja, 'The Role of the United Nations in Preventing and Suppressing Genocide', ibid, 397. In *Nicaragua*, the Court also found that the obligation to respect and to ensure respect for the Geneva Conventions 'does not derive only from the Conventions themselves, but from the general principles of humanitarian law to which the Conventions merely give specific expression' (*Nicaragua v USA*, para 220).

[92] Robert Kolb and Richard Hyde, *An Introduction to the International Law of Armed Conflicts* (Bloomsbury 2008) 288; Marco Longobardo, 'Genocide, Obligations *Erga Omnes*, and the Responsibility to Protect: Remarks on a Complex Convergence' (2015) 19 Intl J HR 1199, 1204; Etienne Henry, 'Alleged Acquiescence of the International Community to Revisionist Claims of International Customary Law (With Special Reference to the *Jus Contra Bellum* Regime)' (2017) 18 Melb J Int'l L 260, 277.

[93] George P Politakis, 'Variations on a Myth: Neutrality and the Arms Trade' (1992) 35 GYBIL 435, 487.

[94] Georg Nolte, *Eingreifen auf Einladung. Zur völkerrechtlichen Zulässigkeit des Einsatzes fremder Truppen im internen Konflikt auf Einladung der Regierung* (Springer 1999) 578.

352 INTERNATIONAL LAW AND THE PRINCIPLE OF NON-INTERVENTION

aid to Pakistan as a consequence of the brutal measures against civilians adopted by the Pakistani army in 1971 against the secessionist East (now Bangladesh).[95] On 17 August 1979, after the publication of a report proving massacres in which Emperor Bokassa was personally involved, the French government suspended all economic aid to the Central African Empire apart from health, education and food, noting that '[à] partir du moment où ont été déclenchées les violences répressives de Bangui, en janvier 1979, exercées sur la population, le gouvernement français a estimé que ces actes, contraires aux droits de l'homme, excluaient le soutien au régime centrafricain'.[96] In 1990, France also stopped all bilateral cooperation and funding to the Haitian authorities '[d]evant l'ampleur des atteintes aux droits de l'homme et l'interruption des libertés publiques'.[97] In the Syrian Civil War, the Assad government, which among other violations used chemical weapons against its own population, initially appeared open to some form of 'coordinate forcible action' with the Western states against ISIL, but the United States turned down the offer and preferred to rely on the collective self-defence of Iraq to justify its military operations in Syria.[98] In February 2019, the United States also stopped certain military assistance to Cameroon over allegations of human rights violations committed by its forces against political opponents under the pretext of fighting the terrorist group Boko Haram.[99] Finally, in 2021 Washington adopted a wide range of restrictive measures against Myanmar and members of its government and military in response to the violent crushing of popular protests following the military coup of February of the same year.[100]

What is not clear, however, is whether this practice is accompanied by the corresponding *opinio juris*, that is, the conviction that supporting or allowing support for a government responsible for IHRL and/or IHL violations would be an internationally wrongful act. In several cases, third-state assistance to a government has in fact continued despite its involvement in the violations under consideration. During the Nigerian Civil War, for instance, the United Kingdom continued to authorize the export of reasonable amounts of arms and ammunition of the same type and quantity that were already being sold to the federal authorities, in spite of the humanitarian crisis in Biafra.[101] The British foreign secretary affirmed that, as neutrality was not applicable, Britain could not stop selling arms to the Nigerian government because this would have resulted in supporting the Biafran rebellion.[102] In the conflict in

---

[95] Ved P Nanda, 'Self-Determination in International Law: The Tragic Tale of Two Cities—Islamabad (West Pakistan) and Dacca (East Pakistan)' (1972) 66 AJIL 321, 324, 334.

[96] Jean Charpentier, 'Pratique française du droit international' (1979) 25 AFDI 905, 909, 963.

[97] Jean Charpentier and Erick Germain, 'Pratique française du droit international' (1990) 36 AFDI 977, 1059.

[98] Claus Kreß, 'The Fine Line Between Collective Self-Defense and Intervention by Invitation: Reflections on the Use of Force against "IS" in Syria' (*Just Security*, 17 February 2015) <www.justsecurity.org/20118/claus-kreb-force-isil-syria/>.

[99] Lesley Wroughton, 'U.S. Halts Some Cameroon Military Assistance Over Human Rights: Official' (*Reuters*, 6 February 2019) <www.reuters.com/article/us-usa-cameroon/u-s-halts-some-cameroon-milit ary-assistance-over-human-rights-official-idUSKCN1PV2Q5>.

[100] Kristen E Eichensehr (ed), 'Contemporary Practice of the United States' (2021) 115 AJIL 527, 558–67.

[101] UK Commonwealth Secretary in the House of Commons, in Charles Rousseau, 'Chronique des faits internationaux' (1968) 72 RGIP 145, 234.

[102] British Foreign Secretary, House of Commons, 13 March 1969, in AHM Kirk-Green, *Crisis and Conflict in Nigeria—A Documentary Sourcebook 1966–1969*, vol 2 (OUP 1971) 363.

Darfur (2003–present), Sudan's government has been assisted in various forms by China, Russia, and Iran (until 2016), even though both the Janjaweed (Arab–African militias employed by the government) and the black African Darfur rebels have committed atrocities.[103] For the US ambassador to the United Nations, the supply of weapons to the Assad government in the Syrian Civil War was 'not technically, obviously, a violation of international law since there's not an arms embargo, but it's reprehensible that arms would continue to flow to a regime that is using such horrific and disproportionate force against its own people'.[104] The United States' policy with regard to Saudi Arabia is also particularly indicative of the absence of *opinio juris*, as it has changed depending on the administration of the day: if President Barack Obama limited the sale of arms and ammunition to the Gulf monarchy in response to the numerous civilian deaths caused by its military operations in the civil war in Yemen, President Donald Trump resumed and increased military cooperation even though IHL violations continued to occur, until his successor, Joe Biden, cut it again.[105]

Even the dispatch of armed forces on the side of governments accused of committing the violations in question has not been criticized on this specific ground.[106] No state, for instance, has claimed that Russia's intervention in support of Bashar al-Assad was unlawful because of the latter's involvement in the commission of war crimes. Although the Bahraini forces had previously launched a raid to clear the Pearl Roundabout in Manama of the pro-democracy protesters camped there, killing four and injuring about 300, in 2011 the Gulf Cooperation Council states intervened in the island state at the request of its king amid the silence of the international community.[107] All that can be said at this stage, therefore, is that

> states seem to be reluctant to explicitly assert a fully fledged right to intervene militarily at the request of a regime held responsible for widespread violations of fundamental human rights, but are equally hesitant to maintain that such a regime has forfeited its power to express a valid consent to a use of force by a foreign state.[108]

As has been seen, this conclusion also applies to lesser forms of intervention.

---

[103] Christine Gray, *International Law and the Use of Force* (4th edn, OUP 2018) 61.

[104] Louis Charbonneau, 'U.S. Condemns Reported Russian Arms Shipment to Syria' (*Reuters*, 31 May 2012) <www.reuters.com/article/uk-syria-arms-russia/u-s-condemns-reported-russian-arms-shipment-to-syria-idUKBRE84U0X020120531>.

[105] John Hursh, 'International Humanitarian Law Violations, Legal Responsibility, and US Military Support to the Saudi Coalition in Yemen: A Cautionary Tale' (2020) 7 JUFIL 122, 125–6.

[106] Erika De Wet, *Military Assistance on Request and the Use of Force* (OUP 2020) 130–5; Seyfullah Hasar, *State Consent to Foreign Military Intervention during Civil Wars* (Brill/Nijhoff 2022) 305–7.

[107] Note of the Secretary General of the Cooperation Council, 23 March 2011, cited in Agatha Verdebout, 'The Intervention of the Gulf Cooperation Council in Bahrain—2011' in Tom Ruys and Olivier Corten (eds), *The Use of Force in International Law. A Case-Based Approach* (OUP 2018) 795, 797.

[108] Kreβ, 'Major Post-Westphalian Shifts', 29.

6. Third-State Assistance to a Government against an Armed Opposition Group Responsible for Violations of IHL during a Civil War

As has been seen in Chapter V, when the situation of internal unrest becomes a civil war the principle of internal self-determination partly displaces that of non-intervention, with the result that third states can no longer send armed forces in support of the incumbent authorities regardless of their request. If, however, the insurgents do not respect IHL, can the government be assisted, the occurrence of a civil war notwithstanding? In other words, does IHL compliance take priority over the principle of internal self-determination?

Sending armed forces in support of a government involved in a civil war cannot be justified as a countermeasure in response to the IHL violations committed by the insurgents, as countermeasures can only be adopted in the case of an internationally wrongful act of a state, not non-state actors. Any justification, therefore, needs to be founded on a customary international law rule preventing the application of the principle of internal self-determination in the scenario under consideration and bringing back the permissibility of intervention by invitation.

An examination of state practice to verify the existence of this customary rule needs to discard cases where the intervention in support of a government occurred in a situation of internal unrest short of civil war, as in such cases intervention upon invitation of the incumbent authorities is at any rate permissible. In 2021, for instance, Rwanda deployed a joint force in Mozambique's Cabo Delgado province 'affected by terrorism and insecurity' and recalled its commitment to the R2P doctrine: the language used by Rwanda suggests that the legal basis of the operation was the request of the Maputo government.[109]

With regard to intervention in civil wars proper, the states sending troops in reaction to the commission of IHL violations by armed opposition groups have been reluctant to rely *sic et simpliciter* on the consent of the incumbent government as a justification for the intervention and/or have frequently emphasized the limited scope of the operation and the non-interference in the merits of the internal struggle for power.[110] When it intervened in the Liberian Civil War in August 1990, for instance, the Economic Community of West African States (ECOWAS) stressed that the Economic Community of West African States Monitoring Group (ECOMOG) force was 'going to Liberia first and foremost to stop the senseless killing of innocent civilian nationals and foreigners, and to help the Liberian people to restore their democratic

---

[109] Republic of Rwanda, 'Rwanda Deploys Joint Force to Mozambique', 9 July 2021 <www.gov.rw/blog-detail/rwanda-deploys-joint-force-to-mozambique>.

[110] Moore distinguishes between intervention to protect human rights before and after the outbreak of 'insurgency': in the former case, it is permissible to intervene at the request of the 'widely recognized government' while, in the latter, criteria that determine the legitimacy of intervention to protect human rights include '(1) an immediate and extensive threat to fundamental human rights, particularly a threat of widespread loss of human life; (2) a proportional use of force which does not threaten greater destruction of values than the human rights at stake; (3) a minimal effect on authority structures; (4) a prompt disengagement, consistent with the purpose of the action; and (5) immediate full reporting to the Security Council and appropriate regional organizations' (John Norton Moore, 'The Control of Foreign Intervention in Internal Conflict' (1969) 9 Va J Intl L 209, 264).

institutions' and that it was 'in no way designed to save one part or punish another.'[111] With regard to the 1994 Operation Turquoise in Rwanda, France declared that there would be no interposition between the warring parties and no taking sides and that the operation had the purpose of saving human lives using force if necessary.[112] Belgium offered analogous arguments and also referred to the consent of both the Kigali government and the Front Patriotique Rwandais to evacuate Belgian nationals from the country.[113] When, in August 2013, the situation in the Central African Republic worsened and assumed genocidal aspects, the transitional authorities that had replaced the Séléka government requested France to intervene, but Paris based its justification for Operation Sangaris on the authorization contained in Security Council Resolution 2127 (2013).[114] The only case where the intervening state appears to have relied exclusively on the consent of the incumbent government is Uganda's intervention in South Sudan in 2013 in support of President Salva Kiir's security forces against units loyal to Deputy President Riek Machar: Uganda invoked the consent of the Juba government for the evacuation of Ugandan nationals and to avert a potential genocide.[115]

The above cases suggest that, unlike terrorist groups,[116] insurgents who commit violations of IHL during a civil war do not entirely forfeit their internal self-determination standing: it is not the group as such but only their unlawful conduct that is sanctioned by the international legal order by bringing back the application of the principle of non-intervention and thus the permissibility of intervention upon the invitation of the incumbent authorities. Differently from the case of counterterrorism intervention, therefore, third-state involvement in the present scenario must be limited to ending the violations of IHL and protecting civilians, and not aimed at keeping the incumbent authorities in power.[117]

---

[111] UN Doc S/21485, 10 August 1990, Annex, 3. According to Nigeria's delegate at the Security Council, 'ECOMOG's mandate is not to take sides, but to reconcile the sides, to restore peace and to create an atmosphere conducive to the resumption of free political activity and, eventually, democratic elections' (S/PV.2974, 22 January 1991, 7). ECOMOG's intervention in Liberia was commended by the UN Security Council (SC Resolutions 788, 19 November 1992, para 1; 813, 26 March 1993, para 2; 856, 10 August 1993, para 6; 866, 22 September 1993, Preamble). In the debates, all delegates apart from that of Burkina Faso supported the operation (S/PV.3138, 19 November 1992).

[112] Jean Charpentier, 'Pratique française du droit international 1994' (1994) 40 AFDI 1003, 1032–3.

[113] Michel Cassese with Jean-Pierre Legrand, 'La pratique des gouvernements et le contrôle des Assemblées de l'Etat fédéral et des entités fédérées belges en matière de droit international (oct. 1993–sept. 1995)' (1997) 30 RBDI 226, 285–6.

[114] See Frédérique Coulée, 'Pratique française du droit international' (2013) 59 AFDI 535, 564–5.

[115] Tom Ruys and Nele Verlinden (eds), 'Digest of State Practice 1 January–30 June 2014' (2014) 1 JUFIL 323, 340–1.

[116] See Chapter V, Section 5.2.

[117] Antonello Tancredi, La secessione nel diritto internazionale (CEDAM 2001) 677; Valentina Grado, Guerre civili e terzi Stati (CEDAM 1998) 308.

356 INTERNATIONAL LAW AND THE PRINCIPLE OF NON-INTERVENTION

7. Third-State Intervention in Support of Insurgents Fighting against a Government Responsible for Violations of IHRL or IHL

Coercion on a government responsible for IHRL and/or IHL violations can be exercised not only by suspending or terminating assistance in its favour, but also by supporting opposition groups in different forms.[118] While such support would not fall under the prohibitive scope of the principle of non-intervention to the extent that it aims to secure compliance with an international obligation of the target state, it might however still be proscribed by other primary rules of international law.

Before exploring this problem, a point needs clarification. It has been maintained that the Friendly Relations Declaration indirectly recognizes a right of 'remedial' secession in extreme cases of oppression accompanied by massive violations of human rights,[119] and some states have occasionally referred to this argument with regard to their armed intervention in secessionist struggles. When it intervened in East Pakistan (1971), for instance, India claimed that, under international law, 'where a mother-State has irrevocably lost allegiance of such a large section of its people as represented by Bangla Desh and cannot bring them under its sway, conditions for the separate existence of such a state comes [*sic*] into being.'[120] Similarly, Russia argued that

> the achievement of the right to self-determination in the form of separation from an existing state is an extraordinary measure and that, in the case of Crimea, it obviously arose as a result of the legal vacuum created by the violent coup against the legitimate Government carried out by nationalist radicals in Kyiv, as well as by their direct threats to impose their order throughout the territory of Ukraine.[121]

In February 2022, President Vladimir Putin also explained that Russia's recognition of the independence of the Donbass People's Republics was mainly motivated by 'a genocide against the millions of people living there'.[122]

---

[118] See Chapter III, Section 8.

[119] The Declaration points out that nothing in it 'shall be construed as authorizing or encouraging any action which would dismember or impair, totally or in part, the territorial integrity or political unity of sovereign and independent States conducting themselves in compliance with the principle of equal rights and self-determination of peoples as described above and thus possessed of a government representing the whole people belonging to the territory without distinction as to race, creed or colour' (GA Res 2625 (XXV), Annex, fifth principle, para 7). See also *Reference re Secession of Quebec* [1998] 2 SCR 217, para 154; African Commission on Human and Peoples' Rights, *Katangese Peoples' Congress v Zaire*, Communication 75/92, Eighth Activity Report 1994–1995, Annex VI, para 6.

[120] UN Doc S/10445, 12 December 1971. Israel was one of the first countries to recognize the new state. Bangladesh, however, 'refused' the recognition in protest against the occupation of the Palestinian territories (Khaled Nasir, 'Time for a Quiet Revolution in Bangladesh–Israeli Relations' (*The Jerusalem Post*, 9 February 2011) <www.jpost.com/Opinion/Op-Ed-Contributors/Time-for-a-quiet-revolution-in-Banglad esh-Israeli-relations>).

[121] UN Doc S/PV.7134, 13 March 2014, 15. See also Russia's written statement in *Accordance with International Law of the Unilateral Declaration of Independence in Respect of Kosovo* (Request for Advisory Opinion) 16 April 2009, para 88 <www.icj-cij.org/case/141>. In Kosovo's case, however, Russia did not believe that, in 2008, the extreme circumstances justifying remedial secession were present (ibid, para 99).

[122] UN Doc S/2022/154, 24 February 2022, Annex, 5.

As noted by the ICJ, however, it remains unclear whether international law does allow secession as a last-resort remedy in extreme cases of oppression.[123] Indeed, states and international organizations have called upon the wrongdoing states to respect international law, but at the same time have endorsed their territorial integrity and the non-interference in the merits of the secessionist conflict.[124] Be that as it may, it is not necessary for our purposes to address this complex problem because, as in wars of national liberation,[125] even if a right to remedial secession did exist in current international law, what would still need to be demonstrated is that third states can adopt forcible or other coercive measures to enforce it.[126]

7.1 The Dispatch of Armed Forces

The issue of sending armed forces in support of opposition groups against a government responsible for gross violations of IHRL and/or IHL overlaps with the *vexata quæstio* of the legality of humanitarian intervention, defined by the IIFFMCG as 'a coercive, notably military action across state borders by a state or a group of states aimed at preventing or ending widespread and grave violations of human rights of individuals other than its own citizens, without the permission of the state in whose territory force is applied'.[127] An examination of all problems raised by the doctrine of humanitarian intervention exceeds the bounds of the present work: the following pages primarily focus on intervention that takes the form of armed support for foreign insurgents.

7.1.1 Arguments in favour of the legality of sending armed forces
The ICISS R2P Report claims that 'the [UN] Charter's strong bias against military intervention is not to be regarded as absolute when decisive action is required on human protection grounds'.[128] Several writers have indeed maintained that humanitarian intervention even without Security Council authorization is lawful in contemporary

---

[123] *Accordance with International Law of the Unilateral Declaration of Independence in Respect of Kosovo* (Advisory Opinion) [2010] ICJ Rep 403, para 82. Only two of the forty states intervening in the ICJ proceedings expressed themselves in favour of a right to remedial secession under customary international law, and nine qualified it as a *sui generis* case (see the survey of state positions in Enrico Milano, 'L'autodeterminazione nei Balcani: Soluzioni ad hoc per casi *sui generis* o consolidamento del principio nel contesto post-coloniale?' in Marcella Distefano (ed), *Il principio di autodeterminazione dei popoli alla prova del nuovo millennio* (Wolters Kluwer/CEDAM 2014) 37, 43).

[124] Tancredi, *La secessione*, 614–5. According to the International Fact-Finding Mission on the Conflict in Georgia (IIFFMCG), '[a] right to external self-determination in form of secession is not accepted in state practice ... The case of Kosovo has not changed the rules' (Report of the Independent International Fact-Finding Commission on the Conflict in Georgia (hereafter IIFFMCG Report), vol I, 141 <www.mpil.de/files/pdf4/IIFFMCG_Volume_I2.pdf>).

[125] See Chapter VI, Section 3.2 and its subsections.

[126] The existence of a right to remedial secession, however, might affect the permissibility of third-state intervention on the side of the oppressive government: if the latter is not entitled to oppose the secession, then third states would also be prevented from assisting it in that endeavour in spite of its request. The considerations developed in Chapter VI, Section 3.1 with regard to intervention in support of a colonial power, therefore, would also apply in the present context.

[127] IIFFMCG Report, vol II, 283 <www.mpil.de/files/pdf4/IIFFMCG_Volume_II1.pdf>.

[128] ICISS R2P Report, para 2.27.

358 INTERNATIONAL LAW AND THE PRINCIPLE OF NON-INTERVENTION

international law, with explanations including a narrow interpretation of Article 2(4) of the UN Charter permitting a use of armed force which is not 'against the territorial integrity or political independence of any state, or in any other manner inconsistent with the Purposes of the United Nations',[129] the formation (or re-emergence) of a customary rule allowing it,[130] state of necessity,[131] and moral considerations.[132]

Some states have also expressed themselves in favour of the legality of unilateral armed intervention on humanitarian grounds, although not always consistently. According to a 1976 US memorandum, for instance, intervention to save nationals and non-nationals in danger in an internal armed conflict occurring in a foreign country is legally justifiable when its government is incapable of protecting them.[133] The document, however, seems to have evacuation operations in mind and does not indicate whether it would also be permissible to intervene if it was exclusively the nationals of the territorial state who are at risk and their government was the source of the threat.[134] Fast-forward thirty years and, in his Nobel Lecture, US President Obama proclaimed that 'force can be justified on humanitarian grounds, as it was in the Balkans, or in other places that have been scarred by war': it is unclear whether the statement reflected his personal view or could be read as the *opinio juris* of the United States.[135] Be that as it may, the 2015 US Law of War Manual explicitly rejects the doctrine of humanitarian intervention.[136]

The position of the United Kingdom is different. In 1984, the Foreign and Commonwealth Office (FCO) still maintained that while 'it cannot be said to be unambiguously illegal ... the case against making humanitarian intervention an exception to the principle of non-intervention is that its doubtful benefits would be heavily outweighed by its costs in term of respect for international law'.[137] In 1992, the British government had a change of heart and claimed that the airstrikes in northern Iraq to

---

[129] Anthony D'Amato, 'The Invasion of Panama Was a Lawful Response to Tyranny' (1990) 84 AJIL 516, 520.

[130] ibid, 523. For Richard Lillich, the doctrine of humanitarian intervention is 'so clearly established under customary international law that only its limits and not its existence is subject to debate' (Richard B Lillich, 'Intervention to Protect Human Rights' (1969) 15 McGill L J 205, 210).

[131] Ole Spiermann, 'Humanitarian Intervention as a Necessity and the Threat or Use of *Jus Cogens*' (2002) 71 Nordic J Int'l L 523, 543. The ILC excluded, however, that a state of necessity, as codified in ARSIWA, can justify humanitarian intervention (Commentary on Art 25 [2001] YB ILC vol II, part two, 84, para 21).

[132] Fernando Tesón, *Humanitarian Intervention: An Inquiry into Law and Morality* (3rd edn, Transnational Publishers 2005) 81; Anthony D'Amato, 'There is No Norm of Intervention or Non-Intervention in International Law' (2001) 7 ILT 33, 35, 40; Harold Hongju Koh, 'Syria and the Law of Humanitarian Intervention (Part II: International Law and the Way Forward)' (*EJIL:Talk!*, 4 October 2013) <www.ejiltalk.org/syria-and-the-law-of-humanitarian-intervention-part-ii-international-law-and-the-way-forward/>.

[133] Memorandum of the Attorney Adviser in the Office of the Department of State's Legal Adviser dated 20 February 1976 in Eleanor C McDowell (ed), *Digest of United States Practice in International Law 1976* (GPO 1977) 6.

[134] ibid.

[135] The White House, Remarks by the President at the Acceptance of the Nobel Peace Prize, 10 December 2009 <https://obamawhitehouse.archives.gov/the-press-office/remarks-president-accepta nce-nobel-peace-prize>.

[136] US Department of Defense, Law of War Manual (June 2015, updated December 2016) 46. <https:// dod.defense.gov/Portals/1/Documents/pubs/DoD%20Law%20of%20War%20Manual%20-%20June%202 015%20Updated%20Dec%202016.pdf>.

[137] Foreign Office, 'Is Intervention Ever Justified?' in Geoffrey Marston (ed), 'UK Materials on International Law 1986' (1986) 57 BYBIL 487, 619.

protect the Kurdish population (Operation Provide Comfort) were carried out 'in exercise of the customary international law principle of humanitarian intervention'.[138] In October 1998, an FCO note circulated to NATO allies in the build-up to Operation Allied Force against Yugoslavia (an intervention reminiscent of those of the European powers in the Ottoman Empire for the protection of Christian minorities)[139] posited that the use of force 'on the grounds of overwhelming humanitarian necessity' is justified even without Security Council authorization as long as certain requirements are met.[140] In August 2013, Britain reaffirmed the right under international law, if the UN Security Council is blocked, 'to take exceptional measures in order to alleviate the scale of the overwhelming humanitarian catastrophe in Syria by deterring and disrupting the further use of chemical weapons by the Syrian regime'.[141] The three conditions are that

(i) there is convincing evidence, generally accepted by the international community as a whole, of extreme humanitarian distress on a large scale, requiring immediate and urgent relief; (ii) it must be objectively clear that there is no practicable alternative to the use of force if lives are to be saved; and (iii) the proposed use of force must be necessary and proportionate to the aim of relief of humanitarian need and must be strictly limited in time and scope to this aim (i.e. the minimum necessary to achieve that end and for no other purpose).[142]

Other states that have at some point supported the legality of humanitarian intervention in more or less explicit terms include Denmark,[143] Sweden,[144] Jamaica,[145] and Poland.[146] Estonia and Belgium also do not rule out unilateral action as a means of last resort to prevent genocide,[147] while New Zealand has limited itself to contending that unilateral humanitarian intervention in reaction to genocide might be 'an emerging customary norm'.[148]

---

[138] Geoffrey Marston (ed), 'UK Materials on International Law 1992' (1992) 63 BYBIL 615, 827. The United States and France, on the other hand, resorted to the argument of implied Security Council authorization (Olivier Corten, *The Law Against War: The Prohibition on the Use of Force in Contemporary International Law* (2nd edn, Hart Publishing 2021) 529).

[139] Neff, *War*, 361.

[140] Geoffrey Marston (ed), 'UK Materials on International Law 1999' (1999) 70 BYBIL 387, 571. After the airstrikes began, they were justified as 'an exceptional measure to prevent an overwhelming humanitarian catastrophe' in Kosovo (UN Doc S/PV.3988, 24 March 1999, 12).

[141] Prime Minister's Office, Chemical Weapon Use by the Syrian Regime—UK Government Legal Position, 29 August 2013, para 4 <www.gov.uk/government/publications/chemical-weapon-use-by-syrian-regime-uk-government-legal-position>.

[142] ibid.

[143] Danish Ministry of Defence—Defence Command Denmark, Military Manual on International Law Relevant to Danish Armed Forces in International Operations (2016) 39–40 <http://web.archive.org/web/20200416112752/https://fmn.dk/eng/allabout/Documents/Danish-Military-Manual-MoD-defence-2016.pdf>. The Manual points out, however, that the R2P doctrine 'does not in itself provide an international law basis for the use of force' (ibid, 40).

[144] UN Doc A/54/PV.7, 21 September 1999, 32.

[145] UN Doc A/C.1/SR.1406, 10 December 1965, para 32.

[146] UN Doc A/54/PV.17, 29 September 1999, 6.

[147] *Allegations of Genocide*, Declaration of Intervention Under Article 63 of the Republic of Estonia, para 45; Declaration of Intervention of the Kingdom of Belgium, para 23.

[148] *Allegations of Genocide*, Declaration of Intervention Pursuant to Article 63 of the Statute of the Court by the Government of New Zealand, para 31.

360 INTERNATIONAL LAW AND THE PRINCIPLE OF NON-INTERVENTION

Certain armed interventions in situations of internal unrest appear to have been justified by the intervening states solely as a reaction to the IHL violations committed by the incumbent authorities. In 1948, Egypt, Syria, Lebanon, and Transjordan militarily intervened in Palestine the day after the proclamation of the State of Israel. The Arab states claimed that it was 'their bounden duty as a Government of an Arab State and a civilized nation to intervene in Palestine with the object of putting an end to the massacres raging there and upholding law and principles recognized among the United Nations'.[149] Egypt pointed out that the intervention was 'with the unequivocal consent of the people of Palestine'.[150] In the Liberian Civil War (1989–97), Burkina Faso's President Blaise Compaoré initially denied sending troops in support of Charles Taylor's Front National Patriotique du Libéria and then confirmed it and accused the Liberian government of atrocities.[151] Britain's position in relation to Operation Provide Comfort and Operation Allied Force has already been mentioned. Belgium and the Netherlands also referred to the doctrine under consideration in the proceedings brought against them by Yugoslavia before the ICJ.[152] On 7 April 2017, the United States launched Tomahawk missiles against a Syrian military airbase in response to a sarin gas attack against the rebel-controlled town of Khan Sheikhoun, which had been allegedly conducted by Assad's forces. Whereas the United States did not offer a legal justification, for the United Kingdom the attack was 'a proportionate response to unspeakable acts that gave rise to overwhelming humanitarian distress'.[153] On 14 April 2018, France, Britain, and the United States again conducted missile strikes on governmental targets in Syria in response to the use of chlorine gas in the Damascus suburb of Douma. Britain justified the strikes by referring to the doctrine of humanitarian intervention.[154] The United States, on the other hand, abstained from providing a formal justification based on international law, while the closest to explaining the attacks in legal terms that France went was the declaration of its foreign minister stating that the operation was 'legitimate' because it aimed to stop a serious violation of international law and to prevent the further use of chemical weapons by the Syrian government.[155]

---

[149] UN Doc S/PV.292, 15 May 1948, 3. See also the Egyptian foreign affairs minister's cablegram to the President of the Security Council, S/743, 15 May 1948.

[150] UN Doc S/PV.292, 10. Syria also referred to the request of 'the majority of the inhabitants of Palestine' the failure to respond to which would leave them to their annihilation (UN Doc S/PV.301, 22 May 1948, 12). Many states, however, condemned the Arab intervention as an act of aggression, with Ukraine stating that 'according to the rules of the international community, each Government has the right to restore order only in its own country' (UN Doc S/PV.292, 25).

[151] F Meledje Djedjro, 'La guerre civile du Libéria et la question de l'ingérence dans les affaires intérieures des États' (1993) 26 RBDI 393, 401–2.

[152] Legality of Use of Force (Yugoslavia v Belgium), Oral proceedings, CR 99/15, 10 May 1999, 15–7; Legality of Use of Force (Yugoslavia v Netherlands), Oral proceedings, CR 99/20, 11 May 1999, paras 40–3. See also PC Tange, 'Netherlands State Practice for the Parliamentary Year 2001–2002' (2003) 34 NYBIL 219, 284–92.

[153] UN Doc S/PV.7919, 7 April 2017, 5. Criticism, however, was raised by Russia, China, and several African and Latin American countries (Gray, International Law, 58).

[154] UN Doc S/PV.8233, 14 April 2018, 6–7.

[155] French Embassy in London, 'Syria — Statement by Jean-Yves le Drian, Minister for Europe and Foreign Affairs', 14 April 2018 <https://uk.ambafrance.org/Action-in-Syria-is-legitimate-says-Foreign-Minister#Syria-Statement-by-Jean-Yves-Le-Drian-Minister-for-Europe-and-Foreign-nbsp>. For the French representative at the Security Council, 'the Charter was not designed to protect criminals. Our action is fully in line with the objectives and values proclaimed from the outset by the Charter of the United

It is worth pointing out that, for the supporters of the legality of humanitarian intervention, only the most serious violations of IHRL and IHL can potentially justify the use of force: states have referred to an 'overwhelming humanitarian catastrophe',[156] 'extreme cases' and 'grave and large-scale violations of fundamental human rights',[157] or 'extreme humanitarian distress on a large scale'.[158] The ICISS R2P Report also considers military intervention permissible only in the case of 'large scale loss of life, actual or apprehended, with genocidal intent or not, which is the product either of deliberate state action, or state neglect or inability to act, or a failed state situation' and 'large scale "ethnic cleansing," actual or apprehended, whether carried out by killing, forced expulsion, acts of terror or rape'.[159] As examples of these extreme situations, the Report lists genocide, crimes against humanity, war crimes, ethnic cleansing, 'the threat or occurrence of large scale loss of life, whether the product of genocidal intent or not, and whether or not involving state action', 'overwhelming natural or environmental catastrophes, where the state concerned is either unwilling or unable to cope, or call for assistance, and significant loss of life is occurring or threatened', and 'situations of state collapse and the resultant exposure of the population to mass starvation and/or civil war'.[160] On the other hand, 'human rights violations falling short of outright killing or ethnic cleansing, for example systematic racial discrimination, or the systematic imprisonment or other repression of political opponents' and 'cases where a population, having clearly expressed its desire for a democratic regime, is denied its democratic rights by a military take-over' do not suffice, in the ICISS's view, to justify armed intervention.[161]

7.1.2 Arguments against the legality of sending armed forces

Far more numerous are the countries which have pronounced themselves against the legality of an armed intervention on humanitarian grounds without Security Council authorization or the consent of the territorial sovereign. After Operation Allied Force, the Group of 77, a coalition of 134 developing states, sent a letter to the president of the General Assembly emphasizing that humanitarian intervention has 'no basis in the UN Charter or in international law'.[162] The fifty-seven states of the Organisation of Islamic Cooperation have also rejected 'the so-called right to humanitarian intervention under whatever name or from whatever source, for it has no basis in the Charter

---

Nations. The Organization's mission is "to establish conditions under which justice and respect for the obligations arising from treaties and other sources of international law can be maintained". This action was indeed necessary in order to address the repeated violations by the Syrian regime of its obligations— obligations stemming from the law, treaties and its own commitments' (UN Doc S/PV.8233, 9).

[156] Prime Minister's Office, Chemical Weapon Use by the Syrian Regime, para 4.
[157] Letter to parliament from the Netherlands' minister of foreign affairs, 30 October 2001, reproduced in Tange, 'Netherlands State Practice', 284–92. The letter cites the examples of genocide and crimes against humanity (ibid, 290).
[158] Danish Ministry of Defence, Military Manual, 40.
[159] ICISS R2P Report, para 4.19, italics omitted.
[160] ibid, para 4.20.
[161] ibid, paras 4.25, 4.26.
[162] Ministerial Declaration, Twenty-Third Annual Meeting of the Ministers for Foreign Affairs of the Group of 77, 24 September 1999, para 69 <www.g77.org/doc/Decl1999.html>. The point was reiterated at subsequent meetings.

362 INTERNATIONAL LAW AND THE PRINCIPLE OF NON-INTERVENTION

of the United Nations or in the provisions of the principles of the general international law'.[163] The same view has been repeatedly expressed by the 120 countries forming the Non-Aligned Movement.[164] For Russia, humanitarian intervention and the responsibility to protect are 'concepts unrecognized in international law'[165] and China's official view is that humanitarian intervention is only permissible when authorized by the Security Council and after an invitation from the state where the intervention should take place has been obtained.[166] Analogous positions have been adopted by other states, including the Association of Southeast Asian Nations (ASEAN) members,[167] Canada,[168] and Switzerland.[169]

To these explicit rejections of the legality of armed intervention on humanitarian grounds without Security Council authorization by states of all geographical and political denominations, one should add that no UN resolution has ever recognized such exception to the prohibition of the use of force and that the Declarations on the Inadmissibility of Intervention and on Friendly Relations both stress that states or groups of states have no right to intervene 'for any reason whatever' in the internal or external affairs of other states.[170] The Helsinki Final Act also cautions that, when acting in the field of human rights and fundamental freedoms, the participating states must act 'in conformity with the purposes and principles of the Charter of the United Nations', including the prohibition of the use of force.[171]

It is also significant that, when they have used armed force in the context of humanitarian crises, in most cases the intervening states have not invoked the doctrine of humanitarian intervention as a legal basis but have relied on less controversial grounds. The provisional records of the Security Council debates on the conflict in East Pakistan in 1971, for instance, show that, while India's initial justifications for its military operations in support of the secessionists also included references to humanitarian intervention in response to the atrocities committed by the Pakistani armed forces against civilians, the published version only mentions the exercise of self-defence against the

---

[163] Final Communique of the Twenty-Seventh Session of the Islamic Conference of Foreign Ministers, Kuala Lumpur, 27–30 June 2000, para 79 <www.oic-oci.org/docdown/?docID=4291&refID=1205>.

[164] See eg the Final Document of the 18th Summit of Heads of State and Government of the Non-Aligned Movement, Baku, 25–26 October 2019, NAM 2019/CoB/Doc.1, para 1012 <https://unidir.org/node/6072>. See also the Declaration of the Special Meeting of the Ministers of Foreign Affairs of the Non-Aligned Movement, Doha, 13 June 2005, UN Doc A/59/880, para 18.

[165] UN Doc S/PV.8472, 26 February 2019, 13.

[166] Björn Ahl, 'China' in *MPEPIL Online* (last updated January 2008) para 12.

[167] Eric Corthay, 'The ASEAN Doctrine of Non-Interference in Light of the Fundamental Principle of Non-Intervention' (2016) 17 Asian-Pacific L & PJ 1, 34–6.

[168] Philippe Kirsch (ed), 'Canadian Practice in International Law at the Department of Foreign Affairs in 1996–97' (1998) 35 CYBIL 349, 362.

[169] Legal Opinion of the International Law Department of Switzerland's Department of Foreign Affairs (6 May 1999), in Lucius Caflisch, 'La pratique suisse en matière de droit international public 1999' (2000) 10 RSDIE 627, 671.

[170] See GA Res 2131 (XX), 21 December 1965, para 1; GA Res 2625 (XXV), Annex, third principle, para 1. The same language appears in Art 19 of the Charter of the Organization of American States (Bogotá, 30 April 1948) 119 UNTS 3. The Declaration on the Definition of Aggression also points out that '[n]o consideration of whatever nature, whether political, economic, military or otherwise, may serve as a justification for aggression' (GA Res 3314 (XXIX), 14 December 1974, Annex, Art 5(1)).

[171] Principle VII(8), Helsinki Final Act.

attacks on Indian airfields launched by Pakistan.[172] Several states condemned the abuses committed by Pakistan, but also the Indian intervention.[173] Tanzania's invasion of Uganda in 1978–9 together with Ugandan exiles resulted in the overthrow of President Idi Amin: in spite of Amin's horrific human rights record, Tanzania relied on self-defence language to justify the operation.[174] In the same years, Vietnam invaded Kampuchea and toppled the genocidal Khmer Rouge regime: like India, it invoked its right of individual self-defence against the incursions of the Khmer Rouge into Vietnamese territory.[175] The UN General Assembly and ASEAN condemned the intervention.[176] When it intervened in the Central African Empire in 1979, France relied on former President David Dacko and Prime Minister Henri Maidou's request to remove a regime that oppressed the population and whose gross human rights violations had been established by an African commission.[177] Several states accused France of violating the principle of non-intervention.[178] Unlike the United Kingdom, the United States and France chose not to rely on the doctrine of humanitarian intervention to justify Operation Provide Comfort in northern Iraq to protect the Kurds from Saddam Hussein's attacks, with Washington invoking an implied authorization to use force contained in Security Council Resolution 688 (1991).[179] In the proceedings before the ICJ in the *Armed Activities* case, Uganda referred to genocidal acts committed in the Democratic Republic of the Congo (DRC)'s territory, but did not use this as a legal basis for its intervention in the Congo Civil War.[180] Even if it had—claimed the

[172] Michael Akehurst, 'Humanitarian Intervention' in Hedley Bull (ed), *Intervention in World Politics* (Clarendon Press 1984) 95, 96. See UN Doc S/10445. Although the flood of ten million refugees and massacres were also mentioned, they were not used as a legal justification (A/PV.2003, 7 December 1971, paras 156, 165; S/10445, 105). India first allowed its territory to be used by the insurgents, then provided arms, and finally directly intervened in support of the secessionist East Pakistan.

[173] Akehurst, 'Humanitarian Intervention', 96–7. GA Res 2793 (XXVI), 7 December 1971, para 1, called upon 'the Governments of India and Pakistan to take forthwith all measures for an immediate cease-fire and withdrawal of their armed forces on the territory of the other to their own side of the India–Pakistan borders'.

[174] Tanzania's President Nyerere claimed: 'It is not my responsibility to overthrow Amin. That is the responsibility of the Ugandans. It was my task to chase him from Tanzanian soil' (Keesing's 1979, 29671). The intervention was not discussed at the main UN organs and was explicitly condemned only by a few African states.

[175] UN Doc S/13011, 8 January 1979, Annex, 2; S/PV.2108, 11 January 1979, paras 126–7. Vietnam argued that a 'clear distinction' should be made between 'the border war started by the Pol Pot–Ieng Sary clique against Viet Nam' and 'the revolutionary war of the Kampuchean people against the dictatorial rule of the Pol Pot–Ieng Sary clique, which is an instrument in the hands of the reactionary ruling circles of Peking' and claimed that it was dealing exclusively with the former in the exercise of its right of self-defence (S/PV.2108, paras 115, 127).

[176] GA Res 34/22, 14 November 1979; UN Doc S/13025, 12 January 1979, Annex, 2. GA Res 34/22 emphasized that the Cambodian people are entitled 'to decide their own future and destiny free from outside interference, subversion or coercion' (para 9). The French representative at the Security Council also stated that '[t]he notion that, because a regime is detestable, foreign intervention is justifiable and forcible overthrow is legitimate is extremely dangerous. That could ultimately jeopardize the very maintenance of international law and order and make the continued existence of various regimes dependent on the judgment of their neighbours' (S/PV.2109, 12 January 1979, para 36). For ASEAN's condemnation, see S/13025, Annex, 2.

[177] Charpentier, 'Pratique française' 1979, 908–10.

[178] David Wippman, 'Military Intervention, Regional Organizations, and Host-State Consent' (1996) 7 Duke J Comp & Intl L 209, 211.

[179] Elinor Buys and Andrew Gardwood-Gowers, 'The (Ir)Relevance of Human Suffering: Humanitarian Intervention and Saudi Arabia's Operation Decisive Storm in Yemen' (2019) 24 JCSL 1, 15.

[180] *DRC v Uganda*, Memorial of the DRC (Merits), 6 July 2000, vol I, para 5.61.

364   INTERNATIONAL LAW AND THE PRINCIPLE OF NON-INTERVENTION

DRC's Memorial—it could have not been a valid justification.[181] NATO did not officially invoke the doctrine of humanitarian intervention to justify its 1999 airstrikes to protect ethnic Albanians in Kosovo: as said, some member states referred to it in the subsequent proceedings before the ICJ and in the Security Council debates,[182] but at the same time pointed out that the Kosovo operation was a response to a *sui generis* situation and could not constitute a precedent for future actions.[183] The 2011 NATO airstrikes in Libya to protect civilians from Muammar Ghaddafi's violence were based on the authorization contained in Security Council Resolution 1973 (2011), and not on the request of the opposition or a right of humanitarian intervention.[184] In the Syrian Civil War, Turkey relied on self-defence for its incursions into its neighbour's territory[185] even though the anti-Assad Syrian National Council claimed that 'the Syrian people would welcome an intervention on the part of Turkey for the protection of civilians'.[186] Finally, while President Putin claimed that the purpose of the 2022 invasion of Ukraine was the protection of 'people who have been subjected to abuse and genocide by the Kiev regime for eight years', he invoked self-defence under Article 51 of the UN Charter as the legal justification of the 'special military operation'.[187]

Absent a specific reliance on the doctrine of humanitarian intervention, therefore, the aforementioned cases of intervention have limited evidentiary value for the identification of customary international law, as legal views cannot be ascribed to states if they do not advance them themselves.[188] All in all, the evident reluctance of states to expressly (let alone exclusively) rely on humanitarian grounds as a legal justification for their use of force, as well as the explicit opposition of at least two permanent members of the UN Security Council and of most states in the 'Global South', have prevented unilateral armed intervention against a government responsible for IHRL and/or IHL violations from becoming 'general practice accepted as law' in the Charter

---

[181]   ibid, paras 5.62–5.69.

[182]   For the United States, for instance, the intervention was 'justified and necessary to stop the violence and prevent an even greater humanitarian disaster' (UN Doc S/PV.3988, 5), while Britain argued that 'on the grounds of overwhelming humanitarian necessity, military intervention is legally justifiable' (S/PV.3988, 12). See also *Legality of Use of Force (Yugoslavia v Belgium)*, Oral proceedings, CR 99/15, 10 May 1999, 15–7; *Legality of Use of Force (Yugoslavia v Netherlands)*, Oral proceedings, CR 99/20, 11 May 1999, paras 40–3.

[183]   See the statements of the Belgian, British, Libyan, Croatian, and American representatives at the Security Council (UN Doc S/PV.5839, 18 February 2008, 9, 14, 15, 16, 19). The intervention was condemned in the Communiqué issued by the Rio Group, an association of twenty-four Latin American and Caribbean states dissolved in 2011 and succeeded by the Community of Latin American and Caribbean States (A/53/884-S/1999/347, 26 March 1999, Annex); and in the statements of Russia, Belarus, and China in the Security Council debates (S/PV.3988, 2–3, 12, 15).

[184]   Olivier Corten and Vaios Koutroulis, 'The Illegality of Military Support to Rebels in the Libyan War: Aspects of *jus contra bellum* and *jus in bello*' (2013) 18 JCSL 59, 64.

[185]   See eg UN Doc S/2015/563, 24 July 2015, 1; S/2016/739, 25 August 2016, 1.

[186]   Ignacio Cembrero, 'La oposición siria acepta que Turquía intervenga para proteger a los civiles' (*El País*, 17 November 2011) <https://elpais.com/internacional/2011/11/17/actualidad/1321556946_531748.html>.

[187]   UN Doc S/2022/154, 6. See the requests for intervention by the Donbass Republics in A/76/740-S/2022/179, 7 March 2022, Annexes III and IV, 145. Similar emphatic language that did not translate into a legal justification was also employed by Russia with regard to its 2008 invasion of Georgia (S/PV969, 28 August 2008, 7).

[188]   *Nicaragua v USA*, para 207.

era.[189] The most solid evidence of this is the consensus reaffirmation by the 2005 World Summit (a meeting held in New York City from 14 to 16 September 2005 as a follow-up to the 2000 UN Millennium Summit and which saw the participation of leaders from all UN member states) that, 'should peaceful means be inadequate and national authorities [be] manifestly failing to protect their populations from genocide, war crimes, ethnic cleansing and crimes against humanity', the international community would be prepared to take collective action only 'through the Security Council, in accordance with the Charter, including Chapter VII'.[190] As interpreted by states, therefore, the R2P doctrine confirms that massive human rights violations are no longer a domestic affair of states shielded by the principle of non-intervention, but does not challenge the existing regime on the use of force.[191]

The ICJ has also been sceptical about the permissibility of armed humanitarian intervention in international law. In *Nicaragua*, it found that 'the protection of human rights, a strictly humanitarian objective, cannot be compatible with the mining of ports, the destruction of oil installations, or again the training, arming and equipping of the *contras*'.[192] Even though the Court did not have the opportunity to pronounce on the merits of the cases brought by Yugoslavia against the NATO member states, it declared itself 'profoundly concerned with the use of force in Yugoslavia' and stated that 'under the present circumstances such use raises very serious issues of international law'.[193] In the recent Order on Provisional Measures in the *Allegations of Genocide* case, the ICJ reiterated that 'it is doubtful that the [Genocide] Convention, in light of its object and purpose, authorizes a Contracting Party's unilateral use of force in the territory of another State for the purpose of preventing or punishing an alleged genocide'.[194] The same can be said of Common Article 1 of the Geneva Conventions and Article 1(1) of Additional Protocol I, that is, the duty 'to ensure respect ... in all circumstances' for the obligations contained in those treaties: whatever the meaning of this provision, what is certain is that, as both the ICRC[195] and the ICJ[196] have pointed out, Common Article 1 does not introduce an exception to Article 2(4) of the UN Charter. This is further confirmed by Article 89 of Additional Protocol I, which cautions that, in the case of serious violations of the Conventions or the Protocol, 'the High Contracting Parties undertake to act jointly or individually, in co-operation with the United Nations and *in conformity with the United Nations Charter*'.[197] Article 3(2)

---

[189] The IIFFMCG also found that state practice and *opinio juris* do not support the claim in favour of the legality of humanitarian intervention without Security Council authorization, 'however morally desirable such a rule might be' (IIFFMCG Report, vol II, 284).

[190] GA Res 60/1, para 139.

[191] The UN Secretary-General's Report on Implementing the Responsibility to Protect confirms that 'the responsibility to protect does not alter, indeed it reinforces, the legal obligations of Member States to refrain from the use of force except in conformity with the Charter' (UN Doc A/63/677, 12 January 2009, para 3).

[192] *Nicaragua v USA*, para 268.

[193] *Legality of the Use of Force (Yugoslavia v France)* (Order on Provisional Measures) [1999] ICJ Rep 363, para 16.

[194] *Allegations of Genocide*, para 59. See also the declarations of intervention in the same proceedings made by Latvia (paras 50–4), Sweden (para 48), Romania (para 43), Poland (para 41), Finland (para 19), Australia (paras 52–3), Portugal (para 40), Norway (para 30), and Cyprus (para 29).

[195] 2016 ICRC Commentary on Common Art 1, para 174.

[196] *Palestinian Wall*, para 159.

[197] Emphasis added.

366 INTERNATIONAL LAW AND THE PRINCIPLE OF NON-INTERVENTION

of Additional Protocol II also warns that the Protocol cannot be used as a justification for any direct or indirect intervention 'in the armed conflict or in the internal or external affairs of the High Contracting Party in the territory of which that conflict occurs'.[198]

It is true that several treaties concluded among African states envisage the intervention of regional and sub-regional organizations in the case of gross human rights violations in a member state, which has led certain authors to claim the existence of a regional rule of customary international law allowing humanitarian intervention by African states in Africa without UN Security Council authorization in derogation of Article 53 of the UN Charter.[199] Under Article 4(h) of the 2002 AU Constitutive Act, in particular, one of the basic principles on which the African Union is founded is 'the right of the Union to intervene in a Member State pursuant to a decision of the Assembly in respect of grave circumstances, namely: war crimes, genocide and crimes against humanity'.[200] Collective humanitarian intervention is also envisaged in the 2000 Economic Community of Central African States (ECCAS) Pact of Mutual Assistance,[201] the 2019 ECCAS Protocol Relating to the Peace and Security Council of Central Africa (COPAX),[202] the 2001 Southern African Development Community (SADC) Protocol on Politics, Defence and Security Co-Operation,[203] the 1999 ECOWAS Protocol Relating to the Mechanism for Conflict Prevention, Management, Resolution, Peace-Keeping and Security,[204] and the 2008 ECOWAS Conflict Prevention Framework.[205] As Olivier Corten notes, however, the main

[198] Art 3(2), Protocol II.

[199] See eg Jeremy I Levitt, 'Pro-Democratic Intervention in Africa' (2006) 24 Wis Int'l LJ 785, 792.

[200] Art 4(h), Constitutive Act of the African Union (Lomé, 11 July 2000) 2158 UNTS 3. This right is reiterated in Art 4(j) of the Protocol Relating to the Establishment of the Peace and Security Council of the African Union (Durban, 9 July 2002), which establishes an implementing mechanism for the Assembly's decisions to intervene (text in <https://au.int/en/treaties/protocol-relating-establishment-peace-and-secur ity-council-african-union>). Art 3(d) of the 2005 AU Non-Aggression and Common Defence Pact also codifies the commitment of the states parties 'to prohibit and prevent genocide, other forms of mass murder as well as crimes against humanity'.

[201] Art 8(2) envisages the intervention of an interposition force 'en rapport avec les belligérants, l'ONU et l'OAU' in case the internal conflict results in the commission of international crimes (Mutual Assistance Pact between Member States of ECCAS (Malabo, 24 February 2000) <www.droitcongolais.info/files/ 0.42.02.00-Pacte-d-assistance-mutuelle-du-24-fevrier-2000-entre-les-Etat-membres-de-la-CEEAC.pdf>.

[202] Under Art 3, ECCAS has the right to intervene in a member state following a decision of COPAX in the case of war crimes, crimes against humanity, and genocide (Protocol Relating to the Peace and Security Council of Central Africa (COPAX) (Libreville, 18 December 2019) <www.labase-lextenso.fr/ sites/lextenso/files/lextenso_upload/protocole_du_copax.pdf>. The intervention is carried out by the Force Multinationale de l'Afrique Centrale (FOMAC) (Art 19(3)).

[203] Art 11(2)(b)(i) provides that the Organ can 'seek to resolve any significant intra-state conflict within the territory of a State Party', such as 'large-scale violence between sections of the population or between the state and sections of the population, including genocide, ethnic cleansing and gross violations of human rights' (SADC Protocol on Politics, Defence and Security Co-operation (Blantyre, 14 August 2001) <www. sadc.int/document/protocol-politics-defence-and-security-2001>).

[204] Under Art 25 of the Protocol, the Mechanism established therein can be triggered, inter alia, '[i]n case of internal conflict ... that threatens to trigger a humanitarian disaster' and '[i]n event of serious and massive violation of human rights and the rule of law' (ECOWAS Protocol Relating to the Mechanism for Conflict Prevention, Management, Resolution, Peace-Keeping and Security (Lomé, 10 December 1999) (2000) 5 JCSL 231).

[205] The Framework affirms that ECOWAS can intervene (militarily if necessary) to protect human security and to exercise the responsibility to prevent, react 'in response to grave and compelling humanitarian disasters', and rebuild (The ECOWAS Conflict Prevention Framework, paras 26, 41).

purpose of these provisions is not to claim rights under customary international law, but to grant an organization the competence to act *under its own internal law.*[206] The treaties in question can also be read as granting forward-looking consent to the intervention of a regional organization in case any of the listed grave circumstances occur in a member state.[207]

Finally, it is important to emphasize that even those states that couched their armed interventions in humanitarian language often stressed that they did not intend to influence the outcome of the internal struggle for power. The British and American governments, for instance, declared that Operation Provide Comfort had an exclusively humanitarian purpose and did not aim to support the Kurds against the Iraqi government or to prejudice the territorial integrity of Iraq.[208] According to the Dutch government, during the conduct of a humanitarian intervention '[t]he implications for the political system of the country in question should be limited to what is necessary in order to achieve the objective of the intervention'.[209] Similar words are contained in the Danish Military Manual.[210] The 2013 UK document published in relation to the chemical attacks in Syria points out that the use of force to avert an overwhelming humanitarian catastrophe 'must be necessary and proportionate to the aim of relief of humanitarian need and must be strictly limited in time and scope to this aim (i.e. the minimum necessary to achieve that end and for no other purpose)'.[211] When airstrikes against governmental targets in Syria in response to the chemical attack in Eastern Ghouta were carried out in April 2018, British Prime Minister Theresa May thus stressed that they were 'not about intervening in a civil war. It is not about regime change'.[212] Even if—and it is a monumental 'if'—armed force was allowed in response to gross IHRL and/or IHL violations committed by a foreign government, therefore, the intervention would have to be restricted to the protection of the community

---

[206] Corten, *The Law*, 346.

[207] Ademola Abass and Mashood A Baderin, 'Towards Effective Collective Security and Human Rights Protection in Africa: An Assessment of the Constitutive Act of the New African Union' (2002) 49 NILR 1, 18–19. See also Chapter IV, Section 4.3 of this book. The 2006 Protocol on Non-Aggression and Mutual Defence in the Great Lakes Region differs from other regional security treaties on two grounds. First, it attributes the responsibility to protect populations from genocide, war crimes, ethnic cleansing, crimes against humanity, and gross violations of human rights not to a regional organization but to the states parties after a decision 'taken collectively, with due procedural notice to the Peace and Security Council of the African Union and the Security Council of the United Nations' (Art 4(8)). Secondly, the responsibility to protect is invoked with regard to violations committed by, or within, 'a State', not necessarily a state party. By doing so, the Great Lakes states appear to claim a responsibility to intervene on the territory of any state even without its consent. Art 10(3), however, cautions that '[n]othing contained in this Protocol shall be construed to be contrary to the provisions of the Pact, the Constitutive Act of the African Union, and the Charter of the United Nations': the only way to construe the Protocol consistently with the UN Charter and with the AU Constitutive Act is to interpret the reference to 'a State' as to 'a Member State', that is, as providing for a case of intervention by invitation. On the Great Lakes Protocol, see Marco Roscini, 'Neighbourhood Watch? The African Great Lakes Pact and *Ius ad Bellum*' (2009) 69 ZaöRV 931.

[208] Grado, *Guerre civili*, 311.

[209] Tange, 'Netherlands State Practice', 291.

[210] Danish Ministry of Defence, Military Manual, 40.

[211] Prime Minister's Office, Chemical Weapon Use by the Syrian Regime, para 4(iii).

[212] Prime Minister's Office, 'PM Statement on Syria: 14 April 2018' <www.gov.uk/government/news/pm-statement-on-syria-14-april-2018>.

interest, namely, the cessation of the violations, and not extend to the merits of the internal struggle.[213]

To conclude, armed coercion to ensure respect for IHRL and/or IHL by a foreign government does not fall under the prohibitive scope of the principle of non-intervention as it does not bear 'on matters in which each State is permitted, by the principle of State sovereignty, to decide freely'.[214] It is however still subject to the prohibition codified in Article 2(4) of the UN Charter: states, therefore, cannot use armed force to avert a humanitarian crisis in another country without its government's valid consent and/or Security Council authorization. Even in that case, third-state armed coercion in the context of a civil war must comply with the principle of internal self-determination: it must thus be limited to stopping the violations in question and not be aimed at influencing the outcome of the conflict.

7.2 Intervention Other than by Sending Armed Forces

Can third states take measures other than sending armed forces in support of opposition groups against a government responsible for violations of IHRL and/or IHL? At the beginning of the Syrian Civil War, the Arab League Summit's Doha Declaration stressed 'the right of each member state, in accordance with its wish, to provide all means of self-defense, including military support to back the steadfastness of the Syrian people and the free army'.[215] At the end of May 2013, the EU arms embargo was also lifted in favour of the Syrian opposition under pressure from France and the United Kingdom.[216] While the European Union did not provide an explicit legal justification for the decision, the Dutch foreign affairs minister claimed that, because of the lack of legitimacy of the Assad government and the broad recognition of the Syrian Opposition Council as the legitimate representative of the Syrian people, the supply of military equipment to the latter, 'in exceptional cases and under strict conditions', would not be contrary to international law.[217]

In the *Nicaragua* case, however, the ICJ found that the arming, training, and equipping of the Contras by the United States were incompatible with the objective of protecting

---

[213] Tancredi, *La secessione*, 677. For Michael Reisman, '[h]umanitarian intervention is a short-term initiative, aimed only at stopping massive and ongoing human rights violations. Once the violations cease, it is no longer justified. In contrast, those responsible for a regime change may try to justify it by invoking past human rights violations, but it is, in fact, future-oriented—it is conducted to change the structure and/or personnel of a government' (W Michael Reisman, 'Why a Regime Change is (Almost Always) a Bad Idea' (2004) 98 AJIL 516, 517).

[214] *Nicaragua v USA*, para 205.

[215] Arab League 24th Summit, Doha Declaration, 26 March 2013 <http://arableaguesummit2013.qatar conferences.org/news/news-details-17.html>.

[216] EU Foreign Affairs Council, Council Declaration on Syria, 27 May 2013 <www.consilium.europa.eu/uedocs/cms_data/docs/pressdata/EN/foraff/137315.pdf>.

[217] Letter dated 4 June 2013, translated and quoted in Tom Ruys, 'The Quest for an Internal *Jus Ad Bellum*: International Law's Missing Link, Mere Distraction, or Pandora's Box?' in Claus Kreß and Robert Lawless (eds), *Necessity and Proportionality in International Peace and Security Law* (OUP 2020) 169, 213 (fn 217). Syria sent several letters to the Security Council protesting against the supply of arms and military equipment to the opposition groups (see eg UN Doc S/2013/533, 6 September 2013; S/2013/766, 27 December 2013).

human rights in the Central American country.[218] For the Court, in particular, arming insurgents can be regarded as a threat or use of force and is therefore submitted to the same prohibitive regime.[219] Indeed, while states have admitted the provision of humanitarian aid in Syria, only a few have explicitly acknowledged the supply of military assistance to the opposition and its counterterrorism purpose has been frequently stressed.[220] Some states have also criticized the arms transfers to the anti-Assad insurgents: Austria, for instance, claimed that it was a breach of the principle of non-intervention and of the prohibition of the use of force, regardless of whether the Damascus authorities had committed international crimes.[221] In the earlier Kosovo crisis, the Swiss Department of Foreign Affairs pointed out that arming foreign insurgents cannot be justified with the protection of human rights because reactions to the violation of *erga omnes* obligations must be peaceful ones.[222] All in all, there is no sufficient 'general practice accepted as law' that justifies a departure from the prohibition contained in Article 2(4) of the UN Charter, not even when the use of force consists in the supply of arms.

A different argument can be made with regard to non-forcible measures, including the supply of funds[223] and non-lethal military equipment to the insurgents[224] as well as their premature recognition as belligerents, government, or 'legitimate representatives' of their people.[225] When adopted in response to the IHRL and/or IHL violations committed by a government, these forms of support for opposition groups are beyond

---

[218] *Nicaragua v USA*, para 268.

[219] ibid, paras 195, 247.

[220] Luca Ferro and Nele Verlinden, 'Neutrality during Armed Conflicts: A Coherent Approach to Third-State Support for Warring Parties' (2018) 17 CJIL 15, 26.

[221] Markus P Beham and Gerhard Hafner, 'Austrian Diplomatic and Parliamentary Practice in International Law: Part II' (2013) ARIEL 313, 373–7.

[222] Legal Opinion of the International Law Department, 671.

[223] EU Council Decision 2013/255/CFSP, for instance, provided that '[w]ith a view to helping the Syrian civilian population, in particular to meeting humanitarian concerns, restoring normal life, upholding basic services, reconstruction, and restoring normal economic activity or other civilian purposes ... the competent authorities of a Member State may authorise the purchase, import or transport from Syria of crude oil and petroleum products' in consultation with the Syrian National Coalition for Opposition and Revolutionary Forces (Art 6, EU Council Decision 2013/255/CFSP of 31 May 2013 concerning restrictive measures against Syria [2013] OJ L 147/14).

[224] Unlike the transfer of weapons, that of non-lethal military equipment has frequently not been supplied covertly and has not met with widespread condemnations, which might suggest a different *opinio juris* in regard to this lesser form of military assistance. In the First Libyan Civil War, for instance, the United Kingdom pointed out that it was not engaged in arming the opposition forces but only in supplying non-lethal equipment to help with the protection of civilian lives and the delivery of humanitarian aid (Jacques Hartmann, Sangeeta Shah, and Colin Warbrick, 'United Kingdom Materials on International Law 2011' (2012) 82 BYBIL 676, 746). The EU's comprehensive embargo on 'arms and related matériel of all types' against Syria also excluded the supply of non-lethal equipment, non-combat vehicles, and technical assistance for the Syrian National Coalition for Opposition and Revolutionary Forces intended for the protection of civilians (Art 1, EU Council Decision 2013/109/CFSP, 28 February 2013 Amending Decision 2012/739/CFSP concerning restrictive measures against Syria [2013] OJ L 58/8). On the provision of non-lethal military equipment to insurgents, see Chapter III, Section 8.1.

[225] During the First Libyan Civil War, for instance, the opposition was recognized by several states as the new government of the North African country while Ghaddafi's forces were still in control of Tripoli. The United States, in particular, recognized the National Transitional Council as 'the legitimate governing authority in Libya' (John R Crook, 'Contemporary Practice of the United States Relating to International Law' (2011) 105 AJIL 775, 780), the United Kingdom as 'the sole governmental authority in Libya' (Katie A Johnston, 'Transformation of Conflict Status in Libya' (2012) 17 JCSL 81, 109), and France as 'the sole repository of governmental authority' (Consulate General of France in Calcutta, 'Libya/National Transitional Council—Statement by Alain Juppé, Minister of Foreign and European Affairs', 7 June 2011 <https://in.amb

370 INTERNATIONAL LAW AND THE PRINCIPLE OF NON-INTERVENTION

the reach of the principle of non-intervention even when they constitute coercion as they do not bear on a matter in which the target state can decide freely, and thus are lawful measures to secure compliance with international law.[226] Should they conflict with other international law obligations, they could constitute countermeasures adopted in response to the previous violation of an *erga omnes* or *erga omnes partes* obligation (to the extent that they meet their substantive and procedural requirements).

8. Intervention in Civil Wars with the Authorization of the UN Security Council in Response to IHRL/IHL Violations

Since the end of the Cold War, the Security Council has been involved on a regular basis in humanitarian crises triggered by civil wars. The Council, in particular, has frequently condemned violations of IHRL and/or IHL as a threat to the peace and has authorized member states to intervene under Chapter VII of the Charter.[227] While the Security Council is not bound by the principle of non-intervention when it uses Chapter VII powers,[228] it still has to comply with the principle of internal self-determination, which prohibits armed intervention aimed at influencing the outcome of a civil war.[229]

It is not surprising, therefore, that the Council 'has shown no disposition to truly take sides in an internal conflict on human rights grounds' and has often emphasized the impartial character of the authorized humanitarian interventions in the context of civil wars.[230] In Operation Restore Hope in Somalia (1992–3), for instance, the only

---

afrance.org/Libya-National-Transitional>). NATO (NATO, 'Statement on Libya', 14 April 2011 <www.nato.int/cps/en/natolive/official_texts_72544.htm>), the Arab League (UN Doc S/2011/137, 15 March 2011, 2), Germany (S/PV.6498, 17 March 2011, 4), and Colombia (S/PV.6498, 7) affirmed that Ghaddafi had lost his legitimacy because of the use of violence against the population but, at least initially, they did not deny his status as the government of Libya. The AU invited the insurgents to occupy the Libyan seat in the Organization only on 20 October 2011 after the United Nations did the same, and emphasized 'the uniqueness of the situation in Libya and the exceptional circumstances surrounding it' (Communique of the 297th meeting of the Peace and Security Council, PSC/PR/COMM/2.(CCXCVII), 20 October 2011, para 4). On the other hand, as the United States and the Netherlands made clear (CarrieLyn D Guymon (ed), *Digest of United States Practice in International Law 2012* (GPO 2013) 281; Tom Ruys and Luca Ferro, 'The Enemy of My Enemy: Dutch Non-Lethal Assistance for "Moderate" Syrian Rebels and the Multilevel Violation of International Law' (2019) 50 NYBIL 333, 363), the Syrian Opposition Coalition (SOC) was recognized by certain states and international organizations as the legitimate representative of the Syrian people, but not as a governmental authority (Stefan Talmon, 'Recognition of Opposition Groups as the Legitimate Representative of a People' (2013) 12 CJIL 219, 221–6). Premature recognitions can be a form of political intervention but do not transfer governmental status, which remains with the incumbent authorities until their attempts to regain control of the country have become virtually hopeless. Even if the opposition had been prematurely recognized as the new government, therefore, third states would still be unable to support it by military means upon its request (Talmon, 'Recognition', 237, 243–4; Olivier Corten and Vaios Koutroulis, 'The Illegality' 65–6; Alessandra Annoni, *Il riconoscimento come atto unilaterale dello Stato* (Jovene 2023) 176).

[226] Art 4, Santiago de Compostela Resolution.
[227] On this practice, see Roscini, 'The United Nations', 332–7.
[228] See Art 2(7), UN Charter.
[229] See Chapter V, Section 6.
[230] David Wippman, 'Change and Continuity in Legal Justifications for Military Intervention in Internal Conflict' (1996) 27 Colum Hum Rts L Rev 435, 473.

NON-INTERVENTION AND RESPECT FOR IHRL AND IHL   371

purpose of the authorization to member states to use 'all necessary means' contained in Resolution 794 (1992) was 'to establish as soon as possible a secure environment for humanitarian relief operations in Somalia'.[231] The Preamble of the resolution paid lip service to the principle of internal self-determination by recalling that 'the people of Somalia bear the ultimate responsibility for national reconciliation and the reconstruction of their own country'.[232] Security Council Resolutions 816 (1993) and 836 (1993) authorized member states to take all necessary measures to enforce the no-fly zones in Bosnia[233] and to support the United Nations Protection Force (UNPROFOR) in performing its mandate to protect the safe areas in Bosnia.[234] NATO pointed out that 'the air strikes foreseen by the Council decision of August 2 are limited to the support of humanitarian relief, and must not be interpreted as a decision to intervene militarily in the conflict'.[235] Resolution 929 (1994) stressed 'the strictly humanitarian character of [Operation Turquoise in Rwanda] which shall be conducted in an impartial and neutral fashion, and shall not constitute an interposition force between the parties'.[236] Resolution 2304 (2016) also decided that the 4,000-member Regional Protection Force to be included in the United Nations Mission in the Republic of South Sudan (UNMISS) 'with the responsibility of providing a secure environment in and around Juba ... and in extremis in other parts of South Sudan as necessary' would carry out its protection mandate impartially.[237]

The risk that states interpret Security Council authorizations broadly, however, is high.[238] During the constitutional crisis in Côte d'Ivoire that led to heavy fighting between the forces of President Laurent Gbagbo and President-elect Alassane Ouattara, for instance, France intervened on the basis of Resolution 1975 (2011) and the request of the Secretary-General in order to protect civilians and repeatedly affirmed that it would not take sides.[239] French and UN Operation in Côte d'Ivoire (UNOCI) forces eventually attacked Gbagbo's stronghold and caused the surrender of his forces and the eventual instalment of Ouattara.[240] Several states criticized the intervention as exceeding the authorization granted in Resolution 1975.[241] The Security Council

---

[231] SC Res 794, para 10. The US representative at the Security Council noted that '[t]he measures authorized by the resolution and supported by my Government have one objective: to achieve a secure environment for the delivery of humanitarian relief to the Somali people in the areas of greatest need' and that '[m]ilitary intervention is no substitute for political reconciliation, and that task belongs firmly in the hands of Somalis' (UN Doc S/PV.3145, 3 December 1992, 36–7).

[232] SC Res 794, Preamble.

[233] SC Res 816, 31 March 1993, para 4; SC Res 836, 4 June 1993, para 10.

[234] SC Res 836, para 10.

[235] NATO Press Statement, 2 August 1993, reproduced in Joyce P Kaufman, NATO and the Former Yugoslavia: Crisis, Conflict, and the Atlantic Alliance (Rowman & Littlefield 2002) 104.

[236] SC Res 929, 22 June 1994, Preamble. France, which led the operation, emphasized that its mandate 'naturally exclude[d] any interference in the development of the balance of military forces between the parties involved in the conflict' (UN Doc S/1994/734, 21 June 1994, 1).

[237] SC Res 2304, para 8. See also SC Res 2327, 16 December 2016, para 7.

[238] Grado, Guerre civili, 344.

[239] SC Res 1975, para 6.

[240] Antonios Tzanakopoulos, 'The UN/French Use of Force in Abidjan: Uncertainties Regarding the Scope of UN Authorizations' (EJIL:Talk!, 9 April 2011) <www.ejiltalk.org/the-un-use-of-force-in-abidjan/>.

[241] Olivier Corten and Agatha Verdebout, 'Les interventions militaires récentes en territoire étranger: Vers une remise en cause du jus contra bellum?' (2014) 60 AFDI 135, 161.

372 INTERNATIONAL LAW AND THE PRINCIPLE OF NON-INTERVENTION

welcomed Ouattara's acquisition of power but did not comment on the interven-tion.[242] Another controversial case is NATO's intervention in the Libyan Civil War in 2011. Resolution 1973 (2011) authorized member states to use 'all necessary measures' exclusively 'to protect civilians and civilian populated areas under threat of attack'.[243] It is doubtful, therefore, that the authorization constituted carte blanche for the subse-quent airstrikes against governmental forces and installations which did not represent a direct threat to civilians and for the supply of arms to the opposition forces. Indeed, the airstrikes would have been justified only if, and to the extent that, they had been strictly functional to the protection of civilians under threat of attack, and the arms transfers only if such arms had been used by the insurgents to protect civilians and not to conduct hostilities against the governmental forces.[244] In their Joint Statement of 14 April 2011, US President Obama, UK Prime Minister David Cameron, and France's President Nicolas Sarkozy did emphasize that their 'duty and mandate under U.N. Security Council Resolution 1973 [was] to protect civilians ... It [was] not to re-move Qaddafi by force'.[245] In the end, however, NATO's intervention in Libya turned into military support for the insurgents and facilitated regime change: as several states noted, therefore, it exceeded the authorization contained in Resolution 1973.[246]

9. Conclusions

In a significant departure from the pre-Charter era, states can now no longer claim that the protection of human rights is an exclusively domestic matter. The use of coercion to ensure respect for them both in time of peace and in armed conflict, therefore, is not prohibited by the principle of non-intervention although it might be proscribed by other primary rules of international law. Coercion can be exercised on a government responsible for IHRL and/or IHL violations in two ways: by refusing, suspending,

---

[242] SC Res 1980, 28 April 2011.
[243] SC Res 1973, para 4. The limited scope of the authorization was stressed by, among others, South Africa (UN Doc S/PV.6566, 27 June 2011, 4), Russia (S/PV.6528, 4 May 2011, 9), China (ibid, 10), Cuba (S/PV.6531, 10 May 2011, 28), and Nicaragua (ibid, 34).
[244] Christian Henderson, 'The Provision of Arms and "Non-Lethal" Assistance to Government and Opposition Forces' (2013) 36 UNSWLJ 642, 658.
[245] Barack Obama, David Cameron, and Nicolas Sarkozy, 'Libya's Pathway to Peace' (*The New York Times*, 14 April 2011) <www.nytimes.com/2011/04/15/opinion/15iht-edlibya15.html>. They also cautioned, how-ever, that 'it is impossible to imagine a future for Libya with Qaddafi in power' (ibid).
[246] Ugo Villani, 'Aspetti problematici dell'intervento militare nella crisi libica' (2011) 5 DUDI 369, 371; Corten and Koutroulis, 'The Illegality', 74–7; Yoram Dinstein, *Non-International Armed Conflicts in International Law* (2nd edn, CUP 2021) 122.

and terminating assistance in its favour, or by supporting opposition groups. As to the former, states can always decline a request for assistance or suspend/terminate existing voluntary cooperation with a foreign government that commits the violations in question but, differently from the case of a colonial or occupying power, have an obligation to do so only if it is required by treaties or Security Council decisions. If an obligation to support the foreign authorities facing internal unrest arises from a treaty and in the absence of a sanction regime decided by the UN Security Council, compliance with such treaty can be suspended and/or terminated even when the grounds codified in the VCLT cannot be invoked: the suspension or termination can constitute a countermeasure adopted in reaction to the breach of an *erga omnes* or *erga omnes partes* obligation, providing that the necessary substantive and procedural requirements are met.

Coercion can also be exercised on a state by supporting opposition groups. Non-military forms of support adopted in response to the IHRL and/or IHL violations committed by the incumbent government are beyond the reach of the principle of non-intervention as they do not bear on a matter in which the target state can decide freely: they are, therefore, lawful measures to secure compliance with international law by the target state. Should they conflict with other international law obligations, they can constitute countermeasures adopted in response to the previous violation of an *erga omnes* or *erga omnes partes* obligation (to the extent that they meet their substantive and procedural requirements). Third states, however, are not permitted to send armed forces or transfer arms to insurgents who are fighting a murderous government, as humanitarian intervention does not constitute an accepted exception to the prohibition of the use of force codified in Article 2(4) of the UN Charter. Such intervention could only lawfully take place with the authorization of the Security Council under Chapter VII of the Charter and consistently with the principle of internal self-determination.

Finally, the fact that an opposition group commits IHL violations does not displace the application of the principle of internal self-determination in civil war. Differently from when it is conducted against terrorist organizations, therefore, third-state armed intervention in this scenario requires not only the consent of the state where the intervention takes place but must also be limited to end the violations in question and to protect civilians, and not be aimed at keeping the incumbent authorities in power.

VIII

The Principle of Non-Intervention in the Information Age: Cyber Operations as a New Means of Coercion in the Domestic Affairs of States

1. Introduction

The Digital Revolution, characterized by the shift from mechanical and analogue electronic technology to digital electronics, started in the second half of the 20th century with the introduction of computers and digital record-keeping but revolutionized most aspects of social life only with the creation of the World Wide Web in 1989. The Digital Revolution has marked the beginning of the Information Age, an era of human civilization defined by access to and control of information.

Among the many consequences of the Digital Revolution is the emergence of a new form of intervention: if computer networks become a society's 'nerve system', incapacitating them may mean paralyzing an entire country. Indeed, the more digitally reliant a state is, the more vulnerable it is to attacks conducted in and through cyberspace.[1] Geographical distance and frontiers are also irrelevant in cyberspace as a target could be hit on the other side of the world in a matter of seconds. To make matters worse, cyber technologies and expertise are relatively easy and cheap to acquire, which allows weaker states and even non-state actors to potentially cause considerable harm to countries with superior conventional military power: although extreme scenarios have not occurred yet, a cyber operation could disable power generators, cut off the military command, control and communication systems, cause trains to derail and airplanes to crash, nuclear reactors to melt down, pipelines to explode, weapons to malfunction, and banking systems to become unavailable. Cyber operations can also be launched to influence public opinion in a foreign country, particularly on the eve of elections and referendums.

It is then hardly surprising that cyber threats have become a major concern of the international community. While the UN Security Council arrived late to the party and held its first-ever open debate on maintaining international peace and security in cyberspace only in June 2021, the General Assembly has adopted a series of annual

---

[1] Cyberspace is '[t]he environment formed by physical and non-physical components to store, modify, and exchange data using computer networks' (Michael N Schmitt (ed), *Tallinn Manual 2.0 on the International Law Applicable to Cyber Operations* (2nd edn, CUP 2017) 564). Technically, cyberspace consists of a physical layer (the hardware used for the transmission of data), a logical layer (the data and software), and a social layer (the human beings who engage in cyber activities): ibid, 12.

International Law and the Principle of Non-Intervention. Marco Roscini, Oxford University Press. © Marco Roscini 2024.
DOI: 10.1093/oso/9780198786894.003.0009

resolutions on information and telecommunications in the context of international security since its 1998–9 session.[2] The Assembly has also established Groups of Governmental Experts (GGE) to examine the impact of developments in information and communication technologies (ICT)[3] and, in December 2018, set up an Open-Ended Working Group (OEWG) tasked with developing rules, norms, and principles of responsible behaviour of states in cyberspace, discussing ways for their implementation, and exploring avenues of institutional dialogue. Unlike the GGE, the OEWG is open to the participation of all UN member states as well as other stakeholders.[4]

No treaty, however, has been adopted so far to specifically regulate cyber operations attributable to states.[5] That said, the lack of ad hoc rules does not mean that cyber operations can be conducted by states in or against other states without restrictions: international obligations that are technology neutral can be presumed to apply in cyberspace unless the contrary is demonstrated.[6] As the International Court of Justice (ICJ) has noted, in particular,

> where parties have used generic terms in a treaty, the parties necessarily having been aware that the meaning of the terms was likely to evolve over time, and where the treaty has been entered into for a very long period or is 'of continuing duration', the parties must be presumed, as a general rule, to have intended those terms to have an evolving meaning.[7]

In recent years, a growing number of states have also expressed their views on a range of issues related to the application of international law in cyberspace: these statements constitute not only verbal practice but also important evidence of *opinio juris*, which can contribute to the formation of customary international law specifically addressing cyber operations conducted by states.[8] True, these position papers and statements still come from a relatively limited number of states, but this is not an insurmountable

---

[2] The first resolution is GA Res 53/70 of 4 January 1999.

[3] Six GGEs have been convened so far. While the first Group, established in 2004, did not produce a substantial report, the second, created in 2009, issued a report in 2010 (UN Doc A/65/201, 30 July 2010). A third and fourth Group met in 2012–13 and 2014–15, respectively, and also adopted final reports containing a set of recommendations (A/68/98, 24 June 2013; A/70/174, 22 July 2015). The 2016–17 Group, which was, inter alia, tasked with studying 'how international law applies to the use of information and communications technologies by states' (GA Res 70/237, 23 December 2015, para 5), reached no consensus on a final report. The last GGE adopted a final report in 2021 (A/76/135, 14 July 2021). More details at <https://disarmament.unoda.org/group-of-governmental-experts>.

[4] GA Res 73/27, 5 December 2018, para 5. In March 2021, the OEWG 2019/2020 adopted its final report (UN Doc A/AC.290/2021/CRP.2, 10 March 2021). In December 2020, the OEWG was renewed for 2021–5. More information at <https://disarmament.unoda.org/open-ended-working-group>.

[5] The Convention on Cybercrime (Budapest, 23 November 2001) 2296 UNTS 167 (Budapest Convention), in particular, does not apply to 'conduct undertaken pursuant to lawful governmental authority' (Council of Europe, Explanatory Report to the Convention on Cybercrime, 23 November 2001, para 38 <https://rm.coe.int/16800cce5b>).

[6] Kubo Mačák, 'Unblurring the Lines: Military Cyber Operations and International Law' (2021) 6 Journal of Cyber Policy 411, 416.

[7] *Dispute Regarding Navigational and Related Rights (Costa Rica v Nicaragua)* (Judgment) [2009] ICJ Rep 213, para 66.

[8] The Cyber Law Toolkit is a regularly updated database that contains, among other things, details on cyber incidents and the national positions on international law in cyberspace: <https://cyberlaw.ccdcoe.org/wiki/Main_Page>.

376 INTERNATIONAL LAW AND THE PRINCIPLE OF NON-INTERVENTION

obstacle to the sedimentation of customary rules: as the International Law Association (ILA) points out, the extensive character of state practice and *opinio juris* is more a qualitative than a quantitative criterion and 'if all major interests ("specially affected States") are represented, it is not essential for a majority of States to have participated (still less a great majority, or all of them)'.[9] While all states have an obvious interest in cyber security, the most digitized ones arguably are those 'specially affected' because they are at the same time the most likely to conduct offensive cyber operations and the most vulnerable to them.

It is starting from these premises that the present chapter examines whether and how the principle of non-intervention applies in cyberspace. It starts by identifying the various types of cyber operations and then discusses which of them can constitute a violation of the principle of non-intervention. To do this, the chapter explores what constitutes domestic jurisdiction and coercion of state in the cyber context. The different effects of cyber operations are then analysed in order to establish when they are coercive. The chapter concludes by addressing the legality of cyber operations in support of an incumbent government and of armed opposition groups in situations of internal unrest. A caveat: to properly understand the arguments developed in the following pages, this chapter should be read together with Chapter III on the content of the principle of non-intervention.

2. The Different Types of Cyber Operations

In spite of the multiplicity of terms employed in the different documents, state operations conducted in or through cyberspace can be distinguished into two main types: cyber exploitation and offensive or defensive cyber attacks. Cyber *exploitation* refers to those operations that access computers, computer systems, or networks without the authorization of their owners in order to exfiltrate information, but without affecting the functionality of the accessed system or amending/deleting the data resident therein.[10] A cyber *attack*, on the other hand, is a cyber operation designed to alter, delete, corrupt, or deny access to computer data or software in order to 1) influence or deceive; 2) disrupt the functioning of the targeted computer, computer system or network, and the physical infrastructure they operate (if any); and/or 3) cause material damage to persons or objects.[11]

Cyber attacks can thus go from relatively innocuous psychological operations, such as website defacement, to acts that cause havoc in electoral campaigns by generating disinformation, or acts resulting in major disruption of services and loss of property and lives. In order to achieve these results, they can target either information systems or infrastructure control systems.[12] The former contain information but do not

---

[9] ILA, Final Report of the Committee on the Formation of Customary (General) International Law, Statement of Principles Applicable to the Formation of General Customary International Law, Report of the Sixty-Ninth Conference (London 2000) 737 <www.ila-hq.org/en_GB/documents/conference-report-london-2000-2>.

[10] Marco Roscini, *Cyber Operations and the Use of Force in International Law* (OUP 2014), 16–17.

[11] ibid, 18.

[12] John Ricou Heaton, 'Civilians at War: Reexamining the Status of Civilians Accompanying the Armed Forces' (2005) 57 AF L Rev 155, 161.

operate physical infrastructures, hence an attack on them causes loss or corruption of data but does not directly result in malfunction of infrastructures or material damage. The latter, of which a common type is Supervisory Control and Data Acquisition (SCADA) systems, operate infrastructures: if corrupted, the consequence will be loss of functionality or even material damage to property or persons.[13] Denial of service (DoS) attacks are different as they do not normally penetrate into a system but aim to inundate the target with excessive calls, messages, enquiries, or requests in order to overload it and force its shut down. When the DoS attack is carried out by a large number of computers organized in botnets, it is referred to as a 'distributed denial of service' (DDoS) attack.[14]

Another important distinction is that between cybercrime and state cyber operations (often inaccurately referred to as 'cyber warfare'). If 'cybercrime', that is, offences against the confidentiality, integrity, and availability of computer data and systems committed by individuals or private entities for personal gain,[15] is primarily a domestic law matter,[16] cyber operations conducted by states in or against other states (be they cyber attacks or cyber exploitation operations) fall under the remit of international law. The applicable legal paradigm, then, depends first and foremost on whether or not the operation is attributable to a subject of international law. It is however notoriously difficult to establish the identity of the author of a cyber operation with sufficient certainty, which significantly complicates the legal process of attributing it to a state under the rules codified in Part One, Chapter II of the International Law Commission's Articles on the Responsibility of States for Internationally Wrongful Acts (ARSIWA). As it is beyond the bounds of this work to discuss the technical, political, and legal complexities of the attribution of cyber operations,[17] the following analysis assumes that the responsibility of a state has been established.

3. The Application of the Principle of Non-Intervention in Cyberspace

There is now broad consensus that sovereignty and the rules flowing from it extend to cyberspace.[18] Indeed, if, in the agricultural age, sovereignty essentially had a

---

[13] ibid. For security reasons, SCADAs are normally 'air gapped' from the internet and the attack can only be delivered from within the closed network or through local installation of malware by agents that have close access to the system.

[14] 'Botnets' (short for 'robot networks'), which are the source of most spam, are networks of infected computers hijacked from their unaware owners by external users: linked together, such networks can be used to mount massive DDoS attacks.

[15] The language is borrowed from Chapter II, Section 1, Title 1 of the Budapest Convention.

[16] States, however, can conclude agreements on judicial cooperation with regard to cybercrime, as in the case of the Budapest Convention.

[17] On this problem, see Marco Roscini, 'Evidentiary Issues in International Disputes Related to State Responsibility for Cyber Operations' (2015) 50 Tex Intl LJ 233.

[18] See Report of the Group of Governmental Experts on Developments in the Field of Information and Telecommunications in the Context of International Security, UN Doc A/68/98, para 20 (UN GGE Report 2013); Report of the Group of Governmental Experts on Developments in the Field of Information and Telecommunications in the Context of International Security, A/70/174, para 27 (UN GGE Report 2015); Report of the Group of Governmental Experts on Advancing Responsible State Behaviour in Cyberspace in the Context of International Security, A/76/135, para 71(b) (UN GGE Report 2021). States have exercised

land-based connotation which later extended, in the mercantile era, to the seas and eventually to airspace, the Digital Revolution has led to new declinations of sovereignty, including 'information sovereignty', 'technological sovereignty', 'data sovereignty', and 'digital sovereignty'.[19] These expressions still do not have generally agreed definitions and are often used interchangeably to refer to a state's exclusive legislative, administrative, and judicial jurisdiction over the cyber infrastructure, actors, or data located on its physical territory or in a platform that enjoys sovereign immunity.[20]

From a textual perspective, the formulation of the principle of non-intervention contained in the Charter of the Organization of American States (OAS), in General Assembly Resolutions 2131 and 2625, and in the Helsinki Final Act is broad enough to allow its application in cyberspace by means of evolutionary interpretation. Article 19 of the OAS Charter, in particular, stresses that the principle 'prohibits not only armed force but also *any other form* of interference or attempted threat against the personality of the State or against its political, economic, and cultural elements'.[21] The relevant paragraphs of General Assembly Resolutions 2131 and 2625 also condemn '*any ... type* of measures to coerce another State in order to obtain from it the subordination of the exercise of its sovereign rights or to secure from it advantages of any kind'.[22] Similarly, Principle VI of the Helsinki Final Act requires the participating

---

sovereignty over the different layers of cyberspace in different ways. China, for instance, has asserted control over 'its' cyberspace by means of the 'Great Firewall', which filters data traffic from abroad, while Russia and Iran aim to physically separate their networks from the World Wide Web (Henning Lahmann, 'On the Politics and Ideologies of the Sovereignty Discourse in Cyberspace' (2021) 32 Duke J Comp & Intl L 61, 80–2).

[19] 'Information sovereignty' refers to the 'information content produced and disseminated by using information and communication technologies and network', while 'technological sovereignty' is aimed at strengthening 'capabilities in developing home-grown technologies in key areas' (World Internet Conference, *Sovereignty in Cyberspace: Theory and Practice* (Version 3.0), 28 September 2021 <www.wici nternet.org/2021-09/28/c_815431.htm>). Data sovereignty appears to indicate that 'a State (or an international organization) can exercise full control over the data it processes (which are not in the public domain), to the exclusion of any (other entity)', whereas digital sovereignty refers to 'a broader form of "sovereign" control that covers not just data but also the hardware and software supply chains ... as well as network infrastructure (cables, routers and switches) and the communications supply chain' (Massimo Marelli, 'The SolarWinds Hack: Lessons for International Humanitarian Organizations' (2022) 104 IRRC 1267, 1273–4).

[20] The UN GGE has pointed out that '[s]tates have jurisdiction over the ICT infrastructure located within their territory' (UN GGE Report 2015, para 28(a)). Germany has also stressed that 'a State retains a right of regulation, enforcement and adjudication (jurisdiction) with regard to both persons engaging in cyber activities and cyber infrastructure on its territory' (UN Doc A/76/136, 13 July 2021, 32).

[21] Charter of the Organization of American States (Bogotá, 30 April 1948) 119 UNTS 3, emphasis added.

[22] GA Res 2131 (XX), 21 December 1965, paras 1 and 2; GA Res 2625 (XXV), 24 October 1970, Annex, third principle, paras 1 and 2, emphasis added. The applicability of the customary rules on non-intervention contained in GA Res 2625 to ICTs has been explicitly affirmed by Brazil (UN Doc A/76/136, 18–19). The 1976 Declaration on Non-interference in the Internal Affairs of States can also cover cyber operations where it condemns 'all forms of overt, subtle and highly sophisticated techniques of coercion, subversion and defamation aimed at disrupting the political, social or economic order of other States or destabilizing the Governments seeking to free their economies from external control or manipulation' (GA Res 31/91, 14 December 1976, para 4). The 1981 Declaration on the Inadmissibility of Intervention and Interference in the Internal Affairs of States recalls '[t]he right of States and peoples to have free access to information and to develop fully, without interference, their system of information and mass media and to use their information media in order to promote their political, social, economic and cultural interests and aspirations, based, inter alia, on the relevant articles of the Universal Declaration of Human Rights and the principles of the new international information order' (GA Res 36/103, 9 December 1981, para 2(I)(c)). Unlike GA Res

NON-INTERVENTION IN THE INFORMATION AGE   379

states 'to refrain from any other act of military, or of political, economic *or other co-ercion*'.[23] In the *Nicaragua* Merits Judgment, the ICJ confirmed that intervention can occur 'with or without armed force'.[24]

In addition, states from all geographical regions and political affiliations, including the Netherlands,[25] Australia,[26] Brazil,[27] Iran,[28] Canada,[29] Denmark,[30] Costa Rica,[31] Italy,[32] Japan,[33] Estonia,[34] Georgia,[35] Norway,[36] the United Kingdom,[37] the United States,[38] France,[39] New Zealand,[40] Romania,[41] Singapore,[42]

2625, however, the broader language contained in the 1976 and 1981 resolutions does not reflect customary international law.

[23] Principle VI, Final Act of the 1st CSCE Summit of Heads of State or Government (Helsinki, 1 August 1975) (1975) 14 ILM 1292, emphasis added.

[24] *Case Concerning Military and Paramilitary Activities in and against Nicaragua (Nicaragua v United States of America)* (Merits) [1986] ICJ Rep 3, para 206 (hereafter *Nicaragua v USA*). See also *Armed Activities on the Territory of the Congo (Democratic Republic of the Congo v Uganda)* (Merits) [2005] ICJ Rep 168, para 164 (hereafter *DRC v Uganda*).

[25] UN Doc A/76/136, 57.

[26] ibid, 5.

[27] ibid, 18–19.

[28] Iran's statement borrows language from GA Res 2625 and affirms that '[a]rmed intervention and all other forms of intervention or attempt to threaten against the personality of state or political, economic, social, and cultural organs of it through cyber and any other tools are regarded as unlawful. No state may compel the other state, by resorting to cyber and other means, to use or encourage to use of political, economic, or any other measures to subject that state in exercising its sovereign rights or guaranteeing concessions from that state' (Declaration of General Staff of the Armed Forces of the Islamic Republic of Iran Regarding International Law Applicable to the Cyberspace, July 2020, Art III(2) <https://nournews.ir/n/53144> (hereafter Iran's statement)).

[29] Government of Canada, 'International Law Applicable in Cyberspace', 2022, paras 22–5 <www.international.gc.ca/world-monde/issues_development-enjeux_developpement/peace_security-paix_securite/cyberspace_law-cyberespace_droit.aspx?lang=eng> (hereafter Canada's position paper).

[30] Jeppe Mejer Kjelgaard and Ulf Melgaard, 'Denmark's Position Paper on the Application of International Law in Cyberspace' (2023) 92 Nordic J Int'l L 1, 1–2 (advance access) (hereafter Denmark's position paper).

[31] Ministerio de Relaciones Exteriores y Culto, Costa Rica's position on the application of international law in cyberspace, 2023, para 19 <https://docs-library.unoda.org/Open-Ended_Working_Group_on_Information_and_Communication_Technologies_-_(2021)/Costa_Rica_-_Position_Paper_-_International_Law_in_Cyberspace.pdf> (hereafter Costa Rica's position paper).

[32] Ministero degli Affari Esteri, 'Italian Position Paper on "International Law and Cyberspace"', 2021, 4–5 <www.esteri.it/MAE/resource/doc/2021/11/italian_position_paper_on_international_law_and_cyberspace.pdf> (hereafter Italy's position paper).

[33] UN Doc A/76/136, 46.

[34] ibid, 25.

[35] Report of Georgia on Resolution 73/27 on Developments in the field of information and telecommunications in the context of international security and Res 73/266 on Advancing responsible State behavior in cyberspace in the context of international security, 1 <https://unoda-web.s3.amazonaws.com/wp-content/uploads/2019/09/UN-73-27-73-266-DEA-and-MOD.pdf>.

[36] UN Doc A/76/136, 68–9.

[37] ibid, 116.

[38] ibid, 139–40.

[39] Ministère des Armées, 'Droit international appliqué aux opérations dans le cyberspace', 9 September 2019, 7 <www.defense.gouv.fr/sites/default/files/ministere-armees/Droit%20international%20appliqué%20aux%20opérations%20dans%20le%20cyberespace.pdf> (hereafter France's position paper).

[40] Department of the Prime Minister and Cabinet, 'The Application of International Law to State Activity in Cyberspace', 1 December 2020, para 9 <www.dpmc.govt.nz/sites/default/files/2020-12/The%20Application%20of%20International%20Law%20to%20State%20Activity%20in%20Cyberspace.pdf> (hereafter New Zealand's position paper).

[41] UN Doc A/76/136, 77.

[42] ibid, 83.

380 INTERNATIONAL LAW AND THE PRINCIPLE OF NON-INTERVENTION

Switzerland,[43] Germany,[44] Chile,[45] Venezuela,[46] Ecuador,[47] Pakistan,[48] Vietnam,[49] China,[50] Egypt,[51] Cuba,[52] Belarus,[53] Poland,[54] the United Arab Emirates,[55] Ghana,[56] Russia,[57] as well as the UN GGE Reports,[58] have explicitly affirmed that the principle of non-intervention applies in cyberspace.[59]

This broad consensus is hardly surprising: if, as shown in Chapter III, during the Cold War the principle's scope was extended in certain documents to cover economic coercion as a consequence of the increasing globalization of financial and trade relations,[60] a further broadening of the principle to include at least certain cyber operations is now necessitated by the interconnectivity of networks and the reliance of modern societies on information systems, which has introduced new ways of impairing state sovereignty. Interestingly, even the Western states, which traditionally have only rarely invoked the principle of non-intervention, are now referring to it in relation to cyber operations, and particularly cyber electoral interferences and disinformation campaigns.[61] This is because Western democracies 'struggle to safeguard their own democratic structures that are under pressure, vulnerable precisely because of their openness'.[62]

The question, therefore, is not if, but *how* the principle of non-intervention applies in cyberspace. Put otherwise, what type of cyber operations does it prohibit? The reader will recall that conduct constitutes a violation of the principle under examination when a state exercises coercion in regard to 'matters in which each State is permitted, by the principle of State sovereignty, to decide freely' (that is, domestic jurisdiction).[63] It is to the application of these two elements in the cyber context that the analysis now turns.

[43] ibid, 88.
[44] ibid, 34.
[45] UN Doc S/2021/621, 1 July 2021, 50.
[46] UN Doc A/AC.290/2021/INF/2, 25 March 2021, 90.
[47] UN Doc A/72/315, 11 August 2017, 6.
[48] UN Doc S/2021/621, 98.
[49] ibid, 12.
[50] ibid, 27. For China, the Five Principles of Peaceful Coexistence (see Chapter II, Section 3) have withstood the test of time and apply in cyberspace (Lixin Zhu and Wei Chen, 'Chinese Approaches to International Law with Regard to Cyberspace Governance and Cyber Operation: From the Perspective of the Five Principles of Peaceful Co-existence' (2022) 20 Baltic YBIL 187, 207).
[51] UN Doc A/74/120, 24 June 2019, 15.
[52] UN Doc A/AC.290/2021/INF/2, 30.
[53] UN Doc A/72/315, 10.
[54] Ministry of Foreign Affairs, 'The Republic of Poland's Position on the Application of International Law in Cyberspace', 2022, 4 <www.gov.pl/web/diplomacy/the-republic-of-polands-position-on-the-applicat ion-of-international-law-in-cyberspace> (hereafter Poland's position paper).
[55] UN Doc S/2023/2, 7 June 2023, 30.
[56] ibid, 36.
[57] UN Doc A/76/136, 79.
[58] See eg the UN GGE Report 2021, paras 70, 71(c).
[59] States with autocratic governments often refer to the broader notion of 'non-interference', which also includes non-coercive activities aimed at destabilizing the internal order of a country. The 'principle of non-interference', however, does not reflect customary international law. See Chapter III, Section 3.
[60] See Chapter III, Section 7.
[61] Lukas Willmer, 'Does Digitalization Reshape the Principle of Non-Intervention?' (2023) 24 GLJ 508, 510–11.
[62] ibid, 520.
[63] *Nicaragua v USA*, para 205.

4. Domestic Jurisdiction and Cyberspace

The impingement on matters in which a state is permitted to decide freely distinguishes coercive cyber operations that breach the principle of non-intervention from those that constitute lawful countermeasures: whereas coercion in the domestic affairs of another states breaches the law, countermeasures are law enforcement mechanisms.[64] Domestic jurisdiction (also referred to, less accurately, as *domaine réservé*) operates in cyberspace no differently than in the analogue realm: it includes all matters where the concerned state is free of international obligations.[65] No matters are 'inherently' domestic: whenever a treaty or customary international law rule requires a certain positive or negative conduct from a state, those to which the obligation is owed and which are injured by its violation can resort to coercive means in order to enforce compliance consistently with the law of countermeasures.[66]

As the OAS Charter, General Assembly Resolutions 2131 and 2625, and the ICJ jurisprudence make clear, the principle of non-intervention protects *all* matters, and *only* those matters, within the domestic jurisdiction of states. Canada, Finland, and New Zealand's position papers on the application of international law in cyberspace, however, conflate the notion of domestic jurisdiction with that of 'inherently sovereign [or governmental] functions'.[67] This view is unsustainable. Indeed, not all matters under a state's domestic jurisdiction are 'inherently sovereign' or 'inherently governmental': what identifies them is rather the fact that they are not regulated by any international law applicable to the concerned state. By the same token, not all inherently sovereign or governmental functions necessarily fall within the domestic jurisdiction of a state: they no longer do so when treaties binding on that state and/or customary international law limit in whole or in part the state's liberty to exercise the function.[68] A violation of the principle of non-intervention, therefore, can occur even when the coercive act does not interfere with the exercise of an inherently governmental function of the target state, as long as the matter falls within its domestic jurisdiction; and a violation of the principle of non-intervention might not occur even if coercion is applied with regard to the exercise of an inherently governmental function of the target state, if that function no longer falls within its domestic jurisdiction.

---

[64] Department of Foreign Affairs, Ireland: Position paper on the application of international law in cyberspace, 2023, para 10 <www.dfa.ie/media/dfa/ourrolepolicies/internationallaw/Ireland---National-Position-Paper.pdf> (hereafter Ireland's position paper).

[65] See Chapter III, Section 5. As has been observed, 'the scope of internal affairs has not changed in the cyber age, but methods of interference have become abundant' (Zhu and Chen, 'Chinese Approaches', 199).

[66] Arts 42, 49–54 ARSIWA.

[67] Ministry for Foreign Affairs, 'International Law and Cyberspace: Finland's National Positions', 15 October 2020, 6 <https://um.fi/documents/35732/0/Cyber+and+international+law%3B+Finland%27s+views.pdf/41404cbb-d300-a3b9-92e4-a7d675d5d585?t=1602758856859> (hereafter Finland's position paper); New Zealand's position paper, para 9; Canada's position paper, para 22.

[68] Michael N Schmitt, 'Autonomous Cyber Capabilities and the International Law of Sovereignty and Intervention' (2020) 96 ILS 549, 560.

5. Coercion of State in Cyberspace

Whether or not a cyber operation breaches the principle of non-intervention ultimately depends on if it *coerces* another state in regard to matters in which it can decide freely.[69] As demonstrated in Chapter III, to be coercive, an act must be designed and able to undermine the agency of the target state and impair its decisional sovereignty.[70] It has also been seen that coercion of state can assume two forms: forcible or dictatorial.[71] *Dictatorial* coercion consists in the binomial 'demands + threats': by causing or prospecting a certain harm, it bends the will of the victim state so as to make it do or not do something.[72] A demand is coercive when it is accompanied by a clear, specific, and credible threat and the threatened harm, whatever its nature, is sufficiently serious.[73] Canada's position paper cites the example of 'a malicious cyber activity that disrupts the functioning of a major gas pipeline, compelling the affected State to change its position in bilateral negotiations surrounding an international energy accord'.[74] Ransomware attacks, examples of which are the 2017 WannaCry attack[75] and the subsequent NotPetya attack,[76] are another type of cyber operation resulting in dictatorial coercion: the hacker hijacks a system so that its users no longer have access to it unless they submit to the hacker's demands. It is not essential that the demands are accepted for the principle of non-intervention to be breached: it is sufficient that the coercive behaviour takes place, whether or not the victim state actually submits to it or decides

---

[69] See Chapter III, Section 3.

[70] ibid.

[71] Chapter III, Sections 3.1 and 3.2.

[72] For the Netherlands, coercion 'means compelling a state to take a course of action (whether an act or an omission) that it would not otherwise voluntarily pursue' with the goal of changing the behaviour of the target state (UN Doc A/76/136, 57). Germany's position paper also affirms that '[c]oercion implies that a State's internal processes regarding aspects pertaining to its *domaine réservé* are significantly influenced or thwarted and that its will is manifestly bent by the foreign State's conduct' (UN Doc A/76/136, 34). A definition of coercion focused on dictatorial interference is also contained in Italy's position paper, according to which a violation of the customary principle of non-intervention occurs 'when a State employs coercive means to compel another State to undertake or desist from a specific action, in matters falling under its domain réservé' (Italy's position paper, 4–5).

[73] Travis Sharp, 'Theorizing Cyber Coercion: The 2014 North Korean Operation Against Sony' (2017) 40 JSS 898, 903, 909.

[74] Canada's position paper, para 24. Norway also gives the example of a cyber operation deliberately causing a temporary shutdown of the target state's critical infrastructure so as to compel that state to take a certain course of action (UN Doc A/76/136, 69).

[75] The attack lasted three days in May 2017, during which it infected the systems of private enterprises and governmental institutions and disrupted, among others, the health service networks in the United Kingdom. It was allegedly conducted by a North Korean hacker, Lazarus. See Attorney General's Office, 'Cyber and International Law in the 21st Century', Speech by the Attorney General Jeremy Wright, 23 May 2018 <www.gov.uk/government/speeches/cyber-and-international-law-in-the-21st-century>.

[76] The attack took place in June 2017 and permanently encrypted computer data from government agencies and the shipping, power, and healthcare sectors in several countries. See Michael Schmitt and Jeffrey Biller, 'The NotPetya Cyber Operation as a Case Study of International Law' (*EJIL:Talk!*, 11 July 2017) <www.ejiltalk.org/the-notpetya-cyber-operation-as-a-case-study-of-international-law/>. It seems that, even though it spread globally, the attack was aimed at Ukraine and 'was probably launched by a state actor or a non-state actor with support or approval from a state' (NATO Cooperative Cyber Defence Centre of Excellence, 'NotPetya and WannaCry Call for a Joint Response from International Community', 30 June 2017 <https://ccdcoe.org/news/2017/notpetya-and-wannacry-call-for-a-joint-response-from-international-community>).

to resist and stoically endure the harm.[77] If they really had been conducted by Russian organs or agents in order to compel Estonia into reversing its decision to move a Soviet war memorial statue to the suburbs of Tallinn, the 2007 DDoS attacks on the Baltic state would have been a good illustration of an attempted case of dictatorial coercion by cyber means and thus of a violation of the principle of non-intervention.[78]

As the case-law as well as the state practice and *opinio juris* analysed in Chapter III demonstrate, the principle of non-intervention prohibits not only dictatorial interferences in the domestic affairs of other states but also *forcible* ones, that is, the exercise of power in the territory of another state without its valid consent or a permissive rule of international law.[79] In this case, the intervening state imposes a certain condition of things on the target state by carrying out the unauthorized act itself instead of compelling someone else to do anything.[80] This would for instance occur when, through a cyber attack, a state takes control of another's networked weapons and weapon systems, such as missiles, satellites, and drones. A further example of violation of the principle of non-intervention resulting from forcible coercion is suggested by Australia:

In order to implement the new laws—including to allow State A's tax office and corporate regulator to monitor and enforce new requirements on companies—State A requires all registered companies to disclose certain information via a government website. State B opposes the reforms because it considers they unfairly impact on the interests of companies from State B operating in State A. In an attempt to prevent State A from implementing the reforms, State B, through its Department of Defence, conducts a series of cyber operations that prevent use of the website and disable government systems of State A's tax office and corporate regulator. As a result, State

---

[77] Costa Rica's position paper, para 24. Art 19 of the OAS Charter and GA Resolutions 2131 and 2625 refer to '*attempted* threats against the personality of the State or against its political, economic, and cultural elements' (emphasis added). As the Argentinian delegate on the Special Committee on Friendly Relations noted, '[e]ven if that State refused to be coerced or intimidated by threats, there might be an intention on the part of the intervening State to coerce the sovereign will of the other State' (UN Doc A/AC.119/SR.28, 23 October 1964, 5, emphasis omitted).

[78] Russell Buchan, 'Cyber Attacks: Unlawful Uses of Force or Prohibited Interventions' (2012) 17 JCSL 211, 225–6.

[79] See Chapter III, Section 3.2. The fact that forcible interferences are also a case of coercion relevant to the determination of a violation of the principle of non-intervention finds confirmation in the views of certain states. The United Kingdom's attorney general, for instance, has suggested that coercion is broader than compelling a state into an act or omission and that it also includes depriving the target state of its 'freedom of control' over matters in which it can decide freely (Attorney General's Office and The Rt Hon Suella Braverman KC MP, 'International Law in Future Frontiers', Speech at Chatham House, 19 May 2022 (hereafter Braverman, 'International Law') <www.gov.uk/government/speeches/international-law-in-fut ure-frontiers>). Disruptive cyber operations could thus be coercive 'even where it might not be possible to point to a specific course of conduct which a State has been forced into or prevented from taking' (ibid). The deprivation of control aspect of coercion in cyberspace has also been emphasized by Australia (UN Doc A/76/136, 57), Canada (Canada's position paper, para 22), and New Zealand (New Zealand's position paper, para 9).

[80] Nicolas Jupillat, 'From the Cuckoo's Egg to Global Surveillance: Cyber Espionage that Becomes Prohibited Intervention' (2017) 42 NC J Int'l L 933, 949 (coercion occurs 'when you have to undergo something being done to you against your will', ie 'when the coercive power uses its position of superiority to do whatever they please despite the victim's lack of consent'). Alteration of data that directly affects a foreign country's systems 'always qualifies as a coercive measure, as there ultimately exists no graver form of interference than performing the action by oneself rather than influencing the target State to do so' (Johann-Christoph Woltag, *Cyber Warfare* (Intersentia 2014) 124).

384 INTERNATIONAL LAW AND THE PRINCIPLE OF NON-INTERVENTION

A is incapable of regulating companies' compliance with the new laws for a substantial period and has no choice but to indefinitely postpone implementation of the new tax reforms. State A also loses significant tax revenue.[81]

The Norwegian Supreme Court has also addressed a case of forcible coercion in cyberspace in the *Tidal* case. In December 2018, the Oslo offices of Tidal (a music streaming company) were searched by the Norwegian authorities to obtain evidence in regard to a case of computer fraud committed by an unknown perpetrator, who allegedly inflated the numbers for some tracks in order to influence the calculation of royalties to certain right holders.[82] During the search, 'source codes' were downloaded from a server based in the United States and stored on a USB stick and the emails of the technical director's Google account were extracted from servers in the Netherlands, Finland, Belgium, and/or Iceland (it is not known in which of these countries the data were actually stored).[83] The Supreme Court qualified the search of data on servers located abroad as a 'coercive measure' and pointed out that 'under international law ... states may exercise coercion only in their own territory ... no state may use coercive measures in the territory of another state without the consent of that state'.[84]

In Chapter III, it has also been seen that, unlike in the case of dictatorial coercion, when the coercing state forcibly engages in unauthorized conduct on foreign territory, intent to coerce is presumed and no demonstration of its existence is required to establish the commission of the wrongful act.[85] The UN GGE, however, has recommended that a state 'should not conduct or knowingly support ICT activity contrary to its obligations under international law that *intentionally* damages critical infrastructure or otherwise impairs the use and operation of critical infrastructure to provide services to the public' without making any differentiations.[86] While it is premature to draw any conclusions, it is entirely possible that, because of the interconnectivity of networks and the high chance of the unintended indiscriminate spread of malware, customary international law will develop a more restrictive special rule that requires evidence of intent to coerce for *any* violations of the principle of non-intervention in cyberspace, including those involving forcible coercion.[87] As Judge Robinson found in another context, intent can be inferred 'from a State's actions, including their gravity, as well as statements made by the State and the relevant context'.[88] The burden of proving its existence rests of course on the state claiming that an intervention has occurred.

---

[81] UN Doc A/76/136, 9.

[82] *Tidal Music AS v The Public Prosecution Authority*, HR-2019-610-A, Case No 19-010640STR-HRET, 28 March 2019, para 3 <www.domstol.no/globalassets/upload/hret/decisions-in-english-translation/hr-2019-610-a.pdf> (hereafter *Tidal*).

[83] ibid, paras 6–7.

[84] ibid, para 40.

[85] See Chapter III, Section 4.

[86] UN GGE Report 2015, para 13(f), emphasis added.

[87] See Nicholas Tsagourias, 'Electoral Cyber Interference, Self-Determination, and the Principle of Non-Intervention in Cyberspace' in Dennis Broeders and Bibi van den Berg (eds), *Governing Cyberspace: Behavior, Power, and Diplomacy* (Rowman & Littlefield 2020) 45, 55.

[88] *Certain Activities Carried Out by Nicaragua in the Border Area (Costa Rica v Nicaragua)* (Merits) [2015] ICJ Rep 807 (hereafter *Costa Rica v Nicaragua*), Separate Opinion of Judge Robinson, para 54. For New Zealand, '[w]hile the coercive intention of the state actor is a critical element of the [the principle of non-intervention], intention may in some circumstances be inferred from the effects of cyber activity' (New Zealand's position paper, para 9).

Having established what coercion of state means in cyberspace, the next step in the analysis is to distinguish the different effects of cyber operations in order to identify those that are capable of bending or replacing the will of the victim state. In particular, four types of operations can be identified: those designed to cause material damage to persons and/or objects; those designed to cause loss of functionality of infrastructure; those exclusively involving the unauthorized access to cyber infrastructure; and those aimed at influencing a decision-making process. These effects are addressed in turn in the next subsections.

5.1 Cyber Operations Causing or Designed to Cause Material Damage to Persons and/or Physical Objects

It is virtually uncontested that, if a cyber attack conducted by a state employed cyber capabilities that cause or are designed to cause material damage to or destruction of property, loss of life, or injury to persons in another state, it would breach the principle of non-intervention. As the German position paper explains, this conclusion is firmly based on kinetic equivalence: cyber operations constitute a prohibited intervention 'if they are comparable in scale and effect to coercion in non-cyber contexts'.[89] In *Nicaragua*, the ICJ found that '[t]he element of coercion, which defines, and indeed forms the very essence of, prohibited intervention, is particularly obvious in the case of an intervention which uses force'.[90]

A cyber operation designed to result in material damage could constitute a forcible interference as in the case of Stuxnet, a computer worm that attacked Iran's industrial infrastructure between 2009 and 2010 with the alleged ultimate purpose of sabotaging the gas centrifuges at the Natanz uranium enrichment facility and delaying the Islamic Republic's nuclear programme.[91] Unlike other worms, Stuxnet did not limit itself to self-replicating, but also contained a 'weaponized' payload designed to give instructions to other programs and is, in fact, the first known use of malicious software aimed to cause material damage by attacking the SCADA system of a national critical infrastructure. Although the exact consequences of the incident have never been conclusively ascertained, the International Atomic Energy Agency reported that Iran stopped feeding uranium into a significant number of gas centrifuges at Natanz.[92]

Cyber operations causing or designed to cause material damage to persons and/or physical objects could also amount to a dictatorial interference when the threat of the infliction or of the continuation of damage is used as leverage to obtain concessions from the victim. As already said, it is not necessary that the cyber operation reaches its objective, it being sufficient that unlawful coercion is exercised, regardless of whether the victim state actually submits to the demands or decides to resist them: even if the coerced conduct does not occur, the harm still materializes and an obligation to

---

[89] UN Doc A/76/136, 34. See also Ireland's position paper, para 9.
[90] *Nicaragua v USA*, para 205.
[91] On Stuxnet, see Marco Roscini, 'Cyber Operations as Nuclear Counterproliferation Measures' (2014) 19 JCSL 133.
[92] Roscini, *Cyber Operations*, 6. In April 2021, Iran sent a letter to the United Nations denouncing another cyber attack against the Natanz fuel enrichment facility (UN Doc A/75/852-S/2021/347, 13 April 2021).

386 INTERNATIONAL LAW AND THE PRINCIPLE OF NON-INTERVENTION

provide full reparation for any consequences that are the proximate effect of the coercing state's conduct arises.[93]

Cyber operations designed to cause material damage to objects and/or persons are not only violations of the general principle of non-intervention but also of the prohibition of the use of force codified in Article 2(4) of the UN Charter. In its *Nuclear Weapons Advisory Opinion*, the ICJ made clear that Articles 2(4), 51, and 42 of the UN Charter 'do not refer to specific weapons. They apply to any use of force, regardless of the weapons employed.'[94] Indeed, there is no reason why the weapons covered by the *jus contra bellum* provisions should necessarily have explosive effects or be created for offensive purposes only: the use of certain dual-use non-kinetic weapons, such as biological or chemical agents, against a state would undoubtedly be treated by the victim state as a use of force under Article 2(4).[95] According to Ian Brownlie, this is so because chemical and biological weapons are commonly referred to as forms of 'warfare' and because they can be used to destroy life and property:[96] both arguments would also suit weaponized malware.

This conclusion finds support in the position papers and statements of states and international organizations on the application of international law in cyberspace, including those of Australia,[97] Brazil,[98] Canada,[99] the United Kingdom,[100] Estonia,[101] Finland,[102] France,[103] Germany,[104] Israel,[105] Italy,[106] NATO,[107] the Netherlands,[108] New Zealand,[109] Norway,[110] Romania,[111] Switzerland,[112] Costa Rica,[113] Poland,[114]

---

[93] See Chapter III, Section 3.1.

[94] *Legality of the Threat or Use of Nuclear Weapons* (Advisory Opinion) [1996] ICJ Rep 226, para 39 (hereafter *Nuclear Weapons*).

[95] As Dinstein suggests, 'cyber ... must be looked upon as a new means of warfare--in other words, a weapon: no less and no more than other weapons' (Yoram Dinstein, 'Cyber War and International Law: Concluding Remarks at the 2012 Naval War College International Law Conference' (2013) 89 ILS 276, 280).

[96] Ian Brownlie, *International Law and the Use of Force by States* (OUP 1963) 362.

[97] UN Doc A/76/136, 5.

[98] ibid, 19.

[99] Canada's position paper, para 45.

[100] UN Doc A/76/136, 116.

[101] Office of the President, 'President of the Republic at the Opening of CyCon 2019', speech, 25 May 2019 <http://web.archive.org/web/20191007093327/https://president.ee/en/official-duties/speeches/15241-president-of-the-republic-at-the-opening-of-cycon-2019>.

[102] Finland's position paper, 6.

[103] France's position paper, 7.

[104] UN Doc A/76/136, 35.

[105] Roy Schondorf, 'Israel's Perspective on Key Legal and Practical Issues Concerning the Application of International Law to Cyber Operations' (2021) 97 ILS 395, 398–9.

[106] Italy's position paper, 8.

[107] NATO, Allied Joint Doctrine for Cyberspace Operations, Allied Joint Publication-3.20, January 2020, 20 <https://assets.publishing.service.gov.uk/government/uploads/system/uploads/attachment_data/file/899678/doctrine_nato_cyberspace_operations_ajp_3_20_1_.pdf>.

[108] UN Doc A/76/136, 58.

[109] New Zealand's position paper, para 7.

[110] UN Doc A/76/136, 69–70.

[111] ibid, 77.

[112] Département Fédérale de Justice et Police (DFJP) et Département Fédéral des Affaires Etrangères (DFAE), 'Avis de droit sur les bases légales des opérations dans les reseaux informatiques par les services du DDPS', JAAC 3/2009, 2 September 2009, 199 <www.bj.admin.ch/bj/fr/home/publiservice/publikationen/berichte-gutachten/2009-10.html> (hereafter Switzerland's position paper).

[113] Costa Rica's position paper, para 36.

[114] Poland's position paper, 5.

Denmark,[115] Ireland,[116] and the United States.[117] These states have explicitly affirmed that cyber operations designed to result in material damage to persons or physical objects are prohibited by Article 2(4) whenever their scale and effects are equivalent to those of a kinetic use of force. Non-binding and non-exhaustive quantitative and qualitative factors have also been suggested in order to establish the kinetic equivalence of the effects.[118]

It is worth recalling that, unlike Article 2(4), the principle of non-intervention only prohibits armed coercion when it bears 'on matters in which each State is permitted, by the principle of State sovereignty, to decide freely'[119] and thus does not rule out the permissibility of cyber operations constituting a use of armed force when adopted by the injured state in response to the violation of an obligation owed to it by the delinquent state. The only cases where resort to armed coercion by kinetic or cyber means is permitted under the UN Charter, on the other hand, are that of self-defence against an armed attack (Article 51) and that authorized by the Security Council under Chapter VII. Even though armed coercion by cyber means to enforce compliance with an international law obligation is beyond the reach of the principle of non-intervention, therefore, it remains unlawful under the *jus contra bellum* rules apart from the two aforementioned exceptions.

5.2 Cyber Operations Causing or Designed to Cause Loss of Functionality of Infrastructure

There is also broad consensus that cyber operations causing or designed to cause loss of functionality of infrastructure with consequent disruption of services but without material damage amount to a breach of the principle of non-intervention whenever they impinge on matters in which a state can decide freely. Indeed, any causation of malfunction to infrastructure located on another state's territory constitutes an extra-territorial exercise of power which, in the absence of the consent of the territorial sovereign or of a permissive rule of international law, amounts to coercion in the form of a forcible interference. Examples provided in state position papers include cyber operations affecting the operation of parliament,[120] preventing the filing of tax returns online,[121] significantly disrupting a state's financial and banking systems[122] or essential medical services,[123] paralysing a 'systemically relevant' company,[124] and 'deliberately

---

[115] Denmark's position paper, 5.
[116] Ireland's position paper, para 18.
[117] UN Doc A/76/136, 137; US Department of Defense, Law of War Manual (June 2015, updated December 2016) 1015.
[118] The Netherlands (UN Doc A/76/136, 58); Norway (A/76/136, 70); Germany (A/76/136, 35–6); Singapore (A/76/136, 83); United States (A/76/136, 137); Denmark (Denmark's position paper, 6); NATO (Allied Joint Doctrine for Cyberspace Operations, 20).
[119] *Nicaragua v USA*, para 205.
[120] Australia (UN Doc A/76/136, 5); Poland's position paper, 4.
[121] Poland's position paper, 4.
[122] Australia (UN Doc A/76/136, 5); United Kingdom (A/76/136, 116); Switzerland's position paper, 204.
[123] United Kingdom (UN Doc A/76/136, 116–17); Japan (A/76/136, 47); United States (A/76/136, 140).
[124] Switzerland (UN Doc A/76/136, 88).

388 INTERNATIONAL LAW AND THE PRINCIPLE OF NON-INTERVENTION

causing ... loss of functionality in ... a state's critical infrastructure, including—for example—its healthcare system, financial system, or its electricity or telecommunications network'.[125] Cyber operations that prevent a country from holding elections by incapacitating electoral machinery, manipulate the vote count, or hack voter databases have also been identified by states as violations of the principle of non-intervention.[126] When these operations aim to compel a state into doing or not doing something, they also constitute coercion in the form of a dictatorial interference.

What is still very controversial is whether cyber operations causing or designed to cause loss of functionality also breach Article 2(4) of the UN Charter. Some states have suggested that a cyber attack that penetrates another state's military systems and cripples its ability to conduct military operations and defend itself amounts to a use of force regardless of whether it results in material damage.[127] An example is the cyber attack allegedly conducted in June 2019 by the United States against the weapons systems used by Iran's Islamic Revolutionary Guard Corps.[128]

With regard to cyber attacks on other infrastructures, I have argued since 2014 that they fall under the scope of Article 2(4) and its customary equivalent if the loss of functionality is permanent or at least significant enough to disrupt 'the backbone of a society's vital functions, services and activities'.[129] Indeed, what matters is that the delivery of critical services is severely disrupted, however this result is achieved: the dependency of modern societies on computers, computer systems, and networks has made it possible to cause significant harm to states through non-destructive means.[130] A week-long cyber attack that shuts down the national grid and leaves millions of people without electricity, cripples the financial market and the transport system, and prevents government communications is thus likely to be treated as a use of force, whether or not material damage ensues.[131] Support for the qualification of a cyber attack causing significant malfunction of critical infrastructures as a use of force can be found in the statements of countries like the Netherlands,[132]

---

[125] New Zealand's position paper, para 10.

[126] France (Ministère des Armées, Manuel de droit des opérations militaires (2 February 2023) 302); Australia (UN Doc A/76/136, 5); New Zealand's position paper, para 10; United Kingdom (A/76/136, 116); Norway (A/76/136, 69); Germany (A/76/136, 35); United States (A/76/136, 140); Finland's position paper, 3; Schondorf, 'Israel's Perspective', 403; Iran's statement, Art III(1); Canada's position paper, para 24; Poland's position paper, 4; Denmark's position paper, 5.

[127] France's position paper, 7; US Department of Defense, Law of War Manual, 1015–16.

[128] Marc Schack, 'Did the US Stay "Well Below the Threshold of War" With its June Cyberattack on Iran?' (EJIL:Talk!, 2 September 2019) <www.ejiltalk.org/did-the-us-stay-well-below-the-threshold-of-war-with-its-june-cyberattack-on-iran/>.

[129] The language is taken from the UN GGE Report 2021, para 43. See Roscini, Cyber Operations, 55.

[130] In his Dissenting Opinion in the 2015 Costa Rica v Nicaragua case, Judge Robinson found that a 'non-violent use of force is not exempted from the prohibition [contained in Art 2(4)]. No shots need be fired, no heavy armaments need be used and certainly no one need be killed before a State can be said to have violated the prohibition' (Costa Rica v Nicaragua, Separate Opinion of Judge Robinson, para 43).

[131] The scenario is inspired by the 'Cyber ShockWave' simulation staged by the Bipartisan Policy Center (Ellen Nakashima, 'War Game Reveals U.S. Lacks Cyber-Crisis Skills' (The Washington Post, 17 February 2010) <https://web.archive.org/web/20130419194959/http://articles.washingtonpost.com/2010-02-17/news/36782381_1_cyber-attack-cyber-coordinator-cyber-shockwave>.

[132] Minister of Defence, 'Keynote HE Ms. Ank Bijleveld MA, Minister of Defence', 20 June 2018 <https://puc.overheid.nl/mrt/doc/PUC_248478_11/1/> ('if a cyber-attack targets the entire Dutch financial system or if it prevents the government from carrying out essential tasks such as policing or taxation ... it would qualify as an armed attack'). In a subsequent document, the Dutch government more cautiously affirmed

Norway,[133] Singapore,[134] Mali,[135] New Zealand,[136] Guatemala,[137] Italy,[138] Denmark,[139] Ireland,[140] Costa Rica,[141] and France.[142] Other states have declared that they are not ready to apply Article 2(4) to non-physical damage[143] or still have to adopt a clear position on the matter,[144] but as far as customary international law is concerned, the trend seems to be going in the direction suggested above.

What distinguishes a cyber operation that breaches Article 2(4) by causing malfunction of infrastructure from one that only constitutes a violation of the principle of non-intervention is the gravity of its scale and effects: the former, unlike the latter, *severely* disrupts the delivery of *critical* services. At least in the cyber context, therefore, a *de minimis* threshold for a violation of Article 2(4) to occur appears to be required by the interconnectivity of networks, the frequency of the operations, and the need to avoid abusive invocations of the right of self-defence.[145] Although it is by no means the exclusive factor, the critical character of the targeted infrastructure is an important

---

that the fact that a cyber operation 'with a very serious financial or economic impact' could be a use of force 'cannot be ruled out' (UN Doc A/76/136, 58).

[133] UN Doc A/76/136, 70 ('a cyber operation causing severe disruption to the functioning of the State such as the use of crypto viruses or other forms of digital sabotage against governmental or private power grid- or telecommunications infrastructure, or cyber operations leading to the destruction of stockpiles of Covid-19 vaccines' as well as 'the use of crypto viruses or other forms of digital sabotage against a State's financial and banking system, or other operations that cause widespread economic effects and destabilisation' could be a use of force in violation of Art 2(4)).

[134] ibid, 84 ('a targeted cyber operation causing sustained and long-term outage of Singapore's critical infrastructure' may in certain circumstances amount to an armed attack, and hence to a use of force).

[135] UN Doc A/64/129/Add.1, 9 September 2009, para 22.

[136] New Zealand's position paper, para 7 (a cyber operation constitutes a use of force when it results, inter alia, in 'significant damage to ... state functioning', although it is not entirely clear whether material damage is also necessary).

[137] Inter-American Juridical Committee, Improving Transparency: International Law and State Cyber Operations—Fifth Report, 7 August 2020, OEA/Ser.Q, CJI/doc. 615/20 rev.1, 19.

[138] Italy's position paper, 8 ('The inclusion of such operations in the scope of the prohibition of the use of force ... could be justified if one considers that, because of the reliance of modern societies on computers, computer systems and networks, cyber technologies have enabled States to cause the interruption of essential services without the need of physical damage').

[139] Denmark does not rule out that 'acts of economic or political coercion can fall within the purview of Article 2(4) of the UN Charter if, for example, a cyber operation resulting in malfunctioning of a State's financial system leads to significant economic damage' (Denmark's position paper, 6).

[140] Ireland's position paper, para 18.

[141] Costa Rica's position paper, para 36. Costa Rica points out that the operating system of the targeted infrastructure must be permanently disabled to constitute an unlawful use of force (ibid).

[142] France's position paper, 7. The paper does not rule out that a cyber operation without physical effects could be a breach of Art 2(4). It also does not exclude that it could amount to an 'armed attack', for instance when it causes significant economic damage or paralyze entire sections of state activity (ibid, 9).

[143] Schondorf, 'Israel's Perspective', 399.

[144] Finland's position paper, 6; Brazil (UN Doc A/76/136, 19).

[145] The debate on the existence of a *de minimis* threshold for a violation of Art 2(4) to occur is not limited to cyber operations: see Tom Ruys, 'The Meaning of "Force" and the Boundaries of the *Jus ad Bellum*: Are "Minimal" Uses of Force Excluded from UN Charter Article 2(4)?' (2014) 108 AJIL 159; Mary Ellen O'Connell, 'The Prohibition on the Use of Force' in Nigel D White and Christian Henderson (eds), *Research Handbook on International Conflict and Security Law* (Edward Elgar 2015) 89, 102–7; Olivier Corten, *The Law Against War: The Prohibition on the Use of Force in Contemporary International Law* (2nd edn, Hart Publishing 2021) 77–85.

element to consider in assessing the severity of the impact of the cyber operation.[146] It is especially helpful to *exclude* that the operation is a use of force: if the targeted infrastructure is not critical, it is highly unlikely that the consequent loss of functionality will affect a state's essential functions and its internal public order. A cyber attack that shuts down a university network, therefore, might be an unlawful intervention in the domestic affairs of a state but not a use of armed force, even if it causes prolonged and severe loss of functionality.

Whether or not a cyber operation exclusively resulting in loss of functionality also amounts to a use of force and not only to a violation of the principle of non-intervention, however, necessarily depends not only on the critical character of the targeted infrastructure, but also on other factors such as the severity of the disruption, its duration, the sophistication of the means employed, the origin of the attack, and the reliance of the victim state on information systems.[147] Although they targeted critical infrastructures (banking and communications), for instance, the aforementioned 2007 DDoS attacks on Estonia caused neither material damage nor serious disruption of services and were arguably a violation of the principle of non-intervention but not of Article 2(4), even if they had been conclusively attributed to a state.

5.3 Cyber Operations Exclusively Involving Unauthorized Extraterritorial Access to Non-Publicly Available Data

Examples of this type of cyber operations include, among others, the unauthorized transborder access to non-publicly available digital evidence by investigative authorities as well as cyber espionage, defined as 'the non-consensual use of cyber operations to penetrate computer networks and systems with the objective of copying confidential data that is under the control of another actor'.[148] Operations to emplace malware or install backdoors in a computer system so as to allow the subsequent unauthorized access also fall in this category. In late 2020, for instance, Russia's Foreign Intelligence Service was accused of inserting malicious code into the Orion software developed by the American company SolarWinds. When SolarWinds inadvertently delivered the backdoor malware as an update to Orion, the operation compromised the data, networks, and systems of, among others, US governmental departments such as Homeland Security and the Treasury and private companies such as FireEye, Microsoft, Intel, Cisco, and Deloitte. The purpose of the operation remains unknown.[149]

---

[146] South Korea has observed that '[c]yberattacks on critical infrastructures including energy, financial, transportation, health, water, and other public services facilities can have devastating security consequences comparable to a heavy kinetic use of force' (UN Doc S/2023/412, 7 June 2023, 54).

[147] France's position paper, 7.

[148] Russell Buchan, *Cyber Espionage* (Hart Publishing 2018) 27.

[149] Saheed Oladimeji and Sean Michael Kerner, 'SolarWinds Hack Explained: Everything You Need to Know' (*WhatIs*, 29 June 2022) <www.techtarget.com/whatis/feature/SolarWinds-hack-explained-Everything-you-need-to-know>. Certain commentators have argued that the SolarWinds attack did not breach the principle of non-intervention as it did not coerce the United States (Kristen E Eichensehr, 'Not Illegal: The SolarWinds Incident and International Law' (2022) 33 EJIL 1263, 1267–9) while others have reached the opposite conclusion (Antonio Coco, Talita Dias, and Tsvetelina van Benthem, 'Illegal: The SolarWinds Hack Under International Law' (2022) 33 EJIL 1275, 1280–1).

NON-INTERVENTION IN THE INFORMATION AGE 391

The legality of this type of cyber operation has been essentially discussed from the perspective of the rule protecting territorial sovereignty: as will be seen, however, a determination of the breach of territorial sovereignty is also important to establish the occurrence of a violation of the principle of non-intervention. Indeed, in the *Nicaragua* case the ICJ found that 'the principle of respect for State [territorial] sovereignty ... is of course closely linked with the principles of the prohibition of the use of force and of non-intervention' and that '[t]he effects of the principle of respect for territorial sovereignty inevitably overlap with those of the principles of the prohibition of the use of force and of non-intervention.[150]

A state can extend its sovereignty over the physical and social layers of cyberspace located on its territory as well as over the information that enters or becomes available through its infrastructure.[151] States disagree, however, on whether a cyber operation involving unauthorized extraterritorial access to non-publicly available data needs to result in harmful effects on the territory of the target state for the latter's sovereignty to be breached. For some, any remote penetration in their communication networks constitutes a violation of their territorial sovereignty, even if no further effects on the territory occur. This is, for instance, the position of France and Iran.[152] Other states, however, disagree and require tangible effects for territorial sovereignty to be encroached, either in the form of material damage, permanent loss of functionality of infrastructure, or at least loss of functionality necessitating repair or replacement of physical components.[153] A middle-ground position is that of those states claiming that a violation of territorial sovereignty occurs when the cyber operation causes 'harmful' effects above a *de minimis* threshold, whether tangible or not, on the territory of the target state.[154] These effects can go from significant but temporary functional impairment of equipment relying on the attacked system and the modification or deletion of information[155] to a mere threat to or destabilization of national

---

[150] *Nicaragua v USA*, paras 212, 251.

[151] Nicholas Tsagourias, 'Law, Borders and the Territorialisation of Cyberspace' (2018) 15 Indonesian J Int'l L 523, 539–40. China, for instance, has defined sovereignty in cyberspace as 'the internal supremacy and external independence that States enjoy, on the basis of their national sovereignty, over the ICT-related infrastructure, entities and activities as well as relevant data and information within their territories' ('China's Views on the Application of the Principle of Sovereignty in Cyberspace' 2021, 1 <http://docume nts.unoda.org/wp-content/uploads/2021/12/Chinese-Position-Paper-on-the-Application-of-the-Princi ple-of-Sovereignty-ENG.pdf>).

[152] France's position paper, 6; Iran's statement, Art II(4). Ireland's position paper also includes 'interference with data', among the effects that a cyber operation encroaching sovereignty might have although it is not clear what is exactly meant by this expression (Ireland's position paper, para 6).

[153] Canada's position paper, para 16.

[154] Germany's position paper, 33; Finland's position paper, 2; Canada's position paper, paras 16–17; Poland's position paper, 3; Denmark's position paper, 4. The Czech Republic also considers that a cyber operation that damages or disrupts 'cyber or other infrastructure with a significant impact on national security, economy, public health or environment' is a violation of sovereignty (Statement by Mr Richard Kadlčák, Special Envoy for Cyberspace, Director of Cybersecurity Department, 11 February 2020, 3 <www.nukib. cz/download/publications_en/CZ%20Statement%20-%20OEWG%20-%20International%20Law%20 11.02.2020.pdf>). For Costa Rica, a breach of sovereignty can occur when a cyber operation causes loss of functionality, including when 'the operating system or database upon which the targeted cyber infrastructure relies stops functioning as intended, as may be the case, for instance, as a result of ransomware.' (Costa Rica's position paper, para 20). Italy's and New Zealand's position papers refer to 'harmful effects' but do not clarify whether this means 'tangible' only or not (Italy's position paper, 4; New Zealand's position paper, para 14).

[155] Finland's position paper, 2; Germany's position paper, 33; Denmark's position paper, 4.

392 INTERNATIONAL LAW AND THE PRINCIPLE OF NON-INTERVENTION

security,[156] but do not include mere rebooting or reinstallation of an operating system.[157] Finally, several states refer to the usurpation of inherently governmental functions as a further effect of cyber operations that might amount to a breach of another state's sovereignty.[158]

It should also be recalled that, for the United Kingdom, there is no separate rule prohibiting cyber conduct below the level of intervention that can be extrapolated from the concept of sovereignty.[159] The United States appears to have adopted a similar position where it has argued that 'a State's remote cyber operations involving computers or other networked devices located on another State's territory do not constitute a per se violation of international law. In other words, there is no absolute prohibition on such operations as a matter of international law.'[160]

This view, however, remains isolated and has been explicitly or implicitly rejected by several states, including Brazil,[161] Canada,[162] China,[163] Norway,[164] Finland,[165] France,[166] Italy,[167] Japan,[168] Bolivia,[169] Guatemala,[170] Guyana,[171] the Netherlands,[172] New Zealand,[173] the Czech Republic,[174] Germany,[175] Romania,[176] Sweden,[177] Ireland,[178] and Switzerland.[179]

My take on this is that the unauthorized remote penetration by a state of the cyber infrastructure located in another state, be it for espionage, collection of evidence, implantation of malware, or other purposes, does not need to result in harmful effects on

---

[156] Iran's statement, Art II(3).

[157] Canada's position paper, para 17.

[158] See eg Denmark's position paper, 4; Finland's position paper, 2; Costa Rica's position paper, para 21.

[159] UN Doc A/76/136, 117.

[160] ibid, 140. The US position, however, has not always been consistent: see, for instance, US Department of Defense, 'An Assessment of International Legal Issues in Information Operations', May 1999, 19 <https://web.archive.org/web/20011103215741/http://www.au.af.mil/au/awc/awcgate/dod-io-legal/dod-io-legal.pdf> ('An unauthorized electronic intrusion into another nation's computer systems may very well end up being regarded as a violation of the victim's sovereignty. It may even be regarded as equivalent to a physical trespass into a nation's territory'). On the ambiguity of the US position on sovereignty, see Russell Buchan, 'When More is Less: The US Department of Defense's Statement on Cyberspace' (*EJIL:Talk!*, 30 March 2020) <www.ejiltalk.org/when-more-is-less-the-department-of-defenses-statement-on-cyberspace/>.

[161] UN Doc A/76/136, 18.

[162] Canada's position paper, para 10.

[163] 'China's Views', 3.

[164] UN Doc A/76/136, 67.

[165] Finland's position paper, 3.

[166] France's position paper, 6–7.

[167] Italy's position paper, 4

[168] UN Doc A/76/136, 46–7.

[169] Inter-American Juridical Committee, Improving Transparency, 29.

[170] ibid.

[171] ibid.

[172] UN Doc A/76/136, 55–6.

[173] New Zealand's position paper, paras 11–12.

[174] Statement by Mr Richard Kadlčák, 2–3.

[175] UN Doc A/76/136, 33.

[176] ibid, 76.

[177] Government Offices of Sweden, 'Position Paper on the Application of International Law in Cyberspace', July 2022, 2 <www.government.se/contentassets/3c2cb6febd0e4ab0bd542f653283b140/swedens-position-paper-on-the-application-of-international-law-in-cyberspace.pdf>.

[178] Ireland's position paper, para 5.

[179] UN Doc A/76/136, 87.

the latter's territory to breach its territorial sovereignty.[180] As Judge Huber famously found in the *Island of Palmas* case, '[s]overeignty in the relations between States signifies independence. Independence in regard to a portion of the globe is the right to exercise therein, *to the exclusion of any other State*, the functions of a State'.[181] From this it follows that a violation of territorial sovereignty occurs—to use the Permanent Court of International Justice's famous words—whenever a state 'exercise[s] its power *in any form* in the territory of another State' without the latter's valid consent or a permissive rule of international law.[182] As shown in Chapter III, the unauthorized extraterritorial exercise of enforcement (or 'executive') jurisdiction is undoubtedly an exercise of 'power',[183] including when it takes the form of the penetration of cyber infrastructure located in another state: no 'general practice accepted as law' has so far determined the emergence of a permissive exception to the *Lotus* principle that excludes all or certain types of cyber operations from the scope of the rule protecting territorial sovereignty.[184] This leads us to the following syllogism: if 1) the extraterritorial non-consensual exercise of power 'in any form' in another state's territory is a violation of its territorial sovereignty; and if 2) the unauthorized access by a state to cyber infrastructure located on the territory of another state is a form of 'exercise of power'; then 3) any such access is a violation of territorial sovereignty whether or not further harmful effects result from it.[185] The fact that the power is exercised remotely does not make any difference: what counts is *where* the concerned infrastructure is, and not *from where* it is accessed.

It is true that most states engage in espionage, either by cyber or more traditional means, but this fact alone does not necessarily mean that such conduct is allowed under customary international law: practice is in itself insufficient to generate customary rules if not accompanied by *opinio juris*.[186] In fact, certain states have expressed

---

[180] Authors who have argued that cyber espionage is a violation of the territorial sovereignty of the target state include Woltag, *Cyber Warfare*, 125–6; Buchan, *Cyber Espionage*, 54; Nicholas Tsagourias, 'The Legal Status of Cyberspace: Sovereignty Redux?' in Nicholas Tsagourias and Russell Buchan (eds), *Research Handbook on International Law and Cyberspace* (2nd edn, Elgar 2021) 9, 22–3; and Kevin Jon Heller, 'In Defense of Pure Sovereignty in Cyberspace' (2021) 97 ILS 1432, 1468–70.

[181] *Island of Palmas Case (Netherland, United States)*, 4 April 1928, 2 RIAA 829, 838, emphasis added.

[182] *The Case of the SS 'Lotus' (France v Turkey)*, Judgment of 7 September 1927, PCIJ Series A No 10, 2, 18, emphasis added. In *Costa Rica v Nicaragua*, the ICJ found that the mere presence of Nicaraguan military personnel on the territory of Costa Rica constituted a violation of the latter's territorial sovereignty (*Costa Rica v Nicaragua*, para 93). For Fausto Pocar, however, while the mere unauthorized presence of military organs of a foreign state is sufficient to encroach on territorial sovereignty, for organs of another nature what is relevant is first and foremost the actual unauthorized exercise of public functions on foreign territory (Fausto Pocar, *L'esercizio non autorizzato del potere statale in territorio straniero* (CEDAM 1974) 111).

[183] See Chapter III, Section 3.2.

[184] UN Doc A/76/136, 18 (Brazil). In literature, see Heller, 'In Defense', 1453 ('sovereignty is a general rule that is not limited to particular means of interfering with a State's exclusive right to control its territory and determine its foreign policy').

[185] The African Union Non-Aggression and Common Defence Pact and the Protocol on Non-Aggression and Mutual Defence in the Great Lakes Region even include 'acts of espionage which could be used for military aggression against a Member State' in their definition of 'aggression' (Art 1 (c)(ix), African Union Non-Aggression and Common Defence Pact (Abuja, 31 January 2005) 2656 UNTS 285; Art 1(3)(i), Protocol on Non-Aggression and Mutual Defence in the Great Lakes Region (Nairobi, 30 November 2006) <https://icglr.org/ova_doc/protocol-on-non-aggression-and-mutual-defence-in-the-great-lakes-region/>.

[186] *North Sea Continental Shelf Cases (Federal Republic of Germany/Denmark; Federal Republic of Germany/The Netherlands)* (Judgment) [1969] ICJ Rep 3, para 77 (hereafter *North Sea Continental Shelf*).

INTERNATIONAL LAW AND THE PRINCIPLE OF NON-INTERVENTION

themselves against the permissibility of unauthorized extraterritorial access to non-publicly available data.[187] The position papers of France and Iran have already been mentioned. China has also endorsed a notion of violation of sovereignty in cyberspace that includes unauthorized access to the ICT infrastructure of another state, cyber espionage, and the theft of important data.[188] Following the global surveillance disclosures of 2013, Brazilian President Dilma Rousseff claimed at the United Nations that US spying on its allies was 'a breach of international law'[189] and the MERCOSUR countries issued a declaration claiming that the US acts of espionage were, *inter alia*, a violation of their sovereignty.[190] In its position paper, Brazil also unsurprisingly claims that the interception of communications is a violation of state sovereignty.[191] Lebanon has accused Israel of intruding in its information and communication networks to conduct monitoring, espionage, and surveillance activities, thus committing '[a] standing violation of the sovereignty of the Lebanese Republic, international law and norms, and the Charter of the United Nations'.[192] Guatemala has additionally noted that sovereignty is violated if a state conducts a cyber operation that 'takes certain information from another State's cyber realm, even when no harm that could affect equipment or the human rights of a person or persons is caused'.[193] Finally, Poland's position paper on the application of international law in cyberspace indicates the theft or public disclosure by a state of data belonging to another state's organs as an example of violation of sovereignty.[194]

Cedric Ryngaert has suggested that, when a cyber operation is conducted by investigative authorities on data stored abroad in order to obtain criminal evidence, the interests of all the concerned states should be balanced against each other in order to establish whether the claim to the extraterritorial exercise of enforcement jurisdiction is reasonable in each specific case.[195] In particular, he posits that '[i]nsofar as the "physical" location of digital data—on a server—may be entirely fortuitous, and may in fact not be known by the territorial State, that State cannot reasonably invoke its territorial sovereignty as a shield against another State's jurisdictional claims over such data'.[196] Ryngaert thus proposes that

> [i]n order to adequately tackle crime in the Internet era, States should be granted more leeway to exercise enforcement—or investigative—jurisdiction over data, regardless of data location ... extraterritorial enforcement jurisdiction [should be] no longer

---

[187] Other states, however, disagree. For Canada, New Zealand, and Switzerland, for instance, cyber espionage is not a breach of territorial sovereignty (Canada's position paper, para 19; New Zealand's position paper, para 14; Switzerland's position paper, 206).

[188] 'China's Views', 2–3.

[189] Julian Borger, 'Brazilian President: US Surveillance a "Breach of International Law"' (*The Guardian*, 24 September 2013) <www.theguardian.com/world/2013/sep/24/brazil-president-un-speech-nsa-surveillance>.

[190] UN Doc A/67/946, 29 July 2013, 2.

[191] UN Doc A/76/136, 18.

[192] UN Doc A/68/703-S/2014/18, 13 January 2014, 2.

[193] Inter-American Juridical Committee, Improving Transparency, 29–30.

[194] Poland's position paper, 3.

[195] Cedric Ryngaert, 'Extraterritorial Enforcement Jurisdiction in Cyberspace: Normative Shifts' (2023) 24 GLJ 537, 543. Several factors can be used to assess such reasonableness (ibid).

[196] ibid, 548.

governed by binary rules (allowed or not allowed). But [it should become] a matter of degree, requiring a granular, contextual assessment. What may be acceptable in some circumstances, may be unacceptable in other circumstances.[197]

In the aforementioned *Tidal* case, for instance, the Norwegian Supreme Court had to determine whether, under the 'principle of sovereignty', the search by investigative authorities in data stored on servers located abroad was an unlawful coercive measure that interfered with another state's exclusive enforcement jurisdiction.[198] After acknowledging that the classic territorial approach to the exercise of enforcement jurisdiction is not without problems in regard to data stored 'in the cloud',[199] the Supreme Court noted that the search was initiated in Norway and conducted 'against a Norwegian company with an office in Norway',[200] it only involved access to the company's data, and no changes were made to the stored data: on this basis, it concluded that its effects on another state were not sufficient to constitute a violation of the principle of sovereignty.[201] As Ryngaert himself points out, however, it would be premature to claim that customary international law presently allows extraterritorial searches on data stored abroad.[202]

Whereas mainstream scholarship asserts that it is only the rule protecting territorial sovereignty that comes into play in this context, I argue that state cyber operations solely designed to remotely access non-public data stored in cyber infrastructure located in another state's territory without its valid consent also fall under the prohibitive scope of the principle of non-intervention: being a non-consensual extraterritorial 'exercise of power', the unauthorized penetration constitutes a case of coercion in the form of a forcible interference as it imposes a certain condition of things (the penetration and consequent acquisition of non-public information) on the target state.[203] The principle of non-intervention and the rule of territorial sovereignty, however, do not entirely overlap: unlike the latter, the former prohibits unauthorized territorial intrusions only when they bear on matters in which the target state can decide freely, and not when they aim to enforce compliance by the target state with its international obligations. If state A were under a treaty obligation to provide certain information to state B but unjustifiably refused to do so, therefore, the principle of non-intervention would not prohibit a cyber operation by state B to coercively obtain the information in question even if it was stored in cyber infrastructure located in state A. Yet the cyber operation would be a breach of state A's territorial sovereignty and state B's responsibility would be precluded only if, and to the extent that, it could be justified as a countermeasure.

Of course, if the competent authority consents to the transborder access of data, the act loses its coercive element and would therefore no longer be an 'intervention'.[204]

---

[197] ibid, 549.
[198] *Tidal*, para 61.
[199] ibid, para 41.
[200] ibid, paras 65, 67.
[201] ibid, para 71.
[202] Ryngaert, 'Extraterritorial Enforcement' 543–4, 549–50.
[203] The UK Attorney General has stated that 'sovereignty and non-intervention are two sides of the same coin' (Braverman, 'International Law').
[204] On the requirements for valid consent, see Chapter IV, Section 4.4 and its subsections.

396 INTERNATIONAL LAW AND THE PRINCIPLE OF NON-INTERVENTION

The question is who exactly is entitled to grant such consent. Under Article 32 of the Budapest Convention on Cybercrime, '[a] Party may, without the authorisation of another Party ... access or receive, through a computer system in its territory, stored computer data located in another Party, if the Party obtains the lawful and voluntary consent of the person who has the lawful authority to disclose the data to the Party through that computer system'.[205] Note, however, that, outside the case of open source data, under customary international law the consent of the 'lawful authority' (be it the user or the internet service provider or another subject) is not sufficient to allow a unilateral transborder search by foreign authorities: the competent *organ* of the territorial state must also authorize the search, without which transborder data access remains unlawful.[206] Article 32(b), therefore, is arguably only opposable to the states parties to the Budapest Convention.[207]

5.4 Cyber Influence Operations

While propaganda activities and election meddling are by no means a new phenomenon,[208] what has changed in the Information Age is their unprecedented scale as, thanks to social media, influence operations can now reach anyone who has a smartphone, a computer, or a tablet, and an internet connection. Two main types of influence operations in and through cyberspace have been identified: hacking and leaking non-public information (*doxing* operations) and the use of information that a state possesses in order to threaten, confuse, or mislead public opinion (*information* operations).[209] Unlike the former, the latter do not involve the unauthorized access of data[210] and have been further divided into *malinformation* operations (the unsolicited

---

[205] Art 32, Budapest Convention.

[206] Jonathan Bourguignon, 'La recherche de preuves informatiques et l'exercice extraterritorial des compétences de l'Etat' in *Internet et le droit international: Colloque de Rouen de la Société Française pour le Droit International* (Pedone 2014) 357, 362–3.

[207] A Council of Europe Report concedes that, in relation to the situations covered in Art 32(b), 'overall, practice, procedures as well as conditions and safeguards vary considerably between different States. Concerns regarding procedural rights of suspects, privacy and the protection of personal data, the legal basis for access to data stored in foreign jurisdictions or "in the clouds" as well as national sovereignty persist and need to be addressed' (Council of Europe, Transborder Access and Jurisdiction: What are the Options?, Report of the Transborder Group of the Cybercrime Convention Committee, 6 December 2012, 58 <https://rm.coe.int/CoERMPublicCommonSearchServices/DisplayDCTMContent?documentId= 09000016802e79e8>). *Contra*, but without much justification, Nicolai Seitz, 'Transborder Search: A New Perspective in Law Enforcement?' (2004–2005) 7 Yale Journal of Law and Technology 23, 45.

[208] On 12 February 1946, for instance, the United States government published a *Blue Book on Argentina*, which detailed Argentina's links with the Nazis. The Department of State ensured wide circulation of the information contained in the *Blue Book* with the purpose of influencing the outcome of the elections in the South American country to be held on 24 February of the same year (Ann Van Wynen Thomas and AJ Thomas, Jr, *Non-Intervention: The Law and Its Import in the Americas* (Southern Methodist University Press 1956) 300).

[209] Barrie Sander, 'Democracy Under the Influence: Paradigms of State Responsibility for Cyber Influence Operations on Elections' (2019) 18 CJIL 1, 5–14. A well-known example of a doxing operation is the Democratic National Committee (DNC)'s email leak: before the 2016 US presidential election, Russia allegedly hacked the DNC's servers and obtained private emails of prominent Democratic Party politicians, which were then leaked to and published by Wikileaks and arguably damaged Hillary Clinton's campaign for the presidency (ibid, 9–10).

[210] ibid, 14.

delivery of factually correct confidential information)[211] and *disinformation* operations (the dissemination of fake or inaccurate news).[212] Botnets, fake accounts, and deep fakes can be used in order to maximize the impact of influence campaigns by deceiving the electorate into believing that they come from insiders, not outsiders.[213]

If it is accepted—as argued above—that any unauthorized access to non-publicly available data stored in cyber infrastructure located in another state's territory constitutes a breach of territorial sovereignty, then doxing operations are also an unlawful intervention whenever they impinge on matters in which the target state can decide freely: the very fact of the non-consensual access to and exfiltration of data is an act of coercion in the form of a forcible interference, regardless of whether or not the obtained information is subsequently used to influence public opinion.[214]

Information operations, on the other hand, involve neither forcible nor dictatorial interferences: merely providing information, be it true or false, to influence someone's decision-making process does not bend the will of the target and, if there is no unauthorized extraterritorial access to data, its will is also not replaced by that of the intervening state.[215] Nicholas Tsagourias, however, has suggested a reinterpretation of the principle of non-intervention. In his view, if the source of legitimate power is popular will, then 'a government's authority and will remain free only when its sourcing is also free'.[216] From this perspective, '[w]hereas the government as the depository of such authority and will is protected by the principle of non-intervention, it is not the primary object of protection as the traditional reading holds, but a derivative one; the primary object of protection are the people and the process of authority and will formation'.[217] Tsagourias thus introduces democratic values in the content of the principle of non-intervention and turns it into a vehicle for democracy promotion.[218] The problem with this view is that distinguishing between governments on the basis of their internal characteristics (in this case, on whether they are the result of free and fair elections) is, in Gerry Simpson's words,[219] a liberal anti-pluralist argument that risks becoming a Trojan horse to legitimize (cyber) intervention aimed at overthrowing non-democratic regimes.[220]

---

[211] ibid, 11. A case of a malinformation operation occurred when Brazilian authorities allegedly shared confidential files in their possession with the Venezuelan opposition in 2017 before a gubernatorial election in order to reputationally damage candidates linked to President Nicolás Maduro (Paula Baldini, Miranda da Cruz, and Rafael Braga da Silva, 'Did Brazil Illegally Intervene in the 2017 Venezuelan Elections?' (*Opinio Juris*, 23 July 2019) <http://opiniojuris.org/2019/07/23/did-brazil-illegally-intervene-in-the-2017-venezue lan-elections>).

[212] Michael N Schmitt, 'Foreign Cyber Interference in Elections' (2021) 97 ILS 739, 746.

[213] This occurred, for instance, during the 2016 US presidential campaign (Jens David Ohlin, *Election Interference: International Law and the Future of Democracy* (CUP 2020) 12).

[214] It is therefore not necessary to investigate whether the influence that doxing operations exercise on the voters is merely persuasive or coercive in order to establish whether the principle of non-intervention has been breached: the act is coercive to the extent that there has been an unauthorized exercise of power by a state on the territory of another to steal information.

[215] The majority of the *Tallinn Manual 2.0* group of experts have noted that 'coercion must be distinguished from persuasion, criticism, public diplomacy, propaganda ... retribution, mere maliciousness, and the like' (Schmitt (ed), *Tallinn Manual 2.0*, 318).

[216] Tsagourias, 'Electoral Cyber Interference', 51.

[217] ibid, 52.

[218] Willmer, 'Does Digitalization', 520.

[219] Gerry Simpson, 'Two Liberalisms' (2001) 12 EJIL 537, 541.

[220] Willmer, 'Does Digitalization', 518.

Ido Kilovaty proposes an alternative reading of the principle of non-intervention, no longer centred on the notion of coercion but on that of disruption.[221] Relying on Myres McDougal and Florentino Feliciano's work,[222] he concludes that doxing operations are a violation of the principle of non-intervention 'when the internal or external process is successfully disrupted by a foreign power acting within cyberspace, and the victim suffers severe domestic or international consequences'.[223] In addition to suffering from a certain indeterminacy (what consequences? how severe?), this argument neglects the fact that disruption can be in itself a form of coercion, either in the form of dictatorial or forcible interference.

Another option is to consider at least disinformation operations, that is, feeding the electorate with false or inaccurate facts, as a new form of coercion of state, namely 'coercive manipulation'.[224] The concept has been so explained:

When evaluating the coerciveness of a fake news story attributable to a foreign power, we must ask two questions: (1) Was the message communicated with the intention of deceiving the target audience into believing a falsehood? (2) Would a reasonable observer judge that the communication was intended to influence the target's decision-making to such an extent that they would be left without a meaningful choice about what to think, and therefore what to do? If the answer to both is in the affirmative, the communication violates the principle of non-intervention.[225]

From this perspective, lying about facts so as to make someone do or not do something can be seen as 'the functional equivalent of coercion' when it leads to exercising control over the victim's behaviour.[226] Indeed, there is only a quantitative, and not qualitative, difference between locking someone in a room (forcible interference), threatening them with violence if they leave the room (dictatorial interference), and falsely claiming that there is a terrorist outside with a suicide vest (coercive manipulation), as in all cases the individual in question will remain in the room without being able to make a meaningful choice.[227] X (formerly Twitter), for instance, could be used by a state to disseminate the wrong information to another state's voters on when and where to vote, or to falsely report an approaching tropical storm so as to deter them from leaving their houses to go to the polls. When manipulation aims to influence the electorate's opinions as in the case of a 'deep fake' that shows a candidate engaging in criminal conduct, and not prevent them from casting their vote, on the other hand, it

---

[221] Ido Kilovaty, 'Doxfare: Politically Motivated Leaks and the Future of the Norm on Non-Intervention in the Era of Weaponized Information' (2018) 9 Harv NSJ 146, 169.

[222] On these authors, see Chapter II, Section 7.2.6.

[223] Kilovaty, 'Doxfare', 173.

[224] Steven Wheatley, 'Foreign Interference in Elections under the Non-Intervention Principle: We Need to Talk About "Coercion"' (2020) 31 Duke J Comp & Intl L 161, 182. The false or inaccurate character of the information can concern not only the reported facts but also its origin and authorship.

[225] ibid, 191–2.

[226] ibid, 181. See also Harold Hongju Koh, 'The Trump Administration and International Law' (2017) 56 Washburn LJ 413, 450; Björnstjern Baade, 'Fake News and International Law' (2018) 29 EJIL 1357, 1363; and Gary P Corn, 'Covert Deception, Strategic Fraud, and the Rule of Prohibited Intervention', Hoover Working Group on National Security, Technology, and Law, Aegis Series Paper No 2005 (18 September 2020) 13–14 <www.hoover.org/sites/default/files/research/docs/corn_webready.pdf>.

[227] Wheatley, 'Foreign Interference', 179; Schmitt, 'Foreign Cyber Interference' 748.

has been suggested that the coercion bar is higher and that it is crossed only if the foreign state's influence operation in support of a candidate dominates social media and thus overwhelms their opponent's campaign.[228]

The notion of 'coercive manipulation' is appealing as it addresses the concerns raised by the scale of cyber influence operations and the unprecedented impact that social media can have in shaping public opinion.[229] Costa Rica, for instance, seems to support this notion where it posits that coercion can occur if 'one State ... deprives another State of the capacity to make free *and informed* choices pertaining to its internal or external affairs [including through] the dissemination of false news ... '.[230] The German position paper also notes that cyber activities targeting foreign elections

> may be comparable in scale and effect to coercion if they aim at and result in a substantive disturbance or even permanent change of the political system of the targeted State, i.e. by significantly eroding public trust in a State's political organs and processes, ... or by dissuading significant groups of citizens from voting, thereby undermining the meaningfulness of an election.[231]

It remains to be seen, however, whether a sufficiently representative majority of states will embrace this line of thinking: some of those that have so far expressed their views on the application of international law in cyberspace have doubted that cyber electoral interferences other than tampering with election machinery and manipulating vote counts can be considered coercive.[232] This reluctance is understandable if one considers that the notion of coercive manipulation might be used by authoritarian states to curb individual freedoms: in March 2022, for instance, Russia blocked Google News from internet users for disseminating 'inauthentic information' on the invasion of Ukraine.[233]

Before concluding, it is worth noting that election meddling can also be an internationally wrongful act if it breaches the principle of self-determination in its internal dimension as formulated in Article 3(e) of the OAS Charter, in the Friendly Relations Declaration, and as reflected in customary international law.[234] This principle, which

---

[228] ibid, 748–9. For Wheatley, this can occur when 'the outside power inundates the information environment in the target state with a single political narrative, drowning out all other voices' (Wheatley, 'Foreign Interference', 189).

[229] Tsagourias, 'Electoral Cyber Interference', 54; Ido Kilovaty, 'The International Law of Cyber Intervention' in Tsagourias and Buchan (eds), *Research Handbook*, 97, 108–9.

[230] Costa Rica's position paper, para 24 (emphasis added). Costa Rica, therefore, considers 'electoral disinformation campaigns seeking to mislead the electorate' as a possible violation of the principle of non-intervention (ibid, para 25).

[231] UN Doc A/76/136, 35.

[232] See Finland's position paper, 3. For Lahmann, there is not yet a rule prohibiting manipulative coercion (Lahmann, 'On the Politics', 106). Another commentator notes that the Western states now seem more prone than during the Cold War to accept a broader notion of intervention that goes beyond the use of armed force and subversive activities so as to also include at least election meddling (Ori Pomson, 'The Prohibition on Intervention under International Law and Cyber Operations' (2022) 99 ILS 180, 216–18).

[233] Alex Hern, 'Russia Blocks Google News after Ad Ban on Content Condoning Ukraine Invasion' (*The Guardian*, 24 March 2022) <www.theguardian.com/world/2022/mar/24/russia-blocks-google-news-after-it-bans-ads-on-proukraine-invasion-content>.

[234] See Chapter V, Section 2. See also Tsagourias, 'Electoral Cyber Interference', 51–6; Jens David Ohlin, 'Did Russian Cyber-Interference in the 2016 Election Violate International Law?' (2017) 95 Tex L Rev 1579, 1594–7.

400 INTERNATIONAL LAW AND THE PRINCIPLE OF NON-INTERVENTION

unlike its external counterpart is not limited in its application to situations of colonialism, racist regimes, and alien occupation, protects a state and its people (intended as the entire population living on the territory of the state) from any external interferences aimed at influencing the outcome of an endogenous process for the choice of the political system: as already noted, while the principle of non-intervention exclusively bans coercive acts, coercion is not required for a violation of that of internal self-determination.[235] Election meddling, therefore, would breach the latter when it is attributable to a foreign state, regardless of whether or not it is considered 'coercive'. That said, one has to concede that election influence operations have a long history and have not normally been condemned on self-determination grounds. As already noted in regard to espionage, however, practice is in itself insufficient to generate customary rules if not accompanied by *opinio juris*.[236]

6. Third-State Cyber Operations in Support of a Government or of Subversive, Terrorist, or Armed Opposition Groups during Civil Strife

It has been seen that one of the rules of application flowing from the general principle of non-intervention is that prohibiting 1) the fomentation and incitement; 2) the organization, assistance, and financing; and 3) the toleration of 'subversive, terrorist or armed activities directed towards the violent overthrow of the regime of another State'.[237] In *Nicaragua*, the ICJ confirmed that 'support for subversive or terrorist armed activities within another State' is a 'particularly obvious' example of coercion.[238] More specifically, support for subversive, terrorist or armed activities can be a form of coercion resulting from either a forcible (for instance, by overthrowing a government) or dictatorial interference (by using the actual or threatened support for an armed opposition group as leverage to obtain certain concessions).

Fomenting and inciting civil strife in another country by cyber means undoubtedly constitutes a violation of the principle of non-intervention. In September 2012, for instance, Azerbaijan denounced a cyber disinformation campaign conducted by the 'Armenian Cyber Army' under the 'direction and control' of Armenia that 'aimed at glorifying terrorists and insulting their victims, as well as at advocating, promoting and inciting ethnically and religiously motivated hatred, discrimination and violence'.[239] Iran has also argued that '[c]yber activities paralyzing websites in a state to provoke internal tensions and conflicts' are a violation of the principle of non-intervention.[240] For Germany, deliberately inciting 'violent political upheaval, riots and/or civil strife

---

[235] See Chapter V, Section 2.
[236] *North Sea Continental Shelf*, para 77.
[237] Chapter III, Section 8.
[238] *Nicaragua v USA*, para 205.
[239] UN Doc A/66/897–S/2012/687, 7 September 2012, 1. Armenia's alleged cyber disinformation campaign against Azerbaijan has been brought before the ICJ, although not from the perspective of the principle of non-intervention (*Application of the International Convention on the Elimination of All Forms of Racial Discrimination (Azerbaijan v Armenia)*, Application instituting proceedings, 23 September 2021, paras 18, 92 <www.icj-cij.org/case/181>).
[240] Iran's statement, Art III(1).

in a foreign country' is a wrongful intervention, particularly when it impedes the orderly conduct of elections.[241] Finland has made a similar point.[242] When spelling out its position on the principle of sovereignty in cyberspace, China has also posited that states cannot 'support or allow separatist forces to undermine other States' territorial integrity, national security and social stability through use of ICTs'.[243] For Costa Rica, '[p]osts inciting individuals ... to disrupt or subvert the internal order of another State may ... breach the principle of non-intervention.'[244] Finally, Poland's position paper affirms that 'a wide-scale and targeted disinformation campaign' can be a violation of the principle of non-intervention 'in particular when it results in civil unrest that requires specific responses on the part of the state'.[245]

As to the organization, assistance, and financing of subversive, terrorist or armed opposition groups, the cyber espionage group Fancy Bear has been accused of infecting, under Russia's instructions, an 'app' used by the Ukrainian armed forces in the armed conflict in Donbass so as to allow the Russian forces to access phone communications and localization data of the Ukrainian artillery.[246] This allegedly facilitated attacks against Ukraine's governmental forces by the secessionists. Several states, including Finland,[247] Germany,[248] Iran,[249] and Switzerland,[250] have explicitly affirmed that cyber operations designed to assist an armed group in another country breach the principle of non-intervention. For Israel, an unlawful intervention can occur even when a state limits itself to supplying information about the cyber vulnerabilities of another state to an armed opposition group.[251] Providing weaponized malware to foreign insurgents and training them to use it to conduct cyber attacks is not only an unlawful intervention but can also be a violation of the prohibition of the use of force.[252] This is the case when the supply of malware and training enables the group to conduct cyber attacks amounting to a use of force, and not only cyber operations below that threshold. A state that funds the cyber operations of a subversive, terrorist, or armed group against a foreign government, on the other hand, could be responsible for a breach of the principle of non-intervention, but not of Article 2(4) and its customary counterpart.[253]

The legal situation of the toleration of cyber subversive, terrorist, or armed activities against another state, on the other hand, is still unsettled. Although not in an internal

---

[241] UN Doc A/76/136, 34–5.
[242] Finland's position paper, 3.
[243] 'China's Views', 2.
[244] Costa Rica's position paper, para 25.
[245] Poland's position paper, 4.
[246] Matteo Fornari, 'Conflitto in Ucraina, orsi fantasiosi e programmi malevoli' (2017) 100 RDI 1156, 1156–7.
[247] Finland's position paper, 3.
[248] UN Doc A/76/136, 34–5.
[249] Iran's statement, Art III(1).
[250] Switzerland's position paper, 200.
[251] Schondorf, 'Israel's Perspective', 403.
[252] *Nicaragua v USA*, para 228. See France's position paper, 7; Switzerland's position paper, 200. An example is the alleged cyber training of members of the Syrian opposition by the US Department of State (Jay Newton-Small, 'Inside America's Secret Training of Syria's Digital Army' (*Time*, 13 June 2012) <http://swampland.time.com/2012/06/13/inside-americas-secret-training-of-syrias-digital-army>).
[253] *Nicaragua v USA*, para 228. But see France's position paper, 7.

unrest context, on 18 October 2016 Ecuador decided to cut off Julian Assange's access to the internet from its London embassy because of the release of documents by Wikileaks impacting the US presidential election campaign: for Marko Milanović, Ecuador 'has essentially expressed its *opinio juris* to the effect that the customary principle of non-intervention requires it to prevent a private actor operating from a place within its jurisdiction from interfering with the electoral process of a third state by leaking the content of a campaign official's private emails'.[254] Certain states, namely the Netherlands, Costa Rica, Denmark, Ireland, and more cautiously Japan, have also claimed the existence of a due diligence customary obligation that requires states to terminate cyber operations against other states originating from their cyber infrastructure,[255] but others have opposed this view, fearing that it might expose them to the injured state's countermeasures for something that they were unable to prevent or not even aware of.[256] The UN GGE 2015 and 2021 reports only include hortatory language and recommend that '[s]tates should not knowingly allow their territory to be used for internationally wrongful acts using ICTs'.[257]

Finally, whether only third-state cyber operations in support of opposition groups are unlawful or also those in support of an incumbent government beset by civil strife is a question that must be answered by applying the principles and rules examined in the previous chapters of this book. As shown, while third states can positively respond to an invitation to intervene, including by cyber means, from a government facing internal unrest short of civil war, the principle of internal self-determination prohibits cyber operations constituting a direct use of armed force in support of any faction when the civil war threshold has been crossed and a process to redefine the political system of a state has been set in motion (other pro-government cyber operations as well as the supply of weaponized malware, however, remain permissible).[258] Even in situations of internal unrest short of civil war, third states are not permitted to conduct any cyber operations in support of a government if the latter is preventing a people from exercising their right to external self-determination.[259]

---

[254] Marko Milanović, 'Ecuador Turns Off Julian Assange's Internet Access' (*EJIL:Talk!*, 19 October 2016) <www.ejiltalk.org/ecuador-turns-off-julian-assanges-internet-access/>.

[255] The Netherlands, UN Doc A/76/136, 59; Costa Rica's position paper, paras 27-9; Denmark's position paper, 7–8; Ireland's position paper, para 12. For Japan, '[o]ne characteristic of cyber operations is the difficulty of making judgment as to attribution to a State. In this respect, the due diligence obligation may provide grounds for invoking the responsibility of the State from the territory of which a cyber operation not attributable to any State originated. It is possible at least to invoke the responsibility of such a State for a breach of its due diligence obligation, even if it is difficult to prove the attribution of a cyber operation to any State' (UN Doc A/76/136, 49).

[256] Among the states that have doubted that a binding rule of due diligence can be transposed to activities in cyberspace under existing law are the United Kingdom (UN Doc A/76/136, 117) and, at least with regard to cyber operations with negligible effects in another state, Canada (Canada's position paper, para 15). For New Zealand, if the due diligence obligation applied in cyberspace, it would need to be restricted to actual, and not constructive, knowledge and involve a reasonableness standard (New Zealand's position paper, para 17).

[257] UN GGE Report 2015, para 13(c); UN GGE Report 2021, norm 13(c), paras 29–30.

[258] See Chapter V, Section 3.2.3.

[259] See Chapter VI, Sections 3.1, 4.

7. Conclusions

As a commentator notes, '[d]igitalization has, at least so far, not so much reshaped the principle of non-intervention, as it has given it a renewed emphasis'.[260] Indeed, it is now virtually uncontested that the application of the principle of non-intervention extends to operations conducted by states in and through cyberspace and even the Western states have been referring to it with an enthusiasm unknown during the Cold War. What remains controversial is exactly what type of cyber operations can be considered coercive so as to fall under its prohibitive scope. The answer depends on the effects that the operations produce or are designed to produce. Those resulting or designed to result in material damage to persons or physical objects or in loss of functionality of infrastructure undoubtedly involve an exercise of power by a state on the territory of another and thus involve coercion in the form of a forcible interference unless they have been validly consented to by the competent organ of the target state. If they aim to compel the target state into doing or not doing something, they also amount to a dictatorial interference. In both cases, they constitute a prohibited intervention whenever they bear on matters in which the target state can decide freely.

Although state practice and *opinio juris* are still limited and unsettled, this chapter has suggested that cyber operations should be considered a breach of territorial sovereignty, and thus—when they bear on matters in which the target state can decide freely—also a violation of the principle of non-intervention, not only when they cause or are designed to cause harmful effects in another state's territory but also when they limit themselves to extraterritorially accessing non-publicly available data without authorization, as in the case of espionage and doxing, as this too involves the non-consensual exercise of power by a state on the territory of another. Disinformation operations, on the other hand, are neither a forcible nor a dictatorial interference but could be seen as a new type of coercion of state ('coercive manipulation'), at least when they disseminate fake or inaccurate information at crucial times in order to prevent the electorate from casting their vote. Finally, cyber operations to foment or incite internal unrest in another country or to support subversive, terrorist, or armed opposition groups against a foreign government are prohibited by the third pillar of the principle of non-intervention. When conducted in support of an incumbent government facing civil strife, cyber operations must be reconciled with the principle of self-determination in both its internal and external dimensions.

---

[260] Willmer, 'Does Digitalization', 521.

General Conclusions

1. History

The principle of non-intervention offers a vantage point from which to analyse the evolution of, and the underlying tensions within, the international legal order. Its study, in particular, constitutes a litmus test to assess the health of its foundational notion, that of sovereignty, of which it is a corollary: as a commentator has observed, '[i]f a state has a right to sovereignty, this implies that other states have a duty to respect that right by, among other things, refraining from intervention in its domestic affairs.'[1] Chapter I showed that the principle of non-intervention originally expressed 'the rejection of a superstate'[2] after the consolidation of national kingdoms *superiorem non recognoscentes* in 15th-century Europe led to the progressive abandonment of the idea of Universal Monarchy. During the 18th century, the principle essentially protected sovereignty as embodied in the person of a God-anointed monarch: it served the absolutist states' purpose to shield themselves from interferences by other states and to consolidate internal sovereignty within their territorial borders after the end of the religious wars in Europe. Intervention, therefore, was conceivable only in support of a legitimate sovereign at his or her request, while support for rebels was in all cases impermissible. The American and French Revolutions violently rejected the idea of the divine right to rule as the source of political legitimacy and replaced it with the consent of the governed as reflected in a social contract. One of the consequences of the turn to popular sovereignty was that the permissibility of intervention came to depend not on compliance with dynastic succession rules and formal transfer of sovereignty, but rather on the factual success of the challenge to the established authority by its subjects.

By the 1830s, the principle of non-intervention, as a balancing mechanism ensuring the co-existence of different forms of political legitimacies in Europe, had become a well-established rule of the *jus publicum europæum* and even those states that were often interfering in the internal affairs of other states, like the Holy Alliance powers, paid lip service to it. While apparently pluralistic, however, the principle was only applied in the intra-European order: it was indeed a corollary of sovereignty, but sovereignty pertained almost exclusively to the European family of nations while relations with the peripheries and semi-peripheries were based on empire.[3] In the second half of the 19th century, a distinction between different situations of internal unrest also emerged. At this point, two factors determined the legality of armed intervention: the context in which the use of force occurred (rebellion/insurrection as opposed to civil

---

[1] RJ Vincent, *Nonintervention and International Order* (Princeton University Press 1974) 14.
[2] ibid, 325.
[3] Christian Reus-Smit, 'The Concept of Intervention' (2013) 39 Rev Intl Stud 1057, 1058.

International Law and the Principle of Non-Intervention. Marco Roscini, Oxford University Press. © Marco Roscini 2024.
DOI: 10.1093/oso/9780198786894.003.0010

war) and the form it took (war or measure short of war). In situations of mere rebellion and insurrection, third states were required to comply with the principle of non-intervention, which essentially entailed that they were prohibited from supporting the insurgents and had the option of assisting the incumbent government upon its request with troops (for some scholars, only by supplying arms and other military *matériel*). The restraining impact of the principle of non-intervention, however, was significantly limited by the fact that—if one accepts the view that war, in this period, was either a right inherent in state sovereignty or an extra-legal phenomenon—a state could have always declared war on that where the internal unrest took place and militarily supported the foreign insurgents. If they decided to intervene without establishing a state of war, however, third states needed to have either a treaty-based right to do so or at least a justification that excused the violation of the fundamental right of independence of the victim state. Self-preservation, in particular, was a catch-all notion that justified action for the protection of both the rights and the essential interests of the intervening states.

In two cases, civil war was treated as an interstate war: when secessionist insurgents had managed to achieve *de facto* statehood and when recognition of belligerency had been granted by the incumbent government and/or by third states. In these cases, the principle of non-intervention was displaced and the same rules that applied to *de jure* wars were triggered, with the consequence that third states had the option of either remaining neutral or becoming involved in the conflict as co-belligerents: whether the latter option was permissible, and on whose side, was determined by the customary and treaty rules on the resort to war in force at the time, and not by the recognition of belligerency.

In the period between the two world wars, states often abstained from supporting governments beset by civil war regardless of whether or not belligerency had been recognized. This attitude was a consequence of the emerging treaty restrictions on the states' *jus ad bellum*, of the limitation of the right of self-preservation to the narrower case of self-defence, and of the progressive emergence of a discrete rule of international law providing for the right of each people to determine their own political system without external interferences. While 'negative equality' with respect to civil wars was undoubtedly a trend detectable in the state practice of the time, it was however not yet an obligation under customary international law: there is no clear evidence of supporting *opinio juris* and treaties had to be concluded to prohibit intervention on any side, the most noticeable examples being the Spanish 'non-intervention agreement' and the General Treaties of Peace and Amity signed by the Central American republics.

In the UN Charter era, the principle of non-intervention has continued to enjoy good health. As shown in Chapter II, not only has it remained the object of scholarly interest, particularly when applied to situations of internal unrest, but it has also been incorporated in a plethora of global, regional, sub-regional, and thematic treaties and it undeniably reflects customary international law. This is hardly surprising: states of all ideological and geographical affiliations, both during and after the end of the Cold War, have considered it a beneficial instrument protecting their individual security interests as well as the general cause of world peace. Conduct inconsistent with the principle has been justified by the intervening states on the basis of alleged exceptions

406 INTERNATIONAL LAW AND THE PRINCIPLE OF NON-INTERVENTION

or has been undertaken covertly, thus confirming the existence of the prohibitive rule. The principle of non-intervention played a particularly important role in the sharply divided world of the Cold War, as it reduced the risks of a nuclear confrontation between blocs.[4] In this period, therefore, the principle was a core component of the law of 'peaceful coexistence' between states with different political and economic systems.[5]

With the fall of the Berlin Wall, the principle of non-intervention started to look outdated.[6] In the 1990s (the 'decade of humanitarianism'), the less confrontational geopolitical scenario made possible armed interventions for the enforcement of community values conducted collectively through the United Nations and/or regional organizations, in particular to maintain or restore international peace and security, to combat international terrorism, and to react to humanitarian crises. This period is thus characterized by a notable decrease in the number of unilateral interventions undertaken by the great powers for the protection of individual interests. When unilateral interventions did occur, the intervening states frequently justified them by invoking the protection of shared normative values.[7]

The consensus, however, was short lived. The demise of the communist bloc did not lead to the global adoption of a single model of political order and the present is once again an ideologically and economically divided world where the principle of non-intervention acts as an instrument to defuse tensions. Even the Western states have been referring to it in recent decades with uncharacteristic enthusiasm: the openness of democratic societies has exposed them to external pressures as a consequence of increasing interconnectivity and large-scale cyber operations to influence public opinion. The idea of non-intervention as a shield from external interferences is now also championed by 'populist' governments.[8] As Martti Koskenniemi notes, today sovereignty

> stands as an obscure representative of an ideal against disillusionment with global power and expert rule. In the context of war, economic collapse, and environmental destruction, in spite of all the managerial technologies, sovereignty points to the possibility, however limited or idealistic, that whatever comes to pass, one is not just a pawn in other people's games but, for better or for worse, the master of one's life.[9]

The same can be said of the principle of non-intervention, which always follows the vicissitudes of sovereignty.

All in all, the legal history of the principle of non-intervention in the last 500 years shows little evidence of historical progression.[10] The frequency of intervention has

---

[4] Sydney Floss, 'Non-ingérence et égalité des États: des principes indépendants des concepts de souveraineté' (2014) 47 RBDI 454, 484; Heike Krieger, 'Populist Governments and International Law' (2019) 30 EJIL 971, 990.

[5] Pierre-Marie Dupuy, 'The Friendly Relations Declaration at 50' in Jorge E Viñuales (ed), *The UN Friendly Relations Declaration at 50: An Assessment of the Fundamental Principles of International Law* (CUP 2020) 362, 363.

[6] Krieger, 'Populist Governments', 990.

[7] S Neil MacFarlane, 'Intervention in Contemporary World Politics', The Adelphi Papers, vol 42, issue 350 (2002) 81.

[8] Krieger, 'Populist Governments', 978–9.

[9] Martti Koskenniemi, 'What Use for Sovereignty Today?' (2011) 1 Asian JIL 61, 70.

[10] MacFarlane, 'Intervention', 20.

been directly proportional to the uniformity of the great powers' ideologies and security interests. When they have shared the same values and interests, they have tended to use them as grounds to intervene in smaller states: in this scenario, respect for the principle of non-intervention depends on compliance by the latter with these common values and interests.[11] When the great powers' mutual relations have been confrontational, on the other hand, the principle of non-intervention has contributed to establishing a balance of power, which has reduced the risk of major conflicts.[12] The intervention pendulum, therefore, has always swung between solidarity and divisiveness and between a statist vision of world order and a communitarian one: tense periods characterized by a strong reliance on the principle have been followed by others where its role has been attenuated to secure compliance with the dominant values and interests.

2. Theory

As seen in Chapter III, during the Cold War several attempts were made at codifying the principle of non-intervention and clarifying its content: regionally, these attempts took place in the framework of the Organization of American States whereas those at the global level were inspired by the communist bloc, which saw them as part of its strategy to gain influence over the Third World countries. What emerges from the examination of the resulting documents is that, in the UN Charter era, treaties, resolutions, and state practice have determined the coexistence of two sets of legal standards, namely, a general principle that prohibits the use of coercion in matters in which each state is permitted to decide freely and a number of rules of application prohibiting specific means and methods of coercion: the prohibition of armed coercion exercised on another state or to deprive peoples of their national identity; the prohibition of economic and political measures designed to obtain the subordination of the exercise of the sovereign rights of the target state to the interests of the coercing state and secure advantages; and the prohibition of organizing, assisting, fomenting, financing, inciting, or tolerating subversive, terrorist, or armed activities directed towards the overthrow of the government of another state, and of interfering in civil strife. While the pillars of the principle of non-intervention prohibiting armed coercion, political coercion in the form of the threat of armed force and premature recognition, and support for subversive, terrorist, and armed activities aimed at overthrowing the government of another state are well established in customary international law, the situation is less clear with regard to economic coercion: because of the inconsistent practice and *opinio juris* of states, we could only conclude that there are indications of a trend towards its inclusion in the customary content of the principle of non-intervention.

The Information Age and the digitization of contemporary societies have also ushered in a new means to intervene in the domestic affairs of other states, that is, cyber operations. As seen in Chapter VIII, whether they fall under the prohibitive scope of the principle under examination depends on their effects. There is now little doubt

---

[11] Gerry Simpson, 'Two Liberalisms' (2001) 12 EJIL 537, 541; Floss, 'Non-ingérence', 486.
[12] Floss, 'Non-ingérence', 486.

that cyber operations resulting or designed to result in material damage to persons or objects or in loss of functionality of infrastructure can constitute an unlawful intervention. This book suggests that cyber operations should also be considered a violation of the principle of non-intervention when they limit themselves to extraterritorially accessing non-publicly available data without the authorization of the competent authorities of the territorial state, as in the case of espionage and doxing. On the other hand, the law is still in flux with regard to disinformation operations: this book posits that they should be seen as a new type of coercion of state at least when they disseminate fake or inaccurate information at crucial times in order to prevent the electorate from casting their vote.

All forms of intervention are characterized by their coercive nature. The analysis conducted in Chapter III demonstrated that, to be coercive, an act must be designed and be able to undermine the agency of the target state and impair its decisional sovereignty. Coercion of state can assume two forms: forcible or dictatorial. Dictatorial coercion consists in the binomial 'demands + threats': by causing or prospecting a certain harm, it bends the will of the victim state so as to make it do or not do something. A demand is coercive when it is accompanied by a clear, specific, and credible threat and the threatened harm, whatever its nature, is sufficiently serious. Forcible coercion, on the other hand, consists in the exercise of power in the territory of another state without its valid consent or a permissive rule of international law. In this case, the coercing state imposes a certain condition of things on the target state by carrying out the unauthorized act itself instead of compelling someone else to do anything. By prohibiting both forms of coercion, the principle of non-intervention protects state sovereignty in all its aspects, that is, decisional and territorial. The existence of an intent to coerce must be demonstrated in the case of dictatorial interferences, while it is presumed in forcible ones.

Coercion, however, constitutes a violation of the principle of non-intervention only when it bears on matters in which each state is permitted to decide freely. The fact that coercion must be exercised in a matter where the target state does not have an obligation under international law to conduct itself in a certain way, that is, in its domestic jurisdiction, is what distinguishes a violation of the principle of non-intervention from a countermeasure: even though it can be coercive, the latter, unlike the former, aims to induce a state that has committed an internationally wrongful act to cease it and provide full reparation. The mere fact that a matter does not belong to a state's domestic jurisdiction does not automatically mean that other states can resort to coercion in regard to it: this would only be permissible when the coercive means are not prohibited by other primary rules of international law or, if they are, when their use is aimed at enforcing compliance by the target state with the breached obligation and all the substantive and procedural requirements under the law of countermeasures are met. The coercing state must also be entitled to react.

Chapter IV examined the role played by consent in the context of the principle of non-intervention. More specifically, from the element of coercion it follows that the principle of non-intervention only prohibits interventions against a state but leaves unaffected those validly consented to by it. Unlike in a neutrality regime, therefore, third states are not required to treat equally the different factions of the civil strife: they can support the incumbent government upon its request and are at the same time prohibited from giving any assistance to opposition groups in spite of their appeal. All in all, the ideologically neutral doctrine of effectiveness continues to be the preferred ground for the identification of the authority entitled to consent to foreign intervention: indeed, history shows that interventionism has always been a by-product of legitimacy doctrines based on religion, ideology, constitutionality, democracy, 'humanrightsism', or other values. In case of rival governmental administrations, the one that was in effective control of the state's territory, population, and apparatus at the beginning of the civil strife continues to be entitled to consent to foreign intervention until it is defeated, or until its resistance becomes merely nominal: the unworkable alternative would be that governmental status shifts from faction to faction depending on the military situation on the field. If the incumbent has been defeated and no other faction has sufficient effective control of the country to be able to claim governmental status, the preferable view is that an intervention to restore a functioning state or protect civilians can only be carried out with the authorization of the Security Council under Chapter VII of the UN Charter.

Consent to intervention constitutes an agreement between the intervening state and that where the intervention takes place and can be granted in writing or orally, publicly or secretly, expressly or implicitly, but cannot be presumed. State practice shows that treaty-based open-ended consent needs to be confirmed before each intervention can validly take place, unless the object and purpose of the treaty is to allow interventions (normally to be undertaken by or through an international organization) if certain events occur even when it is the target state's government that is responsible for them. Furthermore, a state may only consent to intervention on its territory (as consent exclusively operates in the relations between the consenter and the consentee) and only to acts that it could itself lawfully undertake. Last but not least, consent must be valid and the limits attached to it must be respected for it to produce its effects.

3. Interactions

As Christian Tomuschat notes, '[t]o the extent that overriding values are acknowledged by the international community, such values take precedence over the rule of non-intervention'.[13] The UN Charter era, in particular, has seen the emergence and consolidation of new customary rules and principles that have moved away from a purely statist idea of sovereignty and, at least in certain circumstances, have lifted the veil of domestic jurisdiction over the maintenance of internal order. These rules and principles have affected the application of the principle of non-intervention in several ways by shifting the focus from governments to peoples and individuals.

First, when a situation of internal unrest becomes a civil war, the application of the principle of non-intervention is now partly displaced by that of *internal self-determination*. Although it had already been occasionally invoked during the 19th century and had started to consolidate in the period between the two world wars, it is only in the UN Charter era that self-determination becomes a discrete rule of

---

[13] Christian Tomuschat, 'International Law: Ensuring the Survival of Mankind on the Eve of a New Century—General Course on Public International Law' (1999) 281 Recueil des Cours 9, 238.

international law. In its internal dimension, the principle entails that a people have the right to choose and modify their state's political, economic, social, and cultural systems without external interferences and, correspondingly, third states have an obligation to abstain from any interferences in that choice. While not all situations of internal unrest constitute a process for the modification of the political system of a state, this is certainly the case of the most dramatic one, that is, civil wars, defined as those internal armed conflicts where an organized armed opposition group with political objectives controls a portion of the state's territory and has established a *de facto* administration therein. The principle of internal self-determination rules out the permissibility of intervention by invitation and imposes on third states an obligation of negative equality, that is, of abstaining from supporting any party. Under customary international law, however, the obligation of negative equality in civil wars is a qualified one: while it undoubtedly prevents third states from sending armed forces in support of any party, the analysis of state practice and *opinio juris* conducted in Chapter V showed that it does not yet extend to lesser forms of intervention. Incumbent governments, in other words, still maintain a privileged position compared to insurgents even during a civil war. The principle of internal self-determination is also not infringed when the armed intervention in support of an incumbent government beset by civil war has no or only minimal impact on the internal struggle for power, as in the case of evacuation operations and peacekeeping operations; when the insurgents are unlawfully supported by another state, to the extent that the counter-intervention is proportionate to the unlawful support; and when the competent UN organs have certified that the armed opposition group is a terrorist organization and is thus incapable of expressing a people's genuine choice of a political system.

My analysis also demonstrated that the principle of non-intervention continues to apply to forms of internal unrest short of civil war, particularly military coups and mutinies, mercenary attacks, and mob violence. In these cases, third states can intervene in support of the incumbent authorities at their valid request in order to restore internal order, including by sending armed forces. In case of pro-democracy popular uprisings and internal armed conflicts short of civil war, a trend has been detected towards an obligation of negative equality prohibiting direct armed assistance in support of all parties, but it is still premature to conclude that this reflects the *lex lata*.

Secondly, in cases of colonial domination and alien occupation, the principle of *external self-determination* demands that the colonial and occupying powers not prevent the subjugated people from choosing its international status, including by creating a new state if it so wishes. As shown in Chapter VI, therefore, a state breaching this *erga omnes* obligation can no longer hide behind the principle of non-intervention by claiming that the situation is a purely domestic affair. This has two negative consequences for the oppressive government: it can be the object of coercive measures adopted by other states to enforce its compliance with the principle of external self-determination and it cannot receive third-state assistance finalized to the maintenance of the unlawful situation, regardless of its form and of whether or not the unrest has reached the threshold of a civil war. If an obligation to support a colonial or occupying power arises from a treaty of cooperation not specifically finalized at the maintenance of the illegal situation and there is no sanction regime imposed by the UN Security Council, compliance with it can still be suspended and/

or terminated even when the grounds codified in the 1969 Vienna Convention on the Law of Treaties (VCLT) cannot be invoked: the suspension or termination would constitute a countermeasure adopted in reaction to the breach of an *erga omnes* obligation, providing that the necessary substantive and procedural requirements are met.

The principle of external self-determination also has another important consequence. While the principle of non-intervention normally prohibits all assistance to insurgents, consensus formed during the Cold War that at least some support could be granted to a people struggling to free itself from colonial rule or alien occupation. What blocs disagreed on was what type of support was lawful. The opposition of the Western states prevented the formation of a customary rule based on the principle of external self-determination allowing direct or indirect military assistance to national liberation movements. Financial and political support, on the other hand, was considered permissible by the vast majority of states: such measures are not proscribed by the principle of non-intervention when they aim at terminating the unlawful situation as they do not bear on a matter in which the target state can decide freely and, if they were in conflict with other international law obligations, they could constitute countermeasures adopted in response to the violation of an *erga omnes* obligation.

It is important to highlight two differences between the operation of the principles of internal and external self-determination. First, unlike that of an intervention in support of a colonial or occupying power, the illegality of an intervention on the side of a government beset by civil war is not a sanction for a violation of international law committed by the target state, but the result of a normative conflict between the principle of non-intervention and that of internal self-determination in which the latter takes priority as both *lex specialis* and *lex posterior*. The other difference is that the principle of internal self-determination internationalizes a situation of internal unrest only when, and if, the insurgent group becomes strong enough to control parts of the national territory and exercise forms of governance therein, whereas the principle of external self-determination internationalizes the conflict *ab initio* and regardless of the military successes of the armed group.[14] This is because, in the latter case, the struggle is protected in itself by the international legal order as it is functional to the realization of one of its fundamental objectives (the end of colonialism, racist regimes, and alien domination/occupation). In the former, on the other hand, the internal struggle constitutes a mere fact from which, when it reaches the threshold of a civil war, certain legal consequences arise (the obligation of negative equality for third states in order to protect a people's free choice of its political system).

Thirdly and finally, states can no longer claim that the *protection of human rights* is an exclusively domestic matter: the use of coercion to ensure respect for them, therefore, is not prohibited by the principle of non-intervention although it might be proscribed by other primary rules of international law. Chapter VII of the present book showed that coercion can be exercised on a government responsible for international

---

[14] Valentina Grado, *Guerre civili e terzi stati* (CEDAM 1998) 350.

human rights law (IHRL) and/or international humanitarian law (IHL) violations in two ways: by refusing, suspending, or terminating assistance in its favour, or by supporting opposition groups. As to the former, states can always decline a request for assistance or suspend/terminate existing voluntary cooperation with a foreign government that commits the violations in question but, differently from the case of a colonial or occupying power, have an obligation to do so only if it is required by treaties or Security Council decisions. If states are under a treaty obligation to assist the foreign authorities responsible for IHRL and/or IHL violations and in the absence of a sanction regime adopted by the Security Council, non-compliance with this obligation can be justified, even when the grounds codified in the VCLT cannot be invoked, as a countermeasure adopted in response to the violation of an *erga omnes* or *erga omnes partes* obligation.

Third states, on the other hand, are not permitted to send troops in support of or transfer arms to insurgents who are fighting a murderous government, as humanitarian intervention does not constitute an accepted exception to the prohibition of the use of force codified in Article 2(4) of the UN Charter. Such intervention could thus only lawfully take place with the authorization of the Security Council under Chapter VII of the Charter and consistently with the principle of internal self-determination, that is, it must be limited to end the violations in question and to protect civilians and not be aimed at regime change. Non-military forms of assistance for opposition groups adopted in response to the IHRL and/or IHL violations committed by their government, on the other hand, are beyond the reach of the principle of non-intervention even when they are coercive, as they do not bear on a matter in which the target state can decide freely: they are, therefore, lawful measures to secure compliance with international law by the target state. Should they conflict with other international law obligations, these measures would nevertheless be lawful if they constitute countermeasures adopted in response to the previous violation of an *erga omnes* or *erga omnes partes* obligation.

To sum up. Until the internal unrest becomes a civil war, the principle of non-intervention applies with the result that third states may intervene by whatever means on the side of the incumbent authorities at their valid request and may not in any form assist the insurgents. When the unrest becomes a civil war, an obligation of negative equality arises and third states may not send armed forces in support of any faction, whereas lesser forms of assistance for the incumbent authorities remain permissible. Regardless of whether the internal unrest is a civil war, third states may not intervene on the side of a government that prevents a people entitled to external self-determination from exercising it. They also remain prohibited from intervening by using force in support of the national liberation movement, although other forms of support are allowed. Finally, regardless of whether the unrest has become a civil war or not, third states may lawfully stop assistance to a government responsible for IHRL and/or IHL obligations but have no obligation under customary international law to do so. As in the case of external self-determination, third states may not militarily intervene in support of the insurgents against the murderous government, but they may provide other assistance short of the use of armed force.

4. Epilogue

In 1864, Pope Pius IX condemned the principle of non-intervention as one of the errors of the time.[15] All in all, was his a fair assessment? Has the principle in question made a positive contribution to international order or not? Georges Scelle, for one, profoundly disliked the idea of non-intervention and considered it an anarchic principle, a false doctrine born out of the abuses of intervention for political purposes. In Scelle's solidarist view, intervention is a physiological phenomenon in both the domestic and the international legal orders and its lawfulness depends on its purpose, namely, on whether it aims to enforce the law or not.[16] The New Haven School has also attempted to legitimize intervention as an instrument to implement community values.[17] Others, however, have been more sceptical of the beneficial role that intervention can play: from the Italian scholars of the 19th century to the TWAILers of the 20th and 21st, they have all seen it as a means used by the great powers to oppress the weaker states and have considered the principle of non-intervention as an indispensable normative defence against it.[18]

At the end of this book, I prefer to side with those who argue that the principle of non-intervention is neither just nor unjust: as Koskenniemi puts it in *From Apology to Utopia*, 'peace may be associated with intervention as well as non-intervention and even an absolute preference for peace cannot tell us whether intervention should be admitted or not'.[19] The best solution to the problem of non-intervention, therefore, is 'to retain the formal principle but to concede that it may sometimes be morally necessary to breach it—without saying this out loud'.[20] Indeed, a complete abandonment of the principle of non-intervention would likely greenlight the powerful states' pursuit of their own interests at the expense of the weaker ones. At the same time, its attenuation is necessitated by today's global problems (depletion of natural resources, climate change, the risk of nuclear war, cyber security, population growth, just to mention a few), which can only be effectively addressed through cooperation among states and not through obtuse isolationism grounded in populist conceptions of sovereignty.

---

[15] *Syllabus errorum*, 8 December 1864, Proposition LXII.

[16] See Chapter I, Section 10.

[17] See Chapter II, Section 7.2.6.

[18] See Chapter I, Section 10 and Chapter II, Section 7.1.2.

[19] Martti Koskenniemi, *From Apology to Utopia: The Structure of International Legal Argument* (CUP 2006) 498, fn 83. See also Vincent, *Nonintervention*, 344.

[20] Koskenniemi, *From Apology to Utopia*, 501.

Select Bibliography

Books

Alexandrowicz CH, *The Law of Nations in Global History* (D Armitage and J Pitts eds, OUP 2017).

Alvarado Garaicoa T, *Los Principios Internacionales de No Intervención y Autodeterminación* (Dijkman 1962).

Alvarez A, *Le droit international américain* (Pedone 1910).

Anghie A, *Imperialism, Sovereignty and the Making of International Law* (CUP 2004).

Annoni A, *Il riconoscimento come atto unilaterale dello Stato* (Jovene 2023).

Anzilotti D, *Corso di diritto internazionale*, vol III (Athenæum 1915).

Arangio-Ruiz G, *The United Nations Declaration on Friendly Relations and the System of the Sources of International Law* (Sijthoff & Noordhoff 1979).

Armstrong D, T Farrell, and H Lambert, *International Law and International Relations* (CUP 2007).

Baker Sir S, *Halleck's International Law or Rules Regulating the Intercourse of States in Peace and War*, vol I (3rd edn, Kegan Paul, Trench, Trübner & Co 1893).

Balladore Pallieri G, *Diritto internazionale pubblico* (2nd edn, Giuffrè 1938).

Becker Lorca A, *Mestizo International Law* (CUP 2014).

Bedjaoui M, *La revolution algérienne et le droit* (Éditions de l'Association internationale des juristes démocrates 1961).

Bennouna M, *Le consentement à l'ingérence militaire dans les conflits internes* (R. Pichon et R. Durand-Auzias 1974).

Bernard M, *On the Principle of Non-Intervention: A Lecture Delivered in the Hall of All Souls' College* (JH and Jas Parker 1860).

— — *A Historical Account of the Neutrality of Great Britain during the American Civil War* (Longmans, Green, Reader, and Dyer 1870).

Bertotti S, and others, *The Law of War and Peace. A Gender Analysis: Volume One* (Bloomsbury 2021).

Bluntschli JK, *Le droit international codifié* (MC Lardy and A Rivier tr, 5th edn, Guillaumin & Co 1893).

Brownlie I, *International Law and the Use of Force by States* (Clarendon Press 1963).

Buchan R, *International Law and the Construction of Liberal Peace* (Hart 2013).

— — *Cyber Espionage and International Law* (Hart 2019).

Bull H, *The Anarchical Society. A Study of Order in World Public Politics* (4th edn, Macmillian-Red Globe Press 2012).

Calvo C, *Le droit international théorique et pratique*, vol I (4th edn, Guillaumin et al 1887).

Cansacchi G, *Storia dei trattati e politica internazionale. I principii informatori delle relazioni internazionali* (Giappichelli 1965).

Carnazza Amari G, *Nuova esposizione del principio del non intervento* (Caronda 1873).

Cassese A, *Self-Determination of Peoples: A Legal Reappraisal* (CUP 1995).

Castrén E, *Civil War* (Suomalainen Tiedeakatemia 1966).

416 SELECT BIBLIOGRAPHY

Cavaglieri A, *Nuovi studi sull'intervento* (Società Anonima Editrice 1928).

Charlesworth H and C Chinkin, *The Boundaries of International Law: A Feminist Analysis* (Manchester University Press 2000).

Chen TC, *The International Law of Recognition* (LC Green ed, Stevens & Sons 1951).

Chesterman S, *Just War or Just Peace? Humanitarian Intervention and International Law* (OUP 2022).

Chimni BS, *International Law and World Order: A Critique of Contemporary Approaches* (2nd edn, CUP 2017).

Clapham A, *War* (OUP 2021).

Combacau J and S Sur, *Droit international public* (13th edn, LGDJ 2019).

Corten O, *The Law Against War: The Prohibition on the Use of Force in Contemporary International Law* (2nd edn, Hart 2021).

Crawford J, *The Creation of States in International Law* (2nd edn, OUP 2006).

— — *Brownlie's Principles of Public International Law* (9th edn, OUP 2012).

D'Aspremont J, *L'Etat non démocratique en droit international. Etude critique du droit international positif et de la pratique contemporaine* (Pedone 2008).

David E, *Mercenaires et volontaires internationaux en droit des gens* (Editions de l'Université de Bruxelles 1978).

De Guttry A, *Le rappresaglie non comportanti la coercizione militare nel diritto internazionale* (Giuffrè 1985).

Delerue F, *Cyber Operations and International Law* (CUP 2020).

Despagnet F, *Cours de droit international public* (3rd edn, Larose & Tenin 1905).

De Wet E, *Military Assistance on Request and the Use of Force* (OUP 2020).

DeWitt Dickinson E, *The Equality of States in International Law* (Harvard University Press 1920).

Díaz Barrado CM, *El consentimiento, causa de exclusión de la ilicitud del uso de la fuerza, en Derecho Internacional* (Universidad de Zaragoza 1989).

Dinstein Y, *War, Aggression and Self-Defence* (6th edn, CUP 2017).

— — *Non-International Armed Conflicts in International Law* (2nd edn, CUP 2021).

Droetto A, *Pasquale Stanislao Mancini e la scuola italiana di diritto internazionale del secolo XIX* (Giuffrè 1954).

Dupuis C, *Le droit des gens et les rapports des grandes puissances avec les autres État avant le Pacte de la Société des Nations* (Plon-Nourrit 1921).

Elagab OY, *The Legality of Non-Forcible Counter-Measures in International Law* (Clarendon Press 1988).

Fabela I, *Intervention* (Pedone 1961).

Falk RA, *Legal Order in a Violent World* (Princeton University Press 1968).

Fauchille P, *Droit international public*, vol I, Première partie: *Paix* (8th edn, Rousseau & Co 1922).

Fiore P, *Nouveau droit international public suivant les besoins de la civilisation moderne*, vol I (Charles Antoine tr, 2nd edn, A Durand et Pedone-Lauriel 1885).

— — *International Law Codified and Its Legal Sanction or The Legal Organization of the Society of States* (EM Borchard tr, Baker, Voorhis and Company 1918).

Focarelli C, *Introduzione storica al diritto internazionale* (Giuffrè 2012).

Gaeta P, JE Viñuales, and S Zappalà, *Cassese's International Law* (3rd edn, OUP 2020).

Gathii JT, *War, Commerce, and International Law* (OUP 2010).

Grado V, *Guerre civili e terzi Stati* (CEDAM 1998).

Gray C, *International Law and the Use of Force* (4th edn, OUP 2018).

Grewe WG, *The Epochs of International Law* (M Byers tr and rev, Walter de Gruyter 2000).

Hall WE, *A Treatise on International Law* (3rd edn, Clarendon Press 1890).

Hasar S, *State Consent to Foreign Military Intervention during Civil Wars* (Brill/Nijhoff 2022).

SELECT BIBLIOGRAPHY 417

Heffter A-G, *Le droit international public de l'Europe* (Jules Bergson tr and ed, Schrœder and Cotillon 1857).

Henderson C, *The Use of Force and International Law* (CUP 2018).

Historicus, *Letters by Historicus on Some Questions of International Law* (Macmillan 1863).

Hyde CC, *International Law Chiefly as Interpreted and Applied by the United States*, vol I (2nd edn, Little, Brown & Co 1947).

Jouannet E, *The Liberal–Welfarist Law of Nations: A History of International Law* (CUP 2012).

Kolb R, *International Law on the Maintenance of Peace: Jus Contra Bellum* (Edward Elgar 2018).

Koskenniemi M, *The Gentle Civilizer of Nations: The Rise and Fall of International Law 1870–1960* (CUP 2001).

— — *From Apology to Utopia: The Structure of International Legal Argument* (CUP 2005).

— — *To the Uttermost Parts of the Earth. Legal Imagination and International Power, 1300-1870* (CUP 2021).

— — Walter Rech, and Manuel Jiménez Fonseca (eds), *International Law and Empire: Historical Explorations* (OUP 2017).

Lattanzi F, *Garanzie dei diritti dell'uomo nel diritto internazionale generale* (Giuffrè 1983).

Lauterpacht Sir H, *Recognition in International Law* (CUP 1947).

Lawrence TJ, *The Principles of International Law* (3rd edn, Heath & Co 1895).

Le Fur L, *La Guerre d'Espagne et le Droit* (Les Éditions Internationales 1938).

— — *Précis de droit international public* (4th edn, Dalloz 1939).

Lieblich E, *International Law and Civil Wars. Intervention and Consent* (Routledge 2013).

Longobardo M, *The Use of Armed Force in Occupied Territory* (CUP 2018).

Lorimer J, *The Institutes of the Law of Nations: A Treatise of the Jural Relations of Separate Political Communities*, vols I and II (Blackwood and Sons 1883-4).

Maćak K, *Internationalized Armed Conflicts in International Law* (OUP 2018).

Mamiani T, *D'un nuovo diritto europeo* (4th edn, Tipografia Scolastica—Seb. Franco e Figli 1861).

Mancini PS, *Della nazionalità come fondamento del diritto delle genti* (E Jayme ed, Giappichelli 2000).

Martens FF de, *Traité de droit international* (A Léo tr, Librairie A Maresco Ainé, 1883).

Martens GF von, *Précis de droit des gens moderne de l'Europe fondé sur les traités et l'usage*, vol I (Jean Chret Dieterich 1789).

McLaughlin R, *Recognition of Belligerency and the Law of Armed Conflict* (OUP 2020).

McNair L and AD Watts, *The Legal Effects of War* (CUP 1966).

Miele A, *L'estraneità ai conflitti armati secondo il diritto internazionale*, vol II: *La disciplina positiva delle attività statuali* (CEDAM 1970).

Milano E, *Formazione dello stato e processi di state-building nel diritto internazionale. Kosovo 1999-2013* (Editoriale Scientifica 2013).

Moir L, *The Law of Internal Armed Conflict* (CUP 2002).

Neff SC, *War and the Law of Nations* (CUP 2005).

Neuhold H, *The Law of International Conflict. Force, Intervention and Peaceful Dispute Settlement* (Brill/Nijhoff 2016).

Noël J, *Le principe de non-intervention. Théorie et pratique dans les relations inter-américaines* (Editions de l'Université de Bruxelles/Bruylant 1981).

Nolte G, *Eingreifen auf Einladung. Zur völkerrechtlichen Zulässigkeit des Einsatzes fremder Truppen im internen Konflikt auf Einladung der Regierung* (Springer 1999).

Nowak C, *Das Interventionsverbot im Bürgerkrieg: Darstellung eines Wandels durch die Bürgerkriege in Libyen, Syrien, Irak, Jemen und Ukraine seit 2011* (Peter Lang 2018).

Nussbaum A, *A Concise History of the Law of Nations* (rev edn, Macmillan 1954).

418 SELECT BIBLIOGRAPHY

Nys E, *Le droit international: Les principes, les théories, les faits*, vol II (Castagne and Fontemoing 1905).

O'Connell ME, *The Art of Law in the International Community* (CUP 2019).

Oglesby RR, *Internal War and the Search for Normative Order* (Springer 1971).

Olivart El Marqués de, *Del reconocimiento de beligerancia y sus efectos inmediatos* (L Péant é hijos 1895).

Oppenheim L, *International Law: A Treatise*, vol I: *Peace* (2nd edn, Longmans, Green & Co 1912).

— — (ed), *The Collected Papers of John Westlake on Public International Law* (CUP 1914).

Orford A, *Rethinking Humanitarian Intervention: Human Rights and the Use of Force in International Law* (CUP 2003).

— — *International Authority and the Responsibility to Protect* (CUP 2011).

— — *International Law and the Politics of History* (CUP 2021).

Palma L, *Del principio di nazionalità nella moderna società europea* (Editori della Biblioteca Utile 1867).

Pertile M, *La relazione tra risorse naturali e conflitti armati nel diritto internazionale* (CEDAM 2012).

— — *Diritto internazionale e rapport economici nelle guerre civili* (Editoriale Scientifica 2020).

Phillimore Sir R, *Commentaries upon International Law*, vol I (3rd edn, Butterworths 1879).

Picone P, *Comunità internazionale e obblighi «erga omnes»* (Jovene 2006).

Pillet A, *Recherches sur les droits fondamentaux des États dans l'ordre des rapports internationaux et sur la solution des conflits qu'ils font naître* (Pedone 1899).

Pocar F, *L'esercizio non autorizzato del potere statale in territorio straniero* (CEDAM 1974).

Pradier-Fodéré P, *Traité de droit international public*, vol I (Durand et Pedone-Lauriel 1885).

Pustorino P, *Movimenti insurrezionali e diritto internazionale* (Cacucci 2018).

Quadri R, *Diritto internazionale pubblico* (5th edn, Liguori 1968).

Rasilla I de la, *International Law and History: Modern Interfaces* (CUP 2021).

Redaelli C, *Intervention in Civil Wars: Effectiveness, Legitimacy, and Human Rights* (Hart 2020).

Rivier A, *Principes du droit des gens*, vol I (Rousseau 1986).

Romano S, *Corso di diritto internazionale* (CEDAM 1926).

Ronzitti N, *Le guerre di liberazione nazionale e il diritto internazionale* (Pacini 1974).

— — *Diritto internazionale dei conflitti armati* (7th edn, Giappichelli 2021).

Roscini M, *Cyber Operations and the Use of Force in International Law* (OUP 2014).

Roth BR, *Governmental Illegitimacy and International Law* (OUP 1999).

Rougier A, *Les guerres civiles et le droit des gens* (Larose & Forcel 1903).

Rousseau C, *La non-intervention en Espagne* (Pedone 1939).

— — *Droit international public*, vol IV (Sirey 1980).

Ruys T and O Corten, with A Hofer (eds) *The Use of Force in International Law: A Case-based Approach* (OUP 2018).

Ryngaert C, *Jurisdiction in International Law* (2nd edn, OUP 2015).

— — *Selfless Intervention* (OUP 2020).

Sammartino L, *La ricerca di regole applicabili al "commercio" internazionale di armi convenzionali* (Aracne 2021).

Sapienza R, *Il principio del non intervento negli affari interni. Contributo allo studio della tutela giuridica internazionale della potestà di governo* (Giuffrè 1990).

— — *La guerra civile nell'evoluzione del diritto internazionale* (ed.it 2010).

Scarfi JP, *The Hidden History of International Law in the Americas: Empire and Legal Networks* (OUP 2017).

Schmitt C, *Writings on War* (T Nunan tr and ed, Polity 2011).

SELECT BIBLIOGRAPHY 419

Schmitt MN (ed), *Tallinn Manual 2.0 on the International Law Applicable to Cyber Operations* (2nd edn, CUP 2017).

Schwarzenberger G, *International Law as Applied by International Courts and Tribunals*, vol II: *The Law of Armed Conflict* (Stevens & Sons 1968).

Senaratne K, *Internal Self-Determination in International Law: History, Theory, and Practice* (CUP 2021).

Sereni AP, *The Italian Conception of International Law* (Columbia University Press 1943).

Sicilianos L-A, *Les reactions décentralisées à l'illicite: des contre-mesures à la légitime défense* (LGDJ 1990).

Simpson G, *Great Powers and Outlaw States: Unequal Sovereigns in the International Legal Order* (CUP 2004).

Siotis J, *Le droit de la guerre et les conflits armés d'un caractère non-international* (R Pichon et R Duranf-Auzias 1958).

Sivakumaran S, *Non-International Armed Conflicts* (OUP 2012).

Stowell EC, *Intervention in International Law* (John Byrne & Co 1921).

Summers J, *Peoples and International Law* (Brill 2013).

Talmon S, *Recognition of Governments in International Law: With Particular Reference to Governments in Exile* (Clarendon Press 1998).

Tanca A, *Foreign Armed Intervention in Armed Conflict* (Nijhoff 1993).

Tancredi A, *La secessione nel diritto internazionale* (CEDAM 2001).

Tanoviceano J, *De l'intervention au point de vue du droit international* (L Larose et Forcel 1884).

Tesón FR, *Humanitarian Intervention: An Inquiry into Law and Morality* (3rd edn, Transnational Publishers 2005).

Thomas AVW and AJ Thomas, Jr, *Non-Intervention: The Law and Its Import in the Americas* (Southern Methodist University Press 1956).

Vattel E de, *Le droit des gens ou Principes de la loi naturelle appliqués à la conduite et aux affaires des nations et des souverains* (1758), tr by B Kapossy and R Whatmore as *The Law of Nations, Or, The Principles of the Law of Nature, Applied to the Conduct and Affairs of Nations and Sovereigns, with three Early Essays on the Origin and Nature of Natural Law and on Luxury* (Liberty Fund 2008).

Verdebout A, *Rewriting Histories of the Use of Force: The Narrative of 'Indifference'* (CUP 2021).

Verzijl JHW, *International Law in Historical Perspective*, vol I (Sijthoff 1968).

Vidari E, *Del principio di intervento e di non intervento* (Amministrazione del Politecnico 1868).

Vincent R-J, *Nonintervention and International Order* (Princeton University Press 1974).

Walzer M, *Just and Unjust Wars. A Moral Argument with Historical Illustrations* (5th edn, Basic Books 2015).

Westlake J, *International Law*, parts I (Peace) and II (War) (CUP 1904 and 1913).

Wheaton H, *History of the Law of Nations in Europe and America* (Gould, Banks & Co 1845).

— — *Elements of International Law* (WB Lawrence ed, 6th edn, Little, Brown & Co 1855).

Wiesse C, *Le droit international appliqué aux guerres civiles* (B Benda, 1898).

Wilson HA, *International Law and the Use of Force by National Liberation Movements* (Clarendon Press 1988).

Wolff C, *Jus gentium methodo scientifica pertractatum*, vol 2 (Joseph H Drake tr, Clarendon-Humphrey Milford 1934).

Yihdego Z, *The Arms Trade and International Law* (Hart 2007).

Zúñiga LG, *El principio de no intervención* (Tibás 1991).

Book Chapters

Acevedo DE, 'The Haitian Crisis and the OAS Response: A Test of Effectiveness in Protecting Democracy' in L Fisler Damrosch (ed), *Enforcing Restraint: Collective Intervention in Internal Conflicts* (Council on Foreign Relations Press 1993) 119.

Akehurst M, 'Humanitarian Intervention' in H Bull (ed), *Intervention in World Politics* (Clarendon Press 1984) 95.

Anghie A, 'Imperialism and International Legal Theory' in A Orford and F Hoffman (eds), *The Oxford Handbook of the Theory of International Law* (OUP 2016) 156.

Arangio Ruiz G, 'Autodeterminazione (diritto dei popoli alla)' in *Enciclopedia giuridica*, vol IV (Treccani 1988) 1.

Arrighi JM, 'The Prohibition of the Use of Force and Non-Intervention: Ambition and Practice in the OAS Region' in M Weller (ed), *The Oxford Handbook of the Use of Force in International Law* (OUP 2015) 507.

Augusti E, '*L'intervento* europeo in Oriente nel XIX secolo: storia contesa di un istituto controverso' in L Nuzzo and M Vec (eds), *Constructing International Law: The Birth of a Discipline* (Klostermann 2012) 277.

Azarova V and I Blum, 'Belligerency' in *MPEPIL Online* (last updated September 2015).

Barsotti R, 'Insorti' in *Enciclopedia del diritto*, vol XXI (Giuffrè 1971) 796.

Besson S, 'Sovereignty' in *MPEPIL Online* (last updated April 2011).

Bhuta N, 'State Theory, State Order, State System—Jus Gentium and the Constitution of Public Power' in S Kadelbach, T Kleinlein, and D Roth-Isigkeit (eds), *System Order, and International Law: The Early History of International Legal Thought from Machiavelli to Hegel* (OUP 2017) 398.

Buchan R and I Navarrete, 'Cyber Espionage and International Law' in N Tsagourias and R Buchan (eds), *Research Handbook on International Law and Cyberspace* (2nd edn, Edward Elgar 2021) 231.

Bull H, 'Conclusions' in H Bull (ed), *Intervention in World Politics* (Clarendon Press 1984) 181.

—— 'Intervention in the Third World' in H Bull (ed), *Intervention in World Politics* (Clarendon Press 1984) 135.

Burley A-M, 'Commentary on Intervention Against Illegitimate Regimes' in L Fisler Damrosch and DJ Scheffer (eds), *Law and Force in the New International Order* (Westview Press 1991) 177.

Carrera A, 'Tra dovere di obbedienza e diritto di resistenza. La figura del ribelle nel pensiero giuridico di Vattel' in G De Giudici, D Fedele, and EF Malaspina (eds), *Soggettività contestate e diritto internazionale in età moderna* (Historia et ius 2023) 177 <www.historiaetius.eu/uplo ads/5/9/4/8/5943821/de_giudici_ebook.pdf>.

Carter BE, 'Economic Coercion' in *MPEPIL Online* (last updated September 2009).

Chadwick E, 'National Liberation in the Context of Post- and Non-Colonial Struggles for Self-Determination' in M Weller (ed), *The Oxford Handbook of the Use of Force in International Law* (OUP 2015) 841.

Charpentier J, 'Les effets du consentement sur l'intervention' in *Mélanges Séfériadès*, vol II (School of Political Sciences 'Panteios' 1961) 489.

Clark J, 'Debacle in Somalia: Failure of the Collective Response' in L Fisler Damrosch (ed), *Enforcing Restraint: Collective Intervention in Internal Conflicts* (Council on Foreign Relations Press 1993) 205.

SELECT BIBLIOGRAPHY   421

Conforti B, 'The Principle of Non-Intervention' in M Bedhaoui (ed), *International Law: Achievements and Prospects* (UNESCO/Nijhoff 1991) 489.

Crawford E, 'Insurgency' in *MPEPIL Online* (last updated June 2015).

Crawford J, 'Sovereignty as a Legal Value' in J Crawford and M Koskenniemi (eds), *The Cambridge Companion to International Law* (CUP 2012) 117.

— — 'Napoleon 1814–1815: A Small Issue of Status' in I Van Hulle and RCH Lesaffer (eds), *International Law in the Long Nineteenth Century (1776–1914): From the Public Law of Europe to Global International Law?* (Brill 2019) 3.

Demchak CC, 'Economic and Political Coercion and a Rising Cyber Westphalia' in K Ziolkowski (ed), *Peacetime Regime for State Activities in Cyberspace: International Law, International Relations and Diplomacy* (CCDCOE 2013) 595.

Dörr O, 'Use of Force, Prohibition of' in *MPEPIL Online* (last updated September 2015).

Dugard J and D Raić, 'The Role of Recognition in the Law and Practice of Secession' in M Kohen (ed), *Secession: International Law Perspectives* (CUP 2006) 94.

Falk RA, 'Janus Tormented: The International Law of Internal War' in J Rosenau (ed), *International Aspects of Civil Strife* (Princeton University Press 1964) 185.

— — 'Six Legal Dimensions of the United States Involvement in the Vietnam War' in RA Falk (ed), *The Vietnam War and International Law*, vol 2 (Princeton University Press 1969) 216.

— — 'Intervention and National Liberation' in H Bull (ed), *Intervention in World Politics* (Clarendon Press 1984) 119.

Farer TJ, 'A Paradigm of Legitimate Intervention' in L Fisler Damrosch (ed), *Enforcing Restraint: Collective Intervention in Internal Conflicts* (Council on Foreign Relations Press 1993) 316.

Fisher R, 'Intervention: Problems of Policy and Law' in RA Falk (ed), *The Vietnam War and International Law*, vol 1 (Princeton University Press 1968) 135.

Fitschen T, 'Vienna Congress (1815)' in *MPEPIL Online* (last updated January 2015).

Fox GH, 'Intervention by Invitation' in M Weller (ed), *The Oxford Handbook of the Use of Force in International Law* (OUP 2015) 816.

Franck TM, 'Intervention Against Illegitimate Regimes' in L Fisler Damrosch and DJ Scheffer (eds), *Law and Force in the New International Order* (Westview Press 1991) 159.

Friedmann W, 'Intervention, Civil War and the Role of International Law' in RA Falk (ed), *The Vietnam War and International Law*, vol 1 (Princeton University Press 1968) 151.

Frowein JA, 'Self-Determination as a Limit to Obligations under International Law' in C Tomuschat (ed), *Modern Law of Self-Determination* (Nijhoff 1993) 211.

García Robles A, 'La autodeterminación y la non intervención en el derecho internacional e interamericano' in P González Casanova (ed), *No intervención, autodeterminación y democracia en América Latina* (Siglo Veintiuno 1983) 283.

Gill TD, 'Non-Intervention in the Cyber Context' in K Ziolkowski (ed), *Peacetime Regime for State Activities in Cyberspace: International Law, International Relations and Diplomacy* (CCDCOE 2013) 217.

Grant TD, 'Doctrines (Monroe, Hallstein, Brezhnev, Stimson)' in *MPEPIL Online* (last updated March 2014).

Greppi E, 'La diplomatie cavourienne et les nouveaux usages du droit international' in B Cortese (ed), *Studi in onore di Laura Picchio Forlati* (Giappichelli 2014) 403.

— — 'The *Risorgimento* and the "Birth" of International Law in Italy' in G Bartolini (ed), *A History of International Law in Italy* (OUP 2020) 79.

Grote R, 'Westphalian System' in *MPEPIL Online* (last updated June 2006).

Hagemeyer-Witzleb TM, *The International Law of Economic Warfare* (Springer 2021).

422 SELECT BIBLIOGRAPHY

Happold M, 'Economic Sanctions and International Law: An Introduction' in P Eden and M Happold (eds), *Economic Sanctions and International Law* (Hart 2016) 1.

Hargrove JL, 'Intervention by Invitation and the Politics of the New World Order' in L Fisler Damrosch and DJ Scheffer (eds), *Law and Force in the New International Order* (Westview Press 1991) 113.

Henkin L, 'Use of Force: Law and U.S. Policy' in L Henkin and others (eds), *Right v. Might: International Law and the Use of Force* (2nd edn, Council on Foreign Relations Press 1991) 37.

Higgins R, 'Internal War and International Law' in CE Black and RA Falk (eds), *The Future of the International Legal Order*, vol III (Princeton University Press 1971) 81.

— — 'International Law and Civil Conflict' in E Luard (ed), *The International Regulation of Civil Wars* (Thames and Hudson 1972) 169.

— — 'Intervention and International Law' in H Bull (ed), *Intervention in World Politics* (Clarendon Press 1984) 29.

Hinghofer-Szalkay SG, 'Concert of Europe' in *MPEPIL Online* (last updated January 2013).

Hoffman S, 'The Problem of Intervention' in H Bull (ed), *Intervention in World Politics* (Clarendon Press 1984) 7.

Jakjimovska V, 'Uneasy Neutrality: Britain and the Greek War of Independence (1821–1832)' in I Van Hulle and RCH Lesaffer (eds), *International Law in the Long Nineteenth Century (1776–1914): From the Public Law of Europe to Global International Law?* (Brill 2019) 45.

Joyner CC, 'International Law' in PJ Schraeder (ed), *Intervention in the 1980s: U.S. Foreign Policy in the Third World* (Lynne Rienner 1989) 191.

Kamminga MT, 'Extraterritoriality' in *MPEPIL Online* (last updated September 2020).

Keller H, 'Friendly Relations Declaration (1970)' in *MPEPIL Online* (last updated June 2021).

Kilovaty I, 'The International Law of Cyber Intervention' in N Tsagourias and R Buchan (eds), *Research Handbook on International Law and Cyberspace* (2nd edn, Edward Elgar 2021) 97.

Kirkpatrick JJ and A Gerson, 'The Reagan Doctrine, Human Rights, and International Law' in L Henkin and others (eds), *Right v. Might: International Law and the Use of Force* (2nd edn, Council on Foreign Relations Press 1991) 19.

Kohen MG, 'Self-Determination' in JE Viñuales (ed), *The UN Friendly Relations Declaration at 50: An Assessment of the Fundamental Principles of International Law* (CUP 2020) 133.

Kokott J and L Mälksoo, 'States, Sovereign Equality' in *MPEPIL Online* (last updated March 2023).

Koskenniemi M and V Kari, 'Sovereign Equality' in JE Viñuales (ed), *The UN Friendly Relations Declaration at 50: An Assessment of the Fundamental Principles of International Law* (CUP 2020) 166.

Kritsiotis D, 'Topographies of Force' in M Schmitt and J Pejic (eds), *International Law and Armed Conflict: Exploring the Faultlines: Essays in Honour of Yoram Dinstein* (Nijhoff 2007) 29.

— — 'Theorizing International Law on Force and Intervention' in A Orford and F Hoffman (eds), *The Oxford Handbook of the Theory of International Law* (OUP 2016) 655.

— — 'Intervention: Sketches from the Scenes of the Mexican and Russian Revolutions' in K Greenman and others (eds), *Revolutions in International Law: The Legacies of 1917* (CUP 2021) 183.

Kunig P, 'Intervention, Prohibition of' in *MPEPIL Online* (last updated April 2008).

Lamberti Zanardi P, 'Indirect Military Aggression' in A Cassese (ed), *The Current Legal Regulation of the Use of Force* (Nijhoff 1986) 111.

Lantigua DM, 'God, Sovereignty, and the Morality of Intervention outside Europe' in P Slotte and JD Haskell (eds), *Christianity and International Law: An Introduction* (CUP 2021) 91.

SELECT BIBLIOGRAPHY 423

Lattanzi F, 'Autodeterminazione dei popoli' in *Digesto delle discipline pubblicistiche*, vol 2 (4th edn, UTET 1987) 4.

Lesaffer R, 'Kellogg–Briand Pact (1928)' in *MPEPIL Online* (last updated October 2010).

— — 'Too Much History: From War as Sanction to the Sanctioning of War' in M Weller (ed), *The Oxford Handbook of the Use of Force in International Law* (OUP 2015) 35.

Lowe V, 'The Principle of Non-Intervention: Use of Force' in V Lowe and C Warbrick (eds), *The United Nations and the Principles of International Law: Essays in Memory of Michael Akehurst* (Routledge 1994) 66.

Luard E, 'Collective Intervention' in H Bull (ed), *Intervention in World Politics* (Clarendon Press 1984) 157.

Lukashuk II, 'The United Nations and Illegitimate Regimes: When to Intervene to Protect Human Rights' in L Fisler Damrosch and DJ Scheffer (eds), *Law and Force in the New International Order* (Westview Press 1991) 143.

Marauhn T and Ntoubandi ZF, 'Armed Conflict, Non-International' in *MPEPIL Online* (last updated July 2016).

Marchisio S, 'The Unification of Italy and International Law' in G Bartolini (ed), *A History of International Law in Italy* (OUP 2020) 285.

McGoldrick D, 'The Principle of Non-Intervention: Human Rights' in V Lowe and C Warbrick (eds), *The United Nations and the Principles of International Law: Essays in Memory of Michael Akehurst* (Routledge 1994) 85.

Mitrović T, 'Non-Intervention in the Internal Affairs of States' in M Šahović (ed), *Principles of International Law Concerning Friendly Relations and Cooperation* (The Institute of International Politics and Economics, Belgrade & Oceana Publications 1972) 219.

Moore JN, 'Intervention: A Monochromatic Term for a Polychromatic Reality' in RA Falk (ed), *The Vietnam War and International Law*, vol 2 (Princeton University Press 1969) 1061.

Moyn S and U Özsu, 'The Historical Origins and Setting of the Friendly Relations Declaration' in JE Viñuales (ed), *The UN Friendly Relations Declaration at 50: An Assessment of the Fundamental Principles of International Law* (CUP 2020) 23.

Mullerson R, 'Intervention by Invitation' in L Fisler Damrosch and DJ Scheffer (eds), *Law and Force in the New International Order* (Westview Press 1991) 127.

Nanda V, 'Commentary on International Intervention to Promote the Legitimacy of Regimes' in L Fisler Damrosch and DJ Scheffer (eds), *Law and Force in the New International Order* (Westview Press 1991) 181.

Nolte G, 'Secession and External Intervention' in M Kohen (ed), *Secession: International Law Perspectives* (CUP 2006) 65.

— — 'Intervention by Invitation' in *MPEPIL Online* (last updated January 2010).

Oeter S, 'Self-Determination' in B Simma and others (eds), *The Charter of the United Nations: A Commentary*, vol I (3rd edn, OUP 2012) 313.

Orakhelashvili A, 'Governmental Activities on Foreign Territory' *MPEPIL Online* (last updated June 2021).

Otto D, 'Feminist Approaches to International Law' in A Orford and F Hoffman (eds), *The Oxford Handbook of the Theory of International Law* (OUP 2016) 488.

Palmisano G, 'Autodeterminazione dei popoli' in *Enciclopedia del diritto*, vol V (Giuffrè 2012) 82.

Paone P, 'Intervento (diritto internazionale)' in *Enciclopedia del diritto*, vol XII (Giuffrè 1972) 521.

Papa MI, 'Autodeterminazione dei popoli e terzi Stati' in M Distefano (ed), *Il principio di autodeterminazione dei popoli alla prova del nuovo millennio* (Wolters Kluwer/CEDAM 2014) 53.

424 SELECT BIBLIOGRAPHY

Pertile M, 'On the Financing of Civil Wars through Natural Resources: Is There a Duty of Vigilance for Third States on the Activities of Trans-National Corporations?' in FR Jacur, A Bonfanti, and F Seatzu (eds), *Natural Resource Grabbing: An International Law Perspective* (Brill/Nijhoff 2015) 383.

Picone P, 'Interventi delle Nazioni Unite e obblighi *erga omnes*' in P Picone (ed), *Interventi delle Nazioni Unite e diritto internazionale* (CEDAM 1995) 517.

Pitts J, 'Intervention and Sovereign Equality: Legacies of Vattel' in S Recchia and JM Welsch (eds), *Just and Unjust Intervention: European Thinkers from Vitoria to Mill* (CUP 2013) 132.

Pustorino P, 'L'intervento esterno nei conflitti armati interni a sostegno del governo al potere o degli insorti' in E Triggiani and others (eds), *Dialoghi con Ugo Villani* (Cacucci 2017) 191.

Reidel E, 'Human Rights Protection as a Principle' in JE Viñuales (ed), *The UN Friendly Relations Declaration at 50: An Assessment of the Fundamental Principles of International Law* (CUP 2020) 231.

Reisman WM, 'Meddling in Internal Affairs: Establishing the Boundaries on Non-Intervention in a World without Boundaries' in C Giorgetti and N Klein (eds), *Resolving Conflicts in the Law: Essays in Honour of Lea Brilmayer* (Brill/Nijhoff 2019) 98.

Rodley Sir N, ' "Humanitarian Intervention" ' in M Weller (ed), *The Oxford Handbook of the Use of Force in International Law* (OUP 2015) 775.

Rodogno D, 'The European Powers' Intervention in Macedonia, 1903–1908: An Instance of Humanitarian Intervention?' in B Simms and DJB Trim (eds), *Humanitarian Intervention: A History* (CUP 2011) 205.

Roguski P, 'Violations of Territorial Sovereignty in Cyberspace — an Intrusion-based Approach' in D Broeders and B van den Berg (eds), *Governing Cyberspace: Behavior, Power, and Diplomacy* (Rowman & Littlefield 2020) 65.

Ronzitti N, 'Non-ingerenza negli affari interni di un altro Stato' in *Digesto delle discipline pubblicistiche*, vol X (UTET 1995) 159.

— — 'Conflitti armati interni ed intervento di terzi Stati' in I Caracciolo and U Montuoro (eds), *Conflitti armati interni e regionalizzazione delle guerre civili* (Giappichelli 2016) 57.

— — 'Sanctions as Instruments of Coercive Diplomacy: An International Law Perspective' in N Ronzitti (ed), *Coercive Diplomacy, Sanctions and International Law* (Brill 2016) 1.

Rosas A, 'Internal Self-Determination' in C Tomuschat (ed), *Modern Law of Self-Determination* (Nijhoff 1993) 225.

Roscini M, 'Cyber Operations as a Use of Force' in N Tsagourias and R Buchan (eds), *Research Handbook on International Law and Cyberspace* (2nd edn, Edward Elgar 2021) 297.

Salmon J, 'Internal Aspects of the Right to Self-Determination: Towards a Democratic Legitimacy Principle?' in C Tomuschat (ed), *Modern Law of Self-Determination* (Nijhoff 1993) 253.

Sapienza R, 'Autodeterminazione e assetti politici del terzo millennio' in M Distefano (ed), *Il principio di autodeterminazione dei popoli alla prova del nuovo millennio* (Wolters Kluwer/ CEDAM 2014) 165.

Schaller C, 'Siding with Rebels: Recognition of Opposition Groups and the Provision of Military Assistance in Libya and Syria (2011–2014) in H-J Heintze and P Thielbörger (eds), *From Cold War to Cyber War: The Evolution of the International Law of Peace and Armed Conflict over the Last 25 Years* (Springer 2016) 251.

Sender O, 'Coercion', in *MPEPIL Online* (last updated November 2021).

Shaygan F, 'Intervention by Invitation as a Tool of New Colonialism' in James Crawford and others (eds), *The International Legal Order: Current Needs and Possible Responses. Essays in Honour of Djamchid Momtaz* (Brill/Nijhoff 2017) 766.

Simma B and ATh Müller, 'Exercise and Limits of Jurisdiction' in J Crawford and M Koskenniemi (eds), *The Cambridge Companion to International Law* (CUP 2012) 134.

Sinclair Sir I, 'The Significance of the Friendly Relations Declaration' in V Lowe and C Warbrick (eds), *The United Nations and the Principles of International Law: Essays in Memory of Michael Akehurst* (Routledge 1994) 1.

Steinberg JB, 'International Involvement in the Yugoslavia Conflict' in L Fisler Damrosch (ed), *Enforcing Restraint: Collective Intervention in Internal Conflicts* (Council on Foreign Relations Press 1993) 27.

St-Fleur Y, 'L'intervention par invitation d'un État tiers: le consentement au recours à la force contre des combattants étrangers terroristes' in J Crawford and others (eds), *The International Legal Order: Current Needs and Possible Responses. Essays in Honour of Djamchid Momtaz* (Brill/Nijhoff 2017) 783.

Thürer D and T Burri, 'Self-Determination' in *MPEPIL Online* (last updated December 2008).

Tladi D, 'The Duty Not to Intervene in Matters within Domestic Jurisdiction' in JE Viñuales (ed), *The UN Friendly Relations Declaration at 50: An Assessment of the Fundamental Principles of International Law* (CUP 2020) 87.

Toman J, 'La conception soviétique des guerres de libération nationale' in A Cassese (ed), *Current Problems of International Law: Essays on U.N. Law and on the Law of Armed Conflict* (Giuffrè 1975) 355.

Tonolo S, 'Neutralità e non intervento nel diritto internazionale attuale' in D Andreozzi (ed), *Attraverso i conflitti: Neutralità e commercio fra età moderna ed età contemporanea* (Edizioni Università di Trieste 2017) 131.

Tsagourias N, 'Electoral Cyber Interference, Self-Determination, and the Principle of Non-intervention in Cyberspace' in D Broeders and B van den Berg (eds), *Governing Cyberspace: Behavior, Power, and Diplomacy* (Rowman & Littlefield 2020) 45.

— — 'The Legal Status of Cyberspace: Sovereignty Redux?' in N Tsagourias and R Buchan (eds), *Research Handbook on International Law and Cyberspace* (2nd edn, Edward Elgar 2021) 9.

Ungern-Sternberg A von, 'Religion and Religious Intervention' in B Fassbender and A Peters (eds), *The Oxford Handbook of the History of International Law* (OUP 2012) 294.

Vagts D, 'Balance of Power' in *MPEPIL Online* (last updated September 2007)

Verdirame G, 'Sovereignty' in J d'Aspremont and S Singh (eds), *Concepts for International Law: Contributions to Disciplinary Thought* (Edward Elgar 2019) 827.

Verhoeven J, 'Non-intervention: «affaires intérieures» ou «vie privée»?' in *Le droit international au service de la paix, de la justice et du développement. Mélanges Michel Virally* (Pedone 1991) 493.

Villani U, 'Riconoscimento (diritto internazionale)' in *Enciclopedia del diritto*, vol XL (Giuffrè 1989) 633.

Vincineau M, 'Quelques commentaires à propos de la «Déclaration sur l'inadmissibilité de l'intervention et d l'ingérence dans les affaires intérieures des États» (Résolution 36/103 du 9 décembre 1981)' in *Mélanges offerts à Charles Chaumont—Le droit des peoples à disposer d'eux-mêmes. Méthodes d'analyse du droit international* (Pedone 1984) 555.

Watts S, 'Low-Intensity Cyber Operations and the Principle of Non-Intervention' in JD Ohlin, K Govern, and C Finkelstein (eds), *Cyber War: Law and Ethics for Virtual Conflicts* (OUP 2015) 249.

Wedgwood R, 'Commentary on Intervention by Invitation' in L Fisler Damrosch and DJ Scheffer (eds), *Law and Force in the New International Order* (Westview Press 1991) 135.

Wippman D, 'Enforcing the Peace: ECOWAS and the Liberian Civil War' in L Fisler Damrosch (ed), *Enforcing Restrain: Collective Intervention in Internal Conflicts* (Council on Foreign Relations Press 1993) 157.

SELECT BIBLIOGRAPHY

Wippman D, 'Pro-Democratic Intervention' in M Weller (ed), *The Oxford Handbook of the Use of Force in International Law* (OUP 2015) 797.

Wrange P, 'Intervention in National and Private Cyberspace and International Law' in J Ebbesson and others (eds), *International Law and Changing Perceptions of Security: Liber Amicorum Said Mahmoudi* (Brill/Nijhoff 2014) 307.

Wright Q, 'Espionage and the Doctrine of Non-Intervention in Internal Affairs' in RJ Stander (ed), *Essays on Espionage in International Law* (Ohio State University Press 1962) 3.

— — 'Non-Military Intervention' in KW Deutsch and S Hoffman (eds), *The Relevance of International Law: Essays in Honour of Leo Gross* (Schenkman 1968) 5.

Zacharias D, 'Holy Alliance (1815)' in *MPEPIL Online* (last updated December 2007).

Zancla P, 'Contributo alla teoria dell'intervento' in *Studi in onore di Manlio Udina*, vol I (Giuffrè 1975) 884.

Zayas A De, 'Spanish Civil War (1936–1939)' in *MPEPIL Online* (last updated July 2013).

Ziegler KS, 'Domaine Réservé' in *MPEPIL Online* (last updated April 2013).

Ziolkowski K, 'General Principles of International Law as Applicable in Cyberspace' in *Peacetime Regime for State Activities in Cyberspace: International Law, International Relations and Diplomacy* (CCDCOE 2013) 135.

Journal Articles

Abi-Saab GM, 'The Newly Independent States and the Rules of International Law: An Outline' (1962) 8 How LJ 95.

— — 'The Third World and the Future of the International Legal Order' (1973) 29 REDI 27.

— — 'Wars of National Liberation in the Geneva Conventions and Protocols' (1979) 165 Recueil des Cours 353.

Akehurst M, 'Jurisdiction in International Law' (1972–1973) 46 BYBIL 145.

Alabrune F, 'Fondements juridiques de l'intervention militaire française contre Daech en Irak et en Syrie' (2016) 120 RGDIP 41.

— — 'Le cadre juridique des actions militaires menées par la France en Syrie le 14 avril 2018' (2018) 122 RGDIP 545.

Alaimo ML, 'La questione dell'Afghanistan alle Nazioni Unite e il problema del consenso nell'illecito internazionale' (1981) 64 RDI 287.

— — 'Natura del consenso nell'illecito internazionale' (1982) 65 RDI 257.

Alam S, 'Indian Intervention in Sri Lanka and International Law' (1991) 38 NILR 346.

Alfaro RJ, 'The Rights and Duties of States' (1959) 97 Recueil des Cours 91.

Alford NH Jr, 'The Legality of American Military Involvement in Viet Nam: A Broader Perspective' (1966) 75 Yale LJ 1109.

Allain J, 'The True Challenge to the United Nations System of the Use of Force: The Failures of Kosovo and Iraq and the Emergence of the African Union' (2004) 8 Max Planck YB UN L 237.

Allo AK, 'Counter-Intervention, Invitation, Both, or Neither? An Appraisal of the 2006 Ethiopian Intervention in Somalia' (2009) 3 Mizan LR 201.

Aloupi N, 'The Right to Non-Intervention and Non-Interference' (2015) 4 Cambridge J Int'l & Comp L 566.

Amoroso D, 'Il ruolo del riconoscimento degli insorti nella promozione del principio di autodeterminazione interna: considerazioni alla luce della "Primavera Araba"' (2013) 21 Federalismi.it 1 <www.federalismi.it/nv14/articolo-documento.cfm?artid=23420>.

Amvane G, 'Intervention Pursuant to Article 4(h) of the Constitutive Act of the African Union without United Nations Security Council Authorisation' (2015) 15 AHRLJ 282.

Angeles JE, MEP Beltran, and RJA Quitain, 'The International Law Regime Governing Revolutionaries: Status of the MNLF, MILF and Abu Sayyaf in International Law' (2003) 77 Phil LJ 345.

Anghie A, 'The Evolution of International Law: Colonial and Postcolonial Realities' (2006) 27 Third World Quarterly 739.

— — and BS Chimni, 'Third World Approaches to International Law and Individual Responsibility in Internal Conflicts' (2003) 2 CJIL 77.

Ansari MH, 'Some Reflections on the Concepts of Intervention, Domestic Jurisdiction and International Obligation' (1995) 35 IJIL 197.

Apuuli KP, 'Explaining the (Il)legality of Uganda's Intervention in the Current South Sudan Conflict' (2014) 23 African Security Review 352.

Arangio-Ruiz G, 'Human Rights and Non-Intervention in the Helsinki Final Act' (1977) 157 Recueil des Cours 195.

— — 'Droits de l'homme et non intervention: Helsinki, Belgrade, Madrid' (1980) 35 La Comunità internazionale 453.

— — 'Le domaine réservé. L'organisation internationale et le rapport entre droit international et droit interne: cours générale de droit international public' (1990) 225 Recueil des Cours 195.

Asuncion M, I Chao, and J Ocampo, 'The Rise of Interventions to Protect Human Rights in the Waning Years of the 20th Century' (1999) 74 Phil LJ 303.

Audéoud O, 'L'intervention américano-caraïbe à la Grenade' (1983) 29 AFDI 217.

Aust HP, 'Fundamental Rights of States: Constitutional Law in Disguise?' (2015) 4 Cambridge J Int'l & Comp L 521.

Baker Benjamin A, 'Syria: The Unbearable Lightness of Intervention' (2018) 35 Wis Int'l LJ 515.

Balladore Pallieri G, 'L'intervento come istituto giuridico internazionale' (1929–1930) 4 Annali dell'Istituto di Scienze giuridiche, economiche, politiche e sociali della R. Università di Messina 233.

— — 'Quelques aspects juridiques de la non-intervention en Espagne' (1937) 18 RDILC 285.

Bannelier K, 'Military Interventions against ISIL in Iraq, Syria and Libya, and the Legal Basis of Consent' (2016) 29 LJIL 743.

— — and T Christakis, 'Under the UN Security Council's Watchful Eyes: Military Intervention by Invitation in the Malian Conflict' (2013) 26 LJIL 855.

Barrie GN, 'Forcible Intervention and International Law: Legal Theory and Realities' (1999) 116 SALJ 791.

Bassiouni MC, 'Legal Status of US Forces in Iraq from 2003–2008' (2010) 11 Chi J Int'l L 1.

Bastid P, 'La Révolution de 1848 et le droit international' (1948) 72 Recueil des Cours 167.

Beale JH Jr, 'The Recognition of Cuban Belligerency' (1895–1896) 9 Harv L Rev 406.

Beaulac S, 'Emer de Vattel and the Externalization of Sovereignty' (2003) 5 J His Intl L 237.

Ben Achour R, 'Changements anticonstitutionnels de gouvernement et droit international' (2016) 379 Recueil des Cours 397.

Benneh EY, 'Economic Coercion, The Non-Intervention Principle and the Nicaragua Case' (1994) 6 Afr J Intl & Comp L 235.

Benvenisti E, 'Are There Any Inherently Public Functions for International Law?' (2021) 115 AJIL Unbound 302.

Bernstorff J von, 'The Use of Force in International Law before World War I: On Imperial Ordering and the Ontology of the Nation-State' (2018) 29 EJIL 233.

Bettati M, '«Souveraineté limitée» ou «internationalisme prolétarien»? Les liens fondamentaux de la communauté des Etats socialistes' (1972) 8 RBDI 455.

Bianchi A, 'Le recenti sanzioni unilaterali adottate dagli Stati Uniti nei confronti di Cuba e la loro liceità internazionale' (1998) 81 RDI 313.

Bilder RB, 'Comments on the Legality of the Arab Oil Boycott' (1977) 12 Tex Intl LJ 41.

428 SELECT BIBLIOGRAPHY

Bílková V, 'Reflections on the Purpose-Based Approach' (2019) 79 ZaöRV 681.

Blum YZ, 'Economic Boycotts in International Law' (1977) 12 Tex Intl LJ 5.

Boersner D, 'Venezuela ante el intervencionismo en Centroamérica y el Caribe' (1983) 52 Rev Jur UPR 111.

Bohan RT, 'The Dominican Case: Unilateral Intervention' (1966) 60 AJIL 809.

Bond JE, 'A Survey of the Normative Rules of Intervention' (1971) 52 Mil L Rev 51.

Bond Choquette R, 'A Rebuttable Presumption Against Consensual Nondemocratic Intervention' (2016) 55 Colum J Transnat'l L 138.

Boorman JA III, 'Economic Coercion in International Law: The Arab Oil Weapon and the Ensuing Juridical Issues' (1974) 9 JILE 205.

Bourquin M, 'Crimes et délits contre la sûreté des États étrangers' (1927) 16 Recueil des Cours 117.

—— 'La Sainte-Alliance. Une essai d'organisation européenne' (1953) 83 Recueil des Cours 375.

Bowett DW, 'Economic Coercion and Reprisals by States' (1972) 13 Va J Intl L 1.

Brehm M, 'The Arms Trade and States' Duty to Ensure Respect for Humanitarian and Human Rights Law' (2008) 12 JCSL 359.

Brierly JL, 'International Law and Resort to Armed Force' (1930–1932) 4 CLJ 308.

Briggs HW, 'Relations Officieuses and Intent to Recognize: British Recognition of Franco' (1940) 47 AJIL 47.

Brookman-Byrne M, 'Intervention by (Secret) Invitation: Searching for a Requirement of Publicity in the International Law on the Use of Force with Consent' (2020) 7 JUFIL 74.

Brosche H, 'The Arab Oil Embargo and United States Pressure Against Chile: Economic and Political Coercion and the Charter of the United Nations' (1974) 7 Case Western Reserve JIL 3.

Buchan R and N Tsagourias, 'The Crisis in Crimea and the Principle of Non-Intervention' (2017) 19 Int'l Comm L Rev 165.

Bultrini A, 'Reappraising the Approach of International Law to Civil Wars: Aid to Legitimate Governments or Insurgents and Conflict Minimization' (2018) 56 CYBIL 1.

Bundu AC, 'Recognition of Revolutionary Authorities: Law and Practice of States' (1978) 27 Intl & Comp LQ 18.

Butchard PM, 'Territorial Integrity, Political Independence, and Consent: The Limitations of Military Assistance on Request under the Prohibition of Force' (2020) 7 JUFIL 35.

Buys E and A Garwood-Gowers, 'The (Ir)Relevance of Human Suffering: Humanitarian Intervention and Saudi Arabia's Operation Decisive Storm in Yemen' (2018) 24 JCSL 1.

Byrne M, 'Consent and the Use of Force: An Examination of "Intervention by Invitation" as a Basis for US Drone Strikes in Pakistan, Somalia and Yemen' (2016) 3 JUFIL 97.

Cançado Trindade AA, 'The Contribution of Latin American Legal Doctrine to the Progressive Development of International Law' (2015) 376 Recueil des Cours 9.

Carrillo-Santarelli N and C Olarte-Bácares, 'From Swords to Words: The Intersection of Geopolitics and Law, and the Subtle Expansion of International Law in the Consolidation of the Independence of the Latin American Republics' (2019) 21 J His Intl L 378.

Cassese A, 'Le droit international et la question de l'assistance aux mouvements de libération nationale' (1986) 19 RBDI 307.

Castrén E, 'Recognition of Insurgency' (1965) 5 IJIL 443.

Cavaglieri A, 'La questione cretese' (1912) 6 RDI 244, 407.

—— 'Note critiche su la teoria dei mezzi coercitivi al difuori della guerra' (1915) 9 RDI 23.

Cello L, 'The Legitimacy of International Interventions in Vattel's *The Law of Nations*' (2017) 2 Global Intellectual History 105.

Cervell Hortal MJ, 'Ciberinjerencias en procesos electorales y principio de non intervención (una perspectiva internacional y europea)' (2023) 45 REEI 29 <www.reei.org/index.php/revista/num45/articulos/ciberinjerencias-procesos-electorales-principio-intervencion-una-perspectiva-internacional-europea>.

Chaeva N, 'La Russie et la crise syrienne' (2019) 123 RGDIP 203.

Chakste M, 'Soviet Concepts of the State, International Law and Sovereignty' (1949) 43 AJIL 21.

Chan K, 'State Failure and the Changing Face of the *Jus ad Bellum*' (2013) 18 JCSL 395.

Charlesworth H, 'Feminist Reflections on the Responsibility to Protect' (2010) 2 GR2P 232.

Charvin R, 'La doctrine américaine de la «souveraineté limitée»' (1987) 20 RBDI 5.

— — 'A propos de la «question syrienne». Une étape de la politique étasunienne du «Grand Moyen Orient»' (2018) 132 RGDIP 549.

— — 'La question libyenne: ingérences, chaos et décomposition du droit international' (2019) 123 RGDIP 593.

Chaumont C, 'Analyse critique de l'intervention américaine au Vietnam' (1968) 4 RBDI 61.

Chevallier J-J, 'Sainte-Alliance et Société des Nations' (1927) 1 Revue de droit international 9.

Chimni BS, 'Towards a Third World Approach to Non-Intervention: Through the Labyrinth of Western Doctrine' (1980) 20 IJIL 243.

— — 'International Institutions Today: An Imperial Global State in the Making' (2004) 15 EJIL 1.

— — 'The International Law of Jurisdiction: A TWAIL Perspective' (2022) 35 LJIL 29.

Chinkin C, 'A Gendered Perspective to the International Use of Force' (1988–1989) 12 AYBIL 279.

Christakis T and K Bannelier, '*Volenti non fit injuria*? Les effets du consentement à l'intervention militaire' (2004) 50 AFDI 102.

Chukwuka Ofodile A, 'The Legality of ECOWAS Intervention in Liberia' (1994) 32 Colum J Transnat'l L 381.

Clark M, 'A Conceptual History of Recognition in British International Legal Thought' (2017) 87 BYBIL 18.

Cohen JA, 'China and Intervention: Theory and Practice' (1973) 121 U Pa L Rev 471.

Combacau J, 'Pas une puissance, une liberté: la souveraineté internationale de l'Etat' (1993) 67 Pouvoirs 47.

Constantinou A, 'Forcible Activities of Armed Bands as a Case of a Use of Force That Amounts to an Armed Attack in the Context of the Judgment of the ICJ in the *Nicaragua* Case' (1997) 9 Afr J Intl & Comp L 156.

Corten O, 'La licéité douteuse de l'action militaire de l'Ethiopie en Somalie et ses implications sur l'argument de l'«intervention consentie»' (2007) 111 RGDIP 513.

— — 'Déclarations unilatérales d'indépendance et reconnaissances prématurées: du Kosovo à l'Ossétie du Sud et à l'Abkhazie' (2008) 112 RGDIP 721.

— — 'La rébellion et le droit international: le principe de neutralité en tension' (2015) 374 Recueil des Cours 53.

— — 'The Russian Intervention in the Ukrainian Crisis: Was *jus contra bellum* "Confirmed Rather Than Weakened"?' (2015) 2 JUFIL 17.

— — 'L'intervention de la Russie en Syrie: que reste-t-il du principe de non-intervention dans les guerres civiles?' (2018) 53 Quest Intl L 3.

— — 'Is an Intervention at the Request of a Government Always Allowed? From a "Purpose-Based Approach" to the Respect of Self-Determination' (2019) 79 ZaöRV 677.

430 SELECT BIBLIOGRAPHY

— — and Vaios Koutroulis, 'The Illegality of Military Support to Rebels in the Libyan War: Aspects of *jus contra bellum* and *jus in bello*' (2013) 18 JCSL 59.

— — and Agatha Verdebout, 'Les interventions militaires récentes en territoire étranger: vers une remise en cause du *jus contra bellum*?' (2014) 60 AFDI 135.

Corthay E, 'The ASEAN Doctrine of Non-Interference in Light of the Fundamental Principle of Non-Intervention' (2016) 17 Asian-Pacific L & PJ 1.

Coste R, 'Réflexion philosophique sur le problème de l'intervention' (1976) 71 RGDIP 369.

Couzigou I, 'Respect for State Sovereignty: Primacy of Intervention by Invitation over the Right to Self-Defence' (2019) 79 ZaöRV 695.

Criddle EJ, 'Humanitarian Financial Intervention' (2013) 24 EJIL 583.

Croxton D, 'The Peace of Westphalia of 1648 and the Origins of Sovereignty' (1999) 21 The International History Review 569.

Cutler LN, 'The Right to Intervene' (1985) 64 Foreign Aff 96.

D'Amato A, 'The Invasion of Panama Was a Lawful Response to Tyranny' (1990) 84 AJIL 516.

— — 'There is No Norm of Intervention or Non-Intervention in International Law' (2001) 7 ILT 33.

D'Aspremont J, 'The Doctrine of Fundamental Rights of States and Anthropomorphic Thinking in International Law' (2015) 4 Cambridge J Int'l & Comp L 501.

David E, 'Portée et limite du principe de non-intervention' (1990) 23 RBDI 350.

De Cara J-Y, 'The Arab Uprisings Under the Light of Intervention' (2012) 55 GYBIL 11.

Deeks AS, 'Consent to the Use of Force and International Law Supremacy' (2013) 54 Harv Intl LJ 1.

Deinla JS, 'International Law and Wars of National Liberation against Neo-Colonialism' (2014) 88 Phil LJ 1.

Dennis L, 'Revolution, Recognition and Intervention' (1931) 9 Foreign Aff 204.

Desjardins A, 'La doctrine de Monroe' (1896) 3 RGDIP 137.

De Wet E, 'From Free Town to Cairo via Kiev: The Unpredictable Road to Democratic Legitimacy in Governmental Recognition' (2014) 108 AJIL Unbound 201.

— — 'The Modern Practice of Intervention by Invitation in Africa and Its Implications for the Prohibition of the Use of Force' (2016) 26 EJIL 979.

— — 'Reinterpreting Exceptions to the Use of Force in the Interest of Security: Forcible Intervention by Invitation and the Demise of the Negative Equality Principle' (2017) 111 AJIL Unbound 307.

— — 'The African Union's Struggle Against "Unconstitutional Change of Government": From a Moral Prescription to a Requirement under International Law" (2021) 32 EJIL 199.

Dhokalia RP, 'Civil Wars and International Law' (1971) 11 IJIL 219.

Diaconu I, 'La non-immixtion dans les affaires intérieures des États—principe fondamental du droit international contemporain' (1980) 50 RREI 331.

Diallo A, 'Le droit d'intervention de l'Union Africaine au motif de «menace grave à l'ordre légitime»: état des lieux et perspectives de mise en œuvre' (2016) 70 RJPEF 154.

Dinstein Y, 'The *Erga Omnes* Applicability of Human Rights' (1992) 30 AdV 16.

— — 'The Syrian Armed Conflict and Its Singular Characteristics' (2016) 46 Israel YBHR 261.

Doswald-Beck L, 'The Legal Validity of Military Intervention by Invitation of the Government' (1985) 56 BYBIL 189.

Douglass JJ, 'Counterinsurgency: A Permitted Intervention?' (1964) 25 Mil L Rev 43.

Doyle MW, 'A Few Words on Mill, Walzer, and Nonintervention' (2009) 23 Ethics and International Affairs 349.

Dufour G and N Veremko, 'Unilateral Economic Sanctions Adopted to React to An *Erga Omnes* Obligation: Basis for Legality and Legitimacy Analysis? —A Partial Response to Alexandra Hofer's Article' (2019) 18 CJIL 449.

SELECT BIBLIOGRAPHY 431

Dupuy R-J, 'Agression indirecte et intervention sollicitée. A propos de l'affaire libanaise' (1959) 5 AFDI 431.

Eckert A, 'The Non-Intervention Principle and International Humanitarian Interventions' (2001) 7 ILT 49.

Eichensehr KE, 'Not Illegal: The SolarWinds Incident and International Law' (2022) 33 EJIL 1263.

Engelhardt É, 'Le droit d'intervention et la Turquie' (1880) 12 RDILC 363.

Ermacora F, 'Human Rights and Domestic Jurisdiction (Article 2, § 7, of the Charter)' (1968) 124 Recueil des Cours 371.

Esmein A, 'La théorie de l'intervention internationale chez quelques publicistes français du XVIe siècle' (1900) 24 NRHDFE 549.

Fabri P, 'La licéité de l'intervention de la coalition international menée par l'Arabie Saoudite au Yémen au regard des principes de l'interdiction du recours à la force et de non-intervention dans les guerres civiles' (2016) 49 RBDI 69.

Falk RA, 'The United States and the Doctrine of Nonintervention in the Internal Affairs of Independent States' (1959) 5 How LJ 163.

—— 'American Intervention in Cuba and the Rule of Law' (1961) 22 Ohio St LJ 546.

—— 'International Law and the United States Role in the Viet Nam War' (1966) 75 Yale LJ 1122.

—— 'International Law and the United States Role in Viet Nam: A Response to Professor Moore' (1967) 76 Yale LJ 1095.

Farer TJ, 'Harnessing Rogue Elephants: A Short Discourse on Foreign Intervention in Civil Strife' (1969) 82 Harv L Rev 511.

—— 'Foreign Intervention in Civil Armed Conflict' (1974) 142 Recueil des Cours 291.

—— 'Political and Economic Coercion in Contemporary International Law' (1985) 79 AJIL 405.

—— 'Drawing the Right Line' (1987) 81 AJIL 112.

—— 'The United States as Guarantor of Democracy in the Caribbean Basin: Is There a Legal Way?' (1988) 10 HRQ 157.

—— 'Panama: Beyond the Charter Paradigm' (1990) 84 AJIL 503.

Faundez J, 'International Law and Wars of National Liberation: Use of Force and Intervention' (1989) 1 Afr J Intl & Comp L 85.

Fawcett JES, 'Intervention in International Law: A Study of Some Recent Cases' (1961) 103 Recueil des Cours 343.

Fedozzi P, 'Saggio sull'intervento' (1899) 62 Archivio Giuridico 'Filippo Serafini' 3, 247.

Fenwick CG, 'Intervention by Way of Propaganda' (1941) 35 AJIL 626.

—— 'Intervention: Individual and Collective' (1945) 39 AJIL 645.

Fernandes Carvalho Veçoso F, 'Resisting Intervention through Sovereign Debt: A Redescription of the Drago Doctrine' (2020) 1 TWAIL Review 74.

Ferro L, 'Western Gunrunners, (Middle-)Eastern Casualties: Unlawfully Trading Arms with States Engulfed in Yemeni Civil War?' (2019) 24 JCSL 503.

—— 'The Doctrine of "Negative Equality" and the Silent Majority of States' (2021) 8 JUFIL 4.

—— and N Verlinden, 'Neutrality During Armed Conflicts: A Coherent Approach to Third-State Support for Warring Parties' (2018) 17 CJIL 15.

Fidler DP, 'Revolt Against or From Within the West? TWAIL, the Developing World, and the Future Direction of International Law' (2003) 2 CJIL 29.

Fiocchi Malaspina E, '«Toil of the noble world»: Pasquale Stanislao Mancini, Augusto Pierantoni and the International Legal Discourse of 19th Century Italy' (2020) 18 Clio@Thémis: Revue électronique d'histoire du droit <https://journals.openedition.org/cliothemis/350?lang=en>.

Fisler Damrosch L, 'Politics Across Borders: Nonintervention and Nonforcible Influence over Domestic Affairs' (1989) 83 AJIL 1.

432 SELECT BIBLIOGRAPHY

Fitzmaurice Sir G, 'The General Principles of International Law Considered from the Standpoint of the Rule of Law' (1957) 92 Recueil des Cours 1.

Flasch O, 'The Legality of the Air Strikes against ISIL in Syria: New Insights on the Extraterritorial Use of Force against Non-State Actors' (2016) 3 JUFIL 37.

Floeckher A de, 'De la reconnaissance de la qualité de belligérants dans les guerres civiles' (1896) 3 RGDIP 277.

Floss S, 'Non-ingérence et égalité des États: des principes indépendants des concepts de souveraineté' (2014) 46 RBDI 454.

Focsaneanu L, 'Les "cinq principes" de coexistence et le droit international' (1956) 2 AFDI 150.

Fornari M, 'Conflitto in Ucraina, orsi fantasiosi e programmi malevoli' (2017) 100 RDI 1156.

Fortun WC, 'Intervention in Civil Wars Revisited' (1964) 3 Phil ILJ 399.

Franck TM and NS Rodley, 'Legitimacy and Legal Rights of Revolutionary Movements with Special Reference to the Peoples' Revolutionary Government of South Viet Nam' (1970) 45 NYU L Rev 679.

Friedmann W, 'Intervention, Civil War and the Rôle of International Law' (1965) 59 ASIL Proceedings 67.

—— 'Law and Politics in the Vietnamese War: A Comment' (1967) 61 AJIL 776.

—— 'Intervention and the Developing Countries' (1969) 10 Va J Intl L 205.

Frowein JA, 'Collective Enforcement of International Obligations' (1987) 47 ZaöRV 67.

Fry JD, 'Coercion, Causation, and the Fictional Elements of Indirect State Responsibility' (2007) 40 Vand J Transnat'l L 611.

—— 'Dyonisian Disarmament: Security Council WMD Coercive Disarmament Measures and Their Legal Implications' (2008) 29 Mich J Intl L 197.

Garcia-Mora MR, 'International Responsibility for Subversive Activities and Hostile Propaganda by Private Persons against Foreign States' (1960) 35 Ind LJ 306.

García Moreno VC, 'El principio de la no intervención en los conflictos internos de los estados soveranos' (1983) 52 Rev Jur UPR 97.

Garwood-Gowers A, 'The Responsibility to Protect and the Arab Spring: Libya as the Exception, Syria as the Norm?' (2013) 36 UNSWLJ 594.

Gathii JT, 'Neoliberalism, Colonialism and International Governance: Decentering the International Law of Governmental Legitimacy' (2000) 98 Mich L Rev 1996.

Gidel G, 'Droits et devoirs des nations. La théorie classique des droit fondamentaux des États' (1925) 10 Recueil des Cours 537.

Ginsburg G, '"Wars of National Liberation" and the Modern Law of Nations—The Soviet Thesis' (1964) 29 Law and Contemporary Problems 910.

Giuliano M, 'Rilievi sul problema storico del diritto internazionale' (1950) 3 Comunicazioni e studi dell'Istituto di diritto internazionale dell'Università di Milano 106.

Gomulkiewicz RW, 'International Law Governing Aid to Opposition Groups in Civil War: Resurrecting the Standards of Belligerency' (1988) 63 Wash L Rev 43.

Gordon R, 'United Nations Intervention in Internal Conflicts: Iraq, Somalia, and Beyond' (1993-1994) 15 Mich J Intl L 519.

Gorelick RE, 'Wars of National Liberation: *Jus ad Bellum*' (1979) 11 Case Western Reserve JIL 71.

Gowlland-Debbas V, 'The Limits of Unilateral Enforcement of Community Objectives in the Framework of UN Peace Maintenance' (2000) 11 EJIL 361.

Graber DA, 'The Truman and Eisenhower Doctrines in the Light of the Doctrine of Non-Intervention' (1958) 73 Pol Sci Q 321.

Grant TD, 'The Yanukovich Letter: Intervention and Authority to Invite in International Law' (2015) 2 Indon J Int'l & Comp L 281.

Gray C, 'The Limits of Force' (2015) 376 Recueil des Cours 93.

SELECT BIBLIOGRAPHY   433

Greenwood Onuf N, 'The Principle of Nonintervention, the United Nations, and the International System' (1971) 25 International Organization 209.

Gros Espiell H, 'La doctrine du Droit international en Amérique Latine avant la première conference panaméricaine (Washington, 1889)' (2001) 3 J His Intl L 1.

Gross L, 'The Peace of Westphalia, 1648–1948' (1948) 42 AJIL 20.

Guerrero JG, 'La question de l'intervention à la VIe Conférence panaméricaine (janvier 1928)' (1929) 36 RGDIP 41.

Gunewardene RM, 'Indo-Sri Lanka Accord: Invitation or Intervention?' (1991) 3 Sri Lanka J Int'l L 173.

Gurmendi Dunkelberg A, 'A Legal History of Consent and Intervention in Civil Wars in Latin America' (2020) 7 JUFIL 102.

Gutierrez Hermosillo J, 'La intervención y la no intervención' (1967) 3 AHLADI 99.

Hafner G, 'The "Soviet" Intervention in Czechoslovakia (1968)' (2016) ARIEL 27.

Hajjami N, 'Le consentement à l'intervention étrangère. Essai d'évaluation au regard de la practique récente' (2018) 132 RGDIP 617.

Hakimi M, 'Unfriendly Unilateralism' (2014) 55 Harv Intl LJ 105.

Halabi SF, 'Traditions of Belligerent Recognition: The Libyan Intervention in Historical and Theoretical Context' (2012) 27 AU Intl L Rev 321.

Halberstam M, 'The Copenhagen Document: Intervention in Support of Democracy' (1993) 34 Harv Intl LJ 163.

Hammoudi A, 'The International Law of Informal Empire and the "Question of Oman"' (2020) 1 TWAIL Review 121.

Hansohm J and Z Yihdego, 'The South Sudan Crisis: Legal Implications and Responses of the International Community' (2016) 1 Ethiopian YBIL 223.

Harrell PE, 'Modern-Day "Guarantee Clauses" and the Legal Authority of Multinational Organizations to Authorize the Use of Military Force' (2008) 33 Yale JIL 417.

Hartwig M, 'Who Is the Host?—Invasion by Invitation' (2019) 79 ZaöRV 703.

Hathaway OA and others 'Consent-Based Humanitarian Intervention: Giving Sovereign Responsibility Back to the Sovereign' (2013) 46 Cornell Int'l LJ 499.

— — and others 'Consent is Not Enough: Why States Must Respect the Intensity Threshold in Transnational Conflict' (2016) 165 U Pa L Rev 1.

Havercroft J, 'Was Westphalia "All That"? Hobbes, Bellarmine, and the Norm of Non-Intervention' (2012) 1 Global Constitutionalism 120.

Heath KD, 'Could We Have Armed the Kosovo Liberation Army? The New Norms Governing Intervention in Civil War' (1999) 4 UCLA J Int'l L Foreign Aff 251.

Helal MS, 'On Coercion in International Law' (2019) 52 NYU J Intl L & Pol 1.

Heller KJ, 'The Law of Neutrality Does not Apply to the Conflict with Al-Qaeda, and It's a Good Thing Too: A Response to Chang' (2011–2012) 47 Tex Intl LJ 115.

— — 'The Illegality of "Genuine" Unilateral Humanitarian Intervention' (2021) 32 EJIL 613.

Henderson C, 'International Measures for the Protection of Civilians in Libya and Côte d'Ivoire' (2011) 60 Intl & Comp LQ 767.

— — 'The Provision of Arms and "Non-Lethal" Assistance to Governmental and Opposition Forces' (2013) 36 UNSWLJ 642.

— — 'The Arab Spring and the Notion of External State Sovereignty in International Law' (2014) 35 Liverpool LR 175.

— — 'A Countering of the Asymmetrical Interpretation of the Doctrine of Counter-Intervention' (2021) 8 JUFIL 34.

Henderson JC, 'Legality of Economic Sanctions under International Law: The Case of Nicaragua' (1986) 43 Wash & Lee L Rev 167.

434 SELECT BIBLIOGRAPHY

Henkin L, 'The Invasion of Panama Under International Law: A Gross Violation' (1991) 29 Colum J Transnat'l L 293.

Heraclides A, 'Humanitarian Intervention in International Law 1830–1939: The Debate' (2014) 16 J His Intl L 26.

Herik L van den, 'Replicating Article 51: A Reporting Requirement for Consent-Based Use of Force?' (2019) 79 ZaöRV 707.

Hofer A, 'The Developed/Developing Divide on Unilateral Coercive Measures: Legitimate Enforcement or Illegitimate Intervention?' (2017) 16 CJIL 175.

Hollis D, 'The Influence of War; The War for Influence' (2018) 32 Temp Int'l & Comp LJ 31.

Iovane M, 'L'Organizzazione per la Sicurezza e la Cooperazione in Europa e la tutela del principio di autodeterminazione interna' (1998) 53 La Comunità internazionale 460.

Irizarry y Puente J, 'The Doctrines of Recognition and Intervention in Latin America' (1953–1954) 28 Tul L Rev 313.

Isoart P, 'Les conflits du Viêtnam: Positions juridiques des États-Unis' (1966) 12 AFDI 50.

Jamnejad M and M Wood, 'The Principle of Non-intervention' (2009) 22 LJIL 345.

Jessup PC, 'The Spanish Rebellion and International Law' (1937) 15 Foreign Aff 260.

Jiménez P, 'La intervención extranjera en el conflicto angolés y la adecuación a las normas de derecho internacional' (1976) 45 Rev Jur UPR 329.

Jones AG, 'Intervening for Democracy: The Threat or Use of Force and Crisis in The Gambia' (2018) 51 Comp & Int'l LJ S Afr 241.

Joyner CC and MA Grimaldi, 'The United States and Nicaragua: Reflections on the Lawfulness of Contemporary Intervention' (1985) 25 Va J Intl L 621.

Joyner D and M Roscini, 'Is There Any Room for the Doctrine of Fundamental Rights of States in Today's International Law?' (2015) 4 Cambridge J Int'l & Comp L 467.

Jupillat N, 'From Cuckoo's Egg to Global Surveillance: Cyber Espionage that Becomes Prohibited Intervention' (2017) 42 NC J Int'l L 933.

Kattan V, 'To Consent or Revolt? European Public Law, the Three Partitions of Poland (1772, 1793, and 1795) and the Birth of National Self-Determination' (2015) 17 J His Intl L 247.

— — 'Self-Determination in the Third World: The Role of the Soviet Union (1917–1960)' (2023) 8 Jus Gentium: Journal of International Legal History 87.

Keene E, 'International Hierarchy and the Origins of the Modern Practice of Intervention' (2013) 39 Rev Intl Stud 1077.

Kelsen H, 'Théorie Générale du droit international public. Problèmes choisis' (1932) 42 Recueil des Cours 117.

— — 'The Draft Declaration on Rights and Duties of States' (1950) 44 AJIL 259.

Kenny C and S Butler, 'The Legality of "Intervention by Invitation" in Situations of R2P Violations' (2018) 51 NYU J Intl L & Pol 135.

Khayre AAM, 'Self-Defence, Intervention by Invitation, or Proxy War? The Legality of the 2006 Ethiopian Invasion of Somalia' (2014) 22 Afr J Intl & Comp L 208.

Kiessling EK, 'Gray Zone Tactics and the Principle of Non-Intervention: Can "One of the Vaguest Branches of International Law" Solve the Gray Zone Problem?' (2020) 12 Harv NSJ 116.

Kilovaty I, 'Doxfare: Politically Motivated Leaks and the Future of the Norm on Non-Intervention in the Era of Weaponized Information' (2018) 9 Harv NSJ 146.

Kioko B, 'The Right of Intervention under the African Union's Constitutive Act: From Non-Interference to Non-Intervention' (2003) 85 IRRC 807.

Kleczkowska A, 'The Misconception about the Term "Intervention by Invitation"' (2019) 79 ZaöRV 647.

— — 'The Meaning of Treaty Authorisation and *Ad Hoc* Consent for the Legality of Military Assistance on Request' (2020) 7 JUFIL 270.

Klingler J, 'Counterintervention on Behalf of the Syrian Opposition? An Illustration of the Need for Greater Clarity in the Law' (2014) 55 Harv Intl LJ 483.

Kohen M, 'The Principle of Non-Intervention 25 Years after the *Nicaragua* Judgment' (2012) 25 LJIL 157.

Kormanicki T, 'L'intervention en droit international moderne' (1956) 60 RGDIP 521.

Koskenniemi M, 'What Use for Sovereignty Today?' (2011) 1 Asian JIL 61.

Krauss M, 'Internal Conflicts and Foreign States: In Search of the State of Law' (1979) 5 Yale Studies in World Public Order 173.

Kreß C, 'Major Post-Westphalian Shifts and Some Important Neo-Westphalian Hesitations in the State Practice on the International Law on the Use of Force' (2014) 1 JUFIL 11.

— — and Benjamin Nußberger, 'Pro-Democratic Intervention in Current International Law: The Case of The Gambia in January 2017' (2017) 4 JUFIL 239.

Krieger H, 'Populist Governments and International Law' (2019) 30 EJIL 971.

Kriener F, 'Invitation—Excluding *Ab Initio* a Breach of Art. 2(4) UNCh or a Preclusion of Wrongfulness?' (2019) 79 ZaöRV 643.

Kritsiotis D, 'On the Matter of Multiple Legal Justifications for Military Action' (2019) 79 ZaöRV 691.

Kunschak M, 'The African Union and the Right to Intervention: Is There a Need for UN Security Council Authorisation?' (2006) 31 SAYBIL 195.

Kwaka E, 'Internal Conflicts in Africa: Is There a Right of Humanitarian Action?' (1994) 2 AYBIL 9.

Labuda PI, 'UN Peacekeeping as Intervention by Invitation: Host State Consent and the Use of Force in Security Council-Mandated Stabilisation Operations' (2020) 7 JUFIL 317.

Lahmann H, 'On the Politics and Ideologies of the Sovereignty Discourse in Cyberspace' (2021) 32 Duke J Comp & Intl L 61.

Laird A, 'Mali: A Legally Justifiable Intervention by France?' (2012) 10 NZYBIL 123.

Latty F, 'Le brouillage des repères du *jus contra bellum*. A propos de l'usage de la force par la France contre Daech' (2016) 120 RGDIP 11.

Lauterpacht E, 'Notes' (1958) 7 Intl & Comp LQ 102.

Lauterpacht H, 'Revolutionary Activities by Private Persons against Foreign States' (1928) 22 AJIL 125.

— — '"Resort to War" and the Interpretation of the Covenant During the Manchurian Dispute' (1934) 28 AJIL 43.

— — 'Recognition of Insurgents as a *De Facto* Government' (1939) 3 Modern Law Review 1.

Lawson FH, 'Syria's Intervention in the Lebanese Civil War, 1976: A Domestic Conflict Explanation' (1984) 38 International Organization 451.

Lawson G and L Tardelli, 'The Past, Present, and Future of Intervention' (2013) 39 Rev Intl Stud 1233.

Le Mon, CJ, 'Unilateral Intervention by Invitation in Civil Wars: The Effective Control Test Tested' (2002–2003) 35 NYU J Intl L & Pol 741.

Lesaffer R, 'Paix et guerre dans les grands traités du dix-huitième siècle' (2005) 7 J His Intl L 25.

Leurdijk JH, 'Civil War and Intervention in International Law' (1977) 24 NILR 143.

Levitt J, 'Humanitarian Intervention by Regional Actors in Internal Conflicts: The Cases of ECOWAS in Liberia and Sierra Leone' (1998) 12 Temp Int'l & Comp LJ 333.

— — 'The Evolving Intervention Regime in Africa: From Basket Case to Market Place?' (2002) 96 ASIL Proceedings 136.

— — 'Pro-Democratic Intervention in Africa' (2006) 24 Wis Int'l LJ 785.

Lieblich E, 'Intervention and Consent: Consensual Forcible Interventions in Internal Armed Conflicts as International Agreements' (2011) 29 BU Int'l LJ 337.

436 SELECT BIBLIOGRAPHY

— — 'The International Lawfulness of Unlawful Consensual Interventions' (2019) 79 ZaöRV 667.

— — 'Why Can't We Agree on When Governments Can Consent to External Intervention? A Theoretical Inquiry' (2020) 7 JUFIL 5.

Likoti FJ, 'The 1998 Military Intervention in Lesotho: SADC Peace Mission or Resource War?' (2007) 14 International Peacekeeping 251.

Lillich RB, 'Economic Coercion and the International Legal Order' (1975) 51 International Affairs 358.

— — 'Economic Coercion and the "New International Economic Order": A Second Look at Some First Impressions' (1976) 16 Va J Intl L 233.

Lin F-S, 'Subversive Intervention' (1963) 25 U Pitt L Rev 35.

Linarelli J, 'An Examination of the Proposed Crime of Intervention in the Draft Code of Crimes against Peace and Security of Mankind' (1995) 18 Suffolk Transnat'l L Rev 1.

Lingelbach WE, 'The Doctrine and Practice of Intervention in Europe' (1900) 16 Annals of the American Academy of Political and Social Science 1.

Little R, 'Intervention and Non-Intervention in International Society: Britain's Response to the American and Spanish Civil Wars' (2013) 39 Rev Intl Stud 1111.

Lo Giacco L, '"Intervention by Invitation" and the Construction of the Authority of the *Effective Control* Test in Legal Argumentation' (2019) 79 ZaöRV 663.

Longobardo M, '"Super-Robust" Peacekeeping Mandates in Non-International Armed Conflicts under International Law' (2020) 24 SYBIL 42.

Lumsden E, 'An Uneasy Peace: Multilateral Military Intervention in Civil Wars' (2003) 35 NYU J Intl L & Pol 795.

Magi L, 'Sulla liceità dell'intervento militare francese in Mali' (2013) 96 RDI 551.

Mahalingam R, 'The Compatibility of the Principle of Nonintervention with the Right of Humanitarian Intervention' (1996) 1 UCLA J Int'l L Foreign Aff 221.

Mälksoo L, 'The Soviet Approach to the Right of Peoples to Self-Determination: Russia's Farewell to *Jus Publicum Europaeum*' (2017) 19 J His Intl L 200.

Manin A, 'L'intervention française au Shaba (19 mai–14 juin 1978)' (1978) 24 AFDI 159.

Mann FA, 'The Doctrine of International Jurisdiction Revisited after Twenty Years' (1984) 186 Recueil des Cours 9.

Marouda M-D and V Saranti, 'From Ukraine and Yemen to CAR, Mali and Syria: Is Third Country Intervention by Invitation Reshaped in the Aftermath of Recent Practice?' (2016) 3 Ordine internazionale e diritti umani 556 <www.rivistaoidu.net/rivista-oidu-n-3-2016-15-luglio2016/>.

Marxsen C, 'The Crimea Crisis: An International Law Perspective' (2014) 74 ZaöRV 367.

Mastorodimos K, 'Belligerency Recognition: Past, Present and Future' (2014) 29 Conn J Int'l L 301.

Matheson MJ, 'Practical Considerations for the Development of Legal Standards for Intervention' (1983) 13 Ga J Intl & Comp L 205.

Mattessich W, 'Digital Destruction: Applying the Principle of Non-Intervention to Distributed Denial of Service Attacks Manifesting No Physical Damage' (2016) 54 Colum J Transnat'l L 873.

McDougal MS and FP Feliciano, 'The Initiation of Coercion: A Multi-Temporal Analysis' (1958) 52 AJIL 241.

— — and — —, 'International Coercion and World Public Order: The General Principles of the Law of War' (1958) 67 Yale LJ 771.

McNair AD, 'The Law Relating to the Civil War in Spain' (1937) 53 The Law Quarterly Review 471.

Mégret F, 'Are There "Inherently Sovereign Functions" in International Law' (2021) 115 AJIL 452.

Meledje Djedjro F, 'La guerre civile du Libéria et la question de l'ingérence dans les affaires intérieures des États' (1993) 26 RBDI 393.

Mencer G, 'The Principle of Non-Intervention' (1964) 11 RDC 27.

Menon PK, 'Some Thoughts about the Law of Recognition' (1991) 3 Sri Lanka J Int'l L 87.

Milojević M, 'The Principle of Non-Interference in the Internal Affairs of States' (2000) 4 Facta Universitatis 427.

Mirkine-Guetzévitch B, 'L'influence de la Révolution française sur le développement du droit international dans l'Europe orientale' (1928) 22 Recueil des Cours 295.

Moore JN, 'International Law and the United States Role in Viet Nam: A Reply' (1967) 76 Yale LJ 1051.

— — 'The Lawfulness of Military Assistance to the Republic of Viet-Nam' (1967) 61 AJIL 1.

— — 'Law and Politics in the Vietnamese War: A Response to Professor Friedmann' (1967) 61 AJIL 1039.

— — 'The Control of Foreign Intervention in Internal Conflict' (1969) 9 Va J Intl L 205.

— — 'Legal Standards for Intervention in Internal Conflicts' (1983) 13 Ga J Intl & Comp L 191.

Morgenthau, HJ, 'To Intervene or Not to Intervene' (1967) 45 Foreign Aff 425.

Muir JD, 'The Boycott in International Law' (1974) 9 JILE 187.

Murphy C, 'Economic Duress and Unequal Treaties' (1970) 11 Va J Intl L 51.

Nakhimovsky I, 'Carl Schmitt's Vattel and the "Law of Nations" between Enlightment and Revolution' (2010) 31 Grotiana 141.

Nanda VP, 'Self-Determination in International Law: The Tragic Tale of Two Cities—Islamabad (West Pakistan) and Dacca (East Pakistan)' (1972) 66 AJIL 321.

— — 'The Validity of United States Intervention in Panama under International Law' (1990) 84 AJIL 494.

Nasu H, 'Revisiting the Principle of Non-Intervention: A Structural Principle of International Law or a Political Obstacle to Regional Security in Asia?' (2013) 3 Asian JIL 25.

Neff SC, 'The Prerogatives of Violence—In Search of the Conceptual Foundations of Belligerents' Rights' (1995) 38 GYBIL 41.

— — 'The Dormancy, Rise and Decline of Fundamental Liberties of States' (2015) 4 Cambridge J Int'l & Comp L 482.

— — 'Heresy in Action: James Lorimer's Dissident Views on War and Neutrality' (2016) 27 EJIL 477.

Nenadic S, 'The Lawfulness of New Zealand's Military Deployment in Iraq: "Intervention by Invitation" Tested' (2014) 12 NZYBIL 3.

Nesi G, 'Recognition of the Libyan National Transitional Council: When, How and Why' (2011) 21 IYIL 45.

Nolte G, 'Restoring Peace by Regional Action: International Legal Aspects of the Liberian Conflict' (1993) 23 ZaöRV 603.

— — 'The Resolution of the *Institut de droit international* on Military Assistance on Request' (2012) 45 RBDI 241.

Nowak C, 'The Changing Law of Non-Intervention in Civil Wars—Assessing the Production of Legality in State Practice after 2011' (2018) 5 JUFIL 40.

Nowrot K and EW Schabacker, 'The Use of Force to Restore Democracy: International Legal Implications of the ECOWAS Intervention in Sierra Leone' (1998) 14 AU Intl L Rev 321.

Nußberger B, 'Military Strikes in Yemen in 2015: Intervention by Invitation and Self-Defence in the Course of Yemen's "Model Transitional Process" ' (2017) 4 JUFIL 110.

Nuzzo L, 'Da Mazzini a Mancini: il principio di nazionalità tra politica e diritto' (2007) 14 Giornale di Storia costituzionale 161.

Nwogugu EI, 'The Nigerian Civil War: A Case Study in the Law of War' (1974) 14 IJIL 13.

O'Connell ME, 'Continuing Limits on UN Intervention in Civil War' (1992) 67 Ind LJ 903.

438 SELECT BIBLIOGRAPHY

Oglesby RR, 'A Search for Legal Norms in Contemporary Situations of Civil Strife' (1970) 3 Case Western Reserve JIL 30.

Ohlin JD, 'Did Russian Cyber-Interference in the 2016 Election Violate International Law?' (2017) 95 Tex L Rev 1579.

Olivart Marquis de, 'Le différend entre l'Espagne et les États-Unis au sujet de la question cubaine' (1897) 4 RGDIP 577.

Oliver CT, 'The National State and External Coercion: Yesterday and Today and What of Tomorrow?' (1983) 13 Ga J Intl & Comp L 419.

Olivi L, 'La questione sul diritto d'intervento dinnanzi alla scienza' (1880) 24 Archivio giuridico 560.

O'Malley ES, 'Destabilization Policy: Lessons from Reagan on International Law, Revolutions and Dealing with Pariah Nations' (2003) 43 Va J Intl L 319.

O'Rourke VA, 'Recognition of Belligerency and the Spanish War' (1937) 31 AJIL 398.

Osiander A, 'Sovereignty, International Relations, and the Westphalian Myth' (2001) 55 International Organization 251.

Österdahl I, 'The Gentle Legitimiser of the Action of Others' (2019) 79 ZaöRV 699.

Ouchakov N, 'La compétence interne des états et la non-intervention dans le droit international contemporain' (1974) 141 Recueil des Cours 1.

Paddeu F, 'Military Assistance on Request and General Reasons against Force: Consent as a Defence to the Prohibition of Force' (2020) 7 JUFIL 227.

Padelford NJ, 'The International Non-Intervention Agreement and the Spanish Civil War' (1937) 31 AJIL 578.

Parry C, 'Defining Economic Coercion in International Law' (1977) 12 Tex Intl LJ 1.

Partan DG, 'Legal Aspects of the Vietnam Conflict' (1966) 46 BULR 281.

Pearce Higgins A, 'The Monroe Doctrine' (1924) 5 BYBIL 103.

Perkins JA, 'The Right of Counterintervention' (1987) 17 Ga J Intl & Comp L 171.

Peters A, 'Le droit d'ingérence et le devoir d'ingérence — vers une responsabilité de protéger' (2002) 79 RDILC 290.

—— 'Humanity as the A and Ω of Sovereignty' (2009) 20 EJIL 513.

—— 'Introduction. A Century after the Russian Revolution: Its Legacy in International Law' (2017) 19 J His Intl L 133.

—— 'Intervention by Invitation: Impulses from the Max Planck Trialogues on the Law of Peace and War' (2019) 79 ZaöRV 635.

Picone P, Review of Bernd Lindemeyer, *Schiffsembargo und Handelsembargo. Vökerrechtliche Praxis und Zulässigkeit* (1990) 63 RDI 869.

—— Review of Detlev Christian Dicke, *Die Intervention mit wirtschaftlichen Mitteln im Völkerrecht. Zugleich ein Beitrag zu den Fragen der Wirtschaftlichen Souveränität* (1990) 63 RDI 874.

—— 'Unilateralismo e guerra contro l'ISIS' (2015) 98 RDI 5.

—— 'Gli obblighi *erga omnes* tra passato e futuro' (2015) 98 RDI 1081.

—— 'L'insostenibile leggerezza dell'art. 51 della Carta dell'ONU' (2016) 99 RDI 7.

Pierson-Mathy P, 'L'embargo international sur les livraisons d'armes au Portugal' (1973) 9 RBDI 107.

Piirimäe P, 'Just War in Theory and Practice: The Legitimation of Swedish Intervention in the Thirty Years War' (2002) 45 The Historical Journal 499.

Pimont Y, 'La subversion dans les relations internationales contemporaines' (1972) 76 RGDIP 768.

Pinto R, 'Les règles du droit international concernant la guerre civile' (1965) 114 Recueil des Cours 451.

Politakis GP, 'Variations on a Myth: Neutrality and the Arms Trade' (1992) 35 GYBIL 435.

Pomson O, 'The Prohibition on Intervention Under International Law and Cyber Operations' (2022) 99 ILS 180.

Potter PB, 'L'intervention en droit international moderne' (1930) 32 Recueil des Cours 607.

Puma G, 'The Principle of Non-Intervention in the Face of the Venezuelan Crisis' (2021) 79 Quest Intl L 5.

Quigley J, 'The United States Invasion of Grenada: Stranger than Fiction' (1986) 18 U Miami Inter-Am L Rev 271.

— — 'The Reagan Administration's Legacy to International Law' (1988) 2 Temp Int'l & Comp LJ 199.

Reisman WM, 'Old Wine in New Bottles: The Reagan and Brezhnev Doctrines in Contemporary International Law and Practice' (1988) 13 Yale JIL 171.

Reus-Smit C, 'The Concept of Intervention' (2013) 39 Rev Intl Stud 1057.

Riccardi A, 'Sull'esistenza di un obbligo generale di prevenire e reprimere il fenomeno dei *foreign fighters* alla luce della vicenda della guerra civile spagnola' (2017) 72 La Comunità internazionale 213.

Rider Schmeltzer K, 'Soviet and American Attitudes toward Intervention: The Dominican Republic and Czechoslovakia' (1970) 11 Va J Intl L 97.

Rim Y, 'Two Governments and One Legitimacy: International Responses to the Post-Election Crisis in Côte d'Ivoire' (2012) 25 LJIL 683.

Rodogno D, 'European Legal Doctrines on Intervention and the Status of the Ottoman Empire within the "Family of Nations" Throughout the Nineteenth Century' (2016) 18 J His Intl L 5.

Rohlik J, 'Some Remarks on Self-Defense and Intervention: A Reaction to Reading *Law and Civil War in the Modern World*' (1976) 6 Ga J Intl & Comp L 395.

Rojas Castro DE, 'La reconnaissance des gouvernements ibéro-américains. Histoire du droit international et histoire transnationale au XIXe siècle' (2015) 162 Relations internationales 9.

Roldán Barbero J, 'Internal Democracy and International Law' (2018) 22 SYBIL 181.

Rolin-Jaequemyns G, 'Le droit international et la phase actuelle de la question d'Orient' (1876) 8 RDILC 293.

— — 'Note sur la théorie du droit d'intervention. A propos d'une lettre de M. le professeur Arntz' (1876) 8 RDILC 673.

Roncajolo Benítez I, 'El principio de no intervención: consagración, evolución y problemas en el Derecho Internacional actual' (2015) 21 Revista Ius et Praxis 449.

Ronzitti N, 'Wars of National Liberation—A Legal Definition' (1975) 1 IYIL 192.

Roscher B, 'The "Renunciation to War as an Instrument of National Policy"' (2002) 4 J His Intl L 293.

Roscini M, 'Intervention in XIXth Century International Law and the Distinction between Rebellions, Insurrections and Civil Wars' (2020) 50 Israel YBHR 269.

— — and R Labianco, 'The Intersections between the Arms Trade Treaty and the International Law of Foreign Intervention in Situations of Internal Unrest' (2022) 52 Israel YBHR 365.

Rosenau JN, 'Intervention as a Scientific Concept' (1969) 13 J Conflict Resol 149.

Rosenstock R, 'The Declaration of Principles of International Law Concerning Friendly Relations: A Survey' (1971) 65 AJIL 713.

Rostow N, 'Law and the Use of Force by States: The Brezhnev Doctrine' (1981) 7 The Yale Journal of World Public Order 209.

Roth BR, 'The Virtues of Bright Lines: Self-Determination, Secession, and External Intervention (2015) 16 GLJ 384.

Rougier A, 'L'intervention de l'Europe dans la question de Macédoine' (1906) 13 RGDIP 178.

— — 'Théorie de l'intervention d'humanité' (1910) 17 RGDIP 468.

Rucz, C, 'Les mesures unilatérales de protection des droits de l'homme devant l'Institut de droit international' (1992) 38 AFDI 579.

440 SELECT BIBLIOGRAPHY

Ruys T, 'Of Arms, Funding and "Non-lethal Assistance"—Issues Surrounding Third-State Intervention in the Syrian Civil War' (2014) 13 CJIL 13.

—— and L Ferro, 'Weathering the Storm: Legality and Legal Implications of the Saudi-Led Military Intervention in Yemen' (2016) 65 Intl & Comp LQ 61.

—— and —— 'The Enemy of My Enemy: Dutch Non-lethal Assistance for "Moderate" Syrian Rebels and the Multilevel Violation of International Law' (2019) 50 NYBIL 333.

—— and F Rodriguez Silvestre, 'L'Union contre-attaque—La proposition d'instrument anti-coercition (IAC) vue sous l'angle du droit international' (2021) 67 AFDI 143.

—— and C Ryngaert, 'Secondary Sanctions: A Weapon Out of Control? The International Legality of, and European Responses to, US Secondary Sanctions' BYBIL (advance article, 22 September 2020).

Ryngaert C, 'Extraterritorial Enforcement Jurisdiction in Cyberspace: Normative Shifts' (2023) 24 GLJ 537.

Sack AN, 'The Truman Doctrine in International Law' (1947) 7 Law Guild Rev 141.

Sáenz de Santa María A, 'A Right of All Peoples: The Internal Dimension of Self-Determination and Its Relationship with Democracy' (2018) 22 SYBIL 165.

Šahović M, 'Codification des principes du droit international des relations amicales et de la coopération entre les États' (1972) 137 Recueil des Cours 243.

Salmon JA, 'On the Final Text Adopted at the Helsinki Conference' (1976) 23 RCL 59.

Salvati P, 'Intelligence Collection in Time of Peace and International Law' (2013) 68 La Comunità internazionale 285.

—— 'The 2016 US Presidential Election and Russia's (Alleged) Interference Through Cyber Intelligence Collection: A Perspective of International Law' (2017) 72 La Comunità internazionale 7.

Sammartino L, 'Trasferimenti di armi a gruppi armati: Le implicazioni di Diritto Internazionale per le forniture militari ai Peshmerga in Iraq' (2015–2016) 54 RDMDG 117.

Sánchez Legido Á, '¿Podemos armar a los rebeldes? La legalidad internacional del envío de armas a grupos armados no estatales a la luz de los conflictos libio y sirio' (2015) 29 Revista Electrónica de Estudios Internacionales 7 <www.reei.org/index.php/revista/num29/articu los/podemos-armar-rebeldes-legalidad-internacional-envio-armas-grupos-armados-estata les-luz-conflictos-libio-sirio>.

Saul M, 'The Normative Status of Self-Determination in International Law: A Formula for Uncertainty in the Scope and Content of the Right?' (2011) 11 HRLR 609.

Scarfi JP, 'Denaturalizing the Monroe Doctrine: The Rise of Latin American Legal Anti-Imperialism in the Face of the Modern US and Hemispheric Redefinition of the Monroe Doctrine' (2020) 33 LJIL 541.

Scelle G, 'Studies on the Eastern Question' (1911) 5 AJIL 144.

—— 'Règles générales du droit de la paix' (1933) 46 Recueil des Cours 327.

—— 'La guerre civile espagnole et le droit des gens. Les bases du droit positif en matière de guerre civile' (1938) 45 RGDIP 265.

—— 'La guerre civile espagnole et le droit des gens (suite)' (1939) 46 RGDIP 197.

Schachter O, 'Coercion and Self-Determination: Construing Charter Article 2(4)' (1984) 78 AJIL 642.

—— 'The Right of States to Use Armed Force' (1984) 82 Mich L Rev 1620.

Schmidt J, 'The Legality of Unilateral Extra-Territorial Sanctions under International Law' (2022) 27 JCSL 53.

Schmitt MN, 'The Syrian Intervention: Assessing the Possible International Law Justifications' (2013) 89 ILS 744.

—— 'Legitimacy versus Legality Redux: Arming the Syrian Rebels' (2014) 7 JNSLP 139.

— — '"Virtual" Disenfranchisement: Cyber Election Meddling in the Grey Zones of International Law' (2018) 19 Chi J Int'l L 30.

— — 'Autonomous Cyber Capabilities and the International Law of Sovereignty and Intervention' (2020) 96 ILS 549.

Schrijver N, 'The Changing Nature of State Sovereignty' (1999) 70 BYBIL 65.

Schwebel SM, 'Aggression, Intervention and Self-Defence in Modern International Law' (1972) 136 Recueil des Cours 411.

Schwenninger SR, 'The 1980s: New Doctrines of Intervention or New Norms of Nonintervention?' (1981) 33 Rutgers LR 423.

Sciso E, 'La crisi ucraina e l'intervento russo: profili di diritto internazionale' (2014) 97 RDI 992.

Seidl-Hohenveldern I, 'The United Nations and Economic Coercion' (1984) 18 RBDI 9.

— — 'International Economic Law: General Course on Public International Law' (1986) 198 Recueil des Cours 9.

Senaratne K, 'Internal Self-Determination in International Law: A Critical Third-World Perspective' (2013) 3 Asian JIL 305.

Seren AP, 'Il concetto di guerra nel diritto internazionale contemporaneo' (1963) 41 RDI 537.

Shen J, 'The Non-Intervention Principle and Humanitarian Interventions under International Law' (2001) 7 ILT 1.

Shesterinina A, 'Evolving Norms of Protection: China, Libya and the Problem of Intervention in Armed Conflict' (2016) 29 CRIA 812.

Shihata IFI, 'Destination Embargo of Arab Oil: Its Legality under International Law' (1974) 68 AJIL 591.

— — 'Arab Oil Policies and the New International Economic Order' (1976) 16 Va J Intl L 261.

Shitong Q, 'Whither China's Non-Interference Principle?' (2011) 4 European Society of International Law (ESIL) Research Forum 1.

Simon H, 'The Myth of *Liberum Ius ad Bellum*: Justifying War in 19th-Century Legal Theory and Political Practice' (2018) 29 EJIL 113.

Simonen K, 'Premature Recognition and Intervention in Libyan Internal Affairs—Who Had the Right to Decide that Gaddafi Must Go?' (2012) 52 IJIL 421.

Simpson G, 'Two Liberalisms' (2001) 12 EJIL 537.

Skordas A, 'Intervention by Invitation and Its Function: Governance in a Plural Society' (2019) 79 ZaöRV 685.

Smiley W, 'War without War: The Battle of Navarino, the Ottoman Empire, and the Pacific Blockade' (2016) 18 J His Intl L 42.

Smith HA, 'Some Problems of the Spanish Civil War' (1937) 18 BYBIL 17.

Socher J, 'Lenin, (Just) Wars of National Liberation, and the Soviet Doctrine on the Use of Force' (2017) 19 J His Intl L 1.

Sohn LB, 'Gradations of Intervention in Internal Conflicts' (1983) 13 Ga J Intl & Comp L 225.

Souvignet X, 'La Russie et l'ingérence' (2019) 123 RGDIP 39.

Starita M, 'L'intervento francese in Mali si basa su un'autorizzazione del Consiglio di Sicurezza?' (2013) 96 RDI 561.

Stassen JC, 'Intervention in Internal Wars: Traditional Norms and Contemporary Trends' (1977) 3 SAYBIL 65.

Steenberghe R van, 'Les interventions françaises et africaines au Mali au nom de la lutte armée contre le terrorisme' (2014) 118 RGDIP 273.

— — 'Les interventions militaires étrangères récentes contre le terrorisme international. Première partie: fondements juridiques (*jus ad bellum*)' (2015) 61 AFDI 145.

Streit G, 'La question crétoise au point de vue du droit international' (1897) 4 RGDIP 61, 446.

Svicecic M, 'Collective Self-Defence or Regional Enforcement Action: The Legality of a SADC Intervention in Cabo Delgado and the Question of Mozambican Consent' (2022) 9 JUFIL 138.

Szasz PC, 'Role of the United Nations in Internal Conflicts' (1983) 13 Ga J Intl & Comp L 345.

Talmon S, 'Recognition of Opposition Groups as the Legitimate Representative of a People' (2013) 12 CJIL 219.

Tancredi A, 'Sulla liceità dell'intervento su richiesta alla luce del conflitto in Mali' (2013) 96 RDI 946.

— — 'Crisi in Crimea, referendum ed autodeterminazione dei popoli' (2014) 8 DUDI 480.

— — 'The Russian Annexation of the Crimea: Questions Relating to the Use of Force' (2014) 1 Quest Intl L 5.

— — 'A "Principle-Based" Approach to Intervention by Invitation in Civil Wars' (2019) 79 ZaöRV 659.

Teimouri H and SP Subedi, 'Responsibility to Protect and the International Military Intervention in Libya in International Law: What Went Wrong and What Lessons Could Be Learnt from It?' (2018) 23 JCSL 3.

Téllez Núñez A, 'Aproximación multidimensional al régimen de responsabilidad internacional y al principio de non intervención. El problema hermenéutico' (2020) 13 ACDI 79.

Terpstra N, 'Rebel Governance, Rebel Legitimacy, and External Intervention: Assessing Three Phases of Taliban Rule in Afghanistan' (2020) 31 Small Wars & Insurgencies 1143.

Terry PCR, 'Afghanistan's Civil War (1979–1989): Illegal and Failed Foreign Interventions' (2011) 31 PYIL 107.

Tesón FR, 'The Kantian Theory of International Law' (1992) 92 Colum L Rev 53.

— — 'The Vexing Problem of Authority in Humanitarian Intervention: A Proposal' (2006) 24 Wis Int'l LJ 761.

Tomuschat C, 'International Law: Ensuring the Survival of Mankind on the Eve of a New Millennium—General Course on Public International Law' (1999) 281 Recueil des Cours 9.

Townley S, 'Intervention's Idiosyncrasies: The Need for a New Approach to Understanding Sub-Forcible Intervention' (2019) 42 Fordham Int'l LJ 1167.

Toyoda T, 'La doctrine vattelienne de l'égalité souveraine dans le contexte neuchâtelois' (2009) 11 J His Intl L 103.

Treves T, 'La Déclaration des Nations Unies sur le renforcement de l'efficacité du principe du non-recours à la force' (1987) 33 AFDI 379.

Tsagourias N, 'Humanitarian Intervention and Legal Principles' (2001) 7 ILT 83.

— — 'Law, Borders and the Territorialisation of Cyberspace' (2018) 15 Indonesian J Int'l L 523.

Tsouvala N, '"These Ancient Arenas of Racial Struggles": International Law and the Balkans, 1878–1949' (2019) 29 EJIL 1149.

Tuura H, 'Intervention by Invitation and the Principle of Self-Determination in the Crimean Crisis' (2014) 24 FYIL 183.

Tzanakopoulos A, 'The Right to be Free from Economic Coercion' (2015) 4 Cambridge J Int'l & Comp L 616.

Tzimas T, 'Legal Evaluation of the Saudi-Led Intervention in Yemen: Consensual Intervention in Cases of Contested Authority and Fragmented States' (2018) 78 ZaöRV 147.

Ulfstein G and HF Christiansen, 'The Legality of the NATO Bombing in Libya' (2013) 62 Intl & Comp LQ 159.

Ullman R, 'Reflections on Intervention' (1983) 52 Rev Jur UPR 127.

Vashakmadze M, 'Legality of Foreign Military Intervention in International Law: Four Case Studies' (2015) 18 Max Planck YB UN L 462.

Verdebout A, 'The Contemporary Discourse on the Use of Force in the Nineteenth Century: A Diachronic and Critical Analysis' (2014) 1 JUFIL 222.

Verma DP, 'Indo-Sri Lanka Accord: Intervention or Invitation?' (1991) 3 Sri Lanka J Int'l L 153.

Villani U, 'Aspetti problematici dell'intervento militare nella crisi libica' (2011) 5 DUDI 369.

Visser L, 'May the Force Be with You: The Legal Classification of Intervention by Invitation' (2019) 66 NILR 21.

— — 'What's in a Name? The Terminology of Intervention by Invitation' (2019) 79 ZaöRV 651.

— — 'Intervention by Invitation and Collective Self-Defence: Two Sides of the Same Coin?' (2020) 7 JUFIL 292.

Walzer M, 'The Moral Standing of States: A Response to Four Critics' (1980) 9 Philosophy and Public Affairs 209.

Watts S and T Richard, 'Baseline Territorial Sovereignty and Cyberspace' (2018) 22 Lewis & Clark L Rev 771.

Wehberg H, 'La guerre civile et le droit international' (1938) 63 Recueil des Cours 1.

— — 'L'interdiction du recours à la force. Le principe et les problèmes qui se posent' (1951) 78 Recueil des cours 1.

Wentker A, 'Purpose-Based Regulation of Consent to Non-Forcible Operations' (2019) 79 ZaöRV 671.

Werner WG, 'Self-Determination and Civil War' (2001) 6 JCSL 171.

Wheatley S, 'Foreign Interference in Elections under the Non-Intervention Principle: We Need to Talk about "Coercion"' (2020) 31 Duke J Comp & Intl L 161.

Whitton JB, 'La doctrine de Monroe' (1933) 40 RGDIP 5.

Williams JF, 'La doctrine de la reconnaissance en droit international et ses développements récents' (1933) 44 Recueil des Cours 199.

Willmer L, 'Does Digitalization Reshape the Principle of Non-Intervention?' (2023) 24 GLJ 508.

Wilson RR, 'Recognition of Insurgency and Belligerency' (1937) 31 ASIL Proceedings 136.

Winfield PH, 'The History of Intervention in International Law' (1922–1923) 3 BYBIL 130.

— — 'The Grounds of Intervention in International Law' (1924) 5 BYBIL 149.

Wippman D, 'Treaty-Based Intervention: Who Can Say No?' (1995) 62 U Chi L Rev 607.

— — 'Change and Continuity in Legal Justifications for Military Intervention in Internal Conflict' (1996) 27 Colum Hum Rts L Rev 435.

— — 'Military Intervention, Regional Organizations, and Host-State Consent' (1996) 7 Duke J Comp & Intl L 209.

— — 'Pro-Democratic Intervention in Africa' (2002) 96 ASIL Proceedings 143.

Wong I, 'Authority to Consent to the Use of Force in Contemporary International Law: The Crimean and Yemeni Conflicts' (2019) 6 JUFIL 52.

Wood M, 'Assessing Practice on the Use of Force' (2019) 79 ZaöRV 655.

Woolaver H, 'Pro-Democratic Intervention in Africa and the "Arab Spring"' (2014) 22 Afr J Intl & Comp L 161.

— — 'State Failure, Sovereign Equality and Non-Intervention: Assessing Claimed Rights to Intervene in Failed States' (2014) 32 Wis Int'l LJ 595.

— — 'From Joining to Leaving: Domestic Law's Role in the International Legal Validity of Treaty Withdrawal' (2019) 30 EJIL 73.

Woolsey TS, 'The Consequences of Cuban Belligerency' (1896) 5 Yale LJ 182.

Wright Q, 'United States Intervention in the Lebanon' (1959) 53 AJIL 112.

— — 'Legal Aspects of the Viet-Nam Situation' (1966) 60 AJIL 750.

— — 'International Law and the American Civil War' (1967) 61 ASIL Proceedings 50.

Yepes J-M, 'La contribution de l'Amérique Latine au développement du droit international public et privé' (1930) 32 Recueil des Cours 691.

— — 'Les problèmes fondamentaux du droit des gens en Amérique' (1934) 47 Recueil des Cours 1.

Yusuf AA, 'The Right of Intervention by the African Union: A New Paradigm in Regional Enforcement Action?' (2003) 11 AYBIL 3.

444 SELECT BIBLIOGRAPHY

Zamani M and M Nikouei, 'Intervention by Invitation, Collective Self-Defence and the Enigma of Effective Control' (2017) 16 CJIL 663.

Zorgbibe Ch, 'La doctrine soviétique de la "souveraineté limitée' (1970) 74 RGDIP 872.

Zotiades GB, 'Intervention by Treaty Right: Its Legality in Present Day International Law' (1964) 34 Annuaire de l'AAA 153.

Zurbuchen S, 'Vattel's "Law of Nations" and the Principle of Non-Intervention' (2010) 31 Grotiana 69.

Blog Posts

Akande D, 'Self Determination and the Syrian Conflict—Recognition of Syrian Opposition as Sole Legitimate Representative of the Syrian People: What Does this Mean and What Implications Does It Have?' (*EJIL:Talk!*, 6 December 2012) <www.ejiltalk.org/self-determ ination-and-the-syrian-conflict-recognition-of-syrian-opposition-as-sole-legitimate-rep resentative-of-the-syrian-people-what-does-this-mean-and-what-implications-does-it-have/>.

— — 'Would It Be Lawful for European (or other) States to Provide Arms to the Syrian Opposition?' (*EJIL:Talk!*, 17 January 2013) <www.ejiltalk.org/would-it-be-lawful-for-europ ean-or-other-states-to-provide-arms-to-the-syrian-opposition/>.

— — and Z Vermeer, 'The Airstrikes against Islamic State in Iraq and the Alleged Prohibition on Military Assistance to Governments in Civil Wars' (*EJIL:Talk!*, 2 February 2015) <www.ejilt alk.org/the-airstrikes-against-islamic-state-in-iraq-and-the-alleged-prohibition-on-milit ary-assistance-to-governments-in-civil-wars/>.

Barela SJ, 'Cross-Border Cyber Ops to Erode Legitimacy: An Act of Coercion' (*Just Security*, 12 January 2017) <www.justsecurity.org/36212/cross-border-cyber-ops-erode-legitimacy-act-coercion>.

Buchan R and J Devanny, 'Clarifying Responsible Cyber Power: Developing Views in the U.K. Regarding Non-intervention and Peacetime Cyber Operations' (*Lawfare*, 13 October 2022) <www.lawfaremedia.org/article/clarifying-responsible-cyber-power-developing-views-uk-regarding-non-intervention-and-peacetime>.

D'Aspremont J, 'Duality of Government in Côte d'Ivoire' (*EJIL:Talk!*, 4 January 2011) <http://www.ejiltalk.org/duality-of-government-in-cote-divoire/>.

De Sena P and M Starita, 'Fra stato di necessità ed (illecito) intervento economico: il terzo "bail out" della Grecia' (*SIDIBlog*, 4 August 2015) <www.sidiblog.org/2015/08/04/fra-stato-di-necessita-ed-illecito-intervento-economico-il-terzo-bail-out-della-grecia/>.

Ferro L, 'A Libyan Playground for Foreign Powers: Presenting the Case for "Negative Equality"' (*Opinio Juris*, 26 June 2020) <http://opiniojuris.org/2020/06/26/a-libyan-playground-for-foreign-powers-presenting-the-case-for-negative-equality/>.

Goodman R, 'Taking the Weight off of International Law: Has Syria Consented to US Airstrikes?' (*Just Security*, 23 December 2014) <www.justsecurity.org/18665/weight-intern ational-law-syria-consented-airstrikes/>.

— — and M Schmitt, 'Having Crossed the Rubicon: Arming and Training Syrian Rebels' (*Just Security*, 26 September 2014) <www.justsecurity.org/15660/crossed-rubicon-arming-train ing-syrian-rebels/>.

Gurmendi A, 'Estrada Redux: Mexico's Stance on the Venezuela Crisis and Latin America's Evolving Understanding of Non-Intervention' (*Opinio Juris*, 8 January 2019) <http://opin

iojuris.org/2019/01/08/estrada-redux-mexicos-stance-on-the-venezuela-crisis-and-latin-americas-evolving-understanding-of-non-intervention/>.

— — 'The Last Recognition of Belligerency (and Some Thoughts on Why You May Not Have Heard of It' (*Opinio Juris*, 10 December 2019) <http://opiniojuris.org/2019/12/10/the-last-recognition-of-belligerency-and-some-thoughts-on-why-you-may-not-have-heard-of-it/>.

Hasar S, 'Kazakhstan: Another Intervention by Invitation that Played Out as Expected' (*Opinio Juris*, 7 February 2022) <http://opiniojuris.org/2022/02/07/kazakhstan-another-intervent ion-by-invitation-that-played-out-as-expected/>.

Hofer A and L Ferro, 'Sanctioning Qatar: Coercive Interference in the State's Domaine Réservé?' (*EJIL:Talk!*, 30 June 2017) <www.ejiltalk.org/sanctioning-qatar-coercive-interference-in-the-states-domaine-reserve/>.

Hollis D, 'Russia and the DNC Hack: What Future for a Duty of Non-Intervention?' (*Opinio Juris*, 25 July 2016) <http://opiniojuris.org/2016/07/25/russia-and-the-dnc-hack-a-violat ion-of-the-duty-of-non-intervention/>.

Kilibarda P, 'Was Russia's Recognition of the Separatist Republics in Ukraine "Manifestly" Unlawful?' (*EJIL:Talk!*, 2 March 2002) <www.ejiltalk.org/was-russias-recognition-of-the-separatist-republics-in-ukraine-manifestly-unlawful/>.

Kreß C, 'The Fine Line Between Collective Self-Defense and Intervention by Invitation: Reflections on the Use of Force against "IS" in Syria' (*Just Security*, 17 February 2015) <www.justsecurity.org/20118/claus-kreb-force-isil-syria/>.

Lobo M, 'Intervention by Invitation: The German View of Saudi Arabia's Involvement in the Civil War in Yemen' *GPIL—German Practice in International Law online* (20 April 2020) <https://gpil.jura.uni-bonn.de/2020/04/intervention-by-invitation-the-german-view-of-saudi-arabias-involvement-in-the-civil-war-in-yemen/>.

Miklasová J, 'Russia's Recognition of the DPR and LPR as Illegal Acts under International Law' (*Völkerrechtsblog*, 24 February 2002) <https://voelkerrechtsblog.org/russias-recognition-of-the-dpr-and-lpr-as-illegal-acts-under-international-law/>.

Milanovic M, 'Recognition' (*EJIL:Talk!*, 21 February 2022) <www.ejiltalk.org/recognition/>.

Nguyen A, 'The G7's Fear of Economic Coercion through Weaponised Interdependence—Geopolitical Competition Cloaked in International Law?' (*EJIL:Talk!*, 22 June 2023) <www.ejiltalk.org/the-g7s-fear-of-economic-coercion-through-weaponised-interdependence-geopolitical-competition-cloaked-in-international-law/>.

Nussberger B, 'The Post-Election Crisis in The Gambia: An Interplay of a Security Council's "Non-Authorization" and Intervention by Invitation' (*Opinio Juris*, 8 February 2017) <http://opiniojuris.org/2017/02/08/the-post-election-crisis-in-the-gambia-an-interplay-of-a-secur ity-councils-non-authorization-and-intervention-by-invitation/>.

O'Connell ME, 'Drone Attacks on Saudi Aramco Oil Installations' (*EJIL:Talk!*, 17 September 2019) <www.ejiltalk.org/drone-attacks-on-saudi-aramco-oil-installations/>.

Paddeu F and A Gurmendi Dunkelberg, 'Recognition of Governments: Legitimacy and Control Six Months after Guaidó' (*Opinio Juris*, 18 July 2019) <http://opiniojuris.org/2019/07/18/recognition-of-governments-legitimacy-and-control-six-months-after-guaido/>.

Pertile M, 'Sul riconoscimento di governo nella crisi venezuelana: la trasformazione alchemica è completa?' (*SIDIBlog*, 19 May 2019) <www.sidiblog.org/2019/05/19/sul-riconoscimento-di-governo-nella-crisi-venezuelana-la-trasformazione-alchemica-e-completa/>.

Ronzitti N, 'E' lecito armare I ribelli libici?' (*AffarInternazionali*, 1 April 2011) <www.affarint ernazionali.it/archivio-affarinternazionali/2011/04/lecito-armare-i-ribelli-libici/>.

— — 'La pesca in acque libiche in tempo di guerra civile' (*AffarInternazionali*, 19 September 2019) <www.affarinternazionali.it/archivio-affarinternazionali/2019/09/pesca-acque-libiche/>.

SELECT BIBLIOGRAPHY

Schmitt M, 'The United Kingdom on International Law in Cyberspace' (*EJIL:Talk!*, 24 May 2022) <www.ejiltalk.org/the-united-kingdom-on-international-law-in-cyberspace/>.

Svicevic M, 'The Legality of a SADC Intervention in Cabo Delgado in the Absence of Mozambican Consent' (*Opinio Juris*, 2 November 2020) <http://opiniojuris.org/2020/11/02/the-legality-of-a-sadc-intervention-in-cabo-delgado-in-the-absence-of-mozambican-consent>.

Talmon S, 'Meeting with Hong Kong Activist as Interference in China's Internal Affairs?' *GPIL—German Practice in International Law online* (17 November 2020) <https://gpil.jura.uni-bonn.de/2020/11/meeting-with-hong-kong-activist-as-interference-in-chinas-internal-affairs/>.

— — 'Iraq Accuses Germany of Interference in its Internal Affairs' *GPIL—German Practice in International Law online* (25 March 2021) <https://gpil.jura.uni-bonn.de/2021/03/iraq-accuses-germany-of-interference-in-its-internal-affairs/>.

— — 'Iran Condemns German Ambassador's Tweets as Interference in Internal Affairs' *GPIL—German Practice in International Law online* (13 July 2021) <https://gpil.jura.uni-bonn.de/2021/07/iran-condemns-german-ambassadors-tweets-as-interference-in-internal-affairs/>.

Weller M, 'Russia's Recognition of the "Separatist Republics" in Ukraine was Manifestly Unlawful' (*EJIL:Talk!*, 9 March 2022) <www.ejiltalk.org/russias-recognition-of-the-separatist-republics-in-ukraine-was-manifestly-unlawful/>.

Yiallourides C, 'Is China Using Force or Coercion in the South China Sea? Why Words Matter' (*The Diplomat*, 11 July 2018) <https://thediplomat.com/2018/07/is-china-using-force-or-coercion-in-the-south-china-sea/>.

Other Sources

Chatham House, 'The Principle of Non-Intervention in Contemporary International Law: Non-Interference in a State's Internal Affairs used to Be a Rule of International Law: Is It Still?' (28 February 2007) <https://perma.cc/52DL-JSYE>.

Corn GP, 'Covert Deception, Strategic Fraud, and the Rule of Prohibited Intervention', Hoover Working Group on National Security, Technology, and Law, Aegis Series Paper No. 2005 (18 September 2020) <www.hoover.org/sites/default/files/research/docs/corn_webready.pdf>.

Kriener F and L Brassat, 'Quashing Protests Abroad: The CSTO's Intervention in Kazakhstan' Max Planck Institute for Comparative Public Law & International Law (MPIL) Research Paper No. 2023-10, 6 April 2023.

MacFarlane SN, 'Intervention in Contemporary World Politics', The Adelphi Papers, vol 42, issue 350 (2002).

McWhinney E, 'Declaration on the Inadmissibility of Intervention in the Domestic Affairs of States and the Protection of Their Independence and Sovereignty: General Assembly Resolution 2131 (XX), New York, 21 December 1965', United Nations Audiovisual Library of International Law, 2010 <https://legal.un.org/avl/ha/ga_2131-xx/ga_2131-xx.html>.

Moynihan H, 'The Application of International Law to Cyber Attacks. Sovereignty and Non-Intervention' (Chatham House Research Paper 2019) <www.chathamhouse.org/2019/12/application-international-law-state-cyberattacks/3-application-non-intervention-principle>.

Index

For the benefit of digital users, indexed terms that span two pages (e.g., 52–53) may, on occasion, appear on only one of those pages.

abuse of right 164–5n.132
Afghanistan
  Pakistan's intervention in 237–8n.311
  Soviet Union's invasion of 113, 123–4,
    133–4, 167–8, 179–80, 214–15, 224–5,
    231, 240–1, 274–5, 294–5n.360
  Taliban's takeover of 211–12
  US support for the *mujahidin* in 133–4
  Western states' intervention in 133–4,
    231–2, 238n.317, 264–5
African Union (AU) 105–6, 269–70
  interventions by the 105–6, 225–6, 262–3,
    276–7, 334n.170, 366–7
aggression 72, 102n.18, 126, 206, 228–9, 233,
    260–1, 276, 282, 291–2, 296–7, 306, 321–3
  colonialism and alien occupation as acts
    of 324–5, 328–9
  economic coercion as an act of 181n.254
Albania
  foreign intervention in the civil unrest
    in 217–18
  revolution of 1924 in 73
Algerian War of Independence 191–2, 198,
    313n.27, 326n.114, 326n.120
alien domination/occupation 310–14, 327–
    9, 330, 335, 411
  definition of 327–8
  intervention in support of a national
    liberation movement 329, 411, 412
  intervention in support of an occupying
    power 328–9, 410–11, 412
Al-Qaeda 265–6, 270n.177
American Civil War 55, 59–61, 62n.375,
    62n.376
American international law 78, 81
American War of Independence 15, 24–5,
    27–8, 96, 404
  Dutch Republic's recognition of the
    secessionist colonies 25
  France's intervention in the 24–5

Angola
  Civil War in 297
  Cuba's intervention in 238n.312, 261–2,
    294–5n.360
  South Africa's intervention in 217, 261–2,
    316–17, 326–7
  Soviet Union's intervention in 238n.312,
    261–2
apartheid, *see* racist regimes
Arab Spring uprisings 98–9
armed measures short of war 32–4, 35–6,
    70–2, 169n.166, 182–3, 345, 404–5
arms, supply of 68–9, 73, 76–7, 85–6, 92,
    96–7, 189–90, 194, 235–6, 239n.320,
    243–4, 267–8, 278–80, 281, 306, 352–3,
    401, 404–5
  as an armed attack 295n.365
  and the Arms Trade Treaty 190, 350
  duty to prevent the 190, 191–2, 306, 319
  and external self-determination 317–18,
    325–6, 336, 411
  and IHRL/IHL violations 350–3, 368–70,
    373
ASEAN, *see* Association of South-East Asian
    Nations
Association of South-East Asian Nations
    (ASEAN) 107–8, 211–12, 226

Bahrain
  Gulf Cooperation Council's intervention
    in 224–5, 291, 293, 353
  Iran's intervention in 291
balance of power 12–13, 53–4, 96–7, 406–7
Bangladesh's War of Independence 351–2
  India's intervention in 238n.317, 356, 362–4
Barkhane, Operation 260–1, 283, 284
Bay of Pigs operation 98, 191–2, 237–8n.311
Belarus
  possible Russian intervention in 291, 293
  sanctions against 243–4

448 INDEX

Belgian War of Independence 51–2
  France and United Kingdom's intervention
    in the 31–2, 39n.224, 44–5, 48, 53–4
belligerent occupation 327
Bermuda
  British intervention in 285
Bernard, Mountague 28–9, 58–9, 80,
  89–90
blockade 31–2, 33, 59–61, 66, 75–6,
  175n.211, 193, 198
Bodin, Jean 12n.16, 14n.28
Bogotazo Riots 188–9
Bolivian Civil War 69
Bosnia and Herzegovina
  Croatia's intervention in 294–5n.360
  United Nations Protection Force
    (UNPROFOR) in 370–1
Boxers, European powers' intervention
  against the 31–2
Brazil
  revolt of 1893–4 in 63–4, 69
  revolution of 1930 in 68–9
Brezhnev Doctrine 167–8, 169n.163
Brunei
  United Kingdom's intervention in 284–5
Burkina Faso
  France and G5 Sahel states' interventions
    in 283, 292
Burlamaqui, Jean-Jaques 21–2
Burundi
  political crisis of 2015 226
  Zaire's intervention in 285
Byzantine Empire 11n.8

Calvo, Carlos 30
Cambodia
  US ground operations in 220–1, 295n.363
  Vietnam's invasion of 185–6, 214–15,
    215n.134, 227, 238n.317, 240–1, 261
Cameroon
  Chad's intervention in 269–70
  France's interventions in 224–5, 282, 292
  US suspension of military assistance
    for 351–2
CAR, *see* Central African Republic
Caroline incident 37, 66, 72
Carranza Doctrine 30–1
Central African Republic (CAR)
  Cameroon, Gabon, Republic of the Congo,
    and Chad's intervention in the 266, 272

France's interventions in the 227, 256–7,
  266, 287, 354–5
Mission Interafricaine de Surveillance des
  Accords de Bangui (MISAB) 287
Mission Internationale de Soutien à la
  Centrafrique sous Conduit Africaine
  (MISCA) 266
Russia's intervention in the 289
Rwanda's intervention in the 289
South Africa's intervention in the 229–30,
  266, 272
suspension of aid to the 351–2
Chad
  France's interventions in 224–5, 256–7,
    260–1, 272, 284, 292, 294–5n.360
  Libya's interventions in 224–5, 237–
    8n.311, 260–1, 272
  Zaire's intervention in 211, 294–5n.360
Chechnya, armed conflict in 98–9
Chile
  Civil War of 1891 in 62–3, 64–5, 68–9
  US interferences in 179–80
China
  Civil War in 199, 256
  Xinhai Revolution in 73
Civil strife, definition of 196–7, 409–10
Civil war 24n.109, 24n.110, 28, 72
  in the Covenant of the League of
    Nations 75
  difference from non-international armed
    conflict 252–4
  dual-theory of 61n.372
  notion of 2, 17–18, 19–20, 23–4, 55,
    57–67, 196–7, 252–5, 305
  and recognition of belligerency 59–67,
    85–6, 255, 306
  without recognition of belligerency 67–9,
    85–6, 255, 306
co-belligerency 65–7, 93–4, 96–7, 200, 255,
  273, 327, 405
coercion 2–3, 29–30, 34, 115, 145–7, 161–2,
  244, 247–8, 320, 400, 407, 408, 411–12
  and alien domination/occupation 328–9
  armed 29–30, 31–4, 72, 85, 101, 108–9,
    114, 145, 146–7, 148–9, 164, 169–70,
    182–3, 184, 188–9, 195, 407
  attempted 154–5, 382–3, 385–6
  coercive manipulation 398–9, 403
  and consent 151–2, 169–70, 202–3
  in cyberspace 98–9, 178–9, 382–400

and decolonization 152, 326–7
dictatorial 152–5, 158–9, 160–1, 169, 184,
   186–7, 194–5, 382–3, 385–6, 387–8, 397,
   398–9, 400, 403, 408
diplomatic, *see* coercion, political
economic 8, 29–30, 98–9, 103–4,
   105–6, 108–9, 121n.152, 126, 132,
   133, 145, 146–7, 148–9, 150–1, 158–9,
   160–1, 170–86, 187, 188–9, 195, 243–4,
   389n.139, 407
as an element of the principle of non-
   intervention 91–2, 146, 147–58, 161,
   194–5, 202–5, 228, 246, 407
to enforce compliance with IHRL/
   IHL 347–8, 356, 368, 372–3
EU definition of 121n.152, 153, 175–6,
   177–9
forcible 155–8, 169, 186–7, 194–5, 383, 385,
   387–8, 395, 397, 398–9, 400, 403, 408
as a ground for invalidating consent to
   intervention 227–8
in the law of treaties 171, 227–8
political 19–20, 29–31, 72, 85, 103–4,
   108–9, 114, 145, 146–7, 148–9, 150–1,
   158–9, 160–1, 170–86, 179n.242, 188–9,
   195, 369–70n.225, 389n.139, 407; *see
   also* threat of force
Cold War 81, 98–9, 112–13, 143, 153, 194,
   274–5, 314n.34, 342–3, 405–6
debates on the scope of non-intervention
   during the 170–86, 380
interventionist doctrines during
   the 166–9
Collective Security Treaty Organization
   (CSTO) 107–8, 224–5, 291–2
colonial domination 310–27, 328–9, 330,
   335, 410–11
definition of 314–15
link with racist regimes 303–4, 305
self-defence against 324–5
Comoros
African Union's intervention in 334n.170
France's intervention in 287
France and South Africa's intervention
   in 206–7, 224–5, 287
Concert of Europe 41, 43–4, 44n.255
Congo, *see* Democratic Republic of the
   Congo (DRC)
Congo, Republic of
French intervention in the 283, 292

Congress of Vienna 28, 70, 167–8
consent to intervention 2–3, 19–20, 23, 42–4,
   49–50, 51–2, 56–7, 100–1, 135–6, 151–2,
   169–70, 202–5, 244–5, 315–16, 328–9,
   354–5, 408–9
ad hoc 222–6, 234–5, 245, 409
as an agreement 203–4, 219–20, 226–7,
   231–2, 245, 409
Chinese doctrine of 206n.63
in civil wars 151–2, 251, 255–77, 292,
   301–3, 305–6, 330–1, 368, 370–2, 402,
   404–5, 411, 412
and coercion 227–8, 408–9
consent of all factions doctrine 138
consent of any faction doctrine 216–17
by *de facto* or local authorities 207–8
and error, fraud, and corruption 227
form of 219–21, 245
by insurrectional authorities 237–44
and *jus cogens* 228–9
limits to the scope of 232–3, 245, 409
open-ended 222–6, 234–5, 245, 366–7, 409
organ entitled to grant 206–7, 229–30,
   233–4
as a primary or secondary rule 203–5
in situations of anarchy 216–18, 244–5,
   408–9
in situations of internal unrest short of civil
   war 281–93, 305–6, 315–16, 354, 402,
   404–5, 410, 412
timing of 231–2
and UN Security Council
   resolutions 235–6
validity requirements of 226–30, 245, 409
waiver of 231–2
withdrawal of 233–5
continuity of legitimate power, principle 13–
   14, 19, 25, 42, 208
Corsica
Emperor Charles VI's intervention in 15
Cosmopolitan scholarship 131–2
Costa Rica
US intervention in support of 294–5n.360
Côte d'Ivoire
ECOWAS intervention in 261–2
France's intervention in 213–14, 217–18,
   251–2, 256–7, 264, 287, 289, 292, 371–2
political crisis of 2010–1 in 210, 213–14
United Nations Operation in Côte d'Ivoire
   (UNOCI) 264, 289, 303n.408, 371–2

450 INDEX

counter-intervention 80, 90–1, 139–42, 292, 293–8
  in support of an incumbent government 293–6, 306, 409–10
  in support of insurgents 296–8
countermeasures 145–6, 163–4, 169–70, 179–80, 181–2, 195, 243–4, 296n.367, 298, 314, 318–19, 323–4, 325–7, 328–9, 335–6, 346–7, 349, 354, 369–70, 373, 381, 387, 408, 410–12
Crete
  European powers' intervention in 49–50
Crimea
  Russia's occupation of 123–4, 185–6, 202, 320–1, 356
CSTO, see Collective Security Treaty Organization
Cuba
  First Civil War in 62–4, 64n.392
  insurrection of 1851 in 80–1
  revolution of 1953–9 in 278–9n.238
  Second Civil War in 31–2, 48, 49–50n.287, 64–5, 68–9, 80–1
  US interventions after the independence of 82, 83
  US sanctions against 81, 159–60, 171–2, 176–7, 178–80, 248n.13
customary international law, identification of 4–7, 10n.5, 29n.142, 81, 116–18, 120, 135–6, 174–5, 237–9, 254–5, 257, 375–6
cyber operations 2–3, 8
  against Azerbaijan 400–1
  against Estonia 382–3, 390
  causing or designed to cause loss of functionality 387–90, 403, 407–8
  causing or designed to cause material damage 385–7, 403, 407–8
  consent to 395–6
  definitions of 376
  difference from cybercrime 377
  different types of 376–7
  Distributed Denial of Service Attacks (DDoS) 376–7
  DNC hacks 396n.209
  doxing 396–7, 403
  duty to prevent 401–2
  exclusively involving unauthorized extraterritorial access to non-public data 390–6, 403, 407–8
  information operations 396–7, 403, 407–8
  and internal self-determination 399–400
  as a new form of intervention 374
  NotPetya cyber attack 382–3
  ransomware attacks 382–3
  and the rule protecting territorial sovereignty 391–5, 397, 403
  SolarWinds cyber attack 390
  Stuxnet 385
  UN General Assembly and 374–5
  UN Security Council and 374–5
  US cyber operations against Iran's Islamic Revolutionary Guard Corps 388
  as a use of force 386–7, 388–90
  WannaCry cyber attack 382–3
Cyprus
  Turkey's interventions in 224–5
Czechoslovakia
  Warsaw Pact's intervention in 13n.20, 98, 113, 167–8, 224–5, 227, 248n.13, 290–1, 293, 294–5n.360

Darfur, armed conflict in 98–9
decolonization conflicts 98, 113, 139–40, 191–2, 314–27; see also self-determination, external
  intervention in support of a colonial power 315–19, 335–6, 410–11, 412
  intervention in support of national liberation movements 320–7, 336, 411, 412
democracy 130, 132, 133, 179–80, 240–4, 290, 293, 410
  intervention to promote 141, 240–4, 296–7, 361, 397
  and legitimacy of governments 208–9n.81, 240–1
  right to 241, 249–50
Democratic Republic of the Congo (DRC) 236
  Angola, Namibia, and Zimbabwe's intervention in the 264, 294–5n.360
  Belgium's intervention of 1960 in the 206–8, 216–17, 235–6, 238n.315, 335n.176
  Burundi and Rwanda's intervention in the 237–8n.311, 238n.317
  concessions during the Katanga conflict in the 193
  First Shaba War in the 282–3
  Opération des Nations-Unies au Congo (ONUC) 301–2, 332
  Rwanda's intervention in the 237–8n.311, 264

'Safari Club' states' intervention in the 282–3, 292

Uganda's intervention in the 187n.297, 191, 221, 232–3, 234, 237–9

UN Stabilization Mission in the Congo (MONUSCO) 301–2

US and Belgium's intervention in Stanleyville 138–9, 232–3, 239–40, 251–2, 258

US supply of arms and training assistance to the government of the 279n.239

Digital Revolution 374, 377–8, 407–8

Djibouti

French intervention in 283, 292

domaine réservé, see domestic jurisdiction

domestic jurisdiction 13–14, 100–1, 111, 130, 146, 150–1, 161–9, 195, 196–202, 235–6, 244, 246, 247–8, 312–13, 315, 318, 326–7, 328–9, 369–70, 372–3, 408, 409, 411–12

in cyberspace 381

definition of 162–3

Soviet notion of 162–3

Dominican Republic

US interventions between 1916–24 in the 82, 83

US intervention of 1965 in the 98, 217, 258–9

Drago Doctrine 82n.516

Dutch East Indies

UK assistance to the Netherlands in the 316–17

US supply of arms to the Netherlands in the 317n.54

Dutch Revolt 51–2

dynastic legitimacy 12–15, 19, 24, 26–7, 41–2, 44–6, 73, 80, 86, 96, 404

East Germany

Soviet Union's intervention in 98

East Pakistan, *see* Bangladesh

East Timor

Australia, New Zealand, and Portugal's intervention in 288–9

Indonesia's invasion and occupation of 323–4, 328–9

ECCAS, *see* Economic Community of East African States

Economic Community of East African States (ECCAS) 208, 220n.170, 225–6, 276–7, 366–7

Economic Community of West African States (ECOWAS) 106–7, 210, 213–14, 217, 225–6, 261–2, 263–4, 265–6, 276–7, 283, 366–7

ECOWAS, *see* Economic Community of West African States

Electoral interferences 387–8, 396n.208, 398–402, 403, 406, 407–8

El Salvador

Nicaragua's intervention in support of 237–8n.311, 294–5

US intervention in 294–5n.360

Epidamnus, Corcyra and Corinth's interferences in 9

Erga omnes obligations 122–4, 143, 243–4, 298, 312–13, 318–19, 323–4, 326–7, 328–9, 335–6, 342–3, 345–6, 347–8, 349, 368–70, 372–3, 410–12

Estrada Doctrine 86

Ethiopia

armed conflict with Eritrea 332

Cuba and Soviet Union's support for the *Derg* 332

Eritrea's intervention in 271

Tigray War in 98–9, 271

extraterritorial exercise of jurisdiction 155–8, 346, 387–8, 392–3, 394–5

Falkland/Malvinas, Argentina's invasion of the 160–1, 171–2

FARC, *see* Revolutionary Armed Forces of Colombia

feminist scholarship 133–4

Finnish Civil War 70

First World War 70, 88

France

interventions in Africa 98, 222, 224–5, 256–7, 274

July Revolution 44–5, 46

French Revolution 24, 25–8, 42, 96, 404

Austria and Prussia's intervention in the 25–6

British position in relation to the 25–6

Frontline States, South Africa's interventions in the 326n.117

fundamental rights of states 35–40, 72, 88, 102

funding of armed opposition groups 192–3, 278, 280–1, 306, 369–70, 373, 401

duty of vigilance to prevent the 192–4, 306

452 INDEX

funding of national liberation
movements 326–7, 329, 336, 411

Gabon
France's intervention in 206–7, 224–5,
285, 287, 292
Georgia, Russia's intervention in 202, 214–
15, 238n.317
Global North 132
Global South 6, 132, 364–5
Glorious Revolution 15, 16–17, 53n.306
Goa
India's intervention in 323–5
Good Neighbor Policy 82n.517
governments, identification of
democratic legitimacy doctrine 208–
9n.81, 240–1, 408–9
domestic legitimacy doctrine 208–10, 211,
408–9; see also continuity of legitimate
power, principle
effective control doctrine 44–6, 80, 86,
96, 139–40, 211–19, 244–5, 253–4, 404,
408–9
Lauterpacht presumption 215–16, 244–5,
408–9
by the United Nations 218, 219
Great Peloponnesian War 9
Greece
Civil War in 237–8n.311
communist states' intervention in 281–2,
292
United Kingdom's intervention in 281–2
US intervention in 233, 235n.296,
240n.328, 281–2
Greek War of Independence 49–50, 51–2,
59n.356
intervention of United Kingdom, France,
and Russia in the 31–2, 48–9
Grenada
US/OECS intervention in 98, 141, 206–7,
208–9, 217, 219–20, 241, 248n.13, 286,
292
Grotius, Hugo 14n.28, 22–3, 345
Group of 77 226
Guatemala
US, Nicaragua, and Honduras's
intervention in 98, 237–8n.311, 284
Guinea
Liberia and Sierra Leone's involvement in
attacks against 237–8n.311

Guinea-Bissau
Senegal and Guinea's intervention
in 224–5, 283, 292
Gustav III of Sweden, France's support for 15

Haiti
OECS intervention in 213–14, 217–18,
241–2
rebellion of 1888–9 69
US occupation of Haiti in 1915–34 82, 83
Hallstein Doctrine 153, 164–5n.132
Hattousilis III, king of the Hittites 9
Holy Alliance 31–2, 40, 41–8, 78–9, 81–2, 86,
96–7, 167–8, 404–5
Holy Roman Empire 10–12, 12n.18, 15–17,
25–6, 302
Honduras
US intervention in support of 284,
294–5n.360
Hong Kong
landing of a Kuomintang jet fighter in 199
sanctions against China over 178–80,
243–4
humanitarian intervention 14n.28, 38, 48–
51, 90–1, 96–7, 131, 140–1, 158, 237–9,
357–68, 406, 412; see also tyranny,
resistance to
human security 339–40
Hungary
Russia's intervention of 1849 in 42–3
War of Independence 64–5
Warsaw Pact's intervention in 98, 113,
167–8, 214–15, 220n.176, 224–5, 231,
233–4, 290, 293

independence, fundamental right of states
to 36n.200, 37–9, 88–9, 93–4, 96–7, 129
inherently sovereign/governmental
functions 165–6, 381, 391–2
insurrection, definition of 55–7, 76–7
international humanitarian law (IHL) 110–
11, 121–2, 252–3, 320, 327, 337, 343–4
assistance for a government responsible for
violations of 348–53, 357n.126, 372–3,
411–12
compliance with 8, 61–2, 63n.387, 64–5,
67, 69, 179–80, 196–7, 269–71, 272,
302–3, 348–53, 355, 411–12
duty to ensure respect for 343–4, 349–50,
351, 365–6

intervention to ensure compliance with
IHL under UN Security Council
authorization 370-2
intervention in support of insurgents
against a government responsible for
violations of 356-70, 373, 412
violations of IHL as threats to the
peace 344
international human rights law (IHRL) 130,
131, 132, 133, 139-41, 179-80, 196-7,
269-70, 272, 302-3, 318, 337, 347-8,
411-12
assistance for a government responsible for
violations of 348-53, 357n.126, 372-3,
411-12
communist states' position on 342-3
and domestic jurisdiction 340-4, 347-8,
369-70, 411-12
as *erga omnes/erga omnes partes*
obligations 342-3
intervention to ensure compliance with
IHRL under UN Security Council
authorization 370-2
intervention in support of insurgents
against a government responsible for
violations of 356-70, 373, 412
as *jus cogens* norms 341-2
negative equality and 354-5
intervention
against terrorism 298-301, 306, 355,
368-9, 406, 409-10
British doctrine of 46-8, 49, 96-7
in civil wars 88-91, 88n.553, 92-4, 96-7,
135-7, 138, 141-3, 190, 222-3, 250-81,
293-303, 409-10
'cosmopolitan' 346
definition of 29-30
difference from countermeasures 163-4,
381, 408
on grounds of humanity, *see* humanitarian
intervention
on grounds of religion 11-12, 21, 98n.1, 404
Holy Alliance's doctrine of 41-6, 49, 96-7
individual criminal liability for 126-7
intent as an element of 145-6, 158-61,
194-5, 384, 408
and international order 128-34
by invitation 57n.339, 66-7, 88-93, 113,
134-43, 151-2, 167-8, 200, 215-16, 246,
294, 296, 297, 298-9, 354, 361-2, 412

just cause for 92-4, 96
motive as an element of 158, 160-1
Nazi doctrine of 94-5
Oppenheim's definition of 29-30, 32-3
to protect community interests 43-4,
87-8, 90-1, 92-3, 98-9, 129-30, 133,
139-40, 182-3, 345-8, 367-8, 406-7
role of the United Nations in 143, 235-6,
300-3, 306
in self-determination conflicts 137, 141-3,
145-7, 320-1, 326-7, 330, 410-11
Soviet doctrine of 94-5, 113, 167-8, 170, 175
treaty-based 47, 49-50, 56-7, 83-4, 90-1,
96-7, 222-6, 234-5, 245, 366-7, 404-5,
409
with UN Security Council
authorization 217-18, 237-9, 266, 272,
361-2, 370-2
Iran
Soviet Union's interventions in 224-5,
237-8n.311, 334n.174
UK boycott of oil from 179-80
US sanctions against 159-60, 176-7,
179-80
Iraq
French, UK, and US airstrikes to protect the
Kurds in northern 224-5, 227, 367-8
occupation of 231-2
presence of US forces in 266-7
UK and US invasion of 231-2
US and other states' intervention against
ISIL in 266-7
US support for opposition groups
in 240-1
Irish rebellion of 1916 70
ISIL, *see* 'Islamic State'
ISIS, *see* 'Islamic State'
'Islamic State' 185-6, 220-1, 266-7, 268-71,
270n.177, 283, 284, 298-9
Italian School of International Law 90-1
Italian states
Sardinia's interventions in and annexation
of the 52-4, 52n.299, 94n.618

James II, king of England (James VII of Scotland
and James II of Ireland) 16-17, 21
Louis XIV of France's financial support
for 15
William III of Orange-Nassau's
intervention against 16-17, 53n.306

454 INDEX

Jammu and Kashmir National Liberation Front, Pakistan's supply of arms for the 237–8n.311
Johnson Doctrine 166–7
Jordan
 British intervention in 208–9, 235n.296, 284, 290, 292, 293, 294–5n.360
jus in bello, see international humanitarian law (IHL)
jus cogens 122–3, 125–7, 143, 185–6, 200n.32, 222–3, 228–9, 250–1, 312–13, 319, 331n.145, 341–2
jus publicum europæum 12–14, 24, 96–7, 404–5

Kampuchea, *see* Cambodia
Kant, Immanuel 22–3, 345n.48
Katanga 193
Kazakhstan
 CSTO intervention in 224–5, 238n.316, 291–2, 293, 294–5n.360
Kenya
 British intervention in 285
kinetic equivalence 385
Kosovo
 NATO intervention in 227–8, 335n.176, 340–1, 358–9, 362–4, 365–6
 supply of arms to the Kosovo Liberation Army 119n.136, 368–9
Kuwait
 Iraq's invasion of 214–15
Kyrgyzstan
 request for a Russian intervention in 291n.347

Laotian Civil War
 North Vietnam's intervention in the 237–8n.311
 US intervention in the 279n.239, 295n.363
Latin America 20, 28, 31–2, 69, 102, 175, 178–9, 327–8n.126
 reaction to US interventionism 20, 84–6
 US interventions in 20, 31–2, 78–84, 222
 Wars of Independence of the Spanish colonies 38, 41–2, 44–5, 58–60, 79, 96
Latvia
 Soviet Union's invasion and occupation of 154, 166
Lauterpacht, Hersch 29–30, 64–5, 69n.431, 70–1, 191–2, 215–16, 228

law of armed conflict, *see* international humanitarian law (IHL)
League of Arab States 107–8, 261, 268–9
League of Nations 70–1, 75, 81, 100–1
Lebanon
 France's intervention in the Mount Lebanon Civil War 31–2, 49–50
 Syria's intervention in 236, 261, 272
 United Arab Republic's intervention in 237–8n.311, 292
 US intervention in 208–9, 214–15, 282, 284, 294–5n.360
Le Fur, Louis 95
Lesotho
 SADC intervention in 289
 South Africa and other states' interventions in 229n.246, 276–7, 288, 289
liberal scholarship 130–1
Liberation Tigers of Tamil Eelam (LTTE) 121–2, 332–3, 335n.176, *see also* Sri Lanka
Liberia
 Burkina Faso's intervention in 225
 Civil War in 98–9, 236n.300, 262
 ECOWAS intervention in 138n.269, 217, 251–2, 262, 354–5
 Guinea's intervention in 237–8n.311
Libya
 arms embargo on 236n.300, 267–9
 Egypt's intervention in 268–9
 First Civil War in 98–9, 193–4, 211–12, 216, 369n.224
 Government of National Accord (GNA) 193–4, 219, 222–3, 236, 267–9, 279n.240, 280–1, 302
 NATO airstrikes in 238n.319, 251–2, 362–4, 371–2
 oil concessions in 193–4
 Qatar and Sudan's supply of arms to Haftar 237–8n.311
 recognition of the insurgents in 369–70n.225
 Second Civil War in 193–4, 235–6, 267–8
 Turkey's intervention in 224–5, 229–30, 267–8
 US airstrikes against ISIL in 268–9
Lorimer, James 39–40
Louis XIV, king of France 15, 17n.53
Louis XVI, king of France 25–6
Louis XVIII, king of France 26

INDEX 455

Macedonian uprisings
  Austria-Hungary and Russia's intervention in the 49n.283
Malaya
  Australia, New Zealand, and United Kingdom's intervention in 282, 292
Maldives
  India's intervention in 286
Mali
  African-led International Support Mission in Mali (AFISMA) 265n.135, 302
  Chad's intervention in 265-6
  Civil War in 98-9, 215n.136, 216, 265-6
  France's intervention in 265-6, 333
  United Nations Multidimensional Integrated Stabilization Mission in Mali (MINUSMA) 265-6, 302
Mancini, Pasquale Stanislao 51
Manifest Destiny, *see* Polk Corollary
Martens, Georg Friedrich von 23
Metternich, Klemens von 42-4, 49-50
Mexico
  'drug wars' 253
  France's intervention in 80n.501
  revolution of 1910-20 in 68-9, 73
  Ten Tragic Days 45n.262
  Zuloaga insurrection in 45n.265
Mill, John Stuart 37n.209, 47-8
Modena
  Austria's intervention in 42-3
Monroe Doctrine 79-82, 166-7
Mozambique
  Rwanda's intervention in 284, 354
  SADC intervention in 276-7, 292
  South Africa's support of RENAMO in 326n.117
  Tanzania and Zimbabwe's intervention in 294-5n.360
Muscat and Oman
  British intervention in 201-2, 331, 334n.175
Myanmar
  coup of 2021 in 211-12, 243-4, 351-2
  sanctions against 351-2

Namibia, *see* South West Africa
Napoleon I, emperor of the French 26, 39n.224, 40
Napoleon III, emperor of the French 44-5, 53, 54n.317, 80n.501

Napoleonic Wars 28, 41, 42, 43-4
nationalities, principle of 51-4, 90-1, 96-7
national liberation movements 121-2, 143, 237-9, 310, 314n.37, 320-7, 336
  definition of 320
negative equality 57, 70, 73-4, 77-8, 85-6, 88-91, 97, 135-7, 139-40, 143, 251, 255, 272-7, 300-1, 305, 306, 309, 331, 405, 409-10, 411, 412
  and human rights 354-5
  'qualified' 91-2, 222-3, 305-6, 409-10, 412
  in secessionist conflicts 330-4, 336, 405
Nepalese Civil War 279n.239
Netherlands
  Prussia's intervention in the 15
neutrality 23, 27-8, 33-4, 40, 57, 58-69, 70, 76-7, 79, 93-4, 97, 190, 200, 244-5, 255, 273, 290, 306, 327, 331, 405, 408-9
neutralization status 67n.409, 205-6, 226-7
New Haven School, *see* policy-oriented scholarship
New International Economic Order 133
Nicaragua
  armed opposition against Somoza 198
  US economic measures against 81, 159, 160-1, 171-2, 181, 182
  US interventions of 1912 and 1927 in 82
  US support for the Contras in 98, 192, 238n.318, 294-5, 295n.363, 365-6, 368-9
Nigeria
  Civil War in 193, 198, 238n.314, 278, 279n.239, 280
  Multinational Joint Task Force (MNJTF)'s intervention in 269-70
  oil concessions during the Civil War in 193
  UK supply of arms to the government of 352-3
Non-Aligned Movement 112-13, 115, 171, 242-3, 274-5, 320-1, 361-2
non-governmental organizations (NGOs), foreign funding of 186
non-interference 105-6, 107-8, 114, 151
non-intervention
  in African treaties 105-7
  in American treaties 102-5
  application in cyberspace of 377-80, 403
  in Asian treaties 107-8

456 INDEX

non-intervention (*cont.*)
  communist countries' conception
    of 113–14
  as a corollary of sovereignty 39, 96, 121–2,
    161–2, 203, 247, 338, 404–5, 406
  as customary international law 112–20,
    123–4
  difference from the rule protecting
    territorial sovereignty 395
  as an *erga omnes* obligation 122–4, 143
  as an *erga omnes partes* obligation 124
  in European treaties and other
    documents 108–9
  and international organizations 121–2
  as a *jus cogens* norm 125–7, 143
  non-aligned states' conception of 112–13
  as a 'principle' 121–2
  and self-determination 320–1
  stricto sensu 57, 58–9, 65, 70, 76–7, 91–2,
    96–7, 134–5, 139–40, 244–5, 255, 305,
    335–6, 408–9, 412
  in thematic treaties 111–12
  in the UN Charter 100–1
  Western states' conception of 108–9, 114,
    380, 406
non-lethal military equipment, supply
  of 189–90, 369–70
non-recognition 42

OECS, *see* Organisation of East Caribbean
  States
one voice principle 184–5
Organisation of East Caribbean States
  (OECS) 213–14, 217, 219–20, 286
Organisation of Islamic Cooperation 107–8,
  226
Organization of African Unity (OAU) 105–
  6, 217, 261–2, 326n.119
Organization of American States
  (OAS) 102–5, 242–3, 258–9, 275, 407
  intervention by 104–5, 217
Organization of Arab Petroleum Exporting
  Countries' oil embargo 159–60, 179–80
Oriental Crisis
  European powers' intervention in the 42–
    3, 49–50
Ottoman Empire
  interventions in the 5, 32, 38–9, 48–51,
    345, 358–9
  status of minorities in the 50n.288,
    341n.22

Pakistan, US drone strikes in 219–20
Palestinian Territories
  Egypt, Syria, and Transjordan's
    intervention in the 225
  Gaza, Israel naval blockade of 198
  Israel's occupation of the 159–60, 179–80,
    310–12, 328–9
Panama
  US intervention of 1989 in 98, 141, 213–
    14, 225n.214, 241–2
  US intervention against the *Movimento
    Inquilinario* riots in 83n.523
  US intervention in the War of
    Independence of 84
Panama Canal 83, 110, 223n.193, 241–2
Pan-American Conferences 84–6, 102,
  103n.20
Papacy 10–12, 35, 90n.577, 302
Papal States
  Austria's intervention in the 41–2
  France's intervention in the 42–4, 53
  Sardinia's occupation of the 52–4
Papua New Guinea
  peacekeeping force in 333
Paris Commune 68–9
Parma
  Austria's intervention in 42–3
peaceful coexistence 99, 113–14, 117n.121,
  405–6
Peru
  Bolivia's support for Peru during General
    Salaverry's revolt 56–7
  Vivanco insurrection in 67
Piedmont
  Austria's intervention in 41–4
'Pig War' 29–30
Pius IX, Pope 42–3, 43–4n.254, 53, 413
Platt Amendment 83
Poland
  Austria, Prussia, and Russia's intervention
    in 15
  insurrection of 1830–1 in 64–5, 68–9
  January Uprisings of 1863–4 in 63–4
  partition of 1, 15
policy-oriented scholarship 139–42, 148–9,
  398, 413
Polk Corollary 81–2
Portugal
  Liberal Wars in 47, 74n.462
  revolution of 1927 in 73
  sanctions against 310–12, 317–18, 319

positive equality doctrine 137
purpose-based doctrine 138–9

Qatar
  Gulf countries' embargo on 150–1, 159–60, 179–80

racist regimes 169–70, 185–6, 228–9, 303–5, 309–14, 316–17, 317n.54, 319, 330, 411
Ramses II, pharaoh of Egypt 9
Reagan Doctrine 166–7, 169n.163, 240–1
realist scholarship 128–30
rebellion, definition of 17–18, 42, 55–7, 89–90
recognition 14–15, 23, 30, 39–40, 218–19; *see also* non-recognition
  of belligerency 56–7, 59–69, 75–8, 85–6, 95, 97, 185–6, 196–7, 198–200, 255, 405
  of government 61–2, 75–6, 86, 95, 200n.30, 212–13, 216, 218–19
  of insurgency 69–70
  of national liberation movements 326–7, 411
  negatory effects of 184–5
  premature 60–1, 63–4, 147, 156–8, 184–6, 195, 216, 329, 369–70, 407
  of statehood 44–5, 61–2, 79, 238n.314, 356, 356n.120
  by the UN Security Council 219
  in violation of *jus cogens* norms 185–6
Reformation 11–12, 13–14
remedial secession 356–7
reprisals 34, 36n.201, 56n.333, 70–1
Responsibility to Protect (R2P) doctrine 337, 339, 343n.38, 354, 357–8, 361–2, 364–5, 367n.207
Restoration 27–8, 41–6, 74n.462, 167–8
retorsions 164–5n.132, 346–7
Revolutionary Armed Forces of Colombia (FARC) 155–6, 199
rex superiorem non recognoscens in regno suo est imperator 11–12, 404
Rhodesia 185–6, 316–17, 331n.145
  sanctions against 304–5, 310–12, 317–18
Risorgimento 51–4
Roosevelt Corollary 81–2, 83n.520
Russian Civil War 72, 73, 74
Russo-Turkish War of 1877–8 49n.283, 49–50n.287
Rwanda
  Belgium's evacuation operation in 354–5
  Civil War in 236n.300, 344n.46

France's Operation Turquoise in 354–5, 370–1
Uganda's intervention in 237–8n.311

SADC, *see* South African Development Community
Scelle, Georges 87–8, 91–2, 413
Schmitt, Carl 20n.75, 81–2, 94–5, 347
secessionist conflicts 14–15, 25, 55–6, 58–9, 97, 139–40, 193, 301–2
  intervention in 330–5
secondary sanctions 176–7, 181n.254
Second Franco-Hova War 67
Second World War 86
self-defence 36n.201, 37, 70–1n.439, 72, 77–8n.489, 89–90, 93–4, 97, 169–70, 173n.196, 179–80, 214–15, 236, 260–1, 266, 267–8, 270–1, 282, 284, 287–8, 327, 328, 362–4, 386, 387, 389–90, 405
  against colonial and occupying powers 324–5, 329
  collective 141–2, 200, 200n.31, 201–2, 220–1, 237–9, 259–60, 262–3, 264, 265–6, 290–1, 294–5, 297, 324–5, 334n.175
  individual 202n.41, 213–14, 237–9, 261, 262–3, 270–1, 290–1
self-determination 1, 74, 133–4, 139–40, 142–3, 173n.198, 218n.153, 243, 298n.378, 302–3, 305, 306, 332
  Afro-Asian states' position on 324–5
  difference from non-intervention 247–8, 313–14
  external 74, 140–1, 228–9, 309–14, 315–19, 320, 327–8, 330–1, 334–6, 357n.124, 402, 403, 410–11, 412; *see also* decolonization conflicts
  internal 40, 73–4, 88–9, 97, 105, 115, 129, 136–7, 138, 210, 222–3, 236, 246, 247–81, 292–3, 294, 296, 297, 298–9, 300–1, 302–4, 305, 309, 310n.5, 330–1, 333–4, 336, 348n.76, 354, 355, 367–8, 370–1, 373, 399–400, 402, 403, 405, 409–10, 411; *see also* negative equality
  and the prohibition of the use of force 314, 329
  Soviet Union's position on 320–2
  Western states' position on 322–3, 403
self-preservation 23, 24–5, 37, 38, 42–4, 46–8, 49–50, 53–4, 56n.333, 72, 80, 83, 88, 90–1, 96–7, 118–19, 404–5

458 INDEX

Shanghai Cooperation Organization
  (SCO) 107–8
Sierra Leone
  coup of 1997 in 212–13
  ECOWAS intervention in 213–14, 241–2,
    263–4, 287–8, 292
  Guinea's intervention in 224–5, 285
  Liberia's intervention in 237–8n.311
  United Kingdom's intervention in 263–4
  United Nations Mission in Sierra Leone
    (UNAMSIL) 263–4
Solomon Islands
  Australia's intervention in the 288
  Pacific Islands Forum countries'
    intervention in the 288
Somalia
  African Union Mission to Somalia
    (AMISOM) 262–3, 302
  Civil War in 98–9, 212–13, 217–18, 235–6,
    262–3, 302, 344n.46
  Eritrea's intervention in 237–8n.311
  Ethiopia's interventions in 236n.298,
    237–8n.311, 262–3
  Kenya's intervention in 262–3
  Operation Restore Hope in 370–1
Somaliland 207–8
South Africa
  sanctions against 166n.146, 304–5, 310–
    12, 317–18, 319
South African Development Community
  (SADC) 106–7
  interventions by the 225–6, 264, 276–7,
    366–7
South Sudan
  arms embargo on 236n.300, 351n.87
  Uganda's intervention in 269, 272, 354–5
  United Nations Mission in the Republic of
    South Sudan (UNMISS) 370–1
South West Africa 199, 326–7, 328–9
sovereign equality of states 12–13, 18, 23–4,
  101, 121–2, 125, 173n.198, 218; see also
  sovereignty
sovereignty 1, 8, 11–15, 17, 18, 19, 23–4,
  27–8, 36n.199, 36n.200, 38, 63–4, 88–9,
  91–2, 129, 131, 217–18, 241n.337, 247,
  345, 404, 406; see also sovereign equality
  of states
  Chinese doctrine of 113–14
  in cyberspace 377–8, 391–5, 400–1
  decisional 150–1, 177, 194–5, 202–3, 247, 408

and domestic jurisdiction 165–6
and human rights 337, 338–40, 345n.48, 348
limited sovereignty, doctrine of 167–8
and newly independent states 132
popular 26–7, 73, 96, 211, 404
populist conceptions of 413
and self-determination 318
territorial 247, 391–5, 408
transfer of 225–6, 404
Spain
  Carlist Wars in 47, 48n.278, 60n.364, 66, 68–9
  Civil War in 62n.376, 63n.384, 75–8, 95,
    202n.41
  France's intervention in 31–2, 41–3, 47,
    48n.278, 87n.546
Sri Lanka
  India's intervention in 224–5, 332–3,
    335n.176, see also Liberation Tigers of
    Tamil Eelam (LTTE)
subversion
  in cyberspace 400–2, 403
  duty of vigilance to prevent 191–2
  prohibition of 105–6, 107–9, 112–13, 114,
    115, 145–7, 148, 156, 185, 186–94, 195,
    237, 407
Sudan
  Civil War of 1983–2005 in 98–9
  Civil War of 2023-present in 98–9
Sumatran rebellion 199
Syria
  airstrikes against ISIL in 220–1, 266–7,
    294–5n.360, 295n.363
  Civil War in 5, 216, 270–1, 351–2, 358–9
  French, UK, and US missile strikes in
    response to the use of chemical weapons
    in 225, 367–8
  funding of the government during the
    Civil War in 280–1
  funding of the opposition forces during
    the Civil War in 194, 239n.320, 240–1,
    369–70
  Iran's intervention in 270–1
  recognition of the opposition during the
    Civil War in 369–70n.225
  Russia's intervention in 270–1, 353
  supply of arms to the government during
    the Civil War in 279n.239, 280, 352–3
  supply of arms to opposition forces during
    the Civil War in 189–90, 239n.320,
    240–1, 297, 368–9

INDEX 459

supply of non-lethal military equipment to opposition forces during the Civil War in 189–90, 239n.320, 369n.224
Turkey's incursions in 227

Tajikistan
Russia's intervention in 238n.316
Tanganyka
United Kingdom's intervention in 220n.170, 227–8, 285
Tellini, Italy's reprisal in response to the killing of General 71–2
terrorism 114–15, 121–2, 132, 138, 142–3, 145–7, 148, 156, 179–80, 185, 186–94, 195, 219–20, 262–3, 265–71, 283, 291–2, 298–301, 302–3, 306, 333–4, 355, 373, 400, 409–10
definition of 299–301
The Gambia 219
ECOWAS intervention in 210, 213–14, 241–2, 289
Senegal's intervention in 285–6
Third World Approaches to International Law (TWAIL) 132–3, 413
and intervention by invitation 142–3
Thirty Years War 12n.18, 16–17; *see also* Westphalia, Peace of
threat of force 30, 153, 195, 227–8, 407; *see also* coercion, political
Thucydides 9
Timor–Leste, *see* East Timor
Tobar Doctrine 45n.262, 86
Togo
France's intervention in 224–5, 286, 292
Tonga
Australia and New Zealand's intervention in 291, 293
Transnistria
Russia's intervention in 238n.316, 335n.176
Truman Doctrine 166–7, 240–1
Turkey
US support for 235n.296, 240n.328
TWAIL, *see* Third World Approaches to International Law
Two Sicilies, Kingdom of the 53
Austria's intervention in the 41–3
Sardinia's occupation of the 52–3
Spedizione dei Mille in the 53–4, 62n.374
tyranny, resistance to 13–14, 18, 21, 22, 131–2, 241; *see also* humanitarian intervention

Uganda
Tanzania's intervention in 227, 238n.317
United Kingdom's intervention in 285
Ukraine
Maidan Revolution in 208–9, 211–12, 229–30
Russia's invasion of 123–4, 156–8, 179–80, 202, 238n.318, 334n.175, 362–4, 365–6
Russia's support for the Donbass secessionists in 185–6, 237–8n.311, 334n.174, 356, 401
Universal Monarchy 11–12, 11n.12, 404
UN Security Council 5–6, 100–1, 143, 166, 169–70, 179n.236, 189n.308, 193–4, 200, 210n.95, 213–14, 217–18, 219, 225, 235–6, 264, 272, 287–8, 301–3, 306, 318–19, 345–6, 350–1, 370–2, 374–5
use of force, prohibition of 1–2, 5, 101, 106–7, 108–9, 125, 169, 171, 187n.297, 189–90, 191, 197–8, 200, 222–3, 227–8, 239n.320, 244, 247, 294–5, 296, 298, 325–6, 357–8, 368–9, 373, 386, 388–90, 391, 401, 412
difference from non-intervention 169, 387
and external self-determination 314, 320–1, 323–4, 329
in the interwar period 70–2, 97, 405

Vanuatu
Papua New Guinea's intervention in 224–5, 334n.170
Vattel, Emer de 1, 18–21, 22–3, 53n.306, 58–9, 65, 93–4
classification of situations of internal unrest according to 19–20
intervention on the side of an incumbent government according to 20–1
intervention on the side of insurgents according to 21
Venezuela
crisis of 1902–3 in 82, 175n.211
political crisis of 2018 in 178–9, 184–5, 208–9, 211–12, 241–2
sanctions against 81, 175–6, 178–9, 243–4
Vietnam
First Indochina War 199, 201n.36
North Vietnam's intervention in South Vietnam 201–2, 237–8n.311, 296–7
qualification of the armed conflict in 201–2

460   INDEX

Vietnam (*cont.*)
  Second Indochina War 139–40, 142n.306,
    201–2
  US intervention in 139–40, 201–2, 214–
    15, 259–60, 294–5n.360, 295n.363

war 35–6, 60–1
  animus bellandi 33–4, 35–6, 169n.166
  definition of 12–13, 21–2, 32–3
  just causes of 12–13, 13n.24, 14n.28,
    35, 36
  laws and customs of, *see* international
    humanitarian law (IHL)
  state of 31–2, 33–4, 61–2, 65, 67, 69,
    76n.475, 83, 96–7, 404–5
War of Spanish Succession 13n.20
Western Sahara 310–12, 328–9, 329n.140
Westphalia, Peace of 12–13, 15–16
Wheaton, Henry 35, 65–6, 93–4
Wikileaks 401–2
Wilson Doctrine 45n.262

Wolff, Christian 17–18, 19–20, 23–4
  classification of situations of internal
    unrest according to 17–18

Yemen
  Civil War in 98–9, 198–9n.20, 216, 219,
    270, 302
  Gulf Cooperation Council's intervention
    in 232–3, 270, 294–5n.360
  Iran's support to the Houthi in 237–
    8n.311, 270
  North Yemen Civil War 257–8
  US strikes in 219–20, 270
  US support for Saudi Arabia in the Civil
    War in 352–3
Yugoslavia
  UN arms embargo on the
    former 236n.300

Zaire, *see* Democratic Republic of the Congo
  (DRC)